Roger Ebert's
Movie Yearbook
1999

*Other books by Roger Ebert*

An Illini Century

A Kiss Is Still a Kiss

Two Weeks in the Midday Sun: A Cannes Notebook

Behind the Phantom's Mask

Roger Ebert's Little Movie Glossary

Roger Ebert's Movie Home Companion *annually 1986–1993*

Roger Ebert's Video Companion *annually 1994–1998*

Questions for the Movie Answer Man

Roger Ebert's Book of Film: An Anthology

*With Daniel Curley*
The Perfect London Walk

*With John Kratz*
The Computer Insectiary

*With Gene Siskel*
The Future of the Movies: Interviews with Martin Scorsese, Steven Spielberg, and George Lucas

# Roger Ebert's Movie Yearbook 1999

This book is dedicated
to Robert Zonka, 1928–1985.
God love ya.


For information write
Andrews McMeel Publishing,
an Andrews McMeel Universal company,
4520 Main Street,
Kansas City, Missouri 64111.

ISBN 0-8362-6831-8
ISSN 1072-561fl

All the reviews in this book originally appeared
in the *Chicago Sun-Times*.

# Contents

## Acknowledgments

Donna Martin, editor and friend, first suggested this new approach to the annual volume. The design is by Cameron Poulter, the typographical genius of Hyde Park. My thanks to Polly Blair and Julie Roberts, who compiled the electronic manuscript, and Dorothy O'Brien, who assembled the book. I have been blessed with the expert and discriminating copyediting of Avis Weathersbee, Laura Emerick, Jeff Johnson, Jeff Wisser, Christi Kempf, John Barron, Darel Jevens, and Miriam DiNunzio at the *Chicago Sun-Times;* Sue Roush at Universal Press Syndicate; and Michelle Daniel at Andrews McMeel Publishing. Many thanks are also due to the production staff at *Siskel & Ebert,* and to Marsha Jordan at WLS-TV. My gratitude goes to Carol Iwata, my expert office assistant, and to Marlene Gelfond, at the *Sun-Times.* And special thanks and love to my wife, Chaz, for whom I can only say: If more film critics had a spouse just like her, the level of cheer in the field would rise dramatically.

ROGER EBERT


## Key to Symbols

| | |
|---|---|
| ★★★★ | A great film |
| ★★★ | A good film |
| ★★ | Fair |
| ★ | Poor |
| | G, PG, PG-13, R, NC-17: Ratings of the Motion Picture Association of America |
| G | Indicates that the movie is suitable for general audiences |
| PG | Suitable for general audiences but parental guidance is suggested |
| PG-13 | Recommended for viewers 13 years or above; may contain material inappropriate for younger children |
| R | Recommended for viewers 17 or older |
| NC-17 | Intended for adults only |
| 141 m. | Running time |
| 1996 | Year of theatrical release |
| ☞ | Refers to "Questions for the Movie Answer Man." |

# Introduction

This 1999 *Movie Yearbook* includes every review I have written since January 1, 1996, as well as most of the interviews and essays since July 1, 1997, and most of the Movie Answer Man entries published since the book *Questions for the Movie Answer Man* was completed in December 1996.

After thirteen years of annual *Companions*, it was time to face an inescapable fact: The book was bursting at its seams. The most recent volumes reached their physical limit of 1,000 pages and 1,500 reviews. For years, preparing the new volume involved a painful process of triage. For every new review that went in, an old review had to come out. The book could not grow any larger.

This led to two results I was unhappy about. (1) Not all my new reviews were making it into the book. During 1997, for example, I wrote full-length reviews of 264 movies, which means 114 would not have gotten into print. (2) In selecting old reviews to replace, I tended to eliminate the negative reviews, which skewed the book more every year toward positive reviews.

Since I am the only American print critic who writes full-length reviews of virtually every movie of any note that goes into national release [see below], it was a shame there wasn't room in the book for so many of them. In addition to the mainstream studio pictures, I have a particular interest in independent, foreign, art, and documentary films. Since many of those releases never play in many cities, they find their audiences mostly on video; it made sense to include the reviews in a book of this sort.

This reasoning was so sensible, indeed, that Donna Martin, my treasured editor at Andrews McMeel Publishing, suggested this yearbook format two or three years ago. At first I resisted it, because I liked the idea of keeping older reviews in print. But last year, after cutting still another 150 titles to make room for new reviews, I e-mailed Donna that the time had come to embrace her suggestion. The *Companion* was neither a complete reference of older movies, nor a complete collection of my new reviews.

This 1999 edition includes, indeed, many reviews that I wrote between January 1, 1996, and June 30, 1998, that were not in last year's *Video Companion*—about 225, I estimate. (More than 60 percent of the approximately 630 reviews here have never before been in book form.) Next year, we'll cut out the reviews from 1996 and add the latest year, and so on. So the annual volumes will always represent every review I've written for the most recent thirty months.

That means, this year, not only *Titanic* but *Love and Death on Long Island*, not only *L.A. Confidential* but *Bang*, not only *Armageddon* but *Sonatine*. At a time when the mass movie audience is increasingly being driven into a corner by powerful marketing campaigns, it is good to have a choice; good to know that the best movies are not always the ones with the TV spots and the full-page ads.

The 1999 *Yearbook* also includes:

- All the Answer Man entries that are still relevant, arranged by movie title or topic.

The book *Questions for the Movie Answer Man* went into two printings and was a gratifying success, but we thought it would enhance the *Yearbook* to include Qs and As about the latest titles.

- Selections from my film festival coverage. Every year I attend the Cannes, Toronto, Telluride, Hawaii, and Chicago festivals, and many years I also attend the Sundance and Virginia festivals. Every other year, I sail with Dusty Cohl's Floating Film Festival, which next raises anchor in January 2000. I have also attended the Philadelphia, Montreal, Venice, Edinburgh, and Dallas festivals. And indeed in April 1999, I will host my own festival at my alma mater, the University of Illinois at Urbana-Champaign. It will be called the Overlooked Film Festival, and will showcase films I admire that either failed to find distribution, or failed to find the audiences they deserved.
- Those interviews and "think pieces" I've done during the past twelve months. I don't attend as many junkets as I used to, because they're usually not a useful way of getting real information: They've been turned into assembly lines for sound bites, and cater to the "benevolent blurbsters" who can be counted on for peals of ecstasy for every film they see. Sometimes I attend a premiere simply because the film is so widely anticipated (I'm sure I'll be at *Eyes Wide Shut,* for example). Other times, I get interviews during film festivals.

Basically, then, every edition of the *Yearbook* will include a lot of information about the last twelve months in film, plus thirty months of reviews of those recent movies most likely to be found on the shelves of video stores.

* * *

And now for the footnote. I am indeed apparently the only American critic who writes full-length print reviews of virtually every movie of any note that goes into national release. This is true because most newspapers and magazines do not review most of the new films, and those that do employ two, three, or four film critics. When I started at the *Chicago Sun-Times,* I was the only film critic on the staff, and although over the years many excellent critics have written reviews for the paper, I've remained as the paper's only designated film critic.

I could have had more help if I'd wanted it, but I didn't want it. One reason is this *Yearbook.* If it is to be a useful reference, it has to contain all the major and most of the notable minor films of the year. You'd notice it if I took the day off when *Godzilla* opened.

The *Sun-Times* has been a wonderful place to work over the years, not least because it makes generous space available for extended film coverage. On one recent Friday, for example, my paper set aside more than twice as much space for the movies as the *Chicago Tribune.* I am blessed to have the room and the opportunity to review so many movies, and I enjoy the discoveries I make; *Gamera: Guardian of the Universe* is not the kind of movie most critics review, and it's no masterpiece, but I was glad to see it.

* * *

There are, of course, other critics who review most of the new movies, but they're to be found on the World Wide Web, where an excellent critical community flourishes. For those who like to write about the movies, there is no better place to start, and many of the Web-based critics are amateurs in name only, since their reviews are as well conceived and written as a professional's.

* * *

The big news in home video during 1999 will involve the DVD format. DVD discs deliver an astonishing picture to your TV screen—more than twice as good as VHS tapes, and better even than laser discs. But will the format be adopted?

It's already off to a faster start than such consumer electronic introductions as CD players and VCRs. But there's confusion because of two formats: DVD and DVIX. The DVIX discs are purchased at a store and brought home, where you can watch them twice within forty-eight hours after first starting one. Your DVIX machine can then dial a toll-free number to charge you for more viewings, or even sell you the disc. The advantage: Unlike rental tapes and discs, you never have to return it.

The DVD community has declared war on DVIX, fearing another case of format confusion, as happened with VHS and Beta. Because I admire DVD discs, and because I believe home viewers should see and hear the best possible fidelity, I share the concerns of the anti-DVIX faction. But there are two points to keep in mind: DVIX machines will also play standard DVD discs, and the DVIX forces plan a $100 million campaign to introduce their product. That is likely to mean greater and faster market penetration for DVD than would have happened otherwise, and more machines mean more discs and more choices.

Some bothersome questions remain. The DVIX honchos at the studios tend to be drawn from the same small-minded ranks that run the VHS operations, rather than from the laser disc and DVD people who truly know and care about movies. They're marketers, not cinephiles. Although the new discs have room for both a pan-and-scan and a letterbox version of the same movie, the DVIX camp plans to ignore this flexibility and only release in the despised pan-and-scan. This is even crazier than it sounds, because with the introduction of wide-screen High-Def TV sets and new video projectors that can fill a wide screen, letterboxing is coming into its own.

Another question: Will DVIX drive the market, and swamp the value-added DVD discs? Some new DVDs, like many laser discs, include extra bells and whistles like parallel commentary tracks, trailers, outtakes, and supporting material (the Criterion Collection has led in this field).

My guess: In five years, the DVD format will be as widely established as CD audio players, and as the total market grows, so will the market for specialized value-added discs. Laser discs have flourished despite a niche of only about two million players. Think of the market if there were twenty million players for the new digital format.

* * *

My reviews and articles can be found on-line on CompuServe (the go-word is "Ebert") and the World Wide Web (www.suntimes.com/ebert). I hang out in a section of the CompuServe Showbiz Media Forum (the go-word is "Showbiz").

My reviews are also available in the CD-ROM format, as part of Microsoft Cinemania. After the 1997 edition, Microsoft, alas, discontinued this invaluable reference, as part of the elimination of almost all their entertainment and home titles. But as I write, it appears that Cinemania will rise again with a new owner.

* * *

Where should you start in compiling a movie library? Cinemania, when it reappears, is the ideal companion for your Windows 95 or Macintosh machine. On your shelves: *For Keeps,* by Pauline Kael, brings together a generous selection from her many previous books of reviews, providing an overview of the career of the most influential of film critics. The greatly revised and expanded edition of David Thomson's *Biographical Dictionary of Film* is an opinionated, informed, concise summary of hundreds of key careers. The late Ephraim Katz's *Film Encyclopedia* is an invaluable one-volume survey of the world of film. And *Distinguishing Features,* by Stanley Kauffmann, is the latest collection of reviews by the critic whose superb writing and scholarship have distinguished the *New Republic* for decades. Jonathan Rosenbaum's recent book *Movies as Politics* showcases the work of one of the best contemporary critics.

For laser disc fans, there is no better guide than the *Laser Video Disc Companion,* by Douglas Pratt. For the critics who shaped today's film criticism, I recommend the collected works of Kael, Kauffmann, Manny Farber, Andrew Sarris, Dwight Macdonald, James Agee, and Graham Green. On the Web, the best critics include James Berardinelli, Scott Renshaw, Damien Cannon, Harvey S. Karten, Edwin Jahiel, and the excellent writers at Mr. Showbiz and Film.com. The two most valuable resources for finding material on the Web are the Internet Movie Database (http://us.imdb.com/search) and the Movie Review Query Engine at Telerama (http://www.cinema.pgh.pa.us/movie/reviews).

Thanks to the many readers who have written with suggestions and corrections. I can be reached in care of my faithful and patient publishers, Andrews McMeel Publishing, 4520 Main Street, Kansas City, Missouri 64111.

ROGER EBERT

# Reviews

# A

## Absolute Power ★ ★ ★ ½

R, 122 m., 1997

Clint Eastwood (Luther Whitney), Gene Hackman (President Richmond), Ed Harris (Seth Frank), Laura Linney (Kate Whitney), Scott Glenn (Bill Burton), Dennis Haysbert (Tim Collin), Judy Davis (Gloria Russell), E. G. Marshall (Walter Sullivan). Directed by Clint Eastwood and produced by Eastwood and Karen Spiegel. Screenplay by William Goldman, based on the novel by David Baldacci.

Clint Eastwood's *Absolute Power* is a tight, taut thriller with a twist. It's also about a father and daughter, estranged for years, who are finally able to become friends. Not many thrillers slow down to notice relationships, but this one does.

Eastwood stars as Luther Whitney, a burglar who breaks into a mansion in the dead of night and penetrates a hidden room filled with diamonds and cash. He's interrupted in the middle of his work by visitors. Hiding behind a two-way mirror, he sees a man and woman having sex. The play turns rough, the man beats her, the woman stabs him, and two men burst in and shoot her dead.

Eastwood watches, all but his eyes in shadow. He is about to intervene—risking discovery—when the gunshots ring out. He escapes from the mansion down a rope from a third-floor window, carrying with him the deadly knowledge that the woman was the younger wife of an eighty-year-old millionaire, and the man was the president of the United States.

What we have here is a setup that could be developed in a lot of ways. The recent and dreadful *Shadow Conspiracy* detailed a White House plot that was cheerfully absurd. *Absolute Power,* based loosely on a novel by David Baldacci, could have been as silly, but it's not, because Eastwood uses fine actors and a smart script by William Goldman to make it into something more.

A lot of the best qualities come from the thief's relationship with his daughter, Kate (Laura Linney), "the only kid in show-and-tell that got to talk about visiting day." Her dad was in prison most of her childhood, and now, as a prosecutor, she never sees him. But sometimes she senses he's watching her; one of the movie's best scenes has her discovering that he attended her graduation ceremonies. Why did he remain invisible? Having an ex-con for a father would not help her much.

The story behind the murder is developed briskly. Old Walter Sullivan (E. G. Marshall) is a prime backer of the president (Gene Hackman). He was happily married for forty-eight years, but after his wife's death he took a younger wife. The men who burst into the mansion bedroom and shot her were Secret Service agents (Dennis Haysbert and Scott Glenn). The cover-up is being orchestrated by a White House chief of staff (Judy Davis).

Seth Frank (Ed Harris), the cop on the case, immediately notices all sorts of suspicious loose ends: Two shots were fired but only one bullet was recovered, for example, and the gunshot trajectories don't match. He suspects this was more than a simple murder.

Most thrillers depend on chase scenes and shoot-outs. Some of the best scenes in *Absolute Power* involve dialogue. The cop immediately fingers Luther Whitney as a possible suspect (he's one of "only six guys alive" who could have gotten into the mansion), and interviews him at a museum dining room. Eastwood, wearing half-glasses and a cloth cap that accentuate his age, smiles laconically and says, "Go down a rope in the middle of the night? If I could do that, I'd be the star of my AARP meetings."

There is another good scene between Ed Harris and old E. G. Marshall, who tells the policeman the two-way mirror was installed in the bedroom at his wife's suggestion: "She thought I might have liked sitting there. I didn't." His is a poignant character, a self-made man who has spent his life giving money to charity, who has elected a president, and who now fears "I'll go out as the joke of the world."

Eastwood delivers a few nice set pieces as the suspense builds, including a rendezvous with his daughter in a public plaza, while two sets of gunmen train their sights on him. And we get hard-boiled dialogue in the Oval Office, as the president and his merciless chief of staff run the cover-up by ordering the Secret Servicemen to do things not covered in their job description (one is willing, one has qualms). Much depends on a hypocritical speech the president makes, which Luther sees at an airport bar just as he's about to flee the country. In a classic Eastwood moment, the thief's jaw hardens and he decides to stay and fight, rather than give a pass to a heartless liar.

Eastwood as a director is usually eclipsed by Eastwood the actor; he has directed almost twenty films, good enough and successful enough to make him one of Hollywood's top filmmakers, and yet his stardom overshadows that role. Here he creates scenes of pure moviemaking; scenes without dialogue or violence, that work only because we know the characters and because the direction, camera work (by Jack N. Green), and editing (Joel Cox) put them together into suspenseful montages. The opening sequence is especially effective.

But at the end what I remembered most was the relationship between father and daughter. By using this personal story as an arc to draw together the other elements in the film, Eastwood does a difficult thing: He makes a thriller that is not upstaged by its thrills. Luther Whitney is a genuinely interesting, complicated character—not just an action figure. What happens to him matters to us, and that's worth more than all the special effects in the world.

## Addicted to Love ★ ★

R, 101 m., 1997

Meg Ryan (Maggie), Matthew Broderick (Sam), Kelly Preston (Linda), Tcheky Karyo (Anton), Maureen Stapleton (Nana), Nesbitt Blaisdell (Ed Green). Directed by Griffin Dunne and produced by Jeffrey Silver and Bobby Newmyer. Screenplay by Robert Gordon.

I have to train myself to stop expecting plausibility in films. After all, I'm the guy who argues that nothing is implausible in a film if it works, since it's all part of getting the job done. And yet, in the opening scene of *Addicted to Love* I was struggling. Astronomers have a telescope trained on a supernova. Then suddenly it's noon and the chief astronomer (Matthew Broderick) lowers the telescope until he can focus on the woman he loves (Kelly Preston) frolicking in a meadow with the students she teaches.

Huh? I'm thinking. They can see the stars through that telescope at high noon? I should have taken the clue right there. Then I wouldn't have been distracted a little later when Preston announces she wants to leave their small town and spend some time in New York City, and as her commuter plane taxis on takeoff, Broderick races beside it down the runway in his pickup truck, waving good-bye. I think that's against FAA regulations.

So look, I'm not being fair to the movie. It's obviously a romantic fantasy, and only a curmudgeon would nitpick. What bothered me more was that the characters are supposed to be intelligent, and yet they have the maturity of gnats. It is always a problem in a love story when the rival seems more interesting than the hero, and that's what happens here.

But let's back up. Broderick plays Sam, the astronomer, who follows his lifelong love, Linda (Preston), to the big city, where she has gone because she finds small-town life stagnating. Sam soon finds her by canvassing lots of residential hotels until he finds the right one (don't try this yourself unless you have lots of time). Then he discovers Linda is dating a French chef named Anton (Tcheky Karyo). In fact, she's moving in with him.

Sam sneaks into an empty building across the way and, using his astronomer's knowledge of lenses, builds a refracting gadget that projects an image of their apartment onto a wall in his (the technical term for his device is "camera obscura"). Later he bugs their place, so he can relax on his sofa and watch a moving picture of their private life, with sound. Using his scientist's training, he graphs their progress (there is even a chart showing her daily smile quotient) to predict when they will break up.

During this process, a mystery figure on a motorcycle turns up. It is an old rule in movie comedies that whenever a motorcyclist's head and face are completely obscured by a helmet, that motorcyclist is inevitably revealed to be a woman. True again this time: It's Maggie (Meg Ryan), who is the jilted lover of the French chef. Since Maggie and Sam have their losses in common, they team up to try to sabotage the two happy lovers across the way.

Among their tricks: They pull a pickpocket scheme to get lipstick on his collar. They bribe kids to use squirt guns to douse him with perfume. These clues are supposed to make Linda jealous. By this point in the film, I was squirming: What intelligence level is the story pitched at?

Sam eventually inveigles himself into the kitchen of Anton's restaurant as a dishwasher, so that he can masochistically observe his rival at close quarters. This leads to a conversation between the two men in which Anton seems so manifestly wiser and more grown up that I was reminded of a generalization I once heard: "European films are about grown-ups, and American films are about adolescents." Not true in all cases, of course, but it's dramatically true here that Anton has an adult's understanding of the world, and the Sam character thinks he's living in a sitcom.

How much more interesting this situation might have been if they'd forgotten about the reflecting lenses and the practical jokes, and tried to devise a comedy based on personalities and dialogue! That might have even led to an unexpected outcome. Instead, we get a plot so predictable that there cannot be a single person in the audience who doesn't know Broderick and Ryan are destined to fall in love with each other. Not simply destined, but absolutely required to by the bylaws of the Hollywood Code of Clichés.

The actors are very engaging. The production design (including the reflecting lenses) is artful and ingenious. The direction, by Griffin Dunne, is smooth and confident for a first-timer. There are nice supporting roles for Maureen Stapleton, as a wise grandmother, and Nesbitt Blaisdell as Linda's father, Mr. Green, who assigns himself to read her Dear John letters. There is, in fact, a lot of good stuff here, but it's all at the service of an imbecilic approach. It's like bright people got together to make the film and didn't trust the audience to keep up with them. ☞

## Afterglow ★ ★ ★

R, 113 m., 1998

Nick Nolte (Lucky Mann), Julie Christie (Phyllis Mann), Lara Flynn Boyle (Marianne Byron), Jonny Lee Miller (Jeffrey Byron), Jay Underwood (Donald Duncan), Domini Blythe (Helene Pelletier), Yves Corbeil (Bernard Ornay), Alan Fawcett (Count Falco/Jack Dana). Directed by Alan Rudolph and produced by Robert Altman. Screenplay by Rudolph.

Julie Christie has the kind of face you find on the covers of romance novels, and surely one of the reasons she was cast in *Dr. Zhivago* was that she would look so good on the poster. She projects the wounded perfection of a great beauty who has had the wrong sort of luck. In *Afterglow,* only her third role in the 1990s, Alan Rudolph has given her the sort of character she knows inside out: bemused, sad, needful, mysterious.

She plays Phyllis Mann, a former B-movie actress specializing in horror roles, who now lives in Montreal with her husband, Lucky (Nick Nolte), a handyman equally at home with wrenches and wenches. Some great sadness from the past overshadows their marriage, and although Phyllis and Lucky are held together by love and understanding, he philanders, with her tacit permission, among the lonely housewives who phone for his services ("Plumbing and a woman's nature are both unpredictable, and filled with hidden mysteries," he philosophizes).

Nolte plays Lucky not as a sex machine, however, but as a tender, observant man who feels a certain sympathy with the women he has sex with. The deal with his wife is, he can fool around, as long as he doesn't get serious. One day seriousness threatens, when he meets Marianne Byron (Lara Flynn Boyle), a yuppie wife who yearns for the baby her husband will not, or cannot, give her. So deep is her need that she has hired Lucky Mann to convert an extra bedroom into a nursery, even as her cold, arrogant husband, Jeffrey (Jonny Lee Miller, Sick Boy in *Trainspotting*), vows he wants nothing to do with children.

The plot to this point could be the stuff of soap opera, but there's always something askew in an Alan Rudolph film, unexpected notes and touches that maintain a certain ironic distance while permitting painful flashes of human nature to burst through. Imagine a soap in which the characters subtly mock their roles while the actors occasionally break down in grief about their offscreen lives.

*Afterglow* has a script that permits coincidence and contrivance; like many of Rudolph's films *(Choose Me, Trouble in Mind),* it has characters who seem fated to share common destinies. As Lucky Mann falls into the pit created by Marianne's great need, Phyllis meets Jeffrey and allows herself to be drawn toward him in a mixture of curiosity and revenge.

*Afterglow* doesn't depend on a visible style as much as some of Rudolph's films; he seems so interested in the story, which he wrote himself, that he doesn't need to impose directorial distance. That may be because the characters are so poignant. Julie Christie, lounging on a sofa looking at her old horror films, has speeches in which she looks back on Hollywood with the fascination of an accident victim. Nolte's character is not a one-dimensional louse but a man whose sex life may reflect a deep sympathy for women—the same sympathy he feels for his wife, so steeped in sadness.

As for Christie, what's the story with her? She is so familiar a face from her early films *(Darling, McCabe and Mrs. Miller, Far from the Madding Crowd, Shampoo),* but then her career drifted into unessential and forgettable films. Infrequent newspaper interviews reported on her happiness in solitude. Like the character Phyllis, she has a distance on her early career; unlike her, she uses it here to create something fresh and vulnerable. How mysterious and intriguing some performances can be.

## Air Bud ★ ★ ★

PG, 97 m., 1997

Kevin Zegers (Josh Framm), Wendy Makkena (Jackie Framm), Bill Cobbs (Arthur Chaney), Michael Jeter (Norm Snively), Eric Christmas (Judge Cranfield). Directed by Charles Martin Smith and produced by William Vince and Robert Vince. Screenplay by Paul Tamasy and Aaron Mendelsohn.

"Are there ever movies you just hate the idea of going to see?" Yes, I say, there are—but sometimes I'm surprised. It happened again the other night. I dragged myself down to a multiplex to attend a sneak preview of a movie named *Air Bud.* I had seen the trailer, and knew it was about a dog who could play basketball. I was not impatient to see this movie.

I began to have stirrings of hope in the opening scenes, which involved an obnoxious and possibly drunken clown making a fool of himself at a children's party. His act was called "Clown and a Hound," and the dog seemed smarter and nicer than its master, and probably smelled better.

On the highway, the dog's cage bounces out of the clown's pickup, and through a series of adventures the dog makes friends with the young hero of the movie, Josh (Kevin Zegers). Josh has just moved to a small town with his mother (Wendy Makkena) and kid sister. (His father, a test pilot, has been killed in a crash, following the ancient Disney tradition that one dead parent is nice, and an orphan for a hero is best of all.)

Josh is lonely and depressed in the new town, and is an outcast at the junior high school, although eventually he gets to be manager of the basketball team. Could he be a player? He lacks the confidence to try out, although he practices for long hours in an abandoned court he's discovered behind an old church. (The church's notice board carries the ominous legend, EEK AN YE SHAL FIN.)

Josh names the dog Buddy. This is some dog. It has the ability to enter Josh's second-floor bedroom by jumping on a car, climbing a rose trellis, walking across the roof, and jumping in the window. And on the basketball court it turns out to be a star; pass Buddy the ball, and it can bounce it with its nose and make a basket (it doesn't miss once in the entire movie).

The school's aging janitor (Bill Cobbs) turns out to be a New York Knicks star from the 1950s, and when the regular coach is fired, he takes over the team and hands out advice like: "You take that dog. It doesn't give a rat's behind about his point average—he just likes to play the game!" Because by then, of course, Buddy has found the gymnasium, bounded on court during a game, and scored a basket.

There are predictable crises: Will Snively the clown (Michael Jeter) come looking for his dog? Will Josh be promoted from water boy to player? Will the team's mean star and his overzealous dad spoil the fun? The movie touches those bases, but with freshness and energy. And the climactic scenes are not only absurd and goofy but also enormously entertaining. By the end of the film I was quietly amazed: Not only could Buddy play basketball, but I actually cared how the game turned out.

The movie was directed by Charles Martin Smith, himself the star of a much different kind of animal movie, the classic *Never Cry Wolf* (1983). He has the structure of a traditional story here, but makes it seem new with good performances, crisp editing, a lovable dog, and a new twist on the old movie tradition of the "big game." And then the movie just keeps getting better, with a very funny courtroom scene involving a judge (Eric Christmas) who never catches on that the dog is trained to bark when it hears a gavel pounding.

Now, then. Can this dog really shoot baskets? I doubt it. I especially doubt that the dog has a better average from the field than Michael Jordan. But I don't want to know what kind of trickery was used to create the dog's game scenes; whatever it was, it worked. The dog, by the way, wears its own little basketball shoes. Don't let your dog see the movie, or it'll want some. ☞

## Air Force One ★ ★ ½

R, 118 m., 1997

Harrison Ford (President James Marshall), Gary Oldman (Ivan Korshunov), Glenn Close (Vice President Kathryn Bennett), Wendy Crewson (Grace Marshall), Liesel Matthews (Alice Marshall), Paul Guilfoyle (Chief of Staff Lloyd Shepherd), Xander Berkeley (Agent Gibbs), William H. Macy (Major Caldwell), Philip Baker Hall (Attorney General). Directed by Wolfgang Petersen and produced by Petersen, Armyan Bernstein, Gail Katz, and Jon Shestack. Screenplay by Andrew W. Marlowe.

Harrison Ford is one of the most likable and convincing of movie stars, and he almost pulls off the impossible in *Air Force One*. I don't mean he saves the day; I mean he almost saves the movie. Here is a good example of how star power can breathe new life into old clichés—and *Air Force One* is rich with clichés.

You are familiar with the movie's premise because of all the commercials and coming attractions trailers and magazine covers and talk show appearances. You know that Gary Oldman plays the leader of a gang of terrorists who gain control of *Air Force One* as it's flying back home from Moscow. You know it's up to Ford, as President James Marshall, Vietnam combat hero, to battle the terrorists. You know his wife and children are among the hostages—and that he has just vowed that America will never negotiate with terrorists.

So. Since the movie has no macro surprises, does it have any micro ones? Has director Wolfgang Petersen *(Das Boot, In the Line of Fire)* found lots of neat little touches to make the movie work on a minute-by-minute basis, while on the larger scale it slogs to its preordained conclusion?

Sorta, sometimes. There's some neat stuff about *Air Force One*, although I don't know how much of it to believe. (Is it really bulletproof from the inside? Does it really have an escape pod onboard? Is there really a way to parachute out the back hatch? Can you really call Washington from Russia on a cell phone?) Many of the action scenes take place in the bowels of the plane, down in the galley and luggage areas.

There is also a counterplot set in Washington, where the vice president (Glenn Close) learns from the attorney general (Philip Baker Hall) that the president may be technically "incapacitated," and that she should consider taking over. And there are some good action sequences, in which people enter and leave airplanes at an altitude at which the practice is not recommended.

But mostly the movie is stapled together out of ingredients from many, many other films about presidents, terrorists, hijackings, hostages, airplanes, politics, and cat-and-mouse chases. It is inevitable, for example, that the terrorists will separate and go poking around on their own, so that they can be picked off one at a time. It is inevitable that there will be Washington press conferences, so that bones of information can be thrown to the seething press. It is inevitable that there will be personality flare-ups among the lesser politicians, and dire comments by their advisers ("The element of surprise is a formidable weapon").

The movie also resurrects that ancient and dependable standby, the Choosing of the Wires. In countless other movies, the bomb squad hesitates between "Red . . . or black? Red . . . or black?" This is a big-budget movie and presents us with five wires. It's an emergency, and the president needs to decide which two he should connect. See if you can guess the right two colors. The choices are green, yellow, red, white, and blue.

The movie is well served by the quality of the

performances. Close is convincing as the vice president, and Gary Oldman has a couple of effective scenes as the terrorist ("Murder? You took 100,000 lives to save a nickel on the price of a gallon of gas"). And Harrison Ford is steady and convincing as the president, even while we're asking ourselves if a middle-aged chief executive would really be better at hand-to-hand combat than his Secret Service agents.

Some of the special effects scenes are effective, but others are distracting. In a key scene next to an open doorway on the plane, none of the actors convinced me they thought they were standing next to a 30,000-foot drop. (For one thing, they never looked down, which I think is more or less the first thing I would do.) A climactic explosion is less than convincing, visually. And scenes involving a Russian political prisoner are confusing.

*Air Force One* is a fairly competent recycling of familiar ingredients, given an additional interest because of Harrison Ford's personal appeal. At this point, however, I've had enough explosions, showdowns, stunts, and special effects. I saw a movie the other day about a woman in Paris who lost her cat, and know what? It was more exciting than this. At least when the cat got up on the roof, it knew enough to look down. ☞

## An Alan Smithee Film Burn Hollywood Burn no stars

R, 86 m., 1998

Ryan O'Neal (James Edmunds), Coolio (Dion Brothers), Chuck D (Leon Brothers), Eric Idle (Alan Smithee), Richard Jeni (Jerry Glover), Leslie Stefanson (Michelle Rafferty), Sandra Bernhard (Ann Glover), Cherie Lunghi (Myrna Smithee). Directed by Alan Smithee and produced by Ben Myron. Screenplay by Joe Eszterhas.

*An Alan Smithee Film Burn Hollywood Burn* is a spectacularly bad film—incompetent, unfunny, ill-conceived, badly executed, lamely written, and acted by people who look trapped in the headlights.

The title provides clues to the film's misfortune. It was originally titled *An Alan Smithee Film*. Then *Burn, Hollywood, Burn!* Now its official title is *An Alan Smithee Film Burn Hollywood Burn*—just like that, with no punctuation. There's a rich irony connected with the title. "Alan Smithee," of course, is the pseudonym that Hollywood slaps on a film if the original director insists on having his name removed. The plot of *AASFBHB* involves a film so bad that the director wants his name removed, but since his *real* name is Alan Smithee, what can he do? Ho, ho.

Wait, it gets better. The movie was directed by Arthur Hiller, who hated the way the film was edited so much that, yes, he insisted his name be removed from the credits. So now it really *is* an Alan Smithee film. That leaves one mystery: Why didn't Joe Eszterhas, the film's writer, take off his name too?

I fear it is because this version of the film does indeed reflect his vision. Eszterhas is sometimes a good writer, but this time he has had a complete lapse of judgment. Even when he kids himself, he's wrong. "It's completely terrible!" a character says of the film within the film. "It's worse than *Showgirls*!" Of course, Eszterhas wrote *Showgirls*, which got some bad reviews, but it wasn't completely terrible. I was looking forward to explaining that to him this week, but he canceled his visit to Chicago, reportedly because his voice gave out. Judging by this film, it was the last thing to go.

Have you ever been to one of those office parties where the PR department has put together a tribute to a retiring boss? That's how this film plays. It has no proper story line. No dramatic scenes. It's all done in documentary form, with people looking at the camera and relating the history of a doomed movie named *Trio*, which cost more than $200 million and stars Sylvester Stallone, Whoopi Goldberg, and Jackie Chan, who play themselves as if they are celebrity impersonators.

The film stars Eric Idle as Smithee, who eventually burns the print and checks into the Keith Moon Psychiatric Institute in England (ho, ho). Ryan O'Neal plays the film's producer. I love the way he's introduced. We see the back of a guy's head, and hear him saying, "Anything!" Then the chair swivels around and he says "anything!" again, and we see, *gasp!*—why, it's *Ryan O'Neal!* I was reminded of the moment in Mike Todd's *Around the World in 80 Days* when the piano player swivels around and, gasp!—it's *Frank Sinatra!*

These actors and others recount the history of the doomed film in unconvincing sound bites, which are edited together without wit or rhythm. One is accustomed to seeing bad movies, but not incompetent ones. Sophomores in a film class could make a better film than this. Hell, I have a movie here by Les Brown, a kid who looks about twelve and who filmed a thriller in his mother's basement, faking a fight scene by wrestling with a dummy. If I locked you in a room with both movies, you'd end up looking at the kid's.

In taking his name off the film, Arthur Hiller has wisely distanced himself from the disaster, but on the basis of what's on the screen I cannot, frankly, imagine any version of this film that I would want to see. The only way to save this film would be to trim eighty-six minutes.

Here's an interesting thing. The film is filled with celebrities playing themselves, and most of them manifestly have no idea who they are. The only celebrity who emerges relatively intact is Harvey Weinstein, head of Miramax, who plays a private eye—but never mind the role, just listen to him. He could find success in voice-over work.

Now consider Stallone. He reappears in the outtakes over the closing credits. Such cookies are a treat for audiences after the film is over. Here they're as bad as the film, but notice a moment when Stallone thinks he's off camera, and asks someone about a Planet Hollywood shirt. *Then* he sounds like himself. A second later, playing himself, he sounds all wrong. Jackie Chan copes by acting like he's in a Jackie Chan movie, but Whoopi Goldberg mangles her scenes in a cigar bar, awkwardly trying to smoke a stogie. It's God's way of paying her back for telling Ted Danson it would be funny to wear blackface at the Friars' Club. ☞

## Alaska ★ ★ ★

PG, 109 m., 1996

Thora Birch (Jessie Barnes), Vincent Kartheiser (Sean Barnes), Dirk Benedict (Jake Barnes), Charlton Heston (Perry), Gordon Tootoosis (Ben). Directed by Fraser C. Heston and produced by Carol Fuchs and Andy Burg. Screenplay by Andy Burg and Scott Myers.

I've seen back-to-nature adventures like *Alaska* many times before, and yet the movie exercises a real charm. It tells the story of an Alaskan bush pilot whose plane crashes, and of his two children, who travel by kayak, canoe, and foot to rescue him, with the help of a cute polar bear cub. Kids up to a certain age are going to love this movie.

The story is robust and direct. Jessie and Sean, a young sister and brother (Thora Birch and Vincent Kartheiser), have moved to Alaska from Chicago after the death of their mother. Jessie loves it there. Sean misses the hot dogs in Wrigley Field and whines to his dad, "You used to fly 747s. Now you deliver toilet paper." Dad (Dirk Benedict) has a more important job than that; his Piper Supercub is a lifeline to small settlements in the rugged interior.

Sean is well on the path to the local equivalent of juvenile delinquency (the cops have made him clean up some spilled oil with a toothbrush) when tragedy strikes: Their dad's plane disappears in a sudden storm and search planes fail to find the wreckage. There is obviously only one course of action. Jessie and Sean pack their gear and paddle off in a kayak to find their dad themselves.

They're in danger from nature—from wild animals, rapids, waterfalls, and rock-climbing hazards. But *Alaska* also provides two human threats, in the shape of the evil bounty hunter Perry (Charlton Heston) and his witless helicopter pilot, Ben (Gordon Tootoosis). These two specialize in shooting adult polar bears and trapping their cubs; "You have no idea how much my clients in Hong Kong will pay for a live polar cub," Perry says.

When the kids stumble across the poachers' camp and release an imprisoned bear cub, they make a couple of enemies—and also a friend, the cub, which they name "Cubby," no doubt in honor of the bar across the street from Wrigley Field. The cub follows them everywhere, perhaps because it embodies the spirit of the wilderness, or perhaps because it likes the marshmallow pies the kids feed it. While the injured father waits in a plane that slides ever closer to a dangerous cliff, the kids trek through the wilderness, encouraged by a wise old Eskimo ("You two are on a spirit journey") who gives them useful advice: "Trust the bear."

The two bounty hunters provide some comic relief. Perry, sounding suspiciously like the real-life Heston, grouses at one point, "These young people brought up on MTV and video games have no knowledge of the true brutality of nature." There's a truly funny scene that I will not describe except to quote the desperate line, "How much tranquilizer did you put in this dart?" And a Mexican stand-off that deserves to be in a slapstick comedy, involving a bear, a dart gun, a rifle, and a helicopter.

The evil bounty hunter is right about the kids' status in the television generation. At one point Sean prepares to rappel down a mountainside and tells Jessie, "This is how they do it on ESPN." By the end of the film the sister and brother have survived incredible hardships, and in a way I think they deserved a chance to save their father without some aid that comes from a most unlikely source.

*Alaska* was directed by Fraser C. Heston, Charlton's son, with great zest and visual beauty; the landscapes are breathtaking, and the adventure sequences are exciting without being too scary for younger viewers. Thora Birch and Vincent Kartheiser are no-nonsense heroes who seem convincing even at some fairly unlikely moments. As they petted, fed, and wrestled with the bear cub, however, I started hoping for a warning to flash on the screen: "Caution! Kids! Do not try this on your next vacation to Yellowstone!" Trust the bear. But keep the windows rolled up.

## Albino Alligator ★ ★

R, 97 m., 1997

Matt Dillon (Dova), Faye Dunaway (Janet), Gary Sinise (Milo), William Fichtner (Law), Viggo Mortensen (Guy), John Spencer (Jack), Skeet Ulrich (Danny), M. Emmet Walsh (Dino), Joe Mantegna (G. D. Browning). Directed by Kevin Spacey and produced by Brad Krevoy, Steven Stabler, and Brad Jenkel. Screenplay by Christian Forte. Photographed by Mark Plummer.

It's a basic movie situation. Desperate criminals are trapped and surrounded. They have hostages. The hard-boiled cop in charge issues an ultimatum. During a long and exhausting night, the tension builds while the men consider their options. And the hostages try to reason them out of a dangerous decision. In the old days it was always Pat O'Brien as the good Irish cop, a bullhorn to his mouth, shouting out a final ultimatum.

Why did the actor Kevin Spacey choose this formula for *Albino Alligator,* his first film as a director? Maybe because it's fun for the actors, who are required to move through plateaus of emotions. Maybe because by limiting the action mostly to one room, it eliminates distractions and allows for a closer focus. Maybe because he liked the screenplay by Christian Forte—even though it violates that old writer's rule, "Never quote your title in the dialogue."

Spacey does what can be done with the material, but it never achieves takeoff velocity. The heart of the problem, I think, is our suspicion that in real life these situations don't turn into long discussions. The crooks are likely to be too scared, too inarticulate or too confused for the kind of verbal jockeying that occupies most of *Albino Alligator.* The enterprise seems contrived—more like an actor's workshop than a drama.

The story takes place in New Orleans, where we see a group of law enforcers in a stakeout. Three robbers—not the ones the cops are looking for—botch a job at a warehouse and try to make a quick getaway. They have the bad luck to run directly into the police roadblock and a cop is killed (there's a nice shot here of a book of matches; he needed a light at just the wrong time).

In the car are Law (William Fichtner), who is a cold psychopath; Milo (Gary Sinise), who seems more like your high school civics teacher than a criminal; and Dova (Matt Dillon), who is the leader of the gang but not necessarily in control. Two agents are killed when the chase goes wrong, and Milo is injured; the three stumble into an all-night dive poetically named Dino's Last Chance.

Dino is the owner, a phlegmatic old-timer played by M. Emmet Walsh. His bartender is Janet (Faye Dunaway). There are three customers in the bar: a kid playing pool (Skeet Ulrich), a guy in a suit who looks out of place (Viggo Mortensen), and a barfly (John Spencer). They all seem too sober to be drinking at 4 A.M., but if they were like most all-night drinkers, it would take Eugene O'Neill or Charles Bukowski to tell their story.

Dino's is quickly surrounded by cops, led by Browning (Joe Mantegna), who barks the usual orders and issues the usual ultimatums. There's no possible escape; the bar, which is below street level, has no back door and no windows. The criminals are doomed to be caught or killed, unless they come up with a bright idea. They do, sort of.

I will not be giving away plot secrets if I describe at this point the albino alligator connection. According to an anecdote told in the movie, alligators force an albino to go out first in order to flush out the opposition, after which they pounce from ambush. It's ingenious the way Forte's screenplay employs this principle, and interesting the way he develops the characters. Walsh and Dunaway try to reason with the desperadoes; the customers (who are not all exactly who they seem) have a turn; and there's a dynamic within the gang involving Sinise, who begins to think of his Catholic upbringing, Fichtner, who wants to blast everyone away, and Dillon, who tries to keep a level head.

It is all done about as well as it can be done, I suppose. Hostage movies follow such ancient patterns that it's rare to be surprised by one, and this one does have some surprises, none very rewarding. Occasionally the genre will be transformed by brilliant filmmaking, as it was in *Dog Day Afternoon.* Not this time.

## Alien Resurrection ★ ½

R, 109 m., 1997

Sigourney Weaver (Ripley), Winona Ryder (Call), Dominique Pinon (Vriess), Ron Perlman (Johner), Gary Dourdan (Christie), Michael Wincott (Elgyn), Kim Flowers (Hillard), Dan Hedaya (General Perez), Brad Dourif (Gediman). Directed by Jean-Pierre Jeunet and produced by Bill Badalato, Gordon Carroll, David Giler, and Walter Hill. Screenplay by Joss Whedon.

Between *Alien* and *Aliens,* fifty-seven years passed, with Ellen Ripley in suspended animation. Between *Aliens* and *Alien³,* she drifted through space in a lifeboat, before landing on a prison planet. In all three films she did battle with vile alien creatures constructed out of teeth, green sinew, and goo. In *Alien³* she told this life form: "I've known you so long I can't remember a time when you weren't in my life."

I'm telling the aliens the same thing. This is a series whose inspiration has come, gone, and been forgotten. I'm aliened out. The fourth movie depends on a frayed shoestring of a plot, barely enough to give them something to talk about between the action scenes. A "Boo Movie," Pauline Kael called the second one, because it all came down to aliens popping up and going "boo!" and being destroyed.

I found that second film dark and depressing, but skillfully directed by James Cameron *(Terminator II).* I lost interest with the third, when I realized that the aliens could at all times outrun and outleap the humans, so all the chase scenes were contrivances.

Now here is *Alien Resurrection.* Ripley (Sigourney Weaver) is still the heroine, even though 200 years have passed since *Alien³.* She has been cloned out of a drop of her own blood, and is being used as a brood mare: The movie opens with surgeons removing a baby alien from her womb. How the baby got in there is not fully explained, for which we should perhaps be grateful.

The birth takes place on a vast spaceship. The interstellar human government hopes to breed more aliens and use them for—oh, developing vaccines, medicines, a gene pool, stuff like that. The aliens have a remarkable body chemistry. Ripley's genes are all right, too: They allow her reconstituted form to retain all of her old memories, as if cookie dough could remember what a gingerbread man looked like.

Ripley is first on a giant government science ship, then on a tramp freighter run by a vagabond crew. The monsters are at first held inside glass cells, but of course they escape (their blood is a powerful solvent that can eat through the decks of the ship). The movie's a little vague about Ripley: Is she all human, or does she have a little alien mixed in? For a while we wonder which side she's on. She laughs at mankind's hopes of exploiting the creatures: "She's a queen," she says of the new monster. "She'll breed. You'll die."

When the tramp freighter comes into play, we get a fresh crew, including Call (Winona Ryder), who has been flown all the way from Earth to provide appeal for the younger members of the audience. Ryder is a wonderful actress, one of the most gifted of her generation, but wrong for this movie. She lacks the heft and presence to stand alongside Ripley and the grizzled old space dogs played by Ron Perlman, Dominique Pinon, Dan Hedaya, and Brad Dourif. She seems uncertain of her purpose in the movie, her speeches lack conviction, and when her secret is revealed, it raises more questions than it answers. Ryder pales in comparison with Jenette Goldstein, the muscular Marine who was the female sidekick in *Aliens.*

Weaver, on the other hand, is splendid: strong,

weary, resourceful, grim. I would gladly see a fifth *Alien* movie if they created something for her to do, and dialogue beyond the terse sound bites that play well in commercials. Ripley has some good scenes. She plays basketball with a crewman (Perlman) and slams him around. When she bleeds, her blood fizzes interestingly on the floor—as if it's not quite human. She can smell an alien presence. And be smelled: An alien recognizes Ripley as its grandmother and sticks out a tongue to lick her.

These aliens have a lot of stuff in their mouths; not only the tongue and their famous teeth, but another little head on a stalk, with smaller teeth. Still to be determined is whether the littler head has a still tinier head inside of it, and so on. Like the bugs in *Starship Troopers,* these aliens are an example of specialization. They have evolved over the eons into creatures adapted for one purpose only: to star in horror movies.

Mankind wants them for their genes? I can think of a more valuable attribute: They're apparently able to generate biomass out of thin air. The baby born at the beginning of the film weighs maybe five pounds. In a few weeks the ship's cargo includes generous tons of aliens. What do they feed on? How do they fuel their growth and reproduction? It's no good saying they eat the ship's stores, because they thrive even on the second ship—and in previous movies have grown like crazy on desolate prison planets and in abandoned space stations. They're like perpetual motion machines; they don't need input.

The *Alien* movies always have expert production design. *Alien Resurrection* was directed by the French visionary Jean-Pierre Jeunet *(City of Lost Children),* who with his designers has placed it in what looks like a large, empty hangar filled with prefabricated steel warehouse parts. There is not a single shot in the movie to fill one with wonder—nothing like the abandoned planetary station in *Aliens.* Even the standard shots of vast spaceships, moving against a backdrop of stars, are murky here, and perfunctory.

I got a telephone message that *Inside Edition* wanted to ask me about *Alien Resurrection,* and what impact the movie would have on the careers of Weaver and Ryder. Financially, it will help: Weaver remains the only woman who can open an action picture. Artistically, the film will have no impact at all. It's a nine-day wonder, a geek show designed to win a weekend or two at the box office and then fade from memory. Try this test: How often do you think about *Jurassic Park: The Lost World*?

## American Buffalo ★ ★ ½

R, 88 m., 1996

Dustin Hoffman (Teach), Dennis Franz (Don), Sean Nelson (Bobby). Directed by Michael Corrente and produced by Gregory Mosher. Screenplay by David Mamet, based on his play.

Don's antique shop, in *American Buffalo,* has become one of the fundamental spaces of the stage, like Willy Loman's kitchen and Lear's blasted heath and the place, wherever it is, where they wait for Godot. In it, David Mamet created a long day and night in which Don and Teach, and later Bobby, restlessly waited and talked about a job they were going to do, while they uneasily wondered if they should, or could, do it.

The core of *American Buffalo,* and all of Mamet's plays, is in the vernacular of the characters. They have a way of implying just what they're thinking in ways they do not intend. "If I could come up with some of that stuff you were interested in," Teach asks Don, "would you be interested in it?" And "the only way to teach these people is to kill them." And when a gun is introduced into the plot: "God forbid something inevitable occurs."

The shop is a shadowy space filled with objects we cannot imagine much demand for. Don (Dennis Franz) has made it into a sort of warren for himself, and in this film version by Michael Corrente there are alcoves and mezzanines receding into the shadows—caves of tarnished treasure. We gather Don supports himself in ways other than by selling these things. Teach (Dustin Hoffman) hangs out in the store, and the two of them engage in an endless, desultory conversation—talk filled with possibilities, eventualities, potentialities, hypotheses, and folk wisdom. Bobby (Sean Nelson, from *Fresh*), the black kid who works for Don, imperfectly understands the occupation of his employer, but guesses some and wants to know more.

The action in the play involves the possible theft of a coin collection. A man named Fletch may assist them in the crime. Much is made of Fletch: He looms importantly in their regard. When Fletch doesn't turn up as scheduled, various fallback options are explored. "What a day," Don and Teach agree, again and again, as if the day had created them instead of them creating the day.

It is a cliché, but true, that some plays have their real life on the stage. *American Buffalo* is a play like that—or, at least, not a play that finds its life in this movie. I've seen the play more than once, most memorably in London with Al Pacino and J. J. Johnston, and never grown tired of it; the language contains such rich humor just beneath the surface. It's not a comedy (although sometimes we laugh), but an elaborate playwright's joke. Mamet, like one of his characters, invents a labyrinthine, convoluted spiel leading nowhere, and like a magician distracts us with his words while elaborately not producing a rabbit from his hat. The insight, I believe, is that these characters do this every day: Uneasily perched in the darkness of the store, uncomfortable with the light and normality outside, they make plans, and plans, and plans.

On the stage, they are trapped in their space and time. In this film (although the action has been opened up only minimally) they seem less confined. Crucially, they also seem to think their plans are more urgent. Dustin Hoffman somehow seems to be trying too hard, to be making too much of an effort to think his thoughts and speak them. His Teach doesn't seem in on the joke, which is that nothing much is going to happen and Teach sort of knows that.

One doesn't want to see a knowing wink from Teach; it would be wrong for him to tip his hand, to let us see he knows this is dialogue and performance and no payoff. But the wink should be underneath somewhere. At some fundamental level the performance should let us know that Teach has been down this road before—that the road is all there is for Teach. Pacino was able to convey that, but Hoffman has a slight but crucial excess of sincerity.

Dennis Franz, as Don, successfully conveys the notion that he does not much care one way or the other. He exudes a proprietorship over the store and the action: This is his space and he waits here, indefinitely it would seem, while his friends visit him in order to be seen leading their lives. His function is to witness them: Teach exists because Don owns a store and sits in it and provides a foil and an audience. Bobby is not such an important character, but Sean Nelson, who was so powerful as a child actor in *Fresh*, shows here just the right tone: Bobby is not in on the joke, does not know these rituals have been repeated from time immemorial, thinks Don and Teach are substantial beings.

Because the film never really brings to life its inner secrets, it seems leisurely, and toward the end it seems long. It doesn't have the energy or the danger of James Foley's film version of Mamet's *Glengarry Glen Ross*. The language is all there, and it is a joy, but the irony is missing. Or, more precisely, the irony about the irony.

## An American Werewolf in Paris ★

R, 98 m., 1997

Tom Everett Scott (Andy), Julie Delpy (Serafine), Vince Vieluf (Brad), Phil Buckman (Chris), Julie Bowen (Amy), Pierre Cosso (Claude), Thierry Lhermitte (Dr. Pigot), Tom Novembre (Inspector LeDuc). Directed by Anthony Waller and produced by Richard Claus. Screenplay by Tim Burns, Tom Stern, and Waller, based on characters created by John Landis.

Now that *Scream* and *Scream 2* have given us horror film characters who know all the horror clichés, the time has come for a werewolf movie about characters who know they're in a werewolf movie. Not that such an insight would benefit the heroes of *An American Werewolf in Paris*, who are singularly dim. Here are people we don't care about, doing things they don't understand, in a movie without any rules. Triple play.

I was not one of the big fans of John Landis's original 1981 film, *An American Werewolf in London*, but, glancing over my old review, I find such phrases as "spectacular set pieces," "genuinely funny moments," and "sequences that are spellbinding." My review of the Paris werewolves will not require any of those phrases.

The new movie involves three callow Americans on a "daredevil tour" of Europe. Played by Tom Everett Scott (of *That Thing You Do*), Vince Vieluf, and Phil Buckman, they climb the Eiffel Tower by moonlight, only to find a young woman (Julie Delpy) about to leap to her death. They talk, she leaps, and Scott leaps after her, luckily while tethered to a bungee cord. (Hint: Always be sure the other end of a bungee line is tied to something else before tying this end to yourself.)

The girl survives, the lads track her to her home, she has blood on her hands, her friend invites them to a rave club, she's not there, Chris finds her locked in a cell in her basement, the ravers are werewolves, so is she, etc., etc. Please don't accuse me of revealing plot points: In a movie with this title, are you expecting that the girl who leaps from the tower is not a werewolf, her friends are exchange students, and the club is frequented by friendly tourists?

One of the pleasures of a film like this is the ritual explanation of the rules, in which we determine how werewolves are made, how they are killed, and how they spread their wolfiness. Here it doesn't much matter, because the plot has a way of adding new twists (like a serum that makes moonlight unnecessary for a werewolf transformation). By the end of the film, any plot discipline (necessary so that we care about some characters and not the others) has been lost in an orgy of special effects and general mayhem.

But let me single out one line of dialogue. After the three American college students are trying to figure out what happened at the tower, one says, "The kind of girl who jumps off the Eiffel Tower has issues, man." Starting with that line, a complete rewrite could be attempted, in which the characters are self-aware, know the werewolf rules, and know not to make the same mistakes as the characters in *An American Werewolf in London* (not to mention *The Howling, The Howling II: Your Sister Is a Werewolf, Howling III, Howling IV: The Original Nightmare, Howling V: The Rebirth,* and *Howling VI: The Freaks*). I even have a great title for them: *Howler.* ☞

## Amistad ★ ★ ★

R, 232 m., 1997

Morgan Freeman (Theodore Joadson), Anthony Hopkins (John Quincy Adams), Matthew McConaughey (Roger Baldwin), Nigel Hawthorne (Martin Van Buren), Djimon Hounsou (Cinque), David Paymer (Secretary Forsyth), Pete Postlethwaite (Saunders), Stellan Skarsgard (Tappan), Anna Paquin (Queen Isabella), Tomas Milian (Calderon), Austin Pendleton (Professor Gibbs). Directed by Steven Spielberg and produced by Spielberg, Debbie Allen, and Colin Wilson. Screenplay by David Franzoni.

Slavery could, I suppose, be seen largely as a matter of laws and property—at least to those benefiting from it. One of the astonishing facts contained in Steven Spielberg's *Amistad* is that seven of the nine U.S. Supreme Court justices in 1839 were slave-owning southerners. His new film centers on the legal status of Africans who rise up against their captors on the high seas and are brought into a Massachusetts court. Slavery itself is not the issue. Instead, the court must decide whether the defendants were born of slaves (in which case they are guilty of murder) or were illegally brought from Africa (and therefore had a right to defend themselves against kidnapping).

This legal distinction is not made as clear as it could be; the international slave trade had been outlawed by treaties by 1839, but those who were already slaves remained the property of their masters—as did their children. The moral hairsplitting underlying that distinction is truly depraved, but on it depends the defense of Cinque, the leader of the Africans, and his fellow mutineers.

The film opens on the ship *Amistad,* where Cinque (Djimon Hounsou) is able to free himself from shackles and release his fellow prisoners. They rise up against the Spanish crew of the ship, which is taking them from a Havana slave market to another destination in Cuba. The two men who bought them are spared, and promise to guide the ship back to Africa. But they guide it instead into U.S. waters, and the Africans find themselves in an American court.

Luckily, it is a northern court, or they would have little chance at all. They are not at first lucky in their defense team, which is led by Roger Baldwin (Matthew McConaughey), a real estate lawyer who bases his case on property law and only slowly comes to see his clients as human beings. The cause is supported by two Boston abolitionists, a former slave named Joadson (Morgan Freeman) and an immigrant named Tappan (Stellan Skarsgard). And eventually, on appeal, former U.S. president John Quincy Adams (Anthony Hopkins) argues eloquently for the freedom of the men.

*Amistad,* like Spielberg's *Schindler's List,* is not simply an argument against immorality. We do not need movies to convince us of the evil of slavery and the Holocaust. Both films are about the ways good men try to work realistically within an evil system in order to spare a few of its victims. *Schindler's* strategies are ingenious and suspenseful, and lead to a more gripping and powerful film than the legal tactics in *Amistad,* where lawyers in powdered wigs try to determine the origin of men whose language they do not speak.

Entirely apart from the moral issues involved, *Schindler's List* works better as narrative because it is about a risky deception, while *Amistad* is about the search for a truth which, if found, will be small consolation to the millions of existing slaves. As a result, the movie doesn't have the emotional charge of Spielberg's earlier film—or of *The Color Purple,* which moved me to tears.

The moments of greatest emotion in *Amistad* stand outside the main story. They include a horrifying scene where, when food runs low on the ship, the weaker slaves are chained together and thrown over the side to drown so that more food will be left for the rest. And another sequence in which the mechanics of the slave trade are examined, as Africans capture members of enemy tribes and sell them to the slave traders. And a scene where Cinque sees African violets in John Quincy Adams's greenhouse, and is seized with homesickness. And Cinque's memory of his wife left in Africa.

What is most valuable about *Amistad* is the way it provides faces and names for its African characters, who are so often in movies made into faceless victims. The slave called Cinque (his real name is Sengbe Pieh) emerges as a powerful individual, a once-free farmer who has lost his wife and family. We see his wife, and his village, and something of his life; we understand how cruelly he was ripped from his life and ambitions (since it was the policy of slavery to destroy African families, this is especially poignant).

He speaks no English, but learns a little while in prison, and a translator is found who helps him express his dismay at a legal system that may free him but will not affirm the true nature of the crime against him. He learns enough of Western civilization to see its contradictions, as in a scene where he uses an illustrated Bible to explain to a fellow slave how he can identify with Jesus. And there is a touching scene between lawyer and client in which Joadson at last talks to Cinque as a man, and not as a piece in a puzzle. "Give us free!" Cinque cries in a powerful moment in the courtroom, indicating how irrelevant a "not guilty" verdict would be to the real facts of his case.

Djimon Hounsou's performance depends largely on his screen presence, which is formidable. Some of the other performances are disappointing. I was surprised how little importance or screen time was given to the Morgan Freeman character, who in his few scenes indicates the volumes that remain concealed. Matthew McConaughey's character is necessarily unfocused as the defense attorney; he proceeds from moral blindness to a light that surprises no one, and while we are happy for him we are not, under the circumstances, much moved. Nigel Hawthorne plays Martin Van Buren, then the president of the United States, who is revealed as a spineless compromiser who wants only to keep the South off his back; the character is played in the same note as his pathetic old George III, when more shrewd calculation might have been effective.

The heart of the film, really, is in Anthony Hopkins's powerful performance as old John Quincy Adams, who speaks for eleven minutes in defense of the defendants, and holds the courtroom (and the audience) spellbound. It is one of the great movie courtroom speeches. But in praising it, I touch on the film's great weakness: It is too much about the law, and not enough about the victims.

Ever since Spielberg began *Amistad,* the story has been hyped and hailed as a great untold chapter in American history, an event to put beside Nat Turner's uprising. The story of Cinque certainly deserves more attention in textbooks, but it is not an ideal story to make into a film; Nat Turner would have been a better choice for Spielberg. That John Quincy Adams wins his big case is a great achievement for him and a great relief for Cinque and his fellows, but in the sad annals of American slavery it is a rather hollow triumph.

## Anaconda ★ ★ ★ ½

PG-13, 90 m., 1997

Jennifer Lopez (Terri Flores), Ice Cube (Danny Rich), Jon Voight (Paul Sarone), Eric Stoltz (Dr. Steven Cale), Jonathan Hyde (Warren Westridge), Owen Wilson (Gary Dixon), Kari Wuhrer (Denise Kalberg), Vincent Castellanos (Mateo). Directed by Luis Llosa and produced by Verna Harrah, Leonard Rabinowitz, and Carol

Little. Screenplay by Hans Bauer, Jim Cash, and Jack Epps Jr.

"Alone among snakes, anacondas are unique. After eating their prey, they regurgitate in order to eat again."

This information is included in the opening titles of *Anaconda,* and as the words rolled across the screen I heard a chuckle in the theater. It came from me. I sensed with a deep certainty that before the movie was over, I would see an anaconda regurgitate its prey. Human prey, preferably.

*Anaconda* did not disappoint me. It's a slick, scary, funny Creature Feature, beautifully photographed and splendidly acted in a high adventure style. Its snakes are thoroughly satisfying. The most dreaded predator of the Amazon, we learn, the anaconda can grow to forty feet in length, and crushes its prey before engorging it whole (so whole that it eats an entire jaguar, leaving behind only a single poignant eyeball).

These insights into anaconda lore come mostly from a character named Sarone, played by Jon Voight as a slimy river rat with a dangerous gleam in his eye. "This river can kill you in a thousand ways," he intones, and we get the feeling that he can too. The propeller of his boat is broken, and he's rescued by a small expedition that hopes to make a documentary about the People of the Mist—a legendary lost Amazon tribe. "I know them," Sarone says. "They saved my life." And are probably still regretting it.

The leader of the expedition is Terri Flores (Jennifer Lopez, from *Selena*), who will direct the documentary. Ice Cube plays Danny, her cinematographer. Eric Stoltz is Dr. Steven Cale, a scientist. The other members include Jonathan Hyde as their fastidious British narrator, Owen Wilson as the sound man ("ever notice how the jungle makes you horny?"), Vincent Castellanos as the sinister boat pilot, and Kari Wuhrer as a production assistant. If the cast seems large, reflect that some, perhaps many, of these characters are required so that they can be eaten by snakes.

A movie like *Anaconda* can easily be dumb and goofy (see *Piranha*). Much depends on the skill of the filmmakers. Here one of the key players is the cinematographer, Bill Butler, who creates a seductive yet somehow sinister jungle atmosphere. The movie looks great, and the visuals and the convincing sound track and ominous music make the Amazon into a place with presence and personality: It's not a backdrop; it's an enveloping presence.

The acting is also crucial. Director Luis Llosa, whose *Sniper* (1993) was another good thriller set in the jungle, finds the right notes. He gives the members of the expedition plausible backgrounds (Lopez and Ice Cube say they met in the USC film school), and he allows Jon Voight to take some chances with his performance. Voight's river rat is always on the delectable edge of overacting. He sneers, he frowns, he grimaces, he utters ominous pronouncements ("So young—and yet so lethal," he says, as a baby snake sinks its teeth into a fingertip). This is a daring performance: Voight, a serious actor, isn't afraid to pull out the stops as a melodramatic villain, and his final scene, which he plays with a wink, will be remembered wherever great movie exits are treasured.

Now, as for the snakes. Several kinds of snakes are used in the movie: animated, animatronic and, for all I know, real. They are mostly convincing. There are a few moments when we know, if we bother to think about it, that special effects are being used (especially in a scene where a flaming snake attacks). But there are other moments that earn a gasp from the audience, including one where a giant snake captures its falling prey in midair. There are utterly convincing close-ups of an anaconda's head, its bright eyes glistening, its mouth gaping open to reveal fangs, its skin glistening with a terrible beauty. (Those shots are matched by a point-of-view shot from inside the snake, and by another in which we see the snake's belly skin stretched tautly over the body and face of one of its victims.)

The screenplay has nice authentic touches. The Eric Stoltz character lectures on the dangers of going into the water. He's less afraid of the snakes than of "the little catfish that swims up through your urethra, finds a nice warm spot, and spreads its thorny little spines." A scuba diver finds a poisonous wasp in his mouthpiece. An emergency tracheotomy is performed with a pocket knife. There's a mysterious wall built across the river, which they blow up with dynamite which Voight happens to have with him ("always good to be prepared"). And a protest that blowing up the wall will "upset the ecological balance of the river." Yeah, like the wall grew there.

*Anaconda* is an example of one of the hardest kinds of films to make well: a superior mass-audience entertainment. It has the effects and the thrills, but it also has big laughs, quirky dialogue, and a gruesome imagination. You've got to like a film where a lustful couple sneaks out into the dangerous jungle at night and suddenly the guy whispers, "Wait—did you hear that? Silence!"

## Anastasia ★ ★ ★ ½

G, 94 m., 1997

With the speaking voices of: Meg Ryan (Anastasia), John Cusack (Dimitri), Kelsey Grammer (Vladimir), Christopher Lloyd (Rasputin), Hank Azaria (Bartok), Bernadette Peters (Sophie), Kirsten Dunst (Young Anastasia), Angela Lansbury (Dowager Empress Marie), and the singing voices of: Liz Callaway (Anastasia), Lacey Chabert (Young Anastasia), Jim Cummings (Rasputin), Jonathan Dokuchitz (Dimitri). An animated film directed and produced by Don Bluth and Gary Goldman. Screenplay by Susan Gauthier, Bruce Graham, Bob Tzudiker, and Noni White. Songs by Lynn Ahrens and Stephen Flaherty; score by David Newman.

The legend of Anastasia would seem like unlikely inspiration for an animated musical, but *Anastasia* picks and chooses cleverly, skipping blithely past the entire Russian Revolution but lingering on mad monks, green goblins, storms at sea, train wrecks, and youthful romance. The result is entertaining and sometimes exciting—a promising launch for Fox's new animation studio, which has declared war on Disney.

The movie's based loosely on the same speculative story as the 1956 feature film starring Ingrid Bergman; it assumes that when Russia's ruling Romanoff family was murdered in the upheaval of revolution, one child escaped the carnage and survived to make a valid claim for the throne. This was Anastasia (voice by Meg Ryan), beloved granddaughter of the Dowager Empress Marie (Angela Lansbury), who herself escaped to Paris and now wearily rejects one impostor after another.

Young Anastasia is seen wrapped in the warm bosom of her family; then disaster strikes, and she spends years in a cruel orphanage, losing all memory of her earlier days. Then, as a lithe and spirited teenager, she falls into the clutches of two con men named Dimitri (John Cusack) and Vladimir (Kelsey Grammer). They both worked in the royal court and have insider knowledge; their scheme is to tutor an impostor until she can fool the Dowager Empress. The irony, which the movie makes much of, is that this impostor is, in fact, the real thing.

*Anastasia* tells this story within what has become the almost rigid formula of the modern animated feature: The heroine and the hero both have sidekicks, the villain commands nasty little minions, and romance blooms but doesn't get too soppy. Much depends on how colorful the villain is, and the mad monk Rasputin (Christopher Lloyd) is one of the best cartoon villains in a long time. The real Rasputin became infamous for taking so long to die—he was almost unkillable—and this movie version likewise lingers between life and death. His spirit burns on, but his body parts have a disconcerting habit of falling off. His little sidekick Bartok, an albino bat voiced by Hank Azaria, tirelessly screws missing limbs back into place.

Anastasia has a friend, too: her little dog Pooka, who faithfully tags along. Indeed, every important character is assigned a sidekick; Dimitri has Vladimir, and the Dowager Empress has her faithful lady-in-waiting, Sophie (Bernadette Peters). By the movie's end Dimitri wins Anastasia, Vladimir wins Sophie, and I guess we can be relieved that the filmmakers spared us the Bartok-Pooka nuptials.

The film was produced and directed by former Disney artists Don Bluth and Gary Goldman, whose credits include *The Land Before Time* and *An American Tail*. Here they consciously include the three key ingredients in the big Disney hits: action, romance, and music. Only the songs disappoint (why didn't they do the obvious and license the title song from the 1956 film?).

There are three big action sequences: a storm at sea, as Anastasia sleepwalks perilously close to the briny deep; a runaway locomotive and a wreck, as Rasputin's little green goblins sabotage the train carrying Anastasia to Paris; and a final showdown between Rasputin and the forces of good. The action here is alive and energetic, and the train sequence is genuinely thrilling.

What won me over most of all, however, was

the quality of the story: It's clearly set up, so that even younger viewers can understand Anastasia's fate and her hopes. ("I'm not exactly grand duchess material here," she says: "A skinny little nobody with no past and no future.") It gets a couple of neat twists out of the idea of making Anastasia a fraud who isn't a fraud. And the Dowager Empress, as played by Lansbury, creates real pathos with her weariness: How many more frauds must she endure?

Animation is the road less traveled for the movies. Although it offers total freedom over the inconveniences of space, time, and gravity, it's so tricky and difficult that animated features have always been rare—and Disney has always known how to make them best. With *Anastasia*, there's another team on the field.

## Angel Baby ★ ★ ★

NO MPAA RATING, 105 m., 1997

John Lynch (Harry), Jacqueline McKenzie (Kate), Colin Friels (Morris), Deborra-Lee Furness (Louise), Daniel Daperis (Sam), Dave Argue (Dave), Geoff Brooks (Rowan), Humphry Bower (Frank). Directed by Michael Rymer and produced by Jonathan Shteinman and Timothy White. Screenplay by Rymer.

Watching *Shine*, I found myself wondering about the dynamics of the marriage between David and Gillian Helfgott. Could it have been so simple as a loving woman healing a troubled man?

At the same 1996 Sundance Film Festival that introduced *Shine* to North America, there was another Australian film, one that arrived with seven Australian Academy Awards, including best picture, actor, actress, and director. It also dealt with romance and mental illness. Yet somehow it didn't cause the same stir, perhaps because it was the very opposite of a feel-good movie.

Michael Rymer's *Angel Baby* tells the story of Harry and Kate, who meet at an outpatient clinic for mental patients, who fall in love, who seem for a time to be blessed with one another, and who then make the mistake of growing overconfident and discontinuing their medication.

The results are inevitable, but this is not the film of unredeemed dreariness that the story line would suggest; I have noticed in any number of Australian films a pull toward human comedy, an appreciation for the quirks and eccentric fillips of characters who may be doomed but rage cheerfully against the dying of the light. Even in their final downward spiral, Kate (Jacqueline McKenzie) and Harry (John Lynch) see hopeful omens.

But then Kate's whole life is controlled by omens, which she receives from her guardian angel, named Astral. His method of communication is the Australian version of *Wheel of Fortune*. As the letters are turned over and the underlying phrases are revealed, Kate takes careful notes; she learns she's pregnant, for example, when the Australian version of Vanna White turns over letters spelling out "Great Expectations." And she believes it is Astral who is resident in her womb.

The movie avoids many of the clichés often found in pictures about mental illness. The professionals in the film, for example, are sensitive and competent. And in the film's early scenes, it looks as if Harry and Kate might indeed be successful in their quest for love.

Harry is a nice man, who helps his young nephew banish monsters from the bedroom (he draws a magic chalk circle around the kid's bed), and when he's around Kate his face almost always reflects tender concern. She is more out of control; after a careless in-line skater in a mall store cuts her, she grows hysterical at her loss of blood and even licks some of it up off the floor. When they decide to move in together, the choice seems promising, but then they take the fateful decision to stop their medication.

John Lynch is an actor who is ready for wider recognition (you may remember him as a teenager in *Cal*, or as the hunger striker Bobby Sands in *Some Mother's Son*). In *Angel Baby* he has in some ways the more difficult role; Jacqueline McKenzie's Kate is on her own wavelength, but he has to gauge her condition, react to it, and somehow monitor his own health as well. And there is an intensity that goes along with loving anyone who is disturbed—an uncertainty during the happy moments that makes them seem poignant and precious. That's what the movie captures, and that's the tone that prevails even during the harrowing scenes of suffering.

Those who shed tears during *Shine* are likely to be dry-eyed during *Angel Baby*. The movie's only release is a touching fantasy in the last shot. No marriage is simple, and no love story is uncomplicated. Watching this film, I realized that while I admired *Shine* and was moved by it, *Angel Baby* comes closer to dealing honestly with a fraught relationship. As Tolstoy might have written if he had lived longer and seen more movies: All happy endings are the same, but every unhappy ending is unhappy in its own way.

## Angels and Insects ★ ★ ★ ½

NO MPAA RATING, 117 m., 1996

Mark Rylance (William Adamson), Kristin Scott Thomas (Matty Crompton), Patsy Kensit (Eugenia Alabaster), Jeremy Kemp (Sir Harald Alabaster), Douglas Henshall (Edgar Alabaster), Saskia Wickham (Rowena Alabaster), Chris Larkin (Robin Swinnerton), Annette Badland (Lady Alabaster). Directed by Philip Haas and produced by Joyce Herlihy and Belinda Haas. Screenplay by Belinda and Philip Haas.

There are no angels in *Angels and Insects*, only insects, and a strange mid-Victorian family named the Alabasters, who seem to model themselves on insect behavior. The mother is a plump, pale creature, swaddled in yards of white cloth, who collapses on the nearest chair to be fed and coddled by her family. Like a queen bee, she is fecund, pumping out new Alabasters between headaches.

Into this household comes a dour Scots outsider named William Adamson (Mark Rylance). He has returned from ten years in the Amazon, collecting rare specimens, which have all been lost in a shipwreck—all but one precious butterfly, which he presents to Sir Harald Alabaster (Jeremy Kemp), who is obsessed with insects. It is shortly after Darwin's first publications, and Sir Harald is fascinated by the process of natural selection.

So is the film, which is based on a short novel named *Morpho Eugenia*, by A. S. Byatt, and which uses its human characters to play out the ruthless strategies and laws of the insect kingdom. William Adamson is invited to stay as a guest at the Alabasters' country house and organize Sir Harald's insect collection. We cannot help notice that the Alabaster women themselves seem part of an exotic collection; their dresses are made of bright reds and shocking blues, or bold yellows and blacks. In their elaborate hairdos and on their hats they wear flowers, berries, fruits, birds, and even eggs.

The most alluring of the women is the blond, ripe Eugenia Alabaster (Patsy Kensit), with masses of pre-Raphaelite hair. In an early scene she runs sobbing from a ball. Her supercilious brother, Edgar Alabaster (Douglas Henshall), accuses Adamson of having insulted her, but in fact Eugenia is in tears because her fiancé has recently killed himself. Slowly, cautiously, like a potential victim testing a possible web, Adamson positions himself closer to Eugenia, and eventually asks for her hand in marriage. Amazingly, it is accepted—even though he is a penniless man of ordinary family, and she is rich and high-born.

All of this time, a drab little ant has been busily working among the gaudy birds and bees. She is Matty Crompton (Kristin Scott Thomas), a poor young woman who is tutor to the family. She is attracted to Adamson, but he scarcely notices her (she tells him angrily, "You do not know if I am thirty or fifty"). He does notice her superb drawings from nature, however, and her studies of an ant colony.

More of the devious and shocking plot I will not reveal. The story works like the trap of some exotic insect, which decorates the entrances with sweet nectars and soft fragrances, and then prepares an acid bath inside. Notice the countless touches that show the harsh pecking order in mid-nineteenth-century Britain: the servants who turn to face the wall when a master or mistress passes; the cocky arrogance of Edgar, the brother, who feels birth has given him the right to insult his social inferiors; the repressed anger of old Sir Harald, whose insect collection replaces a great many other things he would love to pin wriggling to a corkboard.

The movie has been directed by Philip Haas, and adapted by Haas and his wife, Belinda. They are not shy about using the rich verbal material of their source, A. S. Byatt; butterflies in a conservatory are like "colored air." This is the first film I can remember in which anyone is attacked by moths; Adamson expresses himself in cautious evasions and toadying compliments, like an intellectual Uriah Heep; and when the plot's trap finally springs and a secret is discovered, the movie makes a point of not explaining exactly how that was accomplished. The closest it comes is when Miss Crompton tells Adamson, "There are people in houses who know everything, yet remain invisible."

*Angels and Insects* works best if you're familiar with its world, the country houses of the

British upper classes in the mid-nineteenth century. That world, Henry James has said, was for its fortunate inhabitants the most pleasant that human civilization has produced. Ah, but it had its secrets. *Angels and Insects* is like the dark underside of a Merchant-Ivory film; in one scene, we visit a sunny, pastoral clearing in the woods and lift up a rock to see the plump, slimy little slugs and larvae beneath, dining on each other.

## Anna Karenina ★ ½

PG-13, 108 m., 1997

Sophie Marceau (Anna Karenina), Sean Bean (Count Vronshy), Alfred Molina (Constantin Levin), Mia Kirshner ("Kitty" Scherbatshy), James Fox (Alexi Karenin), Danny Huston (Stiva), Saskia Wickham (Dolly), Fiona Shaw (Lydia Ivanova). Directed by Bernard Rose and produced by Bruce Davey. Screenplay by Rose, based on the novel by Leo Tolstoy.

It's not the story but the style and the ideas that make Tolstoy's *Anna Karenina* a great novel and not a soap opera. There's no shortage of stories about bored rich women who leave their older husbands and take up with playboys. This new screen version of the novel makes that clear by focusing on the story, which without Tolstoy's wisdom is a grim and melodramatic affair. Here is a woman of intoxicating beauty and deep passion, and she becomes so morose and tiresome that by the end we'd just as soon she throw herself under a train, and are not much cheered when she obliges.

The film has been shot on location in Russia; we see St. Petersburg exteriors, country estates, and opulent czarist palaces whose corridors recede to infinity. It all looks wonderful, but the characters, with one exception, are clunks who seem awed to be in the screen adaptation of a Russian classic. The exception is Alexi Karenin, Anna's husband, who is played by James Fox with such a weary bitterness that I found myself caring for him even when he was being cruel to poor Anna.

The story: Anna (Sophie Marceau) and her husband live on a country estate, where their marriage is a dry affair. She goes to the city to counsel her rakish brother, Stiva (Danny Huston), who is treating his wife badly. She meets a slickster named Count Vronsky (Sean Bean), who has a mistress named Kitty (Mia Kirshner) but drops her the moment he sees Anna. He dances with her, she is intoxicated by his boldness, she leaves by train, and he stops the train in the middle of the night to say he must have her, etc. It is not a good sign that while he declares his love we are more concerned about how his horses could have possibly overtaken the train.

Back in the country, Vronsky pursues his idea and Anna succumbs, after a tiny little struggle. Karenin observes what is happening, especially during a steeplechase when Vronsky's horse falls and Anna shrieks with concern that is unseemly in another man's wife. Soon Anna is pregnant by Vronsky, and Karenin, after a lapse (he tries to force himself on her), offers her a deal: If she stays with him and behaves herself, she can keep the child. Otherwise, she gets Vronsky but not the child.

As in all Victorian novels, this crisis leads to a sickbed scene, declarations of redemption and forgiveness, etc., while in the city a parallel romance is developing between the jilted Kitty and the kind but uncharismatic Levin (Alfred Molina). In the novel, Levin stands for Tolstoy and also for the decency the other characters lack.

The challenge of any adapter of *Anna Karenina* is to make Anna sympathetic despite her misbehavior. Sometimes that is done with casting (how could we deny Garbo anything?), sometimes with writing. In this film, it is not done. I never felt sympathy for her, perhaps because Sophie Marceau (from *Braveheart*) makes her such a narcissistic sponge, while Fox makes her husband tortured but understandable. Toward the end, as Anna and Vronsky are shunned by society and live in isolation, she even gets on his nerves, especially after she becomes addicted to laudanum.

There is much more to Tolstoy's story. But not in this bloodless and shallow adaptation. Bernard Rose is a director of talent (his *Paper House* is a visionary film, and his *Immortal Beloved* was a biopic that brought great passion to the story of Beethoven). Here, shooting on fabulous locations, he seems to have lost track of his characters. The movie is like a storyboard for *Anna Karenina,* with the life and subtlety still to be added.

## Anne Frank Remembered ★ ★ ★ ½

PG, 122 m., 1996

Featuring Miep Gies, Hanneli Goslar, and Peter Pfeffer. Narrated by Kenneth Branagh. Diary excerpts read by Glenn Close. A documentary film directed and produced by Jon Blair. Screenplay by Blair.

I would have assumed that the people who helped Anne Frank and her family hide in Amsterdam during the Nazi terror were all long dead—either killed by the Gestapo or claimed by the passage of time. One of the many discoveries in *Anne Frank Remembered* is that Miep Gies, who was Otto Frank's secretary and who supplied the Franks with food and support, was still alive when the film was made, and remembered clearly both the two years of hiding and the ultimate tragedy of the Frank family.

That the world also remembers the Frank family's attempts to save themselves from the Nazis is due, of course, to the journal kept by their daughter, Anne. *The Diary of a Young Girl* has sold 25 million copies, has been translated into many languages, has inspired a play and a movie, and remains as a beacon of memory for a young girl who wrote that she did not want to be forgotten.

*Anne Frank Remembered* assembles rare documentary footage involving the Frank family—including a 1980 interview with Otto, the only family member who survived the death camps. It also has moving interviews with Miep Gies and others. We meet Hanneli Goslar, the last survivor to see Anne Frank alive, and we get a glimpse, through her eyes, of Anne's last days in the Bergen-Belsen concentration camp before she and her sister died of typhus. We also meet Peter Pfeffer, the son of Fritz Pfeffer, one of the others who shared the Franks' hiding place. And we see a meeting—the first in all those years, between Mrs. Gies and the son of the man she tried to save.

These people are all living witnesses to the Holocaust, and also to the remarkable spirit of Anne Frank, who was not a perfect little girl but in many ways a typical one, with crushes on movie stars, flashes of temper, and a completely human desire to publish her diary one day and become famous. In the film's most extraordinary discovery, we see the only existing film footage of Anne Frank, taken one day in 1941 before the Franks went into hiding. There is a wedding party in the street below, and from her window on the third floor, a young girl looks out, smiles, and then turns away. Anne Frank.

*Anne Frank Remembered* has been written and directed by Jon Blair, the same man who made the documentary about Oskar Schindler that helped inspire Steven Spielberg's film. He opens the film by saying he does not want to tell "only" a Holocaust story, and quotes Otto Frank, who said his daughter's diary was not specific to the Jewish experience of the Holocaust, but was a universal message of courage in the face of tyranny. According to the *New York Times,* a study guide prepared by the Anne Frank Center USA for a new translation of the diary makes a point of listing other victims of Hitler's death camps, including his political opponents, resistance fighters, Gypsies, homosexuals, and Jehovah's Witnesses.

But of all of those millions, the one face remembered most clearly by posterity is that of Anne Frank. Her photographs have made her face an instantly recognized image, and her diary, which records an everyday life made extraordinary by its circumstances, fixes a moment in time.

In the film, which is narrated by Kenneth Branagh, we hear Anne Frank's diary entries read by Glenn Close. In the entry quoted at the end of the film, she wrote, "In spite of everything, I still believe that people are really good at heart." One would like to believe she died still believing that, but Hanneli Goslar's memory of Anne in the last days of her life, freezing, starving, weeping, makes that unlikely. All men are not good at heart, but many can be, and if the case were otherwise, life would not be worth the effort. Miep Gies, so ordinary, so quiet-spoken, in her eighties when she was interviewed, risked her life to shelter the Franks, and she must have been one of those Anne was thinking of.

## Antonia's Line ★ ★ ★ ★

NO MPAA RATING, 105 m., 1996

Willeke van Ammelrooy (Antonia), Els Dottermans (Danielle), Jan Decleir (Sebastian), Mil Seghers (Crooked Finger), Marina de Graaf (DeeDee), Jan Steen (Loony Lips), Veerle Van Overloop (Therese), Elsie de Brauw (Lara).

Directed by Marleen Gorris and produced by Hans de Weers. Screenplay by Gorris.

*Antonia's Line* finds its colors in many cultures, and stirs them in the same jolly pot. They should come out muddy brown, but the rainbow endures. The movie incorporates the magic realism of Latin America, dour European philosophies of death, the everyday realities of rural life, a cheerful feminism, a lot of easygoing sex, and a gallery of unforgettable characters. By the time the film is over, you feel you could walk down its village streets and greet everyone by name.

The movie is about a matriarchy founded by a woman named Antonia (Willeke van Ammelrooy), who after World War II returns to her Dutch village. She and her daughter have come back to bury her old mother. It is not an ordinary funeral; the mother sits up in her coffin to sing *My Blue Heaven,* and a statue of Jesus smiles. Later, in the churchyard, a stone angel uses its wing to smite a priest who refused the last rites to a man who sheltered Jews from the Nazis.

Antonia greets her old friends, among them Russian Olga (who runs the café and is an undertaker and midwife), Crooked Finger (who lives in a room with his books and bitterly insists on the futility of life), and Mad Madonna (who utters wild goat cries at the moon because, as a Catholic, she cannot marry her Protestant lover).

There is also Farmer Bas, who comes courting one day with his five sons, and makes a proposal of marriage centering largely on the boys' need for a mother. Antonia finds this underwhelming, but invites him to come over from time to time to do chores, for which she will pay him with hot breakfasts and cups of tea. "I can get those at home," he observes, but he comes anyway, and eventually Antonia tells him, "You can't have my hand, but you can have the rest." They agree that once a week is enough. Antonia doesn't want "all that confusion" in her house, or his, and so they build a little cottage for their meetings.

And so it goes. In fact, the narrator of *Antonia's Line,* Antonia's great-granddaughter, is very fond of reminding us that so it goes; the movie is punctuated with moments where we are assured that season followed season, and crops were planted and harvested, and life went on, and nothing much changed. e. e. cummings's poem "anyone lived in a pretty how town" comes to mind, and has the same sad, romantic, elegiac, pastoral tone.

Generation follows generation. Antonia's daughter, who wants a child but not a husband, auditions candidates for fatherhood. Local matches are made: Loony Lips and DeeDee, who are both retarded, find happiness together. So does the village priest, who one day flings his cassock in the air, shouts, "I'm free!" settles down, and produces a dozen or so children. There are dark days, two of them involving rape, but the women take direct measures: One miscreant is punctured by a pitchfork, and another receives Antonia's curse.

What we remember most of all is the way Antonia's extended family grows. Children and grandchildren, in-laws and outlaws, neighbors, friends, and drifters all come to sit at her long, long dinner table, and all learn the same simple rule, which is to look for the good in others—and to not criticize those who have found a way to be happy without seriously bothering anybody.

One of the most poignant strands in the story involves Crooked Finger (Mil Seghers), who tutors Antonia's brilliant granddaughter Therese, and who is named, I suppose, after the finger that's always holding a place in a book. His room is a shrine to philosophers, and he believes that life is without meaning, that there is no existence after death, that hope is wasted, that God is dead.

Antonia and the others listen to Crooked Finger but do not subscribe to his gloom. They are not religious in a conventional sense, but they're regular churchgoers, because the church provides a weekly gathering of the community—a spiritual version of their communal dinners.

By the end of the film, we have traveled through fifty years of modern life, through trends and controversies, fads, and fashions (the cars in the village are newer every time we see one). These fancies are not as important as the solid, life-affirming values of Antonia, who is embodied by Willeke van Ammelrooy in a remarkable performance. She ages from her thirties to her eighties, always convincingly, and is a substantial, robust, open-faced woman with a warm smile: In Hollywood, she would be considered fat, but we see she is, quite simply, healthy.

The experience of the film lulls us into a strange and wonderful mood: We are told these stories sometimes as inexplicable as a miracle, sometimes as earthy as a barnyard. Beneath them is a philosophy insisting on itself. The filmmaker, Marleen Gorris, believes women have innate understanding and common sense, and that, left to run things, they will right wrongs and encourage sanity. I hope she is right. Even if she is too optimistic, I am glad her movie made me feel hopeful and cheerful. In one of the opening scenes of the film, as Antonia and her daughter walk through the town, a sign on a wall says WELCOME TO OUR LIBERATORS! It is intended for the American troops. But it could, as it turns out, also apply to them.

*Note: The movie won the 1996 Academy Award as best foreign-language film.*

## The Apostle ★ ★ ★ ★

PG-13, 133 m., 1998

Robert Duvall (The Apostle E.F.), Farrah Fawcett (Jessie Dewey), Miranda Richardson (Toosie), Todd Allen (Horace), John Beasley (Brother Blackwell), June Carter Cash (Mrs. Dewey Sr.), Walter Goggins (Sam), Billy Joe Shaver (Joe), Billy Bob Thornton (Troublemaker). Directed by Robert Duvall and produced by Rob Carliner. Screenplay by Duvall.

There's a scene early in *The Apostle* where Robert Duvall, as a Pentecostal preacher from Texas, is having a talk with God, who has to do all of the listening. In an upstairs room at his mother's house, he rants and raves at the almighty, asking for a way to see reason in calamity: His cheating wife is stealing his church from him.

So far, the scene could be in a more conventional film. But then the phone rings, and it's a neighbor, complaining to his mother that someone is "carrying on like a wild man." The call establishes that the preacher lives in a real world, with real neighbors, and not on a sound stage where his life is lived in a self-contained drama. His mother tells the neighbor that her son has talked to God ever since he was a boy and she's not going to stop him now.

*The Apostle* sees its characters in an unusually perceptive light; they have the complexity and spontaneity of people in a documentary. Duvall, who not only plays the preacher but also wrote and directed the film, has seen this preacher—named Eulis "Sonny" Dewey—with great attention and sympathy.

Sonny is different from most movie preachers. He's not a fraud, for one thing; Hollywood tilts toward the Elmer Gantry stereotype. Sonny has a one-on-one relationship with God, takes his work seriously, and in the opening scene of the movie pauses at an auto accident to ask one of the victims to accept Jesus Christ, "who you're going to soon meet." He is flawed, with a quick temper, but he's a good man, and the film is about his struggle back to redemption after his anger explodes.

As the film opens, Sonny is spending a lot of time on the road at revivals (we see him at one of them, made convincing because Duvall cast all the extras from real congregations). His wife (Farrah Fawcett) has taken up with the youth minister, and one night, sitting in a motel room, Sonny figures that out, drives home through the darkness, finds her absent from her bed, and throws a baseball through the minister's bedroom window.

His wife wants out of the marriage. And through legal but shady maneuverings, she also deprives him of his church and his job. Sonny gets drunk, wades into a Little League game being coached by the youth minister, and bangs him on the head with a baseball bat. Then he flees town (there is an overhead shot of his car circling aimlessly around a rural intersection; he has no idea where to go). Eventually he ends up in a hamlet in the Louisiana bayou, where he spends his first night in a pup tent supplied by a man who wants to help him but isn't sure he trusts him.

Sonny changes his name to "The Apostle E.F.," and sets about rebuilding a small rural church given him by a retired black minister. His mostly black congregation is small at first, but grows as the result of broadcasts on the local forty-watt station. We see in countless little ways that Sonny is serious: He wants this church to work, he wants to save souls, he wants redemption. Like the documentary *Say Amen, Somebody,* the film spends enough time at the church services, listening to the music and the preaching, that we get into the spirit; we understand his feelings.

*The Apostle* became something of a legend in independent film circles, because Duvall was so long in getting it made. The major studios turned him down (of course; it's about something, which scares them). So did old associates who had always promised help, but didn't return his calls on this project. As he waited, Duvall must have rewritten the script many times, because it is astonishingly subtle. There isn't a canned and prefab story arc, with predictable stops along the way. Instead, the movie feels as alive as if it's a documentary of things happening right now.

Consider a sequence where the Apostle E.F., who is a man after all, asks the receptionist at the local radio station out on a date. How will he approach her? How does she see him? He wants to find a way to make his desires clear, without offending her. She knows this. As played by Duvall and Miranda Richardson, the sequence is a brilliant observation of social and sexual strategies.

Many of his scenes develop naturally, instead of along the lines of obligatory clichés. A confrontation with his wife, for example, doesn't end as we think it might. And a face-down with a redneck racist (Billy Bob Thornton) develops along completely unexpected lines. The Apostle E.F. is not easy to read; Duvall's screenplay does what great screenwriting is supposed to do and surprises us with additional observations and revelations in every scene.

Perhaps it's not unexpected that Duvall had to write, direct, and star in this film, and round up the financing himself. There aren't that many people in the film industry gifted enough to make such a film, and fewer still with the courage to deal honestly with a subject both spiritual and complex. (Simpleminded spirituality is no problem; consider the market for angels right now.) *The Apostle* is like a lesson in how movies can escape from convention and penetrate into the hearts of rare characters.

## Armageddon ★

PG-13, 150 m., 1998

Bruce Willis (Harry S. Stamper), Billy Bob Thornton (Dan Truman), Ben Affleck (A. J. Frost), Liv Tyler (Grace Stamper), Keith David (General Kimsey), Chris Ellis (Walter Clark), Jason Isaacs (Ronald Quincy), Will Patton ("Chick" Chapple). Directed by Michael Bay and produced by Jerry Bruckheimer, Gale Anne Hurd, and Michael Bay. Screenplay by Jonathan Hensleigh and J. J. Abrams.

Here it is at last, the first 150-minute trailer. *Armageddon* is cut together like its own highlights. Take almost any thirty seconds at random and you'd have a TV ad. The movie is an assault on the eyes, the ears, the brain, common sense, and the human desire to be entertained. No matter what they're charging to get in, it's worth more to get out.

The plot covers many of the same bases as the recent *Deep Impact,* which, compared to *Armageddon,* belongs on the AFI list. The movie tells a similar story at fast-forward speed, with Bruce Willis as an oil driller who is recruited to lead two teams on an emergency shuttle mission to an asteroid "the size of Texas," which is about to crash into Earth and obliterate all life—"even viruses!" Their job: Drill an 800-foot hole and stuff a bomb into it to blow up the asteroid before it kills us.

Okay, say you do succeed in blowing up an asteroid the size of Texas. What if a piece the size of Dallas is left? Wouldn't that be big enough to destroy life on Earth? What about a piece the size of Austin? Let's face it: Even an object the size of that big Wal-Mart outside Abilene would pretty much clean us out, if you count the parking lot.

Texas is a big state, but as a celestial object it wouldn't be able to generate much gravity. Yet when the astronauts get to the asteroid, they walk around on it as if the gravity is the same as on Earth. There's no sensation of weightlessness—until it's needed, that is, and then a lunar buggy flies across a jagged canyon, Evel Knievel–style.

The movie begins with Charlton Heston telling us about the asteroid that wiped out the dinosaurs. Then we get the masterful title card, "65 Million Years Later." The next scenes show an amateur astronomer spotting the object. We see top-level meetings at the Pentagon and in the White House. We meet Billy Bob Thornton, head of Mission Control in Houston, which apparently functions like a sports bar with a big screen for the fans, but no booze. Then we see ordinary people whose lives will be Changed Forever by the events to come. This stuff is all off the shelf—there's hardly an original idea in the movie.

*Armageddon* reportedly used the services of nine writers. Why did it need any? The dialogue is either shouted one-liners or romantic drivel. "It's gonna blow!" is used so many times, I wonder if every single writer used it once, and then sat back from his word processor with a contented smile on his face, another day's work done.

Disaster movies always have little vignettes of everyday life. The dumbest in *Armageddon* involves two Japanese tourists in a New York taxi. After meteors turn an entire street into a flaming wasteland, the woman complains, "I want to go shopping!" I hope in Japan that line is redubbed as "Nothing can save us but Gamera!"

Meanwhile, we wade through a romantic subplot involving Liv Tyler and Ben Affleck. Liv is Bruce Willis's daughter. Ben is Willis's best driller (now, now). Bruce finds Liv in Ben's bunk on an oil platform and chases Ben all over the rig, trying to shoot him. (You would think the crew would be preoccupied by the semidestruction of Manhattan, but it's never mentioned after it happens.) Helicopters arrive to take Willis to the mainland, so he can head up the mission to save mankind, etc., and he insists on using only crews from his own rig—especially Affleck, who is "like a son."

That means Liv and Ben have a heart-rending parting scene. What is it about cinematographers and Liv Tyler? She is a beautiful young woman, but she's always being photographed while flat on her back, with her brassiere riding up around her chin and lots of wrinkles in her neck from trying to see what some guy is doing. (In this case, Affleck is tickling her navel with animal crackers.) Tyler is obviously a beneficiary of Take Our Daughters to Work Day. She's not only on the oil rig, but she attends training sessions with her dad and her boyfriend, hangs out in Mission Control, and walks onto landing strips right next to guys wearing foil suits.

Characters in this movie actually say: "I wanted to say—that I'm sorry," "We're not leaving them behind!" "Guys—the clock is ticking!" and "This has turned into a surrealistic nightmare!" Steve Buscemi, a crew member who is diagnosed with "space dementia," looks at the asteroid's surface and adds, "This place is like Dr. Seuss's worst nightmare." Quick—which Seuss book is he thinking of?

There are several Red Digital Readout scenes, in which bombs tick down to zero. Do bomb designers do that for the convenience of interested onlookers who happen to be standing next to a bomb? There's even a retread of the classic scene where they're trying to disconnect the timer, and they have to decide whether to cut the red wire or the blue wire. The movie has forgotten that *this is not a terrorist bomb,* but a standard-issue U.S. military bomb, being defused by a military guy who is on board specifically because he knows about this bomb. A guy like that, the *first* thing he should know is, red, or blue?

*Armageddon* is loud, ugly, and fragmented. Action sequences are cut together at bewildering speed out of hundreds of short edits, so that we can't see for sure what's happening, or how, or why. Important special effects shots (like the asteroid) have a murkiness of detail, and the movie cuts away before we get a good look. The few "dramatic" scenes consist of the sonorous recitation of ancient clichés ("You're already heroes!"). Only near the end, when every second counts, does the movie slow down: Life on Earth is about to end, but the hero delays saving the planet in order to recite cornball farewell platitudes.

Staggering into the silence of the theater lobby after the ordeal was over, I found a big poster that was fresh off the presses with the quotes of junket blurbsters. "It will obliterate your senses!" reports David Gillin, who obviously writes autobiographically. "It will suck the air right out of your lungs!" vows Diane Kaminsky. If it does, consider it a mercy killing.

## The Arrival ★ ★ ★ ½

PG-13, 109 m., 1996

Charlie Sheen (Zane Zaminski), Ron Silver (Gordian), Lindsay Crouse (Ilana Green), Teri Polo (Char), Tony T. Johnson (Kiki). Directed by David Twohy and produced by Thomas G. Smith and Jim Steele. Screenplay by Twohy.

The planet, we are informed, is warming. The ice caps are melting. Climates are changing. Scientists blame factory smokestacks, car exhausts, and the destruction of the rain forests. *The Arrival* has a more terrifying hypothesis to explain the phenomenon.

In the great paranoid tradition of science fiction, the discovery of this possibility is made by one man who cannot get anyone to listen to him, and who grows desperate as the establishment slams its doors. The man is Zane Zaminski (Charlie Sheen), radio astronomer, who listens for signs of intelligence from outer space. Unlike his colleagues, he's looking in the noisy FM band: "It's like searching for a needle," his partner tells him, "in a haystack of needles." When he picks up an unmistakable signal, Zane takes it gleefully to his boss (Ron Silver), only to be told that the entire intergalactic eavesdropping operation is being scaled down because of budget cutbacks.

Zane's frustration is the engine for a science-fiction film of unusual intelligence that keeps on thinking all the way to the end, springing new surprises and ideas. The movie is as smart as *Mission: Impossible* is dumb. *The Arrival* is always clear about its science, its plot, its characters, and its meaning, unlike *Mission: Impossible,* which is concerned with surface flash, visual impact, and action. (That's not to say *Mission: Impossible* isn't entertaining; I am simply making the comparison.)

Zane is dumped from his job but cannot shake the conviction that he did indeed hear an intelligent signal from another planet. He's the kind of nerd with a goatee and a pocket protector who can duplicate a science lab in his own attic with a couple of good computers and a soldering iron. Aided by a smart black kid from next door (Tony T. Johnson), he soon has his own listening station up and running. His method for duplicating a big government radio telescope is ingenious: He gets a job as a repairman for consumer satellite dishes, secretly wires them into a network, and puts together his own "phased array" to listen to space. I have no idea if this would work, but I like his attitude.

His investigation of the signals leads him to Mexico, where he encounters another scientist, played by Lindsay Crouse. We've seen her in the film's splendid opening sequence, which begins with her sniffing a flower in a meadow and then pulls back to show the meadow surrounded by thousands of square miles of Arctic ice. Together, they speculate about global warming and its possible connection to the strange situations they encounter in a small central Mexico village. At one point, frightened by where her reasoning is leading her, she sighs, "I get so damned apocalyptic when I drink."

Read no further if you plan to see the film.

What I appreciate about *The Arrival* is that it stays with its thesis all the way to the end. It has a chilling hypothesis: Earth is being transformed by an alien species that would prefer the planet a little warmer before moving in. Combining this idea with a touch of *Invasion of the Body Snatchers* and some ambitious special effects, it springs new surprises on us right to the end; the screenplay is by David Twohy, who also directed, and who doesn't run out of steam.

Consider, for example, that clever little spinning globe that seems to work as a vacuum cleaner, sucking everything into another dimension. The job it does on a gigantic radio telescope is one of the best recent examples of special effects. There is a shot when Zane's fiancée (Teri Polo) rolls to the edge of the big dish; at first all we see is its vast white expanse, and then suddenly we see the earth below, spread out beneath her, and the way the shot is constructed makes it into ten seconds of just about perfect cinema.

A lot of movies in this genre break down in the end into a simpleminded series of chases and fights. There are fights and chases in *The Arrival,* but they're generated by the plot and punctuated by fresh revelations and possibilities, so that the movie keeps on thinking and doesn't go on automatic pilot.

*The Arrival* fulfills one of the classic functions of science fiction, which is to take a current trend and extend it to a possible (and preferably alarming) future. Unlike *Species,* which assumed that alien invaders would be monsters (or, if you read the film differently, would send monsters ahead to clear the way for them), *The Arrival* gives its aliens credit for reasoning that we might almost be tempted to agree with. "We're just finishing what you started," one of the aliens tells Zane, referring to the smokestacks, exhausts, rain forests, and so on. "What would have taken you one hundred years will only take us ten." He, or it, has a point.

## Artemisia ★ ★

R, 96 m., 1998

Valentina Cervi (Artemisia), Michel Serrault (Orazio), Miki Manojlovic (Agostino), Luca Zingaretti (Cosimo), Emmanuelle Devos (Costanza), Frederic Pierrot (Roberto), Maurice Garrel (The Judge), Brigitte Catillon (Tuzia). Directed by Agnes Merlet and produced by Patrice Haddad. Screenplay by Merlet.

Most painters draw life studies while looking at nude models. In the secretive opening scenes of *Artemisia,* a young woman uses herself as a model, sketching by candlelight, looking at her own body in a mirror. This is Artemisia Gentileschi, who wants to be a painter but lives at a time when the profession is forbidden to women. She sketches anyway, and when her nude drawings are discovered by the nuns and shown to her father, he responds with pride: "You are the child of a painter."

He is Orazio (Michel Serrault), a professional painter of considerable skills, although his craft is a little behind the new work being done in Florence. It is 1670, the Italian Baroque is flourishing, and he allows his beloved daughter to study in his studio—although he draws the line at letting her view nude males. She is direct and determined, and bribes the fisherman Fulvio with a kiss for letting her draw him.

Artemisia is played by Valentina Cervi, who you may remember as the dark-haired, bright-eyed love child of John Malkovich and Barbara Hershey in *Portrait of a Lady.* She looks older here but is still a coltish teenager, with an eager stride and impulsive courage. You like her right away, because you sense there's no deceit in her: Like all true artists faced with the nude form, she sees not the naughty bits but the technical challenge.

The famous artist Agostino Tassi (Miki Manojlovic) joins her father in carrying out a papal commission. He is more advanced in his work with light and shadow, and she wants to study under him. Tassi wants nothing to do with her until he sees her work. Then he accepts her. "Someday you'll take lessons from me," she tells him. It is foreordained that they will fall in love—and rather touching, since he is a man of the world (she spies on him through a brothel window). He's attracted to her not just for sexual reasons, but because he has literally never met anyone like her before: a woman who thinks for herself, is as talented and ambitious as a man, and says what she believes.

The film follows through on the inevitable consequences of their romance. There is an ecclesiastical trial in which the cardinal in charge, bored with the conflicting testimony, simply has her fingers wound tight with a leather thong until either they are cut off or someone tells the truth. In a sense, she shares the same fate as her sister to the north in *Dangerous Beauty,* another 1998 movie set a century earlier, about a Venetian woman who can be independent only by becoming a courtesan. She can't be a modern woman without her world getting medieval on her.

The difference—and this is the most important difference in the world—is that Artemisia gains her freedom not by selling herself, but by selling her work. She seems to have been the first professional woman artist in the Western world, the first to be commissioned, the first to be admitted to the Academy in Florence, the first to travel to England for employment. Her paintings hang in the museums of Europe, and the critic Harvey Karten says of her painting *Judith Beheading Holofernes* in a Florence gallery: "You don't have to look closely at it to guess that it's the work of a woman painter. Two women are standing over the bearded, defeated general Holofernes, one holding a sword at his neck, the other helping to hold him down to a bed." Not a favorite baroque male fantasy.

*Artemisia* is as much about art as about sex, and it contains a lot of information about techniques, including the revolutionary idea of moving the easel outside and painting from nature. It lacks, however, detailed scenes showing drawings in the act of being created (for that you need *La Belle Noiseuse,* Jacques Rivette's 1991 movie that peers intimately over the shoulder of an artist in love). And it doesn't show a lot of Artemisia's work. What it does show is the gift of Valentina Cervi, who is another of those modern European actresses, like Juliette Binoche, Irene Jacob, Emmanuelle Béart, and Julie Delpy, whose intelligence, despite everything else, is the most attractive thing about her.

## As Good As It Gets ★ ★ ★

PG-13, 138 m., 1997

Jack Nicholson (Melvin Udall), Helen Hunt (Carol Connelly), Greg Kinnear (Simon Bishop), Cuba Gooding Jr. (Frank Sachs), Skeet Ulrich (Vincent), Shirley Knight (Beverly), Yeardley Smith (Jackie). Directed by James L. Brooks and produced by Bridget Johnson and Kristi Zea. Screenplay by Mark Andrus and Brooks.

There's something about Jack Nicholson that makes you want to grin. Maybe the anticipation that you'll see him get away with something. He's the guy who knows the angles. His screen persona was established for all time the moment he told the waitress to hold the chicken salad between her knees. *As Good As It Gets* takes that attitude as far as it will go in the direction it was already headed: He plays an obsessive-compulsive curmudgeon whose communication with the world is mostly limited to insults—not funny ones, but intended to wound.

It is some kind of twisted tribute to Nicholson that he's able to use this dialogue in what is, after all, a comedy. He hurls racist, sexist, homophobic, and physical insults at everyone he meets, and because it's Nicholson we let him; we know there has to be a payback somehow. If you see the movie, ask yourself how Nicholson's tirades would sound coming from any other actor. They'd bring the film to an appalled halt.

Nicholson plays Melvin Udall, a man who crouches in the apartment where he has ground out sixty-two romance novels for women. Asked how he writes the women characters so convincingly, he replies, "I think of a man. And I take away reason and accountability." He hates everyone in the building, and the movie opens with him hurling his neighbor's little dog down the garbage chute. Then he marches out to take his habitual meal in a nearby restaurant, where he lays out his own plastic cutlery.

"Sometimes you must try other people's clean silverware, as part of the fun of eating out," advises Carol the waitress (Helen Hunt). She waits on him but she doesn't like him, and when he makes a disparaging remark about her asthmatic son, she makes him withdraw it or she will never, ever serve him again. Since she's the only waitress who will serve him, and since this is the only restaurant he will eat in, he backs down. (Later, when he's thrown out of the restaurant, there's applause from the regulars.)

We meet Melvin's neighbor, the dog owner. He's a gay artist named Simon (Greg Kinnear), who is beaten up one day by the friends of one of his models. During his recovery, his agent and dealer (Cuba Gooding Jr.) insists that Melvin take care of the little dog, which has been rescued from the garbage. Melvin doesn't want to, but he does, and to his amazement (but not ours) he develops a grudging affection for the mutt.

*As Good As It Gets* was directed by James L. Brooks, whose films *(Terms of Endearment, Broadcast News)* show original characters in unexpected lights. This film, cowritten with Mark Andrus, creates memorable people but is not quite willing to follow them down unconventional paths. It's almost painful, watching the screenplay stretch and contort these characters to fit them somehow into a conventional formula—they're dragged toward the happy ending, screaming and kicking all the way.

If the movie had been either more or less ambitious, it might have been more successful. Less ambitious, and it would have been a sitcom crowd-pleaser, in which a grumpy Scrooge allows his heart to melt. More ambitious, and it would have touched on the underlying irony of this lonely man's bitter life. But *As Good As It Gets* is a compromise, a film that forces a smile onto material that doesn't wear one easily. Melvin is not a man ever destined to find lasting happiness, and the movie's happy ending feels like a blackout, seconds before more unhappiness begins.

Yet there's so much good here, in the dialogue, the performances, and the observation, that the movie succeeds at many moments even while pursuing its doomed grand design. Consider Melvin's decision to arrange for the medical treatment of Carol's son. The little boy suffers agonizing asthma attacks, but through Melvin, Carol is able to find a smarter doctor (Harold Ramis) who can do some good. The material here is right out of a silent weeper: Repentant Scrooge helps poor child to breathe again. But by casting the wonderfully droll Ramis as the doctor and skewing the dialogue just slightly, Brooks makes it new and screwy.

The main story line gets a similar treatment. It becomes clear that Melvin has been destined by the filmmakers to become a better man: First he accepts dogs, then children, then women, and finally even his gay neighbor. But Brooks and Andrus, having blocked out this conventional progression, then write against it, using rich irony so that individual scenes seem fresh even while the overall progress follows ancient custom. When Melvin goes back for a belated visit to his one-time therapist, for example, they give him a perfect line: "How can you diagnose someone as having obsessive-compulsive disorder and yet criticize him for not keeping an appointment?"

There were times, watching *As Good As It Gets,* when I hoped the movie might go over the top into greatness. It had the potential. The pieces were in place. It was sad to see the filmmakers draw back into story formulas. Maybe the studio, mindful of the $50 million price tag, required Brooks to channel his obstreperous material in a safe direction. One can imagine an independent filmmaker, with a smaller budget, taking dialogue and characters like these and following them into the wild blue yonder. One can imagine Brooks, Nicholson, and Hunt doing it too. That's why the film left me with such a sense of lost opportunities.

## The Assignment ★ ★ ★ ½

R, 115 m., 1997

Aidan Quinn (Annibal Ramirez/Carlos), Donald Sutherland (Jack Shaw [Henry Fields]), Ben Kingsley (Amos), Claudia Ferri (Maura Ramirez), Celine Bonnier (Carla), Vlasta Vrana (KGB Head Officer), Liliana Komorowska (Agnieska), Von Flores (Koj). Directed by Christian Duguay and produced by Tom Berry and Franco Battista. Screenplay by Dan Gordon and Sabi H. Shabtai.

*The Assignment* is a canny, tricky thriller that could serve as an illustration of what a similar release, *The Peacemaker*, is not. Both films involve an international hunt for a dangerous terrorist, but *The Peacemaker* is a cartoon and *The Assignment* is intelligent and gripping—and *it has a third act!* Instead of an action orgy, it has more than enough story to see it through to the end and keep us absorbed the whole way. Yes, it ends with a deadly struggle, but as the setting for another stage of the movie's web of deceit.

The film is centered on a CIA plot to discredit and kill Carlos, the feared terrorist who operated for years despite the best efforts of the free world's security agencies to capture him. Donald Sutherland plays Fields, the CIA agent for whom Carlos has become an obsession, and when he finds a U.S. Navy officer named Ramirez (Aidan Quinn) who's a dead ringer for the terrorist, he devises a risky scheme: He'll train Ramirez to impersonate Carlos, then use the double to convince the KGB that their attack dog is disloyal. As a result, Carlos will either be dead or, almost as good, discredited in the eyes of his sponsors.

Fields works with an Israeli named Amos (Ben Kingsley) in training Ramirez, after first using psychological tactics to convince the reluctant navy man to leave his wife and family and become a counterterrorist. (The scene where Fields shows Ramirez a dying child in a hospital is a direct echo of *The Third Man.*) Then the false Carlos is sent into the field to work the deception, which I will not describe.

*The Assignment* is fascinating because its characters can be believed, because there is at least a tiny nugget of truth in the story, and because from the deceptive opening credits, this is a film that creates the right world for these characters to inhabit. Sutherland's CIA man is especially well drawn: "I don't have any family," he says, "and I don't have any friends. The only people I've ever cared about were the ones I've killed."

Quinn plays a dual role, as Ramirez and Carlos, and has some tricky scenes, especially one in which a former lover of Carlos's helps train him sexually so that he will be a convincing bedmate for another of the terrorist's lovers.

The screenplay, by Dan Gordon and Sabi H. Shabtai, has action scenes that grow from the story and are not simply set pieces for their own sake. It's impressive the way so many different story threads come together all at once near the end.

The director, Christian Duguay, is new to me. What he has is a tactile love of film, of images. He and the cinematographer, David Franco, don't use locations so much as occupy them; we visit Jerusalem, Paris, Vienna, Washington, Tripoli, and Moscow (or sets and effects that look like them), and yet the movie's not a travelogue but a story hurtling ahead.

I have seen so many lazy thrillers. They share the same characteristics: Most of the scenes involve the overpriced star, the villain is underwritten, and the plot is merely a setup for the special effects, the chases, and the final action climax. *The Assignment* gives us ensemble work by fine actors, it has a villain of great complexity (developed through the process of imitating him), and at the end there is a tantalizing situation for us to unravel as we leave the theater.

## The Associate ★ ★

PG-13, 114 m., 1996

Whoopi Goldberg (Laurel), Dianne Wiest (Sally), Eli Wallach (Fallon), Tim Daly (Frank), Bebe Neuwirth (Camille), Austin Pendleton (Aesop), Lainie Kazan (Cindy Mason), George Martin

(Manchester). Directed by Donald Petrie and produced by Frederic Golchan, Patrick Markey, and Adam Leipzig. Screenplay by Nick Thiel.

*The Associate* is an uninspired recycling of the *Tootsie* formula, with the fatal error that its Tootsie figure is offscreen most of the time and not lovable when he's onscreen. Can Whoopi Goldberg convincingly play a white man? Only sort of; he looks like a dubious experiment at Madame Tussaud's. Does she make the man into a character we like and care about? Not at all.

The movie stars Goldberg as Laurel, a bright businesswoman who gets discriminated against because she's not a man, so she creates a fictitious man as her invisible partner, and gives him all of her best ideas. This man, named "Cutty," is soon the best-known investment adviser on Wall Street, but he's never seen—he's always out of town or on vacation while Laurel fronts for him.

Eventually it becomes absolutely necessary for people to see Cutty, so Laurel enlists the skills of a friend who's a celebrity impersonator, and appears at public functions as a white man. But not a very interesting or likable man. What people liked about *Tootsie* was Tootsie—her moxie, her personality, her spirit. It wasn't the transvestite plot gimmick that made the movie a success.

On the way to its ungainly third act, *The Associate* scores some good points against the male-dominated hierarchy of the business world. We see Laurel training a man (Tim Daly) who gets the promotion she deserves. We see Daly taking clients to a strip club and closing deals at 3 A.M. after sending Laurel home. We see her quit her job in disgust and open her own firm. And we like the relationship she has with her new secretary (Dianne Wiest), another smart woman lost in the bowels of male power.

We're even sort of amused by elements of the plot, which involve Laurel cycling her own stock tips through the nonexistent Cutty and fooling everyone, even veteran investors. But eventually the monster she's created grows out of control ("Even when I create the perfect man, he ends up stabbing me in the back"). And Laurel has to create a "real" Cutty in order to regain control of the situation.

Dustin Hoffman famously did weeks of tests and almost quit in despair before he finally found the right look for his Tootsie. Robin Williams, as *Mrs. Doubtfire,* wasn't as convincing as Hoffman, but got away with his impersonation. Goldberg's Mr. Cutty, made out of latex and makeup, looks very odd. Maybe Goldberg wanted to play a white man just to prove a point, but if she'd made Cutty a black man she could have made a more provocative point, and probably looked more convincing at the same time.

Even that wouldn't have saved the movie. It has a lot of heart in its scenes between the Goldberg and Wiest characters, but most of the rest of the plot is mechanical—some sitcom, some slapstick, some mistaken identity, and weird scenes where women try to seduce Mr. Cutty while we suspect that in real life what they'd be whispering into his ear would be the name of a good dermatologist.

## August ★ ½

PG, 117 m., 1996

Anthony Hopkins (Ieuan Davies), Kate Burton (Helen), Leslie Phillips (Blathwaite), Gawn Grainger (Dr. Lloyd), Rhian Morgan (Sian), Hugh Lloyd (Prosser), Rhoda Lewis (Mair Davies), Menna Trussler (Gwen). Directed by Anthony Hopkins and produced by June Wyndham-Davies and Pippa Cross. Screenplay by Julian Mitchell, based on *Uncle Vanya* by Anton Chekhov.

"I could have been! I could have done! Now I'm too old!" Uncle Vanya's cry rings down through the years since Anton Chekhov gave it voice. It speaks to a little something in all of us since we could have been and could have done—and might still, we think, placing ourselves a step above poor Vanya.

He is Russian but his plight is universal, which is why the play has been wrenched and recycled into countless shapes and sizes over the years by artists determined to make it their own. I haven't seen *Vanya* done in drag (it is only a matter of time), but in the last two years I have seen it filmed in an abandoned New York theater (Louis Malle's *Vanya on 42nd Street*) and moved to the Australian outback (Michael Blakemore's *Country Life*), and now here it is in Wales, with whiskey replacing the vodka. The despair is just the same.

Anthony Hopkins sets his *August* on a Welsh farm at the turn of the century, and plays the Vanya character, here named Ieuan, an unhappy bachelor who complains "all I do is eat, sleep, and drink." Back for a visit is the loathsome Professor Blathwaite (Leslie Phillips), an art critic who married Ieuan's sister and then, after her death, took a fragrant young wife named Helen (Kate Burton, Richard's daughter). The professor is sickly, although not as sickly as he would like you to think, and treats everyone as his servant.

Ieuan's best friend in the country is Dr. Lloyd (Gawn Grainger), possibly more of a drunk than Ieuan. Both men suffer unrequitedly for Helen. Also living on the farm is Sian (Rhian Morgan), daughter of Blathwaite by the first marriage. She nurtures a secret love for Dr. Lloyd. Downstairs, the characters include Prosser (Hugh Lloyd), a butler who can see no evil in the fraudulent professor, and Gwen (Menna Trussler), the cook, who can see a little evil in just about everyone.

If you've seen the play, you know what's going to happen. (You have to see two or three *Vanyas* to get the relationships straight, but after that it's clear sailing.) The title to the farm has passed to Sian, but for all of these years, the proceeds have gone to support the professor's life in London, where he was (according to himself) doing important work. ("He's retired," Ieuan snaps, "and not one person in the entire world has ever heard of him.")

Now the professor has returned to size up the farm's possibilities. Ieuan thinks he plans to retire there—which fills him with dread (because he hates the professor) and hope (because he loves the professor's wife). Actually, the professor's plans are more sinister, as he explains in a family meeting that is a perfect model of self-centered monstrousness.

*Uncle Vanya,* like all plays about alcoholics, takes place largely at night, when drunken monologues give voice to fears, dreams, and hopeless passions. It would be just as easy to get drunk in the morning and sleep at night, but drinkers tend to start each day with optimistic moderation, and measure out their drinks until count is lost around sundown.

For the uncle, whiskey unleashes decades of hostility. He has worked like a slave under the hot (Welsh/Australian/Manhattan/Russian) sun, trying to make the farm pay so that the professor can live a life of indolence in the city, charming silly girls with ideas they think only they are incapable of understanding, when in fact everyone is. Brooding in the night, nursing his self-pity, lusting for Helen, Ieuan narrows his alternatives to murder and suicide. Both are so attractive he is reluctant to choose.

Since the materials in *Uncle Vanya* are familiar to anyone likely to see this movie, the reason for making yet another version must be to find something new, or to say old things in a fresh way. Hopkins, working from an adaptation by Julian Mitchell, finds nothing new, but by moving the action to his native Wales perhaps he hopes for a different tone. Unfortunately, the characters in *Vanya* are so poetic, morose, proud, and spiteful to begin with that making them Welsh is redundant. Perhaps if he had made them Canadian, or Chinese, new light would have been shed.

Hopkins is a wonderful actor—one of the best—but he needs a director to stand back and assess his performances. In roles as different as Hannibal Lector, C. S. Lewis, and Richard Nixon, he has been able to disappear into characters so completely that even his rages come from different places. Here he seems not new, but simply Anthony Hopkins uneasily trying on a role he is not entirely comfortable with. When he blows up at the professor's bright idea for selling the farm, he seems more comic than outraged; the tone is wrong.

If you must see a *Vanya* (people have such hungers, just as there will always be a market for anchovy paste), I recommend *Vanya on 42nd Street* for the true soul of the play, and *Country Life* for a successful transition to another time and place and mode of behavior; the Australian characters in it seem so entirely Australian that if you didn't know you'd never suspect they had ever been Russian. *August* did not start out as a good idea, and never becomes a better one.

## Austin Powers: International Man of Mystery ★ ★ ★

PG-13, 88 m., 1997

Mike Myers (Austin Powers), Elizabeth Hurley (Vanessa Kensington), Mike Myers (Dr. Evil), Michael York (Basil Exposition), Mimi Rogers (Mrs. Kensington), Robert Wagner (Number Two), Seth Green (Scott Evil), Fabiana Udenio (Alotta Fagina), Charles Napier (Commander Gilmour). Directed by Jay Roach and produced by Suzanne Todd, Demi Moore, Jennifer Todd, and Mike Myers. Screenplay by Myers.

In the opening scenes of *Austin Powers: International Man of Mystery*, the British superagent has nearly won his war against the scheming Dr. Evil. But Evil escapes by boarding a rocket shaped like Bob's Big Boy and going into orbit around Earth—where he will wait, cryogenically frozen, until the time is right to resume his scheme for world domination. To counter this move, Austin Powers has himself frozen, and when Evil returns in 1997, Powers is defrosted too.

That's the simple but productive premise of *Austin Powers*, a funny movie that only gets funnier the more familiar you are with the James Bond movies, all the Bond clones, and countless other 1960s films. The joke is that both Powers and Dr. Evil are creatures of the 1960s, and time has passed them by.

Both roles are played by Mike Myers, who has the same spirit of getting away with something that was so infectious in *Wayne's World*. As Powers, he's a sex-mad male chauvinist pig who tries to seduce a 1990s woman like agent Elizabeth Hurley with words like "groovy," "trendy," and "with-it." He's doing his own thing. In an opening tribute to the immortal *Beyond the Valley of the Dolls*, he throws a party and cries out, "This is my happening and it freaks me out!"

Dr. Evil is similarly time-challenged. With a bald head and a sneer that make him look like a prototypical Bond villain, he pushes buttons to send underlings falling into an incinerator. But he's hopelessly out of touch. During his frozen decades, his operation has moved into legitimate businesses under the direction of Number Two (Robert Wagner), and no longer finds international blackmail profitable. (At one point, when Dr. Evil suggests a scheme involving a million-dollar ransom demand, his board members chuckle as they explain how little a million will buy these days.)

Modern times are not accommodating for these relics from the past. Dr. Evil discovers he has a son named Scott Evil (Seth Green), who resents him for spending all that time in orbit when he should have been performing his parenting duties. They end up at a twelve-step meeting for dysfunctional families.

The movie is based on variations of its theme: James Bond meets Political Correctness. A lot of the laughs come from Elizabeth Hurley, as Vanessa Kensington, liberated feminist British secret agent, who reacts to Austin's seduction techniques as if he were a bug and she should squish him. One of the movie's funniest scenes takes place when Austin frolics nude in their hotel suite: Through elaborate choreography, his private parts are somehow always covered from the camera's point of view, saving the movie's PG-13 rating by a hair, while we find out that the British don't call their breakfast sausages "bangers" for nothing.

The movie, written by Myers and directed by Jay Roach, is smart enough to know the 1960s are funny without being exaggerated. In one sequence, a fashion photographer shoots sixties fashions, and the clothes, which look like outlandish science-fiction fantasies, are in fact identical to costumes worn during posing sessions in Antonioni's *Blow Up* (1967). Movie buffs will have fun cataloging all the references to other movies; I clocked *A Hard Day's Night* and *Sgt. Pepper's Lonely Hearts Club Band* in addition to *BVD* and all the Bond, Matt Helm, and *Our Man Flint* references. And, of course, those who remember Bond's adventures with Pussy Galore will be amused by his female antagonist this time, the sinister Alotta Fagina (Fabiana Udenio).

The cast is well chosen. Michael York is serious business as Basil Exposition, the British spymaster assigned to bring Powers up-to-date. Hurley again shows a nice comic flair (she regards her own sexuality with amusement). Charles Napier, from *BVD*, is the hard-edged Commander Gilmour, all teeth and grim concern. And Seth Green finds the right modern note in totally dismissing everything that his father has worked so long to destroy.

What is best is the puppy-dog earnestness and enthusiasm that Myers brings to his role. He can only imagine how exciting 1997 will be. Just think: When he was frozen, the world was embracing widespread promiscuity, one-night stands, recreational drugs, and mind expansion. He can only imagine what wonderful improvements have come along in the last thirty years.

☞

# B

## Bang ★ ★ ★ ½

NO MPAA RATING, 98 m., 1997

Darling Narita (Woman), Peter Greene (Homeless Man), Michael Newland (Cop), David Allen Graff (Producer), Luis Guizar (Jesus). Directed by Ash and produced by Daniel M. Berger and Ladd Vance. Screenplay by Ash.

*Bang* is a powerful sleeper, convincing, provocative, and exciting—an adventure in "guerrilla filmmaking" that uses an unexpected story device to hold up a mirror to a big American city.

*Bang* tells the story of a desperate young woman who spends a day wearing the uniform of a Los Angeles policeman, and experiences some of the privileges and sorrows that go with being perceived as a cop. Because it's shot in a flat and realistic style, it's curiously convincing: The story doesn't hype manufactured scenes, but considers what might happen in such a situation. I found myself forgetting the structure and artistry, and simply being carried along with the flow.

The movie stars Darling Narita ("her real name," the press notes say) as an unnamed Japanese-American actress, about twenty-five, who has been evicted from her apartment for nonpayment of rent. Homeless and broke, she goes to an audition with a "producer" who drops the names of Julia and Dustin, tells her she looks "like an Asian Meryl Streep with brown hair," and then asks her to join him in a phony love scene. Is he a fake? Probably, but in Hollywood not necessarily.

She flees from the house, and runs into a homeless guy who lives in the bushes (Peter Greene, who played Zed in *Pulp Fiction* and was brilliant in the painful *Clean, Shaven*). He won a bronze medal in the '84 Olympics, he says, although he never takes it out of his brown paper bag.

Angered that she was mistreated, he destroys the producer's mailbox. The cops are called, and an officer leads her into the woods and demands sex. She grabs his gun, forces him to strip, and handcuffs him to a tree. Then she puts on his uniform, drives off on his motorcycle, and the real movie begins.

What would it be like to be a cop? To be hated or treasured by the people on the street, depending on their condition or need? To be seen as a law enforcer, medic, counselor, good guy, bad guy? She finds out.

The story of the making of *Bang* helps explain its curiously convincing quality. The film, written and directed by a British director named Ash ("his real name," the notes say), was shot for only $20,000 on the streets of Los Angeles, without permits or permissions; real L.A. police occasionally got involved in the filming because they thought the film's star was one of their own, and LAPD helicopters circle ominously overhead during some scenes.

What the actors and crew did was to turn up, film a scene quickly, and disappear. Some scenes were improvised on the spot, including one where the "cop" hands out money to homeless men and nearly starts a riot. Others show thought and depth. Despite its budget, *Bang* doesn't look cheap or rushed; that this film cost less than a single costume for *Batman and Robin* is some kind of a parable.

Darling Narita is an actress with a flat, uninflected style (she acts in a movie much like she does in the "audition"). She plays a woman who is depressed and fairly undemonstrative, who gets through scenes by saying as little as possible. The approach creates unexpected tension in a scene like the one where, wearing the uniform, she's eating breakfast in a diner when two real cops join her at her table. Will she be exposed as an impersonator? What can she possibly say? In a more facile movie she'd ad-lib her way out of danger; here, she's nearly speechless, and it plays a lot better.

Two sequences are especially strong. In one, she chases a drug dealer up to a roof, where he threatens to jump. "I'm not a cop!" she shouts, and the scene develops two unexpected but likely surprises. In another lengthy sequence, which is the heart of the movie, her cycle runs out of gas and she gets a lift to the gas station with two Latinos. For once she is able to unwind a little (with a beer and a joint, to their amazement), and then that scene also pays off surprisingly, with great unexpected drama.

The film is filled with other incidents: A run-in with a Japanese-American hooker, who thinks she is being arrested. An encounter with two people she finds making love in the Hollywood Hills. And eventually a return to the real cop, who has spent the day handcuffed to the tree and trying to deal with the homeless man.

*Bang* avoids obvious buildups and payoffs. It takes a simple premise—cop for a day—and treats it not as an excuse for a thriller, but as a window into the everyday life of the city. Its choice as heroine is a good one, because the woman is perceived by others through three lenses: female, Asian, cop. ("Where are you from?" the so-called producer asks. "Here," she says. "No, where are you really from?")

Knowing little about *Bang* before I saw it, except for its reputation as a low-budget film shot guerrilla-style on the streets, I confess I expected flashy sub-Tarantino GenX narcissism. What I didn't expect was a film so well made, so penetrating, so observant. And, like all films that really hold your attention, so entertaining.

## B.A.P.S. no stars

PG-13, 90 m., 1997

Halle Berry (Nisi), Martin Landau (Mr. Blakemore), Ian Richardson (Manley), Natalie Desselle (Mickey), Troy Beyer (Tracy), Luigi Amodeo (Antonio), Jonathan Fried (Isaac), Pierre (Ali). Directed by Robert Townsend and produced by Mark Burg and Loretha Jones. Screenplay by Troy Beyer.

*B.A.P.S.* is jaw-droppingly bad, a movie so misconceived I wonder why anyone involved wanted to make it. As a vehicle for the talents of director Robert Townsend and actors Halle Berry and Martin Landau, it represents a grave miscalculation; I hope they quickly put it behind them.

The title stands for "Black American Princesses." Its two heroines are more like tacky Cinderellas. Berry and Natalie Desselle play vulgar and garish homegirls from Decatur, Georgia, whose artificial nails are eight inches long, whose gold teeth sparkle, and whose hairpieces are piled so high on their heads that the concept passes beyond satire and into cruelty.

There is a thin line between satire and offensiveness, and this crosses it. Its portraits of these two working-class black women have been painted with snobbery and scorn. The actresses don't inhabit the caricatures with conviction. The result is a hurtful stereotype, because the comedy doesn't work to redeem it. We should sense some affection for them from the filmmakers, but we don't—not until they receive a magic Hollywood makeover in the later scenes of the movie, and miraculously lose their gold teeth. The movie invites us to laugh at them, not with them, but that's a moot point since the audience I joined did not laugh at all, except incredulously.

The plot: Berry plays Nisi, a waitress, who hears on MTV about a contest to choose a dancer for a music video and national tour by a rap star named Heavy D. She shares this news with her friend Mickey (Desselle), a hairdresser, and it fits right into their plans for marrying rich guys and living on easy street. So they say good-bye to their shiftless boyfriends and fly to L.A. wearing hairstyles so extreme no one behind them on the airplane can see the movie. Funny? No. It could have been funny, but not when the reaction shots are of annoyed white businessmen asking to change their seats.

In L.A. they're spotted at the audition by a mysterious figure who makes them an attractive offer: room and board in a Bel Air mansion and $10,000. What's the deal? He represents Mr. Blakemore (Landau), a dying millionaire, who has experienced true love only once in his life, many years ago—with Lily, his family's black maid. Nisi will pose as Lily's granddaughter and cheer the old guy in his final days on earth.

There's more to it than that, of course; it's all a scam. But Mr. Blakemore inexplicably takes to the women from the moment he sees them. (Nisi, dressed in pink latex and high heels, looks like a hooker, and Mickey looks like her coach.) The plot later reveals details that make it highly unlikely Mr. Blakemore would even for a second have been deceived by the story, but never mind; the movie's attention span isn't long enough for it to remember its own setup.

Even though the movie fails as a comedy, someone should have told Landau it was intended to be one. He plays Mr. Blakemore with gracious charm and great dignity, which is all wrong; his deathbed scene is done with such clunky sincerity that one fears Landau actually expected audiences to be moved by it. Not in this movie. The cause of his ill health is left a little obscure, and no wonder, because shortly before his dreadful deathbed scene he's well enough to join the women in a wild night of disco dancing. You have not lived until you've seen Martin Landau discoing. Well, perhaps you have.

Another key character is Manley (Ian Richardson), Blakemore's butler, who turns up his nose at the first sight of the women, but inevitably comes to like them. The message of the movie, I guess, is that two homegirls can find wealth and happiness if only they wear blond wigs, get rid of those gold teeth and country vocabularies, and are nice to rich old white men. It gets even better: At one point, the boyfriends from Georgia are flown out to L.A. to share the good luck, and they vow to get their acts together and Plan For Their Futures, in a scene that comes way too late in the film for us to believe or care.

The movie was written by the actress Troy Beyer, who has a small role as a lawyer. What was she thinking of? I don't have a clue. The movie doesn't work, but was there any way this material could ever have worked? My guess is that African-Americans will be offended by the movie, and whites will be embarrassed. The movie will bring us all together, I imagine, in paralyzing boredom.

## Barb Wire ★ ★ ½

R, 98 m., 1996

Pamela Anderson Lee (Barb Wire), Temuera Morrison (Axel), Victoria Rowell (Cora D), Jack Noseworthy (Charlie), Xander Berkeley (Alexander Willis), Steve Railsback (Colonel Pryzer), Udo Kier (Curly), Andre Rosey Brown (Big Fatso). Directed by David Hogan and produced by Brad Wyman, Mike Richardson, and Todd Moyer. Screenplay by Chuck Pfarrer and Ilene Chaiken.

*Barb Wire* takes place in the year 2017—"the worst year of my life," according to Barb. We are in the middle of the second American Civil War. The Congressional Directorate has seized control of America ("They used an HIV derivative named Red Ribbon to wipe out Topeka"), but Barb lives in the last free city, where she runs a nightclub.

Times are hard. So hard, Americans insist on payment in Canadian dollars. Barb steers clear of politics. She's friends with the local police chief, who is on the take, but has a good heart. Then she gets involved in contraband. Some identity lenses are missing. Whoever possesses them can get free passage into Canada. A little guy says he knows where they are. A fat guy offers to buy them. The Congressional Directorate troops, dressed like Nazis, come into Barb's club and tear it apart, looking for them.

You must remember this. It's *Casablanca* recycled. The biggest howler in the credits is the line "based on a story by Ilene Chaiken." Would it have killed Ilene to acknowledge *Casablanca*? True, there are differences, too; in this movie a kiss is not necessarily just a kiss—not when Barb's sex life includes nailing guys through the middle of the forehead with a stiletto heel.

Barb, inspired by a comic-book heroine, is played by Pam Anderson Lee, the "Baywatch" star, in leather, chains, and an industrial-strength WonderBra. As the movie opens, she's on a trapeze, being sprayed by a hose in slow motion, in a scene that reminded me uncannily of the climax of *Behind the Green Door*.

That's when she's posing as a stripper. Later, when she poses as a hooker, it's to gain entry to an apartment so she can blow out the wall and rescue a hostage. Bogie was a wimp compared to Barb, whose personal DNA, if I heard correctly, "holds the antidote to our secret weapon." The movie is wonderfully confusing, but I think that means she could have saved Topeka, whether by preventive intercourse or otherwise I haven't a clue.

Pam Anderson Lee, while not a great actress, is a good sport. She's backlit in endless scenes where, if she could have figured out a way to send her breasts in separately, she could have stayed at home. "Don't call me a babe," she says—a trademark line like "Make my day" or "I'll be back." Everyone who calls her "babe" pays with his life. (One guy tries to light her cigarette, which turns out to be a blow gun, and gets a poison dart between his eyes.)

The parallels with *Casablanca* are fun to spot. The Sydney Greenstreet character, named Big Fatso (Andre Rosey Brown), reclines in the shovel of a Caterpillar tractor at his junkyard, munching on a turkey leg (or maybe an ostrich leg, it's so big) and offering to buy the contact lenses. But Barb has mercy on an idealistic young woman (Victoria Rowell) who is married to a resistance leader, and gives her the lenses. At the end, the heroes board an Air Canada flight.

The one big scene from *Casablanca* that's missing here is the musical showdown, in which the patriots sing the "Marseilles" to drown out the Nazi anthem. Considering that Barb Wire runs a punk leather club, here's today's quiz: What song would be the Congressional Directorate's anthem, and what song would the party-loving S&Msters sing to drown it out?

The movie has been rated "R" for "nudity/sexuality." There is some nudity, mostly weirdly lit. The sexuality involves various forms of foreplay to violence. There is nothing resembling eroticism, except for the dialogue "she's as tender as Tuscan veal." Barb Wire's breasts, winched into place and clamped down by leather and steel costumes, seem as immobile as the similarly shaped fenders on a 1957 Olds Rocket 88. "Look at those guns," a guy says approvingly, not referring to firearms.

There are some strange moments. You know the basic scene where a guy is thrown through a window and we get slow-motion shots from three different angles as he falls to the ground? *Barb Wire* achieves a first by showing a *chair* thrown through a window and descending in slo-mo, etc. Movies like this stir a certain affection in my heart. The filmmakers must have known they were not making a good movie, but they didn't use that as an excuse to be boring and lazy. *Barb Wire* has a high energy level, and a sense of deranged fun. There's as much sheer work in this film as in films ten times as good—which is both encouraging and depressing, I suppose.

## Barney's Great Adventure ★ ★ ★

(Star rating for kids six and under; adults: bring your Walkman)
G, 75 m., 1998

Trevor Morgan (Cody Newton), Diana Rice (Abby Newton), Kyla Pratt (Marcella), George Hearn (Grandpa Greenfield), Shirley Douglas (Grandma Greenfield). Directed by Steve Gomer and produced by Sheryl Leach and Dennis DeShazer. Screenplay by Stephen White.

Since *Barney's Great Adventure* is intended for children six and below, I am writing this review to be read aloud:

Barney has his own movie. Not one of those videos you've watched a hundred times, but a real movie, more than an hour long. If you like him on TV, you'll like him here, too, because it's more of the same stuff, only outdoors and with animals and shooting stars and the kinds of balloons people can go up in.

The main character in the story, after Barney, is a boy named Cody, who is in about the first or second grade. He's just at that age when kids start to have their doubts about dinosaurs who look like large purple stuffed toys. Along with his sister Abby and her best friend, Marcella, he goes to visit Grandpa and Grandma on their farm. Cody doesn't think he'll like the farm, because his grandparents don't have cable TV, so how can he watch Nickelodeon? Plus Grandpa's pigpen is directly below Cody's bedroom window.

But then Barney turns up. He starts as a little toy, and then he becomes about eight feet tall, but looking just the same. He sings a song named "Imagine" and tells Cody that it was Cody's own imagination that made the toy dinosaur become the real Barney.

Cody plays a trick. He stops believing in Barney. Barney disappears. Then Barney plays a trick. He appears again, because *he* believes in Cody! That sort of makes sense.

Barney shows Cody a special wishing star. The star deposits an egg in Grandpa's barn. This is a wishing egg. It has different colored stripes on it. When all the stripes glow, the egg is about to hatch. The kids take the egg to Miss Birdfinch to find out about it.

But the egg gets in a lot of trouble. It falls into the back of a birdseed truck and is hauled off to town. Cody, Abby, and Marcella chase it, and get to be in a parade and see the balloons go up. To get to town they ride a pony.

Barney must not know any new songs, because mostly he sings old ones, like "Twinkle, Twinkle Little Star" and "Old McDonald" and "Clap Your Hands." It's sweet when Grandpa sings "Let Me Call You Sweetheart" to Grandma. Even though this is probably the first time you've heard that song, it's not new, either.

By the end of the movie, Cody believes in Barney, because it's pretty hard not to believe in something that's purple and eight feet tall and standing right there in front of you. The egg hatches and helps everyone have their wishes. Baby Bop and B.J., Barney's friends on television, have small roles. Baby Bop is always looking for her yellow blanket, which she calls a "blan-kee." Don't you think it's time for Baby Bop to get serious about learning to say "blanket"?

## Basquiat ★ ★ ★ ½

R, 108 m., 1996

Jeffrey Wright (Jean Michel Basquiat), Michael Wincott (Rene Ricard), Benicio Del Toro (Benny Dalmau), Claire Forlani (Gina Cardinale), David Bowie (Andy Warhol), Parker Posey (Mary Boone), Dennis Hopper (Bruno Bischofberger), Gary Oldman (Albert Milo), Christopher Walken (The Interviewer), Willem Dafoe (The Electrician). Directed by Julian Schnabel and produced by Jon Kilik, Randy Ostrow, and Sigurjon Sighvatsson. Screenplay by Schnabel.

*"This world to her was but a tragic play. She came, saw, dislik'd, and passed away."*

—inscribed on the tomb of a young girl, Southwark Cathedral, London

Anyone who has ever painted or drawn knows the experience of dropping out of the world of words and time. A reverie state takes over; there is no sensation of the passing of hours. The voice inside our head that talks to us falls silent, and there is only color, form, texture, and the way things flow together.

There is a theory to explain this. Language is centered on the left side of the brain. Art lives on the right side. You can't draw anything as long as you're thinking about it in words. That's why artists are inarticulate about their work, and why it is naive to ask them, "What were you thinking about when you did this?" They may have given it less thought than you have.

Jean Michel Basquiat seems to have spent most of his brief life on the right side of the brain. Only another artist could understand that, and *Basquiat* is the confident and poetic filmmaking debut of the painter Julian Schnabel, who was a friend of Basquiat. As Schnabel remembers him, he is a quiet, often wordless presence, a young man who rarely says what he is thinking and often deliberately chooses to miss the point of a conversation. He is dreamy, sweet, pensive. There are deep hurts and angers, but he often chooses to turn a passive mask to the world.

Basquiat was an important artist in the generation that exhibited in Manhattan's Soho district around 1980. His anonymous work was known earlier: He was a graffiti artist whose neatly printed legends, signed "SAMO," were found all over New York. On April 29, 1979, at a party opening the Canal Zone (a New York art space), Basquiat identified himself as SAMO, and within a short time his paintings were finding collectors.

His work seemed to accumulate on the surfaces he found around him. He painted on boards, walls, canvases, on the dress of his girlfriend, and even on her paintings. His work assembles areas of bold color with more detailed areas of text, figures, designs, and scribbles—blueprints for a world in his mind. He fell into success with astonishing ease. His first sales came after he approached Andy Warhol and the well-known dealer Bruno Bischofberger at a restaurant table, and they bought his decorated postcards.

Basquiat (played by Jeffrey Wright in a performance of almost mystical opacity) was at that time only a few months out of homelessness; he had lived for a time in a cardboard box. Born in New York of middle-class parents, one of them Haitian, he drifted away from home and into a world of his own. Even to his girlfriend, Gina (Claire Forlani), he remained an enigma. His attention was inward; like all drug users, he focused much of the time on how he felt or didn't feel.

As *Basquiat* re-creates it, the New York art world quickly makes Basquiat a star. A dealer named Rene Ricard (Michael Wincott) spots his work at a party, delivers the ancient pitch, "I will make you a star," and does. "You're named SAMO? Sounds famous already. You got a real name?" When he learns that Basquiat also performs in a band, he frets, "Are you Tony Bennett? Do you sing on stage and paint in your spare time?"

Basquiat soon becomes a close friend of Andy Warhol, who in a remarkable performance by David Bowie comes across as preternaturally detached (that's not news) but also as gentle, open, accepting, and instinctively perceptive about new directions in art. When Basquiat is depressed by a magazine article depicting him as Warhol's "mascot," a mutual friend tells him, "Andy has never asked me for a thing except to talk to you about getting off drugs."

That Basquiat will not do. Drugs are the center of his existence. His best friend from the early days, a Puerto Rican painter named Benny Dalmau (Benicio Del Toro), gives him tips ("Don't give anything to Warhol! Trade!"). But Dalmau finally drops him because of his self-destructiveness. His girlfriend finds him nearly dead after an overdose. It is clear to everyone he is in trouble. But by now Basquiat is in a mental land of his own. We learn that his mother is a mental patient, and there is a poignant late scene as he tries to break into the shuttered convent where she once lived; turned away from the chained gates, he wanders the streets in pajamas, aimed at homelessness again.

Schnabel knows the New York art scene intimately (his own paintings appear in the movie as the work of a character played by Gary Oldman), and he shows us the agents, the critics, the collectors, and the dealers (Parker Posey plays Basquiat's dealer Mary Boone, and Dennis Hopper is Bischofberger). He knows the acquisitive greed of collectors, and dealers, and shows Basquiat drawing in plum sauce in the guest book at Mr. Chow's and another guest at the table tearing the page from the book (is it framed on somebody's wall even now?).

Schnabel also has a good ear for the lingo. Racism is not racism, apparently, if it is expressed with the right tone of bored sophistication, and so we hear Basquiat's admirers saying, "This . . . is the real voice of the gutter!" At another point he is described as "the picaninny of the art world." He hears, "There has never been a black painter who was considered important."

Actually, he is a wonderful painter and the right side of his brain is rarely wrong, as he demonstrates in a remarkable scene with Warhol where he fearlessly takes a brush and applies a large white area to one of Warhol's Mobil flying horses. Warhol lets him: "I think you may be right about the white."

But there is always madness there. Schnabel remembers that Basquiat often talked about moving to Hawaii, and shows waves and surfers in the sky above Manhattan. He shows Basquiat painting a stack of car tires, and then seeing them transformed into a flowering tree. At the end, he was wearing boatlike wooden shoes on which he had painted *Titanic*. He died on August 12, 1988. He was twenty-seven years old.

## Batman & Robin ★ ★

PG-13, 126 m., 1997

George Clooney (Batman/Bruce), Chris O'Donnell (Robin/Dick), Arnold Schwarzenegger (Mr. Freeze), Uma Thurman (Poison Ivy), Alicia Silverstone (Batgirl), Michael Gough (Alfred Pennyworth), Pat Hingle (Commissioner Gordon), John Glover (Dr. Jason Woodrue), Elle Macpherson (Julie Madison), Vivica A. Fox (Ms. B. Haven), Jeep Swenson (Bane). Directed by Joel Schumacher and produced by Peter Macgregor-Scott. Screenplay by Akiva Goldsman, based on Batman characters created by Bob Kane and published by DC Comics.

Because of my love for the world of Batman, I went to Joel Schumacher's *Batman & Robin* with real anticipation. I got thrilled all over again by the Gothic towers of Gotham City. I was reminded of how cool the Batmobile is (Batman has a new one), and I smiled at the fetishistic delight with which Batman and Robin put on their costumes, sheathing themselves in shiny black second skins and clamping on lots of belts, buckles, shields, hooks, pulleys, etc. (How much does that stuff weigh? How do they run while they're wearing it?)

But my delight began to fade at about the thirty-minute mark, when it became clear that this new movie, like its predecessors, was not *really* going to explore the bizarre world of its heroes, but would settle down safely into a special effects extravaganza. *Batman & Robin*, like the first three films in the series, is wonderful to look at, and has nothing authentic at its core.

There is a scene that illustrates what I mean. It comes during the dreary central section of the film. Bruce Wayne (George Clooney) dines at home with his fiancée for the past year, Julie Madison (Elle Macpherson). Julie says she would like to spend the rest of her life with Wayne. Bruce hems and haws and talks about his bachelorhood and the complications of his life. Julie looks like she has heard all of this before. The scene is interrupted by an emergency.

Watching it, I realized why it makes absolutely no difference who plays Batman: There's nobody at home. The character is the ultimate Suit.

Garb him in leather or rubber, and he's an action hero—Buzz Lightyear with a heartbeat. Put him in civilian clothes, and he's a nowhere man.

I've always suspected they cast movie Batmans by their chins, which is all you see when the Bat costume is being worn, and Clooney has the best chin yet. But like Michael Keaton and Val Kilmer, he brings nothing much to the role because there's nothing much there. Most of the time he seems stuck for conversation. I think the way to get him started would be to ask about his technological gimmicks. This is a guy who would rather read the Sharper Image catalog than *Playboy.*

The series has been driven by its villains. They make some good memories: Jack Nicholson as the Joker, Danny DeVito as the Penguin, Michelle Pfeiffer as Catwoman, Tommy Lee Jones as Two-Face, Jim Carrey as the Riddler. In *Batman & Robin* we get Arnold Schwarzenegger as Mr. Freeze, a man who can survive only by keeping his body at zero degrees (Celsius? Fahrenheit? absolute?), and Uma Thurman as Poison Ivy, a botanist who turns into a plant and wages war against animals. They earn their places in the pantheon of Batman's enemies, but the screenplay doesn't do them justice: It meanders, and some of the big action sequences are so elaborate they're hard to follow (examples: the one where Freeze's men play hockey with a diamond, and a completely pointless motorcycle chase).

Listening to Schwarzenegger's one-liners ("The iceman cometh!") I realized that a funny thing is happening to the series: It's creeping irresistibly toward the tone of the 1960s TV show. The earlier Batman movies, especially the dark *Batman Returns* (1992), made a break with the camp TV classic and went for moodier tones. But now the puns and punch lines come so fast the action has to stop and wait for them, and although we don't get the POW! and WHAM! cartoon graphics, this fourth movie seems inspired more by the TV series than the Bob Kane comic character.

The plot: Mr. Freeze wants to freeze everybody ("First Gotham—then the World!") while bringing back to life the cryogenically frozen body of his beloved wife. Poison Ivy wants to destroy all animals and free the globe for her new kinds of genetically engineered plants. Ivy attracts Batman and Robin (and every other man in view) with her seductive perfume, and tricks Mr. Freeze into helping her, until he catches on. Thurman plays her with a languid drawl that suggests plants *can* have multiple orgasms.

Among the supporting characters is the faithful old butler, Alfred (Michael Gough), who seems to be dying, and asks poignant questions such as, "For what is Batman but an attempt to control the chaos that sweeps our world?" Midway in the action, Alfred's niece (Alicia Silverstone) turns up and finds herself a job as Batgirl, although the movie can never decide if Robin (Chris O'Donnell) is more attracted to her or to Poison Ivy. Another interesting character is a bionic muscleman named Bane (Jeep Swenson), who is Poison Ivy's pet monster. Chemicals pump his muscles to six times life size, and there are opportunities here for satire on Schwarzenegger's movie roles, but all of them are studiously avoided.

What I'll remember from the film are some of the images, such as the Gotham Observatory, which is inside a giant globe held aloft far above the city streets by a towering statue in the Grecian style. And I will remember Mr. Freeze sadly looking at a little music-box figure of his wife. And Alfred poignantly searching his family tree on his computer. And Ivy's leafy eyebrows.

My prescription for the series remains unchanged: Scale down. We don't need to see $2 million on the screen every single minute. Give the foreground to the characters, not the special effects. And ask the hard questions about Bruce Wayne. There is a moment in the film where we learn that the new telescope in the Gotham Observatory can look at any place on Earth. "Just don't point it at my bedroom," Bruce Wayne chuckles. What is he chuckling about?

## Bean ★ ★ ½

PG-13, 90 m., 1997

Rowan Atkinson (Mr. Bean), Peter MacNicol (David Langley), Pamela Reed (Alison Langley), Sir John Mills (Chairman), Burt Reynolds (General Newton), Harris Yulin (George Grierson). Directed by Mel Smith and produced by Peter Bennet Jones, Tim Bevan, and Eric Fellner. Screenplay by Rowan Atkinson, Richard Curtis, and Robin Driscoll.

Bean is like a malevolent Ace Ventura in slow motion. Remember the Al Capp character who went everywhere with the dark rain cloud hovering over his head? For everyone he meets, Bean is that cloud. Since so many slapstick heroes are relentlessly cheerful or harmless, his troublesome streak is sort of welcome.

Bean, played by Rowan Atkinson, first came to life as the star of a British sitcom that quickly became the most popular comedy show in English-speaking markets all over the world. Only in America, where Bean hides out on PBS, is he relatively unknown. Now comes *Bean* the movie, which arrives in the United States having already grossed more than $100 million in the United Kingdom, Australia, Canada, etc.

Although the United States is the last market to play *Bean*, the film seems to have been tailored with an eye to Yank viewers; most of the action takes place in Los Angeles. The setup is in London, where Bean is employed as a guard at an art gallery and is "easily our worst employee," as the curator says at a board meeting where the first order of business is to fire him. When the ancient chairman (John Mills) vetoes that idea, the board gleefully ships Bean off to America as its representative at the unveiling of *Whistler's Mother*.

The famous painting has been purchased from a French museum by a rich retired general (Burt Reynolds), who is no art lover but hates the idea that the "Frenchies" own America's most famous painting. Bean's task will be to oversee the installation of the painting in L.A. and speak at the unveiling—tasks for which he is spectacularly unequipped.

The Bean character has his roots in the clowns of silent comedy, although few were this nasty. On TV he scarcely speaks at all, preferring wordlike sounds and swallowed consonants, but here he blurts out the odd expression, and in one of the funniest scenes gives a speech before assembled art experts. His adventures are a mixture of deliberate malice and accidental malice. (For example, when he inflates the barf bag on an airplane and pops it above the head of a sleeping passenger, that's malice. But the fact that it was filled with vomit—that was an accident.)

Bean's host in the United States is a young curator (Peter MacNicol), whose wife (Pamela Reed) and children move out of the house after about twenty minutes of Bean. MacNicol hangs in there, as he must: His boss (Harris Yulin) has warned him his job depends on it. Bean goes on a tour of L.A., succeeding in speeding up a virtual-reality ride so that it hurls patrons at the screen, and that's benign compared to what he eventually does to *Whistler's Mother*.

The movie gets in some sly digs as the California museum prepares to market the painting with tie-in products such as T-shirts, beach towels, and beer mugs. But most of the film consists of Bean wandering about, wrinkling his brows, screwing up his face, making sublingual guttural sounds, and wreaking havoc.

Who is Bean, anyway? Like the Little Tramp, he exists in a world of his own, perhaps as a species of his own. He combines guile and cluelessness (he knows enough to use an electric razor on his face, but not enough to refrain from also shaving his tongue). He knows how to perform tasks, but not when to stop (can stuff a turkey, but gets it stuck on his head). And he is not, in any sense, lovable (the movie gets a smile with MacNicol's attempt to tack on one of those smarmy moments where it's observed that Bean means well; he doesn't mean well).

There are many moments here that are very funny, but the film as a whole is a bit too long. Perhaps the half-hour TV form is the perfect length for Bean. When the art gallery episode has closed and the action shifts to a hospital operating room, I had the distinct feeling that director Mel Smith was padding. Maybe there's a rule that all feature films must be at least ninety minutes long. At an hour, *Bean* would have been nonstop laughs. Then they added thirty minutes of stops.

## The Beautician and the Beast ★ ★

PG, 103 m., 1997

Fran Drescher (Joy Miller), Timothy Dalton (Boris Pochenko), Ian McNeice (Grushinsky), Patrick Malahide (Kleist), Lisa Jakub (Katrina), Michael Lerner (Jerry Miller), Phyllis Newman (Judy Miller), Adam LaVorgna (Karl). Directed by Ken Kwapis and produced by Howard W. "Hawk" Koch Jr. and Todd Graff. Screenplay by Graff.

Fran Drescher is a taste I have not acquired, but I concede that one could acquire it. It would help if she made a silent film. Her speaking voice is like having earwax removed with a small dental drill. And yet, doggone it, there's something lovable about her. I picture her making the coffee at Stuart Smalley's AA meetings, or doing the ringside announcements for pro wrestling.

You have seen her on *The Nanny* and on countless talk shows. Most talk show guests say something and then laugh, so you know it's supposed to be funny. She laughs, and then says something, so you know it was supposed to be a laugh and not a respiratory emergency. Not every role would be suitable for her. I cannot visualize her, for example, in *The English Patient,* saying, "Promise you'll come back for me." Or as Sheriff Marge Gunderson in *Fargo,* asking, "So, I guess that was your accomplice in the wood chipper?"

*The Beautician and the Beast* contains a role that seems to have been whipped up out of two parts of Drescher's public persona and one part of nothing else. She plays Joy Miller, who teaches beauty secrets in a Queens night school. After a smoking mishap leads to a wig fire and the school burns down, she is hailed on the front pages as a heroine (for saving the lab rats) and approached by a representative of the obscure central European nation of Slovetzia.

That nation has recently emerged from communism into a dictatorship controlled by Boris Pochenko (Timothy Dalton), a despot who wants to soften his image and thinks maybe importing an American tutor for his children might help. (Pochenko is also the name of the European exile who is killed at the beginning of *Shadow Conspiracy,* but I cannot think of anything to say about this coincidence, other than that they are both named after a popular Japanese pinball game.) Dalton plays the role as if he had somehow found himself the villain in a James Bond film instead of the hero.

Slovetzia is not an advanced nation. There are sheep on the runway of the national airport. Pochenko lives in a castle possibly mortgaged from Young Frankenstein. Joy makes a bad first impression when she is late for her official welcoming ceremony because she hasn't finished her hair and nails.

The dictator (known to his subjects as the "Beast for Life") has three children, who have grown restive under his iron fist while nevertheless managing to speak in American accents after their first few scenes. A daughter is unhappy about her approaching arranged marriage. The son bites his nails. "Don't do that!" Joy tells him. "Do you want to grow a hand in your stomach?"

Joy's wardrobe runs toward day-glo stretch pants and pullover blouses. She is sublimely indifferent to the veiled threats of Pochenko, so he tries unveiled ones, which she tut-tuts away. Meanwhile, she has the castle running like a catering kitchen, and is able to save precious currency reserves by planning a diplomatic reception around frozen Chung King egg rolls.

The trajectory of this story is clear from its title. The beautician will get the beast, and in the subplot Juliet will get her Romeo. The direction is by Ken Kwapis, whose *He Said, She Said* (1991) is invaluable for getting you from John Tesh to the Addams Family in the Kevin Bacon game. Kwapis tries to build suspense where none can possibly exist, which is always an annoyance; is it a crime for a movie to know as much about its story as the audience does?

But there are some genuine laughs here and there, and a certain charm emanates from Fran Drescher, who I suspect is easier to stand in real life than she lets on in her acting. And we are not disappointed in our wait for the Obligatory Transformational Entrance Scene, which all movies like this lead up to. After being an ugly duckling for three-quarters of the movie, the heroine turns up at the top of a staircase looking regal and beautiful, and descends while trying to keep one of those "are they looking at poor little me?" looks on her face.

*The Beautician and the Beast* made me laugh, but each laugh was an island, entire unto itself. They didn't tie together into anything very interesting. Drescher never really seems to be interacting with the other characters. Like Mae West or Groucho Marx, she eyeballs the stiffs while they're talking, and then delivers her zingers. We don't care about her character because we never feel she's really uncertain, insecure, or vulnerable. Here's a woman who will never grow hands in her stomach.

## Beautiful Girls ★ ★ ★ ½

R, 117 m., 1996

Matt Dillon (Tommy Rowland), Noah Emmerich (Michael Morris), Tim Hutton (Willie), Natalie Portman (Marty), Annabeth Gish (Tracy Stover), Lauren Holly (Darian Smalls), Rosie O'Donnell (Gina Barrisano), Max Perlich (Kev), Michael

Rapaport (Paul), Mira Sorvino (Sharon Cassidy), Uma Thurman (Andera), Martha Plimpton (Jan). Directed by Ted Demme and produced by Cary Woods. Screenplay by Scott Rosenberg.

There is a scene in *Beautiful Girls* where a small-town feminist (Rosie O'Donnell) grabs a copy of *Penthouse* from a magazine stand and uses it as a prop while lecturing some of her sheepish male friends on the realities of womanhood. It is not common, she points out, for women to have small hips and large breasts. "Small hips—small breasts. Big breasts—big hips," she explains. By holding onto an unrealistic image of the dream girl they might somehow, someday be able to meet, the guys are denying themselves a good relationship with a real flesh-and-blood woman right here in their hometown.

These are guys who need more than one lesson, and they're going to get more than one lesson. It's an icy February in Knight's Ridge, Massachusetts—a strange time for a high school class reunion, but that's why Willie (Tim Hutton) has returned to town, linking up with his old classmates, including Tommy (Matt Dillon), Paul (Michael Rapaport), and Kev (Max Perlich). The local guys work construction in the summer and plow snow in the winter, and mope over the girls they used to love and the girls they may someday love—all kinds of girls except for the girls they could reasonably love.

Paul, for example, has a crazed obsession for supermodels. His room, in the house he shares with Tommy, is papered with pinups from old swimsuit issues. Supermodels are "bottled promise," he explains. His dog is named Elle Macpherson. While he moons over the inaccessible, he mourns the loss of his longtime girl (Martha Plimpton), who has given up after dating him for years and started going out with another guy. Paul retaliates by plowing snow in front of her garage door.

Tommy has big problems too. He's been going with Sharon (Mira Sorvino), but he still longs for his old high school flame, Darian (Lauren Holly). Sharon is wounded: "How do I feel with you when the best years of your life were in high school?" Darian has married, but still wants to carry on an affair with Tommy. She thinks her husband doesn't know.

For Willie, the Tim Hutton character, life is just as complicated. He has left a girl behind in New York City and come home for a couple of weeks to "sort things out," which is another way of saying that, like all of his buddies, he's terrified by the commitment of marriage. He moves in with his terminally depressed father and brother, and soon finds himself smitten by Marty, the girl next door. The problem is she's only thirteen.

We can see what he sees in her. As played by Natalie Portman (from *The Professional*), she's smart, she's pretty, she sees right through him, and she has a gift with words. Willie is so charmed that when he sees Marty with one of her schoolmates, he complains to a friend: "I'm actually jealous of a twelve-year-old kid on a bike." When Marty sees him with a woman his own age, her comment is priceless: "Two words not in her vocabulary: lunch money."

*Beautiful Girls* is not, however, about a Lolita complex, although when Paul identifies Marty as the "neighborhood Lolita," her response is swift, hilarious, and devastating. What the movie is really about is just what Rosie O'Donnell said in her lecture about *Penthouse;* it's about guys who are so be dazzled by visions of possible bliss that they cannot see, or relate to, the perfectly wonderful women right there in front of them.

The movie was directed by Ted Demme with a light touch that allows the humor to survive in spite of the gloomy thoughts and the bleak, dark, frozen winter landscape. The screenplay by Scott Rosenberg shows the same verbal facility he employs in *Things to Do in Denver When You're Dead,* but this time the dialogue feels more real and less written. Even the big set-pieces, like the monologues by O'Donnell and Rapaport, sound convincing.

What's nicest about the film is the way it treasures the good feelings people can have for one another. They emerge most tenderly in the friendship between Willie and the thirteen-year-old girl. They have crushes on each other for essentially idealistic reasons (each projects a simplicity and perfection that may not be there), and yet they draw apart, ever so tactfully, because they are sensible enough to know that's the right thing to do.

Their relationship is mirrored in all of the others, which are all about idealism and its disappointments. The men insist that women correspond to some sort of universal ideal, and the women sometimes blame themselves when they cannot. But somehow, doggedly, true love teaches its lesson, which is that you can fall in love with an ideal, but you can only be in love with a human being.

### Beautiful Thing ★ ★ ★

R, 90 m., 1996

Glenn Berry (Jamie Gangel), Scott Neal (Ste Pearce), Linda Henry (Sandra Gangel), Tameka Empson (Leah), Ben Daniels (Tony). Directed by Hettie Macdonald and produced by Tony Garnett and Bill Shapter. Screenplay by Jonathan Harvey.

*Beautiful Thing* tells the story of two teenage boys, neighbors in a London high-rise housing project, who gradually become aware that they are homosexual. But a funny thing happens: The most interesting scenes involve the characters around them, who all but steal the movie. The boys' lives contain few surprises (it is clear from the start what the one big surprise is going to be), but from the other characters there is one astonishment after another.

The boys are Jamie (Glenn Berry), an introverted, quiet type, and Ste (Scott Neal), an athlete. Jamie becomes aware that he's drawn to Ste, but does nothing about it until one night when Ste is beaten (as usual) by his alcoholic father, and Jamie's mother takes pity and invites Ste to sleep at their house. Ste and Jamie fairly quickly discover how they feel about each other, and there is a touching scene where they study a copy of *Gay Times* magazine, trying to figure out what they're supposed to know about homosexuality. (They guess that the word "frottage" means a kind of yogurt.)

Their relationship is shown in a fairly simple, sweet way, and we realize that, straight or gay, all teenage first romances have a lot in common, including great wonder inspired by raging hormones and idealism. What is much more interesting is the world they inhabit. The housing project consists of long rows of flats opening onto balconies, and along the balconies the neighbors have established an easygoing, friendly community.

We meet Jamie's mother, Sandra (Linda Henry), a barmaid with a big personality. She's loud, jolly, self-confident, good company. Her relationship with her son seems basically a healthy one, although some might question her hours and her choice in boyfriends. Her current squeeze is Tony (Ben Daniels), a leftover hippie younger than she, who is a good sort, although pot has made him vague. (Meditating on Jamie's situation, he comes up with profundities such as, "I think he should just like . . . move toward getting away from all that.")

The dynamo of the balcony is a young black woman named Leah (Tameka Empson), who lives next door and obsesses about the Mamas and the Papas. She wants, indeed, to be the next Mama Cass, and plays her records at top volume at unexpected hours. "It's not natural," Sandra says. "A girl her age, into Mama Cass." On the other side lives Ste's dysfunctional family, which also includes a violent older brother.

These peripheral characters are the real life of the film. They're quirky, funny, unpredictable. There is nothing really remarkable about Jamie and Ste; the director, Hettie Macdonald, exhausts what she has to say about them by making them gay and having them understand and accept that. But Sandra, Leah, and Tony are colorful adults who are verbal (if not articulate) about their beliefs and desires, and we brighten up every time we see them on the screen.

Although I have never been a gay London teenager, I had the feeling that Jamie and Ste were not understood very deeply by the film, and their behavior wasn't convincing. After they tentatively accept that they are gay, for example, they go to a pub advertised in *Gay Times*, and find drag queens putting on a floor show (one of the songs is "Hava Nagillah"). Here they realize they are not alone in the universe, and even eventually invite Sandra and Tony to go there with them.

Oh, yeah? To begin with, no London teenager is going to be completely in the dark about homosexuality. Not in these times. Nor are most sixteen-year-olds going to find much amusing in a pub full of older men, many of them in drag, a lot of them drunk. Teenagers of any sexuality seek others their age, think thirty-year-olds are "old," and might be a little slow to dig middle-aged men doing Barbra Streisand imitations.

This pub is not going to be the answer to Jamie and Ste's search, and yet there are times, I swear, when the movie actually seems to think that once you come out of the closet, you head straight for the pub and live there happily for the rest of your life. It also contrives a happy ending where Jamie and Ste embrace each other in public in a commons area at the project, while Mama Cass's voice bounces encouragingly off the walls, and neighbors and strangers beam their approval. Also not a likely scenario. The scene where Sandra confronts the truth about Jamie, on the other hand, is well-written and acted; the movie understands her better than her son.

*Beautiful Thing* is essentially a fantasy, a coming-out fable with about the same depth and insight as a romance novel for teenagers. What makes the movie special and worth recommending are those other characters. I'd like to see a whole movie about Leah. I was pleased that Sandra finally got her own pub, and I'd like to see a movie about her managing it. As for Jamie and Ste, they will grow up, and become more complicated, better informed, and less one-dimensional, and the day will come when they will look at a movie like this, smile, and shake their heads in amusement and disbelief.

## Beavis and Butt-Head Do America ★ ★ ★

PG-13, 80 m., 1996

Voice-overs: Mike Judge (Beavis/Butt-Head). Directed by Mike Judge and produced by Abby Terkuhle. Screenplay by Judge and Joe Stillman.

It is impossible to deal with *Beavis and Butt-Head Do America* without first dealing with Beavis and Butt-Head themselves. The real subject of the film is attitude, because B&B are *about* attitude. What actually happens is of little importance, since Beavis and Butt-Head are so stupid and sublimely self-absorbed that the exterior world has little reality except as an annoyance or distraction.

It would be easy to attack B&B as ignorant, vulgar, depraved, repulsive slobs. Of course they are. But that would miss the point, which is that Mike Judge's characters reflect parts of the society that produced them. To study B&B is to learn about a culture of narcissism, alienation, functional illiteracy, instant gratification, and television zombiehood. Those who deplore Beavis and Butt-Head are confusing the messengers with the message.

For B&B, happiness is easily defined. It consists of sitting side by side on a sofa watching television, which they dimly perceive as containing images of food, drink, mayhem, and large breasts. As long as the TV is on and they are supplied with food and drink, B&B see no need to move. They would be as happy in prison, assuming the set was working. (The movie shows an album of old photos of B&B growing up; we see them as infants, toddlers, children, teenagers, etc.—always on the couch, watching TV.)

Early in Mike Judge's *Beavis and Butt-Head Do America,* there is a funny sequence in which their television is stolen. This becomes apparent to B&B after a time, because they realize that they are looking at the place where the TV should be, and it is not there. As this fact sinks in, they grow restless and disturbed. Beavis (or Butt-Head; I forget) tries to reconstruct the crime, and the movie shows a series of shots: (1) broken window, (2) missing TV, (3) footprints leading from window to where TV was, (4) footprints leading out the open door. Then the movie repeats this series of shots a second time, and then a third time, and then the series is broken up into close-ups, for closer study. Eventually the clues are correctly deciphered: The set is not there because it has been stolen! This sequence is brilliant in the way it illustrates the mental capabilities of B&B, who between them have the IQ of a cork.

I said I wasn't sure if Beavis or Butt-Head deconstructed the TV theft. It is, of course, possible to tell them apart in this movie: One wears a Metallica T-shirt, and the other wears an AC/DC T-shirt. Their haircuts differ. And one has a more or less permanent damp patch in his crotch. I am sure students of the TV series can describe subtle differences in their personalities, just as there are said to be viewers who can identify the individual Ninja Turtles. For practical purposes, however, B&B are one personality, split into two so that they will have somebody to talk to.

The plot of the movie involves a deadly biological weapon, which comes into the possession of B&B during a trip in which they encounter normal Americans, including a retired couple touring the West in their camper. Through a series of adventures unnecessary to describe, B&B eventually end up in the Oval Office (and there is a cameo for President Clinton). In between, the health and safety of the nation have been threatened, and B&B have used the retired couple's camper and several other locations for their most inventive and ambitious pastimes, which are masturbating and farting. They have also completely missed the point of everything that has happened to them, everything said to them, and everything around them.

It is impossible to feel any affection for B&B. They aren't lovable goofs, like Bill and Ted (of *Excellent Adventure* fame). Judge has stripped them of all redeeming qualities. Why, then, did *Beavis and Butt-Head Do America* hold my interest, and amuse and stimulate me—why was the movie so much fun? Because B&B represent an extreme version of people we see around us every day, and because the movie is radical and uncompromising: Having identified B&B as an extreme example of grunge, disaffection, and cheerfully embraced ignorance, the movie is uncompromising in its detestation of them.

I make this point because it is widely but wrongly believed that *Beavis and Butt-Head* celebrates its characters and applauds their sublime lack of values, taste, and intelligence. I've never thought so. I believe Mike Judge would rather die than share a taxi ride to the airport with his characters—that for him, B&B function like Dilbert's supervisors in the Scott Adams universe. They are a target for his anger against the rising tide of stupidity.

B&B share another quality with Adams's Dilbert strip: The use of what the French call the "clear line" approach to cartooning and animation. The master of this style, Hergé, used it in his Tin Tin books to create a world of extreme simplicity, in which nothing existed except exactly what was needed to fill the next frame and further the story. (Ernie Bushmiller's "Nancy" strip is another good example.) The movie is not "fully animated" in the sense that *The Lion King* is, but its low-rent animation disguises a sophisticated graphic style and visuals that perfectly suit the material: The movie looks the way it should.

All of this is just another way of saying that the less you're like Beavis and Butt-Head, the more you might like this movie. On the other hand, B&B would probably enjoy it, too—if it was on television. I wonder if they would notice that it was about themselves. ☞

## Bed of Roses ★ ★

PG, 87 m., 1996

Christian Slater (Lewis), Mary Stuart Masterson (Lisa), Pamela Segall (Kim), Josh Brolin (Danny), Brian Tarantina (Randy), Debra Monk (Mom), Mary Alice (Alice), Kenneth Cranham (Simon). Directed by Michael Goldenberg and produced by Allan Mindel and Denise Shaw. Screenplay by Goldenberg.

*Bed of Roses* tells a sappy story about two sad sacks who get more or less what they deserve—each other. It's one of those weepers that might have made sense in the 1930s, with big stars to let us know it was only kidding. But I'm afraid this movie is very serious about its romance, which is so earnest and sweet that I kept hoping at least one of the lovers would turn out to be a slasher.

The film opens with a day in the life of Lisa (Mary Stuart Masterson), a top-level executive whose private life is empty despite the presence (or more usually the absence) of a boyfriend. Both of them are such workaholics that it's convenient to go with a person who has no time for them. One day Lisa gets some news: A man named Stanley has died in Philadelphia. On the same day, she receives a mysterious delivery of flowers from an anonymous admirer.

We learn more about Stanley later: He was Lisa's abusive adoptive father, who raised her after she was abandoned at an airport. Stanley's wife died soon after the adoption; Lisa is a woman with more missing parents than most. (There is even a flashback to little Lisa asking the drunken, sullen Stanley, "When's my birthday?" and him growling, "You don't have a birthday.")

Back to the present. Who are the flowers from? She cross-examines the delivery man, named Lewis (Christian Slater). He claims to know nothing, but later confesses the flowers are from him. He takes long walks at night, you see, to try to forget the pain of his wife and child having died, and one day he saw Lisa standing in her window, and fell in love. Oh, and he owns the florist shop.

Lisa and Lewis are both almost bent with the weight of their misfortunes, but they begin to date, and the progress of their relationship is charted by Lisa's best friend, Kim (Pamela Segall), who is one of those convenient characters put into movies so the heroine will have someone to talk to while providing innermost thoughts that would otherwise have to go into voice-over narration. (At least Segall brings bright energy to the role; we have a feeling that if the flowers had been delivered to Kim, she would have had better things to do than spend three days trying to find out who sent them.)

Far be it from me to reveal what happens as the romance progresses. But I'm serious about thinking one of them would turn out to be a dangerous nut. Usually, in modern movies, romantic setups like this are played so straight only *when* a nasty surprise is going to pop up later. (See *Fatal Attraction.*)

Is he too good to be true? Does her moody exterior conceal dangerous aberrations? Alas, no. The movie hinges on that most reliable of modern romantic clichés, the Fear of Commitment. How can she commit to romance when she has been abused by Stanley and grown up into a workaholic? And how can he commit, when he is afraid all will end in disaster, as it did with his first wife?

Just to give you a sample of the movie's goofiness, the two of them spend their first date delivering flowers. See, even though Lewis owns the shop, he likes to deliver the flowers himself, just to see people's faces light up when they receive them. What a sensitive guy.

The actors are wasted on this material, which moves forward with grave deliberation. Mary Stuart Masterson, who specializes in spunk and fortitude, doesn't seem right as an unfocused, self-pitying loser. And Christian Slater is better as a cool, laconic outsider than as a dreamer with a song in his heart. Maybe one reason they seem unconvincing is that the story lays it on so thick; they're buried by the material.

## Bent ★ ★

NC-17, 104 m., 1997

Clive Owen (Max), Lothaire Bluteau (Horst), Brian Webber (Rudy), Ian McKellen (Uncle Freddie), Mick Jagger (Greta). Directed by Sean Mathias and produced by Michael Solinger and Dixie Linder. Screenplay by Martin Sherman, based on his play.

*Bent* tells a heart-rending love story, set against the backdrop of the Holocaust. I could describe the film in solemn pieties, but that would be too easy. The more deeply it descends into horror, the more alarming its agenda becomes, until finally I'd had enough: The material is not worthy of its setting.

The story involves a Berlin homosexual named Max (Clive Owen), who is swept up in the Nazi madness, forced to kill his lover, sent to a prison camp, and there finds true love with another man. Max has lied to qualify for a yellow star (signifying he is Jewish) instead of a pink one (homosexual). By the end he is proud to wear the pink star, but his decision is staged as a crowd-pleaser.

*Bent* is a movie very much about entertaining its audience (I have not seen the stage play by Martin Sherman). It opens with a gay orgy, hosted by the transvestite Greta (Mick Jagger), where bodies are strewn about in sexual congress. Some of the celebrants are either Nazis, or wear Nazi uniforms as a form of erotic enhancement (whether their own or the audience's is a tricky question).

Max goes home with a handsome young Nazi, and has sex with him to the dismay of Max's lover, Rudy (Brian Webber). It is the time of the purge of gay Nazis; storm troopers burst in to slit the Nazi's throat. Max and Rudy escape, hide in the woods, and are captured after a thrilling action scene. The scene exists for its own sake; the drama is suspended so the audience can thrill to the formula of pursuit.

On a train to prison camp, Max is forced to commit unspeakable acts and betray his friend. The underlying message is, it's every man for himself; the film will refute that. In the camp, Max is assigned to shift rocks from one pile to another. He's joined by Horst (Lothaire Bluteau), whom he met on the train. "Friendship lasts about twelve hours in this place," Horst tells him.

But soon, in the midst of dread and a bitter winter, they find erotic desire stirring, and there is a scene where they stand side by side, with no eye contact, and by describing their feelings verbally are able to arrive at simultaneous orgasm. This scene works like the chase scene: It drops out of the drama to stand alone as entertainment—as eroticism. A better film would have found a way to absorb the sexuality into the underlying theme; both scenes are crowd-pleasers, and so is a closing sequence, which seems staged more as a noble tableaux than as drama at all.

Max's personal victory we of course applaud,

but does the film, with its methods, deserve the sentiment it requests? Sherman's stage version of *Bent* is, I am told, a moving experience. During the film there was scarcely a moment when I wasn't aware of the gears cleverly turning.

## Beyond Silence ★ ★ ★ ½

PG-13, 100 m., 1998

Sylvie Testud (Lara), Tatjana Trieb (Lara as a child), Howie Seago (Martin), Emmanuelle Laborit (Kai), Sibylle Canonica (Clarissa), Matthias Habich (Gregor), Alexandra Bolz (Marie), Hansa Czypionka (Tom). Directed by Caroline Link and produced by Thomas Wobke, Jacob Claussen, and Luggi Waldleitner. Screenplay by Link and Beth Serlin.

*Beyond Silence* is one of those films that helps us escape our box of time and space and understand what it might be like to live in someone else's. It tells the story of Lara, the child of deaf parents, who loves them and has been well raised by them, but must, as all children must sooner or later, leave her nest and fly on her own.

The movie isn't centered on a few manufactured plot points, but gives us a sense of the whole span of the family's life. It's not a sentimental docudrama but a hard and yet loving look at the way these people deal with their issues and incriminations. No one is the hero and no one is the villain; they are all doing the best they can, given the way life has made them.

Lara, played as a child by Tatjana Trieb and as a young woman by Sylvie Testud, moves effortlessly between the worlds of sound and sign. She sits beside the TV set, signing for her parents, and translates for them during a heated meeting with a banker. (At the end of the conference, when the banker says, "Thanks, Lara," she pointedly tells him, "My parents are your customers, not me.") She is not above mischief. At a parent-teacher conference, she shamelessly represses the teacher's critical observations about her schoolwork.

The crucial event in the film is a simple one: Lara's aunt, her father's sister, gives her a clarinet. This is a gift fraught with meaning. In a flashback, we see the father as a young deaf boy, watching as relatives crowd around to applaud his sister's first clarinet recital. Frustrated, he gives voice to a loud, painful noise, and is banished to a bedroom. It is the kind of exclusionary wound that shapes a lifetime, and although the father and sister as children communicated effortlessly, as adults they are cool and distant.

There is a ten-year gap (the actresses are so well matched we hardly notice it), and Lara, now nearly twenty, is encouraged by her aunt to attend music school. Her father is opposed, and there is a bitter argument. Lara, who is a gifted player, sits in with her aunt's group, takes classes, and one day sees a man signing to a boy in a park. She follows them, and is surprised to find that he is not deaf, but the child of a deaf father, and a teacher in a school for the deaf. They fall in love.

All of these events are seen with a particular clarity, as stages in Lara's discovery of herself. The opening shot of the movie places the camera underwater in a frozen pond, as skaters circle on the surface and muffled voices come from far away. The whole movie is a process of breaking through the ice into the air of communication.

*Beyond Silence* was one of the 1998 Academy Award nominees for Best Foreign Film, but I have not mentioned until now that this is a German film, because I know some readers have an irrational prejudice against subtitles. But, really, what language is this film in? The subtitles handle not only the spoken dialogue but also describe the music and the sound effects, like thunder; they are designed to be useful for deaf viewers. If the movie were in English, it would still be subtitled. So little does the movie depend on which language is spoken that Howie Seago, the actor playing the father, is an American (both he and Emmanuelle Laborit, as his wife, are hearing impaired).

The movie is alert to nuances of the politics of deafness. Characters talk about the historical prejudice against sign language in Germany, and Lara's grandmother frets that she was advised not to sign, in order to "force" her son to learn to talk: "If I hadn't listened to that pighead, my hands might be able to fly too."

But *Beyond Silence* is wise and complex about the limitless subject of deafness. It is about how hurts are formed in families and remain for decades. About how parents favor a hearing child over a deaf one. About how Lara and her parents have formed a symbiosis that must be interrupted if she is to have a life of her own. So much hinges on simple things, as when Lara wants her mother to ride a bicycle "like other mothers."

One night on TV, Tom Brokaw asked Harrison Ford if movies have grown mediocre because of their dependence on mindless action and special effects, and I raised up my hands in frustration. If such a question really mattered to Brokaw, he would do a segment about a film like *Beyond Silence,* instead of publicizing the latest mindless 'plex product. Of course, you have to be the kind of person to whom *Beyond Silence* just plain *sounds* more interesting than, say, *Godzilla*. Such people are rare, and to be valued.

## The Big Hit ★

R, 93 m., 1998

Mark Wahlberg (Melvin Smiley), Lou Diamond Phillips (Cisco), Christina Applegate (Pam Shulman), Avery Brooks (Paris), Bokeem Woodbine (Crunch), Antonio Sabato Jr. (Vince), China Chow (Keiko), Lela Rochon (Mistress), Lainie Kazan (Jeanne Shulman), Elliott Gould (Morton Shulman). Directed by Che-Kirk Wong and produced by Warren Zide and Wesley Snipes. Screenplay by Ben Ramsey.

Hollywood used to import movie stars from overseas. Then directors. Then they remade foreign films. Now the studios import entire genres. It's cheaper buying wholesale. *The Big Hit* is a Hong Kong action comedy, directed by Che-Kirk Wong *(Crime Story),* starring an American cast, and written by Ben Ramsey, an American who has apparently done as much time in the video stores as Quentin Tarantino.

The movie has the Hong Kong spirit right down to the deadpan dialogue. Sample:

Hit Man: "If you stay with me you have to understand I'm a contract killer. I murder people for a living. Mostly bad people, but . . ."

Girl He Has Kidnapped: "I'm cool with that."

The characters in these movies exist in a twilight zone where thousands of rounds of ammunition are fired, but no one ever gets shot unless the plot requires him to. The bullets have read the screenplay.

As the film opens, we meet four buddies working out in a health club. They're played by Mark Wahlberg (of *Boogie Nights*), Lou Diamond Phillips, Bokeem Woodbine, and Antonio Sabato Jr. The guys are hunks with big muscles, which we can study during a locker-room scene where they stand around bare-bottomed while discussing Woodbine's recent discovery of masturbation, which he recommends as superior to intercourse, perhaps because it requires only one consenting adult.

Then they dress for work. They're all garbed as utilities workers, with hard hats, tool boxes, and wide leather belts holding wrenches and flashlights. As they saunter down the street to Graeme Revell's pumping sound track, they look like a downsized road company version of the Village People.

The plot: They attack the heavily defended high-rise stronghold of a rich pimp who has just purchased three new girls for $50,000 a head. They break in with guns blazing, and there's an extended action sequence ending with one of the heroes diving out of an upper floor on a bungee cord, just ahead of a shattering explosion. And so on.

They kidnap Keiko (China Chow), the daughter of a rich Japanese executive. Complications ensue, and she ends up in the hands, and later the car trunk, of the leader of the hit men named Melvin Smiley (Wahlberg). This is most likely the first movie in which the hero hit man is named Melvin Smiley. But he does smile a lot because his weakness is, "I can't stand the idea of people who don't like me." You would think a hit man would have a lot of people walking around not liking him, but not if he is a good enough shot.

Keiko falls in love with Melvin with astonishing rapidity. Sure, she tries to escape, but by the end she realizes her future lies with him. Will this complicate Melvin's life? Not any more than it already is.

He has a black mistress (Lela Rochon), who looks at a dismembered body in their bathtub and says, "He's kinda cute." And he has a Jewish fiancée (Christina Applegate), who is Jewish for the sole purpose of having two Jewish parents (Lainie Kazan and Elliott Gould) so they can appear in the middle of the movie like refugees from a Woody Allen picture and provide crudely stereotyped caricatures. Gould makes crass remarks about his wife's plastic surgery, gets drunk, and throws up on Lou Diamond

Phillips, in a scene where both actors appear to be using the powers of visualization to imagine themselves in another movie.

Many more action scenes. Cars explode. Cars are shot at. Cars land in trees. They fall out of trees. Remember those old serials where someone got killed at the end of an installment, but at the beginning of the next installment you see him leap quickly to safety? That trick is played three times in this movie. Whenever anyone gets blowed up real good, you wait serenely for the instant replay.

I guess you could laugh at this. You would have to be seriously alienated from normal human values and be nursing a deep-seated anger against movies that make you think even a little, but you could laugh.

## The Big Lebowski ★ ★ ★

R, 117 m., 1998

Jeff Bridges (The Dude), John Goodman (Walter Sobchak), Julianne Moore (Maude Lebowski), Steve Buscemi (Donny), David Huddleston (The Big Lebowski), Philip Seymour Hoffman (Brandt), Tara Reid (Bunny Lebowski), Ben Gazzara (Jackie Treehorn), John Turturro (Jesus), Sam Elliott (Narrator). Directed by Joel Coen and produced by Ethan Coen. Screenplay by Joel Coen and Ethan Coen.

The Coen brothers' *The Big Lebowski* is a genial, shambling comedy about a human train wreck, and should come with a warning like the one Mark Twain attached to *Huckleberry Finn:* "Persons attempting to find a plot in it will be shot." It's about a man named Jeff Lebowski, who calls himself The Dude, and is described by the narrator as "the laziest man in Los Angeles County." He lives only to go bowling, but is mistaken for a millionaire named The Big Lebowski, with dire consequences.

This is the first movie by Joel and Ethan Coen since *Fargo.* Few movies could equal that one, and this one doesn't—but it's weirdly engaging, like its hero. The Dude is played by Jeff Bridges with a goatee, a pot belly, a ponytail, and a pair of Bermuda shorts so large they may have been borrowed from his best friend and bowling teammate, Walter Sobchak (John Goodman). Their other teammate is Donny (Steve Buscemi), who may not be very bright, but it's hard to tell for sure since he is never allowed to complete a sentence.

Everybody knows somebody like The Dude—and so, rumor has it, do the Coen brothers. They based the character on a movie producer and distributor named Jeff Dowd, a familiar figure at film festivals, who is tall, large, shaggy, and aboil with enthusiasm. Dowd is much more successful than Lebowski (he has played an important role in the Coens' careers as indie filmmakers), but no less a creature of the moment. Both dudes depend on improvisation and inspiration much more than organization.

In spirit, *The Big Lebowski* resembles the Coens' *Raising Arizona,* with its large cast of peculiar characters and its strangely wonderful dialogue. Here, in a film set at the time of the Gulf War, are characters whose speech was shaped by earlier times: Vietnam (Walter), the flower power era (The Dude), and *Twilight Zone* (Donny). Their very notion of reality may be shaped by the limited ways they have to describe it. One of the pleasures of *Fargo* was the way the Coens listened carefully to the way their characters spoke. Here, too, note that when the In & Out Burger shop is suggested for a rendezvous, The Dude supplies its address: That's the sort of precise information he would possess.

As the film opens, The Dude is visited by two enforcers for a porn king (Ben Gazzara) who is owed a lot of money by the Big Lebowski's wife. The goons, of course, have the wrong Lebowski, but before they figure that out one has already urinated on his rug, causing deep enmity: "That rug really tied the room together," The Dude mourns. Walter, the Vietnam vet, leads the charge for revenge. Borrowing lines directly from President Bush on TV, he vows that "this aggression will not stand," and urges The Dude to "draw a line in the sand."

The Dude visits the other Lebowski (David Huddleston), leaves with one of *his* rugs, and soon finds himself enlisted in the millionaire's schemes. The rich Lebowski, in a wheelchair and gazing into a fireplace like Major Amberson in *The Magnificent Ambersons,* tells The Dude that his wife, Bunny (Tara Reid), has been kidnapped. He wants The Dude to deliver the ransom money. This plan is opposed by Maude (Julianne Moore), the Big Lebowski's daughter from an earlier marriage. Moore, who played a porno actress in *Boogie Nights,* here plays an altogether different kind of erotic artist; she covers her body with paint and hurls herself through the air in a leather harness.

Los Angeles in this film is a zoo of peculiar characters. One of the funniest is a Latino bowler named Jesus (John Turturro), who is seen going door to door in his neighborhood on the sort of mission you read about, but never picture anyone actually performing. The Dude tends to have colorful hallucinations when he's socked in the jaw or pounded on the head, which is a lot, and one of them involves a musical comedy sequence inspired by Busby Berkeley. (It includes the first point-of-view shot in history from inside a bowling ball.)

Some may complain that *The Big Lebowski* rushes in all directions and never ends up anywhere. That isn't the film's flaw, but its style. The Dude, who smokes a lot of pot and guzzles White Russians made with half-and-half, starts every day filled with resolve, but his plans gradually dissolve into a haze of missed opportunities and missed intentions. Most people lead lives with a third act. The Dude lives days without evenings. The spirit is established right at the outset, when the narrator (Sam Elliott) starts out well enough, but eventually confesses he's lost his train of thought.

## The Big One ★ ★ ★

PG-13, 96 m., 1998

A documentary directed by Michael Moore and produced by Kathleen Glynn. Screenplay by Moore.

Americans are happy with the economy. Unemployment is at an all-time low. Clinton gets high approval ratings despite scandals because times are good and we don't want to rock the boat.

Swimming upstream against this conventional wisdom, here comes Michael Moore, the proletarian in the baseball cap. In his new documentary, *The Big One,* he crisscrosses the country on a book tour and finds factories closing, corporations shipping jobs overseas, and couples working extra jobs to make ends meet. "It's like being divorced," a mother with three jobs tells him in Centralia, Illinois. "I only see the kids on weekends." Many locals have lost their jobs with the closure of, ironically, the Payday candy bar factory.

Moore became famous overnight in 1989 with his hilarious documentary *Roger and Me,* in which he stalked Roger Smith, president of General Motors, in an attempt to find out why GM was closing its plants in Flint, Michigan, and moving production to Mexico. The movie was filled with cheap shots and media manipulation, and proud of it: Part of the fun was watching Moore turn the imagery of corporate America against itself.

In 1989, though, we were in a slump. Now times are good. Is Moore's message outdated? Not necessarily. If unemployment is low, that doesn't mean the mother in Centralia is prosperous. And what about the workers at Johnson Products in Milwaukee, which celebrated $500 million in profits by closing its factory and moving to Mexico? Moore visits their factory and tries to present them with a "Downsizer of the Year Award" along with his check for eighty cents: "The first hour's wage for a Mexican worker."

He likes to write checks. He creates fictitious committees to make donations to 1996 presidential candidates: Pat Buchanan's campaign cashes a $100 check from "Abortionists for Buchanan," and Moore also writes checks from "Satan Worshippers for Dole," "Pedophiles for Free Trade" (for Perot), and "Hemp Growers for Clinton." Watching Steven Forbes on TV, he notes that the candidate never blinks, and gets an NYU doctor to say, "That's not human."

The occasion for this documentary is Moore's forty-five-city tour to promote *Downsize This!* his best-seller about hard times in the midst of prosperity. We see him lecturing campus crowds, confronting security guards, sympathizing with the striking workers at a Borders bookstore. He's an unapologetic liberal, prounion, anti–fat cat; during an interview with Studs Terkel, he beams beatifically as Studs notes the sixtieth anniversary of the CIO's sit-down strikes against the carmakers.

The movie is smart, funny, and edited cleverly; that helps conceal the fact that it's mostly recycled information. There is little here that *Roger and Me* didn't say first and more memorably. But we get two docs for the price of one: The second one is about book tours, with Moore on a grueling schedule of one city a day, no sleep, endless talk shows and book signings, plus his guerrilla raids on downsizers.

He still wears the gimme caps and the blue jeans with the saggy seats, but the Moore of *Roger and Me* was an outsider, and the Moore of *The Big One* is a celebrity (flight attendants recognize him from his TV show, kids want his autograph). He's rueful about the "media escorts" hired by his publisher to accompany him in every city; at one point, he describes one of his escorts to security guards as a "stalker." She's forcibly led outside the building before the "joke" is revealed; I didn't find it as funny as Moore did.

She is, after all, a working person, too—and so are the security guards Moore banters with as they eject him from factories. Most of them don't even work for the companies they guard, but for temp agencies, and one of the movie's startling statistics is that the largest employer in America is not AT&T, not GM—but Manpower, the hourly temp agency.

Moore's goal in the film is to get at least one corporate big shot to talk to him on camera. He finally lands Phil Knight, CEO of Nike, whose shoes are famously manufactured in Indonesia by workers paid a few dollars a day. Knight is in a no-win situation, but at least he's willing to talk. He doesn't hide behind corporate security.

His case: Shoe factories are good for the Indonesian economy, which in another generation could bootstrap itself into more prosperity. And, "I am convinced Americans do not want to make shoes." But what about Indonesia's genocidal practices against minority groups? Moore asks. "How many people died in the Cultural Revolution?" asks Knight. That's not an answer, but it is a response.

Do Americans want to make shoes? Moore returns to his hometown of Flint and asks citizens to rally if they want a shoe job. It's a cold day, which may have kept the turnout down, but Moore is forced to use low-angle shots to conceal the fact that the crowd of eager shoe workers is not very large. Maybe the issue isn't whether poor Americans want to make shoes, but why poor Americans are charged $150 for a pair of shoes that Indonesians are paid pennies to manufacture.

Moore's overall conclusion: Large American corporations care more for their stockholders than for their workers, and no profit level is high enough to satisfy them. If he'd been able to get more top executives on camera, I have a feeling their response would have been: "Yes. And?"

## The Big Squeeze ★

R, 98 m., 1996

Lara Flynn Boyle (Tanya), Danny Nucci (Jesse), Peter Dobson (Benny), Luca Bercovici (Henry), Michael Chieffo (Inspector), Bert Santos (Manny), Teresa Dispina (Cece). Directed by Marcus De Leon and produced by Zane W. Levitt, Mark Yellen, and Liz McDermott. Screenplay by De Leon.

*The Big Squeeze* opens with a scene involving what I have come to think of as a Teeny-Prole: an actor who looks like a handsome teenage model, playing a character who is allegedly a hardened proletarian. Peter Dobson plays Benny, a young man who is thrown out of a railroad boxcar after cheating in a poker game. Uh, huh. That's how lots of GenXers spend their time.

He rolls down an embankment and into a story that feels like a 1930s screwball comedy but is set in the present day and, even more incredibly, doesn't seem to know it's a comedy. It plays its contrived story perfectly straight, as if events like this could happen.

Benny is a con man. He walks into a bar and meets the two bartenders, Tanya (Lara Flynn Boyle) and Cece (Teresa Dispina). He follows Tanya home, gives her a "diamond" necklace, and then returns to try to pick up Cece. Soon he's in on a promising scam. Tanya, who spots him as a grifter, enlists him to get money out of her husband, Henry (Luca Bercovici). He's a former baseball player who has been paid $130,000 in an injury settlement, and has tried to keep the money a secret from Tanya, who has supported him for years.

Benny's scheme: He discovers that Henry is a devout Catholic, and that the local mission desperately needs $130,000 to complete earthquake repairs. He enlists the help of Jesse (Danny Nucci), a gardener Tanya has moved in with after leaving her husband. They will fake a miracle involving a fast-growing tree. That will inspire Henry to give the money to the mission. They will intercept the money and split it three ways. And, oh yes, there's lots more, including what happens when true believers think it's a real miracle.

I watched this movie with mounting incredulity. The plot is so ungainly that the characters spend a good deal of time just explaining it to one another. Like the miracle tree, it grows and grows. There is a certain naïveté in the film that is beguiling: All of the characters act like unworldly innocents, despite the seamy milieu they inhabit. And they do things like meeting in Union Station for no better reason than that it's an attractive location.

Dobson, as the con man Benny, has a role and screen presence that reminded me of John Cusack in *The Grifters.* But that movie explained why a young man would find himself in a world of crime and deception. *The Big Squeeze* wants us to believe the baby-faced Dobson in a role that essentially requires someone like Harry Dean Stanton or Harvey Keitel—someone rough and worn, battered and experienced. Not that different casting would have saved the plot.

Lara Flynn Boyle has a hapless assignment too. She's good as an icy brunette, but wrong here, where some scenes are too real for the material (as when her husband strikes her) and others are pure fabrication. She is required at one point to fall in love with Jesse, the gardener, and as I was watching their love scenes I could visualize the pages of the script turning, one by one, too slowly: The only reason these characters are in bed with one another, I thought, is because the screenwriter thought he was obligated to put them there.

*The Big Squeeze* is a movie without purpose, conviction, or reward. I can't understand why anyone would want to tell this story—why they liked it, why they thought it would work, why anyone considered it commercial (it's pretty clear the movie was not made for artistic motives). The actors are wrong for the characters, the story is lugubrious, and when I discovered that the movie's original title was *The Body of a Woman,* somehow I wasn't surprised: It makes sense that this material would have started out attached to a title that had nothing to do with it.

## The Birdcage ★ ★ ★

R, 118 m., 1996

Robin Williams (Armand Goldman), Gene Hackman (Senator Keeley), Nathan Lane (Albert), Dianne Wiest (Louise Keeley), Dan Futterman (Val Goldman), Calista Flockhart (Barbara Keeley), Hank Azaria (Agador), Christine Baranski (Katharine). Directed and produced by Mike Nichols. Screenplay by Elaine May.

Hollywood has had a little cottage industry in recent years, turning out American retreads of French films. Now comes the remake of the most seductive target, the comedy *La Cage aux Folles* (1978), which is about a gay man whose son wants him to play it straight for a few days. All of this will be familiar if you've seen the original, or the two sequels, or the Broadway version.

*The Birdcage* isn't about plot, anyway. It's about character, and about the twisted logic of screwball comedy, in which everybody acts the craziest just when they're trying to make the most sense. What makes Mike Nichols's version more than just a remake is good casting in the key roles, and a wicked screenplay by Elaine May, who keeps the original story but adds little zingers here and there ("Live on Fisher Island and get buried in Palm Beach—that way you'll get the best of Florida!").

The movie stars Robin Williams as Armand Goldman, the owner-operator of a drag revue on South Beach. He lives upstairs over his nightclub with Albert (Nathan Lane), the star of the show, who has been his lover for some twenty years. Albert is a basket case, threatened by encroaching age and insecurity, and functions only because Agador (Hank Azaria), the flamboyant houseboy, tranquilizes him with Pirin tablets. ("They're just aspirin with the 'as' scraped off," he confides to Armand.)

A crisis. Armand's son, Val (Dan Futterman), has become engaged (to a girl, I should add), and wants to bring her home to meet his dad, but not "Auntie Albert." The complication is that his fiancée's father is a conservative senator (Gene Hackman), who leads the Coalition for Moral Order and thinks the pope is too controversial and Billy Graham too liberal.

Albert is, of course, devastated that the boy he raised like his own son is turning his back on him. Armand is upset, too, but goes along with a masquerade in which Val's mother (Christine Baranski) will pretend to be Mrs. Goldman. Imagine everything that can go wrong, including the peculiarity of Val having two mothers on stage at the same time, and you more or less have the rest of the movie.

Since the material is familiar, what's a little

amazing is how fresh it seems at times in the hands of the American cast. Robin Williams is the best surprise; in a role that seems written as a license for flamboyance, he's more restrained than in anything he's done since *Awakenings* (1990). Nathan Lane, from Broadway's *Guys and Dolls*, doesn't have quite the semihysterical sincerity that Michel Serrault had in the original, and his impersonation of Val's mother is a little too obvious and over the top, but he works well the rest of the time, especially in his more pensive passages. One problem is that some of his biggest moments (as when he tries to practice walking like John Wayne) are telegraphed from the earlier movie.

Most of the biggest laughs, for me, came from Gene Hackman and Dianne Wiest, as the senator and his wife. Hackman's senator is weathering a crisis (his closest colleague has just died in bed with an underage prostitute), and thinks maybe meeting his new in-laws will promote family values. Wiest, who sees and understands more than her husband but dotes on him, reads the situation in South Beach more quickly, but goes with the flow.

*The Birdcage* is the first time Mike Nichols and Elaine May, who helped define improvisational comedy in the 1950s, have worked together on a movie. What mostly sparkles from their work here is the dialogue, as when the senator's daughter, trying to cast the situation in the best possible light, explains that South Beach is "about two minutes from Fisher Island, where Jeb Bush lives." Or when the Williams character surveys the crowd at his nightclub and whispers to the maître d', "Free coffee for the Kennedys."

## Bliss ★ ★ ★ ½

R, 98 m., 1997

Craig Sheffer (Joseph), Sheryl Lee (Maria), Terence Stamp (Baltazar Vincenza), Spalding Gray (Alfred), Casey Siemaszko (Tanner), Leigh Taylor Young (Redhead). Directed by Lance Young and produced by Allyn Stewart. Screenplay by Young.

*Bliss* is a daring movie not because of the sexuality it contains, but because it is so intent about it. You can snicker about anything sexual in our society, but sex, when it's taken seriously, makes people squirmy, and here's a movie that's grown-up, thoughtful, and surprisingly erotic.

The movie tells the story of two people who are in love with each other, but bring to their marriage many problems that prevent them from having a fulfilling sex life. Joseph (Craig Sheffer) and Maria (Sheryl Lee) are both apprehensive on their wedding day; he knows she's compulsive and neurotic, and while he's ostensibly better adjusted, that may be because he's better at hiding things. Within six months they're telling their problems to a therapist (Spalding Gray), who uses a traditional psychoanalytic approach, and before much longer Maria is sneaking to secret sessions with a sex therapist named Baltazar (Terence Stamp), who "operates on the edge of the law."

The movie is awkward at getting to this point, but once the Stamp character appears on screen, the film finds its rhythm and its confidence, and becomes the story of a search, not for the perfect orgasm, but for the healthiest route in that direction. Because the material is fraught with pitfalls, there's always the danger we might laugh to cover our embarrassment; what's remarkable is how well the actors handle scenes which, in the wrong hands, would have been unplayable.

Lance Young, who wrote and directed the film, moves confidently among enough sex-related topics to fill six months of *Cosmo* covers. Maria fakes her orgasms, Joseph claims he never masturbates, they love each other, but when they try getting closer it's so frightening to Maria that she insists Joseph move out. Eventually a repressed memory surfaces: She was abused by her father, whom she loved, and so she fears love because she fears betrayal. Meanwhile, Joseph has confronted Baltazar in anger but stayed to listen, and is being led through a course of sexual training that includes tantric theories, the art of "injaculation," and yoga breathing exercises while hanging by the heels.

This material could, with just a slight tilt, easily become a Woody Allen movie. Amazing, how good acting can find the truth in well-written material. Although Craig Sheffer and Sheryl Lee are courageous and convincing in very challenging scenes, the key to the film's success is Terence Stamp's performance. His character is written not only at the edge of the law but also at the edge of parody. He lives in an apartment out of *Architectural Digest*, plays violin in the symphony, and believes that the object of sex is bliss (which is nine on his personal scale) and not orgasm (which is down around four). He nevertheless makes the character believable because he plays it with a great and solemn conviction, and very sparingly—there are no unnecessary notes.

I'm sure professional sex counselors will find much to object to in the details of his therapeutic approach. But the details aren't the point. What makes *Bliss* remarkable is that it approaches sex openly and thoughtfully, doesn't fall into soap opera clichés, and avoids all the temptations to turn into a docudrama. It works as the story of these people. It stays focused. When Maria flashes back to episodes of abuse from her childhood, for example, we expect one of those tiresome, obligatory scenes where she confronts her father. Instead, the film accepts this new information, deals with it, and learns from it: The point is to move on, not to extract revenge. (I'm not saying she shouldn't confront her father; I'm saying that scene would be an unnecessary distraction in the progress of this movie.)

The film also avoids the temptation to pit the two therapists against one another. One approach obviously works better than the other for this couple, but when the two therapists meet in a hospital waiting room and learn important information, all the movie does, subtly, is have each man deal with this information in his own jargon. Truth is the objective, not proving who's right or wrong.

Sex is a currency in our society, sold on the basis of glib assumptions and glossy packaging. It's about bodies and functions, not about people. The lessons in *Bliss* are idealistic and romantic, but at the same time unblushingly grounded on specific physical processes and fairly clinical language.

This is Lance Young's first film. I learn from *Box Office* magazine that he went to USC on a golfing scholarship, was a financial analyst, and got into movies as a "production executive." This debut as a writer and director is very impressive. Some moments a more experienced director would have avoided (there are countless better ways to introduce Baltazar than with the silly gimmick involving a telescope at a construction site), and the character of Maria takes too long to be defined. But what's important is that *Bliss* is not an "adult film" but a film for and about adults: It's provocative, and it has a heart.

## Blood and Wine ★ ★ ★ ½

R, 100 m., 1997

Jack Nicholson (Alex Gates), Stephen Dorff (Jason), Jennifer Lopez (Gabrielle), Judy Davis (Suzanne Gates), Michael Caine (Victor Spansky). Directed by Bob Rafelson and produced by Jeremy Thomas. Screenplay by Nick Villiers and Alison Cross, based on a story by Villiers and Rafelson.

*Blood and Wine* is a richly textured crime picture based on the personalities of men who make their living desperately. Jack Nicholson and Michael Caine are the stars, as partners in a jewel theft that goes wrong in a number of ways, each way illustrating deep flaws in the ways they choose to live. It's a morality play, really, but dripping with humid sex and violence.

Nicholson is a Florida wine dealer whose business is going broke, whose wife (Judy Davis) wants to leave him, and whose stepson (Stephen Dorff) hates him. He hooks up with a tubercular British exile (Michael Caine) to steal a million-dollar diamond necklace from the house of some rich people. But it is all so much more complicated than that, and includes Nicholson's sexual liaison with the rich family's nanny (Jennifer Lopez). That's just the setup. The plot gets *really* complicated.

*Blood and Wine* was directed and cowritten by Bob Rafelson, who directed Nicholson's first great picture (*Five Easy Pieces*, 1970) and also worked with him in *The King of Marvin Gardens* (1972), *The Postman Always Rings Twice* (1981), and the unsuccessful *Man Trouble* (1992). This is a return to the tone of their best work; all the major characters are villains or victims. The director Paul Schrader was telling me not long ago that movies have passed out of an existential period and into an ironic period. In that case, *Blood and Wine* is a throwback, because there is nothing ironic about these characters except what finally happens to them. The plot is lurid and blood-soaked beyond description, but is handled seriously as a string of events illustrating the maxim that bad things happen to bad people.

Much of the film's delight depends on what

happens to the diamond necklace after Nicholson and Caine do finally steal it. The theft itself is not so hard. "Rich people are so cheap," the Caine character says. "They'll spend millions on a necklace and lock it in a tin box from Sears." I will not spoil the fun of discovery by describing the travels of the necklace once it is stolen. Instead, I'd like to observe some wonderful actors hard at work.

This is one of Nicholson's best performances, because he stays willingly inside the gritty, tired, hard-nosed personality of Alex Gates, who is failing at love, business, and crime. He nevertheless remains a romantic at heart, and his romance with young Gabrielle (Lopez) is genuine: They love one another, even though she is unwise to believe his stories about how they'll soon be unwinding in Paris. What makes the performance believable is in the details, in the way he tells his stepson to put on a shirt before leaving the house, or in the way he and his wife have a practiced shorthand, condensing all their old arguments into short, bitter trigger-words.

Michael Caine, who can sleepwalk through bad movies, can bring good ones a special texture. Here he is convincing and sardonically amusing as a wreck of a man who chain-smokes, coughs, spits up blood, and still goes through the rituals of a jewel thief because that is what he is. He is capable of sudden violence (pounding Nicholson with a golf club, he observes, "That was an acupuncture point"). But he almost inspires sympathy, as a crook who has labored a long time at a hard profession and has nothing to show for it.

The other roles are given almost equal weight; the supporting characters aren't atmosphere, but crucial to the story, and one sign of the good writing is in the way other relationships (the mother and her son, the son and Gabrielle) affect the outcome of the plot. In a bad crime movie, people do what they do to fit the plot. In a good crime movie, people are who they are, and that determines the plot. Judy Davis, for example, projects a fierce, wounded anger that adds a whole dimension to her marriage; she has given this man her money and trust and seen both thrown away.

Then there is the way Rafelson handles the movie's love triangle, if that is what it can be called. Gabrielle has no way of knowing the relationship between the man she loves and the man she is beginning to love, and Rafelson walks a fine line; when she's forced to choose, we honestly have no way of knowing which way she'll turn.

One early review of this film said it had a "seventies feel." Perhaps that means it takes its plot seriously and doesn't try to deflect possible criticism by hedging its bets, by pretending there is an ironic subtext. I like movies like this: I like the way the actors are forced to commit to them, to work without a net. When Rafelson and Nicholson find the right material, it must be a relief for them to fall back into what they know so well how to do, to handle hard scenes like easy pieces.

## Blues Brothers 2000 ★ ★

PG-13, 121 m., 1998

Dan Aykroyd (Elwood Blues), John Goodman (Mighty Mack McTeer), Joe Morton (Cabel Chamberlain), J. Even Bonifant (Buster), Frank Oz (Warden), Kathleen Freeman (Mother Mary Stigmata), B. B. King (Malvern Gasperon), Aretha Franklin (Mrs. Murphy). Directed by John Landis and produced by Landis, Dan Aykroyd, and Leslie Belzberg. Screenplay by Aykroyd and Landis.

*Blue Brothers 2000* has a lot of good music in it. It would have had more if they'd left out the story, which would have been an excellent idea. The film is lame comedy surrounded by high-energy blues (and some pop, rock, and country and western). And don't stop watching: *after* the end credits James Brown does "Please, Please, Please."

It's as if director John Landis had such good James Brown footage he had to use it, even though there was no room in the main plot line, which mostly involves updates on characters in the original 1980 film. "I always thought there was another story to be told," Landis says in the film's notes. Fine; then tell one.

The first movie opened with Jake Blues (the late John Belushi) getting out of Joliet Prison and going with his brother Elwood (Dan Aykroyd) to the orphanage where they were raised, still presided over by the fearsome Sister Mary Stigmata. The new movie begins with Elwood getting out of prison and seeking out the aging nun, who still whacks Elwood when his manners stray.

Elwood wants to get the old band back together again. Sister Mary has another idea: He should do a little "mentoring" for Buster (J. Even Bonifant), a ten-year-old orphan. Buster gets his own Blues Brothers uniform, plays some harmonica, and gets Elwood charged with kidnapping—but what's he *doing* in this story? Apparently Landis originally conceived the role for Macaulay Culkin. Culkin outgrew it, and Landis should have too.

Seeking out old friends, Elwood goes to a strip joint where he encounters Mighty Mack (John Goodman), a bartender who has a good voice and is enlisted as Jake's replacement. Other band members are added along the way, during an interstate chase orchestrated by a state policeman (Joe Morton) who is more or less Elwood's stepbrother (the dialogue spends a lot of time explaining that "more or less").

The original (much better) film made great use of locations in the Blues Brothers' sweet home Chicago, but this one was shot mostly near Toronto and New Orleans, with a few shots of the Chicago skyline thrown in for effect. (Hint: Bars in Louisiana do not usually advertise that they are "licenced.")

The 1980 movie had neo-Nazi bad guys. This one has a right-wing militia group, with a leader whose pep talks are unnecessarily offensive. I've noticed a disturbing trend recently for lightweight comedies to toss in racist language under the guise of "establishing" the villains. Vile language doesn't require additional currency.

But I stray from the heart of the film, which is good blues music. Just as the 1980 film included show-stopping numbers by Aretha Franklin and Cab Calloway, this one has great musical segments by Aretha ("R.E.S.P.E.C.T."), Eddie Floyd ("634-5789"), John Popper and Blues Traveler ("Maybe I'm Wrong"), Lonnie Brooks and Junior Wells ("Checkin' Up On My Baby"), and the Paul Butterfield Blues Band version of "Born in Chicago."

What is amazing is that the numbers by the guest artists are outnumbered by the Blues Brothers (including little Bonifant), who are backed up by a terrific band. There is food for thought in the sight of the late, great Junior Wells playing backup to a couple of comedians. It's not so much that I didn't enjoy their numbers as that, let's face it, with backup like these guys get, Buddy Hacket and I could be the Blues Brothers.

Jonathan Eig wrote an article in *New Republic* that explains "How the Blues Brothers destroyed the Windy City's musical heritage." It opens in a smoky dive on the South Side where the true blues still live, and then sniffs at the upscale North Side clubs where suburbanites pay $8 entry fees to hear tarted-up and smoothed-down blues.

But surely it has always been thus? The true blues come from, and flourish in, a milieu of hard times—hard emotionally, economically, racially, and not infrequently in lifestyle and substance abuse choices. Move the music to an affluent, paying audience, contract the musicians to two shows a night, mix in some soul and r-&-b to lighten the blues' heavy load, and that's entertainment. The notion that a professional blues musician can be "authentic" on demand (i.e., depressed, angry, bereft, and forlorn) is amusing. It's like they say in the theater: The most important thing is sincerity, and if you can fake that, you've got it made.

What the Blues Brothers do is worse than Eig's complaint about the posh blues clubs. They take a musical tradition and dine out on it, throwing scraps to the real pros. If Junior Wells, Aretha Franklin, Wilson Pickett, John Popper, and James Brown want to sing in a Hollywood musical, they've got to be supporting characters for the brothers.

I don't suggest that Aykroyd and Belushi, in the 1970s, were not providing entertaining musical performances. I do suggest that the Blues Brothers schtick has outlived its usefulness. Watching *Blues Brothers 2000,* I found I had lost all interest in the orphanage, orphans, police cars, nuns, and mentoring. I wanted more music.

It's said that the climactic sequence of *BB2000,* a talent contest assembling many legendary musicians (even an ill-at-ease Eric Clapton), was a legendary jam session. No doubt. I'd love to see it as a concert film. With no chase scenes and no little kids. And really shot in Chicago. Or New Orleans would be okay. Not Toronto. I've heard Toronto called a lot of things, but not the home of the blues.

## Blush ★ ★ ½

NO MPAA RATING, 119 m., 1996

Wang Ji (Qiu Yi), Wang Zhiwen (Lao Pu), He Saifei (Xiao'e), Zhang Liwei (Liu Qing), Wang Rouli (Mrs. Pu), Song Xiuling (Rui Feng), Xing

Yangchun (Mr. Zhang), Zhou Jianying (Mrs. Zhang). Directed by Li Shaohong and produced by Chen Kunming and Jimmy Tan. Screenplay by Ni Zhen and Li Shaohong, based on the novel by Su Tong. In Chinese with subtitles.

There is such a tactile pleasure in the visuals of the Chinese movie *Blush* that only after I thought back carefully through the story did I realize how much better it could have been. It tells the stories of two prostitutes whose brothel is closed after the communist victory of 1949, how the new collectivist society changes them, and how their lives become entwined with the same man. This is a big subject, but the film treats it more like a melodramatic 1940s Hollywood weeper.

Still, what a wonderful look it has! Like almost all recent films from mainland China, *Blush* is so visually sensuous that looking is almost enough. The camera style hasn't been beaten down into lazy TV formulas: The point of view is always thoughtfully chosen; the backgrounds are as important as the foregrounds; there are camera movements that advance the drama by revealing additional elements.

And look at the locations and the use of color. There is a shot in the film that shows a jumble of very old rooftops, jammed at crazy angles toward one another. The stone tiles are dark gray-blue or black, and completely fill the screen. Two women escape from an upper window onto the roof, their bright dresses like the splash of color that helps us see and feel everything else.

Later in the film, the women meet again. One has fled from her own wedding to chase the other down narrow streets. Again, there is the same palate: the old gray stones, damp and dark, and the color of the dresses. These shots and many others (a bridge over a stream through Beijing, a canal with houses built close to it, the interiors of ornate old houses that have been much lived in, a courtyard with views into living quarters) are like living, tactile paintings.

The movie's story has great interest, but not enough depth or detail when we want it. As the movie begins, the prostitutes of the Red Happiness Inn are taken onto canal boats to be moved to a "re-education center." Dressed in their bright silk gowns (again against gray backgrounds), they move calmly, with dignity. But once at the center, a tall, reserved woman named Qiu Yi (Wang Ji) cannot abide the regimentation. She and a younger woman named Xiao'e (He Saifei) try to escape.

Only Qiu Yi makes it. She goes to the house of a rich young man who was her client, and he asks her to move in. Eventually, however, she is forced to leave by the mother, and she begins an odyssey through Beijing that dramatizes how few choices she has. She goes to a convent, shaves her head, and becomes a nun. Eventually the nuns evict her. She goes to a cousin's house, but he will not take her in. She wanders the streets. She could, of course, have taken real work (the other Red Happiness girls work in a textile factory), but she pays the price of becoming an outcast.

Meanwhile, the younger woman, Xiao'e, seeks out the young man that Qiu Yi had been living with and marries him. This man, named Lao Pu (Wang Zhiwen), actually still loves Qiu Yi. His marriage is torn apart by his jealousy and Xiao'e's hysterical demands (they have a screaming match terrifying in its intensity). And then the three lives come together again in an unexpected and bittersweet way.

"Perhaps, after all, I should have stayed with the other girls," Qiu Yi muses at one point. The movie, directed by a woman (Li Shaohong), sometimes seems to argue, however, that marriage is the only real solution to the character's dilemmas, and indeed after Qiu Yi marries Old Feng, owner of a nearby teahouse, things seem to smooth out for her. The movie is not critical of the reforms that upset Qiu Yi's life, but on the other hand it's not critical of her, either; although she never becomes a loyal people's worker, she emerges as the heroine of the story—a survivor who through hard lessons finds happiness at last.

## Bogus ★ ★ ★

PG, 112 m., 1996

Whoopi Goldberg (Harriet Franklin), Gérard Depardieu (Bogus), Haley Joel Osment (Albert), Denis Mercier (Mr. Antoine), Nancy Travis (Lorraine). Directed by Norman Jewison and produced by Jewison, Arnon Milchan, and Jeff Rothberg. Screenplay by Alvin Sargent.

*Bogus* tells the story of a little boy who is orphaned and then finds his life filled with two unconventional parent-substitutes. How unconventional? They're played by Whoopi Goldberg and Gérard Depardieu—Goldberg as the aunt he never knew about, and Depardieu as an imaginary friend, a large, shambling Frenchman, who bounces out of the pages of a coloring book.

The little boy's name is Albert (Haley Joel Osment), and he has grown up in Las Vegas, where his mother (Nancy Travis) was an assistant in the magic act of Mr. Antoine (Denis Mercier), who seems to be a cross between David Copperfield and Cirque du Soleil. It's not an ordinary childhood; he has a baseball autographed by Liza Minnelli. After his mother is killed in a traffic accident early in the film, Mr. Antoine and the other showbiz people meet to decide what is to be done with the child. But the mother has provided for that in her will, naming her African-American foster sister Harriet (Goldberg), who nobody knew about.

Harriet is not thrilled to be given responsibility for a kid. She runs a restaurant supply business out east, knows nothing of showbiz and less about kids, and has a lot on her mind. But she accepts the responsibility because she must, and the morose little boy flies east to his destiny. It is then that Bogus (Depardieu) materializes from the coloring book to become his sidekick, adviser, and confidant.

This mixture of the poignant and the mystical is not new to director Norman Jewison, who in films like *Moonstruck* and *Only You* has found a winsome romanticism that bypasses the pragmatic side of life. Here he works with a story by Alvin Sargent that seems contrived from unlikely inspirations. It is not enough to provide Albert with Whoopi Goldberg as a foster mother and Gérard Depardieu as an imaginary friend: The movie must also allow Harriet to see Bogus, too—and not just see him, but dance "The Continental" with him, in the unlikeliest pas de deux of our age.

*Bogus* is light as a feather. It's a charming, inconsequential fantasy that sidesteps such matters as logic and motivation, and rightly so: This is the sort of beguiling fairy tale that needs as little reality as possible, and I thought it really took off after the stepmother finally saw Bogus too.

A few problems are provided in the third act, as when the homesick Albert travels all by himself to Atlantic City, where Mr. Antoine is performing, and of course there are manufactured moments when it seems the little boy is missing or lost. A crisis like that is necessary, I suppose, in order for there to be a happy ending.

But essentially the movie is about the charm of the actors, especially Goldberg and Depardieu. And it adds still more wonder to the career of Depardieu, who increasingly seems to be costumed in giant's overcoats and shirts made out of draperies. He is an unmade bed with a broken nose, and the biggest French star of his generation, which, in a way, is an even better trick than popping out of a coloring book.

## Boogie Nights ★ ★ ★ ★

R, 152 m., 1997

Mark Wahlberg (Eddie/Dirk), Burt Reynolds (Jack Horner), Julianne Moore (Amber Waves), John C. Reilly (Reed Rothchild), Heather Graham (Rollergirl), Don Cheadle (Buck Swope), Luis Guzman (Maurice T. Rodriguez), Philip Baker Hall (Floyd Gondolli), Philip Seymour Hoffman (Scotty J), Ricky Jay (Kurt Longjohn), William H. Macy (Little Bill), Nina Hartley (Bill's Wife), Robert Ridgely (The Colonel). Directed by Paul Thomas Anderson and produced by Lloyd Levin, John Lyons, Anderson, and Joanne Sellar. Screenplay by Anderson.

Paul Thomas Anderson's *Boogie Nights* is an epic of the low road, a classic Hollywood story set in the shadows instead of the spotlights, but containing the same ingredients: fame, envy, greed, talent, sex, money. The movie follows a large, colorful, and curiously touching cast of characters, as they live through a crucial turning point in the adult film industry.

In 1977, when the story opens, porn movies are shot on film and play in theaters, and a director can dream of making one so good that the audience members would want to stay in the theater even after they had achieved what they came for. By 1983, when the story closes, porn has shifted to video and most of the movies are basically just gynecological loops. There is hope, at the outset, that a porno movie could be "artistic," and less hope at the end.

*Boogie Nights* tells this story through the life of a kid named Eddie Adams (Mark Wahlberg) from Torrance, who is a dishwasher in a San Fernando Valley nightclub when he's discovered by a Tiparillo-smoking pornographer named Jack

Horner (Burt Reynolds). "I got a feeling," Jack says, "that behind those jeans is something wonderful just waiting to get out." He is correct, and within a few months Eddie has been renamed "Dirk Diggler" and is a rising star of porn films.

If this summary makes the film itself sound a little like porn, it is not. Few films have been more matter-of-fact, even disenchanted, about sexuality. Adult films are a business here, not a dalliance or a pastime, and one of the charms of *Boogie Nights* is the way it shows the everyday backstage humdrum life of porno filmmaking. "You got your camera," Jack explains to young Eddie. "You got your film, you got your lights, you got your synching, you got your editing, you got your lab. Before you turn around, you've spent maybe $25,000 or $30,000."

Jack Horner is the father figure for a strange extended family of sex workers; he's a low-rent Hugh Hefner, and Burt Reynolds gives one of his best performances, as a man who seems to stand outside sex and view it with the detached eye of a judge at a livestock show. Horner is never shown as having sex himself, although he lives with Amber Waves (Julianne Moore), a former housewife and mother, now a porn star who makes tearful midnight calls to her ex-husband, asking to speak to her child. When Jack recruits Eddie to make a movie, Amber becomes his surrogate parent, tenderly solicitous of him as they prepare for his first sex scene.

During a break in that scene, Eddie whispers to Jack, "Please call me Dirk Diggler from now on." He falls immediately into star mode, and before long is leading a conducted tour of his new house, where his wardrobe is "arranged according to color and designer." His stardom is based on one remarkable attribute; "everyone is blessed with one special thing," he tells himself, after his mother has screamed that he'll always be a bum and a loser.

Anderson wisely limits the nudity in the film, and until the final shot we don't see what Jack Horner calls "Mr. Torpedo Area." It's more fun to approach it the way Anderson does. At a pool party at Jack's house, Dirk meets the Colonel (Robert Ridgely), who finances the films. "May I see it?" the silver-haired, business-suited Colonel asks. Dirk obliges, and the camera stays on the Colonel's face as he looks, and a funny, stiff little smile appears on his face; Anderson holds the shot for several seconds, and we get the message.

The large cast of *Boogie Nights* is nicely balanced between human and comic qualities. We meet Rollergirl (Heather Graham), who never takes off her skates, and in an audition scene with Dirk adds a new dimension to the lyrics "I've got a brand-new pair of roller skates, you've got a brand-new key." Little Bill (William H. Macy) is Jack's assistant director, moping about at parties while his wife (porn star Nina Hartley) gets it on with every man she can. (When he discovers his wife having sex in the driveway, surrounded by an appreciative crowd, she tells him, "Shut up, Bill; you're embarrassing me.") Ricky Jay, the magician, plays Jack's cameraman. "I think every picture should have its own look," he states solemnly, although the films are shot in a day or two. When he complains, "I got a couple of tough shadows to deal with," Jack snaps, "There are shadows in life, baby."

Dirk's new best friend is Reed (John C. Reilly). He gets a crush on Dirk and engages him in gym talk ("How much do you press? Let's both say at the same time. One, two . . ."). Buck Swope (Don Cheadle) is a second-tier actor and would-be hi-fi salesman. Rodriguez (Luis Guzman) is a club manager who dreams of being in one of Jack's movies. And the gray eminence behind the industry, the man who is the Colonel's boss, is Floyd Gondolli (Philip Baker Hall), who on New Year's Eve 1980 breaks the news that videotape holds the future of the porno industry.

The sweep and variety of the characters has brought the movie comparisons to Altman's *Nashville* and *The Player.* There is also some of the same appeal as *Pulp Fiction,* in scenes that balance precariously between comedy and violence (a brilliant scene near the end has Dirk and friends selling cocaine to a deranged playboy while the customer's friend throws firecrackers around the room). Through all the characters and all the action, Anderson's screenplay centers on the human qualities of the players. They may live in a disreputable world, but they have the same ambitions and, in a weird way, similar values as mainstream Hollywood.

*Boogie Nights* has the quality of many great films, in that it always seems alive. A movie can be very good and yet not draw us in, not involve us in the moment-to-moment sensation of seeing lives as they are lived. As a writer and director, Paul Thomas Anderson is a skilled reporter, who fills his screen with understated, authentic details. (In the filming of the first sex scene, for example, the action takes place in an office set that has been built in Jack's garage. Behind the office door we see old license plates nailed to the wall, and behind one wall of the set, bicycle wheels peek out.) Anderson is in love with his camera, and a bit of a showoff in sequences inspired by the famous nightclub entrance in *GoodFellas,* De Niro's rehearsal in the mirror in *Raging Bull,* and a shot in *I Am Cuba* where the camera follows a woman into a pool.

In examining the business of catering to lust, *Boogie Nights* demystifies its sex (that's probably one reason it avoided the NC-17 rating). Mainstream movies use sex like porno films do, to turn us on. *Boogie Nights* abandons the illusion that the characters are enjoying sex; in a sense, it's about manufacturing a consumer product. By the time the final shot arrives and we see what made the Colonel stare, there is no longer any shred of illusion that it is anything more than a commodity. And in Dirk Diggler's most anguished scene, as he shouts at Jack Horner, "I'm ready to shoot my scene *right now!*" we learn that those who live by the sword can also die by it. ☞

## Booty Call ★ ★ ★

R, 77 m., 1997

Tommy Davidson (Rushon), Vivica Fox (Lysterine), Jamie Foxx (Bunz), Tamala Jones (Nikki). Directed by Jeff Pollack and produced by John Morrissey. Screenplay by Takashi Bufford and Bootsie Parker.

In a world where vulgarity is the new international standard, where everyday speech consists entirely of things you wouldn't want your grandmother to hear, *Booty Call* nevertheless represents some kind of breakthrough. This is the raunchiest sex comedy I can remember—sort of an *Animal House Grosses Out.*

Did I laugh? Sure. Did I recount some of the more incredible episodes to friends? You bet. Is the movie any good? Does goodness have anything to do with it? I walk out of movies like this wishing my parents had sent me to more concerts instead of letting me read *Mad* magazine. I'm astonished at some of the things I laugh at. But laugh I do.

The action follows two couples on a double date. Rushon and Nikki (Tommy Davidson and Tamala Jones) have been dating for a while. Rushon gets Nikki to fix up his friend Bunz (Jamie Foxx) with her across-the-hall neighbor, Lysterine (Vivica Fox). Lysterine ("That's spelled with a 'y,' not an 'i'") is at first not enchanted by the dreadlocked Bunz ("That tarantula-head fool looks like Predator"). But her girlfriend talks her into coming along for the evening.

It is a long and very busy evening (the usually understated MPAA notes "nonstop sexuality, including sex-related dialogue and crude humor, and strong language"). During its course both couples reveal great enthusiasm for sex, but the sex scenes aren't detailed. Well, they're detailed, all right, but not about sex—the details are in the difficulties, the refinements, and what goes wrong or sometimes even right.

Consider, for example, Lysterine's peculiar turn-on. She likes to have sex while her partner does a Jesse Jackson imitation, and Bunz is happy to oblige with highlights from several speeches. (For afterplay, he cools down with Bill Cosby.) Lysterine is also into various kinky implements, props, and costumes. There are times when she enters the bedroom and Bunz reacts like a man about to have an orthoscopic examination.

"Safe sex" is the watchword of both women, and this leads to a scene where Rushon fights with Nikki's pet dog for possession of a condom. Rushon wins. That's funny in itself, but even funnier (and possibly unscripted) is the way the dog continues for the rest of the scene to leap desperately into the air, barking and snapping at the prize held just out of its reach.

This is some dog. It also figures in the funniest single scene in the movie, where it licks Lysterine's toes under the table, and Lysterine thinks it's Bunz. Later, Bunz makes a similar mistake, also involving the dog, which I will not recount here.

One of the movie's positive qualities is its hearty equality of the sexes. This is not about lustful male predators and female victims. All four characters are equally matched, and equally enthusiastic. And all four have a healthy cheerfulness about sexuality. Although the movie is a wall-to-wall exercise in bad taste, it somehow retains a certain innocence; it challenges and sometimes shocks, but for me at least it didn't offend, because its motives were so obviously good-hearted. I was reminded of Mel Brooks's defense of *The Producers:* "This movie rises below vulgarity."

Example: Toward the end of the movie, Rushon finds himself in a hospital about to be operated on. Through a sneaky mix-up in charts, his minor surgery is upgraded to removal of the testicles. Anesthetized and unable to speak, he looks in horror at the surgeon's preparations. His friends can't dissuade the grim doctor from the performance of his mission. Finally they hit upon the magic words that will stop any operation in mid-slice: "He doesn't have any insurance!" (The pre-op preparations lead, a little later, to a truly inspired recycling of the famous line, "Not only am I the president—I'm a client!")

To evaluate this movie, I find myself falling back on my time-tested generic approach. First, I determine what the movie is trying to do and what it promises its audiences they will see. Then, I evaluate how successful it is, and whether audiences will indeed see the movie they've been promised and enjoy it. *Booty Call* is being advertised as a raucous exercise in vulgarity. It is. I laughed. So I must, to be honest and consistent, award it three stars. In an era when so many movies have no taste at all, a movie in bad taste is at least sailing under its true colors.

## The Borrowers ★ ★ ★

PG, 83 m., 1998

John Goodman (Ocious Potter), Jim Broadbent (Pod Clock), Celia Imrie (Homily Clock), Flora Newbigin (Arrietty Clock), Tom Felton (Peagreen Clock), Aden Gillett (Joe Lender), Mark Williams (Exterminator Jeff), Bradley Pierce (Pete Lender), Hugh Laurie (Officer Steady), Raymond Pickard (Spiller), Ruby Wax (Town Hall Clerk), Doon Mackichan (Victoria Lender). Directed by Peter Hewitt and produced by Tim Bevan, Eric Fellner, and Rachel Talalay. Screenplay by Gavin Scott and John Kamps, based on the novels by Mary Norton.

*The Borrowers* is a charming, whimsical family adventure about little people who live in the walls and under the floors of big people's houses, and support themselves by stealing—excuse me, "borrowing"—the necessities of life. Their needs are small: One pea is enough to make a cup of pea soup. They're the ones to blame for all those items that go missing: buttons, cuff links, salt shakers. Ever notice how ice cream disappears from the freezer?

Borrowing and Borrowers are the inventions of the British author Mary Norton, whose books have been adapted twice into TV movies, and now inspire this big-screen, big-budget version with special effects so amusing it's like *Toy Story* has come to life.

As the movie opens, two children of the tiny Clock family (average height: four inches) are on an expedition to the kitchen of the Lenders, the "beings" whose house they inhabit. The kids want ice cream, but things go wrong and one is trapped inside the freezing compartment. It's up to their dad, Pod Clock (Jim Broadbent), to rescue the kid with an emergency trip up the ice-cube chute—and when cubes come crashing down, they look like boulders.

The Lender family is in trouble. An aged aunt left them their house, but after her death the will is missing, and an evil lawyer (John Goodman) plans to destroy the house and build condos. But the Borrower kids get their hands on the will, and the lawyer comes after them with an exterminator.

The plot, and there's a lot more of it, is simply a way to lead us from one wonderfully imagined set after another. Like *The Incredible Shrinking Man* (and Lily Tomlin's shrinking woman), the Clocks live in a world where everyday items look gargantuan: A birthday candle is as big as a torch. Some of the effects will also remind you of *Honey, I Shrunk the Kids,* but the charm comes in the way *The Borrowers* makes its world look like a timeless storybook. The Lenders' new neighborhood looks like a British factory town, for example, but the skyline is an (obvious) matte painting of a metropolis of the future.

The humor is physical. Goodman, as the lawyer, gets a face full of insecticide, is nearly electrocuted, and has all kinds of things bounce off his head. Little Peagreen Clock (Tom Felton) has a harrowing time in a milk bottling plant (he's trapped in a bottle that's filled with milk and capped shut—a challenge for Houdini). Exterminator Jeff (Mark Williams) has a bloodhound that feeds on cheese and stinks up the place. And all of the Clocks face terrifying dangers, as when the kids fall out the bottom of a moving truck, and are almost sucked into a vacuum cleaner.

The film is wisely modest in its scope: It sets up the situation, involves us, has fun with the special effects and the cliffhanging adventures, and is over in eighty-three minutes. If the action and the physical humor are designed to appeal to kids, the look of the film will impress adults who know what to look for. The director, Peter Hewitt, made *Bill & Ted's Bogus Adventure* (1991) and exhibits the same wild visual imagination this time.

Consider the possibilities, for example, when little Peagreen is desperately clinging to a lightbulb, and the evil lawyer turns on the light. How long can he hang on before the bulb heats up? Can his sister rescue him with that spring-loaded retractable tape measure? There's something you don't see every day.

## Bound ★ ★ ★ ★

R, 109 m., 1996

Jennifer Tilly (Violet), Gina Gershon (Corky), Joe Pantoliano (Caesar), John P. Ryan (Mickey Malnato), Christopher Meloni (Johnnie Marconi), Richard Sarafian (Gino Marzzone), Barry Kivel (Shelly). Directed by Larry Wachowski and Andy Wachowski and produced by Andrew Lazar and Stuart Boros. Screenplay by Larry Wachowski and Andy Wachowski.

*Bound* is one of those movies that works you up, wrings you out, and leaves you gasping. It's pure cinema, spread over several genres. It's a caper movie, a gangster movie, a sex movie, and a slapstick comedy. It's not often you think of *The Last Seduction* and the Marx Brothers during the same film, but I did during this one—and I also thought about *Blood Simple* and Woody Allen. It's amazing to discover all this virtuosity and confidence in two first-time filmmakers, Larry and Andy Wachowski, self-described college dropouts still in their twenties, from Chicago.

As the film opens, a tough but sexy woman is moving into a new apartment. She rides the elevator to her floor with what looks like a mobster and his ditzy girlfriend. He's a mobster, all right, but she's not as ditzy as she looks. It's more of an act that gives her immunity in a dangerous environment.

The sexy newcomer is Corky (Gina Gershon), a lesbian who has just finished serving a prison sentence. The mobster is Caesar (Joe Pantoliano), a mid-level functionary in the Chicago crime syndicate. His girlfriend is Violet (Jennifer Tilly), whose lust for their new neighbor is so obvious she might as well just turn herself in to Jerry Springer and get it over with ("Violet—afraid to tell Mafioso boyfriend she's a lesbian").

Violet creates an excuse to meet Corky; she uses the routine about how her ring fell down the sink. In old movies this was a ploy to trap men, but for about ten years I've noticed that the only movie characters who seem to do household tasks anymore are lesbians. There's always a scene early in the movie showing them caulking something.

Passion between the two women is instantaneous, steamy, and kind of funny. Gershon and Tilly are electric together, maybe because they understand the humor of their situation and play the sex for delight instead of for solemn, earthshaking, gynecological drudgery. The movie seems to be shaping up as an erotic popcorn masher, but then the plot thickens and keeps on thickening, twisting the characters and the audience ever tighter into a sticky web of murder, blood, sex, and money.

Violet and Corky have secret tête-à-têtes, and vice versa, and become lovers. Violet whispers that she wants to escape Caesar so the two women can start a new life together. So far she hasn't been able to get Caesar to listen. ("Caesar, I'm leaving!" she announces. "Why?" he whines. "Did I use a good towel?")

Violet tells Corky that a bag man named Shelly (Barry Kivel) is arriving at Caesar's with $2 million in cash. She thinks they should steal the cash, and she needs Corky's help—since as an ex-con, Corky is presumably an expert criminal.

Now the movie turns into a macabre caper comedy of clockwork virtuosity. The plot depends on split-second timing; if anything goes wrong, they could be dead. Of course everything goes wrong. Shelly arrives with the briefcase, and it appears that he's going to get his fingers cut off one at a time. When this scene played at the Toronto Film Festival, people fled from the theater, so be warned. But also know that the movie never goes as far or shows as much as it seems about to; like *Blood Simple,* it takes us to the edge of the unacceptable, peers over wistfully, and tiptoes away.

To describe what happens in the film's brilliant and long-sustained caper sequence would be unfair. Familiar movie devices are made to feel new. Bodies stack up. The cops arrive and there is evidence of murder right in front of them if they only know where to look. The two lovers are in constant danger of exposure and death.

All of this is somehow constructed like a perfect Marx Brothers routine; the briefcase full of money moves around like the pea in a shell game, powerful Mafia bosses arrive from the East Coast and represent certain death for the increasingly desperate Caesar, and there are little tricks involving things like the redial button on a telephone that have the audience gasping with fear and delight.

The movie is a jubilant comeback for Gina Gershon, whose career now takes a U-turn after the unsuccessful *Showgirls.* She brings an edge and intelligence to her character that reminded me a little of Linda Fiorentino in *The Last Seduction.* Jennifer Tilly takes the giggly showgirl act she introduced in Woody Allen's *Bullets Over Broadway* and uses it to hide a steel will. And Joe Pantoliano has some of the trickiest scenes in the movie, bouncing from paranoia to greed to lust to abject fear like a pinball in the wrong machine.

*Bound* is shocking and violent, and will offend some audiences. It's that kind of movie. But it's skillful filmmaking, setting a puzzle that involves time, space, money, and danger, and seeing how many different ways it can be solved.

## Box of Moonlight ★ ★ ★

R, 111 m., 1997

John Turturro (Al Fountain), Sam Rockwell (The Kid), Catherine Keener (Floatie Dupre), Lisa Blount (Purlene Dupre), Annie Corely (Deb Fountain), Alexander Goodwin (Bobby Fountain), Dermot Mulroney (Wick), Mike Stanley (Doob). Directed by Tom DiCillo and produced by Marcus Viscidi and Thomas A. Bliss. Screenplay by DiCillo.

*Box of Moonlight* tells the story of a man who lost the key to living, somewhere along the way. His name is Al Fountain, he's an engineer on an out-of-town factory job, and the foreman describes him as "one of those guys who goes through life like a robot." His wife calls him "Mr. Clockwork" because he always does exactly what he says he will do, precisely when he says he will do it.

John Turturro plays Al as a sad and lonely everyman in white shirts and black slacks. When the factory job is canceled and they're paid their bonuses and sent home, he doesn't go home. He rents a car and stays in the area, and asks the motel clerk if he's ever heard of Splatchee Lake—a place he remembers being taken to when he was a kid. God knows if Al has ever been happy since.

This is a man going through some kind of a crisis. He just got his first gray hair. He is beginning to see things backward: Water runs up into the tap; children pedal their bikes in reverse. He has commitments but no contacts; when he calls home, he doesn't even want to speak to his son, maybe because he has nothing to say to him or anyone else.

Splatchee Lake is a disappointment. An elderly couple tell him it's filled up with formaldehyde: "You step in it and it'll burn your feet off." It's not only nature that fails him. Sex and religion don't help either; he makes a baffling call to a phone sex service, and meets a man who has seen a vision of Jesus in the flames on a billboard barbecue grill.

Then Al meets The Kid (Sam Rockwell), who wears a coonskin cap and lives in a clearing in the woods, which he has decorated to resemble—oh, I dunno, a junkyard run by Daniel Boone. The Kid is a free spirit who encourages Al to shoot at things and go to a bar and break the rules of society. Among The Kid's possessions is a box of moonlight, although whether it has moonlight in it is a question to post alongside the details on the briefcase in *Pulp Fiction.* Eventually a couple of young women (Catherine Keener and Lisa Blount) join the little camp in the clearing, and Al makes sweet love with one of them. That seems kind of unfair to his long-suffering wife (Annie Corely), but maybe it falls under the heading of therapy.

*Box of Moonlight* was written and directed by Tom DiCillo, a filmmaker with a streak of magic realism in him. His *Johnny Suede* starred Brad Pitt as sort of a leftover 1950s icon. His next film, *Living in Oblivion,* made fun of more or less the exact kind of whimsical little indee film *Box of Moonlight* is, but so what? The fact that he knows what he's doing, and how close it is to parody, adds a sort of smile to the material.

There isn't a whole lot of story in *Box of Moonlight*. The film works by setting up Al Fountain as a mope, and then hurling gobs of life at him. Some stick. Turturro is good for the role because he can play both speeds: defeated salaryman, and reawakened dreamer. People keep asking him, "Are you all right?" Too bad about Splatchee Lake.

## The Boxer ★ ★ ★

R, 105 m., 1998

Daniel Day-Lewis (Danny Flynn), Emily Watson (Maggie), Brian Cox (Joe Hamill), Ken Stott (Ike Weir), Gerard McSorley (Harry), Eleanor Methven (Patsy), Ciaran Fitzgerald (Liam), Kenneth Cranham (Matt McGuire). Directed by Jim Sheridan and produced by Sheridan and Arthur Lappin. Screenplay by Sheridan and Terry George.

*The Boxer* is the latest of Jim Sheridan's six rich stories about Ireland, and in some ways the most unusual. Although it seems to borrow the pattern of the traditional boxing movie, the boxer here is not the usual self-destructive character, but the center of maturity and balance in a community in turmoil. And although the film's lovers are star-crossed, they are not blind; they're too old and scarred to throw all caution to the wind.

The film takes place in a Belfast hungering for peace. It stars Daniel Day-Lewis (also the star of Sheridan's *My Left Foot* and *In the Name of the Father*) as Danny Flynn, an IRA member who was a promising boxer until he was imprisoned at eighteen for terrorist associations. Refusing to name his fellow IRA men, he was held captive for fourteen years, and is now back on the streets in a city where Joe Hamill (Brian Cox), the ranking IRA man, is trying to negotiate a truce with the British.

Danny was in love as a young man with Maggie (Emily Watson), Hamill's daughter. After his imprisonment, she married another IRA man, who is now in prison. IRA rules threaten death for any man caught having an affair with a prisoner's wife; Danny and Maggie, who are still drawn to one another, are in danger—especially from the militant IRA faction led by Harry (Gerard McSorley), a hothead who hates Hamill, fears Danny, and sees the forbidden relationship as a way to destroy them both.

Danny Flynn is no longer interested in sectarian hatred. He joins his old boxing manager, an alcoholic named Ike (Ken Stott), in reopening a local gymnasium for young boxers of all faiths. And he goes into training for a series of bouts himself, becoming a figurehead for those in the community who want to heal old wounds and move ahead. The story, which is constructed in a solid, craftsmanlike way by Sheridan and his cowriter, Terry George, balances these three elements—the IRA, boxing, and romance—in such a way that if elements of one goes wrong the other two may fail as well.

Sheridan is a leading figure in the renaissance of Irish films. His directing credits include *My Left Foot* (1989), with Day-Lewis in an extraordinary performance as Christy Brown, the poet who was trapped inside a paralyzed body; *The Field* (1990), which won Richard Harris an Oscar nomination as a man who reclaims land from a rocky coast; and *In the Name of the Father* (1993), nominated for seven Oscars and starring Day-Lewis as a Belfast man wrongly accused of bombings. He also cowrote Mike Newell's comedy *Into the West* (1993) and Terry George's *Some Mother's Son* (1996), about the mothers of hunger strikers in the Maze prison. George is his frequent collaborator.

His films are never exercises in easy morality, and *The Boxer* is more complex than most. Apart from Danny and Maggie, the film's key figure is Joe Hamill, played with a quiet, sad, strong center by Brian Cox as a man who has, in his time, killed and ordered killings—but has the character to lead his organization toward peace. Harry, the bitter militant, lost a child to the British and accepts no compromise; if Danny and Maggie act on their love for one another, they may destroy the whole delicate balance.

Against the political material, the boxing acts as a setting more than a world. We see how hot passions are passed along to a younger generation, how boxing can be a substitute for warfare, and (in an almost surrealistic scene in a black-tie private club in London) how the rich pay the poor to bloody themselves.

What's fascinating is the delicacy of the relationship between Maggie and Danny. Played by two actors who have obviously given a lot of thought to the characters, they know that love is not always the most important thing in the world, that grand gestures can be futile ones, that more important things are at stake than their own gratification, that perhaps in the times they live in romance is not possible. And yet they hunger. Day-Lewis and Watson (from *Breaking the Waves*) are smart actors playing smart people; when they make reckless gestures, it is from despair or nihilism, not stupidity.

The film's weakness is in its ambition: It covers too much ground. Perhaps—I hate to say it—the boxing material is unnecessary, and if the film had focused only on the newly released prisoner, his dangerous love, and the crisis in IRA politics, it might have been cleaner and stronger. There are three fights in the film, and the outcome of all three is really just a distraction from the much more important struggles going on outside the ring.

## Boys ★ ★

PG-13, 89 m., 1996

Winona Ryder (Patty Vare), Lukas Haas (John Baker Jr.), Skeet Ulrich (Bud Valentine), John C. Reilly (Officer Kellogg Curry), Bill Sage (Officer Bill Martone), Matt Malloy (Bartender), Wiley Wiggins (John Phillips), Russell Young (John Van Slieder). Directed by Stacy Cochran and produced by Peter Frankfurt, Paul Feldsher, and Erica Huggins. Screenplay by Cochran.

*Boys* is a low-rent, dumbed-down version of *Before Sunrise*, with a rent-a-plot substituting for clever dialogue. It goes to excruciating lengths to explain why a teenage boy and a slightly older girl would meet and spend most of the night together, and then it gives them nothing of any interest to say.

This is a waste of the talents of Winona Ryder, who can and has played the most intelligent of movie characters (see *The Age of Innocence* and *Little Women*), and of Lucas Haas, who has never played a character quite this shallow, even in his juvenile roles (see his work as the curious young man in *Rambling Rose*).

In *Before Sunrise* (1995), you will recall, two young people met on a train, began to talk, liked each other, and decided to spend a day and night walking around Vienna. As they walked, they talked and we grew to know them. The whole plot structure—the train, the deadline of a flight the next day—was simply a setup for their conversation and was treated with the casualness it deserved. The point of the movie was the smart dialogue, written by Richard Linklater and acted by Ethan Hawke and Julie Delpy.

*Boys* gives us another setup, drenched in melodrama, coincidence, flashbacks, and drama, and thinks we should care about it. We don't. We do care about the two young characters, until it becomes clear that the movie doesn't. This movie goes to a great deal of trouble to explain why two teenagers are able to meet and exchange a series of time-worn clichés about life and love. ("I feel like I wake up with my mind on the wrong channel or something." "I feel like that every day.")

As the movie opens, police arrive at a country mansion to question young Patty Vare (Winona Ryder) about a car that was stolen the night before near a party she attended. She says she knows nothing about the car, and then she goes horseback riding. Cut to a nearby private boys' school, where a young student bursts in and recruits the older John Baker Jr. (Haas) to "borrow" a school car on a mission of mercy.

Baker discovers that his classmates have found a riderless horse and a girl unconscious in a field. The girl, of course, is Patty, and Baker smuggles her into the school to treat her wounds. This process also involves getting her out of that wet blouse and into a dry shirt, of course.

Other upperclassmen, curious and mean, think Baker is hiding a girl somewhere, but soon the two leave the school in order to visit that absolutely inescapable location for all movies without purpose or inspiration, a carnival midway. Yes, they kiss on a merry-go-round. Yes, the older kids follow them there. Yes, a policeman is still curious about Patty; he thinks she knows something about the stolen car and a missing professional baseball player named Bud Valentine.

And she does, as we discover in carefully parceled-out flashbacks, which I would not dream of describing. Given what she knows, it is a little startling that she would be calm enough to engage in cute dialogue with Baker and some snuggling on a hillside near the carnival, which leads, hardly convincingly, to a mild sex scene.

One of the qualities of *Before Sunrise* was its reluctance to rely on plot standbys like a sex scene (the couple spend the night together, but between discreet dissolves that leave it up to us to decide what, if anything, happened). Here the sex seems more obligatory than motivated, and the entire apparatus of the flashbacks, the cops, the missing car, etc., is of no interest.

One curious detail. The movie seems to want to work in material about Baker's relationship with his father, but doesn't know how to do it. There is a brave telephone call in which the son makes a declaration of independence (what he says sounds more like a high school essay than real dialogue), but not long after he's knocking on his parents' door. And when we meet the father, he doesn't fit at all. He's inappropriately hostile, aggressive, and mean, taking up so much psychic space that the movie should have either dealt with him or dropped him.

*Boys* must think audiences are not very bright. Any movie like this faces two choices early in the development process: (1) Make the characters original and interesting, and write them some dialogue worth hearing, or (2) trick up the plot with tired clichés, lurid flashbacks, and phony suspense, throw in a little sex, and have a perfunctory happy ending. *Boys* takes the dumb way out.

A footnote. Before I had seen the film, someone described it to me as "Winona Ryder is hidden in a boys' school." This sounded like a splendid premise for a movie, and I thought of several story possibilities, as indeed you can too. Why is it only the people who *make* the movies who do their thinking on automatic pilot?

## Brassed Off ★ ★ ★

R, 107 m., 1997

Pete Postlethwaite (Danny), Tara Fitzgerald (Gloria), Ewan McGregor (Andy), Stephen Tompkinson (Phil), Jim Carter (Harry), Philip Jackson (Jim), Peter Martin (Ernie), Sue Johnston (Vera). Directed by Mark Herman and produced by Steve Abbott. Screenplay by Herman.

The central image in *Brassed Off* is that of a face: shiny, homely, dead serious. It is the face of a man who earnestly believes he is doing the most important thing in the world. The man's name is Danny, and he is the leader of a brass band made up of coal miners who work at a pit in Grimley, a Yorkshire mining town. The band was founded in 1881, and its rehearsal room is lined with the photographs of past bandmasters, looking down sternly on the current generation of musicians.

It is 1992, and the colliery is about to be closed. The Conservative government made a decision some years earlier to replace coal with nuclear power as a source of fuel, and as a result some 140 pits, representing more than 200,000 miners' jobs, were declared redundant. The closure of a pit means the death of a town, because a village like Grimley depends entirely on the wages of the miners, whose families for generations have gone down in the mines—and played for the band.

*Brassed Off* is a film that views the survival of the town through the survival of the band, and the survival of the band through the eyes of Danny (Pete Postlethwaite), who in some corner of his mind probably believes the mines exist only to supply him with musicians. The movie makes liberal use of storytelling formulas (there is a love story involving young people, and a crisis involving a married couple, and a health crisis involving Danny, a strategic use of "Danny Boy," and a national band contest at the Royal Albert Hall). But Postlethwaite's performance elevates and even ennobles this material.

He loves music. He is stern and exacting about it. His band members may labor in the pits all day, but when they come to rehearsal he expects seriousness and concentration. There is a fourteen-town competition coming up, and then the national finals, and this year he thinks the Grimley Brass Band has a real chance. If the pit closes, it will be a last chance.

Into the rehearsal hall one day comes a pretty young woman named Gloria (Tara Fitzgerald), who asks if she can sit in with her flugelhorn. She can. Her late father had been the band's best flugelhorn player, and her performance of "Rodrigo's Concerto" brings tears to the eyes of some of the band members—and a sparkle to the eye of young Andy (Ewan McGregor, from *Trainspotting*), who had a crush on her in school. Now she has gone away to London, and returned to Grimley (we learn) to make a study about the pit closure.

She pretends to have forgotten Andy, but later admits, "I did know your name—I just didn't want you to think it was etched forever on my brain." The love they felt when they were fourteen blossoms again, until it is revealed that she is working for the other side—for the government agency that would close the mine. She protests that she is on the miners' side and that her study might save the pit, but is told scornfully, "It's just a bloody P.R. exercise. They've already made their decision while you were at bloody college."

Another important figure in the story is Phil (Stephen Tompkinson), Danny's son, who struggles to make ends meet for his wife and large family. He wants to quit the band in order to save paying the dues, but lacks the nerve to tell his father. Phil moonlights as Chuckles the Clown, and brings a quick end to a children's birthday party with an uncontrolled outburst against Margaret Thatcher.

*Brassed Off* is a sweet film with a lot of anger at its core. The writer and director, Mark Herman, obviously believes the Tory energy decisions were inspired by the fact that coal miners voted Labour while nuclear power barons were Conservative. His plot tugs at every possible heartstring as it leads up to a dramatic moment in the Royal Albert Hall, which I will not reveal; it includes a speech against Thatcherism that some British critics found inappropriate, although it's certainly in character for old Danny.

One of the movie's great pleasures is the music itself. Brass bands are maintained by many different British institutions—schools, police forces, military units, coal miners, assembly-line workers—and their crisp music always seems gloriously self-confident. Some of the film's best shots show Pete Postlethwaite's face as he leads the band: his anger when members get drunk and miss notes, and his pride when everything is exactly right.

Acting is not accomplished only with words and emotion. Sometimes it is projected from within, into a stance or an expression. There is not a moment in *Brassed Off* when I did not believe Postlethwaite was a brass band leader—and a bloody good one.

## Breakdown ★ ★ ★

R, 96 m., 1997

Kurt Russell (Jeff Taylor), J. T. Walsh (Red Barr), Kathleen Quinlan (Amy Taylor), M. C. Gainey (Earl), Jack Noseworthy (Billy), Rex Linn (Sheriff Boyd), Ritch Brinkley (Al), Moira Harris (Arleen). Directed by Jonathan Mostow and produced by Martha De Laurentiis and Dino De Laurentiis. Screenplay by Mostow and Sam Montgomery.

*Breakdown* is taut, skillful, and surgically effective, the story of a man who finds himself trapped in a surrealistic nightmare. The story's setup is more entertaining than the payoff; as Hitchcock observed, suspense plays better than action. But the film delivers—right up until a final moment I'll get to later.

Kurt Russell and Kathleen Quinlan star as a Massachusetts couple driving to California through the deserts of the Southwest. They've made two mistakes, as a character later helpfully explains: driving a brand-new red Jeep, and having out-of-state plates. In the middle of nowhere, the car breaks down, or so they think, and they are left at the mercy of the locals.

The locals do not come well advertised. Early in the film, the Jeep nearly sideswipes a dusty black pickup driven by a stringy-haired goon (M. C. Gainey) who looks like he belongs back home in the swamps of *Deliverance.* He later accosts them at a gas station, and Russell floors the Jeep in an attempt to put highway space between them. That may be a mistake during the new car's break-in period; it has an engine meltdown in the desert, and they seem to be at the mercy of the goon until a helpful semi driver (J. T. Walsh) happens along.

Now I will move carefully to conserve plot details. Walsh offers them a ride to a nearby diner, Russell chooses to stay with his car, and Quinlan accepts the offer so she can phone a road service. But when Russell later arrives at the diner, no one there has seen his wife. And when he stops the truck driver for a highway showdown with a deputy sheriff on hand, Walsh convincingly argues he has never seen the woman. Russell narrowly avoids being arrested, and is left standing by the side of his car in the middle of nowhere, baffled and angered by the disappearance of his wife.

The situation at this point resembles the opening dilemma of *The Vanishing* (1988), a brilliant Dutch-French thriller (accept no substitutes; the 1993 U.S. remake is a pale shadow). In that one, a couple paused at a highway rest stop, the woman walked inside, and was never seen again. There is a moment here when Russell stares at a wall of Missing Persons posters in the local sheriff's office, and realizes how common it is for people to disappear into thin air. (The sheriff cheerfully quotes discouraging statistics.)

What happened to his wife? I will tell no more than necessary, but stop reading now if you want total suspense. If *Breakdown* had the courage of *The Vanishing*, which was a chillingly nihilistic film, we would never find out—or, we would discover things we would rather not have known. But this is an American thriller, and so it is preordained that Russell will find himself on a desperate solo struggle to find his wife and save her. (The previews provided a large hint with a shot of him hanging onto a speeding truck's undercarriage.)

In the course of his quest, there are two scenes that don't work as well as they should. One is a scene in a small-town bank, which shows Russell behaving so awkwardly that opportunities for suspense are lost; the director, Jonathan Mostow, seems to have realized that, and cuts away from the bank abruptly without concluding the sequence. Another is a scene where Russell is being pursued by villains and unwisely drives his nice new Jeep down an embankment and into a river. In the TV ads it would power across to the other shore, but in the movie it floats downstream, allowing him to discover, in the vastness of the landscape, a single tiny doughnut wrapper that provides a (unnecessary) clue.

Those scenes raise questions. The others do not. For most of its length *Breakdown* functions so efficiently that we put logic on hold and go with the action. Russell makes a convincing, dogged, weary everyman, and the J. T. Walsh character is given some shades that are interesting (including his relationship with his wife and son).

I'm recommending *Breakdown*, but I have a problem with the closing scene I mentioned above. It involves a situation in which a villain is disabled and powerless—yet a coup de grace is administered. There is (or was) a tradition in Hollywood thrillers that the heroes in movies like this kill only in self-defense. By ending as it does, *Breakdown* disdains such moral boundaries. I noticed, interestingly, that no one in the audience cheered when that final death took place. I felt a kind of collective wince. Maybe that indicates we still have an underlying decency that rejects the eye-for-an-eye values of this film. *Breakdown* is a fine thriller, and its ending is unworthy of it. ☞

## Breaking the Waves ★ ★ ★ ★

R, 158 m., 1996

Emily Watson (Bess), Stellan Skarsgard (Jan), Katrin Cartlidge (Dodo), Jean-Marc Barr (Terry), Udo Kier (Man on the Trawler), Adrian Rawlins (Dr. Richardson), Jonathan Hackett (The Minister), Sandra Voe (Bess's Mother). Directed by Lars von Trier and produced by Vibeke Windelov and Peter Aalbaek Jensen. Screenplay by von Trier.

*Breaking the Waves* is emotionally and spiritually challenging, hammering at conventional morality with the belief that God not only sees all, but understands a great deal more than we give Him credit for. It tells the story of Bess, a simple woman of childlike naïveté, who sacrifices herself to sexual brutality to save the life of the man she loves. Is she a sinner? The grim bearded elders of her church think so. But Bess is the kind of person Jesus was thinking of, I believe, when he suffered the little children to come unto him.

The movie takes place in the 1970s, in a remote northern Scottish village. Bess (Emily Watson), a sweet-faced and trusting girl, is "not quite right in the head," and her close-knit community is not pleased by her decision to marry Jan (Stellan Skarsgard), who works on one of the big oil rigs in the North Sea. But she loves Jan so much that when the helicopter bringing him to the wedding is delayed, she hits him in a fury. He is a tall, gentle man with a warm smile, and lets her flail away before embracing her in his big arms.

She is a virgin, but so eager to learn the secrets of marriage that she accosts her new husband in the powder room at the reception after the ceremony, telling him eagerly, "You can love me now!" And then, "What do I do?" The miracle of sexual expression transforms her, and she is grateful to God for having given her Jan and his love and his body. Meanwhile, downstairs at the ceremony, Jan's shipmate and Bess's grandfather scowl at one another; the shipmate crushes a beer can, and the grandfather picks up a lemonade glass and breaks it in his bloody hand.

We learn a little about Bess, who had a breakdown when her brother died. Her closest friend is her sister-in-law, Dodo (Katrin Cartlidge), a nurse who stays in the remote district mostly because of her. Bess belongs to a strict sect where women do not speak in church, and the sermon over the body at a funeral might be, "You are a sinner and will find your place in hell." Bess's grandfather observes sourly, "We have no bells in our church."

Jan is critically injured in an accident on the rig. He is paralyzed from the neck down, and the local doctor tells Bess he may never walk again. "You don't know Jan!" she says fiercely. One day Jan asks her to find a man and make love to him "for my sake. And then tell me about it." Bess does not like this idea, but she does what Jan asks. Dodo is enraged: "Are you sleeping with other men to feed his sick fantasies? His head's full of scars—he's up to his eyeballs in drugs."

It is indeed never made quite clear why Jan, a good man, has made this request of the woman he loves. That is not the point. The point is that Bess, with her fierce faith, believes that somehow her sacrifice can redeem her husband and even cure him. As his condition grows worse, her behavior grows more desperate; she has herself taken out to a big ship where even the port prostitutes refuse to go because of the way they have been treated there.

The film contains many surprising revelations, including a cosmic one at the end, which I will leave you to discover for yourself. It has the kind of raw power, the kind of unshielded regard for the force of good and evil in the world, that we want to shy away from. It is easier sometimes to wrap ourselves in sentiment and pious platitudes, and forget that God created nature "red in tooth and nail." Bess does not have our ability to rationalize and evade, and fearlessly offers herself to God as she understands him.

This performance by Emily Watson reminds me of what Truffaut said about James Dean, that as an actor he was more like an animal than a man, proceeding according to instinct instead of thought and calculation. It is not a grim performance and is often touched by humor and delight, which makes it all the more touching, as when Bess talks out loud in two-way conversations with God, speaking both voices—making God a stern adult and herself a trusting child. Her church banishes her and little boys in the village throw stones at her, but she tells a doctor, "God gives everyone something to be good at. I've always been stupid, but I'm good at this."

*Breaking the Waves* was written and directed by Lars von Trier, from Denmark, who makes us wonder what kinds of operas Nietzsche might have written. He finds the straight pure line through the heart of a story, and is not concerned with what cannot be known: This movie does not explain Jan's cruel request of his wife because Bess does not question it. It shows people who care about her, such as the sister-in-law and the local doctor, and others who do not: religious bean-counters like the bearded church elders. They understand nothing about their Christianity except for unyielding rules they have memorized, which means they do not understand Christianity at all. They talk to God as if they expect him to listen and learn. At the end of the film they get their response in a great, savage, ironic peal.

Not many movies like this get made because not many filmmakers are so bold, angry, and defiant. Like many truly spiritual films, it will offend the Pharisees. Here we have a story that forces us to take sides, to ask what really is right and wrong in a universe that seems harsh and indifferent. Is religious belief only a consolation for our inescapable destination in the grave? Or can faith give the power to triumph over death and evil? Bess knows. ☞

## Broken Arrow ★ ★

R, 108 m., 1996

John Travolta (Vic Deakins), Christian Slater (Riley Hale), Samantha Mathis (Terry Carmichael), Delroy Lindo (Colonel Max Wilkins), Bob Gunton (Pritchett), Frank Whaley (Giles Prentice), Howie Long (Kelly). Directed by John Woo and produced by Mark Gordon, Bill Badalato, and Terence Chang. Screenplay by Graham Yost.

A lot of stuff gets blown up real good in *Broken Arrow,* including a train, four helicopters, and a mountain, but these brief flashes of special effects don't do much to speed up a slow, talky action thriller that plays like an homage to the Fallacy of the Talking Killer.

The Fallacy, you will recall, occurs when all the bad guy has to do is pull the trigger and his problems are over. Instead, he talks, and talks, until his target escapes from his predicament.

There are also scenes where the two enemies describe their motives and plans to one another, because otherwise neither side would know what to do next and the movie would stop dead in its tracks.

*Broken Arrow,* directed by the Hong Kong cult favorite John Woo, is Woo's big-budget Hollywood debut, after his more modestly priced first U.S. film *Hard Target* (1993). It shows Woo capable of staging noisy fight scenes and spectacular explosions, but he's nowhere near the league of Andy Davis *(The Fugitive)* and Tony Scott *(Top Gun)* when it comes to crafting smart action with intriguing characters and dialogue.

*Broken Arrow* is basically a duel between two military pilots, played by John Travolta and Christian Slater, who are assigned to a top-secret low-altitude training mission with a Stealth bomber. Turns out Travolta is a traitor who plans to kill Slater, steal the bombs, and sell them to a syndicate that plans to blackmail the government.

This is a promising premise, but somehow *Broken Arrow* never really sinks in its teeth and takes it seriously. Consider, for example, the scene where we discover Travolta is not what he seems. He turns to Slater in the cockpit and . . . narrows his eyes. That's right. Narrows them fiercely and intensely. There is a lot of eye-narrowing in Hong Kong chop-socky movies, and there I guess it passes for character development, but here it just looks goofy, as if Travolta were back in that great scene in *Get Shorty,* teaching Danny DeVito lessons in how to look menacing.

One fundamental problem with the movie is that John Travolta is seriously miscast as a nuclear terrorist. Say what you will about the guy, he doesn't come across as a heavy. Watching this film, you understand why Dennis Hopper and Christopher Walken play so many mad bombers: because they can.

The movie laboriously sets up the rivalry between Travolta and Slater in an opening scene, where they're boxing. Travolta tells Slater he "lacks the will to win." *Ping!!* That's the Full Circle Alarm going off, alerting us to the certainty that by the end of this film, Slater will have found the will to win and demonstrated that to Travolta, most likely (are you ready for this?) in a fistfight.

There is such a fight in *Broken Arrow.* Also a series of chase scenes that involve police cars, campers, Hummers, helicopters, mine-shaft elevators, raging rivers, and a runaway train. But always with the suspense undermined by the Talking Killer. As when the two enemies communicate by phone, discussing their plans. Or when Slater actually interrupts the disarming of a nuclear warhead in order to say things on his cellular phone he shouldn't say. (That's quite a phone; it works from the bottom of a copper mine in the middle of Utah.)

At one point, when it looks like Travolta has won, he looks out the door of a railway freight car and sees Slater's helicopter poised right there, with Slater pointing a rifle at him. Does Slater shoot? No, because this is such an ideal opportunity for a Meaningful Exchange of Glances in which the two men can communicate those deep macho vibes without which no action movie can endure. Oh, and I almost forgot the Tagalong, a park ranger played fetchingly by Samantha Mathis, whose purpose is to follow Slater everywhere, help him out, warn him, and take off her shirt as soon as possible.

It goes without saying, I guess, that the nuclear warheads in the movie come equipped with bright red digital readouts, so we can see how many seconds remain before they explode. Down at the old nuclear warhead factory, how, exactly, do the engineers explain the purpose of a digital readout on a bomb? Who will ever see it, except in a mad bomber movie? What purpose does it serve?

In *Broken Arrow,* to be sure, it's indispensable to the plot. If my notes are correct, it is first set to 29 minutes. Then reset to 13 minutes. Then turned off. Then set to 29 minutes again. Then set to 4 minutes. This isn't a bomb; it's a handy plot device to generate the required number of seconds of suspense, whenever required. And of course it comes complete with a handheld remote-control device about the size of a channel changer. Push one button, you arm the bomb. Push another button, you disarm it.

Is this what our tax dollars are being spent for? Isn't there supposed to be some sort of secret code in a locked briefcase in the White House or something? Has it all come down to two guys fighting on a burning train for a channel-surfer? No wonder they narrow their eyes so much. That's what a lot of people do when they're trying real hard to think.

## Broken English ★ ★ ★

NO MPAA RATING, 90 m., 1997

Rade Serbedzija (Ivan), Aleksandra Vujcic (Nina), Julian Arahanga (Eddie), Marton Csokas (Darko), Madeline McNamara (Mira), Elizabeth Mavric (Vanya), Jing Zhao (Clara), Yang Li (Wu), Temuera Morrison (Manu). Directed by Gregor Nicholas and produced by Robin Scholes. Screenplay by Nicholas, Johanna Pigott, and Jim Salter.

*Broken English* opens with news footage of the devastation in Croatia, and then it is three years later and we are in the green, quiet land of New Zealand. A family of Croatians, allowed to immigrate because the mother was born in New Zealand, have moved there. And far from home, the father enforces his unyielding standards on his family; he uses a baseball bat to chase off a man who is necking with one of his daughters.

Fathers who have a jealous obsession with the sex lives of their grown daughters are not new to the movies. But *Broken English* is about more than that. It is about ethnic identity transferred to a place where it cannot find nurture. The father, named Ivan (Rade Serbedzija), still nurses old wounds, and lingers over videotapes from home. He does not want his daughters to associate with the local men—but who else, really, is there for them to date?

The story focuses on Nina (Aleksandra Vujcic), who likes to dress in sexy clothes. She works in a Chinese restaurant, where she's attracted to the Maori cook named Eddie (Julian Arahanga). They fall into a passionate relationship. Meanwhile Ivan broods about the wrongs done to his people and is angered even when the pope visits the war zone to ask for peace and forgiveness. "We've left that madness behind," his wife cries. Ivan has not.

He brings his old mother over from Croatia and holds a feast to welcome her. Nina asks if she can bring "a friend," and Ivan, who has briefly met Eddie, says she can. But resentment against this man of another race is obviously brewing, and when Nina also turns up at the party with two Chinese friends, Ivan says the party has been invaded by "a bloody UN peacekeeping force."

As the Croatian music plays in Ivan's backyard, another festival with music is going on next door in the yard of a large Maori family. The Maoris, of course, have been in New Zealand longer than anybody else, which does not prevent Ivan from resenting the racket they're making. And then Ivan gets a surprise: Although Nina is dating Eddie, she has agreed to marry the Chinese man, who will pay her $16,000 because marriage will give him citizenship. When the would-be groom unwisely drinks too much and announces this fact to Ivan, there is a brief, brutal moment of violence that sets up the final passages of the film.

Like the powerful *Once Were Warriors*, this film is about how old wounds cause new ones, and is about male sexual jealousy mixed with alcoholism. The situation is not original, but the setting makes it seem so, and the director and cowriter, Gregor Nicholas, is alert to nuances of the characters.

Consider, for example, Nina's style. She likes to wear tight leather pants, she likes to appear sexy, and at the feast Eddie notices the way she flirts with her father and all the other men in the family. "Do you always sit on those guys like that?" he asks. She does. And we can intuit that she was taught to act like that at an early age; undeclared, unconsummated incest is a family style.

The acting is sometimes ragged but always effective. Rade Serbedzija, who plays Ivan, played a much different character in *Before the Rain*, a film in which he was the sad-eyed outsider observing ethnic hatreds. Aleksandra Vujcic, a newcomer, is effective as the flashing-eyed woman who wants to break loose from her family while remaining unaware of how closely she is still bound. Julian Arahanga's Maori character is able to find a certain thoughtful detachment from the situation, which leads to a better perspective. And I was touched by Zing Zhao, as the Chinese woman, who wants only to "have a little kiwi." (Temuera Morrison, unforgettable as the brutish husband in *Once Were Warriors*, has a smaller role as Arahanga's friend.)

We assume the movie will end in violence, but Nicholas finds a more thoughtful and probably more realistic conclusion. The underlying subject of the film is what might be called tribalism: The belief that a group depends for its existence on the exclusion and hatred of outsiders. Transplanted far from the ethnic conflicts that have ravaged their homeland, these characters still play the same tired tapes. If there are no Serbs to hate, then they will hate Maoris and Chinese. Of course, such feelings are not limited to Croatians. Serbians in the same situations might act the same. Or Maoris. Or Chinese. And all the rest of us. Tribalism is a universal human trait that has long outlived its usefulness.

## A Brother's Kiss ★ ★ ★

R, 92 m., 1997

Nick Chinlund (Lex), Michael Raynor (Mick), Cathy Moriarty (Doreen), Rosie Perez (Debbie), Justin Pierce (Young Lex), Joshua Danowsky (Young Mick), Marisa Tomei (Missy), John Leguizamo (Drug Dealer). Directed by Seth Zvi Rosenfeld and produced by Bob Potter and E. Bennett Walsh. Screenplay by Rosenfeld.

*A Brother's Kiss* tells the harrowing story of two brothers—one a cop, one a crackhead—on a collision course. We've seen that before. What we haven't seen is how they got where they are; the movie's early scenes are heartbreaking in the way they show the brothers as kids.

They live with their mother, Doreen (Cathy Moriarty), who is at that delicate stage between being a tramp and becoming a hooker—the stage when a woman accepts presents from men, but doesn't exactly charge them. There's a parade of strange men through the East Harlem apartment, and Doreen even has the kids prepare some breakfast eggs for one of them.

She's not an unloving mother. She cares fiercely for them, and would do a better job of parenting if she had money, if she were not an alcoholic, and if she were not slowly dying of diabetes. The kids help her take her insulin shots, and they stir her martinis before they all sit down to a Scrabble game.

One day young Lex (Justin Pierce) and Mick (Joshua Danowsky) are coming home through the park when Mick, the smaller and weaker, is sexually assaulted by an off-duty cop. Lex, already strong as a man, stabs the cop, and this is the act that sets the course for his life: He is sent to reform school, and begins a long slide down into unemployment, drug addiction, and even stealing from his own brother's apartment.

As adults, Mick (Michael Raynor) becomes, curiously, a policeman. He remains a virgin; his sexuality is so confused after that night in the park (which they never mention to one another) that he has hidden his manhood behind a shield. Lex (Nick Chinlund) is a ladies' man, gets a girl (Rosie Perez) pregnant, has a kid, tries working as a bus driver, and eventually finds himself tied to the local dealer (John Leguizamo). Lex's problem is that he does more drugs than he sells, so that the dealer becomes a threat to his life—and to his supply.

*A Brother's Kiss* began life as a one-act play, also starring Chinlund and Raynor. I learn that the writer-director, Seth Zvi Rosenfeld, grew up with Raynor in the area shown in the movie, and Raynor met Chinlund when they were both eleven. So there is history and emotion embedded in the dialogue and performances.

Since what happens to the characters as adults is more or less preordained, what makes the movie work is the conviction of the performances. It's fascinating how Chinlund's character is simultaneously a screw-up and the dominant older brother, while Raynor's is simultaneously the responsible cop and the terrified kid. The roles that life has assigned them do not match their natures, and sooner or later the policeman will find himself in a situation where he has to decide what frightens him more—his brother, or his department superiors.

The supporting cast is good across the board. Marisa Tomei plays a disintegrating cocaine addict, Rosie Perez is touching as a woman who tries to protect her child, and Cathy Moriarty (immortal as Vicky LaMotta in *Raging Bull*) here takes a clichéd role and makes it fresh and heartbreaking. Watching the story of these two brothers, I was reminded of *Angels With Dirty Faces* (1938), with James Cagney and Pat O'Brien as two boys who get in trouble. One is caught, and becomes a killer. The other gets away, and becomes a priest. After the killer is executed, the priest says, "Let's say a prayer for a boy who couldn't run as fast as I could."

## Buddy ★ ★

PG, 84 m., 1997

Rene Russo (Trudy Lintz), Robbie Coltrane (Dr. Lintz), Alan Cumming (Dick), Irma P. Hall (Emma), Peter Elliott (Buddy), Paul Reubens (Professor Spatz), John Aylward (Mr. Bowman), Mimi Kennedy (Mrs. Bowman). Directed by

Caroline Thompson and produced by Steve Nicolaides and Fred Fuchs. Screenplay by Thompson, based on the book *Animals Are My Hobby* by Gertrude Davies Lintz.

*Buddy* is about a woman who is stark raving mad, and the filmmakers don't seem to know it. She lives in a rambling suburban mansion with six geese, five dogs, countless cats, tanks full of fish, a parrot, horses, and two chimpanzees, who she likes to dress up and take to the movies. One day she brings home a baby gorilla named "Buddy."

How does her husband react? Well, he's a doctor, and so he takes out his stethoscope, examines the infant simian, and gravely announces, "double pneumonia." But little Buddy recovers, and soon he is a full-sized gorilla, although the woman insists on treating him as a child (she tells a gorilla expert that a little chicken soup never hurts).

I watched this movie with steadily mounting incredulity. I was trying to find the category for it, and there isn't one. The posters make it look like a madcap family film about a zany couple and their lovable pets. But in a family film you don't expect subtle but unmistakable sexual undertones. Nor is it a serious wildlife film like *Gorillas in the Mist.* Not with Buddy wearing a suit and tie, and the chimps juggling meat cleavers in the kitchen. It could be a study of undiagnosed mental illness, if it weren't shot on perky 1930s sets, scored with upbeat music, and played by the actors like a *Thin Man* movie with Nick and Nora on Prozac.

The film, "based on a true story," stars Rene Russo as Trudy Lintz, who fills her home with animals. Robbie Coltrane plays her chubby, long-suffering and, I must say, remarkably patient husband. His job is to wear three-piece suits and pleasantly say, "Trudy, sweetheart? I wonder if I might have a word with you . . ." (It's inspired casting to put a fat man in this role: He knows a 900-pound gorilla can sit down wherever he wants to, but he always thought *he* was the gorilla.)

The household also includes a cook (Irma P. Hall) whose standard lines ("Don't you do that in my kitchen!") sound strange when addressed to apes, and a butler (Alan Cumming) whose tasks include extricating his mistress from Buddy's death grip by distracting the beast with bowls of milk. He also presumably cleans up around the house, if you get my drift, although that aspect of the situation is not explored.

More than once during the film, I was reminded of John Cassavetes's *Love Streams,* where the deeply disturbed Gena Rowlands character pulls up in a taxi with a duck, a goat, some chickens, a dog, and a parrot, having done a little compulsive shopping at a pet store. The difference is, *Love Streams* knows its heroine is nuts, and *Buddy* doesn't. One of the peculiarities of the film is the vast distance between the movie they've made and the movie they think they've made.

Consider, for example, a sequence where Trudy takes Buddy and the chimps to the Chicago World's Fair. "Sweetheart, I beg you not to take Buddy to the fair," says her sweet husband. "There will be hundreds of people there. He's not used to it." But she persists.

One of the chimps lets Buddy out of his cage and he wanders onto the midway, where there is an unintentionally hilarious sequence showing hundreds of people fleeing and screaming like extras in a *Godzilla* movie, while Buddy ambles about in confusion. (Later that night, Trudy and a cop drive through the empty fairgrounds while she calls "Buddy! Buddy!"—as if a gorilla could remain undetected for hours at a world's fair.)

The story's underlying tragedy, of course, is that Buddy grows up. "He doesn't know his own strength," Trudy says. In one scene he hugs her so tightly we're afraid she'll be crushed. And what about the very peculiar scene where Trudy is asleep in a filmy negligee in her 1930s movie bedroom, and Buddy wanders in? The cutting, the pacing, and the music all suggest, very subtly, that some of the neglected themes in *King Kong* are about to get belated recognition.

Rene Russo plays Trudy as a sweet, resourceful, intelligent woman who is obviously on the edge of screaming hysteria. She smiles, she's the voice of reason, and we're thinking she ought to be shot with tranquilizer darts. Consider the scene where she walks out into the backyard and talks to her animals with a series of shrieks, growls, roars, whistles, and wild, bestial cries. The scene would be odd enough as I've described it. But now imagine it lasting about twice as long as you'd expect.

Robbie Coltrane's husband is a case study in an actor at sea. Why *would* a husband benevolently allow his wife to fill their home with dozens of messy, annoying, and sometimes dangerous animals? If the character were based on Jim Fowler, that would be one thing. But the husband is a doctor who, it appears, doesn't much care about animals one way or another. Coltrane handles this enigma by ignoring it. He addresses his wife always with calm and sweet reason. One day he will probably drop her into a bathtub filled with acid. If he shows the jury this movie, they might let him off with the minimum.

## Bulletproof ★ ★

R, 85 m., 1996

Damon Wayans (Keats), Adam Sandler (Moses), James Caan (Colton), Jeep Swenson (Bledsoe), James Farentino (Captain Jensen), Kristen Wilson (Traci), Larry McCoy (Detective Sulliman), Allen Covery (Detective Jones). Directed by Ernest Dickerson and produced by Robert Simonds. Screenplay by Joe Gayton and Lewis Colick.

*Bulletproof* is one more lap around the same old track: It's a buddy comedy about a cop and a crook, filled with action and stunts and gags and homophobia. That it works as well as it does is because the stars, Damon Wayans and Adam Sandler, have an easy rapport and some good one-liners, and the film is short and manic.

The opening scene is a car chase, so somehow we know we're not in for a lot of character development. Keats and Moses (Wayans and Sandler) are car thieves, who specialize in comic banter during dangerous situations, as when speeding down Hollywood Boulevard pursued by the police.

Veteran cop/buddy viewers can tick off the obligatory scenes: (1) wisecracks with would-be arresting officers; (2) bar scene where cute chick has a towering, bald-headed, tattooed guy in tank top for a boyfriend; (3) ambush in which countless gunmen reveal themselves in moves carefully choreographed to match camera placement and music cues; (4) villain as drug dealer surrounded by henchmen who treat him like cross between corporate giant and spiritual leader.

During a gunfight, Keats is hit in the head by a bullet, and has to undergo physical therapy under the ministrations of the beautiful Traci (Kristen Wilson). He is paralyzed, but soon learns to walk and have sex. Then he's fully recovered and back on the street, enraged at Moses (who he thinks shot him in the head). Moses is also disappointed in him (he thought Keats was his best friend, and didn't know he was an undercover cop).

Keats is after Moses's connection, the big-shot drug dealer (James Caan). He arrests Moses, keeps him in handcuffs most of the time, and then they go on the lam together because they've been betrayed by almost everyone. The director, Ernest Dickerson, now blends nonstop action with weird supporting characters, and gives Sandler room to improvise comic shtick, including a Whitney Houston imitation that parodies a situation in *The Bodyguard*.

The movie's stunt and effects budget must have been considerable. There is another choreographed attack (this time the coordinated bad guys materialize out of the desert in pickup trucks equipped with machine guns), a plane crash, an encounter with a motel clerk from the Twilight Zone, still another choreographed attack, etc. (Drug kingpins in movies always seem to have countless bad guys on their payrolls who are eager to line up and be shot during action sequences.)

Adam Sandler is an actor who benefits from strong direction. He tends, I think, to metamorphose into a stand-up comic at the slightest opportunity, and self-criticism is not one of his traits. I thought after his previous movie *(Happy Gilmore)* that I had seen more or less enough of him for one lifetime, but here he surprised me; he's often funny and not so grating, maybe because he has a character to play. He still insists on lines that work as stand-up but not as dialogue (his definition of seventies porno, for example), but he's learning.

Damon Wayans plays Keats as a sort of closeted bisexual; the dialogue is homophobic, but the undertones suggest his feelings for Moses run a little deeper than simple friendship. Wayans has used veiled gay tones for most of his movie characters (in the "Men on Film" segments on TV's *In Living Color* they were not so veiled). I don't know if it's a choice or a tic. Doth his characters protest too much?

*Bulletproof* isn't good enough to recommend, but it's not bad enough to dismiss. There are a lot of better movies around, to say the least, but if you find yourself watching this one you will be amused—sometimes fitfully, sometimes greatly. I especially liked the motel clerk (Mark Roberts), who uses a few lines of dialogue to suggest *Psycho, Twin Peaks,* and *Motel Hell.*

## Bulworth ★ ★ ★ ½

R, 108 m., 1998

Warren Beatty (Jay Bulworth), Halle Berry (Nina), Don Cheadle (L.D.), Paul Sorvino (Graham Crockett), Jack Warden (Eddie Davers), Sean Astin (Gary), Nora Dunn (Missy Berliner), Laurie Metcalf (Mimi), Oliver Platt (Dennis). Directed by Warren Beatty and produced by Beatty and Pieter Jan Brugge. Screenplay by Beatty.

What it comes down to is a politician who can no longer bring himself to recite the words, "America is standing on the doorstep of a new millennium." Over and over and over again he has repeated the same mindless platitudes, the same meaningless baloney, the same hot air. Now he sits in his office, playing one of his stupid TV commercials on an endless loop. He has not eaten or slept in three days. He is sick to the soul of the American political process.

These do not seem to be the makings of a comedy, but Warren Beatty's *Bulworth* made me laugh, and wince. You realize that if all politicians were as outspoken as Bulworth, the fragile structure of our system would collapse, and we would have to start all over again. The movie suggests that virtually everything said in public by a politician is spin. "Spin control" is merely the name for spin they don't get away with.

Bulworth is a onetime Kennedy liberal (like Beatty himself), an incumbent senator from California who is accused by an opponent of being "old liberal wine trying to pour himself into a new conservative bottle." The joke to Bulworth is that liberal and conservative, Democrat and Republican, are no longer labels that mean much: When it comes to national health care, for example, the insurance companies have both parties in their pockets (and both parties have their hands in the companies' pockets).

Bulworth is in trouble. He hates his job and his life, and has just lost millions in the market. So he puts out a contract on his own life and flies back to California thinking he has three days to live. His impending death fills him with a sense of freedom: At last he is free to say exactly what he thinks, and that's what he does. In a black church, he observes, "We all come down here, get our pictures taken—forget about it." Blacks will never have power within the establishment, he says, until they've spent the money to buy it like the whites do.

Bulworth's campaign manager (Oliver Platt) goes ballistic and hits a fire alarm to end the church service. But an hour later in Beverly Hills Beatty is insulting a mostly Jewish audience of movie moguls: "How much money do you guys really need?" he asks, observing that they produce "mostly crap." And so it goes. "That was good. Really good," he says. He's enjoying political speechmaking for the first time in his life.

Following Bulworth through his conversion is a posse of foxy young black women who pile into his limousine and direct him to an after-hours club, where he samples hip-hop and drugs. Lingering always nearby in the background is an attractive woman named Nina (Halle Berry), who eventually takes him home to her neighborhood, where he sees grade-school kids selling crack, and is treated to the truth of families where everybody has lost someone to gunfire.

*Bulworth* doesn't consist simply of the candidate making insults like a radical Don Rickles. There's substance in a lot of the dialogue, written by Beatty with a debt to the critiques of American society by such as Noam Chomsky. Beatty zeroes in on the myth that government is wasteful and industry is efficient by claiming that government runs Medicare for a fourth of the overhead raked off by insurance companies for equivalent health care. But why don't we have national health care like every other First World country? Because of insurance payoffs, Bulworth is only too happy to explain.

The movie fires shots in all directions. Some of them hit, some of them miss. When Bulworth asks Nina where all the black leaders have gone, her answer is as intelligent and plausible as a year's worth of op-ed columns. But when the movie presents black culture as automatically more authentic and truthful than white, that's a leftover knee-jerk; the use of blacks as repositories of truth and virtue is a worn-out convention in white liberal breast-beating. (There is even a mysterious old black man who follows Bulworth around reciting incantations that are meant, I guess, to be encoded universal truths.) It's better when Bulworth simply abandons political correctness and says what he thinks, however reckless, as when he theorizes that the solution to racial difficulties is for everybody to bleep everybody else until we're all the same color.

*Bulworth* seems to reflect a rising tide of discontent with current American political discourse. Like *Wag the Dog* and *Primary Colors,* it's disenchanted with the state of the system. No wonder. I can remember listening, as a child, to radio debates between those two old warhorses of Illinois politics, Paul Douglas and Everett Dirksen. They simply had at each other, like two opinionated guys talking off the tops of their heads. Now debates, like campaigns, are carefully hedged with rules and regulations designed to ensure that everyone stays timidly within the tradition of "doorsteps of the new millennium," etc.

*Bulworth* is not a perfect movie, nor could it be. It's too messy and takes too many risks. I didn't buy the romance between Bulworth and Nina; it's a recycling of the tired movie convention that a man in a fight for his life can always find time, in three days, to fall in love with a woman half his age. And I didn't much like the movie's ending—not the false ending, and not the real one that follows, either.

But those are minor complaints. *Bulworth* plays like a cry of frustrated comic rage. It's about an archetypal character who increasingly seems to stand for our national mood: the guy who's fed up and isn't going to take it anymore. Funny how in the twenty-two years since we heard those words in *Network,* we've kept right on taking it. ☞

## The Butcher Boy ★ ★ ½

R, 105 m., 1998

Stephen Rea (Da Brady), Fiona Shaw (Mrs. Nugent), Eamonn Owens (Francie Brady), Alan Boyle (Joe Purcell), Aisling O'Sullivan (Annie Brady), Sinead O'Connor (Virgin Mary). Directed by Neil Jordan and produced by Redmond Morris and Stephen Woolley. Screenplay by Jordan and Patrick McCabe, based on the novel by McCabe.

Neil Jordan's *The Butcher Boy* tells the story of a young Irish boy who turns violent and insane under the pressure of a tragic childhood and a sense of betrayal. By the end of the film, when he acts out his murderous fantasies, I was thinking, of course, about the shooting spree by the two young boys in Jonesboro.

This film is, in a sense, optimistic. It suggests that children must undergo years of horrible experiences before they turn into killers. The Jonesboro shooters were apparently more fortunate: more or less normal kids raised with guns, and unable to understand the consequences of their actions. We want to believe violent kids have undergone emotional torments like Francie Brady, the young hero of *The Butcher Boy.* If they haven't, then the abyss is closer than we think.

The film takes place in the early 1960s, in a small town in the west of Ireland. It is narrated by Francie, who is played by the newcomer Eamonn Owens in one of the cockiest and most confident performances I've seen by a young actor. Francie's home life is not happy. His father (Stephen Rea) is a drunk who turns violent, who kicks in the TV, who weeps for the lost innocence of his days before whiskey. His mother (Aisling O'Sullivan) is suicidal; one day Francie comes home from school to find a chair on the kitchen table, and his ma preparing to hang herself.

She has a "breakdown," and is sent to a mental institution, which Francie calls a "garage," because that's where you usually go with a breakdown. He meanwhile clings to the islands of reassurance in his fragile universe, especially his best friend, Joe (Alan Boyle). They hide out in a playhouse near the river, they live in the fantasies of comic books, and Francie feels a fierce, possessive pride in his friend.

Francie's archenemy is the hated Mrs. Nugent (Fiona Shaw), who speaks with an English accent and is a snob and a scold, and seems to delight in persecuting Francie. It's she who turns in Francie and Joe for stealing apples. Francie in his fantasies imagines dire consequences, and is occasionally comforted by the appearance of the Virgin Mary (Sinead O'Connor), who sometimes turns up on TV and is not above using the f-word (although always, to be sure, in a lilting Irish context).

Things fall apart. He's sent to a youth home, where the priest dresses him in girl's clothes before being caught and whisked away to another garage. Francie returns to a job as a butcher boy, cutting up pig carcasses. He has fantasies of nuclear disaster, of humans turned into beasts, of charred corpses. His dad dies, and Francie leaves him in his favorite chair for a long time, until the authorities break in. Joe betrays him and becomes the friend of Mrs. Nugent's hated son.

The closing passages of the film, which is based on a novel by Patrick McCabe, are the logical outcome of what has come before. Jordan doesn't exploit; his tone is one of sad regarding, in which Francie's defiant voice sounds brave and forlorn. This is a kid who keeps up a front while his heart is breaking.

Neil Jordan *(The Crying Game, Michael Collins)* is a strong, passionate director, and *The Butcher Boy* is original work, an attempt to combine magic realism with everyday reality and tie it together with Francie's own brash, defiant personal style (he is not a dumb kid). Yet in some way the movie held me outside; I didn't connect in the way I wanted to, and by the end I was out of sympathy with the material.

Why was this? I can see, objectively, that this is a film of weight, daring, and visual invention. I was in a little awe of young Eamonn Owens's performance. I can understand any praise this film receives, but I cannot feel it. *The Butcher Boy* has been compared to Kubrick's *A Clockwork Orange*, an acknowledged masterpiece that I have also found myself standing outside of. Rationalize as I will, revisit the film as I have, I cannot feel the emotional shift that would involve me in the material: It remains for me an exercise, not an experience (odd that his detached, cerebral *2001* sweeps me so easily into its spell).

Am I simply out of sympathy with Francie? Would I have been more moved by a more realistic approach (like the treatment of the reform school boy in *The Loneliness of the Long-Distance Runner*), rather than this film with miracles and horrific mirages? I can't say. I know there is something substantial here. I can't recommend the film, and yet if it sounds intriguing to you, I certainly think you should see it.

## Butterfly Kiss ★ ★ ★ ½

NO MPAA RATING, 88 m., 1996

Amanda Plummer (Eunice), Saskia Reeves (Miriam), Kathy Jamieson (Wendy), Des McAleer (Eric), Lisa Jane Riley (Danielle), Freda Dowie (Elsie), Paula Tilbrook (Ella), Fine Time Fontayne (Tony). Directed by Michael Winterbottom and produced by Julie Baines. Screenplay by Frank Cottrell Boyce.

"I've looked all up and down these roads for someone to love me," says Eunice, the tortured murderess and pilgrim whose story is told in *Butterfly Kiss.* Later she observes, "Punishment is all I understand." She is a gaunt, angry woman who stalks the roadsides of Britain, bursting into petrol stations to ask the women behind the counter, "Are you Judith?" Then she kills them.

But she doesn't kill Miriam, the slow-witted, hard-of-hearing clerk who sees her splashing herself with gasoline and walks out of the store and sits next to her on a concrete wall, and is kind to her. After they talk quietly, Eunice reaches out and kisses Miriam, who is from that moment completely dazzled by her power. "Mother, Auntie Kathy, a girl at swimming—and Eunice," Miriam remembers. "Those are all the people who have kissed me."

The wounds of mental sickness, loneliness, and need in *Butterfly Kiss* are so deep that we can hardly watch. The two women begin a journey across England, Eunice killing and Miriam mostly cleaning up after her, as we begin to understand how these two deeply scarred, incomplete personalities have somehow found the perfect fit. The writer, Frank Cottrell Boyce, and the director, Michael Winterbottom, show the relationship forming but allow it to be a mystery: What draws these women together, logic is not relevant to it.

Miriam (Saskia Reeves), her long-sleeved sweater buttoned over her clerk's smock, looks like an innocent, sentimental waif. Eunice (Amanda Plummer) looks hard-edged and worn by a lifetime of pain, and one of her small pleasures is to unbutton her blouse to show people that her gaunt body, covered with bruises, is wrapped in chains, her nipples pierced and linked. "She had 17 tattoos," Miriam remembers, in a black-and-white video apparently made by the police at the end of it all. "And they all had a meaning."

Do the chains and piercings hurt? Yes, they do, Eunice says. She wants to be hurt. She is doing penance for her sins. At times she is articulate, wondering why nobody else will punish her. Is she so insignificant that God will let her murder people and not even notice? The movie wisely never explains exactly who she is or where she comes from; this is not a case study but a sad parable.

Who is Judith, the woman she seeks? Some reviews of the film have drawn insights from the biblical Judith, an avenger who beheaded an enemy of the Israelites. Has Eunice found Judith in the Bible, or been loved by her in some real or imagined past? Eunice never lets go of a packet of papers, wrapped in plastic, that contain all the "writings"—the documentation to support whatever madness her mind has thrown up as a bulwark against the world. Her quest for Judith defines her. The first day she meets Miriam, Eunice goes home with her, they make love, and Miriam is happy, one gathers, for the first time in her life. But the next morning the words YOUR NOT JUDITH are written in shaving cream on the mirror, and Eunice is gone.

Miriam chases after her down the highway and finds her shortly after she's murdered again. Miriam helps conceal the body. "I never stopped looking in her for the good," she says in the videotape. Sometimes she seems dimly aware that there may not be very much good. Eunice gets into an argument about dolphins with a man who gives them a lift. He thinks they may be superior to humans. "We must be superior to the dolphins," Eunice says, "since we kill the dolphins." Later there is a frightening sequence when the two women, having stolen a car, give a lift to a homeless father and his daughter, and it seems that even the daughter will not be spared by Eunice. Miriam acts here to save the girl—but her loyalty to Eunice never falters.

The performances have a gravity about them that is unusual in the movies. Amanda Plummer (Honey Bunny in *Pulp Fiction*) plays Eunice with a fierce, if twisted, intelligence: She talks to herself, her eyes roam restlessly, but she always seems aware of exactly what she's done, and is even able to analyze her own actions. Saskia Reeves *(Antonia and Jane)* plays Miriam with acceptance, warmth, and sweetness, but little comprehension: She accepts all of Eunice's horrifying crimes and scars and justifies them, driven by a complicated mix of need, sentimentality, incomprehension, and sexual awakening. The movie's weak point is in the black-and-white videotaped testimony, when Reeves lets Miriam seem more aware, more of a performer, than elsewhere in the film.

The names of the women are shortened in the movie to the suggestive "Mi" and "Eu." Can they be read as parts of a schizophrenic personality? Or is the story to be taken as it is told, as the record of a madwoman and a dim and trusting one, who spend some bleak time together and are able to find a small measure of happiness? I don't know. The movie doesn't defend or glorify them; it simply shows them. How you respond to *Butterfly Kiss* depends on what you bring to it, and how much empathy you are willing to extend to these sad and horrifying women.

# C

## The Cable Guy ★ ★

PG-13, 91 m., 1996

---

Jim Carrey (Cable Guy), Matthew Broderick (Steven), Leslie Mann (Robin), Jack Black (Rick), George Segal (Steven's Father), Diane Baker (Steven's Mother), Ben Stiller (Sam Sweet), Eric Roberts (Eric Roberts). Directed by Ben Stiller and produced by Andrew Licht, Jeffrey A. Mueller, and Judd Apatow. Screenplay by Lou Holtz Jr.

---

We want to like Jim Carrey. A movie that makes us dislike him is a strategic mistake. The opening scenes of *The Cable Guy* are promising; Carrey seems to be playing a variation on his usual hyperkinetic goofball. Then our reaction grows more puzzled: This *is* supposed to be fun, right? By the end, the movie has declared itself as a black comedy about one very deeply troubled cable guy.

I realize I am setting a trap here. I am insisting that Carrey should have played a character more like Ace Ventura or the *Dumb and Dumber* guy. Yet when he did, I didn't give those performances particularly great reviews. True, but Carrey was growing on me. He was defining his comic space and teaching it to audiences, and I was just about there, admiring his talent and boundless energy while wishing it had been better used than in the dreadful *Ace Ventura: When Nature Calls.*

I was primed for *The Cable Guy.* In my mind, I had a notion of how the movie might unfold—a notion nurtured by the ads and previews, which understandably emphasize the madcap zany stuff. The movie is not much like that. The movie character the cable guy most resembles in his psychological profile is Rupert Pupkin, the pathological celebrity hound played by Robert De Niro in Scorsese's *The King of Comedy.* Yet the movie isn't trying to make a statement about the cable guy; it is simply trying for laughs in a way that will not produce them.

The plot centers around a character named Steven (Matthew Broderick), who has just been turned down for marriage by his girlfriend Robin (Leslie Mann). He moves into a bachelor pad and calls for cable service, and Chip Douglas (Carrey) comes pounding on his door (making sure, of course, to arrive very late and while Steven is in the shower). The cable guy is a manic nerd with a lisp and an underslung jaw. He wants to be Steven's friend. He has a lot of trouble pronouncing certain words. "My brother is a speech therapist," Steven says helpfully. The cable guy says, "Tho?"

Soon the cable guy has insinuated himself into Steven's life and is offering detailed advice about life (which he reveals he has learned that morning from the summation at the end of a Jerry Springer program). His strategy for getting Robin to come back: Watch *Sleepless in Seattle* with her. Women are suckers for it. Many of these strategies work, and we're reminded of the relationship in the British comedy classic *School for Scoundrels* (which Carrey should remake) in which a cad teaches one-upmanship to a loser.

But soon the movie drifts into murkier waters. The cable guy has an unhealthy need to be Steven's friend, and he pursues that goal with behavior designed to scare anyone. He's a stalker. He's obnoxious and peculiar and inappropriate and relentless, and we start disliking him. That's when the movie jumps the rails.

The director, Ben Stiller *(Reality Bites),* throws in a lot of gratuitous but funny asides: There's a running gag about a *Court TV* trial involving Hollywood twins whose relationship ends in murder. And in-jokes, as when the cable guy covers his face with fried chicken skin to imitate a scene from *The Silence of the Lambs* (actor Charles Napier, whose face was borrowed by Hannibal Lecter in *Lambs,* turns up here as a cop). And there's a fake TV commercial showing Eric Roberts playing a dual role in *Brother, Sweet Brother,* the docudrama based on the Hollywood trial.

But those are all side trips. The main line of the movie heads into deep trouble. My guess is, it happened accidentally. I don't think the writer, Lou Holtz Jr., wanted to do anything other than write a comedy that would please Jim Carrey fans and justify the star's famous $20 million paycheck. But somehow the logic of the story pushed it in another direction. If the cable guy is a pathological pest, then in the second half of the movie he has to be sicker than in the first.

Maybe it would have worked better if the cable guy had become a real friend to Steven, devising love strategies and Machiavellian schemes to win back Robin and thwart her other suitors. As it is, the movie goes in one direction and the cable guy goes in another, and by the end we aren't really looking forward to seeing Jim Carrey reappear on the screen.

*Note to the producers: There's an old show biz saying that "satire is what closes on Saturday night." To which could be added another: "Black comedy is not what you pay someone $20 million for."*

## Can't Hardly Wait ★ ½

PG-13, 98 m., 1998

Ethan Embry (Preston Meyers), Jennifer Love Hewitt (Amanda Beckett), Lauren Ambrose (Denise Fleming), Peter Facinelli (Mike Dexter), Seth Green (Kenny Fisher), Charlie Korsmo (William Lichter), Jenna Elfman (The Angel), Jerry O'Connell (Trip McNeely). Directed by Deborah Kaplan and Harry Elfont and produced by Jenno Topping and Betty Thomas. Screenplay by Kaplan and Elfont.

There's one character in *Can't Hardly Wait* who is interesting and funny. Maybe it was a mistake to write her in; she makes the other characters look like gnat-brained bozos. Her name is Denise, she is played by Lauren Ambrose, and she has a merry face, a biting tongue, and a sardonic angle on high school. Her classmates look like candidates for *Starship Troopers* or the *Sports Illustrated* swimsuit pictorial.

The early days of June seem to bring a movie like this every year, celebrating the graduation of the senior class and its ejection onto the conveyor belt of life. *Can't Hardly Wait* is a lesser example of the genre, which includes (in descending order of accomplishment) *Say Anything, American Graffiti, Dazed and Confused, Fast Times at Ridgemont High,* and *Porky's.*

The movie lumbers gracelessly from romantic showdowns to deep conversations to bathroom humor. The hero is Preston (Ethan Embry), a would-be writer who has lusted for four years after the class sexpot, Amanda (Jennifer Love Hewitt). He knew their destinies were entertwined when they both ate strawberry Pop Tarts during their first freshman class. But the class jock, Mike (Peter Facinelli), won her instead.

Now it is the night of graduation day, and Mike has dumped Amanda because he plans to move up from high school *girls* to college *women.* At a long (some would say endless) keg party, Preston tries to give Amanda a letter he has written, spilling out his innermost thoughts. This must be some letter. We never get to see what it says, no doubt because a letter good enough to win Amanda would have to be better than anything the screenwriters are capable of writing.

Meanwhile, Mike learns from last year's high school make-out champ, Trip McNeely (Jerry O'Connell), that college women are always talking about serious stuff and dating older guys. Bummer. So he tries to win Amanda back in a scene played before a hushed crowd, but is rejected. That's even though Amanda has earlier wailed, "If I'm not Mike's girlfriend, who am I? Nobody knows me as anything else. I don't even know me as anyone else."

Real poignancy there. My own rule of thumb, in high school and ever after, is that if a woman has little of interest to say, she is likely, over a span of time, to have less and less to say, until finally she will drive you mad. That is true even though she may, as Amanda does, have awesome boobs.

Now take Denise, on the other hand. She gets accidentally locked into the bathroom with Kenny (Seth Green), who talks like a black rap artist even though he's white, and wears goggles and thinks he's cool and will someday no doubt be a radio talk jock. Denise is cute and plucky, and has intelligent lips (don't pretend you don't know what I mean), and kids Kenny's affectations, and remembers that they were best pals until the sixth grade, when he dropped her because, she says, "I was in all the smart classes, and my parents didn't make a lot of money, and you desperately needed to sit at the popular table in the lunchroom."

Denise is the only person in this senior class that anyone of any taste would want to be friends with. Why don't the filmmakers know that? Why do they go through the tired old motions of making Denise the comic relief, and assigning the romantic leads to a couple of clueless rubber stamps?

You tell me. *Can't Hardly Wait* is the kind of movie that somehow succeeds in moving very, very slowly even while proceeding at a breakneck pace. It cuts quickly back and forth between nothing and nothing. It underlines every single scene with a pop song that tells us what the scene is about. It doesn't have the zing of life and subversion that the best high school movies always have. Or, if they don't have them, like *Porky's* didn't, at least they have mercy on us and throw in a shower scene.

## Career Girls ★ ★ ★

R, 87 m., 1997

Katrin Cartlidge (Hannah), Lynda Steadman (Annie), Kate Byers (Claire), Mark Benton (Ricky), Andy Serkis (Mr. Evans), Joe Tucker (Adrian), Margo Stanley (Ricky's Nan), Michael Healy (Lecturer). Directed by Mike Leigh and produced by Simon Channing-Williams. Screenplay by Leigh.

The world of Mike Leigh is one of small victories, painfully earned. His characters don't have lives that are easily transformed; they can't remake themselves overnight as self-help success stories. They're stuck with who they are and what they started out with, and somehow they find the courage to carry out essential upkeeps and improvements.

*Career Girls,* Leigh's first film since the heralded *Secrets and Lies,* is about two thirtyish women who were roommates six years ago, when they were both students at a London college. Now they meet again. Have their lives improved? Yes. Are they where they want to be? No. Are they confident they can get there? Not very.

Annie (Lynda Steadman) takes the train to London to meet Hannah (Katrin Cartlidge), who still lives there. Annie is as taut as a guitar string; she doesn't talk, she jerks the words free from her inhibitions. She's better now, though, than she was on the first day when she came to see Hannah in response to a roommate-wanted ad. In those days Annie had a nasty skin condition that covered half her face, and it wouldn't take a specialist to guess the rash was connected to nerves.

Leigh likes to let scenes develop in their own time. They don't rush to a payoff, because how the characters talk is often more important than their conclusions. Both actresses are highly mannered (or Leigh directs them to be), and as we watch, we're reminded of how smooth and articulate most characters are in the movies—why, you'd almost imagine someone had written out all the words for them to memorize! Not Annie, who seems blazingly self-conscious, and not Hannah, who is so wound up that words come tumbling out like an assault. I was reminded of a good performance in a much different movie—Benicio del Toro's work in *Excess Baggage,* where he also finds a new tone for his dialogue, lazy and coiling. Distinctive speech styles can be an affectation, or they can be a gift from the actor: *Career Girls* is like a workshop on conversational self-defense.

The two women sit and chat, and decide to go out (Hannah is apartment-hunting). They run into some old friends from their school days, including a rental agent named Adrian (Joe Tucker), who uncannily reminded me of the scenes in *Trainspotting* when Renton, the Ewan McGregor character, puts on a suit and tie and works as a real estate agent. Adrian dated one of the roommates and then the other, but doesn't remember either one.

In a hilarious flashback, we see another page from their social life: A drink at a pub with Ricky (Mark Benton), who closes his eyes when he talks, the better perhaps to read the words off the insides of his eyelids. One of Leigh's favorite actors is Timothy Spall, who played the photographer in *Secrets and Lies;* it's not a stretch to see Ricky as a younger version of the same character.

As *Career Girls* advances, we gradually realize that there is not going to be much of a plot to resolve. Annie and Hannah are in midstream. They know where they came from, but it's pretty murky in the direction they're going. They are neither successes nor failures, neither happy nor particularly sad, and they have jobs which, for the moment, focus their lives. They are, in short, like most of the young jobholders in big cities, and to an important degree their self-images are defined by the apartments they live in. (Looking out the window of a high-rise shown by an estate agent, one observes, "You can see the class struggle from up here!")

What is the use of a film like this? It inspires reflection. Strongly plotted films provide a goal and reach it, and we can go home under the impression that something has been accomplished. Mike Leigh's films realize that for most people, most days, life consists of the routine of earning a living, broken by fleeting thoughts of where our efforts will someday take us—financially, romantically, spiritually, or even geographically.

We never arrive in most of those places, but the mental images are what keep us trying.

Annie and Hannah have a game they play in the film. Holding a copy of Emily Brontë's *Wuthering Heights,* they chant "Miss Brontë, Miss Brontë . . ." and then ask her a question, as if she were a Ouija board. Then they stab at a page at random, and read what she says in response.

I recognized the edition they were using: the Penguin English Library paperback, first published in 1965. I have the identical edition on my shelf, so I took it down. "Miss Brontë, Miss Brontë," I chanted, "what is the bottom line on the characters in this movie?" I opened it to page 163, stabbed, and read: "Oh, I'm burning! I wish I were out of doors—I wish I were a girl again, half savage and hardy, and free . . . and laughing at injuries, not maddening under them!"

## Carried Away ★ ★ ★

R, 104 m., 1996

Dennis Hopper (Joseph Svenden), Amy Irving (Rosealee Henson), Amy Locane (Catherine Wheeler), Julie Harris (Joseph's Mother), Gary Busey (Major Wheeler), Hal Holbrook (Dr. Evans), Christopher Pettiet (Robert Henson). Directed by Bruno Barreto and produced by Lisa M. Hansen and Paul Hertzberg. Screenplay by Ed Jones, based on the novel *Farmer* by Jim Harrison.

Joseph was crippled in a farming accident as a young man, and perhaps his lame leg has kept him close to home. He still lives in the farmhouse he was raised in, and has taught for years in the local school. He is realistic about his abilities: "I'm a mediocre teacher and an even worse farmer." For six years he has been dating the widow of his best friend, and maybe one of these years he will even marry her, if his excuses run out.

Then one day a seventeen-year-old girl comes into his life. She is a student whose family has moved to the isolated north woods village where Joseph lives. She is sexually experienced and aggressive, and one day in his barn she tries to seduce her teacher, who is forty-seven. He does the right thing and rejects her, and walks away. Then he comes back, finds her still waiting, and says flatly, "I think we should make love."

This story is told in *Farmer,* the 1976 novel by Jim Harrison that is not so much about sex, or farming, as about taking risks, especially the wrong ones (since they are the only ones that are really dangerous). Joseph is played in the film by Dennis Hopper, in a quiet, studied performance that will come as a surprise to those who know him from his most recent films. The young girl, named Catherine, is played by Amy Locane, and Amy Irving plays Rosealee, the local woman who has been courted so politely all these years.

But Bruno Barreto's *Carried Away* is not simply a love triangle and, although it sets up situations in ways that seem familiar, it doesn't resolve them as we expect. Everyone in the film—even the teenager—is more intelligent and articulate than is usually permitted in American movies, and having gotten themselves into an emotional tangle, they go to work getting themselves out again.

Dennis Hopper has been a movie actor for forty-one years, and for the last ten he has made a lot of money playing crazed villains like the mad bomber in *Speed* and the lizard-man in *Super Mario Brothers.* But he is ambitious to do good work, and when the right role comes along he abandons all thought of paychecks and simply goes with it. That's what he did twice in 1991, in *The Indian Runner* and *Paris Trout,* and here he is again, surprising us with his range.

Joseph is a good man. He teaches as well as he can. He moves slowly through life, not because of his limp, but by preference. When Catherine bares her breasts to him, it is hard to say all that he thinks, but perhaps he considers that she knows better what she is doing than he does, and that if he does not take this mad leap into sexual folly, he will plod without deliverance to his grave. Of course it is wrong. But everything he has been doing that is right is also wrong.

What does the girl want? Her mother is an alcoholic who rarely leaves their home. Her father (Gary Busey) is a retired major who has come to this district to hunt. Catherine wants to go to drama school. She senses that Joseph is the only man in town with much feeling for the arts. And there is the suggestion that this is not the first time she has used sex as a shortcut to an adult life she urgently wants to begin. ("Whatever happened," her father says later, "I have a feeling it was more than half her idea.")

As the private drama unfolds, Joseph faces another crisis. The local school will be merged with a larger one and he will no longer be needed as a teacher. Can he farm? He doubts it. Rosealee wants him to marry her, but Rosealee is caring for her dying mother; and Joseph feels that their romance has become simply a habit. After Catherine helps him remember passion, he bursts in on Rosealee one night, demanding that they make love for once with the lights on, and do other wild things that are not part of their rehearsed repertory.

*Carried Away* is not a neat package. You don't leave it knowing exactly what it was saying, or how it felt about all of the characters (Catherine, unfinished in life, is wisely not defined too carefully). What you do feel is that these people (also including the local doctor, played by Hal Holbrook) were not born yesterday, and have the imagination to figure out what to do next—instead of simply using the standard melodramatic tools of guns and emotional explosions. They get into a painful situation, and then they go to work getting out and seeing if they learned anything.

## Cats Don't Dance ★ ★ ★

G, 69 m., 1997

With the voices of: Scott Bakula (Danny), Jasmine Guy (Sawyer), Natalie Cole (Sawyer's Songs), Ashley Peldon (Darla Dimple), John Rhys-Davies (Woolie), Kathy Najimy (Tillie), Matthew Harried (Pudge), George Kennedy (Mr. Mammoth). Directed by Mark Dindal and produced by David Kirschner and Paul Gertz. Screenplay by Roberts Gannaway, Cliff Ruby, Elana Lesser, and Theresa Pettengill.

The words "Disney" and "animation" fit together so firmly in the public mind that a feature-length cartoon from any other studio has tough going. If it's not Disney, somehow parents don't feel automatically compelled to load up the family van and head for the multiplex.

Warner Bros. has been trying to change that perception, and its *Space Jam,* starring Michael Jordan and Bugs Bunny, was a box-office hit, even though it didn't break through the magic $100 million domestic box-office ceiling. Now the studio is back again, with *Cats Don't Dance,* a cute animated musical about Danny the Song and Dance Cat from Kokomo, Indiana, who hops on a bus to Hollywood in search of stardom, circa 1939.

The movie lacks the strong plotting and vividly defined characters that are typical of Disney movies, and it doesn't start with the death of one or more parents, which seems more or less obligatory in the genre. It plays, indeed, more like an animated version of an old Hollywood musical (there are elements of *Singin' in the Rain,* and the late Gene Kelly is credited with the animated choreography).

The opening is right out of countless showbiz tales. Danny arrives in Hollywood with a seven-day plan that starts with getting an agent and ends with getting the girl. He quickly discovers the hard facts of life: Animal actors aren't much in demand, and humans get all the best jobs.

He's lucky to land a one-liner ("Meow") in a new musical by Darla Dimple (voice by Ashley Peldon), legendary heroine of Mammoth Studios, where the formula for a box-office hit is "Simple! It's Dimple!" He works the meow up into an entire routine, and is in the process of stealing the show when an ominous presence looms high above him: Max, Darla's butler (lifted here, accent and all, from Erich von Stroheim in *Sunset Boulevard*).

Danny (voice by Scott Bakula) makes some new friends, including Woolie (voice by John Rhys-Davies), the elephant who serves as Mammoth's mascot and spends his off-hours playing piano in the gypsy caravan that doubles as his home. (There's nice animation in a scene where Woolie's slightest movement causes his home to tremble alarmingly.) And Danny falls in love with Sawyer (voice by Jasmine Guy, songs by Natalie Cole), a veteran feline actress. But after Max gets him all but blacklisted in Hollywood, he grows disheartened and starts to go back home—only to change his mind, return, and star in a triumphant impromptu production number at the premiere of Darla's new movie. Even the dreaded mogul L. B. Mammoth (voice by George Kennedy) is won over.

This scene, which mirrors *Singin' in the Rain* by making a new star at the cost of an older one, is well handled with a lot of energy. And Mark Dindal, the film's director, creates a fresh look for the animation: not Disney and not Loony Tunes, but a touch of Betty Boop and Max Fleischer. *Cats Don't Dance* is not compelling and it's not a breakthrough, but on its own terms it works well. Whether this will appeal to kids is debatable; the story involves a time and a subject they're not much interested in. But the Randy Newman songs are catchy, the look is bright, the spirits are high, and fans of Hollywood's golden age might find it engaging.

*Note: The movie's curtain-raiser is "Pullet Surprise" (say it out loud), a six-minute color cartoon produced by the legendary animator Chuck Jones, and starring Foghorn Leghorn.*

## Caught ★ ★ ★

R, 109 m., 1996

Edward James Olmos (Joe), Maria Conchita Alonso (Betty), Arie Verveen (Nick), Steven Schub (Danny), Bitty Schram (Amy), Shawn Elliot (Santiago), Bernie and Tommy Abbot (Peter), Sandra Kazan (Bag Lady). Directed by Robert M. Young and produced by Richard Brick and Irwin Young. Screenplay by Edward Pomerantz.

"Fish been very good to me," says Joe, early in *Caught*. He runs a fish market in Jersey City and has a proud policy: "Any customer finds a bone, I give them their money back, plus a quarter." Joe's life is full because he loves fish ("Fish are his life," his wife says, with an irony that Joe doesn't pick up on). This looks like the setup for a story of proletarian bliss, but in fact *Caught* is the most carnal of recent movies, a film that reminds us how movies used to take sex seriously, instead of using it as an excuse for muscular choreography.

For many years Joe (Edward James Olmos) and his wife, Betty (Maria Conchita Alonso), have run their fish store on a street of other small shops. Their marriage would be perfect if only Joe liked sex more and Betty liked fish more. Their only son, Danny (Steven Schub), has moved to Hollywood to seek work as a stand-up comic, and sends back videos of his act, which seem like the rantings of a dangerous lunatic, although his mother proudly calls him "the next Robin Williams."

Into their shop one day steps a young man on the run from the police. His name is Nick (Arie Verveen), and he's not a criminal, just a kid down on his luck. Joe and Betty take pity on him, invite him home for dinner, and eventually offer him a job. The pay isn't great but the deal includes room and board, and Nick is given Danny's old room in the cramped flat where the family lives.

In a sense, Nick is the son Joe and Betty wanted and deserved. The absent Danny is a drugged-out creep who lies, "My agent has Letterman and *Saturday Night Live* fighting over me." But Nick is grateful, friendly, learns fast, and loves the same things Joe and Betty love: fish and sex. With fish it is a slower process, but Joe teaches him patiently, and soon he can bone a chubb in under five minutes, which is "the mark of a fish man."

Sharing the same cramped space with Betty, Nick becomes aware of her as a woman. This is a remarkably easy thing to do when Betty is played by Maria Conchita Alonso, one of the rare actresses who seems to think sex is an occasion to laugh and be grateful—instead of a grim showdown with Darwinian, management, and marketing overtones. Because both Betty and Nick care for Joe, they do not want to cheat, but a deep current of passion grows between them, and after their first illicit lovemaking they become helpless in the face of their obsession, snatching stolen moments while in constant danger of being discovered by Joe.

One of the things that makes *Caught* intriguing is that we don't want them to be discovered—because we care for Joe. As played by Olmos, he is a good man, a little too single-minded, who does not deserve to be hurt. Nick and Betty know this too. "I wish we could tell him—show him—so he could see how wonderful it is," Betty says.

The situation reaches a crisis when the obnoxious Danny returns from Los Angeles with his wife and child. Despite his boasts, he has no prospects and a dim future; he uses a lot of dope and focuses on cruel one-liners, a lot of them aimed at Nick. It takes Danny little time to figure out what's going on between his mother and the new shop assistant, and there is a shocking moment at a picnic when he tricks his mother, who uses her toes to caress her son's leg under the table, thinking it is Nick's.

*Caught* is not the kind of movie we ordinarily expect from Robert M. Young, a director whose films run toward political themes with progressive overtones (his credits include *The Ballad of Gregorio Cortez, Short Eyes, Dominick and Eugene,* and *Triumph of the Spirit*). It's more classic in its undertones; we are reminded of Oedipus.

But there is a special twist to the story, since the villain is the real son, while the symbolic son is more the victim of the irresistible attraction that grows up between himself and Betty, and the father is an innocent bystander. These confused lines of affection and loyalty make for an explosive and complicated crisis, which is surprising in its form and its shocking outcome.

Watching the movie has the fascination of watching a traffic accident; we know there is going to be a crash, cannot stop it, and cannot look away. But Young and his actors are able to lead us to the crash through a process that makes us care about the people it happens to. And they are fearless in showing us the consequences of uncontrolled lust.

When I think of sex in recent movies, I think of a joyless, calculated display of commercialized images, as in such movies as *Striptease, Showgirls*, and all of those yuppie dramas where men are destroyed by mantislike female executives. *Caught* is a throwback to a time when the movies thought about sex more simply, as something that people wanted so much that sometimes it overwhelmed their better senses. And that strong, elemental power, coursing under the surface of the story, gives it a strength that elevates melodrama almost to tragedy.

## Caught Up ★ ★

R, 95 m., 1998

Bokeem Woodbine (Daryl), Cynda Williams (Vanessa), Joseph Lindsey (Billy Grimm), Clifton Powell (Herbert/Frank Lowden), Basil Wallace (Ahmad), Snoop Doggy Dogg (Kool Kitty Kat), LL Cool J (Roger), Tony Todd (Jake). Directed by Darin Scott and produced by Peter Heller. Screenplay by Scott.

*Caught Up* is the first movie directed by Darin Scott, who has written three earlier movies and has produced eight. I suspect he spent those years impatiently stashing away ideas and images for his own first film; *Caught Up* plays like Fibber McGee's closet—it opens and everything but the kitchen sink comes tumbling out. Scott is ambitious and not without talent, but he ought to ration his material a little; there's so much plot it's dizzying.

*Caught Up* stars Bokeem Woodbine as Daryl, a man who dreams of opening his own club to support his girlfriend and their son. He needs $10,000, and a friend offers to get it at the bank. Daryl realizes too late that the withdrawal is a robbery. In prison, Daryl reads Greek philosophy. "You wanna know what those five years were like?" he asks. And when he answers, "Hell!" Scott has flames shoot up from the bottom of the screen. It's that kind of film.

On the outside again, Daryl meets a woman named Vanessa (Cynda Williams, from *One False Move*), who looks uncannily like his former girlfriend (who he is "staying away from" until he has his act together). She tells his fortune (tarot cards are superimposed on the screen) and gets him a job as a limo driver, ferrying dubious people to unsavory destinations.

And then—well, at some point I have to bail out of the plot description because it begins to appear that Daryl is caught in an elaborate web of betrayal and deception, and nobody is quite who or what they seem. We get the rug pulled out from beneath us so many times we stop caring: What's the use of trying to figure things out when the story is toying with us?

Yet the film has qualities. I liked the stylized way the story was told, with narration and flashbacks, visual overlays and special effects. Even those phony flames from hell were entertaining just because the movie was trying something. You could sense the enthusiasm of the director.

What I didn't much like was the device of a mysterious man in black, his face concealed, who follows Daryl and tries to kill him. I didn't like him as a gimmick, and I liked him even less when I heard the ludicrous explanation of who he was and why he was mad. And my patience was running a little thin by the time a body was hurled through a glass window perfectly on cue—timed to be the punch line for dialogue that, of course, no one on the other side of the window could hear. I sort of liked the sulfuric acid scene, though.

*Caught Up* is a film by a man who wanted to make a movie more than he wanted to tell a story. The story is the excuse for visual gizmos and directorial virtuosity. It makes me curious to see Scott's next film, but next time he should remember that if the audience can't care about the characters it has a hard time caring about the style.

## Celestial Clockwork ★ ★ ★

NO MPAA RATING, 85 m., 1996

Ariadna Gil (Ana), Arielle Dombasle (Celeste), Evelyne Didi (Alcanie), Frederic Longbois (Armand), Lluis Homar (Italo), Chantal Aimee (Tina), Alma Rosa Castellanos (Lucila), Dominique Abel (Gaby). Produced and directed by Fina Torres. Screenplay by Torres.

*Celestial Clockwork* is a riotous carnival of music, colors, witchery, sexuality, and magic. It's pitched at approximately the same level of seriousness as *Flying Down to Rio,* and if you approach it in that spirit, it's infectious and funny. The opening scene is lifted from *The Graduate,* the plot recycles *Cinderella,* and some of the visuals seem inspired by Godard and others by Jodorowsky. If Almodovar had made this movie, it would have been hailed as his best work in years.

Because it has been made by a more obscure director, Fina Torres of Venezuela, it will be approached by suspicion in those circles where whimsy needs a pedigree. Too bad. It's rare to find a relatively unknown director with so much style and the confidence to tell a silly story about silly people just for the fun of it.

The movie opens with Ana (Ariadna Gil) deciding at the altar that she cannot marry the man standing next to her. She flees from the church, packs her Maria Callas poster on the way to the airport, and flies from Venezuela to Paris, still in her wedding gown. On her journey, elements of magic realism sneak in: Taxicabs change colors and clouds scurry surrealistically across the sky.

In Paris, she finds a place to stay with four other women from South America, and soon has two jobs, as a cleaning woman and a bakery worker. She dreams of being an opera singer, and sings on a rooftop in the rain—an enchanting moment in a movie filled with music, both Latin and operatic. Soon she has convinced a voice coach to take her as a pupil, and she dreams of auditioning for the great impresario Italo Medica (Lluis Homar), who is casting a film of Rossini's *Cinderella* and needs the perfect unknown.

There are Cinderella-like hurdles to her ambition, including a wicked stepmotherlike figure named Celeste and called La Pirata (Arielle Dombasle), who dreams of being cast for the role and sabotages Ana's chances. But after Ana moves in with a female psychologist, secret African love potions make her the woman's lover, and also cast a spell that leads, indirectly, to the director hearing a cassette of her lovely voice. "Find me that girl!" he orders his flunky, in a line that could have been borrowed from *Singin' in the Rain.*

The movie shows the Latin roommates playing shuffle-the-roomie to fool the immigration police, and has a subplot involving a gay waiter who marries her—providing both the church wedding his parents crave and the visa Ana needs. Meanwhile, inspiration comes when the Callas poster begins to sing.

Much of the movie's charm comes from the glow and charisma of Ariadna Gil, who has a beautiful smile—and just as well, since she smiles so much during the movie. I kept thinking she reminded me of somebody, and finally I figured it out: She looks like a young, nubile Dr. Ruth, and has about the same energy level, not to mention the same open-minded attitude toward sex. True, the plot is silly, but this is a musical comedy and knows it, and brings freshness to its old material.

The movie also benefits from the Latin freedom in color, movement, and music. Sometimes when I'm channel-surfing I'll happen upon one of those variety shows on a Spanish channel where the hostess has big sex-bomb hair and a low neckline and a manic energy level, and I'll think, how come the English channels seem so uptight and slowed down by comparison? *Celestial Clockwork* inspires similar thoughts.

## The Celluloid Closet ★ ★ ★ ½

NO MPAA RATING, 102 m., 1996

Sony Pictures Classics presents a documentary narrated by Lily Tomlin and featuring Tony Curtis, Whoopi Goldberg, Harvey Fierstein, Quentin Crisp, Gore Vidal, Paul Rudnick, Shirley MacLaine, and others. Directed and produced by Rob Epstein and Jeffrey Friedman. Screenplay by Epstein, Friedman, and Sharon Wood.

When was I first aware that a movie character was intended to be homosexual? It must have been in the early 1960s, in the final sequence of Fellini's *La Dolce Vita,* when two transvestites join the sad group that goes to meet the dawn.

What *The Celluloid Closet* makes clear is that I had seen lots of gay characters before then—it's just that the movies never quite identified them as gay or, like a lot of moviegoers, I didn't pick up on the clues. I remember that Peter Ustinov, playing Nero in *Quo Vadis* (1951), struck me oddly in a scene where he collected his tears in a tiny crystal goblet, but maybe I thought that was typical of Roman emperors.

Portrayals of homosexuality were frowned upon until the 1960s by the movie industry's production code and such groups as the Legion of Decency. Yet gays were everywhere in the movies right from the beginning—this documentary shows two men dancing together in a Thomas Edison short named "The Gay Brothers" from 1895—and often they were hidden in plain view. Hollywood knew who was gay and who was not, and there were in-jokes like John Ireland's line to Montgomery Clift in *Red River:* "There are only two things more beautiful than a good gun—a Swiss watch or a woman from anywhere. You ever had a Swiss watch?"

*The Celluloid Closet* is inspired by a 1981 book by Vito Russo, who wrote as a gay man who found he had to look in the shadows and subtexts of movies to find the homosexual characters who were surely there. His book was a compendium of visible and concealed gays in the movies, and now this documentary, which shows the scenes he could only describe, makes it clear Hollywood wanted it both ways: It benefited from the richness that gays added to films, but didn't want to acknowledge their sexuality. In those few films that were frankly about gays, their lives almost always ended in madness or death (there is a montage of gays dying onscreen, of which my favorite from a Freudian point of view is Sandy Dennis as a lesbian in *The Fox,* crushed by a falling tree).

The movie, narrated by Lily Tomlin, contains interviews with a lot of witnesses from the days when gays were in the Hollywood closet. The chat with Gore Vidal has already become famous. He recalls how he was hired by director William Wyler to do rewrites on *Ben-Hur.* One of the film's problems was that there was no plausible explanation for the hatred between the characters played by Charlton Heston and Stephen Boyd. Vidal's suggestion: They were lovers when they were teenagers, but now Ben-Hur (Heston) denies that time and Boyd is resentful. Wyler agreed that would provide the motivation for a key scene, but decided to tell only Boyd, not Heston, who "wouldn't be able to handle it." The film shows the scene, which plays with an amusing subtext.

Sometimes directors deleted gay-themed scenes because of studio or censorship pressure. Tony Curtis is droll as he recalls a scene with Laurence Olivier in Stanley Kubrick's *Spartacus,* where the two men flirted in a hot bath. (The scene was restored when the movie was re-released in the 1990s.)

Is it because we know stars were gay that their scenes play differently this time around? There's a scene from *Pillow Talk* in which Rock Hudson plays a straight man pretending to be gay in order to avoid an entanglement with Doris Day. Does Hudson seem privately amused by the twist? It looks that way (and Mark Rappaport's *Rock Hudson's Home Movies* finds scenes all through Hudson's career where he seems aware of additional levels of possibilities).

*The Celluloid Closet* was directed by Rob Epstein and Jeffrey Friedman, who won Oscars for their two previous gay-themed docs, *The Times of Harvey Milk* and *Common Threads: Stories from the Quilt;* their track record encourages their interview subjects to open up. Playwright and actor Harvey Fierstein recalls that when he was young he always liked the "sissies" in the movies, and Tomlin, narrating a montage that shows how very many sissies there were (from Peter Lorre to Anthony Perkins), says sissies made the other characters seem "more manly or more womanly, by filling the space in between."

*The Celluloid Closet* surveys movies from the earliest times to the present, showing characters who were gay even though the movies pretended not to know (Marlene Dietrich in trousers in *Morocco,* for example, or a musical number named "Ain't There Anyone Here for Love?" in *Gentlemen Prefer Blondes* (1953) in which Jane Russell dances smolderingly through a gym where the bodybuilders studiously ignore her). It gives full due to the groundbreaking movie *The Boys in the Band* and such recent films as *Philadelphia.*

I learn from Brandon Judell, a film critic on the Internet, that the filmmakers weren't able to include one planned sequence because of legal objections. They wanted to show scenes from biopics that turned gays into straights, but couldn't get the rights. Richard Burton's estate refused the rights to show scenes from *Alexander the Great.* Goldwyn wouldn't license clips from *Hans Christian Andersen* (Epstein says, "Somehow they got the idea we were outing Danny Kaye as opposed to Hans Christian Andersen"). Lawyers stepped in at the possibility that the film would identify Cole Porter as homosexual(!). And Charlton Heston refused permission to use scenes from *The Agony and the Ecstasy,* "because he'd done a lot of research for his role and he assured us that Michelangelo was not homosexual." And I suppose Ben-Hur wasn't, either.

## Celtic Pride ★ ★

PG-13, 91 m., 1996

Damon Wayans (Lewis Scott), Daniel Stern (Mike O'Hara), Dan Aykroyd (Jimmy Flaherty), Gail O'Grady (Carol), Adam Hendershott (Tommy), Paul Guilfoyle (Kevin O'Grady), Deion Sanders (Deion Sanders), Bill Walton (Bill Walton). Directed by Tom De Cerchio and produced by Roger Birnbaum. Screenplay by Judd Apatow.

*Celtic Pride* is about a couple of fans who risk divorce and even imprisonment in their enthusiasm for the Boston Celtics. Gym teacher Mike O'Hara (Daniel Stern) and plumber Jimmy Flaherty (Dan Aykroyd) live and breathe basketball (and football, baseball, and hockey), and Mike's wife is leaving him because she can no longer take the mood swings during playoff seasons.

As the movie opens, the Celtics and the Utah Jazz are about to play the sixth game of the NBA championships. Mike and Jimmy have front-row seats, and complex theories of lucky omens (they trade off for odd or even games). The main barrier between the Celtics and the championship is a Utah player named Lewis Scott (Damon Wayans), who is famous for taking fifty shots a game, never passing to his teammates, and having an attitude ("Suddenly, Dennis Rodman doesn't seem so bad").

Utah wins the sixth game. Mike and Jimmy discover that Scott is drinking in a nearby bar. They go there, pose as Jazz fans, and devote themselves to getting him drunk—though they are aghast when Larry Bird walks in and, to keep up their scheme, they have to appear before their hero as fallen-away Celtics fans. One thing leads to another, and soon the two fans have kidnapped Lewis Scott and are holding him captive in Jimmy's apartment.

The best scenes and dialogue in the movie belong to Wayans who, as the veteran player, sizes up the situation and begins to play head games with the two fans. First he accuses them of racism ("Is this backlash for the O. J. Simpson verdict?"). Looking around Jimmy's den at all the autographed balls, framed posters, and sports souvenirs, he tells the "Septic Tank King" he's pathetic: "Do you think Larry Bird has a picture of *you* at home, wrangling a toilet?" Finally he attacks their sexuality, wondering which one is "the man of the couple."

This particular approach has become identified with Wayans, who played one of the outrageously effeminate "Men on Film" on *In Living Color.* In movies like *Major Payne,* where he was a drill sergeant, he did a big business in homophobic insults. Here, they work as a survival strategy in a particular situation, but Wayans shouldn't make gay-bashing a specialty.

*Celtic Pride* is a little too lumbering to really take off as a comedy; the director, Tom De Cerchio, doesn't show a light touch. But there is the germ of an idea here, especially in the scenes where the professional star ridicules two grown men for taking a basketball game so seriously. And then there are some nice reversals in the final scenes, as Mike and Jimmy balance between their sports loyalties and their survival instincts.

But I wish the movie had been a little more focused, a little quicker on its feet. There are a couple of subplots that could have been better developed, one involving a buddy who's a suspicious Boston cop, and another involving a towering Jazz player from Croatia, named, if I heard correctly, Lurch Bronferknocker. The time is ripe for a sharp, wicked sports satire. *Celtic Pride* points the way, but doesn't get there.

## Chain Reaction ★ ★ ½

PG-13, 100 m., 1996

Keanu Reeves (Eddie Kasalivich), Morgan Freeman (Shannon), Rachel Weisz (Lily Sinclair), Fred Ward (FBI Agent Ford), Kevin Dunn (FBI Agent Doyle), Brian Cox (Lyman Earl Collier), Joanna Cassidy (Maggie McDermott), Nicholas Rudall (Dr. Alistair Barkley). Directed by Andrew

**Davis and produced by Davis, Richard Zanuck, and Arne L. Schmidt. Screenplay by J. F. Lawton and Michael Bortman.**

I'm tempted to say that *Chain Reaction* needed more work on its script, but maybe it needed less. The film is so filled with scientific events, chase scenes, and bewildering explanations of the plot that finally, after taking eight pages of notes, I gave up exhausted and just watched the kinetics on the screen. It's not a bad film in individual moments and in the energy of its performances, but it doesn't make a whole lot of sense.

The story: Keanu Reeves plays Eddie Kasalivich, a physics student and machinist (yes, with a machine shop in his apartment) who is working on the University of Chicago Hydrogen Energy Project. He once blew up a science lab, but never mind: "It could have been a good experiment." He is now supervised by the brilliant Dr. Barkley (Nicholas Rudall), an idealist who dreams of energy without pollution.

Barkley is leading Eddie and his beautiful fellow scientist Lily Sinclair (Rachel Weisz) in trying to extract power from water. And early in the movie, after Eddie accidentally finds the exact sound frequency, or something, at which the atoms will separate, or something, they succeed. The big water tank in their lab bounces up and down like a towel dryer in a car wash, hydrogen flames shoot up in the background, and it is announced that there is enough energy in a single glass of water to power the city of Chicago for a week.

This is good news, right? No, it is bad news. When the jubilant scientists try to post their discoveries on the Internet, their effort is thwarted, and later their laboratory disappears in a fireball that levels eight city blocks. Eddie, as it happens, was in the building just before the explosion and discovered that Dr. Barkley had been murdered. Soon he and Lily realize they are being framed as spies who have sold the secrets to the Chinese.

I have not yet mentioned the enigmatic Shannon (Morgan Freeman), head of the "Foundation," who seems to have some role in these events. Or his even more enigmatic associate Collier (Brian Cox), who seems to have taken it upon himself to cause the explosion, although (1) he doesn't want to call attention to the experiment, which leveling eight blocks might tend to do, (2) he wants to possess the means of converting water to energy, yet (3) he has framed Eddie, the only person who knows the secret frequency, and (4) his men are now involved in making Eddie look like a cop killer, so that Eddie may be killed on sight, which would mean Collier wouldn't have the frequency. Here and there in the movie Shannon, the Freeman character, has curious little snippets of dialogue that seem to suggest even he doesn't understand what Collier is up to.

The movie was directed by Andrew Davis, who made that other, much superior chase movie, *The Fugitive.* Despite his impenetrable plot, Davis brings great visual interest to the film in a series of chase scenes set against a chilly winter landscape. He even finds a new twist on that Chicago standby, a pursuit up the Michigan Avenue drawbridge while it is opening. (What the twist is, I'm not sure; it looked like Eddie hid in the gears, but naw, that couldn't be.) Later Eddie and Lily flee to Wisconsin by train, rendezvous with an astronomer, and flee from a police helicopter in an ice boat before turning up in Washington (either the movie doesn't explain how they got to Washington, or I missed it).

All of these chases are well-done, and there is a big extravaganza at the end involving still another gigantic explosion (the escape is by that durable movie standby, the ventilation duct that leads exactly where you need it to lead). There's even literate dialogue in between, although it doesn't hold together or lead anywhere. (Shannon tells Collier, "I wish you wouldn't threaten to kill my scientists right to their faces!") Meanwhile, an FBI agent (Fred Ward) coordinates the hunt for Eddie and Lily, while betting $100 that they're innocent and being framed by the CIA. Don't bet against him.

Trying to get the logic of the movie straight in my mind, I found only confusion. The Foundation is apparently a CIA front, but the CIA doesn't know it. The water-to-energy project is being run by Shannon and Collier, but they don't want to reveal that it has been successful. Why not? Free energy, we are told, would lead to recession, unemployment, and plummeting stock prices. But would it? It seems to me free energy would unleash the greatest era of prosperity in planetary history. By movie's end, I'd seen some swell photography and witnessed some thrilling chase scenes, but when it came to understanding the movie, I didn't have a clue.

## The Chamber ★ ★

R, 130 m., 1996

Chris O'Donnell (Adam Hall), Gene Hackman (Sam Cayhall), Faye Dunaway (Lee Bowen), Robert Prosky (E. Garner Goodman), Raymond Barry (Rollie Wedge), Bo Jackson (Sergeant Packer), Lela Rochon (Nora Stark), David Marshall Grant (Governor McAllister). Directed by James Foley and produced by John Davis, Brian Grazer, and Ron Howard. Screenplay by William Goldman and Chris Reese.

There is an unpleasant way in which *The Chamber* and the previous John Grisham thriller *A Time to Kill* linger over the racism and hate language of their characters. Yes, the racist characters are the villains. But the ugly things they say linger in the air, there to be admired by anyone on their wavelength.

Any subject, including racism, can be the legitimate material of a movie. But I am not happy when I see deep wounds in our society being opened for the purpose of entertainment. *The Chamber* is not a serious movie about anything, and so when characters are allowed to rant at length about their hatred of African-Americans and Jews, repeating the most vile old hate clichés, what I get from the screen is not simply dialogue, but the broadcasting of dangerous language.

Sometimes racially charged language plays a defensible role, as it did in Martin Scorsese's *Casino*, a thoughtful film that dealt with the tension between gangsters of Italian and Jewish descent. But in the two Grisham films this year, I get the queasy feeling that race hate is working like a condiment to add spice to otherwise unremarkable courtroom stories. That's particularly true because the villains in each film (played by Kiefer Sutherland in *A Time to Kill* and Gene Hackman and Raymond Barry in *The Chamber*) are the most colorful characters, overwhelming the more pedestrian heroes played by Matthew McConaughey and Chris O'Donnell.

*The Chamber* tells the story of a young Chicago lawyer named Adam Hall (O'Donnell) who wants to go down south to handle the final appeal of a murderer on Death Row. The killer, a Klan member named Cayhall (Hackman), has been convicted of setting off a bomb in the offices of a Jewish civil rights attorney. The attorney's two young sons were killed; he was maimed and later committed suicide. What the movie reveals fairly quickly is that Adam Hall is Cayhall's grandson. Adam's father also committed suicide—perhaps because of the violent acts he watched Cayhall perform.

The murders took place in the 1960s. Appeals have dragged on for years, but now the time of execution is near. Adam goes south and discovers old family secrets from his aunt (Faye Dunaway), who watched years ago as Cayhall shotgunned a neighboring black man to death. Cayhall quickly discovers who his new attorney really is and reacts with a litany of colorful hate language.

I have heard all of Cayhall's clichés before, but they have actually pretty much disappeared from general use in America, and there will be some younger audience members hearing them for the first time. How will these words affect them? In both *A Time to Kill* and *The Chamber*, the Ku Klux Klan, with its secret meetings and its ghostly costumes, is presented in a way that is technically negative but could seem thrilling. The films portray the Klan as criminal, racist, and anonymous, but those have always been its selling points; it is not portrayed as boring and stupid.

The real subject of *The Chamber* is the family left behind by old Sam Cayhall: his son, a suicide; his grandson, who dreams of a Death Row miracle; his daughter (Dunaway), who has married a local banker and says she's "done pretty well for poor white trash. But when the world finds out I'm Hitler's daughter . . ." Flashbacks show how Cayhall murdered the father of his son's black playmate, traumatizing his children and sending remorse spiraling down through the generations.

Because Cayhall is played by Gene Hackman, an actor who implies decency in his very bones, we know that he will not go to the gas chamber spouting Klan slogans. If the film's purpose had been to present an unredeemable villain, they would have cast Christopher Walken, Dennis Hopper, M. Emmet Walsh, or another actor who can be read as completely hateful. Hackman is a superb actor, but even in his most vile moments here, the musical score undermines the effect by subtly sneaking in feelings of sadness and thoughtfulness. Listen carefully when the grandson tells Cayhall about a fake bomb in his motel room; the music playing under Cayhall's reaction gives away the ending of the movie.

O'Donnell is sincere and focused as the lawyer, but is really too young to bring much more to the role. Since he hates racism, why does he want to defend his grandfather? Because he hates the death penalty more? Or because he hopes for a deathbed conversion? The movie's own attitudes toward the death penalty are confused; Hackman brilliantly delivers a long monologue describing the effect of poison gas on the system, but then the movie suggests some people may deserve that very effect.

There is also some confusion involving Cayhall's relationship with another conspirator named Rollie Wedge (Raymond Barry). Without giving away details, all I can suggest is that Cayhall's loyalty serves the plot, not common sense. And, given the fact that Cayhall has spent years in prison mouthing the language of the Klan, it is inexplicable that the movie has a scene in which he quietly nods a sad farewell to his black fellow inmates on the row. I didn't believe his behavior, and I particularly didn't believe theirs.

In the early days of X-rated movies, they were always careful to include something of "redeeming social significance" to justify their erotic content. Watching *The Chamber*, I was reminded of that time. The attitudes about African-Americans and Jews here represent the pornography of hate, and although the movie ends by punishing evil, I got the sinking feeling that, just like with the old sex films, by the time the ending came around, some members of the audience had already gotten what they bought their tickets for.

## Character ★ ★ ★ ½

R, 114 m., 1998

Fedja van Huet (Katadreuffe), Jan Decleir (Dreverhaven), Betty Schuurman (Joba [mother]), Victor Low (De Gankelaar), Tamar van den Dop (Lorna Te George), Hans Kesting (Jan Maan), Lou Landre (Retenstein), Bernhard Droog (Stroomkoning). Directed by Mike van Diem and produced by Laurens Geels. Screenplay by van Diem.

*Character* oozes with feelings of spite and revenge that grow up between a father and the son he had out of wedlock. It is dark, bitter, and fascinating, as all family feuds are—about hatred so deep that it can only be ended with a knife.

The Dutch winner of this year's Academy Award as Best Foreign Film, it involves the character of Dreverhaven (Jan Decleir), a lone and stony bailiff who exacts stern measures on the poor. One day, and one day only, he enters the room of his housekeeper, Joba (Betty Schuurman). That visit leads to a pregnancy. The man doesn't send his housekeeper into disgrace and abandonment, as we might expect; she freely chooses such a state, preferring it to the prospect of becoming Dreverhaven's wife. "When is our wedding?" the stern man demands of her, from time to time, but she does not answer.

The boy is named Katadreuffe (Fedja van Huet). In school he is taunted as a bastard, and his mother is shouted at in the streets. He grows up with a deep hatred for his father. We learn all of this in flashbacks; the film opens with a confrontation between father and son, and with reasons to suspect that the boy is guilty of his father's murder.

The film is based on a 1938 novel by Ferdinand Bordewijk. It evokes some of the darker episodes of Dickens, and also, in its focus on the grind of poverty and illegitimacy, reflects the twisted stories of family secrets by that grim Victorian, George Gissing. It is essentially the story of a young man growing up and making good, by pluck and intelligence, but all of his success comes out of the desire to spite his father.

"Today, I have been made a lawyer. You no longer exist for me! You have worked against me all my life," the son tells his father in the opening scene. "Or for you," the father replies. For reasons concealed in his own past, he believes that to spare the rod is to spoil the child, and indeed calls in a loan just three days before the son's final examinations, apparently hoping to cause him to fail. "Why don't you leave our boy in peace?" Joba asks Dreverhaven in one of their rare meetings. "I'll strangle him for nine-tenths, and the last tenth will make him strong," the old man replies, carrying Tough Love a shade too far.

The film is set in Rotterdam, in sets and streets suggesting its gloomy turn-of-the century shadows; I was reminded of *M* and other German Expressionist films in which the architecture sneers at the characters. The boy finds work in a law firm, rises to the post of office manager, and even falls in love, with Lorna Te

George (Tamar van den Dop). She perhaps likes him, too, but he is so mired in self-abasement that he cannot declare his love, and he bitterly looks on as she keeps company with another man from the office. When he encounters her in a park some years later, he tells her, "I shall never marry anyone else. I have never forgotten you." For a man like him, masochistic denial is preferable to happiness.

The film is filled with sharply seen characters, including Katadreuffe's friend, an odd-looking man with an overshot lower jaw, who tries to feed him common sense. There are scenes of truly Dickensian detail, as when the father evicts a family from quarters where the rent has not been paid—going so far as to carry their dying mother into the streets himself. (He says she's faking it; he has a good eye.)

The opening scenes, which seem to show a murder, provide the frame, as the young man is cross-examined by the police. The closing scenes provide all the answers, in a way, although there is a lot more about old Dreverhaven we would like to know, including how any shreds of goodness and decency can survive in the harsh ground of his soul.

## Chasing Amy ★ ★ ★ ½

R, 114 m., 1997

Joey Lauren Adams (Alyssa), Ben Affleck (Holden), Jason Lee (Banky), Dwight Ewell (Hooper), Jason Mewes (Jay). Directed by Kevin Smith and produced by Scott Mosier. Screenplay by Smith.

*Chasing Amy* is a romantic comedy about people who write comic books for a living—whose most passionate conversations can involve the sex lives of Archie and Jughead. Kevin Smith, who wrote and directed the movie, makes these characters intense and funny, and it's all in the writing.

We meet his Gen X heroes at a comic-book convention, where they're autographing copies of their book *Bluntman and Chronic*. Holden (Ben Affleck) and Banky (Jason Lee) have been best friends for years, live together, and take their art so seriously that when an obnoxious fan says, "An inker is only a tracer," there's a fight. Then Holden meets Alyssa (Joey Lauren Adams), and during a long dart game in a nearby pub they find that their minds are well matched; Holden assumes that where the minds go the bodies should follow, but what he doesn't realize is that Alyssa is a lesbian.

This could be the setup for an empty-headed sexcom, but Smith is more ambitious and subtle. While the surface of his film sparkles with sharp ironic dialogue, deeper issues are forming, and *Chasing Amy* develops into a film of touching insights. Most romantic comedies place phony obstacles in the way of true love, but Smith knows that at some level there's nothing funny about being in love: It's a dead serious business, in which your entire being is at risk. (That's why lovers can be so funny for the rest of us.)

For Kevin Smith, *Chasing Amy* represents a big step ahead into the ranks of the most interesting new directors. Smith is the legendary guerrilla filmmaker from New Jersey who made the 1994 comedy *Clerks* on a budget of $24,000; his heroes, who worked behind the counters of a convenience store and the video store next door, talked endlessly about sex, life, and videotapes, and because Smith was such a gifted creator of dialogue, the movie worked despite its bargain-basement production values.

His next film was *Mallrats* (1995), a disaster (Smith actually apologized for it at the 1996 Independent Spirit Awards). His mistake was to try to direct an action comedy with stunts and special effects, when in fact his real gift is as a writer. Smith's direction is clunky and basic: He tends to arrange his characters, aim the camera, and let them talk. Visual grace is not yet his strong point, but in a movie like *Chasing Amy*, that is absolutely all right, because his strength is the ability to create characters and give them dialogue that's alive and charged.

Like Quentin Tarantino he is willing to follow his characters into the subjects that obsess them, even if they seem to be straying from the plot. Here we get, for example, a hilarious speech at the ComicCon about the racism and white imperialism of "the holy trilogy" *(Star Wars)*, delivered by a wonderful character named Hooper (Dwight Ewell)—a gay black man whose militant anger is partly a put-on and partly real pain, masked in irony.

There are also well-written speeches of surprising frankness about sex (the plumbing as well as the glory). "Chicks never tell you what to do," Holden complains. He thinks they should handle sex "like CNN or The Weather Channel—providing constant updates."

The main line of the story involves Holden's discovery that Alyssa is gay, and his even more inconvenient discovery that he loves her anyway—loves her, and her wit and personality and piercing chuckling voice with an intensity that reveals to him the vacuity of all his previous loves. He is desperate. And so is Banky, his best friend, who may be also secretly in love with him.

The movie's sneaky in the way it draws us in. We expect the characters to exist at a certain comic level, and they do, but then important things happen to them (love, friendship, and happiness are all threatened—along with all the adjustments of self-image that are necessary if romance is going to be able to leap across the straight/gay divide). Even the most simple characters can be eloquent when their lives are at issue, and these characters aren't simple. Like the clerks in Smith's first film, they're verbal, passionate, and poetic.

There are touching dialogue scenes between Alyssa and Holden, in which they spill out their secrets. In a lesser movie, that would be that. *Chasing Amy* has more up its sleeve. The closing scenes, which I will not reveal, spring deeper psychological surprises, and there is a three-way meeting between Holden, Alyssa, and Banky that is touching and yet written with the skill of a screwball comedy.

Joey Lauren Adams is a discovery as Alyssa: She has the kind of deep voice and conspiratorial smile that make you think she could be a buddy as well as a lover. Ben Affleck's role is tricky—emotionally, he makes the biggest changes—and he always makes us believe him. Jason Lee's sidekick is good at not showing us all his cards; at the end, when it's important to know how he really feels, he doesn't make it easy for us. And Kevin Smith himself appears as Silent Bob, the character he's played in all three of his films. This time Silent Bob opens up, with a heartfelt parable that explains who Amy was, and why she was being chased. ☞

## A Chef in Love ★ ★ ★

PG-13, 95 m., 1997

Pierre Richard (Pascal Ichac), Micheline Presle (Marcelle Ichac), Nino Kirtadze (Cecilia Abachidze), Teimour Kahmhadze (Zigmund Gogoladze), Jean-Yves Gautier, Ramaz Tchkhikvadze (Anton Gogoladze). Directed by Nana Dzhordzhadze and produced by Marc Ruscart. Screenplay by Irakli Kvirikadze and Andre Grall.

When communism comes to the Republic of Georgia, one of its great chefs is philosophical: Marxism will pass away, he observes, but great cuisine will live forever. It is perhaps relevant that the chef making this remark is a Frenchman, who has moved to the Georgian capital of Tbilisi out of love for a woman.

Nana Dzhordzhadze's *A Chef in Love,* which was filmed in Paris and the former Soviet Georgia, paints the chef, named Pascal Ichac, as a great eccentric bon vivant: a man capable of identifying any vintage by its bouquet, of finding a bomb at the opera by his nose alone, of criticizing another chef's recipes by the aromas that float in through an attic window.

In the past he has also been something of an opera singer and, it is rumored, a gigolo on a cruise ship on the Nile.

As we meet Pascal, played by Pierre Richard, he is well into his fifties and looks like a cuddly, fuzzy version of Peter Ustinov. He enters the train compartment of the beautiful Cecilia (Nino Kirtadze), smiles, uncorks a rare vintage, and offers her a glass. It is her favorite wine. He asks for five minutes to prepare something to go along with it. She steps into the corridor for a cigarette. When she returns, he has laid out a feast of hard-cooked eggs, cheese, and fruit, presented on fine china; apparently he assembled it from ingredients in his valise, or perhaps, like all great chefs, he always has a meal in his pocket.

Pascal's story is told in flashbacks, after Cecilia's son, an artist, is given his mother's journal. In it she describes the great love of her life. She was in her twenties, much younger than Pascal when she met him, but she identified immediately with his passion, which was not so much for food as for all the things of life: sex, music, art, living creatures.

For love of Cecilia, he remains in Georgia and opens a restaurant, which thrives until the communist takeover in the early 1920s, when he has to turn it over to the state and run it for the benefit of the new communist bosses. (Cecilia is forced into a union with the piggish local party chief.)

He grows angry and morose, attempts to poison the bosses at a picnic, and is banished to imprisonment in the attic. Never mind; Pascal, sitting unhappily by his garret window, smells what's cooking in the kitchen below, and sends helpful suggestions to the chef (who cannot read—but a young cook can, and the recipes are preserved to become a famous cookbook).

Pascal hates communism not on ideological grounds but because it gets in his way. When he and a party chief get into a bitter exchange, a duel results; after considering guns and knives, they end up throwing bricks at one another. The movie is droll about its forms of violence; when Pascal's enemy wants to murder him, shooting is rejected as too mundane, and the poltroon, having recently read *Hamlet,* decides to pour mercury into his ear.

*A Chef in Love* was Georgia's entry in the foreign film category of the Oscars, and plays as a hymn, somewhat disjointed, to bon vivants everywhere. It also functions, I imagine, to recall decades when it was difficult to get a great meal in Georgia unless you cooked it yourself (Cecilia takes Pascal on a tour of great Georgian cooking in the prerevolutionary era).

Pierre Richard, best known for *The Tall Blond Man with One Black Shoe,* is convincing here at something that is hard for an actor to do: He really seems to be savoring the tastes and aromas of the foods and wines he loves. On TV food commercials, I'm distracted by the sanitary way the models always eat; food disappears into their mouths and they immediately smile, but they never seem to chew or swallow. In addition to his other joyous qualities, old Pascal is an enthusiastic masticator.

## Children of the Revolution ★ ★

R, 102 m., 1997

Judy Davis (Joan), Sam Neill (Nine), F. Murray Abraham (Stalin), Richard Roxburgh (Joe), Rachel Griffiths (Anna), Geoffrey Rush (Welch), Russell Kiefel (Barry), John Gaden (Dr. Wilf Wilke). Directed by Peter Duncan and produced by Tristram Miall. Screenplay by Duncan.

There were some die-hard Western communists who never did get the news that Stalin was a murdering tyrant, and his Soviet Union was not the progressive mecca of their dreams, but a sinkhole of repression, tyranny, and racism. They dreamed on, long after the Hitler-Stalin pact and the show trials and all the other signals that their god had failed. Like true believers in all times and places, they made the fatal error of believing that the ends justified the means. Their error was that Stalin was not even in agreement with them about what the ends were.

*Children of the Revolution* is a satirical comedy about one such true believer in Australia in the late 1940s. Her name is Joan (Judy Davis), she worships Stalin, and she sends him a chatty letter every week. This sets into motion a chain of events that, some twenty years later, brings Australia to within a week of civil war. "The government blamed one man," we're told by the movie's newsreel narration. "He blamed his mother."

Joan's letters find a wide readership. They are read by Australian intelligence agents, Soviet bureaucrats, and finally by Stalin (F. Murray Abraham) himself, who finds them so seductive he invites Joan to the 1952 party congress, and ends up sleeping with her on the last night of his life (the look on her face is priceless when Stalin sneaks an arm around her during a movie screening). Another visitor to her bed during that busy night is a double agent named Nine (Sam Neill). Nine months later, a boy named Joe is born. But is Stalin his father, as Joan insists?

Whoever his biological father is, the man who raises him is Welsh (Geoffrey Rush of *Shine*), a fellow traveler who stands by the fanatic Joan in good times and bad. Joan is played as only Davis could play her, with ferocious intensity and the kind of humorlessness and lack of irony that is needed to believe many forms of fundamentalism.

The fruit of the liaison between Joan and Stalin doesn't fall far from the tree, and when her son, Joe (Richard Roxburgh), grows up, he becomes an agitator who, with more modern causes and methods, is able to bring the government to its fictional crisis.

The film tells this story in many styles. There are newsreels, photo montages, clips from history, and even a musical comedy sequence in which Stalin and his three side men (Khrushchev, Beria, and Malenkov) do a song-and-dance number to "I Get No Kick from Champagne."

It also finds more than one acting approach, ranging from Abraham's barely controlled farce as Stalin to Davis's zealotry to Rush's genial patience.

*Children of the Revolution* is the first film by writer-director Peter Duncan (whose own father was reportedly a lifelong Stalin supporter). It is enormously ambitious—maybe too much so, since it ranges so widely between styles and strategies that it distracts from its own flow. It is specifically Australian in a lot of its material (the Communist Party there was more mainstream and labor oriented and thus respectable than it ever was in the United States), and American audiences, I think, will tend to view it more from the outside, as a curiosity, rather than as a film that speaks to them directly.

## Chungking Express ★ ★ ★

PG-13, 104 m., 1996

Takeshi Kaneshiro (First Cop), Brigitte Lin Ching-Hsia (Woman in Wig), Tony Leung Chiu-Wai (Second Cop), Faye Wang (Faye), Valerie Chow (Flight Attendant). Directed by Kar-Wai Wong and produced by Chan Yi-Kan. Screenplay by Wong.

Quentin Tarantino introduced a screening of *Chungking Express* in July 1995 at UCLA, and confessed that while rewatching it on video, "I just started crying." He cried not because the movie was sad, he said, but because "I'm just so happy to love a movie this much."

I didn't have to take out my handkerchief a single time during the film, and I didn't love it nearly as much as he did, but I know what he meant: This is the kind of movie you'll relate to if you love film *itself*, rather than its surface aspects such as story and stars. It's not a movie for casual audiences, and it may not reveal all its secrets the first time through, but it announces Kar-Wai Wong, its Hong Kong–based director, as a filmmaker in the tradition of Jean-Luc Godard.

He is concerned more with the materials of a story than with the story itself, and he demonstrates that by telling two stories, somewhat similar, that have no obvious connection. He sets the stories in the Hong Kong world of fast-food restaurants, shopping malls, nightclubs, concrete plazas, and pop culture (one of his heroines wears a blond wig and dark glasses, and the other seems addicted to "California Dreamin'" by the Mamas and the Papas). His visuals rhythmically switch between ordinary film, video, and pixilated images, often in slow motion, as if the very lives of his characters threaten to disintegrate into the raw materials of media.

If you are attentive to the style, if you think about what Wong is doing, the movie works. If you're trying to follow the plot, you may feel frustrated. As the film opens, we meet a policeman named He Qiwu (Takeshi Kaneshiro), who wanders the nighttime city, lonely and depressed, pining after a girl who has left him. He gives himself thirty days to find another girl, and uses the expiration dates on cans of pineapple as a way of doing a countdown. A new woman walks into his life: the woman in the wig (Brigitte Lin Ching-Hsia), who is involved in drug deals.

We expect their relationship to develop in conventional crime movie ways, but instead, the film switches stories, introducing a new couple. The first cop hangs out at a fast-food bar, where he notices an attractive waitress (Faye Wang), but she has eyes only for another cop who frequents the same restaurant (Tony Leung Chiu-Wai). He scarcely notices her, but she gets the keys to his apartment, and moves in when he isn't there—cleaning, redecorating, even changing the labels on his canned food. She's playing at being his wife.

Both of these stories, about disconnections, loneliness, and being alone in the vast city, are photographed in the style of a music video, crossed with a little Godard (signs, slogans, pop music) and some Cassavetes (improvised dialogue and situations). What happens to the characters is not really the point; the movie is about their journeys, not their destinations. There is the possibility that they have all been driven to desperation, if not the edge of madness, by the artificial lives they lead, in which all authentic experience seems at one remove.

Tarantino loved this movie so much, indeed, that he signed a deal with Miramax to start his own releasing company, and his first two pickups are *Chungking Express* and another Kar-Wai Wong film. There's a lot of interest in Hong Kong films right now, but it centers more on commercially oriented figures like John Woo and Jackie Chan. Wong is more of an art director, playing with the medium itself, taking fractured elements of crisscrossing stories and running them through the blender of pop culture.

When Godard was hot, in the 1960s and early 1970s, there was an audience for this style, but in those days there were still film societies and repertory theaters to build and nourish such audiences. Many of today's younger filmgoers, fed only by the narrow selections at video stores, are not as curious or knowledgeable, and may simply be puzzled by *Chungking Express* instead of challenged. It needs to be said, in any event, that a film like this is largely a cerebral experience: You enjoy it because of what you know about film, not because of what it knows about life. Tarantino may weep again when he sees the box-office figures.

## Citizen Ruth ★ ★ ★

R, 106 m., 1997

Laura Dern (Ruth Stoops), Swoozie Kurtz (Diane), Kurtwood Smith (Norm Stoney), Mary Kay Place (Gail Stoney), M. C. Gainey (Harlan), Kelly Preston (Rachel), Burt Reynolds (Blain Gibbons), Tippi Hedren (Jessica Weiss), Kenneth Mars (Dr. Charlie), Diane Ladd (Ruth's Mother). Directed by Alexander Payne and produced by Cary Woods and Cathy Konrad. Screenplay by Payne and Jim Taylor.

One of the danger signals of substance abuse, I'm pretty sure, is finding yourself sniffing patio sealant. Ruth Stoops, the heroine of *Citizen Ruth,* gets an even clearer signal: When the arresting cops already know your name, that's a real tip-off you have a problem. Pitiful, bedraggled Ruth (Laura Dern) is a forlorn specimen of hopelessness with more than a dozen arrests for "illegal inhalation." She has just been thrown out by her boyfriend (of one night) and turned away by her brother-in-law, and now she's told she is pregnant.

"You've been found to be an unfit mother four times!" a Tulsa judge informs her. "Uh-uh," Ruth says. "Two times." The judge threatens her with the charge of "felony criminal endangerment of a fetus," but offers to drop the charges if she'll have an abortion. The logic there is difficult to follow, but it's nothing compared to the ideological thicket that Ruth wanders into after her case becomes a national battleground for pro- and antichoice groups.

*Citizen Ruth,* written and directed by Alexander Payne, is a satire with the reckless courage to take on both sides in the abortion debate. There are no positive characters in the film—certainly not Ruth, whose preferred state is oblivion, and who perks up only when both sides start making cash offers. At a time when almost every film has a "market" in mind, here is a movie with a little something to offend anyone who has a strong opinion on abortion. Who's left to buy tickets? Maybe those dwindling numbers who admire movies for their daring and wit, and do not expect to be congratulated and reinforced by the characters on the screen.

The movie is a gallery of sharp-edged, satiric portraits. Thrown into jail, Ruth finds herself sharing the same cell with hymn-singing "Baby Savers" who have been jailed after a protest at an abortion clinic. She is quickly taken under the wings of Norm and Gail Stoney (Kurtwood Smith and Mary Kay Place), who bring her home to a safe environment (safe, that is, until she finds their son's airplane glue). Gail alternates between praise of life and bitter fights with her teenage daughter, who eventually helps Ruth sneak out of the house to a party.

One of the Baby Savers is Diane (Swoozie Kurtz), who reveals herself as a spy for the pro-choice side, and spirits Ruth away to the wilderness retreat she shares with her lesbian lover, Rachel (Kelly Preston), who sings to the Moon. They arrange for Ruth to have an abortion, but by now the Baby Savers have issued a national alert, the network crews are camped out in the parking lot, and the national leaders for both sides have flown into Tulsa to make their stands.

Payne has a good eye for the character traits of zealots who feel the call to run other people's lives. The leader of the choice side, played by Tippi Hedren, is portrayed as so fashionable and sensible that you know it's a cover-up for unspeakable demons lurking beneath. And the leader of the prolifers is played by Burt Reynolds as a sloganeering hypocrite who praises the American family while maintaining a boy toy on his payroll.

There is a point at which this all perhaps grows a little thin; we yearn for someone to cheer for, instead of against. But there is courage in the decision to make Ruth an unredeemed dopehead whose only instinct is to go for the cash. I doubt that the two sides in the debate would actually engage in a bidding war, but that's what satire is for: to take reality and extend it to absurdity.

The movie illuminates the ways in which mainstream films train us to expect formula endings. Most movies are made with the belief that no one in the audience can be expected to entertain more than one idea at a time, at the very most. We are surprised when it develops that there will be no "good side" and "bad side" in the struggle over Ruth, and incredulous when it appears that the movie will not arrive safely in port with a solution to please everyone. Some situations, Payne seems to be arguing, can simply not be settled to everyone's satisfaction. Maybe, for some viewers, that will make this a horror film.

## City Hall ★ ★ ½

R, 112 m., 1996

Al Pacino (Mayor Pappas), John Cusack (Kevin Calhoun), Danny Aiello (Frank Anselmo), Bridget Fonda (Marybeth Cogan), Martin Landau (Judge Stern), Tony Franciosa (Zappati). Directed by Harold Becker and produced by Edward R. Pressman, Ken Lipper, Charles Mulvehill, and Harold Becker. Screenplay by Lipper, Paul Schrader, Nick Pileggi, and Bo Goldman.

*City Hall* begins with a street shooting not unlike those that happen every month in big cities: A detective and a gangster exchange bullets and they're both killed—along with a six-year-old boy unlucky to be caught in the crossfire. Questions arise: Why was the cop at a one-on-one meeting with the nephew of a top Mafia boss? Why was there no backup? Whose bullet killed the kid?

For New York Mayor John Pappas (Al Pacino), this is all in a day's work and he moves smoothly into action, accompanied by his idealistic young deputy mayor, Kevin Calhoun (John Cusack). He visits the cop's widow. He visits the boy's father. He holds a press conference. ("Be sure the *Post* gets the first question.") He promises an investigation. And he delivers—up to a point.

The movie is about what that point is, and what lurks beyond it. Working from a script written in part by Nick Pileggi, a New York investigative reporter, director Harold Becker shows how one hand rubs the other even in the administration of a relatively ethical mayor like Pappas, who is considered a presidential possibility. As Cusack follows the paper trail of the dead mobster's probation report, his suspicions are aroused. How did this violent young man get probation instead of a jail sentence? Was the fix in?

We meet the other players in the game, including Frank Anselmo (Danny Aiello), the political boss of Brooklyn, and Paul Zappati (Tony Franciosa), the Mafia boss whose nephew was shot dead. How and why these people are connected, I leave to the movie to explain. There is never any doubt that they are.

The story is told mostly through the eyes of the Cusack character, an idealist from Louisiana who admires his boss and hopes to learn from him. Much is made by everyone of political lore passed down through the generations; the script reads like a politician's *Bartlett's*, with quotations from Kennedy, Johnson, LaGuardia, and Pericles. Some of the dialogue is awkwardly literary, yet works anyway. ("There is only one man who would have made a good probation officer—Kafka. And he wasn't available.")

The shooting case develops against a backdrop of two other items on the mayor's desk: a demand by Anselmo for a subway stop and an off-ramp in Brooklyn to service a new banking center, and the city's bid for the next Democratic convention. Personality quirks are explored, including Anselmo's deep attachment to the music of Rogers and Hammerstein.

Much is also made of *menshkeit*, a Yiddish expression which, Pappas explains to his deputy, is about the bond of honor between two men—about what happens between the two hands in a handshake. This bond doesn't mean much to Marybeth Cogan (Bridget Fonda), the lawyer for the policeman's association, who defends the dead cop's honor and fights for his widow's pension even as incriminating evidence turns up. Gradually the deputy mayor comes to understand that *menshkeit* is such a powerful concept that it transcends even the law.

*City Hall* covers so much material that at times it feels uncomfortably episodic; although audiences are said to resist films that are "too long," this one might have benefited by more running time. Some scenes are so good we want them to play longer, especially scenes involving the Brooklyn boss meeting with real estate developers, and the mayor planning strategy. There are a few scenes of great power, including one where the Brooklyn boss comes home for lunch in the middle of the day, his wife expresses her concern through the medium of the dish she has cooked, and then the Mafia boss makes an unexpected visit. There is also a strong, although curiously tentative, late scene between the mayor and his deputy.

One scene handled with subtlety involves the mayor's decision to speak at the funeral of the slain child in a Harlem church. His advisers tell him he won't be welcome there. But he goes anyway, and cranks himself up for an oration of unashamed rhetoric. It gets a good response from the congregation, but the mayor knows, and his deputy knows, that it was phony, and the way they carefully avoid discussing it in the limousine taking them away is a delicate use of silence and evasion. Pacino and Cusack are effective together throughout the movie—the older man wise and tough, the younger one eager to learn, but with principles that don't bend.

Many of the parts of *City Hall* are so good that the whole should add up to more, but it doesn't. The subplot involving the lawyer played by Fonda is not necessary, and leads to an extended sequence where they travel by train to Buffalo in the snow, as the movie's momentum is lost. And the movie's shameless upbeat final scene, showing the Cusack character running for office, feels false to all that's gone before—as if the movie was judged too gloomy, and so false cheer was tacked on. Good movies deserve to end with scenes involving what they are about, not what they are not about.

## City of Angels ★ ★ ★

PG-13, 116 m., 1998

---

Nicolas Cage (Seth), Meg Ryan (Dr. Maggie Rice), Dennis Franz (Nathaniel Messinger), Andre Braugher (Cassiel). Directed by Brad Silberling and produced by Dawn Steel and Charles Roven. Screenplay by Dana Stevens.

---

Angels are big right now in pop entertainment, no doubt because everybody gets one. New Age spirituality is Me-oriented, and gives its followers top billing in the soap operas of their own lives. People like to believe they've had lots of previous incarnations, get messages in their dreams, and are psychic. According to the theory of karma, however, if you were Joan of Arc in a past life and are currently reduced to studying Marianne Williamson paperbacks, you must have made a wrong turn.

When there's a trend toward humility and selflessness, then we'll know we're getting somewhere on the spiritual front. That time is not yet. *City of Angels* hits the crest of the boom in angel movies—and like most of them, it's a love story. Hollywood is interested in priests and nuns only when they break the vow of chastity, and with angels only when they get the hots for humans. Can you imagine a movie where a human renounces sexuality and hopes to become an angel?

Still, as angel movies go, this is one of the better ones, not least because Meg Ryan is so sunny and persuasive as a heart surgeon who falls in love with an angel. This is one of her best performances, as Dr. Maggie Rice, who loses a patient early in the film and then, in despair, finds herself being comforted by an angel named Seth (Nicolas Cage). The amazing thing is that she can see him. Angels are supposed to be invisible and hang around in long black coats, looking over people's shoulders and comparing notes at dawn and dusk.

Seth is deeply moved that he is visible to Maggie. He has wondered for a while (which in his case could be millions of years) what it would be like to have a physical body. "Do you ever wonder what that would be like—touching?" he asks another angel. Maggie has a patient named Nathaniel Messinger (Dennis Franz) who is due for a heart operation, and as she operates on him she tips her hand: "No dying, now, Mr. Messinger—not until you give me Seth's phone number."

She knows Seth is special: "Those eyes. The way he looked right down into me." Soon she has him over for dinner, where he slices his finger, but does not bleed. She feels betrayed, and cuts him again. Still no blood. She slaps him: "You freak! Just get out! Get out!" This is jarringly the wrong note, forced and artificial, but required by modern screenplay formulas, which specify that the loving couple must fight and break up so that later they can get back together again.

There are revelations in the story, involving Mr. Messinger and others, that I will leave you to discover. And a surprise development toward the end that the movie sets up so mechanically that it comes as an anticlimax. It's not a perfect movie, and there are times when Cage seems more soppy and dewy-eyed than necessary. But it has a heart, and Meg Ryan convincingly plays a woman who has met the perfect soul mate (as, indeed, she has).

The movie is based on *Wings of Desire,* the great 1988 film by Wim Wenders. But it's not really a remake. It's more of a formula story that benefits from some of Wenders's imagery (solitary angels standing in high places, solemnly regarding humanity) and his central story idea (in his film, an angel played by Bruno Ganz falls in love with a trapeze artist and chooses to become human, with the guidance of a former angel played by Peter Falk).

The Wenders film is more about spirituality. The decision to fall to Earth comes toward the end. In *City of Angels* the angel's decision to fall is, of course, only the necessary theological prelude to the big scene in front of the fireplace ("Do you feel that? And that?"). To compare the two films is really beside the point, since *Wings of Desire* exists on its own level as a visionary and original film, and *City of Angels* exists squarely in the pop mainstream. Using Dwight Macdonald's invaluable system of cultural classification, *Paradise Lost* would be high cult, *Wings of Desire,* would be midcult, and *City of Angels* would be masscult.

Example of the difference: In *Wings of Desire,* an angel simply says, "I learned amazement last night." In *City of Angels,* Seth says: "I would rather have had one breath of her hair, one kiss from her mouth, one touch of her hand, than eternity without it. One." That's too much icing on the cake. Much more effective would have been simply, "I would rather have had one breath of her hair." Period. And then give the audience the pleasure of mentally completing the implications of that statement. By spelling it all out, the dialogue keeps the emotion on the screen, instead of allowing it to unfold in the viewer's imagination.

What I did appreciate is that *City of Angels* is one of the few angel movies that knows one essential fact about angels: They are not former people. "Angels aren't human. We were never human," observes Seth. This is quite true. Angels are purely spiritual beings who predate the creation of the physical universe. That leaves us with the problem of why Seth is male, and attracted to a female, when angels are without gender. But Maggie doesn't seem to have any complaints there in front of the fireplace. ☞

## City of Industry ★ ½

R, 97 m., 1997

Harvey Keitel (Roy Egan), Stephen Dorff (Skip Kovich), Timothy Hutton (Lee Egan), Famke Janssen (Rachel Montana), Wade Dominguez (Jorge Montana), Michael Jai White (Odell), Reno Wilson (Keshaun Brown). Directed by John Irvin and produced by Evzen Kolar and Ken Solarz. Screenplay by Solarz.

*City of Industry* is a performance in search of a movie. Harvey Keitel comes to play, delivering a fully formed and convincing portrait of a professional criminal who wants revenge—and the loot that's been stolen from him. He stalks through a movie that is otherwise so confused even day and night seem interchangeable. In a key daylight scene, he is wounded and nearly blown up, and yet it's night when he crawls into a drainage pipe and out of sight of nearby police and firemen. How much time has passed? How did he get there? No one saw him?

You don't ask questions like that. The movie has been directed by a seasoned pro, John Irvin *(Turtle Diary, A Month by the Lake),* but it has awkward shots in it that a film student wouldn't okay. When motel keys are going to be important, there's a big close-up of keys falling out of Keitel's pocket. When Keitel enters a motel room, the camera keeps panning past the door until it ends in a close-up of a propane tank. Think it will explode? And when a woman points out "Uncle Luke," a Chinese gangster, to Keitel, they're parked in a car on the street—but we get an interior tracking shot, which is an impossible point of view.

Why get bogged down in details? Because the details in this movie bog it down. There are too many characters, sketchily introduced; they often get a setup but not a payoff. When the bad guy (Stephen Dorff) wants to confront some dangerous bad guys, for example, he hires a black gang to back him up. The black gang leader is very interested in what's going down; he obviously wants to rip off some of the players. But there's no follow-through. After a time the movie seems to be going through crime-movie exercises; scenes look competent, but don't flow smoothly into the story.

As the film opens, three guys are planning a Palm Springs diamond robbery (the Russian Mafia drops off hot jewels every April). The thieves are played by Wade Dominguez, Dorff, and Timothy Hutton—who calls in his older brother, played by Keitel. The heist planning process is interesting, although we've seen such scenes many times before. The robbery is a success. And then there is a betrayal that comes with sudden brutality, and is very effective. Keitel is left to even the score.

I like him as an actor, and I like him in this movie: taciturn, dogged, tough. He has some brief tender moments with the wife (Famke Janssen) of one of the robbers, but they don't add up to much, because there's so much other ground to cover. I never quite understood the relationships and roles of the Chinese and black gangsters in the film, and other characters—such as Dorff's lawyer—have scenes that are padding. (I liked it, though, when he offers Keitel a phone number and Keitel simply takes the laptop computer it's in.)

Los Angeles and environs have been photographed so often for so long that it takes a gifted location scout to find new locations. The scout on *City of Industry* does too good a job: Every single scene seems set in a new, exotic, colorful, and unlikely locale, until you wonder how much gas these guys burn, racing from junkyards to strip clubs to motels that look like sets for *The Grapes of Wrath.*

The screenplay, by Ken Solarz, has some nice touches. I like Keitel's line "I'm my own police." And a scene after violence is committed and all the neighbors turn out to have guns. And the laptop business. But the movie plays more like an exercise in *noir* atmosphere and violence than like a story; the pieces are sometimes nice, but they don't fit.

## Clockwatchers ★ ★ ★ ½

PG-13, 96 m., 1998

Toni Collette (Iris), Parker Posey (Margaret), Lisa Kudrow (Paula), Alanna Ubach (Jane). Directed by Jill Sprecher and produced by Gina Resnick. Screenplay by Jill Sprecher and Karen Sprecher.

*Clockwatchers* is a wicked, subversive comedy about the hell on earth occupied by temporary office workers. Hired by the day, fired on whims, they're victims of corporate apartheid: They have no rights or benefits and can't even call their desks their own. They're always looking at Polaroids of someone else's family.

This is a rare film about the way people actually live. It's about the new world of security cameras, Muzak, cubicle life, and hoarding office supplies. "Try not to make too many mistakes," a new temp worker is told. "These forms are expensive." When she botches some forms, she throws them out in the ladies' room to hide her crime. The toilet, indeed, is the only sanctuary in a big office: the refuge, the retreat, the confessional. Only when your underwear is off can you find a space to call your own.

*Clockwatchers* was written by two sisters, Jill and Karen Sprecher, and directed by Jill. I don't have to be psychic to know they've worked as office temps. The Coen, Hughes, and Wachowski brothers make movies about crime and passion, and so do the Sprecher sisters, but their violence is more brutal and direct, like stealing the precious rubber-band ball of Art, the anal-retentive guy in charge of the office supplies.

The movie stars Toni Collette as Iris, the new temp. Frightened and insecure, blinded by the buzzing overhead fixtures like a rabbit in the headlights, she's taken under the wing of Margaret (Parker Posey), a temp who knows the ropes and has a healthy contempt for the office, her bosses, and temp life in general. When she answers someone else's phone, she doesn't take a message, she just leaves the caller on hold until they get bored and hang up: "By the time they find out, you're long gone."

At lunchtime, Margaret leads Iris to the lonely Formica tables in the corner of the cafeteria, where the temps sit huddled together. None of the permanent workers mix with them; it's like they have a disease. Jane (Alanna Ubach) tells Iris: "I used to work in a bank. There was this button on the desk and I kept looking at it every day for a month and finally I just pushed it. It was the alarm. They never tell you anything because they're afraid you'll take their stupid jobs."

Boredom hangs low over the office like a poisonous fog. It's the kind of place where you carve I WAS HERE into the desk, but don't sign your name. Paula (Lisa Kudrow), another temp, is given a business card by a male coworker and it's the same card she's always finding left in the ladies' room, as if the guy's pathetic title and embossed little name would make him sexually irresistible. A new girl is hired, and the temps try to figure out how she got the job as the boss's new permanent assistant. At quitting time, every eye is riveted to the wall clock: They're like third-graders, waiting to be dismissed, so they can go to nearby bars, smoke cigarettes, and be lied to by half-looped junior executives.

Something interesting happens. There is a crime wave. Office supplies and little doodads are missing from people's desks. Who is the thief? Eyes narrow. There's lots of whispering at lunchtime. Security cameras are pointed directly at the desks of the temps: Yeah, like they're going to steal from themselves. One of the girls is fired and gets the last word: "How can you fire me? You don't even know my name!"

I take hope when I see a movie like this, because it means somebody is still listening and watching. Most new movies are about old movies; this one is about the way we live now. *Clockwatchers* is the kind of movie that can change lives by articulating anger; a few of the people who see it are going to make basic changes because of it—they're going to revolt—and ten years from now the Sprecher sisters will get a letter from one of them, thanking them.

There's that, and then there's also the way the movie is so mercilessly funny, because it sees stupidity so clearly. Take Iris's first day on the job, where she's told to sit in a chair and wait, and sits there for hours, until the office manager says, "Why didn't you tell me you were here?" Like it's her fault. Like Iris knew who the stupid office manager was. Like it's not the office manager's job to see if anyone is sitting in the stupid chair. Like at the salary level of a temp, it makes any difference how long she sits there. Like maybe someday, with hard work, good luck, patience, and timing, she can be a big shot like Art, and have her own stupid rubber-band ball.

## Cold Comfort Farm ★ ★ ★

PG, 105 m., 1996

Kate Beckinsale (Flora Poste), Eileen Atkins (Judith Starkadder), Sheila Burrell (Ada Doom), Rufus Sewell (Seth), Ivan Kaye (Reuben), Ian McKellan (Amos Starkadder), Stephen Fry (Mybug), Freddie Jones (Adam Lambsbreath), Joanna Lumley (Mrs. Smiling), Maria Miles (Elfine), Miriam Margoyles (Mrs. Beetle). Directed by John Schlesinger. Produced by Alison Gilby. Screenplay by Malcolm Bradbury.

British fiction is packed with stories of forlorn orphans being shipped out to live with stone-hearted relatives. *Cold Comfort Farm* satirizes those stories. This time the dreadful relatives find their lives in an uproar; they get more than they expect and better than they deserve. The movie, based on the famous comic novel by Stella Gibbons, is dour, eccentric, and very funny, and depends on the British gift for treating madness as good common sense.

As it opens, poor Flora Poste (Kate Beckinsale) has lost her parents and been cast into the cruel world with only one hundred pounds a year ("hardly enough to keep you in stockings and furs," a rich friend observes). She writes to her relatives for a place to live, and receives unencouraging replies (one uncle promises "plenty of hard life surrounded by ruin on all sides"). Finally she decides to accept an invitation to live with the Starkadders, whose Cold Comfort Farm is well named, an oasis of despair in a slough of despond.

The Starkadders are ruled by an invisible matriarch named Ada Doom (Sheila Burrell), who keeps to her room while shrieking that once, years ago, she "saw something nasty in the wood shed." Her daughter Judith (Eileen Atkins) tries to hold hearth and home together with the aid of two seldom bathed sons, Seth (Rufus Sewell) and Reuben (Ivan Kaye). Among the other inhabitants of the cheerless, muddy place are Judith's brother Amos (Ian McKellan), a ferocious preacher, and young Elfine (Maria Miles), who gambols in the wood like a demented Isadora Duncan.

If this were a story by Dickens, poor Flora would immediately begin working her fingers to the bone, pausing only to wipe away a tear while remembering better times. But Flora is a modern heroine, and calmly sets about upsetting all the traditions of Cold Comfort Farm and refurbishing the lives of its inhabitants. By the time Seth has been cleaned up and put in a tuxedo, he is ready to star in the movies, and obviously all the preacher requires is a Ford van, so that he can drive round to the county fairs and stop driving his family crazy.

Flora (invariably referred to as "Robert Poste's child," for reasons eventually revealed) is a bit of a poet and novelist herself. We get a sample of her prose: "The golden orb had almost disappeared behind the interlacing fingers of the hawthorne." She makes friends with a local intellectual (Stephen Fry) who hopes to prove the novels of the Brontë sisters were written by their brother, Branwell. She is happy to discover that the Arts and Crafts movement is flourishing in the district, along with enthusiastic Morris dancing. And she even tackles the problem of the reclusive Mrs. Doom ("How long have you been in there, Aunt Ada?").

One of the gifts of the movie is its physical presence; Cold Comfort Farm and the nearby hamlet of Beershorn Halt are designed and photographed as if vagrants had spent decades defacing a once-charming locale. Beneath the grime and grit, and beyond the animals who crowd up to the family at its dinner table, there is, somehow, a charming place here, and Flora Poste is able to imagine it.

*Cold Comfort Farm* is a departure in style for its director, John Schlesinger, whose credits include *Midnight Cowboy* and *Sunday, Bloody Sunday.* It seems more like the sort of film Chris Noonan might have directed after *Babe.* It takes joy in eccentricity, but it's wicked, too, like *A Fish Called Wanda.*

Kate Beckinsale, last seen in *Much Ado About Nothing,* finds a nice balance between her Flora Poste's native spunk and her instinctive snobbishness, and Atkins provides a center for the film, as the mother determined to keep her strange household together under impossible conditions. *Cold Comfort Farm* is like Thomas Hardy rewritten by P. G. Wodehouse, which is a nice trick if you can pull it off, and the movie does.

## Cold Fever ★ ★ ★

NO MPAA RATING, 85 m., 1996

Masatoshi Nagase (Atsushi Hirata), Lili Taylor (Jill), Fisher Stevens (Jack), Gisli Halldorsson (Siggi), Laura Hughes (Laura), Seijun Suzuki (Grandfather). Directed by Fridrik Thor Fridriksson and produced by Jim Stark. Screenplay by Fridriksson and Stark.

It is an ancient Japanese tradition to pay homage to one's ancestors. It is a modern Japanese tradition to fly to Hawaii for golf. The hero of *Cold Fever,* a Tokyo businessman named Atsushi, is preparing for a golf holiday in the islands when he is shamed by a relative into changing his plans. Instead, he will fly to Iceland, where his parents were drowned in a river some years before.

So begins an odd and beautiful film about a pilgrimage to a desolate land, gripped by winter and inhabited by people whose customs are a mystery not only to the visitor from Japan, but to us. Early in the film, Atsushi (Masatoshi Nagase) is in an airport cab that stops so the driver can visit an isolated farmhouse. The visitor waits in the cab as long as he can bear it and then peeks inside, where a roomful of Icelanders are performing a ritual with sheep and weird musical instruments. What are they doing? We do not have the slightest idea.

Atsushi presses on. He is ill-prepared for a journey in this frigid land, where the sun is a brief finger drawn between the dawn and the dusk. He comes into the possession of a dubious car, an exhausted Citroen, and sets off down roads with alarming signs asking, "Does anyone know you are going this way?" Why his parents chose this landscape as a holiday destination is a question not answered.

But the film finds humor and beauty in its odyssey. It takes the classic form of the road movie and populates it with improbable wanderers in the snow. A woman, for example, who "collects funerals," and photographs them all over the world. An American couple (Lili Taylor and Fisher Stevens) who hitchhike with him, and continue the quarrel their marriage seems to be based on. And an Icelander who repairs cars by singing at them.

The Icelanders sing a lot in this movie, maybe to keep their spirits up, maybe to keep warm. One scene involves a group of barflies who sing American country-and-western songs and drink the "national beverage," which they helpfully explain is called Black Death, while consuming steaming platters of sheep testicles.

Walking into this movie, my knowledge of Iceland was largely limited to (1) it is one of the five Nordic nations, (2) trans-Atlantic flights refueled there in the years before jets, and (3) Bobby Fischer won the World Chess Championship there. What the movie achieves, almost as a side effect, is to portray Iceland as a haunting and beautiful land, where the snow in the moonlight creates such an ethereal landscape that when the spirit of a child appears to guide Atsushi, we are almost not surprised. I can now imagine visiting Iceland—not that it's at the top of my list.

The actor Masatoshi Nagase is an old hand at movies about strangers in strange lands. He was the star of Jim Jarmusch's *Mystery Train* (1989), playing a Japanese tourist in search of Memphis rock 'n' roll shrines. The connection is not a coincidence; *Cold Fever* was produced by Jim Stark, who produced the Jarmusch film. So you could describe this movie as a retread ("Where will we send Nagase this time?"), except that it earns its right to stand alone by taking an ancient formula and rebuilding it with scenes that feel absolutely new. (The director, Fridrik Thor Fridriksson, made *Children of Nature*, which was nominated in the Oscar foreign category in 1991.)

I run into people who ask me what new movies they should see. When I describe a movie like this, they roll their eyes. A Japanese businessman? In Iceland? Yeah, I say, so why don't you go see a movie made out of special effects and explosions? That'll be real new for you. But not as new as a shot in *Cold Fever* where the wind whips across a moonlight landscape and lifts a sheet of snow, which falls back with a sigh.

## Commandments ★ ★

R, 87 m., 1997

Aidan Quinn (Seth Warner), Courteney Cox (Rachel Luce), Anthony LaPaglia (Harry Luce), Shirl Bernheim (Sylvia), Pamela Gray (Melissa Murphy). Directed by Daniel Taplitz and produced by Michael Chinich, Joe Medjuck, and Daniel Goldberg. Screenplay by Taplitz.

In the opening scenes of *Commandments,* Seth Warner's wife drowns at the beach, his house is destroyed by a tornado, and he is struck by lightning while threatening suicide.

Seth, played by Aidan Quinn, has rotten luck. Either that, or God is angry with him. But why? With one parent Jewish and the other Catholic, he seeks answers in both religions, crying out in a synagogue: "Why does God play tricks?" The answer is that God does not—or so at least Einstein assured us. But as Seth tells his brother-in-law, Harry: "If your shoestring breaks every day for two years, it's time to check the Bible."

Things get worse. Seth loses his job. He discovers that his dog's leg was burned by the lightning bolt. Why would God pick on a dog? Or, for that matter, on Seth's innocent wife? His brother-in-law, Harry, doesn't much care. Played by Anthony LaPaglia, he considers Seth such a loser that he thinks Seth might be better off ending it all. But Seth has one last weapon in his battle with heaven: "I'm gonna break every one of the Commandments," he vows, "until I get an answer."

One of the problems with *Commandments* is that I was never sure how seriously I should take Seth's problem. Is this a heavy theological story? Not at all. Is it a comedy, distantly related to *Joe vs. the Volcano*? There are times when it tilts in that direction. But a great deal of the story time is given over to romance, mostly involving the love that grows between Seth and Harry's wife, Rachel (Courteney Cox). That Rachel is also the sister of Seth's dead wife is, given this movie, just one more coincidence.

Of course, Seth may be pursuing his course because of a determination to commit adultery while working his way through the Commandments. But it's not really that, because he loves Rachel. (Harry, meanwhile, has a mistress, which is one relationship too many for a movie that is not about relationships.) Perhaps the writer and director, Daniel Taplitz, began with a heavy *Seven*-type story and then decided it couldn't hurt to work in a little comedy and romance.

The sequence that reminded me the most of *Joe vs. the Volcano* was the ending one, with Seth standing in a lighthouse waiting for a hurricane to strike. Nothing can compel me to tell you where this particular gesture leads, but let me say it suggests possibilities so heavy that the rest of the movie looks irreverent by comparison.

Instead of revealing the ending, let's talk theology. Did Seth's wife drown just so God could prove a point to Seth? Hey, isn't that sort of unfair to her? Is God indeed toying with Seth? The movie makes this pretty clear. If he is, why would he be pleased that Seth is violating the Ten Commandments? Could it be that by breaking them,

Seth is proving he believes in them, and in God? And this pleases God? But . . . why would God give us the Commandments if the only way to send him a message is by breaking them?

I ask these questions not expecting an answer, but only to suggest how weird they seem, coming at the end of a dark comedy about love affairs and suchlike. This is one strange movie; it's as if *When Harry Met Sally* were directed by Ingmar Bergman.

## Con Air ★ ★ ★

R, 115 m., 1997

Nicolas Cage (Cameron Poe), John Cusack (Larkin), John Malkovich (Cyrus the Virus), Steve Buscemi (Garland Greene), Nick Chinlund (Billy Bedlam), Rachel Ticotin (Bishop), Colm Meaney (Malloy), M. C. Gainey (Swamp Thing), Ving Rhames (Diamond Dog), Danny Trejo (Johnny 23), Mykelti Williamson (Baby O). Directed by Simon West and produced by Jerry Bruckheimer. Screenplay by Scott Rosenberg.

Midway in *Con Air*, the Nicolas Cage character observes: "Somehow they managed to get every creep and freak in the universe on this one plane." That's the same thought I was having. The plane—a hijacked flight of dangerous convicts—has so many criminal superstars on it, it's like a weirdo version of those comic books where the superheroes hold a summit conference.

Let's take an inventory. There's the ringleader, Cyrus the Virus (John Malkovich), who cheerfully reports that his last evaluation found him insane. Diamond Dog (Ving Rhames), a black militant who's pretending to be Cyrus's lieutenant until he sees an opening to make his own move. And Johnny 23 (Danny Trejo), so called because of his twenty-three rape victims ("It woulda been Johnny 600 if they knew the whole story").

Plus about ten more creeps—including, of course, Garland Greene (Steve Buscemi), a serial killer with thirty-seven victims, who arrives on board encased in custom-made restraints patterned after Hannibal Lecter's traveling suit. (When Cyrus the Virus sees Greene strapped in a cocoon of leather and steel, he protests, "This is no way to treat a national treasure!" And adds, "Love your work.")

All of these monsters are on board the same flight, a lumbering C-123K troop transport that is taking them to a maximum security prison. Also on board is a good guy: Cameron Poe (Nicolas Cage), an Army Ranger unfairly locked up for eight years for protecting his family from drunken goons. This is his flight home for parole. Sitting next to him is a friend from prison (Mykelti Williamson), a diabetic who must have an insulin shot or die. Among the guards who survive the initial takeover of the plane is Bishop (Rachel Ticotin), who immediately inspires the rapist to change his name to Johnny 24.

That's just the partial roll call of creeps and freaks in the air. On the ground, we meet a good-guy U.S. marshal (John Cusack) and a mad-dog DEA agent (Colm Meaney), whose solution to the problem is to blow the commandeered plane out of the air. This is a big cast, but easy to keep straight, because everyone is typecast and never does anything out of character.

The movie is a solo production by Jerry Bruckheimer, who with his late partner Don Simpson masterminded a series of high-tech special effects extravaganzas *(Beverly Hills Cop, Top Gun, Days of Thunder, Crimson Tide, The Rock). Con Air* is in the same vein, but with less of the dogged seriousness of many action pictures and more of the self-kidding humor of *The Rock*. This is a movie that knows it is absurd, and does little to deny the obvious.

Malkovich has the charisma to hold the plot together, with another of his dry, intellectual villains. Cage makes the wrong choice, I think, by playing Cameron Poe as a slow-witted Elvis type who is very, very earnest and approaches every task with tunnel vision; it would have been more fun if he'd been less of a hayseed. Cusack is limited in many of his scenes to screaming into a phone, which he does with great conviction. Buscemi is a gifted character actor who wisely avoids imitating Anthony Hopkins's Hannibal Lecter, and plays his serial killer as a soft-spoken, reasonable guy. The movie skirts dangerously close to bad taste in a scene where he has tea with a little girl who, we fear, will become his next victim; humor saves the scene, as the toddler leads him in a sing-along of the last song you'd think he knew.

The movie is essentially a series of quick setups, brisk dialogue, and elaborate action sequences. You may have seen most of the high points in the TV commercials: the car being dragged behind the plane, the crash-landing in Las Vegas, and the obligatory shot of humans somehow outrunning fireballs. Still, assembled by first-time director Simon West, a British music video whiz, it moves smoothly and with visual style and verbal wit. It even continues a recent tradition in Nicolas Cage's career (after *Honeymoon in Vegas* and *Leaving Las Vegas*) of finding new ways to crash-land on the Strip.

In a film filled with strange people and bizarre events, here is the strangest and most bizarre: The closing credits, played over "Sweet Home Alabama," include a montage of all the major characters—smiling. Yes, smiling. Cyrus the Virus and Johnny 23 and all the rest, looking like nice guys in a fast-food ad. Apparently the strategy is to leave the audience on an upbeat note. That would require a very short attention span on the part of the audience, but this may be just the movie to assemble that audience.

## Conspiracy Theory ★ ★ ½

R, 129 m., 1997

Mel Gibson (Jerry Fletcher), Julia Roberts (Alice Sutton), Patrick Stewart (Dr. Jonas), Cylk Cozart (Agent Lowry). Directed by Richard Donner and produced by Donner and Joel Silver. Screenplay by Brian Helgeland.

*Conspiracy Theory* cries out to be a small film—a quixotic little indee production where the daffy dialogue and weird characters could weave their coils of paranoia into great offbeat humor. Unfortunately, the parts of the movie that are truly good are buried beneath the deadening layers of thriller clichés and an unconvincing love story.

I can almost guess how this happened. The original screenplay by Brian Helgeland must have been strange and wonderful. It told the story of a New York cabby who combines everything he hears into one grand unified conspiracy theory. Most of the time he's wacko. Sometimes, like a stopped clock, he's on the money. ("I was right!" he says at one point. "But what was I right about?")

This screenplay no doubt attracted widespread attention in Hollywood because of its originality and brilliance. Then it was packaged with major stars (Mel Gibson and Julia Roberts) and an A-list director (Richard Donner, of *Lethal Weapon*). The movie could essentially have been filmed for a few million dollars, but not with talent like that, so it turned into a megaproduction and was lost.

Almost immediately (I'm still weaving my fantasy here) some industry genius decreed that Gibson and Roberts had to fall in love in the movie "because the audience will want to see that." Oh, yeah? Not if it involves such torturous contrivances that whole shards of the plot are torn off and sent flying like rubber off of truck tires. The same genius, or his clone, then decreed that since there was the money for bloated action sequences, of course there had to be some.

Very few action sequences work. Most of them bring movies to a lurching halt. *Conspiracy Theory* is never more interesting than when Gibson is spinning his bizarre theories, and never more boring than when secret agents are rappelling down ropes from helicopters hovering over New York streets. There have been so many action sequences in so many movies that we have lost the capacity for surprise; unless they work as part of the plot, our eyes glaze over because we know the actors have gone out for lunch and we are looking at stuntmen supervised by the second unit.

Anyway. The Gibson character in *Conspiracy Theory* is a wonderful creation, a guy named Jerry Fletcher who has listened to way too much talk radio. Secrets spin from his fertile imagination and into the incredulous ears of his passengers: The right-wing militias, which say they'll defend us from a UN invasion, *are* UN troops. Vietnam was fought over a bet between Howard Hughes and Aristotle Onassis. They rounded up the fathers of all the Nobel Prize winners to extract and freeze their sperm. Oliver Stone is a disinformation specialist who works to discredit conspiracy theories. NASA plans to assassinate the president with an earthquake triggered by the space shuttle. And there is a reason all the goofballs seem to read *Catcher in the Rye*.

This is great stuff, and Gibson, a gifted comic actor, delivers it with a kind of intense, insane conviction. (He would have been fine in the little indee production, except that the mere presence of a big star in a perfect screenplay tends to alter it, in a Hollywood version of the Heisenberg Uncertainty Principle.) Turns out he has an obsession: a Justice Department agent (Julia Roberts) he fell in love with after saving her from a mugging. He tries to tell her all of his conspiracy theories, and she tries to humor him, until one day it appears he may actually be onto something.

More of the plot I will not reveal. Much of it involves Patrick Stewart as a government psychiatrist who spends much of the movie with an injured nose, although not to the effect of Jack Nicholson in *Chinatown*. What's good about the movie are the gritty scenes of the taxi driver's life (including a little homage to *Taxi Driver* in the form of street drummers in Times Square). If the movie had stayed at ground level—had been a real story about real people—it might have been a lot better, and funnier. All of the energy is in the basic material, and none of it is in a romance that is grafted on like an unneeded limb or superfluous organ.

I have no inside knowledge of the production details. Not a smidgen. I'm going entirely on instinct. But all my instincts tell me that major changes were made to the original material in order to suit "audience expectations" about the stars. If you want to experience the anguish of rewrites dictated by knee-jerk bureaucrats, attentively watch the scenes where the movie tries to explain why this woman and this man could arrive at this relationship. It is always painful to see a movie in flight from its strengths.

## Conspirators of Pleasure ★ ★ ★

NO MPAA RATING, 83 m., 1998

Petr Meissel (Peony), Anna Wetlinska (Mrs. Beltinska), Gabriela Wilhelmova (Mrs. Loubalova), Jiři Labus (Kula), Barbora Hrzanova (Mrs. Malkova), Pavel Novy (Beltinsky). Directed by Jan Svankmajer and produced by Jaromir Kallista. Screenplay by Svankmajer.

The opening scene of *Conspirators of Pleasure* shows a man examining the skin magazines in a porno shop and finally selecting one. This will be the most normal moment of sexual behavior in the movie. At home, paging through the magazine, the man's attention is distracted by a large cabinet standing by the wall. The busty girls in the magazine are no competition for whatever it contains. As the man eyes the cabinet's keyhole and nervously licks his lips, we meet some of his neighbors.

His landlady, for example, is involved in stealing straw from a mattress to construct a large dummy. The man who owns the magazine store is building an apparatus that will embrace and caress him while he watches tapes of a pretty newscaster. The newscaster, while she is broadcasting, keeps her feet in a tank so catfish can nibble her toes. Out in the garage, her husband is building devices that will roll up and down his body, alternating nail heads with tickly fluff. Then there is the postwoman, who rolls a loaf of bread into little round balls that she pokes into her nose and ears.

These pastimes reminded me of the films of Luis Buñuel, the great Spanish filmmaker whose characters pleasured themselves in strange ways (a bishop got off by pretending to be a gardener, a man constructed wax dolls and put them into furnaces, and in *Belle de Jour* there was that strange client with his little box; we never saw what was in it, but the women in the brothel wanted nothing to do with it).

*Conspirators of Pleasure* is a film about lonely people who apply the "do-it-yourself" approach to previously unimagined possibilities. By the end of the film, when the first little man has pulped his porno magazines to construct a papier-mâché chicken head, and is flapping about the garden with wings made of old umbrellas, we realize our notions of kinky behavior are seriously deficient. Whether the movie is serious or funny depends, I suppose, on whether you're the toes or the fish.

This is the third feature film by Jan Svankmajer, a Czech who gets around the problem of subtitles by the simple device of having no dialogue in his movie. There are sound effects and music, but no conversations, because these six people are in isolation chambers of their own making. As they tinker busily in their solitary rooms and garages, constructing devices that will give them pleasure, I thought of the great crushing loneliness that must have descended on creatures like Jeffrey Dahmer, who literally stood outside the ordinary consolations of the human race.

And yet *Conspirators of Pleasure* is not an angry or tragic film. It's too matter-of-fact for that. It's not even overtly sexual, because its eroticism takes place inside the imaginations of its characters. It doesn't have an MPAA rating, but I'd love to see how the ratings board would deal with a film that is entirely about masturbation, but has no explicit nudity, no "language," no contact between two people and no intimate touching. Would they rate it "R" because we can see some breasts in the skin mags at the beginning? Films like this subvert the whole notion of ratings by showing that pornography exists in the unseen places of the individual mind.

Svankmajer up until now has been mostly an animator; his short films are seen all over the world. Here he's used living actors, but treats them like the subjects of animation: caricatures whose thoughts are conveyed in broad physical terms. There is a little stop-action animation in the film, but essentially it's as unadorned and straightforward as porno, with people in their rooms, absorbed in their activities. Its lesson, I suppose, is that in the absence of love one turns to technology, which is a small consolation; the characters seem to derive more pleasure out of constructing their toys than using them.

In his end credits, Svankmajer acknowledges the "technical expertise" of a number of people, including de Sade, Sader-Masoch, Freud, and, of course, Buñuel—whose *Un Chien Andalou,* made with Salvador Dali, must have helped inspire *Conspirators of Pleasure.* Svankmajer calls himself a radical surrealist, and like the original surrealists he gains his effects not by abstract fantasies but by taking a skewed new look at everyday reality. So much of this film is practical: how to keep the fish alive under the bed, or what to do with little bread balls after you've used them (the postwoman mails them to the newscaster to feed the fish). All of this ingenuity reminded me of a college friend, the late novelist Paul Tyner, who was studying ads for electric sexual aids when he hit upon the ultimate perversion: plug them in, fit them together, and watch them.

## Contact ★ ★ ★ ½

PG, 150 m., 1997

Jodie Foster (Dr. Eleanor "Ellie" Arroway), Matthew McConaughey (Palmer Joss), James Woods (Michael Kitz), John Hurt (S. R. Hadden), Tom Skerritt (David Drumlin), William Fichtner (Kent Clark), David Morse (Ted Arroway), Angela Bassett (Rachel Constantine), Rob Lowe (Richard Rank). Directed by Robert Zemeckis and produced by Zemeckis and Steve Starkey. Screenplay by James V. Hart and Michael Goldenberg, based on the novel by Carl Sagan.

*"Do you think there are people on other planets?"*

*"I don't know. But if it's just us, it would be an awful waste of space."*

—dialogue from *Contact*

You can hear an echo there of the hopeful, curious voice of the late Carl Sagan, who spoke optimistically of "billions of billions of stars," and argued that if life can exist at all (and it can) then it should presumably be found all over the universe. Sagan's novel *Contact* provides the inspiration for Robert Zemeckis's film, which tells the smartest and most absorbing story about extraterrestrial intelligence since *Close Encounters of the Third Kind.*

It also makes an argument that sounds like pure common sense. Because the universe is so awesomely large, it would hardly be practical for alien beings to go zipping around it in spaceships, tracking down hints of intelligent life. Why wouldn't they simply set up an automated program to scan the skies for signals—and then auto-respond with instructions on how another race (ourselves, for example) could contact *them?* That would be faster, easier, cheaper, and less of a waste of resources, since if we're not capable of following the instructions, we're not ready to meet them.

This idea, so simple, so seductive, inspires the intriguing payoff of *Contact,* which stars Jodie Foster as Dr. Ellie Arroway, a radio astronomer who has dedicated her life to the cosmological field of SETI (Search for Extra-Terrestrial Intelligence). She uses a giant radio telescope in Puerto Rico to scan the skies for signals that might originate from intelligent beings. One clue would be that a series of prime numbers, which can be easily transmitted in a universal code, would be the same everywhere, and would stand out from random radio noise.

The movie is about Ellie's search, but it is also about her mind and personality. It's surprising to find a science-fiction film exploring issues like love, death, and the existence of God; science fiction as a literary form has, of course, explored those subjects for years, but SF movies generally tend toward titles like *Independence Day,* which are about actors being attacked by gooey special effects. (Why do we always assume aliens will be bug-eyed and ugly? The next time you look in the mirror, ask yourself how you'd feel if you were a cat, and Earth was visited by something looking like you.)

Ellie's scientific quest is a lonely one. Her superior, Dr. David Drumlin (Tom Skerritt), tells her the SETI field is tantamount to professional suicide. She's needled ("Hi, Ellie. Still waiting for E.T. to call?"), but her obsession runs deep: With her father (David Morse), she shared the excitement of picking up distant stations on a ham radio outfit. He died while she was still young, and she became convinced that somehow, someday, she could contact him. This conviction is complicated by the fact that she does not believe in God or the supernatural; perhaps her SETI is a displaced version of that childhood need.

In Puerto Rico she meets Palmer (Matthew McConaughey), a young man who does believe in God. They have a brief but tender and important love affair, and then, when the dubious Drumlin pulls the plug on her research, she leaves for New Mexico, and an alternate research site. Before they separate, they talk about a paradox: Pondering the immensity and mystery of the universe, you're tempted to explain it with a concept like God, and yet you wonder if "God" isn't a patronizing simplification. Ellie and Palmer disagree about God; as viewers, we are surprised and pleased that the movie lets them debate the subject. Most Hollywood movies are too timid for theology. Question for discussion: Should man's first emissary to an alien race be required to believe in God? And if so, whose?

Ellie's research project has been all but ended when there's a sudden breakthrough: unmistakably intelligent signals from space! Drumlin, in the manner of all bureaucrats everywhere, conveniently forgets his opposition to SETI and smoothly takes the credit. The signals, which include a startling bounce back of a TV image from Earth, provide a schematic diagram for a machine which, apparently, would allow a representative of the human race to travel to the home of the race that sent the signal.

Zemeckis has filled his movie with intriguing characters, played by good actors. There is, for example, old Hadden (John Hurt), a billionaire incorporating elements of Howard Hughes and Armand Hammer. He follows Ellie's search and commands vast resources of his own. And there are two presidential advisers (James Woods and Angela Bassett), who, in the great tradition of movies about aliens, consider the signals to be a possible threat. And there are others, but I will not describe them, in order to leave key secrets intact.

What happens in the last third of the film, indeed, I will not describe. Some of it you can guess. You may be guessing wrong. Zemeckis uses special effects to suggest the climactic events without upstaging them. (Earlier effects, however, that seemingly incorporate President Clinton into the film, are simply distracting.)

Movies like *Contact* help explain why movies like *Independence Day* leave me feeling empty and unsatisfied. When I look up at the sky through a telescope, when I follow the landing of the research vehicle on Mars, when I read about cosmology, I brush against transcendence. The universe is so large and old and beautiful, and our life as an intelligent species is so brief, that all our knowledge is like a tiny hint surrounded by a void. Has another race been around longer and learned more? Where are they? We have been listening for only a few decades. Space and time are so vast. A signal's chances of reaching us at the right time and place are so remote they make a message in a bottle look reliable. But if one came . . . ☞

## Contempt ★ ★ ★

NO MPAA RATING, 103 m., 1963 (rereleased 1997)

Brigitte Bardot (Camille Javel), Jack Palance (Jeremiah Prokosch ["Jerry"]), Michel Piccoli (Paul Javel), Giorgia Moll (Francesca Vanini), Fritz Lang (Fritz Lang), Jean-Luc Godard (The Assistant Director), Linda Veras (Siren), Raoul Coutard (Cameraman). Directed by Jean-Luc Godard and produced by Georges de Beauregard, Carlo Ponti, and Joseph E. Levine. Screenplay by Godard, based on Alberto Moravia's novel *A Ghost at Noon.*

*Contempt* was Jean-Luc Godard's 1963 attempt at a big-budget, big-star production, and more or less satisfied his curiosity. It was not the direction he wanted to move in, and the rest of his career can be seen, in a way, as a reaction to the experience. Not that the film itself is a compromise; you can see the tension between Godard and his backers right there on the screen, and hear it between the lines of the dialogue in this newly restored 1997 print.

The film is about a failed playwright (Michel

Piccoli) who is hired by a corrupt American producer (Jack Palance) to work on the script of a movie by a great veteran director (Fritz Lang, playing himself). The playwright is married to a sexy former typist (Brigitte Bardot) that the producer has his eye on. The film is going to be based on *The Odyssey*, but Palance has a *Hercules* ripoff in mind, while Lang wants to make an art film.

Many critics have interpreted *Contempt* as a parallel to *The Odyssey*, with Piccoli as Odysseus, Bardot as Penelope, and Palance as Poseidon, but it is just as tempting to see the frustrated screenwriter as Godard, the woman as Godard's then-wife Anna Karina, and the producer as a cross between Joseph E. Levine and Carlo Ponti, who were both attached to the project. There's a scene where Palance views a rough cut of the movie (which looks like stark, modernist wallpaper) and shouts at Lang: "You cheated me, Fritz! That's not what's in the script!"

As Palance hurls cans of film around the screening room, we may be reminded that the film opened with a curious, extended scene in which Bardot's naked (but not explicitly revealed) body is caressed and praised by Piccoli. Insecure, she asks him about her thighs, her arms, her breasts, and he replies in every case that he gazes upon perfection. This sequence was belatedly photographed after the producers screamed at Godard that he had cheated them by shooting a film starring Bardot and including not one nude shot. In revenge, he gave them acres of skin but no eroticism.

Fritz Lang sails through the movie like an immovable object, at one point telling Palance, "Include me out—as a real producer once said." The others carry the real weight of the story. Early in the film, after the disastrous screening, Palance storms out and then offers Bardot a ride to his Roman villa, leaving his secretary and Piccoli to follow behind. Palance makes a pass at Bardot, who turns him down contemptuously, and is then disturbed when Piccoli doesn't seem to defend her as he should—is he trying to provide his wife to the producer?

That leads to the film's second act, an extended marital argument between Piccoli and Bardot, shot in the disconnected cadences of real life; couples do not often argue logically, because what both sides are really asking for is uncritical acceptance and forgiveness. Then comes the third major location, a sensational villa jutting out high above the Mediterranean, its roof reached by a broad flight of steps that look like the ascent to a Greek temple.

Godard's screenplay, based on the novel *A Ghost at Noon* by Alberto Moravia, contains many moments to be savored by those who have enjoyed Godard's long battle with the film establishment. He has the crass producer constantly misquoting or misusing half-understood snippets of Great Quotations, and at one point shouting: "I like gods. I like them very much. I know exactly how they feel."

Lang's character includes details from his own life (we are told the possibly exaggerated story about how Goebbels offered him the German film industry, and he fled Germany on the midnight train). He also frequently seems to be speaking for Godard, who was forced to shoot in CinemaScope, and has Lang say, "CinemaScope is fine for snakes and coffins, but not for people."

Jack Palance is not well cast as the producer; perhaps he was too much of an outsider himself to play a craven money man. He seems ill at ease in many scenes, unconvinced by his own dialogue. Bardot, whose role is emotionally easier to understand, seems very natural. And Michel Piccoli (in his first role!) is persuasive as a man with few talents and great insecurities; his screenwriter is quite different from the typical Piccoli roles of years to come, when he played men who were confident, smooth, devious.

As for Godard, he stays as always a little aloof. All of his films are, in a way, about filmmaking; he breaks the illusion of the fourth wall in order to communicate directly with the audience, usually in such an enigmatic way that he seems to be satirizing the whole idea of communication. He likes mannered shots that call attention to themselves, and here, faced with the great width of the CinemaScope screen, he has moments when he pans slowly back and forth from one side of the room to the other, using an unbroken take but refusing to place both characters on the screen at the same time.

When widescreen movies are shown on TV these days, they are often subjected to the annoying practice of "pan and scan," in which the sides are chopped off and then the camera moves back and forth to show two people who were originally meant to be seen at once. I can only imagine how the "pan-and-scan" process would look if applied to this movie, in which Godard has built his own panning into the wide-screen compositions. The worst scenario: The movie pans in two directions at once.

*Contempt* is not one of the great Godard films, for reasons it makes clear. In a way, it's about its own shortcomings. A drama exists at ground level involving the characters, while the film fights between the tendency to elevate them into art (Lang) or vulgarize them into commerce (Palance). It is interesting to see, and has moments of brilliance (the marital argument, the use of the villa steps), but its real importance is as a failed experiment. *Contempt* taught Godard he could not make films like this, and so he included himself out, and went on to make the films he could make.

## Cop Land ★ ★

R, 104 m., 1997

Sylvester Stallone (Freddy Heflin), Harvey Keitel (Ray Donlan), Ray Liotta (Gary "Figs" Figgis), Robert De Niro (Moe Tilden), Peter Berg (Joey Randone), Janeane Garofalo (Cindy Betts), Robert Patrick (Rucker), Michael Rapaport (Murray Babitch), Annabella Sciorra (Liz Randone), Cathy Moriarty (Rose). Directed by James Mangold and produced by Cary Woods, Cathy Konrad, and Ezra Swerdlow. Screenplay by Mangold.

A reader, Rich Gallagher of Fishkill, New York, writes to ask why they remake only the good movies, not bad ones. Good films don't require remaking, he observes, but what about "promising concepts which were poorly executed for one reason or another?"

Mr. Gallagher could have been writing about *Cop Land*, a movie with such a promising concept, yet so poorly executed that it begs to be remade. The characters are all over the map, there are too many unclear story threads, our sympathies are confused, and there's an unconvincing showdown in which the story's lovingly developed ambiguities are lost.

The premise: A group of New York cops take part-time jobs as transit policemen in order to get around the requirement that they live in the city. They buy houses in a New Jersey hamlet named Garrison, just across the river. Here they can run the show. Many of them have obtained mortgages from a mob-connected bank through the good offices of a cop fondly known as Uncle Ray (Harvey Keitel), who is connected.

The town's police force is headed by the plump and half-deaf Sheriff Freddy Heflin (Sylvester Stallone), who isn't and never will be a "real cop," as Uncle Ray tauntingly reminds him. Also on the force is Cindy Betts (Janeane Garofolo), who pulls over Uncle Ray when he's going 71 in a 25 mph zone, and gets a lecture from him. Ray is so cocky he talks smart to Cindy even though, in the backseat of his car, he's hiding a rookie cop who is wanted for questioning in the deaths of two young men.

As the film opens, the rookie (Michael Rapaport), driving while drunk, thinks he sees a rifle pointed at him by two young black men. Actually, it's not a rifle but The Club—a crucial point so poorly established that many viewers will miss it. The cop fires, the kids are killed, and there's no weapon to be found in their car—especially not after a black ambulance attendant gets into a fight with a white cop he sees trying to plant one. In the confusion, the rookie disappears and Uncle Ray announces he has thrown himself from the bridge.

Already we have enough for a movie, especially after we meet Moe Tilden (Robert De Niro), of the department's Internal Affairs Bureau. But there's more. Another cop, named Figgis (Ray Liotta), nurses an old grudge against Ray. Stallone also has memories; when he was a teenager, he dove into the river to save Liz (Annabella Sciorra), who is now married to a cop named Joey Randone (Peter Berg). Stallone lost the hearing in one ear during that rescue, which is why he's stuck in this small town, settling domestic disturbances—as when the blowzy Rose (Cathy Moriarity) dumps her garbage in front of the Randones' house, because Joey is cheating on her by sleeping with his wife.

The screenplay, by director James Mangold, has the richness and complexity of a novel, but the best movies are more like novellas. All of these characters are seen in such detail that any three of them would make a story. A dozen leave us trying to remember who is who and why. The Stallone character offers the closest thing the movie has to a center, but his sheriff, like some of the other characters, seems to have suffered in the editing. Early in the film, for example, he gets drunk and smashes up a squad car, but then his alcoholism is dropped, and his sadness (because he should have married Liz) is established without being developed.

There are even greater problems with the De Niro character, who has three big scenes without any little scenes to tell us how he got from one point to another. He challenges Stallone to work with him in exposing the crooked cops ("I don't know how you do it, sheriff: all blue and everybody packing!"), and then seems to reject him, and then reverses himself with a line of dialogue that stands out like a sore thumb.

And what about the Keitel character? Keitel has some of the best moments in the movie (especially a barroom speech about separating the men from the boys). But after helping the rookie disappear as a suicide, why does he flaunt him alive at a drunken cop party—especially considering what he wants to do next?

James Mangold wrote and directed *Heavy* (1996), one of the year's best films, a rich character study of a mama's boy and a reckless young waitress. He showed an abundance of talent. And talent is on display, too, in *Cop Land*—in the dialogue, in the way the characters are developed, in the ambition of the story. But clarity is lacking. What is the movie really about? Where is the moral center? Why so many subplots about adulteries and old grudges?

There is a rough balance between how long a movie is, how deep it goes, and how much it can achieve. That balance is not found in *Cop Land*, and the result is too much movie for the running time. Still, all the materials are here for the remake. Two remakes: one about the disappearing rookie cop plot, and the other about the town where all the police live. Maybe even a third one about the garbage war between the cop's wife and his mistress.

## Cousin Bette ★ ★ ★

R, 108 m., 1998

Jessica Lange (Cousin Bette), Bob Hoskins (Mayor Crevel), Elisabeth Shue (Jenny Cadine), Hugh Laurie (Baron Hulot), Kelly MacDonald (Hortense), Aden Young (Wenceslas), Geraldine Chaplin (Adeline). Directed by Des McAnuff and produced by Sarah Radclyffe. Screenplay by Lynn Siefert and Susan Tarr, based on the novel by Honoré de Balzac.

Characters motivated by money are always more interesting than characters motivated by love, because you don't know what they'll do next. Tom Wolfe knew that when he wrote *The Bonfire of the Vanities*, still an accurate satire of the way we live now. Maybe that's why writers from India, where marriages are often arranged, are the most interesting new novelists in English.

The Victorians knew how important money was. The plots of Dickens and Trollope wallowed in it, and Henry James created exquisite punishments for his naively romantic Americans caught in the nets of needy Europeans. And now consider *Cousin Bette*, a film based on one of Balzac's best-known novels, in which France of the mid-nineteenth century is unable to supply a single person who is not motivated more or less exclusively by greed. Wolfe said his *Bonfire* was inspired by Balzac, and he must have had this novel in mind.

The title character, played by Jessica Lange with the gravity of a governess in Victorian pornography, is a spinster of about forty. Her life was sacrificed, she believes, because her family had sufficient resources to dress, groom, and train only one of the girls—her cousin (Geraldine Chaplin). Bette was sent to work in the garden, and the lucky cousin, on her deathbed, nostalgically recalls the dirt under Bette's nails. When the lucky cousin dies, Bette fully expects to marry the widower, Baron Hulot (Hugh Laurie). But the baron offers her only a housekeeper's position.

Refusing the humiliating post, Bette returns to her shabby hotel on one of the jumbled back streets of Paris, circa 1846, where the population consists mostly of desperate prostitutes, starving artists, and concierges with arms like hams. Bette is not a woman it is safe to offend. She works as a seamstress in a bawdy theater, where the star is the baron's mistress, Jenny Cadine (Elisabeth Shue). The rich playboys of Paris queue up every night outside Jenny's dressing room, their arms filled with gifts. Baron Hulot does not own her, but rents her, and the rent is coming due. Bette knows exactly how Jenny works, and uses her access as a useful weapon ("You will be the ax—and I will be the hand that wields you!").

Every night, pretending to sleep, Bette watches as Wenceslas (Aden Young), the handsome young Polish artist who lives upstairs, sneaks into her room to steal the cheese from her mousetrap and a swig of wine from her jug. She offers to support him from her savings (as a loan, with interest, of course), and falls in love with him, only to learn that he has fallen in love with Jenny. ("They say," Jenny unwisely tells Bette, "that he lives with a hag. A fierce-eyed dragon who won't let him out of her sight.")

Meanwhile, the baron is bankrupt and in hock to the moneylenders. His son fires the family servants in desperation. Nucingen, a familiar figure from many of Balzac's novels, lends money at ruinous interest. And the baron's daughter Hortense (Kelly MacDonald) unexpectedly weds Wenceslas, who unwisely allows love to temporarily blind him to Jenny's more sophisticated appeals. Also lurking about is the rich lord mayor of Paris, Crevel (Bob Hoskins), who once offered Hortense 200,000 francs for a look at her body, and is now, because of her desperation, offered a 50 percent discount.

All of these people are hypocrites, not least Wenceslas, who designs small metal decorations and poses as a great sculptor. When the baron, now his father-in-law, underwrites the purchase of a huge block of marble, Wenceslas's greatest gift is describing what he plans to do with it.

This is a plot worthy of *Dynasty,* told by the first-time director Des McAnuff with an appreciation for Balzac's droll storytelling; he treats the novel not as great literature but as merciless social satire, and it is perhaps not a coincidence that for his cinematographer he chose Andrzej Sekula *(Pulp Fiction),* achieving a modern look and pace. The movie is not respectful like a literary adaptation, but wicked with gossip and social satire. ("The nineteenth century as we know it was invented by Balzac," Oscar Wilde said.)

Between 1846, when the movie opens, and 1848, when it reaches a climax, popular unrest breaks out in Paris. Angry proletarians pursue the carriages of the rich down the streets, and mobs tear up cobblestones and build barricades. Balzac's point is that history has dropped an anvil on his spoiled degenerates. But the plot stays resolutely at the level of avarice, and it is fascinating to watch Cousin Bette as she lies to everyone, pulls the strings of her puppets, and distributes justice and revenge like an angry god. By the end, as she smiles upon an infant and the child gurgles back, the movie has earned the monstrous irony of this image.

## The Craft ★ ★

R, 100 m., 1996

Robin Tunney (Sarah), Fairuza Balk (Nancy), Neve Campbell (Bonnie), Rachel True (Rochelle), Skeet Ulrich (Chris), Christine Taylor (Laura Lizzie), Breckin Meyer (Mitt), Nathaniel Marston (Trey). Directed by Andrew Fleming and produced by Douglas Wick. Screenplay by Peter Filardi and Fleming.

In the opening scenes of *The Craft,* a teenage girl and her family move into a vast, crumbling old mansion, overgrown with vines and apparently set within decaying wetlands. An ominous man arrives at the door, holding a snake. Soon he leaves. The teenager, named Sarah (Robin Tunney), decides to go to school even though she doesn't have her uniform yet. Her stepmother drops her off at a Catholic high school in a posh section of Los Angeles. Where, exactly, in Los Angeles are there Gothic mansions in bayou country? Even the La Brea Tar Pits are landscaped.

Never mind. The mansion is essentially making a guest appearance as atmosphere. It establishes a pattern: Many of the scenes in this movie have no attention span, do not remember any of the other scenes, and exist only on their own terms. In the high school, we meet three other teenage girls: Nancy (Fairuza Balk), Bonnie (Neve Campbell), and Rochelle (Rachel True). They are witches. "The fourth is arriving," Nancy intuits. I thought witches came in threes, but no: You need one for each of the four points of the compass.

Sarah has potential. While bored in French class, she balances a pencil on its top and makes it spin by mind-power alone. A boy in the class named Chris (Skeet Ulrich) calls her "snail trail" and is mean to her, but soon she will have him under her spell, and Chris won't be graduating with the rest of his class.

The girls are all outsiders. Their classmates don't like them, which seems strange, since they have messy hair, slather on black lipstick, wear leather dog collars, smoke a lot, have rings piercing many of the penetrable parts of their bodies, sneer constantly and, in short, look like normal, popular teenagers. At St. Benedict's Academy, though, they're known as "The Bitches of Eastwick."

Sarah seems like a nice enough girl, but she grows depressed at being treated in an unfriendly fashion at the new school, and is soon recruited by the witches—who do, in fact, have a lot of magical powers. "As above, so below," they chant, and other stuff, while we witness levitation, clouds of butterflies, telekinesis, and other manifestations of the supernatural.

One thing you have to give them: They're practical, and use witchcraft to deal with their problems. Bonnie has scars from burns, but is able to erase them. Rochelle, who is black, is the subject of racist taunts from a blond girl, whose hair falls out and is replaced by sores. And Nancy transforms herself into a Sarah clone and throws herself (literally, and at high speed) at Chris.

What I have always wondered about supernatural characters in movies is why their horizons are so limited. Here are four girls who could outgross David Copperfield in Vegas, and they limit their amazing powers to getting even. The plot, in short, is beneath our interest.

What is intriguing is that the four actresses succeed in playing their characters as realistic modern teenagers—the underside of the coin from *Clueless.* All four are convincing performers; Balk relishes her character's loathsome behavior, and Rachel True has the sunniest smile since Doris Day. The movie's failure is one of imagination. It tilts too far in the direction of horror and special effects, when it might have been more fun to make a satirical comedy about punk teenagers.

## Crash ★ ★ ★ ½

NC-17, 100 m., 1997

James Spader (James Ballard), Holly Hunter (Dr. Helen Remington), Elias Koteas (Vaughan), Deborah Unger (Catherine Ballard), Rosanna Arquette (Gabrielle), Peter MacNeil (Seagrave). Directed and produced by David Cronenberg. Screenplay by Cronenberg, based on the novel by J. G. Ballard.

If you can imagine the state of mind I'm about to describe, you will understand David Cronenberg's *Crash.* It is that trancelike state when you are drawn to do something you should not do, and have passed through the stages of common sense and inhibition and arrived at critical velocity. You are going to do it.

Such a trance or compulsion is often associated with sex, and is also experienced by shoplifters, gamblers, drug users, stunt men, and others mesmerized by pleasure through risk. All of the key characters in *Crash* live in such a trance; they are hopelessly fascinated by a connection between eroticism and automobile accidents.

Now of course there is no connection between eroticism and automobile accidents. Show me a man who can become aroused while aiming into the oncoming lane at 60 mph, and I will show you a man whose mind is not on the road. Even sadomasochists require a degree of control. The idea of deliberately seeking accidental death in a speeding car is not attractive to anyone; those who seek it want suicide, not ecstasy.

*Crash* is about characters entranced by a sexual fetish that, in fact, no one has. Cronenberg has made a movie that is pornographic in form, but not in result. Take out the cars, the scars, the crutches, and scabs and wounds, and substitute the usual props of sex films, and you'd have a porno movie. But *Crash* is anything but pornographic: It's about the human mind, about the way we grow enslaved by the particular things that turn us on, and forgive ourselves our trespasses.

When a college president makes dirty phone calls, when a movie star or a TV preacher picks up a hooker in a red-light district, we ask: What in the world were they thinking of? The answer is, they were thinking (a) I want to do this, and (b) I can get away with it. *Crash* is a movie that understands that thinking. One of the characters speaks of "a benevolent psychopathology that beckons toward us." It is a strange and insightful film about human sexual compulsion (*Belle de Jour, Peeping Tom,* and *Damage* are others). By deliberately removing anything that an audience member is likely to find even remotely erotic, Cronenberg has brought a kind of icy, abstract purity to his subject.

The movie begins with a woman pressing her breast against the metal of a shiny new airplane. Then she licks the paint, while her lover licks her. This is Catherine Ballard (Deborah Unger). When her husband, James (James Spader), returns home, they compare notes; both risked being discovered having sex in public places. Notice how they talk to one another: It is a point of pride to be cold and detached. That's not because they don't care. It's because they do. They are fascinated by each other's minds, and by the tastes they share.

Soon after, James is involved in a head-on crash. A man in the other car is propelled through the windshield and into James's car, dead. James is badly injured but alive. His eyes lock into the eyes of Helen (Holly Hunter), the woman in the other car. They find themselves in the same hospital ward, walking with canes and braces, trailing their IV bags behind them. After they're released, they happen to meet in the car pound, where they've gone to visit their smashed cars. "Can I give you a lift?" James asks. "I somehow find myself driving again." Soon they narrowly escape another head-on crash, and then they drive directly to an airport garage and have quick, passionate sex.

What's happening here? Take out the crashes and the injuries, and substitute the usual romantic movie story line, and it would be easy to understand this progression. For the first crash, substitute a chance meeting at a party. Have the husband make a fool of himself. Have them meet later by chance. Have them survive a dangerous experience. Let them feel sudden sexual attraction. No one in the audience would bat an eye if there was then a sex scene. It's not what happens that disturbs us; it's their turn-on that turns us off.

More characters are introduced. Vaughan (Elias Koteas) is a photographer who specializes in restaging celebrity car crashes, like the James Dean crash. "Notice that we use no seat belts, padded suits, or roll bars," he tells his small but exclusive audiences. "We rely only on the skill of our drivers." He lives with Gabrielle (Rosanna Arquette), who walks with braces. He works with a stunt driver (Peter MacNeil). He drives a Lincoln Continental similar to the one JFK was riding in when shot.

Soon James, Catherine, and Helen are involved in his scene. It's not an accident these people have found each other, since they share the same tastes and fetishes. They have sex together in most of the possible pairings, including homosexual; the focus is not on the other person, but on the settings and props. There are no moments of healing sanity because the characters are comatose with lust and fascination. They follow their self-destructive courses because they do not want to stop. If you seek to understand them, ignore their turn-ons and substitute your own.

When *Crash* premiered in May 1996 at the Cannes Film Festival, some people fled the theater. The movie played in Canada and Europe to widespread controversy, inspiring polemics both pro and con. Ted Turner, whose Fine Line distributed the film in America, has said he hates it. Certainly it will repel and disgust many viewers.

It's like a porno movie made by a computer: It downloads gigabytes of information about sex, it discovers our love affair with cars, and it combines them in a mistaken algorithm. The result is challenging, courageous, and original—a dissection of the mechanics of pornography. I admired it, although I cannot say I "liked" it. It goes on a bit too long. Afterward, I found myself wishing a major director would lavish this kind of love and attention on a movie about *my* fetishes. ☞

## Critical Care ★ ★ ★

R, 106 m., 1997

James Spader (Dr. Werner Ernst), Kyra Sedgwick (Felicia Potter), Helen Mirren (Stella), Margo Martindale (Connie Potter), Anne Bancroft (Nun), Albert Brooks (Dr. Butz), Jeffrey Wright (Bed 2), Wallace Shawn (Furnaceman). Directed by Sidney Lumet and produced by Steven S. Schwartz and Lumet. Screenplay by Schwartz, based on the book by Richard Dooling.

"I have lettuce in my refrigerator that has a better chance of becoming conscious than this guy," says the young doctor in charge of Bed 5. The patient is in a "persistent vegetative state." One of his daughters wants the hospital to pull the plug. The other daughter wants full life-support measures to be used, especially after it's claimed that her father's trembling hand is using Morse Code to send the message, "If you love me."

Okay, then: If you love him, what do you do? Young Dr. Ernst (James Spader) gets input from old Dr. Butz (Albert Brooks): "What's wrong with Bed 5? He's all paid up and he's got three insurance companies paying off his bills monthly." In other words, keep him alive as long as the money's coming in. But, asks Ernst, should they carry out a procedure to allow the unconscious patient to be fed artificially? Butz is livid: "You think just because someone's going to die soon, we don't need to feed them? I've news for you! We're *all* gonna die! So why should *any* of us eat?"

This kind of collision between ethics and income is at the heart of Sidney Lumet's *Critical Care*, a smart, hard-edged movie about how insurance policies essentially dictate modern medical care. Spader plays Ernst as an exhausted third-year resident who has been a nerd all his life, and is belatedly enjoying an active sex life because the "M.D." after his name has made him attractive to women. Helen Mirren is Nurse Stella, the veteran in charge of the intensive care unit, and Bed 5's two daughters are the sexpot Felicia (Kyra Sedgwick) and the devout Connie (Margo Martindale).

The film is a stimulating mix of medical drama and courtroom showdown, with broad comedy from Brooks, a little sexual blackmail, and a touching subplot involving another terminally ill patient who thinks he is being visited by the devil. Underlining the sense of heightened and limited reality, the ICU in the movie is bathed in white light, like the command deck of a heavenly spaceship, and essentially contains only the two patients and their problems.

The other patient (Jeffrey Wright) has rejected two kidneys and has lost any will to live. He's in pain and despair, and although there is no hope for him, he is being kept alive because the hospital can profitably transplant kidneys into him indefinitely. Nurse Stella sympathizes with him, but he must also deal with the pep talks of the Furnaceman (Wallace Shawn), who tempts him to die, and a good nun (Anne Bancroft), who holds out the hope of reconciliation.

His case is played as a sober counterpoint to the drama in Bed 5, and Mirren is wonderful in her quiet scenes with the dying young man. Spader's Dr. Ernst, meanwhile, is in a tug-of-war between Bed 5's daughters and the alcoholic Dr. Butz ("Just make sure you don't have money for health care and you'll die happy in your own king-sized bed!"). Ernst invites Felicia out to dinner and their relationship progresses, even though he half-heartedly protests that ethics forbid him from discussing her father's case. In a scene cleverly written by Stephen Schwartz, she uses sex to get what she needs.

The devout daughter, Connie, on the other hand, swears her father is communicating with her and will snap out of his coma at any moment. Could either daughter be motivated by the terms of Bed 5's $10 million trust fund? Will Ernst's career be ruined? The movie debates its issues with a sharpness and cynicism not often seen, and steps wrong only once, with Connie's parting line of dialogue, which is an inappropriate clinker.

Of all the characters, I liked Brooks's Dr. Butz the best. He inhabits a cluttered office up under the eaves of the old wing of the hospital, pouring himself drinks out of the office bottle and denying charges that he is a chronic alcoholic. "If I *were* a chronic alcoholic, I'd have, ah . . . whatever you call it." "Short-term memory loss?" asks Ernst.

## The Crucible ★ ★

PG-13, 115 m., 1996

Daniel Day-Lewis (John Proctor), Winona Ryder (Abigail Williams), Paul Scofield (Judge Danforth), Joan Allen (Elizabeth Proctor), Bruce Davison (Reverend Parris), Rob Campbell (Reverend Hale), Jeffrey Jones (Thomas Putnam), Peter Vaughan (Giles Corey), Charlayne Woodard (Tituba). Directed by Nicholas Hytner and produced by Robert A. Miller and David V. Picker. Screenplay by Arthur Miller.

The first scene in *The Crucible* strikes the first wrong note. We are in Salem, Massachusetts, in the year 1692. By the light of a full moon, a minister happens upon a group of adolescent girls, naked, dancing in the forest around a boiling pot of witches' brew. In all the troubled history of Salem, was there ever an event like this? How did the young girls, so carefully protected, slip from their homes? How did they come to be so uninhibited, in a Puritan society, that they could dance naked together? In a movie that will be about false accusations of witchcraft, this is an ominous beginning; if it looks like witchcraft, sounds like witchcraft, and smells like witchcraft, then can it possibly be an innocent frolic of high-spirited young teenagers?

This scene was offstage, wisely, in the original 1952 stage production of Arthur Miller's *The Crucible*. To show it in this new film version is a mistake, because the play is not about literal misbehavior but about imagined transgressions; what one imagines a witch does is infinitely more stimulating and troubling than this child's play.

Miller's play is about religious hysteria fanned by repressed and denied sexual lust. During the course of the action there will be an outbreak of accusations of witchcraft—all of them false, most of them inspired either by sexual revenge or misguided holy ecstasy. When the play was first produced, it was easily decoded as an allegory about the anticommunist frenzy of the McCarthy period. Today, ironically, we have come full circle; we are no longer paranoid about communists, but we are once again paranoid about Satan-worship.

Perhaps every age gets the *Crucible* it deserves. Anyone who has seen the 1996 documentary *Paradise Lost: The Child Murders of Robin Hood Hills* will recognize in its portrait of a small Arkansas town many parallels with this fable about Salem, including those who mask their own doubts in preemptive charges of Satanic conspiracies. (Would Satanism die out altogether if not for the zeal of its opponents in publicizing it?)

At the center of the story of *The Crucible* is one moment of unguarded lust, in which a good man named John Proctor (Daniel Day-Lewis) commits adultery with a saucy wench named Abigail Williams (Winona Ryder), his servant girl. She is one of the naked moonlight dancers, and is furious because she was rejected by a repentant Proctor and dismissed by Proctor's wife, Elizabeth (Joan Allen). After being witnessed in the midnight revels by Reverend Parris (Bruce Davison) and charged with unholy behavior, she counters with accusations against Proctor.

Parris is a narrow man but not a bad one. He brings in a consultant, Rev. Hale (Rob Campbell), who forces one of the other revelers to confess. (She is a slave from Barbados who allegedly tutored the local girls, although it is hard to imagine class and racial barriers being so easily crossed at that time.)

Soon the whole village is abroil with accusations and counteraccusations. Rev. Hale begins to suspect some of the motives, but events have been set inexorably in motion. An experienced witchhunter, Judge Danforth (Paul Scofield), is brought to town, takes an early hard line against witchcraft, and then finds it impossible to back down, even as the evidence seems to be evaporating. He fears losing face—and believes obscurely that *someone* should be punished, lest witchcraft seem to be condoned. This is, of course, the same dilemma faced by all Satan-floggers: Without Satanists to flog, they'd be out of a job.

These threads lead to a climax in which the accused are required to admit to their guilt or be executed. We know all the players—who is guilty, who is innocent, what the issues are—and yet the film's climactic scenes lack a certain urgency. As Proctor waits on the scaffold, making his moral stand, we are less than persuaded. The story has all the right moves and all the correct attitudes, but there is something lacking at its core; I think it needs less frenzy and more human nature.

The characters I believed in most were Elizabeth Proctor, the Rev. Hale, and Judge Danforth. As written and acted, they seem like plausible people doing their best in an impossible situation. Too many of the others seem like fictional puppets. The village girls in general (and Abigail Williams in particular) don't even seem to belong to the seventeenth century; as they scurry hysterically around the village, they act like they've seen too many movies. And as John Proctor, Daniel Day-Lewis has the task of making moral stands that are noble, yes, but somehow pro forma. *The Crucible* is a drama of ideas, but they seem laid on top of the material, not organically part of it.

## Curdled ★ ★

R, 94 m., 1996

Angela Jones (Gabriela), William Baldwin (Paul Guell), Bruce Ramsay (Eduardo), Lois Chiles (Katrina Brandt), Barry Corbin (Lodger), Mel Gorham (Elena), Daisy Fuentes (Clara), Carmen Lopez (Lourdes). Directed by Reb Braddock and produced by John Maass and Raul Puig. Screenplay by Maass and Braddock.

Legend has it that when Quentin Tarantino was making the rounds of film festivals with his *Reservoir Dogs*, he kept running into a short subject by Reb Braddock about a Miami maid service specializing in mopping up crime scenes. Tarantino borrowed that idea as the inspiration for the Harvey Keitel character in *Pulp Fiction* who calmly supervises the cleanup and disposal of dead bodies. And then, as a form of payback QT helped produce *Curdled*, a feature-length version of Braddock's original idea.

*Curdled*, which is not very interesting, provides two more pieces for the Tarantino jigsaw puzzle. (1) It further establishes how much of *Pulp Fiction* was inspired by other movies seen by the fanatic video freak QT, and (2) it shows how brilliantly Tarantino transforms his raw ingredients. The sad thing about *Curdled* is that *Pulp Fiction* does just about everything that can be done with the idea of a murder mop-up service, and does it quickly, comically, and as part of a larger story.

*Curdled*, on the other hand, extends its thin idea to ninety-four minutes and tries to flesh it out with a story and characters who never seem convincing. Although it does a good job of capturing the color and music of Miami, that simply shows that Braddock has a gift with atmosphere and locations. Now he needs a better screenplay.

The film stars the appealing Angela Jones as Gabriela, a woman from Colombia who has been fascinated by dead bodies ever since she saw one hurtling past her window when she was a little girl. Now, grown up and living in Miami, she happily watches TV shows like *Miami DOA* (watch for the mug shot of Tarantino as a killer). The TV news spends a lot of time on the Blue Blood Killer, a serial killer who picks on rich women.

Angela is delighted when she gets a job with the Postforensic Cleaning Service, where the standards are high: "At the end of a job, always be sure to do an Idiot Check to make sure you didn't overlook anything," her supervisor tells her, recalling a customer who wanted a refund after finding overlooked skull fragments under the dining room table. Soon Angela is happily on the job, using high-powered laundry detergents and cleaning aids to cut through the congealed blood.

The movie makes no secret of the identity of the Blue Blood Killer, who we see early on. He's played by William Baldwin as a calm, well-mannered psychopath who makes few errors, but at one crime scene makes a doozy, managing to lock himself inside a wine cellar not far from where Angela is mopping up blood. And wouldn't you know that she also finds a clue—the killer's name, written by a victim before she died.

Angela is as happy cleaning up blood as the models in TV commercials are when a new product cuts the grease twice as fast. She brings her boyfriend to witness the current crime scene, just as the killer has unscrewed some of the bolts inside the wine cellar, and . . .

That's the windup. The delivery leaves a lot to be desired. I liked Angela Jones—she plays a tricky role with the right note of deadpan delight—and I liked the energy with which Reb Braddock tried to force his short subject to work at feature length. It doesn't.

I have a hunch that part of the deal was for QT to produce a feature-length version of Braddock's original short subject, when a better idea might have been to produce an original feature. And don't tell me Braddock doesn't have one stashed away somewhere; anyone who can get a short subject made has a dozen brilliant screenplays he's dying to show you.

# D

## Dadetown ★★

NO MPAA RATING, 93 m., 1996

Jim Pryor (Tom Nickenback), Fred Worrell (Ed Hubble), Edith Meeks (Dorrie Daniel), Ford Slater (Tom Dooley), Bill Garrison (Bill Parsons), Carolynn Hannan (Julie Parsons), Lucia Reed (API Daughter). Directed by Russ Hexter and produced by Jim Carden. Screenplay by Hexter and John Housely.

*Warning: Secrets are revealed throughout this review; read at your own risk.*

A few weeks before I saw Russ Hexter's *Dadetown,* I received e-mail from a friend who told me there was an "amazing" development during the closing credits. Then the film opened at the Nuart theater in Los Angeles—where, according to Kevin Thomas of the *Los Angeles Times,* it played with the warning, "No one will be allowed to leave the theater during the last five minutes of this film." He agreed that it was "essential to stay through the end credits."

All charged up, I saw *Dadetown* and then, somewhat perplexed, watched the closing credits on video a second time. Then I went to the Internet for other input and found a review by the excellent James Berardinelli. He writes: "Whatever you do, don't leave before the final credits have rolled. *Dadetown*'s most startling surprise is reserved for then."

Nothing in the closing credits had surprised me. But before I discuss them in detail, let me describe the movie.

*Dadetown* begins with the information that it started out as a fifteen-minute PBS documentary about the small towns of America. Developments during the shoot, however, inspired the filmmakers to stay longer, watching the town transform itself from a smokestack to a silicon economy. The film works through interviews with locals: town council members, workers at the Gorman metal works, a sheriff's deputy, a store owner, and many others—including spokesmen for API Technologies, a high-tech outfit that has relocated to Dadetown's bucolic upstate New York landscape, with its low taxes and small-town charm.

It's hard to explain exactly what API makes, or does, or is. The initials stand for "American Peripheral Imaging," and the company is "a facility dealing in the transmission of scientific and commercial data." Say again? The spokesman who explains is a little sheepish, as well he might be, since he is fluent only in Corporate PR-Speak.

Dadetown's major employer, pre-API, was the Gorman plant, which during the Second World War won glory by turning out aircraft parts for Grumman. It has since come down a notch or two, and produces "small metal products," which is Euphemistic-speak for paper clips and staples.

The filmmakers visit with Gorman workers who talk with pride about their town and their jobs. And they visit API newcomers, who are moving into new luxury homes and wishing the town had boutiques and maybe a movie theater. Then calamity strikes: Gorman lays off 150 workers in preparation for shutting down. The economics are clear. For the cost of ten tons of paper clips in Dadetown, 120 tons can be made in Asia.

The town is in an uproar. Local elections are affected. A beloved, recently deceased councilman might have agreed to a shady settlement. The Gorman workers are out of jobs. There's a building boom for nice new API homes, but dozens of Gorman workers' homes flood the market. And then we arrive at the famous end titles.

What do they reveal that is so stunning? Read no further unless you want to know . . . that the documentary is a fake. *Dadetown* is a fiction film masquerading as a documentary. It had a script and actors.

I was underwhelmed. I didn't know the secret when I saw the film, but it was clear to me from the film's opening moments that it was fiction—not only because of obvious clues, but because any sophisticated viewer can just plain *tell* by listening closely to the tones and nuances of the dialogue.

The most perplexing and fascinating documentary I have ever seen is Errol Morris's *Gates of Heaven,* about pet cemeteries in California. Its dialogue and developments are so remarkable that many feel it must be fiction. But no, you can sense instinctively that the people on screen are actually talking spontaneously to the camera, and not delivering prepared dialogue, however wonderfully worded. (I checked; the people were real.)

By the same token, I could sense that the actors in *Dadetown* were actors. They are good actors, for the most part, but I believe that no actor is good enough to deliver fictional dialogue as if it is real and get away with it for very long. (Some of Cassavetes's movies come close.) Yet all the reviews I've mentioned preserved the "secret" that the movie was a fake, as if audiences would be astonished by the end credits. As I was watching it, I recalled Barbara Kopple's *American Dream* (1992) about the tragic Hormel strike in Austin, Minnesota. No one who has seen Kopple's documentary footage of displaced workers could mistake similar scenes in *Dadetown* for the real thing.

Apart from my disenchantment with the end titles, I had questions about the film itself. As a fan of Michael Moore's *Roger & Me,* I am, of course, sympathetic to the fates of downsized workers and the sins of runaway manufacturers. But these are not real workers or companies, and so any judgment about *Dadetown* must be based on the information in the film.

Watching it, it occurred to me that making paper clips and staples was not the sort of job many people would choose for a lifetime, if they had alternatives. The film mentions that money is "pouring into Dadetown" as a result of API's expansion, and that there is a building boom. Construction pays better than paper clip assembly lines, and ambitious workers would probably choose to quit Gorman voluntarily to take advantage. Those new yuppies also mean a boom for service industries, and for well-paid plumbers, electricians, and carpenters.

I also doubt it was a tragedy that Dadetown got a boutique (I hope they get a movie theater). The movie's locals basically seem to be saying that they liked the town exactly the way it was and resent all outsiders. That's a touching combination of Norman Rockwell and xenophobia, but modern Americans are forever on the move—*Dadetown*'s pastoral continuity is a sentimental fiction. Many moments ring false; at one point, the API newcomers make a wish list that includes "twenty-four-hour restaurants like Burger King." No town whose economy is based on a paper clip plant would lack fast food; the filmmakers have confused Dadetown with an affluent suburb with snotty zoning laws. (It would have made more sense to have the API folks trying to close down McDonald's.)

*Dadetown* poses as a brave statement in favor of small towns and against what one reviewer called the fascist onslaught of high tech. I see it more as Know-Nothingism and nostalgic sentimentality. Hexter deserves praise for so cleverly making a fake documentary. But somehow I was reminded of a toy cathedral glued together out of matchsticks: Why go to all that trouble just to prove a point, when the real thing is so much more compelling?

Here's my best advice: If *Dadetown* sounds interesting, program a double feature of *Roger & Me* and *Gates of Heaven* and really be amazed. Then, for a view of an American town devastated by downsizing and union-busting, view Barbara Kopple's *American Dream.* All the workers in that film are real.

*Note: Russ Hexter, the young director of* Dadetown, *died unexpectedly not long after the film was finished. He showed great promise here, not least in the imagination to even try such a project.*

## Dangerous Beauty ★ ★ ★ ½

R, 115 m., 1998

---

Catherine McCormack (Veronica Franco), Rufus Sewell (Marco Venier), Oliver Platt (Maffio), Moira Kelly (Beatrice), Fred Ward (Domenico Venier), Jacqueline Bisset (Paola Franco). Directed by Marshall Herskovitz and produced by Herskovitz, Ed Zwick, Arnon Milchan, and Sarah Caplan. Screenplay by Jeannine Dominy.

---

"The life you lead, the freedom you have—will you deny my daughters the same chance?" Not the request every mother would address to a prostitute, but *Dangerous Beauty* makes a persuasive case for the life of a courtesan in sixteenth-century Venice. At a time when Europeans are bemused by our naïveté about dalliance in high places, this is, I suppose, the film we should study. It's based on the true story of Veronica Franco, a well-born Venetian beauty who deliberately chose the life of a courtesan because it seemed a better choice than poverty or an arranged marriage to a decayed nobleman.

Veronica, played by Catherine McCormack with cool insight into the ways of men, is a woman who becomes the lover of many because she cannot be the lover of one. She is in love with the curly-headed Marco (Rufus Sewell), and he with her, but they cannot wed; "I must marry," he tells her, "according to my station and my family's will." Veronica knows this is true, and knows, too, that because her father has squandered the family fortune, she is also expected to marry money.

Shall they then become unmarried lovers? Marco persuasively argues, "God made sin that we might know his mercy." But then Veronica, her virginity lost, could never make a good marriage. Her mother (Jacqueline Bisset) has a better idea. "You cannot marry Marco, but you shall have him! You'll become a courtesan—like your mother used to be."

Veronica's eyes widen, but her mother's logic prevails, and the daughter is launched on a training course in grooming, fashion, and deportment. Her mother even shows her a great Venetian library, off limits to women, but not to Veronica ("Courtesans are the most educated women in the world"). For a courtesan, as for an army recruit, the goal is to be all that she can be. And indeed Veronica is soon the most popular and respected fallen woman in Venice, sought by princes, generals, and merchants, and even dandled on the knee of the cardinal.

The film, directed with great zest by Marshall Herskovitz, positions this story somewhere between a romance novel and a biopic. It looks like Merchant-Ivory but plays like *Dynasty.* And it's set in a breathtakingly lovely Venice, where special effects have been used to empty the Grand Canal of motorboats and fill it with regattas and gondolas. No city is more sensuous, more suited to intrigue, more saturated with secrets.

McCormack plays Veronica as a woman not averse to physical pleasure (the morning after her initiation, she smiles dreamily and asks, "Who's next?"). But sex is not really the point with a courtesan. She provides intellectual companionship for her powerful clients; through her connections she can share valuable pillow talk. And there is high entertainment as she uses poetry for verbal duels with noblemen. Her lover Marco, by contrast, is doomed to marriage with a rich girl who, like all wives of the time, is sheltered and illiterate. "Do you like poetry?" he asks her hopefully on their wedding night. "I know the psalms," she replies.

Veronica's great moment comes when the Turkish fleet seizes Venetian territory and prepares an assault on the city itself. Everything depends on the French king: Will he supply ships for the Venetian cause? The king, young and with a reputation for depravity, visits Venice and singles out Veronica for his night's pleasure. The screenplay, by Jeanine Dominey, who brings a woman's realism to matters of the heart, is pointed.

"What do you yearn for, King Henry?" asks Veronica. "Your tears," he says, pressing a knife to her throat. "I don't think so," she says, and a shadow of doubt crosses his face. "Then what do I yearn for?" he asks. She graces him with a cold smile: "Why don't we find out?" Cut to the next morning, as the doge and other nobles nervously await the king's reappearance. He emerges, settles himself somewhat painfully on a cushion, and says, "You'll get your ships."

Veronica saves the city, but is herself condemned when the plague strikes Venice and the Inquisition blames it on women and heresy. Obviously a woman with so much power must be a witch. In a courtroom scene that I somehow doubt played out quite this way in real life, she defends herself and the life of a courtesan. It is better, she argues, to prostitute herself willingly, for her own gain, than to do so unwillingly in an arranged marriage: "No biblical hell could be worse than a state of perpetual inconsequence."

I am not surprised, as I said, that the screenwriter is a woman. Few movies have been so deliberately told from a woman's point of view. We are informed in all those best-sellers about Mars and Venus, that a man looks for beauty and a woman for security. But a man also looks for autonomy, power, independence, and authority, and a woman in sixteenth-century Venice (and even today) is expected to surrender those attributes to her husband. The woman regains her power through an understanding of the male libido: A man in a state of lust is to all intents and purposes hypnotized. Most movies are made by males, and show women enthralled by men. This movie knows better. ☞

## Dangerous Ground ★ ★

R, 92 m., 1997

Ice Cube (Vusi), Elizabeth Hurley (Karen), Ving Rhames (Muki), Sechaba Morojele (Ernest), Roslyn Morapedi (Vusi's Mother), Thokozani

**Nkosi (Young Vusi). Directed by Darrell James Roodt and produced by Gillian Gorfil and Roodt. Screenplay by Greg Latter and Roodt.**

*Dangerous Ground* begins with a promising idea and runs away from it as fast as it can. The movie is set in South Africa—where, we learn, young Vusi (Ice Cube) was forced to flee when he was thirteen, after being threatened by the police because of his connection to revolutionaries. Now fourteen years have passed, there is a new South Africa under Mandela, and Vusi has returned to his home in the Transkei for the funeral of his father.

This leads to some amusing moments of culture shock, as when Vusi, as the oldest son, is expected to cut the neck of a calf as a sacrifice for his father. He wants no part of it. "I left as an African. I came back as an American," he explains to his younger brother, a disaffected freedom fighter who has found no role in peacetime. Vusi is also more or less at a loss about what to do with his father's spear, which he has inherited.

All he really wants to do is drive his rental car back to the airport and fly home to San Francisco. But it will not be that simple. First Vusi will have to abandon this interesting story about two cultures, and bury himself in a plot that is more or less identical with dozens of other action movies about drug dealers and violent confrontations.

He is asked by his brother and mother to go to Johannesburg and bring back his brother Stephen, who has left home and lost touch, and is rumored to be associating with the wrong types. Vusi reluctantly agrees, and makes the mistake of driving his rented red BMW into Soweto, the giant African township near Jo'burg, where he is carjacked by a black gang that also takes his jacket and his shirt. "Why you botherin' me?" he asks them. "We supposed to be brothers!" That gets a good laugh.

In the city, he tracks his brother to a high-rise apartment that looks recycled out of *Blade Runner*. Stephen isn't there, but Vusi meets his next-door neighbor, Karen (Elizabeth Hurley), who seems to know a lot about him. They meet again later at the strip club where she works as a "dancer," and he finds out Karen is Stephen's girlfriend. He also discovers they are both into cocaine, and that Stephen's disappearance is linked to $15,000 owed to Muki (Ving Rhames), a local drug lord.

The plot is standard issue, but the details are new and intriguing. We see a lot of the new South Africa out of the corners of our eyes: There are scenes shot in discos and high-rises, and even a trip to Sun City, the gambling mecca that is Africa's Vegas. And there is a pointed scene in which Muki commits a gangland assassination in the presence of a white police officer who is on his payroll.

The plot comes adorned with a strong message, probably the work of the director and cowriter, Darrell James Roodt. He shows aspects of the crime wave in urban South Africa, puts in a scene involving white neo-Nazis, is unflinching about drugs and police corruption, and gives the Ice Cube character a pointed line: "You can't fall in the same trap as the black Americans did in the seventies. They got free, and then they got high."

Ice Cube delivers this and other lines with a bluntness that is supposed to pass for a performance, but there's little sense here that he's playing a character—certainly not the "student of African literature and community volunteer" he's described as. He seems more like a tourist who has wandered into an action picture.

Much better are Ving Rhames and Elizabeth Hurley. Rhames has perfected the South African accent and brings a kind of easy charm to his role as a drug lord; he's a sadistic killer, but charming. (*Pulp Fiction* fans will enjoy the first view of him, which shows the back of his neck, this time without the bandage that caused so much discussion after the Tarantino movie. We see the scar the bandage was hiding.)

Hurley takes her generic role and makes it particular. We get a feel for her—rootless, careless, addicted to cocaine—and her reckless lifestyle. She's ditzy in the right way, and doesn't make the mistake of seeming too much at home in the action scenes (it's right that she'd fire at the ceiling in her big moment of gunplay).

*Dangerous Ground* seems to be an attempt to make an American-style action picture and sneak some South African stuff in sideways. That's a doomed approach. Hollywood does Hollywood so well that it's a mistake for overseas filmmakers to even try. Canada could have had a much healthier film industry if it hadn't tried to be a little Hollywood, and the films of Australia and England are thriving right now because they are local, particular, and about something other than canned action scenes.

## Dante's Peak ★ ★ ½

PG-13, 112 m., 1997

Pierce Brosnan (Harry Dalton), Linda Hamilton (Rachel Wando), Jamie Renee Smith (Lauren Wando), Jeremy Foley (Graham Wando), Elizabeth Hoffman (Ruth), Charles Hallahan (Paul Dreyfus). Directed by Roger Donaldson and produced by Gale Anne Hurd and Joseph M. Singer. Screenplay by Leslie Bohem.

*Dante's Peak* is constructed about as skillfully as a disaster movie can be, and there were times when I found it working for me, sort of. But hasn't this genre pretty much been played out to the point of exhaustion? Once you know the premise (volcano, tornado, killer bees), you can guess the story line. Starting in this case with a volcano, we know there will be:

• Ominous portents of doom on a seemingly ordinary day, such as people being boiled alive in a hot springs, too many dead trees in the middle of summer, and alarming seismic activity.

• Everyday folks going about their business, in this case the Dante's Peak Pioneer Day Festival, at which the mayor (Linda Hamilton) accepts the town's *Money* magazine award as the "second best place to live in America."

• Arrival of scientists, including (a) hero scientist, played here by Pierce Brosnan, and (b) pooh-pooh scientist, played by Charles Hallahan, whose job is to dismiss the hero scientist's concerns and tell everyone there is no need for alarm.

• Inevitable subplot involving big corporation that plans to sink millions into the area, but may take its investment elsewhere if it hears rumors that Dante's Peak is about to blow.

• Establishment of friendship, leading to love affair, between hero scientist and town mayor, who comes equipped with a full kit of disaster movie accessories, including children, dog, and gray-haired mother-in-law who refuses to come down from her cabin on the mountainside.

• Mounting alarm, as hero scientist finds dead trees, dead squirrels, brown drinking water, and other early warnings of volcanic doom.

• Town meeting called to prepare for evacuation, but interrupted, of course, by a volcanic eruption.

• Elaborate special effects sequences as citizens flee the town while the mountain roars, ash falls from sky, melting snow causes rivers to rage out of control, a dam bursts, bridges collapse, shock waves flatten forests, etc.

• Gripping human drama involving hero scientist, town mayor, children, dog, and granny, and including flight by four-wheel vehicle, two-wheel vehicle, boat, and foot. Ingenious last-minute scheme to outwit volcanic destruction. (Query: Can a utility vehicle actually ford a river with its engine completely under water?)

• And finally the distribution of poetic justice, which means death of those who scoffed at volcano's fury, survival of those who took it seriously.

• A new dawn. Music swells.

Oh, and of course, the Obligatory Unrelated Opening Crisis, which is defined by *Ebert's Little Movie Glossary:* "In an action movie, the spectacular title sequence that never has anything to do with the rest of the story." It involves a close call the hero had four years earlier on the site of another volcano, and the emotional trauma he suffered there, which can only be repaired this time around.

*Dante's Peak,* written by Leslie Bohem and directed by Roger Donaldson, follows the disaster formula so faithfully that if you walk in while the movie is in progress, you can estimate how long the story has to run. That it is skillful is a tribute to the filmmakers. Roger Donaldson *(Species)* is a good director who pays attention to the human elements even in a fiction machine like *Dante's Peak,* and Gale Anne Hurd, the producer, is a specialist in action films *(Aliens, Alien Nation, The Abyss, Tremors, Terminator 2).* They orchestrate the special effects so that they look and feel real (mostly), and in Brosnan and Hamilton they have actors who play for realism and don't go over the top—never screaming, not even when molten lava sets their truck tires on fire. The sound track is especially effective.

Is it a case, for me, of simply being overfamiliar, right down to my bones, with the ways in which *Dante's Peak* is simply an old movie in new clothing? For a film like this to work, one must be caught up in it. But every time another familiar story element was trotted out (the gun-shy investors, the pooh-poohher, the dog), I was bungeed back to reality.

In one detail I was not disappointed. In my "Movie Answer Man" column there was a discussion of whether a man can outrun an explosive fireball. The conclusion was that it cannot be done in life, but can be done in the movies. A correspondent wrote me with news of a Jaguar that outran a shock wave from Mount St. Helens, while a hapless utility vehicle was fried. This led to much discussion (how far away were the two vehicles? etc.).

In *Dante's Peak,* Pierce Brosnan ominously informs Linda Hamilton, "If the mountain blows, the blast would get here in less than a minute." The mountain blows. We see the shock wave flatten zillions of pine trees, demolish homes and office buildings, etc. Then we see it rolling down the main street of the town, with the heroes trying to outrace it in a truck. I estimate the mountain to be ten miles from the town. If the blast can travel one mile in six seconds, which would be extremely conservative, then it can travel one village block in . . . but never mind. I'd rather think back on the more convincing moments in the movie, as when a volcanologist looks at his computer readout of the mountain's ominous portents and says, "She's just clearing her throat. She hasn't even begun to sing."

## Dark City ★ ★ ★ ★

R, 103 m., 1998

Rufus Sewell (John Murdoch), William Hurt (Inspector Bumstead), Kiefer Sutherland (Dr. Daniel Schreber), Jennifer Connelly (Emma Murdoch), Richard O'Brien (Mr. Hand), Ian Richardson (Mr. Book), Bruce Spence (Mr. Wall), Colin Friels (Walenski). Directed by Alex Proyas and produced by Andrew Mason and Proyas. Screenplay by Proyas, Lem Dobbs, and David S. Goyer.

*Dark City* by Alex Proyas is a great visionary achievement, a film so original and exciting it stirred my imagination like Lang's *Metropolis* or Kubrick's *2001*. If it is true, as the German director Werner Herzog believes, that we live in an age starved of new images, then *Dark City* is a film to nourish us. Not a story so much as an experience, it is a triumph of art direction, set design, cinematography, special effects—and imagination.

Like *Blade Runner,* it imagines a city of the future. But while *Blade Runner* extended existing trends, *Dark City* leaps into the unknown. Its vast *noir* metropolis seems to exist in an alternative time line, with elements of our present and past combined with visions from a futuristic comic book. Like the first *Batman,* it presents a city of night and shadows, but it goes far beyond *Batman* in a richness of ominous, stylized sets, streets, skylines, and cityscapes. For once a movie city is the equal of any city we could picture in our minds; this is the city *The Fifth Element* teased us with, without coming through.

The story combines science fiction with *film noir*—in more ways than we realize and more surprising ways than I will reveal. Its villains, in their homburgs and flapping overcoats, look like a nightmare inspired by the thugs in *M,* but their pale faces would look more at home in *The Cabinet of Dr. Caligari*—and, frighteningly, one of them is a child. They are the Strangers, shape-changers from another solar system, and we are told they came to Earth when their own world was dying. (They create, in the process, the first space vessel since *Star Wars* that is newly conceived—not a clone of that looming mechanical vision.)

They inhabit a city of rumbling, elevated, streamlined trains, dank flophouses, scurrying crowds, and store windows that owe something to Edward Hopper's *Night Owls.* In this city lives John Murdoch (Rufus Sewell), who awakens in a strange bathtub beneath a swinging ceiling lamp, to blood, fear, and guilt. The telephone rings; it is Dr. Schreber (Kiefer Sutherland), gasping out two or three words at a time, as if the need to speak is all that gives him breath. He warns Murdoch to flee, and indeed three Strangers are at the end of the corridor and coming for him.

The film will be the story of Murdoch's flight into the mean streets, and his gradual discovery of the nature of the city and the Strangers. Like many science-fiction heroes, he has a memory shattered into pieces that do not fit. But he remembers the woman he loves, or loved—his wife, Emma (Jennifer Connelly), who is a torch singer with sad eyes and wounded lips. And he remembers . . . Shell Beach? Where was that? He sees it on a billboard and old longings stir.

There is a detective after him, Inspector Bumstead (William Hurt). Murdoch is wanted in connection with the murders of six prostitutes.

Did he kill them? Like the hero of Kafka's *The Trial,* he feels so paranoid he hardly knows. Rufus Sewell plays Murdoch like a man caught in a pinball machine, flipped back into danger every time it looks like the game is over.

The story has familiar elements made new. Even the hard-boiled detective, his eyes shaded by the brim of his fedora, seems less like a figure from *film noir* than like a projection of an alien idea of *noir.* Proyas and his coscreenwriters, Lem Dobbs and David S. Goyer, use dream logic to pursue their hero through the mystery of his own life. Along the way, Murdoch discovers that he alone, among humans, has the power of the Strangers—an ability to use his mind in order to shape the physical universe. (This power is expressed in the film as a sort of transparent shimmering projection aimed from Murdoch's forehead into the world, and as klutzy as that sounds, I found myself enjoying its very audacity: What else would mind power look like?)

Murdoch's problem is that he has no way of knowing if his memories are real, if his past actually happened, if the woman he loves ever existed. Those who offer to help him cannot be trusted. Even his enemies may not be real. The movie teasingly explores the question that babies first ask in peek-a-boo: When I can't see you, are you there? It's through that game that we learn the difference between ourselves and others. But what if *we're* not there, either?

The movie is a glorious marriage of existential dread and slam-bang action. Toward the end, there is a thrilling apocalyptic battle that nearly destroys the city, and I scribbled in my notes: "For once, a sequence where the fire and explosions really work, and don't play just as effects." Proyas and his cinematographer, Dariusz Wolski, capture the kinetic energy of great comic books; their framing and foreshortening and tilt shots and distorting lenses shake the images and splash them on the screen, and it's not "action" but more like action painting.

Proyas was the director of *The Crow* (1994), the visually inspired film that was almost doomed when its star, Brandon Lee, was killed in an accident. I called that film "the best version of a comic book universe I've seen," but *Dark City* is miles beyond it. Proyas's background was in music videos, usually an ominous sign, but not here: His film shows the obsessive concentration on visual detail that's the hallmark of directors who make films that are short and expensive. There's such a wealth on the screen, such an overflowing of imagination and energy, of sets and effects. Often in f/x movies the camera doesn't feel free because it must remain within the confines of what has been created for it to see. Here we feel there's no limit.

Is the film for teenage boys and comic book fans? Not at all, although that's the marketing pitch. It's for anyone who still has a sense of wonder and a feeling for great visual style. This is a film containing ideas and true poignancy, a story that has been all thought out and has surprises right up to the end. It's romantic and exhilarating. Watching it, I thought of the last dozen films I'd seen and realized they were all essentially about people standing around and talking to one another. *Dark City* has been created and imagined as a new visual *place* for us to inhabit. It adds treasure to our notions of what can be imagined.

## Day for Night ★ ★ ★ ★

PG, 115 m., 1973 (rereleased 1997)

Jacqueline Bisset (Julie), Jean-Pierre Aumont (Alexandre), Valentina Cortese (Severine), Jean-Pierre Leaud (Alphonse), Dani (Liliane), François Truffaut (Ferrand), Alexandra Stewart (Stacey), Jean Champion (Bertrand). Directed by François Truffaut and produced by Marcel Bebert. Screenplay by Jean-Louis Richard, Suzanne Schiffman, and Truffaut.

PRODUCER: *Aren't we one big happy family?*
ACTOR: *So are the people in Greek tragedies.*

The actor in this exchange, which comes midway through François Truffaut's *Day for Night,* is overstating his case. He should have said, "So are the people in French farces." He's talking about the sort of family that forms every time a movie shoots and breaks up when it wraps. For several weeks there's a kind of forced community where privacy is rare, everyone is exhausted, and emotional desperation is epidemic.

Truffaut's film, made in 1973 and being revived with a newly-struck 35mm print, is a poem in praise of making movies. Not good movies, not bad movies—movies. It takes place at the Victorine Studio in Nice, in the south of France, which has produced movies since the silent days. Truffaut himself plays Ferrand, the director of a movie named *Meet Pamela,* which is pretty clearly going to be a stinker. Ferrand exhibits not the slightest sign that he knows this, or that he would care if he did; he isn't intended to be a director of ambitious movies (like Truffaut), but a technician in love with the process—with the stunts and special effects, the chemistry between the actors, the daily shooting schedule.

Strange, seeing this movie again in 1997, how much it reminded me of the recent films *Ed Wood* and *Boogie Nights.* Those are both films about people for whom the end product—the film itself—is only the necessary by-product of their real reason to be in the movie business, which is to be on the set. To be making a movie. For a certain kind of emotionally footloose, artistic personality, a movie production is like a homeless shelter: Their basic animal needs are satisfied, they are too tired to see beyond the morning call, and sex, when it comes, is between people who are careful to agree it doesn't mean too much.

When visitors from the real world arrive (husbands, lovers, bankers, journalists), they are provided with a director's chair to sit in, and they watch the action and nod and smile like proud grandparents. They'll never understand. "I'd drop a guy for a film," a character says in *Day for Night.* "I'd never drop a film for a guy."

Truffaut's film is like a little anthology of anecdotes from movie sets. We recognize all the familiar types: The callow, young, love-mad star (Jean-Pierre Leaud); the alcoholic diva past her prime (Valentina Cortese); the sexy romantic lead (Jacqueline Bisset), whose breakdowns are hopefully behind her now that she's married her doctor; and the aging leading man (Jean-Pierre Aumont) who is finally coming to terms with his homosexuality.

There are also the functionaries with supporting roles: the script girl, the stunt man, the producer, the woman who runs the hotel.

During the course of the movie romances end and begin, marriages are threatened and repaired, people lock themselves in their rooms and a cat refuses to lap up the milk on cue. We learn in an offhand way some of the trade secrets of moviemaking, such as how they make it snow in the summertime, how a third-floor balcony can have no building beneath it, and how scenes are shot "day for night" (a filter is used to give the effect of night while shooting in daylight).

The movie is narrated by the Truffaut character. "Shooting a movie is like a stagecoach trip," he says. "At first you hope for a nice ride. Then you just hope to reach your destination." At night he has a dream, in black and white of course, in which he's a small boy going downtown after dark. He reaches through the grating in front of the local theater and steals the eight-by-ten glossy publicity stills for *Citizen Kane.*

Earlier there's a scene where Ferrand and his producer (Jean Champion) shuffle through glossy photos of their actress (Bisset). The parallel is clear. As a youth, Ferrand dreamed of being another Welles, but now he's pleased to simply work in the same industry.

In her review of the film, Pauline Kael wrote that it was "a movie for the movie-struck, the essentially naive—those who would rather see a movie, any movie (a bad one, a stupid one or an evanescent, sweet-but-dry little wafer of a movie like this one), than do anything else." It may not be for them, but it's certainly about them. When Leaud's girlfriend says she's glad to be in Nice with all of its restaurants, he's shocked: "Little restaurants? You must be joking! Don't you know Nice has thirty-seven movies? We can grab a sandwich."

Kael's review is indignant: "I don't share Truffaut's fond regard for the kind of moviemaking that *Meet Pamela* represents." No, but it's possible to share Truffaut's affection for the people who make them. I asked Jeanne Moreau once about one of her famous scenes. She told me she hadn't seen any of her movies, except for a handful at film festivals, where her presence was required. "I get paid to make them," she said. "You get paid to see them."

François Truffaut (1932–1984) was one of the most beloved of filmmakers, a man whose own love of film was obvious in details like the old-fashioned iris shots he borrowed from silent films. (That's a shot where the screen seems to screw down to circle one detail before going to black.) "The most beautiful thing I have seen in a movie theater," he once said, "is to go down to the front, and turn around, and look at all the uplifted faces, the light from the screen reflected upon them."

He was a founder of the New Wave generation—French film critics who celebrated Hollywood's veterans in the 1950s and then made their own films. Truffaut was there at the start, with *The 400 Blows* (1959), *Shoot the Piano*

*Player* (1960), and *Jules and Jim* (1961, starring Moreau—I hope she saw it). In twenty-five years he directed twenty-three films. Why did he make so many? I think because he loved to be on the set. The young actor in *Day for Night* is heartbroken after his girl runs off with the stuntman. Truffaut's character consoles him: "People like us are only happy in our work."

## Daylight ★ ★

PG-13, 109 m., 1996

Sylvester Stallone (Kit Latura), Amy Brenneman (Madelyne Thompson), Viggo Mortensen (Roy Nord), Dan Hedaya (Frank Kraft), Jay O. Sanders (Stephan Crighton), Karen Young (Sarah Crighton), Claire Bloom (Eleanor Trilling), Stan Shaw (George Tyrell). Directed by Rob Cohen and produced by John Davis, Joseph M. Singer, and David T. Friendly. Screenplay by Leslie Bohem.

*Daylight* is the cinematic equivalent of a golden oldies station, where you never encounter anything you haven't grown to love over the years. It stars Sylvester Stallone as a disgraced former chief of the rescue service, who happens to be on the spot when an explosion rips through the Holland Tunnel, sealing both ends and trapping the usual assortment of character actors in the middle. Stallone may have lost a few men in the emergency that got him canned, but he, and only he, knows how to save these lives.

Every group of trapped civilians always includes one hothead who wants to take command, one tearful child, one bickering couple, one heroic guard, a few bad guys who turn out to be good guys, and, yes, one dog. The mommy in one family helpfully reads a description of the tunnel aloud so her family can appreciate the experience they are having, and we can get information crucial to the plot.

The setup: Three trucks loaded with toxic wastes head into the tunnel from Manhattan to New Jersey. They are soon followed by crazed diamond thieves, whose decision to evade police pursuit by driving into the tunnel is not one of your brighter criminal plans. They crash their car into the waste trucks, causing an inferno.

The movie then pays homage to the special effects cliché of the year, the Visibly Approaching Fireball. The best science available informs us that an explosion expands too quickly to be seen at close quarters—but not in the movies, where the occupants of cars have time to see the approaching fireball, scream, and duck behind the dashboard. Presumably the fireball is superhot and consumes all of the oxygen available, although luckily it is not quite hot enough to melt the cast, which is left with "enough air for three hours."

Hello! *Three hours* of air? I eagerly started looking for a red digital readout clock that would count down the minutes and seconds. All disaster movies have one. *Daylight*, alas, doesn't supply a digital readout for the potential asphyxees. But it has several in a crucial sequence where Stallone has to enter the tunnel by lowering himself through a series of four giant exhaust fans. (The fans can be shut down for sixty seconds, but not simultaneously, and only once; not a very flexible capability, eh?)

Stallone has a limited number of seconds to drop through the blades of each one before it starts spinning again. And what's installed on the wall next to *every one* of the four fans? A nice, big, red digital readout clock, that's what—that tells how many seconds until Stallone gets sliced and diced. (The digital clocks were presumably installed by the same spendthrifts who provided emergency lighting in all areas of the tunnel that are sealed off so nobody can enter them.)

Once into the tunnel, Stallone deals with the usual Trapped Civilian Character Dilemmas. A few of the characters are interesting. I liked Stan Shaw, as the tunnel guard who keeps a cool head (although early in the picture, I knew he was making a big mistake when he promised his girlfriend, "I'll give you that bracelet tonight"). Viggo Mortensen has some juicy moments as a business tycoon and hero mountain climber, who always travels with his equipment and announces a plan to climb up a tunnel filled with risky debris. (I knew he was making a big mistake when he promised Stallone, "I *cannot* fail.")

Stallone is good, too, in a thankless role. At one point, when a trapped civilian asks him if they have a chance, I expected him to say, "Calm down, lady. I've done this in a dozen other movies." After the explosion and the fire comes a flood. And a lot of rats. This is the kind of movie where when one rat turns up in an early scene, you know a lot more rats will turn up later. And when they do, your onboard movie computer starts humming, and you successfully predict that if there's an escape route anywhere in the tunnel, those rats will know it.

The only bad guys in the movie are the city officials, who set up a command post and seem to feel it is extremely urgent that they blow up the tunnel before any possible survivors have a chance of escaping. Unwise as this would be, it pales beside the speech of a city official who nixes the plan: "That tunnel is an *artery!* Do you think you can try to redirect half a million people in and out of the city!"

Say what? Does she think the tunnel is *still usable* now that both ends have collapsed and there are fires, floods, and rats in the middle? New York commuters are masochists, sure, but I don't think many of them are going anywhere near that artery again until they see Mayor Guiliani having breakfast with Regis and Kathie Lee right there on the double centerline.

## The Daytrippers ★ ★

NO MPAA RATING, 87 m., 1997

Hope Davis (Eliza D'Amico), Stanley Tucci (Louis, Eliza's Husband), Parker Posey (Jo Malone, Eliza's Sister), Liev Schreiber (Carl, Jo's Boyfriend), Anne Meara (Rita, Eliza's Mother), Pat McNamara (Jim, Eliza's Father), Campbell Scott (Eddie, the Author), Marcia Gay Harden (Libby). Directed by Greg Mottola and produced by Nancy Tenenbaum and Steven Soderbergh. Screenplay by Mottola.

Greg Mottola's *The Daytrippers* begins with a wife who is cleaning house and finds what seems to be a love note to her husband. She is concerned but not hysterical. She takes the note over to her parents' house, and it's her mother who goes ballistic. Soon the entire family has packed into the family station wagon for a journey into New York to track down the husband and confront him. We are taken along for the ride, which is sour, contrived, and whiny.

The problem is with the mother, Rita (Anne Meara). She's an insufferable scold, and since she's onscreen or nearby for almost the entire film, her presence becomes unbearable. It has been said that you should never marry anyone you are not prepared to take a three-day bus trip with. I wouldn't even get into a cab with Rita.

Her daughter Eliza (Hope Davis), who found the note in the first scene, is a good deal saner. So is Eliza's sister Jo (Parker Posey), who is engaged to Carl (Liev Schreiber). Jo and Carl are visiting for Thanksgiving; Carl likes to quote metaphysical poets at breakfast, and is working on a novel about a man with the head of a dog. These four characters pile into a car driven by the dad, Jim (Pat McNamara), who has been married to Rita for years and can therefore be forgiven for almost anything.

The outcome of this journey is going to be predictable and disappointing. Mottola does his best to make the trip itself enjoyable. The five people, jammed unconvincingly in the station wagon on an implausible mission, talk and bicker and put themselves at the mercy of the mother's whims. They stake out the apartment of the husband's suspected mistress, they try to follow him when he comes out, they go to his office and find he's suspiciously taken a day off, they find themselves invited into the house of a complete stranger, and eventually, that evening, they stake out a book party where he's expected to appear.

The husband (Stanley Tucci, from *Big Night*) is a book editor. The party, like some of the other scenes, plays more like a self-contained opportunity for satire than like part of the overall story. Brief appearances by Campbell Scott (also from *Big Night*) and Marcia Gay Harden leave us wondering if their characters might not have made a more promising film.

I can see what Mottola is trying to do, and I'm happy that he tried. He uses the trip into town as an excuse to string together character bits and the kind of unsprung, liberated dialogue that Tarantino used in *Pulp Fiction* and Kevin Smith has fun with in *Chasing Amy*. His film is intended to be liberated from plot; the device of the mission into town is so broad and obvious we can take it ironically, and just enjoy the strange characters and their colorful speech.

That would work if it were not for the Anne Meara character. And here I must be precise. I do not mean to criticize Meara herself. She is, almost by definition, superb at her assignment here, which is to create an insufferable mother. The film's problem is that she does it so well. She nags and whines and delivers little zingers and pushes the buttons of her loved ones so effectively that *The Daytrippers* could have raised a cheer from the audience simply by dumping her on the roadside.

As for the film's surprise ending: I was a little offended by how pat it was, how it expected us to accept it as the wrap-up of what went before. The movie shows a talent at writing characters and dialogue, but it doesn't really seem to have a purpose for being. The one character we do care deeply about, unfortunately, is the one we can't stand.

## Dead Man Walking ★ ★ ★ ★

R, 122 m., 1996

Susan Sarandon (Sister Helen Prejean), Sean Penn (Matthew Poncelet), Robert Prosky (Hilton Barber), Raymond J. Barry (Earl Delacroix), R. Lee Ermey (Clyde Percy), Celia Weston (Mary Beth Percy), Scott Wilson (Prison Chaplain). Directed by Tim Robbins and produced by Jon Kilik, Robbins, and Rudd Simmons. Screenplay by Robbins.

After seeing *Dead Man Walking*, I paused outside the screening to jot a final line on my notes: "This film ennobles filmmaking." That is exactly what it does. It demonstrates how a film can confront a grave and controversial issue in our society, see it fairly from all sides and not take any shortcuts, and move the audience to a great emotional experience without unfair manipulation. What is remarkable is that the film is also all the other things a movie should be: absorbing, surprising, technically superb, and worth talking about for a long time afterward.

The movie begins with a Louisiana nun, Helen Prejean (Susan Sarandon), who works in an inner-city neighborhood. One day she receives a letter from an inmate on Death Row, asking her to visit him. So she visits him. The prison chaplain (Scott Wilson) doesn't think much of her visit, and briefs her on the ways that prisoners can manipulate outsiders. He obviously thinks of her as a bleeding heart. Her answer is unadorned: "He wrote to me and asked me to come."

The inmate, named Matthew Poncelet (Sean Penn), has been convicted along with another man of participating in the rape and murder of two young people on a lover's lane. We see him first through the grating of a visitor's pen, so that his face breaks into jigsaw pieces. In looks and appearance he is the kind of person you would instinctively dread: He has the mousy little goatee and elaborate pompadour of a man with deep misgivings about his face. His voice is halting and his speech is ignorant. He smokes a cigarette as if sneaking puffs in a grade school washroom. He tells her, "They got me on a greased rail to the Death House here."

He wants her to help with his appeal. At one point, he mentions that they don't have anything in common. Sister Helen thinks about that and says, "You and I have something in common. We both live with the poor." His face looks quietly stunned, as if for the first time in a long time he has been confronted with an insight about his life that is not solely ego-driven. She says she will come to see him again, and that she will help him file a last-minute appeal against his approaching execution.

Sister Helen, as played here by Sarandon and written and directed by Tim Robbins (from the memoir by the real Helen Prejean), is one of the few truly spiritual characters I have seen in the movies. Movies about "religion" are often only that—movies about secular organizations that deal in spirituality. It is so rare to find a movie character who truly does try to live according to the teachings of Jesus (or anyone else, for that matter) that it's a little disorienting: This character will behave according to what she thinks is right, not according to the needs of a plot, the requirements of a formula, or the pieties of those for whom religion, good grooming, polite manners, and prosperity are all more or less the same thing.

But wait. The film is not finished with its bravery. At this point in any conventional story, we would expect developments along familiar lines. Take your choice: (1) The prisoner is really innocent, and Sister Helen leads his eleventh-hour defense as justice is done; (2) they fall in love with one another, she helps him escape, and they go on a doomed flight from the law; or, less likely (3) she converts him to her religion, and he goes to his death praising Jesus.

None of these things happen. Instead, Sister Helen experiences all of the complexities, contradictions, and hard truths of the situation, and we share them. In movies like this you rarely see the loved ones of the victims, unless they are presented in hate-filled caricatures of blood lust. Here it is not like that. Sister Helen meets the parents of the dead girl and the father of the dead boy. (The father is seen among packing cases—moving, after a separation from his wife, who felt it was time for them to "get on with their lives," which he can never do.) She begins to understand that Matthew may indeed have been guilty. She has to face the anger of the parents, who cannot see why anyone would want to befriend a murderer ("Are you a Communist?"). There is a scene of agonizing embarrassment, as the girl's parents make a basic mistake about her motives for visiting them.

And there is more. Matthew, we come to realize, is the product of an impoverished cultural background. He has been supplied with only a few clichés to serve him as a philosophy: He believes in "taking things like a man," and "showing people," and there on Death Row he even makes a play for Sister Helen, almost as a reflex. "Death is breathing down your neck," she tells him, "and you're playing your little man-on-the-make games." He parrots a racist statement from his prison buddies in the Aryan Nation, which does his case no good, and later, when he bitterly resents his stupidity in saying those things, we realize he didn't even think about them; nature abhors a vacuum, and racism abhors an empty mind and pours in to fill it.

The movie comes down to a drama of an entirely unexpected kind: a spiritual drama, involving Matthew's soul. Christianity teaches that all sin can be forgiven, and that no sinner is too low for God's love. Sister Helen believes that. Truly believes it, with every atom of her being. And yet she does not press Matthew for a "religious" solution to his situation. What she hopes for is that he can go to his death in reconciliation with himself and his crime. The last half-hour of this movie is overwhelmingly powerful—not least in Matthew's strained eleventh-hour visit with his family, where we see them all trapped in the threadbare clichés of a language learned from television shows and saloon jukeboxes.

The performances in this film are beyond comparison, which is to say that Sarandon and Penn find their characters and make them into exactly what they are without reference to other movies or conventions. Penn proves again that he is the most powerful actor of his generation, and as for Sarandon—in film after film, she finds not the right technique for a character so much as the right humanity. It's as if she creates a role out of a deep understanding of the person she is playing.

Tim Robbins, Sarandon's longtime companion, has directed once before (*Bob Roberts*, an intelligent political drama). With this film, he leaps far beyond his earlier work and makes that very rare thing, a film that is an exercise of philosophy. This is the kind of movie that spoils us for other films because it reveals so starkly how most movies fall into conventional routine and lull us with the reassurance that they will not look too hard, or probe too deeply, or make us think beyond the boundaries of what is comfortable. For years, critics of the movies have asked for more films that deal, say, with the spiritual side of life. I doubt if *Dead Man Walking* was what they were thinking of, but this is exactly how such a movie looks and feels.

## Dear God ★

PG, 112 m., 1996

Greg Kinnear (Tom Turner), Laurie Metcalf (Rebecca Frazen), Maria Pitillo (Gloria McKinney), Tim Conway (Herman Dooly), Hector Elizondo (Vladek Vidov), Roscoe Lee Browne (Idris Abraham), Jon Seda (Claudio Handsome), Anna Maria Horsford (Lucille Barnett). Directed by Garry Marshall and produced by Steve Tisch. Screenplay by Warren Leight and Ed Kaplan.

*Dear God* is the kind of movie where you walk out repeating the title, but not with a smile. It is a limp, lifeless story starring Greg Kinnear as a con man who becomes a do-gooder, and one of its many problems is that he was a lot more entertaining as a con man.

As the movie opens, Kinnear has his arm wrapped in bandages and is hanging out near ATM machines, pretending to be a burn victim in need of a loan. He has other scams, like returning a "lost" bracelet to get a reward and selling bogus airline tickets. That last one gets him arrested by the LAPD and brought up before a judge, who sentences him, horror of horrors, to get a real job.

Kinnear eventually ends up working for the post office, where there's only time to brief him on a few of the rules ("Fragile" is postal for "bounce against walls") before he's assigned to the dreaded Dead Letter Office, where demoralized clerks try to deal with mail addressed to Elvis, the Tooth Fairy, and God.

By now we are slipping inexorably into the realm of cut-rate Capra and can guess what's coming: Kinnear will read some of the letters, be moved by the plight of the writers, and try to change their lives a little. And he will enlist the aid of some of his coworkers, including Laurie Metcalf as a former lawyer, Roscoe Lee Browne as a worker on the verge of retirement, Tim Conway as a former carrier so morose over losing his route that he seems on the verge of going postal, and Hector Elizondo as the supervisor, a Russian immigrant with his own weird approach to things.

Director Garry Marshall, who usually makes sharper and smarter films, lays on schmaltz by the carload as Kinnear and his friends save a man from committing suicide, do a maid's own housework for her, and give a harassed mother of twins her heart's desire: just one evening off. Greg Kinnear, it must be said, holds his own in the film. If it's boring, that's not his fault. The onetime TV talk show host proved, in the remake of *Sabrina*, that he is a sure-enough actor, and here again he has an easy, engaging quality. But the material lets him down with its relentlessly predictable developments.

Their good deeds quickly become a media phenomenon. "Postal Miracles" become so famous that Los Angeles TV stations interrupt their scheduled broadcasting for bulletins from the site of the latest good deed (uh-huh). Everything eventually ends up in court, where Kinnear and his accomplices are charged with "answering God's mail without authorization." The courtroom scene, I am coming to believe, is the last refuge of the screenwriter who needs an ending and does not have one.

There is a book out named *Reel Justice* that examines many famous movies on the basis of how accurate their legal scenes are. I commend *Dear God* to them, as an example of the same fallacy committed by *A Time to Kill*. This is the verdict brought in according to the requirements of the plot, rather than the rules of the law. If a defendant breaks the law, and admits he did it, and it is generally agreed that he did it, then he cannot be found "not guilty." He can be given a light sentence, a tap on the wrist, or fined $1. But the law in non-Kafkaesque nations cannot simply ignore the facts. Not that I cared. It was more like by that point in the film I needed something—anything—to think about.

## Deceiver ★ ★

R, 102 m., 1998

Chris Penn (Braxton), Ellen Burstyn (Mook), Tim Roth (Wayland), Renee Zellweger (Elizabeth), Michael Rooker (Kennesaw), Rosanna Arquette (Mrs. Kennesaw). Directed by Josh Pate and Jonas Pate and produced by Peter Glatzer. Screenplay by Josh Pate and Jonas Pate.

*Deceiver* is a Chinese box of a movie, in which we learn less and less about more and more. It's centered in a police interrogation room, where a rich kid undergoes a lie detector test in connection with the murder of a prostitute. Did he do it? At first it seems he did. Then he turns the tables on the two cops running the polygraph exam, and by the end of the film everyone is a suspect.

Tim Roth stars as Wayland, a Princeton grad and the son of a textile magnate, but currently unemployed. There's no doubt he knew the prostitute, named Elizabeth (Renee Zellweger, from *Jerry Maguire*): He even took her to a black-tie party at his parents' home, and got disowned in the process. But did he cut her into pieces and distribute her throughout Charleston, South Carolina?

The cops are Braxton (Chris Penn) and Kennesaw (Michael Rooker). Their methods are a little crude; they seem intent on helping Wayland fail the test with intimidation and hints he isn't doing too well. Wayland responds with all the cockiness and self-assurance of a man who knows he's not so much a suspect as a character in a movie, taunting the cops with inside information about their private lives.

*Deceiver* has similarities to *Usual Suspects* in the way it coils around its central facts, looking at them first one way and then another. It also has a less obvious parallel with Quentin Tarantino's practice of working arcane knowledge into the dialogue of his characters. Carefully polished little set-pieces are spotted through the film; the action stops for well-informed discussions about Vincent van Gogh, the dangers of absinthe, the symptoms of epilepsy, and the relative intelligence of the two cops.

There wasn't much I could believe. The movie is basically about behavior—about acting, rather than about characters. The three leads and some supporting characters get big scenes and angry speeches, and the plot manufactures big moments of crisis and then slips away from them. It feels more like a play than a movie.

One of the ways it undermines its characters is by upstaging them with the plot. We get several theories about the death of the prostitute, and lots of flashbacks in which Wayland's tortured childhood offers explanations for actions he may or may not have taken. Facts are established, only to be shot down. Having seen the film twice, I am prepared to accept that its paradoxes are all answered and its puzzles solved, although unless you look closely and remember the face of an ambulance driver, you may miss the explanation for one of the big surprises.

The thing is, even after you figure it all out, a movie like this offers few rewards. It's well acted, and you can admire that on a technical level, but the plot is such a puzzle it shuts us out: How can we care about events that the movie itself constantly undercuts and revises? By the time the final twist comes along, it's as if we've seen a clever show in which the only purpose, alas, was to demonstrate the cleverness.

## Deconstructing Harry ★ ★ ★ ½

R, 95 m., 1997

---

Woody Allen (Harry Block), Kirstie Alley (Joan), Richard Benjamin (Ken), Hazelle Goodman (Cookie), Eric Bogosian (Burt), Billy Crystal (Larry), Judy Davis (Lucy), Mariel Hemingway (Beth Kramer), Julie Kavner (Grace), Elisabeth Shue (Fay). Directed by Woody Allen and produced by Jean Doumanian. Screenplay by Allen.

---

Once a year, like clockwork, Woody Allen writes, directs, and usually stars in exactly the film he feels like making. He works on budgets that make this possible—and just as well, given the mugging he's received from critics who think he shouldn't have made *Deconstructing Harry.*

His new movie is vulgar, smutty, profane, self-hating, self-justifying, self-involved, tasteless, bankrupt, and desperate, I've read. Even the kinder reviews turn sour. Here's a quote from David Edelstein of *Slate:* "The result is more rambunctious—and more fun—than any movie he has made in years. What puzzles me is why it still adds up to something so anemic and coldly distasteful." When a film makes me laugh and then I learn that it's vulgar, I'm reminded of Mel Brooks's defense of *The Producers:* "My film rises below vulgarity." That's the *Deconstructing Harry* defense; there is hardly a criticism that can be thrown at Allen that he hasn't already thrown at himself (or his alter ego) in the film.

This is in many ways his most revealing film, his most painful, and if it also contains more than his usual quotient of big laughs. What was it the man said? "We laugh, that we may not cry."

The film stars Allen as Harry Block, a novelist whose material vaguely suggests Philip Roth. Both names represent aspects of the character, who is blocked, and who is seen by many (and sometimes by himself) as Satan. Harry is under attack. His sister-in-law (Judy Davis) cries out that his new book "is totally about us"—about the two of them, and the affair she thought he would keep a secret. He's told he "can't function in life, only in art." We get the sense that many of the lines assigned to characters were first shouted at Allen himself; there's one line in particular that I'm willing to bet originally came from someone close to him: "This little sewer of an apartment where you take everyone's suffering and turn it into gold."

Harry is portrayed as a user and borrower: He uses people, and then borrows the story of how he used them, and uses that too. The movie cuts between real time and fictionalized episodes from his books, in which Harry's clones and surrogates indulge their appetites when and as they can.

Harry himself is a philandering cheater who's been through three wives and six psychiatrists (the Kirstie Alley character made it into both categories). All of this is done in the blackout style of some of Allen's earlier films; unlike the smoother, more carefully constructed recent films, *Deconstructing Harry* is built revue-style, and there's even a fantasy sequence in hell. As in his early films, Allen includes comic material about Judaism, and there are caricatures and stereotypes that may offend, but to those who would call him a self-hating Jew, Allen has the answer right there on the screen: "You're a self-hating Jew!" Harry is told.

The fact is, he's a self-hater, period. He's critical of every possible aspect of himself. And although he defends some of his excesses as necessary to an artist in the creative process, he doesn't let himself off that hook, either: Harry's art, in the film, is seen as juvenile, manipulative, derivative, vulgar, and sometimes cornball. (That it is also funny is the redeeming grace.)

Allen has borrowed his basic story line from *Wild Strawberries,* the 1957 film by his hero, Ingmar Bergman, about an old professor who revisits scenes and memories from a long life as he returns to his alma mater to be honored. In the Harry Block version, the school expelled him and wants to make amends. But he can't get anyone to go along with him on the trip—not a single relative, friend, ex-lover, or wife is interested. He eventually hires a black hooker named Cookie (Hazelle Goodman) to accompany him; like Mira Sorvino's hooker in *Mighty Aphrodite,* she's useful mostly for her nonsexual functions, such as accepting and liking him. (As the trip progresses, he also picks up a friend, played by Bob Balaban, and then kidnaps his son from school to take him along too.)

The film has a richness of comic bits, of which the most original involves Robin Williams as an actor who is concerned that he's losing his focus—and is (he's out of focus in every scene). There's a visit to hell to see the devil (Billy Crystal, who also plays the friend who has stolen Harry's latest mistress). And a fantasy sequence in which a wife finds that her husband has a few little secrets to share, which build slowly: He was married before. And had children. And killed them all. And ate them. The cannibal husband ends with a plea for understanding: "If I tell you why I did it, do you promise not to noodge me?"

Essentially, this is Allen's plea throughout the film. His private life has spilled untidily into the news in the last couple of years; enshrined as a cultural hero, he is now in the uncomfortable position of feeling like a defendant. He explains, he excuses, he evades, and his critics are not satisfied: They want less, or more, or otherwise. But no single Woody Allen film ever sums up everything, or could, and what is fascinating is to watch him, year after year, making the most personal of films, and hiding himself in plain view.

☞

## Deep Crimson ★ ★ ★ ½

NO MPAA RATING, 109 m., 1998

Regina Orozco (Coral Fabre), Daniel Gimenez Cacho (Nicolas Estrella), Marisa Paredes (Irene Gallardo), Patricia Reyes Espindola (The Widow Ruelas), Julieta Egurrola (Juanita Norton), Rosa Furman (The Widow Morrison), Veronica Merchant (Rebecca San Pedro), Sherlyn Gonzales (Teresa). Directed by Arturo Ripstein and produced by Miguel Necoechea and Paolo Barbachano. Screenplay by Paz Alicia Garciadiego.

*Deep Crimson,* macabre and perverse, is based on a true story from the 1940s, about the "Lonely Hearts Killers"—a couple who posed as brother and sister, victimized lonely widows, and then killed them. Their story was told in a 1970 American film, *The Honeymoon Killers,* but now here is Arturo Ripstein with a Mexican version that combines black comedy with horrifying heartlessness. There were walkouts when I saw the film; those who stay will not easily forget it.

The movie opens like a dark comedy by Pedro Almodovar or Luis Buñuel (who Ripstein once worked for as an assistant director). We meet Coral Fabre, played by the opera singer Regina Orozco; she is a sometime embalmer, now caring for an old man and raising two children haphazardly. My diagnosis: hysteria and manic-depression. She answers a lonely hearts' ad from a "Charles Boyer type," and soon meets Nicolas Estrella (Daniel Gimenez Cacho), a vain, bald gigolo who spends hours adjusting his hairpiece before putting on his trench coat, snapping the brim of his fedora, and sailing out to defraud lonely women.

She has sent him a picture of herself when slim. She is fat. "I lose weight when I want to," she tells him. "How lucky to be able to control your body like that!" he says, before trying to flee. She begs him to stay, blaming his distaste on the smell of formaldehyde from her undertaking duties. "I've never been with a gentleman," she weeps. "Do it to me. Just do it—as a favor!" He does, but not as a favor; as she sleeps, he steals the money from her purse and creeps out.

But Coral has seen him from beneath lowered lids. The next day she arrives at Nicolas's apartment with her two children in tow. "I saw you robbing me," she tells him. "Maybe you were charging for excess fat. I came to stay with you. We're made for each other." He demurs, and so she takes decisive action: dumps her kids at an orphanage, enters his apartment when he's not there, reads his phony letters to lonely hearts victims, and when he returns offers him a partnership. They'll pose as brother and sister, and she'll select the victims.

Nicolas, who is as stupid as he is vain, is flattered. ("You gave up your kids for me! Nobody's ever done anything like that before.") Soon they are choosing their victims, but there's a hitch: Coral is not content to simply defraud and rob them. When she eavesdrops as Nicolas makes love to them, or even talks sweet, she grows jealous, and soon they're leaving a trail of corpses behind.

*Deep Crimson* sinks easily into the swamp of human depravity. Coral and Nicolas are demented even when apart; together, they create an amoral composite personality, a world in which soap opera clichés about love are used to excuse unspeakable sins. Ripstein leads us into this world with the seduction of deadpan black humor, and then pulls out the rug in the final scenes, which are truly horrific. As a study in abnormal psychology, *Deep Crimson* would make his master, Buñuel, proud.

The film has a strong effect on its viewers. When I saw it, there was a scene of harm toward a child that sent many audience members racing for the exits. Others feel betrayed because they laughed along with the earlier scenes, only to be blindsided by the cruelty and dark despair of the conclusion.

One thing that engages some viewers is Coral's weight. It is an unspoken rule of female killers in movies that they be thin. "While Coral's plight calls out for some sympathy from the audience, her loathsome obesity prevents us from commiseration," writes Harvey Karten, an Internet critic. Yet here is Ruthe Stein from the *San Francisco Chronicle*, who cites the slender killers played by Faye Dunaway and Linda Fiorentino and then adds of this one: "Anyone in Hollywood who thinks large women can't be sexy should get a load of her."

This disagreement is revealing. Karten is obviously a candidate for urgent briefings by the Fat Acceptance lobby. Stein may find Coral sexy for politically correct reasons, but Nicolas certainly doesn't. The film isn't about appearances at all, but about the way Coral and Nicolas see what they need to see. She sees not a pathetic, toupee-wearing fraud, but Charles Boyer. He sees not a fat embalmer who has dumped her children, but a woman who would make any sacrifice for him. Their mutual weakness is vanity: She can feel she has Charles Boyer as a lover, and he can feel that she sees Boyer when she looks at him. As long as these mutual fantasies are reinforced, the deaths of a few unfortunate widows can be excused.

Ripstein, not well-known in America, is Mexico's most respected director, and in *Deep Crimson* he creates the kind of dangerous film that Americans made more freely in the 1970s (when *The Honeymoon Killers* got reviews similar to this one's). He is unafraid of offending his audience. He is going for hard truths, and approaching them through humor and a willingness to offend. His purpose is to undercut the way that movies glamorize legendary criminals like Coral and Nicolas. Anyone who thought *Bonnie and Clyde* romanticized its killers is likely to feel that the heroes of *Deep Crimson* get what they have coming, without mercy.

## Deep Impact ★ ★ ½

PG-13, 115 m., 1998

Robert Duvall (Spurgeon Tanner), Tea Leoni (Jenny Lerner), Morgan Freeman (President Beck), Elijah Wood (Leo Biederman), Vanessa Redgrave (Robin Lerner), Maximilian Schell (Jason Lerner), Leelee Sobieski (Sarah Hotchner), James Cromwell (Alan Rittenhouse). Directed by Mimi Leder and produced by Richard D. Zanuck and David Brown. Screenplay by Michael Tolkin and Bruce Joel Rubin.

Early in *Deep Impact* we learn that a comet "the size of Mt. Everest" is on a collision course for Earth. There would seem to be two possible outcomes: (1) The comet hits Earth, destroying it, or (2) the comet does not hit Earth, in which case humanity is spared but the audience is denied the sight of lots of special effects. In the first scenario you don't get the obligatory happy ending, and in the second one everyone leaves feeling cheated.

Most doomsday movies avoid this choice by prudently choosing less than apocalyptic events. A volcano, a twister, or a tidal wave can supply lots of terrifying special effects and still leave a lot of people standing. But *Deep Impact* seems to back itself into a corner, and maybe that's why the producers hired not one but two of the brightest writers in Hollywood to work on the project: Bruce Joel Rubin *(Ghost)* and Michael

Tolkin *(The Player)*. Together, they've figured out how to have their cake and eat it too.

How do they do this? I would not dream of revealing their inspiration, although you may be able to figure it out yourself. Meanwhile, you can enjoy the way they create little flashes of wit in the dialogue, which enlivens what is, after all, a formula disaster movie. What's the formula? Assorted archetypal characters are introduced, they're assigned personal problems, and the story cuts between them as the moment of disaster grows closer. I always think it's more interesting if they know from the start that there's a big problem; I get tired of scenes in which they live blissfully unaware of the catastrophe unfolding beneath their feet, or above their heads, or wherever.

*Deep Impact* begins with the obligatory opening precatastrophe, in this case a runaway semi that mows down a Jeep and kills the astronomer who is bringing news of the approaching comet. (The other movie I saw on the same day, *The Horse Whisperer*, also opened with a runaway semi, and indeed I cannot recall a single movie in which a semi on a two-lane road does not careen out of control.)

Then there's a little ritual media-bashing; Tea Leoni plays a reporter for MSNBC who suspects there's more to the story of a cabinet official's resignation. She accuses him of having an affair with a woman named "Ellie," and he gets to say, "I know you're just a reporter, but you used to be a person." (The approved media response to this is, "Look who's talking! A cabinet member!")

Soon she discovers her error; he is resigning not because of Ellie but because of an E.L.E., which is jargon for "Extinction Level Event." He wants to spend more time with his family, and has stocked a yacht with dozens of cases of vitamin-rich Sustain. He must not have been invited to the briefing where it was explained that all surface life would be destroyed by the comet, or the other briefing about the 1,000-foot-tall tidal wave. My guess is the president wanted him out of the cabinet.

The president, played convincingly by Morgan Freeman, goes on TV to break the bad news to the world, and talks of the *Messiah* Project, which will send a manned U.S.-Russian spacecraft to plant nuclear bombs in the comet and blow it up. We meet the *Messiah* crew members, including old Spurgeon Tanner (Robert Duvall), called out of retirement because he once landed on the Moon and might be able to land on the comet.

The younger crew members resent him, we are told, although dissension onboard is never followed up on. The veteran has a nice line about the youngsters: "They're not scared of dying. They're just scared of looking bad on TV." There's another good line at the high school assembly where the kid (Elijah Wood) who codiscovered the comet is honored. A friend tells him, "You're gonna have a lot more sex starting now. Famous people always get more sex." And I liked a line from late in the movie when one hero tells another, "Look on the bright side. We'll all have high schools named for us."

But the movie as a whole is pretty routine. There's a laborious subplot in which Tea Leoni resents her father (Maximilian Schell) for divorcing her mother (Vanessa Redgrave) and marrying a bimbo, and while Redgrave brings a nice sad quality to her scenes, the rest of the subplot plays out suspiciously like a scheme to place two humans in front of a big special effect. There are also some fairly unconvincing scenes in which millions of people try to flee from a city, and all of them are trapped in gridlock except, of course, for the two who are required by the plot to get somewhere fast.

Whether Earth is saved or doomed or neither, I will leave you to discover for yourself. I personally found it easier to believe that Earth could survive this doomsday scenario than that the *Messiah* spacecraft could fly at thousands of miles an hour through the comet's tail, which contains rocks the size of two-car garages, without serious consequences. On the disaster epic scale, on which *Titanic* gets four stars and *Volcano* gets one and a half, *Deep Impact* gets two and a half—the same as *Dante's Peak*, even though it lacks a dog that gets left behind.

## Deep Rising ★ ½

R, 106 m., 1998

Treat Williams (Finnegan), Famke Janssen (Trillian), Anthony Heald (Carlton), Kevin J. O'Connor (Pantucci), Wes Studi (Hanover), Derrick O'Connor (Captain), Jason Flemyng (Mulligan), Cliff Curtis (Mamooli). Directed by Stephen Sommers and produced by Laurence

Mark and John Baldecchi. Screenplay by Sommers.

---

*Deep Rising* could also have been titled *Eat the Titanic!* It's about a giant squid that attacks a luxurious cruise ship in the South China Sea. Like all movie monsters, the squid has perfect timing and always bursts into the frame just when the characters are least expecting it. And it has an unsavory way of dining. "They eat you?" asks one of the survivors. "No—they drink you."

The mechanics for a movie like this were well established in the *Alien* pictures, and *Deep Rising* clones the same formula: Survivors are trapped inside giant vessel. Creature finds its way around air ducts and sewer pipes, popping out of shaft openings to gobble up minor characters (the first victim is sucked down the toilet).

D'ya think they have meetings out in Hollywood to share the latest twists? I've been seeing the same gimmicks in a lot of different pictures. Evidence: No sooner does the snake in *Anaconda* release a slimy survivor from its innards than the squid in *Deep Rising* does the same thing. No sooner is there an indoor Jet Ski chase in *Hard Rain* than there's one in *Deep Rising.* No sooner does a horrible monster crawl out of the air ducts in *Alien Resurrection* than it does so in *Deep Rising.* And last week I saw *Phantoms,* which was sort of *Deep Rising Meets Alien and Goes West.* In that one, the creature emerged from the depths of the earth rather than the sea, but had the same nasty practice of living behind piles of undigested remains.

An effort has been made by Stephen Sommers, writer-director of *Deep Rising,* to add humor to his story, although not even the presence of Leslie Nielsen could help this picture. The hero, Treat Williams, is a freelance power cruiser skipper who hires his craft out to a gang of vile and reprehensible bad guys, led by Wes Studi. They want to hijack a new casino ship on its maiden voyage. The owner of the ship (Anthony Heald) makes several speeches boasting about how stable it is; it can stay level in the water even during a raging tempest. I wonder if those speeches were inserted after the filmmakers realized how phony their special effects look. Every time we see the ship, it's absolutely immobile in the midst of churning waves.

No matter; the creature from the deep attacks the ship, and by the time Williams delivers the pirates, it seems to be deserted. All except for the evil owner, of course, and also a jewel thief (Famke Janssen) who was locked in the brig and survived the carnage.

A movie like this depends much upon the appearance of the monster, which has been designed by f/x wizard Rob Bottin. There is a vast evil squid head, and lots of tentacles (which seem to have minds of their own, and lots of mouths with many teeth). So vicious is the squid, indeed, that only the cynical will ask how it can survive for long periods out of water, or how and why it emits its piercing howl, which goes reverberating through the air shafts.

There's comic relief from Williams's engine room man, Pantucci (Kevin J. O'Connor), who plays the Donald O'Connor role and is always wisecracking in the face of adversity. And an effective supporting performance by Djimon Hounsou, as one of the more fanatic members of the pirate gang (he played Cinque in *Amistad,* and shows a powerful screen presence once again, although on the whole I'll bet he wishes the giant squid movie had come out *before* the Spielberg film).

Bemusing, how much money and effort goes into the making of a movie like this, and how little thought. It's months of hard work—for what? The movie is essentially an *Alien* clone with a fresh paint job. You know something's wrong when a fearsome tentacle rears up out of the water and opens its mouth, and there are lots of little tentacles inside with their own ugly mouths, all filled with nasty teeth, and all you can think is, been there, seen that.

## Deja Vu ★ ★ ★ ½

PG-13, 116 m., 1998

---

Victoria Foyt (Dana), Vanessa Redgrave (Skelly), Stephen Dillane (Sean), Michael Brandon (Alex), Glynis Barber (Claire), Noel Harrison (John Stoner), Anna Massey (Fern Stoner). Directed by Henry Jaglom and produced by John Goldstone. Screenplay by Jaglom and Victoria Foyt.

---

We all look for love like the love in *Deja Vu.* We hardly ever find it. That's why there are movies. We want a love that spans the generations and conquers time, a love so large that only the supernatural can contain it. Here is a movie about a love like that. It makes *City of Angels* look timid.

The story involves an American woman named Dana (Victoria Foyt) on a buying trip to Jerusalem when she is approached by a mysterious older blonde who engages her in conversation. Soon she is revealing all her secrets: Yes, she is engaged, because "being engaged has become a condition of my life," but after six years and no marriage she is not very happy.

The other woman tells her about the love of her life. It was a wartime romance. She was a French Jewish woman; he was an American GI. They planned to wed. He went home "to tell his girlfriend" and never returned. Eventually she got a letter with a photo of the man's first child.

Perhaps, Dana says, he could not find you. The woman smiles sadly. "He knew where to find me. Life had got hold of us." She pauses. "Nothing seemed so real again. In fact, all my life since then has been like a dream." The woman gives her a piece of jewelry—a clip—and disappears, after mentioning that the clip was a gift from the GI, who kept the other one.

Dana heads toward home. When the Chunnel train stops briefly at Dover, she inexplicably gets off instead of going on to London. Above the white cliffs of Dover, she meets a painter named Sean (Stephen Dillane). "Have we met before?" she asks him. He says, "It feels like one of those moments where if you turn the wrong way you regret it forever." It's love at first sight, but they fight it. She's engaged, after all. But then they meet again, by coincidence, at the house of British friends. She discovers he is married.

Her fiancé is Alex (Michael Brandon). His wife is Claire (Glynis Barber). It becomes clear that Dana and Sean are helplessly in love, and their partners react in disbelief and anger, but with a certain civilized restraint. I must not reveal any more. I must say instead that old songs like "The White Cliffs of Dover" and "We'll Meet Again" and "These Foolish Things" are like time machines that can carry love down through the years and can leap from mind to mind, spreading their foolishness and dreams.

*Deja Vu* is not a weepy romantic melodrama, but a sophisticated film about smart people. Foyt and Dillane make convincing lovers not because they are swept away, but because they regard what has happened to them and accept it. When they fall in love, there is a lot at risk: jobs, businesses, which country they live in, the people they're committed to. It takes no trouble at all to fall in love when you're twenty and single. But Dana and Sean must look in their hearts and be sure they cannot live without one another.

The film was directed by Henry Jaglom and written by Jaglom and his star, Victoria Foyt, who is also his wife. Ah-ha, you think, guessing the connection, especially since the movie is dedicated "to the love of my life." But there is another connection coiling down through the years. The trademark of Jaglom's film company is a brief moment of time, showing Orson Welles producing a rainbow out of thin air. Jaglom was one of Welles's close confidants and friends.

In *Citizen Kane,* which Welles made in 1941, there occurs my favorite passage of movie dialogue. Old Mr. Bernstein is talking about the peculiarities of time. "A fellow will remember a lot of things you wouldn't think he'd remember," he says. "You take me. One day, back in 1896, I was crossing over to Jersey on the ferry, and as we pulled out, there was another ferry pulling in, and on it there was a girl waiting to get off. A white dress she had on. She was carrying a white parasol. I only saw her for one second. She didn't see me at all, but I'll bet a month hasn't gone by since that I haven't thought of that girl."

Late in *Deja Vu,* a character tells a similar story, about a woman he once met: "A week hasn't gone by since I last saw her that I haven't thought of her. She was the love of my life."

Yes. And can you, dear reader, think of such a moment too? Perfect love is almost always unrealized. It has to be. What makes those memories perfect is that they produce no history. The woman with the white parasol remains always frozen in an old man's memory. She never grows old, is never out of temper, never loses interest in him, never dies. She exists forever as a promise, like the green light at the end of Gatsby's pier.

Only rarely does the universe wheel around to bring two hearts once again into communion. That's what *Deja Vu* is about. And that explains the two most curious characters in it. They are the old couple (Anna Massey and Noel Harrison) who own the house where Dana and Sean meet by accident. They have been married a very long time, and like to read in bed and eat Mars bars at the same time and be happy to be together. At first you wonder what their scenes mean. Then you understand.

## Denise Calls Up ★ ★

PG-13, 80 m., 1996

Alanna Ubach (Denise), Tim Daly (Frank), Caroleen Feeney (Barbara), Dan Gunther (Martin), Dana Wheeler-Nicholson (Gale), Liev Schreiber (Jerry), Aida Turturro (Linda). Directed by Hal Salwen and produced by J. Todd Harris. Screenplay by Salwen.

*Denise Calls Up* is a great idea. I was going to say it was a "great idea for a movie," but apparently it's not, since the movie, short as it is, grows tiresome before it's over. Maybe it's more of a great idea for a stand-up routine, or a magazine article, or for conversation.

The idea is this: In an age of telephones, pagers, answering machines, beepers, e-mail, appointment schedulers, on-line conferencing, and cybersex, people are too busy to meet with one another. All communications are at arm's length, and the arm in question usually ends in a hand holding a telephone receiver, a computer mouse, or a remote control for the answering machine.

The movie is about a group of seven friends who, we gradually realize, have never met. They keep in touch mostly by phone. As the story opens, one of the characters surveys a groaning buffet table in her apartment, but no one comes to her party. They're all "tied up." It's not that they dislike her or want to hurt her; it's that in-person events rank low on their list of priorities.

This notion, true as it is, doesn't stretch well enough to make a feature film. But Hal Salwen, the writer and director, makes a real try, and there are moments of comic inspiration, as when the friends learn that one of them has died in a car crash: "She was on the car phone at the time, and the crash forced the receiver up her ear and into her brain."

Another funny sequence begins when Marty gets a call from Denise, who is pregnant with his child. Ah, so *they* at least met? Not at all: Marty made a donation to a sperm bank and Denise made a withdrawal. This situation leads to a moment that film fans, weary of obligatory live childbirth scenes, may enjoy: the first movie childbirth by telephone.

Other moments: A mother visits her son, who doesn't answer the door; she can call if she wants to talk to him. A friend sets up two of her friends on a blind date; none of them has ever seen the others. Two would-be lovers have phone sex—and fake their orgasms. It's hard to make appointments even over the phone ("I have my schedule with me—but not my primary schedule"). And a couple talks about how they broke up:

"We didn't really split up, we just sort of drifted apart." "How long has it been since the last time we saw each other?" "Five years."

The basic problem with the film, I think, is that after the comic inspiration wears off, it requires a plot. And although Salwen provides as much of a plot as he can, it's hard to care about a movie story in which none of the characters ever meets one another or really cares about one another. So there you have it: The movie falls under the weight of its own premise.

## The Designated Mourner ★ ★ ★

R, 95 m., 1997

Mike Nichols (Jack), Miranda Richardson (Judy), David de Keyser (Howard). Directed by David Hare and produced by Donna Grey, Mike Nichols, and Hare. Screenplay by Wallace Shawn.

The second time I saw *The Designated Mourner*, I kept my eyes mostly closed, and that was a useful approach. This is not a film so much as a filmed record of an audio performance; the words and the voices carry what is important, and when you open your eyes to look occasionally at the readers, it is like breaking the illusion.

Three people sit behind a table furnished with papers, pencils, cups of water, books. They talk, sometimes to us, rarely to each other, mostly to themselves (or "for the record"). Most of the talking is done by Jack (Mike Nichols), a loquacious journalist who was once married to Judy (Miranda Richardson), the daughter of an intellectual named Howard (David de Keyser). In the unspecified country where they live, a totalitarian regime swept away those who thought too much, finding such men dangerous, and Judy and Howard were among the victims. (This is not the sort of film where it matters that I reveal such details.) Jack is left behind, the "designated mourner for a very special way of life that died."

The film is based on a play by Wallace Shawn, whose works like the screenplay for *My Dinner with André* and the play *Aunt Dan and Lemon* pile up monologues from characters who are looking for something to hang on to. In *The Designated Mourner,* his narrator is an engaging philistine who once agreed with his father-in-law, Howard, that the intellectual life was important—that to understand the poems of John Donne was a valuable achievement. But Jack lost that faith, came to see Howard as an empty vessel, and now seeks to clear his mind of its incessant chatter of secondhand notions, received ideas, and buzzwords. At the end of the play he evokes the ideal of sitting at a café table feeling a gentle evening breeze on his face, and thinking of almost nothing.

Well, is it important to understand the poems of John Donne? I write the question knowing that most people will not be familiar with his poems (although the words "No man is an island" may toll a distant bell). Last night at dinner I found myself next to a woman who talked about the novels of Henry James, which filled me with gratitude, and then about Cynthia Ozick's essays about James, which filled me with amazement—because unless you are lucky enough to live on a university campus, you are likely to do most of your serious reading in solitude.

I feel, stubbornly, that it is important to read Donne and the other masters because they have thought and written at the highest level about what it means to be alive, to be conscious of choices, to consider the approach of death, and to turn those subjects into meditations that are sometimes true, false, cheerful, sad, ironic, bitter, or hopeful. A great writer engages you in a conversation that you are not likely to be able to have with anyone you know.

But we exist under a daily reprieve. We can choose to read John Donne because we live for the moment in a free, stable society that does not make our reading impossible. War, famine, or poverty—the conditions under which most people have always lived—would make reading (not to mention intellectualism) an idle fantasy. *The Designated Mourner* is about a society that does not like readers, and most of its words are spoken by a survivor who stands a little outside and looks wryly at what happened to the members of his circle. He chuckles sometimes at the entire foundation of his idea of himself. His all-important, precious "I" is, he fears, simply a rummage sale of whatever has been shoveled into his memory over the years.

To see this play on a stage would be a pleasure, because then you would be in the same time and space as the actors, and the words would take on the allure of storytelling. To read the play would also be a pleasure, because the scenes being described would take form in your mind. To see this film (directed by David Hare while his stage production was being performed in London with the same actors) is not the best choice. The material suffers by being placed in a frame it is not suited to. It's likely that an audio book of the play or film will be released, and that would be a good way to absorb Shawn's disturbing, introspective, Prufrockian words. I give the film "three stars" as a compromise between its material and the presentation.

At the end, I concluded: It is better to be able to read John Donne than not, but if the tide turns against you, it isn't likely to do you much good. Of course, in a nutshell, that's life.

## Desperate Measures ★ ★

R, 100 m., 1998

Michael Keaton (Peter McCabe), Andy Garcia (Frank Connor), Brian Cox (Jeremiah Cassidy), Marcia Gay Harden (Samantha Hawkins), Erik King (Nate Oliver), Efrain Figueroa (Vargus), Joseph Cross (Matthew Connor), Janel Maloney (Sarah Davis). Directed by Barbet Schroeder and produced by Schroeder, Susan Hoffman, Gary Foster, and Lee Rich. Screenplay by David Klass, Henry Bean, and Neal Jimenez.

*Desperate Measures* opens with the same hook as *Hard Rain:* What looks like a robbery turns out to be an action by the good guys. *Hard Rain* really cheated (hey—they're not robbers; they're armored car drivers!). *Desperate Measures,* which is a better movie, has a better gimmick. A raid is staged on government computers in order to search for the perfect DNA match for a kid who is dying and needs a bone marrow transplant.

Andy Garcia plays a cop named Connor, the father who will do anything to save his son's life. Searching a national database, he discovers that only one man has the proper DNA. He's Peter McCabe (Michael Keaton), a psychopath now in prison after killing four people, including a fellow inmate. Will McCabe agree to become a bone marrow donor? Why should he? Offered the opportunity, he reflects on the alternative: "After all these years of being locked up, I'm given the opportunity to kill again."

But McCabe eventually caves in, after a laundry list of demands including better prison quarters and all the cigarettes he wants. Turns out it's all a trick. Using blueprints available (of course) on the Internet, he plans an elaborate escape from the hospital where he's taken to have the tricky operation. How does he get out of the handcuffs? How does he ward off the effects of anesthesia? It's all here. It's not convincing, but it's here.

All of this is prelude to the movie's real plot, which centers on the fact that McCabe must remain alive in order for his bone marrow to be of any use to little Matthew, the dying kid. McCabe sets people on fire during his escape attempt and uses violence as he flees a police dragnet. And Connor finds himself in the curious position of trying to shield this vicious killer, sometimes with his own body, against fellow policemen who might kill him.

What is the proper morality here? Or, as a police official (Brian Cox) succinctly asks, "How many people are gonna have to die here tonight so that kid of yours can live?" It's a good question, and explored a different way in a more thoughtful movie, it might have generated some genuine drama.

*Desperate Measures* is, unfortunately, only masquerading as a thoughtful movie that's really about something. At heart, it's an action thriller—a chase picture. It has all the usual implausible or impossible stunts, the highway carnage, the jumps off bridges, the slides down laundry chutes, and other feats that make it more of a video game than a drama.

Too bad, because the actors could have brought class to better material. Michael Keaton, an actor who can convincingly project intelligence, is intriguing as McCabe, a thinker who likes to toy with people he can control. Garcia's dilemma as a cop and a father is handled well in a handful of quiet scenes (especially in conversations with pediatrician Marcia Gay Harden), and his son (Joseph Cross) is a smart kid who asks all the right questions at the wrong times.

But the movie would rather jolly along an action audience than play fair with its material, and so we're treated to the usual, standard, obligatory bankrupt action dreck: kinetic energy on autopilot. Too bad. The director, Barbet Schroeder, has made some good movies *(Barfly, Reversal of Fortune, Single White Female).* This time he's a hired gun. He could have made a better movie, I imagine, if the producers had wanted him to, but sometimes that's just not the way it works.

## Devil's Advocate ★ ★ ½

R, 138 m., 1997

Keanu Reeves (Kevin Lomax), Al Pacino (John Milton), Charlize Theron (Mary Ann Lomax), Jeffrey Jones (Eddie Barzoon), Judith Ivey (Mrs. Lomax), Craig T. Nelson (Alexander Cullen), Connie Nielsen (Christabella), Tamara Tunie (Jackie Heath). Directed by Taylor Hackford and produced by Arnon Milchan, Arnold Kopelson, and Anne Kopelson. Screenplay by Jonathan Lemkin and Tony Gilroy.

Most movies about lawyers involve selling their souls to the devil, but *Devil's Advocate* is the first in which the devil gets more dialogue than the lawyers. The movie chronicles the descent of Kevin Lomax (Keanu Reeves), a small-time legal star from Florida, into the depths of the New York big time. Recruited by a powerful Manhattan law firm, he finds himself defending goat killers and real estate tycoons for a boss named John Milton, who offers him a paradise found.

Milton (Al Pacino) is the devil. That is a secret reserved for the second hour of the film, although the title hints it, the posters and TV commercials reveal it, and by the time it arrives Lomax is the only character who hasn't suspected. Charming, persuasive, with a wise little cackle, Milton sends a recruiter to Florida, where Lomax is an undefeated master of picking juries that do not convict. He wants the young man to join his team, and tempts him not on a mountaintop but on a rooftop.

The scene of the first meeting between Milton and Lomax, on a skyscraper roof, scores a stunning visual impact. The production designer, Bruno Rubeo, has created a spectacular effect: a water garden in the sky, with pool surfaces spilling over the edges of the building, so that water and sky seem to meet without any architectural separation. The two men walk perilously close to the edge, as the director, Taylor Hackford, plays with vertigo to suggest that Lomax is being offered all of Manhattan at his feet—and also the possibility of a great and sudden fall.

The young lawyer is impressed. So, at first, is his wife, Mary Ann (Charlize Theron), who can't believe it when Milton offers them a three-bedroom apartment in a luxurious Fifth Avenue co-op. Only Lomax's Bible-quoting mother (Judith Ivey) has her doubts, quoting scripture about Sodom, Gomorrah, and other keywords that pop into the mind when Manhattan is mentioned. Her advice, indeed, seems increasingly sound as the film progresses.

Lomax becomes obsessed with his job, ignoring his wife and drawing closer to a sexy woman at the office (Connie Nielsen). And the wife, obsessed with having a baby, begins to come apart. She has the film's first supernatural vision, when she sees a demon materialize in the face and body of a helpful neighbor (Tamara Tunie), and soon she's begging to go back to Gainesville.

The satanic character is played by Pacino with relish bordering on glee. Reeves in contrast is sober and serious—the straight man. That's the correct choice for his role, but it leaves Pacino with many of the best lines ("I'm maybe the last humanist. The twentieth century was entirely mine. I'm perking!") *Devil's Advocate* is neither fish nor fowl: It is not a serious film about its subject, nor is it quite a dark comedy, despite some of Pacino's good lines. The epilogue, indeed, cheats in a way I thought had been left behind in grade school. And yet there are splendid moments.

I liked the way Hackford used speeded-up photography, as in *Koyaanisqatsi*, to indicate the passage of time; the fact that Milton's office looks the way Satan's might look if he had a great designer; the nice little throwaways, as when the goat killer (Delroy Lindo) apparently causes the prosecutor to have a coughing fit. The casting is good in small roles, including Heather Matarazzo, from *Welcome to the Dollhouse*, as the victim in an early courtroom scene.

But the movie never fully engaged me; my mind raced ahead of the plot, and the John Grisham stuff clashed with the *Exorcist* stuff. Still, I enjoyed Pacino. Looking less deeply wrinkled than of late, his face smooth with satanic self-contentment, he relishes the details, such as that Milton likes to stand in front of fires and always travels by subway. The phantasmagorical final confrontation between the two men, set to the Sinatra version of "It Happened in Monterey," ranges from melodrama to camp ("You're the anti-Christ!" "Whatever."). It includes an extraordinary special effect of a marble bas-relief that comes to life and melts into a licentious orgy. If the whole film were as good as its production design, we'd really have something here.

## The Devil's Own ★ ★ ½

R, 107 m., 1997

Harrison Ford (Tom O'Meara), Brad Pitt (McGuire/Devaney), Margaret Colin (Sheila O'Meara), Rubén Blades (Edwin Diaz), Treat Williams (Billy Burke), George Hearn (Peter Fitzsimmons), Mitchell Ryan (Chief Jim Kelly), Natascha McElhone (Megan Doherty). Directed by Alan J. Pakula and produced by Lawrence Gordon and Robert F. Colesberry. Screenplay by Robert Mark Kamen and Kevin Jarre, based on a story by Jarre.

*"It's not an American story. It's an Irish one."*
—Brad Pitt in *The Devil's Own*

Ah, but that's just where he's wrong. *The Devil's Own* is an American story, to such a degree that American audiences will be able to watch this movie in total ignorance of the history of Northern Ireland, and be none the wiser at the end. Imagine this: One of the key characters is an Irish Republican Army leader who has killed more than twenty men and goes to America to buy guided missiles—and at no point in the movie, to the best of my recollection, are the words "Catholic" or "Protestant" ever uttered, even though sectarian conflict is at the heart of the Troubles.

This is history lite. In the opening scenes, an eight-year-old boy is having dinner with his family when masked men burst into their cottage and shoot his father dead. Flash forward twenty years, and now Francis McGuire (Brad Pitt) has been cornered in a Belfast hideout. There's a shoot-out with police and British troops, and then he escapes out the back way (with hundreds of men, as the British somehow didn't think of the rear door). We know the father was shot by either British troops or Protestant militants (the movie doesn't bother to say), and we gather McGuire is in the IRA. But the issues involved between the two sides are never mentioned, even obliquely; for all we learn, he's avenging his father's death and that's it.

Soon he's in America, where an Irish-American judge gets him a place to live, in the basement of an honest cop named Tom O'Meara (Harrison Ford). O'Meara knows nothing about the past of the man, now calling himself Rory Devaney. He's just being a good Samaritan. Ask yourself this: How many cops, knowing what they know about the dangers of modern society, would allow a complete stranger with no job to live under the same roof with the cop's wife and daughters?

But don't ask. O'Meara is simply being a nice guy. Soon we learn that Devaney has lots of money for buying guided missiles from a creep named Billy Burke (Treat Williams). And we learn that O'Meara is a very good cop, honest and unswerving. There are several scenes in which we see him avoiding the use of force and condemning cops who shoot first and ask questions later. When his partner (Rubén Blades) does just that, it forces a crisis of conscience—but it doesn't pay off; it simply sets up the cop's determination, later in the film, to bring in Devaney alive.

Both Pitt and Ford have criticized this film because, they say, it started shooting without a completed screenplay. I can believe that. Consider that Pitt, while nominally the villain, is seen in an attractive light, while a British intelligence operative is seen as a sleazeball, and yet Ford, fearing the sleazeball wants to kill Pitt, dedicates himself to bringing him in alive—so he can be brought to trial by the sleazeball for crimes which the IRA, of course, considers to be justified acts of war. The moral reasoning in the film is so confusing that only by completely sidestepping it can the plot work at all.

And sidestep it does. Harrison Ford and Brad Pitt are enormously appealing and gifted actors, and to the degree that the movie works, it's because of them. Using all the gifts of the actor's craft, they're able to sell scenes that don't make sense and don't add up. Even in a final confrontation, they're so convincing that only later do we ask ourselves, hey, did Devaney really plan to sail across the North Atlantic Ocean in a leaky old tugboat?

*The Devil's Own* (what does the title mean?) plays better if you don't give it a single thought and just let the knee-jerk cues dictate your emotions. Handsome guy's father is killed, so he fights back (for personal, not political reasons). Nice-guy cop likes Irish kid, but gets frosted when bad guys (British? Irish turncoats?) invade his home looking for kid. Cop wants to arrest kid, yet doesn't want to see him gunned down by British creeps. All criminals deserve their rights, cop believes; fine, except what opinion, if any, does cop have about terrorism or the presumed use of missiles against civilian targets? (Cop never, during entire movie, expresses any opinion about long history of struggle involving British, Northern Irish, and IRA.)

I've got a notion for a quick rewrite: Leave out Ireland altogether and make it a revenge picture. Or deal with Ireland intelligently, as *In the Name of the Father, Michael Collins,* and *Cal* have. Either way, the film should make it clear whether it considers the Brad Pitt character to be a hero or villain. My best guess is he's a villain given a moral touch-up because he's also a movie star. He may be a cold-blooded terrorist, but he's our cold-blooded terrorist, and, saints preserve us, isn't he a likable lad?

## Diabolique ★ ★

R, 108 m., 1996

Sharon Stone (Nicole), Isabelle Adjani (Mia), Chazz Palminteri (Guy Baran), Kathy Bates (Shirley), Spalding Gray (Simon Veach), Alan Garfield (Leo Kazman), Adam Hann-Byrd (Erik). Directed by Jeremiah Chechik and produced by Marvin Worth and James G. Robinson. Screenplay by Don Roos.

*Diabolique* isn't a remake of the classic 1955 French thriller so much as a repudiation of it. It takes the famous original ending—which audiences were urged not to reveal—and discards its elegance and wit in favor of a ludicrous struggle in which one character gets a rake embedded in the skull and a policewoman gives her blessing to a homicide. Film lovers should study the two *Diaboliques* side by side in order to see how the Hollywood assembly line trashed its treasure from the past.

"Don't be a devil," the 1955 film pleaded in its

closing credits. "Don't ruin the interest your friends could have in this film. Don't tell them what you saw." The warning was timely, because *Diabolique* depends on a plot reversal that comes as a complete surprise. We know *something* is coming—but not that! The movie depended, too, on its sense of brooding evil, as murder comes to a third-rate provincial boarding school occupied by a shady cast of characters.

The 1996 *Diabolique* begins promisingly and at times is almost a line-by-line, even shot-by-shot, remake of Henri-Georges Clouzot's film. Since the original was so cleverly constructed, that's not a bad idea. (Hitchcock wanted to buy the rights and remake it, but the authors of the original book wrote *Vertigo* for him instead.) If the whole movie had been a faithful remake, I would have had no complaints. But alas, *after* the surprise ending of the original story, the new version adds another surprise ending, and then another. The final scenes suggest that the filmmakers have contempt for the intelligence and taste of the audience. They throw in slasher elements and violate the logic of two important characters just for a cheap payoff.

As the film opens, we meet a stingy bully named Guy Baran (Chazz Palminteri), who runs a shabby boarding school owned by his timid wife, Mia (Isabelle Adjani). Guy has been having an affair with a tough teacher named Nicole (Sharon Stone), who walks around with a cigarette stuck in her mug and makes biting remarks. (A crew making a promotional film "wants to shoot the kitchen crew," and Nicole says, "Take a number.") The cast is not the problem with the film; the acting would have distinguished a worthier screenplay. Stone finds an acid edge to Nicole, and I liked the way, when Mia asked "Am I alive?" she answered, "No, you're dead. This is Heaven, and I'm the Virgin Mary." Adjani, as the weak young wife, is vulnerable and impressionable. And Palminteri seems admirably contemptible.

But their context is missing. The school was carefully established in the 1955 film, but here the students are a backdrop of faceless extras. The remake also throws overboard two colorful teachers (played here by Spalding Gray and Alan Garfield). In the original, they added to the school's fog of corruption. Here, they disappear after a brief duet. Modern movies spend lots of money on their stars and want to keep them in the center of the screen as much as possible, so supporting characters and atmosphere get shoved aside.

We learn gradually that Mia and Nicole now both have reason to hate Guy, and that together they plan to murder him. The murder and its grisly techniques are *not* the surprise you're not supposed to reveal. Guy is drowned according to plan in a bathtub and his body dumped in the school pool, so that when he's discovered it will be assumed he got drunk and fell in. Then his body seems to disappear from the pool. Is he really dead or not?

Enter a police inspector (Kathy Bates), who wanders into the case before it really is a case, and stays around asking questions. Bates is a wonderful actress, but her role has been mutilated. The inspector in the original *Diabolique* was the inspiration for Peter Falk's *Colombo* character—right down to the shabby raincoat, the constant cigar, and the absentminded questions. Bates is not given any of that material to work with, and her final scene in the film makes a travesty of the character.

Now I must tread carefully. I will try not to give away crucial details, and yet still complain about them. If you see the movie, remember afterward a particular shot of Guy after he has been drowned in the tub. The women have covered his body with a shower curtain, turned out the light, left the room and locked the door. Now we see Guy underwater, a tiny bubble escaping from his mouth. This shot is cheating.

There's more cheating in the final scenes. The elegance of the original was in the way the inspector saw through the plot and orchestrated its conclusion. The movie ended on a note of grim, macabre irony. But not here, where everyone appears onstage for a silly struggle, an evil character suddenly develops a sentimental side, and the inspector not only condones a crime, *but does so on the basis of knowledge there is no way, at that point, she could have possessed!*

A few years ago there was a brilliant European thriller named *The Vanishing.* It was just about perfect. Then it was remade into an American film in which the dead leaped from graves, a heroic woman slammed a killer over the head with a shovel and the original ending—so final, so sad, so faultless—was trashed. Now comes *Diabolique,* and it gets the same treatment. Why bother to remake *Diabolique* if you don't love it?

Why not just remake a slasher movie and let the dead rest in peace?

### Different for Girls ★ ★ ★

R, 101 m., 1997

Steven Mackintosh (Kim Foyle), Rupert Graves (Paul Prentice), Miriam Margolyes (Pamela), Saskia Reeves (Jean), Charlotte Coleman (Alison), Neil Dudgeon (Neil), Nisha K. Nayar (Angela), Lia Williams (Defense Solicitor). Directed by Richard Spence and produced by John Chapman. Screenplay by Tony Marchant.

The unexamined mystery at the heart of *Different for Girls* is—what, exactly, does Paul see in Kim? Paul is a rowdy motorbike messenger who roars through the streets and punk clubs of London. Kim, whose name was once Karl, is a postoperative transsexual. "I am straight, you know," Paul tells Kim. "So am I," she replies.

They knew each other sixteen years ago at a boarding school, and the opening titles include a flashback to those days. Karl is taunted in the shower by his gay-bashing schoolmates, and Paul gallantly comes to the rescue. When they meet again after a minor traffic accident, Paul recognizes the former Karl almost at once, but Kim—as she now is—at first denies they knew each other.

Of course, they did. But in what way? Was Paul (Rupert Graves) sexually attracted in his school days? Or is he fascinated only now by the unexplored country of gender swapping? He asks Kim (Steven Macintosh) out for lunch, and then causes a scene that cuts the date short (deliberately, Kim senses). He apologizes with flowers and asks her out again, but it's clear he's deeply conflicted: He is attracted to this mannish woman, but reluctant to admit it, to her or to himself.

*Different for Girls* follows the time-honored conventions of the romantic comedy, in which opposites attract despite obstacles. Paul is macho, he already has a girlfriend, he likes loud music, he gets drunk. Kim wants to blend in and disappear. Even her clothes give that message: She wears the sort of conservative fashions a nun might choose as civilian garb. If it's a mystery what Paul thinks of her, it's a puzzle why she's attracted to him. Immature and reckless, he lands them both in jail one night by exposing himself in public (not as a sexual act, but to make a point during a drunken rant).

The movie's effect depends on the performance by Mackintosh, as Kim. The actor does not look persuasively feminine, and indeed many of the other characters in the movie immediately read Kim as a transvestite. But the point of the movie is not deception, as it was in *The Crying Game*. It is self-discovery. Kim considers herself a woman born into a man's body, and explains herself patiently to Paul: the confusion, the counseling, the gender reassignment surgery, the hormones. As Kim explains the changes in her body, Paul discovers to his horror that he has grown aroused. And here is the interesting question: Is Paul aroused by Kim's description of her breasts and hips, or by the fact that the description comes from someone Paul used to know as a man?

"I always thought you was gay," Paul says. "So did I," Kim says. We believe Kim. But what about Paul, who drops his current girlfriend in a second to circle with fascination around this person he has nothing in common with? If the movie had explored the dynamic of Paul's attraction, it might have been more honest. Instead, it moves sideways into an unnecessary subplot involving Kim's sister (Saskia Reeves) and her husband, an army career officer (Neil Dudgeon), haunted by his infertility. The obvious point is that there is more to being a man (or a woman) than reproduction. But we knew that.

As Kim, Mackintosh's performance finds and holds the right notes of shyness, determination, privacy, and love. Yes, Kim is attracted to Paul—probably because she always was, even in prep school. Attracted not by the swashbuckling, irresponsible lifestyle, but by the good heart that inspired Paul to come to the rescue. Despite her sex change, Kim is less complicated than Paul: What you see is what you get with her, while Paul doesn't know how to present himself or how to give.

Transsexuality is so new as a subject for films that the movie can be excused, I suppose, for thinking it is about Kim. But I wish *Different for Girls* had explored Paul's struggle with his own feelings. Is he attracted to Kim because it gives him an excuse to date a boy who is a girl? Or is he attracted to the good feminine and human qualities Kim definitely has? Or it is simply fascination with Kim's redefinition of herself? The movie ends on a conventional romantic note, leaving all of those questions unasked. Here is one of those rare films where the sequel would be infinitely more intriguing than the original.

### The Disappearance of Garcia Lorca ★ ★ ★

R, 109 m., 1997

Esai Morales (Ricardo), Edward James Olmos (Lozano), Andy Garcia (Federico García Lorca), Jeroen Krabbe (Colonel Aguirre), Giancarlo Giannini (Taxi), Miguel Ferrer (Centeno), Marcela Walerstein (Maria Eugenia), Eusebio Lazaro (Vicente Fernandez). Directed by Marcos Zurinaga and produced by Enrique Cerezo and Marcos Zurinaga. Screenplay by Zurinaga, Juan Antonio Ramos, and Neil Cohen, based on the books *The Assassination of Federico Garcia Lorca* and *Federico Garcia Lorca: A Life* by Ian Gibson.

Near the beginning of *The Disappearance of Garcia Lorca*, a teenage boy attends an opening night in Madrid in 1934—a performance of a work by the poet and playwright Federico García Lorca. Twenty years later he recalls, "That night I learned that poetry could be an act of violence." Backstage, he is introduced to the poet, who asks, "How old are you?" "Fourteen," he replies. "So am I," says the poet, adding, "Remember me."

Not long after, García Lorca is dead, another victim of the Spanish civil war. He had thought perhaps he was too visible to be assassinated by the forces of the fascist rebel Franco, but he was wrong. And ever since there has been a veil of mystery around the questions of how García Lorca was killed, and by whom.

This movie, based on two books by Ian Gibson, is a reconstruction and speculation, told through the eyes of the young boy, Ricardo, who moves with his family to Puerto Rico, and tells his father one day in 1954 that he intends to return to Spain and try to find out what happened. For his father, all of that is in the past and, with Franco still in power, best left there. But the boy, now grown to manhood and played by Esai Morales, returns anyway, and begins to unravel the secrets of the death.

García Lorca, played by Andy Garcia, is seen in the movie as an artist whose very existence is a challenge to the insurgents. What is often forgotten about Spain, because it reverses the usual pattern, is that the elected government was left-wing, and the rebels were fascists; Franco was supported by Hitler and Mussolini, and the air battles in Spain were seen by historians as a dress rehearsal for the Luftwaffe.

To the rebels, the famous poet was a symbol, and his poetry like a red flag at a bullfight. But García Lorca was also well connected, with influence, with powerful friends. There is a scene in the movie where he strides confidently from a house to where some military men are beating his friend; he thinks his prestige will be enough to stop them, but he is wrong, and a fascist goon named Centeno (Miguel Ferrer) slugs him in the stomach. García Lorca does not quite realize even after this event that his society has changed fundamentally, that a new class is taking power, that he is doomed.

Returning to Spain in 1954, Ricardo meets a publisher named Lozano (Edward James Olmos), who is bringing out a handsome edition of García Lorca's works. "But . . . didn't you arrest him?" Ricardo asks. Lozano replies, "You're a brave man, Ricardo. No one else has been brave enough to say that to me." Lozano did sign the arrest order, and was possibly present at the death, along with others who would now rewrite their roles in history.

The lesson apparently is that poets who are alive are a threat to repression, but dead poets can be safely embalmed as national treasures or legends. The film is also about how the secrets of the past still hold their power for revenge, if they are exposed, and in 1954 there are many people still alive who know how and why García Lorca was killed—people whose current lives cannot accommodate that knowledge, so that Ricardo's quest is a threat.

Ricardo enters a Madrid where there are suspicious eyes and ears everywhere, and a taxi driver (Giancarlo Giannini) may be a friend or a spy. Where nothing is simple, and people who thought they had sufficient reason in 1934 to side with the fascists and the Third Reich no longer wish their association to be recalled. The movie is a murder investigation, really, except that Ricardo will also be discovering things about his own origin that he does not suspect.

Do people read García Lorca today? Or poetry in general? Not many, I suppose. I took down my book of his poems and read some of them after seeing the movie, and felt the passion. But

García Lorca is perhaps more important today as a symbol than as a poet, and this film is really not so much about him as about memory and history—about how poets are given most of their power not by those who love them, but by those who fear them.

## Doctor Dolittle ★ ★ ★

PG-13, 90 m., 1998

Eddie Murphy (Dr. John Dolittle), Ossie Davis (Archer Dolittle), Oliver Platt (Dr. Mark Weller), Peter Boyle (Calloway), Richard Schiff (Dr. Gene Reiss), Kristen Wilson (Lisa), Jeffrey Tambor (Dr. Fish), Kyla Pratt (Maya). Directed by Betty Thomas and produced by John Davis, David T. Friendly, and Joseph M. Singer. Screenplay by Nat Mauldin and Larry Levin.

*Doctor Dolittle* is a gross-out movie, yes, and it's going to be criticized by those who can't believe it got a PG-13 rating. Like Eddie Murphy's previous film, *The Nutty Professor*, it has a lot of jokes about bodily functions. It breaks some new ground, with a scene where the Murphy character gives the kiss of life to a rat, and when a pigeon makes a low-level bombing run at Oliver Platt's nostrils. And of course, there's the scene where the Murphy character, as a little boy, learns from his dog why dogs sniff each other's behinds, and then tries the same tactic in checking out the new school principal.

Is this material a mistake? I don't think so. Kids have a healthy interest in bodily functions, and if you don't believe me, ask Captain Mike, who runs a kiddie playland in Sawyer, Michigan, and gives away an amazing number of Whoopee Cushions as free prizes. Too many adults have a tendency to confuse bad taste with evil influences; it's hard for them to see that the activities in *Doctor Dolittle,* while rude and vulgar, are not violent or antisocial. The movie will not harm anyone, and in the audience I saw it with, lots of parents and kids seemed to be laughing together.

The movie stars Murphy as John Dolittle, who as a child could talk to the animals (there's a gem of an opening scene in which he chats matter-of-factly with his dog, whose voice is by Ellen DeGeneres, about what dogs think about people). The boy grows out of this stage, however, and even goes through an animal-hating phase before he knocks his head in a car accident and regains his inner ear for animals.

By now Murphy is grown up, a famous doctor whose partner (Platt) is in a lather to sell out their medical operation to an HMO. But Murphy gets seriously distracted by his new insights into animals, and on the night of a big business meeting he's more interested in emergency treatment for an ailing tiger from the zoo. There's also trouble with his despairing family, which has him committed to a mental institution.

Murphy is essentially the straight man in the movie; most of the laughs belong to the animals, who are brash and outspoken—especially Rodney the guinea pig, voiced by Chris Rock. Albert Brooks finds a nice long-suffering note as the ailing tiger, and Reni Santoni and John Leguizamo have some nice zingers as the laboratory rats who are brought back to life by Dolittle's first aid: "You want gratitude? Get a hamster." Some of the animals are real. Most of them are creations of the Jim Henson muppet builders. All of them look real enough, and there's some nice physical humor in a scene where Rodney gets drenched, dries itself out under a blower, and then enjoys a quick massage.

Murphy, I think, finds the right strategy in acting opposite this menagerie: He's mostly quiet, calm, not trying too hard for laughs; the overall tone of the movie, despite the gross material, is one of sweetness and gentleness. Sure, a lot of the stuff is in bad taste, but I'll never forget Mel Brooks's defense of one of his movies: "Vulgar? It rises *below* vulgarity."

## Don't Look Back ★ ★ ★

NO MPAA RATING, 96 m., 1967 (rereleased 1998)

A documentary directed by D. A. Pennebaker and produced by Albert Grossman, John Court, and Leacock-Pennebaker Inc. With Bob Dylan, Joan Baez, Bob Neuwirth, Donovan, Tito Burns, and Albert Grossman.

What a jerk Bob Dylan was in 1965. What an immature, self-important, inflated, cruel, shallow little creature, lacking in empathy and contemptuous of anyone who was not himself or his lackey. Did we actually once take this twerp as our folk god?

I scribbled down these and other observations as I watched the newly restored print of *Don't Look Back,* the 1967 documentary about Dylan's 1965 concert tour of England. And I was asking myself: Surely I didn't fall for this at the time? I tried to remember the review I wrote when the movie was new. Was I so much under the Dylan spell that I couldn't see his weakness of character?

Take the two scenes, for example, where he mercilessly puts down a couple of hardworking interviewers who are only trying to do their job (i.e., give Dylan more publicity), while a roomful of Dylan yes-men, groupies, and foot-kissers join in the jeers. I was chilled by the possibility that I reacted to these scenes differently the first time around, falling for Dylan's rude and nearly illiterate word games as he pontificates about "truth."

I hurried home and burrowed into my files for the 1967 review of *Don't Look Back,* and was relieved to discover that, even then, I had my senses about me. "Those who consider Dylan a lone, ethical figure standing up against the phonies will discover after seeing this film," I wrote, "that they have lost their hero. Dylan reveals himself, alas, to have clay feet like all the rest of us. He is immature, petty, vindictive, lacking a sense of humor, overly impressed with his own importance and not very bright." Thank God I was not deceived. I gave the movie three stars, and still do, for its alarming insights.

Of course there is the music. Always the music. I'm listening to "Highway 61 Revisited" as I write these words. I like his music, and I like his whiny, nasal delivery of it; it speaks to the eternal misunderstood complainer in all of us. I remember the thrill we all felt as undergraduates when we first heard "Blowin' in the Wind." Of course, at the time we thought *we* were the answer, my friends, but we were young and hadn't seen this movie.

As a musician, Dylan has endured and triumphed. Perhaps he has also grown and matured as a human being, and is today a nice guy with an infectious sense of humor and a certain soft-spoken modesty. Or maybe not. I don't know. What I do know is that D. A. Pennebaker's 1967 film, which invented the rock documentary, is like a time capsule from just that period when Sgt. Pepper was steamrollering Mr. Tambourine Man. "You don't ask the Beatles those questions, do you?" Dylan says to one reporter. To which the only possible answer was, Bob, you just don't know the half of it.

Another irony is that a true folk goddess, Joan Baez, with her remarkable voice, presence, and soul, tags along during the early scenes, barely acknowledged by Dylan. She brings a glow to the film by singing "Love Is a Four-Letter Word" in a hotel room one night, and then disappears from the film, unremarked. My guess is that she'd had enough.

The movie is like a low-rent version of the rock concert documentaries that would follow. Dylan is badgered by a room full of journalists at a press conference—but it's a small room, with only half a dozen reporters. He insults them, lacking the Beatles' saving grace of wit. He's mobbed by fans—hundreds, not thousands. He fills Royal Albert Hall, not Wembley Stadium. He reminds me of that mouse floating down the Chicago River on its back, signaling for the drawbridge to be raised.

Sometimes you simply cannot imagine what he, or the filmmakers, were thinking. "How did you start?" he's asked at a press conference. Cut to a scene in a southern cotton field. Dylan stands in front of a pickup truck with some old black field hands sitting on it. He sings a song. Are we supposed to think he rode the rails and bummed in hobo jungles and felt proletarian solidarity with the workers, like Woody Guthrie, Pete Seeger, or Ramblin' Jack Elliott? I was reminded of Steve Martin in *The Jerk* saying, "I was born a poor black child." The field hands break into grateful applause, as the scene dissolves into a thunderous London concert ovation. Give us a break.

If Dylan sees this rerelease, I hope he cringes. We were all callow once, but it is a curable condition. A guy from *Time* magazine comes to interview him. "I know more about what you do just by looking at you than you'll ever be able to know about me," Dylan tells him, little suspecting how much we know just by looking at him. He suggests that the magazine try printing the truth. And what would that be? "A photo of a tramp vomiting into a sewer, and next to it a picture of Rockefeller," suggests the man described in a recent review as "one of the most significant artists of the second half of the twentieth century." Significance I will grant him. More than we knew.

## Donnie Brasco ★ ★ ★ ½

R, 121 m., 1997

Al Pacino (Lefty Ruggiero), Johnny Depp (Joe/Donnie), Michael Madsen (Sonny), Bruno Kirby (Nicky), Anne Heche (Maggie), James Russo (Paulie), Andrew Parks (Hollman). Directed by Mike Newell and produced by Mark Johnson, Barry Levinson, Louis DiGiaimo, and Gail Mutrux. Screenplay by Paul Attanasio, based on the book *Donnie Brasco: My Undercover Life in the Mafia,* by Joseph Pistone and Richard Woodley.

Norman Mailer told us tough guys don't dance, but in the movies it's mostly tough guys who do dance. We're so leery of close emotional bonds between men that the movies are only comfortable showing them if the guys are cops, jocks, soldiers, or Mafioso. Beneath everything else, *Donnie Brasco* is the story of two men who grow to love one another within the framework of a teacher-student relationship. It's not about sex. It's about need.

The movie opens in a New York coffee shop that's a hangout for the mob. A young guy named Donnie (Johnny Depp) comes in and talks disrespectfully to an older guy named Lefty (Al Pacino). Lefty can't believe his ears: "You're calling me a dumbski? You know who you're talkin' to? Lefty from Mulberry Street!" As if that means anything.

Actually, though, it means a lot to Donnie Brasco, whose real name is Joe Pistone, and who is an undercover agent for the FBI. He gradually wins Lefty's trust, and it becomes clear that Lefty badly needs someone to trust; he has cancer, his son is a junkie, and his mob career is going nowhere. Donnie is a good-looking kid who listens well, and Lefty desperately needs to be a mentor. In another world he would have been your favorite high school teacher.

"If I say you're a friend of mine, that means you're connected," Lefty explains to Donnie. "If I say you're a friend of ours, that means you're a made guy. If I introduce you, I'm responsible for you. Anything wrong with you, I go down."

The movie is based on a 1978 book inspired by the real "Donnie Brasco" case (its author is still living in the government protection program). The story plays like a companion to *GoodFellas,* with the same lore, the same fierce Mafia code, the same alternation between sudden violence and weird comedy. (At one point Lefty is summoned to a meeting with his boss and expects to be killed. Instead, he's given a present—a lion, because he likes to watch wild animals on videos.)

The British director Mike Newell, whose biggest hit was *Four Weddings and a Funeral,* might seem like a strange choice for this material, but he's the right one because the movie is not really about violence or action, it's about friendship. We can see immediately why Lefty is drawn to Donnie, but it takes a little longer to see why Donnie begins to like Lefty. After all, a guy risks his life because he trusts you, you can't help feeling like a rat if you're double-crossing him.

Michael Madsen plays the boss Lefty reports to. He's tall, tough, relentless—and scared, too, because when he gets bumped up a notch, the job includes a $50,000 monthly payment to the guy above him. A lot of the time these guys spend time hanging around their social club, playing cards, and complaining that business is bad. In this movie Mafia guys don't get away with anything: With them it's work, work, work, just like with everybody else.

Donnie has some ideas for them, including a club in Florida that he thinks might make them some money. But opening night goes wrong, and although they suspect a stoolie in their midst, what they do not suspect is that a rival mob faction was responsible. Everytime I see a Mafia movie, I wonder how any Mafiosi can still be alive, given the rate of sudden, violent attrition and the willingness to shoot first and find out the rest of the facts later.

The Florida project and the other jobs are a backdrop for the relationship between Donnie and Lefty, which is complicated because the FBI agent has a wife and kids squirreled away in the suburbs, where they go for weeks at a time without hearing from him. He can't even tell them what he does (nor would they believe him). "I pretend I'm a widow," his wife tells him.

Eventually all of the threads, personal and criminal, come down to one moment when Lefty either will or will not act on what he knows, or thinks he knows. As the two men face their moment of truth, we are reminded what fine acting the movie contains. We expect it from Pacino, who is on ground he knows well, and who is poignant and gentle as a man who is "just a spoke in the wheel," a loyal soldier who lives and dies by the rules. For Johnny Depp, *Donnie Brasco* breaks new ground; he seems a little older here, a little wearier, and he makes the transition from stoolie to friend one subtle step at a time.

The violence in this movie is gruesome (a scene involving the disposal of bodies is particularly graphic). But the movie has many human qualities, and contains what will be remembered as one of Pacino's finest scenes. At an important moment in his life, he puts some things in a drawer. He starts to leave, then thinks again, turns back, and leaves the drawer ajar. What this implies and how it plays creates the perfect ending for the film, which fades to black—only to start up again with unnecessary footnotes. No matter; I'll remember that scene.

## Double Team ★ ★

R, 90 m., 1997

Jean-Claude Van Damme (Jack Quinn), Mickey Rourke (Stavros), Dennis Rodman (Yaz), Natacha Lindinger (Katherine), Paul Freeman (Goldsmythe), Jay Benedict (CIA Agent Brandon), Rob Diem (Dieter Staal). Directed by Tsui Hark and produced by Moshe Diamant. Screenplay by Don Jakoby and Paul Mones.

*Double Team* is one of the most preposterous action films ever made, and I do not mean that as a criticism. It will give you some notion of this movie's strangeness if I tell you that Dennis Rodman does not play the most peculiar character.

Oh, he's the weirdest *looking*, all right. But consider what Mickey Rourke's villain does: Burning for vengeance on Jean-Claude Van Damme, he captures Van Damme's newborn son and puts the tot in the center of the Roman Coliseum, surrounded by land mines and threatened by a prowling tiger. "If you live, you'll know your son," he shouts. "If not—I'll raise him as my own."

Van Damme plays Jack Quinn, a counterterrorist operative recruited for one last assignment. Scribbling madly in the dark, I got down the highlights of his briefing. If you read closely, you may notice a contradiction between the fourth and sixth sentences: "You're a hunter, Jack. You miss the game. Stavros is bad. And we want him alive. We've got a Delta team prepped and waiting for you at Antwerp. Face it, Jack—you can't retire until he dies."

In Antwerp, Van Damme meets Yaz (Rodman) in an omnisexual club in the red-light district, and Rodman sets him up with weapons from such a formidable workshop that Van Damme calls him "Santa." Rodman: "I may not have reindeer, but I do have the best elves in the business." Stavros (Rourke) is also in Antwerp, and takes his child to an amusement park, where the kid is killed in a shoot-out.

Stavros escapes, and as punishment Van Damme is banished to the Colony, a think tank for those "too valuable to kill—too dangerous to set free." Determined to escape and rejoin his pregnant wife, Van Damme cuts off his thumbprint to fool a security device. His getaway is done via aerial stunts, and indeed all the stunt work and special effects are impressive; the direction is by Tsui Hark of Hong Kong, famous for the *Chinese Ghost Story* films.

The trail leads to Rome. Van Damme is joined by Rodman. They jump from a plane without parachutes and land inside a giant basketball, although I'm none too clear about how it inflated around them. Meanwhile, Stavros kidnaps Van Damme's wife and sets a trap for him involving a bomb disguised as a baby. The movie is moving so fast here that the poor wife has her big childbirth scene reduced to a cameo (someone shouts "Push! Push!" as a battle rages around her).

Rodman analyzes the situation: "It's time to get off the bench. The best defense is a strong offense." Van Damme is desperate to find his wife. Rodman comes to the rescue. He just happens to be on friendly terms with an order of monks whose subterranean database can track down missing persons. This leads to a trip through the Catacombs and a scene where Rodman throws a human skull at a detonator, misses, and says, "Oops! Air ball!" Then come the baby and the tiger.

The movie is a typical international action thriller, with as little dialogue as possible (to make dubbing easier). The structure is simple: setup scene, action, stunts, next setup, etc. Van Damme was better in his last two movies *(Timecop* and *Sudden Death)* because he had more to do: Here he's at the mercy of the jam-packed plot.

And Dennis Rodman? He does a splendid job of playing a character who seems in every respect to be Dennis Rodman. He seems at home on the screen, he's confident, and in action scenes he'll occasionally do a version of the high-spirited hop-skip-and-jump he sometimes does on the court. He looks like he's having fun, and that's crucial for a movie actor. His agent should have told him, though, that if you can't be the hero, be the villain. That's always a better role than the best friend.

## Down Periscope ★ ★ ★

PG-13, 93 m., 1996

Kelsey Grammer (Tom Dodge), Lauren Holly (Emily), Rob Schneider (Marty Pascal), Harry Dean Stanton (Howard), Bruce Dern (Admiral Graham), Rip Torn (Admiral Winslow), William H. Macy (Captain Knox), Ken Hudson Campbell (Buckman), Toby Huss (Nitro), Harland Williams (Sonar). Directed by David S. Ward and produced by Robert Lawrence. Screenplay by Hugh Wilson, Andrew Kurtzman, and Eliot Wald.

*Down Periscope* plays so much like a sitcom it may even inspire one, especially since it has two of the key requirements: an easygoing father figure, and action largely confined to one set. It's about a troublesome navy officer (Kelsey Grammer) who is finally given command of his own submarine, an ancient 1958 diesel model he refers to as "the USS *Rustoleum*." His task: Engage in a war game to see if one of these old boats could penetrate the modern nuclear navy and attack an American harbor.

As plots go, this one is perhaps a harbinger of things to come. Now that the evil empire has collapsed, there's a shortage of enemies in Hollywood; the list is basically down to fanatic terrorists and neo-Nazis. So why not copy Pogo and declare that we have met the enemy, and the enemy is us?

Grammer plays Tom Dodge, a gifted but problematic officer who is known throughout the navy for two feats: brushing against a Soviet submarine in a near-collision, and getting drunk afterward and having the words WELCOME ABOARD tattooed on precisely that place we must not mention in a family newspaper.

Now Admiral Winslow (Rip Torn) promotes him to sub commander, growling, "I want a pirate, damnit! One with a tattoo on his bleep!" Winslow complains that the Russkies are selling their old subs to places like Iraq and Libya, and he's afraid a renegade commander could launch a suicide mission against a U.S. port. To test his theory, he wants Tom Dodge to take an old Stingray out of mothballs and try it himself.

That's the premise. Next comes the Introduction Scene, obligatory in this genre, in which we meet the key supporting players, such as the manic first officer, the goofy radar man, the slovenly cook, and the goofball. We also meet Lt. Emily Lake (Lauren Holly), who is part of a program to test the use of women on submarines. She gets privacy, and no doubt has her dreams much enhanced, by hanging her hammock between the torpedoes.

The heavy is another admiral, played by the dependable Bruce Dern, as a foaming-at-the-mouth egoist who screams, "I've never lost a war game!" and does all he can to humiliate Dodge. The stakes are high: First, Dodge's sub needs to send up flares in Charleston Harbor. Then, with the live torpedoes secretly supplied by Winslow, he needs to blow up an old junker ship in Norfolk Harbor.

The navy usually goes by the book, and so does this movie. But it works anyway, and generates a certain charm by not trying too hard, and depending on the actors to sell their characters. Grammer is laid-back and likable. Rob Schneider is perhaps a little over the top as the mutinous mad-dog first officer. The radar operator (Harland Williams) wears his baseball cap with the bill bent up, like Huntz Hall, but has such good ears that when somebody drops his change on another sub, he reports, "a quarter and two dimes!" For the benefit of an eavesdropping nuclear sub, he convincingly imitates the love coos of two whales having sex.

The movie raises a few tiny logical questions. When the sub hides between the screws of a supertanker going into Norfolk Harbor, isn't that risky? What if the tanker is damaged and floods the East Coast with oil? And when our guys fire those two torpedoes at the target ship—what if they miss and blow up a dockside chowder house?

These questions are best suppressed for the full enjoyment of the film. Another disappointment: Early in *Down Periscope*, Dodge takes the sub down to 500 feet, which is below its depth limit, to "test" it. Gaskets blow and the hull creaks alarmingly. As far as I'm concerned, this setup creates a moral obligation on the part of the filmmakers to take the sub down to at least

600 feet later in the film. No luck. But I liked the movie anyway.

## Dragonheart ★ ★ ★

PG-13, 108 m., 1996

Dennis Quaid (Bowen), Sean Connery (Voice of Draco), David Thewlis (Einon), Pete Postlethwaite (Gilbert), Dina Meyer (Kara), Jason Isaacs (Felton), Brian Thompson (Brok), Lee Oakes (Young Einon), Wolf Christian (Hewe). Directed by Rob Cohen and produced by Raffaella De Laurentiis. Screenplay by Charles Edward Pogue.

Rob Cohen's *Dragonheart* is one of the most sublimely silly movies I have ever seen. Since it combines its silliness with special effects that are, quite simply, sublime, I must resist the urge to take easy shots at it. (And when it comes to offering easy shots, this movie is a sitting duck—or dragon.)

The film takes place—oh, I dunno, sometime between the age of King Arthur and the invention of flush toilets. It stars Dennis Quaid as Bowen, last of the professional dragon slayers, and Sean Connery as the voice of Draco, the last of the dragons. Obviously, once Bowen slays Draco, they're both out of business.

There's a neat little standoff where Draco has Bowen between his jaws, but Bowen has his sword aimed straight through the roof of Draco's mouth at his brain, and they decide that as reasonable beings they should discuss this thing further. (Bowen eases the situation by picking Draco's teeth clean of the remains of one of the dragon's earlier victims.) Eventually their truce leads to a partnership in a phony dragon-slaying scam.

Is *Dragonheart* then some sort of prehistoric *Naked Gun* movie, with Quaid in the Leslie Nielsen role? Not at all. It takes itself seriously—easily as seriously as, say, Ray Harryhausen's *Clash of the Titans* or *The Golden Voyage of Sinbad.* It's swashbuckling adventure, blood-soaked romance, and villainous cretins against colorful heroes. And it has remarkable special effects. The dragon, a winged beast with a hide as studded as a Harley-Davidson jacket, isn't cheated in fuzzy long shots, but is right there on the screen next to Quaid. And when it talks, its lips are perfectly synched with Connery's voice, and its facial expressions are astonishingly subtle. As a creation of special effects, Draco is up there with E.T., and has more screen time.

The story. Early in the film, Bowen is trying to teach the elements of chivalry to the uncouth young prince Einon. But the lad is a bad apple. Then his father the king is slain, the prince is seriously wounded, and his mother the queen (Julie Christie—yes, Julie Christie) takes him to the dragon's lair, where the lad's life is saved, although not without a sacrifice by the dragon that provides much of the meaning of the movie's last fifteen minutes.

Time passes. Einon (David Thewlis, from *Naked*) has pledged to Draco that his conduct will follow the Old Code, but he grows up as a sadistic lout, and soon Bowen and Draco are leading a revolt of the peasants against his unsavory reign. (Here is one of the movie's several immortal exchanges: "The peasants are revolting!" "They've always been revolting! Now they're rebelling!")

One of the strange elements of the movie is the way the dragon seems to share the same language and values as the human characters. Draco has lines like, "When there are no more dragons to slay, how will you make a living, knight?" And "Dreams die hard, and you hold them in your hand long after they have turned to dust"—which is pretty philosophical for a dragon. Also good for a quotable line or two is a monk named Gilbert (Pete Postlethwaite), whose dialogue seems limited to selections from *Bartlett's Familiar Quotations.* I noted "Pride goeth before a fall" and "Turn the other cheek." Not terribly original, until you remember that Gilbert is working at least five hundred years before the King James version of the Bible.

The movie's climax, involving deep metaphysical details I will not reveal, is heavy in symbolism, cosmology, and poetic justice. It is also as goofy as the rest of the film, but by then I had long since forgiven *Dragonheart* its excesses. A movie like this is some kind of a test for moviegoers. While no reasonable person over the age of twelve would presumably be able to take it seriously, there is nevertheless a lighthearted joy to it, a cheerfulness, an insouciance, that recalls the days when movies were content to be fun. Add that to the impressive technical achievement that went into creating the dragon, and you have something to acknowledge here. It isn't great cinema, but I'm glad I saw it.

## Dream With the Fishes ★ ★ ★

R, 96 m., 1997

David Arquette (Terry), Brad Hunt (Nick), Cathy Moriarty (Aunt Elise), Kathryn Erbe (Liz), Patrick McGaw (Don), J. E. Freeman (Joe, Nick's Father), Timi Prulhiere (Michelle), Anita Barone (Mary), Allyce Beasley (Sophia). Directed by Finn Taylor and produced by Johnny Wow and Mitchell Stein. Screenplay by Taylor.

Desperation sometimes brings with it a certain clarity. Early in *Dream With the Fishes,* a character is balanced on a bridge, ready to commit suicide by throwing himself off, when he's interrupted by a stickup man who asks for his wristwatch: "Since you're going to be dead in a few minutes anyway, what use will it be to you?"

The would-be suicide is named Terry (David Arquette). The stickup guy is Nick (Brad Hunt). "Could I have some privacy?" Terry asks. That's ironic, since in the movie's opening scenes we've seen that Terry is a Peeping Tom who spies on his neighbors with binoculars, and his favorite subjects are Nick and his girlfriend Liz (Kathryn Erbe).

From this unlikely Meet Cute, *Dream With the Fishes* generates a free-ranging road and buddy movie that, with its use of drugs and counterculture spirit, could be a seventies production—made when characters could slip through a movie without carrying a lot of plot along with them.

Terry climbs down off the bridge after Nick paints an unpleasant picture ("Hitting the water from this height, it will be like hitting concrete"). Nick makes a better offer: In return for the watch, he'll give Terry enough pills to finish himself off. But the offer is a fraud, the pills are vitamins, and the two opposites gradually, warily, become friends. If this sounds too easy, it doesn't feel that way in Finn Taylor's movie, because the screenplay goes for an edgy, elegiac tone, and we suspect that both men are carrying more secrets than they're willing to reveal.

Motivated by Nick's deteriorating health and a bargain the two of them strike, they embark on a journey. There are adventures in the spirit of the old road movies, an unplanned robbery, and even an acid trip involving a cop who pulls his gun and shoots some doughnuts dead. Their destination is Nick's childhood home, where his father, Joe (J. E. Freeman), slams the door on him. Joe has apparently had enough of his son for one lifetime, and after he finally lets his son into the house we guess the nature of their relationship from a painful shoulder-butting contest.

Freeman is good as the cool, distant father: a hard case himself, and fed up with his son. Allyce Beasley, as Nick's mother, is weary of her son's lifelong screwups, but more loving. Where he finds acceptance and some understanding, however, is with his Aunt Elise (Cathy Moriarty), a former stripper with a blowzy friendliness. Eventually Liz, the apprehensive, tattoo-obsessed girlfriend, catches up with them.

The story provides a deadline in the form of Nick's health. But the surface is as meandering as a 1970s road movie: Colorful characters materialize, do their thing, and shrink in the rear-view mirror. Taylor's screenplay is skillful in the way it presents us with Nick and Terry, who are equally unlikable, and subtly humanizes them, while Kathryn Erbe gradually modulates Liz, Nick's girlfriend, so that beneath her fearsome surface we begin to sense shadows and softness.

*Dream With the Fishes* is a first film, and shows some of the signs of unchained ambition. Its visual style can be a distraction, beginning with the grainy, saturated look of a music video, and then leveling out into flat realism, then getting fancy again. Although many directors have tried using contrasting visual styles to control the tone of a film (switching between black and white and color is an old technique), what usually happens is that we get sidetracked by the style changes, and the mood is broken. Better, I think, to choose a look for a film and stick with it, unless there are persuasive reasons to experiment.

There is also a plot point, involving the wife Terry says he lost in a car crash, that is resolved a little awkwardly. That strand shows signs of having survived from a first draft, maybe because Taylor needed some quick motivation. His finished film creates enough of an arc for Terry that the wife is not needed. How *Dream With the Fishes* works is that the road-movie and buddy-movie formulas slowly dissolve from around Nick and Terry, who by the end of the movie stand revealed in three dimensions; it's like the cinematic equivalent of what sculptors call the lost-wax method.

## D3: The Mighty Ducks ★

PG, 104 m., 1996

Emilio Estevez (Gordon Bombay), Jeffrey Nordling (Coach Orion), David Selby (Dean Buckley), Heidi Kling (Casey), Joshua Jackson (Charlie), Joss Ackland (Hans), Elden Ryan Ratliff (Fulton), Shaun Weiss (Goldberg), Jack White (Coach Wilson). Directed by Robert Lieberman and produced by Jordan Kerner and Jon Avnet. Screenplay by Steven Brill and Jim Burnstein.

*D3: The Mighty Ducks* is the first movie title I've seen that correctly predicts its grade on the *Entertainment Weekly* scorecard. The Mighty Ducks, Minnesota's underdog kid hockey team, are back again in a third version of more or less the same story: Evil, petty, vindictive, mean-spirited, cheating, lying snobs try to stop them, but the Ducks, after first dealing with cockiness, infighting, pride, anger, and a new coach, redeem themselves in the big match.

"You've never heard of the Anaheim Mighty Ducks?" asks Charlie, the team's top scorer. "They named a pro team after us!" He uses this as a pickup line with a cute brunette. Maybe it would have worked even better if he'd added, "And the same company that owns the team produced all three *Mighty Duck* movies in a transparent exercise of cross-promotion!"

As the movie opens, the state champion Ducks have all been given scholarships to snobby Eden Hall, a private academy with a hockey program so good that they have more flags hanging from the ceiling of their arena than a used car lot on Washington's birthday. Not everyone is happy about these newcomers, who bring blacks, Asians, Jews, fat kids, and even a girl into the famous hockey program, which is apparently otherwise made up mostly of rich white snobs.

Leading the bigots is the sneering Dean Buckley (David Selby), who tries everything he can think of to sink the scholarships. And then there's the varsity coach (Jack White), who is capable of pep talks to his boys like: "They don't belong in our school. Now show them why!"

The Ducks are devastated as the movie opens to discover that beloved Coach Bombay (Emilio Estevez) won't be with them anymore. Bombay, the hot-shot lawyer who began coaching them as a form of court-ordered community service, has moved on to the Junior Goodwill Games. Their new coach is a former pro player named Coach Orion (Jeffrey Nordling), who lectures on defense.

"I'm a scorer," sniffs the star player, Charlie (Joshua Jackson). We've seen more than one movie and can guess where *that* kind of talk will lead, although we are not prepared for the way the script delivers with a bludgeon rather than a scalpel: The Ducks go out to a 9–0 lead, but don't play defense, and so their opponents then score nine straight goals to tie the match.

The movie's desperation can be seen in several totally contrived scenes of which the most obvious shows the fat kid losing control while on inline skates, and rolling away while Charlie speeds to rescue him. The kid, screaming piteously for help, rolls down a flight of stairs, into city traffic, past snarling dogs, etc., while sometimes skating on one leg, knocking over garbage cans, etc., and finally flying through the air and somehow landing just as Charlie is able to save him. The problem here is that only one of the best inline skaters in the world could have possibly performed well enough to do all of these stunts; we wonder who the movie is trying to fool.

Most of the dramatic scenes involve a feud between the freshman Ducks and the snob varsity, who stick them with the bill at an expensive private club, leading to the first movie scene since the 1930s in which we are asked to believe that the penniless diners could work off their bill by washing dishes. Other time-killers include a scenic trip to the Mall of America, and a curious side plot involving old Hans (Joss Ackland), who has followed the team since the beginning, always believed in them, and listens to their games on the radio while shaking his head sadly at their follies.

Hans is a familiar kind of movie fixture: A character obviously doomed to die before the end of the film. I've gotten to where I can spot them in their first shots, and I whisper, "He's gonna die!" to my wife, who tells me to be quiet and watch the movie.

At the end of the film, there is skullduggery involving the Ducks' free scholarships, which of course can be settled if they win a big match and if Coach Bombay comes back to practice his formidable legal skills. Everyone in the movie seems to agree that athletic skill is the only criterion for scholarships at Eden Hall, a school where I cannot remember anyone ever taking any classes, although my attention may have wandered.

Will there be a *D4*? Do ducks quack?

# E

## Eddie ★ ½

PG-13, 88 m., 1996

Whoopi Goldberg (Eddie), Frank Langella (Wild Bill Burgess), Dennis Farina (Coach Bailey), Richard Jenkins (Assistant Coach Zimmer), Lisa Ann Walter (Claudine), John Benjamin Hickey (Joe Nader), Troy Beyer (Beth Hastings), John Salley (Nate Wilson). Directed by Steve Rash and produced by David Permut and Mark Burg. Screenplay by Jon Connolly, David Loucka, Eric Champnella, Keith Mitchell, Steve Zacharias, and Jeff Buhai.

*Eddie* begins with Whoopi Goldberg playing a limousine dispatcher who does a play-by-play of Knicks games over the radio to her drivers. It ends with Whoopi as the coach of the New York Knicks, who are headed for the playoffs. This sounds like a sensational scenario, but alas, almost everything in between is recycled out of lightweight sports-movie clichés, and the movie never captures the electricity and excitement of the real NBA. For more authenticity about high-stakes basketball you'd have to go back to William Friedkin's *Blue Chips* (1994).

Goldberg plays Eddie, a vocal, demonstrative superfan whose seats are in the nosebleed section but who captures the eye of Wild Bill Burgess (Frank Langella), the flamboyant Texan who has just bought the Knicks. Wild Bill, who introduces himself to the fans in Madison Square Garden by riding onto the court on a horse wearing basketball shoes, is a student of the bottom line. He wants his coach (Dennis Farina) to showboat a little more, but Farina says he's no cheerleader, and quits.

Wild Bill has already seen something of Eddie (she was his limo driver in from the airport, and later he rigged a contest to make her honorary coach for a game). Now he appoints her acting coach at the bargain-basement price of $50,000, and before long she's guiding the Knicks out of a nineteen-game losing streak and into playoff contention. That's not surprising, since Hollywood firmly believes that any amateur can coach any sport better than any professional (see *Sunset Park*).

Goldberg is a high-energy performer, and you can see she's having fun with the role. But it never really digs in and deals with the realities of a woman fan coming out of the stands to coach a team. (The closest it gets is when a breathless TV reporter asks her, "How does it feel to be a woman?")

The movie has a lot of pro basketball players in it, who mostly do a good job of playing sanitized, toned-down versions of real-life athletes. The movie might have had more fun being more real. I didn't for a moment believe the Knicks would (a) accept a fan as their coach, or (b) act on her advice. And I wasn't much impressed by the coaching, either; Eddie runs up and down the sidelines shouting "Defense!" and "Hit the open man!"—which just about anyone would be happy to do for $50,000 a year.

The film looks as if some shots were grabbed at real games, and then dialogue scenes were added later in close-ups with extras. The result is fairly convincing visually, although I doubt if the Garden has had that many empty seats in many a year.

Of the pro players doing guest shots, John Salley of the Chicago Bulls has the best dramatic moment, explaining to Eddie that she has to pay more attention to the players' personal problems if she wants to blast them out of their funk. The L.A. Clippers' Malik Sealy plays a player named Stacy Patton, who always refers to himself in the third person. The Indiana Pacers' Dwayne Schintzius plays a Russian import named Ivan, who knows three words of English (and seems to know only the corresponding three words in Russian), and the Utah Jazz' Greg Ostertag plays a player so dim he doesn't ever quite understand why he should win one for the Gipper. Dennis Rodman, still in a San Antonio uniform, has a walk-by and some dialogue.

Since you can see all of these players doing more dramatic, amusing, and intelligent things on basketball courts during the regular season, there is little reason to see them scaled down for the innocuous fantasy of *Eddie*. The movie's underlying plot doesn't amount to much, either, with Wild Bill as the evil capitalist who wants to sell the team to St. Louis. How Eddie counters this desire is something I will not reveal, except to say I seriously doubt that there is a single referee in the NBA who would let her get away with it.

## The Edge ★ ★ ★

R, 118 m., 1997

Anthony Hopkins (Charles Morse), Alec Baldwin (Robert Green), Elle Macpherson (Mickey Morse), Harold Perrineau (Stephen), L. Q. Jones (Styles), Kathleen Wilhoite (Ginny), David Lindstedt (James), Marc Kiely (Mechanic). Directed by Lee Tamahori and produced by Art Linson. Screenplay by David Mamet.

*The Edge* is like a wilderness adventure movie written by David Mamet, which is not surprising, since it *was* written by Mamet. It's subtly funny in the way it toys with the clichés of the genre. Too subtle, apparently, for some; I've read a couple of reviews by critics who think director Lee Tamahori *(Once Were Warriors)* misses the point of the Mamet screenplay and plays the material too straight. But if he'd underlined every laugh line and made the humor as broad as *The Naked Gun*, would that have made a better picture? Not at all.

Although Mamet, a poet of hard-boiled city streets, is not usually identified with outdoor action films, *The Edge* in some ways is typical of his work: It's about con games and occult knowledge, double-crosses and conversations at cross-purposes. Its key scenes involve two men stalking each other, and it adds to the irony that they are meanwhile being stalked by a bear. "Most people lost in the wild die of shame," the older character tells the younger. "They didn't do the one thing that could save their lives—thinking."

The setup: Billionaire Charles Morse (Anthony Hopkins) flies his private plane into the Alaskan wilderness so that fashion photographer Robert Green (Alec Baldwin) can photograph Morse's wife, a famous model (Elle Macpherson). Leaving the wife behind at a lodge, the two men and a photographer's assistant fly farther into the bush, and when the plane crashes and the pilot is killed, the three survivors are left to face the wilderness.

At this point we can easily predict the death of the assistant (Harold Perrineau). He's an African-American, and so falls under the BADF action movie rule ("The Brother Always Dies First"). The redeeming factor in this case is that Mamet knows that, and is satirizing the stereotype instead of merely using it. His approach throughout the movie is an amused wink at the conventions he lovingly massages.

Now Charles and Bob are left alone in the dangerous wild. Charles luckily is a very bright man, who just happens to have been reading the book *Lost in the Woods*, and has the kind of mind that absorbs every scrap of information that floats into it. Before the movie is over he will fashion a compass from a paper clip, build a bear trap, make fire from ice, and explain how you can use gunpowder to season meat.

Charles is also smart enough to suspect that Bob has been having an affair with his wife. "So, how you planning to kill me?" he asks. The catch is that each man needs the other to survive, and so a murder, if any, must be postponed or carefully timed.

The movie contains glorious scenery, quixotic Mamet conversations, and of course the obligatory action scenes. Even in generating tension, the movie toys with convention. As a bear pursues them, the men desperately bridge a deep chasm with a log, and hurry to cross it—not sitting down and scooting as any sensible person would, but trying to walk across while balancing themselves, like the Escaping Wallendas. Meanwhile, the bear, which often seems to have its tongue in its cheek, stands on the far edge and shakes the log with both paws.

There are a couple of bear-wrestling matches and a big showdown with the beast, but the movie doesn't lose its mind and go berserk with action in the last half-hour, as most action films seem to. (One of the enduring disappointments for the faithful moviegoer is to see interesting characters established in the first two acts, only to be turned into action puppets in the third.) It is typical of Mamet that he could devise his plot in such a way that the climactic payoff would be not bloodshed, but the simple exchange of a wristwatch.

*Footnote: Having successfully negotiated almost its entire 118 minutes,* The Edge *shoots itself in the foot. After the emotionally fraught final moments, just as the audience is savoring the implications of what has just happened, the screen fades to black and we immediately get a big credit for "Bart the Bear." Now Bart is one helluva bear (I loved him in the title role of* The Bear*), but this credit in this place is a spectacularly bad idea.*

## Ed's Next Move ★ ★ ★

R, 88 m., 1996

Matt Ross (Eddie Brodsky), Callie Thorne (Lee Nicol), Kevin Carroll (Ray Obregon), Ramsey Faragallah (Dr. Banargee), Nina Sheveleva (Elenka), Jimmy Cummings (Raphael). Directed by John Walsh and produced by Sally Roy. Screenplay by Walsh.

*Ed's Next Move,* a sweet and quietly funny love story, is the kind of movie that seems to be meandering, and then it sneaks up on you. It begins as the story of a museum-quality nerd: a rice geneticist from Wisconsin who is so organized in his mid-twenties that he even has his cemetery plot bought and paid for. He moves to New York and swims into the orbit of a young singer who does Liz Phair–type songs about the irony of banality. They kiss.

By the time they kiss, I wanted them to kiss. That's how I realized the movie was working. In some of the earlier passages I'd been unconvinced, but the movie builds quietly but very surely toward a point at which we like these characters, we worry about them, and (always the fatal step) we recognize elements of ourselves.

The movie stars Matt Ross as Eddie Brodsky, who knows a lot about rice but will never, at his present rate of progress, get any thrown at him at a church door. Callie Thorne is Lee Nicol, a New Yorker who regards Wisconsin as a word association test for which the answer is "cheese." Kevin Carroll plays Ray, Eddie's first roommate, a ladies' man who tries to give him advice about women and the ways of the world. Ed complains, "You allow for things I can't even pronounce."

It goes without saying that Ed and Ray spend a lot of time sitting in the kinds of diners that have Formica countertops and waitresses who write orders down on green guest checks. All single men in the movies hold most of their conversations in diners, maybe because putting them across a booth from one another is a perfect way to explain a dialogue scene in which the faces are close enough for a two-shot without anybody getting any funny ideas. Just in recent weeks, I've witnessed heartfelt diner discussions between single men in *Swingers* and *Things to Do in Denver When You're Dead,* and then of course there was the mother of all guys-in-diners scenes in *Heat.*

Ed and Ray discuss topics such as the origin of "nitty gritty" and the types of Arctic fauna. The diner is run by a friendly Jewish woman who introduces Ed to such exotic foods as bagels and borscht; one of the film's underlying themes is the way the Wisconsin kid learns the ropes in the big city.

One thing he needs to know more about is the mind of a woman. His telephone conversations with Lee sound like they were memorized in a foreign language. She looks at him sometimes as if he's a pod person. On their first date, Ed kills some mice and she leaves, and he is deeply despondent, and Ray explains, "Let's just say first dates go better when nothing dies."

The movie was written and directed by John Walsh, who told a Toronto film festival crowd he financed it with credit cards after a friend tipped him off about lots of extra 35mm stock left over from the filming of *Smoke.* (That film's director, Wayne Wang, used very long shots, so if an actor lost it early in a scene, there were nice film tags left over.) The movie doesn't betray its low-budget origins. It looks as good as it needs to, and sounds wonderful; Walsh has a gift with dialogue. We get the kinds of lines new lovers use when they are at a loss to explain their chemistry: "If Raymond Carver and Hoagy Carmichael had gotten together, they would have sounded like us." And quiet, funny little exchanges ("You smell like cookies." "It's a perfume that I made myself.").

*Ed's Next Move* is a comedy, not a docudrama, and yet it's more accurate about romance than many more serious movies. For one thing, it is driven by dialogue and social uncertainty, rather than by testosterone. For every romance that begins with a Mickey Rourke type slamming a Kim Basinger type up against an alley wall in the rain, there are a thousand, I suppose, that begin when your cat throws up a fur ball in the lap of the woman you're trying to impress.

## The Education of Little Tree ★ ★ ★

PG, 117 m., 1998

Joseph Ashton (Little Tree), Graham Greene (Willow John), James Cromwell (Granpa), Tantoo Cardinal (Granma), Mika Boorem (Little Girl), Leni Parker (Martha), Rebecca Dewey (Dolly), William Rowat (Henry). Directed by Richard Friedenberg and produced by Jake Eberts.

Screenplay by Friedenberg, based on the novel by Forrest Carter.

*The Education of Little Tree* is another fine family movie that will no doubt be ignored by the fine families of America. The notion that there is a hungry audience for good family entertainment, nurtured by such dreamers as the critic Michael Medved, is a touching mirage. American families made it a point to avoid *The Secret Garden, The Little Princess, Shiloh,* and even *Rocket Man,* and I fear they'll also shield their offspring from *The Education of Little Tree.* Too bad. If children still exist whose imaginations have not been hammered into pulp by R-rated mayhem like *Starship Troopers,* this film will play as a magical experience.

The film tells the story of a half-Cherokee orphan who eludes the clutches of his prim white aunt and is raised in the wilderness of the Great Smoky Mountains by his grandparents. Granma (Tantoo Cardinal) is Cherokee; Granpa (James Cromwell) was "born white, but learned to see through Cherokee eyes." In a series of vignettes that add up to life's lessons, they teach Little Tree (Joseph Ashton) his school lessons, the poetry of nature, and a lot of common sense.

The film, set in the 1930s, of course sentimentalizes the wisdom of Native Americans—who, after decades in which they could do no right in the movies, now can do no wrong. Even Granpa's occupation—distilling and selling moonshine—is seen as a sort of public service for the local population, who don't have the money for store-bought booze. But for Little Tree, life in his grandparents' small cabin is an idyll: He learns of nature, of the seasons, of dogs and frogs, and the mysteries of life and death. More insights are provided by an Indian neighbor, played by Graham Greene.

The movie has its share of suspense and action, especially when "revenooers" come tramping through the woods looking for the still (the loyal dog Blue Boy holds them at bay while the boy crashes through the undergrowth rescuing a sack of granpa's equipment). And when the grandparents lose custody of the boy because of the moonshine business, there is a sequence set in a place called the Notched Gap Indian School, which is less a school than a reformatory, trying to cure its students of the notion that they are Indians. Little Tree looks through a window at the star that Granma told him to keep in sight, and knows that it looks down on her too. Granpa takes more direct action.

The film is quietly well acted. James Cromwell, as Granpa, proves here, as he did as the farmer in *Babe* and the police chief in *L.A. Confidential,* that despite his unmistakable physical presence he can play characters who are completely different from one another. What I liked here was the way Granpa is allowed to be sweet and light from the start; the movie avoids the usual cliché in which the older man is stiff and unbending, and only gradually yields. There is a touching sequence where we fear deeply for him. Tantoo Cardinal, as Granma, has a presence and conviction that gives freshness to her dialogue, which on the page might have looked rather simplistic. And Joseph Ashton, as Little Tree, is another of those young actors who is fresh and natural on camera; I believed in his character.

The movie arrives with some baggage. It is based on a book by Forrest Carter, which was first identified as autobiographical, and then, after a literary scandal, moved across the page from the *New York Times* nonfiction best-seller list to the "fiction" column. In the process it was revealed that Carter was in fact a man named Asa Carter, who had links to white supremacist groups and wrote speeches for George Wallace in his preenlightened days. What journey Asa made on his way to becoming Forrest might make a good movie, too; in *The Education of Little Tree* he wrote a story that has the elements in it for a strong, unusual, affecting drama. Anyone can find redemption.

I began on a note of pessimism, fearing that families will not embrace this wholesome PG-rated film. That would be a shame. My best guess is that more nine-year-olds will see *Scream 2* than *Little Tree.* The loud, violent, cartoonish entertainment that's pumped into the minds of kids cannot be creating much room for thought and values. It's all sensation. Movies like *Little Tree* are the kinds that families can discuss afterward. There are truths to be found in them. And questions. Somehow the noisy action junk never leaves any questions (except about the future of our civilization).

## 8 Heads in a Duffel Bag ★ ★

R, 97 m., 1997

Joe Pesci (Tommy Spinelli), Andy Comeau (Charlie), Kristy Swanson (Laurie Bennett), Todd Louiso (Steve), George Hamilton (Dick Bennett), Dyan Cannon (Annette Bennett), David Spade (Ernie). Directed by Tom Schulman and produced by Brad Krevoy, Steve Stabler, and John Bertolli. Screenplay by Schulman.

*8 Heads in a Duffel Bag* sounds, I know, like a miniseries inspired by *Bring Me the Head of Alfredo Garcia.* But the movie's roots are in screwball comedy, and occasionally it does approach the zaniness it yearns for. It stars Joe Pesci as a gangster whose mission is to deliver the heads of eight gangsters to a man in San Diego who will accept them, not unreasonably, as evidence that their owners are dead.

Pesci's duffel bag is switched at an airport with an identical bag owned by Charlie (Andy Comeau), a medical student headed for a Mexican vacation with his fiancée. He has enough problems. His beloved, named Laurie (Kristy Swanson), is no longer sure she wants to marry him. Under the influence of her alcoholic mother (Dyan Cannon) and deeply tanned father (George Hamilton), she has changed. "Look at you!" Charlie cries. "Six months at home and you've mutated from a fun-loving free spirit into . . . into . . . Nancy Reagan!"

Spinelli, the Pesci character, has twenty-four hours to find those heads. Using clues in Charlie's bag, he visits the kid's fraternity house and tortures two of his frat brothers (David Spade and Todd Louiso) to find out Charlie's vacation plans. I've seen a lot of torture methods in the movies, but never one as ingenious as this: He makes them put on their stethoscopes, and then bangs the little metal discs together. They talk.

Meanwhile, in Mexico, Charlie has discovered the heads in his bag. So has the resort's pet dog, who sniffs out the secret and would have gotten more laughs if they'd cast a truly funny dog, like a Chihuahua. Spinelli and the fraternity brothers fly to Mexico for the climax, which involves at one point as many as fourteen heads, I believe, along with much debate about whether it's murder if you thaw out a cryogenically frozen person.

Joe Pesci is the best thing in the movie; he's funny every moment he's on the screen. None of the other characters is fully realized, and the two most promising—played by Hamilton and Cannon—aren't onscreen enough. Andy Comeau, as Charlie, doesn't generate the madness the role requires. He seems merely frenzied when he needs to seem crazed. For screwball comedy to work, there has to be a frightening intensity in the characters. The plots are always threatening to spin out of control, and their single-minded urgency is needed to keep the story grounded. Everyone here, except Pesci, is just a little too comfortable.

Pesci has a lot of scenes that strike just the right note, as when he gets into a fight with a flight attendant over whether he can put his oversize bag into the overhead compartment. Consider his dilemma: He's desperate because the heads need to be in San Diego. He's trapped because if he protests too much they'll throw him off the plane. Anger and ferocity lurk just beneath the surface, but he can't explode or he'll get in trouble with the airline. Pesci finds a great actor's solution to the scene: He's not fighting with the attendant, he's fighting with himself. (Jim Carrey did the same sort of thing in *Liar Liar.*)

He has other good scenes, including one in which George Hamilton's mother gets on his nerves, and he sends her on a quick tour of the Mexican mountains. But the others in the cast aren't at his level, and scenes that should be funnier (as when a blind laundress pops a head in the dryer) lack focus and a payoff. We also get an unnecessary Mexican youth gang, which surrounds Charlie and laughs maniacally while calling him a gringo, simply because every single time a gringo gets lost in Mexico it is written in the clouds that he must be surrounded and laughed at maniacally. (Did this cliché start with Alfonso Bedoya in *The Treasure of the Sierra Madre,* or is it even older?)

*8 Heads in a Duffel Bag,* written and directed by Tom Schulman, takes a lot of chances, and if they'd all worked it might have been a great comedy—its combination of Mafia logic and grotesque humor might have propelled it toward the success of a triumph like *Bound.* But it doesn't scale those heights. It stops at the foothills, and only Pesci continues, climbing on alone.

## The Eighth Day ★ ★ ★

NO MPAA RATING, 118 m., 1997

Daniel Auteuil (Harry), Pascal Duquenne (Georges), Miou-Miou (Julie), Isabelle Sadoyan (Georges's Mother), Henri Garcin (Company Director), Michele Maes (Nathalie), Laszlo Harmati (Luis Mariano), Helene Roussel (Julie's Mother), Fabienne Loriaux (Fabienne), Didier De Neck (Fabienne's Husband). Directed by Jaco Van Dormael and produced by Philippe Godeau. Screenplay by Van Dormael.

*The Eighth Day* teaches a lesson that everybody piously agrees with and nobody practices: We must embrace simplicity and freedom, give ourselves room to breathe, and shake off the shackles of the lockstep world. In the movie, evil is represented by a faceless giant corporation, photographed in cold shades of gray and blue. Goodness is embodied in a character who has Down syndrome and approaches life directly, with great delight. During the course of the story he will teach the lesson of freedom to Harry, a harassed executive.

There is nothing to quarrel with here, but we must be careful before we sign up for freedom. I applaud it, but if I miss too many deadlines while embracing joy and freedom, I will find myself without a job. You, dear reader, can read my review and likewise subscribe to freedom. But if you are like me, reading the paper is a blessed oasis of private time in the morning before you must race out of the house and rejoin the rat race.

I've seen a lot of movies where simple characters teach complex ones how to relax and enjoy life. *Rain Man* is an obvious example. Offhand, I can't recall a movie where a character starts out unfettered and free, and the movie teaches him that he needs to punch a time clock. I guess nobody would buy a ticket to that movie.

The hero of *The Eighth Day* is Georges, played by Pascal Duquenne, a professional actor in Belgium who has Down syndrome. Since the death of his mother, Georges has lived in an institution that looks like a pleasant place. He has a sweetheart there, and some friends, and in his dreams he's comforted by his mother. One day a lot of the patients prepare for visits. Georges has no one to visit, but he packs his bag and sets off across the fields, his destination uncertain.

The movie's other central character is Harry (Daniel Auteuil), whose corporate job is to teach his company's faceless minions how to fake a smile. He is consumed by unreleased anger. His wife (Miou-Miou) has left him, he is under orders not to approach her home, and although his daughters are allowed to visit him, he forgets they're coming. They wait at the train station and then take the next train home, furious.

Harry's life is not worth living. In a touching scene, he addresses a chair as if his wife were sitting in it. He drives out recklessly into the rain, inviting suicide, and kills a big dog that has accompanied Georges. He is at a loss what to do. The police are no help. Eventually he finds himself saddled with Georges, and after they bury the dog they find themselves sharing life together for a few days. Harry wants nothing more than to get rid of Georges. In real life, of course, that would take only a phone call, but this is a movie.

Georges lives in a world where fantasy and reality pass back and forth through the membrane of his perceptions. He takes things literally. He believes that after you cut the grass, you should comfort it. He is visited by a singing Mexican cowboy from a Technicolor musical. When he hears the word "Mongoloid," he imagines a world of Mongols with Chinese hats and pigtails. He responds directly and without affectation to whatever happens. He embraces life. He goes with the flow. Whatever.

You now have everything you need to imagine the movie. It is about Harry's gradual alienation from his corporate prison, and about the lessons Georges can teach him. About how the two men become friends. There is even a scene late in the film where Georges is reunited with some of his former fellow patients, and they commandeer a bus and drive it wildly through the streets; such an adventure is more or less obligatory for a story like this.

Watching *The Eighth Day,* I felt contradictory impulses. On the one hand, I was acutely aware of how conventional the story was. On the other, I was enchanted by the friendship between Harry and Georges. Auteuil is a fine actor, and so is Duquenne, who belongs to a Brussels experimental theatrical troupe and approaches every scene with a combination of complete commitment and utter abandon. These two men shared the Best Acting prize at the 1996 Cannes Film

Festival, and indeed it would be impossible to honor one without the other.

What I also liked was the visual freedom that the director, Jaco Van Dormael, brings to the screen. We see the most unexpected sights here: busy little ladybugs, and an ant being trapped inside a vacuum cleaner, and Georges walking on water, and scenes of flying and drifting, clouds and fantasies, dreams and rest. The single most enchanting moment in the film is an overhead shot, looking straight down on the two men after one has said "in a minute," and then for exactly sixty seconds they pause, and wait, and experience a minute, so that we can too.

*The Eighth Day* could have been a better film. Its message is too easy. It could have dealt more deeply with these characters. One can choose to reject its easy sentimentality. I eventually chose not to. I opened myself to it. Went with the flow. Whatever.

## Emma ★ ★ ★

PG, 121 m., 1996

Gwyneth Paltrow (Emma Woodhouse), Jeremy Northam (Mr. Knightly), Toni Collette (Harriet Smith), Greta Scacchi (Mrs. Weston), Alan Cumming (Reverend Elton), Juliet Stevenson (Mrs. Elton), Ewan McGregor (Frank Churchill), Polly Walker (Jane Fairfax), Sophie Thompson (Miss Bates), Phyllida Law (Mrs. Bates). Directed by Douglas McGrath and produced by Patrick Cassavetti and Steven Haft. Screenplay by McGrath, based on the novel by Jane Austen.

The British read the novels of Trollope during the London blitz because his stories of Victorian life distracted them from the V-2 rockets. Maybe that helps explain the current popularity of movies based on the novels of Jane Austen: In an impolite age, we escape to the movies to see good manners.

*Emma* is the fourth recent version of an Austen novel, after *Persuasion, Sense and Sensibility,* and the TV adaptation of *Pride and Prejudice.* (As a bonus, the Beverly Hills comedy *Clueless* was based on the same story.) It is not about very much—about the romantic intrigues of a small group of people who will all more or less have to marry one another sooner or later, if they haven't already.

Either you are in sympathy with this material or you are not. I had to smile at an undergraduate's review of the movie posted on the Internet, which complains that "a parade of 15 or 20 or 8 billion supporting characters waltzes through the scenes. Each is called Mister or Miss or Mrs. Something, and each of them looks and acts exactly the same (obnoxious)."

I am not sure you can look obnoxious, but never mind. It may be that young people in a permissive age do not have sympathy for a movie in which a busybody matchmaker spends her days trying to pair off unwilling candidates for matrimony. Yet in its high spirits and wicked good humor, *Emma* is a delightful film—second only to *Persuasion* among the modern Austen movies, and funnier, if not so insightful.

Gwyneth Paltrow sparkles in the title role, as young Miss Woodhouse, who wants to play God in her own little patch of England. You can see her eyes working the room, speculating on whose lives she can improve. She takes as a project Harriet Smith (Toni Collette), a respectable young woman of imperfect pedigree, insisting that she marry the Reverend Elton (Alan Cumming). Miss Smith would much sooner marry a local farmer, but Emma won't hear of it. When the poor farmer sends Miss Smith a letter of proposal, she shows it to Emma, who sniffs, "It is a good letter. One of his sisters must have helped him."

Miss Smith is so uncertain of herself that she turns down the farmer, only to discover that the reverend doesn't love her—he loves Miss Woodhouse ("I have never cared for Miss Smith," he tells Emma, "except as your friend"). This should be a lesson for Emma, but she'll need more than one.

Stories like this are about manners, nuance, and the way that one's natural character tugs against the strict laws of society. In a time when most people traveled little and diversion was largely limited to local parties, three-volume novels, and church services, gossip was the great pastime. Local characters were prized because they gave you someone to talk about, and *Emma* has its share, most delightfully Mrs. Elton (Juliet Stevenson), who praises herself incessantly by quoting others (of her musical talent, she says, "I myself don't call it great. I only know that my friends call it so").

Other local color is provided by Miss Bates and her deaf mother, Mrs. Bates. (They are played by Sophie Thompson and Phyllida Law, who are Emma Thompson's sister and mother.) Miss Bates says everything three times and Mrs. Bates never hears it, and when Emma is unforgivably rude to poor Miss Bates it is the upright Mr. Knightly (Jeremy Northam), her brother-in-law, who dresses her down, giving her a stern lecture on her responsibilities under the class system.

Emma thinks of Knightly as a brother. She is interested in the reverend not at all. There is a dashing young bachelor in the neighborhood named Frank Churchill (Ewan McGregor) who seems cast as her beau (he rescues her when her carriage gets mired in the river, and again when she is threatened by gypsies). But he has other plans, too, and in the fullness of time Austen sees that everyone gets what they deserve, or in Emma's case perhaps rather more.

## The Empire Strikes Back ★ ★ ★ ★

PG, 127 m., 1980 (rereleased 1997)

Mark Hamill (Luke Skywalker), Harrison Ford (Han Solo), Carrie Fisher (Princess Leia), Billy Dee Williams (Lando Calrissian), Anthony Daniels (C-3PO), Frank Oz (Yoda), David Prowse (Darth Vader), James Earl Jones (Vader's Voice), Alec Guinness (Ben [Obi-Wan] Kenobi). Directed by Irvin Kershner and produced by Gary Kurtz. Screenplay by Leigh Brackett and Lawrence Kasdan, based on a story by George Lucas.

*The Empire Strikes Back* is the best of three *Star Wars* films, and the most thought-provoking. After the space opera cheerfulness of the original film, this one plunges into darkness and even despair, and surrenders more completely to the underlying mystery of the story. It is because of the emotions stirred in *Empire* that the entire series takes on a mythic quality that resonates back to the first and ahead to the third. This is the heart.

The film was made in 1980 with full knowledge that *Star Wars* had become the most successful film of all time. If corners were cut in the original budget, no cost was spared in this one, and it is a visual extravaganza from beginning to end, one of the most visionary and inventive of all films.

Entirely apart from the story and the plot, the film is worth seeing simply for its sights. Not for the scenes of space battle, which are more or less standard (there's nothing here to match the hurtling chase through the high walls of the Death Star). But for such sights as the lumbering, elephantlike Imperial Walkers (was ever a weapon more impractical?). Or for the Cloud City, on its spire high in the sky. Or for the face of a creature named Yoda, whose expressions are as convincing as a human's, and as subtle. Or for the dizzying, vertiginous heights that Luke Skywalker dangles over, after nearly plunging to his death.

There is a generosity in the production design of *The Empire Strikes Back*. There are not only the amazing sights before us, but plenty more in the corners of the screen, or everywhere the camera turns. The whole world of this story has been devised and constructed in such a way that we're not particularly aware of sets or effects—there's so *much* of this world that it all seems seamless. Consider, for example, an early scene where an Empire "probe droid" is fired upon on the ice planet Hoth. It explodes. We've seen that lots of times. But then hot pieces of it shower down on the snow in the foreground, in soft, wet plops. That's the kind of detail that George Lucas and his team live for.

There is another moment. Yoda has just sent Luke Skywalker into a dark part of the forest to confront his destiny. Luke says a brave farewell. There is a cut to R2-D2, whirling and beeping. And then a cut back to Yoda, whose face reflects a series of emotions: concern, sadness, a hint of pride. You know intellectually that Yoda is a creature made by Frank Oz in a Muppet shop. But Oz and Lucas were not content to make Yoda realistic. They wanted to make him a good actor too. And they did; in his range of wisdom and emotion, Yoda may actually give the best performance in the movie.

The worst, I'm afraid, is Chewbacca's. This character was thrown into the first film as window dressing, was never thought through, and as a result has been saddled with one facial expression and one mournful yelp. Much more could have been done. How can you be a space pilot and not be able to communicate in any meaningful way? Does Han Solo really understand Chew's monotonous noises? Do they have long chats sometimes?

Never mind. The second movie's story continues the saga set up in the first film. The Death

Star has been destroyed, but Vader, of course, escaped, and now commands the Empire forces in their ascendancy against the rebels. Our heroes have a secret base on Hoth, but flee it after the Empire attack, and then the key characters split up for parallel stories. Luke and R2-D2 crash-land on the planet Dagobah and Luke is tutored there by Yoda in the ways of the Jedi and the power of the Force. Princess Leia, Han Solo, Chewbacca, and C-3PO evade Empire capture by hiding their ship in plain sight, and then flee to the Cloud City ruled by Lando (Billy Dee Williams), an old pal of Han's and (we learn) the original owner of the Millennium Falcon, before an unlucky card game.

There are a couple of amusing subplots, one involving Han's easily wounded male ego, another about Vader's knack of issuing sudden and fatal demotions. Then comes the defining moment of the series. Can there be a person alive who does not know (read no further if you are that person) that Luke discovers Darth Vader is his father? But that is not the moment. It comes after their protracted (and somewhat disorganized) laser-sword fight, when Luke chooses to fall to his death rather than live to be the son of Vader.

He doesn't die, of course (there is a third movie to be made); he's saved by some sort of chute I still don't understand, only to dangle beneath the Cloud City until his rescue, and a conclusion that only by sheer effort of will doesn't have the words "To be continued" superimposed over it.

Perhaps because so much more time and money was spent on *The Empire Strikes Back* in the first place, not much has been changed in this restored and spruced-up 1997 rerelease. I do not recall the first film in exact detail, but learn from the *Star Wars* Web pages that the look of the Cloud City has been extended and enhanced, and there is more of the Wampa ice creature than before. I have no doubt there are many improvements on the sound track, but I would have to be a dog to hear them.

In the glory days of science fiction, critics wrote about the "sense of wonder." That's what *The Empire Strikes Back* creates in us. Like a lot of traditional science fiction, it isn't psychologically complex or even very interested in personalities (aside from some obvious character traits). That's because the characters are not themselves—they are us. We are looking out through their eyes, instead of into them, as we would in more serious drama. We are on a quest, on a journey, on a mythological expedition. The story elements in the *Star Wars* trilogy are as deep and universal as storytelling itself. Watching these movies, we're in a receptive state like that of a child—our eyes and ears are open, we're paying attention, and we are amazed.

## The End of Violence ★ ★

R, 122 m., 1997

Andie MacDowell (Paige), Bill Pullman (Mike), Gabriel Byrne (Ray), Traci Lind (Cat), Loren Dean (Detective Doc Block). Directed by Wim Wenders and produced by Deepak Nayar, Wenders, and Nicholas Klein. Screenplay by Klein.

Some of the key scenes in Wim Wenders's *The End of Violence* involve a man who sits high above Los Angeles in the Griffith Park observatory, spying on the city through a network of secret TV cameras. Of course, he doesn't need to be high (he can sit anywhere and watch the screens), but the detail is significant; Wenders may be evoking an echo of *Wings of Desire* (1988), the great film in which he imagined lonely angels in Berlin, looking down at the lives of men.

Wenders revisited that image to much less effect in *Faraway . . . So Close* (1993), and now here it is again, with the mysterious observer (Gabriel Byrne) free to watch but powerless to intercede, and not always sure what he is seeing. One of the things he sees is the violent abduction of a Hollywood producer (Bill Pullman), who is kidnapped by paid thugs, for reasons that will gradually become clear. These two character threads—the producer and the voyeur—will continue through the film, but there is a lot of other stuff, not all of it necessary. Wenders has always liked to make very long films, and at 122 minutes, *The End of Violence* may not be long enough to do justice to all of his ideas.

The movie in its present form, although reedited since an unsuccessful screening at Cannes, is essentially a mess. Films work best when audiences are absorbed by the flow. Although there is pleasure in trying to untangle puzzles and mysteries, that's not what we get here; instead, like archaeologists, we're given incomplete shards of a work and asked to imagine the whole.

Many of the scenes involving the Pullman character are, however, sharp-edged and on target. We see him first sitting on the lawn of his expensive home, dealing with the world through telephones, computers, and fax machines. When his wife (Andie MacDowell), who is in the same house, wants to talk to him, she calls him. "I'm leaving you," she says. "I'll get right back to you," he says, putting her on hold and then forgetting all about her as he hurries to the hospital room of an injured stunt woman.

This blinkered Hollywood mentality is illuminated again, hilariously, after the producer is kidnapped and tries to buy his own freedom. "I wanna give you a million dollars," he says. "In points." They aren't buying. Eventually Pullman finds himself free and under the protection of the Mexican family that tends his lawn. He lets his beard grow, puts on gardener's clothes, and avoids a citywide manhunt because by becoming Mexican, he has made himself invisible.

There is more. A subplot involves a secret government plan to use the surveillance cameras to control crime and violence in Los Angeles, and Byrne, sad-faced and thoughtfully musing as only he can be, tries to piece together what he knows about his job, and what he guesses. Everything comes together, somewhat unconvincingly, at the end.

Wim Wenders is a gifted and poetic filmmaker whose reach sometimes exceeds his grasp. It helps when he has some kind of clear narrative thread to organize his material—as he did in *Kings of the Road* (1976), where two men confront their problems within the conventions of a road movie, or *Paris, Texas* (1984), with Harry Dean Stanton as an amnesiac trying to piece together the pieces of his life. Those films had goals, as did the search for the sharing of loneliness in *Wings of Desire*.

*The End of Violence*, on the other hand, doesn't seem sure what it is about, or how it is about it. There is an abundance of ideas here, but they're starting points, not destinations. Wenders is able to invest individual scenes with a feeling of urgency and importance, but at the end there is a certain emptiness, a feeling that the movie has not really been pulled together.

## The English Patient ★ ★ ★ ★

R, 160 m., 1996

Ralph Fiennes (Almasy), Juliette Binoche (Hana), Willem Dafoe (Caravaggio), Kristin Scott Thomas (Katharine Clifton), Naveen Andrews (Kip), Colin Firth (Geoffrey Clifton), Julian Wadham (Madox), Kevin Whately (Hardy). Directed by Anthony Minghella and produced by Saul Zaentz. Screenplay by Minghella, based on the novel by Michael Ondaatje.

Backward into memory, forward into loss and desire, *The English Patient* searches for answers that will answer nothing. This poetic, evocative film version of the novel by Michael Ondaatje circles down through layers of mystery until all of the puzzles in the story have been solved, and only the great wound of a doomed love remains. It is the kind of movie you can see twice—first for the questions, the second time for the answers.

The film opens with a prewar biplane flying above the desert, carrying two passengers in its open cockpits. The film will tell us who these passengers are, why they are in the plane, and what happens next. All of the rest of the story is prologue and epilogue to the reasons for this flight. It is told with the sweep and visual richness of a film by David Lean, with an attention to fragments of memory that evoke feelings even before we understand what they mean.

The "present" action takes place in Italy, during the last days of World War II. A horribly burned man, the "English patient" of the title, is part of a hospital convoy. When he grows too ill to be moved, a nurse named Hana (Juliette Binoche) offers to stay behind to care for him in the ruins of an old monastery. Here she sets up a makeshift hospital, and soon she is joined by two bomb disposal experts and a mysterious visitor named Caravaggio (Willem Dafoe).

The patient's skin is so badly burned it looks like tortured leather. His face is a mask. He can remember nothing. Hana cares for him tenderly, perhaps because he reminds her of other men she has loved and lost during the war. ("I must be a curse. Anybody who loves me—who gets close to me—is killed.") Caravaggio, who has an interest in the morphine Hana dispenses to her patient, is more cynical: "Ask your saint who he's killed. I don't think he's forgotten anything."

The nurse is attracted to one of the bomb disposal men, a handsome, cheerful Sikh officer named Kip (Naveen Andrews). But as she watches him risk his life to disarm land mines, she fears her curse will doom him; if they fall in love, he will die. Meanwhile, the patient's memories start to return in flashes of detail, spurred by the book that was found with his charred body—an old leather-bound volume of the histories of Herodotus, with drawings, notes, and poems pasted or folded inside.

I will not disclose the crucial details of what he remembers. I will simply supply the outlines that become clear early on. He is not English, for one thing. He is a Hungarian count named Laszlo de Almasy (Ralph Fiennes) who, in Egypt before the war, was attached to the Royal Geographic Society as a pilot who flew over the desert, making maps that could be used for their research—which was the cover story—but also used by English troops in case of war.

In the frantic social life of Cairo, where everyone is aware that war is coming, Almasy meets a newly-married woman at a dance. She is Katharine Clifton (Kristin Scott Thomas). Her husband, Geoffrey (Colin Firth), is a disappointment to her. Almasy follows her home one night, and she confronts him and says, "Why follow me? Escort me, by all means, but to follow me . . ." It is clear to both of them that they are in love. Eventually they find themselves in the desert, part of an expedition, and when Geoffrey is called away (for reasons that later are revealed as good ones), they draw closer together. In a stunning sequence, their camp is all but buried in a sandstorm, and their relief at surviving leads to a great romantic sequence.

These are the two people—the count and the British woman—who were in the plane in the first shot. But under what conditions that flight was taken remains a mystery until the closing scenes of the movie, as do a lot of other things, including actions by the count that Caravaggio, the strange visitor, may suspect. Actions that may have led to Caravaggio having his thumbs cut off by the Nazis.

All of this back story (there is much more) is pieced together gradually by the dying man in the bed, while the nurse tends to him, sometimes kisses him, bathes his rotting skin, and tries to heal her own wounds from the long war. There are moments of great effect: one in which she plays hopscotch by herself. A scene involving the nurse, the Sikh, and a piano. Talks at dusk with the patient, and with Caravaggio. All at last become clear.

The performances are of great clarity, which is a help to us in finding our way through the story. Binoche is a woman whose heart has been so pounded by war that she seems drawn to its wounded as a distraction from her own hurts. Fiennes, in what is essentially a dual role, plays a man who conceals as much as he can—at first because that is his nature, later because his injuries force him to. Thomas is one of those bright, energetic British women who seem perfectly groomed even in a sandstorm, and whose core is steel and courage. Dafoe's character must remain murkier, along with his motives, but it is clear he shelters a great anger. And Andrews, as the bomb disposal man, lives the closest to daily death and seems the most grateful for life.

Ondaatje's novel has become one of the most widely read and loved of recent years. Some of its readers may be disappointed that more is not made of the Andrews character; the love between the Sikh and the nurse could provide a balance to the doomed loves elsewhere. But the novel is so labyrinthine that it's a miracle it was filmed at all, and the writer-director, Anthony Minghella, has done a creative job of finding visual ways to show how the rich language slowly unveils layers of the past.

Producers are not always creative contributors to films, but the producer of *The English Patient*, Saul Zaentz, is in a class by himself. Working independently, he buys important literary properties *(One Flew Over the Cuckoo's Nest, Amadeus, The Unbearable Lightness of Being, At Play in the Fields of the Lord)* and savors their difficulties. Here he has created with Minghella a film that does what a great novel can do: Hold your attention the first time through with its story, and then force you to think back through everything you thought you'd learned, after it is revealed what the story is *really* about. ☞

## Eraser ★ ★ ★

R, 115 m., 1996

Arnold Schwarzenegger (Eraser/John Kruger), Vanessa Williams (Lee Cullen), James Caan (Robert Deguerin), James Coburn (Beller), Robert Pastorelli (Johnny C). Directed by Charles Russell and produced by Arnold and Anne Kopelson. Screenplay by Tony Puryear and Walon Green.

It helps to have a short attention span while watching *Eraser,* the Arnold Schwarzenegger picture. Consider, for example, a sequence late in the film, where Arnold is shot through the left shoulder. He grabs his shoulder and grimaces. From the bullet's point of entry, we guess his shoulder bone is broken and there is a lot of muscular damage.

Immediately afterward, Arnold is in a fight to the death with the villain (James Caan) on top of a shipping container that has been lifted high in the air by a crane. The heroine (Vanessa Williams) is also on the container, and she falls off. But Arnold is able to grab her in mid-air. He holds her with his right hand, and supports the weight of both of them with his left hand and arm.

That's a neat trick after a bullet has shattered your shoulder. But wait. If you think way back to the movie's second big action sequence near the beginning of the film, Arnold and Vanessa are the targets of a nail bomb, which explodes, driving a spike completely through Arnold's right hand—the one he later holds Williams with. A guy like that, he could play basketball on bad ankles for weeks.

How does he do it? I guess he has plumb forgotten the spike through his hand. There have been a lot of distractions, like being attacked by alligators at the New York Zoo and falling out of an airplane without his parachute and shooting at a Boeing 727 with a handgun in mid-air. Arnold is amazingly serene under this stress. After he shoots the alligator through the head, he tells it, "You're luggage!"

The plot of *Eraser* involves Vanessa Williams as Lee Cullen, who stumbles across evidence that a secret cabal inside the U.S. government is illegally exporting advanced weapons systems. In particular, they're selling the "rail gun." What is a rail gun? Allow the movie's director, Charles Russell, to explain: "Rail guns are hypervelocity weapons that shoot aluminum or clay rounds at just below the speed of light."

Uh, huh. Just below the speed of light? Which is 186,000 miles a second? What happens to aluminum and clay rounds shot at that speed? They don't pulverize or anything, do they? That muzzle velocity doesn't cause overheating or anything, I suppose? At least there's no recoil when the bullets leave the guns at just below the speed of light. I know that because at one point Arnold holds a rail gun in each hand (including the injured right one) and fires them simultaneously.

What is amazing is that Charles Russell wants us to believe these guns are plausible. "These guns," he elaborates in the press notes, "represent a whole new technology in weaponry that is still in its infancy, though a large-scale version exists in limited numbers on battleships and tanks. They have incredible range. They can pierce three-foot-thick cement walls and then knock a canary off a tin can with absolute accuracy." If I read this correctly, he is talking here about the battleship model. My curiosity is awakened. To hell with the secret government plot—I want to see the U.S. Navy shooting clay bullets at just beneath the speed of light through three-foot cement walls at canaries. And I want to stay for the credits: "No canaries were harmed during the filming of this motion picture."

But I digress. *Eraser* is actually good action fun, with spectacular stunts and special effects (I liked the sequence where Arnold shoots it out with the Boeing 727) and high energy. Arnold plays his usual heroic character, an ace operative in the federal witness protection program, and Vanessa Williams is a good sport, running and jumping and fighting and shooting and kicking and screaming and being tied to chairs and smuggling computer discs and looking great.

There is fun, too, when Arnold contacts an old friend named Johnny C (Robert Pastorelli) from the witness protection program. Johnny is an ex-Mafia guy now working in a drag bar. When Arnold finds out the illegal arms are being shipped from docks controlled by the union, Johnny goes to his uncle, Tony Two-Toes, who looks unkindly on anybody moving anything through the docks without union sanction. Soon Johnny, Tony Two-Toes, and other mafiosi are spying on a Russian ship that's being loaded. They have the following conversation:

Tony Two-Toes: "Those dirty commies!"

Underling: "They're not commies anymore. They're a federation of independent liberated states."

Tony: "Don't make me hurt you, Mikey."

*Eraser* is more or less what you expect, two hours of mindless nonstop high-tech action, with preposterous situations, a body count in the dozens, and Arnold introducing a new trademark line of dialogue (it's supposed to be "Trust me," but I think "You're luggage" will win on points). Thinking back over the film, I can only praise the director's restraint in leaving out the canary.

## Escape from L.A. ★ ★ ★ ½

R, 100 m., 1996

Kurt Russell (Snake Plissken), Stacy Keach (Malloy), Steve Buscemi (Map to the Stars Eddie), Peter Fonda (Pipeline), George Corraface (Cuervo Jones), Bruce Campbell (Surgeon General), Valeria Golino (Taslima), Pam Grier (Hershe), Cliff Robertson (President), A. J. Langer (Utopia). Directed by John Carpenter and produced by Debra Hill and Kurt Russell. Screenplay by Carpenter, Hill, and Russell.

John Carpenter's *Escape from L.A.* is a go-for-broke action extravaganza that satirizes the genre at the same time it's exploiting it. It's a dark vision of a postapocalyptic Los Angeles—leveled by a massive earthquake, cut off from the mainland by a flooded San Fernando Valley, and converted into a prison camp for the nation's undesirables.

Against this backdrop Carpenter launches a special effects fantasy that reaches heights so absurd that there's a giddy delight in the outrage. He generates heedlessness and joy in scenes like the one where the hero surfs on a tsunami wave down Wilshire Boulevard and leaps onto the back of a speeding convertible. It's as if he gave himself license to dream up anything—to play without a net. This is the kind of movie *Independence Day* could have been if it hadn't played it safe.

The production reunites Carpenter with actor Kurt Russell and producer Debra Hill, who also made his *Escape from New York* (1981). They wrote the script together (reportedly starting right after the 1994 earthquake), and it combines adventure elements with a bizarre gallery of characters and potshots at such satirical targets as plastic surgery, theme parks, agents, and the imperial presidency.

As the movie opens in the year 2013, "Los Angeles Island" is no longer part of the United States, but a one-way destination for "immorals and undesirables," who are offered an option at the deportation office: They can choose instant electrocution instead. The island is controlled by Cuervo Jones (George Corraface), a Latino revolutionary who has a big disco ball mounted on the trunk of his convertible. The United States is ruled by a president for life (Cliff Robertson), who has moved the capital to his hometown of Lynchburg, Virginia. Now his rebellious daughter Utopia (A. J. Langer) has hijacked *Air Force Three* and fled to Los Angeles with the precious black box that contains the codes controlling the globe's energy-transmission satellites.

The president and his chief henchman (Stacy Keach) need to get that black box back. So they track down outlaw Snake Plissken (Kurt Russell), who saved an earlier president from the prison city of New York. His assignment: Go in, get the box, kill the girl, and return within ten hours before he dies of a virus they've helpfully infected him with as an added inspiration.

Movies like this depend on special effects, costumes, and set design to create their worlds out of scratch, and *Escape from L.A.* is wall-to-wall with the landmarks of a postearthquake L.A. We see the Chinese theater, the Hollywood Bowl, and a beached ocean liner, and the showdown takes place in an amusement park intended, I think, to suggest Disneyland's Main Street USA. Snake finds his way through the deadly wilderness with a series of guides, including Pipeline (Peter Fonda), a has-been surfer; Taslima (Valeria Golino), a beautiful but doomed street person; Map to the Stars Eddie (Steve Buscemi), who is the "guy to see" about anything; and the exotic Hershe (Pam Grier), a transsexual Snake once knew back in Cleveland, where he/she was known as Carjack.

Meanwhile, the clock is ticking, and Snake has been supplied with that indispensable device for all action thrillers, a digital readout that tells him how much time he has left to live. At the end, when Snake has only twenty minutes to find Cuervo Jones, grab the black box, and seize the daughter, Hershe suggests they get to Pasadena in a hurry by using hang gliders. Whose heart is so stony it can resist the sight of Kurt Russell and Pam Grier swooping down out of the sky, automatic weapons blazing, in an attack on Disneyland?

Who, for that matter, can resist some of the other stops along the way, including Snake's encounter with a colony of "surgical failures," who have had one plastic surgery too many and can survive only by obtaining a steady supply of fresh body parts? Or by the sight of San Fernando Valley used-car signs peeking above the waves? Or by a chase scene that involves motorcycles, cars, trucks, horses, machine guns, and boleros?

*Escape from L.A.* took some courage for Carpenter, Russell, and Hill to make; they had to hope that moviegoers would accept a special effects picture with a satiric sense of humor. Yes, there are laughs in *Independence Day,* but they're fairly obvious and don't sting. *Escape from L.A.* has fun with the whole concept of pictures like itself. It goes deliberately and cheerfully over the top, anchored by Russell's monosyllabic performance, which makes Clint Eastwood sound like Gabby Hayes.

Futuristic Los Angeles fantasies have uneven histories at the box office; neither *Blade Runner* nor *Strange Days* did all that well in their initial theatrical releases. But *Escape from L.A.* has such manic energy, such a weird, cockeyed vision, that it may work on some moviegoers as satire and on others as the real thing. That could lead to some interesting audience reactions. John Carpenter as a filmmaker has been all over the map, from the superb *(Halloween)* to the weirdly offbeat *(Christine, Starman),* to the dreary *(Village of the Damned).* This time he simply tears the map up; the implications of his final scene are breathtaking. Good for him.

## The Evening Star ★ ½

PG-13, 129 m., 1996

Shirley MacLaine (Aurora Greenway), Bill Paxton (Jerry Bruckner), Juliette Lewis (Melanie Horton), Miranda Richardson (Patsy Carpenter), Marion Ross (Rosie), George Newbern (Tommy Horton), MacKenzie Astin (Teddy Horton), Jack Nicholson (Garrett Breedlove), Donald Moffat (Hector Scott), Ben Johnson (Arthur Cotton). Directed by Robert Harling and produced by David Kirkpatrick, Polly Platt, and Keith Samples. Screenplay by Harling, based on the novel by Larry McMurtry.

*The Evening Star* is a completely unconvincing sequel to *Terms of Endearment* (1983). It tells the story of the later years of Aurora Greenway (Shirley MacLaine), but fails to find much in them worth making a movie about. It shows every evidence, however, of having closely scrutinized the earlier film for the secret of its success. The best scenes in *Terms* involved the death of Aurora's daughter, Emma, unforgettably played by Debra Winger. Therefore, *The Evening Star* has no less than three deaths. You know you're in trouble when the most upbeat scene in a comedy is the scattering of ashes.

The movie takes place in Houston, where Aurora lives with her loyal housekeeper Rosie (Marion Ross) and grapples unsuccessfully with the debris of her attempts to raise her late daughter's children. The oldest boy (George Newbern) is in prison on his third drug possession charge. The middle boy (MacKenzie Astin) is shacked up with a girlfriend and their baby. The girl, Melanie (Juliette Lewis), is on the brink of moving to Los Angeles with her boyfriend, a would-be actor. (The absence of their father, Flap, played in the first movie by Jeff Daniels, is handled with brief dialogue.)

Aurora has broken up with the general (Donald Moffat), who lives down the street, but he is still a daily caller, drinking coffee in the kitchen with Rosie and offering advice. The next-door neighbor, in the house that used to be owned by the astronaut (Jack Nicholson), is now the genial Arthur (the late Ben Johnson), who also pays Rosie a great deal of attention. And still on the scene is Patsy (Miranda Richardson), Emma's best friend, now one of Aurora's confidantes.

All of these people live together in the manner of 1950s sitcoms, which means they constantly walk in and out of each other's houses and throw open the windows to carry on conversations with people in the yard. I don't know about you, but if I had to live in a neighborhood where all of my friends and neighbors were hanging out in the kitchen drinking my coffee and offering free advice and one-liners all day long, I'd move. Let them go to Starbucks.

Rosie, a lovable busybody, notices that Aurora has fallen into a depression, and tricks her into seeing a therapist, Jerry (Bill Paxton). Aurora tells him that she is still seeking "the great love of my life." Anyone who has slept with an astronaut played by Jack Nicholson and can still make that statement is a true optimist. Soon, amazingly, the much-younger Jerry violates all the rules of his profession and asks her out, and we get one of those patented movie scenes designed to show how a rich older lady is the salt of the earth: She takes him to a barbecue joint named the Pig Stand, where she knows everybody by name (this is probably one of the danger signals of alcoholism).

Now we're in for a series of scenes showing how colorful Aurora is, and sure enough, before long she actually crawls in through Jerry's window. The explanation for Jerry's fascination with her, when it finally arrives, is no less inane for being predictable. (I dislike most movie scenes where new characters are dragged onscreen for one shot, just to provide a punch line.)

Developments. Melanie, the granddaughter, wants to move to L.A. with her boyfriend, Bruce. Rosie and old Arthur start dating. The general gets into a snit because Aurora is dating Jerry. Rosie decides to marry Arthur. ("Nobody else has ever told me they loved me. Besides, I'll just be next door.") When Rosie gets sick, Aurora reveals her credentials as a control freak by actually going into Arthur's house and carrying Rosie back to her own house, in the rain.

As a counterpoint to these events, Aurora rummages in a closet and comes up with a roomful of diaries, photo albums, old dance cards, theater programs, and journals, which collectively suggest set decorators and prop consultants on an unlimited budget. And the astronaut (Nicholson) turns up again, briefly, adding a shot in the arm. "I'm still looking for my true love," Aurora tells him, and he replies, with the movie's best line, "There aren't that many shopping days until Christmas."

*Terms of Endearment* was about a difficult relationship between two strong-willed women, the MacLaine and Winger characters. Juliette Lewis, as the granddaughter, is available for similar material here, and indeed her performance is the most convincing in the movie, but the script marginalizes her, preferring instead a series of Auntie Mame–like celebrations of Aurora, alternating with elegiac speeches and clunky sentiment.

Sequels are a chancy business at best, but *Evening Star* is thin and contrived. Even the music has no confidence in the picture: William Ross's score underlines every emotion with big nudges, and ends scenes with tidy little flourishes. The title perhaps comes from *Crossing the Bar*, by Tennyson, who wrote:

*Sunset and evening star,*
*And one clear call for me!*
*And may there be no moaning of the bar,*
*When I put out to sea . . .*

His bar, of course, was made of sand, and is not to be confused with the Pig Stand. In *Evening Star*, however, there is a great deal of moaning when anyone puts out to sea.

## Event Horizon ★ ★

R, 97 m., 1997

Laurence Fishburne (Captain Miller), Sam Neill (Weir), Kathleen Quinlan (Peters), Joely Richardson (Stark), Richard T. Jones (Cooper), Jack Noseworthy (Justin), Jason Isaacs (D.J.), Sean Pertwee (Smith). Directed by Paul Anderson and produced by Lawrence Gordon, Lloyd Levin, and Jeremy Bolt. Screenplay by Philip Eisner.

The year is 2047. A rescue mission has been dispatched to the vicinity of Neptune, where seven years earlier a deep space research vessel named *Event Horizon* disappeared. As the rescue ship *Lewis and Clark* approaches, its sensors indicate the temperature on board the other ship is very cold. No human life signs are detected. Yet there are signs of life all through the ship—some other form of life.

*Event Horizon* opens with a lot of class. It has the detailed space vessels moving majestically against the background of stars, it has the deep rumble of the powerful drives, it has sets displaying persuasive technology, and it even has those barely audible, squeaky, chattering voice-like noises that we remember from *2001*, which give you the creepy feeling that little aliens are talking about you.

I love movies like this. I got up and moved closer to the screen, volunteering to be drawn in. I appreciate the anachronistic details: Everybody on board the rescue ship smokes, for example, which is unlikely in 2047 on a deep space mission where, later, the $CO^2$ air scrubbers will play a crucial role. And the captain (Laurence Fishburne) wears a leather bomber jacket, indicating that J. Peterman is still in business half a century from now. I liked all of that stuff, but there wasn't much substance beneath it.

What happened to the ship named *Event Horizon*? Dr. Weir (Sam Neill) may know. He designed the ship's gravity drive, which looks uncannily like a smaller version of the machine in *Contact,* with three metal rings whirling around a central core. The drive apparently creates a black hole and then slips the ship through it, so that it can travel vast distances in a second.

Dr. Weir performs the obligatory freshman-level explanation of this procedure, taking a piece of paper and showing you how far it is from one edge to the other, and then folding it in half so that the two edges touch, and explaining how that happens when space curves. The crew members nod, listening attentively. They're a highly trained space crew, on a mission where space and time are bread and butter, yet they apparently know less about quantum theory than the readers of this review. It's back to Physics 101 for them.

So, okay, where did the ship go for seven years, and what happened while it was there? Why is the original crew all dead? Unfortunately, *Event Horizon* is not the movie to answer these questions. It's all style, climax, and special effects. The rules change with every scene.

For example, early in the film the *Lewis and Clark* approaches the *Event Horizon* through what I guess is the stormy atmosphere of Neptune, with lots of thunder, lightning, and turbulence. But once those effects are exploited, the rest of the movie takes place in the calm of space. And although we are treated to very nice shots of Neptune, the crew members never look at the planet in awe, or react to the wondrous sight; like the actors standing next to the open airplane door in *Air Force One,* they're so intent on their dialogue that they're oblivious to their surroundings.

The obvious inspiration for *Event Horizon* is a much better film, Andrei Tarkovsky's *Solaris* (1972), where a space station orbits a vast planet. The planet in that film is apparently alive, and creates hallucinations in the minds of the orbiters, making them think they're back on Earth with their families. Same thing happens in *Event Horizon,* where the crew members hallucinate about family members they miss, love, or feel guilty about. But while Tarkovsky was combining the subconscious with the Gaia hypothesis, *Event Horizon* uses the flashbacks mostly for shocks and false alarms (hey, that's not really your daughter under the plastic tent in the equipment room!).

Because sensors picked up signs of life all over the ship, we assume it has been inhabited by a life form from wherever the ship traveled. But this possibility is never resolved. One of the crew members approaches the gravity drive, which turns into something resembling liquid mercury, and he slips through it and later returns, babbling, "It shows you things—horrible things—the dark inside me from the other place. I won't go back there!"

Perhaps Dr. Weir has the answers. But then again, perhaps not. Without revealing too much of the ending, let me say that Weir presumably knows as little from personal experience about what lies on the other side of the gravity drive as anyone else in the movie. He has not been there. That makes one of his most dramatic statements, late in the film, inexplicable. But then perhaps it doesn't matter. The screenplay creates a sense of foreboding and afterboding, but no actual boding.

It is observed darkly at one point that the gravity drive is a case of man pushing too far into realms where he should not go. There is an accusation that someone has "broken the laws of physics," and from the way it's said, you'd assume that offenders will be subject to fines or imprisonment. Of course there are no "laws" of physics—only observations about the way things seem to be. What you "break," if you break anything, is not a law but simply an obsolete belief, now replaced by one that works better. Deeply buried in *Event Horizon* is a suspicion of knowledge. Maybe that's why its characters have so little of it.

## Everyone Says I Love You ★ ★ ★ ★

R, 101 m., 1997

Alan Alda (Bob), Woody Allen (Joe), Drew Barrymore (Skylar), Goldie Hawn (Steffi), Julia Roberts (Von), Tim Roth (Charles Ferry), Lukas Haas (Scott), Gaby Hoffmann (Lane), Natasha Lyonne (D.J.), Edward Norton (Holden), Natalie Portman (Laura), David Ogden Stiers (Holden's Father). Directed by Woody Allen and produced by Jean Doumanian and Robert Greenhut. Screenplay by Allen.

Sometimes, when I am very happy, I sing to myself. Sometimes, when they are very happy, so do the characters in *Everyone Says I Love You,* Woody Allen's magical new musical comedy. I can't sing. Neither can some of Allen's characters. Why should that stop them? Who wants to go through life not ever singing?

Here is a movie that had me with a goofy grin plastered on my face for most of its length. A movie that remembers the innocence of the old Hollywood musicals and combines it with one of Allen's funniest and most labyrinthine plots, in which complicated New Yorkers try to recapture the simplicity of first love. It would take a heart of stone to resist this movie.

Allen's most inspired decision was to allow all of his actors to sing for themselves, in their own voices (all of them except for Drew Barrymore, who just plain can't sing). Some of them are accomplished (Alan Alda, Goldie Hawn, Edward Norton). The rest could hold their own at a piano bar. Allen knows that the musical numbers are not about performance or technical quality or vocal range; they're about feeling.

"Cuddle Up a Little Closer." "My Baby Don't Care for Pearls." "Looking at You." "I'm Through With Love." "I'm a Dreamer." "Makin' Whoopee." "Enjoy Yourself, It's Later Than You Think." These are songs that perhaps suffer a little when they're sung too well (just as trained opera singers always overdo it in musical comedy). They're for ordinary, happy voices, and from the first moment of the film, when Edward Norton turns to Drew Barrymore and sings "Just You, Just Me," the movie finds a freshness and charm that never ends.

The story involves a lot of Allen's familiar elements. His character, named Joe, is unlucky in love; he's a writer who lives in Paris, where his French girlfriend Giselle has just dumped him. He contemplates suicide, and debates the wisdom of taking the Concorde to New York before killing himself (with the time gain, he could get an extra three hours of stuff done and still be dead on schedule).

He returns to New York to be comforted by his best friends, who are his first wife, Steffi (Goldie Hawn), and her current husband, Bob (Alan Alda). The extended family is a yours, mine, and ours situation. D.J. (Natasha Lyonne) is Joe's daughter with Steffi. She serves as the narrator. Then there are Skylar (Drew Barrymore), who has just gotten engaged; Scott (Lukas Haas), who has the family concerned with his newfound conservatism; and his sisters Lane (Gaby Hoffman) and Laura (Natalie Portman), who are just discovering boys and have unfortunately discovered the same one.

The plot is simultaneously featherweight and profound, like a lot of Allen's movies: Big questions are raised and then dispatched with a one-liner, only to keep eating away at the hero until an eventually happy ending. Most of the questions have to do, of course, with unwise or inappropriate romances.

Joe decides to get away from it all by taking his daughter D.J. to Venice. Here we get one of the movie's loveliest moments, Allen singing "I'm Through With Love" on a balcony overlooking the Grand Canal. Of course he is not; soon after, he sees the enticing Von (Julia Roberts) in Venice, and falls in love at first sight. Amazingly, D.J. is able to supply him with useful insights into this mystery woman. D.J.'s best friend's mother is Von's psychiatrist, and the kids have eavesdropped on therapy sessions, so D.J. knows Von's likes (Tintoretto) and dislikes (her current husband), and coaches her father. This is, of course, dishonest and unethical, and delicious.

Joe's inside knowledge makes him irresistible to Roberts, although their romance is doomed from the start. Meanwhile, D.J. falls in love with a gondolier and announces an impending marriage. Back in New York, Holden (Edward Norton) has bought an engagement ring for Skylar (while the salesmen at Harry Winston's celebrate in a song and dance). Also meanwhile, Steffi, a liberal who wears her heart on her sleeve, arranges the release of a prisoner (Tim Roth) she thinks has been unfairly treated, and he steals Skylar's heart, for a time, anyway—and also contributes to an unusual dinner party.

Oh, there's more. Including the scene where Skylar accidentally swallows her $8,000 engagement ring and is told by the doctor examining the X rays, "I could have got it for you for $6,000." And a miraculous cure for Scott's conservatism. And a fanciful song-and-dance scene involving some ghosts in a funeral home. And the absolutely wonderful long closing sequence, which begins at a New Year's Eve party in Paris where everyone is dressed like Groucho Marx.

Steffi's family is visiting Paris, and at dawn she and Joe walk off alone to the café where their romance started many years ago. Was their divorce a mistake? Should Steffi dump Bob and come back to Joe? At dawn in a romantic café in Paris all sorts of seductive ideas can occur, but the movie segues away from hard decisions and into a dance number involving Allen and Hawn on the banks of the Seine, Goldie floating effortlessly in a scene that combines real magic with the magic of the heart.

Watching that scene, I thought that perhaps *Everyone Says I Love You* is the best film Woody Allen has ever made. Not the most profound, or the most daring, or the most successful in every one of its details—but simply the best, because he finds the right note for every scene, and dances on a tightrope between comedy and romance, between truth and denial, between what we hope and what we know.

Not many musicals are made these days. They're hard to do, and the fashion for them has passed. This one remembers the musicals of the 1930s, the innocent ones starring Astaire and Rogers, or Powell and Keeler, and to that freshness it adds a sharper, contemporary wit. Allen knows that what modern musicals are missing is not the overkill of multimillion-dollar production numbers, or the weight of hit songs from the charts, but the feeling that some things simply cannot be said in words and require songs to say them. He is right. Attempt this experiment: Try to say "Cuddle up a little closer, baby mine" without singing. Can't be done. Should rarely be attempted.

## Eve's Bayou ★ ★ ★ ★

R, 109 m., 1997

Jurnee Smollett (Eve Batiste), Meagan Good (Cisely Batiste), Samuel L. Jackson (Louis Batiste), Lynn Whitfield (Roz Batiste), Debbi Morgan (Mozelle Batiste Delacroix), Jake Smollett (Poe Batiste), Ethel Ayler (Gran Mere), Diahann Carroll (Elzora), Vondie Curtis Hall (Julian Grayraven). Directed by Kasi Lemmons and produced by Caldecot Chubb and Samuel L. Jackson. Screenplay by Lemmons.

"Memory is a selection of images, some elusive, others printed indelibly on the brain. The summer I killed my father, I was ten years old."

With those opening words, *Eve's Bayou* coils back into the past, into the memories of a child who grew up in a family both gifted and flawed, and tried to find her own way to the truth. The words explain the method of the film. This will not be a simpleminded story that breathlessly races from A to B. It is a selection of memories, filtered through the eyes of a young girl who doesn't understand everything she sees—and filtered, too, through the eyes of her older sister, and through the eyes of an aunt who can foretell everyone's future except for her own.

As these images unfold, we are drawn into the same process Eve has gone through: We, too, are trying to understand what happened in that summer of 1962, when Eve's handsome, dashing father—a doctor and womanizer—took one chance too many. And we want to understand what happened late one night between the father and Eve's older sister, in a moment that was over before it began. We want to know because the film makes it perfectly possible that there is more than one explanation; *Eve's Bayou* studies the way that dangerous emotions can build up until something happens that no one is responsible for and that can never be taken back.

All of these moments unfold in a film of astonishing maturity and confidence; *Eve's Bayou*, one of the very best films of the year, is the debut of its writer and director, Kasi Lemmons. She sets her story in Southern Gothic country, in the bayous and old Louisiana traditions that Tennessee Williams might have been familiar with, but in tone and style she earns comparison with the family dramas of Ingmar Bergman. That Lemmons can make a film this good on the first try is like a rebuke to established filmmakers.

The story is told through the eyes of Eve Batiste, played with fierce truthfulness by Jurnee Smollett. Her family is descended from a slave, also named Eve, who saved her master's life and was rewarded with her freedom and with sixteen children. In 1962, the Batistes are the premiere family in their district, living in a big old mansion surrounded by rivers and swampland. Eve's father, Louis (Samuel L. Jackson), is the local doctor. Her mother, Roz (Lynn Whitfield), is "the most beautiful woman I ever have seen." Her sister, Cisely (Meagan Good), is on the brink of adolescence, and the apple of her father's eye; Eve watches unhappily at a party and afterwards asks her father, "Daddy, why don't you ever dance with me?" Living with them is an aunt, Mozelle (Debbi Morgan), who has lost three husbands, "is not unfamiliar with the inside of a mental hospital," and has the gift of telling fortunes.

Dr. Batiste is often away from home on house

calls—some of them legitimate, some excuses for his philandering. He is a weak but not a bad man, and not lacking in insight: "To a certain type of woman, I am a hero," he says. "I need to be a hero." On the night that her father did not dance with her, Eve steals away to a barn and falls asleep, only to awaken and see her father apparently making love with another man's wife. Eve tells Cisely, who says she was mistaken, and the doubt over this incident will echo later, on another night when much depends on whether Cisely was mistaken.

Lemmons surrounds her characters with a rich setting. There is a marketplace, dominated by the stalls of farmers and fishermen, and by the presence of a voodoo woman (Diahann Carroll) whose magic may or may not be real. Certainly Aunt Mozelle's gift is real; her prophecies have a terrifying accuracy, as when she tells a woman her missing son will be found in a Detroit hospital on Tuesday. But Mozelle cannot foresee her own life: "I looked at each of my husbands," she says, "and never saw a thing." All three died. So when a handsome painter (Vondie Curtis Hall) comes into the neighborhood and Mozelle knows she has found true love at last, she is afraid to marry him, because it has been prophesied that any man who marries her will die.

The film has been photographed by Amy Vincent in shadows and rich textures, where even a sunny day contains dark undertones; surely she looked at the Bergman films photographed by Sven Nykvist in preparing her approach. There is a scene of pure magic as Mozelle tells Eve the story of the death of one of her husbands, who was shot by her lover; the woman and the girl stand before a mirror, regarding the scene from the past, and then Mozelle slips out of the shot and reappears in the past.

There is also great visual precision in the scenes involving the confused night when the doctor comes home drunk, and Cisely goes downstairs to comfort him. What happened? We get two accounts and we see two versions, and the film is far too complex and thoughtful to try to reduce the episode to a simple formula like sexual abuse; what happens lasts only a second, and is charged with many possibilities for misinterpretation, all of them prepared for by what has gone before.

*Eve's Bayou* resonates in the memory. It called me back for a second and third viewing. It is a reminder that sometimes films can venture into the realms of poetry and dreams.

## Evita ★ ★ ★ ½

PG, 134 m., 1997

Madonna (Eva Peron), Antonio Banderas (Che), Jonathan Pryce (Juan Peron), Jimmy Nail (Agustin Magaldi), Victoria Sus (Dona Juana), Julian Littman (Brother Juan), Olga Merediz (Blanca), Laura Pallas (Elisa), Julia Worsley (Erminda). Directed by Alan Parker and produced by Robert Stigwood, Parker, and Andrew G. Vajna. Screenplay by Parker and Oliver Stone, based on the musical *Evita,* with music by Andrew Lloyd Webber and lyrics by Tim Rice.

*Evita* allows the audience to identify with a heroine who achieves greatness by—well, golly, by being who she is. It celebrates the life of a woman who begins as a quasi-prostitute, marries a powerful man, locks him out of her bedroom, and inspires the idolatry of the masses by spending enormous sums on herself. When she sings: "They need to adore me—to Christian Dior me," she's right on the money.

I begin on this note not to criticize the new musical *Evita* (which I enjoyed very much), but to bring a touch of reality to the character of Eva Peron, who, essentially, was famous because she was so very well known. Her fame continued after her death, as her skillfully embalmed body went on to a long-running career of its own, displayed before multitudes, spirited to Europe, fought over, prayed over, and finally sealed beneath slabs of steel in an Argentine cemetery. Eva Peron lived only until thirty-three, but she went out with a long curtain call.

She was not an obvious subject for a musical. Andrew Lloyd Webber and Tim Rice, who wrote the stage version of *Evita* and whose songs are wall-to-wall in the movie, must have known that; why else did they provide a key character named Che Guevera (onstage) and Che (onscreen), to ask embarrassing questions? "You let down your people, Evita," he sings. She let down the poor, shirtless ones by providing a glamorous facade for a fascist dictatorship, by salting away charity funds, and by distracting from her husband's tacit protection of Nazi war criminals.

Why, then, were Webber and Rice so right in choosing Eva Peron as their heroine? My guess is that they perfectly anticipated *Evita*'s core audience—affluent, middle-aged, and female. The musical celebrates Eva Peron's narcissism, her furs and diamonds, her firm management of her man. Given such enticements, what audience is going to quibble about ideology?

For years I have wondered, during "Don't Cry for Me, Argentina," why we were not to cry. Now I understand: We need not cry because (a) Evita got everything out of life she dreamed of, and (b) Argentina should cry for itself. Even poor Juan Peron should shed a tear or two; he is relegated in the movie to the status of a "walker," a presentable man who adorns the arm of a rich and powerful woman as a human fashion accessory.

All of these thoughts, as I watched Alan Parker's *Evita,* did not in the least prevent me from having a good time. I suspect Parker has as many questions about his heroine as I do, and I am sure that Che (Antonio Banderas) and Juan Peron (Jonathan Pryce) do—not to mention Oliver Stone, coauthor of the screenplay. Only Evita herself, magnificently embodied by Madonna, rises above the quibbles, as she should; if there is one thing a great Evita should lack, it is any trace of self-doubt. Here we have a celebration of a legendary woman (for those who take the film superficially), and a moral tale of a misspent life (for those who see more clearly).

Certainly Alan Parker is a good director for this material. He has made more musicals than his contemporaries, not only *Bugsy Malone, Fame,* and *The Commitments,* but especially *Pink Floyd—The Wall,* one of the great modern musicals, where he uses similar images of marching automatons. Working with exteriors in Argentina and Hungary and richly detailed interior sets, he stages Evita's life as a soap opera version of *Triumph of the Will,* with goose-stepping troops beating out the cadence of her rise to glory.

The movie is almost entirely music; the fugitive lines of spoken dialogue sound sheepish. Madonna, who took voice lessons to extend her range, easily masters the musical material. As important, she is convincing as Evita—from the painful early scene where, as an unacknowledged child, she tries to force entry into her father's funeral, to later scenes where the poor rural girl converts herself into a nightclub singer, radio star, desirable mistress, and political leader.

There is a certain opaque quality in Madonna's Evita; what you see is not exactly what you get. The Che character zeroes in on this, questioning her motives, doubting her ideals, pointing out contradictions and evasions. Yet for Evita there are no inconsistencies, because everything she does is at the service of her image. It is only if you believe she is at the service of the poor that you being to wonder. Listen closely as she sings:

*For I am ordinary, unimportant*
*And undeserving*
*Of such attention*
*Unless we all are*
*I think we all are*
*So share my glory.*

The poor, in other words, deserve what Evita has, so her program consists of her having it and the poor being happy for her. After all, if she didn't have it, she'd be poor too. In other words: The lottery is wonderful, just as long as I win it.

Banderas, as Che, sees through this; his performance is one of the triumphs of the movie. He sings well, he has a commanding screen presence, and he finds a middle ground between condemnation and giving the devil her due. He is "of the people" enough to feel their passion for Evita, and enough of a revolutionary to distrust his feelings.

Jonathan Pryce, as the dictator, remains more difficult to read. He is grateful for the success Evita brings him (her broadcasts free him from prison, her campaigns win his elections, her fame legitimatizes his regime). But there is a quiet little scene where he knocks on her locked bedroom door and then shuffles back to his own room, and that scene speaks volumes for the haunted look in his eyes.

The music, like most of the Webber/Rice scores, is repetitive to the point of brainwashing. It's as if they come up with one good song and go directly into rehearsals. The reason their songs become hits is that you've heard them a dozen times by the end of the show. But Parker's visuals enliven the music, and Madonna and Banderas bring it passion. By the end of the film we feel like we've had our money's worth, and we're sure Evita has.

### Excess Baggage ★ ★ ★
PG-13, 98 m., 1997

Alicia Silverstone (Emily), Benicio Del Toro (Vincent), Christopher Walken (Ray), Jack Thompson (Alexander), Harry Connick Jr. (Greg), Nicholas Turturro (Stick), Michael Bowen (Gus), Robert Wisden (Detective Sims). Directed by Marco Brambilla and produced by Bill Borden and Carolyn Kessler. Screenplay by Max D. Adams, Dick Clement, and Ian La Frenais.

Alicia Silverstone, she of the blond locks and quick intelligence, was perfectly cast in *Clueless* as a popular girl who tries to pull all the strings, and gets a few of her own pulled in return. She was such a hit in the film that she formed her own production company while still in her teens, and there were cover stories hailing her as the next . . . I dunno . . . Winona Ryder? Grace Kelly?

She was wonderful in that film, but could she pick another hit? Certainly her agents advised her to take the role of Robin's girlfriend in *Batman and Robin,* where she looked unconvincing, uncomfortable, and a size larger than the costume. Now she is back in a starring role in *Excess Baggage,* a film she coproduced. She's okay in it, but no better than okay. Benicio Del Toro steals it with his performance as a car thief who becomes an unwilling kidnapper.

Silverstone plays Emily, a rich kid who fakes her own kidnapping in order to attract her father's attention. She locks herself in the trunk of her own car, expecting to be rescued quickly, but her plans go wrong when Del Toro's thief, named Vincent, steals the car. At his chop shop, he is amazed to find her in the trunk, and even more amazed when she refuses to be intimidated.

There's a shade of *The Ransom of Red Chief* here, as the kidnapping victim turns into more trouble than she's worth. Vincent's partner, Greg, played by Harry Connick Jr., is possibly smarter and certainly unwilling to get anywhere near a kidnapping, although his situation grows more difficult after they succeed in misplacing $200,000 in mob money.

The architecture of the plot will be familiar. We have Jack Thompson as the wealthy, distant father named Alexander, Christopher Walken as Uncle Ray, Alexander's Mr. Fixit, and handy MacGuffins like the mob money that obviously exist only as tools for the plot. One inspiration may have been enough for this movie; why not set up the phony kidnapping and the carjacking and then play out the plot based on the personalities of the characters, instead of penciling in all the clichés? (At one point, Emily is unhappy with Vincent in a rural diner and stages a scene indicating he has mistreated her, and three very big and ominous guys stand up slowly to come and settle Vincent's hash and defend the little lady. I'm thinking, no diner in a movie is complete without those three guys.)

Despite the elements I could have done without, the movie is often very funny, and a lot of the credit goes to Benicio Del Toro, who creates a slow-talking, lumbrous character who's quite unlike his image in *The Usual Suspects.* Here he has a dash of Brad Pitt and a touch of city-style cornpone; he's one of those guys who cultivates a personal style as a way of giving himself time to think.

The plot creates some fairly involved reasons why Emily and Vincent have to hit the road together, and why Alexander and Uncle Ray never quite figure out what they're up against. Many scenes are based on misunderstandings, and Del Toro grows funnier as he grows more ingenious and desperate in trying to think his way out of a situation he only vaguely comprehends. And Silverstone, as I said, is okay, although she's still coasting here on the success of *Clueless.* Maybe that movie was so entertaining that no follow-up could satisfy us; maybe next time she'll find the perfect role again. *Hint:* It will probably not be in any script containing the words "mob," "kidnapping," "ransom," and "millionaire."

### Executive Decision ★ ★ ★
R, 129 m., 1995

Kurt Russell (David Grant), Steven Seagal (Lt. Col. Travis), Halle Berry (Jean), John Leguizamo (Rat), Oliver Platt (Cahill), Joe Morton (Cappy), David Suchet (Nagi Hassan), Marla Maples (Flight attendant), J. T. Walsh (Senator). Directed by Stuart Baird and produced by Joel Silver. Screenplay by Jim Thomas and John Thomas.

*Executive Decision* is a gloriously goofy mess of a movie about a hijacked airliner and a plot to poison, yes, "the entire eastern seaboard of the United States." (Why doesn't anybody ever poison the western seaboard?) It's the kind of thriller where it's fun to chortle over the plot—a movie for people who are sophisticated enough to know how shameless the film is, but fun-loving enough to enjoy its excesses and manic zeal.

This is the kind of film that supplies subtitles on the screen with such helpful information as (over a shot of the Parthenon) "Athens, Greece." And with dialogue like "I take back every rust-picking, squid-eating thing I've ever said about Squabbies." And with Marla Maples in an almost nonspeaking role as a flight attendant who has three speeds: dedicated, concerned, and deeply concerned. If she decides to continue her acting lessons, I hope she gets a teacher who tells her that, in the movies, experienced actors do *not* try to "mirror emotion" in their facial expressions, because it always comes across as overacting.

The movie stars Kurt Russell as an American intelligence expert, who, in his first scene, is taking flying lessons. Since we know the movie is about a hijacked 747, we can predict with 100 percent certainty that by the end of the film he will be called upon to fly the 747. But first we meet Steven Seagal as a colonel in charge of a U.S. commando unit, which tries to capture a large store of stolen Russian nerve gas, but arrives too late. That's because, as Russell surmises, the toxic gas is on board the hijacked airliner heading for Dulles Airport.

The hijacking is a cover by the clever Islamic terrorist Nagi Hassan (David Suchet), who is actually using the airplane to smuggle the gas into the United States. Can you think of an easier way to get a shipment of contraband into the country than by hijacking a 747 with four hundred people on board? I can, and so can the entire South American drug industry. But never mind. The plane is airborne, flying toward America, and a brilliant but unstable designer (Oliver Platt) hatches a risky plan to have a Stealth bomber sneak up underneath the 747 so that a big airtight tube can be attached to an entry hatch, and American soldiers can climb on board and overpower the terrorists.

Seagal leads the strike force, with Russell and Platt reluctantly coming along for the ride. And at this point the movie succeeded in *really* surprising me, because, while trying to board the plane, Seagal is sucked out of the tube and into the jet stream, no doubt to fall five miles while screaming the very same word that Butch and the Kid shouted when they jumped off that cliff. Any movie prepared to kill off Steven Seagal in the first twenty minutes is prepared for anything, and so I perked right up.

The plot shows the U.S. strike force secreting itself in the bowels of the ship, spying on the hijackers with hidden video cameras, and using laptop computers and lots of ingenuity to try to defuse the nerve gas bomb. (The bomb disposal expert, Joe Morton, cracks a vertebra and spends most of the movie with his head duct-taped to a splint.) We get all the obligatory scenes about whether to clip the red wire or the blue wire.

In the passenger section, Hassan comes across as a fanatic bent on destroying millions of lives. His fellow hijackers think the mission is to force the release of one of their leaders, but after the leader is released, Hassan reveals that his original demands were only a cover for his real plans. A moderate among his followers steps forward, shouts, "This has nothing to do with Islam!" and is shot. His function is to get the filmmakers off the hook: Hassan is a fanatic, see, and not to be taken as typical of his coreligionists. (It would have been easy to make the terrorists members of a nonsectarian movement, and I wish they had; what purpose does it serve to slander a religion?)

As the emergency develops, we meet a publicity-seeking U.S. senator (J. T. Walsh), one of the passengers, who is reminded by an aide, "Remember how much good press Jesse Jackson got for freeing the hostages?" And Kurt Russell is able to enlist a heroic flight attendant (Halle Berry) in his counterattack. She gets the movie's single funniest moment when she discovers, in the terrorist's jacket, a map labeled "Washington, D.C." The map is singularly unhelpful, since all it shows is a dot identified as "Washington," surrounded by concentric circles of, I guess, spreading toxic gases.

The late Hollywood producer Ross Hunter, who died just as this movie was going into release, once explained to me the secret of the airliner-in-trouble genre. This was in 1970, when he produced *Airport*. "The thing is," he said, "all these people get in the airplane and go up, and then something happens, and it doesn't look like they'll be able to get down again. Who can't identify with that?" Hey, don't look at me.

## Eye for an Eye ★

R, 101 m., 1996

Sally Field (Karen McCann), Kiefer Sutherland (Doob), Ed Harris (Mack McCann), Beverly D'Angelo (Dolly Green), Joe Mantegna (Detective Denillo), Charlayne Woodard (Angel Kosinsky). Directed by John Schlesinger and produced by Michael I. Levy. Screenplay by Amanda Silver and Rick Jaffa, based on *Eye for an Eye,* a novel by Erika Holzer.

*Eye for an Eye* is a particularly nasty little example of audience manipulation, leading to a conclusion that, had I accepted it, would have left me feeling unclean. It's about an ordinary woman who is led to seek blood revenge in a plot where the deck is stacked so blatantly it's shameless. It's ironic that this movie was released at the same time as *Dead Man Walking.* Both are about killers and their victims, and both are, in a way, about the death penalty. *Dead Man Walking* challenges us to deal with a wide range of ethical and moral issues. *Eye for an Eye* cynically blinkers us, excluding morality as much as it can, to service an exploitation plot.

The movie stars Sally Field as Karen, a mother whose teenage daughter is raped and killed in a particularly horrifying scene early in the movie. The daughter calls for help, and Karen actually hears the attack over the telephone—and then tries to race home, gets stuck in traffic, and is trapped in a nightmare scene where other drivers refuse her request to use a mobile phone. She arrives at a crime scene.

Karen is shattered, and turns for comfort to her husband (Ed Harris) and their young daughter. Meanwhile, a smart cop (Joe Mantegna) quickly catches a suspect named Doob (Kiefer Sutherland). All the evidence points to him, even the DNA and semen samples. But Doob gets off on a stupid technicality, and then Karen grows obsessed. She joins a support group for survivors (their motto: "You show me your heartbreak and I'll show you mine"). And through them she is introduced into a shadowy network of those who have chosen to take the law into their own hands.

She trails Doob. He is a mean, nasty, brutish man who smokes all the time, has tattoos, needs a shave, and kicks dogs. When he becomes aware she is following him, he visits a playground at her young daughter's school and terrorizes the little girl. Karen goes ballistic, turns to her group's secret advisers for help, buys a weapon, and takes shooting and martial arts lessons. Meanwhile, we watch, through the film's omnipotent point of view, as Doob assaults and murders another victim.

So let's keep this straight. Doob is definitely and without the shadow of a doubt a killer. As audience members, we have seen what no jury can ever see, Doob in the act of killing. He is also a thoroughly despicable, worthless human being. Therefore, he deserves to be killed—right? And Field is justified in murdering him—right?

The film complicates things just a little with the presence in the support group of Angel Kosinsky (Charlayne Woodard), who suspects what Karen may be up to. Angel is a black lesbian, which is perfectly all right with me, although the movie had already tried to manipulate me in so many ways that I was seeking a shabby motive for her character when none was probably intended. (Were the filmmakers trying to show they were broad-minded liberals except when it comes to well-deserved revenge?) There are also two quirky scenes where Field, newly energized by her martial arts training, beats up an innocent bystander and later, elated by the experience, has such aggressive sex with her mild husband that he can't believe it.

This movie is intellectually corrupt because it deliberately avoids dealing with the issues it raises. Unlike *Dead Man Walking,* which is a courageous attempt to show various points of view about the death penalty, this movie is one of those hypothetical cases where everything is skewed to lead up to the conclusion the filmmakers demand. All the right cards are dealt. We know for a fact the guy is guilty. It is demonstrated he will and does kill again. He is a vile monster, a villain to make the skin crawl. Now comes the final straw—the ending of the movie, which I will not reveal, is a complete cop-out because it neatly finds a way to throw meat to the audience while technically, at least, leaving the Sally Field character off the hook.

Movies like *Eye for an Eye* cheapen our character, by encouraging us to indulge simplistic emotions—to react instead of analyzing. It provides a one-in-a-million situation and tries to teach us a lesson from it; thoughtful audience members will be aware they're not being treated fairly. This is filmmaking at the level of three-card monte. If you don't believe me, see *Dead Man Walking*. As you consider the two movies, you may be inspired to painful conclusions about good and bad art.

## Eye of God ★ ★ ★

R, 84 m., 1998

Martha Plimpton (Ainsley Dupree), Kevin Anderson (Jack), Hal Holbrook (Sheriff Rogers), Nick Stahl (Tommy Spencer), Mary Kay Place (Clair Spencer), Chris Freihofer (Les Hector), Woody Watson (Glen Briggs), Richard Jenkins (Parole Officer). Directed by Tim Blake Nelson and produced by Michael Nelson and Wendy Ettinger. Screenplay by Nelson.

Rural Oklahoma. Town named Kingfisher. Ainsley sits in the convenience store by the road, watching strangers on their way through. She works in a hamburger shop. She's lonely. Through a magazine, she gets into correspondence with a prisoner, and when he gets out he comes to see her. They get married.

This time and place are evoked with quiet, atmospheric shots in Tim Blake Nelson's *Eye of God*, a film in which dreams seem to yearn toward a place where they can grow. Kingfisher is a boring place which is a boring drive from other places just as boring. Ainsley (Martha Plimpton) likes people and would like to know more of them, but her opportunities are limited and her desperation makes her see the ex-convict as salvation.

Well, he looks wholesome enough. Jack (Kevin Anderson) is straightforward and sincere, looks her in the eye, tells her how he found Jesus in prison. At first their marriage looks like it will work. Then his controlling side takes over. He doesn't want her working. Doesn't want her hanging out at the truck stop. Doesn't want her to leave the house, indeed, except to go to church with him on Sunday. It's ironic: Her life was empty and barren before, and by marrying him, she's losing what little variety she was able to find.

The film tells this story in flashes of action, intercut with another story involving a local fourteen-year-old named Tommy (Nick Stahl) whose mother gassed herself. Now he lives with an aunt who can't control him. He's trapped in the town too. *Eye of God* works in a fractured style, telling both films out of chronological order, cutting between them in a way that's disorienting at first, as it's meant to be.

Perhaps there's a clue to the editing in the title. The eyes of god exist outside time and don't need to see stories in chronological order, because they know the beginning, middle, and end before the story begins or the characters even exist. *Eye of God* sees its story in the same way: as events that are so interlocked by fate that, in a way, they don't have to happen one after another because they will all happen eventually.

Continuity of sorts is supplied by the sheriff (Hal Holbrook), who provides a narration of sorts, beginning with the story of Abraham and Isaac: How did the son feel as he saw his father poised to kill him? He finds Tommy wandering by the roadside, covered with blood, in one of the first shots of the film. It's not his blood, but whose is it? He doesn't seem able to talk.

Another outside observer is Jack's parole officer (Richard Jenkins), who tells Ainsley something she should have known before she got married: Jack was in prison for beating a woman nearly to death—a woman who was carrying his child, as, before long, Ainsley is.

Martha Plimpton's performance is the center of the movie, quiet and strong. She plays a capable woman for whom life has not supplied a role. I've often seen her playing bright, glib city girls (that was her first big role, in *Shy People*). As Ainsley, she isn't tragically shy and lonely; it's more that she's waiting patiently for her life to begin, with less and less evidence that it's about to.

The villain in the film is not exactly Jack. Like an animal, he behaves according to his nature, and the way to deal with him is to stay away from him. The movie is more about Ainsley's luck than Jack's behavior. Somebody always marries these jerks, but you gotta hope it's not you.

# F

## Face/Off ★ ★ ★

R, 140 m., 1997

John Travolta (Sean Archer), Nicolas Cage (Castor Troy), Joan Allen (Eve Archer), Gina Gershon (Sasha Hassler), Alessandro Nivola (Pollux Troy), Dominique Swain (Jamie Archer), Nick Cassavetes (Dietrich Hassler), Harve Presnell (Victor Lazzaro). Directed by John Woo and produced by David Permut, Barrie Osborne, Terence Chang, and Christopher Godsick. Screenplay by Mike Werb and Michael Colleary.

There is a moment in *Face/Off* when Sean Archer (John Travolta), a member of a secret FBI antiterrorist team, confronts the comatose body of Castor Troy (Nicolas Cage), his archenemy, in the hospital. "You're keeping him alive?" he asks incredulously. "Relax," says a medical technician. "He's a turnip." To prove it, she puts out her cigarette on Troy's arm. Troy won't feel a thing when his face is surgically removed in order to be transplanted to Archer's skull, so the FBI man can enter prison disguised as Troy and get information about a deadly biological bomb.

That exchange of faces and identities is the inspiration for *Face/Off*, the new John Woo action thriller that contains enough plot for an entire series. It's a gimme, for example, that as gravely injured as he may be, Troy will snap out of his coma and force a doctor to transplant Archer's face onto his own bloody skull—so that the lawman and the outlaw end up looking exactly like each other.

This is an actor's dream, and Travolta and Cage make the most of it. They spend most of the movie acting as if they're in each other's bodies—Travolta acting like Cage and vice versa. Through the plot device of a microchip implanted in his larynx, Travolta is allegedly able to sound more like Cage—enough, maybe, to fool the terrorist's paranoid brother, who is in prison and knows the secret of the biological weapon.

The movie is above all an action thriller. John Woo, whose previous American films include *Broken Arrow* with Travolta, likes spectacular stunts in unlikely settings, and the movie includes chases involving an airplane (which crashes into a hangar) and speedboats (which crash into piers and each other). There are also weird settings, including the high-security prison where the inmates wear magnetized boots that allow security to keep track of every footstep.

The high-tech stuff is flawlessly done, but the intriguing elements of the movie involve the performances. Travolta and Cage do not use dubbed voices, and don't try to imitate each other's speaking voices precisely when "occupying" each other's bodies. Instead, knowing that the sound of a voice is created to some degree by the larynx of his host body, they provide suggestions of each other's speech and vocal patterns, along with subtle physical characteristics. The movie's premise is that only the faces change—so each actor also finds ways to suggest that he is not the original inhabitant of his body. (Troy as Archer at one point refers unhappily to Archer's "ridiculous chin," and the fact that it's Travolta playing Cage criticizing Travolta is typical of the spins they put on the situation.)

For the Archer character, who begins inside Travolta's body and then spends most of the movie inside Cage's, the challenge is to fool a convict brother so suspicious that even when faced with the face of his own brother, he's cautious. For Troy, it's even trickier: He goes home to Archer's family, including his wife (Joan Allen) and confused teenage daughter (Dominique Swain), and has to convince them he's the husband and father they know. The wife in particular is surprised by the renewed ardor of a husband whose thoughts, for years, have been on revenge rather than romance. (Meanwhile, Archer as Troy is confronted by Troy's girlfriend, played by Gina Gershon.)

Woo, who became famous for his Hong Kong action pictures before hiring on in Hollywood, is a director overflowing with invention. He works here with an original screenplay by Mike Werb and Michael Colleary, which explores the strange implications of the face swap. One of the issues they touch on involves how much our appearance shapes our personality: If sweet, shaggy John Travolta looked like angular, sardonic Nicolas Cage, would he act any differently?

The summers of 1996 and 1997 were dominated by big-budget special-effects extravaganzas. Interesting that Cage was in three of them: *The Rock, Con Air*, and now *Face/Off*. He brings a quirkiness to the material that's useful. Given the undeniable fact that the plot of *Face/Off* is utterly absurd, it would be strange to see a traditional action hero playing it straight. Cage adds a spin. And here I was about to write: "For example, when he first sees Travolta's teenage daughter, he quips, 'The plot thickens.'" But, of course, it is *Travolta* who sees Travolta's teenage daughter, because it is Travolta playing the Cage character. You see what thickets this plot constructs; it's as if Travolta adds the spin courtesy of Cage's personality, while Cage mellows in the direction of Travolta. Better to conclude that the two actors, working together, have devised a very entertaining way of being each other while being themselves.

This business of exchanged identities is, of course, not new to drama. Shakespeare enjoyed having characters play each other (see *Twelfth Night*), and in Chinese and Japanese plays it's common for masks to be used to suggest identity swaps. Here, using big movie stars and asking them to play each other, Woo and his writers find a terrific counterpoint to the action scenes: All through the movie, you find yourself reinterpreting every scene as you realize the "other" character is "really" playing it.

## FairyTale: A True Story ★ ★ ★

PG, 99 m., 1997

Florence Hoath (Elsie Wright), Elizabeth Earl (Frances Griffiths), Paul McGann (Arthur Wright), Phoebe Nicholls (Polly Wright), Peter O'Toole (Sir Arthur Conan Doyle), Harvey Keitel (Harry Houdini). Directed by Charles Sturridge and produced by Wendy Finerman and Bruce Davey. Screenplay by Ernie Contreras, based on a story by Albert Ash, Tom McLoughlin, and Contreras.

In 1917, two young English girls produced photographs that showed fairies. The photographs were published in a national magazine by Sir Arthur Conan Doyle, creator of Sherlock Holmes and an ardent spiritualist, and he vouched for their authenticity. The "Cottingley fairies" created an international sensation, though there were many doubters. Many years later, when they were old ladies, the girls confessed that the photos were a hoax.

That much is true. *FairyTale: A True Story* fudges so much of it that it should not really claim to be true at all. Not that it really matters. The movie works as a fantasy, and as a story of little girls who fascinate two of the most famous men of the age—Conan Doyle and the magician Harry Houdini, an outspoken debunker of all forms of spiritualism.

Early in the film we see a performance of *Peter Pan* that sets the stage, I think, for the movie's confusion between fantasy and reality. There is a point in the play where the children in the audience are asked, "Do you believe in fairies?" They all shout "yes!" and then the coast is clear for fairies to appear. There is the implication that if they shouted "no!" there would be no fairies, although no audience has been bold enough to test this.

In the movie, too, the fairies appear to those who believe in them. Are they real? Yes, Virginia. The film centers on twelve-year-old Elsie Wright (Florence Hoath) and eight-year-old Frances Griffiths (Elizabeth Earl), who has come to live with her cousin; her father is "missing" in the war in France, and she thinks she knows what that means. Elsie has also had a loss; her brother died not long ago. So both children are primed for belief in the other world, and one day they take a camera into the garden and return with film which, when developed, shows fairies.

Elsie's mother (Phoebe Nicholls), a member of the Theosophical Society, takes the photos to a society official, and soon they find their way into the hands of Conan Doyle (Peter O'Toole), who declares them the real thing, and finds an expert who declares them "as genuine as the king's beard." Harry Houdini (Harvey Keitel) is not convinced, and after escaping from the Chinese water torture tank, he joins Doyle in a visit to the girls' rural home.

Doyle publishes the photos, a journalist tracks down the location where they were taken, and soon the meadows are being trampled by nutcases brandishing cameras and butterfly nets. Meanwhile, Frances continues to worry about her missing father, and the girls gain consolation from the fairies.

Yes, there are fairies. We see them. We see them even when there are no humans around, which I suppose is a sign either that (a) they really exist, or (b) "we believe in fairies!" The fairies are sprites dressed like Arthur Rackham illustrations for children's books, and they flit about being fairylike. (It is often the case that fairies and elves, etc., are so busy expressing their fairyness and elvehood that they never have time to be anything else—like interesting characters, for example.)

The movie is absorbing from scene to scene, and has charm, but it is a little confusing. Not many children, for example, will leave the theater being quite sure who Houdini and Doyle are. And not many adults will know exactly where Houdini stands on the issue of fairies. There's a scene where he skulks around in the family darkroom, looking for evidence. And another where he speaks to the children as one trickster to another, telling them he never reveals secrets, and they shouldn't either.

"I see no fraud here," the movie Houdini says. This is a line that would have the real Houdini doing back flips in his grave. Houdini dedicated the last decades of his life to revealing the tricks of mediums and spiritualists, and would of course have seen fraud. Even *we* can see fraud; although an expert says the photos could have been faked "by an operator of consummate skill," they were in fact (stop reading if you don't want to know) faked by the little girls. They simply put cutouts of drawings from a children's book in front of the camera—as any but the most gullible can see. Examine the originals for yourself on the Web at www.parascope.com/articles/0397/ghosto8.htm.

I wish *FairyTale* had been clearer in its intentions. There are scenes in the movie suggesting the girls were sneaky deceivers, and others suggesting the fairies were real. What are we to assume? That Elsie and Frances committed fraud in an area that coincidentally was inhabited by fairies? Children are not likely to be concerned with these questions, and will view the movie, I suspect, as being about kids who know stuff is real even though adults don't get it.

## Faithful ★ ★ ½

R, 91 m., 1996

Cher (Margaret), Chazz Palminteri (Tony), Ryan O'Neal (Jack), Paul Mazursky (Dr. Susskind), Amber Smith (Debbie), Elisa Leonetti (Maria), Mark Nassar (Maria's Boyfriend). Directed by Paul Mazursky and produced by Jane Rosenthal and Robert De Niro. Screenplay by Chazz Palminteri.

It's a hell of a note: "Two people get married in church and one of them hires a stranger to kill the other." This dialogue comes midway in *Faithful,* a story about a faithless husband (Ryan O'Neal) who hires a hit man (Chazz Palminteri) to murder his wife (Cher). The fact that this comes midway will give you a clue to the construction of the film, which is more about dialogue than it is about husbands, wives, or killers.

The film is based on a stage play by Palminteri, and has been filmed by Paul Mazursky with a few attempts to open up the action, such as a shopping trip by Cher and a glimpse of O'Neal at work (he's having an affair with a younger woman). But mostly the action takes place inside the couple's enormous home, where every room becomes another set after Palminteri breaks in, ties Cher to a chair, and waits for the signal to kill her.

The signal will be two rings of the telephone; O'Neal plans to call home after he's safely in Connecticut with an airtight alibi. I don't think much of it as a signal. What if somebody else calls and hangs up, or what if O'Neal changes his mind? The phone signals get more complicated after Palminteri calls his shrink (played by Mazursky), who is to call back and ring only once. A few more callers, and this plot would require Groucho Marx.

When I said the movie was mostly about dialogue, I mean that seriously. There is never a moment when we think Cher is in serious danger, or that there's any likelihood Palminteri will kill her. The rules are too well established in plots like this. The killer starts talking to his victim, they begin to like one another, and one thing leads to another. Only rarely, as in *Bulletproof Heart,* with Anthony LaPaglia and Mimi Rogers, is there a surprise at the end.

Palminteri is good with dialogue, and the exchanges he's written for the hit man and target are clever in their twists, as when Cher tries to save herself by attempting to (a) seduce Palminteri, (b) convince him that she hired him, not her husband, (c) bribe him, and (d) hire him to kill her husband after he kills her. They even talk about love. "I was in love once," Palminteri tells her. "What happened?" "It didn't work out. I had to kill her father."

Then O'Neal returns home, and Palminteri has some fun with various stage techniques, such as the puzzle of the missing person; the third act keeps us in doubt about what has happened, and why, and to whom, while Cher and O'Neal deconstruct their marriage. *Faithful* is the kind of movie that's diverting while you're watching it, mostly because of the appeal of the actors, but it evaporates the moment it's over, because it's not really *about* anything. Nothing is at stake, the relationships are not three-dimensional enough for us to care about them, and it's likely that nobody will get killed. That leaves the physical presences of the actors and the wit of the dialogue—enough for a play, but not for the greater realism of a movie.

## Fallen ★ ★ ½

R, 120 m., 1998

Denzel Washington (John Hobbes), John Goodman (Jonesy), Donald Sutherland (Lieutenant Stanton), Embeth Davidtz (Gretta Milano), James Gandolfini (Lou), Elias Koteas (Edgar Reese). Directed by Gregory Hoblit and produced by Charles Roven and Dawn Steel. Screenplay by Nicholas Kazan.

*Fallen* is the kind of horror story I most enjoy, set in ordinary and realistic circumstances, with a villain who lives mostly in our minds. Movies like this play with our apprehensions, instead of slamming us with freaky special effects. By suggesting that the evil resides in the real world, they make everything scary; one of the movie's best moments is supplied by a pop machine.

Denzel Washington stars as John Hobbes, a detective who works with his partner, good old Jonesy (John Goodman), on murder cases. The film opens with a flashback ("I want to tell you about the time I almost died"), and then cuts to Death Row, where a vicious killer (Elias Koteas) faces the gas chamber. Hobbes is among the witnesses as the poison capsule drops, and the killer uses his dying breath to sing "Time Is on My Side." And then, this is curious, there is a POV shot from above the dead man's head, and we wonder whose point of view it could possibly be.

Having established the possibility of the supernatural, *Fallen* is at pains to center Hobbes firmly in a real world. The screenplay, by Oscar nominee Nicholas Kazan *(Reversal of Fortune)*, shows us Hobbes at home (he lives with his brother and nephew) and at work (Jonsey is a good pal, but a lieutenant played by Donald Sutherland seems to know more than he says). The story develops along the lines of a police procedural, with the cops investigating some strange murders, including a corpse left in a bathtub while the killer apparently enjoyed a leisurely breakfast.

Hobbes notices an incredible coincidence: The dead man in the bathtub is the same man who walked past him last night, drawing his attention by his singular manner. Now that's strange. And strange, too, are other developments, including the verdict of a linguist that the gas chamber victim's words, on a videotape, were spoken in ancient Aramaic, a language he had no way of knowing.

There is a connection between all these threads, which we discover along with Hobbes. (The audience, indeed, discovers it before Hobbes—but we have the advantage, because we know he's in a horror movie and he doesn't.) Among the characters Hobbes encounters on his search for missing threads, the most interesting is the daughter (Embeth Davidtz) of a cop who committed suicide after being accused of the kinds of offenses that Hobbes himself now seems to face. "If you value your life, if there's even one human being you care about," she tells him, "walk away from this case." Did her father leave a warning behind? What is the meaning of the word *Alazel*, scrawled on the wall of the basement where he killed himself?

Denzel Washington is convincing as a cop, but perhaps not the best choice for the role of Hobbes, which requires more of a *noir* personality. There's something essentially hopeful and sunny about Washington, and the best *noir* heroes encounter grim news as if they were expecting it. There should be, at the core of the protagonist in any *noir* story, guilt and shame, as if they feel they deserve what's happening to them. Washington plays Hobbes more like a conventional hero, and doesn't internalize the evil.

As for the rest of the characters, perhaps they are as they seem, perhaps not, at any given time. The evil presence in the film moves from person to person, and there is a chase scene in a crowd that is eerily effective, because there's no way to tell who the pursuer is. See the film, and you'll understand.

*Fallen* was directed by Gregory Hoblit, who also made *Primal Fear* (1996). Both films contain characters who are not as they seem, and leads who are blindsided by them. *Fallen* reaches further, but doesn't achieve as much; the idea is better than the execution, and by the end, the surprises become too mechanical and inevitable. Still, for an hour *Fallen* develops quietly and convincingly, and it never slips down into easy shock tactics. Kazan writes plausible, literate dialogue and Hoblit creates a realistic world, so that the horror never seems, as it does in less ambitious thrillers, to feel at home.

## Fallen Angels ★ ★ ★

NO MPAA RATING, 96 m., 1998

Leon Lai (Wong Chi-Ming, the killer), Takeshi Kaneshiro (He Zhiwu), Charlie Young (Cherry), Michele Reis (The Agent), Karen Mok (Baby), Toru Saito (Sato, the manager), Chen Wanlei (Father), Kong To-Hoi (Ah-Hoi). Directed by Wong Kar-Wai and produced by Kar-Wai and Jeff Lau. Screenplay by Kar-Wai.

*Fallen Angels* is the latest work from the Hong Kong wild man Wong Kar-Wai, whose films give the same effect as leafing through hip photo magazines very quickly. It's a riff on some of the same material as his *Chungking Express* (1996), about which I wrote, "You enjoy it because of what you know about film, not because of what it knows about life."

I felt transported back to the 1960s films of Godard. I was watching a film that was not afraid of its audience. Almost all films, even the best ones, are made with a certain anxiety about what the audience will think: Will it like it? Get it? Be bored by it? Wong Kar-Wai, like Godard, is oblivious to such questions and plunges into his weird, hyper style without a moment's hesitation.

To describe the plot is to miss the point. *Fallen Angels* takes the materials of the plot—the characters and what they do—and assembles them like a photo montage. At the end, you have impressions, not conclusions. His influences aren't other filmmakers, but still photographers and video artists—the kinds of artists who do to images what rap artists are doing to music when they move the vinyl back and forth under the needle.

The people in his films are not characters but ingredients, or subjects. They include a hit man and his female "manager," who share separate dayparts in a hotel room that seems only precariously separate from the train tracks outside. (She scrubs the place down before her shift, kneeling on the floor in her leather minidress and mesh stockings.) There is also a man who stopped speaking after eating a can of outdated pineapple slices (pineapple sell-by dates were also a theme in *Chungking Express*). He makes a living by "reopening" stores that are closed for the night, and has an uncertain relationship with a young woman who acts out her emotions theatrically. There is another woman wandering about in a blond wig, for no better purpose, I suspect, than that *Chungking Express* also contained such a character.

Does it matter what these people do? Not much. It is the texture of their lives that Wong is interested in, not the outcome. He records the frenetic, manic pace of the city, exaggerating everything with wide-angle lenses, hand-held cameras, quick cutting, slow motion, fast motion, freeze frames, black and white, tilt shots, color filters, neon-sign lighting, and occasionally a camera that pauses, exhausted, and just stares.

That exhausted camera supplies the movie's best moment. The hit man (Leon Lai) has just wiped out a roomful of gamblers. He runs into the street and boards a commuter train. The man behind him is—good God!—a junior high school classmate, now an insurance salesman. The classmate chatters about insurance policies and his own impending marriage, handing the killer an invitation ("fill in your name"). The camera framing holds the killer in left foreground, his face frozen into a rictus of unease and dislike, his eyes turned away, as the classmate rattles on and on.

Finally the classmate asks for the hit man's card, which he supplies ("Ah! You have your own business!"). Then he asks to see a photo of his wife. The hit man supplies a photo of a black woman and a child. On the sound track, narration tells us he paid the woman five dollars to pose with him, and bought the kid an ice cream. The scene is telling us, I think, that in this society even a hit man feels obligated to be able to produce a business card and family photos on request.

A structure emerges uneasily from the film's unceasing movement. We watch the "midnight shopper" as he visits his old father and videotapes him cooking a steak. We see an inflatable doll being slammed in a refrigerator door. We see all-night cafés and hurtling traffic and a man riding a dead pig.

It's kind of exhausting and kind of exhilarating. It will appeal to the kinds of people you see in the Japanese animation section of the video store, with their sleeves cut off so you can see their tattoos. And to those who subscribe to more than three film magazines. And to members of garage bands. And to art students. It's not for your average moviegoers—unless, of course, they want to see something new.

## Family Name ★ ★ ★

NO MPAA RATING, 89 m., 1998

A documentary directed by Macky Alston and produced by Selina Lewis. Screenplay by Alston and Kay Gayner.

*Family Name* tells a story that could have been written by Faulkner. It coils back through the secrets of the South to find if there is a connection between two large families with the uncommon name of Alston. One family is white, the other black. As the film opens, both are having their family reunions only a week and a few miles apart in North Carolina. Neither family knows about the other reunion.

"When I was growing up in Durham," remembers Macky Alston, who is white, "I noticed that many of my black schoolmates had the same last name that I did." When Macky is thirty, living in New York, he decides to make a documentary about what that might mean. He finds two other Alston families, both black, living not far away, and his investigation begins with them and then moves south.

Slavery is the great shame of the nation, and like all shameful things it is not much talked about within families touched by it. The Alstons, Macky finds, "were one of the largest slaveholding families in the state." But the time itself is on the edge of living memory. His father's grandfather owned slaves. There are two very old sisters, light-skinned enough to pass as white, whose family name is also Alston, and who remember their grandparents, who were slaves.

Are the Alstons related by blood? "In slave time," one of the black Alstons tells him, "they knew everything that happened, and they never talked about it." Whose children were whose, even across racial lines, was known but not recorded, and the tombstones of old family cemeteries contain tantalizing hints but never the facts.

*Family Name,* which begins like a family album, develops into a fascinating detective story as Macky follows leads. He discovers old courthouse records, visits cemeteries, finds documents in unexpected places. He begins to focus on a great-great-great-great-grand-uncle named Chatham Jack, who may have had mixed children, and who in his old age, it was said, always "kept a couple of little black children around to sit on his feet when they got cold." Is Jack's blood in both branches of the Alston family?

Tracing descendants down through the years, Macky finds black Alstons of distinction. One, Spinky Alston, was a well-known painter during the Harlem Renaissance. His father, Primus, was a light-skinned man—and not a slave. Was Primus descended from Chatham Jack? Amazingly, Macky finds that Spinky's sister, Rousmaniere, is still alive. But what does she remember?

Another African-American branch includes a professional storyteller named Charlotte, whose ex-husband, Fred, is a classical musician. Coincidentally, Fred and their son Jeff are also interested in traveling south to explore their roots. In living rooms and on front porches, in old baptismal records and birth certificates and wills, there are possibilities and conjectures but no facts. Macky tries to narrow down the possibilities—to see if only one scenario will fit his findings.

But there is much more going on here. For one thing, Macky is gay, and this fact has been withheld from his own grandmother. So in his own life he has experienced the way that secrets work. Must he tell her? And Macky's parents? What secrets do they hide? The trails seem to grow warmer, and a chance remark by an ancient survivor might provide the crucial clue. By the end of the film, we sit in astonishment at the unexpected turn the story has taken. *Family Name* begins by seeking the secrets of a family, and the secrets it discovers cause us to question the very definition of a family. If blood is thicker than water, then perhaps love is thicker even than blood.

## Fargo ★ ★ ★ ★

R, 98 m., 1996

Frances McDormand (Marge Gunderson), William H. Macy (Jerry Lundegaard), Steve Buscemi (Carl Showalter), Peter Stormare (Gaear Grimsrud), Harve Presnell (Wade Gustafson), Kristin Rudrud (Jean Lundegaard), John Carroll Lynch (Norm Gunderson). Directed by Joel Coen and produced by Ethan Coen. Screenplay by the Coens.

*Fargo* begins with an absolutely dead-on familiarity with small-town life in the frigid winter landscape of Minnesota and North Dakota. Then it rotates its story through satire, comedy, suspense, and violence, until it emerges as one of the best films I've seen. To watch it is to experience steadily mounting delight, as you realize the filmmakers have taken enormous risks, gotten away with them, and made a movie that is completely original, and as familiar as an old shoe—or a rubber-soled hunting boot from L.L. Bean, more likely.

The film is "based on a true story" that took place in Minnesota in 1987.* It has been filmed on location, there and in North Dakota, by the Coen brothers, Ethan and Joel, who grew up in St. Louis Park, a suburb of Minneapolis, and went on to make good movies like *Blood Simple*, *Miller's Crossing*, and *Barton Fink*, but never before a film as wonderful as this one, shot in their own backyard.

To describe the plot is to risk spoiling its surprises. I will tread carefully. A car salesman named Jerry Lundegaard (William H. Macy) desperately needs money for a business deal—a parking lot scheme that can save him from bankruptcy. He is under the thumb of his rich father-in-law (Harve Presnell), who owns the car agency and treats him like a loser. Jerry hires a couple of scrawny lowlifes named Showalter and Grimsrud (Steve Buscemi and Peter Stormare) to kidnap his wife (Kristin Rudrud), and promises to split an $80,000 ransom with them. Simple enough, except that everything goes wrong in completely unanticipated ways, as the plot twists and turns and makes a mockery of all of Jerry's best thinking.

Showalter is nervous, sweaty, talkative, mousy. Grimsrud is a sullen slug of few words. During the course of the kidnapping, he unexpectedly kills some people ("Oh, Daddy!" says Showalter, terrified). The bodies are found the next morning, frozen beside the highway in the barren lands between Minneapolis and Brainerd, Minnesota, which is, as we are reminded every time we see the hulking statue outside town, the home of Paul Bunyan.

Brainerd's police chief is a pregnant woman named Marge Gunderson (Frances McDormand). She talks like one of the MacKenzie Brothers, in a Canadian-American-Scandinavian accent that's strong on cheerful folksiness. Everybody in the movie talks like that, with lines like "You're dern tootin'." When she gets to the big city, she starts looking for a place with a good buffet.

Marge Gunderson needs a jump to get her patrol car started in the morning. But she is a gifted cop, and soon after visiting the murder site, she reconstructs the crime—correctly. Eyewitnesses place two suspects in a tan Ciera. She traces it back to Jerry Lundegaard's lot. "I'm a police officer from up Brainerd," she tells him, "investigating some malfeasance."

Jerry, brilliantly played by Macy, is a man weighed down by the insoluble complexities of the situation he has fumbled himself into. He is so incompetent at crime that, when the kidnapping becomes unnecessary, he can't call off the kidnappers, because he doesn't know their phone number. He's being pestered with persistent calls from GMAC, inquiring about the illegible serial number on the paperwork for the same missing tan Ciera. He tries sending faxes in which the number is smudged. GMAC isn't fooled. Macy creates the unbearable agony of a man who needs to think fast, and whose brain is scrambled with fear, guilt, and the crazy illusion that he can somehow still pull this thing off.

*Fargo* is filled with dozens of small moments that make us nod with recognition. When the two low-rent hoods stop for the night at a truck stop, for example, they hire hookers. Cut to a shot of bored mercenary sex. Cut to the next shot: They're all sitting up in bed, watching "The Tonight Show" on TV. William H. Macy, who has played salesmen and con men before (he's a veteran of David Mamet's plays), finds just the right note in his scenes in the auto showroom. It's fascinating to watch him in action, trying to worm out of a lie involving an extra charge for rustproofing.

Small roles seem bigger because they're so well written and observed. Kristin Rudrud has few scenes as Jerry's wife, but creates a character out of them, always chopping or stirring something furiously in the kitchen. Their teenage son, who excuses himself from the table to go to McDonald's, helps establish the milieu of the film with a bedroom that has a poster on its wall for the Accordion King. Marge, discussing a hypothetical killer who has littered the highway with bodies, observes matter-of-factly, "I doubt he's from Brainerd." Harve Presnell is a typical self-made millionaire in his insistence on delivering the ransom money himself: He earned it, and by God if anyone is going to hand it over, it'll be him. He wants his money's worth. And on the way to the violent and unexpected climax, Marge has a drink in her hotel buffet with an old high school chum who obviously still lusts after her, even though she's married and pregnant. He explains, in a statement filled with the wistfulness of the downsizable, "I'm working for Honeywell. If you're an engineer, you could do a lot worse."

Frances McDormand has a lock on an Academy Award nomination with this performance, which is true in every individual moment, and yet slyly, quietly over the top in its cumulative effect. The screenplay is by Ethan and Joel Coen (Joel directed, Ethan produced), and although I have no doubt that events something like this really did take place in Minnesota in 1987, they have elevated reality into a human comedy—into the kind of movie that makes us hug ourselves with the way it pulls off one improbable scene after another. Films like *Fargo* are why I love the movies.

**The Coen brothers later admitted that they made up the "true story" attribution.* ☞

## Fast, Cheap & Out of Control ★ ★ ★ ★

PG, 82 m., 1997

Dave Hoover (Animal Trainer), George Mendonca (Topiary Gardner), Ray Mendez (Mole-Rat Specialist), Rodney Brooks (Robot Scientist). Directed by Errol Morris and produced by Morris, Julia Sheehan, Mark Lipson, and Kathy Trustman.

Life is a little like lion taming, wouldn't you say? Here we are in the cage of life, armed only with a chair and a whip, trying to outsmart the teeth and the claws. If we are smart enough or know the right lore, sometimes we survive, and are applauded.

Errol Morris's magical film *Fast, Cheap & Out of Control* is about four people who are playing the game more strangely than the rest of us. They have the same goal: to control the world in a way that makes them happy. There is a lion tamer, a man who designs robots, a gardener who trims shrubs so they look like animals, and a man who is an expert on the private life of the naked mole rat.

Morris weaves their dreams together with music and images, into a meditation. To watch the movie is to reflect that no matter how hard we work, our lives are but a passing show. Maybe Rodney Brooks, the robot scientist from MIT, has the right idea: We should develop intelligent robots that can repair themselves, and send them out into the universe as our proxies. Instead of a few incredibly expensive manned space missions, why not send up thousands of robots that are fast, cheap, and out of control—and trust that some of them will work?

Consider the lifework of George Mendonca, who is a topiary gardener, and must sometimes reflect that he has spent fifty years or more practicing an art that most people cannot even name. What is a topiary? A shrub that has been trained, clipped, and trimmed in such a way that it looks like a giraffe, or a bear, or a geometric shape. That is not in the nature of shrubs, and Mendonca, who is in his seventies, reflects that a good storm could blow his garden away, and that the moment he stops clipping, nature will go to work undoing his art. There is a beautiful slow-motion shot of him in the rain, at night, walking past his creations as if he, too, were a topiary waiting to be overcome by nature.

And consider Ray Mendez. Here is a happy man. When he first learned of the discovery of the naked mole rat, he felt the joy of a lottery winner. There are not supposed to be mammals like this. They have no hair and no sweat glands because they live always in a controlled environment—their tunnels beneath the African savanna, where they organize themselves like insects. Mendez lives with mole rats in his office, and creates museum environments for them. That means he has to ask himself a question no scientist before him has ever asked: What makes a mole rat happy? So that they can tell the members of one colony from another, they roll cheerfully in their communal feces—but where do they like to do that? In a room at the end of a tunnel system or in the middle? Like the architect of a luxury hotel, Mendez wants his guests to feel comfortable.

Dave Hoover is a lion tamer. He goes into a cage with animals whose nature it is to eat him. He outsmarts them. He explains why animal trainers use chairs: Not to hold off a savage beast, but to confuse it. "Lions are very single-minded. When you point the four legs of a chair at them, they get confused. They don't know where to look, and they lose their train of thought."

Hoover has lived his life in the shadow of a man he readily acknowledges as his superior: Clyde Beatty, the famous animal trainer who also starred in movie serials and radio programs. "There will never be another Clyde Beatty," he says, as we watch images from *Darkest Africa,* a serial in which Beatty and a little fat kid in a loincloth do battle in a hidden city with soldiers who wear large cardboard wings. It is clear that Beatty captured Hoover's imagination at an early age—that Hoover is a lion tamer because Beatty was, so that, in a way, Hoover is carrying out Beatty's programming just as Rodney Brooks's robots are following instructions, and the mole rats are crapping where Ray Mendez wants them to.

Morris's film assembles these images not so much as a documentary might, but according to musical principles: Caleb Sampson's score creates a haunting, otherworldly, elegiac mood that makes all of the characters seem noble and a little sad. The photography uses a lot of styles and textures, from 35mm to Super 8, from film to the handheld feel of home video. The cinematographer is Robert Richardson, who achieved a similar effect for Oliver Stone in *JFK* and *Natural Born Killers.* (Morris adds the year's most memorable end credit: "Mole Photography Sewercam by Roto Rooter.")

Errol Morris has long since moved out of the field of traditional documentary. Like his subjects, he is arranging the materials of life according to his own notions. They control shrubs, lions, robots and rats, and he controls them. *Fast, Cheap & Out of Control* doesn't fade from the mind the way so many assembly-line thrillers do. Its images lodge in the memory. To paraphrase the old British beer ad, Errol Morris refreshes the parts the others do not reach. ☞

## Father's Day ★

PG-13, 102 m., 1997

Robin Williams (Dale Putley), Billy Crystal (Jack Lawrence), Julia Louis-Dreyfus (Carrie), Nastassja Kinski (Colleen), Charlie Hofheimer (Scott). Directed by Ivan Reitman and produced by Reitman and Joel Silver. Screenplay by Lowell Ganz and Babaloo Mandel, based on the film titled *Les Comperes* by Francis Veber.

*Father's Day* is a brainless feature-length sitcom with too much sit and no com. It stars two of the brighter talents in American movies, Robin Williams and Billy Crystal, in a screenplay cleverly designed to obscure their strengths while showcasing their weaknesses.

The story is recycled out of a 1983 French film named *Les Comperes,* as part of a trend in which Hollywood buys French comedies and experiments on them to see if they can be made in English with all of the humor taken out. The discussion about this one seems to have been limited to who got to play the Gérard Depardieu role.

Billy Crystal won, I think. At least he's the one who is a master of the sudden, violent head-butt, which is supposed to be amusing because he's a high-powered lawyer and so nobody expects him to be good at head-butting. As the movie opens, he gets an unexpected visit from a woman (Nastassja Kinski) he knew seventeen years ago. She's now happily married, but needs to tell him something: They had a son, the son has disappeared, she's desperate, and she needs his help in finding him.

Robin Williams plays an unsuccessful performance artist from San Francisco who is at the point of suicide when his phone rings. It's Kinski, with the same story: Seventeen years ago, they had a son, who is now missing, etc. She tells both men to be on the safe side, in case one doesn't want to help. But both men are moved by her story, and by the photograph she supplies of a lad who looks born to frequent the parking lots of convenience stores.

At this point, it is inconceivable that the following events will not transpire: (1) The two men will discover they're both on the same mission. (2) They'll team up, each one secretly convinced he's the real father. (3) They'll find the son, who doesn't want to be saved. (4) They'll get involved in zany, madcap adventures while saving him, preferably in San Francisco, Reno, and places like that. (5) The married one (Crystal) will lie to his wife about what he's doing, and she'll get suspicious and misread the whole situation.

Will the movie get all smooshy at the end, with the kind of cheap sentimentality comedians are suckers for, because they all secretly think they embody a little of Chaplin? You betcha. This movie could have been written by a computer. That it was recycled from the French, by the team of Lowell Ganz and Babaloo Mandel is astonishing, given the superior quality of their collaborations like *Parenthood* and *City Slickers*.

Williams and Crystal are pretty bad. You can always tell a lazy Robin Williams movie by the unavoidable scene in which he does a lot of different voices and characters. This time, nervous about meeting his son, he tries out various roles in front of a mirror. All right, already. We know he can do this. We've seen him do it in a dozen movies and on a hundred talk shows. He's getting to be like the goofy uncle who knows one corny parlor trick and insists on performing it at every family gathering. Crystal is more in character most of the time—more committed to the shreds of narrative that lurk beneath the movie's inane surface.

The kid, played by Charlie Hofheimer, is another weak point. He's not much of an actor—not here, anyway, in material that would have defeated anybody—but the movie doesn't even try to make his character interesting. That would upstage the stars, I guess. An indication of the movie's lack of ambition is its decision to surround the runaway with clichés: His girlfriend has run off with a rock singer, he follows her, Crystal and Williams follow him into the mosh pits of rock concerts and to the band's engagement in Reno, etc. There's even a gratuitous drug dealer, hauled into the plot so he can threaten the kid about a missing $5,000. Would it have been too much to motivate the kid with something besides sex, drugs, and rock 'n' roll? Do we need a drug dealer in this innocuous material?

And what about poor Julia Louis-Dreyfus? She has the thankless role of Crystal's wife. When Crystal and Williams drag the kid into a hotel room for a shower, she misunderstands everything she hears on the phone and thinks her husband is showering with strange men and boys. Later she turns up while he's telephoning her, and he talks into the phone, not realizing her answers are coming from right behind him. This will be hilarious to anyone who doesn't know how telephones work.

The people connected with this movie are among the brighter talents in Hollywood. Ivan Reitman is the director; Ganz and Mandel have a great track record; Williams and Crystal are so good they could improvise a better movie than this. Here's a promising starting point: Two comics get stuck in doomed remake of French comedy and try to fight their way free.

## Fear and Loathing in Las Vegas ★

R, 128 m., 1998

Johnny Depp (Raoul Duke), Benicio Del Toro (Dr. Gonzo), Ellen Barkin (Waitress), Gary Busey (Highway Patrolman), Cameron Diaz (Blond TV Reporter), Lyle Lovett (Musician at Matrix Club), Flea (Musician). Directed by Terry Gilliam and produced by Laila Nabulsi, Patrick Cassavetti, and Stephen Nemeth. Screenplay by Gilliam, Tony Grisoni, Tod Davies, and Alex Cox, based on the book by Hunter S. Thompson.

Hunter S. Thompson's *Fear and Loathing in Las Vegas* is a funny book by a gifted writer, who seems gifted and funny no longer. He coined the term "gonzo journalism" to describe his guerrilla approach to reporting, which consisted of getting stoned out of his mind, hurling himself at a story, and recording it in frenzied hyperbole.

Thompson's early book on the Hells Angels described motorcyclists who liked to ride as close to the line as they could without losing control. At some point after writing that book, and books on Vegas and the 1972 presidential campaign, Thompson apparently crossed his own personal line. His work became increasingly incoherent and meandering, and reports from his refuge in Woody Creek, Colorado, depicted a man lost in the gloom of his pleasures.

Ah, but he was funny before he flamed out. *Fear and Loathing in Las Vegas* is a film based on the book of the same name, a stream-of-altered-consciousness report of his trip to Vegas with his allegedly Samoan attorney. In the trunk of their car they carried an inventory of grass, mescaline, acid, cocaine, uppers, booze, and ether.

That ether, it's a wicked high. Hurtling through the desert in a gas-guzzling convertible, they hallucinated attacks by giant bats, and "speaking as your attorney," the lawyer advised him on drug ingestion.

The relationship of Thompson and his attorney was the basis of *Where the Buffalo Roam*, an unsuccessful 1980 movie starring Bill Murray as the writer and Peter Boyle as his attorney. Now comes *Fear and Loathing in Las Vegas*, with Johnny Depp and Benicio Del Toro. The hero here is named Duke, which was his name in the original Thompson book and is also the name of the Thompson clone in the *Doonesbury* comic strip. The attorney is Dr. Gonzo. Both Duke and the Doctor are one-dimensional walking chemistry sets, lacking the perspective on themselves that they have in both the book and the strip.

The result is a horrible mess of a movie, without shape, trajectory, or purpose—a one-joke movie, if it had one joke. The two characters wander witlessly past the bizarre backdrops of Las Vegas (some real, some hallucinated, all interchangeable) while zonked out of their minds. Humor depends on attitude. Beyond a certain point, you don't have an attitude; you simply inhabit a state. I've heard a lot of funny jokes about drunks and druggies, but these guys are stoned beyond comprehension, to the point where most of their dialogue could be paraphrased as "eh?"

The story: Thompson has been sent to Vegas to cover the Mint 400, a desert motorcycle race, and stays to report on a convention of district attorneys. Both of these events are dimly visible in the background; the foreground is occupied by Duke and Gonzo, staggering through increasingly hazy days. One of Duke's most incisive interviews is with the maid who arrives to clean the room he's trashed: "You must know what's going on in this hotel! What do you think's going on?"

Johnny Depp has been a gifted and inventive actor in films like *Benny and Joon* and *Ed Wood*. Here he's given a character with no nuances, a man whose only variable is the current degree he's out of it. He plays Duke in disguise, behind strange hats, big shades, and the ever-present cigarette holder. The decision to *always* use the cigarette holder was no doubt inspired by the Duke character in the comic strip, who invariably has one—but a prop in a comic is not the same thing as a prop in a movie, and here it becomes not only an affectation but a handicap: Duke isn't easy to understand at the best of times, and talking through clenched teeth doesn't help. That may explain the narration, in which Duke comments on events that are apparently incomprehensible to himself on screen.

The movie goes on and on, repeating the same setup and the same payoff: Duke and Gonzo take drugs, stagger into new situations, blunder, fall about, wreak havoc, and retreat to their hotel suite. The movie itself has an alcoholic and addict mind-set, in which there is no ability to step outside the need to use and the attempt to function. If you encountered characters like these on an elevator, you'd push a button and get off at the next floor. Here the elevator is trapped between floors for 128 minutes.

The movie's original director was Alex Cox, whose brilliant *Sid & Nancy* showed insight into the world of addiction. Maybe too much insight—he was replaced by Terry Gilliam *(Brazil, Time Bandits)*, whose input is hard to gauge; this is not his proudest moment. Who was the driving force behind the project? Maybe Depp, who doesn't look unlike the young Hunter Thompson but can't communicate the genius beneath the madness.

Thompson may have plowed through Vegas like a madman, but he wrote about his experiences later, in a state which, for him, approached sobriety. You have to stand outside the chaos to see its humor, which is why people remembering the funny things they did when they were drunk are always funnier than drunks doing them.

As for Depp, what was he thinking when he made this movie? He was once in trouble for trashing a New York hotel room, just like the heroes of *Fear and Loathing in Las Vegas*. What was that? Research? After River Phoenix died of an overdose outside Depp's club, you wouldn't think Depp would see much humor in this story—but then, of course, there *isn't* much humor in this story.

## Feeling Minnesota ★ ★ ★

PG-13, 95 m., 1996

Keanu Reeves (Jjaks), Vincent D'Onofrio (Sam), Cameron Diaz (Freddie), Delroy Lindo (Red), Courtney Love (Waitress), Tuesday Weld (Nora), Dan Aykroyd (Ben), Levon Helm (Bible Salesman). Directed by Steven Baigelman and produced by Danny DeVito, Michael Shamberg, and Stacey Sher. Screenplay by Baigelman.

*Feeling Minnesota* is about people you are happy to meet in the movies although they would make you acutely uncomfortable in life. Everyone in the film is a lowlife of one description or another, and when a woman is insulted by being told she should have the word SLUT tattooed on her, perhaps this is no more than the truth: She makes love to her new husband's brother at her wedding, and later makes love to him again in a car, right after his mother's funeral (which does not reflect so well upon him either, come to think of it).

To be sure, she has only married her husband in the first place as a punishment—for him. Her name is Freddie (Cameron Diaz) and she is forced to marry Sam (Vincent D'Onofrio) by Red (Delroy Lindo), a drug kingpin who believes that Sam, his accountant, has stolen money from him. To find out why it would be a punishment to marry a woman played by Cameron Diaz, you will have to see the movie.

A flashback establishes that Sam and his brother Jjaks (Keanu Reeves) have been fighting since childhood. At the wedding, they engage in a vicious game of rock-scissors-paper. Soon Sam is boozing heavily and Jjaks is off to the bathroom for a torrid session with Freddie. And not long after that, Jjaks and Freddie go on the lam, which makes Sam and Red intensely unhappy. Freddie talks about the bliss to be found in Las Vegas, "where you get all you can eat for $4, and all of the towels smell like Downy fabric softener." What more could you ask?

If these characters were played at the level where they exist, *Feeling Minnesota* would be a docudrama of despair, depravity, and bad hygiene. Remember that documentary *Brother's Keeper,* about the illiterate brothers who all bunked together in the same shack and didn't bathe for months and were mighty fond of their animals? That's the milieu Jjaks and Sam come from, really. But Hollywood cleans them up real nice, and casts them as Reeves and D'Onofrio, and assumes that a world-class beauty like Diaz would consider it a step up to drop Sam for Jjaks, "who likes to spend all of his free time in prison."

And you know what? That's exactly how it works. By taking characters from the bottom of the barrel and casting them with beautiful people, Hollywood is able to create that ageless alchemy in which we equate physical beauty with personal worth, and so of course we want Freddie to dump Sam (who looks like an incipient Orson Welles) for Jjaks (who has a nice smile).

The movie was written and directed by Steven Baigelman, who must have gotten his characters all out of books and other movies, since I think it unlikely he could travel from their milieu to a movie contract in one lifetime. What he does with them is kind of nice. He creates a whimsical, grungy reality in which whenever the steamy love affair threatens to get boring, it is interrupted by an action scene. (I can remember back when action scenes got boring and were interrupted by steamy love scenes, but then that was back in the days when audiences liked sex more than guns.)

Cameron Diaz is the discovery here. I first became aware of her in *The Mask,* where she was a sex siren in a gown that looked spray-painted onto her almost cartoonishly perfect curves. Now, after seeing her in movies like *Last Supper* and *She's the One,* and in this lead role in *Feeling Minnesota,* I realize she has range and comic ability and is not only a sex bomb; she looks so warmly down-to-earth in these other films, indeed, that instead of praising a sex bomb for being able to play real, we should, I suppose, congratulate a real woman on being able to create the siren in *The Mask.*

D'Onofrio is as always a substantial screen presence; he seems to block more of the sun than most actors, and has to be dealt with. You can't simply dismiss him with plot details. Reeves is very likable, and this film, coming after the enchanting *A Walk in the Clouds,* establishes him as one of the most gifted romantic leads of his generation.

So these people, with their talent and beauty, take dogpatch material and redeem it. It's intriguing, why young filmmakers are so fascinated by the sleazier aspects of life; maybe they think this material lends them an authenticity they otherwise lack. The tension between the slimefest milieu and the charm of the performances is maybe what makes *Feeling Minnesota* work; in its own way, this is as much a fantasy as *James and the Giant Peach.*

## Female Perversions ★ ★ ★ ½

R, 119 m., 1997

Tilda Swinton (Eve Stephens), Amy Madigan (Madelyn Stephens), Karen Sillas (Renee), Frances Fisher (Annunciata), Laila Robins (Emma), Paulina Porizkova (Langley Flynn), Clancy Brown (John), Dale Shuger (Ed). Directed by Susan Streitfeld and produced by Mindy Affrime. Screenplay by Julie Hebert and Streitfeld, based on the book by Dr. Louise J. Kaplan.

There is a scene early in *Female Perversions* where a woman attorney is summarizing her case in a courtroom. Her body language indicates her aggressive intelligence: She uses abrupt, decisive movements. Her language is crisp and definitive. As she talks, the camera uses close-ups to indicate what the judge and the male attorneys are noticing: the neckline of the white blouse beneath her business suit, the slit in her skirt, her high-heeled shoes.

Is this a scene illustrating male chauvinist piggism? Not at all. The attorney is precisely aware of the impression she is making. She is a gender warrior who is fiercely ambitious (she's in line for a judgeship) and fiercely competitive (she throws away a lipstick when she sees another woman using the same shade). The woman, whose name is Eve (Tilda Swinton), is rising in the legal world and succeeding at romance, too—she has a relationship with a male executive that involves twisted sex in his office with the door unlocked.

All of her accomplishments are driving her mad. And *Female Perversions,* uneven and sometimes infuriating, is one of the most provocative films I've seen about the complications of being female in the modern world. It opens with a quote by the feminist scholar Louise J. Kaplan, who says that the roles women are required to play in our society are in themselves a form of perversion. And throughout the movie we see graffiti scrawled on billboards and benches, saying things like, "Perversion scenarios are about desperate need."

They are in Eve's case. Sex for her is a form of hunger, and she is less interested in the other person than in the sudden, savage gratification of her needs (which include the need to dominate, to be desired, to be admired). While continuing her relationship with the male executive, she picks up a woman psychiatrist (Karen Sillas) in an elevator, and they become lovers, too—until the other woman calls it off, saying she moved towns precisely to get out of "this kind" of a relationship.

Eve is on the edge of disintegrating. She hears voices criticizing her appearance, her sexuality, her clothing, and makeup. She fantasizes that she is being tormented by looming male figures. There are imaginary scenes with a rope, which is sometimes phallic, sometimes suggests bondage, sometimes seems to be a lifeline. There are also fantasy scenes in which a vast Earth Mother type exhorts Eve to express her inner femaleness, or whatever. The fantasy scenes in general seem unnecessary; the movie could have stayed with realism.

But the central story is compelling. Eve's sister Madelyn (Amy Madigan) lives in a semirural town, and is finishing her Ph.D. thesis (on a small Mexican village where the women rule—"and as a result get fat, which is what happens in a matriarchy"). Eve dresses in power business suits; Madelyn dresses in shirts and jeans, and has a shoplifting problem. Eve, concerned that a scandal might derail her judgeship, goes to defend Madelyn and finds that she is probably guilty—and has been shoplifting for a long time.

"It's erotic," Madelyn tells Eve. She does it because she finds fulfillment and release. The danger of being caught is part of it. Eve lectures and berates her, but of course Eve's own turn-ons include the danger of being caught while having sex in her lover's office. Is there any difference? Yes: Eve has more to lose.

Madelyn's friends in the small town include a woman who runs a bridal store (Laila Robins); a stripper (Frances Fisher); and a young adolescent tomboy named Ed (Dale Shuger), who loathes her body because of menstruation and is into self-mutilation. The scenes in their household have a quirky fascination of their own; sort of a *Bagdad Cafe* atmosphere. These characters represent an obvious attempt to get still more female role models into the film (and I must not overlook Paulina Porizkova, who plays the lawyer poised to get Eve's old job if she becomes a judge).

The film might have been better served by scaling back to more obvious material about women's roles and absorbing its ideology into the story of Eve and Madelyn. But it's aggressively thought-provoking all the same. It sees so clearly how confused Eve is, how she plays her various roles so well and yet cannot allow them to fit together or make her happy.

The film was directed and cowritten by Susan Streitfeld, who was a high-powered agent (her clients have included Daniel Day-Lewis, Jennifer Jason Leigh, Juliette Binoche, and Joanne Whalley). She knows the business world firsthand. The Kaplan book that inspired the film is theory, not fiction; the story comes from Streitfeld and Julie Hebert, and has a raw power that is impossible to dismiss. Tilda Swinton, who played the androgynous title character in *Orlando,* creates a character perfectly poised between perfection and madness, and Amy Madigan, always persuasive, plays a character who has her problems all more or less figured out, and finds that's not much help. This is the kind of movie you can't stop thinking about.

## Fetishes ★ ★ ★

NO MPAA RATING, 90 m., 1997

---

A documentary directed by Nick Broomfield and produced by Broomfield and Michelle D'Acosta.

---

Howard Stern has his moments of insight, and one came while he was discussing the murder of Mistress Hilda, a fifty-eight-year-old French-born dominatrix whose body was found in her New York apartment surrounded by whips, chains, and the other tools of her craft. It's often said, Stern observed, that the clients of S&M parlors are powerful men. "It's the wimps and the weaklings who are the rapists," he added.

It makes a certain amount of sense. Some men, deprived of a sense of power, compensate by assaulting the weaker. Others, uncomfortable because they have so much power, pay to have someone take command. Certainly the second part of that scenario is borne out by *Fetishes,* a documentary by Nick Broomfield that is fascinating, horrifying, funny, and sad.

Broomfield is the BBC documentarian who specializes in films about sex for cash. Early in his career he made a doc about a Nevada brothel, and two years ago he made *Heidi Fleiss: Hollywood Madam,* a version of that famous case in which Fleiss emerges more sinned against than sinning. *Heidi Fleiss* was one of the year's best films, an unblinking portrait of the manipulation of one person by another. *Fetishes* is not as powerful a film because it lacks the drama of a woman going to jail while the deeper corruption of her lover goes unpunished. But it provides an unblinking portrait of the S&M world that is joked about on late-night talk shows but rarely seen—certainly not in this detail.

Broomfield, who travels light, works with a cameraman and acts as his own sound man. He enters a situation and records it while it is happening, making no attempt to conceal his mike and camera. He spent two months in Pandora's Box, described as an upscale Manhattan S&M brothel where the clients pay up to $1,000 to have the dominatrixes enact elaborate physical and mental fantasies for them.

Is "brothel" the right word? The women insist they never, ever have sex with their clients. The woman in charge is Mistress Raven, who must have a snapshot of Cher tacked up next to her vanity mirror. She is intelligent, articulate, thoughtful. She explains the rationale behind her operation. Then we see her and the other women at work on their clients.

Surprisingly, some of the men are willing to be shown on screen, and although many are masked or concealed, it is probably possible to identify some of them. Why are they so reckless? Perhaps it's part of the thrill of humiliation. They submit to physical and psychological torture here, and some of the most painful sequences involve racial humiliation: a Jew who pays to have a woman play a Nazi, an African-American who wants to be treated like a slave, a white cop who wants to be treated like a black criminal.

Other fantasies are (more? less?) conventional. A stockbroker wears an expensive rubber suit that is airtight, except for a breathing tube that is controlled by his mistress. A man licks a woman's shoes. There are even women who pay to be submissive. Various domestic and toilet scenarios are enacted. There are some whips and chains, although most of the sessions deal more with the mind, or restraint, than with actual physical punishment.

Why do these men pay for such experiences? Mistress Raven and the other women have their theories. The men feel under unbearable pressure of various kinds: professional, personal, sexual. It is a vast relief for them to hand over control, to embrace the blamelessness of the victim. Raven notes with amusement an obvious paradox: It is the client, not the dominatrix, who has the real power, because he pays the money and writes the script, and both he and the woman do exactly what he desires.

There is a subtext to the movie, which emerges subtly. What Raven and her women do is hard work. Transference takes place. The men arrive with tensions and compulsions, responsibilities and hang-ups, and leave them at Pandora's Box—on the shoulders, or the psyches, of the women. At the end of the day, Raven says, she's exhausted, worn down by the weight of the gloom and guilt she has taken on board. She doesn't know how much longer she can stand it. One wonders if after a hard day's work she yearns for someone else to take her reins.

## Fierce Creatures ★ ★ ½

PG-13, 93 m., 1997

John Cleese (Rollo Lee), Jamie Lee Curtis (Willa Weston), Kevin Kline (Vince McCain), Kevin Kline (Rod McCain), Michael Palin (Bugsy Malone), Ronnie Corbett (Reggie Sealions), Carey Lowell (Cub Felines), Robert Lindsay (Sydney Small Mammals). Directed by Robert Young and Fred Schepisi and produced by Michael Shamberg and John Cleese. Screenplay by Cleese and Iain Johnstone.

Having worked under the proprietorship of the media baron Rupert Murdoch, I was receptive to the satirical version of him presented in *Fierce Creatures,* where a Murdochian tycoon wonders if he could buy the satellite TV rights to all of the executions in China. Nor did I blink at a scene where a new employee turns up to program his station, only to learn he has sold it that very morning. At that level, corporations change hands faster than the rest of us unload used cars.

The Murdoch figure in *Fierce Creatures,* named McCain (Kevin Kline), is a blustering bully who demands that all of his properties return an annual profit of at least 20 percent. That includes a zoo he has recently acquired, more or less by accident, in England. He assigns a man named Rollo Lee (John Cleese) to run the zoo, and Lee immediately orders that it will feature only dangerous animals—since they're the best at boosting ticket sales. All other animals must be shot.

This is a funny idea, especially when filtered through the apoplectic character Cleese created on *Fawlty Towers* and essentially repeats here. Autocratic, shortsighted, and short-tempered, Rollo orders his staff to start shooting the harmless animals, and when they balk he determines to do it himself.

The staff, a grab bag of eccentric animal lovers, unsuccessfully try to convince him all of the animals are dangerous. ("The meercat is known as the piranha of the desert! It can strip a corpse clean in three minutes!") Although Rollo's executions do not proceed precisely on schedule, a greater threat to his reign is presented by the arrival of old McCain's son Vince (Kline, in a dual role) and Willa Weston (Jamie Lee Curtis), the deposed programmer. Vince desperately hopes to take over the zoo and increase its profits in order to prove himself to his cruel and distant father. Willa wants a share of the glory, and both Vince and Rollo want a share of her generous charms, displayed in the kind of wardrobe that might result if women's business suits were designed by Frederick's of Hollywood.

Kline, Cleese, Curtis, and Michael Palin (as a hapless animal lover) are reassembled here for the first time since the brilliant comedy *A Fish Called Wanda* (1988). Few movies can hope to be that funny. *Fierce Creatures* is not. It lacks the hair-trigger timing, the headlong rush into comic illogic that made *Wanda* so special. But it does have a charm of its own, and moments of wicked inspiration (regarding the problem of shooting the harmless animals: "It's a pity this isn't Texas; we could charge people to do it for us").

One of the problems may be the dual role by Kevin Kline. Although multiple roles sometimes work (as in Eddie Murphy's family dinner scene in *The Nutty Professor*), they're more often a distraction. Part of my mind is forever trying to see through the trick. I'm observing that they're usually not in the same frame at the same time—and when they are, I'm thinking about how it was done. That brief lack of focus is deadly to the concentration needed for perfect comic timing.

There's also a subtle failure of timing in some of the slapstick sequences, as when a dead body is being dealt with toward the end. Slapstick doesn't consist merely of rushing around frantically; it has a clockwork logic, in which every element must be in position at precisely the right moment. This is so hard to do that it's a miracle when it works; it involves almost musical cadences. *Fierce Creatures* doesn't quite click.

Still, I'm fond of the movie. I like its use of lust and greed, always the most dependable elements of comedy, and I like the way Jamie Lee Curtis demonstrates how a low-cut dress can shift the balance of power in almost any room.

## The Fifth Element ★ ★ ★

PG-13, 127 m., 1997

Bruce Willis (Korben Dallas), Gary Oldman (Zorg), Ian Holm (Cornelius), Milla Jovovich (Leeloo), Chris Tucker (Ruby Rhod), Luke Perry (Billy), Brion James (General Munro), Tommy "Tiny" Lister Jr. (President Lindberg). Directed by Luc Besson and produced by Patrice Ledoux. Screenplay by Besson and Robert Mark Kamen.

*The Fifth Element* is one of the great goofy movies—a film so preposterous I wasn't surprised to discover it was written by a teenage boy. That boy grew up to become Luc Besson, director of good smaller movies and bizarre big ones, and here he's spent $90 million to create sights so remarkable they really ought to be seen.

That's not to say this is a good movie, exactly. It's more of a jumble that includes greatness. Like *Metropolis* or *Blade Runner,* it offers such extraordinary visions that you put your criticisms on hold and are simply grateful to see them. If Besson had been able to link those sights with a more disciplined story and more ruthless editing, he might have really had something.

The movie begins in "Egypt, 1914," that birthplace not only of civilizations but of countless horror and occult films. Inside an ancient tomb, scientists gather at the site of an event that took place (we learn) centuries earlier. Four crucial stones, representing the four elements, had been kept here until a spaceship, looking something like a hairy aerodynamic pineapple, arrived to take them away, one of its alien beings intoning in an electronically lowered voice, "Priest, you have served us well. But war is coming. The stones are not safe on Earth anymore."

Deep portentous opening omens almost invariably degenerate into action sequences. But *The Fifth Element* cuts quickly to another extraordinary scene, New York City in the mid-twenty-third century. The futuristic metropolis, constructed at enormous cost with big, detailed models and effects, is wondrous to behold. It looks like Flash Gordon crossed with those old *Popular Mechanics* covers about the flying automobiles of the future. Towers climb to the skies, but living conditions are grungy, and most people live in tiny modular cells where all the comforts of home are within arm's reach.

Meanwhile, Earth is threatened by a giant pulsating fiery object that is racing toward the planet at terrific speed. "All we know is it just keeps getting bigger," one scientist reports. Ian Holm plays an astrophysicist who significantly observes, "It is evil—evil begets evil."

What is this object? What rough aliens are slouching toward Earth in its wake? And how to stop it? Man's hopes may lie with Leeloo (Milla Jovovich), cloned from a single unworldly cell, who comes into existence with flaming red hair already dark at the roots (those cells remember everything). Leeloo is clad in a garment that looks improvised from Ace bandages but gets no complaints from me (the costumes are by Jean-Paul Gaultier, whose favorite strategy as a designer is to start by covering the strategic places and then stop).

Military-industrial types want to employ Leeloo for their own ends; they observe her from behind unbreakable glass. She breaks the glass, grabs a general's privates, and dives through what looks like a wall of golden crumpled aluminum foil, racing outside to a ledge high in the clouds. She leaps, but is saved from dashing her genes out on the pavements far below by crashing through the roof of a taxi driven by Korben Dallas (Bruce Willis), who seems to have been ported directly here from the cab in *Pulp Fiction.*

Leeloo holds unimaginable powers, but she needs help, and Korben befriends her. Soon the future of the universe is in their hands as the movie unfolds the rest of the story. The "fifth element" of the title, we learn, is the life force itself—that which animates the inanimate (the other four elements are earth, air, fire, and water). Leeloo represents this element. Arrayed against her is a vast antilife force, a sort of black hole of death. Every 5,000 years, a portal opens between the universes where these two forces live; the evil force can slip through unless the five elements are correctly deployed against it. The pulsating fireball in space is the physical manifestation of the dark force.

Involved with mankind in this approaching battle are two alien races: the Mondoshawan, who live inside great clunky armored suits (that was their hairy pineapple) and the Mangalores, whose faces can be pictured by crossing a bulldog, a catfish, and an alderman. The Mangalores are in the hire of the sinister Zorg (Gary Oldman), who supports the evil force despite the fact that (as nearly as I can figure) it would destroy him along with everything else.

Now if this doesn't sound like a story dreamed up by a teenager, nothing does. The *Star Wars* movies look deep, even philosophical, in comparison, but never mind: We are watching *The Fifth Element* not to think, but to be delighted. Besson gives us one great visual conceit after another. A concert, for example, starring a towering alien diva whose skin shines with a ghostly blue light, and who has weird ropes of sinew coming out of her skull. And a space station that seems to be a sort of intergalactic Vegas, in which a disc jockey (Chris Tucker) prances about hosting an endless TV show. And spaceship interiors that succeed in breaking the *Star Wars/Trek* mold and imagining how an alien race might design its command deck.

The movie is a triumph of technical credits; the cinematographer is Thierry Arbogast, the production designer is Dan Weil, and the special effects are by Digital Domain, which created the futuristic Mars in *Total Recall.* And remember that Besson conceived of these sights, and had the audacity to believe his strange visions could make a movie.

For that I am grateful. I would not have missed seeing this film, and I recommend it for its richness of imagery. But at 127 minutes, which seems a reasonable length, it plays long. There is way too much of the tiresome disc jockey character late in the movie when the plot should be focused on business. Sequences are allowed to drag on, perhaps because so much work and expense went into creating them. The editor, Sylvie Landra, is ultimately responsible for the pacing, but no doubt Besson hovered over her shoulder, in love with what he had wrought. A fierce trimming would preserve what makes *The Fifth Element* remarkable, and remove what makes it redundant. There's great stuff here, and the movie should get out of its own way.☞

## Fire ★ ★ ★

NO MPAA RATING, 104 m., 1997

Shabana Azmi (Radha), Nandita Das (Sita), Ranjit Chowdhry (Mundu [servant]), Kulbushan Kharbanda (Ashok), Jaaved Jaaferi (Jatin), Kushal Rekhi (Biji), Alice Poon (Julie). Directed by Deepa Mehta and produced by Bobby Bedi and Mehta. Screenplay by Mehta.

Deepa Mehta's *Fire* arrives advertised as the first Indian film about lesbianism. Among other recent Indian productions (according to the *Hindu,* the national newspaper) are films about tranvestism, eunuchs, sadomasochism, and male homosexuality. Along with Mira Nair's *Kama Sutra, Fire* seems to be part of a new freedom in films from the subcontinent.

Both of these films, directed by women, resent a social system in which many women have no rights. Neither is an angry polemic; the directors cloak their anger in melodrama, in romance, in beautiful photography, and in the sort of gentle sexuality that is often more erotic than explicit scenes, if only because it allows us to watch the story without becoming distracted by the documentary details.

*Fire* is about a beautiful young woman named Sita (Nandita Das), who marries into a New Delhi family that runs a sundries and video store. The entire family lives above the store: her husband, Jatin (Jaaved Jaaferi); her brother-in-law, Ashok (Kulbushan Kharbanda); his wife, Radha (Shabana Azmi); the ancient matriarch, Biji (Kushal Rekhi); and Mundu (Ranjit Chowdhry), the servant, who watches over the old woman during the day. Mundu's favorite pastime is masturbating enthusiastically to videos he sneaks upstairs from the store; a stroke has rendered Biji speechless, but she has a little bell that she rings furiously at him.

It is an arranged marriage between Sita and

Jatin, insisted on by Ashok because the family needs children and his wife can give him none. ("Sorry, no eggs in ovary," the doctor explains.) Jatin, a modern young man with few serious beliefs, religious or otherwise, has gone along with the marriage but flaunts his mistress, Julie (Alice Poon), a Chinese woman. When Sita discovers Julie's photo in her husband's wallet, he is less than apologetic: "Julie is so smart, so special, so pretty—you should meet her!"

It is only a matter of time until the two wives, Sita and Radha, are sharing their unhappiness while looking out over the city from a rooftop veranda. Radha is alienated from her husband—who, depressed by her sterility, follows the teachings of a swami who advises chastity. Sita is devastated that her husband does not love her. One day, simply and directly, she kisses the older woman, and the next day the older woman dresses her hair, and soon they are in each other's arms, I think, although the sex scenes are shot in shadows so deep that censors will be more baffled than offended.

It is, of course, the Indian context that gives this innocent story its resonance. Lesbianism is so outside the experience of these Hindus, we learn, that their language even lacks a word for it. The men are not so much threatened as confused. Sita and Radha see more clearly: Their lives have been made empty, pointless, and frustrating by husbands who see them as breeding stock or unpaid employees.

The film has a seductive resonance. Women do a better job of creating art about sex, I think, because they view it in terms of personalities and situations, while men are distracted by techniques and results. The two women are very beautiful, gentle, and sad together, and the movie is all but stolen by Chowdhry, as the servant who lurks constantly in the background providing, with his very body language, a comic running commentary.

## Fireworks ★ ★ ★

NO MPAA RATING, 103 m., 1998

Takeshi Kitano (Yoshitaka Nishi), Kayoko Kishimoto (Miyuki [Nishi's wife]), Ren Osugi (Horibe), Susumu Terajima (Nakamura), Tetsu Watanabe (Junkyard Owner), Hakuryu (Yakuza Hitman), Yasuei Yakushiji (Criminal). Directed by Takeshi Kitano and produced by Masayuki Mori, Yasushi Tsuge, and Takio Yoshida. Screenplay by Kitano.

It has been said that Western art is the art of putting in, and Oriental art is the art of leaving out. The Japanese film *Fireworks* is like a Charles Bronson *Death Wish* movie so drained of story, cliché, convention, and plot that nothing is left except pure form and impulse. Not a frame, not a word, is excess. Takeshi Kitano, who made it, must be very serene or very angry; only extreme states allow such a narrow focus.

Kitano, who wrote, directed, and edited the film, stars in it as Nishi, a man whose only two emotional states are agony and ecstasy. As the film opens, he is a policeman whose young daughter died not long ago; now his wife is dying of leukemia. During a stakeout, his partner Horibe (Ron Osugi) suggests he go visit his wife in the hospital. He does, and while he is gone another cop is killed and Horibe is so badly wounded that he will spend his life in a wheelchair.

A cop movie would have dwelled on the action. *Fireworks* reveals what happened only gradually, and at first we even misunderstand the source of the bullets. The movie is not about action, but about consequences and states of mind. Nishi leaves the police force, and we learn, abruptly, that he is deep in debt to yakuza loan sharks. How? Why? Unimportant. All of those scenes that other films find so urgent are swept away here. When punk yakuza collectors arrive in a noodle shop to try to get money from Nishi, he stabs one in the eyeball with a chopstick so suddenly and in a shot so brief that we can hardly believe our eyes.

Nishi cares deeply for his wife, Miyuki (Kayoko Kishimoto), and wants to spend time with her. He robs a bank to raise the necessary cash. They do childish things together, like playing with the kite of a girl they meet on the beach. Sometimes they dissolve in laughter. But when a stranger laughs at Miyuki for trying to water dead flowers, Nishi brutally beats him. And when more collectors arrive from the yakuza, Nishi explodes again.

The pattern of the movie is: ordinary casual life, punctuated by sharp, clinical episodes of violence. Nishi hardly speaks (there is little dialogue in the film), and his face shows almost no expression (reportedly because of injuries to Kitano in a motorcycle crash). He is like a blank slate that absorbs the events in the film without giving any sign that he has registered them. When he attacks, he gives no warning; the wrong trigger word releases his rage.

Nishi is therefore, I suppose, psychotic, a dangerous madman. To read his behavior any other way, as "protecting his wife," say, would be childish. Sane people do not behave like this. And his wife, who hardly says six words in the movie, and who seems unaffected by his brutal behavior, shares the family madness. But that isn't really the point: This is not a clinical study, but a distillation of attitudes. In Kitano's bipolar universe, you are happy when the world leaves you alone, and when it doesn't, you strike back.

Against this swing of yin and yang there is a steadying character: Horibe, the man in the wheelchair. He paints naive and yet colorful and disturbing pictures of people with the faces of flowers. At one point his wheelchair is at the edge of the sea, and we anticipate suicide as the tide washes in, but he is a man who has found some accommodation with life, and will endure. Nishi, on the other hand, has adopted such an inflexible and uncompromising attitude toward the world that it will, we feel, sooner or later destroy him.

The film is an odd viewing experience. It lacks all of the narrative cushions and hand-holding that we have come to expect. It doesn't explain, because an explanation, after all, is simply something arbitrary the story has invented. *Fireworks* is a demonstration of what a story like this is *really* about, fundamentally, after you cut out the background noise.

## The First Wives Club ★ ★

PG, 104 m., 1996

Bette Midler (Brenda), Goldie Hawn (Elise), Diane Keaton (Annie), Dan Hedaya (Morty), Victor Garber (Bill), Stephen Collins (Aaron), Maggie Smith (Gunilla), Sarah Jessica Parker (Shelly), Bronson Pinchot (Duarto), Jennifer Dundas (Chris). Directed by Hugh Wilson and produced by Scott Rudin. Screenplay by Robert Harling, based on the novel by Olivia Goldsmith.

*The First Wives Club* is a creepy revenge comedy about three women who are dumped by their husbands. They don't get mad, they get even. Well, they get mad too. The film opens at college in 1969, when four new graduates vow eternal friendship. They don't stay in touch, however, and it takes the suicide of one to bring the other three together at her funeral.

They are all now in their forties. There is Brenda (Bette Midler), who helped her husband build up a chain of electronics stores, only to be dumped for a cute young thing. And Elise (Goldie Hawn), the actress, who has fought age to a standstill with plastic surgery but moans, "In Hollywood, women have only three ages: Babe, District Attorney, and Driving Miss Daisy." And Annie (Diane Keaton), who deludes herself that her husband, who runs an ad agency, is going to come back after their "trial separation."

The story, based on a novel by Olivia Goldsmith, follows them as they grow increasingly disenchanted with men (that doesn't take much) and band together to pull assorted scams and blackmails in order to get what is rightfully theirs, which in each case means their husband's business.

Once you have this structure figured out, there's not much more to think about in the movie, which alternates heartfelt talks with slapstick and sitcom situations. You need a short attention span in order to be touched by the true confession scenes and still be able to believe a sequence in which the three heroines break into the penthouse office of one husband, and escape detection by crawling onto a window washer's platform, which hurtles toward the earth.

Of the three main characters, Elise, the desperate actress played by Goldie Hawn, is the most fun. She has had some success in the movies, fears it is mostly behind her, and has a husband (Victor Garber) who got a free ride to the top as a "producer" because he was married to her. Now he has a very young new bimbo and wants half their assets and monthly alimony.

What's best about the Hawn character is the forthright way the dialogue deals with her dilemma. The first time we see her, she's begging her plastic surgeon for more collagen in her lips: "I want Tina Turner! Jagger! Fill 'em up!" Her first public appearance is at the funeral, wearing lips that look like they belong in neon above Times Square. She denies to her friends that she's had any plastic surgery at all, but finally admits, "I have been freshened up a little bit." She drinks too much, wants sympathy from bartenders, and moans, "Sean Connery's 300 years old and he's *still* a stud."

Annie, the Keaton character, is still being taken advantage of by her husband (Stephen Collins). He even has sex with her immediately before asking for a divorce ("it was sort of a good-bye kiss"). Her daughter (Jennifer Dundas) announces early in the film that she's a lesbian, which sets up an unlikely and forced visit by the three women to a lesbian bar. It's an example of the film's expediency and superficiality that the daughter, searching for a quick put-down for her dad, later uses the announcement of her lesbianism as a glib exit line.

Brenda, the Midler character, was some of the brains and a lot of the effort behind the success of the chain of stores owned by her husband (Dan Hedaya), but "now that he's a celebrity" (because he appears in his own TV ads), she's been dumped too. She functions as the most together of the three friends, the planner and steadying influence.

The movie is heavy on incident but light on plot; the Diane Keaton character, who narrates, uses voice-over bridges to get us from one setup to another. And then there's a very protracted happy ending that goes on and on. First there's a party where every single possible loose end is sewn up (even those we didn't care about), and then the three heroines sing "You Don't Own Me," in a sequence that owes more to self-congratulation than entertainment. There is undoubtedly a movie to be made about this material: a different movie.

## Fled ★ ★

R, 105 m., 1996

Laurence Fishburne (Piper), Stephen Baldwin (Dodge), Will Patton (Gibson), Robert John Burke (Pat Schiller), Robert Hooks (Lieutenant Clark), Victor Rivers (Santiago), David Dukes (Chris Paine), Ken Jenkins (Warden Nichols). Directed by Kevin Hooks and produced by Frank Mancuso Jr. Screenplay by Preston A. Whitmore II.

*Fled* is a movie without a brain in its head, and it borrows cheerfully from lots of other movies, but at least it has the integrity to acknowledge its sources. In a setup sequence, two convicts, chained together, escape from a work gang and plunge through the wilderness. Where should they head? Not for the state line: "Didn't you see *The Fugitive*?" one says. "The first thing Tommy Lee Jones did was set up road blocks at the state line!" Later, they mention *Deliverance, The Godfather* and *The Fly.*

The convicts are Piper (Laurence Fishburne), a tough guy who knows his way around, and Dodge (Stephen Baldwin), a computer hacker who shouldn't have been on the chain gang in the first place. As they continue their escape, we learn background details. Dodge stole millions from a corporation that's a front for the Cuban-American Mafia, and now he has a computer disc that both the feds and the crooks want desperately.

Chained together, splashing through creeks and sliding over waterfalls, Piper and Dodge remind us of Sidney Poitier and Tony Curtis in Stanley Kramer's *The Defiant Ones* (1958). But this isn't going to be a parable about blacks and whites learning to get along. To avoid that possibility, the screenplay manufactures two utterly senseless fights for them. One, in the middle of their escape, takes place in the catch basin of a storm drain—so they can splash a lot, I guess.

I was unable to understand why these two desperate characters who had never met before, being chased by men who want to kill them, would be compelled to pause in their flight to beat each other senseless. At least the screenplay provides them with a durable cliché as a closer. After the fight, Dodge says, "Now we're even," and Piper hits him one more time and says, "No ... *now* we're even." When it comes to dialogue, there's nothing like the golden oldies.

The movie is sort of a comedy, I guess, although a violent one. Some scenes seem to have wandered over from a *Naked Gun* remake. As they're running through the woods chained together, Dodge complains that he's being jerked around "like a rag doll," and (as helicopters circle overhead and men with guns and dogs march through the woods) gives a little speech about how "We got to run to the same rhythm!" Piper, so help me God, pulls out a harmonica and plays a little tune, to establish the rhythm.

Scenes like that seem strange in a movie that also includes much shooting, many explosions, cold-blooded murder, and a torture sequence in which Dodge is suspended from a ceiling by a man who explains the "Chinese death of a thousand cuts." Judging by the length and depth of the first cut, not many victims make it to 1,000.

Other dialogue isn't funny, just awkward. Sample: Gibson (Will Patton), an Atlanta cop who suspects the two guys are being set up, tells a federal marshal, "I think they're more like pawns than hostages." The marshal says, "And I think you're more like a Hardy Boys mystery than real life." And Gibson ripostes, "And I think you're just spittin' in the wind." Such dialogue aside, Patton is very good in the movie, creating a three-dimensional character right there in the middle of flatland.

So, the performances are not to blame. Laurence Fishburne brings an authority to his role that the screenplay doesn't really deserve, and Stephen Baldwin is okay as the hacker, although it would have been entertaining to make him more of a nerd. The picture is good-looking, too, and director Kevin Hooks creates the same kind of flat-out pacing that made his *Passenger 57* (1992) fun to watch. But what were they going for here? The tone is all over the map. The movie should have been funnier, or more serious. Instead, whenever *Fled* gets something going in either direction, it undermines it.

## Flipper ★ ★

PG, 96 m., 1996

Elijah Wood (Sandy), Paul Hogan (Porter), Chelsea Field (Cathy), Isaac Hayes (Buck), Jonathan Banks (Dirk Moran), Jason Fuchs (Marvin), Jessica Wesson (Kim). Directed by Alan Shapiro and produced by James J. McNamara and Perry Katz. Screenplay by Shapiro.

Strange how many movies there are about friendships between young boys and friendly aquatic mammals. Whales, dolphins, and seals are noble creatures, but somewhat limited when it comes to drama; their big scenes mostly involve gazing longingly at their human pals while emitting various clicks and squeals. I am reminded of an Irish friend who assured me lobsters make the perfect pets "because they don't bark, and they know the secrets of the deep."

*Flipper* arrives on the heels, or fins, of *Free Willy* and *Free Willy 2,* which were about a friendly whale, and *Andre,* about a family that adopts a baby seal. It is not the best of class. Like the original 1963 movie and the TV series, it expects us to be endlessly amused by a dolphin that does things that are endless but not amusing.

As the movie opens, Sandy (Elijah Wood), a teenager from Chicago, has been sent to spend the summer with his Uncle Porter (Paul Hogan, of *Crocodile Dundee*) on one of the Florida Keys. Porter is a free spirit who runs a fishing boat, flirts with Cathy, a local shopkeeper (Chelsea Field), and blowtorches Spaghetti-Os whenever he grows hungry.

This would seem like a great setup for a kid from the city, especially since Kim (Jessica Wesson), a cute babe about his age, hangs around on the beach. But Sandy is embittered by his parents' divorce, and angry because he'll be missing a Red Hot Chili Peppers concert. (Any kid who would rather attend a Chili Peppers concert than spend the summer sailing with Crocodile Dundee and meeting babes should be sealed in a sensory deprivation chamber until his mind clears.) Finally Sandy makes friends with Flipper, and becomes only half-sullen.

The first time we see dolphins in the movie, they are gamboling carefree in the waves. Then the evil charter boat captain Dirk Moran (Jonathan Banks) starts shooting at them because they're eating the bait of his ugly rich customers. Sandy befriends Flipper, who follows him back to shore, hangs around the pier, gurgles, clicks, plays catch with him, and becomes his buddy.

Meanwhile, something is affecting the fishing, and Cathy, a former marine biologist, discovers the ocean waters are polluted. How can that be? One night Sandy and Kim see the evil Dirk dumping hazardous-waste containers into the sea. (We know they contain hazardous waste because each fifty-five-gallon drum is helpfully labeled "Hazardous Waste.")

Sandy and Uncle Porter give this news to Sheriff Buck (Isaac Hayes—yes, Isaac Hayes), who needs proof. So Marvin (Jason Fuchs), Cathy's owl-eyed little nerd of a son, constructs the "Flip-O-Cam," an underwater video camera that Flipper uses to scout the sea bed, while an evil hammerhead shark lurks hungrily. At about this point—while Flipper is holding the camera in his mouth, photographing the fifty-five-gallon drums and then signaling his discovery by hitting a tennis ball with his nose—I began to ask myself why the producers didn't have him revise the screenplay too.

The movie ends with a particularly unconvincing special-effects shot showing Flipper escorting a boat toward the horizon. The dolphin looks animated and artificial, leaping like clockwork out of the waves. By then I was resigned to the possibility that the filmmakers didn't really have their hearts in their work. What can you say to people who give us a hammerhead shark, dump Dirk in the water, and then don't let the shark eat him? Have they no sense of cinema?

## Flirt ★ ★

NO MPAA RATING, 85 m., 1996

New York: Bill Sage (Bill), Martin Donovan (Martin), Parker Posey (Emily). Berlin: Dwight Ewell (Dwight), Geno Lechner (Greta), Peter Fitz (Doctor). Tokyo: Miho Nikaidoh (Miho), Kumiko Ishizuka (Naomi), Chikako Hara (Yuki). Directed by Hal Hartley and produced by Ted Hope. Screenplay by Hartley.

I should like Hal Hartley's *Flirt* a lot more than I do, since it illustrates one of my favorite mantras: "A film is not about what it is about, but how it is about it." A good film or a bad film can be made about anything. Therefore, to dismiss (or praise) a film solely because of its subject matter, it is not necessary to see it. That is why people who make statements beginning with the words "I don't like films about . . ." are idiots, or censors.

What *Flirt* does is tell the same story three different times, in three different countries, in three slightly different ways. Thus it proves my point. All three stories are "about" the same thing—a flirtatious lover trying to decide between two enticing partners. By telling the story three times, Hartley invites us to see the story as simply the occasion for the exercise of his art. Which of the versions, we can ask, tells the story best?

The "New York" section of the film involves a man who ends up explaining, "I was shot by the husband of a woman I thought I might be in love with." The "Berlin" section involves a gay man who explains, "I was shot by the wife of a man I thought I might be in love with." In "Tokyo," the milieu changes to the intrigues in a dance troupe, but the dynamic is essentially the same.

In each story, a character is about to leave town and asks a new lover: "Do we have a future together?" In each story, the new lover asks for time, and calls another lover, trying to decide between the two. In each story, three bystanders give advice. In each story, there is a telephone conversation involving much use of the word "no," and a shooting, and a scene in an emergency room.

As an idea, I like it. It would be useful in a film class. I will refer to it in other reviews. It illustrates a point and an approach. It took nerve to make. Hartley keeps pushing the edges of the envelope. But it's not much fun to watch.

Sitting in the theater, I found myself musing about the theory of "memes" floated by Richard Dawkins in his famous book *The Selfish Gene*. Memes are like genes, except they are composed of information, not DNA. He suggests that just as genes can contain the recipes for producing people, or cauliflowers, so memes contain information that can be combined to produce culture.

I have greatly oversimplified, of course, but the point is: Does *Flirt* have a Darwinian argument to make? Is it showing us three competing meme-groups, all beginning in much the same place on an evolutionary tree, just as in Mendel's garden there might be three pea patches? Are they in a struggle for survival of the fittest? The memes involved are all familiar to consumers of popular culture. They include (a) a love triangle, (b) the jealous partner, (c) a journey of separation, (d) a shooting, (e) the emergency room, and (f) the answer to the question, "What happened to you?" (Of course, each meme is made up of countless tinier memes, like "drink," "telephone," "wound," "makeup," etc.)

These memes can express themselves in different guises (English, German, Japanese, gay, straight). To a moviegoer from Mars who had never seen human beings before and knew nothing of our sexuality, they might look to be the same story. The Martian would not notice that one of the men in Berlin is black, and almost everyone in Tokyo is Japanese; to a Martian these differences would be just as invisible as three very slightly different frogs might be to us. In the very long run, however, the fittest frog is likely to find its descendants still in the pond. And is one of these similar stories more likely to survive, and be told more often and inspire more other stories, than the others?

I will not keep you in suspense: I do not know. But I suppose questions something like this are what Hal Hartley wants us to ask. I do not, in other words, think he expects us to say, "What a fascinating story! I want to see it told twice again—once in Berlin, once in Tokyo!" He has created a cultural experiment, an exercise in storytelling and moviegoing. Like many another cultural experiments (minimalist art, *Finnegan's Wake*, the *Chicago Tribune*'s new Friday section), it is more amusing to talk about than to experience. I'm going to dine out on *Flirt* for a long time. I won't need to see it again; I'll remember.

## The Flower of My Secret ★ 1/2

R, 100 m., 1996

Marisa Paredes (Leo), Juan Echanove (Angel), Imanol Arias (Paco), Carmen Elias (Betty), Rossy De Palma (Rosa), Chus Lampreave (Mother), Joaquin Cortes (Antonio), Manuela Vargas (Blanca). Directed by Pedro Almodovar and produced by Agustine Almodovar. Screenplay by Pedro Almodovar.

Are the heroines of Pedro Almodovar's films often, in one way or another, stand-ins for him? That's a common enough critical theory, and if there's truth in it, then his *The Flower of My Secret* suggests intriguing possibilities. The Spanish director's new film tells the story of Leo, a woman who writes trashy but wildly popular romantic novels under a pseudonym. They pay well, but she despises them—hates them so much she adopts another pseudonym in order to write an article attacking them.

Does Almodovar feel the same way about his own career? I hope not, because his previous films, while uneven and not always successful, have at least exhibited a cheerful anarchic trashiness that would bring life to this new and more serious film.

I was reminded while watching it of the Henry James story "The Next Time," about two novelists—a popular writer who wants to be serious but is not good enough, and a serious writer who wants to be popular but is simply too good. Almodovar's strength lies in his popular entertainments, and perhaps he should get nowhere near drama except with his tongue in his cheek.

Leo (Marisa Paredes), the film's key character, is rich because of her steamy potboilers, but not happy. Her husband, Paco (Imanol Arias), believes there is no hope for their marriage, and we are inclined to agree, since he has joined a peacekeeping mission to Bosnia simply to get away from her. Leo is depressed, drinks too much ("Drinking is all I am really good at"), tries to commit suicide, and discovers unhappy truths about Paco and herself.

Almodovar approaches her story through the stories of others. We meet Leo's ailing mother, and Leo's sister, who has sacrificed her own life to caring for their unpleasant parent. We meet Leo's best friend, who is having a secret affair with Paco. We learn that Leo's maid, one of the few pillars of her shaky existence, is about to bail out. The tone is set in an opening scene that seems real but turns out to be an educational film for potential organ donors.

When these people meet, they talk and talk and talk. They weep, they wave their arms, they throw themselves onto convenient pieces of furniture. We have the materials here for a comedy, but not the willingness, and gradually the awful suspicion dawns that Almodovar himself, like Leo, is tired of his success and despairs that his producers will ever let him do something "serious."

One must be grateful for the gifts one is given, and Almodovar has been given irony and cynicism, hyperbole and irreverence. He does not seem to have been given seriousness and deep purpose, but then he has never needed them until now. *The Flower of My Secret* is likely to be disappointing to Almodovar's admirers, and inexplicable to anyone else.

## Flubber ★

PG, 92 m., 1997

Robin Williams (Professor Phillip Brainard), Marcia Gay Harden (Sara Jean Reynolds), Christopher McDonald (Wilson Croft), Wil Wheaton (Bennett Hoenicker), Raymond Barry (Chester Hoenicker), Clancy Brown (Smith), Ted Levine (Wesson), Edie McClurg (Martha George), Jodi Benson (Weebo's Voice). Directed by Les Mayfield and produced by John Hughes and Ricardo Mestres. Screenplay by Hughes and Bill Walsh.

How absentminded do you have to be before they begin clinical testing? This question may occur to the more cynical members of *Flubber*'s audience, as the movie's hero succeeds in forgetting his wedding day for the third time in a row. In this remake of the 1961 hit, Robin Williams plays the absentminded professor who accidentally invents flubber ("Flying rubber! Flubber!") and saves his college, his career, and his romance.

Flubber is a substance that somehow magnifies energy, bouncing faster and higher than it should. Barely drop it, and it rebounds crazily off the walls. *Flubber* the movie seems to be made out of antiflubber; you drop it, and it stays on the floor. Although the movie may appeal to kids in the lower grades, it's pretty slow, flat, and dumb.

Williams stars as Professor Phillip Brainard, who must be related somehow to Professor Ned Brainard, the role originally played by Fred MacMurray in *The Absent-Minded Professor* and *Son of Flubber* (1963). He tinkers in his basement laboratory, creating marvelous inventions that are usually stolen by the scheming Wilson Croft (Christopher McDonald), who now wants to steal flubber—and Brainard's fiancée. She's Sara Jean Reynolds (Marcia Gay Harden), president of the university where Brainard teaches. It's a school about to go bankrupt.

Maybe Brainard keeps forgetting his wedding day because he already has all the woman a techhead like him could possibly want. He's accompanied everywhere by a levitating electronic sidekick named Weebo (voice by Jodi Benson), who has a seductive, womanly tone and a pop-up screen that illustrates her comments with clips from old TV shows. She's kind of like a cross between phone sex and an e-mate.

Weebo advises and encourages the professor, and keeps his appointment calendar. The movie makes much of how the patent on flubber might save the university, while overlooking the obvious fact that Weebo is the sort of personal digital assistant that would sell millions of units in the first year.

No matter. There's a villain on the scene—the scheming millionaire Chester Hoenicker (Raymond Barry), whose son Bennett (Wil Wheaton) just failed Brainard's class. Chester dispatches two goons named Smith and Wesson (Clancy Brown and Ted Levine) to spy on Brainard, and they observe his great new flying rubber just before flubber-covered golf and bowling balls bounce off their heads. (These two prowlers are clones of the bad guys in the *Home Alone* movies, also scripted by *Flubber* writer John Hughes.)

All of this is pretty slow going. Williams plays Brainard straight and steady, with a few whimsical asides, and the special effects team has fun with flubber, making it into a malleable green substance that can take any shape, and at one point forms itself into a song-and-dance number. There's also a flubberized basketball game, and a flubber-powered automobile, which Brainard pilots through the sky without, somehow, creating the magical effect you'd expect.

The suspense hinges on whether he can save flubber from Croft, fight off Smith and Wesson, marry the girl, and save the university. Call me perverse, but just once, just for the sheer novelty value, I'd like one of these movies to end with the hero losing the rights to his invention, while the bad guy marries the girl and the school goes belly-up.

## Fly Away Home ★ ★ ★ ½

PG, 110 m., 1996

Jeff Daniels (Thomas Alden), Anna Paquin (Amy Alden), Dana Delany (Susan Barnes), Terry Kinney (David Alden), Holter Graham (Barry Strickland), Jeremy Ratchford (Glen Seifert), Deborah Verginella (Amy's Mother), Michael J. Reynolds (General). Directed by Carroll Ballard and produced by John Veitch and Carol Baum. Screenplay by Robert Rodat and Vince McKewin, based on the autobiography by Bill Lishman.

*Fly Away Home* tells the story of a thirteen-year-old girl who solos in an ultralight aircraft to lead a flight of pet geese from Canada to the American South. Although her father optimistically describes this adventure as "safer than driving on the highway," I think the statistics he's thinking of apply to scheduled commercial airlines, not to planes that come in a box and you put them together yourself.

As I was watching the film, I couldn't help thinking of little Jessica Dubroff, who was killed along with her father and her flight instructor while trying to fly across the United States. There are some eerie echoes, as Amy (Anna Paquin), the heroine of *Fly Away Home,* flies from Ontario to North Carolina without even using any maps. (Her briefing consists of her father marking pencil lines on charts while saying, "Okay . . . here's us . . . and here's, like, Florida."

And yet finally I had to put away such thoughts and embrace the movie for what it is, a splendid fantasy. As the story opens, Amy's mother is killed in a car crash in New Zealand (that nicely accounts for Oscar-winner Paquin's accent). She goes to live with her father in Canada.

He's played by Jeff Daniels as a nutty inventor who sculpts dinosaurs, flies airplanes and gliders, and ended his marriage by insisting on building a full-scale model of the Lunar Landing Module. ("Hey, the real one is still parked on the Moon. So we need another one down here, right? Every home should have one. That's when you and your mom left. She thought I was crazy.")

Amy is not long on the Ontario farm when bulldozers start to rip through the nearby woods. We know from other movies that bulldozers always mean cash-mad property developers who want to tear down paradise and put up a parking lot. Amy rescues some goose eggs from the carnage, incubates them in her dresser drawer, and soon has fluffy little goslings following her around the house.

Dad being the kind of guy he is, of course this is fine with him. It is also fine with his girlfriend, Susan (Dana Delaney), and his goofy brother, David (Terry Kinney), who turns up to lend a hand. The evil local wildlife agent arrives to explain that the geese are the "property of the Crown," and their wings must be clipped to prevent them from being a nuisance, etc., and Amy beans him with a large pot. He exits muttering imprecations, and soon it develops that the geese, or maybe Amy, have a problem.

The geese think Amy is their mother, and they learn everything—how to fly, how to migrate—from their parents. So it is up to Amy to teach them. Lucky for her that her dad builds ultralight aircraft! Soon Amy is aloft, coaxing the birds into the air, and when the problem arises that geese need to fly south in the winter, of course Amy and her dad hit upon the idea of leading them there in their little airplanes.

All of this sounds, I suppose, like a daffy retread of *Free Willy* or one of those other movies in which small children befriend noble animals. But *Fly Away Home* is not quite that simple. The movie was directed by Carroll Ballard, who in *The Black Stallion* (1979) and *Never Cry Wolf* (1983) made two visionary films about man and nature. A former cinematographer himself, he works with the great cameraman Caleb Deschanel to make the film visually uplifting, and the story is quirky enough and the dialogue so fresh and well acted that this film rises above its genre.

There are individual shots here almost worth the price of admission: Amy on a lawn tractor, leading a parade of geese; the father soaring in his experimental planes, which always seem to land in semicontrolled crashes; Amy and her dad setting off across Lake Ontario; and a stunning shot in which the towers of Baltimore materialize from the mist, and office workers see the little girl and her geese flying past their windows.

Of course at the end of their flight awaits another evil property developer and more monstrous bulldozers, and the movie supplies an artificial deadline (if geese don't turn up to use their winter quarters by November 1, the trees fall). That sort of contrivance is obligatory, I guess. What I will remember is the photography, and the bliss (just this side of madness) with which the Jeff Daniels character invents his foolhardy schemes. I am also grateful to finally have seen a movie during which I could legitimately whisper, "Hey! You can't send a kid up in a crate like that!"

## Follow Me Home ★ ★ ★

NO MPAA RATING, 102 m., 1998

Alfre Woodard (Evey), Benjamin Bratt (Abel), Jesse Borrego (Tudee), Steve Reevis (Freddy), Calvin Levels (Kaz), Tom Bower (Larry), John Allen Nelson (Perry). Directed by Peter Bratt and produced by Bratt, Irene Romero, and Alan Renshaw. Screenplay by Bratt.

After *Follow Me Home* was turned down by every mainstream distributor in America, a new distribution plan was conceived: It would be booked one theater at a time around the country, with a discussion scheduled after almost every screening. For the last year this difficult, challenging film has found audiences in that way. There is a lot to discuss afterward.

The film is about four graffiti mural artists who pile into a van and head cross-country from Los Angeles to Washington with a plan to cover the White House with their paintings. In an age when Cristo wraps up buildings, this is perhaps not as far-fetched as it sounds, although I imagine they'll have trouble getting a National Endowment grant through Congress.

The artists include an African-American, an American Indian, and two Chicanos; on their odyssey most of the people they meet are white weirdos. One is reminded of the ominous rednecks encountered by the hippie motorcyclists in *Easy Rider*. The whites are stereotyped in broad, unfair strokes, but then the movie throws you off balance by throwing in one decent white guy and one redeemable one, and by making one of the painters into a fulminating cauldron of prejudice. By the end, you realize *Follow Me Home* isn't making a tidy statement about anything, but is challenging the audience to make up its own mind: to view racial attitudes and decide where they come from and what lies beneath them.

The writer-director, Peter Bratt, might almost have taken *Easy Rider* as his model—the parts that work, and the other parts too. Some of his dialogue scenes are too long and disorganized, but then suddenly everything snaps together in a scene of real power.

Consider, for example, a scene in a diner where a waitress feels she's been mistreated by one of the men (she is right). The owner comes out, lays a shotgun on the table, and delivers a lecture about their right to free speech and his right to bear arms. What is this scene about? A racist gun owner? Not necessarily, or entirely. The four men in the booth have different ways of seeing the situation, and the scene is about styles of intimidation.

Along the road, the men encounter whites wearing various costumes. There's a white guy who dresses like an Indian; they steal his antique tomahawk. Later, they encounter three white guys dressed in uniform for a U.S. Cavalry reenactment. Are they so inflamed they mistake the men of color for savage redskins? The development and outcome of this scene is hard to believe, but since it builds into magic realism, belief isn't the point. It's about a battle between two myths: the white myth of taming the West, and the black/Indian myth of soul power.

A key character in the film, encountered midway, is an African-American woman played by Alfre Woodard. She takes a lift from the guys, and gets angry when one of them can think of no words for a woman except "whore" and "bitch." Her powerful speech ("Look at me! I am a woman!") quiets him, and later woman power saves them all.

The personal styles of the four painters are all different. The black guy (Calvin Levels) is an intellectual, vegetarian, and pacifist, who uses terms like "patriarchal theocracy." The Indian guy (Steve Reevis) is a recovering alcoholic (a little stereotyping there?). The leader of the expedition, Tudee (Jesse Borrego), is the idealist whose vision brought them together. His cousin Abel (Benjamin Bratt) is angry at everyone, especially women. Are they a cross section? No, just a collection.

Watching the film, I resented the broad caricatures of whites. Then I reflected that broad caricatures of blacks were a feature of movies for decades and decades; just their luck that when a generation of black filmmakers arrives, stereotyping has gone out of style. I don't think Bratt is a racist, however: He's an instigator. He's putting highly charged material on the screen and standing back to see what happens. Most movies are too timid to deal in such controversy.

*Follow Me Home* is being shown in just the right way. It needs that discussion afterward. It doesn't come as a package that you can wrap up and take home. It's open-ended. It shows how films can cut, probe, and wound. It can awaken a sense of fair play in the audience. And in its fantasy and symbolism, it evokes a mystery level, beneath explanation. Most movies are over when they're over. This one is only beginning.

## Fools Rush In ★ ★ ★

PG-13, 106 m., 1997

Matthew Perry (Alex Whitman), Salma Hayek (Isabel Fuentes), Jon Tenney (Jeff), Carlos Gomez (Chuy), Tomas Milian (Tomas), Siobhan Fallon (Lanie), John Bennett Perry (Richard), Jill Clayburgh (Nan). Directed by Andy Tennant and produced by Doug Draizin. Screenplay by Katherine Reback.

In actual fact, of course, angels rush in where fools fear to tread. And that's what happens to Alex Whitman, a fairly unexciting builder of nightclubs, when Isabel Fuentes comes into his life. Alex comes from Manhattan, where he leads the kind of WASP life that requires Jill Clayburgh as his mother. He's in Las Vegas to supervise the construction of a new club when he crosses paths with Isabel, a Mexican-American camera girl at Caesar's, who believes in fate: "There is a reason behind all logic to bring us to the exact same time and place."

The reason, which may be the oldest one in the world, leads them to the same bed for a one-night stand, which both insist they "never" do. But then Isabel disappears for three months, returning unexpectedly one day for a visit during which she asks for saltines (always an ominous sign) before telling Alex she is pregnant.

*Fools Rush In* is a sweet, entertaining retread of an ancient formula, in which opposites attract despite all the forces arrayed to push them apart. Alex (Matthew Perry of *Friends*), who has been fleeing from the same marriage-minded girl "since first grade," decides that Isabel is "everything I never knew I always wanted." Isabel, who also has a suitor in pursuit, knows only that Alex is the man she loves.

Of course there will be roadblocks to their union, although most of them occur after they're married (they get hitched almost immediately in a wedding chapel on the Strip, with an Elvis impersonator as witness). Isabel tearfully decides the marriage cannot work, and tells him, "I ask only that you meet my parents—so when the baby comes they can at least say they met you." She invites him over for dinner, which consists of a backyard barbecue for about one hundred guests, complete with a mariachi band. Alex tries to get in the spirit, despite ominous glares by suspicious male relatives who suspect (correctly) his designs on her.

Much of the rest of the movie consists of misunderstandings that threaten to destroy their potential happiness. There is a movie convention that whenever a lover sees a loved one from afar in a situation that can be wrongly interpreted, it is always interpreted in exactly the wrong way, with no questions asked. That leads to Isabel disappearing on occasion ("we are too different and always will be"), and Alex disappearing on other occasions (she wants to live in Vegas and finish her book of desert photography, he has to work in New York, he lies, she feels betrayed, etc.). "To you," she shouts, "a family is something you put up with on national holidays."

They fight about everything. Even religion. Are they really married after the farce at the wedding chapel? Not according to her parents, who want a Catholic ceremony, or his parents, who are Protestant. ("Presbyterian is not a religion!" she cries.) When she wants him to give up his New York job, he counterattacks: "This is something I waited my whole life for, and I'm not giving it up because I put a $5 ring on your finger in front of Elvis."

All of this manipulation comes with the territory. What makes *Fools Rush In* entertaining is the energy of the performances—especially Salma Hayek's. Until now she's mostly been seen as the partner of gunslingers in action thrillers *(Desperado, From Dusk to Dawn);* here she reveals a comic zestfulness that reminds me of Maria Conchita Alonso. She's one of those women who is sexier in motion than in repose, sexier talking than listening, and should stay away from merely decorative roles.

I also liked the way her parents were portrayed. Tomas Milian is all bluster and ultimatums, but with a tender heart. For some reason the studio's publicity material does not supply the name of the actress playing her mother, even though this is one of the key performances in the movie, and played with a combination of great romance and pragmatism (yes, she agrees, her daughter wants to stay in Vegas near her family—"but your husband has a family to support"). Clayburgh and John Bennett Perry, as his parents, are more narrowly drawn, but that's because of the angle of the movie. (Someday we will get excitable WASPs and dour Mexicans, but not yet.)

By the end, by the time of the obligatory childbirth scene, I was surprised how involved I'd become. Yes, the movie is a cornball romance. Yes, the plot manufactures a lot of standard plot twists. But there is also a level of observation and human comedy here; the movie sees how its two cultures are different and yet share so many of the same values, and in Perry and Hayek it finds a chemistry that isn't immediately apparent. That's a nice touch. Most movies about opposites who attract do not really start out with opposites. (Consider the obviously perfectly compatible Michelle Pfeiffer and George Clooney in *One Fine Day.*) In *Fools Rush In,* they are opposite, they do attract, and somehow in the middle of the formula comedy there is the touch of truth.

## For Richer or Poorer ★ ★

PG-13, 119 m., 1997

Tim Allen (Brad Sexton), Kirstie Alley (Caroline Sexton), Jay O. Sanders (Samuel Yoder), Michael Lerner (Phil Kleinman), Wayne Knight (Bob Lachman), Larry Miller (Derek Lester), Miguel A. Nunez Jr. (Frank Hall), Megan Cavanagh (Levinia Yoder). Directed by Bryan Spicer and produced by Sid Sheinberg, Bill Sheinberg, and Jon Sheinberg. Screenplay by Jana Howington and Steve Lukanic.

Kirstie Alley and Tim Allen are warm and appealing, and good with the zingers after years of practice on sitcoms. Watching them work in *For Richer or Poorer,* I admired their sheer professionalism. The plot is a yawner, another one of those "fish out of water" formula jobs complete with car chases and jokes about cow manure. But they succeed somehow in bringing a certain charm to their scenes, and they never miss with a laugh line.

Allen plays a Trumpian real estate magnate (how I love the word "magnate"), who is celebrating his tenth wedding anniversary by unveiling his latest scheme for a theme park: "Holyland—inspired by God himself." Alley, his wife, works the crowd for investors, but is fed up with the marriage and wants out. Before they get a chance to file for divorce, however, they find themselves in deep doo-doo with the IRS; Allen's accountant has stolen $5 million and made it look like a tax fraud.

These developments naturally make a car chase necessary, and after Alley coincidentally jumps into the back of the Yellow Cab that Allen has stolen, they head for the back roads and end up in Intercourse, Pennsylvania (joke), the center of an Amish community. They need to hide out somewhere, and Allen has studied the movie *Witness,* so they pass themselves off as long-lost Amish cousins from Missouri and move in with a farm family headed by Jay O. Sanders.

What happens during their stay on the farm can be imagined, in broad outline, by anyone who cares to give it a moment's thought, or perhaps less. The city slickers are put to work on farm chores ("Look, honey—it's 4:45 A.M.! We must have overslept!"). Allen is assigned to train a gigantic horse, and Alley tries to fake needlepoint lessons. All routine.

What does work are (a) their personal charm, which invests a lot of these assembly-line scenes with cheerful enthusiasm, and (b) one-liners in the screenplay by Jana Howington and Steve Lukanic. Trying to explain why he doesn't have an Amish beard, Allen stumbles and Alley volunteers: "Lice!" Allen says it was a very brief infestation. "Minute lice," says Alley. I laughed. I also liked Alley's bright idea that the Amish try dressing in a color other than black, and the fashion show she stages for the elders.

But the movie isn't convinced that it's really about its story. It doesn't stay within the logic of the characters. People change their basic natures for a laugh. (Example: The old hatchet-wielding grandfather who wakes them every morning, and then unconvincingly lets them sleep late one day.) There's a romance between two of the local young people, who are seen so one-dimensionally, often at a distance, that they might as well wear name cards saying "Soppy romantic subplot." And the IRS agents who chase the couple, led by the usually reliable Larry Miller, are made into shallow buffoons and kept that way.

And yet there were laughs. Enough of them that I resented it when the movie got softhearted and sentimental at the end. I like a comedy that goes for the jugular and takes no prisoners. If you must see a comedy involving the Amish, I recommend *Kingpin.* It's in terrible taste, but that's part of the fun. *For Richer or Poorer,* on the other hand, has an attack of sincerity just when it needs it the least.

## For Roseanna ★ ★ ★

PG-13, 99 m., 1997

Jean Reno (Marcello), Mercedes Ruehl (Roseanna), Polly Walker (Cecilia), Mark Frankel (Antonio), Giuseppe Cederna (Father Bramilla), Renato Scarpa (Dr. Benvenuto), Luigi Diberti (Capestro), Roberto Della Casa (Rossi). Directed by Paul Weiland and produced by Paul Trijbits, Alison Owen, and Dario Poloni. Screenplay by Saul Turteltaub.

Death inspires a certain logic that can seem very funny if seen from a safe distance. *For Roseanna* tells the story of a woman who believes she has weeks, if not days, to live, and of her loving husband, who wants to observe her dying wish—

to be buried in the village cemetery with their child. It is not a simple matter; since the tightrope walker fell from the rope, there are only three graves left.

The village is in Italy—a movie Italy where everyone speaks English with an Italian accent. The international cast populates a picturesque location just around the corner, I imagine, from the location of *Enchanted April*. Every time I see a movie like this, I find myself thinking, to hell with the movie, I want to go there on vacation.

The dutiful husband is named Marcello (Jean Reno), as well he might be, since this is the kind of role Marcello Mastroianni could have performed in his sleep. He's a friendly but worried trattoria owner whose fear that the cemetery will fill up leads him to a desperate death-prevention campaign in which he directs traffic in the town square, grabs cigarettes out of the mouths of smokers, and even lies that a coma victim in the hospital has regained consciousness and asked for the soccer scores.

Reno, who played a cold, skilled killer in *The Professional*, is here a warm everyman, besotted with love. His wife, Roseanna, is played by Mercedes Ruehl, who may be surprised to find herself as a housewife in Italy but rises to the occasion. She doesn't appear terribly ill; perhaps she suffers from Ali MacGraw's Disease, first identified in *Love Story*, where the only symptom is that the patient grows more beautiful until finally dying.

Her heart is weak. She wants to stage-manage from the grave, and is obsessed with making plans for those who will have to carry on without her. Her husband, for example, should marry her sister Cecilia (Polly Walker). Fine, except that they don't much like each other, and besides, Cecilia falls in love with Antonio (Mark Frankel), the nephew of the rich landowner Capestro (Luigi Diberti), who has caused all the trouble in the first place by refusing to sell the village more land to expand the cemetery. Why is Capestro such a killjoy? Because he and Marcello have been enemies for years. It may have something to do with an old feud over a bicycle race, but there are also deeper currents and old loves that have not died.

We now have all the pieces in place for a good-hearted farce, in which lovers will be split up and united, misunderstandings will nearly lead to tragedy, and death will be feared, avoided, and confronted. There's enough going on that we hardly need the escaped kidnapper, although his final act of vengeance against the man who wronged him does show a certain ingenuity.

*For Roseanna* isn't of much consequence, perhaps, and the gears of the plot are occasionally visible as they turn. But it's a small, sweet film that never tries for more than it's sure of, and the actors find it such a relief to be playing such good-hearted characters that we can almost feel it. Of course, we're sure that with a setup like this the movie must have a sad ending. That only adds to the fun.

## Four Days in September ★ ★

R, 113 m., 1998

Alan Arkin (Charles Burke Elbrick), Pedro Cardoso (Fernando/Paulo), Fernanda Torres (Maria), Luiz Fernando Guimaraes (Marcao), Claudia Abreu (Renee), Nelson Dantas (Toledo), Matheus Nachtergaele (Jonas), Marco Ricca (Henrique). Directed by Bruno Barreto and produced by Lucy Barreto. Screenplay by Leopoldo Serran.

A quiet sadness hovers over *Four Days in September*, the story of young Brazilian revolutionaries who are described even by a government torturer as "innocent kids with big dreams." Based on a memoir by one of a group who kidnapped the American ambassador in 1969, the film examines the way that naive idealists took on more than they could handle.

The movie opens with newsreel footage of demonstrations against a military junta that overthrew the democratic government of Brazil, suspended freedoms, and ran a reign of terror. After the free press was shut down, a group of students decided that kidnapping the ambassador would be one way to get attention for their demands to release political prisoners.

In most movies about political terrorists, the characters are hard-edged and desperate, and the planning is incisive. Not here. The October 8 Revolutionary Movement uses the time-tested system of being sure no one in a cell knows the names of the others (that's also a way of concealing how few cells there may be). But two of the members conceal their friendship, and when one is captured by the police, it doesn't take long to make him talk.

Meanwhile, Paulo (Pedro Cardoso), the most intelligent and uncertain of the kidnappers, forms a bond with the kidnapped American (Alan Arkin). Guarding him for long hours, Paulo feels a certain gentleness toward the older man, who maintains his own dignity. Since Paulo may be called on to shoot the ambassador, this leads to an impossible situation.

The movie cuts between the kidnappers and the police, showing both sides more or less aware of the other's moves. Indeed, there's an amateurish air about the whole situation. As the terrorists wait to intercept the ambassador's Cadillac, a woman looking out her window finds them suspicious and tries to warn the police, who ignore her. And, incredibly, after two cops knock on the gang's hideout, Paulo is able to follow them back to headquarters and eavesdrop at a window to find out how much they know.

These are not brilliant revolutionaries. They're found by the cops because of their large orders of take-out food ("If only they had learned to cook!" a cop says), and at one point, as they wait uneasily inside the house where they're holding the ambassador, the sound track is filled with the same mournful passage from Mascagni's "Cavalleria Rusticana" that opens Scorsese's *Raging Bull.* The tone is not one of determination, but of regret.

I suppose the purpose of the film is to humanize both sides. It succeeds only to a degree. We can sense what the film wants to say better than the film can say it. Political terrorism may be justified in some situations (when it's your revolution, you call it heroism), but these callow students are in over their heads. And making the police and torturers into more human characters doesn't excuse them. Although the kidnapping did result in the release of some political prisoners, it's unclear whether it sped the day of Brazil's return to democracy. And for the participants, in retrospect, it may have been an unwise strategy.

*Four Days in September* was directed by Bruno Barreto, best known in America for *Dona Flor and Her Two Husbands.* Its screenplay, by Leopoldo Serran, is based on the book by Fernando Gabeira (who took the revolutionary name Paulo). He is now an elected official, and we sense a mixture of pride and regret in his memories. Films of the 1960s *(Z, The Battle of Algiers)* were sure of their sympathies. Costa-Gavras's *State of Siege* (1973), about the kidnapping and killing of an American official in Uruguay, was uncompromising in its portrait of U.S. interference in another country's politics.

It was also more clear in its consideration of the choice facing the kidnappers, who stood to lose whether they killed the official or not. This film is more muddled, and by the end we are not quite sure what we feel—or, in the final scene, what the young revolutionaries feel, either. The point of view is that of a middle-aged man who no longer quite understands why, as a youth, he was so sure of things that now seem so puzzling.

## 4 Little Girls ★ ★ ★ ★

NO MPAA RATING, 102 m., 1997

A documentary directed by Spike Lee and produced by Lee and Sam Pollard.

Spike Lee's *4 Little Girls* tells the story of the infamous Birmingham church bombing of September 15, 1963, when the lives of an eleven-year-old and three fourteen-year-olds, members of the choir, were ended by the explosion. More than any other event, that was the catalyst for the civil rights movement, the moment when all of America could look away no longer from the face of racism. "It was the awakening," says Walter Cronkite in the film.

The little girls had gone to church early for choir practice, and we can imagine them, dressed in their Sunday best, meeting their friends in the room destroyed by the bomb. We can fashion the picture in our minds because Lee has, in a way, brought them back to life through photographs, through old home movies, and especially through the memories of their families and friends.

By coincidence, I was listening to the radio not long after seeing *4 Little Girls,* and I heard a report from Charlayne Hunter-Gault. In 1961, when she was nineteen, she was the first black woman to desegregate the University of Georgia. Today she is an NPR correspondent. That is what happened to her. In 1963, Carole Robertson was fourteen, and her Girl Scout sash was filled with merit badges. Because she was killed that day, we will never know what would have happened in her life.

That thought keeps returning: The four little girls never got to grow up. Not only were their lives stolen, but their contributions to ours. I have a hunch that Denise McNair, who was eleven when she died, would have made her mark. In home videos, she comes across as poised and observant, filled with charisma. Among the many participants in the film, two of the most striking are her parents, Chris and Maxine McNair, who remember a special child.

Chris McNair talks of a day when he took Denise to downtown Birmingham, and the smell of onions frying at a store's lunch counter made her hungry. "That night I knew I had to tell her she couldn't have that sandwich because she was black," he recalls. "That couldn't have been any less painful than seeing her with a rock smashed into her head."

Lee's film re-creates the day of the bombing through newsreel footage, photographs, and eyewitness reports. He places it within a larger context of the southern civil rights movement, the sit-ins and the arrests, the marches, the songs, and the killings.

Birmingham was a tough case. Police commissioner Bull Connor is seen directing the resistance to marchers and traveling in an armored vehicle—painted white, of course. Governor George Wallace makes his famous vow to stand in the schoolhouse door and personally bar any black students from entering. Though they could not know it, their resistance was futile after September 15, 1963, because the hatred exposed by the bomb pulled all of their rhetoric and all of their rationalizations out from under them.

Spike Lee says he has wanted to make this film since 1983, when he read a *New York Times Magazine* article by Howell Raines about the bombing. "He wrote me asking permission back then," Chris McNair told me in an interview. "That was before he had made any of his films." It is perhaps good that Lee waited, because he is more of a filmmaker now, and events have supplied him a denouement in the conviction of a man named Robert Chambliss ("Dynamite Bob") as the bomber. He was, said Raines, who met quite a few, "the most pathological racist I've ever encountered."

The other two victims were Addie Mae Collins and Cynthia Wesley, both fourteen. In shots that are almost unbearable, we see the bodies of the victims in the morgue. Why does Lee show them? To look full into the face of what was done, I think. To show racism's handiwork. There is a memory in the film of a big, burly, white Birmingham policeman who in the aftermath of the bombing tells a black minister, "I really didn't believe they would go this far."

The man was a Klansman, the movie says, but in using the word "they" he unconsciously separates himself from his fellows. He wants to dissociate himself from the crime. So did others. Before long even George Wallace was apologizing for his behavior and trying to define himself in a different light. There is a scene in the film where the former governor, now old and infirm, describes his black personal assistant, Eddie Holcey, as his best friend. "I couldn't live without him," Wallace says, dragging Holcey in front of the camera, insensitive to the feelings of the man he is tugging over for display. Why is that scene there? It's sort of associated with the morgue photos, I think. There is mostly sadness and regret at the surface in *4 Little Girls*, but there is anger in the depths, as there should be.

## Free Willy 3: The Rescue ★ ★ ★

PG, 89 m., 1997

Jason James Richter (Jesse), August Schellenberg (Randolph Johnson), Annie Corley (Drew), Vincent Berry (Max Wesley), Patrick Kilpatrick (John Wesley). Directed by Sam Pillsbury and produced by Jennie Lew Tugend. Screenplay by John Mattson.

Willy the whale spends most of his time at sea and underwater in *Free Willy 3: The Rescue,* and I liked him that way—as a whale rather than a toy. The movie is more interested in its human characters and in the issue of whale hunting than in whether Willy knows how to shake its head for "yes" and "no." There is a majesty to whales that the second *Willy* movie trivialized. Part three returns to some of the human elements that made the first movie so good.

As the film opens, Jesse (Jason James Richter) has signed on for the summer as an intern aboard a whale study vessel whose crew includes Randolph (August Schellenberg), his wise old friend from the earlier movies, and the oceanographer Drew (Annie Corley). Jesse rigs the onboard sound system to play a harmonica tune he knows will attract Willy, who is now free, gamboling in the waves of the Pacific Northwest and about to become a father.

Jesse has grown up (people keep asking him how old he is), and the movie supplies a new kid for the story: Max (Vincent Berry), still in grade school. He's thrilled when he learns that his dad (Patrick Kilpatrick) will take him along on his fishing boat—but saddened when he sees that the boat is secretly, and illegally, harpooning whales.

Max's dad, named John Wesley, is not a bad man, although he is doing a bad thing. He's a loving father who promises his son, "I'll teach you everything I know." And he speaks sadly of the days when hunting whales meant bringing light to the world—back when whale oil was used for lamps. Today, fetching $200 a pound, whale meat is secretly exported to Japan for sushi, but hunting them "means the right to earn a living."

Max, wide-eyed and silent, keeps his peace. But then he meets Jesse, and the two boys have a moonlight meeting on board the fishing ship during which Jesse simply and eloquently tells Max why it's wrong to hunt whales. Later, Max has a conversation on morality with his dad, who is hard-pressed to defend what he does.

Meanwhile, the research vessel is tagging Orca whales with little suction-cup devices that I, for one, doubt would last five minutes before being torn off by water pressure. The evil whalers have nabbed Jesse's signal and are using it to lure Willy to his doom. And Max falls overboard and in a magical moment finds himself eyeball-to-eyeball with Willy, who saves him (although this is not the "rescue" of the title).

*Free Willy 3: The Rescue* is filled with sparkling nature cinematography by Tobias Schliessler, and looks great. I assume some of the shots are special effects and that not all of the whales are real, but it's all done so seamlessly that it's convincing. And although the movie has elements of real-life adventure that are improbable, it's essentially grounded in real life. Smart kids will enjoy it.

There was publicity after the first movie revealing that the Orca used in the film had later been transferred to an aquarium and was anything but free. This film ends with a phone number offering more information on that and other whales. And the movie itself is more realistic and serious; the whales here are inspirations for kids, instead of pets. Will there be a *Free Willy 4*? Perhaps; Max has some growing up to do. What's interesting is that the series has grown up too.

## Freeway ★ ★ ★ ½

R, 102 m., 1997

Kiefer Sutherland (Bob Wolverton), Reese Witherspoon (Vanessa Lutz), Amanda Plummer (Ramona Lutz), Michael T. Weiss (Larry [Stepdad]), Brooke Shields (Mimi Wolverton), Wolfgang Bodison (Detective Breer), Dan Hedaya (Detective Wallace), Bokeem Woodbine (Chopper). Directed by Matthew Bright and produced by Brad Wyman and Chris Hanley. Screenplay by Bright.

If Little Red Riding Hood were alive today, she would find that the wolves are bigger and badder, and she'd need to be a lot more resourceful to stay alive. That is the lesson (if it has a lesson) of *Freeway*, a dark comic excursion into deranged pathology. The movie retells the Grimm fairy tale in a world of poor white trash, sexual abuse, drug addiction, and the "I-5 Killer," who prowls the freeways in search of victims.

Written and directed by Matthew Bright, who wrote the teenagers-in-trouble saga *Guncrazy*, it plays like a cross between the deadpan docudrama of *Henry: Portrait of a Serial Killer* and the berserk revenge fantasy of *Switchblade Sisters*. It seems aimed at people who loved *Pulp Fiction* and have strong stomachs. Like it or hate it (or both), you have to admire its skill, and the over-the-top virtuosity of Reese Witherspoon and Kiefer Sutherland as the girl and the wolf.

The opening scenes play like updated Dickens, in which warped outlaws inhabit a lair. The heroine, Vanessa (Witherspoon), is struggling, at fifteen, to sound out such sentences as "The cat drinks milk." After school she meets her mother, Ramona (Amanda Plummer), on the corner where her mom works as a hooker. They return home to Ramona's current husband, Larry (Michael T. Weiss), a stepdad who complains: "Hey, me and your momma both spent the whole day in line getting rent vouchers, and we could use a little consideration."

The Lutz family idyll is interrupted by a narcotics raid. The cops share a little family history: "There's some bad blood between her mom and grandma, on account of she threw a chemical on her face or something." The parents are taken to jail, and a youth officer is assigned to take Vanessa to a youth home; thinking quickly, she handcuffs the officer to the bed, steals her car, and hits the road—on her way to grandmother's house, of course. She packs a handgun given her by her boyfriend.

After a car fire, she's befriended by Bob Wolverton (Sutherland), who has all the right moves to sound like a helpful child psychiatrist. Vanessa confides in him ("It looks like my stepfather's next parole officer ain't even been born yet") and opens her cheap wallet to show him a snapshot of her real father (the photo is of Richard Speck). Bob treats her to dinner and an attempted sexual assault, and chops off her ponytail before she asks if Jesus is his savior, empties the handgun into him, and throws up. She sees a shooting star, a sign from heaven that she did the right thing, and after imprisonment and escape she crosses the border into Mexico, where she works as a hooker in Tijuana until she's arrested.

Am I giving away too much of the plot? Not at all. There's a lot more. And *Freeway* isn't about what happens so much as about Bright's angle on the material; this is like a story based on the most disquieting and disgusting experiences of the most hapless guests on the sleaziest daytime talk shows.

Sutherland, who has played great villains before, outdoes himself this time. Turns out he was not killed by the gunshot wounds, but only wounded in all the most inconvenient places. The doctors patch him together into a Halloween monster whose face was shot away, who speaks through a hole in his throat, and whose other infirmities and amputations are too distressing to catalog. Backed by his all-American wife, Mimi (Brooke Shields—yes, Brooke Shields), he appears on television to lead a campaign against coddling such human garbage as Vanessa. Of course, Mimi does not know Bob is the I-5 Killer.

Occasionally an unsuspecting innocent will stumble into a movie like this and send me an anguished postcard, asking how I could possibly give a favorable review to such trash. My stock response is Ebert's Law, which reads: "A movie is not about what it is about. It is about how it is about it." *Freeway* is a hard-edged satire of those sensational true-crime reports that excite the prurient with detailed re-creations of unspeakable events. We have a great appetite in this country for books, TV shows, and movies about serial killers, perverted hermits, mad bombers, and pathological torturers—just so long as their deeds are cloaked in moralistic judgments. We pant over the pages before closing the book and repeating, with Richard Nixon, "But . . . that would be wrong."

*Freeway* illuminates our secret appetites. Like all good satire, it starts where the others end. And its actors wisely never ever act as if they're in on the joke. Reese Witherspoon (who had her heartbreaking first kiss in the wonderful movie *Man in the Moon*) is as focused and tightly wound here as a young Jodie Foster; she plays every scene as if it's absolutely real. Sutherland plays his early scenes with the complete confidence of a man walking in the trance of his obsession. His bizarre wounds make him a figure of parody in the later scenes, but he plays them, too, with complete conviction. All the way up to the end—which is, shall we say, not only predictable but obligatory.

## The Frighteners ★

R, 106 m., 1996

Michael J. Fox (Frank Bannister), Trini Alvarado (Lucy Lynskey), Peter Dobson (Ray Lynskey), John Astin (The Judge), Jeffrey Combs (Milton Dammers), Dee Wallace Stone (Patricia Bradley), Jake Busey (Johnny Bartlett), Chi McBride (Cyrus), Jim Fyfe (Stuart). Directed by Peter Jackson and produced by Jamie Selkirk and Jackson. Screenplay by Fran Walsh and Jackson.

Incredible, the amount of work that went into *The Frighteners*. And appalling. Anyone who appreciates special effects, computer animation, or movie makeup will regard this movie with awe. There's not a shot that doesn't suggest infinite pains and patience; complex makeup was painstakingly applied to actors for shots that were then married to special effects in order to create a screen filled with gory images.

But all of that incredible effort has resulted in a film that looks more like a demo reel than a movie—like the kind of audition tape a special effects expert would put together, hoping to impress a producer enough to give him a real job. Peter Jackson, who directed *The Frighteners* (and 1994's much better *Heavenly Creatures*), qualifies on the basis of this film for any special effects movie you can imagine, just as long as it's about something.

One of the more excruciating experiences for any movie lover is to sit through a movie filled with frenetic, nonstop action in which, however, nothing of interest happens. *The Frighteners* is a film like that—a film that compels me to break my resolution never to quote Shakespeare's "full of sound and fury, signifying nothing." It's like watching a random image generator.

The plot involves a professional ghostbuster named Bannister (Michael J. Fox), who is not quite the fraud we think him to be. True, he haunts funerals, offering his services to the bereaved, who might want to contact (or avoid) loved ones on the other side. But Bannister isn't just pulling a con game. He can really see ghosts. In fact, he lives with three of them: Judge (John Astin), Cyrus (Chi McBride), and Stuart (Jim Fyfe). They're spirits who have not quite gathered the will to become definitively dead, and so they hang around spooking people to drum up business for Bannister.

The story takes place in a town described as the mass murder capital of the nation. Among its residents is the hapless Patricia (Dee Wallace Stone), who has lived for years as the virtual captive of her mother (Julianna McCarthy) in the old local sanitarium, the site of a gruesome mass murder. Now a new death wave has broken out, and Bannister, because he hangs out at funerals, is a prime suspect. The beautiful window Lucy (Trini Alvarado) believes in Bannister, who grimly tells her, "I've got to have an out-of-the-body experience and have it now!"

His plan: Induce death, do some quick heroics on the other side, and get back before irreversible brain damage sets in. His attempt to do this sets up the central section of the movie, in which the special effects go truly berserk. The walls seem filled with people behind them, who make the wallpaper ripple and bulge. Spectral manifestations pop out of the woodwork. There is a villain who is mostly skeleton, his flesh having rotted but not his malevolence. And his ghost friends come and go, transparent but involved.

The movie is like an anthology of devices from other thrillers about the spirit world. We get squirt guns filled with holy water, we get black goo oozing out of hell, we get ectoplasm in car trunks, we get lots of religious symbolism. (Why is Catholicism the only religion appropriate to exorcism in the movies?) Everything comes to a shrieking climax in the old sanitarium, where the moldering chapel holds the key to the past, and a would-be mass murderer, perhaps overcome with Olympic fever, cries out, "This record should be held by an American!"

It is better, I think, to sit through a movie where nothing happens than one in which everything happens. Last year I reviewed a nine-hour documentary about the lives of Mongolian yak herdsmen, and I would rather see it again than sit through *The Frighteners.*

## From Dusk Till Dawn ★ ★ ★

R, 108 m., 1996

Harvey Keitel (Jacob Fuller), George Clooney (Seth Gecko), Quentin Tarantino (Richard Gecko), Juliette Lewis (Kate Fuller), Cheech Marin (Guard, Chet, Carlos), Fred Williamson (Frost), Salma Hayek (Santanico Pandemonium), Michael Parks (Texas Ranger). Directed by Robert Rodriguez and produced by Gianni Nunnari and Meir Teper. Screenplay by Quentin Tarantino.

*From Dusk Till Dawn* resembles one of those mythological creatures stitched together out of two different species, like a bull with a man's torso. In this case, we get half of a hostage movie and half of a vampire gore-fest. The transition is instantaneous. For about an hour, we follow the story of two mad-dog killers and their victims, and then suddenly a stripper in a Mexican bar turns into a vampire, and off we go.

Genre-hopping like that is a specialty of the movie's writer, Quentin Tarantino, whose work sometimes resembles channel-surfing. Robert Rodriguez, the director of *From Dusk Till Dawn,* can only be said to throw himself into the same spirit, heart and soul. This is one of those movies you might like or you might hate, but you won't be able to deny its crazy zeal.

Actually, a lot of people will hate half of the movie and like the other half. Those who loved the invention of Tarantino's dialogue in *Pulp Fiction* will like the first half, especially a brilliant pretitle sequence featuring Michael Parks as a Texas Ranger who creates a whole world out of a little dialogue. Those who liked the shootouts in Rodriguez's *El Mariachi* and *Desperado* will like the second half, which is nonstop mayhem in a scuzzy bikers' and truckers' strip joint, with lots of vampires, exploding eyeballs, cascading guts, and a weapon made out of a powered wooden stake (I guess you could call it a Pneumatic Vampire Drill).

I liked the first half best. After the title sequence, we get to know the central characters, Seth and Richard Gecko (George Clooney and Tarantino). They've robbed a bank and left a trail of dead and wounded (all toted up by a TV news reporter's digital carnage readout). Richard has helped Seth break out of prison, and now they're heading for the Mexican border with the bank loot, and Richard, who is a rabid loony, is blasting everyone in sight, including innocent bystanders.

Holed up in a sleazebag motel, they take hostages: a former Baptist minister (Harvey Keitel) and his children (Juliette Lewis and Ernest Liu). The minister has left the church after the death of his wife, leaving an opening for another of Tarantino's passages of theological dialogue. Now the minister and his kids are heading south in a mobile home the Geckos hope to hide in while crossing the border.

The minister is inclined to cooperate with the desperadoes. His son thinks he knows better: "Dad—I watch the reality shows!" The charm of the dialogue in these scenes has a lot of competition from the state-of-the-art mayhem, which leaves blood and brains spattered everywhere. Rodriguez doesn't make it very real, though, wisely handling the death of a harmless bank teller in flashes too quick to be seen, since more detail would sink the macabre mix of violence and humor.

In Mexico, the mobile home wheels up to the Titty Twister, a scroungy strip joint with a bizarre decor (this goes next door to Jack Rabbit Slim's in the Tarantino Mall). The doorman is played by Cheech Marin, who also plays two other roles, popping up so often he doesn't need the vampire plot to qualify as undead. The kidnappers and their victims go inside to await a rendezvous for a money drop, and that's when the vampire plot begins.

All I can really say about the last thirty minutes of the film is, if you liked *Dawn of the Dead,* you'll like this. The plot is forgotten as Rodriguez goes for violence and special effects, including people who morph into hideous creatures in the middle of the barroom brawl. There's also an outbreak of vampirism among the leading characters, in scenes owing something to *Assault on Precinct 13* and *Night of the Living Dead.*

*From Dusk Till Dawn* is a skillful meat-and-potatoes action extravaganza with some added neat touches. *E.R.*'s George Clooney, making his big-screen starring debut, shows admirable restraint in going along with the craziness without being overwhelmed by it. The good things in the movie—especially some of the dialogue—are so much better than the rest that you wish Rodriguez and Tarantino had tried to triumph over this material, instead of merely delivering it. It's a pro job, but these guys can do better.

## From the Journals of Jean Seberg ★ ★ ★ ½

NO MPAA RATING, 97 m., 1996

Mary Beth Hurt (Jean Seberg). Written, produced, and directed by Mark Rappaport.

If it is true, as Jean-Luc Godard once said, that "cinema history is the history of boys photographing girls," then one task of movie historians should be to find out what happened to the girls in the process. Mark Rappaport, who uses the Godard quote in his new film *From the Journals of Jean Seberg,* takes it to heart in a unique way. He presents Seberg as the narrator of her own life.

Seberg died in 1979, hounded to suicide by the FBI, which planted poisonous items about her in a gossip column. Since she was not available to play herself, Rappaport uses the actress Mary Beth Hurt (who looks a little like Seberg might have) to play her. And the movie's narration is all spoken by "Seberg," in the first person.

Some of it may be based on things she said or thought. Most of it, including her comments on women in the movies, politics, and her fellow actresses, is invention. Rappaport's mixture of fact and fiction is more audacious than Oliver Stone's *Nixon*—but the movie makes it perfectly clear that it is using both history and imagination, and the result is a tough, intelligent look at the grueling job of being one of those girls photographed by the boys.

Seberg's was a life that had a storybook beginning and a tragic ending. She was a seventeen-year-old "unknown"—that wonderful Hollywood word for anyone not a movie star!—when Otto Preminger found her in Iowa and cast her in his 1957 film *Saint Joan*. She received merciless reviews, but Preminger, determined to be proven right in his choice, starred her again in *Bonjour Tristesse* (1959). That film was a powerful influence on Godard, who quickly cast Seberg in his first film, *Breathless,* launching her career as a star who worked both in Europe and America, in both French and English, in a series of films that were mostly marginal at the box office. (Her biggest hit was her last film of consequence, *Airport,* in 1970.)

Jean Seberg would seem to have had little to complain about, at least at first. To be plucked from obscurity at seventeen and find your picture on the cover of *Life* magazine is something many teenagers dream about. But Otto Preminger was not the perfect mentor for an Iowa girl thrust into the spotlight. "He was a charming conversationalist at dinner and a sadist on the set," Seberg says. That quote may be from life; I had dinner with him many times and visited many of his sets, and it is absolutely true. He specialized in humiliating women in front of his crews.

For *Saint Joan,* Seberg was actually tied to a stake for the burning scene, and, in the take used in the movie, was accidentally burned. "Why *was Life* magazine there to document the day I was burned?" she asks (for let us adopt the convention that the dialogue is Seberg's own words). Did Otto stage the accident for publicity? Nobody knows. But Otto was a master of publicity, and by the time *Saint Joan* opened the whole world was waiting, with knives sharpened, to attack her performance—not because they hated her, but because it was such a temptation to prove Preminger wrong.

Undeterred, Preminger immediately cast her in *Bonjour Tristesse,* the first of many movies in which she would play the younger woman to an older male lover. Why Seberg? Rappaport uses an audacious device to "screen test" other actresses in some of her roles—superimposing famous heads, such as Barbra Streisand and Audrey Hepburn, over Seberg's own. Thus we see Streisand singing "People" while burning at the stake, and Hepburn playing opposite David Niven in *Bonjour Tristesse.* This doesn't quite duplicate the fantasy of making the identical movie with different stars, but it's certainly original.

Seberg in the 1960s appeared in such films as *Lilith* (her best role), *A Fine Madness,* and *Paint Your Wagon,* during which she had an affair with Clint Eastwood. At the time she was still married to Romain Gary, a second-rate French writer, bearded, twenty years her senior, who fancied himself a director and directed her in two movies where the male lead was an older man wearing Gary's beard style. In these movies much was the fault of her character's sexual problems. ("Men love to make movies about women driven mad by sexuality.")

By the 1970s, Seberg, who was drinking and using drugs, had drifted into a left-wing political orbit, and attracted the attention of the reptilian J. Edgar Hoover, who set his agents to spy on her; they leaked to *Los Angeles Times* columnist Joyce Haber an item that she was pregnant by a Black Panther. She was found dead in a parked car in Paris in 1979, still pregnant (the baby was white).

This biographical material is presented side-by-side with a larger critique of the period, its actresses, and its movies. Seberg, we learn, was "the first actress to return the hard stare of the camera lens. In that sense, she was the first modern movie star." But her eyes had nothing to express; they were a cipher, Rappaport says, and proves it by showing us other, more expressive eyes, including Ingrid Bergman's. There is also a side excursion into the career of Jane Fonda ("She apologized for her politics in 1988, but in the 1970s, did she ever apologize for being a bimbo?"), and a general discussion of how women are used in, and by, the movies.

Rappaport's stylistic approach in this film is fascinating, and may be infuriating to some viewers. He takes whatever is at hand, presses it to his needs, makes up what he doesn't know, and relies heavily on the technique of showing us movie clips while telling us what to see in them. He did much the same thing in his little-seen *Rock Hudson's Home Movies,* which reexamined Hudson's career with a voice-over narration providing a gay-oriented analysis of his movies. At the end of both films, we don't know exactly what to believe, but we have been challenged to reinterpret what we see on a screen, and to read a movie as a record of much more than simply its story.

Of course, *From the Journals of Jean Seberg* is Rappaport doing to Seberg what the other boys did, photographing a girl and turning it to his own purposes. But at least he's on her side.

## The Full Monty ★ ★ ★

R, 95 m., 1997

Robert Carlyle (Gaz), Tom Wilkinson (Gerald), Mark Addy (Dave), Steve Huison (Lomper), Paul Barber (Horse), Hugo Speer (Guy), Lesley Sharp (Jean), Emily Woof (Mandy), Deirdre Costello (Linda). Directed by Peter Cattaneo and produced by Uberto Pasolini. Screenplay by Simon Beaufoy.

"A few more years and men won't exist," mourns one of the unemployed workers in *The Full Monty*. Sheffield was once a thriving British manufacturing town known for its steel, but now its mills are closed and the men hang about all day in the gloomy job center, where there are no jobs to be found. Their remaining functions in life seem limited to drinking, getting into mischief, and avoiding child support payments they can't afford.

From this grim working-class prospect, *The Full Monty* creates a lovable comedy, as the men decide to go where the work is. The Chippendale dancers have recently entertained a full house at a local club, including most of the wives, mothers, daughters, sisters, and girlfriends of the unemployed workers. If the Chippendales can make hundreds or thousands of pounds by stripping down to their Speedos, why can't some local blokes make a few quid by going all the way—the "full monty"?

They're led by Gaz, a determined, inventive man played by Robert Carlyle (he was the alarming Begbie in *Trainspotting*). For dance lessons they turn in desperation to their former foreman, Gerald (Tom Wilkinson). He's always lorded it over them, but is now reduced to haunting the jobs center and trying to keep it a secret from his wife that he's out of work: He's too proud to tell her, and one of the movie's best scenes is when he lets down his guard and confesses his financial desperation.

Can he teach them to dance? Sort of, and some of the funniest scenes come during auditions and rehearsals. Their troupe, as it forms, includes Guy (Hugo Speer), who can't dance but will be the star when the Speedos come off; Lomper (Steve Huison), who is young and suicidal; and Horse (Paul Barber), a middle-aged black man with a bad hip, who explains, "me break-dancing days is probably over, but there's always the funky chicken."

The director, Peter Cattaneo, takes material that would be at home in a sex comedy, and gives it gravity because of the desperation of the characters; we glimpse the home life of these men, who have literally been put on the shelf, and we see the wound to their pride. *The Full Monty* belongs in the recent tradition of bittersweet films from Britain that depict working-class life: movies like *The Snapper* and *The Van*, based on Roddy Doyle books; *Raining Stones*, about an unemployed man desperate to buy his daughter's communion dress; and *Brassed Off*, which was also about an industry shutting down and leaving its community stranded.

Robert Carlyle might seem like a strange choice to play Gaz, if you remember him only from *Trainspotting*, but one of his first roles was in Ken Loach's *Riff-Raff*, which took place mostly on a construction site where the workers, itinerants, lived off the land. He has a daring here, as if he's walking on a wire and won't fall if he doesn't look down. He doesn't know himself if his plan has been inspired by courage or bravado.

*The Full Monty* is about more than inventiveness in the face of unemployment: It's about ordinary blokes insisting that their women regard them as men—job or no job. If they're reduced to stripping to pay the bills, well, a lot of women know all about that. This is the undertone, and yet the movie develops a broad, healthy band of humor; it's bawdy, but also gentle and goodhearted, and I felt affection for the characters.

The film's last shot is not hard to guess, although less explicit than some audiences will expect. It was applauded at the screening I attended, but I wish there had been another scene afterward. It's not what you do, it's how you feel about it, and I wanted to see a payoff (triumph, maybe, or more likely relief) on the faces of the men. ☞

## The Funeral ★ ★ ★

R, 99 m., 1996

Christopher Walken (Ray), Chris Penn (Chez), Annabella Sciorra (Jean), Isabella Rossellini (Clara), Vincent Gallo (Johnny), Benicio Del Toro (Gaspare), Gretchen Mol (Helen), John Ventimiglia (Sali). Directed by Abel Ferrara and produced by Mary Kane. Screenplay by Nicholas St. John.

*The Funeral* is about the kind of gangsters the Corleone family might have become if they had all gone to college. It's a film where violence is delayed by conversations about morality, where the younger brother has left-wing sympathies and strange kinks, where the leader of the family protests, "I have ideas. I read books."

This is not to say it is an intellectual movie about professorial gangsters. What it really means is that its characters, members of a mob family in New York, are more tortured than they might otherwise have been because they know more and think more. Ignorance may not always be bliss, but it is sometimes more comfortable than insight.

As the movie opens, Johnny Tempio (Vincent Gallo), the youngest of three brothers, has been brought home dead from a shooting. Greeting his corpse are his older brothers, Ray (Christopher Walken) and Chez (Chris Penn), and the women of the family, played by Annabella Sciorra and Isabella Rossellini. Chez is a hot-blooded bartender, so enraged by the death that he attacks a flower delivery man and goes berserk at the side of the coffin. Ray is more dangerous, slick, and controlled.

The death of the brother must be avenged, but first it is important that we understand how Johnny brought about his own doom, and how it may have been fated by deep currents within his own family. "The only way anything is going to change," a priest observes, "is if this family has a total reversal."

The director, Abel Ferrara, uses flashbacks to lead us back up to the murder, showing Johnny as a misfit even within a family of misfits, a mobster assigned to work with a mob-connected union, who attends a workers' meeting and perhaps even feels some sympathy with the communists who are haranguing it. He has odd tastes for a young man; at a stag party, he passes over the prostitutes who are available in order to choose the old, fat madam.

Ferrara has tried this before, crossing a genre movie with sneaky intellectual side-currents. His *China Girl*, about race hatred on the divide between Little Italy and Chinatown, was based on *Romeo and Juliet.* His *The Addiction,* a vampire movie, was set within the milieu of a graduate school of psychology (a vampire struck her victims at a party celebrating a doctorate). Here we have gangsters who brood and judge and apply moral standards. Chez, the "nicest" brother despite his temper, tries to give a young girl $5 and send her home because he wants to rescue her from prostitution. She holds out for $10. He gives her $20, "because you just sold your soul."

The family's libidos have crossed paths with the woman of a rival gangster, played by Benicio Del Toro, and that leads to violence, but not directly (nothing is direct in this film). Flashbacks, murky memories, and oblique but knowing comments by the women hint of shocking secrets, and Ferrara draws a veil back just long enough for us to observe and speculate, but not long enough for us to be sure of what we should conclude.

The movie doesn't give us a traditional ending, or indeed a satisfactory one; *The Funeral* sets up more dilemmas than it can solve. Much of the movie's appeal is in the acting. Chris Penn won the Best Supporting Actor award at the 1996 Venice festival (where the film won the special jury prize), but his performance seemed to me well within his reach.

The actor I kept my eye on was Walken, who has an ability to hold his characters aloof from commitment; we're not sure how much is real, and how much is an act or strategy that could suddenly reverse itself. He, too, is an intellectual here, and there is a scene where, holding an ax, he considers killing a character he knows does not really deserve to die. He arrives at a logical conclusion: "Since you're never going to forget this—you leave me no choice." The guy is doomed not for what he did, but because of what the Walken character has done in response to it.

Abel Ferrara's material is some of the darkest now being used in American film—hard *noir.* His version of *Invasion of the Body Snatchers* was frightening in a way that turned the two earlier versions of the film into parables. His *Bad Lieutenant* gave us one of Harvey Keitel's most unsettling performances, as a man so fundamentally twisted that he made conventional movie villains look like pretenders. Now here is a gangster movie that does not want setups or payoffs like traditional gangster movies. Other gangster movies focus on crime families. Ferrara links his family with its currently fashionable companion word, dysfunctional.

# G

## Gabbeh ★ ★ ★

NO MPAA RATING, 75 m., 1997

Shaghayegh Djodat (Gabbeh), Abbas Sayahi (The Uncle), Hossein Moharami (The Old Man), Roghieh Moharami (The Old Woman). Directed by Mohsen Makhmalbaf and produced by Khalil Doroudchi and Khalil Mahmoudi. Screenplay by Makhmalbaf.

*Gabbeh* is a fable, clear on the surface, tangled in the shadows, told by a Persian carpet. As the film opens, an old couple in Iran pause by a stream to wash their rug, or "gabbeh," and we see that it is decorated with a portrait of a young woman and a man on horseback. "Who are you?" the old woman asks the girl on the rug, and the girl steps out of the rug and answers her question.

She is Gabbeh. She lived with her nomadic people in the desert, and was in love with the young horseman. But it was decreed that she could not marry until her uncle did—and, at fifty-seven, he was still single. Meanwhile, the horseman followed her through the desert, and at night, as Gabbeh sat with her family around the fire, she heard him making wild wolf cries at the moon.

*Gabbeh* is the thirteenth film directed by Mohsen Makhmalbaf, but the first I have seen. He was imprisoned as a youth in the Shah's Iran for his fundamentalist Islamic beliefs, but this is not the film of an unyielding person. By choosing Gabbeh to tell her own story, he sides with her, and therefore against tradition. It is all very well to wait until the old uncle marries, but in the meantime there is the call of the heart in the blood of the young. I am reminded of a talk show I saw once featuring Louis Farrakhan, who voiced his opposition to interracial romance, but then sighed and spread his hands palms upward, and said, "But the young people—what can you say to them?"

The young people depicted on the rug may have a connection with the present day, but that is a secret for the film to reveal. More to the point is its visual richness. Makhmalbaf uses not only the glories of nature—the desert landscape and sky—but also man's own use of color, and there is a scene where the old uncle talks of color, and the colors magically appear as he names them. In other scenes, we see the wildflowers from which the dyes come, to color the threads of the rug.

There is no shyness here about bold primary colors, and I was reminded of Zhang Yimou's *Ju Dou* (1989), with its scenes set in a workshop where bolts of cloth are dipped into vats of bright colors. There is a kind of voluptuousness that comes with seeing color boldly splashed across the screen, and we are reminded that modern art direction, with its prudently controlled palates, may be too timid or "tasteful" to give us that pleasure.

Is there a message here about the society where the film is set? Probably there is more of an attitude, a feeling that universal human desires cannot be denied. Certainly one can imagine a film asking us to sympathize with the fifty-seven-year-old uncle, whose life has been made a misery because of his niece's desire for romance. Love is the preoccupation of the young for no doubt sound Darwinian reasons.

*Gabbeh* is a simple film. There is hardly more to say about it than I have said. Yet it remains in the memory in a way that more thickly plotted films do not. It teaches a lesson: that there can be more to a movie than episodes and events, that a film can stand back from the micromanagement of small bits of time, and show us the sweep of a life and the long, slow seasons of a heart. Movies like this work like meditation or music, to nudge us toward the important.

## The Game ★ ★ ★ ½

R, 128 m., 1997

Michael Douglas (Nicholas van Orton), Sean Penn (Conrad van Orton), Deborah Kara Unger (Christine), James Rebhorn (Jim Feingold), Carroll Baker (Ilsa), Peter Donat (Sam Sutherland), Armin Mueller-Stahl (Anson Baer). Directed by David Fincher and produced by Steve Golin and Cean Chaffin. Screenplay by John Brancato and Michael Ferris.

The opening scenes of *The Game* show Michael Douglas as a rich man in obsessive control of his life. The movie seems to be about how he is reduced to humility and humanity—or maybe that's just a trick on him. The movie is like a control freak's worst nightmare. The Douglas character, named Nicholas van Orton, is surrounded by employees who are almost paralyzed by his rigid demands on them. "I have an Elizabeth on line three," says one secretary, and then a second adds, "Your wife, sir."

"I know," he says coldly. We have the feeling that if the second secretary had not spoken, he would have replied, "Elizabeth who?" His underlings are in no-win situations. It is, in fact, his ex-wife; at age forty-eight, van Orton lives alone in the vast mansion where his father committed suicide at the same age. His birthday evening consists of eating a cheeseburger served on a silver tray and watching CNN.

Van Orton's younger brother Conrad (Sean Penn) visits him and announces a birthday present: The Game, which is "sort of an experiential Book of the Month Club." Operated by a shadowy outfit named Consumer Recreation Services, The Game never quite declares its rules or objectives, but soon van Orton finds himself in its grasp, and his orderly life has become unmanageable. "It will make your life fun again," he is promised, but that's not quite how he sees it, as a functionary (James Rebhorn) leads him through the sign-up process.

Soon everything starts to fall apart. His pen leaks. His briefcase won't open. Food is spilled on him in a restaurant. He is trapped in an elevator. The level of chaos rises. He finds himself blackmailed, his bank accounts are emptied, he wanders like a homeless man, he is left for dead in Mexico, he is trapped inside a cab sinking in a bay.

Of course, many of the physical details of what happens to him are implausible or even impossible, but so what? The events are believable in the sense that events can be believed in a nightmare: You can hardly worry about how a horror has been engineered when you're trapped inside it.

The mounting campaign of conspiratorial persecution is greeted by van Orton with his usual style of cold contempt and detachment: He knows all the angles, he thinks, and has foreseen all the pitfalls, and can predict all the permutations. But he finds he is totally wrong. Even those few people he thinks he can trust (including a waitress played by Deborah Kara Unger—or is she a waitress?) may be double agents. There is even the possibility that The Game is a front for a well-planned conspiracy to steal his millions. Michael Douglas, who is superb at playing men of power (remember his Gordon Gekko in *Wall Street*) is reduced to a stumbling, desperate man on the run (remember his unemployed engineer in *Falling Down*).

*The Game,* written by John Brancato and Michael Ferris, is David Fincher's first film since *Seven,* and projects the same sense of events being controlled by invisible manipulation. This time, though, there's an additional element: Van Orton is being broken down and reassembled like the victim of some cosmic EST program. And it is unclear, to him and to us, whether The Game is on the level, or a fraud, or perhaps spinning out of control.

The movie's thriller elements are given an additional gloss by the skill of the technical credits and the wicked wit of the dialogue. When van Orton's brother asks, "Don't you think of me any more?" he shoots back, "Not since family week at rehab." And when his ex-wife asks if he had a nice birthday, he answers, "Does Rose Kennedy have a black dress?"

The film's dark look, its preference for shadows, recalls *Seven* and also Fincher's *Alien 3*. The big screen reveals secrets and details in dark corners; on video, they may disappear into the murk. Like *Seven,* the plotting is ingenious and intelligent, and although we think we know the arc of the film (egotist is reduced to greater humility and understanding of himself), the film doesn't progress in a docile, predictable way; for one thing, there is the real possibility that The Game is not an ego-reduction program, but a death plot.

Douglas is the right actor for the role. He can play smart, he can play cold, and he can play angry. He is also subtle enough that he never arrives at an emotional plateau before the film does, and never overplays his process of inner change. Indeed, one of the refreshing things about the film is that it stays true to its paranoid vision right up until what seems like the very end—and then beyond it, so that by the time the real ending arrives, it's not the payoff and release so much as a final macabre twist of the knife.

## Gamera: Guardian of the Universe ★ ★ ★

NO MPAA RATING, 96 m., 1997

Tsuyoski Ihara (Yoshinari Yonemori), Akira Onodera (Naoya Kusanagi), Ayoko Fujitani (Asagi Kusanagi), Shinobu Nakayama (Matumi Nagamine). Directed by Shusuke Kaneko and produced by Yasuyoshi Tokuma. Screenplay by Kazunori Ito.

*Gamera: Guardian of the Universe* is precisely the kind of movie that I enjoy despite all rational reasoning. How, you may ask, can I possibly prefer this Japanese monster film about a jet-powered turtle to a megabudget solemnity like *Air Force One*? It has laughable acting, a ludicrous plot, second-rate special effects, and dialogue like, "Someday, I'll show you around monster-free Tokyo!" The answer, I think, is that *Gamera* is more fun.

There's a learning process that moviegoers go through. They begin in childhood without sophistication or much taste, and like *Gamera* more than *Air Force One* because flying turtles are obviously more entertaining than U.S. presidents. Then they grow older and develop "taste," and prefer *Air Force One*, which is better made and has big stars and a more plausible plot. (Isn't it more believable, after all, that a president could single-handedly wipe out a planeload of terrorists than that a giant turtle could spit gobs of flame?) Then, if they continue to grow older and wiser, they complete the circle and return to *Gamera* again, realizing that while both movies are preposterous, the turtle movie has the charm of utter goofiness and, in an age of flawless special effects, it is somehow more fun to watch flawed ones.

*Gamera* is not a good movie, but it is a good moviegoing experience. I am reminded of Pauline Kael's wise observation: The movies are so seldom great art that we should not go unless we can appreciate great trash. I am satiated, for the time being, by terrorists and fireballs and bomb threats and special effects, and my eyes yearn for new sights, such as a giant radioactive bat trapped inside a baseball dome and emitting green rays. (There is even a voluptuous pleasure to be derived from simply typing the *words* "emitting green rays.") Please, mister, show me something new.

Gamera has starred in nine films in thirty-two years, but has never attained the stardom of Godzilla, perhaps because of speciesism, which prejudices us to prefer dinosaurs to turtles. Gamera lives for much of the time beneath the ocean (or, as the movie refers to it, "The Pacific-Ocean of Death!"), where he shows up on radar screens as a giant atoll. But when Gamera is needed, the atoll begins to glow, and (I can't stop myself) emits rays. And then Gamera flies through the skies, powered by jet outlets on its underside.

Now, then. Considering that Gamera never needs to refuel, we must assume he is organic and not mechanical. Therefore, the jet blasts come not from burning petrol, but from the by-products of organic material. This is not a matter of shame for the Japanese, who are more frank about bodily processes, and even have a best-selling children's book named *The Gas We Pass*. Yes, Gamera is powered by farts.

The plot. A 10,000-year-old bat named Gyaos has aroused itself from slumber and attacks Tokyo. Scientists use floodlights to lure it into a baseball stadium, where they stand in the dugout shouting lines like, "Take your posts!" But only Gamera is a match for Gyaos, and soon the two flying creatures are engaged in a fierce battle that extends even to outer space. (How does a bat fly in space? Don't ask me. I still don't know how Gyaos flies in the air, since it has no moving wings.)

I have referred to Gyaos as a bat, but at one point, after being severely pummeled by Gamera, it drops several eggs the size of minivans on the streets of Tokyo. Bats are mammals and do not lay eggs, I think, so perhaps (a) Gyaos is a bird, (b) bats do lay eggs, or (c) those are turtle eggs, and the movie is about Mrs. Gamera.

There is, strictly speaking, no need for human characters in *Gamera: Guardian of the Universe*, since the creatures are self-contained in their age-old enmity. But the movie does provide us with four observers, including Asagi (Ayoko Fujitani), a teenage girl who seems able to read Gamera's mind, and carries a glowing stone that helps her do that, I think. Late in the film, there is a big close-up of the girl's eyes, and then Gamera's eyes, and then a blob of energized spirit is exchanged somehow, and Gamera is able to live to fight again another day. Studying the film's press releases, I discover that Ayoko Fujitani is Steven Seagal's daughter, and I punch my fist into the air, and cry "Yesssss!"

## Gang Related ★ ★ ★

R, 111 m., 1997

James Belushi (Divinci), Tupac Shakur (Rodriguez), Lela Rochon (Cynthia), Dennis Quaid (William ["Joe"]), James Earl Jones (Arthur Baylor), David Paymer (Elliot Goff), Wendy Crewson (Helen Eden), Gary Cole (Richard Simms). Directed by Jim Kouf and produced by John Bertolli, Brad Krevoy, and Steven Stabler. Screenplay by Kouf.

The two cops in *Gang Related* are like that vaudeville act where the guy tried to keep the plates spinning on the poles. They've made a bad mistake and are desperately trying to conceal it, but their cover-up keeps coming to pieces—they're forced into improvisations and intimidations while the truth seems to march inexorably straight at them.

The movie, which stars Jim Belushi and the late Tupac Shakur as the cops, is a skillful police procedural all the way up until the end, which doesn't quite work. It doesn't cheat with lazy action or chase scenes; the writer-director, Jim Kouf, knows he has a good story to tell and he tells it. And he employs a large and skilled supporting cast; most modern movies, having paid their stars big salaries, keep them onscreen all the time, but *Gang Related* is more like a classic Warner Bros. *film noir* with a lot of colorful speaking roles.

Belushi and Shakur are Divinci and Rodriguez, police partners who operate a scam in which they sell drugs, collect the money, and kill the buyers—thus ridding the city of scum and making themselves rich at the same time. When the movie opens, they've offed ten dealers, but their luck turns bad with their eleventh victim, who is an undercover agent for the DEA.

Because they "investigated" the man's shooting death in the first place, they're assigned to find his killer. And they start shopping for someone to frame—finally settling on a wet-brained homeless man called Joe (Dennis Quaid), who doesn't remember much, and agrees to confess in return for a drink. Divinci is also able to persuade him he actually did commit the murders. It looks like a neat package, but this witness will bring nothing but trouble.

These events are told against a rich backdrop formed by many other characters, including a stripper (Lela Rochon) who sometimes sleeps with Divinci, and who he asks to be a witness against "Joe." And there are others—police captains, federal agents, bail bondsmen, and finally a spirited prosecutor (Wendy Crewson), a public defender (David Paymer), and a famous lawyer (James Earl Jones) who is a surprise entry into the case. Dennis Quaid, unrecognizable at first, does a quietly effective job of disappearing into the role of a shattered man (although his last scene is highly unlikely). The only doubtful casting decision is Rochon as the stripper; she seems too much like a classy ingenue. The movie would have benefited from an older, more streetwise actress (that would also make the romance with the cop more plausible).

For most of the film, I sat in quiet amazement: I was witnessing a complex, well crafted, clearly told story, in a screenplay that moved well and had dialogue that sounded colorful without resembling a Quentin Tarantino clone. Modern screenplays are often so tired in their conventions, using action to replace characters and events. The fascination of *Gang Related* is in the way we understand exactly what the two cops are trying to do, and what they're up against. Even the courtroom scenes aren't recycled clichés but use the personalities of the players to develop genuine tension—they're like a reminder of what a charged silence can feel like.

It is refreshing that the film has no heroes. It's a story about flawed people. Like a novel by Georges Simenon, it is fascinated by criminal psychology and wants to see how certain types function under great stress. It gives the audience credit for being interested in human nature; we don't need a conventional hero to identify with because we identify with the guilt, desperation, and greed of these two cops. We are incapable of doing what they did, but not incapable of feeling what they feel.

Belushi and Shakur work well together; the film, dedicated to the murdered rap artist, is proof (along with *Gridlock'd* earlier this year) that he had an authentic talent. Instead of forcing the two characters into molds, Kouf lets them develop: Belushi's Divinci is not a shallow villain, but a truly amoral man who gives little pep talks to his dubious partner. Shakur's Rodriguez is a problem gambler with a juice enforcer after him, and he struggles with a troublesome conscience. They have a funny, scary scene together where Belushi asks, "Okay—what's the worst-case scenario?" as they're already facing the worst possible case.

I was not persuaded by the film's ending. It's too much of a shaggy dog story; this material deserves more than an ironic twist and a blackout. The film is otherwise so well crafted that I am tempted to wonder if the ending was imposed on Kouf by a lockstep studio executive. I can imagine any number of endings that could have emerged organically from the material, but this one couldn't, and doesn't.

I have a little meter that runs in my mind during a movie, with an imaginary needle that points at a number of stars between one and four. *Gang Related* wavered high for most of its running time, and only settled down to "three" because of the unsatisfying closing scenes. It's one of the best pure police procedurals I've seen in a long time.

## Gattaca ★ ★ ★ ½

PG-13, 112 m., 1997

Ethan Hawke (Vincent/Jerome), Uma Thurman (Irene), Jude Law (Jerome/Eugene), Alan Arkin (Detective Hugo), Loren Dean (Anton), Gore Vidal (Director Josef), Xander Berkeley (Lamar), Tony Shalhoub (German), Elias Koteas (Antonio). Directed by Andrew Niccol and produced by Danny DeVito, Michael Shamberg, and Stacey Sher. Screenplay by Niccol.

What is genetic engineering, after all, but preemptive plastic surgery? Make the child perfect in the test tube and save money later. Throw in perfect health, a high IQ, and a long life span, and you have the brave new world of *Gattaca,* in which the bioformed have inherited Earth, and babies who are born naturally get to be menial laborers.

This is one of the smartest and most provocative of science-fiction films, a thriller with ideas. Its hero is a man who challenges the system. Vincent (Ethan Hawke) was born in the old-fashioned way, and his genetic tests show he has bad eyesight, heart problems, and a life expectancy of about thirty years. He is an "In-Valid," and works as a cleaner in a space center.

Vincent does not accept his fate. He never has. As a child, he had swimming contests with his brother, Anton (Loren Dean), who has all the right scores but needs to be saved from drowning. Now Vincent dreams of becoming a crew member on an expedition to one of the moons of Saturn. Using an illegal DNA broker, he makes a deal with a man named Jerome (Jude Law), who has the right genes but was paralyzed in an accident. Jerome will provide him with blood and urine samples and an identity. In a sense, they'll both go into space.

*Gattaca* is the remarkable debut of a writer-director from New Zealand, Andrew Niccol, whose film is smart and thrilling—a tricky combination—and also visually exciting. His most important set is a vast office where genetically superior computer programmers come to work every day, filing into their long rows of desks like the office slaves in King Vidor's *The Crowd* and Orson Welles's *The Trial.* (Why are "perfect" human societies so often depicted by ranks of automatons? Is it because human nature resides in our flaws?) Vincent, as "Jerome," gets a job as a programmer, supplies false genetic samples, and becomes a finalist for the space shot.

The tension comes in two ways. First, there's the danger that Vincent will be detected; the area is swept daily, and even an eyelash can betray him. Second, there's a murder; a director of the center, who questions the wisdom of the upcoming shot, is found dead, and a detective (Alan Arkin) starts combing the personnel for suspects. Will a computer search sooner or later put together Vincent, the former janitor, with "Jerome," the new programmer?

Vincent becomes friendly with Irene (Uma Thurman), who works in the center but has been passed over for a space shot because of low scores in some areas. They are attracted to one another, but romance in this world can be dangerous; after kissing a man, a woman is likely to have his saliva swabbed from her mouth so she can test his prospects. Other supporting characters include Gore Vidal as a mission supervisor and Tony Shalhoub as the broker ("You could go anywhere with this guy's helix under your arm").

Hawke is a good choice for the lead, combining the restless dreams of a "Godchild" with the plausible exterior of a lab baby. The best scenes in the movie involve his relationship with the real Jerome, played by Law as smart, bitter, and delighted to be sticking it to the system that has grounded him. (He may be paralyzed from the waist down, but after all, as the movie observes, you don't need to walk in space.) His drama parallels Vincent's, because if either one is caught they'll both go down together.

Science fiction in the movies has recently specialized in invasions by aliens, but the best of the genre deals with ideas. At a time when we read about cloned sheep and tomatoes crossed with fish, the science in *Gattaca* is theoretically possible. When parents can order "perfect" babies, will they? Would you take your chances on a throw of the genetic dice, or order up the make and model you wanted? How many people are prepared to buy a car at random from the universe of all available cars? That's how many, I suspect, would opt to have natural children.

Everybody will live longer, look better, and be healthier in the Gattacan world. But will it be as much fun? Will parents order children who are rebellious, ungainly, eccentric, creative, or a lot smarter than their parents are? There's a concert pianist in *Gattaca* who has twelve fingers. Don't you sometimes have the feeling you were born just in time? ☞

## George of the Jungle ★ ★ ★

PG, 92 m., 1997

Brendan Fraser (George), Leslie Mann (Ursula Stanhope), Thomas Haden Church (Lyle Van de Groot), Richard Roundtree (Kwame), Greg Cruttwell (Max), Abraham Benrubi (Thor), Holland Taylor (Beatrice Stanhope), Kelly Miller (Betsy). Directed by Sam Weisman and produced by David Hoberman, Jordan Kerner, and Jon Avnet. Screenplay by Dana Olsen and Audrey Wells, based on characters developed by Jay Ward.

It was a strange experience, watching *George of the Jungle*. The movie would meander along, not going very much of anywhere, and then—pow!—there'd be an enormous laugh. More meandering, and then pow! again. Instead of spreading the laughter out and making a movie that was moderately funny from beginning to end, they concentrated the laughs, and made a movie that is sort of funny some of the time, and then occasionally hilarious.

Consider, for example, the character of Shep, the elephant. Shep looks like an elephant and is played by an elephant (named Tai), but Shep thinks it's a dog. George of the Jungle has trained him that way. When Shep first came bounding through the jungle and slid to a halt and sat on its haunches, barking and panting and wagging its tail, I was blindsided by laughter. And when George demonstrated Shep's ability to fetch by throwing a stick (actually a log), the joke only got funnier.

Then there's an Ape, named Ape, whose voice is dubbed by John Cleese, and who sounds and behaves exactly like George's British butler. I liked the way he looks down his glasses at people, and explains situations in a reserved and very proper tone, like Jeeves might. He's the funniest ape since those gorillas who drank the martinis in *Congo*.

George himself is pretty funny too. He's played by Brendan Fraser, who has bulked up and perfected a facial expression that can best be described as sheeplike goodwill. George has approximately the IQ of his namesake on Jay Ward's famous TV cartoon series, and makes the same mistakes, swinging on vines and crashing into trees.

The movie, which is live action and tries for the look and feel of a cartoon, involves a rich American girl named Ursula Stanhope (Leslie Mann) who goes on an expedition in the jungle, hears of a mysterious white ape, meets George, falls for him, and spends the rest of the movie trying to get out of her engagement to the society snob Lyle Van de Groot (Thomas Haden Church).

George meanwhile knows nothing of the ways of women, doesn't realize she likes him, and turns desperately to Ape for tips on how to woo her. Ape suggests baring his fangs, uprooting grass, beating his chest, and all the other usually dependable approaches, but when they don't work, he's adaptable: He gives his young master a copy of *Coffee, Tea or Me?* and says it contains all of the answers.

The screenplay by Dana Olsen and Audrey Wells makes some obligatory stops (we know more or less what will happen at the society functions in San Francisco, and we guess the fate of the wedding cake), but the movie is good-natured, slightly vulgar (in a mild Jim Carrey way) and well played by actors who are certainly good sports. Among the other cast members are Richard Roundtree, many years down the road from *Shaft in Africa*, as Kwame, an African leader, and Greg Cruttwell and Abraham Benrubi as two expedition members with vile plans of their own.

Is *George of the Jungle* a great movie? No.

But it was well positioned for the silly season, when we'd had just about all of the terrorist explosions we needed for one summer. I recommend a spin-off: a Saturday morning cartoon series about an elephant who thinks he's a dog. Think of all the things a dog could do if he had a trunk, and you'll get the idea.

## Georgia ★ ★ ★ ½

R, 117 m., 1996

Jennifer Jason Leigh (Sadie), Mare Winningham (Georgia), Ted Levine (Jake), Max Perlich (Axel), John Doe (Bobby), John C. Reilly (Herman), Jimmy Witherspoon (Trucker), Jason Carter (Chasman). Directed by Ula Grosbard and produced by Grosbard, Barbara Turner, and Jennifer Jason Leigh. Screenplay by Turner.

*Georgia* is a movie about Sadie, but it is no mistake that it's named after her sister. Sadie is one of those emotional black holes that occupy the center of many families, a victim who sucks all love and concern down into the oblivion at her center. As Georgia observes wearily near the end of the film: "Sadie's pain must be fed. And we're all here to serve."

We first see Sadie (Jennifer Jason Leigh) working as a motel maid and sneaking drinks from the pint bottle hidden under her towels. She leaves town with a blues singer named Trucker (Jimmy Witherspoon), whose multiple personalities make him a little hard to please. Sadie dumps him and turns up at a folk concert in Seattle that stars her sister, Georgia (Mare Winningham). Georgia is a little like Joan Baez in her country-and-western period—serene, together, with a pure voice.

You can tell these sisters have a long history together, and it has always been the same story: Georgia as the perfect one, married, with two kids, not only a singing star but also a good cook and a port in the storm. And needy Sadie, with her lank hair, her raccoon eye makeup, and her tattoos, desperately circling her, admiring her, loving her too much, and then spinning away out of control into booze and drugs.

It is tempting to say Jennifer Jason Leigh often plays characters like Sadie, but that would be too easy. Leigh has made a career out of down-and-out, self-destructive women, always played with unflinching courage, but each one is different. Sadie is a particular case, the kind of alcoholic or addict who expects her friends and family to give and give and give, who is never comforted, who is an open psychic wound, and who toys with them by pretending to be "better" and then going out and using or drinking again, as the whole spiral starts over.

It is easy to say that if Sadie sobered up her life would get better, but it is not that simple. She has done such deep damage that she needs first sobriety, and then a long time of healing. She is too impatient for that process. *Georgia* is not a simple plotted movie about descent and recovery, but a complex, deeply knowledgeable story about how alcoholism and mental illness really are family diseases; Sadie's sickness throws everybody off, and their adjustments to it don't make them healthier people. Is it possible, for example, that Georgia chose her laid-back, supportive, but distanced husband (Ted Levine) because she wanted someone as unlike Sadie as possible?

The film watches Sadie as she attempts to be a singer, like her sister. She joins a struggling rock band that plays in half-empty bars (and at a wedding where it is spectacularly out of place), and she makes friends with the drummer, Herman (John C. Reilly), who is on dope and forgets gigs and is finally fired by the band's leader (John Doe). Sadie is not a talented singer, but she sometimes can be an effective performer, in the Janis Joplin mode: She goes beyond singing, into the public display of pain and grief so intense the audience wants to look away.

What a woman like this usually needs is an enabler—a more competent person who will get sucked into the vortex of sickness and help her stay sick through misguided attempts to help her. She finds one, big-time, in naive young Axel (Max Perlich), who comes to deliver a pizza and stays to become her lover and husband. He thinks she is a great star. He himself is a quiet, friendly innocent who has "a high respect for women," and can say of his old car, "That's my treasure. Very much so."

The movie was directed by Ula Grosbard *(Straight Time)*, and written by Barbara Turner, Leigh's mother, and they make an interesting choice: Instead of alternating musical sequences with dramatic scenes, they develop a lot of the drama *during* onstage performances. That process creates the film's best single scene, as Georgia invites Sadie onstage during a concert and Sadie does a long, out-of-control version of Van Morrison's "Take Me Back" that grows so painful and embarrassing Georgia finally makes it a duet to steer it back toward sanity. This song is the whole story of their relationship. ("Was I great, or was I great?" Sadie says. "I wish I'd been there.")

Sadie tries detox ("I'm having trouble with the 'God as we understand him' part"), but this is not the kind of movie with a happy ending in which she emerges, sober and cheerful. Like *Leaving Las Vegas* (an even more harrowing story), it is about a person who has lost, not sobriety or control, which can be found again, but hope, which once lost can stay lost—barring a miracle.

## Get on the Bus ★ ★ ★ ★

R, 122 m., 1996

Ossie Davis (Jeremiah), Charles S. Dutton (George), Andre Braugher (Flip), Richard Belzer (Rick), Thomas Jefferson Byrd (Evan Thomas Sr.), Harry Lennix (Randall), Isaiah Washington (Kyle), Roger Guenveur Smith (Gary), De'Aundre Bonds (Junior), Hill Harper (Xavier), Gabriel Casseus (Jamal), Wendell Pierce (Wendell). Directed by Spike Lee and produced by Reuben Cannon, Barry Rosenbush, and Bill Borden. Screenplay by Reggie Rock Bythewood.

Spike Lee's *Get on the Bus* is a movie made in haste and passion, and that may account for its uncanny effect: We feel close to the real, often unspoken, issues involving race in America without the distance that more time and money might have provided. The film follows a group of about twenty black men on a cross-country bus trip to the Million Man March on October 16, 1995, and it opens exactly one year later.

Lee made the movie quickly, after fifteen black men invested in the enterprise. He shot in 16mm and video, always in and around the bus, using the cross section of its passengers to show hard truths, and falsehoods too. If the movie's central sadness is that we identify with our own group and suspect outsiders, the movie's message is that we have been given brains in order to learn to empathize.

There are all kinds of men on the bus. The tour leader (Charles S. Dutton) will be an inspiration and a referee. Another steadying hand is supplied by the oldest man on board, Jeremiah (Ossie Davis), a student of black history who delights in informing white cowboys that a black cowboy invented steer wrestling.

Also on board are a father (Thomas Jefferson Byrd) and his young son (De'Aundre Bonds), who have been shackled together by a court order; the irony of going to the march in chains is not lost on the others. An ex Marine (Isaiah Washington), who is gay, boards the bus with his lover (Harry Lennix) and they're singled out for persecution by a homophobic would-be actor (Andre Braugher). And a light-skinned man (Roger Guenveur Smith) is revealed as a cop assigned to South Central. Then there's a UCLA film student (Hill Harper), who is shooting a video documentary. And a member of the Nation of Islam (Gabriel Casseus), in black suit, bow tie, and dark glasses, who says not one word during the journey.

During the course of the trip, conversations will be philosophical, humorous, sad, nostalgic, angry, and sometimes very personal. The homosexual couple provokes the hostility of the gay-hater; prejudice knows no color line. That's true, too, in the attitudes toward the cop, whose skin is so light that he could pass, and who, it is revealed, became a cop in part because his black father, also a cop, was killed ("yes," he says, "by a brother").

"The man says he's black, he's black," pronounces Ossie Davis. But then the cop himself is revealed to have blinkers on. Another man reveals he's a former gang member, "cripping since I smoked a guy on my thirteenth birthday," but that now he does social work with "kids at risk." No matter; the cop warns him: "When we get back to L.A., I'm going to have to arrest you."

For many white people, a distressing element of the Million Man March was the racial slant of its convener, Louis Farrakhan, who has made many anti-Semitic and antiwhite slurs. Lee could have ducked this area, but doesn't. When the bus breaks down, the replacement driver (Richard Belzer) is a Jewish man who keeps quiet as long as he can, and then speaks out about Farrakhan's libels against Jews. "At least my parents did their part," he says; they were civil rights activists. He cites Farrakhan's statements that Judaism is a "gutter religion" and "Hitler was a great man." After some of the tour members recycle old clichés about Jewish landlords, the Belzer character says, "I wouldn't expect you to drive a bus to a Klan meeting," and walks away from the bus at a rest stop. Dutton takes over driving.

This is, I think, a forthright way to deal with Farrakhan's attitudes; the bus driver expresses widely felt beliefs in the white community and acts on his moral convictions. For the men on the bus, quite simply, "this march is not about Farrakhan." We expect that the Nation of Islam member will speak up to defend his leader, but he never does, and his silence, behind his dark glasses, acts as a powerful symbol of a religion that none of the other men on the bus seem to relate to, or even care much about.

As the journey continues, Lee brings in other characters who illustrate the complexity of race in America. There is a satiric cameo by Wendell Pierce as a prosperous Lexus dealer, who boards the bus in mid-journey and puffs on a cigar while airily expressing self-hating clichés about blacks. Then, in Tennessee, the reason for the march comes into sharp focus when the bus is pulled over by white cops. They bring a drug-sniffing dog on board, and treat the men in a subtle but unmistakably racist way. When the cops leave, Lee gives us a series of close-ups of silent, thoughtful faces: Every black man in America has at one time or another felt charged by the police with the fact of being black.

What makes *Get on the Bus* extraordinary is the truth and feeling that go into its episodes. Spike Lee and his actors face one hard truth after another, in scenes of great power. I have always felt Lee exhibits a particular quality of fairness in his films. *Do the Right Thing* was so even-handed that it was possible for a black viewer to empathize with Sal, the pizzeria owner, and a white viewer to empathize with Mookie, the black kid who starts the riot that burns down Sal's Pizzeria.

Lee doesn't have heroes and villains. He shows something bad—racism—that in countless ways clouds all of our thinking. *Get on the Bus* is fair in the same sense. It is more concerned with showing how things are than with scoring cheap rhetorical points. This is a film with a full message for the heart, and the mind.

## Getting Away with Murder ★ ★

R, 91 m., 1996

Dan Aykroyd (Jack Lambert), Lily Tomlin (Inga Mueller), Jack Lemmon (Mueller/Luger), Bonnie Hunt (Gail Holland), Brian Kerwin (Marty Lambert), Jerry Adler (Judge). Directed by Harvey Miller and produced by Frank Price and Penny Marshall. Screenplay by Miller.

I think about the twists and loops of the plot in *Getting Away with Murder* and, yes, I can see how it could have been a good comedy—a dark, ironic one, but funny. But then I think about the subject matter and my heart sinks. Here is a film that tries to find comedy in the Holocaust, and it looks in the wrong places, in the wrong way, and becomes a sad embarrassment.

I know that anything *can* be funny. I remember the "Springtime for Hitler" production number from Mel Brooks's *The Producers*, and I smile even after twenty-nine years. But humor depends on tone, timing, and even on taste, and when a comedy starts on the wrong foot, it is hard to regain balance. *Getting Away with Murder* tells the story of an ethics professor named Lambert (Dan Aykroyd), who lives next door to a kindly old man named Mueller (Jack Lemmon). Lambert plays drums in a local Dixieland band, and one night in a club he meets Gail (Bonnie Hunt), who likes his drumming, and him. A few nights later, they Meet Cute again, when Gail, a doctor, treats his wounds after a fight. There's chemistry. They fall in love.

Meanwhile, the FBI comes calling, because it suspects that Mueller may in fact be Karl Luger, the Beast of Berkau, a fugitive Nazi war criminal responsible for the deaths of hundreds of thousands. (Warning: I am now going to discuss plot points.) Lambert can't believe it at first, but convincing evidence is presented. Then Luger is freed on a technicality. The ethics professor, deeply affronted that this monster can walk free, poisons the apples on his tree, and the old man eats one and dies.

Then it appears (the warning still applies) that the old man was innocent after all. Lambert decides to make moral amends, punishing himself by calling off his marriage to Gail, and again by marrying Mueller's rather pathetic daughter, Inga (Lily Tomlin). And then . . . but I will give away no more, as the plot zigs and zags to its conclusion.

*Getting Away with Murder* is a black comedy, yes, but not a deep one, with a savage message that might justify its subject. It wants basically to be an evening's entertainment at your local theater. And that is why I find it inexcusable that the Lemmon character was made into a death camp commandant. (Try to imagine him as the Ralph Fiennes character in *Schindler's List,* fifty years later.) The movie twists and turns in its search for laughs, but it keeps coming back to those hundreds of thousands of . . . victims, the movie calls them, since for some reason it seems reluctant to use the word "Jews." And the weight of their deaths quiets any hope that the movie could be funny.

It would have been so easy to change just a few words, here and there, and make this into a different movie. Instead of a concentration camp commander, why couldn't old Mueller be a mad Nazi scientist, a guy with a ray beam to cut a hole in the ozone layer? Why tie his evil to real events? Not long ago I gave a negative review to the film *Don't Be a Menace in South Central While Drinking Your Juice in the Hood.* That was the comedy that satirized the genre of hood movies like *Boyz N the Hood* and *Menace 2 Society.* I found a lot of its humor—about drugs, teenage parents, crime, and illiteracy—to be not very funny. Now I feel the same way about *Getting Away with Murder,* which is technically a better-made movie, but generates the same dismay.

It's important to make this clear. I believe *any* subject can be appropriate for a film. I believe any subject can work as a comedy. I am not easily offended. But if a film is going to find jokes in inner-city poverty or the Holocaust, it needs two things these films lacked: (1) a reason, and (2) an approach. A subject is not funny just because we declare it so. The logic of the comedy must supply us with an angle of approach. And when the subject is fraught with emotion, the comedy must find the tone and strategy to sell itself.

There are no rules here, just subjective responses. All a critic can do is report his feelings. I did not feel it was funny to watch hi-jinks about the guilt or innocence of the Beast of Berkau. Oh, I suppose it all could somehow have been made funny, but not by the people who made this movie.

## The Ghost and the Darkness ★ ½

R, 104 m., 1996

Michael Douglas (Remington), Val Kilmer (John Patterson), Brian McCardie (Starling), John Kani (Samuel), Tom Puri (Abdullah), Tom Wilkinson (Beaumont), Emily Mortimer (Helena Patterson), Bernard Hill (Dr. Hawthorne), Henry Cele (Mahina). Directed by Stephen Hopkins and produced by Gale Anne Hurd, Paul Radin, and A. Kitman Ho. Screenplay by William Goldman.

*The Ghost and the Darkness* is an African adventure that makes the Tarzan movies look subtle and realistic. It lacks even the usual charm of being so bad it's funny. It's just bad. Not funny. No, wait . . . there is one funny moment. A bridge builder takes leave of his pregnant wife to go to Africa to build a bridge, and she solemnly observes, "You must go where the rivers are."

The bridge man, named Patterson, is played by Val Kilmer in a trim modern haircut that never grows an inch during his weeks in the bush. He is soon joined by a great white hunter named Remington (Michael Douglas), whose appearance is that of a homeless man who has somehow got his hands on a rifle. If this were a comic strip, there would be flies buzzing around his head.

The men meet up in Uganda, where a big push is on to complete a railroad faster than the Germans or the French. The owner of the rail company is a gruff tycoon who boasts, "I'm a monster. My only pleasure is tormenting those people who work for me." He is too modest. He also torments those who watch this movie.

Work on the railroad bridge is interrupted by a lion attack. Patterson spends the night in a tree and kills the lion. There is much rejoicing. Then another lion attacks. Eventually it becomes clear that two lions are on the prowl. They are devilishly clever, dragging men from their cots and even invading a hospital to chew on malaria patients. "Man-eaters are always old and alone, but not these two," Remington intones solemnly.

The rest of the movie consists of Patterson and Remington sitting up all night trying to shoot the lions, while the lions continue their attacks. At the end we learn that these two lions killed 135 victims in nine months. The movie only makes it seem like there were more, over a longer period.

Many scenes are so inept as to beggar description. Some of the lion attacks seem to have been staged by telling the actors to scream while a lion rug was waved in front of the camera. Patterson eventually builds a flimsy platform in a clearing, tethers a baboon at its base, and waits for the lions. Balanced on a wooden beam, he looks this way. Then that. Then this. Then that. A competent editor would have known that all this shifting back and forth was becoming distracting. Then a big bird flies at him and knocks him off the beam, and right into a lion's path. Lesson No. 1 in lion hunting: Don't let a big bird knock you into the path of a lion.

A narrator at the beginning of the film has informed us, "This is a story of death and mystery." The mystery is why these particular lions behaved as they did. I don't see why it's a mystery. They had reasons anyone can identify with. They found something they were good at and grew to enjoy it. The only mystery is why the screenwriter, William Goldman, has them kill off the two most interesting characters so quickly. (They are Angus, the chatty man on the spot, and an African with a magnificently chiseled and stern face.)

In the old days this movie would have starred Stewart Granger and Trevor Howard, and they would have known it was bad but they would have seemed at home in it, cleaning their rifles and chugging their gin like seasoned bwanas. Val Kilmer and Michael Douglas never for a second look like anything other than thoroughly unhappy movie stars stuck in a humid climate and a doomed production. I hope someone made a documentary about the making of this film. Now *that* would be a movie worth seeing.

## Ghost in the Shell ★ ★ ★

NO MPAA RATING, 82 m., 1995

Directed by Mamoru Oshii and produced by Yoshimasa Mizuo, Shigeru Watanabe, Ken Iyadomi and Mitsunisu Ishikawa. Screenplay by Kazunori Ito.

In the Japanese animated film *Ghost in the Shell*, the "shell" refers to bodies both artificial and organic, and the "ghost" refers to individual identity. Ghosts can move from organic to inorganic bodies, but an inorganic body cannot generate its own ghost; identity is a uniquely human trait. Then a very advanced computer program breaks through, attaining self-consciousness and independence. It moves freely through the Internet, becoming known as the Puppet Master, "the greatest hacker of all time."

The film is set in the next century, when humans coexist with cyborgs, who are part human, part machine, and part computer. The Puppet Master describes itself as "a living, thinking entity who was created in the sea of information." It once occupied a "real" body, but was tricked into diving into a cyborg, and then its body was murdered. Now it exists only in the electronic universe, but is in search of another body to occupy—or share.

*Ghost in the Shell* is not in any sense an animated film for children. Filled with sex, violence, and nudity (although all rather stylized and detached), it's another example of "anime," animation from Japan aimed at adult viewers—in this case the same college-age audience that reads *Heavy Metal* and the other slick comic zines. Anime has been huge in Japan for years, but is now making inroads into the world market; this film was coproduced with British money and includes a song performed by U2, "One Minute Warning," that runs nearly five minutes under apocalyptic images.

The movie has in common with a lot of traditional science fiction the tendency of characters to talk in concepts and abstract information. Sample dialogue: "Aside from a slight brain augmentation, your body's almost entirely human." Or, "If a cyber could create its own ghost, what would be the purpose of being human?" Or (my favorite), "You're treated like other humans, so stop with the angst!"

The lead character is a shapely woman named Major Motoko Kusanagi, who is a cyborg and runs an intelligence operation. Her unit is assigned to investigate an evil foreign operative who wants political asylum, but soon the case leads into contact with the Puppet Master, the "most dreaded cyber-criminal of all time." The major and other characters can change shapes, become invisible, and dive into the minds of others—which places them not so much in the future as in the tradition of Japanese fantasy, in which ghosts have always been able to do such things.

There is much moody talk in the movie about what it is to be human. All of the information accumulated in a lifetime, we learn, is less than a drop in the ocean of information, and perhaps a creature that can collect more information and hold onto it longer is more than human. In describing this vision of an evolving intelligence, Corinthians is evoked, twice: "For now we see through a glass, darkly; but then face to face: now I know in part; but then shall I know even as also I am known." At the end of the film, Puppet Master invites the major to join him face to face in his brave new informational sea.

The movie uses the *film noir* visuals which are common in anime, and it shares that peculiar tendency of all adult animation to give us females who are (a) strong protagonists at the center of the story, and (b) nevertheless almost continuously nude. An article about anime in *Film Quarterly* suggests that to be a "salary man" in modern Japan is so exhausting and dehumanizing that many men (who form the largest part of the animation audience) project both freedom and power onto women, and identify with them as fictional characters. That would help explain another recent Japanese phenomenon, the fad among (straight) teenage boys to dress like girls.

*Ghost in the Shell* is intended as a breakthrough film, aimed at theatrical release instead of a life on tape, disc, and in campus film societies. The ghost of anime can be seen here trying to dive into the shell of the movie mainstream. This particular film is too complex and murky to reach a large audience, it's not until the second hour that the story begins to reveal its meaning. But I enjoyed its visuals, its evocative sound track (including a suite for percussion and heavy breathing), and its ideas.

## Ghosts of Mississippi ★ ★ ½

PG-13, 123 m., 1996

Alec Baldwin (Bobby DeLaughter), Whoopi Goldberg (Myrlie Evers), James Woods (Byron De La Beckwith), Craig T. Nelson (Ed Peters), Susanna Thompson (Peggy Lloyd DeLaughter), Virginia Madsen (Dixie DeLaughter), Lucas Black (Burt DeLaughter), Joseph Tello (Drew DeLaughter), Alexa Vega (Claire DeLaughter). Directed by Rob Reiner and produced by Reiner, Frederick Zollo, Nicholas Paleologos, and Andrew Scheinman. Screenplay by Lewis Colick.

In June 1963, Medgar Evers, a Mississippi NAACP leader, was shot dead while standing in his driveway. A man named Byron De La Beckwith was charged with the crime, but went free after two all-white juries reached deadlocks.

Although De La Beckwith was clearly the killer, at that time and place he was impossible to convict; there is an obvious parallel with the O. J. Simpson verdict. So poisoned was the atmosphere in the Mississippi courtroom that at one point the state's governor, Ross Barnett, actually walked up to De La Beckwith and shook his hand.

All of this is remembered with fidelity in Rob Reiner's *Ghosts of Mississippi,* which tells the story of how a white prosecutor named Bobby DeLaughter reopened the case in 1989 and eventually won a conviction against De La Beckwith, who had spent the intervening years all but openly boasting about the killing. Justice was finally served, to the relief (and amazement) of Myrlie Evers, Medgar's widow, who sought all that time to bring her husband's killer back into a courtroom.

This is a moving story, but it's not a particularly compelling one in *Ghosts of Mississippi,* which plays like a TV docudrama and doesn't generate the emotional intensity of such similar films as *Mississippi Burning* and *A Time to Kill.*

Maybe it focuses on the wrong characters. The movie is seen through the eyes of DeLaughter (Alec Baldwin), who does his job well, and at some hazard—but his story is more of a legal procedural than a human drama. The emotional center of the film should probably be Myrlie Evers (Whoopi Goldberg), who cradled her bleeding husband as he died that night, her weeping and frightened children around her. But the role is underwritten to such a degree that Myrlie never really emerges except as an emblem, and Goldberg plays her like the guest of honor at a testimonial banquet. There's no juice.

That's partly Goldberg's fault (this is not one of her better performances), but mostly the fault of the filmmakers, who see their material through white eyes and use the Myrlie character as a convenient conscience. Many of the scenes between DeLaughter and Mrs. Evers take place on the telephone, where the white lawyer reports that he's doing the best he can, and the widow says, "Uh, huh," and doubts it. It doesn't help that a crucial piece of evidence—the court-certified transcript of the original trial—seems to be missing, and DeLaughter is stymied for months before Mrs. Evers belatedly reveals that she has it. (She says she didn't trust it to anyone; hadn't she heard of Kinko's?)

The movie's most convincing character is Byron De La Beckwith, the old racist, who is made by that splendid actor James Woods into a vile, damaged man. Woods goes for broke. De La Beckwith has a shifty, squirmy hatefulness; being a racist is a source of great entertainment to him, and he expresses his ideas with glee. We detest the character from beginning to end, but we react to it; the movie's other characters are more emblems than people.

There's an underlying issue here. This movie, like many others, is really about white redemption. As Godfrey Chesire points out in his review in *Variety:* "When future generations turn to this era's movies for an account of the struggles for racial justice in America, they'll learn the surprising lesson that such battles were fought and won by square-jawed white guys."

Maybe Hollywood believes that racially charged plots play better at the box office with white stars in the leads. It isn't enough that white southerners practiced segregation and racism for decades; now they get to play the heroic roles in their dismantling. Movies like this underline the rarity of work like Tim Reid's *Once Upon a Time . . . When We Were Colored,* which portrayed a self-sufficient black southern community that had its own worth and reality apart from white society.

In *Ghosts of Mississippi,* white society is seen perceptively. We learn once again about the establishment's White Citizens Councils and their shady links with the Ku Klux Klan. The movie uses DeLaughter's first wife, Dixie (Virginia Madsen), as a link to the past through her father, "the most racist judge in Mississippi." We learn that the newly enlightened white community has ghosts it prefers to keep in the closet: "You're dealing with the past. In the state of Mississippi, that's not where you want to be." Old-timers use revealing word choices, referring to Evers as "the civil rights leader that got himself shot."

All of that is well done, but where are the black people? Myrlie Evers functions as a conscience who is usually offscreen. Other black characters are found mostly in crowd scenes. What we get, really, is self-congratulation: Whites may have been responsible for segregation, but by golly, aren't we doing a wonderful job of making amends?

Alan Parker's *Mississippi Burning* (1988) was criticized for making white FBI agents into heroes of the civil rights era when the real FBI was conspicuous by its lack of enthusiasm for that assignment. But that film paid its way with great performances and tremendously moving drama. *Ghosts of Mississippi* generates nowhere near as much passion. It closes a chapter in history, but scarcely brings it to life.

## G.I. Jane ★ ★ ★ ½

R, 125 m., 1997

Demi Moore (Lieutenant Jordan O'Neil), Viggo Mortensen (Master Chief Urgayle), Anne Bancroft (Senator DeHaven), Jason Beghe (Royce), Scott Wilson (C. O. Salem), Lucinda Jenney (Blondell), Morris Chestnut (McCool), Josh Hopkins (Flea), James Caviezel (Slovnik). Directed by Ridley Scott and produced by Roger Birnbaum and Suzanne Todd. Screenplay by Danielle Alexandra and David Twohy.

"I'm not interested in being some poster girl for women's rights," says Lt. Jordan O'Neil, played by Demi Moore in *G.I. Jane.* She just wants to prove a woman can survive Navy SEAL training so rigorous that 60 percent of the men don't make it. Her protest loses a little of its ring if you drive down Sunset Boulevard in Los Angeles, as I did the other night, and see Demi Moore in a crewcut, glaring out fiercely from the side of an entire office building on one of the largest movie posters in history. Well, the lieutenant is talking for herself, not Moore.

Jordan O'Neil is a navy veteran who resents not being allowed into combat during the Gulf War. Now there's a move under way for full female equality in the fighting forces. Its leader,

Senator DeHaven (Anne Bancroft), wants no more coddling: "If women measure up, we'll get 100 percent integration." O'Neil is selected as a promising candidate, and reports for SEAL training after a farewell bubble bath with her lover, a fellow navy officer named Royce (Jason Beghe).

Now come the scenes from the movie that stay in the memory, as O'Neil joins a group of trainees in a regime of great rigor and uncompromising discomfort. The shivering, soaking-wet, would-be SEALS stand endlessly while holding landing rafts over their heads, they negotiate obstacle courses, they march and run and crawl, they are covered with wet, cold mud, and then they do it all over again.

There is a bell next to the parade ground. Ring it, and you can go home. "I always look for one quitter on the first day," barks Master Chief Urgayle (Viggo Mortensen), "and that day doesn't stop until I get it." He gets it, but not from O'Neil.

Urgayle is an intriguing character, played by Mortensen to suggest depths and complications. In an early scene he is discovered reading a novel by J. M. Coetzee, the dissident South African who is not on the navy's recommended reading list, and in an early scene he quotes a famous poem by D. H. Lawrence, both for its imagery (of a bird's unattended death) and in order to freak out the trainees by suggesting a streak of subtle madness.

The training sequences are as they have to be: incredible rigors, survived by O'Neil. They are good cinema because Ridley Scott, the director, brings a documentary attention to them, and because Demi Moore, having bitten off a great deal here, proves she can chew it. The wrong casting in her role could have tilted the movie toward *Private Benjamin,* but Moore is serious, focused, and effective.

Several of the supporting roles are well acted and carefully written (by Danielle Alexandra and David Twohy). Anne Bancroft is brisk, smart, and effective as the powerful U.S. senator. And consider Salem, the commanding officer, played by Scott Wilson. In an older movie he would have been presented as an unreconstructed sexist. This movie is smart enough to know that modern officers have been briefed on the proper treatment of female officers, and that whatever their private views they know enough about military regulations and the possibility of disciplinary hearings that they try to go by the book.

Salem makes some seemingly helpful remarks about menstruation that are not quite called for (by the time a navy woman gets to SEAL training, she has undoubtedly mastered the management of her period). But neither he nor Master Chief Urgayle are the enemy: They are meant to represent the likely realities a woman might face, not artificial movie villains.

There is a villain in the film. I will not reveal the details, although after the film is over you may find yourself asking, as I did, whether the villainous acts were inspired more by politics and corruption, or by the demands of the plot.

The plot also rears its head rather noticeably in the closing scenes, when the SEAL group finds itself in a situation much more likely to occur in a movie than in life. There is a battle sequence that is choreographed somewhat uncertainly by Scott, so that we cannot quite understand where everyone is or what is possible, and as a result the SEALS come across as not particularly competent. But by now we're into movie payoff time, where the documentary conviction of the earlier scenes must give way to audience satisfaction.

Demi Moore remains one of the most venturesome of current stars, and although her films do not always succeed, she shows imagination in her choice of projects. It is also intriguing to watch her work with the image of her body. The famous pregnant photos on the cover of *Vanity Fair* can be placed beside her stripper in *Striptease,* her executive in *Disclosure,* and the woman in *Indecent Proposal,* who has to decide what a million dollars might purchase; all of these women, and now O'Neil, test the tension between a woman's body and a woman's ambition and will. *G.I. Jane* does it most obviously, and effectively.

## The Gingerbread Man ★ ★ ★

R, 115 m., 1998

Kenneth Branagh (Rick Magruder), Embeth Davidtz (Mallory Doss), Robert Downey Jr. (Clyde Pell), Daryl Hannah (Lois Harlan), Tom Berenger (Pete Randle), Famke Janssen (Leeanne), Mae Whitman (Libby), Jesse James (Jeff), Robert Duvall (Dixon Doss). Directed by Robert Altman and produced by Jeremy

Tannenbaum. Screenplay by Al Hayes, based on an original story by John Grisham.

The ominous approach of Hurricane Geraldo drenches the opening scenes of Robert Altman's *The Gingerbread Man* in sheets of rain and darkness at noon. John Grisham, who wrote the story, named the hurricane well, for like a week's episodes of the television program, the movie features divorce, adultery, kooky fringe groups, kidnapped children, hotshot lawyers, drug addiction, and family tragedy. That it seems a step up from sensationalism is because Grisham has a sure sense of time and place, and Altman and his actors invest the material with a kind of lurid sincerity.

As the film opens, a lawyer named Magruder (Kenneth Branagh, Georgia accent well in hand) has won a big case and driven back to his Savannah law offices for a celebration. Awaiting him in Georgia are his faithful assistant Lois (Daryl Hannah), his faithless estranged wife, Leeanne (Famke Janssen), and his office staff, not excepting the muddled private investigator Clyde (Robert Downey Jr.). After a catered office party at which he drinks too much, Magruder leaves for his car, only to find a woman outside in the rain, screaming after her own departing car. This is Mallory Doss (Embeth Davidtz), who was a waitress at the party, and now believes her car to be stolen.

Magruder offers her his cell phone and then a ride home, where, to their amazement, they find her stolen car. Her door is unlocked, the lights are on, a TV is playing, and she hints darkly that this sort of thing has happened before. It may be the work of her father, who belongs to a "group." Weeping and lashing out at her absent parent, Mallory absentmindedly undresses in front of Magruder, and as thunder and lightning tear through the sky they engage in what is categorically and unequivocally a sexual relationship.

Neat touch in the morning: Magruder prods Mallory's prone body and, getting no response, dresses and leaves, while we wonder if she's dead and he will be framed with the crime. Not at all. A much more complex plot is afoot, and only after the movie is over do we think back through the plot, trying to figure out what the characters planned in advance, and what was improvised on the spot.

Grisham's story line resembles one of those Ross Macdonald novels from thirty years ago, in which old sins beget new ones, and the sins of the fathers are visited on the children. Altman's contribution is to tell the story in a fresh and spontaneous way, to use Branagh's quickness as an actor to make scenes seem fresh. Consider the scene where Magruder, tired and hung over, returns to his office the next morning, marches grimly past his staff toward his office, and asks for "Some of that . . . you know." As his door closes, one secretary turns to another: "Coffee." It's just right: Hangovers cause sufferers to lose track of common words, and office workers complete the boss's thoughts. Lois, the Hannah character, is especially effective in the way she cares for a boss who should, if he had an ounce of sense, accept her safe harbor instead of seeking out danger.

Grisham's works are filled with neo-Nazis, but when we meet Mallory's dad he's hard to classify. Dixon Doss (Robert Duvall) is a stringy, unlovely coot, and his "group" seems to be made up of unwashed and unbarbered old codgers, who hang around ominously in a clubhouse that looks like it needs the Orkin man. In a cartoon they'd have flies buzzing about their heads. In a perhaps unintentional touch of humor, the codgers can be mobilized instantly to speed out on sinister missions for old Doss; they're like the Legion of Justice crossed with Klan pensioners.

Magruder has lots on his hands. He feels protective toward Mallory and assigns Clyde (Downey) to her case; Clyde's method of stumbling over evidence is to stumble all the time and hope some evidence turns up. Magruder's almost ex-wife, who is dating his divorce lawyer, is in a struggle with him over custody, and Magruder finds it necessary to snatch his kids from their school, after which the kids are snatched again, from a hideaway motel, by persons unknown, while the winds pick up and walls of rain lash Savannah.

It's all atmospheric, quirky, and entertaining: the kind of neo-*noir* in which old-fashioned characters have updated problems. There is something about the South that seems to breed eccentric characters in the minds of writers and directors; the women there are more lush and conniving, the men heroic and yet temptable, and the villains Shakespearean in their depravity. Duvall, who can be a subtle and controlled actor (see *The Apostle*), can also sink his fangs into a role like this one and shake it by its neck until dead. And then there's Tom Berenger as Mallory's former husband, who seems to have nothing to do with the case, although students of the Law of Economy of Characters will know that no unnecessary characters are ever inserted into a movie—certainly not name players like Berenger.

From Robert Altman we expect a certain improvisational freedom, a plot that finds its way down unexpected channels and depends on coincidence and serendipity. Here he seems content to follow the tightly plotted maze mapped out by Grisham; the Altman touches are more in dialogue and personal style than in construction. He gives the actors freedom to move around in their roles. Instead of the tunnel vision of most Grisham movies, in which every line of dialogue relentlessly hammers down the next plot development, *The Gingerbread Man* has space for quirky behavior, kidding around, and murky atmosphere. The hurricane is not just window dressing, but an effective touch: It adds a subtle pressure beneath the surface, lending tension to ordinary scenes with its promise of violence to come.

## Girl 6 ★ ★

R, 110m., 1996

Theresa Randle (Girl 6), Isaiah Washington (Shoplifter), Spike Lee (Jimmy), Debi Mazar (Girl 39), Jenifer Lewis (Boss No. 1 [Lil]), John Turturro (The Agent), Madonna (Boss No. 3), Quentin Tarantino (Director No. 1), Naomi Campbell (Girl 75). Directed and produced by Spike Lee. Screenplay by Suzan-Lori Parks.

I am prepared to suspend a great deal of disbelief while I am watching a movie, but during *Girl 6* I found it difficult to believe that a phone sex girl would get addicted to her job. To the money, sure. To the power over the men who call her, perhaps. But to the sex?

Even though Spike Lee's *Girl 6* was written by a woman, it seems conceived from the point of view of a male caller who would like to believe that the woman he's hiring by the minute is enjoying their conversation just as much as he is. Jennifer Jason Leigh's phone sex girl in Robert Altman's *Short Cuts* was much more realistic as she chatted on the phone in the midst of a family uproar.

Spike Lee is a great director, but his strong point is not leading expeditions into the secret corners of the female psyche. *Girl 6* opens with its star, a would-be actress played by Theresa Randle, reading dialogue used by the character Nola Darling in Lee's first film, *She's Gotta Have It*. That was a film about a woman who satisfied her own sexual needs while remaining bemused by her male suitors. So, in a sense, is *Girl 6*. In a way, both films are about emotional transvestites: The women in them relate to sex in ways more commonly associated with men.

As the movie opens, the future Girl 6 is a struggling actress. Lee shows her struggles in a series of recycled clichés. She auditions for a lustful director (Quentin Tarantino, continuing his world tour of other directors' movies). She gets a job passing out brochures on the street. She works as a bored coat-check girl. She's fired by her acting coach because she can't afford the payments. Okay, we get the idea: She's broke and desperate, and needs to make some money.

But before we continue with her odyssey, let's take another look at that auditioning scene with Tarantino. He eventually asks her to unbutton her blouse because he wants to see her breasts. She does not want to. It would diminish and humiliate her. She is angry and tearful. But he claims he's making a big movie with major stars ("Denzel . . . Wesley . . .") and so she does finally unbutton and expose her breasts. Now if Lee is saying Tarantino is a cretin for making her do this, then logically he shouldn't let us see her breasts even if Tarantino can. But he does. What we have here is a scene about a woman being shamed by exposing herself, and the scene is handled so that she exposes herself. That puts Lee in the same boat with the lecher.

That scene is emblematic of the basic problem of the film: It's about a woman exposing herself for male entertainment, even though it pretends to be about men exposing themselves for female employment. Spike Lee makes a big deal in his press notes about how all of the male callers to Girl 6 are photographed in high-def video, which is then transferred to film, while Girl 6 is photographed in 35mm film: "The overall effect is one of diminishing each man's power, while the 35mm look and texture of the women heightens their strength."

Uh, huh, but it's the guys who are paying, and Girl 6 who is delivering. And consider the scene early in the film where she gets so turned on while talking to a man that her heavy breathing attracts a crowd around her phone cubicle. Call me a cynic, but I believe most phone sex girls do it for the money, and while they may take pride in their technical proficiency, their emotional lives take place when the phone is on the hook.

In the film, Girl 6 is first auditioned for phone sex by a dirty-talking woman bar owner (Madonna), but eventually finds a berth in a cozy, well-organized operation run by a good businesswoman (Jenifer Lewis). There's a subplot about how Girl 6's former husband (Isaiah Washington), a shoplifter, still wants to be with her. But Girl 6 prefers her callers. Some of them are weird, like the guy who masturbates while talking about the money he's making, or the guy who says he's pulling out his pubic hairs with a monkey wrench.

But then there's Bob. Girl 6 gets to like Bob. He becomes a regular caller. And then—this is hard to believe—she agrees to meet him in person. Is this wise? Is it plausible? Of course—but only in the fantasies of a phone sex client. And then Bob stands her up, which is, I suspect, the opposite of what would really happen.

Meanwhile, Lee introduces other half-realized ideas into the film. Girl 6 is seen in the dress and hairstyles of many African-American screen icons (Dorothy Dandridge, Pam Grier, the daughter on *The Jeffersons*). Her dress-up scenes are intercut with old clips. To what purpose? I'm not sure. I hope it's nothing so mundane as to show that she can be many things to many people. There is also a subplot with her friendly neighbor (Spike Lee), who cautions her and likes her but serves no particular purpose in the plot.

*Girl 6* is Spike Lee's least successful film, and the problem is twofold: He doesn't really know and understand Girl 6, and he has no clear idea of the film's structure and purpose. If he'd been able to fix the second problem, he might have been able to paper over the first one. Strongly told stories have a way of carrying their characters along with them. But here we have an undefined character in an aimless story. Too bad.

## Girls Town ★ ★ ★

R, 90 m., 1996

Lili Taylor (Patti), Bruklin Harris (Angela), Anna Grace (Emma), Aunjanue Ellis (Nikki), Ramya Pratt (Tomy), Asia Minor (Marlys), Guillermo Diaz (Dylan), Shondalon (Teacher). Directed by Jim McKay and produced by Lauren Zalaznick. Screenplay by McKay, Denise Casano, Anna Grace, Bruklin Harris, and Lili Taylor.

Near the beginning of *Girls Town* there is a scene where two high school girls have a heart-to-heart talk while sprawled on a bed, reading a journal. It's one of those moments when the whole future seems filled with promise, even if the destinies are different: Emma (Anna Grace) and Nikki (Aunjanue Ellis) talk about their school plans, and Emma is quietly surprised that Nikki, who is going to Princeton, still hasn't signed up for housing.

The next day Nikki's delay is easier to understand. She has committed suicide. Her closest friends cannot comprehend, and during a visit to Nikki's home they steal her journal and read it for themselves, discovering that Nikki has been raped while working as an intern at a local magazine.

This information simmers beneath the surface of *Girls Town* as we learn more about Nikki's three friends, who are Patti (Lili Taylor), Angela (Bruklin Harris), and Emma. They are tough but not hardened, self-defined outsiders with a strong feminist code they don't talk much about. Their racial balance (two whites, two African-Americans) shows their willingness to stand outside the cliques of high school and choose their friends instead of letting teenage society dictate to them. Angela and Emma are headed for college; Patti, a single mother, "has been let back so many times that what is she now? Forty?"

During the course of the film the young women will talk a lot, in conversations that sound natural and unforced; I understand the screenplay was developed partly through improvisations by the actors. They realize they never really knew Nikki, even though they thought she was their best friend, and they reveal their own secrets. Emma reveals that she has also been raped. Patti, who has a shaky relationship with Eddie, the loser father of her child, observes,

"They wanna have sex with you, you don't want to have sex with them, they gonna get it. You call that rape, I been raped by about every guy I been out with."

The girls paint a mural in Nikki's memory, and while it provides some consolation it is finally not enough. Gradually, fueled by the logic of their conversations, many of them held on the roof of the dugout on the school's baseball field, the three decide on more direct measures. They vandalize the car of the classmate who raped Emma, and then they decide to go after the smug and uncaring older man who raped Nikki.

The bare bones of the plot of *Girls Town* are not much more subtle than the events in a 1970s exploitation picture like the recently (and unnecessarily) revived *Switchblade Sisters.* But nuance is everything, and the movie's qualities are in the performances and dialogue. We hear the convincing sound of smart teenage girls uncomfortably trying to discover and share the truth about themselves, and we sense the social structure of the school in scenes (usually in the women's washroom) where the three confront their "popular" classmates.

In every high school there are always "popular" students and various groups of outsiders. It is always thought better to be "popular." One of the lessons of *Girls Town* is that popularity is based on the opinion of others, while an outsider chooses that status based on her opinion of herself. We see Patti, Emma, and Angela behaving unwisely and recklessly in *Girls Town,* but we also see them growing, and trying themselves, and discovering who they are. It is a painful process—so painful, many people never do it. I would like to see another movie in three or four years, about what has happened to these angry, gifted friends.

## The Godfather ★ ★ ★ ★

R, 175 m., 1972 (rereleased 1997)

Marlon Brando (Vito Corleone), Al Pacino (Michael Corleone), James Caan (Sonny Corleone), Richard S. Castellano (Clemenza), Robert Duvall (Tom Hagen), Sterling Hayden (McCluskey), John Marley (Jack Woltz), Richard Conte (Barzini), Al Lettieri (Sollozzo), Diane Keaton (Kay Adams), Abe Vigoda (Tessio), Talia Shire (Connie), Gianni Russo (Carlo Rizzi), John Cazale (Fredo Corleone), Rudy Bond (Cuneo), Al Martino (Johnny Fontane), Morgana King (Mamma Corleone), Lenny Montana (Luca Brasi), John Martino (Paulie Gatto), Alex Rocco (Moe Greene), Tony Giorgio (Bruno Tattaglia). Directed by Francis Ford Coppola and produced by Albert S. Ruddy. Screenplay by Coppola and Mario Puzo, based on Puzo's novel.

*The Godfather* is told entirely within a closed world. That's why we sympathize with characters who are essentially evil. The story by Mario Puzo and Francis Ford Coppola is a brilliant conjuring act, inviting us to consider the Mafia entirely on its own terms. Don Vito Corleone (Marlon Brando) emerges as a sympathetic and even admirable character; during the entire film, this lifelong professional criminal does nothing that we can really disapprove of.

During the movie we see not a single actual civilian victim of organized crime. No women trapped into prostitution. No lives wrecked by gambling. No victims of theft, fraud, or protection rackets. The only police officer with a significant speaking role is corrupt.

The story views the Mafia from the inside. That is its secret, its charm, its spell; in a way it has shared the public perception of the Mafia ever since. The real world is replaced by an authoritarian patriarchy where power and justice flow from the godfather, and the only villains are traitors. There is one commandment, spoken by Michael (Al Pacino): "Don't ever take sides against the family."

It is significant that the first shot is inside a dark, shuttered room. It is the wedding day of Vito Corleone's daughter, and on such a day a Sicilian must grant any reasonable request. A man has come to ask for punishment for his daughter's rapist. Don Vito asks why he did not come to him immediately.

"I went to the police, like a good American," the man says. The godfather's reply will underpin the entire movie: "Why did you go to the police? Why didn't you come to me first? What have I ever done to make you treat me so disrespectfully? If you'd come to me in friendship, then this scum that ruined your daughter would be suffering this very day. And, if by chance, an honest man like yourself should make enemies . . . then they would become my enemies. And then they would fear you."

As the day continues, there are two more

séances in the godfather's darkened study, intercut with scenes from the wedding outside. By the end of the wedding sequence, most of the main characters will have been introduced, and we will know essential things about their personalities. It is a virtuoso stretch of filmmaking: Coppola brings his large cast onstage so artfully that we are drawn at once into the godfather's world.

The screenplay of *The Godfather* follows no formulas except for the classic structure in which power passes between the generations. The writing is subtly constructed to set up events later in the film. Notice how the request by Johnny Fontane, the failing singer, pays off in the Hollywood scenes; how his tears set up the shocking moment when a mogul wakes up in bed with what is left of his racehorse. Notice how the undertaker is told, "some day, and that day may never come, I will ask a favor of you . . ." and how when the day comes the favor is not violence (as in a conventional movie), but Don Vito's desire to spare his wife the sight of his son's maimed body. And notice how a woman's "mistaken" phone call sets up the trap in which Sonny (James Caan) is murdered: It's done so neatly that you have to think back through the events to figure it out.

Now here is a trivia question: What is the name of Vito's wife? She exists in the movie as an insignificant shadow, a plump Sicilian grandmother who poses with her husband in wedding pictures, but plays no role in the events that take place in his study. There is little room for women in *The Godfather.* Sonny uses and discards them, and ignores his wife. Connie (Talia Shire), the don's daughter, is so disregarded her husband is not allowed into the family business. He is thrown a bone—"a living"—and later, when he is killed, Michael coldly lies to his sister about what happened.

The irony of the title is that it eventually comes to refer to the son, not the father. As the film opens, Michael is not part of the family business, and plans to marry a WASP, Kay Adams (Diane Keaton). His turning point comes when he saves his father's life by moving his hospital bed, and whispers to the unconscious man: "I'm with you now."

After he shoots the corrupt cop, Michael hides in Sicily, where he falls in love with and marries Appolonia (Simonetta Stefanelli). They do not speak the same language; small handicap for a Mafia wife. He undoubtedly loves Appolonia, as he loved Kay, but what is he thinking here? That he can no longer marry Kay because he has chosen a Mafia life? After Appolonia's death and his return to America, he seeks out Kay and eventually they marry. Did he tell her about Appolonia? Such details are unimportant to the story.

What is important is loyalty to the family. Much is said in the movie about trusting a man's word, but honesty is nothing compared to loyalty. Michael doesn't even trust Tom Hagen (Robert Duvall) with the secret that he plans to murder the heads of the other families. The famous "baptism massacre" is tough, virtuoso filmmaking: The baptism provides him with an airtight alibi, and he becomes a godfather in both senses at the same time.

Vito Corleone is the moral center of the film. He is old, wise, and opposed to dealing in drugs. He understands that society is not alarmed by "liquor, gambling . . . even women." But drugs are a dirty business to Don Vito, and one of the movie's best scenes is the Mafia summit in which he argues his point. The implication is that in the godfather's world there would be no drugs, only "victimless crimes," and justice would be dispatched evenly and swiftly.

My argument is taking this form because I want to point out how cleverly Coppola structures his film to create sympathy for his heroes. The Mafia is not a benevolent and protective organization, and the Corleone family is only marginally better than the others. Yet when the old man falls dead among his tomato plants, we feel that a giant has passed.

Gordon Willis's cinematography is celebrated for its darkness; it is rich, atmospheric, expressive. You cannot appreciate this on television because the picture is artificially brightened. Coppola populates his dark interior spaces with remarkable faces. The front line—Brando, Pacino, Caan, Duvall—are attractive in one way or another, but the actors who play their associates are chosen for their fleshy, thickly lined faces—for huge jaws and deeply set eyes. Look at Abe Vigoda as Tessio, the fearsome enforcer. The first time we see him, he's dancing with a child at the wedding, her satin pumps balanced on his shoes. The sun shines that day, but never again: He is developed as a hulking presence who implies the possibility of violent revenge.

Only at the end is he brightly lit again, to make him look vulnerable as he begs for his life.

The Brando performance is justly famous and often imitated. We know all about his puffy cheeks, and his use of props like the kitten in the opening scene. Those are actor's devices. Brando uses them but does not depend on them: He embodies the character so convincingly that at the end, when he warns his son two or three times that "the man who comes to you to set up a meeting—that's the traitor," we are not thinking of acting at all. We are thinking that the don is growing old and repeating himself, but we are also thinking that he is probably absolutely right.

Pacino plays Michael close to his vest; he has learned from his father never to talk in front of outsiders, never to trust anyone unnecessarily, to take advice but keep his own counsel. All of the other roles are so successfully filled that a strange thing happened as I watched this restored 1997 version: Familiar as I am with Robert Duvall, when he first appeared on the screen I found myself thinking, "There's Tom Hagen."

Coppola went to Italy to find Nino Rota, composer of many Fellini films, to score the picture. Hearing the sadness and nostalgia of the movie's main theme, I realized what the music was telling us: Things would have turned out better if we had only listened to the godfather.

## Godzilla ★ ½

PG-13, 138 m., 1998

Matthew Broderick (Dr. Niko Tatopoulos), Jean Reno (Philippe Roche), Maria Pitillo (Audrey Timmonds), Hank Azaria (Victor [Animal] Palotti), Kevin Dunn (Colonel Hicks), Michael Lerner (Mayor Ebert), Harry Shearer (Charles Caiman), Arabella Field (Lucy Palotti), Vicki Lewis (Dr. Elsie Chapman), Doug Savant (Sergeant O'Neal), Malcolm Danare (Dr. Mendel Craven). Directed by Roland Emmerich and produced by Dean Devlin. Screenplay by Devlin and Emmerich, based on the character Godzilla in films by Toho Co. Ltd.

CANNES, France—Going to see *Godzilla* at the Palais of the Cannes Film Festival is like attending a satanic ritual in St. Peter's Basilica. It's a rebuke to the faith that the building represents. Cannes touchingly adheres to a belief that film can be intelligent, moving, and grand. *Godzilla* is a big, ugly, ungainly device designed to give teenagers the impression they are seeing a movie. It was the festival's closing film, coming at the end like the horses in a parade, perhaps for the same reason.

It rains all through *Godzilla,* and it's usually night. Well, of course it is: That makes the special effects easier to obscure. If you never get a clear look at the monster, you can't see how shoddy it is. Steven Spielberg opened *Jurassic Park* by giving us a good, long look at the dinosaurs in full sunlight, and our imaginations leapt up. *Godzilla* hops out of sight like a camera-shy kangaroo.

The makers of the film, director Roland Emmerich and writer Dean Devlin, follow the timeless outlines of many other movies about Godzilla, Rodan, Mothra, Gamera, and their radioactive kin. There are ominous attacks on ships at sea, alarming blips on radar screens, and a scientist who speculates that nuclear tests may have spawned a mutant creature. A cast of stereotyped stock characters is introduced and made to say lines like, "I don't understand—how could something so big just disappear?" Or, "Many people have had their lives changed forever!" And then there are the big special effects sequences, as Godzilla terrorizes New York.

One must carefully repress intelligent thought while watching such a film. The movie makes no sense at all except as a careless pastiche of its betters (and, yes, the Japanese *Godzilla* movies are, in their way, better—if only because they embrace dreck instead of condescending to it). You have to absorb such a film, not consider it. But my brain rebelled and insisted on applying logic where it was not welcome.

How, for example, does a 300-foot-tall creature fit inside a subway tunnel? How come it's sometimes only as tall as the tunnel, and at other times taller than high-rise office buildings? How big is it, anyway? Why can it breathe fire but hardly ever makes use of this ability? Why, when the heroes hide inside the Park Avenue tunnel, is this tunnel too small for Godzilla to enter, even though it is larger than a subway tunnel? And why doesn't Godzilla just snort some flames down there and broil them?

Most monster movies have at least one

bleeding-heart environmentalist to argue the case of the monstrous beast, but here we get only Niko Tatopoulos (Matthew Broderick), an expert on the mutant earthworms of Chernobyl, who seems less like a scientist than like a placeholder waiting for a rewrite ("insert more interesting character here"). It is he who intuits that Godzilla is a female. (You would think that if a 300-foot monster were male, that would be hard to miss, but never mind.) The military in all movies about monsters and aliens from outer space always automatically attempts to kill them, and here they fire lots of wimpy missiles and torpedoes at Godzilla, which have so little effect we wonder how our tax dollars are being spent. (Just once, I'd like a movie where they train Godzilla to do useful tasks, like pulling a coaxial cable across the ocean floor, or pushing stuck trains out of tunnels.)

In addition to the trigger-happy Americans, there is a French force, too, led by Jean Reno, a good actor who plays this role as if he got on the plane shouting, "I'm going to Disneyland!" All humans in monster movies have simpleminded little character traits, and Reno's obsession is with getting a decent cup of coffee. Other characters include a TV newswoman (Maria Pitillo) who used to be the worm man's girlfriend, a determined cameraman (Hank Azaria), a grim-jawed military leader (Kevin Dunn), and a simpering anchorman (Harry Shearer). None of these characters emerges as anything more than a source of obligatory dialogue.

Oh, and then there are New York's Mayor Ebert (gamely played by Michael Lerner) and his adviser, Gene (Lorry Goldman). The mayor, of course, makes every possible wrong decision (he is against evacuating Manhattan, etc.), and the adviser eventually gives thumbs-down to his reelection campaign. These characters are a reaction by Emmerich and Devlin to negative Siskel and Ebert reviews of their earlier movies *(Stargate, Independence Day)*, but they let us off lightly; I fully expected to be squished like a bug by Godzilla. Now that I've inspired a character in a Godzilla movie, all I really still desire is for several Ingmar Bergman characters to sit in a circle and read my reviews to one another in hushed tones.

There is a way to make material like *Godzilla* work. It can be campy fun, like the recent *Gamera, Guardian of the Universe*. Or hallucinatory, like *Infra-Man*. Or awesome, like *Jurassic Park*. Or it can tap a certain elemental dread, like the original *King Kong*. But all of those approaches demand a certain sympathy with the material, a zest that rises to the occasion.

In Howard Hawks's *The Thing*, there is a great scene where scientists in the Arctic spread out to trace the outlines of something mysterious that is buried in the ice, and the camera slowly pulls back to reveal that it is circular—a saucer. In *Godzilla*, the worm expert is standing in a deep depression, and the camera pulls back to reveal that he is standing in a footprint—which he would obviously already have known. There might be a way to reveal the astonishing footprint to the character and the audience at the same time, but that would involve a sense of style and timing, and some thought about the function of the scene.

There is nothing wrong with making a *Godzilla* movie and nothing wrong with special effects. But don't the filmmakers have some obligation to provide pop entertainment that at least lifts the spirits? There is real feeling in King Kong fighting off the planes that attack him, or the pathos of the monster in *Bride of Frankenstein*, who was so misunderstood. There is a true sense of wonder in *Jurassic Park*.

*Godzilla*, by contrast, offers nothing but soulless technique: A big lizard is created by special effects, wreaks havoc, and is destroyed. What a cold-hearted, mechanistic vision, so starved for emotion or wit. The primary audience for *Godzilla* is children and teenagers, and the filmmakers have given them a sterile exercise when they hunger for dreams. ☞

## Going All the Way ★ ★ ★

R, 110 m., 1997

Jeremy Davies (Sonny Burns), Ben Affleck (Gunner Casselman), Amy Locane (Buddy Porter), Rose McGowan (Gale Ann Thayer), Rachel Weisz (Marty Pilcher), John Lordan (Elwood Burns), Jill Clayburgh (Alma Burns), Lesley Ann Warren (Nina Casselman). Directed by Mark Pellington and produced by Tom Gorai and Sigurjon Sighvatsson. Screenplay by Dan Wakefield, based upon his novel.

One problem with a lot of coming-of-age movies is that the characters seem too old and confident for their problems. Even the Dustin Hoffman character in *The Graduate* seems a little too ironically plugged in, as if he's aware of the movie's subtext. But the characters in *Going All the Way* ring true: They're callow and limited, their motivation is centered on their genitals, and yet they burn with idealism, with fevered fantasies of their own eventual triumph.

The movie, based on Dan Wakefield's novel, is set in Indianapolis soon after the Korean War. Two recently discharged veterans meet on the train home: Sonny Burns (Jeremy Davies), a shy, secretive bundle of insecurity, and Gunner Casselman (Ben Affleck), the golden-boy type. Gunner was a high school sports hero and Sonny was an overlooked nerd; Sonny fully expects Gunner to ignore him, but Gunner amazingly seeks him out, and they become friends.

What happened? Gunner obviously went through a spiritual awakening while stationed overseas ("I never really thought about anything until I got to Japan," he confides, and "Those Zen riddles really made me think"). He seeks out Sonny, no doubt, because he assumes the class nerd was thinking deep thoughts while Gunner was scoring touchdowns. Sonny was actually spending much of his time masturbating, but no matter; soon the two friends are discussing *The Catcher in the Rye*, and Gunner, reading *The Lonely Crowd*, decides he's "inner-directed."

Sonny thinks of little but women. He has a loyal high school girlfriend named, ominously, Buddy (Amy Locane). She's reliable, cheerful, friendly, and sexually available (too available for the 1950s period, I think). Sonny's mother (Jill Clayburgh) enthusiastically promotes marriage, while his father (John Lordan) speaks approvingly of the excellent pension plan at Eli Lilly.

But Sonny doesn't want to get married or go to work for the local pharmaceutical corporation. He wants to wrap his arms around a woman who can fuel his skin magazine–inspired fantasies—like Gunner's sexpot mom (Lesley Ann Warren), for example, or Gayle Ann Thayer (Rose McGowan), the best friend of Gunner's sexy new Jewish girlfriend Marty Pilcher (Rachel Weisz). Gunner's mother, who obviously has incestuous feelings for her son, is jealous of Marty and feeds her son vile anti-Semitic fantasies, but Gunner is his own man and chooses his own course in life.

Not so with Sonny, who is impotent with the women he desires and finds Buddy boring even though, therefore, he can perform with her. During the course of a long summer, it becomes clear to Gunner and Sonny that their future lies outside Indianapolis—lies, instead, amid the gleaming towers of Manhattan, where they will find glory, fame, and lotsa women.

*Going All the Way* is a deeper, more clever film than it first seems. Much of its strength depends on the imploding performance of Jeremy Davies, who swallows his words, ducks his head, squirms away from parental domination, and vaguely knows he must escape home for his own survival. (It says everything that he still has baseball trading cards tacked to the headboard of his bed, and hides his skin magazines in the boxes of his childhood board games.) I'm a decade younger than the characters in this movie, but I grew up in a time and place not far from the film's psychic setting. I recognized much. And here I am, amid the gleaming towers of Chicago.

## Good Burger ★ ★

PG, 94 m., 1997

Kel Mitchell (Ed), Kenan Thompson (Dexter Reed), Sinbad (Mr. Wheat), Abe Vigoda (Otis), Shar Jackson (Monique), Dan Schneider (Mr. Bailey), Jan Schwieterman (Kurt Bozwell), Ron Lester (Spatch). Directed by Brian Robbins and produced by Mike Tollin, Robbins, Heath Seifert, and Kevin Kopelow. Screenplay by Dan Schneider and Kopelow.

*Good Burger* was not made for me, and if I say I didn't much enjoy it, that wouldn't be useful information. The movie was made for daytime viewers of Nickelodeon, and it's a spin-off from a character first seen in the cable channel's *All That* comedy series—Ed, a fast-food worker whose life and dreams are dominated by his love for his work, and whose catchphrase, "Welcome to Good Burger," is as well known to kids as "Where's the beef?" is at the other end of the age spectrum. The movie's stars, Kel Mitchell and Kenan Thompson, also appear on another Nickelodeon series, *Kenan and Kel*.

Good Burger is a small, independent burger stand in the middle of a vague urban landscape (I'm not even sure what state it's supposed to be in—California, probably). Ed (Mitchell) is the counter guy, and he's made the position behind the cash register into his personal sacred ground; when he's late to work the whole operation is paralyzed. As the movie opens, he gets a new coworker named Dexter (Thompson), who desperately needs to earn money because he was driving without a license and crashed into a car much beloved by his teacher, Mr. Wheat (Sinbad).

Dexter was not born to work at the fast-food trade, but he and Ed become good friends, and some of Ed's spirit rubs off. Then a crisis strikes: A gargantuan Mondo Burger stand is opened right across the street. With its towers and searchlights, it looks vaguely like the 20th Century-Fox logo, and it's managed by a neo-Nazi named Kurt (Jan Schwieterman), who predicts Good Burger will soon be history.

The plot involves Ed saving the Good Burger stand by inventing a secret sauce, and Kurt scheming to get his hands on it; meanwhile Ed and Dexter become pals with Otis (Abe Vigoda), arguably the world's oldest fast-food employee, who through a series of mishaps must be rescued from the Demented Hills Asylum. There's also a sweet little romantic subplot involving Monique (Shar Jackson), who has a crush on Ed—to no avail, since burgers are his life. Among the supporting characters is Spatch (Ron Lester), who likes to squash flies on his forehead.

Kel Mitchell, as Ed, provides the heart of the movie, creating an asexual otherworldly character who is protected by his strangeness. Asked "How does ten bucks sound to you?" he crumples the bill next to his ear to find out. Asked "You know what would look great on these corn dogs?" he replies, "A turtleneck?" He wears his Good Burger hat at all times, even in the shower, and at one point thinks it makes him look like a nurse. It's impossible not to like him.

But to understand this movie on its intended level, it's necessary, I think, to be between four and eleven years old and know about the characters from TV. The movie is innocent, good-hearted, colorful, and energetic, but it doesn't have the kind of sophistication that allowed the Pee-wee Herman movies to break out of their primary kiddie audiences and appeal to adult viewers. It's a kid movie, plain and simple. It didn't do much for me, but I am prepared to predict that its target audience will have a good time. I'm giving it two stars. If I were eight, I might give it more.

## Good Will Hunting ★ ★ ★

R, 125 m., 1997

Matt Damon (Will), Robin Williams (Sean McGuire), Ben Affleck (Chuckie), Minnie Driver (Skylar), Stellan Skarsgard (Lambeau), John Mighton (Tom), Rachel Majowski (Krystyn), Colleen McCauley (Cathy), Casey Affleck (Morgan), Cole Hauser (Billy). Directed by Gus Van Sant Jr. and produced by Lawrence Bender. Screenplay by Matt Damon and Ben Affleck.

It must be heartbreaking to be able to appreciate true genius, and yet fall just short of it yourself. A man can spend his entire life studying to be a mathematician—and yet watch helplessly while a high school dropout, a janitor, scribbles down the answers to questions the professor is baffled by. It's also heartbreaking when genius won't recognize itself, and that's the most baffling problem of all in *Good Will Hunting*, the smart, involving story of a working-class kid from Boston.

The film stars Matt Damon as a janitor at MIT, who likes to party and hang around the old neighborhood, and whose reading consists of downloading the contents of whole libraries into his photographic memory. Stellan Skarsgard (the husband in *Breaking the Waves*) plays Lambeau, the professor, who offers a prize to any student who can solve a difficult problem. The next morning, the answer is written on a blackboard standing in the hall.

Who claims credit? None of the students do. A few days later, Lambeau catches Will Hunting (Damon) at the board, and realizes he's the author—a natural mathematical genius who can intuitively see through the thorniest problems. Lambeau wants to help Will, to get him into school, maybe, or collaborate with him—but before that can take place, Will and some buddies are cruising the old neighborhood and beat up a guy. Will also hammers on the cops a little and is jailed.

He's a tough nut. He sees nothing wrong with spending his whole life hanging out with his friends, quaffing a few beers, holding down a blue-collar job. He sees romance in being an honest bricklayer, but none in being a professor of mathematics—maybe because bricklaying is work, and, for him, math isn't.

*Good Will Hunting* is the story of how this kid's life edges toward self-destruction, and how four people try to haul him back. One is Lambeau, who gets probation for Will with a promise that he'll find him help and counseling. One is Sean McGuire (Robin Williams), Lambeau's college roommate, now a junior college professor who has messed up his own life, but is a gifted counselor. One is Skylar (Minnie Driver), a British student at Harvard who falls in love with Will and tries to help him. And one is Chuckie (Ben Affleck), Will's friend since childhood, who tells him: "You're sitting on a winning lottery ticket. It would be an insult to us if you're still around here in twenty years."

True, but Will doesn't see it that way. His reluctance to embrace the opportunity at MIT is based partly on class pride (it would be betraying his buddies and the old neighborhood) and partly on old psychic wounds. And it is only through breaking through to those scars and sharing some of his own that McGuire, the counselor, is able to help him. Robin Williams gives one of his best performances as McGuire, especially in a scene where he finally gets the kid to repeat, "It's not my fault."

*Good Will Hunting* perhaps found some of its inspiration in the lives of its makers. The movie was cowritten by Damon and Affleck, who did grow up in Boston, who are childhood friends, and who both took youthful natural talents and used them to find success as actors. It's tempting to find parallels between their lives and the characters—and tempting, too, to watch the scenes between Damon and Driver with the knowledge that they fell in love while making the movie.

The Will Hunting character is so much in the foreground that it's easy to miss a parallel relationship: Lambeau and McGuire are also old friends, who have fought because of old angers and insecurities. In a sense, by bringing the troubled counselor and the troublesome janitor together, the professor helps to heal both of them.

The film has a good ear for the way these characters might really talk. It was directed by Gus Van Sant *(Drugstore Cowboy, To Die For)*, who sometimes seems to have perfect pitch when it comes to dialogue; look at the scene where Matt and Skylar break up and say hurtful things, and see how clear he makes it that Matt is pushing her away because he doesn't think he deserves her.

The outcome of the movie is fairly predictable; so is the whole story, really. It's the individual moments, not the payoff, that makes it so effective. *Good Will Hunting* has been rather inexplicably compared to *Rainman*, although *Rainman* was about an autistic character who cannot and does not change, and *Good Will Hunting* is about a genius who can change, and grow, if he chooses to. True, they can both do quick math in their heads. But Will Hunting is not an idiot savant or some kind of lovable curiosity; he's a smart man who knows he's smart but pulls back from challenges because he was beaten down once too often as a child.

I'm writing this review just after hearing remarks by friends of the late comedian Chris Farley, by friends who tried to help him and failed. *Good Will Hunting* knows how that goes. Here is a character who has four friends who all love him and want to help him, and he's threatened by their help because it means abandoning all of his old, sick, dysfunctional defense mechanisms. As Louis Armstrong once said, "There's some folks, that, if they don't know, you can't tell 'em." This movie is about whether Will is one of those folks. ☞

## Grace of My Heart ★ ★ ½

R, 120 m., 1996

Illeana Douglas (Denise/Edna), John Turturro (Joel Millner), Eric Stoltz (Howard Caszatt), Matt Dillon (Jay Phillips), Patsy Kensit (Cheryl Steed), Jennifer Leigh Warren (Doris Shelley), Bruce Davison (John Murray). Directed by Allison Anders and produced by Ruth Charny and Daniel Hassid. Screenplay by Anders.

*Grace of My Heart* tells the story of a young woman who wants to be a singer, ends up as a songwriter, and traces in her career the history of pop music from the last gasp of Tin Pan Alley in the late 1950s through the psychedelic era of the early 1970s. In its general arc, although not in the details, this is a career like Carole King's, and it ends with that emblem of a personal artistic statement, a concept album.

The heroine, played winningly by Illeana Douglas, is born Edna Buxton but renamed Denise Waverly. She comes from a rich Philadelphia family, and frets under her mother's coaching: For a song contest, she's made to wear a "wedding dress" and ordered to sing "You'll Never Walk Alone." But backstage she trades dresses with another contestant and sings "Hey, There (You with the Stars in Your Eyes)," which as songs go is not a quantum leap from her original choice but is good enough to win her the contest, a trip to New York, and a "recording contract."

The contract, of course, evaporates, and Edna is near despair when she's discovered by an agent named Joel (John Turturro, wearing a hairpiece of bountiful generosity). He likes her writing better than her singing, moves her into a wedge-shaped office in the Brill Building barely large enough to hold a piano, and puts her to work. Soon she's composing for new groups and has a few hits.

She meets people. One of her early collaborators and lovers is Howard (Eric Stoltz), who introduces her to the notion that songs can be about something other than June, moon, stars, and love. He also introduces her to experiences that will someday help inspire that concept album—things like lying and cheating. She has a crush on a music critic and broadcaster (Bruce Davison) who, alas, really only wants to be friends. Joel also teams her up with a British newcomer (Patsy Kensit), and although they dislike each other at first they become friends and collaborate on a hit for a female vocalist who hides some surprising secrets behind her hair spray.

Time marches on. Tin Pan Alley goes out of business and the Brill Building era ends as singers start writing their own songs. Denise moves to Malibu and becomes the wife of Jay Phillips (Matt Dillon), a character loosely modeled on the Beach Boys' Brian Wilson. He inspires her with his arrangements and studio wizardry, but frightens her with his increasing paranoia ("What happened to my tapes?"), and one day he takes their kids to town and manages to forget them.

There's more, including a hippie funeral and an interlude at a commune in the mountains above Palm Springs, before the concept album, all filled with material written and sung by Denise herself, announces the end of her artistic journey. And always there's Joel as the old friend with good advice (Turturro's character is so sensible and perceptive, indeed, that the bad hairpiece must be his ironic statement, not an oversight).

This is the outline for an interesting movie, and indeed a lot of *Grace of My Heart* is involving and well-done backstage material. But the story goes on too long and covers too much ground. The director, Allison Anders, falls into a predictable narrative rhythm. We get a scene, and then the song it inspires, and then another scene, and then the song it inspires, and so on. And the series of relationships goes on just long enough to make us wonder if Denise is simply collecting one of each type in the musical world.

There's some good music in the film. Instead of recycling hits from the period, Anders and her collaborators create sound-alikes, which are written by such as Elvis Costello, Burt Bachrach, Carol Bayer Sager, Los Lobos, and Leslie Gore. Occupying almost every scene, Illeana Douglas makes a convincing witness to the transition from "Your Hit Parade" to Woodstock. It's a big role and she's equal to it—but is the movie? I would have preferred a more limited story that went deeper, instead of a docudrama that covers so much ground, so relentlessly, that we weary. By the end, I was beginning to think maybe young Edna should have sung "You'll Never Walk Alone" after all.

## Gravesend ★ ★

R, 85 m., 1997

Tony Tucci (Zane), Michael Parducci (Ray), Tom Malloy (Chicken), Tom Brandise (Mikey), Macky Aquilino (Jo-Jo). Directed and produced by Salvatore Stabile. Screenplay by Stabile.

"I'm proud of where I came from," the narrator of *Gravesend* tells us near the end of the film. Since he has shown us not one single thing to be proud of, I can only assume he's setting us up for the sequel. The movie's characters are stupid and brutish, and spend their nights getting into fights every fifteen minutes, possibly because they can think of nothing else to do.

Gravesend, we learn, is a Brooklyn neighborhood, little known because its residents "usually claim to be from Bensonhurst or Coney Island." I have no doubt that many of its streets and people are delightful, but such delights have been denied us by the writer-director of the film, Salvatore Stabile, who wants to share a memory of the night that four of his buddies somehow wound up with three bodies in the trunk of their car, and that was only for starters.

There are possibilities for humor here, and rich characters. I am reminded of movies like *New Jersey Drive, Straight Out of Brooklyn, Spike of Bensonhurst,* and *True Love.* But the lives of these four friends are lived at a monotonous level; they lack the words and perhaps the concepts for pastimes more challenging than drinking, smoking dope, holding aimless arguments, and getting into meaningless fights. Even *this* material could be made amusing, but not here, where the characters seem to circle in loops of their own devising.

And yet *Gravesend* has good things to be said about it, and the most astonishing is that it was made for a reported $5,000, which is $3,000 less than the previous record holder, Robert Rodriguez, spent on *El Mariachi.* Stabile made the film when he was nineteen, found backers to put up postproduction cash, and impressed so many people with his raw talent that *Gravesend* is "An Oliver Stone Presentation" and the director, now twenty-two, has two projects under contract with Steven Spielberg.

Stabile probably has good films in him. *Gravesend,* made with limited resources, shows that. It also gives hints of the ways he'll be able to find humor in tough characters. The most entertaining performance in the movie is by Macky Aquilino, as Jo-Jo the junkie, a janitor and drug dealer who the four friends ask for a favor: They need to dispose of a body. His price, after negotiation: "$500, and a thumb."

Cars with bodies in their trunks tend to attract trouble in the movies, and Stabile has fun with a tow-truck operator and a cop, who both want to get their hands on the car. He also writes in a lot of unsuccessful Tarantinoesque dialogue, including arguments about math problems and lottery odds, and whether Walter Cronkite or Hugh Downs is the host of *20/20.* There are flashes of life here, a feeling of immediacy in the camera style, a lot of energy—and promise. But not yet the movie he's probably capable of; I have a feeling anyone with the wit to make a movie for $5,000 can write characters more worth knowing than these.

## Grease ★ ★ ★

PG, 112 m., 1978 (rereleased 1998)

John Travolta (Danny), Olivia Newton-John (Sandy), Stockard Channing (Rizzo), Jeff Conaway (Kenickie), Barry Pearl (Doody), Michael Tucci (Sonny), Kelly Ward (Putzie), Didi Conn (Frenchy). Directed by Randal Kleiser and produced by Robert Stigwood and Allan Carr. Screenplay by Bronte Woodard, based on the original musical by Jim Jacobs and Warren Casey.

*Grease,* a 1970s celebration of nostalgia for the 1950s, is now being resurrected as 1970s nostalgia. But no revival, however joyously promoted, can conceal the fact that this is just an average musical, pleasant and upbeat and plastic.

The musical is being revived not because it is invaluable, but because it contains an invaluable cultural icon: the singing, dancing performance of John Travolta. It is now clear that, slumps or not, comebacks or not, Travolta is an important and enduring movie star whose presence can redeem even a compromised *Grease.* This is not one of his great films, and lacks the electricity of *Saturday Night Fever* or the quirky genius of *Pulp Fiction,* but it has charm. If Travolta lacks the voltage of Elvis Presley (his obvious role model for this film), at least he's in the same ballpark, and Elvis didn't make such great movies, either.

The story, smoothed out and set in southern California, involves a greaser named Danny (Travolta) who has a sweet summertime romance with Sandy, an Australian girl (Olivia Newton-John; making her character Australian was easier than coaching her American accent). When summer ends, they part forever, they think, only to find themselves at the same school, where Danny's tough-guy image makes it hard for him to acknowledge the squeaky-clean Sandy.

The film re-creates a 1950s that exists mostly in idyllic memory (for an alternative version, see *Rebel Without a Cause).* There are hot rods, malt shops, school dances, songs from the original Jim Jacobs and Warren Casey musical, and new songs, written to fit the characters. It's fun, yes, but it doesn't lift off the screen; the only element that bears comparison with the musicals of the Golden Age is Travolta's performance, although in the 1950s at MGM he would have been best friend, not star.

One problem I always have watching the movie is that all the students look too old. They're supposed to be sixteen or seventeen, I guess, but they look in their late twenties, and don't seem comfortable as teenagers. One of my favorite performances is by Stockard Channing, as Rizzo, the tough girl who forges ahead heedlessly after the condom breaks. She's fun, but were there sixteen-year-old girls like that in the 1950s? Call me a dreamer, but I don't think so.

The movie's worth seeing for nostalgia, or for a look at vintage Travolta, but its underlying problem is that it sees the material as silly camp: It neuters it. Romance and breaking up are matters of life and death for teenagers, and a crisis of self-esteem can be a crushing burden. *Grease* doesn't seem to remember that. *Saturday Night Fever* does.

## Great Expectations ★ ★ ★

R, 111 m., 1998

Ethan Hawke (Finnegan Bell), Gwyneth Paltrow (Estella), Anne Bancroft (Ms. Dinsmoor), Hank Azaria (Walter Plane), Chris Cooper (Joe), Robert De Niro (Prisoner/Lustig), Josh Mostel (Jerry Ragno). Directed by Alfonso Cuaron and produced by Art Linson. Screenplay by Mitch Glazer, based on a novel by Charles Dickens.

This is not, says Finn, the way the story really happened, but the way he remembers it. That is how everyone tells the stories that matter to them: Through their own eyes, rewritten by their own memories, with bold underscores for the parts that hurt. Finn's story is the life of a poor boy who falls in love with a rich girl who has been trained since childhood to break the hearts of men.

This tale has been borrowed from Charles Dickens's *Great Expectations*, where it is told in less lurid images and language, to be sure, but with the same sense of an innocent boy being lured into the lair of two dangerous women. That the women are lonely, sad, and good at heart makes it bittersweet. "What is it like not to feel anything?" Finn shouts at Estella after she has abandoned him. Of course, if you cannot feel anything, that is exactly the question you cannot answer.

The story has been updated by director Alfonso Cuaron, who moves it from Victorian England to a crumbling neo-Gothic mansion in Florida. It stars Ethan Hawke as Finn (Pip in the book), and Gwyneth Paltrow as Estella, the beautiful niece of the eccentric millionairess Ms. Dinsmoor (Anne Bancroft). Their paths cross in one of those backwaters of Florida that have been immortalized by writers like Elmore Leonard and John D. MacDonald, where creeping condos from the north have not yet dislodged small fishing shacks and the huge masonry pile of Paradiso Perduto, which once was a glittering showplace but is now engulfed in trees and creepers, and falling into decay.

Finn lives with his sister Maggie and "her man," Joe (Chris Cooper), who raises him after Maggie disappears. One day he is seen by Ms. Dinsmoor, who invites him to Paradiso Perduto to play with her niece. The two children are about ten. Finn is a gifted artist, and as he sketches the young girl, the old crone perceives that he will eventually fall in love with the girl, and sees her chance for revenge against men.

The original of Ms. Dinsmoor is, of course, Dickens's Miss Havisham, one of the most colorful and pathetic characters in Dickens, who was left stranded on her wedding day by a faithless lover. This version of *Great Expectations* spares us the sight of her wedding cake, covered in cobwebs after the decades (in Florida, tiny visitors would make short work of that feast). But it succeeds in making Ms. Dinsmore equally sad and venomous, and Anne Bancroft's performance is interesting: Despite the weird eye makeup and the cigarettes, despite the flamboyant clothing, she is human, and not without humor. "That's the biggest cat I've ever seen," Finn says on his first visit. "What do you feed it?" She waits for a beat. "Other cats," she says.

Paradiso Perduto and its inhabitants reminded me of *Grey Gardens*, the 1976 documentary about two relatives of Jackie Onassis, who lived in a decaying mansion in East Hampton with countless cats. There is the same sense of defiance: If I was once young, rich, and beautiful, these women say to the world, see what you have made of me! Cuaron, whose previous film was *The Little Princess*, brings a touch of magic realism to the setting, with weeping willows, skies filled with seabirds, and a scene where Finn and

Estella dance to "Besame Mucho" while Ms. Dinsmore looks on, cold-eyed.

Time passes. The young actors who played Finn and Estella are replaced by Hawke and Paltrow, who meet again at the mansion after several years, and share a sudden kiss at a water fountain, which is cut between backlit shots from moving cameras so that it seems more orgiastic than most sex scenes. After this romantic spark Estella again dances away, and the story continues some years later in New York, where a mysterious benefactor offers to bankroll Finn's show at an important gallery, and Estella again appears on the scene, this time with a hapless fiancé/victim named Walter in tow.

*Great Expectations* begins as a great movie (I was spellbound by the first thirty minutes), but ends as only a good one, and I think that's because the screenplay, by Mitch Glazer, too closely follows the romantic line. Dickens, who of course had more time and space to move around in, made it the story of a young man's coming of age, and the colorful characters he encountered—from the escaped prisoner of the opening scenes (played here by Robert De Niro) to good old, proud old Joe. The moment this movie declares itself as being mostly about affairs of the heart, it limits its potential.

And yet the film is a successful translation of the basic material from one period and approach to another. Especially in the early Florida scenes, it seems timeless. Hawke and Paltrow project that uneasy alertness of two people who know they like one another and suspect they'll regret it. But the subplot involving the escaped prisoner doesn't really pay off (it feels more like a bone thrown to Dickens than a necessity of the plot). And I am not quite sure that any good artist can create only when he's in sync with the girl of his dreams: Some artists paint best when their hearts are broken, and most artists paint no matter what, because they have to.

*Great Expectations* doesn't finish at the same high level that it begins (if it did, it would be one of the year's best films), but it's visually enchanted; the cinematographer, Emmanuel Lubezki, uses lighting and backlighting like a painter. And the characters have more depth and feeling than we might expect in what is, underneath everything, a fantasy. There's great joy in a scene where Finn sweeps Estella out of a restaurant and asks her to dance. And sadness later as she observes that Ms. Dinsmore's obsessions have become her own.

## Gridlock'd ★ ★ ★

R, 91 m., 1997

Tim Roth (Stretch), Tupac Shakur (Spoon), Thandie Newton (Cookie), Charles Fleischer (Mr. Woodson), Howard Hesseman (Blind Man), Elizabeth Pena (ER Nurse), James Pickens Jr. (Supervisor), John Sayles (Cop 1), Eric Payne (Cop 2), Tom Towles (D-Reper's Henchman), Tom Wright (Koolaid). Directed by Vondie Curtis Hall and produced by Damian Jones, Paul Webster, and Erica Huggins. Screenplay by Hall.

It is possible to imagine *Gridlock'd* as a movie of despair and desperation, but that would involve imagining it without Tupac Shakur and Tim Roth, who illuminate it with a gritty, goofy comic spirit. This is grim material, but surprisingly entertaining, and it is more cause to mourn the death of Shakur, who gives his best performance as Spoon, a musician who wants to get off drugs.

Spoon and his friend Stretch (Roth) arrive at this decision after rushing Spoon's girlfriend, Cookie (Thandie Newton), to an emergency room, comatose after a drug overdose. The three of them have a jazz trio. Ironically, she's the clean liver, always eating veggieburgers and preaching against smoking. While Cookie hovers in critical condition, Spoon and Stretch spend a very long day trying to find a rehab program they can turn themselves in to.

The heart of the movie is their banter, the grungy dialogue that puts an ironic spin on their anger and fear. Tim Roth is a natural actor, relaxed in his roles, with a kind of quixotic bemusement at life's absurdities. Shakur matches that and adds an earnestness: In their friendship, Spoon is the leader and thinker, and Stretch is the sidekick who will go along with whatever's suggested. It's Spoon who decides to kick, telling his friend (in a line that now has dark undertones), "Lately I feel like my luck's been running out."

Writer-director Vondie Curtis Hall, making his directing debut after a TV acting career on *Chicago Hope* and other shows, combines the hard-edged, in-your-face realism of street life with a conventional story that depends on stock characters: evil drug dealers, modern Keystone Kops, colorful eccentrics. The movie isn't as powerful as it could have been, but it's probably more fun: This is basically a comedy, even if sometimes you ask yourself why you're laughing.

That's especially true in a scene that moviegoers will be quoting for years. Spoon, desperate to get into an emergency room and begin detox, convinces Stretch to stab him. As the two friends discuss how to do it (and try to remember which side of the body the liver is on), there are echoes of the overdose sequence in *Pulp Fiction*. What Tarantino demonstrated is that with the right dialogue and actors you can make anything funny.

The daylong duel with the drug dealers and the encounters with suspicious cops work like comic punctuation. In between is the real life of the movie: the friendship of the two men and their quest to get into rehab. They circle endlessly through a series of Detroit social welfare agencies that could have been designed by Kafka: They find they can't get medicards without being on welfare, can't get into detox without filling out forms and waiting ten days, can't get into a rehab center because it's for alkys only, can't get the right forms because an office has moved, can't turn in the forms because an office is about to close. If this movie reflects real life in Detroit, it's as if the city deliberately plots to keep addicts away from help.

In movies about stupid bureaucracies, the heroes inevitably blow up and start screaming at the functionaries behind the counters. Hall's script wickedly turns the tables: The clerks shout at Spoon and Stretch. Elizabeth Pena plays an ER nurse who maddeningly makes them fill out forms while Cookie seems to be dying. When Spoon screams at her, she screams back, in a monologue that expresses all of her exhaustion and frustration. Later, at a welfare center, an overworked clerk shouts back: "Yeah, we all been waiting for the day you come through that door and tell us you're ready not to be a drug fiend. After five, ten years, you decide this is the day, and the world stops for you?"

This material is so good I wish we'd had more of it. Maybe Hall, aiming for a wider audience, hedged his bets by putting in scenes where the heroes, the drug dealers, and the cops chase each other on foot and in cars around downtown Detroit. Those scenes aren't plausible and they're not about anything.

Much better are the moments when the two friends sit, exhausted, under a mural of the great outdoors, and talk about how they simply lack the energy to keep on using drugs. Or when Spoon remembers his first taste of cocaine in high school: "I didn't even know what it was. Everybody else was throwin' up. But for me it was like going to the Moon." Or when they watch daytime TV and do a running commentary. Or when they're almost nabbed for a murder they didn't commit.

Still, maybe Hall made the smart bet by positioning this story halfway between real life and a crime comedy. The world of these streets and tenements and hospitals and alleys is strung out and despairing, and the human comedy redeems it. By the time a guy is trying to help his friend by stabbing him, we understand well enough what drugs will lead you to. For the premiere audience at the Sundance Film Festival, *Gridlock'd* played like a comedy, with big laughter. Too bad Tupac couldn't be there.

## Grosse Pointe Blank ★ ★ ½

R, 106 m., 1997

John Cusack (Martin Q. Blank), Minnie Driver (Debi Newberry), Alan Arkin (Dr. Oatman), Dan Aykroyd (Mr. Grocer), Joan Cusack (Marcella), Jeremy Piven (Paul Spericki), Hank Azaria (Lardner), Barbara Harris (Mary Blank). Directed by George Armitage and produced by Susan Arnold, Donna Arkoff Roth, and Roger Birnbaum. Screenplay by Tom Jankiewicz, D. V. DeVincentis, Steve Pink,and John Cusack, based on a story by Jankiewicz.

John Cusack is one of those rare actors who can convincingly look as if he is thinking about words of many syllables. He seems smart, and that's crucial for the character he plays in *Grosse Pointe Blank,* because like so many really smart people this one is clueless about matters of the heart. Cusack plays Martin Q. Blank, a professional assassin who is more articulate while discussing his kills with a shrink than while explaining to his high school sweetheart why he stood her up at the prom.

As the movie opens, he's preparing to do a job with a high-powered rifle, while simultaneously discussing his busy schedule with his office manager (played by his sister, Joan Cusack). She thinks he should attend his tenth high school reunion in the Detroit suburb of Grosse Pointe, Michigan. He thinks not. He misses on the assassination attempt, however, and that leads to an interesting coincidence: He can redeem himself by pulling a job in Detroit—killing two birds, so to speak, with one stone.

He discusses his plight with his psychiatrist (Alan Arkin), a man alarmed to learn he has a hit man for a client. "I don't think what a person does for a living is necessarily who he is," Blank observes reassuringly, but the shrink gives the impression of a man constantly holding himself in readiness to take a bullet.

Cusack plays Blank as a man who entered his chosen profession with good skills and high spirits, but is now beginning to entertain doubts about its wisdom as a lifelong career. He has no qualms about killing people (someone has to do it, and as a character in the film observes, it's a "growth industry"). But for him, it's getting to be the same old same old. Against his better judgment, he caves in and heads for Michigan.

Grosse Pointe may hold the key to why Martin's life seems on hold. Unfinished business waits for him there: a woman named Debi (Minnie Driver), whom he loved in high school, but stood up at the senior prom. Tooling through town in a rented car, he hears her voice on the radio and is soon peering through the window of the local radio station. She's a DJ, who smoothly segues into asking her listeners how she should feel when her prom date turns up ten years late.

Another major player in Martin's life is Mr. Grocer (Dan Aykroyd), also a professional assassin, who wants Martin to join a union he is forming: "We could be working together again, for chrissakes! Making big money! Killing important people!" He is also in Grosse Pointe, possibly on the same assignment, and soon Blank and Grocer are seated uneasily across from one another at a diner, both armed and both dangerous, mostly to one another.

The film takes the form but not the feel of a comic thriller. It's quirkier than that. The underlying plot, which also involves Martin being shadowed by assorted mysterious types who want to kill him, is not original. But the screenplay, by Cusack, Tom Jankiewicz, and others, uses that story as a backdrop for Martin Blank's wry behavior. It's not often that a film about professional killers has a high school reunion dance as its centerpiece, and rarer still that the hero kills someone during the dance and disposes of the body in the school boiler.

I enjoyed the exchanges between Cusack and Driver, as the couple on a long-delayed date. Affection still smolders between them, and it was sexy the way Driver casually put an arm around Cusack's shoulders, her hand resting possessively on the back of his neck. I liked the dialogue, too, and the assortment of classmates they encounter; have you ever noticed that whatever odd qualities your friends had in school seem to grow as the years go by?

Despite these qualities, the movie for me is a near miss. One of the problems is the conclusion, in which things are resolved with an elaborate action sequence. This sequence may have been intended ironically, but the gunshots are just as loud as if they were sincere. Too many movies end like video games, with characters popping up and shooting each other. *Grosse Pointe Blank*, which takes such a detached view toward killing and has such an articulate hero, could have done better.

## Guantanamera ★ ★ ★

NO MPAA RATING, 104 m., 1997

Carlos Cruz (Adolfo), Mirtha Ibarra (Georgina), Raul Eguren (Candido), Jorge Perugorria (Mariano), Pedro Fernandez (Ramon), Luis Alberto Garcia Novoa (Tony), Conchita Brando (Aunt Yoyita), Suset Perez Malberti (Iku). Directed by Tomas Gutierrez Alea and Juan Carlos Tabio and produced by Gerardo Herrer. Screenplay by Eliseo Alberto Diego, Alea, and Tabio.

Cuba may languish under a bankrupt and dour political system, but it is after all a Caribbean island—filled with life, color, and invention. *Guantanamera* celebrates Cuban paradoxes in a cheeky little comedy about two romances that endure through the years.

This is the last film by Tomas Gutierrez Alea, the sly satirist who insisted he was a loyal Cuban even while making comedies indicating there was a great deal in his native land that he found overripe for improvement. He died while making it; the direction was taken over by his collaborator, the writer Juan Carlos Tabio, and it stars his widow, Mirtha Ibarra.

The film's target is mindless, pigheaded bureaucracy. The weapons it brings to bear against it are romance, sexuality, and irreverence. The film opens in the small town of Guantanamera, where Yoyita, a famous singer (Conchita Brando) has returned to a heroine's welcome after fifty years in Havana. She is reunited with Candido (Raul Eguren), the lover of her youth, and as they gaze upon each other their old love is rekindled—placing too great a stress on poor Yoyita's heart.

The dead singer is the aunt of Georgina (Ibarra), the long-suffering wife of a local bureaucrat named Adolfo (Carlos Cruz). He is a humorless tyrant with a mad scheme for transporting corpses. Instead of putting a dead body into a hearse at this end and taking it out at the other, he believes the body should be transferred to a different vehicle at every provincial border, spreading the petrol costs around. Elementary math suggests that everyone would end up with essentially the same gas bill, but no matter—Adolfo is a zealot backed by the power of his office.

Adolfo, Georgina, and the grieving old Candido set off on a journey to return the body to the family plot, and that provides *Guantanamera* with the excuse for a road comedy that also documents in zestful detail how sanity survives in the everyday life of today's Cuba. As they hit the road, we meet two truck drivers, the womanizing Mariano (Jorge Perugorria) and the devout Ramon (Pedro Fernandez). They pilot a big vehicle over ill-kept rural roads, providing not only a delivery service but also a sort of lifeline; hitchhikers jump on and off, messages are sent, gossip is exchanged, and Mariano has a lover in every hamlet (some of them as devious as he is).

The truck drivers and the mourners encounter one another, and we learn that Mariano was once Georgina's student, when she was a university teacher. She touched his idealism, he inspired her hope, and now circumstances conspire to draw them back into one another's arms—although there are obstacles, such as the buffoon Adolfo, and Mariano's taste for women who are younger and juicer than the sexy but mature Georgina.

There is fascination everywhere in the frames of *Guantanamera*. In the sides and backgrounds of his shots, Alea has made an unwitting (or perhaps a very witting) documentary. We see a poor economy where black markets flourish, where every yard is home to vegetables and chickens, where shops want U.S. dollars instead of Cuban currency, where meaningless paperwork slows every transaction to a crawl—and provides a constant temptation for bribery.

Let's indulge in some idle speculation—a little harmless decoding. Adolfo represents, perhaps, the crushing weight of the socialist bureaucracy. Mariano and Georgina, when they were younger, represented the hope of workers and intellectuals; now, in middle age, they wonder if they can recapture their exhausted idealism. On the road, they are surrounded by the vitality and humor of everyday Cuba. There is hope—if only the country can break loose from its obsession with finding new ways to cart around the cadavers of its past.

## Guimba the Tyrant ★ ★ ★

NO MPAA RATING, 93 m., 1996

Falaba Issa Traore (Guimba), Bala Moussa Keita (Mambi), Habib Dembele (Sambou, the Griot), Lamine Diallo (Jangine), Mouneissa Maiga (Kani), Helene Diarra (Meya), Fatoumata Coulibaly (Sadio), Cheick Oumar Meiga (Siriman). Directed by Cheick Oumar Sissoko and produced by Idrissa Ouedraogo. Screenplay by Sissoko.

As *Guimba the Tyrant* opens, a dictator is instructing his son in the methods of despotism: "Your goal is to dominate men. Be cruel and merciless. Only tyranny suits them. And marry a woman coveted by all." The son, a dwarf named Jangine, is much less interested in his father's political theories than in his advice about women. He has been intended since birth to marry the beautiful Kani. But on a visit to his betrothed, he conceives a great lust for her mother, the voluptuous Meya. "Father," he cries, "I love big women! With big rumps!"

The father, Guimba, does not want to hear this. He has his hands full, flogging his subjects and expropriating their lands. He orders his son to marry Kani, or else. But Jangine is a spoiled little despot, and one day when Guimba comes riding back into the city, he finds his son flat on his back in the dust, crying, "I want Meya! Right now!"

Solomon would have been proud of Guimba's solution to this problem: Since his son wants to marry the mother, he himself will marry the beautiful daughter. There is a slight technicality—the mother is already married—but Guimba banishes her husband. To discourage potential suitors for the beautiful Kani, the tyrant sends his page through the town announcing, "All future suitors of Kani will be castrated!"

Guimba is the ruler of a mythical African nation in precolonial times, but African audiences have had little difficulty in reading the movie as a parable about recent events in the nation of Mali, where the dictator Moussa Traore was overthrown in 1991 after sponsoring a reign of terror. The film's writer and director, Cheick Oumar Sissoko, was active in the underground movement against Traore, and also has disagreements with the current regime of Alpha Oumar Konare, which did not encourage the making of *Guimba*.

The film is a riotously colorful, irreverent satire on the ways of tyrants, told in the style of the "griots," or village storytellers, who are part of West African tradition. The story begins and ends with a griot plucking a stringed instrument while walking by a river and recounting the fall of Guimba. In these scenes he is formal and restrained, but in the heat of the story his narration grows excited and fanciful, and it is tempting to see parallels with today's rap artists and their verbal improvisations.

The story takes place in a village of great beauty, made of concrete that has been colored ochre by the local sand. Like all fables, it occupies the entire attention of all of the characters, who have no occupations other than their task of following the events and playing their parts in them.

Guimba (Falaba Issa Traore) rules this village with an iron hand, sometimes springing from his throne to personally beat those who defy him. So great is the pressure of his villainy that he wears a headdress shielding his face from the sun. His son, Jangine (Lamine Diallo), is three feet tall but struts around town like the boss's son, which he is. All he has to do is raise a finger and his lackeys bring him a woman. Three fingers, three women. The local people are very tired of this, and as one wife is dragged away to serve Jangine's pleasure, her husband beats his head against a wall.

Guimba seems to exercise total power, but in fact there are magic spells that can defeat him. When the tyrant banishes Meya's husband, Mambi, he seeks out a band of hunters who live outside the village (and who perhaps represent exiled opponents of the Malian regime). Siriman, leader of this band, has magic so powerful he can turn day to night, and soon there is a duel to the death between the tyrant and his enemies.

*Guimba the Tyrant* won the grand prize at the 1995 Fespaco festival, held every other year in Burkina Faso and considered the most important artistic gathering on the continent. It was also honored for its extraordinary costumes by Kandjoura Coulibaly—costumes so colorful and fanciful that if you're at all interested in African fabrics and designs, they alone make the movie worth seeing.

In interviews, Cheick Oumar Sissoko has said that his purpose was not to make a good American film or a good French film, but a good African film, and he describes the African tradition of discursive narrative as his inspiration. A good storyteller does not stay in the same tone throughout his tale, but is serious, sarcastic, fanciful, and absurd as the spirit moves him, and the film is told in the same way. Some scenes are played straight, some are fantasies, some are riotous action, some are comic, some are bluntly realistic. (James Joyce's *Ulysses* also uses such a mixture of styles.)

The result is a film that is confusing at times, but becomes clear at the end after you see where all the pieces fit. The subtitles, which stick to the dialogue and ignore background or context, might have been more helpful at times. But the story is straightforward, the visual style is glorious, and there is boundless energy and optimism in this fable of a tyrant overthrown.

# H

## **Habit** ★ ★ ★

NO MPAA RATING, 112 m., 1997

Larry Fessenden (Sam), Meredith Snaider (Anna), Aaron Beall (Nick), Patricia Coleman (Rae), Heather Woodbury (Liza), Jesse Hartman (Lenny), Marcus A. Miranda (Segundo), Herb Rogers (Slimman), Hart Fessenden (Sam's Dad), Lon Waterford (Mr. Lyons). Written, directed, and edited by Larry Fessenden and produced by Dayton Taylor.

Are we all agreed—all of us except for Anne Rice—that there is no such thing as a vampire? Yes? And yet the children of the darkness prey on our imaginations, and there is something inexplicably erotic about vampirism. *Habit,* a sad and haunting film by Larry Fessenden, is a modern vampire story, or maybe it's not. Maybe, in a way, the hero is drinking his own blood.

Fessenden stars as Sam, an alcoholic whose life is in disrepair. He spends every waking moment drinking, suggesting a drink, or recovering from a drink. His life reflects the discontinuous reality of the advanced alcoholic for whom life is like being in a room where the lights go on and off unexpectedly. He more or less lives in a bar in Greenwich Village, although he has an explanation: "I'm the manager four days a week."

Sam's girlfriend, Liza (Heather Woodbury), has moved out. She's still friendly, but has grown tired of waiting for him to decide to do something about his drinking. His best friend is Nick (Aaron Beall), who wanders around town in a long overcoat, clutching a bottle inside a paper bag and affecting theatrical speech.

One night at a party, very drunk, Sam finds himself talking to an attractive brunette named Anna (Meredith Snaider). She's one of those women who look at you so attentively you feel self-conscious. Anna looks too attractive for Sam, who is missing some front teeth, needs a shave, and is slurring his words. But one thing leads to another, and eventually he finds himself having sex at her hands and waking up in a park in the morning with a bloody lip.

He keeps losing track of Anna, but no matter: She has a way of turning up. Sex with her is great ("It's like having hot milk run through your veins"), but he keeps finding little bites and cuts here and there on his body. And he keeps on drinking. "I'm just not feeling right," he complains. Nick blithely explains that Sam's poor health may be because of "a change in the weather."

Now then. Is Anna a vampire? Or not? Fessenden's movie is a sly exercise in ambiguity. More than one explanation fits all of the events in the film, even those we see with our own eyes. Of all the recent vampire movies *(Interview With the Vampire, The Addiction, Nadja),* this one is the only one to suggest that the powerful symbolism of vampirism could create results even in the absence of causes. You could be killed by vampires even if they do not exist.

The movie is done in a flat, realistic tone that is perfectly suited to the material. Fessenden, Snaider, Beall, and Patricia Coleman (as Nick's girlfriend) are all naturalistic actors who find a convincing everyday tone; Snaider is particularly good at controlling a role that was almost doomed to be overacted. And Woodbury, as the ex-girlfriend, supplies the right note of cool, detached sanity.

I have received a lot of mail from those who feel I need to have David Lynch's *Lost Highway* explained to me. Their explanations are invariably detailed and serenely confident, even though none of them agree. One correspondent, who has obviously never read a single one of my reviews except for *Lost Highway,* lectured me that I should be more open to the experimental and not limit myself to praising formula films. I wrote to him privately in colorful detail; publicly, to him and his kind, I recommend *Habit,* which in the subtlety of its ambiguity reveals *Lost Highway* as an exercise in search of a purpose.

Fessenden, who wrote, directed, acted, and edited this film, is a talent to watch. That he is able to see himself with such objectivity is almost frightening; there is not a shred of ego in his performance. Wandering about the streets, coat flapping open, aimless, sad, drinking without even remembering why, his Sam is an ideal vampire's victim, because he takes so long to catch on. But then, of course, perhaps that's because there is no such thing as a vampire.

## Hamlet ★ ★ ★ ★

PG-13, 238 m., 1997

Kenneth Branagh (Hamlet), Derek Jacobi (Claudius), Julie Christie (Gertrude), Kate Winslet (Ophelia), Richard Briers (Polonius), Charlton Heston (Player King), Nicholas Farrell (Horatio), Michael Maloney (Laertes), Timothy Spall (Rosencrantz), Reece Dinsdale (Guildenstern), Billy Crystal (First Gravedigger), Gérard Depardieu (Reynaldo), Richard Attenborough (English Ambassador), John Gielgud (Priam), Robin Williams (Osric), Rosemary Harris (Player Queen), Judi Dench (Hecuba), Jack Lemmon (Marcellus), Brian Blessed (Ghost), John Mills (Old Norway). Directed by Kenneth Branagh and produced by David Barron. Screenplay adapted by Branagh from the play by William Shakespeare.

There is early in Kenneth Branagh's *Hamlet* a wedding celebration, the Danish court rejoicing at the union of Claudius and Gertrude. The camera watches, and then pans to the right to reveal the solitary figure of Hamlet, clad in black. It always creates a little shock in the movies when the foreground is unexpectedly occupied. We realize the subject of the scene is not the wedding, but Hamlet's experience of it. And we enjoy Branagh's visual showmanship: In all of his films, he reveals his joy in theatrical gestures.

His *Hamlet* is long but not slow, deep but not difficult, and it vibrates with the relief of actors who have great things to say and the right ways to say them. And in the 70mm version, it has a visual clarity that is breathtaking. It is the first uncut film version of Shakespeare's most challenging tragedy, the first 70mm film since *Far and Away* in 1992, and at 238 minutes the second-longest major Hollywood production (one minute shorter than *Cleopatra*). Branagh's Hamlet lacks the narcissistic intensity of Laurence Olivier's (in the 1948 Academy Award winner), but the film as a whole is better, placing Hamlet in the larger context of royal politics and making him less a subject for pity.

The story provides a melodramatic stage for inner agonies. Hamlet (Branagh), the prince of Denmark, mourns the untimely death of his father. His mother, Gertrude, rushes with unseemly speed into marriage with Claudius, her husband's brother. Something is rotten in the state of Denmark. And then the ghost of Hamlet's father appears and says he was poisoned by Claudius.

What must Hamlet do? He desires the death of Claudius but lacks the impulse to action. He despises himself for his passivity. In tormenting himself he drives his mother to despair, kills Polonius by accident, speeds the kingdom to chaos, and his love, Ophelia, to madness.

What is intriguing about *Hamlet* is the ambiguity of everyone's motives. Tom Stoppard's *Rosenkrantz and Guildenstern Are Dead* famously filtered all the action through the eyes of Hamlet's treacherous school friends. But how does it all look to Gertrude? To Claudius? To the heartbroken Ophelia? The great benefit of this full-length version is that these other characters become more understandable.

The role of Claudius (Derek Jacobi) is especially enriched: In shorter versions, he is the scowling usurper who functions only as villain. Here, with lines and scenes restored, he seems more balanced and powerful. He might have made a plausible king of Denmark, had things turned out differently. Yes, he killed his brother, but regicide was not unknown in the twelfth century, and perhaps the old king was ripe for replacement; this production shows Gertrude (Julie Christie) as lustfully in love with Claudius. By restoring the original scope of Claudius's role, Branagh emphasizes court and political intrigue instead of enclosing the material in a Freudian hothouse.

The movie's very sets emphasize the role of the throne as the center of the kingdom. Branagh uses costumes to suggest the nineteenth century, and shoots his exteriors at Blenheim Castle, seat of the Duke of Marlborough and Winston Churchill's childhood home. The interior sets, designed by Tim Harvey and Desmond Crowe, feature a throne room surrounded by mirrored walls, overlooked by a gallery, and divided by an elevated walkway. The set puts much of the action onstage (members of the court are constantly observing) and allows for intrigue (some of the mirrors are two-way, and lead to concealed chambers and corridors).

In this very public arena Hamlet agonizes, and is observed. Branagh uses rapid cuts to show others reacting to his words and meanings. And he finds new ways to stage familiar scenes, renewing the material. Hamlet's most famous soliloquy ("To be, or not to be . . .") is delivered into a mirror, so that his own indecision is thrust back at him. When he torments Ophelia, a most private moment, we spy on them from the other side of a two-way mirror; he crushes her cheek against the glass and her frightened breath clouds it. When he comes upon Claudius at his prayers and can kill him, many productions imagine Hamlet lurking behind a pillar in a chapel. Branagh is more intimate, showing a dagger blade insinuating itself through the mesh of a confessional.

One of the surprises of this uncut *Hamlet* is the crucial role of the play within the play. Many productions reduce the visiting troupe of actors to walk-ons; they provide a hook for Hamlet's advice to the players, and merely suggest the performance that Hamlet hopes will startle Claudius into betraying himself. Here, with Charlton Heston magnificently assured as the Player King, we listen to the actual lines of his play (which shorter versions often relegate to dumb-show at the back of the stage). We see how ingeniously and cleverly they tweak the conscience of the king, and we see Claudius's pained reactions. The episode becomes a turning point; Claudius realizes that Hamlet is on to him.

As for Hamlet, Branagh (like Mel Gibson in the 1990 film) has no interest in playing him as an apologetic mope. Branagh is an actor of exuberant physical gifts and energy (when the time comes, his King Lear will bound about the heath). Consider the scene beginning, "Oh, what a rogue and peasant slave am I . . . ," in which Hamlet bitterly regrets his inaction. The lines are delivered not in bewilderment but in mounting anger, and it is to Branagh's credit that he pulls out all the stops; a quieter Hamlet would make a tamer *Hamlet.*

Kate Winslet is touchingly vulnerable as Ophelia, red-nosed and snuffling, her world crumbling about her. Richard Briers makes Polonius not so much a foolish old man as an adviser out of his depth. Of the familiar faces, the surprise is Heston: How many great performances have we lost while he visited the Planet of the Apes? Billy Crystal is a surprise, but effective, as the gravedigger. But Robin Williams, Jack Lemmon, and Gérard Depardieu are distractions, their performances not overcoming our shocks of recognition.

At the end of this *Hamlet,* I felt at last as if I was getting a handle on the play (I never expect to fully understand it). It has been a long journey. I read it in high school, underlining the famous lines. I saw the Richard Burton film version, and later Olivier's. I studied it in graduate school. I have seen it on stage in England and America (most memorably in Aidan Quinn's punk version, when he sprayed graffiti on the wall: "2B=?"). Zeffirelli's version with Gibson came in 1990. I learned from them all.

One of the tasks of a lifetime is to become familiar with the great plays of Shakespeare. *Hamlet* is the most opaque. Branagh's version moved me, entertained me, and made me feel for the first time at home in that doomed royal court. I may not be able to explain *Hamlet,* but at last I have a better idea than Rosencrantz and Guildenstern. ☞

## The Hanging Garden ★ ★ ★

R, 98 m., 1998

Chris Leavins (Sweet William), Troy Veinotte (Teenage Sweet William), Kerry Fox (Rosemary), Sarah Polley (Teenage Rosemary), Seana McKenna (Iris), Peter MacNeill (Whiskey Mac), Joe S. Keller (Fletcher), Joan Orenstein (Grace). Directed by Thom Fitzgerald and produced by Louise Garfield, Arnie Gelbart, and Fitzgerald. Screenplay by Fitzgerald.

There is a character named William who appears in *The Hanging Garden* at three different ages: as an eight-year-old who is terrified of his father; as a fat fifteen-year-old; and as a twenty-five-year-old, now thin, who has returned for his sister's wedding. The peculiar thing is that the characters sometimes appear on the screen at the same time, and the dead body of the fifteen-year-old hangs from a tree during many of the scenes.

Well, why not? It may be magic realism, but isn't it also the simple truth? Don't the ghosts of our former selves attend family events right along with our current manifestations? Don't parents still sometimes relate to us as if we were children, don't siblings still carry old resentments, aren't old friends still stuck on who we used to be? And don't we sometimes resurrect old personas and dust them off for a return engagement? Aren't all of those selves stored away inside somewhere?

The movie opens on a wedding day. Rosemary (Kerry Fox, from *An Angel at My Table*), who has already started drinking, struggles with her wedding dress and vows she won't show herself until her brother arrives. Her brother, Sweet William (Chris Leavins), does eventually arrive, late, and is about 150 pounds too light to fit into the tux his mother has rented for him. He was fat when he left home. Now he is thin, and gay. We learn that his first homosexual experience was with Fletcher (Joe S. Keller), the very person Rosemary is planning to marry.

The family also includes Whiskey Mac (Peter MacNeill), the alcoholic patriarch, and Iris (Seana McKenna), the mother, who seems like a rock of stability. It's no accident that all the family members are named for flowers; Whiskey Mac poured all of his love and care into his garden, while brutalizing his family. His treatment of his overweight, gay son led the boy to hang himself in one version of reality, and to run away in another, so that when the twenty-five-year-old returns home the body of the fifteen-year-old is still hanging in the garden.

But I am not capturing the tone of the movie, which is not as macabre and gloomy as this makes it sound, but filled with eccentricity. The family members, who live in Canada's Maritime provinces, have survived by becoming defiantly individual. This is going to be one of those weddings where the guests look on in amazement.

The writer-director, Thom Fitzgerald, moves easily through time, and we meet the teenage version of Sweet William (Troy Veinotte) and Rosemary (Sarah Polley, from *The Sweet Hereafter*) as they form a bond against their father. Fitzgerald never pauses to explain his time-shifts and overlaps, and doesn't need to. Somehow we understand why a 300-pound body could be left hanging from a tree for ten years. It isn't really there, although in another sense, of course, it is.

Like many movies about dysfunctional families, *The Hanging Garden* involves more dysfunction than is perhaps necessary. There is the grandmother, who is senile but still has good enough timing to shout "I do!" out the window at the crucial moment in the marriage. And the tomboy little sister, Violet, who bitterly resents having to be the flower girl. And for all the secrets I have suggested, there are others that will surprise you even at the end—including a great big one that I doubt really proves anything.

The heart of the movie is its insight into the way families are haunted by their own history. How the memory of early unhappiness colors later relationships, and how Sweet William's persecution at the hands of his father hangs in the air as visibly as the corpse in the garden.

The movie is Canadian, and joins a list of other recent Canadian films about dread secrets, including *Exotica, The Sweet Hereafter*, and *Kissed*. Although there's a tendency to lump Canadian and American films together into the same cultural pool, the personal, independent films from Canada have a distinctive flavor. If Americans are in your face, Canadians are more reticent. If a lot of American movies are about wackos who turn out to share conventional values at the core, Canadian characters tend to be normal and pleasant on the surface, and keep their darker thoughts to themselves. I don't know which I prefer, but I know the Canadians usually supply more surprises.

## Happy Gilmore ★ ½

PG-13, 92 m., 1996

Adam Sandler (Happy Gilmore), Christopher McDonald (Shooter), Julie Bowen (Virginia), Frances Bay (Grandma), Carl Weathers (Chubbs), Alan Covert (Otto), Robert Smigel (IRS Agent), Bob Barker (Bob Barker), Richard Kiel (Gallery Giant). Directed by Dennis Dugan and produced by Robert Simonds. Screenplay by Tim Herlihy and Adam Sandler.

*Happy Gilmore* tells the story of a violent sociopath. Since it's about golf, that makes it a comedy. The movie, the latest in the dumber and dumbest sweepstakes, stars Adam Sandler as a kid who only wants to play hockey. He hits the puck so hard he kills his father, who is in the act of filming a home movie. Actually, he kills his father's camera, but it's a small point.

Happy can't skate very well, and when he's not chosen for the hockey team, he beats up the coach. Life seems to hold no future for him. After his father's death he is taken in by his beloved grandmother (Frances Bay), and then a crisis strikes: The IRS seizes Grandma's house and possessions. How can Happy possibly earn $275,000 to pay all of the back taxes?

During a visit to a golf driving range, he discovers a hidden talent. He can hit the ball hundreds of yards, straight as an arrow. He's taken under the arm of a veteran golf pro named Chubbs (Carl Weathers), who tries to teach him the game, but it's Happy's tendency to explode and pound his clubs into the ground when he misses a shot. (Chubbs retired from the Tour when a one-eyed alligator bit off his hand in a water trap; he is now forced to use a flimsy wooden hand, which he grasps with his real hand, which is clearly outlined beneath his shirt sleeve. No prizes for guessing that the alligator will turn up again.)

Happy's long game is great, but his short game stinks. He goes on the Tour, where the defending champion, Shooter McGavin (Christopher McDonald), becomes his archenemy. They go mano-a-mano for weeks, in a series of golf scenes that are too heavy on golf for nongolfers, and too irrelevant to the ancient and honorable game for those who follow it. At a pro-am tourney, Happy teams up with Bob Barker, whose fight scene seems longer in the preview trailer than in the movie.

The Happy Gilmore character is very strange. I guess we are supposed to like him. He loves his old Grandma, and wins the heart of a pretty PR lady (Julie Bowen), who tries to teach him to control his temper. Yet, as played by Sandler, he doesn't have a pleasing personality: He seems angry even when he's not supposed to be angry, and his habit of pounding everyone he dislikes is rather tiring in a PG-13 movie. At one point, he even knocks the bottom off a beer bottle and goes for Shooter.

It was a Heineken's beer, I think. The label was a little torn. Maybe nobody paid for product placement. *Happy Gilmore* is filled with so many plugs it looks like a product placement sampler in search of a movie. I probably missed a few, but I counted Diet Pepsi, Pepsi, Pepsi Max, Subway sandwich shops, Budweiser (in bottles, cans, and Bud-dispensing helmets), Michelob, Visa cards, Bell Atlantic, AT&T, Sizzler, Wilson, *Golf Digest,* the ESPN sports network, and Top-Flite golf balls.

I'm sure some of those got in by accident (the modern golf Tour has ads plastered on everything but the grass), but I'm fairly sure Subway paid for placement, since it scored one Subway sandwich eaten outside a store, one date in a Subway store, one Subway soft drink container, two verbal mentions of Subway, one Subway commercial starring Happy, a Subway T-shirt, and a Subway golf bag. Halfway through the movie, I didn't know what I wanted more: laughs or mustard.

## Hard Eight ★ ★ ★ ½

R, 93 m., 1997

Philip Baker Hall (Sydney), John C. Reilly (John), Gwyneth Paltrow (Clementine), Samuel L. Jackson (Jimmy). Directed by Paul Thomas Anderson and produced by Robert Jones and John Lyons. Screenplay by Anderson.

The man's face is sad and lined, and he lights cigarettes as if he's been living in casinos for centuries. He has a deep, precise voice: We get a quick impression that he knows what he thinks, and says what he believes. His name is Sydney, and he has found an unshaven young bum dozing against the wall of a coffee shop and offered him a cup of coffee and a cigarette.

Why? The answer to that question is the engine behind the first half of *Hard Eight.* I am not sure it is ever fully answered, or needs to be. Sydney (Philip Baker Hall) is a man who has been gambling for a long time, and knows a lot about the subject, and shares his knowledge with the kid because—well, maybe just because he has it to share.

The kid is named John (John C. Reilly). He needs $6,000 to bury his mother, and has lost everything. Step by step, Sydney teaches him some ropes. How to start with $150 and recycle it through the casino cashier cages until he seems to have spent $2,000 in the casino and is given a free room. This opening sequence is quietly fascinating: I like movies that show me precisely how to get away with something. At the end of the process, it's funny how John, now that he's in his own room, becomes the genial host. "Free movies on TV?" he asks Sydney. "Drink from the mini-bar?"

Two years pass. Sydney and John are still friends, John dressing like Sydney and even ordering the same drinks. We begin to understand more about the older man. He is a gentleman, with a deep courtesy. He watches the waitress Clementine (Gwyneth Paltrow) flirt with a table of drunks, asks her if she "has" to do that to keep her job, and says, "You don't have to do that with me."

John and Clementine become a couple, even though it's clear Clemmie does some hooking on the side. John also makes a friend of an ominous man named Jimmy (Samuel L. Jackson), whom Sydney doesn't trust. "What do you do?" Sydney asks him. "I do some consulting, security, help out on busy nights," Jimmy says. "Parking lot?" says Sydney. "No, I'm inside," Jimmy says, but Sydney's shot has found its target.

By this point in the film, its writer-director, Paul Thomas Anderson, has us so hooked that we're watching for the sheer pleasure of the dialogue and the acting. Anderson has a good ear. Sydney says precisely what he means. John's statements are based more on hope than reality. Clementine says what she thinks people want to hear. Jimmy likes to say things that are probably not true, and then look at you to see if you'll challenge him. All of them live in the twenty-four-hour days of Reno, where gambling is like a drumbeat in the back of everything they do.

There turns out to be a kind of a plot (a customer doesn't pay Clementine $300, and John gets violent and then calls Sydney to help him out of a mess). There is even a secret from the past, although not the one we expect. But the movie isn't about a plot. It's about these specific people in this place and time, and that's why it's so good: It listens and sees. It observes, and in that it takes its lead from Sydney, who is a student of human nature and plays the cards of life very, very close to his vest.

Philip Baker Hall has been in the movies since 1975, and has been on a lot of TV shows, even *Seinfeld*. He's familiar, in a way: He looks middle-aged and a little sad. And grown-up. Many Americans linger in adolescence, but Hall is the kind of man who puts on a tie before he leaves the house. In 1984, he gave one of the great performances in American movies, in a one-man show, playing Richard Nixon in Robert Altman's *Secret Honor*. Here is another great performance. He is a man who has been around, who knows casinos and gambling, who finds himself attached to three people he could easily have avoided, who thinks before he acts.

Movies like *Hard Eight* remind me of what original, compelling characters the movies can sometimes give us. Like David Mamet's *House of Games* or Mike Figgis's *Leaving Las Vegas*, or the documentary *Crumb*, they pay attention to the people who inhabit city nights according to their own rules, who have learned from experience, and don't like to make the same mistake twice. At one point, when Clementine asks him a question, Sydney says, "You shouldn't ask a question like that unless you know the answer." It's not so much what he says as how he says it.

## Hard Rain ★

R, 98 m., 1998

Morgan Freeman (Jim), Christian Slater (Tom), Randy Quaid (Sheriff), Minnie Driver (Karen), Ed Asner (Charlie), Michael Goorjian (Kenny), Dann Florek (Mr. Mehlor), Ricky Harris (Ray). Directed by Mikael Salomon and produced by Mark Gordon, Gary Levinsohn, and Ian Bryce. Screenplay by Graham Yost.

*Hard Rain* is one of those movies that never convince you their stories are really happening. From beginning to end, I was acutely aware of actors being paid to stand in cold water. Suspension of my disbelief in this case would have required psychotropic medications.

Oh, the film is well made from a technical viewpoint. The opening shot is a humdinger, starting out with a vast flood plain, zooming above houses surrounded by water, and then ending with a close-up of a cop's narrowing eyes. But even then, I was trying to spot the effects—to catch how they created the flood effect, and how they got from the flood to the eyes.

Funny how some movies will seduce you into their stories while others remain at arm's length. *Titanic* was just as artificial and effects-driven as *Hard Rain*, and yet I was spellbound. Maybe it was because the people on the doomed ship had no choice: The *Titanic* was sinking, and that was that.

In *Hard Rain*, there is a bad guy (Morgan Freeman) who *has* a choice. He wants to steal some money, but all during the film I kept wondering why he didn't just give up and head for dry ground. How much of this ordeal was he foolish enough to put up with? Water, cold, rain, electrocutions, murders, shotguns, jet ski attacks, drownings, betrayals, collisions, leaky boats, stupid and incompetent partners, and your fingertips shrivel up: Is it worth it?

The film opens in a town being evacuated because of rising flood waters. There's a sequence involving a bank. At first we think we're witnessing a robbery, and then we realize we are witnessing a pickup by an armored car. What's the point? Since the bankers don't think they're being robbed and the armored truck drivers don't think they're robbing them, the sequence means only that the director has gone to great difficulty to fool us. Why? So we can slap our palms against our brows and admit we were big stupes?

By the time we finally arrived at the story, I was essentially watching a documentary about wet actors at work. Christian Slater stars as one of the armored truck crew. Randy Quaid is the ambiguous sheriff. Morgan Freeman is the leader of the would-be thieves, who have commandeered a power boat. Ah, but, I hear you asking, why was it so important for the armored car to move the cash out of the bank before the flood? So Freeman's gang could steal it, of course. Otherwise, if it got wet, hey, what's the Federal Reserve for?

Minnie Driver plays a local woman who teams up with Slater so that they can fall in love while saving each other from drowning. First Slater is in a jail cell that's about to flood, and then Driver is handcuffed to a staircase that's about to flood, and both times I was thinking what rotten luck it was that *Hard Rain* came so soon after the scene in *Titanic* where Kate Winslet saved Leonardo DiCaprio from drowning after he was handcuffed on the sinking ship. It's bad news when a big action scene plays like a demonstration of recent generic techniques.

Meanwhile, Morgan Freeman's character is too darned nice. He keeps trying to avoid violence while still trying to steal the money. This plot requires a mad dog like Dennis Hopper. Freeman's character specializes in popping up suddenly from the edge of the screen and scaring the other characters, even though it is probably pretty hard to sneak up on somebody in a powerboat. Freeman is good at looking wise and insightful, but the wiser and more insightful he looked, the more I wanted him to check into a motel and order himself some hot chocolate.

*Hard Rain* must have been awesomely difficult to make. Water is hard to film around, and here were whole city streets awash, at night and in the rain. The director is Mikael Salomon, a former cameraman, who along with cinematographer Peter Menzies Jr. does a good job of making everything look convincingly wet. And they stage a jet ski chase through school corridors that's an impressive action sequence, unlikely though it may be.

I was in Los Angeles the weekend *Hard Rain* had its preview, and went to talk to the cast. I found myself asking: Wasn't there a danger of electrocution when you were standing for weeks in all that water with electrical cables everywhere? That's not the sort of question you even think about if the story is working. Hey, how about this for a story idea? An actor signs up for a movie about a flood, little realizing that a celebrity stalker, who hates him, has been hired as an electrician on the same picture.

## Harriet the Spy ★ ★

PG, 102 m., 1996

Michelle Trachtenberg (Harriet), Rosie O'Donnell (Ole Golly), Vanessa Lee Chester (Janie Gibbs), Gregory Smith (Sport), J. Smith-Cameron (Mrs. Welsch), Robert Joy (Mr. Welsch), Eartha Kitt (Agatha K. Plummer), Don Francks (Harrison Withers), Eugene Lipinski (George Waldenstein). Directed by Bronwen Hughes and produced by Marykay Powell. Screenplay by Douglas Petrie and Theresa Rebeck, based on the novel by Louise Fitzhugh.

Harriet M. Welsch shakes up her pop bottle to make it fizz, closes her eyes, and makes a wish: "I wanna see the whole world, and I wanna write down everything." She becomes a junior Thomas Wolfe, prowling her neighborhood with a treasured notebook and making entries about the man with all the cats, the woman with the weird garden, and the goings-on at the Chinese restaurant.

Harriet is the heroine of one of the most popular modern books for children, Louise Fitzhugh's *Harriet the Spy*, which has sold 2.5 million copies and served, I gather, as a great inspiration. On a book review page on the Web, adult women write in to testify to Harriet's influence: The book made one want to become a writer, another to become a journalist, and a third (who did not read it as carefully) to become a private eye.

Now here is the movie, made in cooperation with Nickelodeon and aimed at kids about the same age as Harriet, who is in the sixth grade.

It is not a very technically accomplished movie—the pacing is slow and there are scenes that seem amateurish—but since Harriet doesn't intend to inspire anyone to become a movie critic, perhaps it will work a certain charm for its target audience.

Certainly Michelle Trachtenberg, who plays Harriet, makes a plucky young neighborhood snoop. She stands on piles of abandoned furniture to peer through dusty windows, and climbs up on a roof to spy on the man with the cats, who has named them all after jazz greats.

Harriet writes down everything in her journal, in bold, confident printing that a graphologist would say reveals her need to spell things out very clearly for those who may not be as swift as she is, a category that includes her parents. They live in a house that looks like it was produced in a collision between the Arts and Crafts movement and shop class, and spend most of their time being vaguely alarmed by their prodigy.

Luckily, Harriet has a more understanding adult in her life—her nanny, named Golly (Rosie O'Donnell), who tells her, "There are as many ways to live as there are people in this world, and each one deserves a closer look." Harriet bonds with Golly, but one night Golly and a gentleman admirer take Harriet along on a dinner date, they get home late, the parents are hysterical, and Golly leaves: "It's the right time."

Harriet now approaches a period of crisis. She creeps on her tummy across the landing to spy on her parents, she makes detailed entries in her notebook, and she gets into a conflict with her classmates, who start their own counterspy operation. What with one thing and another, Harriet finds herself covered with blue paint and ordered by her parents to stop with the notebook.

Harriet counterattacks with a hit list of her enemies and her plans of revenge. We get the idea that as an adult she would not be someone we'd want as a sister-in-law. But she is a likable kid, who makes friends with strange local legends like Agatha K. Plummer (Eartha Kitt). And her fantasy world allows an escape from the ho-hum life at school, where the lessons seem to consist largely of showing the girls a film named *Girl to Woman,* and the boys a film named *Boy to Man* ("This is an actual photograph of a boy's vocal cords.")

The materials are here for a better film. The director, Bronwen Hughes, has made one more suited for the after-school slot on Nickelodeon than for theatrical release, where it simply isn't in the same league with *The Secret Garden* or *The Little Princess* (whose Vanessa Lee Chester plays a best pal again this time). Still, sometimes the materials of a movie like this work on audiences not much concerned with style or polish. Harriet is a good role model, a smart, curious girl who keeps her eyes open and writes everything down.

## Hate (La Haine) ★ ★ ★

NO MPAA RATING, 93 m., 1996

Vincent Cassel (Vinz), Hubert Kounde (Hubert), Said Taghmaoui (Said), Karim Belkhadra (Samir), Edouard Montoute (Darty), Francois Levantal (Asterix), Solo Dicko (Santo). Directed by Mathieu Kassovitz and produced by Christophe Rossignon. Screenplay by Kassovitz.

*"Society is like a man falling off a building. As he passes each floor, he calls out, 'So far, so good!'"*

—story quoted in *Hate*

Mathieu Kassovitz is a 29-year-old French director who in his first two films has probed the wound of alienation among France's young outsiders. His film *Hate* tells the story of three young men—an Arab, an African, and a Jew—who spend an aimless day in a sterile Paris suburb, as social turmoil swirls around them and they eventually get into a confrontation with the police. If France is the man falling off the building, they are the sidewalk.

In Kassovitz's first film, *Café au Lait* (1994), he told the story of a young woman from the Caribbean who summons her two boyfriends—one African, one Jewish—to announce that she is pregnant. That film, inspired by Spike Lee's *She's Gotta Have It,* was more of a comedy, but in *Hate,* also about characters who are not ethnically French, he has painted a much darker vision.

In America, where for all our problems we are long accustomed to being a melting pot, it is hard to realize how monolithic most European nations have been—especially France, where Frenchness is almost a cult, and a political leader like Le Pen can roll up alarming vote totals with his anti-Semitic, anti-immigrant diatribes. The

French neo-Nazi right wing lurks in the shadows of *Hate*, providing it with an unspoken subtext for its French audiences. (Imagine how a moviegoer from Mars would misread a film like *Driving Miss Daisy* if he knew nothing about Southern segregation.)

The three heroes of *Hate* are Vinz (Vincent Cassel), Jewish, working-class; Hubert (Hubert Kounde), from Africa, a boxer, more mature than his friends; and Said (Said Taghmaoui), from North Africa, more lighthearted than his friends. That they hang out with each other reflects the fact that in France friendships are as likely to be based on class as race.

These characters inhabit a world where much of the cultural furniture has been imported from America. They use words like "homeboy." Vinz gives Said a "killer haircut, like in New York." Vinz does a De Niro imitation ("Who you talkin' to?"). There's break-dancing in the movie. Perhaps they like U.S. culture because it is not French, and they do not feel very French, either.

During the course of less than twenty-four hours, they move aimlessly through their suburb and take a brief trip to Paris. They have run-ins with the cops, who try to clear them off a rooftop hangout that has become such a youth center it even has its own hot-dog stand. They move on the periphery of riots that have started after the police shooting of an Arab youth. When his younger sister's school is burned down, Vinz's Jewish grandmother warns, "You start out like that, you'll end up not going to temple."

What underlies everything they do is the inescapable fact that they have nothing to do. They have no jobs, no prospects, no serious hopes of economic independence, no money, few ways to amuse themselves except by hanging out. They are not bad kids, not criminals, not particularly violent (the boxer is the least violent), but they have been singled out by age, ethnicity, and appearance as probably troublemakers. Treated that way by the police, they respond—almost whether they want to or not.

As a filmmaker, Kassovitz has grown since his first film. His black-and-white camera is alert, filling the frame with meaning his characters are not aware of. Many French films place their characters in such picturesque settings—Paris, Nice—that it is easy to see them as more colorful than real. But the concrete suburbs where Kassovitz sets his film (the same sterile settings that were home to Eric Rohmer's cosmically different *Boyfriends and Girlfriends* in 1987) give back nothing. These are empty vistas of space—architectural deserts—that flaunt their hostility to the three young men, as if they were designed to provide no cover.

The film's ending is more or less predictable and inevitable, but effective all the same. The film is not about its ending. It is not about the landing, but about the fall. *Hate* is, I suppose, a Generation X film, whatever that means, but more mature and insightful than the American GenX movies. In America we cling to the notion that we have choice, and so if our GenX heroes are alienated from society, it is because they choose to be—it's their "lifestyle." In France, Kassovitz says, it is society that has made the choice.

## Hav Plenty ★ ½

R, 92 m., 1998

Christopher Scott Cherot (Lee Plenty), Chenoa Maxwell (Havilland Savage), Hill Harper (Michael Simmons), Tammi Katherine Jones (Caroline Gooden), Robinne Lee (Leigh Darling), Reginald James (Felix Darling). Directed by Christopher Scott Cherot and produced by Cherot and Robyn M. Greene. Screenplay by Cherot.

I've grown immune to the information that a movie is "a true story," but when a movie begins with that promise *and* a quote from the Bible, I get an uneasy feeling. And when it starts with a "true story," a Bible quote *and* clips from home movies, *and* photos of several main characters, I wonder if I'm watching a movie or a research project. Amateur writers love to precede their own prose with quotations. I don't know whether they think it's a warm-up or a good luck charm.

*Hav Plenty* is basically an amateur movie, with some of the good things and many of the bad that go along with first-time efforts. Set in a comfortable milieu of affluent African-Americans, it's ostensibly the autobiographical story of its writer-director, Christopher Scott Cherot, who plays a homeless writer named Lee Plenty. As the movie opens, he's cat-sitting for a woman named Havilland Savage (Chenoa Maxwell), who has just broken up with a famous musician. She's with her family in Washington, D.C., for New Year's Eve, and invites him to come down and join them, and he does. (So much for the cat.) At the end of the movie, there's a thank-you to "the real Havilland Savage," and I gather most of the things in the movie actually happened, in one way or another. How else to account for an episode involving the offscreen explosion of a toilet?

Cherot plays Lee Plenty as a smart young man of maddening passivity. The plot essentially consists of scenes in which Havilland's best friend Caroline throws herself at Plenty, who rebuffs her. Then Havilland's sister, who has only been married for a month, throws herself at Plenty, but he rebuffs her too. Then Havilland herself throws herself at Plenty, and he does his best to rebuff her. Although we see the beginning of a sex scene, he eventually eludes her too. The movie ends with a scene at a film festival at which Plenty speaks after the premiere of a film that is a great deal like this one.

As a young man I would have been quite capable of writing and starring in a movie in which three beautiful women threw themselves at me. I would have considered this so logical that I would not have bothered, as Cherot does not bother, to write myself any dialogue establishing myself as intelligent, charming, seductive, etc. I would assume that the audience could take one look at me and simply intuit that I had all of those qualities. So I can accept that the homeless Lee Plenty character is irresistible, even to a newlywed and to a beautiful, rich ex-fiancée of a big star. What I cannot accept is that he fights them all off with vague excuses and evasions. "He's not gay," the women assure each other. That I believe. But either he's asexual, or exhibiting the symptoms of chronic fatigue syndrome.

*Hav Plenty* is not a film without charm, but, boy, does it need to tighten the screws on its screenplay. The movie's dialogue is mostly strained, artificial small talk, delivered unevenly by the actors, who at times seem limited to one take (how else to account for fluffed lines?). There are big setups without payoffs, as when Hav's grandmother insists, "You're going to marry him!" And nightmare dream sequences without motivation or purpose. And awkward scenes like the one where the newlywed sister tells her husband that something went on between her and Plenty. The husband enters the room, removes his jacket to reveal bulging muscles, and socks poor Plenty in the stomach. This scene illustrates two of my favorite obligatory cliches: (1) The husband is told only enough of the story to draw exactly the wrong conclusion, and (2) all muscular characters in movies always take off outer garments to reveal their muscles before hitting someone.

*Hav Plenty* is basically a three-actress movie; Cherot, as the male lead, is so vague and passive he barely has a personality (listen to his rambling explanations about why he "doesn't date"). All three actresses (Chenoa Maxwell as Hav, Tammi Katherine Jones as Hav's best friend, and Robinne Lee as the married sister) have strong energy and look good on the screen. With better direction and more takes, I suspect they'd seem more accomplished in their performances. But *Hav Plenty* is more of a first draft than a finished product.

## He Got Game ★ ★ ★ ½

R, 131 m., 1998

Denzel Washington (Jake Shuttlesworth), Ray Allen (Jesus Shuttlesworth), Milla Jovovich (Dakota Burns), Rosario Dawson (Lala Bonilla), Hill Harper (Coleman "Booger" Sykes), Zelda Harris (Mary Shuttlesworth), Ned Beatty (Warden Wyatt), Jim Brown (Spivey). Directed by Spike Lee and produced by Jon Kilik and Lee. Screenplay by Lee.

Spike Lee brings the spirit of a poet to his films about everyday reality. *He Got Game*, the story of the pressures on the nation's best high school basketball player, could have been a gritty docudrama, but it's really more of a heartbreaker about a father and his son.

Lee uses visual imagination to lift his material into the realms of hopes and dreams. Consider his opening sequence, where he wants to establish the power of basketball as a sport and an obsession. He could have given us a montage of hot NBA action, but no: He uses the music of Aaron Copland to score a series of scenes in which American kids—boys, girls, rich, poor, black, white, in school and on playgrounds—play the game. All it needs is a ball and a hoop; compared to this simplicity, Jerry Seinfeld observes, when we attend other sports we're cheering laundry.

This opening evocation is matched by the closing shots of *He Got Game*, in which Lee goes beyond reality to find the perfect way to end his film: His final image is simple and very daring, and goes beyond words or plot to summarize the heart of the story. Seeing his films, I am saddened by how many filmmakers allow themselves to fall into the lazy rhythms of TV, where groups of people exchange dialogue. Movies are not just conversations on film; they can give us images that transform.

*He Got Game* is Lee's best film since *Malcolm X* (1982). It stars Denzel Washington as Jake, a man in prison for the manslaughter of his wife (we learn in a flashback that the event was a lot more complicated than that). His son, Jesus (Ray Allen), is the nation's top prospect. The state governor makes Jake an offer: He'll release him for a week, and if he can talk his son into signing a letter of intent to attend Big State University, the governor will reduce Jake's sentence.

The son is not happy to see Jake ("I don't have a father. Why is there a stranger in the house?"). He still harbors deep resentment, although his sister, Mary (Zelda Harris), has understood and forgiven. Jesus (named not after Christ but after a basketball player) is under incredible pressure. Recruiting offers arrive daily from colleges, and even his girlfriend Lala (Rosario Dawson) is involved; aware that she's likely to be dropped when Jesus goes on to stardom, she's working with a sports agent who wants the kid to turn pro ("He's a friend of the family," she keeps saying, as if her family would just happen to have a high-powered agent as a pal).

Spike Lee's connections with pro ball have no doubt given him a lot of insight into what talented high school players go through. There's a scene in *Hoop Dreams* where he exhorts all-stars at a summer basketball camp to be aware of how they're being used. In *He Got Game*, the temptations come thick and fast: job offers, a new Lexus, $10,000 from his own coach, even a couple of busty "students" who greet him in a dorm room with their own recruiting techniques.

Jake, on the other hand, faces bleak prospects. He moves into a flophouse next door to a hooker (Milla Jovovich) who is beaten by her pimp. Gradually they become friends, and he tries to help her. He also tries to reach his son, and it's interesting the way Lee and Washington let Jake use silence, tact, and patience in the process. Jake doesn't try a frontal assault, maybe because he knows his son too well. Finally it all comes down to a one-on-one confrontation in which the son is given the opportunity to understand and even pity his father.

This is not so much a movie about sports as about capitalism. It doesn't end, as the formula requires, with a big game. In fact, it never creates artificial drama with game sequences, even though Ray Allen, who plays for the Milwaukee Bucks, is that rarity, an athlete who can act. It's about the real stakes, which involve money more than final scores, and showmanship as much as athletics.

For many years in America, sports and big business have shared the same rules and strategies. One reason so many powerful people are seen in the stands at NBA games is that the modern game objectifies the same kind of warfare that takes place in high finance; while "fans" think it's all about sportsmanship and winning, the insiders are thinking in corporate and marketing metaphors.

*He Got Game* sees this clearly and unsentimentally (the sentiment is reserved for the father and son). There is a scene on a bench between Jesus and his girlfriend in which she states, directly and honestly, what her motivations are, and they are the same motivations that shape all of professional sports: It's not going to last forever, so you have to look out for yourself and make all the money you can. Of course, Spike Lee still cheers for the Knicks, and I cheer for the Bulls, but it's good to know what you're cheering for. At the end of *He Got Game*, the father and son win, but so does the system.

## Heaven's Prisoners ★ ★

R, 132 m., 1996

---

Alec Baldwin (Dave Robicheaux), Kelly Lynch (Annie Robicheaux), Mary Stuart Masterson (Robin Gaddis), Eric Roberts (Bubby Rocque), Teri Hatcher (Claudette Rocque), Vondie Curtis Hall (Minos P. Dautrieve), Badja Djola (Batist), Samantha Lagpacan (Alafair). Directed by Phil Joanou and produced by Albert S. Ruddy, Andre E. Morgan, and Leslie Greif. Screenplay by Harley Peyton and Scott Frank.

---

If Louisiana did not exist, Hollywood would need to invent it. In fact, Louisiana *does* exist and Hollywood *still* needs to invent it. Consider *Heaven's Prisoners,* such an overwrought and high-strung example of melodramatic excess that they should have scheduled rest breaks for the actors. The movie has plot enough for three films, although still not quite enough to make sense of this one.

I will attempt a concise plot summary: Retired rogue cop. Plane crash. Scuba air tanks run dry. Cute little Salvadoran orphan. Bait shop. Drug runner. Furniture stripper. Federal agent. Recovering alcoholic. Bad guy named Bubba Rocque ("One of those guys who was always eating light bulbs and pushing thumb tacks into his kneecaps"). Bar named Smilin' Jack's. Rainy night massacre. Local Mafia don. Stripper who gets fingers broken, leaves for Key West. Bubba's wife, nude on balcony. Shoot-out in the French Quarter. Fight on a streetcar. A beating on the bayou. An electrocution in a bathtub. Sex scenes. Revenge scenes. All of this *and* a scene where a character tastes the ring of moisture left by a cold drink and identifies who must have been drinking it, even though gin cannot permeate glass and the moisture would have been, according to the best theories of condensation, pure water.

All the movie is really missing is a zydeco band and a mess of rice and beans. The former cop is Dave Robicheaux (Alec Baldwin), who retired from the force after a couple of guys got killed. Now he runs a bait shop and charter service with his wife (Kelly Lynch), the furniture stripper. Bubba Rocque (I like the spelling of the last name) went to high school with Dave, which qualifies Dave to say, with fierce conviction, the immortal line "I *know* Bubba Rocque!" Bubba (Eric Roberts) is now the kind of guy who has a boxing ring set up on the lawn of his plantation, so he can go a couple of rounds before cocktails. Bubba's wife (Teri Hatcher) meanwhile stands naked on the balcony, boldly challenging Dave to go where no man has gone before, except for every other man in the parish.

So venomous is the atmosphere of evil in this movie that it permeates everything, which is the only way to account for Mary Stuart Masterson (the shining light of *Fried Green Tomatoes* and *Benny & Joon*) as the stripper. To be sure, she has a heart of gold, but then strippers, on the average, are always just about the nicest people in the movies where they appear.

Everyone works very hard in this movie, and at a certain level it is possible to appreciate the simple craft and gusto that went into it. Eric Roberts is a splendid and complex villain, with his corn-rowed hair, his lazy drawl, and his wife as his cross to bear in life. Alec Baldwin is cool, earnest, and menacing as the hero, although I have seen him on the stage in *A Streetcar Named Desire* and feel he will agree this is not his best work. The photography by Harris Savides strikes a nice balance between the humid and the tumid, and Phil Joanou *(State of Grace, Final Analysis)* is tireless in his determination to get through four hours of material in two hours and twelve minutes flat.

But the material is so absurd that when the characters try to become believable, they only cast it in stark relief. Somehow a movie like this demands *worse* acting. It's unsettling when the actors know the back-stories of their characters better than the audience knows the front-stories.

## Heavy ★ ★ ★ ½

NO MPAA RATING, 105 m., 1996

Pruitt Taylor Vince (Victor), Liv Tyler (Callie), Shelley Winters (Dolly Modino), Deborah Harry (Delores), Joe Grifasi (Leo). Directed by James Mangold and produced by Richard Miller. Screenplay by Mangold.

Pete and Dolly's restaurant is the kind of place where the regulars step behind the counter to help themselves to another cup of coffee, and in that gesture you sense it is their home. It is certainly home for Dolly, for her fat son Victor, and for Delores, who has been a waitress there for fifteen years. It's home in the sense that their lives have been invested there, and they have nothing better to turn to.

You've been in places like this. You sit over a second cup of coffee and people-watch, trying to guess the secrets of the sad-eyed waitress and the drunk at the bar and the pizza cook who looks like he's serving a sentence. You don't guess the true horror of the place, which is that there are no secrets, because everyone here knows all about everyone else, inside and out, top to bottom, and has for years.

Dolly (Shelley Winters) sits in an easy chair in the kitchen, complaining about her health and citing the vague sayings of her dead husband, Pete. Delores (Deborah Harry) had an affair with Pete years ago, but Pete and the affair were both so meaningless that even Dolly can hardly stir herself to resentment. Leo (Joe Grifasi), who plants himself at the bar every night, is a nice-looking middle-aged guy who circles his drink protectively with his forearms, while his eyes follow Delores and he uneasily balances the hazards of a relationship against the certainty of another drink. Delores pours Leo's drinks and ponders the fact that there are exactly two men in the whole world she seems likely to ever have sex with: Leo and Victor, the mama's boy. And Victor makes pizza and says nothing, and his eyes dart back and forth like a wounded animal looking to make a break.

This situation has continued for years when Dolly, who knows exactly what she's doing, introduces a new element. She hires another waitress, Callie (Liv Tyler), a tall, coltish college girl whose sexuality wakens all of the sleepers. Victor dreams of romance with her. Leo entertains possibilities. Delores considers her Dolly's "revenge" for the long-ago affair with Pete. Callie is more or less oblivious to their furiously humming thoughts; she has her hands full learning to wait tables.

James Mangold's *Heavy* is basically about Victor. Pruitt Taylor Vince plays him almost without words and usually without expression: He has been emotionally slapped down so many times that like a whipped cur he slinks into his corner of the kitchen and makes pizza, his little eyes peering out through the food shelf at Callie as she waits on customers. Delores sees this and makes her move, in a scene where sheer mechanical sexual need (not romance, love, or lust) is expressed as bluntly and sadly as in any movie I can remember.

These people are so lonely. There is the night Leo gets too drunk to go home. Dolly and Victor bring him to their place, where he shares Victor's bedroom and the thin consolations of pornography. There is the way Victor prepares his mother's breakfast every morning, under the steady hail of her running commentary. The way that a vast change in his life hardly budges his routine. The way a mislaid photograph becomes the emblem of an entire other life that Victor will never live.

Odd, how the heart finds hope. When we are weighing the possibility of love with someone, we do not compare their reality with our reality. We compare their reality with our need, so there is always a perfect fit. Is Victor foolish to dream of Callie? Yes, but in the long run Callie will be lonely too. In fifteen years, she may be just like Delores. And Delores will still be like Delores. And Leo will still be drinking and plotting his next move. We pay for our coffee and leave. We're not like that.

## Heidi Fleiss, Hollywood Madam ★ ★ ★ ★

NO MPAA RATING, 106 m., 1996

A documentary featuring Heidi Fleiss, Ivan Nagy, Madam Alex, Victoria Sellers, Cookie, Daryl Gates, L'Hua Reid, and others. Directed and produced by Nick Broomfield.

*Eventually we'll never know each other. Probably very soon.*

—Heidi Fleiss on Ivan Nagy

Oh, the face of evil can be charming. Remember Hannibal Lecter. Or consider, in the real world, the case of Ivan Nagy. He is a sometime Hollywood movie director who was also—if you can believe his detractors—a pimp, a drug dealer, and a police informer who betrayed his lover while still sleeping with her. He has an impish little smile that he allows to play around his face, and it implicates you in his sleaze. "Come on," the smile suggests, "who are we kidding? We're all men of the world here; we know this stuff goes on."

Ivan Nagy was a key player in the life of Heidi Fleiss, the *Hollywood Madam*, who was sentenced to three years for procuring prostitutes for an A-list of top Hollywood players and free-spending Arabs. Heidi was not an innocent when she met Nagy. At sixteen, she was already the lover of the millionaire financial swindler Bernie Cornfield. But it was Nagy who (according to the legendary Madam Alex) "sold" Heidi to Alex for $500, then used her as a mole to take over Alex's thriving call girl operation. And it was Nagy who eventually turned Heidi over to the police—again, if Madam Alex can be believed.

What is intriguing about *Heidi Fleiss, Hollywood Madam* is that no one can necessarily be believed. This is an endlessly suggestive, tantalizing documentary in which the young life of Heidi Fleiss is reflected back at us from funhouse mirrors: now she is a clever businesswoman, now a dupe, now a cynical hooker, now an innocent wrapped around the little finger of a manipulative hustler. Watching the film, we hear several versions of the same stories. Someone is lying, yes—but is anyone telling the truth?

Nick Broomfield is an enterprising documentary filmmaker for the BBC who tracks his prey with a lightweight camera and sound equipment that can hear around corners. This film is the record of his six months on the case of Heidi Fleiss. She might seem like an insignificant, even pathetic figure, but by the time Broomfield is finished, she has become a victim, and almost sympathetic, if only in contrast with the creatures she dealt with. She wanted to be bad, but had absolutely no idea what she was getting into. "As much bravado as she displays, to me she's still a little kid," her mother tells Broomfield.

Her *mother* participated in this documentary? Most certainly. And so did Heidi and Nagy and Victoria Sellers (Peter's daughter and Heidi's best friend) and Madam Alex and former Los Angeles police chief Daryl Gates. They participated because Broomfield paid them to talk. Madam Alex counts out her cash carefully, and we see Gates pocketing $2,500 before submitting to Broomfield's questions.

What we learn is that Alex was for many years the most successful madam in Los Angeles. Arrested for tax evasion, she got off with probation after an LAPD detective testified she was a valuable police informant. She allegedly used Nagy, a filmmaker with a respectable front, to obtain airline tickets for her since she couldn't get a credit card. Perhaps he also located cocaine for her clients. She says Nagy "sold" her Heidi, at around the age of twenty, and that Heidi helped Nagy steal away her empire. Heidi was the front, but Nagy was always the power and the brains.

Nagy says Madam Alex was "one of the most evil women I've met in my life." He smiles. He asks Broomfield, "Do I look like I need $500?" Then he sells him a home video of himself and Heidi. In the video, he tries to get her to take off her clothes, and she observes with concern but not alarm that "some green stuff" is coming out of that part of a man's anatomy he least desires to produce green stuff. A man who would sell that video needs $500.

Broomfield finds Mike Brambles, an LAPD detective (now in jail for robbery), who says Heidi's problem was that she was a bad police informant. She didn't cooperate, and so Nagy set her up to take the fall. Heidi doesn't seem to know if this is true. She describes her business (her clients wanted "typical untouched Southern California eighteen-year-old girls-next-door. No high heels. Blondes, blondes, blondes"). She is realistic ("A lot of times they'd hire us just to watch them do drugs"). She confesses to always having been attracted to older men ("Over forty, they're all the right age to me").

There is talk of a shadowy Israeli named Cookie, who everyone in the film seems frightened of. If Nagy is the power behind Heidi, is Cookie behind everything? No one will say. Broomfield is tireless in poking his nose, and camera, into these lives. During one visit to Alex he finds her maid using incense to purify the apartment against evil spirits. Nagy conducts a tour of his art collection. Heidi is interviewed in front of her bookshelf, which contains a set of the Great Books of the Western World: Did she buy them or did a client trade them in?

At the end of the film, after Heidi has been found guilty and is going to prison, and she has every reason to hate Nagy, there is a remarkable scene. Nagy calls her on the phone and lets us eavesdrop as he sweet-talks her. You can tell she still falls for him. Nagy smiles to the camera, helplessly: "There you go," he says. Charming.

## Hercules ★ ★ ★ ½

G, 93 m., 1997

With the voices of: Tate Donovan (Hercules [Herc]), Susan Egan (Megara [Meg]), James Woods (Hades), Rip Torn (Zeus), Danny DeVito (Philoctetes [Phil]), Samantha Eggar (Hera), Bobcat Goldthwait (Pain), Matt Frewer (Panic), Paul Shaffer (Hermes). Directed by John Musker and Ron Clements and produced by Musker, Clements, and Alice Dewey. Screenplay by Musker, Clements, Bob Shaw, Don McEnery, and Irene Mecchi.

The wonder is that it took Disney so long to get to the gods of Greek mythology. *Hercules* jumps into the ancient legends feetfirst, cheerfully tossing out what won't fit and combining what's left into a new look and a lighthearted style.

Starting with a day-glo Olympian city in the clouds, and using characters based on the drawing style of the British illustrator Gerald

Scarfe, this new animated feature has something old (mythology), something new (a Pegasus equipped with helicopter blades), something borrowed (a gospel singing group) and something blue (the flaming hair of Hades, which turns red when he gets mad—it works like a mood ring).

Hercules, known as Herc, is a rather different character here than in the pages of *Bullfinch's Mythology.* There, you may recall, he murdered his wife and children. Here he's a big, cute hunk who's so clumsy he knocks over temples by accident, but you gotta love the guy.

In fact, as film critic Jack Matthews has pointed out, the Disney storytellers have merged the Hercules of myth with the modern-day superhero Superman: In both *Hercules* and the Superman story, the hero has otherworldly origins, is separated from his parents, is adopted by humble earthlings, and feels like a weirdo as a kid before finally finding his true strength and calling.

It's getting to be an in-joke, how Disney shapes the story in every new animated feature to match its time-tested underlying formula. The hero is essentially an orphan. There is a colorful villain who schemes against him. There are two twirpy little characters who do a double act (in *The Lion King* they were the friendly Timon and Pumbaa; here they're the scheming Pain and Panic). There are trusted sidekicks and advisers (not only the faithful Pegasus, but also a little satyr named Phil who signs up as a personal trainer). And there's a sexy dame who winds up in the hero's arms, although not without difficulties.

Is Disney repeating a formula? No more than mythology always repeats itself; as Joseph Campbell taught George Lucas, many of the eternal human myths have the same buried structures, and Disney's annual animated features are the myths of our time.

Although I thought 1996's *Hunchback of Notre Dame* was a more original and challenging film, *Hercules* is lighter, brighter, and more cheerful, with more for kids to identify with. Certainly they can care about Herc (voice by Tate Donovan), child of a god and a human, who must leave his father, Zeus (Rip Torn), in heaven and toil among the mortals to earn his ticket back to paradise. Herc stumbles through adolescence as the clumsy "Jerkules" before a statue of his father comes to life and reads him the rules. His tutor will be the satyr Philoctetes (Danny DeVito), who, like all the best movie trainers, advises his student to do as he says and not as he does.

Playing on the other team is Hades, Lord of the Underworld, voiced by James Woods with diabolical glee and something of the same verbal inventiveness that Robin Williams brought to *Aladdin* (Hades to Fate: "You look like a fate worse than death"). Hades is assisted by the two little form-shifting sidekicks Pain and Panic (Bobcat Goldthwait and Matt Frewer), who are able to disguise themselves in many different shapes while meddling with Herc's well-being. Another one of Hades' weapons is the curvaceous Megara (Susan Egan), known as Meg, who is assigned to seduce Herc but ends up falling in love with the lug.

The movie has been directed by John Musker and Ron Clements, who inaugurated the modern era of Disney animation with the inspired *Little Mermaid* (1989) and also made *Aladdin* (1992). The look of their animation has a new freshness because of the style of Gerald Scarfe, famous in the United Kingdom for his sharp-penned caricatures of politicians and celebrities; the characters here are edgier and less rounded than your usual Disney heroes (although the cuddly Pegasus is in the traditional mode). The color palate, too, makes less use of basic colors and stirs in more luminous shades, giving the picture a subtly different look that suggests it is different in geography and history from most Disney pictures.

What *The Little Mermaid* began and all of the subsequent Disney animation features have continued is a sly combination of broad strokes for children and in-jokes and satire for adults. It's hard to explain, for example, why a black female gospel quintet would be singing the legend of Hercules in the opening sequence (returning later to add more details), but the songs (by Alan Menken and David Zippel) are fun, and probably more entertaining than the expected Greek chorus. Other throwaways: lines like "get ready to rumble"; images like Pegasus outfitted by Phil like an LAPD helicopter; Herc's promotion of his own prehistoric exercise video; an arch saying OVER 500,000,000 SERVED"; Hades offering two burning thumbs "way up for our leading lady"; Hermes (Paul Shaffer) observing the preening gods and quipping, "I haven't seen so much love in one room since Narcissus looked at himself"; and quick little sight gags like a spider hanging from the nose of Fate, who disposes of it in a spectacularly unappetizing way.

Will children like this subject matter, or will they find Greek myth unfamiliar? I think they'll love it. And in an age when kids get their heroes from TV instead of books, is Hercules any more unfamiliar than Pocahontas (or Aladdin or the Hunchback, for that matter)? A riffle through *Bullfinch's Mythology* suggests dozens more Disney plots, all safely out of copyright. Next: *Ulysses*?

## High School High ★ ½
PG-13, 86 m., 1996

Jon Lovitz (Mr. Clark), Tia Carrere (Victoria), Louise Fletcher (Mrs. Doyle), Mekhi Phifer (Griff), Malinda Williams (Natalie), Guillermo Diaz (Paco), Lexie Bigham (Two Bags), Gil Espinoza (Alonzo). Directed by Hart Bochner and produced by David Zucker, Robert LoCash, and Gil Netter. Screenplay by Zucker, LoCash, and Pat Proft.

*High School High* opens with a big laugh ("produced by the producer formerly known as David Zucker"), and goes downhill. Zucker, associated with the *Naked Gun* movies, wants to do the same thing here for the urban high school genre, but the movie makes two mistakes: (1) it isn't very funny, and (2) it makes the crucial error of taking its story seriously and angling for a happy ending.

Jon Lovitz stars as Mr. Clark, a teacher at the posh Wellington Academy (the switchboard operator answers the phone with, "Are you white?"). Then he finds himself at the inner-city Marion Berry High School, where on the statue out in front the flag has been replaced by a crack pipe. Bumper stickers boast, "Proud Parent of a D Average Student." Career Day offers two choices, the Marines or the Michigan Militia.

His only friend in the school is Victoria, played by the fetching Tia Carrere as an optimist who believes in education and even in Mr. Clark. The classroom is the usual collection of rebellious louts, and of course the principal is an uncaring martinet (played by Louise Fletcher, the original Nurse Ratchet). But through the help of one student who cares (Mekhi Phifer) Clark is able to inspire great changes.

Movies like this depend on wall-to-wall laughs, and more laughs on the back walls. In the best of the genre, almost everything is a joke in one way or another. Here the targets are easy, and after some potshots, the movie begins an inexorable drift into actually trying to follow its plot to its logical conclusion. You get the feeling with some of the Zucker films that after every draft they cracked a whip over the writers and said, "More! Fifty percent more gags!" Not here.

## Homage ★ ★ ½
R, 97 m., 1996

Blythe Danner (Katherine Samuel), Frank Whaley (Archie Landrum), Sheryl Lee (Lucy Samuel), Bruce Davison (Joseph), Danny Nucci (Gilbert). Directed by Ross Kagan Marks and produced by Elan Sassoon and Mark Medoff. Screenplay by Medoff.

Frank Whaley has appeared in at least twenty movies, mostly with high profiles *(Pulp Fiction, Broken Arrow)*, but he works quietly, insinuating himself into a scene instead of stealing it. Only in the last couple of years have I started to notice his work, as he moved up to leads playing a certain type: the helpful, self-effacing, flattering new arrival in your life who wants to take it over.

In *Swimming With Sharks* (1995) he was the new personal assistant to a powerful, obnoxious producer (Kevin Spacey). Now, in *Homage*, he plays Archie, a strange young man with a Ph.D. in math, who applies for a summer job as an assistant on a New Mexico ranch. Imagine his excitement when he discovers that Katherine, the ranch owner (Blythe Danner), is being visited by her daughter Lucy (Sheryl Lee), who plays the lead in a trash TV show.

The show is named *Banyon's Band*. She plays a detective who's a hooker and works with four street kids to solve crimes. Archie is a student of the series, and also of the low-budget soft-core films Lucy has made, which he studies in the privacy of his room. For the mother, Archie looks like a real find ("I'll balance your soil"). Lucy is not so sure. As she hangs around the house wearing see-through blouses and getting drunk, Archie tries to insinuate himself. He's writing a screenplay, he confides, that's just for her.

Whaley is scary in this role. He delivers the kind of smooth, well-practiced compliments that mark anger and envy—and lust, in this case. He eavesdrops a lot. He knows that Katherine and Lucy do not have a happy relationship, that Lucy has been off drugs four months but is drinking heavily, that Katherine is exhausted by the emotional demands of her troubled daughter. And Archie thinks, foolishly, that since the three of them are on a ranch miles from nowhere, maybe Lucy will want to become his lover. Or maybe Katherine. She's good-looking, and a true groupie will settle for proximity if the real thing isn't reachable.

The celebrity stalker plot could have generated tension and suspense, but the director, Ross Kagan Marks, and the writer, Mark Medoff, have decided to make the movie unnecessarily artsy by starting with the climax and working back. Someone is killed in the opening shots. We know the victim and the killer, and so the movie becomes a flashback rather than a developing crisis. That can work, but it doesn't work here, and it denies Whaley the opportunity to conceal his sinister side, since the secret is out.

There are two key supporting characters. Bruce Davison, always persuasive, is the hard-boozing local public defender who once loved Katherine himself, and Danny Nucci is the Mexican-American jail guard. Archie, described in a news report as a "demented Einstein," practices his sarcasm on both of them: He's a verbal bully who wants to find out how far he can push them, and does.

Medoff, who wrote *Children of a Lesser God*, adapted this screenplay from his play *The Homage That Follows*. I don't know if the play used the same flashback structure, but the theater depends more on performance than story, so it would have been less distracting there. The play would also have been spared Marks's flash-cuts of coming events, which are a distraction.

Intact at the center of the film are the performances: Whaley, creepily ingratiating; Lee, depressed and angry; and Danner, who in a way enjoys having a fan, since her daughter has so many. If this material had been untangled and told from beginning to end, I think it would have added up to more. I have nothing against movies that begin at the end (consider *Citizen Kane*), but they need to earn that technique instead of simply using it to add a little art where none is needed.

## Home Alone 3 ★ ★ ★

PG, 103 m., 1997

Alex D. Linz (Alex), Olek Krupa (Beaupre), Rya Kihlstedt (Alice), Lenny Von Dohlen (Jernigan), David Thornton (Unger), Haviland Morris (Karen), Kevin Kilner (Jack), Marian Seldes (Mrs. Hess). Directed by Raja Gosnell and produced by John Hughes and Hilton Green. Screenplay by Hughes.

"Call me hard-hearted, call me cynical, but please don't call me if they make *Home Alone 3*."

These words, from my review of *Home Alone 2*, now have to be eaten. To my astonishment, I liked the third *Home Alone* movie better than the first two; I'm even going so far as to recommend it, although not to grown-ups unless they are having a very silly day. This movie follows the exact formula of the first two, but is funnier and gentler, has a real charmer for a hero, and provides splendid wish-fulfillment and escapism for kids in, say, the lower grades.

There is even a better rationale for why the hero is left home alone. Played by a winning newcomer named Alex D. Linz, who seems almost too small for a middle initial, the kid gets the chicken pox. His dad is out of town on business, his mom has an emergency at the office, and his brother and sister are at school. So he's left home alone with a beeper number, a fax number, a cell phone number, the number of Mrs. Hess across the street, and dialing "911" as a fallback position.

The subplot has already been set into motion. An international spy ring has stolen a computer chip, and because of an exchange of identical bags at the San Francisco airport, the toy truck containing the chip has ended up at Mrs. Hess's house. Four spies fly to Chicago on the same plane with Mrs. Hess, and have four hours on board to search for the bag, but somehow they fail to find it, and end up deciding to burglarize every house on little Alex's block.

This is going to a lot of extra trouble, in my opinion. They use walkie-talkies, computer programs, surveillance vans, a fake baby buggy and other props in order to be as inefficient and conspicuous as possible, and of course Alex, using his telescope from an attic window, spots them. (Why they never spot Alex up there is the kind of question you're not supposed to ask.)

After he calls the cops twice but no burglars are found, Alex realizes it's up to him. He rigs a lot of elaborate booby traps, just like in the first two movies, and the last forty-five minutes of the film consist of nonstop pratfalls as the bad guys fall for every last trap. As I observed in my review of *Home Alone*, these are the kinds of traps that any eight-year-old could devise if he had a budget of tens of thousands of dollars and the assistance of a crew of movie special effects people.

So, okay. I know the formula, and so does the movie (written, like the first two, by John Hughes). Forewarned and forearmed as I was, why did I actually like *Home Alone 3*? It was partly because of little Alex Linz, who has a genuinely sweet smile on his face as he watches his traps demolish the bad guys. I don't know if he'll have a career like his predecessor, Macaulay Culkin (for his sake, I sort of hope not), but he has the same glint in his eye.

And the booby traps, while painful, are funnier this time. Sure, people fall down dumbwaiters and through floors, and get hit on the head with dumbbells and flower pots, and end up in the frozen swimming pool, but the direction by Raja Gosnell somehow sidesteps the painfulness and makes it okay. The stunts at the end are more pure slapstick and less special effects. And the result is either more entertaining than in the first two films, or I was having a very silly day.

## Homeward Bound II: Lost in San Francisco ★ ★

G, 89 m., 1996

Michael J. Fox (Chance's Voice), Ralph Waite (Shadow's Voice), Sally Field (Sassy's Voice), Sinbad (Riley's Voice), Carla Gugino (Delilah), Robert Hays (Bob Seaver), Kim Greist (Laura Seaver), Veronica Lauren (Hope), Kevin Chevalia (Jamie), Benj Thall (Peter), Max Perlich (Dogcatcher). Directed by David R. Ellis and produced by Barry Jossen. Screenplay by Chris Hauty and Julie Hickson.

The 1993 movie *Homeward Bound: The Incredible Journey* told the story of three pets, two dogs and a cat, who feel they have been abandoned when their human family boards them and goes on a trip to San Francisco. So they escape, and return home across a mountain range, through incredible hardships, while surviving waterfalls and battling mountain lions. It was a pleasant movie and, for what it was, I enjoyed it.

Now comes *Homeward Bound II: Lost in San Francisco*, in which the human family decides to go on a camping trip, and the animals are stranded in the city. That more or less exhausts the permutations, I think, and I expect *Homeward Bound III* will send both humans and animals to Alcatraz.

The movie uses the human characters only briefly, at the beginning and end of the film. The rest of the time, we see and hear the animals, who are gifted with human voices, and who talk without moving their mouths—by telepathy or ventriloquy, I reckon. The animals are Chance, the frisky youngster (voice by Michael J. Fox); Sassy, the fastidious cat (Sally Field); and Shadow, the wise golden retriever (Ralph Waite replaces the late Don Ameche).

These animals don't just talk. They're chatterboxes. Chance in particular seems to have learned the English language from old Jughead comic books, and says things like, "Dogs rule, cats drool" and "Okay, pal—you're toast!" At one point, Chance even steals a Frisbee and uses it to shelter his new girlfriend from the rain, a cognitive feat that is well beyond your average dog. These are not average dogs, however, and after watching them in action for half an hour, I wondered why they didn't simply raise some money by running a game of three-card monte on a street corner, and then take a taxi home.

In the first film, the pets were threatened by the dangers of nature. This time, the dangers of the big city almost overwhelm them. They are followed everywhere by a couple of loutish dogcatchers. And eventually they're befriended by a pack of city dogs, who, of course, have urban black accents. The pack's leader is Riley (voice by Sinbad), who distrusts humans, and it is up to Shadow and Chance to explain that people can sometimes be okay. There is also a love affair between Chance and a city dog named Delilah (Carla Gugino), who, of course, does not have an urban black accent. I leave it to deeper thinkers than me to figure out what the filmmakers are trying to tell us with these choices.

My own feeling is that I have had enough talking animals for the time being. The first movie was good-hearted and I liked it, but since then *Babe* has raised the bar, with animals that not only talk more realistically, but say things that are wittier and more pungent. Of course, as Ed McMahon was always arguing with Johnny Carson, pigs are smarter than horses, so maybe they're smarter than cats and dogs too. They certainly seem to have better agents.

## Hoodlum ★ ★ ★

R, 130 m., 1997

Laurence Fishburne (Bumpy Johnson), Tim Roth (Dutch Schultz), Vanessa L. Williams (Francine Hughes), Andy Garcia (Lucky Luciano), Cicely Tyson (Stephanie St. Clair), Chi McBride (Illinois Gordon), Clarence Williams III (Bub Hewlett), William Atherton (Thomas E. Dewey). Directed by Bill Duke and produced by Frank Mancuso Jr. Screenplay by Chris Brancato.

The business of crime is as much business as crime, as Scorsese demonstrated in *Casino* by centering his story on a gangster who was essentially an accountant and oddsmaker. Now Bill Duke's *Hoodlum* looks into the way the Mafia muscled into the black-run policy racket in Harlem in the 1930s; this is a "gangster movie" in a sense, but it is also about free enterprise, and about how, as the hero says when asked why he didn't go into medicine or law, "I'm a colored man, and white folks left me crime."

Of course, that is not quite the whole story, but by the time Bumpy Johnson (Laurence Fishburne) says it, it's true of him: He's a smart ex-con, returned to the streets of Harlem during its prewar renaissance, when music, arts, and commerce flourished along with the numbers game. He hooks up with old friends, including Illinois Gordon (Chi McBride), who masks his feelings with jokes and introduces him to a social worker, Francine Hughes (Vanessa Williams). Francine sees the good in Bumpy, and encourages him to make something of himself, but Bumpy defends his career choice: "The numbers provide jobs for over 2,000 colored folks right here in Harlem alone. It's the only homegrown business we got."

The game is run by Stephanie St. Clair (Cicely Tyson), known as the Queen of Numbers. She's from the islands, elegant, competitive. She takes on Bumpy as her lieutenant. The mob has up until now let Harlem run its own rackets, but Dutch Schultz (Tim Roth) moves in, trying to take over the numbers. His nominal boss is the powerful Lucky Luciano (Andy Garcia), who disapproves of Schultz because of the way he dresses ("You got mustard on your suit"), and is inclined to stand back and see what happens. He doesn't mind if Schultz takes over Harlem, but is prepared to do business with the Queen and Bumpy if that's the way things work out.

One thing that has kept the Mafia from attaining more power in America is that it has a tendency to murder its most ambitious members; the guys who keep a low profile may survive, but are not leadership material. Imagine a modern corporation run along the same lines. Bumpy is the far-sighted strategist who sees that it's better to talk than fight; Dutch is the thug who itches to start shooting.

This is Bill Duke's second period film set in Harlem, after *A Rage in Harlem* (1991). He likes the clothes, the cars, the intrigue. (In both films, interestingly, he didn't film in Harlem, finding better period locations in Cincinnati for *Rage* and in Chicago for *Hoodlum*.) He builds up to some effective set-pieces, including a massacre that interrupts a trip to the opera; in the payoff, Bumpy and the Queen listen to an aria while he has blood on his shirt.

The film's argument is that the policy racket, like many legitimate homegrown black businesses, was appropriated by whites when it became too powerful. The streets of inner-city America are lined with shuttered storefronts while their former customers line up at Wal-Mart. And, yes, there is an element of racism involved: When I was growing up in Champaign-Urbana in the 1940s and 1950s, the richest black man in town was said to be Wardell Jackson, the reputed local numbers czar. Whites had no problem with the numbers (some played), but they couldn't stop talking about how a black man could make all that money.

Duke and his screenwriter, Chris Brancato, don't make *Hoodlum* into a violent action film, although it has its bloody shoot-outs, but into more of a character study. Schultz is painted as a crude braggart, Lucky Luciano is suave and insightful, and the most intriguing figure among the white characters is crime-fighter Thomas Dewey, who ran for president in 1948 as a reformer, but is portrayed here, in scenes sure to be questioned in many quarters, as a corrupt grafter. (Schultz observes that he is paying off Dewey at the same time the famed prosecutor is getting headlines for trying to put him in jail.)

Bumpy Johnson is played by Fishburne as someone who could have had a legit career, and he's torn when Francine, the social worker, cools toward him because of his occupation. Illinois Gordon, his best friend, also asks hard and idealistic questions, especially after a funeral. By creating these two characters, the screenplay gives Bumpy somewhere to turn and someone to talk to, so he isn't limited to action scenes. As Stephanie St. Clair, Cicely Tyson models her character on real women of the period, who were tough, independent, and used men without caving in to them.

*Hoodlum* is being marketed as a violent action picture, and in a sense it is. But Duke has made a historical drama as much as a thriller, and his characters reflect a time when Harlem seemed poised on the brink of better things, and the despair of the postwar years was not easily seen on its prosperous streets. Was the policy game all that bad? Sure, the odds were stiff, but a couple of times a week, someone had to win. These days, it's called the lottery.

## Hope Floats ★ ★

PG-13, 114 m., 1998

Sandra Bullock (Birdee Pruitt), Harry Connick Jr. (Justin Matisse), Gena Rowlands (Ramona Calvert), Mae Whitman (Bernice Pruitt), Michael Pare (Bill Pruitt), Cameron Finley (Travis), Kathy Najimy (Toni Post). Directed by Forest Whitaker and produced by Lynda Obst. Screenplay by Steven Rogers.

*Hope Floats* begins with a talk show where a woman learns that her husband and her best friend are having an affair. Devastated, she flees from Chicago with her young daughter, and moves back in with her mother in Smithville, Texas. Everybody in Smithville (and the world), of course, witnessed her public humiliation. "Why did you go on that show in the first place?" her mother asks. "Because I wanted a free makeover," she says. "Well, you got one."

The victim's name is Birdee Pruitt (Sandra Bullock), and she was three-time Queen of Corn in Smithville. But she doesn't type and she doesn't compute, and her catty former classmate, who runs the local employment agency, tells her, "I don't see a listing here for prom queen." Birdee finally gets a job in a photo developing lab, where the owner asks her to make extra prints of any "interesting" snapshots.

This material could obviously lead in a lot of different directions. It seems most promising as comedy or satire, but no: *Hope Floats* is a turgid melodrama with the emotional range of a sympathy card.

Consider the cast of characters in Smithville. Birdee is played by Bullock as bewildered by her husband's betrayal (even though he's such a pig that she must have had hints over the years). Birdee's mother, Ramona (Gena Rowlands), is a salt-of-the-earth type who's able to live in a rambling Victorian mansion *and* keep her husband in a luxurious retirement home, despite having no apparent income. Birdee's daughter, Bernice (Mae Whitman), is a little drip who keeps whining that she wants to live with Daddy, despite overwhelming evidence that Daddy is a cretin. And then there's Justin (Harry Connick Jr.), the old boyfriend Birdee left behind, who's still in love with her and spends his free time restoring big old homes. (There is no more reliable indicator of a male character's domestic intentions than when he invites the woman of his dreams to touch his newly installed pine.)

*Hope Floats* is one of those screenplays where everything that will happen is instantly obvious, and yet the characters are forced to occupy a state of oblivion, acting as if it's all a mystery to them. It is obvious that Birdee's first husband is a worthless creep. And that Justin and Birdee will fall in love once again. And that Bernice will not go home to live with Daddy and his new girlfriend. And that the creeps who are still jealous of the onetime Corn Queen will get their comeuppance. The only real mystery in the movie is how Birdee keeps her job at Snappy Snaps despite apparently ruining every roll of film she attempts to process (the only photo she successfully develops during the entire movie is apparently done by magic realism).

I grow restless when I sense a screenplay following a schedule so faithfully that it's like a train conductor with a stopwatch. Consider, for example, the evening of tender romance and passion between Birdee and Justin. What comes next? A fight, of course. There's a grim dinner scene at which everyone stares unhappily at their plates, no doubt thinking they would be having a wonderful time—if only the screenwriter hadn't required an obligatory emotional slump between the false dawn and the real dawn.

I watch these formulas unfold, and I reflect that the gurus who teach those Hollywood screenwriting classes have a lot to answer for. They claim their formulas are based on analysis of successful movies. But since so many movies have been written according to their formulas, there's a kind of self-fulfilling prophecy going on here. Isn't it at least theoretically possible that after a man and a woman spend an evening in glorious romantic bliss, they could still be glowing the next day?

*Hope Floats* was written by Steven Rogers and directed by Forest Whitaker *(Waiting to Exhale)*. It shows evidence of still containing shreds of earlier drafts. At one point, for example, Birdee accuses her mother of embarrassing her as a child with her "roadkill hat and freshly skinned purse." Well, it's a good line, and it suggests that Gena Rowlands will be developed as one of the ditzy eccentrics she plays so well. But actually she's pretty sensible in this movie, and the line doesn't seem to apply.

There's also the problem that the sweet romantic stuff coexists uneasily with harsher scenes, as when little Bernice discovers her daddy doesn't want her to move back in with him. The whole TV talk show setup, indeed, deals the movie a blow from which it never recovers: No film that starts so weirdly should develop so conventionally. Sandra Bullock seems to sense that in her performance; her character wanders through the whole movie like a person who senses that no matter what Harry Connick thinks, she will always be known as the Corn Queen who got dumped on TV.

## The Horse Whisperer ★ ★ ★

PG-13, 160 m., 1998

Robert Redford (Tom Booker), Kristin Scott Thomas (Annie MacLean), Scarlett Johansson (Grace MacLean), Sam Neill (Robert MacLean), Dianne Wiest (Diane Booker), Chris Cooper (Frank Booker), Cherry Jones (Liz Hammond), Ty Hillman (Joe Booker). Directed by Robert Redford and produced by Redford and Patrick Markey. Screenplay by Eric Roth and Richard LaGravenese, based on the novel by Nicholas Evans.

*The Horse Whisperer* is about a man of great patience faced with a woman, a child, and a horse in great need of it. It evokes the healing serenity of the wide-open spaces, and while I suspect that an unhappy New Yorker who moves to Montana is likely to become an unhappy Montanan, I concede that the myth is comforting. In films going back to *Jeremiah Johnson*, Robert Redford has shown that he has a real feeling for the West—he's not a movie tourist—and there is a magnificence in his treatment here that dignifies what is essentially a soap opera.

The story, from the best-selling novel by Nicholas Evans, involves a riding accident that leaves a horse named Pilgrim crippled, and a girl named Grace (Scarlett Johansson) so badly injured that part of her leg must be amputated. The girl's parents are high-powered Manhattanites: The father (Sam Neill) is a lawyer, and the mother, Annie (Kristin Scott Thomas), is clearly modeled on editor Tina Brown.

Their farm workers believe the horse should be put down (it's fearful and skittish), but Annie reads about a famed "horse whisperer" named Tom Booker who heals troubled animals. Booker (Redford) turns her down over the phone, but she's a type-A compulsive who decides to drive both the horse and her daughter to Montana and confront him directly. Her daughter fears "no one will ever want me" with only one leg; if the horse heals, Annie thinks, maybe Grace will heal too.

That's the setup. The heart of the film is in Big Sky country, where Tom Booker runs a cattle ranch with his brother Frank (Chris Cooper) and Frank's wife, Diane (Dianne Wiest). Tom was married once; it was love at first sight, but it didn't last because his city-born wife found the ranch had "too much space for her." Now he's famed for using patience and a gentle touch with difficult horses.

How does horse whispering work? As nearly as I could tell, Tom stares at the horse until the horse gets the idea. Eventually the horse succumbs to its need for love and acceptance. These methods work equally well with women, as both Grace and Annie discover; the girl's anger dissolves, and her mother, a brittle workaholic, finds her hyper personality dissolving in the mountain air—as she falls in love with Tom.

To describe the plot in this way makes it sound cornier than it feels. The elements are borrowed from elsewhere; there's a touch of *The Bridges of Madison County* in the married woman's love for a man who represents freedom, and a touch of *My Friend Flicka* and its sequel, *Thunderhead*, in the treatment of a rebellious horse.

But Redford, as director and star, relates to the underlying themes of the story, which is about city versus country, and responsibility versus passion. The very lifestyle of Redford's ranch is a character in the movie; his plump, cheerful sister-in-law is a contented contrast to Annie, the rail-thin New Yorker who tries to control everything (fretting about her daughter's hospital care, she vows, "I'm going to get to know all the nurses' names"). There are big meals, long hours, and head-clearing rides on the range.

This life has imbued Tom Booker with an empathy that allows him to identify with pain, and for me the best scenes in the movie involved his careful touch with Grace. She's sullen and withdrawn at first, but he insists that Pilgrim will be ridden again—and Grace will ride him. He handles her with respect, and there's a nice moment when he asks her to drive the ranch pickup. She can't drive, she says. "No time like the present to start," he says.

The scenes between Tom and Annie are more problematic. Both adults begin to see the other as the ideal mate they've always been looking for. Love grows between them in unspoken words and quick glances, and eventually it appears that Annie is destined to leave her husband and stay on the ranch with the Bookers. She has fallen so much under the spell of the West that when she's fired from her magazine job, she hardly seems to notice. And Tom sees in her what he needs to see in a woman—what he saw in his wife, until she left.

"This is me," Tom tells her, looking around at the ranch. "This is where I belong. Could you live here?" Yes, says Annie, she could. Maybe that's because she sees the West in terms of a Redford film. Before she burns her bridges, I'd advise her to see *City Slickers.* I never felt much chemistry between Scott Thomas and Redford; their characters are in love with the idea of one another, not with each other's bodies and souls. And so Redford and his writers, Eric Roth and Richard LaGravenese, were correct to supply their story with a different ending than Nicholas Evans's climax.

What works is the beauty of the western country, the tactful way Tom deals with Grace, and the touching scenes in which the damaged horse is healed. The story moves a little too slowly, but it respects its characters, and even the lawyer from New York, when he finally arrives out west, turns out to be a person of insight and intelligence (his confession to his wife is really more touching than anything Tom says to her). *The Horse Whisperer* treads on the brink of contrivance, but the honesty of its feelings pulls it through.

## The Horseman on the Roof ★ ★ ★

R, 118 m., 1995

Juliette Binoche (Pauline de Theus), Olivier Martinez (Angelo Pardi), Pierre Arditi (Mr. Peyrolle), Francois Cluzet (The Doctor), Jean Yanne (The Peddler), Claudio Amendola (Maggionari), Carlo Cecchi (Guiseppe), Christiane Cohendy (Mme. Peyrolle). Directed by Jean-Paul Rappeneau and produced by Rene Cleitman. Screenplay by Rappeneau, Nina Companeez, and Jean-Claude Carriere.

*The Horseman on the Roof* is a rousing romantic epic about beautiful people having thrilling adventures in breathtaking landscapes. Hollywood is too sophisticated (or too jaded) to make movies like this anymore; it comes from France, billed as the most expensive movie in French history.

It's a grand entertainment, intelligently written, well researched, set in the midst of a nineteenth-century cholera epidemic. A newcomer named Olivier Martinez stars, as an Italian patriot named Angelo Pardi who has escaped to France from the Austrian invaders who have overrun the north of his own country. There he encounters the beautiful Pauline de Theus (Juliette Binoche), wife of a French noble, who bravely seeks her older husband in the plague- and terror-ridden land.

Of course these two people are destined to fall in love. But the movie wisely delays the inevitable; it's as coy as *The African Queen* in the way its two lead characters share adventures and danger while denying, to each other and to themselves, that a strong attraction is growing between them.

Pauline was sixteen, the daughter of a country doctor, when she married her husband, who was forty years older. Now she wants to return to the quarantined areas of France, where the cholera epidemic lays waste whole villages, to find him. Angelo comes along to aid and protect her, and their quest is told in scenes of action, adventure, and fascinating historical detail.

The most memorable visuals in the movie involve the cholera epidemic—its victims, the panic it inspires, and especially the carrion birds that stalk fearlessly among the dead and dying. (At one point Pauline is attacked by a bird and observes, "They don't fear men since they have started to eat them.")

There are scenes here that reminded me of similar moments in *Restoration* (1995), another lavishly produced period film about a world in the grip of disease. At one point Angelo pauses in a village to drink from a well and is attacked and nearly killed by the villagers, convinced he is a well-poisoner. In another scene a mayor's elegant dinner party is reduced to anarchy by the merest suggestion that someone at the table might be contagious.

Eventually, still seeking her husband, Pauline voluntarily goes into quarantine—into a vast makeshift hospital set aside for the dying and their loved ones—and Angelo follows her. The scenes here are fearful and touching, and we learn a little of the crude medical resources, mostly based on ignorance, that were being used against cholera. Not much was known about how germs spread disease, but in one scene, after the characters have possibly been contaminated, they rub alcohol on their skin and set it briefly alight to kill the bacteria.

But the movie is mostly about adventure and romance, not hospital wards, and there are thrilling stunt and special-effects sequences, directed by Jean-Paul Rappeneau with an eye for the small detail as well as the vast canvas (Angelo escapes from a mob by fleeing over rooftops, and his progress is intercut by the movements of an inquisitive little cat, which follows him fearlessly and curiously).

Martinez, as the hero, is a new leading man in the style of the young Jean-Paul Belmondo, who starred in films like *Cartouche*. Binoche usually plays sophisticated young women of the world (she was the woman gripped by sexual passion in Philip Kaufman's *Unbearable Lightness of Being* and Louis Malle's *Damage*, and the composer's widow in Krzysztof Kieslowski's *Blue*). This time she is much simpler—a woman loyal to her husband, for whom duty is a higher calling than passion.

Her reserve, and the instinctive chivalry of Angelo, create a sexual tension between them that is more interesting because it is not acted upon. Their restraint sets the stage for an eventual development all the more romantic because it is based on love and faith, not carnal satisfaction.

*The Horseman on the Roof* was produced by the French in an attempt to recapture their own domestic market from the inroads of Hollywood's big-budget romantic action extravaganzas. Whether it can find the same audiences in North America is more doubtful; the movie may be too broad for the art-house crowd and too subtitled for everyone else. But it satisfies an old hunger among moviegoers: It is pure cinema, made of action, beauty, landscape, and passion, all played with gusto and affection.

## Hotel de Love ★ ★ ½

R, 96 m., 1997

Aden Young (Rick Dunne), Saffron Burrows (Melissa Morrison), Simon Bossell (Stephen Dunne), Pippa Grandison (Alison Leigh), Ray Barrett (Jack Dunne), Julia Blake (Edith Dunne), Peter O'Brien (Norman), Belinda McClory (Janet). Directed by Craig Rosenberg and produced by Michael Lake and David Parker. Screenplay by Rosenberg.

"I fell in love even before I saw her," Stephen, the hero of *Hotel de Love*, tells us. He walked into a party when he was a teenager, felt love, turned and saw Melissa, and that was that. Unfortunately, while walking across the room toward her, he was interrupted for a moment and his twin, Rick, started chatting her up. That was that. Melissa and Rick dated until Melissa moved on with her life, and then years passed like a heartbeat.

These days Stephen (Simon Bossell) sells stocks, and Rick (Aden Young) manages the Hotel de Love, an establishment for which "tacky" would be high praise. It's a honeymoon hotel in which every room illustrates a different theme: one is for soccer fans, one looks like a tropical rain forest, one seems to be a cave. The hotel even has a tiny waterfall named Niagara Smalls.

One day Melissa (Saffron Burrows) returns and checks into the hotel, radiant. She plans to marry the fairly uninteresting Norman (Peter O'Brien). Neither Stephen nor Rick approve of this plan, although Rick has never known that his twin also loved Melissa.

Stephen is not a young man of great self-confidence. He has small twitches, so fast you almost miss them, and a way of bottling up his emotions until they come popping out in a rush. "I love you!" he blurts to Melissa at the door of her room before running away. He turns up so often for such lightning declarations that she eventually calls them "drive-by 'I-love-yous.'" What, he wonders, does Melissa possibly see in Norman the human coat hanger? "Norman and I discuss ideas and philosophies," she explains. "That is not love," Stephen says. "That is a book group."

*Hotel de Love* is an Australian film in the current tradition of such films, which means that everyone seems secretly peculiar while trying to appear friendly and normal. Australian movies make a particular specialty of dad and mum, who seem to have spent years perfecting a dysfunctional mutual symbiosis. Jack and Edith Dunne, the parents of the twins, have also checked into the hotel—to renew their vows or kill each other in the attempt, it would appear.

The key player in this drama, although at first we don't realize it, is Alison (Pippa Grandison), a palmist and fortune-teller who is Rick's girlfriend as the movie opens and eventually becomes Stephen's friend. She's a dark, lively brunette, who befriends poor Stephen as he carries his hopeless torch for Melissa. Of course, Stephen is destined to eventually notice that true love is right there under his nose, but that will require a lot of deep thought, not to mention the movie's prologue and epilogue, to accomplish.

*Hotel de Love* is a pleasant and sometimes funny film, without being completely satisfying. It is too twee. Too many lines are said for their cuteness, too many exchanges sound like a comedy routine, and the movie works too earnestly at being daffy. Melissa never convinces me she deserves ten years of anybody's obsession, while Alison is worth a good fifteen. I also grew impatient at a subplot involving anonymous love poems. The one character I wanted more of was the hotel's owner, who plays cocktail piano in the lobby and has a song for every occasion—including ones the characters don't quite realize they are having.

## House Arrest ★

PG, 108 m., 1996

Jamie Lee Curtis (Janet Beindorf), Kevin Pollak (Ned Beindorf), Kyle Howard (Grover), Amy Sakasitz (Stacey), Jennifer Love Hewitt (Brooke Figler), Russell Harper (T. J. Krupp), Christopher McDonald (Donald Krupp), Jennifer Tilly (Cindy Figler). Directed by Harry Winer and produced by Judith A. Polone and Winer. Screenplay by Michael Hitchcock.

We live in a hard age. Once they made innocent movies like *The Parent Trap,* in which twins conspired to get their divorced parents back together. Now we get movies like *House Arrest* in which the kids discover their parents are separating, and lock them in the basement until they wise up. John Grisham, who fears that serial killers might be influenced by the movies, can now start worrying that America's children will become parentnappers.

As *House Arrest* opens, the Beindorf children, Grover and Stacey, have just finished editing a fancy home video celebrating their parents' eighteenth wedding anniversary. It has neat titles, jump cuts, tilt shots, and optical effects; Grover is obviously only minutes away from a contract with MTV. The Beindorfs look at the video and decide this is the right time to spring the bad news: They're separating.

Grover (Kyle Howard) sees that immediate action is called for. He enlists Stacey (Amy Sakasitz) in planning a fake "anniversary party" in the basement. As the parents, Janet and Ned (Jamie Lee Curtis and Kevin Pollak), admire the crepe paper hung from the ceiling, they hear the sound of the stairway door being nailed closed. They are captives until they agree to stay married.

You would think this is the sort of scheme that would quickly be discovered. You would be wrong. Everyone in the Beindorfs' town is capable of believing anything a kid can say over the phone, and the only person who discovers the plan is the school bully, T. J. Krupp (Russell Harper). He thinks it's a great idea, and turns up with *his* parents. Word spreads, and soon several other parents are in the basement, including local party mom Cindy Figler (Jennifer Tilly), who seems to think she's one of the kids.

In a different movie, in a different universe, this situation might have led to an interesting film. I am reminded of Luis Buñuel's great *The Exterminating Angel* (1962), which began with a house party. At the end of the evening, none of the guests could bring themselves to leave. Curious. The door was wide open, but . . . they preferred to bed down in the living room. Strange. Day followed day, and they took up permanent residence, breaking through walls to get water from the pipes. As bears, sheep, and disembodied hands stalked through their haunted space, civilization decayed into anarchy.

*The Exterminating Angel* is an "art film," but actually it is easier to understand and immensely more entertaining than *House Arrest*, which wants only to pander to the lowest common denominator, and fails. The director, Harry Winer, and the writer, Michael Hitchcock, cannot think of anything for their characters to do or say that they have not seen previously on a sitcom.

Not only do they recycle predictable events, they don't even think to raise them to another level of ingenuity. Ned Beindorf, who is an architect and remodeled the home, suddenly recalls an abandoned laundry chute. Anyone who has a laundry chute and seals it up belongs on the funny farm, but never mind; the desperate parents rip out the plasterboard and send Jamie Lee Curtis shinnying up the chute like Clint Eastwood in *Escape from Alcatraz*.

Which brings me to my point: Why didn't the filmmakers think of spoofing old prison-break movies, from *Stalag 17* to *The Great Escape*, instead of wasting time on long dialogues between the parents and their outlaw offspring?

We realize perhaps ten minutes into this film, with a sinking heart, that it will contain a Lesson, and that the Lesson will be the one Hollywood has taught so many times before: We need to slow down and listen to one another, and not be workaholics, and not be driven by success, but put our loved ones first. Such a strategy would, of course, be a blueprint for professional suicide in Hollywood itself, where maniacal, egotistical, narcissistic overachievement is how you relax. But people always want what they don't have, and that may explain why Hollywood wants to teach us this Lesson so much more than we want to learn it.

Why must that be? Why must every character, line of dialogue, development, and situation in this movie be taken from the dusty old pegboard of weary clichés? Why, oh why, must there even be a kindly old police chief across the street with binoculars? Isn't there some way this plot could have broken free of its lockstep progress to a tedious conclusion and given us something we haven't seen before? The cast has some bright people in it. I'll bet that while they were sitting in that basement waiting for the next shot to be lit, they were amusing themselves by inventing sardonic variations on the dreck they were about to perform. Is there anyone in Hollywood bright enough to figure out that sardonic variations almost always gross *better* than dreck?

## The House of Yes ★ ★ ½

R, 86 m., 1997

Parker Posey (Jackie-O), Josh Hamilton (Marty), Tori Spelling (Lesly), Freddie Prinze Jr. (Anthony), Genevieve Bujold (Mrs. Pascal), Rachael Leigh Cook (Young Jackie-O), David Love (Voice of Young Marty). Directed by Mark Waters and produced by Beau Flynn and Stefan Simchowitz. Adapted for the screen by Waters, based on the stage play by Wendy MacLeod.

It's just . . . that we've never had a guest before." Not what you want to hear when you're the guest. On a stormy Thanksgiving night in 1983, in a Virginia suburb, Marty Pascal brings home his fiancée to meet his family. They include his twin sister, who calls herself Jackie-O; his kid brother, Anthony (who reveals she's their first guest); and his mother, who tells her children, "I look at you people and wonder, how did you ever fit in my womb?"

*The House of Yes* exists somewhere between *Long Day's Journey into Night* and *The Addams Family*, as the story of a damaged family that has somehow struggled along until the introduction of a stranger brings all of its secrets crawling into the light. As the story opens, Jackie-O (Parker Posey) is disturbed to learn from Anthony (Freddie Prinze Jr.) that their brother, Marty (Josh Hamilton), is bringing a friend home for the holiday. She is even more ominously alarmed when Marty introduces Lesly (Tori Spelling) and announces that they are engaged.

Few actresses can smolder from beneath lowered brows more dramatically than Parker Posey, and she receives this news with ill-concealed dismay. Her mother, Mrs. Pascal (Genevieve Bujold), does little to reassure their guest: "Jackie and Marty belong to each other. Jackie's hand was holding Marty's penis when they came out of the womb." Anthony, who loses no time visiting Lesly in the guest room, has hopes of talking her out of his brother and into sleeping with him. Outside, the storm rages.

The film's opening scenes intercut actual TV footage of Jacqueline Kennedy's tour of the White House with Jackie-O's parallel tour of her family's home. The real Mrs. Kennedy is surprisingly simpering in the old footage; her memory is not well served by repeating the broadcast. Jackie-O, whose wardrobe copies Mrs. Kennedy's, later turns up in the same pink dress and pillbox hat that the president's wife wore on the fatal trip to Dallas. She reveals that she and her brother often play a game reenacting the shooting, with ketchup and pasta as props for blood and brains.

It's clear fairly soon that Marty and Lesly will never be married and may indeed not last the night. After Anthony's visit to Lesly's room, Jackie-O goes up for a chat ("Where's the wildest place you've ever made love?"). Marty tells the family he met Lesly behind the counter at a Donut King store ("She smells like powdered sugar"). As played well by Tori Spelling, she reads the situation quickly and responds appropriately, by trying to get the hell out of the house. The best exchange between Lesly and Jackie-O comes when the sister says, "Pretend he's not my brother," and Lesly answers quickly, "I do."

The arc of the movie is not hard to predict. The dialogue, adapted by director Mark Waters from Wendy MacLeod's stage play, is smart and terse, with a lot of back-and-forth word play, most of it driven by Jackie-O, who is played by Posey as smart, dark, and fresh out of an institution. When the film was over I was not particularly pleased that I had seen it; it was mostly behavior and contrivance. While it was running, I was not bored.

## The Hunchback of Notre Dame ★ ★ ★ ★

G, 95 m., 1996

With the voices of: Tom Hulce (Quasimodo), Demi Moore (Esmeralda), Tony Jay (Frollo), Kevin Kline (Phoebus), Paul Kandel (Clopin), Jason Alexander (Hugo [Gargoyle]), Charles Kimbrough (Victor [Gargoyle]), Mary Wickes (Laverne [Gargoyle]), David Ogden Stiers (Archdeacon). Directed by Gary Trousdale and Kirk Wise and produced by Don Hahn. Screenplay by Tab Murphy, Bob Tzudiker, Irene Mecchi, Noni White, and Jonathan Roberts, based on an animation story by Tab Murphy from the Victor Hugo novel *Notre Dame de Paris.*

When I first heard about the project, I wondered if *The Hunchback of Notre Dame* could possibly work as a Disney animated feature—if the fearsome features and fate of its sad hero Quasimodo would hold audiences at arm's length. When I saw the preview trailers for the film, with its songs about "Quasi," I feared Disney had gone too far in an attempt to popularize and neutralize the material. I was wrong to doubt, and wrong to fear: *The Hunchback of Notre Dame* is the best Disney animated feature since *Beauty and the Beast*—a whirling, uplifting, thrilling story with a heart-touching message that emerges from the comedy and song.

The story involves the lonely life of the deformed Quasimodo (voice by Tom Hulce), born a "monster" and thrown down a well before being rescued and left to be raised by the priests of Notre Dame Cathedral in Paris. The vast, gloomy, Gothic shadows of the cathedral become his playground, and his only friends are three stone gargoyles. But his life changes on the day of the Festival of Fools, when he ventures out of the cathedral, is elected "King of the Fools," and then hears Clopin, king of the gypsies, gasp: "That's no mask!"

Quasimodo is made a captive by the mob and tied down at the orders of the heartless Judge Frollo, but is rescued by the gypsy girl Esmeralda (voice by Demi Moore). He rescues her in turn, giving her sanctuary inside the cathedral. And then he finds himself in the center of a battle to save the gypsies of Paris from Frollo's troops, led by Phoebus (voice by Kevin Kline), captain of the guard. But Phoebus is not a bad man, and besides, he has fallen in love with the fiery Esmeralda. But . . . so has Quasimodo.

This is not such a simple story. There are depths and shadows to it, the ending cannot be simple, and although the heroes may live ever after, it may not be happily. This is the first Disney animated film I can recall with two heroes who both love the girl, which makes heartbreak inevitable.

The movie is forthright in its acceptance of Quasimodo's appearance ("You've got a look that's all your own, kid"), and doesn't look away from his misshapen face. One of Alan Menken's songs even looks on the bright side: "Those other guys that she could dangle / All look the same from every boring point of view—You're a surprise from any angle . . ."

But Quasimodo is an enormously sympathetic character; we grow accustomed to his face. And we follow him into a series of locations in which the Disney animators unveil some of their most breathtaking visual inventions. The Festival of Fools is a riotous celebration in the shadow of Notre Dame. Then Quasi finds himself in the gypsies' Court of Miracles, in the catacombs beneath Paris, for a display of animation and music that is breathtaking in its freedom over time and space.

The cathedral itself is a character in the film, with its rows of stone saints and church fathers, and its limitless vaults of shadows and mystery. Quasimodo moves through its upper reaches like a child on a jungle gym, and there are scary sequences in which he and his friends risk dashing their brains out on the stones below. The thing that animation can do better than any other film form is show human movement freed from the laws of gravity, and as Quasi clambers up and down the stone walls of Notre Dame, the camera swoops freely along with him creating dizzying perspectives and exhilarating movement.

The buried story of the film—the lesson some younger viewers may learn for the first time—is that there is room in the world for many different kinds of people, for hunchbacks and gypsies as well as for those who scornfully consider themselves the norm. Judge Frollo wants to rid Paris of its gypsies, and assigns Phoebus to lead the genocide, but the captain instinctively feels this cannot be right. And when he meets Esmeralda, gypsies suddenly gain a human face for him, and he changes sides.

As for Quasimodo, who has lived so long in isolation, there is a kind of release in discovering the gypsies ("Were you once an outcast too?"). He understands that he is not unique in being shunned, that the need to create outsiders is a weakness of human nature.

*The Hunchback of Notre Dame*, directed by Gary Trousdale and Kirk Wise, is a high point in the renaissance of Disney animation that began in 1989 with *The Little Mermaid*. It blends Menken's songs, glorious animation, boundless energy and the real substance of the story into a movie of heart and joy. More than *Aladdin* or *The Lion King*, certainly more than *Pocahontas*, it is as good for its story and message as for its animation. It reminds us, as all good animation does, that somehow these cartoons of lines and colors and movements can create a kind of life that is more archetypal, more liberating, than images that are weighed down by human bodies and the gravity that traps them.

## Hurricane Streets ★ ★

R, 88 m., 1998

Brendan Sexton III (Marcus), Isidra Vega (Melena), Carlo Alban (Benny), David Roland Frank (Chip), Antoine McLean (Harold), Lynn Cohen (Lucy), Damian Corrente (Justin), L. M. Kit Carson (Mack), Jose Zuniga (Kramer). Directed by Morgan J. Freeman and produced by Galt Niederhoffer, Gill Holland, and Freeman.

*Hurricane Streets* takes place on the Lower East Side of New York, where its five characters, all fourteen or fifteen, commute to their crimes on bicycles. They're petty thieves who hang out in a secret clubroom and earn spending money by shoplifting CDs and athletic shoes, which they sell at a discount on playgrounds. It's only a matter of time until they graduate to more serious and dangerous things (indeed, it's a little hard to believe, in today's world, that they're not already drug couriers).

The group is racially mixed. The story mostly concerns a white kid, Marcus (Brendan Sexton III), whose mother is in prison and whose grandmother is raising him, after a fashion (she owns a bar, and that's where she holds his birthday party). Marcus dreams of someday moving to New Mexico with his mother, after she gets out on probation, but he doesn't have all the information about when that will be. Meanwhile, he meets a Latina girl named Melena (Isidra Vega) and dates her despite the opposition of her father.

The kids are on the brink of big trouble. The cops know who they are and what they're doing. They're ready to graduate to auto theft and burglary, and their days of stealing food from convenience stores are soon going to resemble a time of innocence. Their story may sound similar to *Kids, Fresh, Straight Out of Brooklyn,* and other films about tough street kids, but *Hurricane Streets* is mild by comparison—more of a love story than a sociological drama. The kids seem relatively harmless and normal, and the plot depends not on impending tragedy but on unlikely coincidences, including one that leads to a very unlikely death.

If you saw *Welcome to the Dollhouse,* the wonderful film about a junior high school girl in the midst of unpopular geekhood, you may remember Brendan Sexton III, the actor who plays Marcus here. In that film he tormented the heroine; that was his way of showing affection, and when he makes a date to "rape" her, she shows up for it—although clearly neither one knows exactly what to do then. Here he's an unlikely hero, a sad sack who drifts through a fairly clueless existence with little of the intelligence that made the characters in *Fresh* and those other films so interesting. His story is sad, yes, but he is not very compelling as its hero.

There was a time, I suppose, when *Hurricane Streets* would have been seen as a harrowing slice of life. So many better films have told the stories of alienated young street kids, alas, that this one seems relatively superficial. The dialogue sounds written, not said, and the twists in the plot are unconvincing (the characters are always able to turn up where and when they're needed).

*Hurricane Streets* won the Best Director and Best Cinematography at the 1997 Sundance Film Festival. And the "Audience Award." That means the audience preferred it to *In the Company of Men, Chasing Amy, Kissed, Suburbia,* and *love jones.* Strange.

## Hush ★ ★

PG-13, 95 m., 1998

Jessica Lange (Martha), Gwyneth Paltrow (Helen), Johnathon Schaech (Jackson), Nina Foch (Alice Baring), Debi Mazar (Lisa), Kaiulani Lee (Sister O'Shaughnessy), David Thornton (Gavin), Hal Holbrook (Dr. Hill). Directed by Jonathan Darby and produced by Douglas Wick. Screenplay by Darby and Jane Rusconi.

*Hush* is the kind of movie where you walk in, watch the first ten minutes, know exactly where it's going, and hope devoutly that you're wrong. It's one of those Devouring Woman movies where the villainess never plays a scene without a drink and a cigarette, and the hero is inattentive to the victim to the point of dementia.

Gwyneth Paltrow stars as Helen, a New York career woman who's in love with Jackson (Johnathon Schaech). He takes her home to Virginia to meet his mother, Martha (Jessica Lange), and see the family spread, named Kilronan—a famous horse farm with a main house that looks like Thomas Jefferson either designed it or meant to. The house is large, elaborately decorated, and eerie, but then we knew it would be eerie because the music over the opening titles is "Hush, Little Baby," and that's a song used only in horror films.

Martha is a controlling woman, possessive about her beloved son. She prepares separate bedrooms for them. "It's a Catholic thing," Jackson explains, but when Martha accidentally finds the naked Helen in her son's bed she doesn't seem very perturbed, and I suspect the Catholic theme is there only because Hollywood traditionally depends on the church for props and atmosphere whenever true evil needs to be evoked.

It's a big house, with no servants. "She can't keep 'em," sniffs feisty old Alice (Nina Foch), Jackson's paternal grandmother, who lives in a nursing home and is prepared to talk to anyone, anytime, about Martha's devious ways. The youngsters are deep into lust, which seizes them at inopportune moments, so that they make love on the floor of the entry hall one night, while Martha observes from a shadowed landing.

Is Martha jealous of Helen's sexual relationship with her son? Not at all. She's a horse woman. "Started as a stable girl," Alice tells Helen, supplying a graphic explanation of the ways in which a woman like Martha not only breeds horses in the figurative sense, but is right there in the middle of the fray when a mare needs calming or a stallion needs guidance. Martha devises a way to inspire the young couple to leave New York and move to Kilronan, and we gather she hopes to breed a male heir to Kilronan by Jackson, out of Helen. Once she has one, of course, Helen may become unnecessary.

The general outlines of this scheme are visible early in the film, and the details grow more graphic, right up until a "push! push!" childbirth scene that is given a whole new spin. What's frustrating is that little of the evildoing would be possible if Jackson behaved at any moment like a normal, intelligent person. He consistently does the wrong thing just because the film needs him to.

The plot lumbers on its way to setting up the finale. Martha deviously tells Helen one thing and Jackson another, and we can hear the screenplay creaking in her dialogue. She spreads rumors that could be corrected in an instant if anyone bothered. The old family doctor (Hal Holbrook) is called upon for specialized information that is so transparently dangerous that the audience snickers.

And then credulity breaks down totally. I will step carefully here, to preserve some secrets. I was amazed by the sequence of events after Jackson leaves the big horse race and speeds home to the rescue, only to never go near his possibly dying wife. I was astonished by her miraculous recovery, so that she could preside over a denouement that's not only wildly implausible but probably medically impossible.

The film's most intriguing element is the performance by Jessica Lange, who by *not* going over the top provides Martha with a little pathos to leaven the psychopathology. That side of her doesn't seem consistent with her demented behavior at a crucial moment, but then consistency is not the film's strong point.

## Hype! ★ ★ ★

NO MPAA RATING, 84 m., 1997

A documentary film featuring The Mono Men, The Walkabouts, Pearl Jam, Soundgarden, and others. Directed by Doug Pray and produced by Steven Helvey.

"There's so much rain in Seattle," a pioneer of grunge rock observes, "that it was logical to go down to the basement." Grunge began with basement and garage bands playing in local clubs, and became a media event just when it was ripe for the *Spinal Tap* treatment. The popularity of Nirvana and the suicide of its lead singer Kurt Cobain gave it notoriety; *Rolling Stone* ran a fashion layout on flannel shirts, Joan Rivers posed in grunge outfits for *Vanity Fair*, and a local publicist made up a phony glossary of Grunge Speak that the *New York Times* fell for lock, stock, and barrel.

A smart, ironic documentary named *Hype!* charts the rise of grunge and its enormous impact on the Seattle scene (at the height of the phenomenon, *Spin* magazine was gushing, "Seattle is to the rock and roll world what Bethlehem is to Christianity"). Local types are more sardonic. Art Chantry, who designed grunge posters and album covers, observes: "A lot of occult stuff takes place here. The first flying saucers were sighted in the Pacific Northwest. This is the serial killer capital of the world. The Manson family used to vacation up this way."

What grunge did in the mid-eighties was take heavy metal, punk, and old-time rock 'n' roll and put it together into a sound that was looser and more fun than a lot of the music on the national scene. A local label named Sub-Pop, realistically observing that none of the Seattle bands were known outside town, promoted its label instead of its bands. Sub-Pop flew a British journalist into town, he toured the clubs, and wrote an influential article for the UK music magazine *Melody Maker*, and soon, the movie says, "bands that had never played live professionally were being signed up by labels."

*Hype!* doesn't put down the music; it likes grunge but is amused by the way publicity and image took over, turning a local movement into a commodity. Bands like Pearl Jam, Soundgarden, Mudhoney, and Nirvana are seen performing, but there's also early video footage of obscure club bands, including one where a drummer falls onto a guitarist and the band keeps playing. Nothing stopped a performance, photographer Charles Peterson remembers; audiences and band members would drink together, often during a performance, and fans came to party, not criticize (he contrasts Seattle crowds with sniffy New Yorkers saying, "I think they just missed a note").

By the end, in the early 1990s, "Pearl Jam" was the answer to a question on *Jeopardy!*, and Kurt Cobain's Nirvana was one of the hottest bands in the country. Then Cobain, who had a history of drug problems, killed himself. In such cases it is always said that the publicity and the pressure got to him, but actually, of course, the drugs got to him. There is touching footage of a candlelight vigil at the Space Needle in his honor—and in a way his story is still playing out through his wife, Courtney Love, who got her own act together, emerged as a powerful actress in *The People vs. Larry Flynt*, and may be the most important figure produced by the period, if not by the music. (See *Kurt & Courtney*.)

Pearl Jam's Eddie Vedder is probably the key musical figure from grunge, and in *Hype!* he comes across as intelligent and thoughtful. While acknowledging that the grunge phenomenon was dissipated by its fame (it was most at home in small local clubs), he sounds like the survivor of a war or a shipwreck: "It will be a tragedy if we don't do something with this." But, of course, they did.

*Hype!* has been directed by Doug Pray and photographed by Robert Bennett, who give you a real sense of the music and its excitement, while at the same time keeping a certain distance as journalists. They find funny, articulate local observers—producers, journalists, musicians, fans, publicists—who lived through the scene and kept it in perspective. Producer Steve Helvey says the whole thing reminds him of Baby Huey, waddling around making delightful discoveries: The record labels waddled to Austin, Texas, and Athens, Georgia, and then they waddled to Seattle and waddled on to Minneapolis: "We were just like part of that process."

# I

## I Know What You Did Last Summer ★

R, 100 m., 1997

Jennifer Love Hewitt (Julie James), Sarah Michelle Gellar (Helen Shivers), Ryan Phillippe (Barry Cox), Freddie Prinze Jr. (Ray Bronson), Muse Watson (Fisherman), Bridgette Wilson (Elsa Shivers), Anne Heche (Melissa Egan), Johnny Galecki (Max). Directed by Jim Gillespie and produced by Neal H. Moritz, Erik Feig, and Stokely Chaffin. Screenplay by Kevin Williamson.

The best shot in this film is the first one. Not a good sign. *I Know What You Did Last Summer* begins dramatically, with the camera swooping high above a dark and stormy sea, and then circling until it reveals a lonely figure sitting on a cliff overlooking the surf. The shot leads us to anticipate dread, horror, and atmospheric gloominess, but, alas, it is not to be.

Like so many horror films, this one is set on a national holiday—the Fourth of July. (Christmas and Graduation Day are also popular, although Thanksgiving now seems reserved for movies about dysfunctional families.) In a small North Carolina town, a beauty pageant ends with Helen (Sarah Michelle Gellar) being crowned the Croaker Queen. (The reference is to a fish, but the pun is intended, I fear.) Blinking back tears of joy, she announces her plans: "Through art, I shall serve my country."

We meet her friends: her obnoxious, rich boyfriend, Barry (Ryan Phillippe); her brainy best friend, Julie (Jennifer Love Hewitt); and Julie's boyfriend, Ray (Freddie Prinze Jr.). Barry is a jerk who likes to get in fights and drive while drunk ("Can you say 'alcoholic'?" Julie asks him). They build a bonfire on the beach and debate the old urban legend about the teenage couple who found the bloody hook embedded in their car door. And then, on the way home, they strike a shadowy figure walking in the road.

In a panic, they dump him into the sea, even though he is not quite dead at the time. They're afraid to go to the police and risk reckless manslaughter charges. ("This is your future, Julie," Barry screams at her.) Helen then goes off to New York for her showbiz career, and Julie heads for college, but by the next summer they're back home again, pale, chastened, and racked by guilt.

That's when one of them gets a note that says, "I know what you did last summer." As they panic and try to find out who sent it—who knows what they did—the movie loses what marginal tension it has developed, and unwinds in a tedious series of obligatory scenes in which nonessential characters are murdered with a bloody hook wielded by the Fisherman, a macabre figure in a long slicker and a rubber rain hat.

"This is a fishing village," one of the friends says. "Everybody has a slicker." Yes, but not everybody wears it ashore, along with the hat, during steamy July weather. Only the Fisherman does. And since the movie doesn't play fair with its Fisherman clues, we're left with one of those infuriating endings in which (danger! plot spoiler ahead!) the murders were committed by none of the above.

The ads make much of the fact that *I Know What You Did Last Summer* is from "the creators of *Scream*." That means both scripts are by Kevin Williamson. My bet is that he hauled this one out of the bottom drawer after *Scream* passed the $100 million mark. The neat thing about *Scream* was that the characters had seen a lot of horror films, were familiar with all the conventions, and knew they were in a horror-type situation. In *I Know*, there's one moment like that (as the two women approached an ominous house, they observe ominously, "Jodie Foster tried this . . ."). But for the rest of the movie they're blissfully unaware of the dangers of running upstairs when pursued, walking around at night alone, trying to investigate the situation themselves, going onto seemingly empty fishing boats, etc.

After the screening was over and the lights went up, I observed a couple of my colleagues in deep and earnest conversation, trying to resolve twists in the plot. They were applying more thought to the movie than the makers did. A critic's mind is a terrible thing to waste.

## I Shot Andy Warhol ★ ★ ★ ½

NO MPAA RATING, 103 m., 1995

Lili Taylor, (Valerie Solanas), Jared Harris, (Andy Warhol), Stephen Dorff, (Candy Darling), Martha

Plimpton (Stevie), Danny Morgentstern (Jeremiah), Lothaire Bluteau (Maurice Girodias), Michael Imperioli (Ondine), Reg Rogers (Paul Morrissey). Directed by Mary Harron and produced by Tom Kalin and Christine Vachon. Screenplay by Harron and Daniel Minahan.

When Andy Warhol mused that in the future everyone would be famous for fifteen minutes, he could not have anticipated that Valerie Solanas would earn her fame by shooting him. To be fair, she did it only as a last resort; God knows she tried everything else to get Andy to make her famous. Now her life and crime are dramatized in *I Shot Andy Warhol*, which Warhol might have found the perfect movie title, combining as it does the deadpan, the sensational, and name-dropping.

Solanas walked into the Factory, Warhol's studio, on June 3, 1968, pulled out a gun that was given to her by a man she met in a mimeo shop, and fired on America's most famous artist. "Jesus Christ, now she's shot somebody," one of Warhol's assistants says. (One expects Warhol to summon his strength and gasp, "Not just *somebody*.") When the police ask her why she did it, she says she has "a lot of real involved reasons." She sure does.

In following the life of Valerie Solanas from her wounded childhood to her moment of vindication, director Mary Harron and actress Lili Taylor go inside the mind of a woman who was deranged and possibly schizophrenic, and follow the logic of her situation as she sees it, until her act is revealed as the inevitable result of what went before.

Solanas, who was abused as a child and worked her way through college as a prostitute, comes across as a gifted woman who never quite loses a wry sense of humor. After a short career on her college paper (she writes columns arguing that females can reproduce without males and should do so), Valerie takes on Manhattan; she writes plays, does readings in luncheonettes, and is befriended by Candy Darling (Stephen Dorff), a transsexual who takes her for the first time to the Factory.

Warhol (Jared Harris) finds her as interesting as he finds anything. He puts her in one of his movies *(I, a Man)*, and she emotes on a staircase of the Chelsea Hotel—too hot for Warhol's cool. She writes a play and hopes Warhol will produce it, but her precious typed playscript is tossed behind a sofa at the Factory, and when no one will return it to her, Solanas begins to get angry.

At this point, she is essentially a bag lady, living and writing on the roof of a building, and supporting herself by prostitution and by selling copies of her radical lesbian feminist polemic, the *S.C.U.M. Manifesto*. The initials stand for "The Society for Cutting Up Men." Her friends, including a sometime lover named Stevie (Martha Plimpton), try to help her, but no one in this self-obsessed world really sees her, listens to her, and cares.

Harron, a first-time director who cowrote the screenplay with Daniel Minahan, does two remarkable things in her movie: She makes Solanas almost sympathetic and sometimes moving and funny, and she creates a portrait of the Factory that's devastating and convincing. Warhol emerges as a man whose entire being—intelligence, sexuality, artistry—seems concentrated in his detached, bemused gaze. (If Andy ever got a tattoo, I hope it read "I like to watch.") He fears personal contact; he snaps pictures and makes tapes of the people around him, and I imagine him later, alone, arranging those documents as an entomologist might pin butterflies to a corkboard.

Solanas, on the other hand, is passionately engaged in her life. She says she hates men, but depends on two to make her famous: Warhol, and Maurice Girodias (Lothaire Bluteau), the publisher of the Olympia Press, who prospered in the 1950s and 1960s by publishing pornography with literary pretensions, and literature with pornographic pretensions. (His list ranged from *Lolita* and *The Ginger Man* to *Harriet Marwood, Governess.*)

Of all the literary dinners ever shared by authors and their publishers, the encounter between Solanas and Girodias must rank as the most unlikely. Solanas wanted a publisher for her manifesto; Girodias wanted to find a new trend to ride, now that porn was becoming commonplace. Desperately poor, Solanas signed a contract that gave her an immediate cash payment, and then became obsessed with the (correct) notion that Girodias planned to steal her work for a pittance.

Everywhere she looked, more presentable feminists seemed to be taking her ideas and running with them. Watching bra-burners on

TV, Valerie complains, "They got their message from me." She bombards the Factory for the return of her play. Brushed off by Warhol, told by Candy Darling that she's been "excommunicated," Solanas walks into the Factory and starts shooting.

Lili Taylor plays Solanas as mad but not precisely irrational. She gives the character spunk, irony, and a certain heroic courage (the sight of her typing on her rooftop, the wind rustling the pages of her manuscript, is touching). *Variety* calls Taylor "the first lady of the indee cinema," and in one independent film after another *(Mystic Pizza, Dogfight, Household Saints, Arizona Dream, Bright Angel, Short Cuts)* she has proven herself the most intelligent and versatile of performers. If you had to look at all of the films of one actor who has emerged in the last ten years, you would run less chance of being bored with Lili Taylor than anyone else.

Some audience members, I'm sure, will not be in sympathy with *I Shot Andy Warhol.* They will find it the story of a pathetic madwoman who shot an emotional eunuch. And so it is. But not any madwoman and not any eunuch, and that is the gift art can bestow: to show us the person beneath the skin, and to reveal that even the strangest behavior is often simply a strategy for obtaining what we all require, love and recognition.

## The Ice Storm ★ ★ ★ ★

R, 112 m., 1997

Kevin Kline (Ben Hood), Joan Allen (Elena Hood), Henry Czerny (George Clair), Sigourney Weaver (Janey Carver), Jamey Sheridan (Jim Carver), Christina Ricci (Wendy Hood), Tobey Maguire (Paul Hood), Elijah Wood (Mikey Carver), Adam Hann-Byrd (Sandy Carver), David Krumholtz (Francis Davenport), Michael Cumpsty (Reverend Philip Edwards). Directed by Ang Lee and produced by Ted Hope, James Schamus, and Lee. Screenplay by Schamus, based on the novel by Rick Moody.

*The Ice Storm* takes place as an early winter storm descends on Connecticut, casting over Thanksgiving a shroud of impending doom. In a wooded suburb, affluent adults stir restlessly in their split-level homes, depressed not only by their lives but by their entertainments and even by their sins. Their teenage children have started experimenting with the same forms of escape: booze, pot, and sex.

The Hood family is held together by quiet desperation. Ben (Kevin Kline) is having an affair with a neighbor (Sigourney Weaver). His wife, Elena (Joan Allen), is a shoplifter who is being hit on by a longhaired minister. The children sip wine in the kitchen. Young Wendy Hood's grace before Thanksgiving dinner is to the point: "Thanks for letting us white people kill all the Indians and steal all their stuff." Ben and Elena observe later, "The only big fight we've had in years is about whether to go back into couples therapy."

The film, based on a novel by Rick Moody, has been directed by Ang Lee, whose previous credit was an adaptation of Jane Austen's *Sense and Sensibility.* Both films are about families observing protocol and exchanging visits. Only the rules have changed. When Ben Hood visits Janey Carver (Weaver) for an adulterous liaison, he wanders into Janey's rec room to find his own daughter, Wendy (Christina Ricci), experimenting with Janey's son Mikey (Elijah Wood). Wendy, who is fourteen, has also conducted an exploratory session with Mikey's kid brother, Sandy. The father asks his daughter what she's doing there. She could as easily have asked him.

The early 1970s were a time when the social revolution of the 1960s had seeped down, or up, into the yuppie classes, who wanted to be "with it" and supplemented their martinis with reefers. The sexual revolution is in full swing for the characters in this movie, leading to Ben Hood's lecture to his son on the facts of life: "Masturbating in the shower wastes water and electricity." When Janey Carver finds her son and the Hood girl playing "I'll show you mine if you'll show me yours," her response is a bizarre speech on Margaret Mead's book about coming of age in Samoa.

The literate, subtle screenplay by James Schamus cuts between the children and their parents, finding parallels. Paul takes the train into the city to visit the apartment of the girl he likes; he sneaks sleeping pills into the drink of his rival to put him out of the picture, but she, of course, wants a pill of her own, and passes out. Meanwhile in New Caanan, the adults are attending a "key party," which turns into a sort of race: Can they swap their wives before they pass out?

Elena Hood even finds Philip, the longhaired minister (Michael Cumpsty), there. "Sometimes the shepherd needs the comfort of the sheep," he explains tolerantly. She answers: "I'm going to try hard not to understand the implications of that."

There is a sense of gathering tragedy, symbolized in one scene where a child balances on an icy diving board over an empty pool. When disaster does strike, it releases helpless tears for one of the characters; we reflect on how very many things he has to cry about. Despite its mordant undertones, the film is often satirical and frequently very funny, and quietly observant in its performances, as when the Weaver character takes all she can of Kline's musings about his dislike of golf, and finally tells her lover: "You're boring me. I have a husband. I don't feel the need for another."

They all feel the need for something. What we sense after the film is that the natural sources of pleasure have been replaced with higher-octane substitutes, which have burnt out the ability to feel joy. Going through the motions of what once gave them escape, they feel curiously trapped. ☞

## If Lucy Fell ★

R, 93 m., 1996

Sarah Jessica Parker (Lucy), Eric Schaeffer (Joe MacGonaughgill), Ben Stiller (Bwick), Elle MacPherson (Jane), Scarlet Johansson (Emily), James Rebhorn (Simon). Directed by Eric Schaeffer and produced by Brad Krevoy, Steve Stabler, and Brad Jenkel. Screenplay by Schaeffer, based on a story by Schaeffer and Tony Spiridakis.

There is an affectation that I find particularly annoying, and that is when people choose to perform at a level below their natural intelligence. Teenage boys sometimes do that when they feel the need to be obnoxious; they lose all sense of manner and style, and go into lout mode. Usually this also involves eating while holding a fork like a shovel.

It's not often you find this voluntary dimwittedness in a movie, but *If Lucy Fell* offers a depressing example in the case of Joe MacGonaughgill (Eric Schaeffer), one of the least appealing characters ever offered for the public's entertainment. He's an artist who has, for the last two or three years, been sharing an apartment with a therapist named Lucy (Sarah Jessica Parker). Now they are both pushing thirty, and make a pact: Either they both find true love in twenty-eight days, or they jump off the Brooklyn Bridge. (I found myself hoping they would not find love, because the only way for a premise this stupid to redeem itself would be, of course, in their deaths.)

Lucy is fairly smart—too smart to be in this movie, for starters. But she talks to Joe on his level. "Joe," she asks, "would you drink my spit?" She continues by describing in great detail exactly what consistency and texture the spit would have, and how it would dribble before being ingested by Joe. This kind of geek dialogue is supposed to show that the characters are maintaining an ironic distance from conventional social rules. All that's missing is the irony. Joe is the kind of person who seriously believes this is a pickup line: "I have herpes. But not downstairs."

Joe and Lucy both meet possible candidates for love. For Lucy, it is an action painter named Bwick (Ben Stiller), who seems to have random malfunctions at the level where the speech and movement centers of the mind do their work. For Joe, it is Jane (Elle MacPherson), the tall beauty who lives next door and conducts most of her life—undressing, kissing her dates—in front of an open window.

Joe has been spying on her and painting her for years, and puts on a gallery show of his work. Jane comes to the show, is amused, and allows herself to be picked up by Joe, even though he has a white ring around his mouth because of unwise use of sunblocker during a session at a tanning salon. Joe cannot believe his good fortune. She is fragrant and friendly, and soon he has her against a wall with her shirt off, and is expressing misgivings about the Mickey Rourke position. But then . . . she spoils it all by revealing she *knew* he was watching her. Joe leaves in dismay.

His dismay is nothing compared to ours. Couldn't he have borne his disappointment at least long enough for her to take off her bra? I know this is an unworthy and even a sexist sentiment, but is it fair for a movie to bore us for an hour with the arid predicaments of two woefully uninteresting characters, and then take Elle MacPherson's shirt off, and then bail out on scruples? I felt like the rat that spent three days stumbling through a maze, and all it got for its reward was a chlorophyll gumball.

Eric Schaeffer not only plays Joe MacGonaughgill, but also wrote and directed this movie. Earlier, he made a film called *My Life's in Turnaround.* That film had walk-ons from Phoebe Cates and Martha Plimpton. He cast Sarah Jessica Parker in this film after meeting her in a cab he was driving. He is obviously a lot better with women than Joe MacGonaughgill.

It is so incredibly hard to get an independent film made that Schaeffer deserves credit simply for the fact that these films exist. He is obviously a smart guy. Why does he play dumb? What's with the goofy blue hats he wears throughout the film? And the doofus haircut? And the self-referential dialogue? And why does he betray himself at the end with lines like, "You figured out the girl in your heart isn't the girl in your dreams," when he should be jumping off the bridge?

I'd like to see a Schaeffer movie in which he plays a guy as smart as he is; in which he takes the risk of wanting to make a good film, instead of hiding behind irony. It's okay to feel. It's okay to think. It's okay to be sincere. It's okay to be a moral perfectionist, too, but that doesn't mean you shouldn't give Elle MacPherson at least twenty-four hours before kicking her out of your life.

## I'm Not Rappaport ★ ★ ½

PG-13, 135 m., 1997

Walter Matthau (Nat Moyer), Ossie Davis (Midge Carter), Amy Irving (Clara Gelber), Martha Plimpton (Laurie Campbell), Craig T. Nelson (The Cowboy), Boyd Gaines (Pete Danforth), Guillermo Diaz (J.C.), Elina Lowensohn (Clara Lemlich), Ron Rifkin (Feigenbaum), Marin Hinkle (Hannah). Directed by Herb Gardner and produced by John Penotti and John Starke. Screenplayby Gardner, based on his play.

If *I'm Not Rappaport* had been a little more like *My Dinner With André* and a little less like *Grumpy Old Men*, I would have liked it more. It's impossible to *dislike* the film; it stars two immensely warm performers, Walter Matthau and Ossie Davis, in an extended riff on two guys sitting on a park bench. But if they'd stayed on the bench and just talked—talked for two solid hours—it might have been more successful. Instead, writer-director Herb Gardner loses faith in his original impulse and adds plot—way too much plot—to force the movie into more conventional channels.

Imagine an old Jewish left-winger and an old African-American janitor, both about eighty, both articulate and with senses of humor, sitting on a bench and free-associating about where life has taken them and what they learned on the journey. There are scenes like that in *I'm Not Rappaport,* and they're the heart of the movie, as they were of Gardner's 1986 Tony-winning play. When Nat (Matthau) and Midge (Davis) talk, it's like verbal music. We could listen all night.

Now add: A tenant committee that wants to take away Midge's job. A daughter who wants Nat committed to an old folks' home. A lonely girl who's trying to get off drugs. A sinister drug dealer who considers the park his turf. A mugger. And Nat leading the shoppers in a grocery store on a strike against higher prices. Every time one of these developments appears on the screen, it feels yanked in by the scruff of its neck. I could believe, at least, the attempt to retire old Midge (his building is going co-op, etc.), but when Nat impersonates a Mafia don in an attempt to scare off the drug dealer, it's sitcom time: Why contrive material like this when the fundamental idea is so promising?

Matthau has by now ripened into the most engaging old guy in the movies; he's had a long time to do that, since it is hard to remember a movie in which he seemed particularly young. Davis, whose background is on the stage and in less frequent films, is a little more complicated: He's not an "old guy" but a particular character who lets you know he's seen a lot and drawn his conclusions. Here and in Spike Lee's *Get on the Bus,* he has an almost oracular authority.

Together, sitting on the bench, their characters use conversational material they've been rehearsing for years. "You listen to me," Nat says. "I was dead once. I know things." Midge tells Danforth, the head of the tenant's committee: "You givin' me bad guy news, tryin' to look like a good guy doin' it." Nat lives in his fantasies and pretends to be several different people (a Cuban, a gangster, the head of a consumer agency). Midge steadfastly holds to his identity as the only man alive who can get his building's boiler to work. They're wonderful together, and when they use the park band shell to try out their version of the vaudeville act with the punch line "I'm not Rappaport," there is an effortless grace at work.

The other actors in the film are good at what they do, but I wish it had not been done. Martha Plimpton is the art student, fresh out of rehab. Amy Irving is touching as the daughter who wonders if Nat should live on his own any longer. Guillermo Diaz is menacing as a mugger, and Craig T. Nelson, as Cowboy, the drug dealer, plays a man who ruthlessly defends his business. But all of these people and the plot twists they inspire are simply not necessary.

Two old guys, sitting on a bench, talking for two hours. That's my rewrite.

## In and Out ★ ★ ★

PG-13, 92 m., 1997

Kevin Kline (Howard), Joan Cusack (Emily), Tom Selleck (Peter Malloy), Debbie Reynolds (Berniece), Wilford Brimley (Frank), Matt Dillon (Cameron), Bob Newhart (Mr. Halliwell), Gregory Jbara (Walter), Shalom Harlow (Sonya). Directed by Frank Oz and produced by Scott Rudin. Screenplay by Paul Rudnick.

You're a high school English teacher in a small Indiana town, watching the Academy Awards with your fiancée, when one of your former students wins the Oscar. He won for playing a gay soldier, and in his acceptance speech, he thanks a lot of people, including you, his teacher—"who," he volunteers, "is gay."

This comes as news to the fiancée. Also to the teacher, named Howard (Kevin Kline). Also to his father (Wilford Brimley) in the same town, who tells his wife: "We used to mow our lawn. No more!" Also to the high school principal (Bob Newhart), who will eventually try to fire Howard. Also to the players on the football team that Howard coaches, although one of them says there are two places where it's okay to be gay: "Prison and space, where they kind of float into each other while they're weightless."

*In and Out* is a lighthearted, PG-13–rated comedy about homosexuality, so innocuous you can easily imagine it spinning off into a sitcom. Its opening moments were inspired by the moment on the Oscarcast when Tom Hanks won as best actor for *Philadelphia,* and thanked his own gay high school drama teacher. The story goes that producer Scott Rudin, watching the broadcast, imagined a different outcome to the story, and pitched it to screenwriter Paul Rudnick, who under the pen name Libby Gelman-Waxner writes a funny column for *Premiere* magazine.

The result is one of the jollier comedies of the year, a movie so mainstream that you can almost watch it backing away from confrontation, a film aimed primarily at a middle-American heterosexual audience. Thirty years ago this movie would have been controversial. Now it's simply funny.

Kevin Kline is almost always a dependable comic actor, an everyman who tries to keep his dignity while his life falls apart. Here he's well matched with Joan Cusack, as Emily, the fiancée, who has lost dozens or hundreds of pounds under the inspiration of Richard Simmons, in order to slim down for marriage to Howard; she's had a crush on him for years. Now, on the eve of the wedding, her whole world has come crashing down, and even the parish priest is astonished that during a three-year courtship she has never once slept with her intended.

Howard tries to fix that. "But I'm *not* gay!" he thunders, crashing into her bedroom in a belated display of macho lust. One of the plot mysteries is why the former star pupil (a witty, wry performance by Matt Dillon) would have said so on national TV. No matter; Howard becomes the center of a media blitz, and a celebrity gossip journalist played by Tom Selleck arrives in town to host a TV special documenting the real story.

Selleck's character is gay—and cheerfully prepared to assure everyone of that fact. He also assumes Howard is gay, despite his protestations. So does the high school principal, whom Newhart plays as a man so inhibited that when he speaks, everything of importance is implied by long, agonized pauses.

*In and Out* is a lot of fun, an audience-pleaser that creates characters that only become more likable the more the plot digs in. Rudnick is a gifted screenwriter whose 1995 *Jeffrey* was not as relaxed about sexuality as this film is. The director and sometime Muppeteer Frank Oz *(Little Shop of Horrors)* knows that while the predictable is the death of comedy, its closest relative, the inevitable, is essential.

Only the ending bogs down. There's a scene in the high school auditorium that could have been recycled directly from a Frank Capra movie, and without giving it away, I will say that it is too long, too lugubrious, and too cloyingly uplifting. On the other hand, the movie takes a cheap shot at Barbra Streisand that's so funny it will probably make even her laugh, and in a year when good comedies seem as hard to make as ever, *In and Out* is one of the best. ☞

## In Love and War ★ ★

PG-13, 115 m., 1997

Sandra Bullock (Agnes Von Kurowsky), Chris O'Donnell (Ernest Hemingway), Mackenzie Astin (Henry Villard), Emilio Bonucci (Domenico Caracciolo), Ingrid Lacey (Elsie "Mac" MacDonald), Margot Steinberg (Mabel "Rosie" Rose), Colin Stinton (Tom Burnside), Ian Kelly (Jimmy McBride). Directed by Richard Attenborough and produced by Dimitri Villard and Attenborough. Screenplay by Allan Scott, Clancy Sigal, and Anna Hamilton Phelan.

Ernest Hemingway went to the First World War like a kid going to summer camp. It sounded like a lot of fun; he wouldn't have missed it for the world. Early in *In Love and War,* he gets his fun and his war all boiled down into a few minutes. He arrives at the front lines, is thrilled by first sight of the enemy, and then a shell strikes nearby and he is surrounded by mud and body parts.

A wounded man screams for help, Hemingway races to carry him to safety and is shot in the leg. In a field hospital, amputation looks like the best bet, but Hemingway says he would rather be dead than lose a leg. He tells this to a nurse named Agnes, who convinces the doctor to spare his leg. During his long convalescence, they fall in love.

Although Hemingway's love affairs were well charted during a long and publicized life, the specifics of this one escaped notice until Agnes von Kurowsky died in the 1980s, and a cache of love letters to Hemingway came to light. He was eighteen. She was twenty-six. In his mind, it was all planned that she would follow him back to the States and they would marry and live in his father's cabin in the woods and she'd "be making the old place spic and span, while I write great words."

This prospect on reflection did not appeal to von Kurowsky, who wrote him breaking off their engagement. She later married a doctor she met in the war. If Hemingway's biographers did not know of this early romance, Hemingway himself certainly remembered it, and wrote about it in *A Very Short Story,* which takes less than two pages to express his bitterness. Describing what is obviously the same event—the nurse caring for his wound, the wartime love affair—he ends with a few terse sentences about receiving a letter in which she says it was boy-girl love, not man-woman love. A few days later, he says, he got VD from a woman he met in the Loop and took on a cab ride through Lincoln Park. End of story.

Not, as they say, a pretty picture, but Richard Attenborough's *In Love and War* doesn't use the Hemingway angle and indeed could be about someone else altogether. There is little feeling here for the man and writer Hemingway would become, and the movie is essentially the story of a romance between a naive kid and a woman who liked him—maybe even loved him—but was too wise to risk her life on his promises of future glory.

Chris O'Donnell plays Hemingway and Sandra Bullock is Agnes von Kurowsky. Their relationship seems more sentimental than passionate; to recycle a Hemingway phrase that perhaps became more notorious than he would have liked, the earth does not shake. It is hard enough to make a movie about a love affair without a future, and harder still when the audience agrees that maybe it doesn't need a future. Eight years is a big age difference, especially between eighteen and twenty-six, and although great love can certainly transcend it, this is not great love.

There are some problems, also, with the way the love affair is depicted. The movie chooses not to deal with two realities that might have made it more interesting: Hemingway at eighteen was probably sexually inexperienced, and sex before marriage in 1918 was not treated as casually as it is today. The screenplay by Allan Scott, Clancy Sigal, and Anna Hamilton Phelan chooses not to reflect those conditions, and so when Ernest and Agnes make love for the first time in the little pensione down by the railroad station, it is a conventional movie scene, not one specific to these characters.

"I wanted this to be the most beautiful place on God's earth," he says, realizing the pensione is little other than a brothel. "Then close your eyes," she says. Hemingway would have been reaching for his blue pencil. Then again, maybe not, as the earth shook.

I am always suspicious of stories that take on significance because of events that happen after they're over (". . . and that little boy grew up to be—George Washington!"). *In Love and War* is not much interested in Ernest Hemingway's subsequent life and career, and even in its treatment of this early period it doesn't deal with such themes as his macho posturing, his need to prove himself, his grandiosity. Hemingway creates a more interesting (and self-revealing) character in his own stories of the war.

As for Agnes von Kurowsky, she comes across in the Bullock performance as sweet, competent, and loving. She must have reflected, after Hemingway was shipped home, on her choices between marrying a wealthy doctor, or keeping things "spic and span" for a kid trying to become a novelist while living in his dad's cabin. And as she read about Hemingway in the papers, did she sometimes regret the decision she had made? Not if she read the same stories the rest of us have.

## In the Company of Men ★ ★ ★ ★

R, 93 m., 1997

Aaron Eckhart (Chad), Stacy Edwards (Christine), Matt Malloy (Howard), Michael Martin (Coworker 1), Mark Rector (John), Chris Hayes (Coworker 2), Jason Dixie (Intern), Emily Cline (Suzanne). Directed by Neil LaBute and produced by Mark Archer and Stephen Pevner. Screenplay by LaBute.

Now here is true evil: cold, unblinking, reptilian. The character Chad in *In the Company of Men* makes the terrorists of the summer thrillers look like boys throwing mud pies. And for every Chad there is a Howard, a weaker man, ready to go along, lacking the courage to disagree and half intoxicated by the stronger will of the other man. People like this are not so uncommon. Look around you.

The movie takes place in the familiar habitats of the modern corporate male: hotel corridors, airport "courtesy lounges," corporate cubicles, and meeting rooms. The men's room is an invaluable refuge for private conversations. We never find out what the corporation makes, but what does it matter? Modern business administration techniques have made the corporate environment so interchangeable that an executive from Pepsi, say, can transfer seamlessly to Apple and apply the same "management philosophy" without missing a beat.

Chad (Aaron Eckhart) and Howard (Matt Malloy) have been assigned for six weeks to a regional office of their company. Waiting for their flight, they talk. Chad is unhappy and angry because he's been dumped by his girlfriend ("The whole fade-out thing"). He proposes a plan: "Say we were to find some girl vulnerable as hell . . ." In their new location, they'll select a young woman who doesn't look like she has much of a social life. They'll both shower her with attention—flowers, dinner dates—until she's dizzy, and then, "out comes the rug, both of us dropping her!"

Chad explains this plan with the blinkered, formal language of a man whose recreational reading consists of best-selling primers on excellence and wealth. "Life is for the taking—is it not?" he asks. And, "Is that not ideal? To restore a little dignity to our lives?" He hammers his plan home in a men's room, while Howard, invisible behind a cubicle door, says he guesses he agrees.

The "girl" they choose for their target turns out to be deaf—a bonus. Her name is Christine (Stacy Edwards). She is pleasant, pretty, articulate; it is easy to understand everything she says, but Chad is cruel as he describes her to Howard: "She's got one of those voices like Flipper. You should hear her going at it, working to put the simplest sounds together." Chad makes a specialty of verbal brutality. Christine is not overwhelmed to be dating two men at once, but she finds it pleasant, and eventually she begins to really like Chad.

*In the Company of Men,* written and directed by Neil LaBute, is a continuing series of revelations, because it isn't simply about this sick joke. Indeed, if the movie were only about what Chad and Howard do to Christine and how she reacts, it would be too easy, a one-note attack on these men as sadistic predators. The movie deals with much more and it cuts deeper, and by the end we see it's about a whole system of values in which men as well as women are victims, and monstrous selfishness is held up as the greatest good.

Environments like the one in this film are poisonous, and many people have to try to survive in them. Men like Chad and Howard are dying inside. Personal advancement is the only meaningful goal. Women and minorities are seen by white males as unfairly advantaged. White males are seen as unfairly advantaged by everyone else.

There is an incredibly painful scene in *In the Company of Men* where Chad tells a young black trainee, "They asked me to recommend someone for the management training program," and then requires the man to humiliate himself in order to show that he qualifies. At first you see the scene as racist. Then you realize Chad and the trainee are both victims of the corporate culture they occupy, in which the power struggle is the only reality. Something forces both of them to stay in the room during that ugly scene, and it is job insecurity.

On a more human level, the story becomes poignant. Both Howard and Chad date Christine. There is an unexpected emotional development. I will not reveal too much. We arrive at the point where we thought the story was leading us, and it keeps on going. There is another chapter. We find a level beneath the other levels. The game was more Machiavellian than we imagined. We thought we were witnessing evil, but now we look on its true face.

What is remarkable is how realistic the story is. We see a character who is depraved, selfish, and evil, and he is not a bizarre eccentric, but a product of the system. It is not uncommon to know personally of behavior not unlike Chad's. Most of us, of course, are a little more like Howard, but that is small consolation. "Can't you see?" Howard says. "I'm the good guy!" In other words, I am not as bad as the bad guy, although I am certainly weaker.

Christine survives, because she knows who she is. She is deaf, but less disabled than Howard and Chad, because she can hear on frequencies that their minds and imaginations do not experience. *In the Company of Men* is the kind of bold, uncompromising film that insists on being thought about afterward—talked about, argued about, hated if necessary, but not ignored. "How does it feel right now, deep down inside?" one of the characters asks. The movie asks us the same question.

## Independence Day ★ ★ ½

PG-13, 145 m., 1996

Will Smith (Captain Steven Hiller), Bill Pullman (The President), Jeff Goldblum (David), Mary McDonnell (Marilyn), Judd Hirsch (Julius), Margaret Colin (Constance), Randy Quaid (Russell), Robert Loggia (General Grey), Brent Spiner (Dr. Okun), Harvey Fierstein (Marty). Directed by Roland Emmerich and produced by Dean Devlin. Screenplay by Emmerich and Devlin.

The best shot in *Independence Day* is one of the first ones, of a vast shadow falling across the lunar surface. Visitors have arrived from beyond the solar system, and soon their presence is detected in our skies. Their ship is pretty big: "One-fourth the size of the Moon!" a scientist gasps, and although an object that size in near-Earth orbit might be expected to cause tidal waves, this is not a movie that slows down for the small details.

As the president of the United States and an assortment of other stock movies types look on, the mother ship dispatches smaller saucers (only fifteen miles across) to hover menacingly above Earth's cities. Do they come in peace? Don't make me laugh. As David (Jeff Goldblum), a broadcast technician and computer whiz, soon discovers, they are using our own satellite system to time an attack.

*Independence Day* is not just an inheritor of the 1950s flying saucer genre, it's a virtual retread—right down to the panic in the streets, as terrified extras flee toward the camera and the skyscrapers frame a horrible sight behind them. Like those old B movies, the alien threat is intercut with lots of little stories involving colorful characters who are chosen for their ethnic, occupational, and sexual diversity: Representing the human race here are not only David the techhead and the president, but also assorted blacks, Jews, Arabs, Brits, exotic dancers, homosexuals, cute kids, generals, drunken crop dusters, frizzy-haired scientists, tight-lipped defense secretaries, and the McLaughlin Group. There is not a single character in the movie who doesn't wear an invisible label.

Although the special effects in *Independence Day* are elaborate and pervasive, they aren't outstanding. The giant saucers are a dark, looming presence at the top of a lot of shots, big but dull, and the smaller "fighter" saucers used by the aliens are a disappointment—clunky, squat little gray jobs that look recycled out of ancient Rocket Men of Mars adventures.

When the aliens attack, there are shots of the White House and the Empire State Building getting blowed up real good, but if these creatures can field a spaceship a fourth the size of the Moon, why do they bother engaging in aerial dogfights with the U.S. Air Force? And why don't they blow up everything at once? Or knock out the Internet with a neutron bomb, instead of simply causing snow and static on TV screens? And why don't the humans react more? At one point, the news comes that New York, Washington, and Los Angeles have been destroyed, and is there grief? Despair? Anguish? Speculation about what that will mean for professional sports? Not a bit; the characters nod and hurry on to the next scene.

We're not supposed to ask such questions, I know. We're supposed to get wrapped up in the story, and there are some neat ideas in the movie—especially the revelation that Area 51, the government's "secret" base north of Las Vegas, actually does harbor that alien spaceship everybody believes the feds captured in New Mexico in 1947. The spaceship and some embalmed aliens are guarded far below the earth, and the underground lab is run by the long-haired Dr. Okun (played by none other than Brent Spiner, who is Data on *Star Trek: The Next Generation*). Okun is your classic mad scientist type, complaining "They don't let us out much," and telling the president, "Guess you'd like to see the big tamale, eh?"

As the president readies Earth's response, it is clear much will depend on a jerry-built solution by David, who Goldblum plays as a hemming and hawing genius. His plan, after he devises it, depends on fighter ace Steven Hiller (Will Smith) for its delivery.

But what Goldblum comes up with I cannot reveal here. No, I insist. I only observe that it is a wonder these aliens have traveled across uncounted light-years of space, and yet have never thought of a computer virus protection program. (My own theory is that any aliens who could be taken in by this particular plan probably arrived here after peddling a long time across space on bicycles.)

For all of its huge budget, *Independence Day* is a timid movie when it comes to imagination. The aliens, when we finally see them, are a serious disappointment; couldn't they think of anything more interesting than octopus men? If an alien species ever does visit Earth, I, for one, hope they have something interesting to share with us. Or, if they must kill us, I hope they do it with something we haven't seen before instead of with cornball ray beams that look designed by the same artists who painted the covers of *Amazing Stories* magazine in the 1940s. Still, *Independence Day* is in the tradition of silly summer fun, and on that level I kind of liked it, as, indeed, I kind of like any movie with the courage to use the line, "It's the end of the world as we know it."

☞

## Infinity ★ ★ ★

PG, 119 m., 1996

Matthew Broderick (Richard Feynman), Patricia Arquette (Arline Greenbaum), Peter Riegert (Mel Feynman), Dori Brenner (Tutti Feynman), Peter Michael Goetz (Dr. Hellman), Zeljko Ivanek (Bill Price), Matt Mulhern (Gate Guard), Joyce Van Patten (Aunt Ruth). Directed by Matthew Broderick and produced by Joel Soisson, Michael Leahy, Patricia Broderick, and Matthew Broderick. Screenplay by Patricia Broderick.

Richard Feynman was one of the most interesting men our century has produced. As a very young man, he did theoretical work at Los Alamos on the project to develop an atomic bomb. In 1960, he gave a speech so famous it is known simply as "Feynman's Talk," in which he described a new science of nanotechnology—the manipulation of very, very small things.

Not only was it possible to write the complete contents of the *Encyclopedia Britannica* on the head of a needle, he said, but the contents of every book ever written could be stored in a space the size of a dust mote. (This speech helped point the way to the tiny microprocessors on silicon chips which made modern computers possible.) Near the end of his life, conducting a simple experiment with a glass of ice water, he solved the mystery of the *Challenger* space-shuttle disaster. Feynman, who won the Nobel Prize in Physics in 1965, died in 1988.

I was at first disappointed that *Infinity*, the

new film based on his early years, pays relatively little attention to Feynman's science. Here it follows an old tradition; movies about great men tend to concentrate on when they were young and in love, rather than when they were middle-aged and doing their most important work. (It is a great relief when the subject, like Mozart, dies while still young.)

*Infinity* follows Feynman (Matthew Broderick) from the late 1930s until the mid 1940s, a time during which he met and courted his first wife, Arline Greenbaum (Patricia Arquette). He was born brilliant and was not shy to admit it; on one of his first dates with Arline, he bets a Chinese merchant that he can solve problems in his head faster than the man can use his abacus.

A graduate of MIT, now studying at Princeton, Feynman has long been in love with Arline. Marriage, they thought, could wait—and would have to because they had no money. Then two things changed all that. Feynman was offered a job in the top-secret research project at Los Alamos, and Arline became seriously ill with tuberculosis.

In those days TB was a hushed-up illness; patients went to sanitariums to recover, placing their lives on hold. In the film, Feynman and his love are not sure they have time to spare. She may die. And he knows as well as anyone that the developing war may bring untold disaster. Over his parents' objections, they get married despite her illness. Feynman leaves for New Mexico, and at the first opportunity sends for Arline, who becomes a patient in a hospital in Albuquerque.

Broderick and Arquette have a sweet, unforced chemistry as the young couple, who try their best to lead normal lives in an abnormal situation (in one scene, they barbecue steaks on a grill on the front lawn of the hospital). For Feynman, almost everything is an experiment; he pounces around her hospital room, testing the limits of the human nose. (His theory: We could sniff out things a lot better if we paid more attention to the process.)

The project at Los Alamos takes on a shadowy unreality as a backdrop to their married life. I vividly remember the great documentary *The Day After Trinity*, about the development of the bomb, and in the backgrounds of some shots I could guess what was happening in the real world of the Manhattan Project. But the film, directed by Broderick and written by his mother, Patricia, is more concerned with their inner landscapes.

Eventually the love story won me over. I could see that *Infinity* was not going to be about Feynman's science but about his heart, but then the film had never promised to be anything else. Maybe the problems of these two small people didn't amount to a hill of beans in the crazy world they were living in—but they mattered to Richard and Arline, and at the center of the story is the way a brilliant scientist, who can figure out almost anything, can't make the slightest dent in the ultimate reality of death.

*Infinity* is a sweet story about smart people, and depends for its effect on the bittersweet knowledge that their happiness is transitory. There are moments when they seem to sense some higher power, as when they hold a picnic in a kiva—one of the dwellings hewn out of rock faces by early cliff-dwelling Indians. And others when sorrow strikes, as when Richard buries his face in Arline's clothes to remember her powder and perfume. It is a small story, and a touching one.

## Intimate Relations ★ ★

R, 105 m., 1997

Rupert Graves (Harold Guppy), Julie Walters (Marjorie Beasley), Matthew Walker (Stanley Beasley), Laura Sadler (Joyce). Directed by Philip Goodhew and produced by Angela Hart, Lisa Hope, and John Slan. Screenplay by Goodhew.

"I'd rather be dead than brazen," Mrs. Beasley tells her husband when he pleads for "relief" in *Intimate Relations.* We already suspect that she might have the opportunity to be both. The film peeks behind the respectable lace curtains of a British village where Marjorie Beasley is a landlady, her husband, Stanley, is a one-legged war veteran, and their teenage daughter, Joyce, is too smart for her own good.

Into their uneasy idyll one day comes the hapless Harold Guppy (Rupert Graves), who is looking for a room to rent. "Call me 'Mom,'" Mrs. Beasley (Julie Walters) tells him firmly. Conducting a tour of the house, she is quite clear about the sleeping arrangements: "Mr. Beasley and I keep separate rooms for medical purposes."

Harold is a bit of a case study himself. Until recently in the merchant marine, he has some shady skeletons in his closet, but seems friendly enough, and enjoys the reasonable rent, good food, and all-around hospitality, especially from "Mom," who embraces him hungrily in the hallways and creeps silently into his room at night.

But not quite silently enough, because Joyce (Laura Sadler) pops in right after her, and demands to join them in bed. "It's my birthday," she explains. "That's not decent!" Harold protests. "I'm her mother," Marjorie says, concerned that Joyce might betray them to Mr. Beasley (Matthew Walker), who by this hour of the night is usually deep in an alcohol-induced snooze.

*Intimate Relations* tells a story that resembles in some respects pornography, although it suggests that if one ever did find oneself in such a situation it would be a great deal more bother than it was worth. Mother and daughter alternate visits to the handsome young Mr. Guppy, Dad begins to harbor dark suspicions, and "Mom" panics when it appears that Harold may be prepared to escape into the army.

*Intimate Relations* is about the same sort of repressed sexual goofiness that found an outlet in *Heavenly Creatures,* the New Zealand film about the two close friends who committed murder together, or *The Young Poisoner's Handbook,* about the earnest young man whose chemistry experiments went entirely too far. Its deadpan humor is entertaining, up to a point, but that point is passed before the movie is quite at its halfway point, and then we're left watching increasingly desperate people who are trapped by each other's madness. At the end I was not sure quite what it was all about, and neither, I am sure, was Mr. Guppy.

## Inventing the Abbotts ★ ★

R, 120 m., 1997

Joaquin Phoenix (Doug Holt), Billy Crudup (Jacey Holt), Will Patton (Lloyd Abbott), Kathy Baker (Helen Holt), Jennifer Connelly (Eleanor Abbott), Michael Sutton (Steve), Liv Tyler (Pamela Abbott), Joanna Going (Alice Abbott). Directed by Pat O'Connor and produced by Ron Howard, Brian Grazer, and Janet Meyers. Screenplay by Ken Hixon, based on the story by Sue Miller.

*Inventing the Abbotts* is a film that seems to have been made in a time machine. Not only the picture's story but also its values and style are inspired by the 1950s. It's like a subtler, more class-conscious *Peyton Place,* and if the same movie had been made forty years ago with Natalie Wood, Sandra Dee, Troy Donahue, and Ricky Nelson, it could have used more or less the same screenplay (minus the four-letter words).

The film seems indirectly inspired by Welles's *Magnificent Ambersons.* It's about the Abbotts, a rich family whose parties and wealth dominate a small Midwestern town, and about a local working-class boy who has made the family his "addiction." He eventually conquers all three of the Abbott girls, while his younger brother lusts after one and loves another, but lacks his courage.

The movie is narrated by the younger brother, Doug Holt (Joaquin Phoenix). He tends to repeat himself, finding countless different ways to say that his upwardly mobile brother Jacey Holt (Billy Crudup) has always been more confident and successful—especially around the Abbott girls. The oldest is Alice (Joanna Going), the official "nice girl," who gets pregnant, gets married, gets divorced, and gets Jacey, in that order. The middle is Eleanor Abbott (Jennifer Connelly), the official "bad girl," who gets sent away to stewardess school for her exploits. The youngest is Pam (Liv Tyler), and she's also the nicest, and the one Doug really likes, although he also lusts after Eleanor.

To understand the three Abbott girls and the two Holt brothers it helps to understand their world. They live in Haley, Illinois, a town of maybe 20,000, dominated by a steel desk factory owned by Mr. Abbott (Will Patton). Years ago, Mr. Abbott and the boys' father were friends. But then Abbott allegedly cheated Holt out of a valuable patent for sliding desk drawers, and then Holt died when he drove his DeSoto roadster onto a frozen lake on a stupid $20 bet. Soon after, rumors raced through town that Mr. Abbott was spending way too much time consoling the new widow Holt (Kathy Baker).

This is the kind of material that might have graced a mid-1950s Universal-International weeper—maybe one adapted from a John O'Hara best-seller filled with descriptions of country clubs. Even then it would have had more energy. *Inventing the Abbotts* seems slow and almost morose, and the director, Pat O'Connor, shows none of the cheerful love of human nature that enlivened his *Circle of Friends* (1995), the smart and touching picture about young love in 1950s Ireland.

The picture is haunted by a story problem: It isn't about anything but itself. There's no sense of life going on in the corners of the frame. The characters, completely preoccupied by the twists of the plot, have no other interests. Mr. Abbott is one of those 1950s dads whose sole functions in life are to drive gas guzzlers, stand behind a big desk, smoke a lot of cigarettes, and tell teenage guys to stay away from his daughters. Kathy Baker is more dimensional as Mrs. Holt—she has some touching scenes—but her life, too, has been completely defined by what happened with the Abbotts in the past, what is happening with the Abbotts now, and what, I fear, will happen with the Abbotts in the future.

The film's art direction is uncanny. It doesn't look like a period picture; it looks like a movie that was actually shot in 1955. Looking at the old cars and the storefronts and the front yards and the clothes, I was reminded of *Young at Heart* or *A Summer Place*. The actors do their best, and are sometimes quite appealing, but the story is so lugubrious there's nowhere they can go with it. And it's a shame the most interesting Abbott girl (the Jennifer Connelly character) is shipped out of town just after she delivers the movie's best line. ☞

## It's My Party ★ ★ ★

R, 110 m., 1995

Eric Roberts (Nick Stark), Gregory Harrison (Brandon Theis), Margaret Cho (Charlene Lee), Bruce Davison (Rodney Bingham), Lee Grant (Nick's Mother, Amalia), George Segal (Nick's Father, Paul), Devon Gummersall (Andrew Bingham), Marlee Matlin (Nick's Sister, Daphne), Roddy McDowall (Damian Knowles), Olivia Newton-John (Lina Bingham). Directed by Randal Kleiser and produced by Joel Thurm and Kleiser. Screenplay by Kleiser.

*It's My Party* is gentle and very sad, the story of a man who discovers that he has a short time to live and throws a party of family and friends, so that he can say good-bye before committing suicide. The story is not so concerned with his disease or his decision as with recording the emotional tones that surround it, and watching the film is uncannily like going through the illness, death, and memorial service of a loved one.

The dying man is Nick Stark (Eric Roberts). He has been HIV-positive for eight years. Now he experiences a series of small, troubling signs. He forgets his keys. He drops a barbell at the gym. "Get the scan," a friend says, and he does, and the test finds lesions on his brain. The full name of his condition is progressive multifocal leukoencephalopathy, and it is depressing to discover that some of his friends can rattle that term right off.

Nick, a designer, was the lover for many years of Brandon (Gregory Harrison), a TV director, but they broke up after Nick tested positive. Painful flashbacks show them fighting over their house and dog; Brandon brought most of the money to the relationship, and so it was Nick who moved out to a little frame house where the final party will be held. Telling his closest friends (including Charlene, played by Margaret Cho) that it is "time for Plan B" and he wants to die "while I am still me," he goes through his Rolodex, making an invitation list: "Dead . . . dead . . . dull . . . dead."

The centerpiece of the movie is Roberts's performance as the dying man. This is a quieter, gentler Eric Roberts than I've seen before. As the friends and family start to gather, he tries to comfort them, bringing to each one what he senses they need. There is some laughter and a few macabre jokes, but basically the party (which stretches to two days because of some latecomers) consists of Nick at the epicenter, brave and sweet, surrounded in the corners of the rooms by many worried and sad conversations.

"Gay people get to choose their own families," one of Nick's friends says, "and he chose us." His natural family is also there: Lee Grant as his Greek mother, George Segal as his Jewish father, and Marlee Matlin as his sister. It is clear in a conversation they have that his father never accepted Nick's homosexuality, and buried that and other issues in lifelong alcoholism. The father tries to apologize, awkwardly.

The key event of the party is the arrival of Brandon, the former lover. Nick's friends are hostile to him: They think he has his nerve. But Charlene invited him because she senses that Nick will be happy to see him, and although there is still anger and resentment, she is right.

"When he got sick, I guess I got scared," Brandon confesses.

The idea of voluntary suicide, much in the news because of Dr. Kevorkian, is treated here not as an issue but as an accepted choice. In another flashback, we see how Nick and others helped a friend of theirs who chose to kill himself. They leave him to die, and the next day they go to deal with the body, only to discover that he is not yet quite dead. So they follow through. This scene will cause the most discussion after the film, and indeed within the film Roddy McDowall plays a Catholic who argues that only God should decide when we die.

For Nick, whose vision is blurring and whose memory is fading, the choice seems clear. By the end of the film, in a quiet, understated way, director and writer Randal Kleiser has created a genuine family feeling. This is not one of those overplotted constructions in which every character poses a problem, and the screenplay assigns solutions. It's more three-dimensional and realistic, showing how death, for all of its sadness, can sometimes create joy if people are given the opportunity to affirm what they feel for one another. It is not an end, but a passage. And some things finally get said that needed to be said a long time earlier.

# J

## **Jack** ★ ½

PG-13, 117 m., 1996

Robin Williams (Jack Powell), Diane Lane (Karen Powell), Brian Kerwin (Brian Powell), Jennifer Lopez (Miss Marquez), Bill Cosby (Lawrence Woodruff), Fran Drescher (Dolores Durante), Adam Zolotin (Louis Durante), Todd Bosley (Edward). Directed by Francis Ford Coppola and produced by Ricardo Mestres, Fred Fuchs, and Coppola. Screenplay by James DeMonaco and Gary Nadeau.

In his choice of characters, Robin Williams seems more comfortable playing soloists—people set apart by special skills or problems. Remember him in *Jumanji*, trapped in time. Or in *Popeye*, where "I yam what I yam." Or in *Mrs. Doubtfire*, crossing the gender line. Or consider his unclassifiable characters in *The Fisher King* and *Toys*.

Williams seems most at home in bodies that don't quite fit. Maybe that's why he had so much fun doing the voice for the genie in *Aladdin*. He must have been the first choice for Francis Ford Coppola's *Jack*, where he plays a boy who is aging at four times the normal rate. He is born, fully developed, after a two-month pregnancy, and at the age of ten he looks exactly like a forty-year-old man.

The notion of a boy trapped in a man's body has been done before, by Tom Hanks in *Big*, for example. *Jack* brings it poignancy, because the situation isn't caused by magic, but by medical reasons; it's obvious Jack may not turn twenty. (His condition is not inspired by a real disease, but was created by the filmmakers.)

Williams works hard at seeming to be a kid inside a grown-up body, and some of his inspirations work well. But he has been ill-served by a screenplay that isn't curious about what his life would *really* be like. Francis Coppola brought great pathos to a similar situation in his *Peggy Sue Got Married* (1986), where a forty-three-year-old woman (Kathleen Turner) found herself inside her own teenage body. He found scenes that dealt truly with the crushing fact that we float on a current of time. In *Jack*, he and his writers, James DeMonaco and Gary Nadeau, go for more obvious payoffs.

The setup: As a device to make the story simpler and more dramatic, Jack is essentially kept out of society until he's ten. A tutor (Bill Cosby) comes to his home every day, and Jack has no ordinary contact with other kids. The movie explains this through the concerns of his uptight mom (Diane Lane), but finally the tutor and the dad (Brian Kerwin) prevail, and he goes to school.

Of course the other kids don't accept him. Well, why should they? He's got a receding hairline. (His dad teaches him to shave during the film, which seems odd, since by my calculations he should have been doing that since he was about four.) When he sits down on his first day in fifth grade, the desk isn't big enough, it collapses beneath him, and my heart sank: Why would anyone the size of Robin Williams try to sit in a fifth-grade chair except to produce a slapstick gag?

Eventually the kids accept him (he's a good basketball center), and then they find he has other uses—he can buy *Penthouse*, for example. But instead of using *Penthouse* as the springboard for observations about the ambivalence of boys that age to sex, the movie goes for a payoff in which a tree house collapses. (The next time I see a tree house collapse or a character fall through several floors of an old building, I'm going to picket the prop union.)

There is one scene in the movie that works, is true, and does illuminate Jack's human dilemma, and that's the scene where he gets a crush on his teacher (Jennifer Lopez) and plies her with a bag of red Gummi Bears before asking her to the school dance. (She's the only female in view who is tall enough to dance with him.) The way the teacher tactfully and gently handles this situation is an illustration of a path the whole movie could have taken, had it been more ambitious.

But *Jack* doesn't want to be a great movie. It only wants to pluck the usual heartstrings and provide the anticipated payoff. Far from being able to empathize with the thought processes of a ten-year-old, the filmmakers place him in situations they can imagine but a kid probably couldn't. I intensely disliked a subplot involving a schoolmate's trampy mother (Fran Drescher), which leads to a scene in a bar that doesn't work and doesn't belong, but does illustrate the ancient principle that every time there is a bar in a movie, there is a fight.

Who was this movie made for? Kids, maybe, who will like the scene where Jack passes himself off as the school principal (although the scene could have been written with smarter dialogue). But if this is a kids' movie, go for kids' reference points. Or if it's for adults, then it shouldn't have been constructed as a sitcom. My best guess is that the premise blinded everyone. Robin Williams is a ten-year-old in a forty-year-old's body? Great! When do we start shooting? If anyone dared to bring up the possibility of a better screenplay, he was probably shouted down: In the delirium of high concept, it doesn't pay to rain on the parade—no, not even if flowers might afterward grow.

## Jack and Sarah ★ ★ ★

R, 110 m., 1996

Richard E. Grant (Jack), Samantha Mathis (Amy), Judi Dench (Margaret), Ian McKellen (William), Cherie Lunghi (Anna), Eileen Atkins (Phil), Imogen Stubbs (Sarah), David Swift (Michael). Directed by Tim Sullivan and produced by Pippa Cross, Simon Channing-Williams, and Janette Day. Screenplay by Sullivan.

We begin with the presence of Richard E. Grant. He smiles but is somehow shifty. He doesn't seem like a leading man in a comedy about raising a baby. He isn't smooth, dependable, and cuddly. He is, in fact, edgy and short-tempered, and appallingly self-centered. No Hollywood casting director would think twice before rejecting him for the lead in *Jack and Sarah*. That is why he makes such an interesting choice, and why the movie rises above its formula origins to become perversely interesting.

You may have seen Grant before, although his name may not come immediately to mind. He was the costar of *Withnail & I* (1987), as a desperately bitter, angry, unemployed actor. In *How to Get Ahead in Advertising* (1989), his misery was so great that it produced a boil on his shoulder that eventually developed a mind of its own. In *The Player, Bram Stoker's Dracula*, and *The Age of Innocence* he played varieties of ominous twits. Not, in other words, the kind of warmhearted Hugh Grantish, Dudley Moorish, Richard Dreyfussian lead you would expect in a movie about a selfish egotist who learns to love.

Why is Grant not the expected choice? His face is too long. His eyes are too frank. His mouth is too wry. These are, of course, excellent attributes for an actor, and will give him longevity; Richard Grant will be playing intriguing roles long after Hugh Grant has been consigned to kindly godfathers. But they are not qualities we associate with fuzzy parent-figures.

Grant has, in fact, received some negative reviews for this film—mostly, I think, because he forces viewers to come to terms with him, instead of allowing them to settle into a comfortable cocoon of mindless sitcom reassurance. His presence forces the movie to be about something other than its clichés, which are many, and by the end I had become involved in his character's struggle to become a nice person.

Grant plays Jack, a London lawyer who snarls at the workmen rehabbing his home, gets into an ill-advised fight with someone clamping his car (or, as we say here, getting the Denver Boot), and is so intense and competitive that during a natural childbirth class with his pregnant wife, Sarah (Imogen Stubbs), he goes into sympathetic labor. Soon it is time for the baby to be born, an event he misses, having fallen down the stairs and gone unconscious to the hospital in the same ambulance as his wife. (You can see how a casting director would think of Dudley Moore.)

It is not betraying too much of the plot, I hope, to reveal that Sarah dies in childbirth. This happens very early on, as a setup for the central plot, which involves Jack's struggle to become a good parent, love his little daughter Sarah, and transform himself into an acceptable human being.

He is assisted in this struggle by Amy (Samantha Mathis), an American working as a waitress in London; he rescues her from the restaurant and hires her to be Sarah's nanny. And he is helped by William (Ian McKellen), an alcoholic derelict who cleans himself up nicely and more or less appoints himself the household butler. Assorted grandparents also come into the picture, particularly those wonderful actresses Judi Dench, as his mother, and Eileen Atkins, as his stepmother. They dote on little Sarah, and hope Jack will become a good father—if such a thing is possible.

If you muse a bit on the characters I've described, you will no doubt be able to fashion a very good guess about what eventually happens. That's why Richard Grant is so important to the movie. The screenplay, by Tim Sullivan (who also directs), is straight off the assembly line. But by casting against type, by finding an actor whose very presence insists he is not to be disregarded, the movie works in spite of its conventions. Grant makes general scenes into particular ones, and adds suspense by generating doubt about whether his character will respond according to formula. *Jack and Sarah* is almost perverse in the way it backs into its cheerful outcome; first the heart transplant, then the heart.

## The Jackal ★ ½

R, 119 m., 1997

Bruce Willis (The Jackal), Richard Gere (Declan Mulqueen), Sidney Poitier (Preston), Diane Venora (Valentina Koslova), Mathilda May (Isabella). Directed by Michael Caton-Jones and produced by James Jacks, Sean Daniel, and Kevin Jarre. Screenplay by Jarre and Chuck Pfarrer, based on *The Day of the Jackal* by Kenneth Ross.

*The Jackal* is a glum, curiously flat thriller about a man who goes to a great deal of trouble in order to create a crime that anyone in the audience could commit more quickly and efficiently. An example: Can you think, faithful reader, of an easier way to sneak from Canada into the United States than by buying a sailboat and entering it in the Mackinaw-to-Chicago race? Surely there must be an entry point somewhere along the famous 3,000-mile border that would attract less attention than the finish line of a regatta.

To be sure, the Jackal (for it is he) has the money to buy the boat. He is charging $70 million to assassinate the head of the FBI—half now, half payable on completion. He's hired by the head of the Russian Mafia, who, like many a foreigner with extra change in his pocket, doesn't realize he is being overcharged. There are guys right here in town, so I have heard, who would do a whack for ten grand and be happy to have the business.

*The Jackal* is based on the screenplay of Fred Zinnemann's 1973 classic *The Day of the Jackal.* That was a film that impressed us with the depth of its expertise: We felt it knew exactly what it was talking about. *The Jackal,* on the other hand, impressed me with its absurdity. There was scarcely a second I could take seriously.

Examples: In the Washington, D.C., subway system, the Jackal jumps across the tracks in front of a train to elude his pursuers. The train stops, exchanges passengers, and pulls out of the station. Is it just possible, do you suppose, that in real life after a man jumps across the tracks, the train halts until the situation is sorted out?

Or, how about the scene where the Jackal parks his van in a garage and paints the hatch handle with a deadly poison? One of his enemies touches the handle, convulses, and dies an agonizing death. Is that a good way to avoid attention? By being sure there's a corpse on the ground next to your van?

Or, how about the scene early in the film where a fight breaks out on cue, and then stops immediately after a gunshot is fired? Bad handling of the extras here by the assistant director: Everybody in a bar doesn't start or stop fighting at once. Even in the movies there are always a few guys who delay before joining in, or want to land one last punch at the end. These barflies are as choreographed as dancing Cossacks.

The Jackal is played by Bruce Willis as a skilled professional killer who hires a man to build him a remote-controlled precision gun mount. The man unwisely asks the kind of questions that, in his business, are guaranteed to get you killed. Hint: If you should find yourself doing business with a man who wants to pay cash for a device to hold, move, and aim a rifle capable of firing 100 explosive rounds before the first one hits its target—hey, don't go into a lot of speculation about what he may be planning to do with it.

On the Jackal's trail is the deputy head of the FBI (Sidney Poitier), who enlists the help of an IRA terrorist (Richard Gere). The IRA man is a federal prisoner, released into Poitier's custody to lead them to his lover, a Basque terrorist (Mathilda May), who knows what the Jackal looks like. The other major character is a Russian-born agent named Valentina (Diane Venora), whose character trait (singular) is that she lights a cigarette every time she is not already smoking one. I kept waiting for her to be killed, so that a last puff of smoke could drift from her dying lips as her fingers relaxed their grip on her lighter.

There was never a moment in *The Jackal* where I had the slightest confidence in the expertise of the characters. The Jackal strikes me as the kind of overachiever who, assigned to kill a mosquito, would purchase contraband insecticides from Iraq and bring them into the United States by hot-air balloon, distilling his drinking water from clouds and shooting birds for food.

Without giving away too much of the plot, I would like to register one dissent on the grounds of taste. There is a scene making a target out of a character clearly intended to be Hillary Clinton (hints: She is blond, fiftyish, the wife of the president, and is dedicating the New Hope Children's Hospital). The next time Bruce Willis or Richard Gere complains about the invasion of their privacy by the media, I hope someone remembers to ask them why their movie needed to show the first lady under fire.

## Jackie Brown ★ ★ ★ ★

R, 154 m., 1997

Pam Grier (Jackie Brown), Samuel L. Jackson (Ordell Robbie), Robert Forster (Max Cherry), Bridget Fonda (Melanie), Michael Keaton (Ray Nicolette), Robert De Niro (Louis Gara), Michael Bowen (Mark Dargus), Chris Tucker (Beaumont Livingston), Lisa Gay Hamilton (Sheronda), Tommy "Tiny" Lister Jr. (Winston), Hattie Winston (Simone), Aimee Graham (Billingsley Sales Girl). Directed by Quentin Tarantino and produced by Lawrence Bender, Richard N. Gladstein, Paul Hellerman, Elmore Leonard, Bob Weinstein, and Harvey Weinstein. Screenplay by Tarantino, adapted from the novel *Rum Punch* by Elmore Leonard.

I like the moment when the veins pop out on Ordell's forehead. It's a quiet moment in the front seat of a van, he's sitting there next to Louis, he's just heard that he's lost his retirement fund of $500,000, and he's thinking hard. Quentin Tarantino lets him think. Just holds the shot, nothing happening. Then Ordell looks up and says, "It's Jackie Brown."

He's absolutely right. She's stolen his money. In the movies, people like him hardly ever need to think. The director has done all their thinking for them. One of the pleasures of *Jackie Brown*, Tarantino's new film based on a novel by Elmore Leonard, is that everybody in the movie is smart. Whoever is smartest will live.

Jackie (Pam Grier) knows she needs to pull off a flawless scam or she'll be dead. Ordell (Samuel L. Jackson) will pop her, just like that guy they found in the trunk of the car. So she thinks hard, and so do her bail bondsman (Robert Forster) and the ATF agent (Michael Keaton). Everyone has a pretty good idea of exactly what's happening: They just can't figure it out fast enough to stay ahead of Jackie. The final scenes unfold in a cloud of delight, as the audience watches all of the threads come together.

This is the movie that proves Tarantino is the real thing, and not just a two-film wonder boy. It's not a retread of *Reservoir Dogs* or *Pulp Fiction* but a new film in a new style, and it evokes the particular magic of Elmore Leonard—who elevates the crime novel to a form of sociological comedy. There is a scene here that involves the ex-con Louis (Robert De Niro) and Ordell's druggie mistress (Bridget Fonda) discussing a photograph pinned to the wall, and it's so perfectly written, timed, and played that I applauded it.

Tarantino has a lot of scenes that good in this movie. The scene where one character lures another to his death by tempting him with chicken and waffles. The scene where a nagging woman makes one suggestion too many. The scene where a man comes around in the morning to get back the gun a woman borrowed the night before. The moment when Jackie Brown uses one line of dialogue, perfectly timed, to solve all of her problems.

This movie is about texture, not plot. It has a plot, all right, but not as the whole purpose of the film. Jackie Brown, forty-four years old, is an attendant on the worst airline in North America and supplements her meager salary by smuggling cash from Mexico to Los Angeles for Ordell, who is a gun dealer. Beaumont (Chris Tucker), one of Ordell's hirelings, gets busted by an ATF agent (Keaton) and a local cop (Michael Bowen). So they know Jackie is coming in with $50,000 of Ordell's money, and bust her.

Ordell has Jackie bailed out by Max Cherry (Robert Forster), a bondsman who falls in love the moment he sees her, but keeps that knowledge to himself. Jackie knows Ordell will kill her before she can cut a deal with the law. Maybe she could kill Ordell first, but she's not a killer, and besides, she has a better idea. The unfolding of this idea, which involves a lot of improvisation, occupies the rest of the movie.

At the heart of the story is the affection that grows between Jackie and Max. In a lesser thriller, there would be a sex scene. Tarantino reasonably believes that during a period when everyone's in danger and no one's leveling about their real motives, such an episode would be unlikely.

Max silently guesses part of what Jackie is up to, and provides a little crucial help. Jackie takes the help without quite acknowledging it. And their attraction stays on an unspoken level, which makes it all the more intriguing.

In *Jackie Brown,* as in *Pulp Fiction,* we get the sense that the characters live in spacious worlds and know a lot of people (in most thrillers the characters only know one another). Ordell has women stashed all over southern California, including a dim runaway from the South who he keeps in Glenwood, which he has told her is Hollywood. Max Cherry has a partner (Tiny Lister) who is referred to long before he goes into action.

The sides of the film's canvas are free to expand when it's necessary. If Tarantino's strengths are dialogue and plotting, his gift is casting. Pam Grier, the goddess of 1970s tough-girl pictures, here finds just the right note for Jackie Brown; she's tired and desperate. Robert Forster has the role of a career as the bail bondsman, matter-of-fact about his job and the law; he's a plausible professional, not a plot stooge.

Jackson, as Ordell, does a harder, colder version of his hit man in *Pulp Fiction,* and once again uses the word "nigger" like an obsession or a mantra (that gets a little old). De Niro, still in a longtime convict's prison trance, plays Louis as ingratiatingly stupid. Bridget Fonda's performance is so good it's almost invisible; her character's lassitude and contempt coexist with the need to be high all the time.

A lot of crime films play like they were written by crossword puzzle fans who fill in the easy words and then call the hotline for the solution. (The solution is always: Abandon the characters and end with a chase and a shoot-out.) Tarantino leaves the hardest questions for last, hides his moves, conceals his strategies in plain view, and gives his characters dialogue that is alive, authentic, and spontaneous. You savor every moment of *Jackie Brown.* Those who say it is too long have developed cinematic attention deficit disorder. I wanted these characters to live, talk, deceive, and scheme for hours and hours. ☞

## Jackie Chan's First Strike ★ ★ ★

PG-13, 88 m., 1997

Jackie Chan (Jackie), Jackson Lou (Tsui), Chen Chun Wu (Annie), Bill Tung (Uncle Bill), Jouri Petrov (Colonel Yegorov), Grishajeva Nonna (Natasha). Directed by Stanley Tong and produced by Barbie Tung. Screenplay by Tong, Nick Tramontane, Greg Mellott, and Elliot Tong.

Here is crucial dialogue from early in *Jackie Chan's First Strike:* "It's me! I found new suspect!"

"Who is he?"

"I don't know!"

Right there you have the beauty of the Jackie Chan movies. He always finds the suspect. And he never quite knows what he's doing. In its exotic locations and elaborate stunts, this could be a James Bond movie, if Bond were a cheerful Hong Kong cop who bumbles into the middle of the action by accident and fights his way out in sheer desperation.

Chan is said to be the world's top action star—except in the United States, which has resisted most of his forty-plus pictures. Now he is engaged in a campaign to conquer this last frontier; in 1996 we got *Rumble in the Bronx* and *Supercop,* and in 1997 we got *Jackie Chan's First Strike* and *Thunderbolt.* All are dubbed in English, mostly by Chan and the other actors themselves.

What makes him popular is not just his stunts (he is famous for doing them all himself) but his attitude to them: After a downhill ski chase in his shirtsleeves, his teeth chatter. When he's submerged in an icy lake, he desperately rubs his hands together for warmth. He wants our sympathy. And there is a sporting innocence in the action: Chan never uses a gun, there is no gore and not much blood, and he'd rather knock someone out than kill him.

The plot of *Jackie Chan's First Strike* is surrealistic. Chan plays a Hong Kong cop named Jackie, who is assigned to follow the mysterious Natasha on a flight to the Ukraine (he carefully makes a note every time she goes to the airplane toilet). In the snow-covered Ukraine, he stumbles into a plot involving conspirators who want to steal the warhead of a nuclear missile.

Chan follows them into a forbidden military area. He sees a warning sign and shouts to his superiors over his cell phone, "It says trespassers will be shot!" "That's just for kids," his boss assures him. Then we get the downhill ski sequences, including one in which Jackie skis off the side of a hill and grabs the runners of a helicopter. To be sure, it's not a very big hill and the helicopter is pretty close—but then we reflect that this is a real stunt, not a special effect, and we're impressed by Chan's skill and determination to entertain.

The "new KGB" surfaces, explains that the nuclear warhead is now in Australia, and that they are cooperating with the Hong Kong police. They will dispatch Jackie to Brisbane—by submarine, which seems a rather slow way to get there. In Australia, Chan meets Annie (Chen Chun Wu), whose job is to enter an oceanarium tank to feed the sharks, and whose brother has stolen the warhead, which she hides for him in the shark tank.

This situation, of course, requires Chan to spend a lot of time just barely escaping being eaten by sharks, while snatching breaths of oxygen from his enemies' scuba tanks. At one point my notes read: "New Russian Mafia terrorists fire rocket grenade at Chinese funeral in Brisbane," which will give you the general idea, if you can also imagine the scene where a guy forces Jackie to strip while singing "I Will Follow You," and then dresses him in a clown suit, after which Jackie tries to operate a cellular phone while wearing porpoise flippers. A little later, Jackie incapacitates a foe by flipping him into a tank filled with "toxic sea creatures," which attach themselves to his body like mean little pincushions.

Jackie Chan is an acquired taste. His movies don't have the polish of big-budget Hollywood extravaganzas, the dialogue sounds like cartoon captions, and as the plot careens from Hong Kong to the Ukraine to Australia we realize that it was probably written specifically to sell well in Russia and Down Under. But Chan himself is a graceful and skilled physical actor, immensely likable, and there's a kind of Boy Scout innocence in the action that's refreshing after all the doom-mongering, blood-soaked Hollywood action movies. It's as if the movie has been made of, by, and for thirteen-year-old boys, and while you watch it you feel like one.

## James and the Giant Peach ★ ★ ★

PG, 80 m., 1995

Paul Terry (James), Susan Sarandon (Spider), Richard Dreyfuss (Centipede), Simon Callow (Grasshopper), Pete Postlethwaite (Old Man), Miriam Margolyes (Aunt Sponge/Glowworm), David Thewlis (Earthworm). Directed by Henry Selick and produced by Denise Di Novi and Tim Burton. Screenplay by Karey Kirkpatrick, Jonathan Roberts, and Steve Bloom.

Almost all Disney animated films involve dead or absent parents, whose departure frees their little heroes to become independent adventurers. But *James and the Giant Peach* wipes out the parents with so much glee it almost seems like an inside joke. The movie opens with a pastel, soft-focus live-action sequence, in which little James lives an idyllic life by the seaside with his loving mom and dad. All is perfect. And then—bam! Both parents are gobbled up by a giant rhinoceros. So much for them.

James (Paul Terry) is immediately packed off to a miserable life with his horrid relatives, Aunt Sponge and Aunt Spiker, who work him like a slave, mock him, and feed him fish heads—when he's lucky. The lonely little boy draws his dreams on a paper bag and makes it into a hot-air balloon, sending it floating by candlepower.

A mysterious old man (Pete Postlethwaite) finds the paper bag and returns it filled with countless little green crocodile tongues. James spills the bag, and some of the tongues hop away, but one enchants an old peach tree on the aunts' property and a giant peach starts growing.

His aunts sell tickets to the attraction, but then the starving James eats a bite of the peach, along with a crocodile tongue, and that unleashes the peach's magic, as the movie cuts from live action to animation.

We now follow a cartoon James, who clings to the peach for dear life as it rolls down the hill, picking up a picket fence that winds around its circumference. He discovers that the peach is inhabited by colorful insects, including a centipede, a ladybug, a spider, a grasshopper, a glowworm, and an earthworm. All are friendly—but not the fearsome mechanical steam shark that comes along and tries to gobble them all up. They're saved by seagulls, who lift the peach into the sky on silken threads from the glowworm, and the movie's odyssey begins.

*James and the Giant Peach* is the second collaboration between producer Tim Burton *(Batman)* and director Henry Selick. Their first was *The Nightmare Before Christmas* (1993). Both films use stop-action animation, a technique in which three-dimensional puppets are moved ever so slightly from one frame to the next, giving the illusion of movement. Drawings, animation, and real life are combined in the settings.

The technique is not new. It was used in the earliest days of film and flourished in the 1920s and 1930s, when Willis O'Brien used it for the special-effects monsters in *The Lost World* (1925) and *King Kong* (1933). Ray Harryhausen advanced the technique in a series of adventure epics from *Mighty Joe Young* (1949) through *Clash of the Titans* (1981), but it has always been used sparingly, because it takes such infinite pains to do correctly, and because kids grew accustomed to the flat cartoon world of traditional animation.

What Selick and Burton have done with it, however, brings stop-motion to a new plateau. The movements of their characters are so fluid, compared to the slight jerkiness of older stop-motion, that I wonder if computers have been used to smooth out some of the motion. If not, then their achievement is even more amazing. All of the creatures, especially the colorful insects that share James's journey, are brought to vivid life, and the fact that we can see realistic textures—like the cloth in some of the costumes—gives the illusion an eerie quality halfway between reality and invention.

As for the movie, based on a familiar children's book by Roald Dahl, it will, I think, entertain kids for whom stop-motion animation is the last thing they're thinking about. The peach, carried by seagulls, drifts far north to the Arctic Circle, where there is a frightening underwater adventure on a sunken pirate ship (the villains torture the centipede on the rack). But James finally arrives at his destination in New York, where still more adventures await him (and the rhino attacks again). Oh, and there are some songs.

## Jane Eyre ★ ★ ★ ½

PG, 113 m., 1995

William Hurt (Rochester), Charlotte Gainsbourg (Jane Eyre), Joan Plowright (Mrs. Fairfax), Anna Paquin (Young Jane), Geraldine Chaplin (Miss Scatcherd), Billie Whitelaw (Grace Poole), Maria Schneider (Bertha), Fiona Shaw (Mrs. Reed), Elle Macpherson (Blanche Ingram). Directed by Franco Zeffirelli and produced by Dyson Lovell. Screenplay by Hugh Whitemore and Zeffirelli.

In *Jane Eyre* can be found all of the elements of the modern Gothic romance novel, which fills the paperback racks with countless versions of the same story. The covers give the game away: In the foreground a wide-eyed heroine, hair flying, bodice torn, flees from a forbidding Gothic manor. In the manor a light shines in one window, high in a tower. In the background a dark, sinister man glowers enigmatically. Additional elements, such as horses, children, dogs, governesses, willow trees and tombstones are optional.

What made *Jane Eyre* work so well as a novel by Charlotte Brontë, and in three previous film versions, is the classic purity of the two central characters. Jane (played here by Charlotte Gainsbourg) is plain, severe, dressed in somber clothes, an unwanted orphan whose unhappy days at boarding school have been followed by employment at the forbidding Thornfield Hall. And Mr. Rochester (William Hurt), the master of the hall, is tall, dark, handsome, glowering, deep-voiced, and enigmatic. These two anchors—the uncertain young girl and the distant, potentially threatening older man—can be found in almost every Gothic story, and it doesn't take a Freud to plunder the subtext.

The new *Jane Eyre* has been directed and cowritten by Franco Zeffirelli, the Italian director of films and opera, who is drawn to English literature; he made the Taylor-Burton *Taming of the Shrew* in 1967, a classic *Romeo and Juliet* in 1968, and Mel Gibson's 1990 *Hamlet*. The first two of those films were bursting with life and color, but *Hamlet* had a gloomier, damper texture, and with *Jane Eyre*, Zeffirelli has banished brightness and created a cold, gray world where, as the dialogue has it, "The shadows are as important as the light."

This is the right approach. Jane Eyre's world

must seem an ominous and forbidding place, charged with implied sexuality. In a sense, Jane's environment *is* sexuality—which surrounds her, misunderstood and unacknowledged. The movie creates the right visual atmosphere of deep shadows and gloomy interiors; the cinematographer, David Watkin, who also shot Zeffirelli's *Hamlet,* makes Thornfield Hall into a place where Jane's bedchamber is sunny and bright, but the spaces controlled by Rochester are ominous.

As played by Charlotte Gainsbourg, Jane's wide mouth and deep-set eyes make her look in the mirror with despair. After her unhappy childhood and adolescence, she has come to Thornfield to teach a young girl who is Rochester's ward, and she is a prim, dark figure in the background at his fancy-dress balls. As Blanche (Elle Macpherson), Rochester's snobby blond fiancée, observes, "You can always tell a governess at first glance. They're plain—in a very special way."

For Jane Eyre, Thornfield is a happy place, despite Rochester's enigmatic comings and goings. As a young orphan (played by Anna Paquin, the Oscar-winner from *The Piano*), she was hated by her aunt ("I have done what I could for the girl, but she has a willful, obstinate nature") and sent to a strict, cruel school. But there her spirit is not broken. When the headmaster labels her a liar and asks if she knows how to avoid going to hell, she replies: "Keep well and not die, sir."

At Thornfield Hall, the household is ruled by the kindly Mrs. Fairfax (Joan Plowright), and Jane's duty is to be governess for little Adele Varens (Josephine Serre), whose relationship to Rochester is unexplained. There is another employee at the hall, Grace Poole (Billie Whitelaw), whose duties are mysterious, but are perhaps connected to the disturbing screams that are sometimes heard in the middle of the night from a locked room in a far wing.

The key to the story is Jane's romantic attraction to Rochester—whom she fears to approach. Does he like her? Dislike her? Notice her? Rochester, so often away, does not explain himself. (One of his rare sallies: "You are not naturally austere any more than I am naturally vicious.") But one night when Jane saves him from a mysterious fire and is soaked in the process, he gives her his cloak to wrap herself in, and as she pulls it around herself, they both realize a divide has been crossed.

What I liked about this version is that Zeffirelli is true to the characters. Rochester never really melts, and Jane Eyre is spared the obligatory glamour shot when she takes her hair down and we realize she was really beautiful all along (Joan Fontaine starring in the 1944 version, opposite Orson Welles's Rochester). This is a romance between two troubled, wounded people, and by playing it that way, Zeffirelli makes it touching, when it could have been recycled Gothic Lite.

*Note: Jean Rhys wrote a novel called* Wide Sargasso Sea *that dealt with Rochester's life in Jamaica, and the first Mrs. Rochester. In 1993, it was made into a good film, erotic and atmospheric, by John Duigan.*

## Jerry Maguire ★ ★ ★

R, 135 m., 1996

Tom Cruise (Jerry Maguire), Cuba Gooding Jr. (Rod Tidwell), Renee Zellweger (Dorothy Boyd), Jay Mohr (Bob Sugar), Bonnie Hunt (Laurel Boyd), Regina King (Marcie Tidwell), Kelly Preston (Avery Bishop), Jerry O'Connell (Frank Cushman). Directed by Cameron Crowe and produced by James L. Brooks, Laurence Mark, Richard Sakai, and Crowe. Screenplay by Crowe.

There are a couple of moments in *Jerry Maguire* when you want to hug yourself with delight. One comes when a young woman stands up in an office where a man has just been fired because of his ethics, and says, yes, she'll follow him out of the company. The other comes when she stands in her kitchen and tells her older sister that she really, truly loves a man with her whole heart and soul.

Both of those moments involve the actress Renee Zellweger, whose lovability is one of the key elements in a movie that starts out looking cynical and quickly becomes a heart-warmer.

The man she follows, and loves, is Jerry Maguire (Tom Cruise), a high-powered professional sports agent who has so many clients he can't really care about any of them. He spends most of his time as a road warrior, one of those dogged joggers you see in airports, racking up the frequent-flier miles in pursuit of the excellence they read about in pinbrained best-sellers. One night he has a panic attack in a lonely hotel room, and writes a memo titled "The Things We Think and Do Not Say."

One of the things he thinks is that agents should be less concerned about money and more concerned about their clients. That gets him a standing ovation in the office, but a few days later, when he's fired, he understands why agents do not say those things they think. Maguire stages a grandstand exit (his decision to take along the office goldfish plays awkwardly, however). But when he asks who's walking out with him, only Dorothy, an accountant he's met just once at the airport, stands up and says she believes in him.

Dorothy is a widow with a cute little son (maybe just a mite too cute). She also has an outspoken older sister, played by Bonnie Hunt with her usual exuberance and ironic cheer (she's almost always a delight to watch). The sisters live together in a house where the living room seems to be semipermanently filled by a kvetching self-help group for divorced women, who spend all of their time talking about men. Someone should tell them that resentment is just a way of letting someone else use your mind rent-free.

Only one client doesn't dump Maguire when the agency boots him out. That's Rod Tidwell (Cuba Gooding Jr.), a wide receiver for Arizona, who resents the crappy waterbed commercials Maguire puts him in, but sticks with him anyway. Rod's wife, Marcie (Regina King), is her husband's shrewdest defender and biggest fan, and their marriage is a true love story—in contrast to Maguire's failing engagement to the power-mad Avery Bishop (Kelly Preston).

Avery is soon out of the picture, Dorothy begins to look less like an accountant and more like the most wonderful woman in the world, and under the influence of his ennobling new feelings, Jerry helps Rod learn to play from the heart and not just from the mind and the pocketbook. And somewhere along in there I began to feel that writer-director Cameron Crowe had bitten off more than he really needed to chew. The screenplay knows enough about sports agents to make that the subject of the whole film, and enough about romance, too, but there are so many subplots that *Jerry Maguire* seems too full: Less might have been more.

Still, the film is often a delight, especially when Cruise and Zellweger are together on the screen. He plays Maguire with the earnestness of a man who wants to find greatness and happiness in an occupation where only success really counts. She plays a woman who believes in this guy she loves, and reminds us that true love is about idealism. (Remember Franklin McCormick years ago on the all-night radio? "I love you because of who you are—and who I am when I am with you.")

The actual sports scenes are more predictable (right down to and including the big play that settles the season). But Cuba Gooding Jr., so strong in *Boyz N the Hood,* is fine here in a much different role, and finally the movie is about transformation: about two men who learn how to value something more important than money, and about two women who always knew.

## Jingle All the Way ★ ★ 1/2

PG, 89 m., 1996

Arnold Schwarzenegger (Howard Langston), Sinbad (Myron Larabee), Phil Hartman (Ted Maltin), Rita Wilson (Liz Langston), Robert Conrad (Officer Hummell), Martin Mull (DJ), Jake Lloyd (Jamie Langston), James Belushi (Mall Santa). Directed by Brian Levant and produced by Chris Columbus, Mark Radcliffe, and Michael Barnathan. Screenplay by Randy Kornfield.

*Jingle All the Way* was inspired, I suspect, by that panic a few years ago when they ran out of Cabbage Patch dolls. As the movie opens, little Jamie Langston is watching the TurboMan show on TV, and of course he wants the TurboMan action figure for Christmas, complete with all its accessories. Jamie's dad, Howard, is a busy businessman (Arnold Schwarzenegger) who says he has already purchased the doll—but lies, and whose adventures while trying to find a TurboMan provide the movie's plot.

There was once a time when family movies at Christmastime were about kindly old St. Nick and peace on earth, but as Christmas struggles to widen its lead in the holiday shopping sweepstakes, products and not sentiments are what turn kids on. Jamie (Jake Lloyd) wants the doll. His mother, Liz (Rita Wilson), is mad at her husband for always being too busy for family responsibilities. And so Howard goes out in desperation to do battle with half the other fathers in Minneapolis, who are also looking for TurboMan.

At the first store he goes to, he meets a manic postal worker named Myron (Sinbad), who rants against the sinister forces that are forcing us to compete for goods and services, and explains, "I know what I'm talking about because I went to junior college for a semester and studied psychology. I'm out there." Howard will meet Myron again and again during the course of this long day, but the movie never quite figures out if he's a friend, a villain, or a figure of fun, and so he's used interchangeably, and confusingly, in all of those roles.

Howard's biggest adventure comes at the Mall of America, where they're raffling off the last TurboMen at double the retail price (somehow I imagine that last detail was looped in later, and not shouted out inside the mall itself). A kid gets the last numbered ball, Howard chases him through one of those McDonald's-style jungle gyms, and eventually gets mauled by mothers who pound him with their purses while he protests, unforgettably, "I'm not a pervert! I yust vas looking vor a TurboMan doll!"

More of the plot I should not tell. Some of it involves the Langstons' helpful next-door neighbor (Phil Hartman), who has his eyes on Liz, and is one of those guys so deeply into Christmas that he rents a reindeer and puts up Christmas lights on *your* house. (Schwarzenegger is eventually attacked by the reindeer, and later makes up with it and gives it beer, in a scene that will not be used at his AFI tribute.)

The climax of the movie uses lots of special effects and swooping around and kids in peril and close calls, all of them done well and the swooping with great humor. The climax includes not one, but two of the inevitable kiddie movie clichés: A kick to the groin administered by the little hero, and the big hero saying, "Yesssssss!"

I liked a lot of the movie, which is genial and has abundant energy, but on the other hand I was sort of depressed by its relentlessly materialistic view of Christmas, and by the choice to go with action and (mild) violence over dialogue and plot. Audiences will like it, I am sure, but I have to raise my hand in reluctant dissent and ask, please, sir, may we have some more goodwill among men? Even TurboMen?

## johns ★ ★ ★

R, 96 m., 1997

Lukas Haas (Donner), David Arquette (John), Arliss Howard (John Cardoza), Keith David (Homeless John), Christopher Gartin (Crazy Eli), Josh Schaefer (David), Wilson Cruz (Mikey), Terrence Dashon Howard (Jimmy the Warlock), Elliott Gould (Manny). Directed by Scott Silver and produced by Beau Flynn and Stefan Simchowitz. Screenplay by Silver.

*johns*, a movie about male prostitutes in Los Angeles, has a moment that offers a key to the film: Tourists offer a hustler $20 to pose in a snapshot with them. They want to show the folks back home that they've not only seen the sights, they've met the locals.

There was a time when most people didn't know men sold sex, and didn't want to know. Now the cruising underworld is the stuff of movies, songs, novels, and fashion ads that are easy to decode. *johns* dramatizes the lifestyle at the same time it tells a cautionary tale: "Young man! Stay off of the streets!" (Sing to the tune of "YMCA.") The audience, like the tourists, gets to meet the locals while keeping a safe distance. That's because the hustling world is sentimentalized here, filtered through a lens of romanticism.

The movie stars Lukas Haas and David Arquette as Donner and John, who work Santa Monica Boulevard, nurtured by their dreams: John wants to spend his twenty-first birthday in a luxury hotel room, and Donner wants them both to take the bus to Branson, Missouri. Donner is gay and loves John; John says he's straight and working only for the money, and he does have a girlfriend, although the relationship is fleeting and chancy.

The film's symbolism is established early, when we learn that John's birthday is Christmas Day. He wears a stolen Santa hat for much of the film, and in an encounter with a violent client he picks up the marks of a crown of thorns. More symbolism: Three characters in the movie are named John, and all of the clients, of course, are called "johns," perhaps indicating that everyone is in the same boat. (Donner's name reminds me of the notorious Donner Party, suggesting still more parallels.)

Christ symbolism makes me apprehensive in a movie; it tips the ending, and besides, most

Christ-figures die for their own sins, not for ours. But *johns* overcomes the undergraduate symbol-mongering of its screenplay with a story that comes to life in spite of itself, maybe because the actors are so good, or maybe because the writer-director, Scott Silver, has documentary roots that correct for his overwriting.

Silver does a good job of capturing the unsprung rhythm of the street. Although one of the characters is always asking what time it is, that never really matters; time is what he sells, not what he passes. The characters form a loose-knit community at the mercy of strangers in cars. They may spend hours together and then not see each other for a week. We meet some of the street regulars: Crazy Eli (Christopher Gartin), for example, who spouts wild theories, and Homeless John (Keith David), who turns up from time to time like John the Baptist, with support and encouragement.

Working from stories he got from real life, Silver shows his heroes encountering a series of johns: one turns suddenly violent, one (well-played by Elliott Gould) is a kindhearted guy who sneaks in some action while his family is out shopping, one is an old man with peculiar tastes who wants to know "who in the Sam Hill" Donner thinks he is.

There is some underlying urgency: John has stolen $300 that belongs to a drug dealer (Terrence Dashon Howard), and now the dealer and his bodyguard are looking for him. He wants to use the $300 for his hotel room. Will he get his dream before the dealer gets the money? There is an ominous sign: His "lucky sneakers" are stolen at the beginning of the movie. Nothing bad could happen to him while he was wearing them, but now . . .

David Arquette and Lukas Haas find the right note for their characters: They have plans and dreams, but vague ones, and they're often sort of detached, maybe because their lives are on hold in between johns. They have fallen into a lifestyle that offers them up during every waking moment for any passing stranger. They do it for money, but it pays so badly they can't save up enough to stop. What the johns are really paying them for is not sex, but availability: to remain homeless and permanently on call.

## The Journey of August King ★ ½

PG-13, 92 m., 1996

Jason Patric (August King), Thandie Newton (Annalees), Larry Drake (Olaf Singletary), Sam Waterston (Mooney Wright), Sara-Jane Wylde (Ida Wright), Eric Mabius (Hal Wright), Bill Whitlock (Samuel), Muse Watson (Zimmer). Directed by John Duigan and produced by Nick Wechsler and Sam Waterston. Screenplay by John Ehle.

John Duigan's *The Journey of August King* tells the story of a lonely man, returning to his rural home from the market, who encounters an escaped slave woman and decides to help her. He tells her what he is doing is "against the law," but he does it anyway, in part because of guilt over a dead wife he was unable to help, and in part because she is helpless and harmless and he feels sorry for her. Later, there is an element of affection, although the film is over before we see what it might lead to.

The movie stars Thandie Newton as the escaped slave, named Annalees, and Jason Patric as August King, whose wife died in childbirth. The other major character is Olaf Singletary (Larry Drake), the slave owner who has posted a reward for Annalees. He is a cruel man and master, but not when it comes to Annalees: "She was my ray of light," he says, and not for the reason we might at first assume.

The movie sets its story in the photogenic forests of North Carolina, and does a good job of establishing its time, the early nineteenth century. Its characters are well played, and Thandie Newton (so wonderful in Duigan's *Flirting*) is so simple and effective here that you remember the affectations of her slave girl in *Jefferson in Paris* and wish you could transfer this performance to that movie.

The movie is good-hearted, earnest, and handsome to look at. But it is boring. The pacing, which is meant to be thoughtful, is lethargic. The silences grow longer than the moods they are intended to establish. The relationship between Annalees and August could have generated a great deal more tension than it does, perhaps if August had been made not quite so good, so that he had to struggle more to do the right thing.

Duigan is an interesting director. His credits

include *Flirting* (which I urge you to rent) and *Sirens* (for which many people required no urging). Here I think he's made a film filled with good intentions, but without the dramatic charge necessary to make it compelling.

## Jude ★ ★ ★

R, 123 m., 1996

Christopher Eccleston (Jude Fawley), Kate Winslet (Sue Bridehead), Liam Cunningham (Phillotson), Rachel Griffiths (Arabella), June Whitfield (Jude's Aunt), Ross Colvin Turnbull (Little Jude), James Daley (Jude as a Boy). Directed by Michael Winterbottom and produced by Andrew Eaton. Screenplay by Hossein Amini, based on the novel *Jude the Obscure* by Thomas Hardy.

Thomas Hardy's bleak and shocking novel *Jude the Obscure*, published in 1895, told the story of a stonemason who dreamed of becoming a scholar, but was crushed by the British social system, by fate, and by his own rotten luck. The novel created such an uproar when it was published that Hardy never wrote another one, retreating into his poetry and an old age of rural seclusion.

Now it has been filmed as *Jude*, an angry saga that just barely manages to find a bittersweet ending by overlooking the novel's final pages—which are even grimmer, if you can believe it, than the sad events we see on the screen. Only the energy of the leading actors and the glory of the photography rescue the film from the slough of despond—and in a way, Hardy might have thought, that's cheating. The novel argues that with society and conventional morality arrayed against you, there's not much you can do.

The movie stars Christopher Eccleston as Jude Fawley, a stonemason from a small village whose tutor, Phillotson, takes him to the top of a hill and shows him the towers of Christminster (which is meant to be Oxford). "If you want to do anything in your life, Jude," he tells him, "that's where you have to go." But the boy has few opportunities and no money, and soon he is courting Arabella (Rachel Griffiths), a pig farmer's daughter. They make love in a barn, their passion accompanied by the noises of the animals. She thinks she is pregnant, they marry, and their marriage is symbolized in a scene where Arabella dresses a pig carcass while he studies Greek and Latin.

Arabella, played by Griffiths as a sturdy, lusty woman with plans of her own, abandons Jude when she believes she is not pregnant, and leaves for Australia. Jude goes to Christminster, where he falls in love at first sight with his cousin, Sue (Kate Winslet, from *Sense and Sensibility*) and follows her to a socialist meeting. He studies for his entrance exams, and takes her to meet Phillotson (Liam Cunningham), who offers her a teaching job.

Jude's hopes of gaining admission to Christminster are dashed by the class system; not many self-taught manual laborers were accepted into British universities at the time, and there is a poignant scene where Jude, rejected as a scholar, defiantly recites the Creed in Latin in a pub, to an audience of drunken proles who mock his learning.

Sue wants to marry Jude, but when he reveals he's already married, she marries Phillotson on the rebound. The marriage doesn't work, and Phillotson himself observes, "I think you are one person split in two." Soon Sue and Jude are living together in sin, and Sue's refusal to even pretend to be married causes them to become outcasts: Jude loses a job at a church, they are thrown out of lodgings, and eventually they're reduced to selling pastries at street fairs.

In the meantime, Jude has adopted a son by Arabella (who was pregnant after all), and had two more by Sue—allowing his solemn-faced boy to watch during one childbirth. The couple sink into poverty and despair, moving from one bolt-hole to another, while the older son looks on quietly. The tone of the film is set in the opening black-and-white sequence, where Eduardo Serra's photography places small figures on a horizon and composes the shot so that a vast, dark, wet field of mud and rocks looms up to a sliver of sky. He and the director, Michael Winterbottom, create a convincing period landscape and townscape for "Wessex," the fictional county where Hardy's novels are set: Shops and cottages, streets and markets look beautiful as compositions, but the film gradually reveals its world as one with no comfort for the outcasts of this story.

What was Hardy arguing in his novel? Many of his books were about ordinary working-class people whose best efforts were not enough to escape the trap set for them by society. They labored, they dreamed, and the establishment slapped them down like troublesome flies. Yet despite the fact that Hardy was writing at a time when a socialist critique of his society was being fashioned, he doesn't seem to have a political message: Hardy was not a reformer but a mourner.

*Jude* is the second film I've seen by Winterbottom, whose *Butterfly Kiss* (1996) was a searing fable about a woman who was a schizophrenic killer, and the simpleminded girl she dominated and loved during a murder spree. Hardy supplies appropriate material for him. On the basis of these films, he is angry, clearheaded, and with a sure visual sense. And his casting gives personalities to the characters. Eccleston you may recall as one of the yuppie killers in *Shallow Grave*, Griffiths was the heroine's saucy girlfriend in *Muriel's Wedding*, and Winslet shows her range again this time, making Sue into a sassy, defiant woman who would rather be right than happy. Together they take a difficult story and make it into a haunting film.

## Jungle 2 Jungle ★

PG, 111 m., 1997

---

Tim Allen (Michael), Sam Huntington (Mimi), JoBeth Williams (Patricia), Lolita Davidovich (Charlotte), Martin Short (Richard), Valerie Mahaffey (Jan), LeeLee Sobieski (Karen), Frankie Galasso (Andrew). Directed by John Pasquin and produced by Brian Reilly. Screenplay by Bruce A. Evans and Raynold Gideon.

---

There is a scene early in *Jungle 2 Jungle* that indicates how brainless the movie is. Before I explore its delights, I must make you familiar with the premise. A Manhattan commodities broker journeys up the Amazon to obtain a divorce from the wife he has not seen in many years. She works now among the Indians. The broker is astonished to find that he has a son, who has been raised by his estranged wife in the jungle. The son now wants to return to New York with his father because he has promised the tribal chief he will bring back the fire from the torch atop the Statue of Liberty.

Now, as we rejoin our story, the broker (Tim Allen) and his son (Sam Huntington) arrive at Kennedy Airport, and here is the brainless part: The boy, who is about thirteen, is still dressed for the jungle. He wears only a loincloth and some feathers and suchlike; no shirt or shoes. If memory serves, he carries his deadly dart blowgun, which is the sort of thing you're not allowed to have on an aircraft, but never mind: Did either of this child's parents stop to consider that perhaps the lad should have jeans and a sweatshirt for a 3,000-mile air journey? Such garments are available in Brazil. I know; I've been there. I flew upstream in a plane with pontoons and landed on the Amazon above Belem without seeing a single person in a loincloth, although I saw many Michael Jordan T-shirts.

But no, the parents didn't stop to think, and that is because they *don't think*. Why don't they think? Because no one is allowed to think in this movie. Not one single event in the entire plot can possibly take place unless every character in the cast has brains made of Bac-O-Bits.

The plot of *Jungle 2 Jungle* has been removed from a French film called *Little Indian, Big City*. The operation was a failure and the patient dies. The only reason I am rating this movie at one star while *Little Indian, Big City* got no stars is that *Jungle 2 Jungle* is too mediocre to deserve no stars. It doesn't achieve truly awful badness, but is sort of a black hole for the attention span, sending us spiraling down into nothingness.

Most of the comic moments come from the "fish out of water" premise, or "FOW," as Hollywood abbreviates it (you know your plot's not original when it has its own acronym). The kid has been raised in the jungle, and now, in the city, he tries to adapt. There are many jokes involving his pet tarantula, which he has brought along with him, and his darts, which Allen uses to accidentally put his fiancée's cat to sleep.

The fiancée is played by Lolita Davidovich, who is supposed to be a successful businesswoman, but dresses as if she aspires to become a lap dancer. The joke is that she doesn't like the idea of her future husband having a jungle boy. Additional jokes involve Martin Short, who plays Allen's associate and has stolen Jim Jarmusch's hairstyle although not his wit. There are also some Russian Mafia guys, who march in and out like landlords in a Three Stooges comedy.

*Little Indian, Big City* (1996) got many if not most of the year's worst reviews, but when I heard it was being remade with Tim Allen, I must confess I had some hope: Surely they would see how bad the premise was and repair it? Not a chance. This movie has not learned from the mistakes of others, and like a lemming follows *Little Indian* over the cliff and into the sea.

## Junk Mail ★ ★ ★

NO MPAA RATING, 83 m., 1998

Robert Skjaerstad (Roy), Andrine Saether (Line), Per Egil Aske (Georg), Eli Anne Linnestad (Betsy). Directed by Pal Sletaune and produced by Petter Boe and Dag Nordahl. Screenplay by Jonny Halberg and Pal Sletaune. In Norwegian with English subtitles.

Roy is not someone you would want to know. Or stand very close to. Or get your mail from. He brings new aromas to the concept of grunge. He is a mailman in Oslo who reads any letters that look interesting, and then delivers them smeared with cold spaghetti that he eats out of cans. He dumps junk mail into a cave by the railroad tracks. He's so low on the mailman evolutionary chain that even if you crossed him with Kevin Costner in *The Postman*, the result would frighten dogs.

Roy stumbles into the life of Line, a hearing-impaired woman who lives on his route. One day she forgets and leaves her house keys in the lock of her mailbox. He lets himself in, sniffs around, tastes some of her food, looks through her drawers and hears a message from "Georg" on her answering machine: "We did it together. You were as much a part of it as I was."

On another day he returns, falls asleep, and hides under the bed when she comes home early. Hearing nothing after a while, he finds her underwater in the bathtub. He saves her from suicide, calls an ambulance, and escapes. In a nightclub, he meets a blowzy, bosomy blonde in leopard-skin pants, who is long past her sell-by date. He takes her back to Line's apartment, knowing of course that it will be unoccupied. The blonde gets drunk, vomits, and throws things around.

I've been hearing about *Junk Mail* ever since the 1997 Sundance festival. People would mention it with that little smile that suggests a lot is being left unsaid. It's a film about a voyeur, and it appeals to the voyeur in us: We don't like Roy or approve of him, but we watch fascinated because he lives so casually outside the rules. He's the kind of guy who will steal candy from a patient in a coma.

Every once in a while I recommend a film and get an indignant postcard from someone informing me the characters were *disgusting.* I invariably agree. Roy, for example, is disgusting. So is Line (she and Georg mugged a security guard, who is the man in the coma). So is Georg. So is the leopard-skin blonde. In Norway, a land we think of as wholesome and enlightened, it is almost a relief to discover they still have room for a few token outcasts.

But why, oh why, the postcard always continues, should we pay our good money to see a film about *such disgusting people?* The postcards never have a return address, or I would write back arguing that my review described the film accurately, so why did they go? I might even cite Ebert's Law, which teaches us: "A film is not about what it is about. It is about how it is about it." Films about disgusting people can be amusing and interesting, or they can be worthless. But they are not bad simply because of their subject matter. Subjects are neutral. Style is all.

Consider, for example, that Roy does not kill anyone. What are his worst crimes? He is a bad mailman. He eats cold spaghetti out of a can. He needs a bath and a shave. He shouldn't sneak into that poor woman's apartment, although at least he saves her from suicide instead of simply sneaking out again. Compare Roy with—oh, I dunno, how about Art, the FBI guy played by Bruce Willis in *Mercury Rising*? Art also needs a bath and a shave. He kills countless people, speeds dangerously down the streets of Chicago, is associated with explosions and fires, and participates in a shoot-out at an old folks' home. He is a much more alarming specimen than Roy, even if he is the good guy—and yet no one sent me a postcard describing him as *disgusting.*

Why not? It is not because of the behavior or the values, but because of the hygiene. Roy is not attractive, muscular, and well coordinated. He is a scuzzy loser. If he were in a cartoon, flies would be buzzing around his head. And yet we are more likely to meet Roy than Art, because Roy exists in the world and Art exists only in a cinematic machine called a thriller. Roy wants love too. He asks Line out for a cup of coffee. He shares a few meager secrets about his existence with her. And at the end, when the bad guys come, he tries to protect her, just as Art tries to protect Stacy and the cute little autistic kid in *Mercury Rising*. What more can a hero do?

*Junk Mail* is a first film by Pal Sletaune, who has plunged headfirst into a world of rain, mud, desolate cityscapes, sickly greens, depressing blues, and sad struggling people. His mailman is not admirable, but he is understandable. And at least he doesn't have a hole in the back of his head, so that a director can stick in a key and wind him up.

## The Juror ★ ★

R, 120 m., 1996

Demi Moore (Annie Laird), Alec Baldwin (The Teacher), Joseph Gordon-Levitt (Oliver, Annie's son), Anne Heche (Juliette), James Gandolfini (Eddie), Matt Craven (Warren). Directed by Brian Gibson and produced by Irwin Winkler and Rob Cowan. Screenplay by Ted Tally and George Dawes Green.

*The Juror* tells the story of a woman who volunteers, almost eagerly, to serve on the jury in the trial of a Mafia godfather accused of murder. This is the sort of cross in life that many people happily would not bear, but not Annie Laird. When the judge asks her if she's read about the case, she says, no—but she's heard about it from her son. And she knows enough to know the defendant is said to be "the big SpaghettiO" in the mob.

She says that, and worse, in an open courtroom, with the defendant and his henchmen sitting right there. Wouldn't her mother's instincts at least advise her not to mention her child? Is she a complete stupid-o? She's asking for it, and she gets it, in a movie that could have maybe been wrung down into a nice little thriller, but ends up long-winded and rambling.

Annie, played by Demi Moore, is a sculptor whose art consists of building boxes that you stick your hand into to feel the strange things inside. Many observations could be made about this choice of work, but I will not make any of them. Almost before she's home from the jury hearing, a Mafia operator named the Teacher (Alec Baldwin) is inside her house, photocopying family pictures and phone numbers, and feeling up the artwork. The next day he surfaces as a so-called art buyer, who drops a check for $24,000 at her gallery and asks her out to dinner.

The Teacher doesn't fool around. He tells Annie that unless she says two little words—"not guilty"—terrible things will happen to her son and her friends. She believes him and votes not to convict, but that's only the beginning of her nightmare.

This Teacher is a piece of work. He is suave, he is cultivated, he quotes Lao-tse, he can talk knowledgeably about art, he builds puppets, and he is a psychopathic killer. He's obviously the smartest man in the mob (smarter than the godfather's son, that's for sure), and he gets off by psychologically manipulating his victims instead of just intimidating them.

Annie is foolish enough to think that maybe she can outsmart him. This does not work. In two really unnecessarily ugly scenes, the Teacher shows her how he could run down her child—and he forces her best friend to first have sex with him, then kill herself. Watching that second scene, I was wondering exactly what thought process went into the theory that it was necessary to the movie.

Without revealing plot twists, I will say that the movie goes on a long while—a very long while—after the trial is over, and that a trip to the jungles in Guatemala is unnecessary, to put it mildly. In the midst of all this psychological carnage, Demi Moore maintains uncanny self-possession, especially if you compare her work with the scorched-earth performance of Sally Field in the oddly similar *Eye for an Eye*, which came out just a few weeks earlier.

Both movies have the same buried plot: Mom fears child will be killed by violent nut, so takes the law into her own hands. I found *Eye for an Eye* offensive in its manipulative arguments for vigilante justice. *The Juror* didn't bother me as much because the heroine doesn't deliberately choose her course; she has it forced upon her. It's an almost invisible distinction, I grant you, but this movie submerges its philosophy in the conventions of a thriller, while *Eye for an Eye* plays like an ad for handguns.

A performance that caught my eye is by

James Gandolfini, as Eddie, the Teacher's sidekick. He has a very tricky role as a Mafia soldier who is about as sympathetic as a man can be who *would,* after all, kill you. His line readings during a couple of complicated scenes are right on the money (watch the careful way he learns from the Teacher about the death of Annie's friend). If the movie had been pitched at the level of sophistication and complexity that his character represents, it would have been a lot better. Of course, it would have been a different movie too. I could have lived with that.

# K

## Kama Sutra ★ ★

NO MPAA RATING, 114 m., 1997

Indira Varma (Maya), Sarita Choudhury (Tara), Ramon Tikaram (Jai Kumar), Naveen Andrews (Raj Singh), Rekha (Rasa Devi), Khalik Tyabji (Biki), Arundhati Rao (Annabi), Surabhi Bhansali (Young Maya). Directed by Mira Nair and produced by Nair and Lydia Dean Pilcher. Screenplay by Helena Kriel and Nair.

*Kama Sutra* is a lush, voluptuous tale told in sixteenth-century India, about two young women who grow up to pleasure a king—one as his wife, the other as his courtesan. To find a film like this from the 1960s, made by a man, would be one thing; to find it made in 1997 by Mira Nair is more startling. Nothing in her previous work (the great film *Salaam Bombay!* and two good films, *Mississippi Masala* and *The Perez Family*) prepared me for this exercise in exotic eroticism.

The heroine of the story is a servant girl named Maya (Indira Varma), who has always lived in the shadow of her childhood friend, the well-born Princess Tara (Sarita Choudhury, from *Mississippi Masala*). When Tara is betrothed to the king, Raj Singh (Naveen Andrews), Maya slips into his chamber on the night before the wedding and seduces him. The next day she taunts her rival: "All my life I have lived with your used things. Now something I have used is yours forever."

Maya is exiled from the village by the bitter Tara and drifts from town to town until she falls beneath the gaze of a sculptor (Ramon Tikaram). She becomes his lover and model, until he decides she cannot be both at the same time, and unwisely (in my opinion) prefers her as his model. She then meets a wise older woman (Rekha) who runs a school for courtesans based on the ancient book *Kama Sutra*, or *Lessons in Love*.

This book is known in the West mostly for its exhaustive (and exhausting) lists of sexual positions, and for its carefully delineated caressing techniques. (Concerning the pressing of the nails against the body, for example, I have always much preferred the subtle "leaf of the blue lotus" technique to the more abrupt "jump of a hare.") But there is much in the book beyond technique: It is a work of art, dance, and philosophy, and Maya proves a good student, telling her teacher: "I want to learn the rules of love and how to use them. And if I can't use them on the one I love, I will use them on the ones I don't."

She does indeed become accomplished as a courtesan, and eventually drifts back into the orbit of the royal court; the king takes her as his lover, and then there are boudoir intrigues involving the sculptor, whom Maya still loves. Nair has prepared the screenplay with great attention to the mores of the time (doctors arrived in the chambers of women covered with a cloth, for example, which provides the means for a lover's escape just in the nick of time).

The movie's story is really just the occasion for the scenes of eroticism, but it must be said that those scenes have a beauty and solemnity that is quietly impressive. And the two actresses are great beauties; Varma, with her lithe model's figure, is the more conventional, but there is much to be said for Choudhury's full lips and deep eyes, and the cinematography by Declan Quinn places them in painterly compositions that have a sensuous quality of their own.

The problem, in the end, is that *Kama Sutra* really adds up to very little. The story is contrived and unconvincing, the psychology is shallow, and moments of truth are passed over for moments of beauty. The film is entrancing to regard, but I expected more from Mira Nair, and I was disappointed. She is better than this work.

## Kansas City ★ ★ ★

R, 110 m., 1996

Jennifer Jason Leigh (Blondie O'Hara), Miranda Richardson (Carolyn Stilton), Harry Belafonte (Seldom Seen), Michael Murphy (Henry Stilton), Dermot Mulroney (Johnny O'Hara), Steve Buscemi (Johnny Flynn), Brooke Smith (Babe Flynn), Jane Adams (Nettie Bolt). Directed by Robert Altman and produced by Altman, Matthew Seig, and David C. Thomas. Screenplay by Altman and Frank Barhydt.

Robert Altman has often seemed impatient with the conventional ways of making a movie. At seventy-one, he is still the most iconoclastic and experimental of major American filmmakers. Ambitious young directors want to make slick formula hits that mimic one another, but Altman tries to make it new every time. Sometimes he strikes out, but he always goes down swinging.

His originality and invention pay off in *Kansas City*, his thirty-first film—a memory of the wide-open Depression era, circa 1934, when Boss Tom Pendergast ruled, jazz flourished, and the city boasted the largest red-light district in the country. Altman tells a fairly straightforward story about a gun moll who kidnaps a politician's wife, but there's a lot more to the film than its story.

Altman grew up in Kansas City—he was nine in 1934—and he has a lot of memories, first— and secondhand, about a colorful period that always seemed to have a jazz sound track. He remembers the "cutting contests" in which soloists would duel on stage, and I think he wants to make this movie a cutting contest too. The story is intercut with performance footage from the "Hey Hey Club," and as jazz musicians try to top one another it's as if the actors are doing the same thing in their arena.

The movie opens with a tough gangster's girl named Blondie (Jennifer Jason Leigh) faking her way into a mansion and kidnapping Carolyn Stilton (Miranda Richardson), whose husband is a powerful Democrat. Blondie's plan: Hold the wife to force the husband to use his influence in order to free the moll's husband, a gangster named Johnny O'Hara (Dermot Mulroney). That is going to take a lot of influence, because O'Hara has been so unwise as to stick up the best customer of the local black gambling boss, Seldom Seen (Harry Belafonte). O'Hara has added insult to injury by pulling his stickup in blackface: "You've been held up by Amos 'n Andy," a customer chortles to Seldom.

This story by itself is fairly thin; it might have held together for the length of a 1930s B movie, which is probably what Altman was thinking of when he wrote it. But the story is not really what *Kansas City* is about. As counterpoint, Altman gathered some of the best living jazz musicians, put them on a set representing the Hey Hey Club, and asked them to play period material in the style of the Kansas City jazz giants (Count Basie, Coleman Hawkins, Jay McShann, Lester Young, etc.). He filmed their work in a concert documentary style, and intercuts it with another narrative, involving a hard-boiled political hack (Steve Buscemi) who is rounding up drunks and drifters and buying their votes on Election Day.

What he asks of the actors (those who are "soloists" anyway) is not realism but the same kind of playful show-off performances he's getting from the musicians. And to understand the acting, it's helpful to begin with the music. The one scene everyone will remember from this movie is an extended exchange of solos involving Hawkins (Craig Handy), Young (Joshua Redman), and Ben Webster (James Carter). The music is terrific and so is the energy level, as the musicians not only celebrate their own styles but quote and borrow from one another, and weave elements of other songs into the one they're playing.

Understand that, and you see what Jennifer Jason Leigh is doing in the key performance in *Kansas City*. Her reference point is the movie star Jean Harlow (at one point she even takes Mrs. Stilton to the movies). Leigh, as "Blondie," wants to look like her and talk like her ("Park it, sister!" she tells her captive). This is not so farfetched. The screenwriter Ben Hecht, who wrote such gangster classics as *Scarface* (1932), was once asked how he knew how gangsters talked. "I made it up," he said. "The gangsters went to the movies and copied the characters on the screen."

Leigh and Richardson, as the moll and the socialite, have their own verbal duel in counterpoint to the musical duel at the Hey Hey Club. Richardson is taking laudanum most of the time, causing her grasp of the situation to remain hazy, and some of the musicians are no doubt high too. Harry Belafonte, showing a hard-edged side not often revealed in his performances, plays Seldom Seen as a wise, canny, proud black gangster who is annoyed by Johnny O'Hara's crime but angered by his blackface caper. But like a musician, he plays through, or from, his feelings: He begins a joke in the film and continues it during a murder.

The film does a good job of re-creating the period—not just in clothes, cars, and advertising signs, which go without saying, but in the look of interiors and in the tone of the colors. I was reminded at times of Altman's other movie about Depression-era gangsters, *Thieves Like Us* (1974), also set in the lower Midwest. It was a time when the props that defined this century—

cars, movies, radio, cigarettes, publicity—were sort of new, and people were still getting used to them.

Today people who smoke think they should stop. In the 1930s, people who smoked thought they were participating in a new kind of personal expression, in a glamour they learned from the screen and identified with. In *Kansas City* it's not just Blondie who thinks she could be a movie star. All of the characters act as if somebody might come along someday and make a movie about them. And Altman, who made the movie, gets his chance to sit in at last on one of those cutting sessions.

## Kazaam ★ ½

PG, 93 m., 1996

Shaquille O'Neal (Kazaam), Francis Capra (Max), Ally Walker (Alice), Marshall Manesh (Malik), James Acheson (Nick), Fawn Reed (Asia Moon), John Costelloe (Travis), JoAnne Hart (Mrs. Duke). Directed by Paul M. Glaser and produced by Scott Kroopf, Glaser, and Bob Engelman. Screenplay by Christian Ford and Roger Soffer.

*Kazaam* is a textbook example of a film deal in which adults assemble a package that reflects their own interests and try to sell it to kids. How else to explain a children's movie where the villains are trying to steal a bootleg recording so they can sell pirated copies of it? What do kids know, or care, about that?

The movie stars Shaquille O'Neal, the basketball player, as Kazaam, a genie who is released from captivity in an old boom box, and has to perform three wishes for a little kid (Francis Capra). Right there you have a wonderful illustration of the movie's creative bankruptcy. Assigned to construct a starring vehicle for Shaq, the filmmakers looked at him, saw a tall bald black man, and said, "Hey, he can be a genie!" At which point, somebody should have said, "Okay, that's level one. Now let's take it to level three."

Shaq has already proven he can act (in *Blue Chips*, the 1994 movie about college basketball). Here he shows he can be likable in a children's movie. What he does not show is good judgment in his choice of material; this is a tired concept, written by the numbers. Kids old enough to know about Shaq as a basketball star will be too old to enjoy the movie. Younger kids won't find much to engage them. And O'Neal shouldn't have used the movie to promote his own career as a hopeful rap artist; the soundtrack sounds less like music to entertain kids than like a trial run for a Shaq album.

The plot: A wrecking ball destroys an old building, releasing a genie who is discovered by a kid named Max (Capra). The rules are he gets three wishes. The twist is the genie doesn't much like people, having made no friends in 5,000 years and having spent most of that time cooped up in bottles, lamps, radiators, etc. The other twist is the kid doesn't much trust people because his father has disappeared.

The genie, however, helps the kid find his father, only to find out the father is involved in an illegal music pirating operation. The father is not quite ready to go straight, but eventually, after some action sequences involving an evil gang, he realizes that his future depends on living up to his son's expectations.

Uncanny, how much this plot resembles *Aladdin and the King of Thieves*, a Disney made-for-video production. In that one, Aladdin has never known his father, but an oracle in an old lamp tells him where the father is to be found, and the helpful blue genie helps him go there. His father is the king of the thieves, it turns out, and may not be entirely ready to go straight. But after some action sequences involving the evil gang of thieves, the father realizes that he must live up to his son's expectations, etc.

Did anybody at Disney notice they were making the same movie twice, once as animation, once as live action? Hard to say. The animated movie at least has the benefit of material that fits the genre, much better songs, a colorful graphic style, and another outing for the transmogrifying genie with the voice by Robin Williams. *Kazaam*, on the other hand, by being live action, makes the bad guys too real for the fantasy to work, and the action sequence feels just like the end of every other formula movie where the third act is replaced by fires and fights.

There are several moments in the movie when fantasy and reality collide. One comes when the genie astonishes the kid with a room full of candy, which cascades out of thin air. I was astonished too. Astonished that this genie who had been bottled up for most of the last 5,000 years would supply modern off-the-shelf candy in its highly visible commercial wrappers:

M&Ms, etc. Does the genie's magic create the wrappers along with the candy, or does the genie buy the candy at wholesale before rematerializing it?

There is also the awkwardness of the relationship between the genie and the kid, caused by the need to make Kazaam not only a fantasy figure, but also a contemporary pal who can advise the kid, steer him straight, and get involved in the action at the end. Genies are only fun in the movies if you define and limit their powers. That should have been obvious, but the filmmakers didn't care to extend themselves beyond the obvious commercial possibilities of their first dim idea. As for Shaquille O'Neal, given his own three wishes, the next time he should go for a script, a director, and an interesting character.

## Kicked in the Head ★ ½

R, 90 m., 1997

Kevin Corrigan (Redmond), Linda Fiorentino (Megan), Michael Rapaport (Stretch), James Woods (Uncle Sam), Burt Young (Jack), Lili Taylor (Happy), Olek Krupa (Borko). Directed by Matthew Harrison and produced by Barbara De Fina. Screenplay by Kevin Corrigan and Harrison.

*Kicked in the Head* is one of those movies where you wish the story were about the supporting characters. There are three of them worthy of features of their own: Uncle Sam (James Woods), the hero's con man relative, Megan (Linda Fiorentino), an airline attendant who has an enigmatic one-night stand with the hero, and Stretch (Michael Rapaport), a self-styled beer distribution czar.

In a generally underwritten (and yet too talky) movie, these New Yorkers are so intriguing we want to know more about them. Unfortunately, the movie isn't about them. It involves some time in the life of Redmond (Kevin Corrigan), an aimless young man who spends a lot of his time writing bad poetry about the meaning of life.

The plot, such as it is, involves Uncle Sam sending Redmond to drop off some cocaine at an elevated stop. Cocaine is, of course, the handiest MacGuffin of our time; introduce it into a plot, and you don't have to explain motivations. The dope drop turns into a gun battle in which countless shots are fired but nobody is hit, and then Redmond embarks on an odyssey that takes him into the orbits of Stretch (who runs Stretch's Beer-o-Rama) and Jack (Burt Young), the guy who gave Uncle Sam the cocaine. (Young's character has a great line, even though it is not remotely plausible: "I like organized—with a 'g,' like in 'phlegm.'")

The nearest thing to a sustained relationship takes place between Redmond and Fiorentino, as a woman he sees crying on a train, and hopes to console. Fiorentino plays the character as a milder version of her man-eater in *The Last Seduction*. Wary, wounded, and cynical, she sleeps with Redmond for reasons having little to do with the plot and much to do, perhaps, with Kevin Corrigan, who cowrote the screenplay, wanting to give himself a good scene.

Well, there is a good scene (at an airline bar), but when Fiorentino exits, the interest leaves too, because we care about her, not him. That's true all through the movie, as the colorless Redmond plays straight man to Stretch (Rapaport does some hilarious riffs on the glories of beer distribution), Woods ("This is my dentist's car. He asked me to watch it for him"), and Burt Young's Russian hit man (who carefully looks up menacing threats in his phrase book).

I've seen the film twice, and there's one scene that played differently the two times. It's a long dialogue exchange between Redmond and Stretch at the beer depot. It's clear the scene is semi-improvised, and there were times when Rapaport seemed to be smiling inappropriately, going out of character to let us see the actor playing with the process. That bothered me the first time, but not the second, because by then I knew the characters weren't as interesting as the actors struggling with the material.

## Kids in the Hall: Brain Candy ★

R, 89 m., 1996

David Foley (Marv, Psychiatrist, Suicidal Businessman, and New Guy), Bruce McCullouch (Alice, Cisco, Cop, White Trash Man, and Grivo), Kevin McDonald (Chris Cooper, Chris's Dad, and Doreen), Mark McKinney (Don Roritor, Simon, German Patient, Nina Bedford, Cabbie, and White Trash Woman), Scott Thompson (Mrs. Hurdicure, Baxter, Wally, Malek, The Queen, and Clemptor). Directed by Kelly Makin and produced by Lorne Michaels. Screenplay by Norm

Hiscock, Bruce McCulloch, Kevin McDonald, Mark McKinney, and Scott Thompson.

Did somebody, maybe me, forget to push my laugh button before *The Kids in the Hall: Brain Candy* began? It's a comedy, and I know people who think it's a funny one, and intellectually I can appreciate some of the stuff they're trying to do—but, of course, intellectual appreciation is deadly to comedy, which needs to originate at a more elemental level of the being, and arrive at the mind only after the laughter begins. On that more visceral level, I found it less a comedy than a curiosity.

The Kids are a Canadian comedy troupe that had its origins in Second City–style improv, migrated to Canadian television, and can be seen almost daily on the Comedy Central cable channel. They're all men, and play the female roles in drag, but I learn from their Web page that this is more a matter of necessity than choice: The troupe included women in the early days, but the women's "careers took off too quickly and they would go solo." So the men decided to put an end to that by playing all of the roles themselves.

The female characters are played "straight," in the sense that we're supposed to relate to them as women, not men in drag. (The Web site goes on to explain helpfully that one of the Kids is gay, one is bi, one is married, one is curious, and one lists a preference that cannot be printed in a family newspaper. Ah, the Web, what a boon to the scholar.) Although the Kids are apparently trying to say something about the role of women in society, they are saying it in the same way that a woman in the role would say it; they're not using drag itself as a way to comment.

The movie's not a series of sketches, but a story about a drug named Gleemonex, which does more or less what Prozac does, but better, and with a lot more side effects. The drug has been invented by a scientist working for Roritor Pharmaceuticals, which has a laboratory that looks like a high school chem lab, and a boardroom that looks recycled out of *The Hudsucker Proxy.* The drug has been invented by a company scientist who thinks it needs more testing, but management wants to market the drug immediately to save the company from bankruptcy.

This story is told in counterpoint with several others (the Kids play a bewildering variety of roles), and we meet some of the people who might be aided by Gleemonex—which, among other things, recaptures happy memories. The movie's strategy is to create slices of ordinary North American family life and then add a twist, as when a happy family tells a visitor, "Dad's upstairs masturbating to gay porn." Or when a promo man complains, "The nipples of Mother Hype have run dry." Or when a happy character explains, "I haven't felt this good since they said it's not malignant." Or when . . . but enough.

The effect of the drug, it's claimed, is to "make it feel like it's 72 degrees in your head all the time." The upstairs dad takes it and realizes he is homosexual, and celebrates with his family in the musical number "I'm Gay! (He's Gay!)." Punk rockers become positive and upbeat on Gleemonex. An overworked office slave grows cheerful as he recalls his own happiest memory, involving adding a bodily fluid to the boss's coffee. And there are a lot of disease jokes, including a music video about a character named Cancer Boy.

Reader, I did not laugh. I felt the Kids were too busy being hip and ironic to connect at the simpler level where comedy lives. They were brought down by their own self-protective devices. It's not cool to seem to want to be funny, and so the modern strategy is to adopt the pose that you are funny by not seeming to want to be funny. That's what the performers do. The audience laughs because the performers are being hip by trying to be funny without seeming to try to be funny. Thus everybody has an irony orgy and goes home, if not satisfied, at least unexposed as unhip. It seemed to me there were two or three superfluous levels of attitude between the Kids and their material. A laugh can penetrate a lot of things, but not a solid block of cool.

## Killer: A Journal of Murder ★ ★

R, 91 m., 1996

James Woods (Carl Panzram), Robert Sean Leonard (Henry Lesser), Ellen Greene (Elizabeth Wyatt), Cara Buono (Esther Lesser), Robert John Burke (R. G. Greiser), Steve Forrest (Warden Charles Casey), Jeffrey De Munn (Sam Lesser), Christopher Petrosino (Richard Lesser). Directed by Tim Metcalfe and produced by Janet Yang and Mark Levinson. Screenplay by Metcalfe, based on the book by Thomas E. Gaddis and James O. Long.

In the annals of serial killers, where the relentless parade of inhuman acts blurs the distinctions, Carl Panzram has a niche of his own as one of the most vicious, degenerate criminals of his time. After beating a prison worker to death, he was hanged in 1930, pausing on his way to the gallows long enough to dash off a note to opponents of capital punishment: "The only thanks you or your kind will ever get from me for your efforts on my behalf is that I wish you all had one neck and I had my hands on it."

*Killer: A Journal of Murder* is the fuzzy-headed story of a prison guard who befriended Panzram, who tried to understand what made such a violent man the way he was. The guard, Henry Lesser, came from a middle-class family that could not comprehend his career choice. Soon we begin to understand. After Panzram is punished for an escape attempt by being beaten, Lesser feels sympathy and slips him a dollar bill, which would buy a lot of smokes and candy bars. Soon Lesser gives Panzram writing supplies; the journal Panzram wrote was kept by Lesser for many years, who found a publisher for it around 1960. In it, Panzram recounts a lifetime of carnage. In alternating chapters, two crime reporters document the truth of most of his claims.

The film *Killer: A Journal of Murder* opens with the memories of Lesser as an old man. He seems to recall Panzram with nostalgia, as a man who could have redeemed himself, who needed only to be understood. Then the movie flashes back to the young Lesser (Robert Sean Leonard), who goes to work at Leavenworth and first meets the killer (James Woods).

Gradually the two men become—not friends exactly, but bound together in tentative trust. The film was written and directed by Tim Metcalfe, who found a copy of Panzram's journal in a used book store, read it, and spent five years getting it onto the screen. He does not, however, ask the right questions about Lesser, and the film softens some hard edges.

Why did Lesser choose work as a prison guard, and why was he immediately and strongly attracted to the most evil man in the prison? Why not choose a more deserving prisoner? Is there a whiff of grandiosity here, a desire to seem saintly by facing up to the worst the human race has to offer? Is it the Stockholm syndrome, with the guard playing the role of hostage? Although Panzram is nominally the prisoner, he is so brilliant and ruthless that there are many times when he could have killed or injured Lesser. Is Lesser responding gratefully (even erotically) to his reprieve?

Metcalfe's casting of James Woods as the killer is a good choice, and Woods gives a powerful, searing performance. He does not compromise Panzram or soften him. But the movie does, by withholding information. The real Panzram is well documented in crime references, and he led quite a life: He was born in 1891, was in trouble with the law from the age of eight, burned down a reformatory at the age of fourteen, and at sixteen began a practice of sodomizing men at gunpoint (he counted more than 1,000). He burned churches in Montana, committed armed robberies in Oregon, worked in oil fields in South America and set oil rigs on fire for the hell of it, returned to the United States, stole $40,000 from the home of former president William Howard Taft, bought a yacht, hired ten sailors to crew it, blew their brains out, dumped them in the sea, was arrested for burglary, escaped prison again, went to Africa, sodomized and killed a twelve-year-old, hired six porters to accompany him on a crocodile hunt, killed the porters and fed them to the crocodiles, and . . . but you get the idea. He sang a little ditty on the gallows.

The movie is less than forthcoming about this life; its purposes are served by being vague about the details (although it does set the tally at twenty-one murders). It needs to humanize Panzram. Perhaps no one is completely irredeemable. But Panzram was a monster and prison was his destiny. If Lesser had sought out a different prisoner for his sympathy, *Killer* might have been more convincing. By choosing Panzram, Lesser places his own motives in a curious light: Was he attracted to evil? Was he excited by proximity to it, by his own invulnerability to such a dangerous man? Some people are.

I have just seen *Butterfly Kiss*, a British film about two women. One of them is an unhinged psychopath who stalks the motorways of Britain, killing people. The other is a dim young woman who feels sympathy for this lonely drifter. After she is sexually initiated by the killer (who is only the fourth person in her life to kiss her), she follows along on the trail of carnage, "always trying to find the good in her."

*Butterfly Kiss* is straightforward about three things that *Killer* doesn't acknowledge. (1) It understands that sexual tension, whether overtly expressed or not, exists in such a relationship. (2) It understands that the "good" partner in such a pairing might be fulfilling deep and sick needs. (3) It understands that evil on this scale is impenetrable to normal minds; that serial killers and those attracted to them are involved in a mystery that the rest of us will never really understand.

If you want to understand what's going on in *Killer,* see *Butterfly Kiss.* It will deconstruct the earlier film for you, while itself remaining opaque and disturbing—as it should.

## Kiss Me, Guido ★ ★

R, 99 m., 1997

Nick Scotti (Frankie), Anthony Barrile (Warren), Anthony DeSando (Pino), Craig Chester (Terry), Dominick Lombardozzi (Joey Chips), Molly Price (Landlady), Christopher Lawford (Dakota), David Deblinger (Actor With No Name). Directed by Tony Vitale and produced by Ira Deutchman and Christine Vachon. Screenplay by Vitale.

If you can believe that an aspiring actor who studies De Niro movies doesn't know what "GWM" means in a singles ad, then you can believe just about everything in *Kiss Me, Guido,* a movie that gives you lots to believe. It's a mistaken-identity comedy about a straight guy from the Bronx who answers an ad in an alternative weekly and ends up with a gay roommate in the Village.

"Guy With Money, right?" asks Frankie (Nick Scotti), who hangs around the family pizzeria in the Bronx but dreams of someday becoming an actor. His brother Pino (Anthony DeSando) is not much help; while Frankie was studying De Niro, Pino was obviously studying Travolta and Stallone, and yearns for disco to make a comeback and provide him with the stage on which he was intended to strut.

*Kiss Me, Guido* is a movie with a lot of funny one-liners, but no place to go with them. Like a thirty-minute sitcom, it acts like you already know all the characters and are just happy to have fresh dialogue. It's as if all of the deeper issues have been settled in previous episodes. And yet, also like a sitcom, it's kind of fun as it slides past. Here is a movie that was born to play on television.

Frankie and Warren (Anthony Barrile), his gay roommate-to-be, are both walking wounded: They've recently been unlucky in love. That would give them something in common, except that Frankie is so naive he doesn't even figure out what "GWM" means after he's watching a Julie Andrews movie with one. Not even Warren's chummy peroxided friend Terry (Craig Chester) rings any bells.

The plot device involves a play that Warren is scheduled to star in. He twists an ankle, and through reasoning that is entirely plot-driven, Frankie is picked to substitute for him—in a play about gay lovers, written and directed by Warren's ex-roommate (Christopher Lawford). But . . . can Frankie actually bring himself to kiss another man, as the role requires? Hey, didn't the great Al Pacino himself do that in *Dog Day Afternoon*?

The performances have energy and charm; the movie may be a launching pad for the careers of several actors, especially Scotti and DeSando, who has some funny moves as the Italian stallion brother. If only it had been written a little smarter. There's a scene early in the film where Frankie and Warren talk for the first time on the phone, and their dialogue is all at cross-purposes; everything is misunderstood. Dialogue like that always depresses me, because it's so artificial: You have to be almost as smart to get everything wrong as to get everything right.

I wish that Tony Vitale, the writer and director, had taken a long look at his screenplay and said, "Okay, let's assume he *knows* what 'GWM' means. What would happen then?"

## Kiss or Kill ★ ★ ★

R, 96 m., 1997

Frances O'Connor (Nikki), Matt Day (Al), Chris Haywood (Hummer), Barry Otto (Adler Jones), Andrew S. Gilbert (Crean), Barry Langrishe (Zipper Doyle), Max Cullen (Stan). Directed by Bill Bennett and produced by Bill Bennett and Jennifer Bennett. Screenplay by Bill Bennett.

There has never been a movie where a middle-aged couple go on the run, pursued by teenage cops. This is the sort of thing that's so obvious it never occurs to anybody. All lovers on the run are young. All cops are older. That's because road movies are to late adolescence what monster movies are to kids: a way of exorcising unease.

Little kids identify with monsters because, like Godzilla, they feel uncoordinated and misunderstood. Moviegoers in their teens and twenties identify with road movies because, like their fugitive heroes, they feel a deep need to leave home, to flee adult regimentation, to exist outside organized society, to make their own rules. The genre requires them to commit crimes before going on the lam, but that's just a technicality—required in order to explain why the cops are chasing them.

*Kiss or Kill* is a rare revisionist road movie. It breaks with the genre in three key ways. (1) Although Nikki and Al, the young lovers, are indeed criminal, they spend most of the movie suspecting each other of their crimes. (2) The rebels and nonconformists they meet on the road are all middle-aged or old. (3) The cops are wry practical jokesters—the coolest characters in the movie. I've seen countless road movies, but this one felt different, as if it had an unbalanced flywheel.

The movie takes place in Australia, which in the American imagination is becoming a place like Texas, inhabited by freewheeling eccentrics with too much space on their hands. It opens with a genuinely shocking moment, which I will not reveal, that helps explain why Nikki (Frances O'Connor) grows up with a twisted view of life. As an adult, she teams up with her boyfriend, Al (Matt Day), to pull a scam: She picks up businessmen in bars, returns to their hotels with them, slips pills into their drinks, and then lets Al into the room. They steal whatever they can. Because the businessmen are married, they usually don't call the cops.

So, how many pills did Nikki put into the drink of her latest victim? This is important because the man is unexpectedly dead. Nikki and Al find a video in his briefcase, exposing Zipper Doyle (Barry Langrishe), a local sports hero, as a pedophile. She unwisely calls Zipper's office and makes shrill threats into the answering machine. Nikki and Al go on the run, heading from Adelaide to Perth across the well-named Nullarbor Plain, a reach of the outback where every motel is a shout of defiance against the void.

Nikki and Al do not trust each other very much; maybe Nikki will never trust anybody. Al wonders if she deliberately killed the businessman. Soon Nikki wonders how a motel owner died. Pursued by two cops and the venomous Zipper Doyle, they leave a trail of bodies and robberies behind them—but the crimes take place offscreen, and in a series of getaway cars, they stew in paranoia and suspicion, and we're left to guess which of them (if either) committed the crimes.

Like all road movies, this one serves as a clothesline for colorful characters. There's a drunken motel manager (Max Cullen) who mutters darkly about "unphantomable tunnels under the desert." And a couple who live on an abandoned nuclear test site ("it's very private here") and make handmade jewelry. And the two detectives (Chris Haywood and Andrew S. Gilbert) who have a long, deceptive conversation in a coffee shop that could have been written by David Mamet.

The endings of road movies are usually their least satisfactory elements. There are two possibilities for the characters: die a spectacular death, or get a daytime job. The first choice is preferable, I suppose. Can you imagine Bonnie and Clyde on parole, doing spin-control on Barbara Walters and Larry King? Thelma and Louise, maybe.

## Kiss the Girls ★ ★ ★ ½

R, 117 m., 1997

Morgan Freeman (Alex Cross), Ashley Judd (Kate McTiernan), Cary Elwes (Nick Ruskin), Alex McArthur (Sikes), Tony Goldwyn (Will Rudolph), Jay O. Sanders (Kyle Craig), Bill Nunn (Sampson), Gina Ravera (Naomi Cross), Brian Cox (Chief Hatfield). Directed by Gary Fleder and produced by David Brown and Joe Wizan. Screenplay by David Klass, based on the novel by James Patterson.

"Is there a better actor in America than Morgan Freeman?" Pauline Kael once asked, to which one could add, is there one with more authority?

Freeman has a rare presence on the screen, a specific gravity that persuades us. He never seems to be making things up. He never seems shallow, facile, or unconvinced, and even in unsuccessful films like *Chain Reaction* (1996), he doesn't go down with the ship: You feel he's authentic even as the film sinks around him.

In *Kiss the Girls,* Freeman's performance is more central than his work in the movie this one is clearly inspired by, *Seven* (1995). He is the lead, at the center of the story, and that gives it a focus that the buddy aspects of *Seven* lacked. Once again he plays a policeman on the trail of a kinky serial killer, and once again the shadows are deep and the antagonist is brilliant and the crimes are supposed to send some kind of a twisted message. But the movie's not a retread; it's original work, based on a novel by James Patterson, about a criminal who (the Freeman character intuits) is not killing his victims, but collecting them.

Freeman plays Alex Cross, a forensic psychologist with the Washington, D.C., police, who becomes involves in a series of kidnappings in Durham, North Carolina, when his own niece (Gina Ravera) is abducted. He flies to Durham and calls on the police department, where he's kept waiting for hours until he finally bursts into the office of the chief. (In a movie that is generally convincing, this scene played like boilerplate.) The kidnap targets are being taken by a man who signs himself "Casanova," and one of his victims is found dead—tied to a tree and "left for the critters to find."

Cross wonders why there aren't more bodies, and theorizes that Casanova is a collector who kills only when he feels he must. The other victims, including his niece, must still be alive somewhere. His theory is proven when a local doctor named Kate (Ashley Judd) is abducted but escapes after making contact with several other captives in some kind of subterranean warren of cells.

The cop and the doctor become a team during the rest of the movie, working together as the trail leads to the West Coast, and unraveling surprises that it is not my task to reveal. David Klass, the screenwriter, gives Freeman and Judd more specific dialogue than is usual in thrillers; they sound like they might actually be talking with one another and not simply advancing plot points. And what Freeman brings to all of his scenes is a very particular attentiveness. He doesn't merely listen; he seems to weigh what is told him, to evaluate it. That quality creates an amusing result sometimes in his movies, when other actors will tell him something and then (you can clearly sense) look to see if he buys it.

Ashley Judd's debut, *Ruby in Paradise,* established her among the most convincing actresses of her generation, and *Normal Life* (1996), disgracefully relegated to video by a clueless studio, was one of the year's best films. She can't always transcend genre material (what was she doing in *A Time to Kill*?), but when it's well written and directed with care, as it is here, we find we care about her even in a scene of revelation toward the end that could have been handled more subtly.

*Kiss the Girls* was directed by Gary Fleder, whose first feature, *Things to Do in Denver When You're Dead* (1996), showed talent but a little too much contrivance. Here he's more disciplined and controlled, with a story where the shadows and nuances are as scary as anything else. Fleder has said that he and his cinematographer, Aaron Schneider, studied the work of Gordon *(Prince of Darkness)* Willis, whose photography for *The Godfather* and other pictures often uses a few overhead key lights on crucial elements and leaves the rest in darkness. Here (as in *Seven*) we get a consistent sense of not being able to see everything we think we want to.

When the film is over and we know all of its secrets, here's one we'd like to know more about: What exactly is the dynamic of the relationship between the two most twisted members of the cast? But being left with such a question is much more satisfactory than being given the answer in shorthand Freudian terms. What we're also left with is the real sense of having met two very particular people in the leads. Freeman and Judd are so good you almost wish they'd decided not to make a thriller at all—had simply found a way to construct a drama exploring their personalities.

## Kissed ★ ★ ★

NO MPAA RATING, 78 m., 1997

Molly Parker (Sandra Larson), Peter Outerbridge (Matt), Jay Brazeau (Mr. Wallis), Natasha Morley (Young Sandra). Directed by Lynne Stopkewich and produced by Dean English and Stopkewich. Screenplay by Stopkewich and Angus Fraser, based on the story "We So Seldom Look on Love" by Barbara Gowdy.

"When life turns into death, I've seen bodies shining like stars," says Sandra, who tells her story in *Kissed.* "Each of them has its own wisdom, innocence, happiness, grief. I see it."

From early childhood, Sandra has been obsessed with dead things. She and a playmate would find dead birds and bury them, but then, "after dark I'd go back and give them a proper burial." In a ritual by flashlight, she rubs her body with the dead bird in what she calls "the anointment."

In her late teens, working for a florist, she makes a delivery to a funeral home, absorbs the atmosphere, and states simply, "I'd like to work here." The mortician is happy to show her around. Opening the door to the embalming room, he says with plump satisfaction, "This is where it all happens." Soon she is working there.

*Kissed* is about a necrophile, but in its approach it could be about spirituality or transcendence. Sandra, played with a grave intensity by Molly Parker, does things that are depraved by normal standards, but in her mind she is performing something like a sacrament. The dead are so lonely. When she comforts them with a farewell touch from the living, the room fills with light, and an angelic choir sings in orgasmic female voices.

*Kissed* was, needless to say, one of the most controversial films at the Toronto and Sundance film festivals. Mostly people talked about how Lynne Stopkewich, its writer and director, had gotten away with it. One would think there was no way to film this material without disgusting the audience—or, worse, making it laugh at the wrong times. Stopkewich does not disgust, and when there are laughs, she intends them (there is a quiet mordant humor trickling through the film). What is amazing, at the end, is that we feel some sympathy for Sandra, some understanding.

Humans seem to be hard-wired at an early age into whatever sexuality they eventually profess. There is little choice in the matter. Most are lucky enough to fall within the mainstream, but for those who are attracted to obscure fetishes, it is a question of acknowledging their nature, or denying themselves sexual fulfillment. Of course some compulsions are harmful to others, and society rightly outlaws them; but the convenience of necrophilia, as the joke goes, is that it requires only one consenting adult.

In the case of Sandra, her sexuality seems to be bound up with her spirituality. She feels pity for the dead bodies in her care. Stopkewich makes it clear that sex does take place, but like many women directors she is less interested in the mechanics than in the emotion; the movie is not explicit in its sexuality, although there is a scene about embalming techniques that is more detailed than most of the audience will require. In Sandra's mind, she is helping the dead to cross over in a flood of light to a happier place: Her bliss gives them the final push.

Then Sandra, who has never dated in a conventional way, meets a young man in a coffee shop. His name is Matt (Peter Outerbridge). She is stunningly frank with him. "Why would you want to be an embalmer?" he asks. "Because of the bodies," she says. "I make love to them." He is fascinated. Soon she finds a notebook he is keeping, a sexual journal cross-indexed with obituaries from the local paper.

"It's not about facts and figures!" she says. "It's about crossing over."

"I have to do it," he vows.

"I *need* to do it," she tells him. "It's not something you force yourself to do."

If Sandra's obsession is occult and unnatural, Matt's is much more common: His male pride becomes involved in pleasing the woman he loves, and he finds himself in competition with the dead. Jealousy—and jealousy's accomplice, love—drive him. But how can he possibly compare to his rivals?

*Kissed* is a first film by Stopkewich, who is thirty-two and lives in Vancouver. Talking about the film at Sundance, she said she read the original story, "We So Seldom Look on Love," by Barbara Gowdy, in a book of erotica for women.

"It haunted me. Sandra is in charge of her sexuality. Although she is a fringe dweller, she achieves something we all search for. We're all looking for transcendence." Oddly enough, this is a feeling the movie largely succeeds in conveying, although there is perhaps an insight in something else Stopkewich said: "At the end of the shoot, every single person working on the film said they would choose cremation."

## Kissing a Fool ★
R, 105 m., 1998

David Schwimmer (Max Abbott), Jason Lee (Jay Murphy), Mili Avital (Samantha Andrews),

Bonnie Hunt (Linda), Vanessa Angel (Natasha), Kari Wuhrer (Dara), Frank Medrano (Cliff Randal), Bitty Schram (Vicki Pelam). Directed by Doug Ellin and produced by Tag Mendillo, Andrew Form, and Rick Lashbrook. Screenplay by James Frey and Ellin.

One of the requirements of TV sitcoms is that the characters live in each other's pockets. They pop into their friends' apartments at any time of day or night, and every development becomes the subject of a group discussion. That works fine on *Seinfeld,* but on the big screen it looks contrived. Consider, for example, the new comedy *Kissing a Fool* in which none of the characters behave at any moment like any human being we have ever met.

The movie involves situations that wouldn't even exist if it were not for the tortuous contortions of the plot. Jay (Jason Lee) introduces his best friend, Max (David Schwimmer), to Sam (Mili Avital), the woman who is editing his book—even though Jay loves Sam himself. Why does he do this? Otherwise there wouldn't be a role for Max, who is such a hapless shmoe that the only reason Sam dates him is because the plot requires her to. It's crashingly obvious to everyone in the audience, but not to anyone in the movie, that Jay and Sam will eventually realize that they are really in love with one another. When we're that much smarter than the characters, you have to wonder why they aren't buying tickets to watch us.

The film begins at a wedding, with a kiss between two newlyweds. Because the shot is obviously and laboriously contrived to conceal the face of one of the newlyweds, we in the audience of course know immediately that there is a reason for this. Could it be that the two people who are getting married are not the two people the movie will spend the next ninety minutes pretending are going to get married?

At the wedding, we meet Linda (Bonnie Hunt), who runs the publishing company where Sam is editing Jay's book. Linda is the film's narrator. She tells two obnoxious guests at the wedding the whole story of how the newlyweds wound up at the altar. She tells this story without ever once using both of their names, and as she picks her way through a minefield of synonyms and vague adverbial evasions, we get downright restless. Obviously, she's concealing something. And we know what it is, so who's she kidding?

Why is this story, pea-brained to begin with, filtered through the annoying device of a narration? Maybe because the filmmakers thought we would be delighted at the wonderful surprise they are concealing for the last shot. I wonder: Do they know anyone that dumb in their own lives, or do they just think the rest of us are clueless?

Sitcoms like to supply their characters with physical props, and so poor Bonnie Hunt is required to hold a cigarette in every single scene she appears in. And not any cigarette. A freshly lit one, in her right hand, held in the air roughly parallel to her ear. I hope they had a masseuse to give her shoulder rubs between takes. Ms. Hunt, who I hope is suing her agent, does what she can with a character whose IQ is higher than those of the other three characters combined.

Max, the Schwimmer character, plays a WGN sportscaster who thinks Australia is in Europe. Sam and Jay immediately compare notes about charming little trattorias in Florence. Max is obviously not the right choice for this woman, but the movie explains their attraction as first love—a love so strong that Max is actually moved to take his toothpick (sitcom prop) out of his mouth when he sees her.

We are then made to endure a lame contrivance in which Max grows fearful that Sam will not remain faithful to him, and so enlists Jay to attempt to seduce her—as a test. Not since Restoration comedy has this plot device been original, but in *Kissing a Fool* it is taken so seriously that it leads to moments of heartfelt dismay, carefully cued by the sound track, and one of those "darkness before the dawn" sequences in which it appears, for a teeth-gnashing instant, that the right people will not end up together. One character, in dismay, goes into a bar and orders four vodkas at once; the movie doesn't even know how drinkers drink.

If James Frey and the director Doug Ellin, who wrote this screenplay, didn't have an outline from a script workshop tacked to the wall in front of them, then they deserve an Oscar for discovering, all by themselves, a basic story formula that was old, tired, and moronic long before they were born.

I like the title, though. *Kissing a Fool.* They got that right.

## Kolya ★ ★ ★ ½
PG-13, 105 m., 1997

Zdenek Sverak (Louka), Andrej Chalimon (Kolya), Libuse Safrankova (Klara), Ondrez Vetchy (Mr. Broz), Stella Zazvorkova (Mother), Ladislav Smoljak (Mr. Houdek), Irena Livanova (Nadezda), Lilian Mankina (Aunt Tamara). Directed by Jan Sverak and produced by Eric Abraham and Sverak. Screenplay by Zdenek Sverak.

In Prague in 1988, Russian trucks rumble through the streets and Czechs make an accommodation with their masters, or pay a price. Louka pays a price. Because in a moment of unwise wit he wrote a flippant answer on an official form, he has been bounced out of the philharmonic and now scrapes by playing his cello at funerals and repairing tombstones.

Life has consolations. A parade of young women visits his "tower," an apartment at the top of a rickety old building. At fifty-five, Louka (Zdenek Sverak) looks enough like Sean Connery to make hearts flutter, and he has the same sardonic charm. But he is broke and needs a car, and so he listens when his grave digger pal makes an offer. The pal's Soviet niece must get married or she'll be sent back to Russia, where she does not want to go. The niece and her chain-smoking aunt will pay Louka to go through a phony marriage.

Against his better judgment, he does. Then the niece skips to West Germany to join a former boyfriend, leaving behind her five-year-old son, Kolya (Andrej Chalimon). The aunt dies, and Louka is stuck with the kid. This puts a severe cramp in his love life (the kid is delivered in the middle of a would-be seduction), and besides, he knows nothing about kids, and this one speaks only Russian, a language Louka has on principle refused to learn.

The outlines of this story are conventional and sentimental (is there any doubt he will come to love the child?). What makes *Kolya* special is the way it paints the details. Like the films of the Czech New Wave in the late 1960s, it has a cheerful, irreverent humor, and an eye for the absurdities of human behavior. Consider Louka's old mother, who refuses to care for the child because she will not have a Russian in the house, and watch the scene where Russian army trucks stop outside her cottage and the kid hears his native language and runs out happily to talk to the soldiers.

Consider, too, the bureaucracy, faithful to the Soviets. Louka is subjected to a grilling by a hard-nosed official who suspects, correctly, that the marriage was a sham, but the tone of the interview is much altered because Kolya refuses to stay outside and draws pictures all during the interrogation; his evident love for his "stepfather" is a confusing factor.

Quirky details are chosen to show the gradual coming together of Louka and Kolya. The cellist drags the kid to the funerals where he plays, and the kid watches open-eyed as the musicians play and the soloist sings. It is perhaps not surprising that his first words of Czech are the 23rd Psalm. But look at Louka's face when he realizes the kid is using a puppet theater to stage a cremation.

There are many women in Louka's life, but one becomes special: Klara, played by Libuse Safrankova. He ropes her in to helping him care for the child, and eventually something fairly wonderful happens, and at fifty-five Louka finds a way to break out of the trap of his routine. His new freedom is shown against a backdrop of the end of the Cold War, as the Berlin Wall drops, the Russians leave town, and joyous Czechs take to the streets, chanting "It's finally over!" Louka is placed in the center of the celebrants, where he sees, of course, his former bureaucratic interrogator now part of the joyous crowd.

*Kolya* was written by its star, Zdenek Sverak, and directed by his son, Jan. It is a work of love, beautifully photographed by Vladimir Smutny in rich deep reds and browns, with steam rising from soup and the little boy looking wistfully at the pigeons on the other side of the tower window. It is said that American audiences are going to fewer foreign films these days. Missing a film like *Kolya*, winner of a 1997 Golden Globe, would not be a price I would be willing to pay.

## Krippendorf's Tribe ★ ★
PG-13, 94 m., 1998

Richard Dreyfuss (James Krippendorf), Jenna Elfman (Veronica), Natasha Lyonne (Shelly), Gregory Smith (Mickey), Carl Michael Lindner (Edmund), Lily Tomlin (Ruth Allen). Directed by Todd Holland and produced by Larry Brezner.

Screenplay by Charlie Peters, based on the book by Frank Parkin.

Is it possible to recommend a whole comedy on the basis of one scene that made you laugh almost uncontrollably? I fear not. And yet *Krippendorf's Tribe* has such a scene, and many comedies have none. I was reminded of the dead parakeet that had its head taped back on in *Dumb and Dumber.* A scene like that can redeem a lot of downtime.

The scene in *Krippendorf's Tribe* involves the backyard fakery of a primitive circumcision ritual. But I am getting ahead of the story. The movie stars Richard Dreyfuss as James Krippendorf, an anthropologist who has gone to New Guinea, utterly failed to find a lost tribe, and returned to his campus, having spent all of his grant money. Now it is time to produce results, of which he has none.

Krippendorf has two small sons and a teenage daughter; his wife died in New Guinea, but she's handled so remotely in the film that I wonder why they bothered with her. No matter. Back home, Krippendorf has descended into sloth and despond, and pads about the house aimlessly. Then an enthusiastic colleague named Veronica, played with zest and wit by Jenna Elfman, pounds on his door with a reminder that he is to lecture on his findings that very night.

Krippendorf's lack of any findings takes on a whole new meaning when his department head informs him that another colleague will do prison time for misappropriating grant money. Terrified, Krippendorf improvises a lecture in which he claims to have found a lost tribe. He even produces one of its artifacts—a sexual aid, he claims, although sharp eyes might recognize it as a toy space shuttle, belonging to one of his sons who left it in the oven.

Krippendorf has promised home movies of the lost tribe, which, in desperation, he has named the Shelmikedmu, after his children Shelly, Mike, and Edmund. At home, he fakes the footage, dressing his children up like New Guinea tribesmen and intercutting their romps in the backyard with actual footage from his trip. It's at about this point that he hits on the inspiration of the circumcision ritual, which his two boys enter into with such zeal that the scene takes on a comic life of its own.

The movie as a whole isn't that funny. It introduces characters and doesn't really develop them. Lily Tomlin, for example, is Krippendorf's rival. She is given various props, including a pet monkey and an adoring female admirer, and then packed off to New Guinea, where the movie seems to forget her between brief remote appearances. David Ogden Stiers is likewise misused as a video producer who is brought onstage and then never really used. I did like Jenna Elfman's work as Veronica, who towers over Dreyfuss and eventually becomes an accomplice in the deception. Comic momentum threatens to build up during a late scene at a banquet, where the university's aged benefactor unexpectedly discovers the secret of the fraud. But the movie can't find that effortless zaniness that good screwball comedy requires. Dreyfuss and Elfman change into and out of a tribal disguise, and we can see how it's meant to be funny, but it isn't. *Krippendorf's Tribe* contains that one scene that reminds us of what great comedy can play like, and other scenes that don't benefit from the reminder.

## Kundun ★ ★ ★
PG-13, 128 m., 1997

Tenzin Yeshi Paichang (Dalai Lama, age two), Tulku Jamyang Kunga Tenzin (Dalai Lama, age five), Gyurme Tethong (Dalai Lama, age twelve), Tenzin Thuthob Tsarong (Adult Dali Lama), Tencho Gyalpo (Dalai Lama's Mother), Tsewang Migyur Khangsar (Dalai Lama's Father), Lobsang Samten (Master of the Kitchen), Sonam Phuntsok (Reting Rinpoch). Directed by Martin Scorsese and produced by Barbara De Fina. Screenplay by Melissa Mathison.

At a midpoint in Martin Scorsese's *Kundun*, the fourteenth Dalai Lama reads a letter from the thirteenth, prophesying that religion in Tibet will be destroyed by China—that he and his followers may have to wander helplessly like beggars. He says, "What can I do? I'm only a boy." His adviser says, "You are the man who wrote this letter. You must know what to do."

This literal faith in reincarnation, in the belief that the child at the beginning of *Kundun* is the same man who died four years before the child was born, sets the film's underlying tone. *Kundun* is structured as the life of the fourteenth Dalai Lama, but he is simply a vessel for a larger life or spirit, continuing through centuries. That is the film's strength, and its curse. It provides a deep spirituality, but denies the Dalai Lama humanity; he is permitted certain little human touches, but is essentially an icon, not a man.

*Kundun* is like one of the popularized lives of the saints that Scorsese must have studied as a boy in Catholic grade school. I studied the same lives, which reduced the saints to a series of anecdotes. At the end of a typical episode, the saint says something wise, pointing out the lesson, and his listeners fall back in amazement and gratitude. The saint seems to stand above time, already knowing the answers and the outcome, consciously shaping his life as a series of parables.

In *Kundun,* there is rarely the sense that a living, breathing, and (dare I say?) fallible human inhabits the body of the Dalai Lama. Unlike Scorsese's portrait of Jesus in *The Last Temptation of Christ,* this is not a man striving for perfection, but perfection in the shape of a man. Although the film is wiser and more beautiful than Jean-Jacques Annaud's recent *Seven Years in Tibet,* it lacks that film's more practical grounding; Scorsese and his writer, Melissa Mathison, are bedazzled by the Dalai Lama.

Once we understand that *Kundun* will not be a drama involving a plausible human character, we are freed to see the film as it is: An act of devotion, an act even of spiritual desperation, flung into the eyes of twentieth-century materialism. The film's visuals and music are rich and inspiring, and like a Mass by Bach or a Renaissance church painting, it exists as an aid to worship: It wants to enhance, not question.

That this film should come from Scorsese, master of the mean streets, chronicler of wise guys and lowlifes, is not really surprising, since so many of his films have a spiritual component, and so many of his characters know they live in sin and feel guilty about it. There is a strong impulse toward the spiritual in Scorsese, who once studied to be a priest, and *Kundun* is his bid to be born again.

The film opens in Tibet in 1937, four years after the death of the thirteenth Dalai Lama, as monks find a young boy who they sense may be their reincarnated leader. In one of the film's most charming scenes, they place the child in front of an array of objects, some belonging to the thirteenth, some not, and he picks out the right ones, childishly saying, "Mine! Mine! Mine!"

Two years later, the monks come to take the child to live with them and take his place in history. Roger Deakins's photography sees this scene and others with the voluptuous colors of a religious painting; the child peers out at his visitors through the loose weave of a scarf, and sits under a monk's red cloak as the man tells him, "You have chosen to be born again."

At his summer palace, he sees dogs, peacocks, deer, and fish. He is given a movie projector, on which a few years later he sees the awful vision of Hiroshima. Soon the Chinese are invading Tibet, and he is faced with the challenge of defending his homeland while practicing the tenets of nonviolence. There is a meeting with Chairman Mao at which the Dalai Lama hears that religion is dead and can no longer look in the eyes of a man who says such a thing. He focuses instead on Mao's polished Western shoes, which seem to symbolize the loss of older ways and values.

The film is made of episodes, not a plot. It is like illustrations bound into the book of a life. Most of the actors, I understand, are real Tibetan Buddhists, and their serenity in many scenes casts a spell. The sets, the fabrics and floor and wall coverings, the richness of metals and colors, all place them within a tabernacle of their faith. But at the end I felt curiously unfulfilled; the thing about a faith built on reincarnation is that we are always looking only at a tiny part of it, and the destiny of an individual is froth on the wave of history. Those values are better for religion than for cinema, which hungers for story and character.

I admire *Kundun* for being so unreservedly committed to its vision, for being willing to cut loose from audience expectations and follow its heart. I admire it for its visual elegance. And yet this is the first Scorsese film that, to be honest, I would not want to see again and again. Scorsese seems to be searching here for something that is not in his nature and never will be. During *The Last Temptation of Christ,* I believe Scorsese knew exactly how his character felt at all moments. During *Kundun,* I sense him asking himself, "Who is this man?"

## Kurt & Courtney ★ ★ ★

NO MPAA RATING, 99 m., 1998

A documentary directed by Nick Broomfield and produced by Tine Van Den Brande and Michael D'Acosta.

Nick Broomfield does not like Courtney Love. Neither do some of the other people in her life. In Broomfield's rambling, disorganized, fascinating new documentary named *Kurt & Courtney,* Love's father teases us with the possibility that she could have killed her rock star husband, Kurt Cobain. An old boyfriend screams his dislike into the camera. A nanny remembers there was "way too much talk about Kurt's will." A deranged punk musician says, "She offered me fifty grand to whack Kurt Cobain." A private eye thinks he was hired as part of a cover-up.

Broomfield is a one-man band, a BBC filmmaker who travels light and specializes in the American sex 'n' violence scene. After an exposé of the evil influences on Hollywood madam Heidi Fleiss, and an excursion into a Manhattan S&M parlor *(Fetishes),* he takes his show to the Pacific Northwest to examine the unhappy life and mysterious death of Cobain—the lead singer of the grunge rock band Nirvana, apparently dead by his own hand.

Did Cobain really kill himself? No fingerprints were found on his shotgun, we're told, and the movie claims his body contained so many drugs it was unlikely he could have pulled the trigger. Broomfield's film opens with Love as a suspect, only to decide she was probably not involved, and the movie ends in murky speculation without drawing any conclusions. It's not so much about a murder investigation as about two people who won fame and fortune that only one was able to handle. Cobain probably did kill himself, but it was a defeat as much as a decision; he could no longer endure his success, his drug addiction, and his demanding wife.

When Courtney met Kurt, we learn, Cobain was already a star; she was lead singer in a second-tier local band. In 1992, in her words, "We bonded pharmaceutically over drugs." In the words of a friend, she came into his life and in a three-year period took over everything. Then, as Kurt descended, lost into drugs, she got her own act together, and after his death in 1994 she won a Golden Globe nomination for *The People vs. Larry Flynt* and, in the doc's closing scenes, is a presenter of a "freedom of information" banquet of the L.A. chapter of the ACLU. As she takes the stage, it is impossible not to think uneasily of *A Star Is Born.*

Broomfield is not objective. He's in the foreground, narrating everything. The real subject of his films is what he goes through to shoot them. We learn that Courtney refused permission to use her music or Kurt's (no kidding), and he tells us what songs he "would have used" over certain scenes. He hires paparazzi to stalk Love into a recording studio, and at the end, at the ACLU event, he barges onto the stage, grabs the microphone, and accuses her (accurately) of making implied death threats against journalists. One gathers that the ACLU, focusing on the message of *The People vs. Larry Flynt* and desiring a high-profile star for their benefit, invited Love a little prematurely.

In all of Broomfield's films, you meet people you can hardly believe exist. El Duce, for example, the punker who claims Love offered him money to kill Cobain, is a character out of Fellini, or hell. At the end of the movie, we are not surprised to learn he died after stumbling into the path of a train, but we are astonished to learn he was in his mid-thirties; he looks like a well-worn fifty-year-old bouncer. Love's father, a former manager for the Grateful Dead, has written two books about Kurt's death, both of them unflattering to his daughter, and speaks of buying pit bulls "to put peace into our house." Assorted old friends, flames, and hangers-on make appearances that seem inspired by the characters in Andy Warhol's *Chelsea Hotel.* Only Kurt's Aunt Mary, who plays tapes of him singing joyously as a child, seems normal.

Why did Kurt Cobain die? Because of his drug use, obviously, from which everything else descended, including his relationship with Courtney. He was filled with deep insecurities that made him unable to cope with the adulation of his fans; he was far too weak for Love's dominating personality; drugs and booze led to chronic stomach pain, and when he climbed over the wall of his last rehab center, he was fleeing to his death.

We learn from one of his old girlfriends that Cobain was acutely sensitive to how scrawny he was. We see a skeletal self-portrait. "He wore lots and lots of layers of clothing to make himself look heavier," she says. It is one of the film's many ironies that the grunge rock fashion statement, with its flannel shirts beloved by millions, may have come about because Kurt Cobain was a skinny kid.

# L

## La Ceremonie ★ ★ ★

NO MPAA RATING, 111 m., 1997

Sandrine Bonnaire (Sophie), Isabelle Huppert (Jeanne), Jacqueline Bisset (Catherine), Jean-Pierre Cassel (Georges), Virginie Ledoyen (Melinda), Valentin Merlet (Gilles). Directed by Claude Chabrol and produced by Marin Karmitz. Screenplay by Chabrol and Caroline Eliacheff, based on the novel *A Judgement in Stone* by Ruth Rendell.

French gangsters had a word for the events leading up to death by guillotine. They called it "la ceremonie." Claude Chabrol's icy, ruthless new film is also about ceremony—about the patterns of life that divide a rich French family and their strange new housekeeper. Unlike most ceremonies, it ends with an unexpected outcome.

The film opens with Catherine, a pleasant, cultured French art dealer of a certain age (Jacqueline Bisset) interviewing a new housekeeper named Sophie (Sandrine Bonnaire). She explains the job: She lives with her husband and children in an isolated rural district, but Sophie will be free to visit the town from time to time. Sophie agrees, and presents a letter of recommendation from her previous employer. There is something subtly wrong about the way Sophie does this; we feel it but don't understand it.

We meet the rest of the family: the father, Georges (Jean-Pierre Cassel), the attractive twentyish daughter Melinda (Virginie Ledoyen), the younger son Gilles (Valentin Merlet). They live in an elegant but not ostentatious country house, furnished in good taste, with many books and artworks; the wintry classical music on the sound track sets the mood.

Sophie is an excellent housekeeper, but not much company. She stays to herself in her room, staring impassively at the TV. The family agrees, "So far, she's been wonderful." They offer to let her drive the car into town, but she cannot drive. They offer driving lessons, but she says she cannot see well. They offer an eye exam, but she avoids the appointment and buys some cheap ready-made glasses as a cover. One day when the husband calls home asking about a file on his desk, Sophie hangs up the phone and pretends they were disconnected.

We guess her secret before the family does. One day in town she buys some chocolates and presents a 100-franc note. "Do you have any change?" asks the clerk. "No," says Sophie. "Yes you do!" says the clerk, rudely snatching her purse and counting out the coins. (The scene helps establish the film's view of class; the bourgeoisie shopkeeper would do that with a servant girl, but never with a middle-class customer.) By now we know Sophie cannot read or count; she is illiterate or dyslexic.

Sophie makes a friend in the village who can read all too well: the postmistress, Jeanne (Isabelle Huppert), who opens all of Georges's mail. He hates her. She returns the feeling. Sophie and Jeanne become fast friends and learn things about one another. Jeanne was once charged with killing her retarded child, but explains to Sophie, "It's not true . . . she killed herself . . . there's no proof." Jeanne teases Sophie: "I know something about you." She produces a newspaper clipping linking Sophie to a fire that killed fifteen people. Once again, there was no proof. The two girls hug each other with delight and collapse on the bed, giggling like conspirators. It is the scariest moment in the movie.

Now all of the elements are in place: Sophie's deep vulnerability, Jeanne's ability to instigate, the growing resentment of the girls toward the family. Only the family seems oblivious; life for them seems so refined and orderly as they settle down for an evening of watching Mozart on television.

Claude Chabrol has made about fifty films since 1958, when he was one of the figures in the French New Wave. Most of them involve crime, all of them involve pathological or obsessive behavior, and the number of them worth seeing is impressive. *La Ceremonie,* he has said, is a Marxist film about class struggle, but perhaps it is more of a Freudian film, about the scarcely repressed sexuality of Jeanne and Sophie, and the ways it is expressed against a family that represents for both of them a hated authority.

Watching the film, you think maybe you know where it's headed. Or maybe not. Not every ceremony ends in the way we anticipate. (Who would guess, never having attended a Mass, that flesh and blood are consumed—and not just symbolically, according to believers?) Certainly from the family's point of view their opera has an unexpected outcome. The actors include old hands who have worked with Chabrol before (Huppert was unforgettable in his *Violette Noziere*) and strike the right note: No one in this movie should act as if he knows how it ends. And no one does.

## L.A. Confidential ★ ★ ★ ★

R, 138 m., 1997

Kevin Spacey (Jack Vincennes), Russell Crowe (Bud White), Guy Pearce (Ed Exley), James Cromwell (Dudley Smith), Kim Basinger (Lynn Bracken), David Strathairn (Pierce Patchett), Ron Rifkin (D.A. Ellis Loew), Danny DeVito (Sid Hudgens). Directed by Curtis Hanson and produced by Arnon Milchan, Hanson, and Michael Nathanson. Screenplay by Brian Helgeland and Hanson, based on the novel by James Ellroy.

*Confidential* was a key magazine of the 1950s, a monthly that sold millions of copies with its seamy exposés of celebrity drugs and sex. I found it in my dad's night table and read it breathlessly, the stories of reefer parties, multiple divorces, wife-swapping, and "leading men" who liked to wear frilly undergarments. The magazine sank in a sea of lawsuits, but it created a genre; the trash tabloids are its direct descendents.

Watching *L.A. Confidential*, I felt some of the same insider thrill that *Confidential* provided: The movie, like the magazine, is based on the belief that there are a million stories in the city, and all of them will raise your eyebrows and curl your hair. The opening is breathlessly narrated by a character named Sid Hudgens (Danny DeVito), who publishes *Hush-Hush* magazine and bribes a cop named Jack Vincennes (Kevin Spacey) to set up celebrity arrests; Jack is photographed with his luckless victims, and is famous as the guy who caught Robert Mitchum smoking marijuana.

It's Christmas Eve 1953, and Bing Crosby is crooning on the radio as cops pick up cartons of free booze to fuel their holiday parties. We meet three officers who, in their way, represent the choices ahead for the LAPD. Vincennes, starstruck, lives for his job as technical adviser to *Badge of Honor*, a *Dragnet*-style show. Bud White (Russell Crowe) is an aggressive young cop who is willing to accommodate the department's relaxed ethics. Ed Exley (Guy Pearce) is a straight arrow, his rimless glasses making him look a little like a tough accountant—one who works for the FBI, maybe.

Ed is an ambitious careerist who wants to do everything by the book. His captain, Dudley Smith (James Cromwell), kindly explains that an officer must be prepared to lie, cheat, and steal—all in the name, of course, of being sure the guilty go to jail. Captain Smith likes to call his men "good lads," and seems so wise we can almost believe him as he administers little quizzes and explains that advancement depends on being prepared to give the "right answers."

*L.A. Confidential* is immersed in the atmosphere and lore of *film noir*, but it doesn't seem like a period picture—it believes its *noir* values and isn't just using them for decoration. It's based on a novel by James Ellroy, that lanky, sardonic poet of Los Angeles sleaze. Its director, Curtis Hanson *(Bad Influence, The Hand That Rocks the Cradle)*, weaves a labyrinthine plot, but the twists are always clear because the characters are so sharply drawn; we don't know who's guilty or innocent, but we know who should be.

The plot involves a series of crimes that take place in the early days of the new year. Associates of Mickey Cohen, the L.A. mob boss, become victims of gangland-style executions. A decomposing body is found in a basement. There's a massacre at an all-night coffee shop; one of the victims is a crooked cop, and three black youths are immediately collared as suspects, although there's evidence that police may have been behind the crime.

We meet a millionaire pornographer named Pierce Patchett (David Strathairn). He runs a high-class call girl operation in which aspiring young actresses are given plastic surgery to make them resemble movie stars; one of them is Lynn Bracken (Kim Basinger), who has been "cut" to look like Veronica Lake. Bud White, the Crowe character, tracks her down, thinking she'll have info about the decomposing corpse, and they fall almost helplessly in love ("You're the first man in months who hasn't told me I look just like Veronica Lake").

At this point, perhaps an hour into the movie, I felt inside a Raymond Chandler novel: not only because of the atmosphere and the dialogue, but also because there seemed to be no way all of these characters and events could be drawn together into a plot that made sense. Not that I would have cared; I enjoy *film noir* for the journey as much as the destination.

But Hanson and his cowriter, Brian Helgeland, do pull the strands together, and along the way there's an unlikely alliance between two cops who begin as enemies. The film's assumption is that although there's small harm in free booze and a little graft, there are some things a police officer simply cannot do and look himself in the mirror in the morning.

The film is steeped in L.A. lore; Ellroy is a student of the city's mean streets. It captures the town just at that postwar moment when it was beginning to become self-conscious about its myth. Joseph Wambaugh writes in one of his books that he is constantly amazed by the hidden threads that connect the high to the low, the royalty to the vermin, in Los Angeles—where a hooker is only a role from stardom, and vice, as they say, versa.

One of the best scenes takes place in the Formosa Cafe, a restaurant much frequented in the 1940s by unlikely boothfellows. Cops turn up to question Johnny Stompanato, a hood who may know something about the Cohen killings. His date gives them some lip. "A hooker cut to look like Lana Turner is still a hooker," one of them tells her, but Jack Vincennes knows better: "She is Lana Turner," he says with vast amusement.

One of the reasons *L.A. Confidential* is so good, why it deserves to be mentioned with *Chinatown,* is that it's not just plot and atmosphere. There are convincing characters here, not least Kim Basinger's hooker, whose quiet line, "I thought I was helping you," is one of the movie's most revealing moments. Russell Crowe *(Proof)* and Guy Pearce *(The Adventures of Priscilla, Queen of the Desert)* are two Australian actors who here move convincingly into star-making roles, and Kevin Spacey uses perfect timing to suggest his character's ability to move between two worlds while betraying both (he has a wonderful scene where he refuses to cooperate with a department investigation—until they threaten his job on the TV show).

Behind everything, setting the moral tone and pulling a lot of the plot threads, is the angular captain, seemingly so helpful. James Cromwell, who was the kindly farmer in *Babe,* has the same benevolent smile in this role, but the eyes are cold, and in his values can be seen, perhaps, the road ahead to Rodney King. *L.A. Confidential* is seductive and beautiful, cynical and twisted, and one of the best films of the year.

## Land and Freedom ★ ★ ★

NO MPAA RATING, 109 m., 1995

Ian Hart (David), Rosana Pastor (Blanca), Iciar Bollain (Maite), Tom Gilroy (Lawrence), Marc Martinez (Vidal), Frederic Pierrot (Bernard). Directed by Ken Loach and produced by Rebecca O'Brien. Screenplay by Jim Allen.

The key fact about the Spanish Civil War is that the fascists banded together, while the factions of the Left fought among themselves. The war, often called a dress rehearsal for World War II, began after Leftists legally won victories at the Spanish polls. The fascist forces of Generalissimo Franco, backed by army units, landowners, and the church, declared war to overthrow them. Franco got aid from his soul brothers Hitler and Mussolini, while the Left was denied aid by the democracies of the West, which were shy of antagonizing Germany.

Volunteers from all over the world went to Spain to fight Franco, and were romanticized by Hemingway and others, although it was George Orwell, in his book *Homage to Catalonia,* who saw clearly that the true agenda of the Communists was to defeat their presumed allies, the socialists and anarchists, even at the cost of losing the war against Franco.

Ken Loach's *Land and Freedom* tells this story through the eyes of one young man, a British Communist who volunteers to fight in Spain for fairly simpleminded reasons, including knee-jerk politics and the fact that he'll get a free train ticket to travel there. The man's name is David, and he's played by Ian Hart, who previously played John Lennon in two films *(The Hours and Times and Backbeat),* and was perhaps cast by Lynch for the same reasons he made a good Lennon: He seems idealistic, visionary, romantic, and not terribly realistic.

Loach is the most class-conscious of filmmakers, and in a recent group of movies he has created some memorable working-class heroes. *Riff-Raff* was about construction workers, *Raining Stones* was about an unemployed man's determination to buy a first communion dress for his daughter, and the searing *Ladybird, Ladybird* was about a war between an angry, hostile mother and the social services.

Those were all up close portraits. *Land and Freedom* is a completely different kind of film, a broad-scale view of the fighting in Spain, in which David sometimes seems just a means of navigating between the points Loach wants to make. There is a personal story, yes, involving David's infatuation with a former prostitute named Blanca (Rosana Pastor), who fights by his side but loves another man. In one of the movie's best scenes, David's unit attacks a fascist-held village, and when its defenders take civilians as hostages, he (rightly) can't shoot them, and Blanca's lover is killed. In the rough-hewn camaraderie of war, David and Blanca settle naturally at one another's side; war cannot pause to mourn the dead.

The Franco forces had the advantage of being led by experienced military officers. Their troops followed orders and were disciplined. The Left in Spain, on the other hand, was a chaotic experiment in varieties of democracy, consensus, political education, and ideology, and hardly a decision was taken without exhaustive debate. *Land and Freedom* has been criticized in some circles for what I think is its most useful scene, in which David's militia unit stops everything to have a lengthy debate about how some land, recently occupied, should be farmed. Some feel it should be collectivized, Soviet-style. Others feel each worker should have his own little plot. "I work my land my way," a peasant argues, but ideology prevails. All of the histories of the war, most notably Hugh Thomas's classic *The Spanish Civil War*, emphasize how the forces of the Left seemed more adept at political infighting, debate, and intrigue than at organizing and fighting.

*Land and Freedom* is less satisfying than it could have been, because David is unsophisticated about his own politics and motives. But as a record of how idealism was swamped by the rising Nazi tide—in which the bombing of Guernica, for example, was a field test for Nazi aerial warfare strategies—it is unique among films about Spain.

## The Land Girls ★ ★ ½

R, 112 m., 1998

Catherine McCormack (Stella), Rachel Weisz (Ag), Anna Friel (Prue), Steven Mackintosh (Joe Lawrence), Tom Georgeson (Mr. Lawrence), Maureen O'Brien (Mrs. Lawrence), Gerald Down (Ratty). Directed by David Leland and produced by Simon Relph. Screenplay by Keith Dewhurst and Leland, based on the novel *Land Girls* by Angela Huth.

*The Land Girls* tells the story of the Land Army, the volunteer force of civilians raised in England during World War II to take the place of farmworkers who enlisted in the armed forces. The movie takes place during a green, wet winter on a beautiful farm in Dorset, where three "land girls" from the city are sent to become farm laborers.

Their lessons begin, predictably, with the challenge of milking cows. Mr. Lawrence (Tom Georgeson), the farmer, is unimpressed: "It's not an army—it's just an excuse for a lark!" But the girls learn quickly and work hard, and in one way or another all three are attracted to Joe Lawrence (Steven Mackintosh), the farmer's son.

Prue (Anna Friel), who before the war was a hairdresser, is the boldest of the girls, and tells Agatha (Rachel Weisz), who is a Cambridge graduate but still a virgin at twenty-six, she should seize her opportunity with Joe. "Fornication? With him? He's unspeakable!" "So what?" Ag thinks it over and approaches Joe in all seriousness: "I'll come straight to the point. Would you mind giving me a go?"

Joe would not. He is more seriously attracted, however, to Stella (Catherine McCormack from *Dangerous Beauty*), who is engaged to a pilot. She tries to remain loyal to her man, but Joe has an appeal that's apparently irresistible to the women in the movie, although less compelling to the audience.

What happens to the characters is more or less predictable (we guess there will be some setbacks, some wartime tragedies, some angry partners, and weepy reunions). What I liked about the movie—what I preferred to the romances and relationships, indeed—was the look of the film, its sensual evocation of the British countryside in winter.

The cinematographer, Henry Braham, uses a

saturated, high-contrast color style that makes the woods look dark and damp and the grass wet, cold, and green. The vast skies are that lonely and yet reassuring shade that watercolorists call Payne's gray. Farmer Lawrence loves his land, which he tramps morning and night in the company of his dog, Jack. His wife (Maureen O'Brien) loves it just as much, and acts as a quiet influence on his temper.

In one of the best sequences in the movie, Farmer Lawrence tells a government official he will not plow his east meadow, no matter how much the land is needed for wartime crops. "You should see this field in the spring," he tells Stella. "It's beautiful—just beautiful." He remembers courting his wife there. But Stella, stung in love and by what she perceives as the farmer's dislike, fires up the tractor one morning and plows it. This act of rebellion is what wins the farmer's respect.

I'll remember that scene, and another one where the land girls wait for the mailman to arrive, and one of them balances on a rail of the farm gate, like a figurehead in the mist. More than with most movies, I felt the reality of the rural setting, the earth beneath the grass, the closeness of the animals to their masters. But the story itself seemed thin in comparison: flirtations, broken hearts, bittersweet regret, all pretty routine.

## Larger Than Life ★½

PG, 93 m., 1996

Bill Murray (Jack Corcoran), Janeane Garofalo (Mo), Matthew McConaughey (Tip Tucker), Linda Fiorentino (Terry Bonura), Anita Gillette (Mom), Keith David (Hurst), Pat Hingle (Vernon), Lois Smith (Luluna), Jeremy Piven (Walter). Directed by Howard Franklin and produced by Richard B. Lewis, John Watson, and Pen Densham. Screenplay by Roy Blount Jr., based on a story by Densham and Garry Williams.

Curious, how in such a disappointing comedy, Bill Murray manages to dash off a hilarious warm-up. The opening scenes of *Larger Than Life,* showing him as a third-rate motivational speaker, are right on target, with one zinger after another aimed at after-dinner speakers who promise to remake your life with touchy-feely slogans.

Murray plays Jack Corcoran, whose trademark slogan is "Get Over It!" He shows a banquet crowd how to unleash its hidden abilities by calling for volunteers to make a human pyramid. His clients include the American Motion Upholstery Association (reclining chairs), but his agents promise him some bigger fees, real soon. Meanwhile, he's preparing to get married, urged on by his mom (Anita Gillette), who has always told him his father drowned while saving helpless children.

Not true. A telegram arrives informing him of his father's death. "You mean I had a father all these years?" he wails, and his mother explains she left her husband because he was "irresponsible." Maybe he was. The old man was a circus clown. Jack's inheritance includes a pile of bills and a trained elephant named Vera.

Most of *Larger Than Life* involves Jack's attempts to move Vera entirely across the United States to California, where the elephant will end up either as the victim of a sadistic animal trainer (Linda Fiorentino) or as part of a breeding herd being shipped to Sri Lanka by an environmental activist (Janeane Garofolo). The formula for road movies, even those involving elephants, includes colorful characters encountered along the way, and two of the bright spots in a dim screenplay are provided by an old carny named Vernon (Pat Hingle) and his tattooed wife, Luluna (Lois Smith). They knew and loved Jack's father and teach Jack some commands that (sometimes) make Vera perform an amazing repertory of tricks. They also advise him to avoid the straight life and become a carny, not a rube.

Jack's adventures with transporting Vera include a train journey, followed by an attempt to maneuver a semi-trailer truck. And we meet Tip Tucker (Matthew McConaughey), a manic semi owner-operator with weird theories about everything in American society, especially school lunch programs. He pursues Jack and Vera cross-country after they misuse his truck. At the end of the journey, Jack has to decide between the circus and the zoo for Vera—and, in a way, for himself.

The materials are here to make a good comedy, I guess. The screenplay is by Roy Blount Jr., a funny writer. But the energy isn't there. Murray often chooses to play a laid-back, detached character, but this time he's so detached he's almost absent. He chooses to work in a low key, and the other actors, in matching his energy level, make a movie that drones instead of humming. Comedy is often about people who are passionately frustrated in goals they're convinced are crucial. Here Jack hardly seems to care, as he and Vera mosey along cross-country, bemused rather than bedazzled by their adventures.

The sad thing is, there are the fixings for another comedy, probably a much better one, right there in the opening scenes. Motivational speakers are ripe for satire. The bookshelves groan with self-improvement volumes, all promising to explain the problems of your universe, and their solution, in a few well-chosen rules. An honest bookstore would post the following sign above its "self-help" section: "For true self-help, please visit our philosophy, literature, history, and science sections, find yourself a good book, read it, and think about it."

Murray's portrait of an inspirational speaker is right on target and filled out with lots of subtle touches of movement and dialogue, and there is humor, too, in the way his audiences will go along with his insane schemes (like the human pyramid), as if being able to balance three people on your back would solve your problems at work. This whole section of the movie is inspired; Murray should star in the movie of *The Dilbert Principle.* As for the elephant portions of the movie: They say an elephant never forgets, which means that I have an enormous advantage over Tai, who plays Vera, because I plan to forget this movie as soon as convenient.

## Last Dance ★ ★ ½

R, 103 m., 1996

Sharon Stone (Cindy Liggett), Rob Morrow (Rick Hayes), Randy Quaid (Sam Burns), Peter Gallagher (John Hayes), Jack Thompson (The Governor), Jayne Brook (Jill), Pamala Tyson (Legal Aid Attorney), Skeet Ulrich (Billy). Directed by Bruce Beresford and produced by Steven Haft. Screenplay by Ron Koslow, based on a story by Haft and Koslow.

*Last Dance* stars Sharon Stone as a woman who has spent twelve years on Death Row after being convicted of two murders. Now her appeals seem exhausted and her execution date draws near. A state-appointed attorney looks into her case and thinks there are grounds for appeal. But the state governor is a hard-liner who almost never grants stays of execution. And the woman herself doesn't much prefer a life sentence to death.

This is potentially powerful material, and the movie handles it thoughtfully. It makes a good showcase for Stone, who wants to be taken seriously as more than Hollywood's favorite femme fatale. She does a good job of disappearing into the role; there are no leftover glamour touches or star turns, and I was reminded a little of Susan Hayward's Oscar-winning work in *I Want to Live!* (1958). After Stone's interesting work in *Casino* and *Diabolique,* it is a reminder of how easy it is to stereotype an actress on the basis of a few famous sex-and-violence roles, and how unfair.

But the movie suffers from one inescapable misfortune: It arrived while *Dead Man Walking* was still fresh in our memory. That film was an unquestioned masterpiece, containing some of the best writing, acting, and directing of recent years. *Last Dance* can't stand up against it. Too many of its scenes are based on conventional ideas of story construction. We can see the bones beneath the skin.

Stone's heroine, Cindy, is a poor white—a disadvantaged child of an abusive home, who was exposed to sex and drugs at an early age and was on crack continuously for two days before she committed murder, a fact not brought up at her trial. There are other circumstances about the murders that might also have interested a jury, but she received a poor defense, missed a chance at a plea bargain, and now faces death by lethal injection.

Her lawyer is named Rick Hayes (Rob Morrow, from *Quiz Show*). He's not much of a legal brain. He got his state job because his brother (Peter Gallagher) is an aide to the governor. His boss (Randy Quaid), wonders what kind of an applicant turns up late for a job appointment with wine on his breath.

There are two famous convicts on Death Row: Cindy, and a black man named John Henry Reese (Charles Dutton), who has masterminded an effective campaign to get his sentence commuted. "How they gonna go and kill a man who's been on the *New York Times* best-seller list?" he asks. The governor (Jack Thompson) is a defender of the death penalty, but it appears if he pardons anybody, it will be the other convict and not Cindy.

She doesn't much care. She distrusts everybody, is disillusioned with appeals, doesn't want to spend the rest of her life in prison, and refuses to fight for her own life. Rick tries to break down her reserves, and eventually does so ("What have you got to lose?"). But these scenes owe more to movie conventions than to psychological truth. By helping her, he's helping himself, and finding the self-respect he lost as a kid growing up in the shadow of a successful older brother.

The movie has a few scenes that really should have been rewritten before filming. One is the unconvincing moment when Rick awkwardly confronts the governor in the worst possible way, at the worst possible moment, to demand clemency for his client. Another is when Cindy's former boyfriend attacks Rick during a prison interview; the scene plays as action, not drama. And why is it that all movies about execution always hinge on a phone call—and the call never comes until seconds before midnight? What are judges waiting for? What if they get a busy signal? Why can't they call in at 11:30? Because they're the creatures of the plot mechanics, that's why.

Among the very best scenes in *Last Dance* are those leading up to the possible execution. Rick buys Cindy a dress she can wear into the death chamber, and as she unpacks it, the moment becomes very moving. And then there is the matter-of-fact way the prison officials go about their duties. "This is hard for everyone," the warden says, not very helpfully, "but together, we're going to get through it."

Stone can be proud of her work in this movie, but the material is simply not as good as it needs to be after *Dead Man Walking*. That film reinvented the Death Row genre, saw the characters and the situation fresh, asked hard questions, and found truth in its dialogue. *Last Dance*, by comparison, comes across as earnest but unoriginal. It might have seemed better if it hadn't been released in the shadow of *Dead Man Walking*, but we'll never know.

## The Last Days of Disco ★ ★ ★ ½

R, 112 m., 1998

Chloe Sevigny (Alice), Kate Beckinsale (Charlotte), Chris Eigeman (Des), MacKenzie Astin (Jimmy), Matt Keeslar (Josh), Robert Sean Leonard (Tom), Jennifer Beals (Nina), Matthew Ross (Dan). Directed by Whit Stillman and produced by Edmon Roch and Cecilia Kate Roque. Screenplay by Stillman.

*The Last Days of Disco* is about people who *would* like to belong to the kinds of clubs that would accept them as members. It takes place in "the very early 1980s" in Manhattan, where a group of young, good-looking Ivy League graduates dance the night away in discos.

Unlike the characters in *Saturday Night Fever*, who were basically just looking for a good time, these upwardly mobile characters are alert to the markers of social status. *New York* magazine is their textbook, and being admitted to the right clubs is the passing grade.

The movie is the latest sociological romance by Whit Stillman *(Metropolitan, Barcelona)*, who nails his characters with perfectly heard dialogue and laconic satire. His characters went to good schools, have good jobs, and think they're smarter than they are. "Alice, one of the things I've noticed is that people hate being criticized," says Charlotte, who seems quietly proud of this wisdom. They are capable of keeping a straight face while describing themselves as "adherents to the disco movement."

Alice (Chloe Sevigny, from *Kids*) is the smartest member of the crowd, and definitely the nicest. She has values. Her best friend, Charlotte (Kate Beckinsale), only has goals: to meet the right guys, to be popular, to do exactly what she imagines someone in her position should be doing. Both girls are regulars at a fashionable disco. Charlotte is forever giving poor Alice advice about what to say and how to behave; she says guys like it when a girl uses the word "sexy," and a few nights later, when a guy tells Alice he collects first editions of Scrooge McDuck comic books, she faithfully observes that she has always found Uncle Scrooge sexy.

As the movie opens, a junior ad executive named Jimmy Steinway (MacKenzie Astin) has just failed to get his boss into the club (he was wearing a brown suit). Jimmy goes in anyway.

Alice and Charlotte, working as a team (Charlotte is the coach), forcibly introduce themselves. During the opening scenes we meet other regulars, including Des (Christopher Eigeman), the floor manager, who gets rid of girls by claiming to be gay, and who has his doubts about the club's management ("To me, shipping cash to Switzerland in canvas bags doesn't sound legal"). Other regulars include Josh (Matthew Keeslar), who casually mentions that he's an assistant district attorney, and Tom (Robert Sean Leonard), who has a theory that "the environmental movement was spawned by the rerelease of *Bambi* in the late 1950s."

During the movie these people will date each other with various degrees of intensity. Charlotte's approach is to take no hostages; she invites the D.A. to dinner at a time when she doesn't even have an apartment, and then rents one. A real-estate agent explains the concept of a "railroad flat" to her (you have to walk through both bedrooms and the kitchen to get to the bathroom, but the flat has two hall doors, so the best way to get from the front to the back is to walk down the hall).

If Scott Fitzgerald were to return to life, he would feel at home in a Whit Stillman movie. Stillman listens to how people talk and knows what it reveals about them. His characters have been supplied by their Ivy League schools with the techniques but not the subjects of intelligent conversation, and so they discuss *Lady and the Tramp* with the kind of self-congratulatory earnestness that French students would reserve for Marx and Freud. (Their analysis of the movie is at least as funny as the Quentin Tarantino character's famous deconstruction of *Top Gun* in the movie *Sleep With Me.*)

Stillman has the patience to circle a punch line instead of leaping straight for it. He'll establish something in an early scene and then keep nibbling away until it delivers. The guy who dumps girls by claiming to be gay, for example, eventually explains that he always thought he was straight until, one day, he felt "something different" while watching Jim Fowler on *Wild Kingdom.*

The movie has barely enough plot to hold it together; it involves drugs and money laundering, but it's typical of Stillman that most of the suspense involves the young D.A. fretting about a romantic conflict of interest. The underlying tone of the film is sweet, fond, and a little sad: These characters believe the disco period was the most wonderful period of their lives, and we realize that it wasn't disco that was so special, but youth. They were young, they danced, they drank, they fell in love, they learned a few lessons, and the music of that time will always reawaken those emotions.

It's human nature to believe that if a club admits people like you, you will find the person you are looking for inside. The problem with that theory is that wherever you go, there you are. At the end of *The Last Days of Disco,* as the club scene fades, people are hired to stand outside and pretend they have been turned away. When they get off work, what clubs do they go to? So it goes.

## Last Man Standing ★

R, 103 m., 1996

Bruce Willis (John Smith), Bruce Dern (Sheriff Ed Galt), William Sanderson (Joe Monday), Christopher Walken (Hickey), David Patrick Kelly (Doyle), Michael Imperioli (Giorgio Carmonte), Karina Lombard (Felina), Ned Eisenberg (Fredo Strozzi), Alexandra Powers (Lucy Kolinski). Directed by Walter Hill and produced by Hill and Arthur Sarkissian. Screenplay by Hill, based on a story by Ryuzo Kikushima and Akira Kurosawa.

*Last Man Standing* is such a desperately cheerless film, so dry and laconic and wrung out that you wonder if the filmmakers ever thought in any way that it could be . . . fun. It contains elements that are often found in entertainments—things like guns, gangs, and spectacular displays of death—but here they crouch on the screen and growl at the audience. Even the movie's hero is bad company.

The movie stars Bruce Willis as a man who says his name is John Smith, and who arrives at the Texas town of Jericho during Prohibition. It is a strange town: The buildings suggest a Western from the 1880s, the cars suggest the late 1920s, and there are two local bootlegging gangs who have arrived at an uneasy truce. And that's it. Near as I could tell, there are *no* other non-gang residents of Jericho except for the undertaker, the sheriff, and the bartender.

"I won't say business has been good lately," the

bartender tells John Smith, who walks in for a drink. No kidding. Who do the bootleggers sell their booze to? Is Jericho simply a distribution point? Then why are there two virtual armies of gangsters, one imported from Chicago, wearing fedoras and business suits and hanging around ominously?

I'm missing the point, I know. *Last Man Standing* is not intended as a realistic portrait of anything. The credits announce a screenplay by Ryuzo Kikushima and Akira Kurosawa, and some filmgoers will recognize the plot outlines from Kurosawa's *Yojimbo* (1961). Well, Kurosawa has inspired other good American movies (his *Seven Samurai* was remade as *The Magnificent Seven* and *Yojimbo* itself loosely inspired *A Fistful of Dollars*), but here the attempt to move the story from Japan to Texas seems pointless, because the movie made from it isn't Kurosawa, or a Western, or a gangster movie, or anything else other than a mannered, juiceless, excruciatingly repetitive exercise in style.

The director is Walter Hill. When he's in good form, he makes films like *48 HRS* and the neglected *Geronimo* (1993). When he's not in top form, he makes male action mythology like *Wild Bill* (1995). What he almost always shows are violent men living in a society that doesn't give them much opportunity to do anything other than kill one another.

*Last Man Standing* takes that story line to its ultimate refinement. Following in the footsteps of Kurosawa's samurai tale, Willis arrives in a strange town with no history and few plans ("Drunk or sober, I had no complaints—even if I did get my hands dirty on the way"). He discovers local power is divided between the Strozzi gang (led by Ned Eisenberg) and the Doyle gang (led by David Patrick Kelly). He decides to end their uneasy truce in order to make money from the resulting chaos.

Both gangs have some interesting lieutenants. Strozzi is saddled with Giorgio Carmonte (Michael Imperioli), son of a Mafia chief in Chicago. Doyle has the dreaded Hickey (Christopher Walken), said to be so tough that at fifteen he burned down an orphanage and enjoyed watching the "little kids go up like candles."

Smith packs two guns, shoots them at the same time, and never misses. Early in the film he is drawn on by twelve men and kills them all before they can hit him. When he's offered $1,000 to work for Doyle ("a day or a week?") he responds, "I'm worth it. I'm good." The jealous Walken character leaps up, sprays the room with machine gun bullets and says, "That good?" Uh, how good is that?

His plan is to work for one side, weaken it, then work for the other side, weaken it, and eventually set up a war in which he will be the only survivor. And there is a woman involved. Doyle stole her from her mother and child, and dotes on her. To look upon her is a capital crime in Jericho. Smith befriends the woman and in other ways reveals that he is not entirely accurate when he says, "I have no conscience."

This story line is roughly borrowed from *Yojimbo,* as is the friendship with the local innkeeper, although in the Kurosawa movie the town was divided between clans selling saki and silk, not booze. It makes no difference, because the story reduces itself to macho posturing, boasting, threats, sudden outbursts of gunfire, a mounting body count, and the hero's weary narration.

Even the look of the film is arid. Hill and his cinematographer, Lloyd Ahern, have sought to drain the color and life from the images. Many scenes look exactly like those unfortunate early-1960s films where the color has faded, leaving only reds, browns, and shadows. Dust covers everything. Nothing is beautiful. All seems tired, worn, exhausted. The victory at the end is downbeat, and there is an indifference to it. This is such a sad, lonely movie.

## The Last Supper ★ ★ ★

R, 92 m., 1995

Cameron Diaz (Jude), Jonathan Penner (Marc), Courtney B. Vance (Luke), Ron Eldard (Pete), Ron Perlman (Norman Arbuthnot), Annabeth Gish (Paulie), Nora Dunn (Sheriff Stanley), Charles Durning (Reverend Hutchens). Directed by Stacy Title and produced by Larry Weinberg and Matt Cooper. Screenplay by Dan Rosen.

*I disapprove of what you say, but I will defend to the death your right to say it.*

—Voltaire

Everybody in *The Last Supper* disapproves of that sentiment, and if anybody is going to die it will indeed have to be Voltaire. The movie is a savage satire about intolerance. By the end, its liberal heroes are arguing about whether they've killed and buried ten or eleven right-wingers in their back garden, but the movie isn't about Left and Right, it's about those on any side who do not understand freedom of speech.

Amazing, really, how many Americans do not support that first freedom. There is a fever abroad in the land to limit our freedom to communicate, and I was not surprised to discover that Senator James Exon, the author of the Internet "decency" bill, was unable the other day to answer even the simplest questions about how it should be implemented. The great thing is to ban things, not define them or understand them.

Strange. We never think to limit our own freedoms. Only other people's. Consider the five Iowa graduate students in *The Last Supper.* They share a house together, eat communal meals and are all proudly left-wing. One day a stranger gives a lift to one of their friends, and they invite him to stay for dinner. The stranger, a truck driver named Zac (Bill Paxton), turns out to be a virulent racist ("Hitler had the right idea"). He's also a Desert Storm veteran, and when one of the liberal students makes a wisecrack ("Was that really a war? I thought it was a Republican commercial"), Zac demonstrates how true patriots defend their ideas by holding a knife to a student's throat and breaking an arm. In the struggle that results, Zac is killed.

After the students bury him in the back garden, they get to thinking: "What if you could have killed Hitler, before he was Hitler? Think of the lives you could have saved." The idea is seductive, and the left-wingers feel heady after their taste of violence. "The conservatives are effective," one of them complains. "They do things. All we do is buy animal-friendly mascara."

They plan a series of dinner parties, inviting carefully selected right-wingers. One of the carafes of wine on the table contains arsenic. They listen carefully during the dinner conversation. Their guests include a homophobe ("Homosexuality is the disease. AIDS is the cure"), a male chauvinist pig ("I doubt most rape is really rape"), an antiecologist, a book-burner, and others who eventually find their glasses being refreshed from the poisoned carafe. One guy comes in wearing a swastika and is polished off before dinner: "I told him it was happy hour. Why waste the food?"

This elimination process has a certain perverse appeal, but goes on too long once we've grasped the story's structure. The left-wingers are as intolerant as their guests, but can't see that because they're blinded by their own self-righteousness. That's why it's a mistake to see *The Last Supper* as being against either political wing: It's against all those who believe their opinions are so correct that those who disagree should be silenced.

The five students make a lively group. They're played by Cameron Diaz, Ron Eldard, Annabeth Gish, Jonathan Penner, and Courtney B. Vance, all of whom share the crucial skill of seeming smart enough to know better, which is important (if they were stupid, we could forgive them). The guests are played in a series of sharp-tongued cameos by such as Charles Durning, Mark Harmon, and Jason Alexander. And the film is stolen at the end by Ron Perlman, as a Rush Limbaugh clone who savors his expensive cigar and talks leisurely circles around his antagonists while seeing right through their plot.

If the movie is a little too long and a little too repetitive, it is nevertheless a brave effort in a timid time, a Swiftian attempt to slap us all in the face and get us to admit that our own freedoms depend precisely on those of our neighbors, our opponents, and yes, our enemies. Those who limit another's freedom of speech create a nation in which freedom can be limited—and what goes around, comes around. You would think Americans would understand that. Senators, especially.

## Lawn Dogs ★ ½

R, 101 m., 1998

Mischa Barton (Devon), Sam Rockwell (Trent), Kathleen Quinlan (Clare), Christopher McDonald (Morton), Bruce McGill (Nash), Eric Mabius (Sean), David Barry Gray (Brett), Miles Meehan (Billy). Directed by John Duigan and produced by Duncan Kenworthy. Screenplay by Naomi Wallace.

John Duigan's *Lawn Dogs* is like a nasty accident at the symbol factory. Pieces are scattered all over the floor, as the wounded help each other to the exits. Some of the pieces look well made and could be recycled. We pick up a few of them, and put them together to see if they'll fit. But they all seem to come from different designs.

The movie isn't clear about what it's trying to say—what it wants us to believe when we leave. It has the form of a message picture, without the message. It takes place in an upscale Kentucky housing development named Camelot Gardens, where the $300,000 homes sit surrounded by big lawns and no trees. It's a gated community; the security guard warns one of the "lawn dogs"—or yard workers—to be out of town by 5:00 P.M.

In one of the new houses lives ten-year-old Devon (Mischa Barton), who has a scar running down her chest after heart surgery. Her insipid parents are Morton (Christopher McDonald) and Clare (Kathleen Quinlan). Morton plans to run for office. Clare has casual sex with local college kids. And Trent (Sam Rockwell) mows their lawn.

Devon is in revolt, although she doesn't articulate it as interestingly as the heroine of *Welcome to the Dollhouse.* She wanders beyond the gates, finds Trent's trailer home in the woods, and becomes his friend. There are unrealized undertones of sexuality in her behavior, which the movie never makes overt, except in the tricky scene where she asks Trent to touch her scar. He has a scar, too; here's a new version of you show me yours and I'll show you mine.

The people inside Camelot Gardens are all stupid pigs. That includes the security guard, the parents, and the college kids, who insult and bully Trent. Meanwhile, Trent and Devon spend idyllic afternoons in the woods, being friends, until there is a tragic misunderstanding that leads to the death of a dog and even more alarming consequences.

Nobody makes it into the movie just as an average person. Trent's dad is a Korean vet whose lungs were destroyed by microbes in the K rations, and who is trying to give away his American flag collection. Trent is the kind of guy who stops traffic on a one-lane bridge while he strips, dives into the river, and walks back to his pickup boldly nude. Devon is the kind of little girl who crawls out onto her roof, throws her nightgown into the sky, and utters wild dog cries at the Moon.

All of these events happen with the precision and vivid detail of a David Lynch movie, but I do not know why. It is easy to make a film about people who are pigs and people who are free spirits, but unless you show how or why they got that way, they're simply characters you've created. It's easy to have Devon say, "I don't like kids—they smell like TV." But what does this mean when a ten-year-old says it? It's easy to show good people living in trailers and awful people living in nice homes, but it can work out either way. It's easy to write about a father who wants his little girl to have plastic surgery so her scar won't turn off boys, and then a boy who thinks it's "cool." But where is it leading? What is it saying? Camelot Gardens is a hideous place to live. So? Get out as fast as you can.

## The Leading Man ★ ★ ★

R, 96 m., 1998

Jon Bon Jovi (Robin Grange), Lambert Wilson (Felix Webb), Anna Galiena (Elena Webb), Thandie Newton (Hilary Rule), Barry Humphries (Humphrey Beal), David Warner (Tod), Patricia Hodge (Delvene), Diana Quick (Susan). Directed by John Duigan and produced by Bertil Ohlsson and Paul Raphael. Screenplay by Virginia Duigan.

*The Leading Man* begins as a backstage story about the London theater world, and then a little Hitchcockian intrigue edges into the frame. The movie's about "Britain's greatest living playwright," a bedeviled middle-aged man with a wife and a mistress, both angry with him. A Hollywood sex symbol, who is starring in his new play, offers to solve all his problems by seducing the wife.

This is a little like Hitchcock's setup in *Strangers on a Train,* where an outsider sees a need and volunteers to meet it—at a price. The neat trick in *The Leading Man* is that we never quite understand the movie star's complete plan. Why is he doing this (apart from getting the husband's license to seduce the wife?). What else does he have in mind?

The movie star, Robin Grange, is played by the rock musician Jon Bon Jovi, who is convincing as a man who is completely confident of his ability to seduce any woman, anywhere, anytime. Like Richard Gere, he has a way of looking at a woman as if they're both thinking the same thing. The playwright, Felix Webb (Lambert Wilson), is one of those men for whom romantic intrigue is hardly worth the trouble: His wife is bitter at his treatment of his family, and his mistress is tired of listening to his promises about how someday, very soon, he will leave his wife. He can't be happy anywhere.

Felix's problems come to a boil during rehearsals for his new play, which stars both Robin and Hilary (Thandie Newton), his mistress. It also stars two dependable British veterans, played by David Warner and Patricia Hodge, who have seen backstage affairs before, and will see them again, and simply turn up to do their jobs. (While the younger actors are doing nervous deep-breathing exercises before the curtain goes up, Warner's character listens to cricket and plays solitaire.)

The playwright could be leading a very happy life. He has a big, old house on the banks of the Thames, down from Hammersmith Bridge, where his happy children play in the garden while his wife, Elena (Anna Galiena), steeps in resentment (one night as he sleeps she takes a scissors and chops off his famous forelock). Elena is younger than Felix, and Hilary is younger still, living with roommates who race out to dance clubs and are amused by the fogey she has taken into her bed. But here's a twist: The young girl is steadfast and sincere in her love for him, and not portrayed as a flirt or a siren.

Robin, the American, quickly sees what Felix thinks is a secret, his affair with his leading lady. Robin makes the great man an offer: He will seduce Elena, clearing the field. "It would be doing a favor for a friend," he explains. "Besides, I've seen her photographs. She's a beautiful woman."

So she is, and a faithful one, up to a point. But Robin studies his quarry carefully, making lists of the books she reads and the music she listens to (these details are not very convincing), and discovering her own secret—she is also a playwright, but her writing is hidden in the shadow of Felix's great reputation. He can help her, but is something sinister concealed in Robin's helpfulness? Robin is also growing closer to his costar, Hilary. Does he plan to take both women away from the playwright? And what about the gun he likes to play with?

The film, directed by John Duigan and written by his sister Virginia, is completely familiar with its showbiz world. Virginia is married to the director Bruce Beresford, and Duigan himself has long been linked romantically with Newton, whom he directed in the wonderful film *Flirting* (1992). Little biographical details—like Newton's degree from Oxford—are lifted from life.

But the climax does not, I'm afraid, do justice to the setup. Hitchcock, having brought the gun and the matching love triangles onstage, would have delivered. Still, Duigan keeps us interested right up to the overwrought final developments, and his portrait of the London theater world is wry and perceptive. The way he uses the actor Barry Humphries as the director of Felix's play, and Warner and Hodge as the seasoned pros, adds a certain ironic perspective to all the heavy breathing in the foreground.

## Leave It to Beaver ★ ★ ★

PG, 88 m., 1997

Christopher McDonald (Ward), Janine Turner (June), Cameron Finley (Beaver), Erik von Detten (Wally), Adam Zolotin (Eddie), Barbara Billingsley (Aunt Martha), Ken Osmond (Eddie Sr.), Frank Bank (Frank). Directed by Andy Cadiff and produced by Robert Simonds. Screenplay by Brian Levant and Lon Diamond, based on the TV series created by Bob Moser and Joe Connelly.

*Leave It to Beaver* is a gentle, good-hearted movie about an eight-year-old who sighs, "I used to want to be a kid the rest of my life, but lately I just want to get it over with." Beaver Cleaver despairs of ever being as smart, as popular, as talented, and (especially) as old as his teenage brother, Wally, and all of his schemes to evolve in that direction seem doomed. Even when he finally gets the bicycle of his dreams, he's allowed to ride it only on the sidewalk: He's a "flat-lander."

The movie is based on the popular TV series. I've never watched a single episode of the series all the way through, but like most Americans I have a working knowledge of the Cleavers: Ward and June and their sons Beaver and Wally, and Wally's friend, the conniving Eddie Haskell. They lead the kinds of lives in which all problems can be solved in 22.5 minutes of program time; faced with an eighty-eight-minute movie, they almost run out of plot.

But the film is disarmingly charming, and, like *Good Burger*, pitched at young audiences. Whether they'll want to see it is a good question; kids these days seem to tilt more toward violent action pictures. I was surprised to find myself seduced by the film's simple, sweet story, and amused by the sly indications that the Cleavers don't live in the 1950s anymore.

In a way, all sitcom families are profoundly mad. They must be, to generate so many shallow emergencies, to talk only in one-liners, and to never leave the room without a punch line. *Leave It to Beaver* suggests a certain dark component to the Cleaver's sunniness, as in a moment when Ward (Christopher McDonald) experiences suppressed apoplexy after learning that the Beaver has "lost" his new bike, or in another moment when we learn that June (Janine Turner), who always wears pearls and heels while vacuuming, may know it's a turn-on for her husband.

They live in a time suspended between 1957 and 1997. The cars look new, but they still use glass milk bottles. As the film opens, Beaver (Cameron Finley) wants a bike as badly as his father wants him to join the school football team. Easy, says Eddie Haskell (Adam Zolotin): Pretend to join the team, and your dad will buy you the bike.

The Beaver is so much smaller than the other team members that giving him a uniform seems like a form of child abuse. But he does join the team, briefly, and he does get the bike—only to have it stolen by a mean kid. Much of the plot involves the Beaver's attempts to get the bike back, and to conceal from his father that he's not playing in any games because of homework difficulties.

When he finally does get in a game (because of a rule that everybody on the bench has to play at least a little), he's on his way to scoring a touchdown when a kid from the other team shouts, "Throw me the ball," and he does. This, of course, causes him bottomless shame and remorse, and stirred ancient memories of my own about falling for such tricks—and practicing them. Meanwhile, there's a parallel plot involving Wally (Erik von Detten) and Eddie—kind of a romantic triangle, in which Wally coaches Eddie on how to win a girl, while the girl secretly has a crush on Wally.

The dialogue, by Brian Levant and Lon Diamond, has some nice moments: "For a second he had the same kind of blubbering look he had when the lights came up at the end of *The Lion King*." Or, when older brother Wally is asked to accompany the Beaver to school on the new bike: "I get it—you don't want some truck turning the Beaver into road kill." Or, when the hostile girl rejects Eddie's advances: "Take another step, and I'll file a restraining order."

It's all sort of low-key, and innocent, and depends on the guileless charm of young Cameron Finley, whose needs are simple: He only wants to be loved, respected, and understood, and doesn't know yet that he'll feel that way for the rest of his life.

## Les Miserables ★ ★ ½

PG-13, 129 m., 1998

Liam Neeson (Valjean), Geoffrey Rush (Javert), Uma Thurman (Fantine), Claire Danes (Cosette), Hans Matheson (Marius). Directed by Bille August and produced by Sarah Radclyffe and James Gorman. Screenplay by Rafael Yglesias, based on the novel *Les Miserables* by Victor Hugo.

*Les Miserables* is like a perfectly respectable Classics Illustrated version of the Victor Hugo novel. It contains the moments of high drama, clearly outlines all the motivations, is easy to follow, and lacks only passion. A story filled with outrage and idealism becomes somehow merely picturesque.

Liam Neeson stars as Jean Valjean, and the movie makes its style clear in an early scene where he stands, homeless and hungry, at the door of a bishop, and says: "I am a convict. My name is Jean Valjean. I spent nineteen years at hard labor. On my passport I am identified as a thief." And so on. "I know who you are," replies the bishop, but not before the audience has been spoon-fed its briefing. Valjean is taken in, fed and sheltered, and tries to steal the bishop's silver. In one of the most famous episodes from Hugo's novel, the bishop tells the police he *gave* the tramp the silver, and later tells Valjean: "I've ransomed you from fear and hatred and now I give you back to God." There was a similar scene in Claude Lelouch's 1995 *Les Miserables*, which intercut passages from the novel with a story set during World War II; it was touching, but this version feels more like a morality play.

Valjean sells the silver, gets a job in a provincial factory, and uses the nest egg to buy the factory. As we rejoin him some years later, he is the local mayor, respectable and beloved, trying to teach himself to read and write. Then fate reenters his life in the person of Inspector Javert (Geoffrey Rush), a police official who recognizes him from his years at hard labor and wants to expose him: In this world, if you once do something wrong, you are banished forever from the sight of those lucky enough not to have been caught.

Consider, in the same light, poor Fantine (Uma Thurman), fired from the factory and forced into prostitution because it is discovered she has a child out of wedlock. Valjean discovers her plight (he was unaware of the firing), nurses her through a fatal illness, and promises to care for the child. Thurman's performance is the best element of the movie.

With the unyielding Javert forever at his back, Valjean takes his money and flees to Paris, taking refuge in a convent he had once (foresightedly) given money to. There he and the child, Cosette, spend ten years. Then Cosette, now a young woman played by Claire Danes, yearns for freedom; Valjean, against his better wisdom, takes a house for them. Cosette falls for the fiery radical Marius (Hans Matheson), who is being tailed by the police, which puts Javert once more onto the trail of poor Valjean.

Javert is the kind of man who can say with his dying breath, "I've tried to lead my life without breaking a single rule." He means it, and will never cease his pursuit of Valjean, even though the other man, as mayor, spared his job: "I order you to forgive yourself." As Javert pursues his vendetta against a man who has become kind and useful, Marius leads the mobs to the barricades, which look a lot here as they do in the stage musical.

That musical, by the way, is a long time coming. This is the second movie made of *Les Mis* during a decade when the "musical version" has been promised annually. There is, I think, an obvious person to direct it: Alan Parker, whose *Evita* and *Pink Floyd the Wall* show he is one of the few modern filmmakers who understands musicals. In the meantime, this dramatic version is by the Danish director Bille August, whose work *(Pelle the Conqueror, The Best Intentions* from the Bergman screenplay, *The House of the Spirits),* while uneven, has shown a juiciness and complexity.

Here we have a dutiful, even respectable, adaptation that lacks the rabble-rousing usually associated with *Les Miserables.* The sets and locations are handled well, the period looks convincing, but the story is lame. When Cosette pleads with her father to leave the convent, she sounds more like a bored modern teenager than a survivor of murderous times. ("Don't leave the cab!" he tells her on their first venture into the world, so of course she immediately does.)

Her father could, of course, settle all her objections with a few words of explanation, but in the great movie tradition of senselessly withholding crucial information, he refuses to; it must have been difficult for Neeson to maintain that expression of fearful regret in scene after scene. Rush, in his first major role since *Shine,* somehow doesn't project the fevered ethical madness that drives Javert; he comes across more as a very stubborn bore.

It's hard to make a period picture come alive, but when it happens *(Restoration, Dangerous Beauty, Amistad)* we feel transported back in time. *Les Miserables* only made me feel transported back to high school history class.

## Les Voleurs (The Thieves) ★ ★ ★ ½

R, 117 m., 1996

Catherine Deneuve (Marie), Daniel Auteuil (Alex), Laurence Cote (Juliette), Benoit Magimel (Jimmy), Fabienne Babe (Mireille), Didier Bezace (Ivan), Julien Riviere (Justin), Ivan Desny (Victor). Directed by Andre Techine and produced by Alain Sarde. Screenplay by Techine and Gilles Taurand.

I have been staring at the wall, trying to figure out how to describe *Les Voleurs* without giving away the entire plot. With a lot of movies, you can safely withhold a detail or two and still give a good idea of the story. But here is a film constructed like a pile of pick-up sticks. Pull out one and the game is over.

The director and cowriter is Andre Techine, who is fascinated by the secrets and ancient wounds within families. His previous film *Ma Saison Preferee* starred Catherine Deneuve and Daniel Auteuil as a brother and sister locked into a volatile mutual obsession. Both actors appear again this time, as a cop named Alex and a philosophy professor named Marie—and both are in love with the same young woman.

Who is she? I will step carefully. She is a tomboy named Juliette (Laurence Cote) whom

Alex meets for the first time after she's arrested for shoplifting. He lets her off. He sees her again one day when he visits the sleazy nightclub run by his brother, Ivan (Didier Bezace). If Alex is a cop, Ivan is a robber. And Ivan is in business with Jimmy (Benoit Magimel), who is Juliette's brother.

And there are more connections, weaving back and forth through family connections and time. But since the movie is about the gradual revelation of those connections, I dare not say more. They come out, one at a time, in a story told in the north of France, in winter, in shots so wet and gray the cold almost seeps from the screen.

The movie is so tricky to describe because it starts in the middle, as a small boy discovers in the middle of the night that his father is dead. Then it flashes backward and forward to explain what led up to that moment. The strategy is interesting because it shows us the assumptions we make about families, and why they may be wrong. One of the characters in the film is particularly chilling in a scene where the little boy asks for the truth about his father, and is told, "A job backfired," and is satisfied. But I cannot tell you who that character is without giving away an important secret.

What can we discuss? What about Catherine Deneuve? Her character stands off to one side of the main action—she is connected only through her affair with the young girl, and later through meetings with the cop who is having a loveless affair with the same girl ("We were united by a feeling of mutual contempt"). The first time we see her, she's telling her students that humans naturally exploit one another. Yet she seems determined not to exploit Juliette, and even gives her freedom at a time when it might have been wiser to appeal to her feelings.

Deneuve continues to fascinate. She has a timeless beauty, and avoids stereotyping by consistently playing against it, as unexpected characters in offbeat stories; consider that her career, now in its fortieth year, has embraced *Belle de Jour, The Hunger, The Umbrellas of Cherbourg,* and *Indochine.* She seems wise, as if her beauty has encouraged strangers to open up to her, and she has remembered what they taught her.

Here she understands that some deep current within Juliette—a fierce bond with her criminal brother, perhaps, or a need to punish herself—has drawn the young woman into a lethal situation. Why does Juliette go along on a dangerous theft? Maybe she hopes to be killed. Or to prove herself "good as a man." Or to compete with her brother. Eventually Juliette's two older lovers—the cop and the professor—call a truce and talk it over between themselves, wondering if they can help her.

Meanwhile, the story circles. There are various narrators, of which the most intriguing is the little boy who starts the film. At one point he finds and hides a revolver, and we confidently expect that it will be used before the end of the film. But what happens is more unexpected, and scarier.

*Les Voleurs* doesn't have the Hollywood kind of ending, where everything is sorted out by who gets shot. It is about the people, not their plot. It is about how the sins of the fathers are visited on the sons and the grandsons. The more you think about the little twist at the end, the more you understand what the whole movie was about. Techine involves us in a subtle, gradual process of discovery; each piece changes the relationship of the others. He is so wise about these criminals, he makes the bad guys in most American films look like cartoon characters.

## Liar Liar ★ ★ ★

PG-13, 86 m., 1997

Jim Carrey (Fletcher Reede), Maura Tierney (Audrey Reede), Justin Cooper (Max Reede), Cary Elwes (Jerry), Jennifer Tilly (Samantha Cole), Amanda Donohoe (Miranda), Swoosie Kurtz (Dana Appleton). Directed by Tom Shadyac and produced by Brian Grazer. Screenplay by Paul Guay and Stephen Mazur.

I am gradually developing a suspicion, or perhaps it is a fear, that Jim Carrey is growing on me. Am I becoming a fan? In *Liar Liar* he works tirelessly, inundating us with manic comedy energy. Like the class clown who'll do anything for a laugh, Carrey at one point actually pounds himself with a toilet seat. And gets a laugh.

The movie is a high-energy comeback from 1996's dismal *The Cable Guy,* which made the mistake of giving Carrey an unpleasant and obnoxious character to play. Here Carrey is likable and sympathetic, in a movie that will play for the whole family, entertaining each member on a different level (he's a master at combining slapstick for the kids with innuendo for the grown-ups).

Carrey plays a yuppie lawyer whose career is on the rise but whose wife (Maura Tierney) has divorced him and whose five-year-old son (Justin Cooper) no longer believes a word he says. "My dad's a liar," the kid says in class. "You mean a *lawyer,*" the teacher says. The kid shrugs. Whatever. Carrey is so wrapped up in cases that he even misses the kid's birthday party. So the kid closes his eyes and blows out the candles on the cake and makes a wish: He hopes that for one day his dad won't tell a lie.

The wish comes true. It is, of course, impossible to be a lawyer (or any other form of adult) if you are not prepared to lie, and so the day goes badly. He's defending the respondent in a big-bucks divorce case; his client (Jennifer Tilly) is a buxom sex bomb who is charged with one count of adultery but insists, somewhat proudly, that the actual count is closer to seven. This is not the sort of information you want to give to an attorney who cannot lie.

The screenplay, by Paul Guay and Stephen Mazur, takes this simple premise and applies it to the lawyer's workday. I can imagine the idea getting old really fast with a lesser actor, but Carrey literally throws himself into the story. Struggling to force himself to tell a lie, he goes mano-a-mano with a blue felt-tip pen. He tries to say it's red. He fails. His rubber face contorts itself in agony, but he *cannot* tell a lie.

There's trouble in the courtroom. "How are you today, counselor?" asks the judge. "I'm a little upset about a bad sexual episode last night," he replies. He can't even plead his client's case, since he knows it's false. As the judge and courtroom look on, Carrey climbs the walls and rolls on the floor, and finally escapes to the men's room, where in an astonishing display of comic energy he mugs himself, hoping to get the case continued until tomorrow.

The movie orchestrates one situation after another in which he has to tell the truth. "Do you know why I pulled you over?" a traffic cop asks. "That depends on how long you were following me," Carrey says. In one of the best sequences, he disrupts a partners' meeting at his law firm by telling the complete truth about everyone present.

The movie has been directed by Tom Shadyac, who also did *Ace Ventura: Pet Detective,* and it's mostly content to plant the camera and watch as Carrey goes bananas. He's a remarkable physical comedian. At one point, during a truth-telling session with his son, the kid twists his mouth out of shape and asks, "If I keep making this face, will it get stuck that way?" Absolutely not, says Carrey: "In fact, some people make a good living that way." ☞

## A Life Less Ordinary ★ ★

R, 90 m., 1997

Ewan McGregor (Robert), Cameron Diaz (Celine), Ian Holm (Naville), Delroy Lindo (Jackson), Holly Hunter (O'Reilly), Dan Hedaya (Chief Gabriel), Stanley Tucci (Elliot). Directed by Danny Boyle and produced by Andrew Macdonald. Screenplay by John Hodge.

*A Life Less Ordinary* is from the team that gave us *Shallow Grave* and *Trainspotting,* so maybe it's a penance that their characters this time are angels and lovers, rather than body snatchers and druggies. See, ma? We're good lads at heart.

The film expends enormous energy to tell a story that is tedious and contrived. It begins in heaven's police station, where Chief Gabriel (acting on orders from the top) dispatches two angels to Earth to engineer a romance. It appears that God is displeased by the divorce rate.

We meet the two lovers that heaven plans to unite. Robert (Ewan McGregor) is a janitor. Celine (Cameron Diaz) is a millionaire's daughter who amuses herself by using a handgun to shoot apples off the head of her fiancé (Stanley Tucci). (She misses, and a friend observes, "He'll live, but he'll never practice orthodontics again.")

Robert works for her father's company, and when he's replaced by robots, he seizes one of the squat little machines and tries to smash it against the wall of the chairman's office. The millionaire (Ian Holm) calls security, Robert grabs one of the guards' guns, and at a crucial point Celine kicks the gun back into his grasp—maybe because she hopes he will kidnap her, which he does.

The film then settles into a formula familiar from two other recent films, *Excess Baggage* and *Nothing to Lose.* The kidnapper and his victim grow friendly, and eventually become conspirators. Robert turns out to be inept at making threatening phone calls, and Celine starts with helpful hints and ends up stage-managing the kidnapping herself. ("That's all I am to you," he complains bitterly. "Your latest kidnapper—a fashion accessory!")

All of this is being manipulated, in a sense, by two angels, Jackson (Delroy Lindo) and O'Reilly (Holly Hunter). For reasons unclear to me, they are hired by the millionaire to track down his daughter and the kidnapper, and the movie develops into a long, unhinged chase sequence in which the angels act more like cops than matchmakers. By this point I was well past caring.

After the anarchic glee of *Trainspotting*, this film is a move toward the mainstream by the team of director Danny Boyle, producer Andrew Macdonald, and writer John Hodge. It's a conventional movie that never persuades us it needed to be made. Most films with angels depend more on supernatural intervention than character development, but in this case the film seems completely confused about the nature the intervention should take, and so are we. The plot's a mess, the characters flail about in scenes without points, and the more we see of Cameron Diaz and Ewan McGregor the more we yearn for a nice, simple little love story—say, about the rich girl who falls in love with the Scots janitor and gets along just fine without any angels.

## Little Indian, Big City   no stars

PG, 90 m., 1995

Thierry Lhermitte (Stephan Marchado), Patrick Timsit (Richard), Ludwig Briand (Mimi-Siku), Miou Miou (Patricia), Arielle Dombasle (Charlotte), Sonia Vollereaux (Marie), Tolsty (Pavel). Directed by Herve Palud and produced by Louis Becker and Thierry Lhermitte. Screenplay by Palud and Igor Aptekman.

*Little Indian, Big City* is one of the worst movies ever made. I detested every moronic minute of it. Through a stroke of good luck, the entire third reel of the film was missing the day I saw it. I went back to the screening room two days later to view the missing reel. It was as bad as the rest, but nothing could have saved this film. As my colleague Gene Siskel observed: "If the third reel had been the missing footage from Orson Welles's *The Magnificent Ambersons*, this movie *still* would have sucked." I could not have put it better myself.

*Little Indian, Big City* is a French film (I will not demean the fine word "comedy" by applying it here). It is not in French with English subtitles, however. It has been dubbed into English, a canny move, since the movie is not likely to appeal to anyone who can read. The dubbing means that awkward, hollow-sounding words emerge from the mouths of the characters while they flap their lips to a different rhythm. In an attempt to make the English dubbing match the length of the French dialogue, sentences are constructed backward and the passive voice pops up at random. People says things like, "You have a son—you hear?"

The character speaking that last line is the mother (Miou Miou) of a boy of about twelve. She was once married to the film's hero (Thierry Lhermitte), but left him thirteen years ago when she was pregnant because he spent too much time on the telephone. She fled to the Amazon, and has raised her child while living with an Indian tribe. Now the father has flown to the rain forest to find his wife, so they can be divorced, and he can marry the stupidest woman on earth.

The hero did not know he had a son—you hear? Now he meets him. The son, named Mimi-Siku (Ludwig Briand), wears a cute breechcloth, carries a bow and arrow, has a mask painted on his face, and kills snakes by biting them. His mother is an intelligent, sensitive soul who loves the environment and the rain forest. She is the only person in the jungle who speaks English (or French, in the original), and so if her son learned to speak it, he learned it from her. I guess it was her idea of a joke to teach him pidgin English, so that he says things like, "Me no able read." I guess she didn't teach him to read, either. She is depicted as a kind of a secular saint.

Mimi-Siku is so good with a blowgun that he can kill a fly with a dart, and often does so. He has a hairy pet spider. His father brings him back to Paris, where the movie get worse. The father has a business partner who never knows what to wear, and so always wears the same thing the father wears. Ho, ho. They go to business meetings in matching ties. Hee, hee. The partner has a daughter, and soon the son is bouncing in a hammock with a nubile twelve-year-old and telling his father, "Me like you—love only one female." I doubt if the relationship will last, since the boy is prettier than the girl.

Later (or perhaps earlier, since it was in the third reel) Mimi-Siku climbs barefoot up the Eiffel Tower. This feat is handled so ineptly by the film that it has neither payoff nor consequence. He does it, and then the movie forgets it. Meanwhile, the father is doing a business deal with some shady Russians who speak in dubbed accents and drink vodka and seem to be wearing Khrushchev's old suits. The father's fiancée (Arielle Dombasle) chants mantras, plans a New Age wedding, and wants her guru to live with them. I think she's in such a hurry to get married because she's afraid the collagen injections in her lips might shift. By the end of the film, father and son have bonded and cooked a fish by the side of the expressway. And the father has learned to kill a fly with a dart.

If you, under any circumstances, see *Little Indian, Big City*, I will never let you read one of my reviews again.

## Little Men ★ ½

PG, 98 m., 1998

Michael Caloz (Nat Blake), Mariel Hemingway (Jo Bhaer), Ben Cook (Dan), Ricky Mabe (Tommy Bangs), Chris Sarandon (Fritz Bhaer), Kathleen Fee (Narrator). Directed by Rodney Gibbons and produced by Pierre David and Franco Battista. Screenplay by Mark Evan Schwartz, based on the novel by Louisa May Alcott.

In my review of *Little Women* (1994), I wrote, "the very title summons up preconceptions of treacly do-gooders in a smarmy children's story." I was relieved to report, however, that the movie itself was nothing of the sort; it was a spirited and intelligent retelling of the Louisa May Alcott classic. Now, alas, comes *Little Men*, which is indeed about treacly do-gooders in a smarmy children's story.

Although younger children may enjoy the movie on a simple and direct level, there's little depth or texture to make it interesting for viewers over the age of, say, about ten. It's all on one note. The adults are all noble and enlightened, the boys are all basically good, and the story is all basically a sunny, innocent fable.

The year is 1871. The "little women" have all grown up, according to a narrator who tells us far more than she should have to. Jo (Mariel Hemingway) has married Fritz Bhaer (Chris Sarandon), and together they run Plumfield School, a country home for wayward or orphaned boys.

To Plumfield comes the Boston street urchin Nat (Michael Caloz) and, not long after, his best friend Dan (Ben Cook). There they find love, acceptance, and such lessons as, "If a pie has twelve pieces and three-quarters of them are served at dinner, how many pieces are left?" All of the boys scribble industriously on their chalkboards to solve the puzzle, although since several of them are later involved in a game of poker, they would seem to have the necessary skills for mental calculation.

Plumfield has limited funds, and perhaps cannot afford to keep Dan. And then Dan causes some problems, as when he sponsors the secret poker game (complete with beer and cigars) and it almost results in Plumfield being burned down. Apart from such hitches, Plumfield is an ideal haven, with pillow fights scheduled every Saturday night, and the narrator informs us that "the feeling that someone cared for him made that playroom seem like heaven for the homeless child."

There is a certain complexity in Fritz, Jo's husband, who recalls that his grandmother taught him to think before he spoke by cutting the end of his tongue with her scissors. His idea of punishment is to have the boys cane him, a practice that will not withstand a single moment's more thought than the movie gives it. He rumbles suspiciously about Dan, but Dan "has the makings of a fine man," Jo declares, and although another boy is sent away for stealing, Dan survives the poker, beer, and cigar scandal.

There is a horse at Plumfield. Only one, untamed and unruly. In an early scene, we see the hired man trying to tame it. We know with complete certainty that Dan was born to tame that horse, which indeed is waiting (all saddled up) when the lad's rebellious spirit requires such a test.

I have no doubt that Louisa May Alcott wrote something resembling this plot, although nothing in it sends me hurrying to the bookshelf. *Little Men* is an example of the kind of movie that wins approval because of what it doesn't have, not for what it has. It is wholesome, blameless, positive, cheerful, well photographed, and nicely acted (especially by Ben Cook), and it has a PG rating. But, man, is it smarmy.

## Live Flesh ★ ★ ★ ½

R, 101 m., 1998

Liberto Rabal (Victor Plaza), Francesca Neri (Elena), Javier Bardem (David), Angela Molina (Clara), Jose Sancho (Sancho). Directed by Pedro Almodovar and produced by Agustin Almodovar. Screenplay by Pedro Almodovar, based on the novel by Ruth Rendell.

Pedro Almodovar's *Live Flesh* is the kind of overwrought melodrama, lurid and passionate, that I have a weakness for. It dives in headfirst, going for broke, using the entire arsenal of coincidence, irony, fire, and surprise. It's about cops, lovers, paralysis, prostitution, adultery, deception, and revenge, and it is also surprisingly tender in its portrait of a man who gets into a lifetime of trouble just because he wants to make a woman happy.

Because it is by Almodovar, that Spanish poet of the perverse, none of these elements are come by easily. Victor, the hero, is born on a bus, the child of a prostitute, with a madam as midwife (the Madrid bus company gives him a lifetime pass). Twenty years pass and we find him ringing the doorbell of Elena, a woman he has met only briefly. He recalls their brief encounter at a disco: "The guy you had sex with in the toilet—remember?" She does, but wants nothing to do with him. She's waiting for her drug dealer and all Victor has brought her is a pizza.

But Victor is stubborn. His encounter with Elena was his first sexual experience, and he is doe-eyed with desire to know her better. She's in no condition to be known. They argue, the cops are called, and a gun discharges, striking a young cop and paralyzing him. Flash forward: Victor, in prison, is surprised to see that the cop is now a wheelchair basketball star, and Elena, cheering from the sidelines, has cleaned up her act and is now his devoted wife. Meanwhile, Victor rots behind bars, an innocent man.

Innocent, yes, because he did not fire the gun. In the struggle, it was the other cop—the alcoholic Sancho (Jose Sancho)—who pulled the trigger and hit his young partner, David (Javier Bardem). Why? Because he suspected David of having an affair with his wife, Clara. Of course, it is only a matter of time until Victor, released from prison, is having an affair with Clara himself.

Don't be concerned if you have not quite followed every twist and turn of this convoluted story. Almodovar makes it clear as it unfolds; his screenplay is based on a novel by Ruth Rendell, the British mistress of plots that fold back upon themselves. Another source for the film's style is Douglas Sirk, the master of 1950s Hollywood melodrama, whose films Almodovar claims to have seen hundreds of times, and who manufactured melodramatic plots with the ingenuity of chess puzzles.

Almodovar's films are often intended as put-ons. This one may be, too, but it's played more or less straight (for him, anyway). The actors understand that in melodrama of this sort, the slightest suggestion of irony is fatal, and they play everything with desperate intensity, while inhabiting screens so filled with bright colors it's a wonder they don't wince.

For Victor (Liberto Rabal), life has not been fair. But his luck changes when, after being released from prison, he goes to visit the grave of his mother. There he meets Clara (Angela Molina), an older woman, and after a strictly routine night of love he pleads inexperience and begs her to teach him everything she knows. She proves to be a gifted teacher. His long-term plan is to spend one night with the cruel Elena, proving himself the world's greatest lover and leaving her sobbing for more. Many men dream of such scenarios, but few have Victor's dedication to the necessary training regimen.

There are many other coincidences in the film, which I will not reveal. Some we can anticipate; others are complete surprises. It's interesting how Almodovar anchors the story so concretely in a real world, with everyday jobs and concerns; in the midst of jealousy and lust, the characters somehow retain a certain depth and plausibility. I especially liked the work of Molina, a frequent actress in Almodovar's films, as an older woman whose experience and wisdom have not been enough to protect her from a brutish husband.

And Javier Bardem takes a refreshing approach to the role of the paralyzed ex-cop: Of all the men in the movie, he has the strongest physical presence and the greatest menace. There's a scene where he goes in his chair to call on the young ex-convict, and the way he enters the room and establishes himself makes him the aggressor, not the handicapped one.

Movies like *Live Flesh* exist for the joy of telling their stories. They recall a time before high romance was smothered by taste. They don't apologize for breathless energy and cheerful implausibility, and every time a character walks into a room we feel like bracing ourselves for a new shock. Almodovar cannot be called "sincere" on the basis of this film—there's still a satirical glint in his eye—but by choosing to stick with the story and downplay his usual asides, nudges, and in-jokes, he's made a *film noir* of great energy.

## The Locusts ★ ★ ½

R, 124 m., 1997

Kate Capshaw (Mrs. Potts), Jeremy Davies (Flyboy), Vince Vaughn (Clay), Ashley Judd (Kitty), Paul Rudd (Earl), Daniel Meyer (Joel), Jessica Capshaw (Patsy), Jessie Robertson (Ellen). Directed by John Patrick Kelley and produced by Brad Krevoy, Steve Stabler, and Bradley Thomas. Screenplay by Kelley.

Watching *The Locusts* was like being whirled back in a time warp to the 1950s—to the steamiest and sultriest new work by William Inge or Tennessee Williams about claustrophobic lust in a twisted family. This is the kind of movie that used to star Paul Newman or William Holden, Kim Novak or Natalie Wood or Elizabeth Taylor, with Sal Mineo as the uncertain kid who's lost in confusion and despair.

Even the big emotional outbursts seem curiously dated. When the alcoholic, resentful, sluttish mother wants to wound her hated and helpless son, for example, what does she do? Staggers out into the rain and castrates his beloved bull, of course. And when it's truth time, the family secret seems almost inevitable.

The movie is not bad so much as it's absurd. I never felt I was in the hands of incompetent or untalented filmmakers, and indeed on the basis of *The Locusts,* I anticipate the next film by John Patrick Kelley, its writer-director. He has a talent for rhythm, for mood, for Gothic weirdness. This is his first film, and perhaps in trying to fill it with as much atmosphere and passion as possible, he allowed it to become overwrought.

He also has a gift for casting, and the highest praise I can give the performers here is to say they measure up to the 1950s icons I can so easily imagine in the roles. Kate Capshaw is wonderful as Mrs. Potts, the sultry widow who runs a Kansas feed lot, circa 1960, and takes one of her ranch hands into her bed every night. Vince Vaughn, from *Swingers,* is far from the fleshpots of Hollywood in this second role, as Clay, a drifter with a secret in his past, who turns up in town and is soon parked on lover's lane with Ashley Judd, as Kitty, the warmhearted local girl who wants to heal his soul. And Jeremy Davies is touching and brave in the role of Flyboy, Mrs. Potts's son, who has the full gamut of 1950s symptoms: He feels guilty about his father's suicide, he has spent eight years in an institution getting shock treatment, and now he shuffles around the house as a cowering, mute servant.

All of these characters are created in bold, confident performances of well-written roles. I liked the way Kitty, the Ashley Judd character, cuts to the chase in her dialogue, telling Clay, "So now we're going to skip the sex and go straight to the brooding?" And Kate Capshaw, her cigarette seen glowing through the porch screens on hot summer nights, brings a certain doomed poignancy to the role of a woman whose consolations are whiskey and hired studs.

Because the movie is in some ways so good, it's a shame it's so utterly, crashingly implausible. It's like an anthology of clichés from the height of Hollywood's love affair with Freud. Of course Clay is running away from a tragedy in his past, and of course Kitty wants to heal him, and of course Mrs. Potts knows a lot more than she's telling about Flyboy, and of course there will eventually be a showdown between the widow and her new hired hand.

But listen carefully when Clay tells Kitty what happened back in Kansas City. Ask yourself if Clay wasn't perhaps a mite careless in allowing that incredible chain of events. And ask yourself about the exact chronology of impregnation in the Potts household, and how its menfolk sorted it out. And remind yourself of the old theatrical rule that if a gun comes onstage in the first act it must be discharged in the third, and ask how that applies to the grisly early scene in which Clay learns how a bull becomes a steer.

There are small, quiet scenes here, however, that are just right. I was moved by Jeremy Davies in a scene where Flyboy pins one of Clay's *Playmate* foldouts to a bathroom mirror, lights an unfamiliar cigarette, and engages in conversation with the pinup (he thinks she will be interested in hearing about his bull). I admired the real pain Capshaw brought to her final scenes. And there is a wonderful moment when Kitty teaches Flyboy to dance, and then says, "Thank you for the date. It was the best one I ever had." And Flyboy has a spastic little gesture of joy.

*The Locusts* is not successful. Its material is so overwrought and incredible, so curiously dated, that it undermines the whole enterprise. But it was not made carelessly or cynically, it shows artists trying to do their best, and its makers had ambition. You can sense they wanted to make a great film, and that is the indispensable first step to making one—a step most films do not even attempt.

## Lone Star ★ ★ ★ ★

R, 136 m., 1996

Chris Cooper (Sam Deeds), Elizabeth Pena (Pilar), Kris Kristofferson (Charlie Wade), Joe Morton (Delmore Payne), Ron Canada (Otis Payne), Clifton James (Hollis Pogue), Matthew McConaughey (Buddy Deeds), Miriam Colon (Mercedes Cruz), Frances McDormand (Bunny), Stephen Mendillo (Cliff), Stephen J. Lang (Mikey). Directed by John Sayles and produced by R. Paul Miller and Maggie Renzi. Screenplay by Sayles.

John Sayles's *Lone Star* contains so many riches it humbles ordinary movies. And yet they aren't thrown before us to dazzle and impress: It is only later, thinking about the film, that we appreciate the full reach of its material. I've seen it twice, and after the second viewing I began to realize how deeply, how subtly, the film has been constructed.

On the surface, it's pure entertainment. It involves the discovery of a skeleton in the desert of a Texas town near the Mexican border. The bones belong to a sheriff from the 1950s, much hated. The current sheriff suspects the murder may have been committed by his own father. As he explores the secrets of the past, he begins to fall in love all over again with the woman he loved when they were teenagers.

Those stories—the murder and the romance—provide the spine of the film and draw us through to the end. But Sayles is up to a lot more than murders and love stories. We begin to get a feel for the people of Rio County, where whites, blacks, Chicanos, and Seminole Indians all remember the past in different ways. We understand that the dead man, Sheriff Charlie Wade, was a sadistic monster who strutted through life, his gun on his hip, making up the law as he went along. That many people had reason to kill him—not least his deputy, Buddy Deeds (Matthew McConaughey). They exchanged death threats in a restaurant shortly before Charlie disappeared. Buddy became the next sheriff.

Now Charlie's skull, badge, and Masonic ring have been discovered on an old army firing range, and Buddy's son, Sam Deeds (Chris Cooper), is the sheriff on the case. He wanders through town, talking to his father's old deputy (Clifton James), and to Big Otis (Ron Canada), who ran the only bar in the county where blacks were welcome, and to Mercedes Cruz (Miriam Colon), who runs the popular Mexican restaurant where the death threat took place.

Along the way, Sam does a favor. A kid has been arrested for maybe stealing car radios. He releases him to the custody of his mother, Pilar (Elizabeth Pena). He is pleased to see her again. Pilar and Sam were in love as teenagers, but their parents forced them to break up, maybe because both families opposed a Mexican-Anglo marriage. Now, tentatively, they begin to see each other again. One night in an empty restaurant, they play "Since I Met You Baby" on the jukebox and dance, having first circled each other warily in a moment of great eroticism.

All of these events unfold so naturally and absorbingly that all we can do is simply follow along. Sayles has made other films following many threads (his *City of Hope* in 1991 traced a tangled human web through the politics of a New Jersey city). But never before has he done it in such a spellbinding way; like Faulkner, he creates a sure sense of the way the past haunts the present, and how old wounds and secrets are visited upon the survivors.

*Lone Star* is not simply about the solution to the murder and the outcome of the romance. It is about how people try to live together at this moment in America. There are scenes that at first seem to have little to do with the main lines of the story. A school board meeting, for example, at which parents argue about textbooks (and are really arguing about whose view of Texas history will prevail). Scenes involving the African-American colonel (Joe Morton) in charge of the local army base, whose father was Big Otis, owner of the bar. Another scene involving a young black woman, an army private, whose interview with her commanding officer reveals a startling insight into why people enlist in the army. And conversations between Sheriff Deeds and old widows with long memories.

The performances are all perfectly eased together; you feel these characters have lived together for a long time and known things they have not spoken about for years. Chris Cooper, as Sam Deeds, is a tall, laconic presence who moves through the film, learning something here and something there and eventually learning something about himself. Cooper looks a little like Sayles; they project the same watchful intelligence.

As Pilar, Elizabeth Pena is a warm, rich female presence; her love for Sam is not based on anything simple like eroticism or need, but on a deep, fierce conviction that this should be her man. Kris Kristofferson is hard-edged and mean-eyed as Charlie Wade, and there is a scene where he shoots a man and then dares his deputy to say anything about it. Wade's evil spirit in the past is what haunts the whole film and must be exorcised.

And then there is so much more. I will not even hint at the surprises waiting for you in this film. They're not Hollywood-style surprises—or yes, in a way, they are—but they're also truths that grow out of the characters; what we learn seems not only natural, but instructive, and by the end of the film we know something about how people have lived together in this town, and what it has cost them.

*Lone Star* is a great American movie, one of the few to seriously try to regard with open eyes the way we live now. Set in a town that until very recently was rigidly segregated, it shows how Chicanos, blacks, whites, and Indians shared a common history, and how they knew each other and dealt with each other in ways that were off the official map. This film is a wonder—the best work yet by one of our most original and independent filmmakers—and after it is over and you think about it, its meanings begin to flower.

## The Long Kiss Goodnight ★ ★ ½

R, 120 m., 1996

Geena Davis (Samantha/Charly), Samuel L. Jackson (Mitch Henessey), Yvonne Zima (Caitlin Caine), Craig Bierko (Timothy), Tom Amandes (Hal), Patrick Malahide (Perkins), David Morse (Luke/Daedalus), Brian Cox (Nathan). Directed by Renny Harlin and produced by Harlin, Shane Black, and Stephanie Austin. Screenplay by Black.

*The Long Kiss Goodnight* is a cinematic comic book, a series of "biff!-*bam!*-whack!" action episodes, all more or less impossible, surrounding the larger-than-life characters. I liked it in the same way I might like an arcade game: It holds your attention until you run out of quarters, and then you wander away without giving it another thought.

Geena Davis, a good sport if ever there was one, stars as a woman who thinks she's a soccer mom named Samantha when actually she's a trained government assassin named Charly. She has forgotten her real identity because of "what the doctors call focal retrograde amnesia." She leads a quiet life in a small town, playing Mrs. Santa in the Christmas parade, until a TV broadcast and a violent car wreck begin to bring back her past.

Certainly it's a clue to her past life when she kills a deer by breaking its neck with her bare hands. And how about the kitchen scene when Samantha chops a carrot as if she'd never seen a knife before, and suddenly Charly takes over like a human veg-a-matic, pulverizing vegetables and then for her encore throwing a tomato in the air and skewering it to the wall with a deftly thrown knife. "Chefs do that," she explains to her stunned daughter and boyfriend.

She's hired a fly-by-night private eye (Samuel L. Jackson) to track down her past, and he turns up clues that lead to a full-scale war with the U.S. intelligence establishment. Without giving away too much of the plot (as if, heh, heh, there was much of a plot), I'll say that bad guys thought she was dead and now want to kill her, and she has to defend herself while having flashbacks to violent episodes in her past life.

The movie is put together like a Top 40 radio station, in which you get ten minutes of hits and then have to listen to somebody talking for ninety seconds. The dialogue serves only to separate and set up the action scenes. Sooner or later they're actually going to advertise one of these movies with the line, "Less talk and more action!" It's the kind of film where when the mother undergoes a personality change and decides she does love her little daughter after all, she shouts that information—*"I love her!!"*—over the noise of battle. Leave out those three words and the movie's central human dilemma would be misplaced.

Geena Davis has gone on the talk shows to explain that she personally performed all, or most, or many, of her stunts in the movie. For example, that's really her being blown out of a window and flying through the air. My message is: Geena, give yourself a break. I looked really closely as you were blown out the window, and it all happened so fast that I couldn't even be sure it was you—so why not let a stunt woman do it? That's what they're paid for.

The explosion scene allowed me to enjoy one more example of the latest way in which action movies suspend the laws of physics. Davis and Jackson actually outrun a flaming fireball that chases them down a corridor. I've seen that done in a lot of movies lately, and I've got news for them: It can't be done. (It also cannot be done on a motorcycle, although Keanu Reeves does it in *Chain Reaction,* or in the Chunnel, although Tom Cruise does it in *Mission: Impossible.*)

The movie is Hitchcockian in its use of famous locations. The climax involves a truck-bomb that is supposed to blow up the bridge at Niagara Falls, and at one point Samantha/Charly actually uses a dead body as a counterweight to lift her into the sky so she can shoot it out with a helicopter under the "Welcome to Canada" arch. Yep. And wouldn't you know that when the truck explodes, Jackson and Davis get to outrun another fireball, this time in a car, although that can't be done, either.

Anyway, Geena Davis and Samuel L. Jackson prove they're game in this movie, as they trade quips in the breaks between special-effects sequences. And the action is what we expect: sensational, violent, and loud. The target audience is apparently fourteen-year-old boys and those who have not forgotten how to think like fourteen-year-old boys, a group that apparently includes millions of filmgoers who like to see stuff blowed up real good. I admired it as an example of craftsmanship, but what a lot of time and money to spend on something of no real substance.

## Lost Highway ★ ★

R, 135 m., 1997

Bill Pullman (Fred Madison), Patricia Arquette (Renee/Alice), Balthazar Getty (Pete Dayton), Robert Blake (Mystery Man), Gary Busey (Bill Dayton), Robert Loggia (Mr. Eddy/Dick Laurent), Natasha Gregson Wagner (Sheila), Richard Pryor (Arnie), Michael Massee (Andy), Jack Nance (Phil). Directed by David Lynch and produced by Deepak Nayar, Tom Sternberg, and Mary Sweeney. Screenplay by Lynch and Barry Gifford.

David Lynch's *Lost Highway* is like kissing a mirror: You like what you see, but it's not much fun and kind of cold. It's a shaggy ghost story, an exercise in style, a film made with a certain breezy contempt for audiences. I've seen it twice, hoping to make sense of it. There is no sense to be made of it. To try is to miss the point. What you see is all you get.

That's not to say it's without interest. Some of the images are effective, the sound track is strong and disturbing, and there is a moment Hitchcock would have been proud of (although Hitchcock would not have preceded or followed it with this film). Hope is constantly fanned back to life throughout the story; we keep thinking maybe Lynch will somehow pull it off until the shapeless final scenes, when we realize it really is all an empty, stylistic façade. This movie is about design, not cinema.

It opens with two nervous people living in a cold, threatening house. They hate or fear each other, we sense. "You don't mind if I don't go to the club tonight?" says the wife (Patricia Arquette). She wants to stay home and read. "Read? Read?" he chuckles bitterly. We cut to a scene that feels inspired by a 1950s roadhouse movie (*Detour,* maybe), showing the husband (Bill Pullman) as a crazy hep-cat sax player. Cut back home. Next morning. An envelope is found on their steps. Inside, a videotape of their house (which, architecturally, resembles an old IBM punch card).

More tapes arrive, including one showing the couple asleep in bed. They go to a party and meet a disturbing little man with a white clown face (Robert Blake), who ingratiatingly tells Pullman, "We met at your house. As a matter of fact, I'm there right now. Call me." He does seem to be at both ends of the line. That mirrors another nice touch in the film, which is that Pullman seems able to talk to himself over a doorbell speakerphone.

Can people be in two places at once? Why not? (Warning: Plot point coming up.) Halfway through the film, Pullman is arrested for the murder of his wife and locked in solitary confinement. One morning his guard looks in the cell door, and—good God! It's not the same man inside!

Now it's a teenager (Balthazar Getty). The prison officials can't explain how bodies could be switched in a locked cell, but have no reason to hold the kid. He's released and gets his old job at the garage. A gangster (Robert Loggia) comes in with his mistress, who is played by Patricia Arquette. Is this the same person as the murdered wife? Was the wife really murdered? Hello?

The story now focuses on the relationship between Getty and Loggia, a ruthless but ingratiating man who, in a scene of chilling comic violence, pursues a tailgater and beats him senseless ("Tailgating is one thing I can't tolerate"). Arquette comes to the garage to pick up the kid ("Why don't you take me to dinner?") and tells him a story of sexual brutality involving Loggia, who is connected to a man who makes porno films. This requires a scene where Arquette is forced to disrobe at gunpoint and stand naked in a roomful of strange men; an echo of Isabella Rossellini's humiliation in Lynch's *Blue Velvet.*

Does this scene have a point? Does any scene in the movie have a point? *Lost Highway* plays like a director's idea book in which isolated scenes and notions are jotted down for possible future use. Instead of massaging them into a finished screenplay, Lynch and collaborator Barry Gifford seem to have filmed the notes.

Is the joke on us? Is it our error to try to make sense of the film, to try to figure out why protagonists change in midstream? Let's say it is. Let's say the movie should be taken exactly as is, with no questions asked. Then what do we have? We still have just the notes for isolated scenes. There's no emotional or artistic thread running through the material to make it seem necessary that it's all in the same film together. The giveaway is that the characters have no interest apart from their situation; they exist entirely as creatures of the movie's design and conceits (except for Loggia's gangster, who has a reality, however fragmentary).

Luis Buñuel, the Spanish surrealist, once made a film in which two actresses played the same role interchangeably, in the appropriately titled *That Obscure Object of Desire* (1977). He made absolutely no attempt to explain this oddity. One woman would leave a room, and the other would reenter. And so on.

But when Lynch has Patricia Arquette apparently play two women (and Bill Pullman and Balthazar Getty perhaps play the same man), we don't feel it's a surrealistic joke. We feel—I dunno, I guess I felt jerked around. Lynch is such a talented director. Why does he pull the rug out from under his own films? I have nothing against movies of mystery, deception, and puzzlement. It's just that I'd like to think the director has an idea, a purpose, an overview beyond the arbitrary manipulation of plot elements. He knows how to put effective images on the screen, and how to use a sound track to create mood, but at the end of the film our hand closes on empty air.

## Lost in Space ★ ½

PG-13, 130 m., 1998

Matt LeBlanc (Major Don West), Gary Oldman (Dr. Zachary Smith), William Hurt (Professor John Robinson), Mimi Rogers (Maureen Robinson), Heather Graham (Judy Robinson), Lacey Chabert (Penny Robinson), Jack Johnson (Will Robinson). Directed by Stephen Hopkins and produced by Mark W. Koch, Hopkins, and Akiva Goldsman. Screenplay by Goldsman.

*Lost in Space* is a dim-witted shoot-'em-up based on the old (I hesitate to say "classic") TV series. It's got cheesy special effects, a muddy visual look, and characters who say obvious things in obvious ways.

If it outgrosses the brilliant *Dark City,* the previous science-fiction film from the same studio, then audiences must have lost their will to be entertained.

The TV series was loosely modeled on the novel *The Swiss Family Robinson,* about a family shipwrecked far from home and using wit and ingenuity to live off the land. I loved that book, especially its detailed description of how the family made tools, machines, and a home for themselves, and trained the local animals.

The movie doesn't bother with such details. After a space battle that is the predictable curtain-raiser, and a quick explanation of why and how the Robinson family is setting off for a planet called Alpha Prime, the film takes place mostly on board their saucer-shaped ship, and involves many more space battles, showdowns, struggles, attacks, hyperspace journeys, and exploding planets. In between, the characters plow through creaky dialogue and exhausted relationship problems.

Imagine the film that could be made about a family marooned on a distant planet, using what they could salvage from their ship or forage from the environment. That screenplay would take originality, intelligence, and thought. *Lost in Space* is one of those typing-speed jobs where the screenwriter is like a stenographer, rewriting what he's seen at the movies.

The story: Earth will not survive another two decades. Alpha Prime is the only other habitable planet mankind has discovered. Professor John Robinson (William Hurt) and his family have been chosen to go there and construct a hypergate, to match the gate at the Earth end. Their journey will involve years of suspended animation, but once the other gate is functioning, humans can zip instantaneously to Alpha Prime.

There needs to be a hypergate at both ends, of course, because otherwise there's no telling where a hyperdrive will land you—as the Robinsons soon find out. Also on board are the professor's wife, Maureen (Mimi Rogers), their scientist daughter, Judy (Heather Graham), their younger daughter, Penny (Lacey Chabert), and their son, Will (Jack Johnson), who is the brains of the outfit. The ship is piloted by ace space cadet Don West (Matt LeBlanc), and includes an intelligent robot who will help with the tasks at the other end.

Oh, and lurking below deck is the evil Dr. Zachary Smith (Gary Oldman), who wants to sabotage the mission, but is trapped on board when the ship lifts off. So he awakens the Robinsons, after which the ship is thrown off course and seems doomed to fall into the Sun.

Don West has a brainstorm: They'll use the hyperdrive to zap right *through* the Sun! This strategy of course lands them in a galaxy far, far away, with a sky filled with unfamiliar stars. And then the movie ticks off a series of crises, of which I can enumerate a rebellious robot, an exploding planet, mechanical space spiders, a distracting romance, and family issues of trust and authority.

The movie might at least have been more fun to look at if it had been filmed in brighter colors. Director Stephen Hopkins and his cinematographer, Peter Levy, for some reason choose a murky, muted palate. Everything looks like a drab brown suit or a cheap rotogravure. You want to use some Windex on the screen. And Bruce Broughton's musical score saws away tirelessly with counterfeit excitement. When nothing of interest is happening on the screen, it just makes it worse when the music pretends it cares.

Of the performances, what can be said except that William Hurt, Gary Oldman, and Mimi Rogers deserve medals for remaining standing? The kids are standard-issue juveniles with straight teeth and good postures. And there is a monkeylike little alien pet who looks like he comes from a world where all living beings are clones of Felix the Cat. This is the kind of movie that, if it fell into a black hole, you wouldn't be able to tell the difference.

## The Lost World: Jurassic Park ★ ★

PG-13, 134 m., 1997

Jeff Goldblum (Dr. Ian Malcolm), Julianne Moore (Dr. Sarah Harding), Pete Postlethwaite (Roland Tembo), Arliss Howard (Peter Ludlow), Richard Attenborough (John Hammond), Vince Vaughn (Nick Van Owen), Vanessa Lee Chester (Kelly Curtis), Peter Stormare (Dieter Stark), Harvey Jason (Ajay Sidhu), Richard Schiff (Eddie Carr), Thomas F. Duffy (Dr. Robert Burke), Joseph Mazzello (Tim), Ariana Richards (Lex). Directed by Steven Spielberg and produced by Gerald Molen and Colin Wilson. Screenplay by David Koepp, based on the novel by Michael Crichton.

Where is the awe? Where is the sense that if dinosaurs really walked the earth, a film about them would be more than a monster movie?

Where are the ooohs and ahhhs? *The Lost World: Jurassic Park* demonstrates even more clearly than *Jurassic Park* (1993) that the underlying material is so promising it deserves a story not written on autopilot. Steven Spielberg, a gifted filmmaker, should have reimagined the material; should have seen it through the eyes of someone looking at dinosaurs, rather than through the eyes of someone looking at a box-office sequel.

The movie is well done from a technical viewpoint, yes. The dinosaurs look amazingly real, and we see them plunge into the midst of 360-degree action; a man on a motorcycle even rides between the legs of a running beast. It can be said that the creatures in this film transcend any visible signs of special effects, and seem to walk the earth. But the same realism isn't brought to the human characters, who are bound by plot conventions and action formulas, and scripted to do stupid things so that they can be chased and sometimes eaten by the dinosaurs.

Maybe it was already too late. Perhaps the time to do the thinking on this project was before the first film, when all the possibilities lay before Spielberg. He should have tossed aside the original Michael Crichton novel, knowing it had given him only one thing of use: an explanation for why dinosaurs might walk among us. Everything else—the scientific mumbo-jumbo, the theme-park scheme—was already just the recycling of other movies. We know the tired old plot lessons already, about man's greed and pride, and how it is punished, and why it does not pay to interfere with Mother Nature.

Why not a pseudodocumentary in which the routine plot elements are simply ignored, and the characters venture into the unknown and are astonished and frightened by what they find? There are moments in the first *Jurassic Park* that capture a genuine sense of wonder, the first time we see the graceful, awesome prehistoric creatures moving in stately calm beyond the trees. But soon they are cut down to size by a plot that has them chasing and scaring the human characters, as in any monster movie.

*The Lost World* is even more perfunctory. The plot sets up a reason for a scientist (Jeff Goldblum) to return to an island where dinosaurs survive. His girlfriend (Julianne Moore) is already there. He takes along an equipment specialist and a "video documentarian" (who comes equipped with a tiny tourist toy of a video camera and doesn't seem sure how to use it). They land on the island, are soon photographing prehistoric creatures, and so careless is the screenplay that the newcomers to the plot are not even allowed to express their amazement the first time they see their prey.

Much of the film, especially the action scenes, is shot at night in the rain. I assume that's to provide better cover for the special effects; we see relatively few dinosaurs in bright light, and the conceit is taken so far that even the press conference announcing a new dinosaur park in San Diego is held in the middle of the night. The night scenes also allow Spielberg to use his most familiar visual trademark, the visible beams from powerful flashlights, but apart from that touch Spielberg doesn't really seem present in the picture: This feels like the kind of sequel a master hands over to an apprentice, and you sense that although much effort was lavished on the special effects, Spielberg's interest in the story was perfunctory.

Here's the key to the movie's weakness: Many elaborate sequences exist only to be . . . elaborate sequences. In a better movie they would play a role in the story. Consider the drawn-out episode of the dangling research trailer, for example, which hangs over a cliff while the characters dangle above a terrifying drop and a hero tries to save the trailer from falling while a dinosaur attacks. This is only what it seems to be, an action sequence. Nothing more. It doesn't lead into or out of anything, and is not necessary, except to fill screen time. It plays like an admission that the filmmakers couldn't think of something more intriguing involving the real story line.

Consider, too, the character of Goldblum's daughter (Vanessa Lee Chester). Why is she here? To be placed in danger, to inspire contrived domestic disagreements, and to make demands so that the plot can get from A to B. At one point, inside the trailer, she gets frightened and says urgently that she "wants to go someplace real high—right now! Right now!"

So Goldblum and another character put her in a cage that lifts them above the forest, after which Goldblum must descend from the cage, after which I was asking why they had ascended in it in the first place. (Early in the film it is established that the girl is a gymnast; later the film observes the ancient principle that every gymnast in a movie sooner or later encounters a bar.)

There are some moments that work. Pete Postlethwaite, as a big game hunter who flies onto the island with a second wave of dinosaur mercenaries, doesn't step wrong; he plays a convincing, if shallow, character, even if he's called upon to make lengthy speeches in speeding jeeps, and to utter arty lines about "movable feasts" and having "spent enough time in the company of death." He alone among the major characters seems convinced he is on an island with dinosaurs, and not merely in a special-effects movie about them.

The film's structure is weird. I thought it was over, and then it began again, with a San Diego sequence in which Spielberg seemed to be trying to upstage the upcoming *Godzilla* movie. The monster-stepping-on-cars sequences in the Japanese import *Gamera: Guardian of the Universe* are more entertaining. And can we really believe that a ship could ram a pier at full speed and remain seaworthy?

The problem with the movie is that the dinosaurs aren't allowed to be the stars. They're marvelously conceived and executed, but no attempt is made to understand their fearsomeness; much of the plot hinges on mommy and daddy T-Rexes exhibiting parental feelings for their offspring. Must we see everything in human terms? At one point one character tells another, "These creatures haven't walked the earth for tens of millions of years, and now all you want to do is shoot them?" Somebody could have asked Spielberg the same question.

## Love Always ½ ★

R, 90 m., 1997

Marisa Ryan (Julia Bradshaw), Moon Zappa (Mary Ellen), Beverly D'Angelo (Miranda), Michael Reilly Burke (Mark Righetti), James Victor (Sean), Mick Murray (Will Bradshaw), Doug Hutchinson (James), Beth Grant (Stephanie). Directed by Jude Pauline Eberhard and produced by Isaac Artenstein. Screenplay by Eberhard and Sharlene Baker.

"You are like a cluster bomb that explodes in a thousand different ways at once," the heroine is told in *Love Always.* As opposed to a cluster bomb that doesn't? I dunno. This movie is so bad in so many different ways you should see it just to put it behind you. Let's start with the dialogue. Following are verbatim quotes:

—"Someday you'll love somebody with all the intensity of the Southern Hemisphere."

—"There's a Starbuck-free America out there!"

—"To be young and in love! I think I'm gonna head out for some big open spaces."

—"Like sands in an hourglass, these are the days of our lives. That's the way the cookie crumbles."

—"Watch your back."

And my favorite, this advice from the heroine's girlfriend (Moon Zappa) as she sets out on her hitchhike odyssey across America: "Follow your intestines."

Does Jude Pauline Eberhard, the writer and director, intend these lines to be funny? Does this film belong in one of those funky festivals where people understand such things? Alas, I fear not. *Love Always* is sincere in addition to its other mistakes.

The movie tells the story of Julia Bradshaw (Marisa Ryan), an intrepid San Diego woman who finds herself in a series of situations that have no point and no payoff, although that is the screenplay's fault, not hers. Early in the film, for example, she goes to the racetrack and her horse comes in, and she says "Yes!" and rides her bike home along the beach, and we never really find out why she was at the track, but no matter, because before long the film goes to visit an amateur theatrical and we see an *entire* "rooster dance," from beginning to end, apparently because film is expensive and since they exposed it they want to show it.

The rooster dance also has nothing to do with the film, which properly gets under way when Julia gets a postcard from her onetime lover Mark, asking her to come to Spokane so he can marry her. This information is presented by filling the screen with a big close-up of the postcard, which Julia then reads aloud for us. Soon we find her in the desert with a bedroll on her back, posing photogenically on the windowsill of a deserted house so that interesting people can brake to a halt and offer her rides.

Her odyssey from San Diego to Spokane takes her via a wedding in Boston. That's a road movie for you. At one point along the way she shares the driving with a woman who is delivering big ceramic cows to a dairy. After Julia drops a ceramic calf and breaks it, she drives the truck to Vegas to get another calf, but when she gets there the ceramic cow lady's husband tells her the dairy canceled the order, so Julia wanders the Strip in Vegas, no doubt because the Road Movie Rule Book requires at least one montage of casino signs.

Back on the road, Julia meets a band of women in a van. They are the Virgin Sluts. They dress like models for ads for grunge clubs in free weeklies in the larger cities of smaller states. She is thrilled to meet them at last. She also meets a make-out artist, a sensitive photographer, and a guy who is convinced he has the movie's Dennis Hopper role. On and on her odyssey goes, until finally she gets to Spokane, where she finds out that Mark is a louse, as we knew already because he didn't send her bus fare.

## Love and Death on Long Island ★ ★ ★ ½

PG-13, 93 m., 1998

John Hurt (Giles De'Ath), Jason Priestley (Ronnie Bostock), Fiona Loewi (Audrey), Sheila Hancock (Mrs. Barker), Maury Chaykin (Irving), Gawn Grainger (Henry), Elizabeth Quinn (Mrs. Reed), Linda Busby (Mrs. Abbott). Directed by Richard Kwietniowski and produced by Steve Clark-Hall and Christopher Zimmer. Screenplay by Kwientniowski, based on the novel by Gilbert Adair.

A creaky British writer, who has lived for decades in a cocoon of his books and his musings, locks himself out of the house one day in the rain. He takes refuge in a nearby movie theater, choosing a film based on a novel by Forster. After a time he murmurs, "This isn't E. M. Forster!" And he begins to collect his coat and hat so that he can leave.

Indeed it is not Forster. The film is *Hotpants College II,* about the hijinks of a crowd of randy undergraduates. But as the writer, named Giles De'Ath, rises to his feet, he sees an image that causes him to pause. The camera slowly zooms in on his face, illuminated by the flickering light reflected from the screen, as he stands transfixed by the sight of a young actor named Ronnie Bostock.

It is this moment of rapture that gives *Love and Death on Long Island* its sly comic enchantment. Giles De'Ath, played by John Hurt as a man long settled in his dry and dusty ways, has fallen in love with a Hollywood teen idol, and his pursuit of this ideal leads him stumbling into the twentieth century. He finds that films can be rented, and goes to a video store to obtain two other Ronnie Bostock titles, *Tex Mex* and *Skidmarks.*

Dressed like an actor playing T. S. Eliot, discussing the titles with the clerk as if he were speaking to a librarian in the British Museum, he rents the tapes and brings them home, only to find that he needs a VCR. He purchases the VCR, and has it delivered to his book-lined study, where the delivery man gently explains why he will also require a television set.

At last, banishing his housekeeper from his study, Giles settles down into a long contemplation of the life and work of Ronnie Bostock. He even obtains teenage fan magazines (the cover of one calls Bostock "snoggable!"), and cuts out Ronnie's photos to paste them in a scrapbook, which in his elaborate cursive script he labels "Bostockiana." He sneaks out to dispose of the magazines as if they were pornography, and daydreams of a TV quiz show on which he would know all the answers to trivia questions about Ronnie (Favorite author: Stephen King. Favorite musician: Axel Rose).

These opening scenes of *Love and Death on Long Island* are funny and touching, and Hurt brings a dignity to Giles De'Ath that transcends any snickering amusement at his infatuation. It's not even perfectly clear that Giles's feelings are homosexual; he has been married, now lives as a widower, and there is no indication that he has (or for that matter had) any sex life at all. At lunch with his bewildered agent, he speaks of "the discovery of beauty where no one ever thought of looking for it." And in a lecture on "The Death of the Future," he spins off into rhapsodies about smiles (he is thinking only about Ronnie's).

There is something here like the obsession of the little man in *Monsieur Hire,* who spies adoringly on the young woman whose window is opposite his own. No physical action is contemplated: Sexual energy has been focused into the eyes and the imagination. The cinema of Ronnie Bostock, Giles believes, "has brought me into contact with all I never have been."

It is always a disappointment when fantasies become real; no mere person can equal our imaginings. Giles actually flies to Long Island, where he knows Bostock has a home, and sets out to find his idol. This journey into the new land is not without hazards for the reclusive London writer, who checks into a hot-sheets motel and soon finds himself hanging out at Chez D'Irv, a diner where the owner (Maury Chaykin) refers to almost everything as "very attractive."

But eventually Giles does find his quarry. First he meets Audrey (Fiona Loewi), Ronnie's girlfriend, and then Ronnie himself, played by Jason Priestley with a sort of distant friendliness that melts a little when Giles starts comparing his films with Shakespeare's bawdy passages. The film doesn't commit the mistake of making Ronnie stupid and shallow, and Audrey is very smart; there's a scene where she looks at Giles long and hard, as his cover story evaporates in her mind.

I almost wish Giles had never gotten to Long Island—had never met the object of his dreams. The film, directed by Richard Kwietniowski and based on a novel by the British film critic Gilbert Adair, steps carefully in the American scenes, and finds a way to end without cheap melodrama or easy emotion. But the heart of the film is in Giles's fascination, his reveries about Ronnie's perfection.

There is a scene in *Hotpants College II* in which Ronnie reclines on the counter of a hamburger joint, and his pose immediately reminds Giles of Henry Wallis's famous painting *The Death of Chatterton,* in which the young poet is found dead on his bed in a garret. Thomas Chatterton was to the eighteenth century as Bostock is to ours, I suppose: sex symbol, star, popular entertainer, golden youth. It's all in how you look at it.

## Love and Other Catastrophes ★ ★

R, 79 m., 1997

Alice Garner (Alice), Frances O'Connor (Mia), Matthew Dyktynski (Ari), Matt Day (Michael), Radha Mitchell (Danni), Suzi Dougherty (Savita), Kim Gyngell (Professor Leach). Directed by Emma-Kate Croghan and produced by Stavros Andonis Efthymiou. Screenplay by Yael Bergman, Croghan, and Helen Bandis, based on a story by Efthymiou.

*Love and Other Catastrophes* is one of those first films that makes you long for the second one. Shot in seventeen days on lunch money, it's a campus comedy about love, roommates, professors, sex, and paying your overdue library fine so you can switch departments. There's a lot of potential charm here, but the director, Emma-Kate Croghan, is so distracted by stylistic quirks that the characters are forever being upstaged by the shots they're in.

The movie has been described as a Generation X film from Australia, although most of the students seem young enough to belong to that unnamed generation that has come along since X. True Xers, I think, are now thirtyish, and if you're twentyish you'd no more want to be described as an Xer than a hippie would want to be called a beatnik. Time flies; the generational nicknames ought to keep up with it.

The film's central characters are two roommates: Mia (Frances O'Connor), a lesbian who's breaking up with her girlfriend, and Alice (Alice Garner), who has a crush on one guy while another guy has a crush on her. The other potential romantic partners: Danni (Radha Mitchell), who in retaliation against Mia is seeing another woman; Ari (Matthew Dyktynski), the sort of playboy that Alice likes; and Michael (Matt Day), shy and inarticulate, who is in love with Alice.

All of these people are, of course, terminally cool about their sexuality. That's too bad, because a little uncertainty and doubt can make a great contribution to a comedy (see Kevin Smith's *Chasing Amy,* in which the hero's discovery that the girl he loves is a lesbian leads to inspired dialogue and deeply heartfelt misunderstandings). To put it another way, the characters in *Love and Other Catastrophes* don't seem *needy* enough to require a movie about them; they're self-contained as they are.

The amusing stuff in the movie has to do with campus bureaucracy. Most campuses, everywhere in the world, are run not by their faculties but by two ubiquitous types of staff members: (1) part-time or dropout students who affect a studied disdain for their jobs, and (2) local clerical employees who follow all of the rules as a form of sadism. Alice's best scenes involve her thesis ("Doris Day: Feminist Warrior"), which is four years past due, and her cinema professor (Kym Gyngell), who eats a doughnut in every single scene. (They must not have Dunkin'

Donuts shops in Australia, since no company works harder at placing its products in movie scenes, and yet these doughnuts are merely generic.)

Meanwhile, Mia is trying to change departments, but first must pay a library fine, which requires her to shuttle from one uninterested bureaucrat to another in a frustrating process that reminded me of the similar but better scenes in *Gridlock'd*. These academic crises are the counterpoint to the challenges in their sex lives.

The characters are all bright and edgy, and I expect to see them again in movies that feel more finished. *Love and Other Catastrophes* affects a visual style in the same spirit of the unreadable graphics of many new magazines, where typefaces slam up against each other and yellow print is put on brown backgrounds. The whole movie seems to have been subtly tinted brown, scenes play more like sketches for scenes, and there is a general air of self-congratulation on how clever everyone is.

Movies like this are intensely interesting to the people in them, just as people like this are intensely interesting to one another. Outsiders (moviegoers, say) are justified in asking what larger appeal the characters have. I admit they have some interest: I would like to know more about them, and if the movie had told me more, I might have liked it more. Emma-Kate Croghan has talent or she wouldn't have been able to get this movie made. Now she needs time and money. And a less insistent style. And a better screenplay.

## love jones ★ ★ ★

R, 110 m., 1997

Larenz Tate (Darius), Nia Long (Nina), Bill Bellamy (Hollywood), Isaiah Washington (Savon), Lisa Nicole Carson (Josie), Bernadette Clarke (Sheila), Khalil Kain (Marvin). Directed by Theodore Witcher and produced by Nick Wechsler and Jeremiah Samuels. Screenplay by Witcher.

*love jones* is a love story set in the world of Chicago's middle-class black artists and professionals—which is to say, it shows a world more unfamiliar to moviegoers than the far side of the Moon. It is also frankly romantic and erotic, and smart; this is the first movie in a while where the guy quotes Mozart and the girl tells him he's really thinking of Shaw.

The movie stars Nia Long as Nina, a professional photographer, and Larenz Tate as Darius, a novelist. After an opening montage of great black and white Chicago scenes (Nina's photographs, we learn), they Meet Cute at the Sanctuary, a club inspired by the various venues around town for poetry slams, cool jazz, and upscale dating. His moves are smooth: He meets her, walks to the mike, and retitles his poem "A Blues for Nina," reading it to her across the smoky room. She likes that. "Maybe next week you'll write something for me," he says. They engage in flirt-talk. "There are other things than sex," she tells him. Like what? he wants to know. She takes a pen and writes "love" on his wrist.

As their relationship develops, we see it in the context of the world they live in, a world of African-American artists, writers, teachers, and intellectuals. The film's writer-director, Theodore Witcher, says he wanted to suggest a modern Chicago version of the Harlem Renaissance, but this is the 1920s filtered through modern eyes, and some of the parties they attend have conversation that sounds like hip campus faculty talk.

The relationship between Darius and Nina proceeds, but not smoothly. Is it just a sex thing? They talk about that. She's on the rebound from her last man, and tells Darius "the timing is bad," but it starts looking pretty good. And their chemistry, as characters and actors, is hot. There's a sensuous scene where they go to her place, and she loads her camera and tells him to strip, and shoots him while he's teasing her. This nicely turns the gender tables on the famous *Blow Up* scene where the photographer made love through his camera.

Witcher's screenplay is not content to move from A to B to love. There are hurt feelings and misunderstandings, and Nina goes to New York at one point to see her former fiancé and find out if there's still life in their relationship. I didn't buy that New York trip; it seemed clear to me that Darius was her love, and if she was merely testing him, why take a chance of losing a good thing? Darius starts seeing another woman, she starts dating his best friend, and a completely avoidable misunderstanding develops.

I felt frustrated, but I was happy to. When movie characters inspire my affection so that I want them to stay together when they don't, that shows the movie's working. And there is a very nice sequence when they both end up at a party with other people, and see each other across the room, and are hurt.

These two characters are charismatic. There's electricity when they go on a date to the weekly Steppin' ball hosted by Herb Kent the Cool Gent, who plays himself. Steppin' is a Chicago dance style that comes out of jitterbug, cooled down, and as we watch this scene we get that interesting feeling when a fiction film edges toward documentary and shows us something we haven't seen before.

Nia Long and Larenz Tate are destined for more starring roles. They embody qualities we associate with Whitney Houston and Denzel Washington: They're fresh, have a sense of humor, and are almost implausibly good-looking. It's hard to believe that Tate—so smooth, literate, and attractive here—played the savage killer O-Dog in *Menace II Society.* Nia Long was Brandi, one of the girlfriends, in *Boyz N the Hood. love jones* extends their range, to put it mildly.

Witcher has a good eye for locations. You can see Loop skyscrapers in the backgrounds of a lot of shots, so you know this is Chicago, but movies haven't shown us these neighborhoods before. Scenes are set in Hyde Park, on the near North Side, and in between. As the characters move from coffee bars to record stores to restaurants to the Sanctuary, we realize how painfully limited the media vision of urban black life is. Why do the movies give us so many homeboys and gangstas and druggies and so few photographers, poets, and teachers?

The title is spelled all lower case. That kind of typography was popular in avant-garde circles from the 1920s through the 1950s, on everything from book covers to record album jackets. I think Witcher is trying to evoke the tone of that period when bohemia was still somewhat secret, when success was not measured only by sales, when fictional characters wrote novels instead of computer programs and futures contracts. There is also a bow to the unconventional in the ending of his film. Many love stories contrive to get their characters together at the end. This one contrives, not to keep them apart, but to bring them to a bittersweet awareness that is above simple love. Some audience members would probably prefer a romantic embrace in the sunset, as the music swells. But *love jones* is too smart for that.

## Love Serenade ★ ★ ★

R, 101 m., 1997

Miranda Otto (Dimity Hurley), Rebecca Frith (Vicki-Ann Hurley), George Shevtsov (Ken Sherry), John Alansu (Albert Lee), Jessica Napier (Deborah), Jill McWilliam (Curler Victim), Ryan Jackson (Boy on Ride), Sabrina Norris (Beautiful Baby). Directed by Shirley Barrett and produced by Jan Chapman. Screenplay by Barrett.

"I've come to Sunray to escape the hustle and bustle of the big city," Ken Sherry explains. He says that like he says everything else, in a dry, flat voice that defies you to believe him. He is the new disc jockey at the local radio station, a fifty-watt operation in a ramshackle hut where all the songs are still on vinyl. He has been divorced three times.

Dimity and Vicki-Ann Hurley live next door to the house he's rented. They are unspeakably thrilled to think that a big radio personality like Ken Sherry (George Shevtsov) would come all the way from Brisbane to live in their moribund corner of the Australian outback. Until he arrived, the only way to pass the time was to go fishing. They offer him a fish. He says he doesn't eat fish. Then how about a chicken casserole?

The opening scenes of *Love Serenade* play like a definition of the kind of movie that fascinates me. I like films with a very specific sense of place, with characters who are defiantly individual, with plots it is impossible to anticipate. There is the suggestion that *Love Serenade* will be some kind of a love triangle, with both sisters competing for the disc jockey's attention—but something about Ken Sherry's implacable, insolent, lazy personality suggests that he has secrets we have not even remotely guessed.

Australian films love to create strange characters. Movies like *Sweetie, Muriel's Wedding,* and *Strictly Ballroom* were populated by people whose lives seem made out of pop fantasies and sheer desperation. The Hurley girls are like that. Vicki-Ann (Rebecca Frith) works in a hair salon (the Hairport), and Dimity (Miranda Otto) is a waitress at the downtown Chinese restaurant, where the owner, Albert Lee (John Alansu), sings "Wichita Lineman" in a mournful baritone. When Ken Sherry walks into the restaurant, Dimity breathlessly blurts out, "Excuse me for interfering, but my sister Vicki-Ann is looking for a boyfriend and we live right next door to you!" Sherry regards her like a specimen on a microscope slide: "What about you? Are *you* looking for a boyfriend?"

She is. Their seduction scene is the least erotic in the history of movies. They discuss whether fish have souls and if they can go to heaven. He speaks about how lonely he is. She offers to ease his loneliness. He remains so impassive that his seduction technique seems to involve challenging women to make him notice them. (The long-faced George Shevtsov plays the character with such snaky detachment that even while we're watching this film we want to see him in others.)

Vicki-Ann, who believes the theory that the way to a man's heart is through his stomach, has adopted the casserole method of seduction, and is shattered to learn that her kid sister has scored first, using more direct methods. But soon both sisters have enjoyed, or endured, or survived Ken Sherry's charms. And peering out from behind their blinds or peeking over the top of the backyard fence, they remain fascinated by his lifestyle. What does he do in there? What is he like?

The film gives an almost physical sense of the small town of Sunray. The sisters meet for lunch at a picnic table in an exhausted park. The main street is almost always deserted. A creek bed is dried up. The sun beats down. The buildings seem to wince in its heat. The radio station is the local outpost, however attenuated, of the glamorous world of show business. Ken Sherry pulls the microphone closer and dedicates songs to "broken dreams." He plays the kind of 1970s songs favored by lounge acts.

And then there is a secret, gradually revealed, about the deejay. Is it strange? Very strange. Does it provide the film with an ending that could not under any circumstances have been guessed? It does. Is it necessary? I don't know. The flat, ironic, desperate but hopeful lives of the sisters might have supplied all the humor the movie needed, and Ken Sherry was certainly odd enough before the final revelations. Still, I am always grateful when a movie shows me something I have never seen before. And in this case, something I shall undoubtedly never see again.

## Love! Valour! Compassion! ★ ★ ★

R, 115 m., 1997

Jason Alexander (Buzz Hauser), Randy Becker (Ramon Fornos), Stephen Bogardus (Gregory Mitchell), John Glover (John and James Jeckyll), John Benjamin Hickey (Arthur Pape), Justin Kirk (Bobby Brahms), Stephen Spinella (Perry Sellars). Directed by Joe Mantello and produced by Doug Chapin and Barry Krost. Screenplay by Terrence McNally, based on his play.

In its structure, Terrence McNally's *Love! Valour! Compassion!* is as old-fashioned as a nineteenth-century three-act play. A group of friends meet for a June weekend in a country house. In midsummer, they meet again. At summer's end, they meet a third time. In the first act the characters are introduced and their problems are established. In the second, there is conflict and crisis. In the third, truth and resolution. When this play won its 1994 Tony Award, it wasn't for technical innovation.

In content, too, the material is not original. All of the friends are gay men, and during the course of the drama some of their relationships will dissolve and some will strengthen, and new ones will form. And the specter of AIDS will hover over the drama, which is one of the ways these characters must be different from, say, the characters in *The Boys in the Band*. In crisis, some of the characters will behave well and others badly, and there will be a bittersweet conclusion in which we discover that some will die and others will live, some will be happy and others will remain sad and lonely.

As a formula, this will do nicely for any set of characters of your choice. The dramatic arc is so traditional it's almost reassuring. Yet *Love! Valour! Compassion!* has power and insight, and perhaps what makes it strong is its disinterest in technical experiments: It is about characters and dialogue, expressed through good acting—the very definition of the "well-made play."

Joe Mantello, who directed the play off-Broadway and makes his film debut here, is more concerned with recording the performances than with visual innovation. He allows himself small flashes of wit (one of the characters, packing his bag, throws in flannel shirts, Winstons, and handcuffs).

But basically he's at the service of the material, which builds firmly and observantly into a touching record of human life—not gay, but universal, since the real issues in the play do not depend on sexuality but on character.

"I hope you appreciate the details," says the narrator, Gregory (Stephen Bogardus), taking us on a tour of his rambling Victorian lakeside home. He's proud of the architecture and the furnishings. He is a successful choreographer, and lives there with his lover, Bobby (Justin Kirk), who is blind. We see some of the guests arriving, including the acerbic, lonely British composer John Jeckyll (John Glover), who observes acidly, "What kind of statement do you think a choreographer is making about his work when he lives with a blind person?"

John has a new boyfriend along, named Ramon (Randy Becker), who is a darkly handsome hunk. Other guests include Buzz (Jason Alexander), who has memorized countless Broadway musicals and quotes them compulsively; and Perry (Stephen Spinella) and Arthur (John Benjamin Hickey), who will celebrate their fourteenth anniversary this summer.

Ramon, of course, is the equivalent of the loaded gun which, brought onstage in the first act, must eventually fire. In an early scene that will not puzzle Freudians, he encounters the blind Bobby feeling a tree, and silently places himself in Bobby's way. Soon the two of them are grappling passionately in the kitchen at night, and when Bobby confesses his infidelity to Gregory, their relationship is shaken. That will not be the last of the mischief provoked by Ramon, although he is not a bad person, simply a young one more concerned with pleasure than commitment.

The relationship between John and Ramon is exclusively a sexual one, we see; John is a bitter misanthrope who likes to stand apart from the others, smoking and brooding. In midsummer he gets a call from his twin, James, an AIDS sufferer who needs help and arrives to join the house party. Both characters are played by Glover, who won a Tony for this dual role on Broadway and contributes the two best performances in the film.

It's almost impossible to play a dual role without falling into the *Parent Trap* syndrome, in which the audience spends most of the movie trying to spot the secrets of the trick photography and camera angles, but Glover does it: Both of the Jeckyll brothers are so well acted that we believe in them as individuals, even when they have scenes together.

James is the sweet twin, the one everyone likes. John has spent a lifetime mired in resentment. "You got the good soul; I got the bad one," John tells James, and in a strong late scene: "What's the secret of unconditional love? I'm not going to let you die with it." But it is Buzz (Alexander) who finds and shares that secret, and the movie's best single scene is a quiet conversation on a shaded porch between Buzz and James.

*Love! Valour! Compassion!* has, of course, been compared to *The Boys in the Band* because of their obvious similarities, but there are as many differences, and one of them is crucial: This story is not about homosexuality, but about homosexuals. The 1970 movie was the first frank big-studio treatment of uncloseted gays, and much of the movie was preoccupied with how they "got" to be gay, and how they felt about being gay, and how they "accepted" their homosexuality, etc.—an encounter group with drinks served. In *Love! Valour! Compassion!* the characters' sexuality is the air they breathe, the natures they were given; the point is not how they make love, but simply how they love, or fail to love.

There is still ground to be broken and depths to be discovered in drama about homosexuals. There will eventually be a play like this in which one of the characters need not be an expert on the works of Ethel Merman and Gertrude Lawrence, and none of the characters will perform in tutus. The most successful film explorations of homosexuality so far have been about lesbians *(Lianna, The Incredibly True Adventures of Two Girls in Love)*. Perhaps that's because women, as a gender, prefer to begin with a relationship and move on to sexuality, while men usually approach it the other way around. But *Love! Valour! Compassion!* is a touching and perceptive film, about themes anyone can identify with: loneliness, jealousy, need, generosity.

## Love Walked In ★ ★

R, 90 m., 1998

Denis Leary (Jack Hanaway), Terence Stamp (Fred Moore), Aitana Sanchez-Gijon (Vicki Rivas), Danny Nucci (Cousin Matt), Moira Kelly (Vera), Michael Badalucco (Eddie Bianco), Gene

Canfield (Joey), Marj Dusay (Judith Moore). Directed by Juan J. Campanella and produced by Ricardo Freixa. Screenplay by Campanella, Lynn Geller, and Larry Golin, based on a novel by Jose Pablo Feinmann.

*Love Walked In* proves something that nobody ever thought to demonstrate before: You can't make a convincing *film noir* about good people. *Noir* is about weakness and temptation, and if the characters are going to get soppy and let their better natures prevail, what's left? Has there ever been a thriller about resisting temptation?

The movie has two other problems: It requires the female lead to behave in a way that's contrary to everything we know about her. And it intercuts the action with an absurd parallel story, a fantasy the hero is writing. He hopes to become a novelist, but on the basis of this sample he should stick to playing the piano. Oh, and the filmmakers should have guessed that the big ending, where the hero falls out of a tree, would inspire laughs just when the movie doesn't need any.

Yet the elements are here for a decent *film noir.* There is, first of all, good casting. Denis Leary plays Jack, a world-weary pianist in a fleapit lounge named the Blue Cat. Aitana Sanchez-Gijon is Vicki, his wife, a songstress who has a way with the pseudo-Gershwin tunes Jack writes. And Terence Stamp, he of the penetrating blue eyes and saturnine features, is a rich man named Moore who frequents the lounge and whose desire stirs for Vicki. Leary has been in a lot of movies lately *(The Real Blonde, Wag the Dog)*, but this is the one where he really emerges: He began as a comedian learning to act, but now you can see that he has the stuff, that given a good script he could handle an important role.

Aitana Sanchez-Gijon (Keanu Reeves's love in *A Walk in the Clouds*) is also just right; you can see how this situation could have been rewritten into a workable *noir.* But neither she nor any other actress could convincingly handle the scenes where she is required to mislead Moore. Women don't work that way. Oh, a femme fatale might, but the whole point is that Vicki's heart is in the right place.

The setup: Jack and Vicki are desperately poor after ten years of touring crummy clubs. (Strange, since they're talented.) Jack's old buddy Eddie (Michael Badalucco), now a private eye, turns up and reveals he's been hired by Moore's jealous wife to get the dirt on him. Since Moore has the hots for Vicki, Eddie says, why not blackmail him—which would rescue Vicki and Jack from poverty row: "You guys have the real thing. All you need is a little dough to complete the picture."

This is a classic *noir* suggestion. And in a different kind of film we'd believe it when Jack suggests this plan to Vicki. But we never sense that Vicki is that kind of girl. She's wounded when she first hears the plan; Jack says she'd only have to "make out" with Moore long enough for Eddie to take photos, and Vicki shoots back, "Make out? How much? Second base? Third? Home run?" But she goes along with the scheme, even though the movie lacks any scene or motivation to explain her change of heart—or indeed, any way of telling what she's really thinking most of the time. Her character is seen entirely from the outside, as an enigma, and maybe that's exactly what she was to the writer-director, Juan J. Campanella.

As for Jack, his character is confusingly written, and it doesn't help that he constantly interrupts the action with cutaways to a parallel story, which he narrates with Rod Serlingesque solemnity. The plot whips itself into a frenzied payoff, with thunder and lightning on cue, as Jack finds himself out on a limb in a scene that would be plausible, unfortunately, only if played by John Belushi in *Animal House.*

*Love Walked In* has the right moves for *noir:* the melancholy, the sexiness, the cigarettes, the shadows. But you have to believe in the characters and their capacity for evildoing. These characters act like they saw *Double Indemnity* on TV once and thought they could do that stuff themselves, and were wrong.

## Lumière & Company ★ ★ ★

NO MPAA RATING, 88 m., 1996

A documentary directed by Sarah Moon. Artistic director Anne Andreu.

A couple of years ago, some 150 film directors were challenged to play the same game. The rules: They were to film a continuous shot, no more than fifty-two seconds in length, in no more than three takes, with no artificial light and no synchronized sound. Forty great film directors agreed to those conditions. And they all used exactly the same camera: The actual camera originally used by the Lumière brothers at the dawn of the cinema, in 1895.

"I feel like crossing myself," one of the directors says, looking at the simple wooden box within which the first film was shot. Called the "Cinématographe," it is about a foot square, with a crank on one side. It was restored by Philippe Poulet of the Museum of Cinema in Lyon, and he also provided the film, with only two sprocket holes per frame, just as the Lumières used.

*Lumière & Company,* the film that resulted from this project, is both more and less than you would expect. The forty brief films are often wonderful, and always revealing in the way they show professional directors working on what amounts to a haiku. The surrounding footage is uneven. It is amusing sometimes to see the directors setting up their shots, but when they're asked to answer such questions as "Why do you film?" and "Is the cinema mortal?" the answers tend toward hyperbole or, worse, shrugs.

Some of the directors tell little stories. Zhang Yimou shows a couple dressed in Peking Opera garb, dancing atop the great wall of China, and then tearing off their costumes to reveal punk rock clothes. Jacques Rivette shows a little girl in a square, surrounded by in-line skaters and strolling newspaper readers ("It's too short!" complains the author of those four-hour French extravaganzas). Wim Wenders shows his angels from *Wings of Desire,* revisiting Berlin. Jaco Van Dormael of Brussels shows an enthusiastic kiss between two lovers who have Down's syndrome.

Nadine Trintignant puts the camera on a wheelchair to make a dolly shot showing the courtyard of the Louvre, the classic architecture in the background replaced by the glass pyramid in the foreground. Merchant and Ivory show a nineteenth-century street scene, and then dolly to reveal a McDonald's. Regis Wargnier asks the late president François Mitterand which images above all he remembers from the cinema, and as he walks past the camera, we hear him say, "A Hungarian film . . . people were dancing . . ."

Two directors shoot at the site of the bomb blast at Hiroshima. One shows a little girl trying to weigh herself. One shows an attempt to film the great pyramid. Liv Ullmann's film is of the great cinematographer Sven Nykvist filming the camera as it films him. John Boormann visits the set of Neil Jordan's *Michael Collins* and has three actors (Liam Neeson, Aidan Quinn, and Stephen Rea) gaze wonderingly into the camera.

Claude Lelouch's film is ambitious: As lovers kiss while revolving on a turntable, a moving platform behind them shows them being filmed by crews with equipment representing the transition from the Lumières' Cinématographe to more advanced cameras, to 35mm, to sound, to video. Alain Corneau introduces color by hand-tinting a gypsy dance.

Throughout the film there are glimpses of the Lumières' own films, many of them street scenes simply recording the wonder of what something looked like on a given day 100 years ago. Patrice Leconte shows their famous shot of a train arriving at a station, and then photographs the same station a century later: It now has gained a terminal, but the train (the Eurostar express) races past without stopping.

What the Lumières did above all was to capture moments in time in a medium that for the first time made that possible. The film opens with their shot of a baby stumbling over a step on a sidewalk. Later, Costa-Gavras shows passersby gazing in wonder into the lens. And Spike Lee makes a home movie of his baby daughter, prompting her to say "Da-da." He prompts her again and again, and she smiles happily but mutely at the camera as we grow aware of the fifty-two seconds ticking away. Finally she produces a "Da" in the nick of time. A trouper.

The Lumière camera produces an image with a slight flicker, caused by the slower shutter speed. And slight variations in speed, because no two operators crank it at the same rate. Except for the modern props, the new films look 100 years old. Or the old films look new. "The cinema is pieces of time," Orson Welles said. Here is a film of those pieces.

# M

## Ma Vie en Rose ★ ★ ★

R, 88 m., 1998

Georges Du Fresne (Ludovic), Michele Laroque (Hanna), Jean-Philippe Ecoffey (Pierre), Helene Vincent (Elisabeth), Julien Riviere (Jerome), Cristina Barget (Zoe), Gregory Diallo (Thom), Erik Cazals De Fabel (Jean). Directed by Alain Berliner and produced by Carole Scotta. Screenplay by Chris vander Stappen and Berliner.

Ludovic is a seven-year-old boy who likes to dress in girl's clothes, not so much because he likes the clothes as because he is convinced he is a girl. It all seems very clear. After he learns about chromosomes, he explains to his parents that instead of the female XX chromosomes he was intended to get, he received the male XY after "my other X fell in the garbage."

Ludovic's parents have just moved to a suburb of Paris that looks for all the world like a set for *Ozzie and Harriet.* Ominously, they live next door to his father's boss. A barbecue is planned to welcome the newcomers, and it's at this party that Ludovic makes his dramatic entrance, dressed in pink. The adults, who would not have looked twice at a little girl wearing jeans and sneakers, are stunned. "It's normal until seven," Ludovic's mother explains bravely. "I read it in *Marie-Claire.*"

*Ma Vie en Rose* offers gentle fantasy, and a little hard reality, about Ludovic's predicament. He is convinced he is a girl, knows some sort of mistake was made, and is serenely intent on correcting it. Soon he's making the arrangements for a play "marriage" with Jerome, his best friend, who lives next door and is therefore, unluckily, the boss's son. Since the boss is a blustering bigot, this is not a good idea. Indeed, most of the adults in the movie seem like members of the Gender Role Enforcement Police.

The film is careful to keep its focus within childhood. It's not a story about homosexuality or transvestism, but about a little boy who thinks he's a little girl. Maybe Ludovic, played by a calmly self-possessed eleven-year-old named Georges Du Fresne, will grow up to be gay. Maybe not. That's not what the movie is about. And the performance reflects Ludovic's innocence and naïveté; there is no sexual awareness in his dressing up, but simply a determination to set things right.

The movie is about two ways of seeing things: the child's and the adult's. It shows how children construct elaborate play worlds out of dreams and fantasies, and then plug their real worlds right into them. Ludovic's alternate universe is ruled by his favorite TV personality, named Pam, who dresses like a princess and has a boyfriend named Ken and flies about the house with her sparkling magic wand. It also contains his beloved grandmother. In this world Ludovic is sort of an assistant princess, and we can see how his worship of Pam has made him want to be just like her.

Adults, on the other hand, see things in more literal terms and are less open to fantasy. No one is threatened by a girl who dresses like a boy, but the father's boss is just one of the people who sees red whenever Ludovic turns up in drag. This innocent little boy is made to pay for all the gay phobias, fears, and prejudices of the adult world.

Because *Ma Vie en Rose (My Life in Pink)* is a comedy, however, the going never gets too heavy. Ludovic is taken to a psychiatrist, he is shouted at by his (mostly sympathetic) parents, he is a figure of mystery to his three well-adjusted siblings, and he is a threat to the stability of his neighborhood. Since it's one of those sitcom neighborhoods where everyone spends a lot of time out on the lawn or gossiping over the driveways, what happens to one family is the concern of all.

*Ma Vie en Rose* is the first film by Alain Berliner, a Belgian, who worked from the original screenplay of Chris vander Stappen, herself a tomboy who got a lot of heat as a child. There are clearly important personal issues at work beneath the surface, especially for Ms. vander Stappen, who identifies herself as a lesbian, but they skate above them. And there is a certain suspense: Surely Ludovic cannot simply be humored? Simply allowed to dress as a girl? Or can he?

## Maborosi ★ ★ ★ ★

NO MPAA RATING, 110 m., 1997

Makiko Esumi (Yumiko), Takashi Naitoh (Tamio, Second Husband), Tadanobu Asano (Ikuo, First

Husband), Gohki Kashiyama (Yuichi, Yumiko's Son), Naomi Watanabe (Tomoko, Tamio's Daughter), Midori Kiuchi (Michiko, Yumiko's Mother), Akira Emoto (Yoshihiro, Tamio's Father), Mutsuko Sakura (Tomeno). Directed by Hirokazu Kore-Edaand produced by Naoe Gozu. Screenplay by Yoshihisa Ogita, based on a story by Teru Miyamoto.

*Maborosi* is a Japanese film of astonishing beauty and sadness, the story of a woman whose happiness is destroyed in an instant by an event that seems to have no reason. Time passes, she picks up some of the pieces, and she is even distracted sometimes by happiness. But at her center is a void, a great unanswered question.

The woman, named Yumiko, is played by the fashion model Makiko Esumi. Models are not always good actresses, but Esumi is the right choice for this role. Tall, slender, and grave, she brings a great stillness to the screen. Her character speaks little; many shots show her seated in thought, absorbed in herself. She is dressed always in long, dark dresses—no pants or jeans—and she becomes after a while like a figure in an opera that has no song.

She is twenty when we meet her. She is happily, playfully married to Ikuo (Tadanobu Asano). They have a little boy, and there is a sunny scene where she bathes him. Then an inexplicable event takes place, and she is left a widow. Five years pass, and then a matchmaker finds a husband for her: Tamio (Takashi Naitoh), who lives with his young son in an isolated fishing village. At twenty-five, she starts her life again.

This is the first film by Hirokazu Kore-Eda, a young Japanese director whose love for the work of the great Yasujiro Ozu (1903–1963) is evident. Ozu is one of the four or five greatest directors of all time, and some of his visual touches are visible here. The camera, for example, is often placed at the eye level of someone kneeling on a tatami mat. Shots begin or end on empty rooms. Characters speak while seated side by side, not looking at one another. There are many long shots and few close-ups; the camera does not move, but regards.

In more obvious homage, Kore-Eda uses a technique which Ozu himself borrowed from Japanese poetry: the "pillow shot," inspired by "pillow words," which are words that do not lead out of or into the rest of a poem but provide a resting place, a pause or punctuation. Kore-Eda frequently cuts away from the action to simply look for a moment at something: a street, a doorway, a shop front, a view. And there are two small touches in which the young director subtly acknowledges the master: a characteristic tea kettle in the foreground of a shot, and a scene where the engine of a canal boat makes a sound so uncannily similar to the boat at the beginning of Ozu's *Floating Weeds* (1959) that it might have been lifted from the sound track.

But what, you are asking, do these details have to do with the movie at hand? I mention them because they indicate the care with which this beautiful film has been made, and they suggest its tradition. *Maborosi* is not going to insult us with a simpleminded plot. It is not a soap opera. Sometimes life presents us with large, painful, unanswerable questions, and we cannot simply "get over them."

There isn't a shot in the movie that's not graceful and pleasing. We get an almost physical sensation for the streets and rooms. Here are shots to look for:

The first husband walking off cheerfully down the street, swinging an umbrella. Yumiko's joy in bathing the baby. A child playing with a ball on a sloping concrete courtyard. Yumiko and her second husband sitting in front of an electric fan in the hot summertime, too exhausted to make love any longer. Yumiko, wearing a deep blue dress, almost lost in shadow at a bus stop. A funeral procession, framed in a long shot between the earth, the sea, and the sky. And a reconciliation seen at a great distance.

*Maborosi* is one of those valuable films where you have to actively place yourself in the character's mind. There are times when we do not know what she is thinking, but we are inspired with an active sympathy. We want to understand. Well, so does she. There's real dramatic suspense in the first scenes after she arrives at the little village. Will she like her new husband? Will their children get along? Can she live in such a backwater?

It's lovely how the film reveals the answers to these questions in such small details as a shot where she walks out her back door into the sunshine. Underneath these immediate questions, of course, lurk the bigger ones. "I just don't understand!" she says. "It just goes around and around in my head!" Her second husband offers an answer of sorts to her question. It is based on an experience fishermen sometimes have at sea, when they see a light or mirage that tempts them farther from shore. But what is the reason for the light?

## Mad City ★ ★ ½

PG-13, 120 m., 1997

John Travolta (Sam), Dustin Hoffman (Brackett), Mia Kirshner (Laurie), Alan Alda (Hollander), Robert Prosky (Lou Potts), Blythe Danner (Mrs. Banks), William Atherton (Dohlen). Directed by Constantin Costa-Gavras and produced by Arnold Kopelson and Anne Kopelson. Screenplay by Tom Matthews.

*Mad City* arrives with the last thing a movie about journalism needs—last year's news. It's about the media feeding frenzy that erupts when a museum guard takes hostages. A TV newsman is one of them, the news channels carry the story around the clock, the museum is ringed with cops and cameras, and we get lots of scenes showing the vanity and hypocrisy of anchormen. This is not news.

It's time to admit the obvious: The public enjoys sensational journalism, and the media are only giving them what they demand. People who say they deplore paparazzi journalism are approximately as sincere as smokers who lecture you on how bad their habit is.

*Mad City* might have been more fun if it had added that extra spin—if it had attacked the audience as well as the perpetrators. It's too predictable: A media circus springs up when the museum guard, a likable everyman played by John Travolta, creates a hostage crisis and finds himself bonding with a TV newsman (Dustin Hoffman). The movie is obviously inspired by *Ace in the Hole,* the knife-edged 1951 satire by Billy Wilder, about a man trapped in a cave, and the broken-down newsman (Kirk Douglas) who spins out the crisis to rescue his own career. But while Wilder's movie was smart and ironic, *Mad City* is dumbed down into a roundup of the usual suspects: the old-fashioned news director, the egotistical network star, the young intern on the make, etc. Costa-Gavras, who directed the film, should have remembered that satire depends on exaggeration, not attack.

As the film opens, Hoffman is at the museum to cover a story when Travolta walks in and demands a hearing with his boss (Blythe Danner). He's been fired from his low-wage job and wants it back. The guard is not too bright, and has brought along a duffel bag containing a shotgun and sticks of dynamite—to get her attention, he says. Soon he has inadvertently taken a group of children hostage and accidentally shot his best friend, another guard. He's having the kind of day Jim Carrey might have scripted.

Hoffman was once a network star, but after running afoul of an egomaniacal anchor (Alan Alda), he's been exiled to the sticks. This is the big story that can rebuild his career. He stays inside the museum, broadcasting from a battery-powered lapel mike, and over the course of long hours and nights he becomes friends with the hapless guard, who only wanted his job back, and is terrified that now his wife will be mad at him.

Hoffman's performance is on target, and would have served a better screenplay. Alan Alda has some well-observed moments as the star anchorman. There are nice little digs, as when it's suggested to Travolta that Thursday prime time would be the best time to surrender, ratings-wise. But the movie makes its points early and often, and the Travolta character, too familiar from similar roles in *Phenomenon, Michael,* and *White Man's Burden,* keeps playing the same scene: remorse, confusion, resolve.

What I liked was a lot of screenwriter Tom Matthews's dialogue for the Hoffman character, who in effect turns into the guard's unofficial media adviser: "That's your jury pool out there," he tells him. The movie knows what it wants to do, but lacks the velocity for liftoff. There is no moment where satire and human nature meet in perfect union, as there is in *Ace in the Hole,* when Kirk Douglas advises the wife of the trapped man to get herself photographed while praying in church, and she replies, "I don't pray. Kneeling bags my nylons."

## Mad Dog Time no stars

R, 93 m., 1996

Richard Dreyfuss (Vic), Gabriel Byrne (Ben London), Ellen Barkin (Rita Everly), Jeff Goldblum (Mick Holliday), Diane Lane (Grace), Gregory Hines (Jules Flamingo). Directed by Larry Bishop and produced by Judith Rutherford James. Screenplay by Bishop.

*Mad Dog Time* is the first movie I have seen that does not improve on the sight of a blank screen viewed for the same length of time. Oh, I've seen bad movies before. But they usually made me *care* about how bad they were. Watching *Mad Dog Time* is like waiting for the bus in a city where you're not sure they have a bus line.

The plot: A gangster boss (Richard Dreyfuss) is released from a mental hospital and returns to a sleazy nightclub to take over control of his organization. He has been gone long enough that a long list of gangsters would like to have his job, led by Jeff Goldblum, who has been conducting an affair with Dreyfuss's girlfriend (Diane Lane) and her sister (Ellen Barkin). The girls share the last name of Everly, so they're the Everly sisters—get it? Ho, ho, ho. God, what rich humor this movie offers!

Other candidates for Dreyfuss's throne include characters played by Gabriel Byrne, Kyle McLachlan, Gregory Hines, Burt Reynolds, and Billy Idol. The way the movie works is, two or three characters will start out in a scene and recite some dry, hard-boiled dialogue, and then one or two of them will get shot. This happens over and over.

"Vic's gonna want everybody dead," a character says at the beginning, in what turns out to be a horrible prophecy. Vic is the Dreyfuss character. Goldblum is named Mick, and Larry Bishop, who directed this mess, is Nick. So we get dialogue that thinks it's funny to use Vic, Nick, and Mick in the same sentence. Oh, hilarious.

I don't have any idea what this movie is about—and yet, curiously, I don't think I missed anything. Bishop is the son of the old Rat Packer Joey Bishop, who maybe got him a price on the songs he uses on the sound track, by Dean Martin, Sammy Davis, and Frank Sinatra (Paul Anka sings "My Way," which was certainly Bishop's motto during the production).

What were they thinking of? Dreyfuss is the executive producer. He's been in some good movies. Did he think this was a script? (Not a bad script—a script at all?) The actors perform their lines like condemned prisoners. The most ethical guy on the production must have been Norman Hollyn, the editor, because he didn't cut anybody out, and there must have been people willing to do him big favors to get out of this movie.

*Mad Dog Time* should be cut up to provide free ukulele picks for the poor.

## Madadayo ★ ★ ★

NO MPAA RATING, 134 m., 1998

Tatsuo Matsumura (Hyakken Uchida), Kyoko Kagawa (Uchida's wife), Hisashi Igawa (Takayama), George Tokoro (Amaki). Directed by Akira Kurosawa and produced by Hisao Kurosawa. Screenplay by Akira Kurosawa.

Made in 1993 when he was eighty-three, *Madadayo* is possibly the last film by the Japanese master Akira Kurosawa, who is the greatest living filmmaker. And yet the very title of the film argues otherwise; it means "not yet!" That is the ritual cry that the film's old professor shouts out at the end of every one of his birthday parties, and it means that although death will come and may be near, life still goes on.

This is the kind of film we would all like to make, if we were very old and very serene. There were times when I felt uncannily as if Kurosawa were filming his own graceful decline into the night. It tells the story of the last two decades in the life of Hyakken Uchida, a writer and teacher who retires in the war years of the early 1940s. He was the kind of teacher who could inspire great respect and affection from his students, who venerate him and, as a group, help support him in his old age.

In Japan they have a tradition of "living national treasures"—people who because of their gifts and knowledge are treated like national monuments. Uchida is such a man, who has taught all his life and now finds that his books are selling well enough that he can move with his wife to a pretty little house, and sit in the entranceway: "That will be my study, and at the same time I will be the gatekeeper."

Kurosawa's career has itself spanned some sixty years, and the titles of his films are spoken with awe by those who love them. Consider that the same man made *Rashomon, Yojimbo, Ikiru, The Seven Samurai, The Hidden Fortress, Red Beard, Throne of Blood, Kagemusha, Ran,* and twenty-five more. His movies have been filled with life and spectacle, but here, in *Madadayo,* he has made a film in the spirit of his near-contemporary Yasujiro Ozu, whose domestic dramas are among the most quietly observant and contemplative of all films.

Very little happens in *Madadayo.* The old man (Tatsuo Matsumura) and his wife (Kyoko Kagawa) are feted by his students on his sixtieth birthday, and go to live in the fine little house. The house is destroyed in an air raid. They move to a little hut, hardly more than a room and a half, and there the professor also sits in the doorway and writes. His students come to see him, and every year on his birthday they have the ritual party at which he downs a big glass of beer and cries out "not yet!"

The students conspire to find the professor a larger house. Then something very important happens. A cat named Nora wanders into their house, and the professor and his wife come to love it. Nora disappears. The professor is grief-stricken. Leaflets are circulated, and his students, now middle-aged businessmen, scour the neighborhood for Nora, without success. Then another cat walks into their house, and the wound is healed.

At the professor's seventy-seventh birthday dinner, we see that things have changed. The early events were held Japanese-style, with men only. Now women are present, too: wives, daughters, even grandchildren, in a Western-style banquet room. And still the cry is "not yet!"

Like Ozu, Kurosawa is content to let his camera rest and observe. We never quite learn what sorts of things the professor writes (the real Uchida was in fact a beloved essayist), but we know he must be a great man because his students love him so. We learn few intimate details about his life (not even, if I recall, his wife's first name). We see him mostly seated in his front door, as a stranger might.

Like his students, we are amused by his signs forbidding visitors and warning away those who would urinate on his wall. We learn about the burglar-proofing strategies in his first, larger, house: He leaves a door open, with a sign saying "Burglar's Entrance." Inside, signs indicate "Burglar's Passage," "Burglar's Recess Area" and "Burglar's Exit." He guesses right that burglars would prefer to operate in a house that grants them more anonymity.

The movie is as much about the students as the professor, as much about gratitude and love as about aging. In an interview at the time of the film's release, Kurosawa said his movie is about "something very precious, which has been all but forgotten: the enviable world of warm hearts." He added, "I hope that all the people who have seen this picture will leave the theater feeling refreshed, with broad smiles on their faces."

## Madame Butterfly ★ ★ ★

NO MPAA RATING, 129 m., 1996

Ying Huang (Cio-Cio-San), Ning Liang (Suzuki), Richard Troxell (Pinkerton), Richard Cowan (Sharpless), Jing-Ma Fan (Goro), Constance Hauman (Kate Pinkerton), Christopheren Nomura (Prince Yamadori). Directed by Frederic Mitterrand and produced by Daniel Toscan Du Plantier and Pierre-Olivier Bardet. Screenplay by Mitterrand, based on the opera by Giacomo Puccini.

Puccini's *Madame Butterfly* is one of the cruelest stories ever told. In nineteenth-century Japan, an American Navy officer named Pinkerton marries a fifteen-year-old girl named Cio-Cio-San, never intending to take his vows seriously. He leaves this Butterfly behind, promising to return. When he does finally return, it is to discover his bride has borne him a child. The officer has in the meantime married "a real American bride," and visits Butterfly *with his new wife* so that they can take her child from her and raise him as an American. *And* Pinkerton gets to sing a sad song at the end.

This is such heartlessness that my eyes are more likely to well up with anger than with the sorrow which is the approved emotion while attending *Madame Butterfly.* I would like, just once, to hear Pinkerton's toadying friend clear his throat and ask, "Ah, excuse me, old man, but wouldn't it be rather easier on Butterfly if you left your new wife behind on the ship?"

The moral imbalance in the opera is so extreme that it provides a way to measure racial attitudes, for there was once a time when some audiences felt sorry for Butterfly, yes, but felt that Pinkerton was, after all, really only doing the right thing.

This beautiful new film version of *Madame Butterfly* is not a revisionist approach; it films Puccini's opera more or less as it was intended to be seen, and of course that is what we want (I am not looking forward to the Baz Luhrmann version, with Pinkerton as the leader of a motorcycle gang, and Butterfly as the daughter of a Korean grocer in the Bronx). The approach is traditional, the pace is attentive, and yet the emotion is still all there, and when Pinkerton's carriage comes rolling up with his new family inside, my blood boils.

The key casting decision is Butterfly, and the filmmakers have discovered a new face for the role of Cio-Cio-San, a twenty-seven-year-old Chinese singer named Ying Huang. She has said in interviews that she will never sing the role on the stage because her voice is not big enough, but in the more intimate spaces of this film, it fills all the corners. She may not look fifteen, but she does look young and defenseless, and in the later scenes, as the depth of Pinkerton's betrayal sinks in, she exhibits true pathos.

Pinkerton is played by another newcomer, Richard Troxell, who made his professional debut only in 1993. His voice is splendid and his manner assured, and he does not betray by one flick of an eyelid what a monster Pinkerton is. That is the correct approach, I suppose; one tiny glimmer of insight and Pinkerton is lost.

Films of operas have two avenues open to them: cast for the voices, or cast for the faces. There must almost always be a compromise in one direction or the other. There is a stage performance of *Butterfly* on laser disc starring a soprano who has a magnificent voice but is old enough to be Butterfly's grandmother. Watching the disc, I don't care; she is a superb actress, and once I accept that I am watching a stage performance of great music, Puccini sweeps all quibbles aside.

This *Butterfly*, however, is essentially a film, and benefits from Ying Huang's fresh face and manner. She has several moving scenes with her servant, Suzuki (Ning Liang), also well cast, and it is touching to see doubt creeping into her eyes as Suzuki asks, "Have you ever heard of a foreign husband returning?"

The film has been directed by Frederic Mitterrand (nephew of the late French president), who intercuts his crisp color photography with old newsreels of the U.S. fleet visiting Japan around the turn of the century. He uses shots of the Stars and Stripes and Puccini's sly quotations from the "Star-Spangled Banner" to set up an ironic contrast between Butterfly's trust in America and Pinkerton's betrayal of that faith. And of course there are the great sorrowful arias that have become among the most familiar of all operatic music.

From the narrow point of view of its musical quality, this *Madame Butterfly* is not at the level you would find in a first-class opera house. But as a treatment of the story, as an evocation of the emotions of love and the wound of betrayal, it is close to Puccini's intentions, and very moving.

## The Man in the Iron Mask ★ ★ ½

PG-13, 117 m., 1998

Leonardo DiCaprio (King Louis/Phillippe), Jeremy Irons (Aramis), John Malkovich (Athos), Gérard Depardieu (Porthos), Gabriel Byrne (D'Artagnan), Anne Parillaud (Queen Anne), Judith Godreche (Christine), Peter Sarsgaard (Raoul). Directed by Randall Wallace and produced by Wallace and Russell Smith. Screenplay by Wallace, based on the novel by Alexandre Dumas.

On the island of St. Marguerite, offshore from Cannes of all places, still stands the rude stone fortress where the Man in the Iron Mask spent his lonely days. I have sat below his window while the owner of the little Italian trattoria assured me that the man in the mask was no less than the twin brother of Louis XIV, held there because the state could not tolerate another claimant to the throne.

No one knows who the man in the mask was, but his dangerous identity must have been the whole point of the mask, so the twin brother theory is as good as any. *The Man in the Iron Mask* is "loosely based" on the Dumas novel, and includes a return appearance by the Three Musketeers. They come out of retirement in a scheme to rescue France from the cruel fist of the young, spoiled king.

Louis XIV and his brother are played by Leonardo DiCaprio in a dual role, his first film since *Titanic*. He looks well fed as the despotic ruler and not particularly gaunt, for that matter, as the man in the mask. As the film opens, he presides over a court that lives in decadent luxury, while mobs riot for bread in the streets. The beautiful Christine (Judith Godreche) catches his eye, and since she's engaged to the young Raoul (Peter Sarsgaard), the king sends Raoul off to war and makes sure he gets killed there.

The death of Raoul enrages his father, Athos (John Malkovich), one of the original musketeers, who enlists his comrades Aramis (Jeremy Irons) and Porthos (Gérard Depardieu) in a plan for revenge. Also involved, on the other side, is the original fourth musketeer, D'Artagnan (Gabriel Byrne), who remains loyal to Louis XIV and the twins' mother, Queen Anne (Anne Parillaud).

This setup, easy enough to explain, takes director Randall Wallace too long to establish, and there are side plots, such as the king's war against the Jesuits, that will confuse audiences. There was once a time when everyone had heard of the musketeers and the Man in the Iron Mask, but history these days seems to start with the invention of MTV, and those not familiar with the characters will take some time to get oriented.

The screenplay by Wallace (who wrote *Braveheart*) is not well focused, and there are gratuitous scenes, but finally we understand the central thread: The musketeers will spring the Man in the Iron Mask from captivity, and secretly substitute him for his brother. The actual mechanics of their plan left me shaking my head with incredulity. Does anyone think Jeremy Irons is large enough to smuggle Leonardo DiCaprio past suspicious guards under his cloak? Wallace should have dreamed up a better plan.

The substitution of the king and his twin is accomplished at a fancy dress ball, where the conspirators drive Louis XIV wild with fear by convincing him he sees iron masks everywhere. But the movie, alas, limits itself to the action in the plot—escapes, sword fights, the frequent incantation "all for one and one for all"—and ignores the opportunity to have more fun with the notion of a prisoner suddenly finding himself king.

Leonardo DiCaprio is the star of the story without being its hero, although his first emergence from the mask is an effective shot. The three musketeers are cast with big names (Irons, Malkovich, Depardieu), but to my surprise the picture is stolen by Gabriel Byrne, who has the most charisma and is the most convincing. His scenes with Parillaud (from *La Femme Nikita*) are some of the best in the movie. Once all the pieces of the plot were in place, I was at least interested, if not overwhelmed; I could see how, with a rewrite and a better focus, this could have been a film of *Braveheart* quality instead of basically just a costume swashbuckler. ☞

## The Man Who Knew Too Little ★

PG, 95 m., 1997

Bill Murray (Wallace Ritchie), Peter Gallagher (James Ritchie), Joanne Whalley (Lori), Alfred Molina (Boris), Richard Wilson (Daggenhurst). Directed by Jon Amiel and produced by Arnon Milchan, Michael Nathanson, and Mark Tarlov. Screenplay by Robert Farrar and Howard Franklin, based on the novel *Watch That Man* by Farrar.

The funniest thing about *The Man Who Knew Too Little* is the title; that melancholy truth develops with deadening finality as the movie marches on. The movie develops endless permutations on an idea that is not funny, until at last, in desperation, we cry, "Bring on some dancing Cossacks!" and it does.

Bill Murray stars, as Wallace, a clueless American tourist, visiting London to see his brother (Peter Gallagher). The brother is a banker throwing a big business dinner, so to get rid of Wallace he buys him a ticket to the "Theater of Life," a troupe that works on the city streets and involves one audience member at a time in a real-life drama.

Wallace, alas, answers a pay phone at the wrong time and finds himself involved in a real spy drama instead of a fake theatrical one. This leads to no end of misunderstandings, and when I say "no end," please assume a tone of despair mixed with exhaustion.

The movie is simply not funny. It is clever, yes. Based on a book by Robert Farrar, it concocts conversations that all have the same thing in common: They can be taken both ways. So Wallace means one thing and the spies think he means another, and on and on and on and on and on.

When he is funny, Bill Murray is very funny. But he needs something to push against. He is a reactor. His best screen characters are passive aggressive: They insinuate themselves unwanted into ongoing scenarios. Here he's the center of the show, and all of the other characters are carefully tailored to fit precisely into the requirements of his misunderstanding, like pieces of a jigsaw.

There are sequences here dripping with desperation, like the whole business involving the window ledge. The dancing Cossack scene involves many Chinese dolls, one containing a bomb with a red digital readout (RDR). Here is a movie gasping for diversions, and does it think of any gags involving the RDR? It does not. It never even clearly establishes how we can *see* the RDR, since it is inside the doll. Or maybe (sound of critic's palm smacking against forehead) that's the joke.

## Mandela ★ ★ ★

NO MPAA RATING, 120 m., 1997

A documentary on the life of Nelson Mandela, directed by Jo Menell and Angus Gibson and produced by Jonathan Demme, Edward Saxon, and Menell.

Nelson Mandela is one of the great men of our century. The leader of South Africa's banned African National Congress, he was condemned in 1964 to life imprisonment on Robben Island, off Cape Town. As he entered the prison, he believed "the way you are treated by prison authorities depends on your demeanor." Such was his demeanor that while imprisoned he became the obvious choice to lead his country, and was eventually released to lead a successful campaign that replaced white rule.

*Mandela,* a new documentary, charts his life from obscure beginnings to the Nobel Prize, and focuses on his steadfast vision of a multiracial South Africa where all would live together peacefully. When I spent 1965 as a student at the University of Cape Town, most people, black and white, believed the apartheid system would end in a bloody civil war. That there was a peaceful, democratic exchange of power is a tribute above all to Mandela's moral leadership.

But it was also because of the courage and imagination of F. W. de Klerk, the white South African president who freed Mandela from prison, lifted the ban on the ANC, and then ran against Mandela in a general election—and lost, as he knew he would. The two men shared the Nobel Peace Prize in 1993.

I mention de Klerk because this film essentially writes him out of the story; it so simplifies the transfer of power in South Africa that it plays more like a campaign biography than a documentary. Why did de Klerk arrive at his decision? Civil unrest and international economic sanctions forced his hand, we are told, and then we see de Klerk informing the South African Parliament that his government had reached an irreversible decision to free Mandela and hold multiracial elections.

The actual story of the events leading to the election is more complicated and interesting than that. Yes, South Africa suffered from economic sanctions. But it could have survived for many years before caving in; it forged clandestine trading arrangements with countries ranging from China to Israel, and its diamonds still found their way onto the fingers of brides all over the world. Civil unrest was widespread, but South Africa had a fearsome array of police and military forces to counter it. If South Africa had chosen, apartheid might still be its law.

What happened was a political miracle. Mandela's unswerving moral and political strength coincided with the growing conviction within the ruling Nationalist Party (and its secret lodge, the Broderbund, and the quasi-official Dutch Reformed Church) that apartheid was, simply, wrong. While de Klerk's predecessor, F. W. Botha, pledged eternal white defiance, de Klerk and other younger ministers instituted secret contacts with Mandela, and the new future of South Africa was hashed out in meetings over a period of years.

De Klerk, when he became president, wanted to free Mandela immediately. Mandela insisted he be "the last man off" of Robben Island; his colleagues and fellow political prisoners had to be freed first, and the ANC had to be recognized as a legitimate political party, not a terrorist underground. Mandela, essentially running a government in exile, moved into the prison warden's house, and often made secret trips elsewhere in South Africa. One famous story tells of a hot day when Mandela's government driver stopped outside a store to buy cold soda, and the world's most famous political prisoner was left alone in the car. He could have simply walked away. But he realized he was more useful to the cause as a prisoner.

None of those events are told in *Mandela,* which simplifies the transfer of power into a fable of black against white, and all but implies that de Klerk was unwilling to see power change hands. The hope for the new South Africa's future lies in multiracialism, and its foundation story is a good place to start.

Still, what a fascinating portrait this film paints of Mandela! Named "Nelson" by a teacher who did not like his tribal name, Mandela was one of nine children of a polygamist father who had four wives (how did Mandela feel about that? The movie doesn't ask). When his father died, the bright boy was adopted by a chief, and prepared to become counselor to the king. He ran away to Johannesburg in the early 1940s to escape an arranged marriage, and had soon moved into the Soweto Township home of Walter Sisulu, who with Oliver Tambo would join him in leading the ANC.

Mandela worked hard to support himself while studying for the law, became a lawyer, and was soon a key leader of the ANC. His cause was never "black power," but "one man, one vote." That led him to Robben Island, and for thirteen years he did hard physical labor in a limestone quarry while continuing to lead classes and discussion groups among his fellow prisoners.

The film has many revealing personal touches: his childhood fear, during a circumcision ceremony, that he would not be as "forthright and strong" as the other boys. His wry imitation of a teacher repeating, "I am a descendant of the famous Duke of Wellington." His memories of hunting animals on the veld. His passion for his second wife, Winnie Mandela, in hundreds of tender letters written from prison—and his anguished decision to divorce her. There are amusing glimpses of Mandela under the guidance of personal aides, including a maternal Indian woman who advises him on wardrobe (he feels choked when he wears a tie).

*Mandela* delivers a powerful emotional charge in its closing scenes of the Nobel Prize and Mandela's election victory. Today the new South Africa offers the best hope for a new Africa. Its engine might be able to pull the train of corrupt regimes to the north and lead the way to reform. Mandela's South Africa seems to be working, despite worrisome crime rates. It is one of the most inspiring stories of our time. But there is more to it than *Mandela* chooses to tell.

## Manny and Lo ★ ★ ★ ½

R, 90 m., 1996

Mary Kay Place (Elaine), Scarlett Johansson (Amanda [Manny]), Aleksa Palladino (Laurel [Lo]), Paul Guilfoyle (Mr. Humphreys), Glenn Fitzgerald (Joey), Cameron Boyd (Chuck), Novella Nelson (Georgine), Angie Phillips (Connie). Directed by Lisa Krueger and produced by Dean Silvers and Marlen Hecht. Screenplay by Krueger.

Many children remember their mother by her favorite perfume. When Amanda and Laurel want to remember theirs, they spray the sheets with Arrid Extra Dry. She long ago left them to the care of foster homes, but now that they're on the lam and in trouble, they could use some advice. "What would Mom tell us?" asks Manny. "Depends," says Lo. "Is she drunk, or stoned?"

Lo, who is sixteen, has just run away from one foster home and taken her eleven-year-old sister from another, "so that our family can be together again." Also because she did not much like sleeping in a garage. Jump-starting cars, sleeping in model homes, stealing groceries, they stay on the move. They don't have much to leave behind, although Lo visits her boyfriend, a monster truck driver, and he is able to tear his mind away from the truck long enough to provide her with perfunctory sex and a blouse she doesn't like, either.

Eventually it becomes clear that Lo is pregnant. She doesn't have a clue about what to do next, except to "settle down" somewhere. They find an unlocked cabin at the end of a lonely road, move in, and hang around the baby supply store in the nearby village, where a clerk named Elaine (Mary Kay Place) seems to know everything there is to know about birthing babies. So, they kidnap her.

And it is then that the movie's real story begins. This is not even remotely a *Thelma and Louise*–type saga about two women on the run, but a much different kind of story, about two girls who need a mother—and maybe about an older woman who needs two girls.

Although Elaine is kept under constant watch and hobbled at the ankles so she can't run away, it eventually becomes clear that she doesn't much want to run away. Other things become clear, too, which I will not describe, because one of the pleasures of the movie is the way it reveals its characters in sudden, unexpected, defining acts.

The movie is narrated by Manny (Scarlett Johansson). We get the notion she may be writing this all down for a story, and indeed of the two she would be the writer: At eleven she is wise, observant, and knows how to keep a secret. Lo (Aleksa Palladino) is more impulsive and probably not as smart, although she was smart to pick Elaine as her "hostage," since Elaine does seem capable of helping her through this pregnancy.

The movie is serious about its characters, but with sidelong glances at the absurdity of the situation ("I used to think, *no way* can you give your kid to your hostage"). It was written and directed by Lisa Krueger, who developed it at Robert Redford's Sundance Institute, and seems to have taken advantage of the Sundance emphasis on script; the movie depends on character, not melodrama, and is so sly about revealing its ultimate destination that you realize it must have been through many subtle rewrites.

That's especially true of the character of Elaine, which Place develops so gradually that we're never sure until the end quite what we know about her. She is firm with the girls, and rather angry at first, and promises them that everyone she knows will come looking for her. She delivers little lectures on physical and emotional growth. What is happening beneath her surface is only gradually revealed.

What I like about movies like this is the way they keep us involved right up until the end. There is no formula that we can project; *Thelma and Louise* was clearly heading for an act of self-destruction, but here we have no idea what to expect, except (inevitably) the birth of a child. It's also interesting the way Krueger develops a hidden theme. Only after *Manny and Lo* is over do we really understand what it's about.

## Margaret's Museum ★ ★ ★ ½

R, 118 m., 1997

Helena Bonham Carter (Margaret MacNeil), Clive Russell (Neil Currie), Craig Olejnik (Jimmy), Kate Nelligan (Catherine), Kenneth Welsh (Angus), Andrea Morris (Marilyn). Directed by Mort Ransen and produced by Ransen, Christopher Zimmer, Claudio Luca, and Steve Clark-Hall. Screenplay by Gerald Wexler and Ransen, based on stories by Sheldon Currie.

The opening shot of *Margaret's Museum* looks like a painting by Andrew Wyeth of a little clapboard cottage in a sea of grass on a cliffside. Two visitors drive up to visit the "museum," and a moment later one runs from the house, screaming. Then a title card takes us back "three years earlier."

As openings go, this one plays like it belongs on another film. That it doesn't gradually becomes clear. We are in the mining town of Glace Bay on Cape Breton Island in Nova Scotia, in the late 1940s, where the coal pits take a terrible toll in life and limb—and where Margaret (Helena Bonham Carter) and her family live in half a house because the earth subsided into a mine shaft beneath the other half.

Margaret scrubs floors at the hospital. One day a strapping tall fellow named Neil (Clive Russell) walks into a restaurant, half-drunk, and begins to serenade her with big bagpipes. She scorns men but likes this one, and brings him home to meet her bitter mother (Kate Nelligan), who has buried a husband and a son after pit disasters, and cares for a father whose lungs are so filled with dust that he needs to be regularly slammed on the back ("Don't forget to thump your grandfather!").

*Margaret's Museum* is the story of the people who must make their living from the cold-hearted, cost-conscious mining company, but it isn't like other films with similar themes *(Sons and Lovers, The Molly Maguires,* or *Matewan).* It's quirkier and more eccentric, and has a thread of wry humor running through it. The dialogue, inspired by the short stories of Sheldon Currie, shows that Celtic wit has traveled well to the new land. (When Margaret encourages her younger brother to ask his girl to the Sunday dance, he replies, "They're not supposed to dance on Sunday." She tells him, "They're not supposed to work. Dancing's not work." And he replies, "They're Protestant, aren't they? For them, it's work.")

Most of the movie is the love story of Margaret and Neil. He towers above her slight frame and threatens to force them all out of the house with his drinking, his buddies, and his songs. But he listens when she protests, and mends his ways. Soon he has built her the curious house near the sea, using parts scrounged around town. (The bedroom, with walls and a ceiling made from old windows, is going to be bloody cold in a Nova Scotia winter.)

As Margaret's mother, Nelligan is hard and dour, and can see no point in a life that snatches all of your loved ones away from you. "I'll have five sons and three daughters," Margaret tells her. "I can hear them in the bagpipe, screaming to be born." Her mother's predictions about the fates of these unborn infants are blood-chilling.

The margins of the movie are filled with colorful characters. With old grandfather, who coughs and writes his song requests on a notepad. With Uncle Angus (Kenneth Welsh), who dreams of sparing his nephew a life in the mines, and works double shifts in hopes that if he just once sees Toronto, he'll see there is a different life waiting for him. With the pit manager, who orders his red-haired daughter (Andrea Morris) not to see Margaret's brother (Craig Olejnik). The daughter and the brother perform their own marriage ceremony, solemnly, before two candles in a root cellar.

The destination of the film may be guessed by some, but I will not reveal it, nor how it contributes to Margaret's museum and its sign, THE COST OF COAL. What is surprising about the film is not its ending, but how it gets there. Helena Bonham Carter might seem an unlikely candidate for this role (she took it in preference to the lead in *Breaking the Waves*), but she is just right—plucky, sexy, bemused, glorious in a scene where Neil sneaks her into the miner's cleaning area and she takes the first hot shower of her life. Russell, as Neil, is sort of a rougher-hewn Liam Neeson, strong, gentle, and poetic. And Nelligan is astounding in the way she allows her humanity to peek out from behind the mother's harsh defenses. *Margaret's Museum* is one of those small, nearly perfect movies that you know, seeing it, is absolutely one of a kind.

## Marius and Jeannette ★ ★

NO MPAA RATING, 1998

Ariane Ascaride (Jeannette), Gerard Meylan (Marius), Pascale Roberts (Caroline), Jacques Boudet (Justin), Frederique Bonnal (Monique), Jean-Pierre Darroussin (Dede), Laetitia Pesenti (Magali), Miloud Nacer (Malek). Directed by Robert Guediguian and produced by Gilles Sandoz. Screenplay by Guediguian and Jean-Louis Milesi. In French with English subtitles.

*Marius and Jeannette* is a sentimental fantasy of French left-wing working-class life, so cheerful and idealized that I expected the characters to break into song; they do all dance together, in the forecourt of a shuttered cement factory. Set in a blue-collar district of Marseilles, it plays like a sitcom spin-off of *Carmen,* with everyone popping in and out of each other's houses and lives, while all personal emergencies are handled in public, collectively.

The director, Robert Guediguian, has visited this territory before; his 1980 film *Last Summer* dealt with workers in the same factory when it was still in operation. Now the jobs have fled to Malaysia, the workers tell each other, although they are none too sure where that is, and they sit outside their doors in beach chairs, unemployed but unbowed.

The movie's heroine is Jeannette (Ariane Ascaride, the director's wife). She's raised two kids by different fathers, and as the movie opens she tries to steal cans of paint from the factory. She's stopped by a security guard, Marius (Gerard Meylan), who limps around in an orange one-piece suit, patrolling the ruins. "My house will collapse without a paint job!" Jeannette shouts, calling him a fascist. The next day, he delivers the cans to her door, and that's the beginning of a romance.

Well, we like these two people, and that's the argument for liking the movie. Jeannette is irredeemably cheerful and upbeat, a pal to her children, a no-nonsense figure in jeans and a Levi's jacket. Sample dialogue: "You're beautiful," she tells her teenage daughter Magali, who tries on a lacy minidress. "But I look cheap," the daughter says. "Yes, but it suits you." "If I wear this I'll be pregnant before I get to the end of the street," Magali says. Jeannette smiles: "I'd like to be a grandma."

Not your typical mother, eh? Jeannette combines elements of old-time leftist idealism with the hippie commune spirit. She and her neighbors live in each other's pockets; they occupy a little courtyard with windows that open onto a common space, and even the most intimate matters are freely discussed. They also laugh a lot—too much, I thought. At one point the neighbor's husband lands in the hospital after getting drunk and throwing rocks at right-wing political posters. The rocks bounce back and hit him in the head. At this news everyone laughs so uproariously that they have to wipe away the tears. I didn't believe I was looking at laughter: It looked more like overacting in response to the screenplay instruction, "They laugh uncontrollably."

There must be an arc in all romances, a darkness before the dawn. Marius and Jeannette fall in love, but then he unexpectedly disappears, and the movie falls back on that most ancient of clichés, that in wine there is truth. The neighborhood guys get him drunk, and he confesses his innermost fears and insecurities. There is also an unnecessary and unmotivated bar brawl. Then, in a tactic that takes communal living too far, they haul him unconscious back to Jeannette's bed.

Meanwhile, Jeannette conducts her private war against the bosses. She's a checkout clerk at a supermarket, where the chair hurts her back (she should try standing up like an American grocery clerk). She shouts at the manager, "The Gestapo could have used these chairs for torture!" Since the movie is set much too late for Jeannette to have had any experience of World War II, this seems more like a dated, ritualized left-wing attribution of fascism to all the enemies of the workers.

By the end of the film, I was fed up. Yes, I liked Jeannette and Marius as individuals; they're a warm, attractive, funky couple on the shores of middle age who find happiness. But the movie forces its politics until it feels like a Pete Seeger benefit. And, hey, I like Pete Seeger. It's just that the love story of *Marius and Jeannette* is at an awkward angle to the politics, and the lives and dialogue of these characters seem impossibly contorted to reflect the director's politics.

## Mars Attacks! ★ ★

PG-13, 100 m., 1996

Jack Nicholson (President James Dale/Art Land), Glenn Close (First Lady Marsha Dale), Annette Bening (Barbara Land), Pierce Brosnan (Professor Donald Kessler), Danny DeVito (Rude Gambler), Martin Short (Jerry Ross), Sarah Jessica Parker (Nathalie Lake), Michael J. Fox (Jason Stone), Rod Steiger (General Decker), Tom Jones (Tom Jones). Directed by Tim Burton and produced by Burton and Larry Franco. Screenplay by Jonathan Gems, based on the "Mars Attacks!" trading cards by Topps.

First he made *Ed Wood,* a tribute to the man fondly recalled as the worst movie director of all time. Now Tim Burton seems to have made a tribute to Wood's work. *Mars Attacks!* has the look and feel of a schlocky 1950s science-fiction movie, and if it's not as bad as a Wood film, that's not a plus: A movie like this should be a lot better, or a lot worse. The movie plays like one of those fifties movies that are *not* remembered as cult classics.

*Mars Attacks!* opens with an image worthy of Buñuel: A herd of flaming cattle, running down a country lane (see note below). What set them afire? We see the first of the movie's many flying saucers, designed in perfect imitation of those fuzzy photos in old UFO books—the ones that looked like either alien spacecraft or anodized aluminum ceiling light fixtures, take your pick.

Earth is soon under attack from a vast fleet of Martian invaders, and the U.S. president (Jack Nicholson) takes advice from a few of the many big stars in the film: Martin Short as his publicity consultant, Rod Steiger as his nuke-'em military adviser, Pierce Brosnan as a scientific adviser, Glenn Close as the first lady, and Paul Winfield as a Colin Powell look-alike who runs the Joint Chiefs.

Watching Nicholson deliver his televised fireside chat with the nation about the impending saucer attack, I wondered, why is this supposed to be funny? Burton has made a common mistake: He assumes it is funny simply to *be doing* a parody, when in fact the material has to be funny in its own right. It isn't funny *that* Jack Nicholson is the president—it's only funny if the writing makes the role comic. Peter Sellers was funny in *Dr. Strangelove* (one of this movie's many inspirations) because the story was funny. *Mars Attacks!* is not so much a comedy as a replica of tacky old saucer movies—not so much a parody as the real thing.

The action also takes place in Las Vegas, where Nicholson, in an unsuccessful and unnecessary dual role, plays a casino owner with a boozy girlfriend (Annette Bening). Also in Vegas, we meet Jim Brown as a former heavyweight champion, now dressed like a gladiator and employed as a casino greeter. He has many telephone conversations with his estranged wife, played by Pam Grier as a character so realistic and plausible that apparently Burton forgot to tell her she was in a comedy. Also in Vegas: Danny DeVito, playing a gambler in a role of complete inconsequence. And Tom Jones, playing himself and thus impossible to parody.

The third locale is a trailer park in rural Kansas, where gun nut Joe Don Baker presides over a brood including his mother (Sylvia Sidney) and his son (Lucas Haas). Many of these people are eventually fried by the Martians, whose ray guns look suspiciously like the high-volume water guns you can buy in upscale toy shops. Their victims look briefly like X-ray pictures of themselves, which is funny one (1) time, but is used as a visual gag many (many) times.

The movie was obviously expensive, and Burton lingers too long on the dollars in the screen. The massing of the Martian fleet continues long after we've gotten the point, for example, and the animated Martians would be funnier if we saw a lot less of them. Later, when mankind discovers a secret weapon against the Martians, it's amusing to see one of the eggheaded creatures pop his skull and coat the inside of his space helmet with green oatmeal. But it happens again and again.

The Martians, supplied by animation, have laughter possibly inspired by Beavis and Butt-Head. They're so stupid it's hard to figure out how they achieved space travel, but that's not the kind of question one is supposed to ask during a movie like this.

*Mars Attacks!* was inspired by a series of old Topps bubble-gum cards. The art direction is first-rate in creating the kinds of saucers and aliens that graced the covers of my precious old issues of *Imagination Science Fiction* magazine (which was downscale and ran bug-eyed monsters that Analog and F&SF would have never touched). But the movie plays more like a series of pictorial representations of old sci-fi situations than like a story. And the actors bring little joy to the material. Joe Don Baker and Pierce Brosnan are the exceptions; many of the other actors don't seem in on the joke, and Nicholson doesn't look like he's having a good time.

Ed Wood himself could have told us what's wrong with this movie: The makers felt superior to the material. To be funny, even schlock has to believe in itself. Go to a video store and look for *Infra-Man* or *Invasion of the Bee Girls* and you will find movies that lack stars and big budgets and fancy special effects, but are funny and fun in a way that Burton's megaproduction never really understands.

*Note: Special effects. No living animals were barbecued during the production of this film.*

## Marvin's Room ★ ★ ★ ½

PG-13, 98 m., 1997

Meryl Streep (Lee), Leonardo DiCaprio (Hank), Diane Keaton (Bessie), Robert De Niro (Dr. Wally), Hume Cronyn (Marvin), Gwen Verdon (Ruth), Hal Scardino (Charlie), Dan Hedaya (Bob), Margo Martindale (Dr. Charlotte), Cynthia Nixon (Home Director). Directed by Jerry Zaks and produced by Scott Rudin, Jane Rosenthal, and Robert De Niro. Screenplay by Scott McPherson, based on his stage play.

There is a line of dialogue that occurs late in *Marvin's Room* and contains the key to the whole film. It is spoken by a woman who has put her life on hold for years to care for a father who "has been dying for twenty years—slowly, so that I won't miss anything." Has her life been wasted? She doesn't believe so. She says: "I've been so lucky to have been able to love someone so much."

The woman's name is Bessie (Diane Keaton). She lives in Florida with her still-dying father, Marvin (Hume Cronyn), and a dotty aunt (Gwen Verdon), who wears some kind of medical device that is always opening the garage door. Bessie has discovered that she has cancer, but that her life might be saved by a bone marrow transplant. The only candidates for donors are Lee (Meryl Streep), a sister she has not seen in years, and Lee's two children. If they are to be of any help, some old wounds will have to be reopened.

Lee lives in Ohio, where her precarious life has recently taken an upturn; she's received her degree in cosmetology. It has also taken a downturn; her older son, Hank (Leonardo DiCaprio), has just burned down the house. Her younger son, Charlie (Hal Scardino), has reacted to this development as he reacts to most, by burying his nose in a book. Lee visits Hank in an institution, where he proudly reports, "They're not strapping me down anymore!" "Don't abuse that privilege," she tells him. The two sisters have not so much as exchanged Christmas cards in years, for reasons which they would certainly not agree on.

In broad outlines, this story goes on the same shelf with *What's Eating Gilbert Grape?*, another drama about a malfunctioning family (also starring DiCaprio). Both have children who are the captives of chronically housebound parents; both have a child whose behavior is unpredictable and perhaps dangerous; both have a rich vein of bleak humor; both are about the healing power of sacrifice.

One of the big differences between the films, for a viewer, is that *Marvin's Room* has so much star power: not only Streep and Keaton, but also Robert De Niro, as a detached, apologetic doctor whose attempts to sound reassuring are always alarming. (How many spins can a doctor put on the words "test results"?) The famous faces make it difficult at first to sink into the story, but eventually we do; the characters become so convincing that even if we're aware of Keaton and Streep, it's as if these events are happening to them. (De Niro never becomes that real, and neither does Dan Hedaya, who is brilliant as his problematic brother, but that doesn't matter because they function like the fools in a tragedy.)

Lee piles Hank and Charlie into the car for the drive down south, during which she keeps Hank (on release from a juvenile home) on a very short chain. (Having burned down the house, he naturally is not allowed matches, so when he wants to smoke she has Charlie, the ten-year-old, light his cigarette.) When she first sees Bessie, there is bluntness and disbelief: Both have aged by twenty years, except in each other's minds—and in their own.

Once the sisters are reunited, the material boils down into a series of probing conversations, and we sense the story's origin as a play. (It was written by Scott McPherson, and first produced at the Goodman Theater in Chicago in 1990; McPherson wrote a version of the screenplay before he died in 1992.) The stage origins, although we sense them, are not a problem because these two women *need* to talk to one another. There is a lot to say, and director Jerry Zaks lets them say it.

How do families fall apart? Why do many have one sibling who takes on the responsibilities of maintaining the "family home" and being the caregiver, while others get away as far and fast as they can? Is one the martyr and are the others taking advantage? Or does everyone get the role they really desire?

What *Marvin's Room* argues is that Lee, by fleeing the sick people at home, may have shortchanged herself, and that Bessie, "chained" to the bed of her slowly dying father, might have benefited. Or perhaps not; perhaps Lee was constitutionally incapable of caring for her father and was better off keeping out of the way. There is a point in *Marvin's Room* where such questions inspired parallel questions in my own mind; all families have illness and death, and therefore all families generate such questions.

Is one of the three visitors from Ohio a match for the transplant operation? Will Bessie live? Will her father die? The true depth of *Marvin's Room* is revealed in the fact that the story is not about these questions. They are incidental. The film focuses instead with the ways the two sisters deal with their relationship—which they both desperately need to do—and the way the sons learn something, however haphazardly, about the difference between true unhappiness and the complaints of childhood.

Streep and Keaton, in their different styles, find ways to make Lee and Bessie into much more than the expression of their problems. Hal Scardino has some wonderful moments as the "good" boy of a mother who is a borderline control freak (watch how he meticulously eats a potato chip just as she instructs). DiCaprio on his good days is one of the best young actors we have. Here he supplies the nudge the story needs to keep from reducing itself to a two-sided conversation; he is the distraction, the outside force, the reminder that life goes on and no problem, not even a long dying, is forever.

## Masterminds ½ ★

PG-13, 106 m., 1997

Patrick Stewart (Raif Bentley), Vincent Kartheiser (Ozzie), Brenda Fricker (Principal Maloney), Brad Whitford (Miles Lawrence), Matt Craven (Jake), Annabelle Gurwitch (Helen), Jon Abrahams (K-Dog), Katie Stuart (Melissa). Directed by Roger Christian and produced by Robert Dudelson and Floyd Byars. Screenplay by Byars, based on a story by Byars, Alex Siskin, and Chris Black.

Patrick Stewart, best known for his work on *Star Trek,* is an actor of effortless class and presence, and *Masterminds* is like an obstacle course he has to run. Can he make it from beginning to end of this dreadful movie without lowering himself to its level of idiocy? Or will he go down with the material? The answer to that question provides the only suspense and nearly the only interest in one of the worst films of the year.

The premise: Young Ozzie (Vincent Kartheiser) is a computer hacker who has been exiled for life from the exclusive Shady Glen School. His father threatens to send him to a military academy. He has his bedroom rigged with motion detectors and spends his days downloading pirated software.

He takes his little sister, Melissa (Katie Stuart), to the school, which is walled and guarded like the CIA, and talks his way past the security guard. Inside, he confronts the bossy principal (Brenda Fricker) and the ominous Raif Bentley (Patrick Stewart), the school's newly-hired chief of security, who has been brought on staff mostly because of the recent depredations of Ozzie.

To make a long but shallow story into a short but no less shallow one, it turns out that Bentley plans to kidnap ten of the kids, whose parents are among the richest people in America. And Ozzie, locked inside the school during a hostage crisis, uses his skills as a hacker and troublemaker to battle the evil scheme.

More than that you do not need to know, since already in your mind you are conjuring up images of air shafts, abandoned boiler rooms, hacked computers, obscure electrical connections, and ways to commandeer the school's public address system. The details run together in my mind. I lost all interest. I stopped taking notes on my Palm Pilot and started playing the little chess game.

Since we have all seen this movie several times (all of the pieces have been assembled from better films, but then there are few worse films to borrow from), the sole remaining interest comes from the presence of Patrick Stewart. He is clipped, trim, precise, wise. He narrows his eyes impressively. He is a good actor, and no doubt signed up for this movie for the same reason as everyone else involved: A case of mass hallucination in which the screenplay appeared to be for another film.

Does Stewart emerge unsullied? Very nearly. I give him credit for that. Right up until almost the very end of the film, he retains a certain poise and dignity. But then (do not read further if you intend to see this film) he is placed in a situation that, I submit, no actor could survive. Not De Niro. Not Olivier. He is made to take little Melissa hostage and then engage in a high-speed chase with Ozzie through a sewer system, using souped-up dune buggies.

If you go to see *Masterminds,* do not by any means walk out early. You must stay, simply to appreciate Stewart's expression as he struggles with the little hostage who is trying to jump off his dune buggy. I cannot read lips or minds, but I intuit that what he is saying, if only as an interior monologue, runs along the lines of, "Beam me the hell up outta here!"

## The Matchmaker ★ ★ ★

R, 96 m., 1997

Janeane Garofalo (Marcy), David O'Hara (Sean), Jay O. Sanders (McGlory), Denis Leary (Nick), Milo O'Shea (Dermot). Directed by Mark Joffe and produced by Tim Bevan, Eric Fellner, and Luc Roeg. Screenplay by Karen Janszen, Louis Nowra, and Graham Linehan, based on a screenplay by Greg Dinner.

I attempted once in a review to write that the Irish "have the gift of gab," and was reprimanded by an editor who told me this was an unwarranted and possibly offensive generalization about an ethnic group.

That editor has moved on and a new regime rules, which allows me to risk offending readers of Irish descent by stating that, yes, the Irish do indeed often express themselves with freedom and an innate poetry.

Some Americans, especially northerners and those involved in political campaigns, also have a certain vocal style, which might be described as "cutting out the crap and getting to the bottom line." And one of the pleasures of *The Matchmaker* is to hear these two styles in conflict. Milo O'Shea, that twinkly professional Irishman, has enormous fun expounding on his theories of romance, and Janeane Garofalo, who has a built-in blarney detector, cuts to the chase.

The movie stars Garofalo as Marcy, an aide to the fatuous Senator McGlory from Massachusetts (Jay O. Sanders), who is behind in his campaign for reelection and dispatches her to Ireland to round up some ancestors so he can visit them.

This is not her idea of a good time. In Ireland, on a bus to McGlory's ancestral village of Ballinagra, she finds herself surrounded by ebullient women who seem on the brink of song. "Do men and women have to travel separately in Ireland?" she asks grumpily, only to discover she is en route to the village's annual matchmaking festival, at which unattached men and women size up the opposition.

In Ballinagra, the hotel facilities are primitive ("a little bijou," is how the clerk puts it), the locals seem to be speaking in code, the customs are incomprehensible, and the local color is seductive.

There have been a lot of good-hearted comedies from Ireland in recent years, and many of them argue more or less the same thing: Instead of watching the telly and cowering behind locked doors, we'd be better off among people who know each other and enjoy singsongs in pubs. I am always persuaded by this argument.

In Ballinagra, Marcy meets Sean (David O'Hara), a former journalist who has retreated to this rural backwater in order to work on a book. He is not her idea of sophistication, especially when he has a Kleenex stuck up his nostril because of a nosebleed. They strike uneasy sparks.

Meanwhile, the professional matchmaker Dermot (Milo O'Shea) drums up customers for his other business, Turbo Tans, and keeps an eye on Marcy and Sean. He senses a certain chemistry there, and when a competitor bets him £100 he can't match them up, he takes the bet and contrives to send them to one of the isolated Aran Islands, where, he says, lives the only genealogist in Ireland capable of tracing the senator's ancestors.

The scenes on the island are magnificent. The scenery is wild and forbidding, the sea is awesome, the people are suspicious at first and then quickly friendly, and in no time Marcy finds herself judging the song contest at the local pub. (Sample lyrics: "In eighteen hundred and forty-one, my corduroy britches I put on.")

Whether Marcy and Sean will find love, I leave you to discover. Whether the senator will personally arrive on the scene, I leave you to predict. Whether the action returns to America, I reluctantly confirm, since the Irish center of the film is so charming we feel distracted by the bookends.

*Matchmaker* might have been better if it hadn't shoehorned in the Massachusetts scenes, but it could hardly be more entertaining in its Irish material. Garofalo, fresh from the magical *Truth About Cats and Dogs,* is one of the most engaging actresses around. We relate with her cynical intelligence and the warmth of her smile as she makes observations such as, "The basis of any friendship is that the two people not hate each other." Somehow we are not surprised that this is the only romantic comedy in which a downhearted lover attempts suicide by tanning.

## Matilda ★ ★ ★

PG, 100 m., 1996

Mara Wilson (Matilda), Danny DeVito (Mr. Wormwood), Rhea Perlman (Mrs. Wormwood), Embeth Davidtz (Miss Honey), Pam Ferris (Trunchbull), Paul Reubens (FBI Agent), Tracey Walter (FBI Agent No. 2), Brian Levinson (Michael). Directed by Danny DeVito and produced by DeVito, Michael Shamberg, Stacey Sher, and Liccy Dahl. Screenplay by Nicholas Kazan and Robin Swicord, based on the book by Roald Dahl.

Roald Dahl was by all accounts a singularly unpleasant person, which may explain why he wrote stories that are so fascinating to children. He nursed the grudges of childhood, he distrusted adults, and he was unmoved by false sentimentality. Kids may not feel cuddled by his books, but they sense Dahl is the real thing: He's writing out of strong emotion and not just to be cute.

Consider the character of Trunchbull in the darkly comic new film *Matilda.* Trunchbull must be a woman, because she is someone's aunt, but she is never called "Miss"—and we see at once that "Mrs." would be out of the question. She was a champion shot-putter and hammer-thrower in the 1972 Olympics, we learn, before moving on to her current career as the school principal and dominatrix at Trunchbull Hall, a fearsome grade school with the motto "When you are having fun you are not learning."

To this school comes the heroine of the story, Matilda Wormwood (Mara Wilson), a very, very smart little girl whose parents neglect her when they are not insulting her. Matilda, left at home alone all day, has taught herself to read and walked to the library where by the time she is six she has read not only *Heidi* and *Ivanhoe* but also *For Whom the Bell Tolls* and *Moby Dick*. When she tells her parents (Danny DeVito and Rhea Perlman) she's old enough to go to school, her dad replies: "Nonsense! Who would sign for the packages?" But when he meets the redoubtable Trunchbull he announces that he has at last found the right school for Matilda.

Trunchbull, played by Pam Ferris with great zest and well-hidden but genuine humor, is not a nice person. "Sit down, you squirming worm of vomit!" she says to the hapless Matilda at one point, and later calls her "You villainous sack of dog slime!" When a cute little blond girl dares to wear her hair in pigtails, Trunchbull seizes the child by the pigtails, swings her around and hurls her through the air like a hammer in the Olympics—and, of course, the movie does not neglect to show her narrowly missing a spike fence before landing safely in a flower bed.

This is the kind of villainess children can enjoy, because she is too ridiculous to be taken seriously and yet really is mean and evil, like the witch in *Snow White*. And since most children have at one time or another felt that their parents are not nice enough to them, they may also enjoy the portrait of Matilda's parents. Mr. and Mrs. Wormwood and their older son spend all of their time gobbling food and watching television, and when Matilda says she would rather read, her incredulous father cries, "Read? What do you want to read for when you got a perfectly good TV set right here?"

Trunchbull Hall is a school that would have appalled Dickens. Children are punished by solitary confinement in a steamy closet with nails sticking through the walls. But redemption comes in the person of a saintly teacher, Miss Honey (Embeth Davidtz), who is amazed when little Matilda does difficult math problems in her head, and eventually becomes her guardian and best friend.

*Matilda* is not in any sense a "children's movie," although older children will probably like it a lot. It is a dark family comedy about stupid parents, cruel teachers, and a brave little girl, and it is no surprise to find that Danny DeVito not only stars in it but directed it. Consider that his previous directing credits include *Throw Momma from the Train* and *The War of the Roses*, and you sense that he has some kind of deep, mordant fascination for dysfunctional families (the family life in his *Hoffa* was not exactly functional, either).

There is never a moment (except toward the happy ending) that we sense DeVito is anything other than quite serious about this material. He goes with Roald Dahl's macabre vision. Whatever it was that hurt Dahl so deeply, he never forgave it, and his children's stories (like *James and the Giant Peach* and *Charlie and the Chocolate Factory*) are driven by it. DeVito seems to vibrate on the same wavelength. *Matilda* doesn't condescend to children, it doesn't sentimentalize, and as a result it feels heartfelt and sincere. It's funny too.

## Maybe . . . Maybe Not ★ ★ ★

R, 100 m., 1996

Til Schweiger (Axel), Katja Riemann (Doro), Joachim Krol (Norbert), Rufus Beck (Waltraud), Antonia Lang (Elke), Armin Rohde (Horst). Directed by Sonke Wortmann and produced by Bernd Eichinger. Screenplay by Wortmann, based on the comic books by Ralf Konig.

Conventional box office has it that there are more movies about lesbians than about gay men because both men and women, gay and straight, will go to lesbian movies, but only gay men will attend movies about gay men. This is no doubt because straight men, foolishly optimistic, dream that two lesbians are only killing time until a man comes along, while all women, ever realistic, know an unavailable man when they see one. (This assumes that movie audiences want to identify with lovers on the screen, which is a pretty safe bet.)

No such theories explain the popularity of movies in which a straight man finds himself in a homosexual situation because of a series of misunderstandings. There are enough of these now to form a subgenre, including, of course, *La*

*Cage aux Folles* and its American remake, *The Birdcage*. My theory: Many straight men are intrigued by the gay lifestyle, but are paranoid about revealing their interest. They welcome movies that provide them with an excuse: "Hey, it's a comedy, and the guy got into this situation by accident (ho, ho)."

The legendary folk singer Bob Gibson skewered this dodge neatly in his song about a man who hires a transvestite hooker, discovers his mistake, and decides to make the best of it: "She was a he, but what the hell, honey—since you've already got my money . . ."

The German film *Maybe . . . Maybe Not* opens with scenes designed to establish Axel, its hero, as so straight he could be Ollie North's roommate. Making eye contact with a promising woman in a club, he sneaks her aside for a quickie, only to be discovered by his girlfriend. He shouts, "I can explain! It's not what you think!" but it is, and she's outta there. She ejects him from her apartment, he's broke and homeless, and after asking every woman he knows for a place to stay (while "Just a Gigolo" plays on the sound track), he ends up attending a gay party with a friend named Walter. After doing as many double takes as the material can possibly provide, he ends up going home with Norbert, a nice guy, plain but friendly, who offers him a place to stay.

In the movie's central passages, Axel (Til Schweiger) operates as a surrogate for the straight audience. What he sees (and is shocked or surprised by), we see. One big difference between the men in *Maybe . . . Maybe Not* and those in *Cage* and *Birdcage* is that you can definitely imagine these men having sex, while the gay men in the earlier films seemed to get off primarily by shocking the bourgeoisie.

Axel's girlfriend, Doro (Katja Riemann), inevitably turns up pregnant shortly after throwing him out, and so she is cautiously receptive to his pleas that she take him back again. But the movie uses all of the devices of screwball comedy to give her the idea that he might actually have turned gay after all. How else to explain Axel in bed with Norbert? Or Axel nude in a closet? Or the suggestive voices she hears on the telephone?

*Maybe . . . Maybe Not* was an enormous box-office hit in Germany, where Til Schweiger has become a star. Then Schweiger went to Hollywood, seeking to follow in the footsteps of Arnold Schwarzenegger, John-Claude Van Damme, Antonio Banderas, and other Euro-hunks. If he can speak English, he can make it: He's handsome, he's got an easy, unforced acting style, and he can do comedy. (The ability to smile at themselves is at the center of Schwarzenegger's and Banderas's appeal, and the inability is what limits Van Damme's choice of roles.)

This movie, while not a comic masterpiece, is very funny in places, and unexpectedly affecting in other places, especially in its view of everyday events in a gay lifestyle. The gay characters are exaggerated, but then comedy is exaggeration. By the end of the film, conventional values are asserted, and straight audiences can leave having survived their walk on the wild side. Only the most thoughtful among them will wonder if Axel is completely ready to settle down to that lifetime of bliss with Doro.

## Me and My Matchmaker ★ ★ ★

NO MPAA RATING, 55 m., 1996

A documentary about Irene Nathan, directed by Mark Wexler and produced by Hajira Majid. Screenplay by Wexler and Robert DeMaio.

The more you know about watching films, the better *Me and My Matchmaker* will seem to you. You need to register the nuances to see what a strange and subtle thing happens during the filming of this documentary, as the filmmaker loses control over his situation and is drawn into the emotional force field of his subject. The key events in the movie take place in the pauses during conversations, in quiet gestures and looks, in word choices that seem slightly unexpected.

As the film opens, Mark Wexler, a successful photojournalist, is thirty-nine and single. He decides to make a documentary about Irene Nathan, a Chicago matchmaker who arranges meetings between Jewish singles and says that more than 200 marriages have resulted from her introductions, leading to only four divorces. Does Wexler choose this subject because he thinks it will make a good film, or because it is a way to meet women without admitting that's what he's doing? An excellent question.

Irene Nathan, sixtyish, is an intelligent, calm, penetrating woman who has, we learn, degrees in clinical psychology and gerontology. A Dolly

Levi she isn't. We see her interviewing potential clients. Some are good catches, like the former stock trader who runs a bagel company. Others have less compelling credentials, like the bachelor who hopefully tells her he has "a TV set and 150 different tapes."

Her price is $400 for a year of introductions and advice. "They think if it costs $400, they should get Robert Redford," she sighs. But she tries to identify with her clients. "You like boxing?" she says to a sportsman. "Oh, I'd like to try that." She tells Mark she'd like to "get you off lonesome street and into the arms of the proper girl." Unfortunately, Mark is only half-Jewish (his father, Haskell, is the famous cinematographer), and not religious: "You'd have to convert," she says.

So far the film has played like a straightforward documentary: Irene is the subject and Mark is the filmmaker. But Irene breaks the fourth wall and talks directly to Mark—ignoring his attempt to use the camera as a prop and shield. Mark meets a few of Irene's clients and follows them with his camera, even starting to date one, Nancy. Eventually he tells her it's not working out. "I see your pattern," Irene says: "A few kicks, and a clean getaway."

Wexler flies to California for his mother's birthday, and to get some distance from the film. On the beach at Malibu, he meets Sherry, forty-three, and they are strongly attracted to one another. "I'd love to meet her," Irene says. Sherry flies to Chicago, where Irene tells her, "My No. 1 priority is to see Mark married."

As she prepares a meal for them, Sherry observes, "This is very funny. This is like a mother and son thing." Irene says quietly, "Actually, we're lovers." Cut to Sherry doing a very peculiar double take. Exit Sherry.

"I didn't like her," Irene tells Mark. "I didn't like anything about her. A face is a mask. If you marry the most beautiful girl in the world and she turns out to be a bitch and a nag, she is gonna look like the ugliest thing that was ever dug up."

*Me and My Matchmaker* never quite says what conclusions it is discovering. We can draw our own. The movie is narrated by Wexler, who does not have a career ahead of him doing voice-overs; he sounds stilted, like he's reading. But he is the right person for this sound track, because he's arriving at insights about himself.

Through Irene, he meets Terry, and likes her. They date, although Irene disapproves ("She came to me to find a Jewish man to marry"). At one point Terry looks into Mark's camera and says, "Maybe you're just doing this to meet women."

"Am I?" Mark asks himself. "The documentary has turned into something else—or does Irene have something to do with it?" She does. "Something strange has happened between us," Irene tells him. "I felt a connection with you that first day we met." If he meets the right girl, "When you get married, is she going to take my place?"

Watching the last ten minutes of the film is like walking on eggshells. Mark is obviously a hit-and-run specialist, who has spent his life in a perfectionist's quest for the unattainable "goddess." Irene has seen all this before, and understands Mark. But does she understand herself?

The film is amazing and touching in the way it allows people to reveal themselves on camera, to think aloud. After it's over, we stand back and review what happened. A man started to make a documentary about someone else, and ended by making a documentary about himself. Irene turned into the filmmaker and Mark turned into the subject. And there is more. In the last moments of the film we are reminded that the heart is indeed a lonely hunter, and that the hunt never ends.

## Meet the Deedles ★ ½

PG, 90 m., 1998

Steve Van Wormer (Stew Deedle), Paul Walker (Phil Deedle), A. J. Langer (Jesse Ryan), John Ashton (Captain Douglas Pine), Dennis Hopper (Frank Slater), Eric Braeden (Elton Deedle), Richard Lineback (Crabbe), Robert Englund (Nemo). Directed by Steve Boyum and produced by Dale Pollock and Aaron Meyerson. Screenplay by Jim Herzfeld.

The cult of stupidity is irresistible to teenagers in a certain mood. It's a form of rebellion, maybe: If the real world is going to reject them, then they'll simply refuse to get it. Using jargon and incomprehension as weapons, they'll create their own alternate universe.

All of which is a tortuous way to explain *Meet the Deedles,* a movie with no other ambition than to create mindless slapstick and generate a series in the tradition of the *Bill and Ted* movies. The story involves twin brothers Stew and Phil Deedle (Steve Van Wormer and Paul Walker), slackers from Hawaii who find themselves in the middle of a fiendish plot to sabotage Old Faithful in Yellowstone National Park.

As the movie opens, Stew and Phil are hanging beneath a balloon being towed above the Hawaiian surf, while being pursued by a truant officer on a Jet Ski. Soon they're called on the carpet before their millionaire father (Eric Braeden), who snorts, "You will one day take over the entire Deedles empire—and you are surf bums!" His plan: Send them to Camp Broken Spirit, a monthlong experience in outdoor living that will turn them into men.

Through plot developments unnecessary to relate, the Deedles escape the camp experience, are mistaken for Park Ranger recruits, come under the command of Ranger Pine (John Ashton), and stumble onto the solution to a mysterious infestation of prairie dogs.

Now prairie dogs can be cute, as anyone who has seen Disney's *The Living Prairie* nature documentary can testify. But in large numbers they look alarmingly like herds of rats, and the earth trembles (slightly) as they scurry across the park. Why so many prairie dogs? Because an evil ex-ranger named Slater (Dennis Hopper) has trained them to burrow out a cavern around Old Faithful, allowing him to redirect the geyser's boiling waters in the direction of New Faithful, to which he plans to sell tickets.

Hopper lives in the cavern, relaxing in his E-Z-Boy recliner and watching the surface on TV monitors. His sidekicks include Nemo, played by Robert Englund, Freddy of the *Nightmare on Elm Street* pictures. At one point he explains how he trained the prairie dogs, and I will add to my permanent memory bank the sound of Dennis Hopper saying, "Inject kibble into the dirt, and a-tunneling they would go." Study his chagrin when the Deedles employ Mentholatum Deep Heat Rub as a weapon in this war.

While he schemes, the Deedles fumble and blunder their way through ranger training, and Phil falls for Jesse (A. J. Langer), the pretty stepdaughter of Ranger Pine. There are a lot of stunts, involving mountains, truck crashes, and river rapids, and then the big showdown over Old Faithful. The Deedles relate to everything in surfer terms (plowing into a snowbank, they cry, "We've landed in a Slurpy!").

I am prepared to imagine a theater full of eleven-year-old boys who might enjoy this movie, but I can't recommend it for anyone who might have climbed a little higher on the evolutionary ladder. The *Bill and Ted* movies had a certain sly self-awareness that this one lacks. Maybe that's a virtue. Maybe it isn't.

## Men in Black ★ ★ ★

PG-13, 98 m., 1997

Tommy Lee Jones (K), Will Smith (J), Linda Fiorentino (Laurel), Vincent D'Onofrio (Edgar), Rip Torn (Zed), Tony Shalhoub (Jeebs), Siobhan Fallon (Beatrice). Directed by Barry Sonnenfeld and produced by Walter F. Parkes and Laurie MacDonald. Screenplay by Ed Solomon.

There is a moment in *Men in Black* when a grim government official shows a wall chart of "every alien on Earth." We're not too surprised to see some of the faces on display: Sylvester Stallone, Al Roker, Newt Gingrich, Dionne Warwick. (When the movie comes out on video, I'll use freeze frames to capture the rest.) Wicked little side jokes like that are the heart and soul of *Men in Black* (or *MiB*, as it is already being called, no doubt in the movie title-as-software tradition of *ID4*).

A lot of big-budget special-effects films are a hair this side of self-parody and don't know it. *Men in Black* knows it and glories in it; it's a refreshing Bronx cheer aimed at movies that think $100 million budgets equal solemnity. This is not a film about superheroes, but the adventures of a couple of hardworking functionaries whose assignment is to keep tabs on the sizable alien population of the United States.

Tommy Lee Jones, never more serious, unsmiling, and businesslike, stars as K, the veteran agent of Division 6, whose members dress, as William Morris agents used to, in black suits and black ties. The agency is headed by Zed (Rip Torn), who grows alarmed at the latest threat to Earth's sovereignty, and assigns K a young assistant code-named J (Will Smith).

Their biggest problem materializes when a flying saucer strikes the truck of a hillbilly named Edgar (Vincent D'Onofrio), and the alien inside occupies his body, none too comfortably.

Imagine Orson Welles in a suit of armor and you will have a rough approximation of how easily the Edgar-alien inhabits his skin.

The running gag in the movie is that almost anyone could be an alien; the film begins on the Mexican border, where Jones takes charge of a group of lawmen who have nabbed some illegal aliens, and picks out the one who is *really* an alien: a fantastical, blobby, bug-eyed monster with a realistic human face mask.

The special effects are by Industrial Light and Magic, and the aliens are by Rick Baker, perhaps Hollywood's greatest creator of monsters. Here he goes hog-wild. Instead of being asked to create one alien race, he's been assigned to create a galaxy-full, and every one is a new surprise. There were times I thought we were seeing the new seven dwarfs: Slimy, Gooey, Icky, Creepy, Sticky, Barfy, and Pox.

The plot (if there can be said to be one, and if I understood it) involves Edgar's scheme to somehow use a captured galaxy to conquer Earth. Although aliens would presumably be more advanced than we laggards on Earth, many of these aliens seem to have advanced only to the approximate level of the Three Stooges, and are vanquished by a series of bizarre weapons employed by J and K (you may have seen the previews: "Any idea how to use this?" "None whatsoever").

Linda Fiorentino, still looking for the right role to follow her triumph in *The Last Seduction*, hasn't found it here—but her hard-bitten coroner will do nicely as an intermediate step. Performing autopsies on some of these creatures is a process much like dissecting very old spinach lasagna.

The movie makes good use of a lot of New York landmarks (there's a chase through the Guggenheim, a flying saucer lands in Shea Stadium, and another one has been disguised as an exhibit at the 1964 World's Fair). Director Barry Sonnenfeld (*The Addams Family* and its sequel) shows a cheerful willingness in the movie's first hour or so to completely cut loose from all conventions of dreary storytelling and simply let the story follow the laughs and absurdities. Writer Ed Solomon, who on the basis of this irreverent screenplay could probably play all three of the critics on MST3K, deflates one sci-fi pomposity after another.

When the plot finally does click in, it slows down the trajectory a little, but not fatally. *Men in Black* expands on the tradition of big-budget action pictures that at least have the wit to know how silly they are. ☞

## Men With Guns ★ ★ ★ ★

R, 128 m., 1998

Federico Luppi (Dr. Fuentes), Damian Delgado (Domingo, the Soldier), Dan Rivera Gonzalez (Conejo, the Boy), Tania Cruz (Graciela, the Mute Girl), Damian Alcazar (Padre Portillo, the Priest), Mandy Patinkin (Andrew), Kathryn Grody (Harriet). Directed by John Sayles and produced by R. Paul Miller and Maggie Renzi. Screenplay by Sayles.

*Men With Guns* tells the story of a doctor in an unnamed Central American country who makes a trip into the rain forest to visit the young medical students he trained some years earlier. They were supposed to fan out among the Indian villages, fighting tapeworm and other scourges. The doctor has reason to believe many of them have been killed.

The doctor's journey is enlarged by John Sayles into an allegory about all countries where men with guns control the daily lives of the people. Some of the men are with the government, some are guerrillas, some are thieves, some are armed to protect themselves, and to the ordinary people it hardly matters: The man with the gun does what he wants, and his reasons are irrelevant—unknown perhaps even to himself.

The film takes the form of a journey, sometimes harrowing, sometimes poetic. It has a backbone of symbolism, as many great stories do. As the doctor moves from the city to the country, from the shore to the mountains, he also moves through history. We see the ruins of older civilizations that lived in this land, and we see powerless villagers moved here and there according to arbitrary whims. They are killed by the military for helping the guerrillas, and killed by the guerrillas for helping the military, and their men are killed simply because they are men without guns. There is no suggestion that either military or guerrillas have any larger program than to live well off the spoils of power.

The doctor (Federico Luppi), tall and white-haired, has a grave dignity. He is not an action hero, but a man who has been given a pass in life;

while he has lived comfortably in the capital with a nice practice, his country's reality has passed him by. As he ventures into the countryside, he gathers four traveling companions. There is an army deserter, now a thief, who first steals from him, then joins him. A former priest ("his church calls it liberation theology, but he preferred to liberate himself"). A young boy who knows the area better than any of them and has an uncanny ability to judge the essence of a situation. And a woman who has not spoken since she was raped.

The critic Tom Keogh suggests that there is an element of *The Wizard of Oz* in the doctor and his companions, who need a heart, a voice, and courage. There are also suggestions of *Treasure of the Sierra Madre* and other stories in which a legendary goal—Oz, gold, El Dorado—is said to be hidden further on. In this case the travelers begin to hear about a village named "The Circle of Heaven," which is so high on a mountain and so deep in the trees that the helicopters cannot find it, and people live free. Sayles tells his story in a series of vignettes—encounters on the road, stories told, flashbacks of earlier experiences, a touch of magic realism.

From time to time, the travelers and their journey are interrupted by two other characters, chatty American tourists (Mandy Patinkin and Kathryn Grody) who are looking for "antiques" and haven't a clue about the reality of the land and people behind them.

The tourists serve a satirical purpose, but I found myself seeing them in a different light. From time to time, reviewing a movie, I'll say the leading characters were shallow but the people in the background seemed interesting. In that sense, *Men With Guns* is about the background. Sayles finances his own films. If he had taken this script to a studio executive, he no doubt would have been told to beef up the American tourist roles and cast the roles with stars. The film would have become an action sitcom with Indians, doctors, priests, and orphans in the background as local color.

If you doubt me, look again at *Medicine Man* (1992), with Sean Connery in the rain forest, or *Anaconda* (1997), with snake-hunters up the Amazon. In my bemusement, every time the American tourists turned up, I thought of them as visitors from the phantom Hollywood revision of this material: magic realism of a different sort. It's as if Sayles is saying, "Here's what the studios would have made this movie into."

When the history of the century's films is written, John Sayles will stand tall as a director who went his own way, made his own films, directed and edited them himself, and operated completely outside the traditional channels of distribution and finance. When we hear Francis Coppola's lament that he has to make a John Grisham film in order to make one of his "own" films, we can only reflect that Sayles has demonstrated that a director can be completely independent if he chooses.

*Men With Guns* is immensely moving and sad, and yet because it dares so much, it is an exhilarating film. It frees itself from specific stories about *this* villain or *that* strategy to stand back and look at the big picture: at societies in collapse because power has been concentrated in the hands of small men made big with guns. I understand guns in war, in hunting, in sport. But when a man feels he needs a gun to leave his house in the morning, I fear that man. I fear his fear. He believes that the only man more powerless than himself is a dead man.

## Mercury Rising ★ ★

R, 108 m., 1998

Bruce Willis (Art Jeffries), Alec Baldwin (Kudrow), Miko Hughes (Simon), Chi McBride (Bizzi Jordan), Kim Dickens (Stacey), Robert Stanton (Dean), Bodhi Pine Elfman (Leo). Directed by Harold Becker and produced by Brian Grazer and Karen Kehela. Screenplay by Lawrence Konner, Ryne Douglas Pearson, and Mark Rosenthal, based on the novel by Pearson.

*Mercury Rising* is about the most sophisticated cryptographic system known to man, and about characters considerably denser than anyone in the audience. Sitting in the dark, our minds idly playing with the plot, we figure out what they should do, how they should do it, and why they should do it, while the characters on the screen strain helplessly against the requirements of the formula.

The movie begins with the two obligatory scenes of most rogue lawman scenarios: (1) Opening hostage situation, in which the hero (Bruce Willis) could have saved the situation if not for his trigger-happy superiors; (2) The calling on the carpet, in which his boss tells the lawman he's being pulled off the job and assigned to grunt duty. "You had it—but the magic's gone," the boss recites. Willis's only friend is a sidekick named Bizzi Jordan (Chi McBride), who has, as is the nature of sidekicks, a wife and child, so that the hero can gaze upon them and ponder his solitude.

Experienced moviegoers will know that in the course of his diminished duties, Willis (playing an FBI man named Jeffries) will stumble across a bigger case. And will try to solve it single-handedly, while he is the object of a police manhunt. And will eventually engage in a hand-to-hand struggle with the sinister man behind the scheme. This struggle will preferably occur in a high place (see "Climbing Killer," from *Ebert's Little Movie Glossary*). Plus, there's a good bet the hero will enlist a good-looking woman who will drop everything for a chance to get shot at while by his side.

The new twist this time is explained by the evil bureaucrat (Alec Baldwin) in one of several lines of dialogue he should have insisted on rewriting: "A nine-year-old has deciphered the most sophisticated cipher system ever known—and he's autistic!?!" Yes, little Simon (Miko Hughes) looks at a word game in a puzzle magazine, and while the sound track emits quasi-computeristic beeping noises, he figures out the code concealed there, and calls the secret phone number, causing two geeks in a safe room to leap about in dismay.

Agents are dispatched to try to kill the kid and his parents, who live in Chicago. FBI agent Jeffries comes late to the scene, eyeballs the dead parents, immediately intuits it wasn't really a murder-suicide ("How's a guy that's so broke afford a $1,500 handgun?"), and then finds Simon hiding in a crawl space. Putting two and two together (without beeping noises), he deduces that Simon knows a secret, and powerful people want to destroy him.

The movie then descends into formula again, with obligatory scenes in which the police guard is mysteriously pulled off duty in a hospital corridor (see *The Godfather*), and Jeffries runs down corridors with the kid under his arm while evil agents demonstrate that no marksman, however well trained, can hit anyone important while there's still an hour to go. (The David Mamet movie *The Spanish Prisoner*, which is as smart as *Mercury Rising* is dumb, has the hero ask a markswoman: "What if you had missed?" and supplies her with the perfect answer: "It would be back to the range for me!")

The movie's greatest test of credibility comes when Jeffries, object of a citywide manhunt, walks into a restaurant in the Wrigley Building, meets a complete stranger named Stacey (Kim Dickens), and asks her to watch the kid for him while he goes on a quick mission. Of course Stacey agrees, and cooperates again when the agent and the kid turn up at her house in the middle of the night and ask for a safe place to stay. Before long, indeed, she's blowing off a business trip to Des Moines because, well, what woman wouldn't instinctively trust an unshaven man in a sweaty T-shirt, with an autistic kid under his arm and a gun in his belt—especially if the cops were after him?

What is sad is that the performances by Willis, Dickens, and young Miko Hughes are really pretty good—better than the material deserves. Willis doesn't overplay or overspeak, which redeems some of the silly material, and Dickens somehow finds a way through the requirements of her role that allows her to sidestep her character's wildly implausible decisions.

But what happened to Alec Baldwin's BS detector? Better replace those batteries! His character utters speeches that are laughable in any context, especially this one: "You know," he says, "my wife says my people skills are like my cooking skills—quick and tasteless." And listen to his silky speech in the rain as he defends his actions.

Here are the two most obvious problems that sentient audiences will have with the plot. (1) Modern encryption cannot be intuitively deciphered, by rainmen or anyone else, without a key. And (2) if a nine-year-old kid can break your code, don't kill the kid; kill the programmers.

## Metro ★ ★ ★

R, 117 m., 1997

Eddie Murphy (Scott Roper), Michael Rapaport (Kevin McCall), Carmen Ejogo (Ronnie Tate), Michael Wincott (Michael Korda), Denis Arndt (Captain Frank Solis), Art Evans (Lieutenant Sam Baffert), Donal Logue (Earl), Paul Ben-Victor (Clarence Teal). Directed by Thomas Carter and produced by Roger Birnbaum. Screenplay by Randy Feldman.

In formula action pictures, there are always setup scenes early in the movie that trigger payoff scenes later on. *Metro* is a movie so preoccupied with its chases, stunts, and special effects that it never gets around to the payoffs. That's not a criticism, just an observation. Leave out the setups *and* the payoffs, and you'd have wall-to-wall action, which is the direction I suspect we're heading in.

*Metro* stars Eddie Murphy in a muscular, energetic performance as Roper, a star hostage negotiator for the San Francisco Police Department. He's the guy who walks unarmed into the bank where the robber is holding a gun to a hostage's head, and gets the guy talking. Murphy has always been a good talker, and he has fun with some of this dialogue. Taking a bag of doughnuts in to a manic madman, Roper explains, "I'm duty-bound under my oath as a negotiator to take out this wounded man." And does.

This opening scene of course has nothing to do with the rest of the movie. Action movies always start in the middle of a crisis, establish the hero, and then move into the story. Usually the early crisis is followed by a quiet domestic scene (Roper meets his former girlfriend) and the introduction of the police chief, etc., before another crisis develops. Oh, and the cop has to meet his New Partner.

*Metro* makes all the early stops, which makes it interesting that it never doubles back to refer to them again. For example:

1. Roper gets a new partner named McCall (Michael Rapaport) who is a marathon runner, can lip-read, is a sharpshooter, etc., but has never done hostage negotiations before. The formula calls for the veteran to resent the kid and make it hard for him. Not here. Roper asks his chief for a raise, gets it, and takes the kid to the racetrack.

2. After a friend of Roper's is killed by Korda (Michael Wincott), the movie's homicidal diamond thief, Roper vows revenge. Then, of course, the chief Takes Him Off the Case. Roper continues to chase the guy anyway—no one says a word to reprimand him, and his badge and gun are never taken away.

3. In a mock-up of a grocery store, Roper uses department store mannequins to represent stickup guys, and rehearses his new partner in the methods of handling such a situation. This will inevitably pay off when the kid has to handle such a situation, right? Wrong.

4. Roper is seen as a compulsive gambler. This will have something to do with the plot, right? Wrong again. It's a meaningless character detail.

5. Roper's girlfriend, Ronnie (Carmen Ejogo), has left him for a baseball star. The two men meet briefly, and coldly, at her apartment. Then she gets back with Roper. The baseball player will turn up later, angry and possibly dangerous, right? Nope; he's never seen again.

These aren't loose threads, because the plot doesn't matter anyway. They're simply punctuation marks between the extravagant stunt scenes. The reason to see *Metro* is because it has two ingenious action sequences. One occurs when Korda, fleeing Roper, leaps aboard a San Francisco streetcar and kills the driver. The streetcar speeds downhill out of control, crashing into dozens of cars, and Roper and McCall chase it in a vintage Cadillac before Roper jumps onto the streetcar and McCall steers the Caddy broadside in front of it, slowing it before it plows into dozens of victims at the bottom of the slope.

This is, of course, impossible (the Caddy's tires don't even blow after scraping sideways for a couple of thousand yards), but so what? It's fun, and skillfully directed by Thomas Carter. And there's an ingenious scene later in the film where Ronnie, the hapless girlfriend, is strapped to a piece of machinery that functions in exactly the same way that sawmills did in old silent movies: If Roper takes his hand off the red button, the girl will be cut in two. If he doesn't, he'll be killed. Neat.

The movie also has fun with horror movie clichés. Ronnie keeps closing her bathroom mirror so we can see the killer behind her—and the movie's music swells ominously, but there's no killer. She calls for her dog, and the dog doesn't come. More swelling music. But the dog isn't dead. And *Metro* should get a gold star for being the first movie in the history of San Francisco to stage a chase through Chinatown without having the cars get stuck in the middle of a parade. On the debit side, after Roper knows the villain has escaped jail and vowed revenge, he lets Ronnie go back into her apartment alone. "I'll be right back," she says, when, as the characters in *Scream* observe, hardly anyone who says that ever is.

The movie works well on its chosen level. The

big action scenes are cleverly staged and Eddie Murphy is back on his game again, with a high-energy performance and crisp dialogue. Rapaport makes a good foil—stalwart, with good reaction shots—and Wincott is a smart, creepy killer. There are some nice twists. Perhaps it is even a good thing that this is the first cop buddy movie that uses all the clichés from the first half of the formula and none from the second. It's not like I missed them.

## Michael ★ ★ ★

PG, 105 m., 1996

John Travolta (Michael), Andie MacDowell (Dorothy Winters), William Hurt (Frank Quinlan), Bob Hoskins (Vartan Malt), Robert Pastorelli (Huey Driscoll), Jean Stapleton (Pansy Milbank), Teri Garr (Judge Esther Newberg). Directed by Nora Ephron and produced by Sean Daniel, Ephron, and James Jacks. Screenplay by Ephron, Delia Ephron, Pete Dexter, and Jim Quinlan.

I don't have the exact figures on this, but I'll bet there's not a star in Hollywood who wouldn't jump at the opportunity to play an angel in a movie. What other kind of character (they secretly think) could more completely reflect their true hidden qualities? So popular are angels in Hollywood that one out of every thirty entries in the Microsoft Cinemania CD-ROM mentions them somewhere, and just this season John Travolta, Denzel Washington, and Dolly Parton have played them in new movies.

Travolta's angel is the scruffiest. He needs a shave, smokes a lot, eats his breakfast cereal using the backhanded steam-shovel spoon grip, and lives in the office of the Milk Bottle Motel, somewhere in rural Iowa. He is discovered there, in *Michael,* by three sensation-mongering reporters from a Chicago supermarket scandal sheet, after they get a postcard from the sweet little old lady (Jean Stapleton) who owns the motel.

Is he an angel? Vartan Malt (Bob Hoskins), the editor of the *National Mirror,* doesn't much care, as long as he has wings and will pose with Sparky, the little dog that is the paper's beloved mascot. (Sparky has already posed with President Clinton, Santa Claus and, very recently, Elvis.)

Sparky's master, much less popular with the paper than the dog, is Huey Driscoll (Robert Pastorelli), a disgraced former reporter for the *Chicago Tribune* who was fired for socking the managing editor. (One of the screenplay writers is Jim Quinlan, formerly of the *Chicago Sun-Times,* so perhaps a little displacement is going on here.) Huey's investigative partner is Frank Quinlan (William Hurt), a laid-back type who realizes the only way to survive a job like his is with perpetual bemusement.

As Huey and Frank are preparing to leave for Iowa, they're saddled with a newcomer: Dorothy Winters (Andie MacDowell), thrice-divorced "angel expert," whom the editor assigns to join the reporting team. All of this is curiously muted; one expects the editor of a trash tabloid to not only be apoplectic (as Hoskins usually is) but also sleazy and corrupt. Not a chance. I actually had the impression that this editor and his staff more or less believed the stories they published, in a way, sort of.

The heart of the movie takes place in Iowa, and is hard to describe, because it consists more of mood than of plot. The movie evokes Michael as a character of whimsical, petulant, brilliant, perplexing charm. Travolta plays the angel as a tourist who has grown fond of Earth during many previous visits, and regrets that this one is his last blast: "There are only so many visits allowed." Michael's previous visits to Earth have been eventful. On one of them, he explains, "I invented standing in line." Learning that the three visitors are reporters, he says, "I'm a writer, too." "What did you write?" they ask. "Psalm 85. Of course, they weren't numbered then."

Michael's relationship with Pansy Milbank (Stapleton) is based on fondness and comfortability, and maybe a slightly more spiritual bond; it's left to the audience to discover exactly why he chose that rural motel for his earthly arrival. His mission, he says, is to help Frank rediscover his heart, and Frank does, with the help of Dorothy. Like so many movie lovers, they quarrel all the way into each other's arms.

A lot of the good things in the movie are charmingly inconsequential, as when MacDowell sings a Randy Newman song about pie, or when Travolta starts dancing to "Chain of Fools" in a roadhouse, and all of the women are drawn magically onto the floor with him. The closing scenes are a wink at movie clichés; without revealing what happens to little Sparky, I will say that his eventual fate will be easily predictable for any student of movie dogs.

*Michael* doesn't set up big drama or punch up big moments. It ambles. Travolta, using the same offhand ease that worked in *Phenomenon,* works his magic on the humans without even seeming to have his mind much on his job. He's more concerned with his farewell tour of Earth's pleasures. There's even an offscreen scene where he apparently does have hanky-panky with a judge (Teri Garr). Angels, of course, have no sexual feelings, but tell that to the angel. Or the judge.

## Michael Collins ★ ★ ★

R, 138 m., 1996

Liam Neeson (Michael Collins), Aidan Quinn (Harry Boland), Julia Roberts (Kitty Kiernan), Stephen Rea (Ned Broy), Alan Rickman (Eamon De Valera), Ian Hart (Joe O'Reilly), Richard Ingram (British Officer), John Kenny (Patrick Pearse). Directed by Neil Jordan and produced by Stephen Woolley. Screenplay by Jordan.

"History will record the greatness of Michael Collins," the Irish president and patriot Eamon De Valera said as an old man in 1966, "and it will be recorded at my expense." Yes, and perhaps justly so, but even "Dev" could hardly have imagined this film biography of Collins, which paints De Valera as a weak, mannered, sniveling prima donna whose grandstanding led to decades of unnecessary bloodshed in, and over, Ireland.

*Michael Collins* paints a heroic picture of the Irish Republican Army's inspired strategist and military leader, who fought the British Empire to a standstill and invented the techniques of urban guerrilla warfare that shaped revolutionary struggles all over the world. Played by Liam Neeson in a performance charged with zest and conviction, Collins comes across as a clear-sighted innovator who took the IRA as far as it could reasonably hope to go, and then signed a treaty with the British that was, he argued, "the best we can hope for at this moment in time."

The treaty established an Irish Free State, but it preserved the division of Ireland into north and south, and it fell short of the independent republic the IRA had been fighting for. Collins felt that additional negotiations over a period of years could eventually produce those gains; he and his comrades were weary of bloodshed.

But De Valera (played with shifty conceit by Alan Rickman) refused to support the treaty, and his decision led to an Irish civil war and, indirectly, to the assassination of Collins. And today IRA bomb blasts still rock London, and the peace that Collins hoped for has come only from time to time.

Was De Valera (who led Ireland in various offices for most of the years between 1932 and 1973) really responsible for all these tragic consequences? Some argue so, but others will find that *Michael Collins,* in need of an Irish villain to balance the British enemy and explain the death of Collins, makes Dev into a weaker and more devious man than he ever was. The film even implies, without quite saying so, that Dev was aware of, or at least not adverse to, the plot against Collins.

Such questions will be much debated in Ireland, where the minutiae of IRA politics and strategy are a cottage industry. For audiences elsewhere in the world, the facts in *Michael Collins* will be less interesting than the characters and the myths, and on that basis Neil Jordan's movie functions well, giving us a folk hero known throughout Ireland as "The Big Fella," who even with a price of £10,000 on his head was able to bicycle through Dublin in immunity.

Partly that was because few knew, until he went to London to negotiate the peace treaty, quite what Michael Collins looked like. There is a scene in the movie where Collins audaciously presents himself at midnight to British Army headquarters, says he is an informer, gains entrance, and works with an insider (Stephen Rea) to copy out secret information on British security forces.

The film, which has the look and feel of authenticity, opens with a one-sided British victory over IRA troops that tried to occupy Dublin's Main Post Office. Collins sees, correctly, that if the IRA adopts conventional tactics it will be destroyed by the British troops, and so he argues for a strategy in which IRA men melt into the crowds, are indistinguishable from civilians, and disappear after sudden strikes. This approach is good enough to force the British to the negotiating table (despite the intransigence of Churchill), even though De

Valera continues to argue for more conventional methods; he seems to feel diminished by not leading a proper-looking army.

The movie moves confidently when it focuses on Collins and his best friend and co-strategist Harry Boland (Aidan Quinn). But it falters with the unnecessary character of Kitty Kiernan (Julia Roberts), who is in love with both men, and they with her. "I was ahead by a length," Harry tells her in one scene. "Now where am I?" She shakes her head: "It's not a race, Harry. You without him . . . him without you . . . I can't imagine it." The movie uses the scenes with Kitty to provide obligatory romantic interludes between war and strategy, but even though Kitty was a historical character, we never feel the scenes are necessary; they function as a sop to the audience, not as additional drama.

Collins, who died at thirty-one, was arguably the key figure in the struggles that led to the separation of Ireland and Britain. He was also, on the basis of this film, a man able to use violence without becoming intoxicated by it. The film argues that if he had prevailed, Ireland might eventually have been united, and many lives might have been saved. We will never know. But De Valera was right. History has judged Collins at his expense.

## Microcosmos ★ ★ ★ ★

G, 77 m., 1997

A documentary directed by Claude Nuridsany and Marie Perennou and produced by Galatee Films, Jacques Perrin, Christophe Barratier, and Yvette Mallet. Screenplay by Nuridsany and Perrenou.

There are so many different insect species that there's a famous biologists' quip: Essentially *all* species are insects. Their biomass—the combined weight of the creepy-crawly things—is many times greater than the combined weight of everything else that swims, flies, walks, and makes movies. Insects are the great success story on planet Earth; they were here before we arrived and will remain long after we've gone, inhabiting their worlds of mindless and intricate beauty.

Children, being built nearer to the ground and having more time on their hands, are close observers of ants and spiders, caterpillars and butterflies. Adults tune them out; bugs are things you slap, swat, step on, or spray. *Microcosmos* is an amazing film that allows us to peer deeply into the insect world, and marvel at creatures we casually condemn to squishing. The makers of this film took three years to design their close-up cameras and magnifying lenses, and to photograph insects in such brilliant detail that if they were cars we could read their city stickers.

The movie is a work of art and whimsy as much as one of science. It uses only a handful of words, but is generous with music and amplified sound effects, dramatizing the unremitting struggle of survival that goes on in a meadow in France. If a camera could somehow be transported to another planet, there to photograph alien life forms, would the result be any more astonishing than these invasions into the private lives of snails and bees, mantises and beetles, spiders and flies?

Where did these forms come from? These legs—two, four, six, a thousand? Eyes like bombardiers' turrets? Giant pincers? Honeyed secretions? Metamorphosis from a wormy crawling thing into a glorious flying thing? Grasshoppers that look like plants, and beetles that look like ants? Every one of these amazing creatures represents a successful Darwinian solution to the problem of how to reproduce and make a living. And so do we.

One beautiful creature after another takes the screen. There is a parade of caterpillars. A dung beetle, tirelessly moving his treasure. Two snails engaging in a long and very loving wet kiss. Spiders methodically capturing and immobilizing their prey (what a horrible fate; does the victim understand what has happened to it?). Ants construct lives of meticulous order and then a hungry bird comes along and gobbles up thousands of them. More ants construct more anthills, flawless in design and function, and then the hills are bombed by raindrops that look to them as big as beach balls.

There is a fight to the death between two beetles, and their struggle looks as gargantuan as the battling dinosaurs in *Jurassic Park*. There are tiny insects who live in, on, and for the nectar supplied by plants that are perfectly designed for them. Ladybugs seem so ill-designed to fly that every takeoff looks like a clumsy miracle; do they get sweaty palms? Overhead there is a towering canopy of jungle foliage, consisting of the grasses and flowers of the meadow.

*Microcosmos* is in a category of its own. There is no other film like it. If the movies allow us to see places we have not been and people we do not know, then *Microcosmos* dramatically extends the range of our vision, allowing us to see the world of the creatures who most completely and enduringly inhabit Earth.

Sometimes the close-up cameras are almost embarrassingly intimate; should we blush to see these beings engaged in their crucial daily acts of dining, loving, fighting, being born, and dying? You may leave this movie feeling a little like a god. Or like a big, inelegant and energy-inefficient hunk of clunky design. Of course, we're smart and they're not. We know the insects exist, and they don't know we exist. Or need to.

## Midnight in the Garden of Good and Evil ★ ★ ½

R, 154 m., 1997

Kevin Spacey (Jim Williams), John Cusack (John Kelso), Jack Thompson (Sonny Seiler), The Lady Chablis (Herself), Alison Eastwood (Mandy Nichols), Irma P. Hall (Minerva), Paul Hipp (Joe Odom), Jude Law (Billy Hanson). Directed by Clint Eastwood and produced by Eastwood and Arnold Stiefel. Screenplay by John Lee Hancock, based on the book by John Berendt.

*Midnight in the Garden of Good and Evil* is a book that exists as a conspiracy between the author and the reader: John Berendt paints a portrait of a city so eccentric, so dripping with Southern Gothic weirdness, that it can't survive for long when it's removed from the life-support system of our imagination. Clint Eastwood's film is a determined attempt to be faithful to the book's spirit, but something ineffable is lost just by turning on the camera: Nothing we see can be as amazing as what we've imagined.

The book tells the story of a New York author who visits Savannah, Georgia, is bewitched, and takes an apartment there. Gradually he meets the local fauna, including a gay antiques dealer, a piano bar owner of no fixed abode, a drag queen, a voodoo sorceress, a man who keeps flies on leashes, a man who walks an invisible dog, and the members of the Married Women's Card Club. The plot grows labyrinthine after the antiques dealer is charged with the murder of a young hustler.

Berendt introduces these people and tells their stories in a bemused, gossipy fashion; he's a natural storyteller who knows he has great stories to tell and relishes the telling. He is not, however, really a major player in the book, and the movie makes a mistake by assigning its central role to a New York writer, now named John Kelso, through whose hands all of the action must pass.

There is nothing wrong with the performance by John Cusack except that it is unnecessary; if John Lee Hancock's screenplay had abandoned the Kelso character and just jumped into the midst of Savannah's menagerie with both feet, the movie might have had more energy and color. Or if Kelso had been a weird character, too, that might have helped; he's written and played as a flat, bland witness, whose tentative love affair with a local temptress (Alison Eastwood) is so abashed we almost wonder if he's ever dated before.

Berendt's nonfiction book (the credits inexplicably call it a novel) circulates with amusement and incredulity among unforgettable characters. But the screenplay whacks the anecdotal material into shape to fit the crime-and-courtroom genre. A doped-up young bisexual hothead (Jude Law) is introduced in two overplayed scenes, and then found dead on the floor of the antiques dealer's office. His death inspired an unprecedented four trials in real life, which the movie can be excused for reducing to one—but as the conventions of courtroom melodrama take over, what makes Savannah unique is gradually lost sight of. Jack Thompson gives a solid performance as Sonny Seiler, the defense attorney, but he's from Grisham territory, not Savannah.

The characters in the book live with such vivid energy that it's a shame we see them only in their relations with Kelso, the quiet outsider (there's hardly a scene in the movie of the locals talking to each other without the Yankee witness). Kevin Spacey plays Jim Williams, the antiques dealer, who holds two Christmas parties—one so famous that *Town & Country* magazine has assigned Kelso to cover it, and another, the night before, "for bachelors only." Spacey's performance is built on a comfortable drawl, perfect timing, a cigar as a prop, and the actor's own twinkling warmth: We like Jim

Williams so much we're surprised we don't see more of him. "What money I have," he explains, "is about eleven years old. Yes, I am 'nouveau riche'—but it's the 'riche' that counts."

Kelso also encounters The Lady Chablis, a drag queen played by the real Lady Chablis, who specializes in shocking the bourgeoisie. She has some one-liners that are real zingers, but her big scene—crashing the black debutante ball to embarrass Kelso—is a scene so lacking in focus and structure that it brings the movie to a halt. My guess is that The Lady Chablis would be well known to the black middle class of Savannah (where everybody knows everybody), and the blank stares she gathers make you realize the scene lacks setup, purpose, and payoff.

Another colorful character in the book is Joe Odom, who makes himself at home as an unpaid (and unauthorized) "house-sitter" in historic mansions, supporting himself as the host of the longest-running house party in Georgia. He's a charmer who has the misfortune to be dating Mandy Nichols (Alison Eastwood), and so the movie has to hustle him out of sight to free Mandy for her frictionless dalliance with Kelso—who mutters vaguely about his "track record" in romance, and has to be instructed to kiss her after their first date. What's the point?

Much is made of Minerva (Irma P. Hall), the voodoo priestess, who casts hexes against the prosecuting attorneys and leads midnight forays into local cemeteries. In the book some local residents, Jim Williams included, halfway believe in her magic; in the movie, she comes across more as a local eccentric.

In a way, the filmmakers faced the same hopeless task as the adapters of Tom Wolfe's *The Bonfire of the Vanities.* The Berendt book, on best-seller lists for three years, has made such a vivid impression that any mere mortal version of it is doomed to pale. Perhaps only the documentarian Errol Morris, who specializes in the incredible variety of the human zoo, could have done justice to the material.

Still, I enjoyed the movie at a certain level simply as illustration: I was curious to see The Lady Chablis, and the famous old Mercer House where the murders took place, and the Spanish moss. But the movie never reached takeoff speed; its energy was dissipated by being filtered through the deadpan character of Kelso. They say people who hadn't read *The Bonfire of the Vanities* liked the movie more than those who knew the book. Maybe the same thing will happen with *Midnight.*

## Mimic ★ ★ ★ ½

R, 104 m., 1997

Mira Sorvino (Susan Tyler), Jeremy Northam (Peter Mann), Alexander Goodwin (Chuy), Giancarlo Giannini (Manny), Charles S. Dutton (Leonard), Josh Brolin (Josh), Alix Koromzay (Remy), F. Murray Abraham (Dr. Gates). Directed by Guillermo Del Toro and produced by Bob Weinstein, B. J. Rack, and Ole Bornedal. Screenplay by Matthew Robbins and Del Toro, based on the short story "Mimic" by Donald A. Wolheim.

There is a sense in which *Mimic* is exactly the same movie as *Event Horizon,* which is exactly the same movie as *The Relic,* which like many other movies was descended from *Alien,* which itself was the child of a well-established horror tradition.

All of these movies, and there are hundreds more, follow a formula in which a pseudoscientific setup in the opening act leads to a series of scenes in which the heroes are trapped (in a subway system, spaceship, tunnel, etc.) with a new and terrifying monster in a form not previously known to man, and the monster leaps out of hiding at them in ways long known to special-effects technicians.

One does not attend *Mimic* hoping for more than a few new twists on the durable old idea; such movies, like thrill rides at parks, work every single time if they have been well planned and constructed. But *Mimic* is superior to most of its cousins, and has been stylishly directed by Guillermo Del Toro, whose visual sense adds a certain texture that makes everything scarier and more effective. It's not often that a movie like this can frighten me, but I was surprised how effective *Mimic* was.

The film begins with ominous reports of a plague that has devastated Manhattan, claiming mostly young children. It is spread by cockroaches, and Mira Sorvino plays a scientist named Susan Tyler who, with her colleagues, is able to use genetic engineering to create the "Judas Breed," a designer bug (half-mantis, half-termite) that can mimic cockroaches, infiltrate their strongholds, and kill them. Soon the plague has ended, three years have passed, and apparently those new little bugs (which were supposed to be sterile) have kept right on evolving.

This is all pretty standard stuff. Originality is in the details. Del Toro, whose movie *Cronos* (1992) was about a nasty little antique metal vampire bug, creates thrills by manipulating human nature. We're all squeamish about sticking our hands into unseen dark places where something might bite us. We're all concerned when we see children who don't know they're in danger. We're instinctively frightened when an entity looks like one thing and suddenly reveals itself as something else.

Del Toro touches all of those bases. The hand reaching into darkness had me sliding down in my seat. I liked the two little kids who are bug collectors and know their way around the subway system. And there's a shoeshine man's kid who clicks spoons together in such a way that he mimics the clicking sounds of the Judas Breed. That sets up an expectation that sooner or later the kid will send the wrong (or right) message by accident. Tactical suspense like that is hard to create, but effective: As Hitchcock pointed out, it's more fun to wait for a payoff than to see one.

As for the insect predators, what they have learned to mimic, and how they do it, provides one of the best payoff shots in the movie. There is also a visual intrigue in the locations. Instead of locking us forever into dark, claustrophobic tunnels, Del Toro creates an abandoned subway station with a vaulted ceiling and overhead windows; we could be somewhere on the Paris Metro. There's a shot where a character, trapped below, can look up and see people walking in the daylight above—so close, and so far away. And an old subway car provides a useful prop.

Mira Sorvino's casting in the role of the scientist has been questioned in some quarters, perhaps because she is remembered as the ditzy hooker in Woody Allen's *Mighty Aphrodite*. But here she comes across as the smart but unfocused graduate student who knows everything and hopes she got it right. (I liked the scene where she grabs insect goo and tells her friends, "Here! Rub it all over yourself!") Jeremy Northam plays her husband, also a scientist; Charles S. Dutton is a subway guard with a lot of information about the underground system, and Giancarlo Giannini is the shoeshine man.

There are expected payoffs, yes, and the usual scenes where a false shock is followed by a real one. *Mimic* is a loyal occupant of its genre. But Del Toro is a director with a genuine visual sense, with a way of drawing us into his story and evoking the mood with the very look and texture of his shots. He takes the standard ingredients and presents them so effectively that *Mimic* makes the old seem new, fresh, and scary.

## The Mirror Has Two Faces ★ ★ ★

PG-13, 126 m., 1996

Barbra Streisand (Rose Morgan), Jeff Bridges (Gregory Larkin), Lauren Bacall (Hannah Morgan), George Segal (Henry Fine), Mimi Rogers, (Claire), Pierce Brosnan (Alex), Brenda Vaccaro (Doris), Austin Pendleton (Barry). Directed by Barbra Streisand and produced by Streisand and Arnon Milchan. Screenplay by Richard LaGravenese, based on the film *Le Miroir a Deux Faces.*

Barbra Streisand's new film *The Mirror Has Two Faces* approaches the subject of marriage warily and with wit, like a George Bernard Shaw play; two articulate people talk circles around love for two acts before falling exhausted before the biological imperative in the third. Streisand plays Rose, a professor of literature who has more or less given up on her marriage prospects, when she meet Gregory (Jeff Bridges), a man she really likes. He really likes her too. The key words are "really likes," which are not the same as "really loves."

Rose, fortyish in the movie, is in the dumps because of the marriage of her sister (Mimi Rogers) to a handsome new husband (Pierce Brosnan). Rose's own dating circle seems to be limited to a nerd with an infectious grin (Austin Pendleton). Her sister, in desperation, answers a lonely hearts ad, and Rose and Gregory find themselves out on a date together.

Gregory is the kind of man who believes he cannot function well if he's in love. In an awkward and unconvincing early scene, he is giving a talk on mathematical theory when he spots his ex-wife in the audience, falters, blathers, and flees from the stage. Desperate, he calls a phone sex line (for advice, not sex) and that leads to his lonely hearts ad and the big first date with Rose, at which he exclaims "Beautiful!" as he looks at the sound waves on an oscilloscope while attending a concert.

Later, they discuss prime numbers. He is amazed by how smart she is. She is amazed by how much she is attracted to him. So attracted that when he proposes marriage she agrees to his terms: no sex, no physical affection, just "a meeting of two minds"—respect and friendship and none of that messy stuff to get in the way. This works for a while, until she gets carried away and puts on a sexy nightgown, and he locks himself in the bathroom.

The screenplay, by Richard LaGravenese, based on an earlier French film, is like a Shaw play—*Pygmalion*, in fact, except that this Higgins has nothing to teach his Eliza, and she has everything to teach him. It's rare to find a film that deals intelligently with issues of sex and love, instead of just assuming that everyone on the screen and in the audience shares the same popular culture assumptions.

It's rare, too, to find such verbal characters in a movie, and listening to them talk is one of the pleasures of *The Mirror Has Two Faces.* There is a wonderful scene in which Rose and her mother (Lauren Bacall) discuss beauty. We see a photograph of Bacall at about the age of twenty, and we see Bacall now, beautiful in a different way but old, and the daughter asks, "How did it feel? Being beautiful?" "It was wonderful," her mother says, and we get the eerie and magical sense that we are hearing Streisand and Bacall discussing this. The mother then produces a photo of a cute baby, which Streisand assumes is of her sister. But it's a picture of herself. "You were such a beautiful baby," the mother says, and Rose says, "Thanks for showing me this picture, Mom." It is a great scene.

It leads to a dependable movie cliché, in which Rose transforms herself through exercise, wardrobe, and makeup, into a beauty. Gregory has left after the awkward sex showdown, but now he wants to come back, and she thinks maybe she can seduce him. Transformation scenes are standard in the movies, but this one pays off in an unexpected way, leading to a payoff the movie works hard for, and earns.

Some quibbles. Where is Streisand's family from? Streisand speaks with her usual New York accent, Bacall sounds mid-Atlantic, and Mimi Rogers sounds WASP as the sister. And although the Streisand character is articulate and intelligent in most scenes, her intelligence level falters in the key scene intended to establish it, as she lectures her Columbia lit students. She comes across more like an inspirational after-dinner speaker with a stand-up comic's style than like a literature professor; in today's better schools, the students would quickly pass the word that she was a lightweight showboat.

On balance, though, this is a moving and challenging movie, fascinated by the murky depths that separate what people want from what they say they want and what they think they should want.

## Mission: Impossible ★ ★ ★

PG-13, 105 m., 1996

Tom Cruise (Ethan Hunt), Jon Voight (Jim Phelps), Emmanuelle Béart (Claire), Henry Czerny (Kittridge), Jean Reno (Krieger), Ving Rhames (Luther), Kristin Scott-Thomas (Sarah Davies), Vanessa Redgrave (Max). Directed by Brian De Palma and produced by Tom Cruise and Paula Wagner. Screenplay by David Koepp and Robert Towne.

I'm not sure I could pass a test on the plot of *Mission: Impossible.* My consolation is that the screenwriters probably couldn't, either. The story is a nearly impenetrable labyrinth of post–Cold War double-dealing, but the details hardly matter; it's all a setup for sensational chase sequences and a delicate computer theft operation, intercut with that most reliable of spy movie standbys, the midnight rendezvous under a streetlamp in a chilly foreign capital.

Tom Cruise stars as Ethan Hunt, professional spy, whose assignment, which he chooses to accept, is to prevent the theft of a computer file containing the code names and real identities of all of America's double agents. It's not enough to simply stop the guy; Cruise and his team (also including Jon Voight, Kristin Scott-Thomas, and Emmanuelle Béart) are asked to photograph the enemy in the act of stealing the information, and then follow him until he passes it along. This process involves a checklist of cold war spycraft and clichés: eyeglasses with built-in TV cameras, concealed microphones, laptop computers, agents in elaborate disguise, exploding cars, knifings, shootings, bodies toppling into a river, etc.

Because *Mission: Impossible* was directed by Brian De Palma, a master of genre thrillers and sly Hitchcockian wit *(Blow Out, Body Double),* it's a nearly impossible mission to take the plot seriously. He is more concerned with style than story, which is wise, since if this movie ever paused to explain itself it would take a very long time. There are so many double-reverses in the first half-hour that we learn to accept nothing at face value (not even faces, since they may be elaborate latex masks). And the momentum of the visuals prevents us from asking logical questions, such as, is physically copying a computer file onto another disc the only way to steal it? (My colleague Rich Elias has written that the obvious solution for the CIA would have been to hire Robert Redford's team from *Sneakers* to commit an on-line theft.)

*Mission: Impossible* is all slick surface and technical skill. The characters are not very interesting (except for Vanessa Redgrave, as an information broker, and Jon Voight, who expresses a touching world-weariness in a film too impatient for weariness of any kind). The plot is impossible to follow. The various strategies of Cruise and his allies and foes don't stand up under scrutiny. And none of that matters. This is a movie that exists in the instant, and we must exist in the instant to enjoy it. Any troubling questions from earlier in the film must be firmly repressed.

De Palma is expert at sustained nonverbal action sequences, and there are three in the film: the opening scenario at the diplomatic reception; a delicate act of computer theft; and a chase in which a helicopter follows the high-speed London-Paris train into the Chunnel with Cruise and a bad guy clinging to the top of it.

The computer theft scene will ring a bell with anyone who has seen *Rififi* (1954) or *Topkapi* (1964), both by Jules Dassin, who became famous for his extended theft sequences done in total silence. *Topkapi* also used the device of suspending a thief from a hole in the ceiling to avoid antitheft devices on the floor. This time, De Palma gives us a computer "safe room" rigged so that alarms will sound at any noise above a certain decibel level, any pressure on the floor, any change in temperature. Cruise hangs in a harness while carefully inserting a blank disc and making a copy of the file.

Of course it's convenient that the decibel level is set high enough that it isn't triggered by the noise of a computer copying a disc—which is precisely what it should be guarding against. Convenient, too, that the infrared rays guarding the ceiling hatch can be so conveniently dealt with. And very convenient for the audience that the rays are made visible to a normal eye. If you want to see infrared rays *really* exploited in a heist movie, have a look at *Grand Slam* (1968).

If the heist has been done before and better, not even the James Bond films have ever given us anything quite like the ending chase sequence, with a bad guy in a helicopter flying into the Chunnel linking Britain to France. Earlier it's been established that the train through Britain is traveling so fast that Cruise, clinging to it, might easily be blown off. This will cheer the film's British viewers, who can forget for a moment that the Chunnel train goes that fast only on the French side, since the high-speed tracks on the British side have not yet been completed. (Inaugurating the Chunnel, François Mitterand wickedly described a traveler "speeding through France and then enjoying a leisurely view of the British countryside.") No matter. The train goes fast, and the helicopter follows it right under the Channel, and De Palma's special effects (by Industrial Light and Magic) are clever for obscuring the scale involved, since a helicopter's blades would obviously not fit into the tunnel—but then why am I quibbling, since the whole stunt is obviously impossible?

The bottom line on a film like this is that Tom Cruise looks cool and holds our attention while doing neat things that we don't quite understand—doing them so quickly and with so much style that we put our questions on hold and go with the flow. When the movie is over, it turns out there wasn't anything except the flow. Our consolation, I guess, is that we had fun going with it.

## Mr. Holland's Opus ★ ★ ★ ½

PG, 143 m., 1996

Richard Dreyfuss (Glenn Holland), Glenne Headly (Iris Holland), Jay Thomas (Bill Meister), Olympia Dukakis (Principal Jacobs), W. H. Macy (Vice Principal Wolters), Alicia Witt (Gertrude Lang), Jean Louisa Kelly (Rowena Morgan). Directed by Stephen Herek and produced by Ted

Field, Michael Nolin, and Robert W. Cort. Screenplay by Patrick Sheane Duncan.

High school teachers seem locked in time to us; we seem like part of a flowing stream to them. My teachers are frozen in the late 1950s, an innocent time when high school portals had quotations from Milton carved over the doorways and no metal detectors. But to them, the Class of 1960 was one of ten, twenty, thirty, or more classes passing through their hands, and even though Coach Smith did assure us at our tenth reunion that "there was never another class like you," we had the suspicion that he said that at all the reunions.

*Mr. Holland's Opus* tells the story of thirty years in the life of a high school music teacher named Glenn Holland, who takes the job in the first place as a temporary measure. His real work, he believes, is to compose music. Teaching is just a way to pay some bills. He realizes only gradually that it is, in fact, his destiny. (As they say, "What you're doing instead of your real job *is* your real job.")

As the movie opens, Holland (Richard Dreyfuss) and his wife, Iris (Glenne Headly), are a couple fueled by his heady ambitions. He will be a great composer, of that he is sure, but then financial realities make him take the teaching job, where the hard-edged principal (Olympia Dukakis) looks him over sternly and reads him as a man for whom teaching has no seriousness.

God knows the school needs a music teacher. At his first meeting with the high school orchestra, he finds they play badly. How badly? I didn't recognize the first four notes of Beethoven's Fifth Symphony. (By the end of the film, a successor to this orchestra has so improved that it sounds for all the world like a Hollywood recording stage filled with professional session musicians under the baton of Michael Kamen.)

Meanwhile, the Hollands have a baby, to Iris's delight and Glenn's somewhat more muted pleasure—which turns to coldness when he discovers his son, named Cole, is deaf. Holland almost takes it as a personal affront that his son will not be able to hear the great opus that he still clings to as his ultimate vision.

Year follows year, and it is one of the pleasures of *Mr. Holland's Opus,* like *Forrest Gump,* that the characters live through many of the watershed events of three decades: the assassination of Kennedy, the war in Vietnam, the plague of drugs and school violence, and the cost-cutting measures that eventually eliminate programs like Mr. Holland's music classes. (The day American high schools admit that "electives" like music, art, and drama are as important as sports will be the day they value culture as much as entertainment for the alums.)

Every teacher has his favorite students, and Mr. Holland has several. One is a hopelessly untalented band member (Alicia Witt). Mr. Holland is not able to make her talented, but he is able to restore her self-esteem, and she reappears many years later as a woman who learned much more than music in his class. Another is a beautiful and talented student (Jean Louisa Kelly) who has her sights set on showbiz, and who falls in love with Mr. Holland, who must walk a delicate emotional tightrope with an end not always in sight.

Although much of the movie involves Mr. Holland helping his students to mature, the character of the son, Cole, provides a counterpoint: a way for Mr. Holland to grow up, too, and accept both his son and his life. Some of the scenes between them are painful, and a later scene, where Mr. Holland sings John Lennon's "Beautiful Boy" to Cole, is very moving.

Richard Dreyfuss, who is sometimes too exuberant, here finds the right tones for Mr. Holland, from youthful cocksureness to the gentle insight of age. His physical transformations over thirty years are always convincing. Glenne Headly has a more thankless role as his wife, but watch her handle the scene where she suddenly sees something she had not suspected, and intuitively knows how to deal with it. The supporting cast is all strong, especially Jay Thomas as the football coach who becomes Holland's lifelong friend.

Watching this film, falling into its rhythm, appreciating its sweep, I could not help but remember my own high school teachers. Sitting here at the keyboard, I began a list of their names, only to realize that you have your own list. Amazing, how clearly I remember their excellence, and their patience. One anecdote will do. Stanley Hynes, who taught us Shakespeare, always addressed us as "Mr." and "Miss," as a college teacher would do, and somehow that brought a greater seriousness to *Macbeth* and *Julius Caesar,* which were uncharted new worlds for us. Modifying the curriculum to make it more "contemporary" and "relevant" is doing an injustice to students, whose lives will become relevant to the exact degree that high school encourages them to outgrow themselves, and escape from the contemporary into the timeless. Mr. Hynes knew that. So does *Mr. Holland's Opus.*

## Mr. Jealousy ★ ★ ½

R, 103 m., 1998

Eric Stoltz (Lester Grimm), Annabella Sciorra (Ramona Ray), Chris Eigeman (Dashiell Frank), Carlos Jacott (Vince), Marianne Jean-Baptiste (Lucretia), Brian Kerwin (Stephen), Peter Bogdanovich (Dr. Poke), Bridget Fonda (Irene). Directed by Noah Baumbach and produced by Joel Castleberg. Screenplay by Baumbach.

Lester Grimm, the hero of *Mr. Jealousy,* is the kind of guy who can grow so obsessed with a girl that he shadows her all the time, hiding in shrubbery to see where she goes and what she does—until she drops him because he never seems to be around. His insecurity started early. At fifteen, he took a girl to a movie and an Italian restaurant on what he thought was a perfectly acceptable date, only to spot her later at a party, making out with a twenty-four-year-old club promoter.

Ever since, Lester (Eric Stoltz) has been tormented by images of his dates in the arms of other guys. Who did they date before they met him? How did they feel about their former lovers? How do they still feel? At thirty-one, Lester is still single, and working as a substitute teacher of Spanish, a language he does not speak. He is dating Ramona (Annabella Sciorra), who conducts museum tours and is getting her doctoriate in abstract expressionism. Can he trust her? Did she have a life before he met her?

She sure did. She used to date Dashiell Frank (Chris Eigeman), "the generation-defining writer" whose novels speak powerfully to Generation Xers. When Ramona and Dashiell accidentally encounter one another, Lester's jealousy is inflamed by their air of easy affection, and he starts following Dashiell. Discovering that the writer is a member of a therapy group, Lester signs up for the same group—not under his own name, but as "Vince," the name of his best friend (Carlos Jacott).

That's the setup for Noah Baumbach's film, which, like his observant *Kicking and Screaming* (1995), is about characters who are too old for college but unready for real life. Baumbach has a good ear for how these characters talk, but the unforced originality of his earlier film is joined here by homages to other directors; he gets the iris shots and narration from Francois Truffaut, the nebbishy insecurity from Woody Allen and Henry Jaglom, and the self-analytical dialogue from Whit Stillman. I'm not bothered by his homage to them so much as I miss his confidence in himself.

That earlier film nailed the characters and the dialogue so accurately that you remembered people exactly like that; indeed, you recalled *being* like that. *Mr. Jealousy* pumps in more plot, and I'm not sure that's the right decision. Mistaken identities and mutual misunderstandings can only be taken so far before the plot seems to be leading the characters. That's okay in farce, but in more thoughtful comedies the characters should appear to be making their decisions entirely unprompted by the requirements of the genre.

Baumbach is a gifted filmmaker, however, and many of his scenes are just right, including a sequence where Dashiell, the writer, reads a story to the group and Lester thinks it must be based on Dashiell's relationship with Ramona. He challenges the writer to "reveal more about his characters," and learns what he didn't want to know, that the original of the woman in the story "was a bit of a tart."

Well, was she? Ramona strikes us as sensible and restrained, and discriminating enough in her relationships that she probably shouldn't even be dating Lester. But we begin to sense uneasily that a story arc is being shaped here, and that the movie will require Lester to almost lose Ramona, and for secrets to be revealed and emotional showdowns to be arrived at, and for events to replace insights.

Eric Stoltz, who also starred in *Kicking and Screaming,* is well cast as Lester; he has a quiet intelligence matched with a kind of laconic earnestness about himself. Chris Eigeman, a veteran of Stillman's films, finds and holds a difficult note as a writer who is young and famous without being any more insufferable as a result than is absolutely necessary. Annabella Sciorra does a good job of creating the kind of woman who puts up with a lot from a guy if she likes him; she has her own life, doesn't need to live through his, and only gradually realizes that in a quiet, elusive way he is stark staring mad.

*Mr. Jealousy* isn't quite successful, but it does provide more evidence of Baumbach's talent. So many young filmmakers aim merely for success, and throw anything at us that they think we'll buy. Only a few are trying to chronicle their generation, listening to how it talks and watching how it behaves. That number includes the Whit Stillman of *The Last Days of Disco,* the Richard Linklater of *subUrbia,* the Kevin Smith of *Chasing Amy,* and the Nicole Holofcener of *Walking and Talking. Mr. Jealousy* shows that Baumbach is the real thing, but he needs to focus.

## Mr. Magoo ½★

PG, 97 m., 1997

Leslie Nielsen (Mr. Magoo), Kelly Lynch (Luanne), Matt Keeslar (Waldo), Nick Chinlund (Bob Morgan), Stephen Tobolowsky (Agent Chuck Stupak), Ernie Hudson (Agent Gus Anders), Jennifer Garner (Stacey Sampanahoditra), Malcolm McDowell (Austin Cloquet). Directed by Stanley Tong and produced by Ben Myron. Screenplay by Pat Proft and Tom Sherohman.

Magoo drives a red Studebaker convertible in *Mr. Magoo,* a fact I report because I love Studebakers and his was the only thing I liked in the film. It has a prescription windshield. He also drives an eggplantmobile, which looks like a failed wienermobile. The concept of a failed wienermobile is itself funnier than anything in the movie.

*Mr. Magoo* is transcendentally bad. It soars above ordinary badness as the eagle outreaches the fly. There is not a laugh in it. Not one. I counted. I wonder if there *could* have been any laughs in it. Perhaps this project was simply a bad idea from the beginning, and no script, no director, no actor, could have saved it.

I wasn't much of a fan of the old cartoons. They were versions of one joke, imposed on us by the cantankerous but sometimes lovable nearsighted Magoo, whose shtick was to mistake something for something else. He always survived, but since it wasn't through his own doing, his adventures were more like exercises in design: Let's see how Magoo can walk down several girders suspended in midair, while thinking they're a staircase.

The plot involves Magoo as an innocent bystander at the theft of a jewel. Mistaken as the thief, he is pursued by the usual standard-issue CIA and FBI buffoons, while never quite understanding the trouble he's in. He's accompanied on most of his wanderings by his bulldog and his nephew, Waldo, of which the bulldog has the more winning personality.

Magoo is played by Leslie Nielsen, who could at the very least have shaved his head bald for the role. He does an imitation of the Magoo squint and the Magoo voice, but is unable to overcome the fact that a little Magoo at six minutes in a cartoon is a far different matter than a lot of Magoo at ninety minutes in a feature. This is a one-joke movie without the joke. Even the outtakes at the end aren't funny, and I'm not sure I understood one of them, unless it was meant to show stunt people hilariously almost being drowned.

I have taken another look at my notes, and must correct myself. There is one laugh in the movie. It comes after the action is over, in the form of a foolish, politically correct disclaimer stating that the film "is not intended as an accurate portrayal of blindness or poor eyesight." I think we should stage an international search to find one single person who thinks the film is intended as such a portrayal, and introduce that person to the author of the disclaimer, as they will have a lot in common, including complete detachment from reality.

## Mr. Nice Guy ★ ★ ★

PG-13, 90 m., 1998

Jackie Chan (Jackie), Richard Norton (Giancarlo), Gabrielle Fitzpatrick (Diana), Miki Lee (Miki), Karen McLymont (Lakeisha), Vince Poletto (Romeo), Barry Otto (Baggio), Sammo Hung (Cyclist). Directed by Sammo Hung and produced by Chua Lam. Screenplay by Edward Tang and Fibe Ma.

Jackie Chan's *Mr. Nice Guy* was originally titled *No More Mr. Nice Guy,* which would also have worked; as the film opens he's a smiling chef on a TV show, and as it closes he's single-handedly destroying a house with a giant piece of earthmoving equipment. Still, I like the new title, because Chan *is* a nice guy, with his infectious grin, potato nose, and astonishing physical comedy.

In a seminar last year at the Hawaii Film Festival, I compared some of Chan's action sequences to work by Buster Keaton. That may seem like a stretch, but look at his films and it's obvious Chan is more in the tradition of silent comedy than of the chop-socky genre. He kids himself, he pretends to be in over his head, and he survives by luck and skill instead of brute force.

In *Mr. Nice Guy*, he's the innocuous bystander who gets involved only to save a pretty girl, and wanders into a drug war by accident. The plot is a clothesline for the action sequences. A TV reporter (Gabrielle Fitzpatrick) has a videotape incriminating some drug lords. The bad guys want it back. They chase her. Jackie helps her. The bad guys become convinced Jackie has the tape. They chase both of them. Jackie's TV show assistant (Karen McLymont) turns up and gets chased too. Jackie's girlfriend from Hong Kong (Miki Lee) flies into town. Then the bad guys chase Jackie and all three women.

Sample dialogue. Goon tells boss: "I'm sorry, boss. We didn't get the tape, and four of our guys got blown up!" Boss tells goon: "Get the tape or you'll never be seen again." So far, so good, but then the boss grabs the goon's tie and starts slapping him on his face with the end of it, and this is so unexpected and weirdly goofy that it gets a laugh.

The plot is an excuse for sight gags, physical humor, stunts, and exquisite timing. There are big action ballets, but one of my favorite moments is a quieter one that happens so fast you'll miss it if you blink. Jackie is holding a gun he knows is not loaded. He comes around a corner and is face-to-face with a bad guy, also with a gun. The guy points the gun at Jackie. Jackie hands his own gun to the guy. The guy looks at the gun he's been given, and Jackie simply takes the other gun, as if in trade. Then the guy shoots Jackie—but with the unloaded gun. It's like a three-card monte trick. I think I've left out a couple of steps, but you get the idea: The logic of the physical movements drives the drama.

Another neat sequence: Jackie is demonstrating cooking skills in a shopping center by flipping bite-sized pieces of crepes twenty yards into the mouths of his fans. A bad guy steps in front of a fan, and intercepts one of the bites. Jackie grins and flips him another bite. This time it's a fiery pepper. Okay, so this isn't Antonioni.

The big action sequences involve runaway horses, a chase through a shopping center, the use of a crane, and an escape across a steel beam high in the air. Some of the stunts are amazing. That giant earthmoving vehicle, for example, has wheels that look twelve feet high. In one shot, as a wheel approaches Jackie to crush him, he keeps himself away from it—by pushing off with his feet against the moving wheel to scoot himself along on his back. Get that one wrong, and you have tire treads where your face used to be.

There's a stunt, too, where Jackie is hanging out the side of a moving carriage, about to fall, and braces himself by running sideways, as it were, down the side of a passing trolley car. Hard to describe, and almost impossible to do, but for Chan it's a throwaway, a few seconds in length.

The movie ends, as always, with credit cookies showing outtakes of Jackie landing wrong and nearly getting creamed. They prove what we know, that he does his own stunts. You watch how good he is and how hard he works, and you're glad his plots are an afterthought, because you don't want anything distracting from his sheer physical exuberance.

## Mrs. Brown ★ ★ ★ ½

PG, 103 m., 1997

Judi Dench (Queen Victoria), Billy Connolly (John Brown), Geoffrey Palmer (Henry Ponsonby), Antony Sher (Disraeli), Gerald Butler (Archie Brown), Richard Pasco (Doctor Jenner), David Westhead (Prince of Wales). Directed by John Madden and produced by Sarah Curtis. Screenplay by Jeremy Brock.

"Honest to God," the man tells the woman, "I never thought to see you in such a state. You must miss him dreadfully." Between ordinary people, ordinary words. Between a commoner and a queen, sheer effrontery. How can this bearded man, a Scotsman who oversees Queen Victoria's palace at Balmoral, have the gall to look her in the eye and address her with such familiarity?

The atmosphere in court is instantly tense and chilling. But the man, John Brown, has caught the queen's attention and cut through the miasma of two years' mourning for her beloved consort, Prince Albert. The little woman—a plump pudding dressed all in black—looks up sharply, and a certain light glints in her eyes. Before long she is taking Brown's advice that she must ride out daily for the exercise and the fresh air.

*Mrs. Brown* is a love story about two strong-willed people who find exhilaration in testing one another. It is not about sexual love, or even romantic love, really, but about that kind of love based on challenge and fascination. The film opens in 1864, when Queen Victoria (Judi Dench), consumed by mourning, has already been all but invisible to her subjects for two years. Her court coddles and curtseys to her, and that's what she expects: A nod or a glance from her can subdue an adviser.

Her household thinks perhaps riding might help her break out of her deep gloom, and import John Brown (Billy Connolly), a Scotsman in a kilt, who arrives with one of the queen's horses and is promptly ignored. Not to be trifled with, he stands at attention in her courtyard next to the horse. The next day he is there again. Proper behavior would have him waiting, docile and invisible, in the stables. "The queen will ride out if and when she chooses," Victoria informs him.

"And I intend to be there when she is ready," Brown informs Victoria.

Nobody in her life had spoken to her in this way, except perhaps for the beloved Albert. A charge forms in the air between them. Victoria is a complex and observant woman, who knows exactly what he is doing, and is thrilled by it: Queens perhaps grow tired of being fawned upon. Soon Brown and the queen are out riding, and soon the color has returned to her cheeks, and soon Brown is offering advice on how she should manage her affairs, and soon the household and the nation are whispering that this beastly man Brown is the power behind the throne.

"Mrs. Brown," they called her behind her back. Her son the Prince of Wales (David Westhead) is enraged to find that at Brown's order the smoking room is to be closed at midnight ("Mr. Brown needs his rest," the queen serenely explains). Brown takes her riding in the country and they call at a humble cottage, and the queen is offered Scotch whisky. The national newspapers raise their eyebrows. Finally the prime minister, Benjamin Disraeli (Antony Sher), pays a visit to see for himself what is happening in the royal household.

Judi Dench has long been one of the reigning stars of the London stage. She often plays strong-willed, intelligent women. She has never been much interested in the movies, although she did play "M" in a Bond film. This is her first starring role. She is wonderful in it, building the entire character on the rock of utter self-possession, and then showing that character possessed by another. Entrenched behind her desk, dressed in mourning, coils of braids framing her implacable face, she presents such a formidable facade that it is curiously erotic when Brown melts through it.

Billy Connolly is also little known in films; he is a stand-up comic, I learn, although here he has the reserve and self-confidence that most stand-up comics lack almost by definition. There is a manliness to him, a robust defiance of the rules. He also drinks too much, and although he seems for a long time able to hold it, one of the movie's subtle themes is that the better he gets to know the queen the less sure he is of how be should proceed.

Would there be, could there be, physical sex between them? Almost certainly not. But they both tacitly recognize that they might enjoy it. The queen is not an attractive woman, but she is powerful, and power is thrilling; in one key scene Brown swims naked in the highlands, intoxicated by his closeness to the throne. Victoria is like a movie nun-like Deborah Kerr in *Black Narcissus*—in being all the more intriguing because forbidden.

*Mrs. Brown* was written by Jeremy Brock and directed by John Madden, whose first film, the torturous *Ethan Frome,* gave little promise of his confidence here. The movie is insidious in its methods, asking us to see what is happening beneath the guarded surfaces. The behavior of a queen and her servant is so minutely dictated by rules and customs that they may look much the same when breaking them as when following them. So much depends on the eyes.

## Mrs. Dalloway ★ ★ ★ ½

PG-13, 97 m., 1998

Vanessa Redgrave (Mrs. Dalloway), Natascha McElhone (Young Clarissa), Rupert Graves

**(Septimus Smith), Michael Kitchen (Peter Walsh), Alan Cox (Young Peter), Sarah Badel (Lady Rosseter [Sally]), Lena Headey (Young Sally), John Standing (Richard Dalloway), Robert Portal (Young Richard), Amelia Bullmore (Rezia Smith). Directed by Marleen Gorris and produced by Stephen Bayly and Lisa Katselas Pare. Screenplay by Eileen Atkins, based on a novel by Virginia Woolf.**

In many lives there is a crossroads. We make our choice and follow it down to the present moment. Still inside of us is that other person, who stands forever poised at the head of the path not chosen. *Mrs. Dalloway* is about a day's communion between the woman who exists and the other woman who might have existed instead.

The film's heroine muses that she is thought of as "Mrs. Dalloway" by almost everybody: "You're not even Clarissa any more." Once she was young and fair, and tempted by two daring choices. Young Peter would have been a risk, but he was dangerous and alive. Even more dangerous was Sally, with whom flirtation threatened to develop into something she was unwilling to name. Clarissa took neither choice, deciding instead to marry the safe and sound Richard Dalloway, of whom young Peter sniffed, "He's a fool, an unimaginative, dull fool."

Now many years have passed. Mrs. Dalloway is giving a party. The caterer has been busy since dawn, the day is beautiful, and she walks through Hyde Park to buy the flowers herself. So opens Virginia Woolf's famous 1923 novel, which follows Clarissa Dalloway for a day, using the new stream-of-consciousness technique James Joyce was experimenting with. We will follow her through until the end of her party, during a day in which no one she meets will know what she's really thinking: All they will see is her reserved, charming exterior.

The novel stays mostly within the mind of Clarissa, with darts into other minds. Film cannot do that, but *Mrs. Dalloway* uses a voice-over narration to let us hear Clarissa's thoughts, which she never, ever, shares with anybody else. To the world she is a respectable, sixtyish London woman, the wife of a Cabinet official. To us, she is a woman who will always wonder what might have been.

Vanessa Redgrave so loved the novel that she commissioned this screenplay by Eileen Atkins, an actress who has been involved in a lot of Woolf-oriented stage work. Redgrave, of course, seems the opposite of a woman like Clarissa Dalloway, and we assume she has few regrets. But we all wonder about choices not made, because in our memories they still glow with their original promise, while reality is tied to the mundane.

As the film makes its way through Clarissa's day, there are flashbacks to long-ago summers when young Peter (Alan Cox) was courting young Clarissa (Natascha McElhone), and young Sally (Lena Headey) was perhaps courting her, too, although the movie is cagier about that than the novel. But Woolf is too wise to let Peter and Sally remain in the sunny past of memory. They both turn up on this day.

In middle age, Peter (Michael Kitchen) is rather pathetic, just returned from what seems to have been an unsuccessful romance and career in India. And Sally (Sarah Badel) is now the distinguished Lady Rosseter. There is a wonderful scene where Peter and Sally find a quiet corner of the party, and he tells her of Clarissa, "I loved her once, and it stayed with me all my life, and colored every day." Sally nods, keeping her own thoughts to herself. We gather that Sally, in middle age, may be practicing the same sort of two-track thinking that Clarissa uses: Both women see more sharply, and critically, than anyone imagines, although with Sally we must guess this from the outside.

There is another crucial character in the film. Unless you've read the novel you may have trouble understanding his function. This is Septimus Warren Smith (Rupert Graves), who in an early scene watches as a friend is blown up in the no-man's-land of the trenches in France. Now five years or more have passed, but he suffers from shell shock, and has a panic attack outside a shop where Clarissa pauses. She sees him, and although they never meet, there is a link between them: Both have seen beneath the surface of life's reassurance, to the possibility that nothing, or worse than nothing, lurks below. Woolf is suggesting that World War I unleashed horrors that poisoned every level of society.

The subtext of the story is suicide. Woolf is asking what purpose is served by the decisions of Clarissa and Septimus to go on living lives that they have seen through. A subtle motif throughout the film is the omnipresence of sharp fence railings—spikes, like life, upon which one could be impaled.

The director, Marleen Gorris, previously made the Oscar-winning Dutch film *Antonia's Line,* about a woman who makes free choices, survives, and prevails. Here is the other side. It's surprising that Gorris, who was so open about Antonia's sexuality, is so subtle about the unspoken lesbianism in Woolf's story, but it's there for those who can see it.

More important is the way she struggles with form, to try to get an almost unfilmable novel on the screen. She isn't always successful; the first act will be perplexing for those unfamiliar with the novel, but Redgrave's performance steers us through, and by the end we understand with complete, final clarity what the story was about. Stream-of-consciousness stays entirely within the mind. Movies photograph only the outsides of things. The narration is a useful device, but so are Redgrave's eyes, as she looks at the guests at her party. Once we have the clue, she doesn't really look at all like a safe, respectable, middle-aged hostess. More like a caged animal—trained, but not tamed.

## Mrs. Winterbourne ★ ★ ½

PG-13, 104 m., 1996

Shirley MacLaine (Grace Winterbourne), Ricki Lake (Connie Doyle), Brendan Fraser (Bill/Hugh Winterbourne), Miguel Sandoval (Paco), Loren Dean (Steve DeCunzo), Peter Gerety (Father Brian), Jane Krakowski (Christine), Debra Monk (Lieutenant Ambrose). Directed by Richard Benjamin and produced by Dale Pollock, Ross Canter, and Oren Koules. Screenplay by Phoef Sutton and Lisa-Maria Radano.

Some movies require what the critics call "the willing suspension of disbelief." *Mrs. Winterbourne* requires disbelief to be hoisted by a heavy-duty crane and detonated. I was happy to perform this duty, however, since the movie is charming, if as evanescent as those cookie wrappers you get at Italian restaurants—where after you light them they fly up for a moment of glory and then disintegrate into invisible specks.

The movie stars Ricki Lake in her first movie role since her transformation into a daytime TV talker. One of her qualities is a no-nonsense warmth, and she uses it here in the story of Connie Doyle, an unhappy girl who runs away from home and lands in New York City. She's befriended by a louse named Steve (Loren Dean), who introduces her to a life of "no flowers, but lots of stolen car radios." When she is pregnant, he throws her out, and later, as she stands homeless in the rain beneath his window, tosses her a quarter.

Poor Connie. She drifts to Grand Central Station, gets a ticket from a friendly stranger, boards a train, and meets a friendly and charitable young man named Hugh (Brendan Fraser). Hugh is traveling with his own pregnant wife, and in a moment of girl-to-girl talk, the wife allows Connie to try on her wedding ring. Then the train crashes, Hugh and his wife are killed, and when Connie wakes up she is on the luxurious estate of Hugh's family, the Winterbournes. They have never met Hugh's wife, and, of course, because of the ring they think Connie is the wife and soon-to-be mother of the Winterbourne heir.

That's the setup. Read no further if you want to spare yourself certain plot details—although if you close your eyes and meditate, I am sure you can predict with amazing accuracy what happens for the rest of the movie, especially if I tell you that the late Hugh has an identical twin brother named Bill (also played by Fraser).

The estate is ruled by the wise Mrs. Winterbourne (Shirley MacLaine), a widow who was herself not the soul of respectability when she married into the family. She is ill, and welcomes a new grandchild, and soon, wouldn't you know, Bill and Connie are dancing the tango in the kitchen, and marriage is proposed.

There are a few hitches along the way. Bill develops certain suspicions about Connie, but shelves them because of how she handles a crucial scene involving Mrs. Winterbourne's will. And then there is the problem of the evil Steve, who might be interested in blackmailing a future Mrs. Winterbourne.

What's best about the movie are the human qualities of the actors. Shirley MacLaine has a few lines so sensible I'm sure she must have edited them herself. Ricki Lake has a direct, blunt honesty that is appealing, although I think her romance would be more plausible if she'd been slightly more polished. Brendan Fraser is solid as the lover who sees through deception and out the other side. And there are some nice moments with Paco (Miguel Sandoval), the gay Cuban chauffeur, who considers himself a Winterbourne of sorts and tells the weeping Connie, "If bad things are going to happen, let them happen here."

*Mrs. Winterbourne* has the kind of plot that might have distinguished an old Hollywood tearjerker, and in fact it did: *No Man of Her Own* (1951), with Barbara Stanwyck. It is old-fashioned manipulated romantic melodrama, where coincidence is a condition of the universe. Because it is light and stylish and good-hearted, it is quite possible to enjoy, in the right frame of mind, on an empty night when you need something to hurl at the gloom.

## Mon Homme ★ ★

NO MPAA RATING, 95 m., 1998

Anouk Grinberg (Marie), Gérard Lanvin (Jeannot), Valeria Bruni-Tedeschi (Sanguine), Olivier Martinez (Jean-Francois), Sabine Azema (Berangere), Dominique Valadie (Gilberte), Mathieu Kassovitz (First Client), Jacques Francois (Second Client). Directed by Bertrand Blier and produced by Alain Sarde. Screenplay by Blier. In French with English subtitles.

"What I sell is true love," says the heroine of Bertrand Blier's *Mon Homme.* "With me they hear the music." She says her name is Marie (Anouk Grinberg) and she is the hooker of a john's dreams: "I should pay you," she tells one client. As the film opens, we find her sitting outside a hotel ("This is where I spin my web"), explaining how much she enjoys prostitution. "Ever thought of being paid for it?" she asks a matron who is passing by. The matron has. In no time at all, Marie has talked her into turning her first trick.

Blier's films are often about men in the service of their sexual needs. *Too Beautiful for You* (1988) starred Gérard Depardieu as a man who leaves his elegant wife for the dowdy secretary who obsesses him. The Oscar winner *Get Out Your Handkerchief* (1977) starred Depardieu as a man who despairs of satisfying his wife. In *Mon Homme,* Blier in a sense has cast the male role with a woman: Marie calls the shots, satisfies herself, sleeps with whom she wants, and gets paid for it.

But her life is not perfect until one day she discovers a derelict sleeping near a garbage heap. She brings him home, feeds him (leftover veal stew; French refrigerators never contain old pizzas and doggie bags from the Chinese restaurant). Then they make love. Grinberg is awesome in suggesting her passion; the earth shakes because she's shaking it. There is a small detail that's just right: the way she bites his chin through his beard. Jeannot (Gérard Lanvin) is expert and enduring. She bathes him, shaves him, and asks him to be her pimp and take all her money.

He: What if you want money?

She: I'll ask you for it.

He: And if I refuse?

She: Then you'll be a real pimp.

I wouldn't go so far as to say there are *no* hookers like this in Paris, but Blier may have found the only one.

I was distracted, during their lovemaking, by the thought that a homeless man, found on a garbage heap, would be aromatic. Shouldn't she have bathed him before sex? But a moment's thought reveals that Marie is not being entirely truthful about her needs: It is not so much that she loves sex and prostitution as that she's a masochist, as Jeannot intuits when he slaps her after she has given him stew, sex, and what he concedes is a rather nice red wine. ("Like the smack?" She nods. Later, good fellow that he is, he instructs her on how to duck when she senses a slap on its way.)

If Blier had been true to the logic of the story, he would have followed Marie's compulsions to their bitter end. Instead, he spins off into Jeannot's story, as the new pimp (who cleans up nicely) who seduces a manicurist, names her Tangerine, and tries to set her up in business. Tangerine, who thinks with her mouth open, does not have enough wit for the game, and soon Jeannot is being slapped around by the cops; in France, it is legal to be a prostitute but not to be a pimp.

The film drifts away into developments, fantasies, whimsy, and conceit. Its energy is lost. Blier has a strong central character and abandons her rather than accept the inescapable implications of her behavior. I do not argue that prostitutes cannot be happy (indeed, I have here a letter from a prostitute taking me to task for calling all the characters in *Boogie Nights* sad). But I argue that Marie is not happy, and that Blier's view of women and their sexuality is so narrow that he simply cannot accommodate that inconvenience.

## Money Talks ★ ★ ★

R, 92 m., 1997

Charlie Sheen (James Russell), Chris Tucker (Franklin Hatchett), Paul Sorvino (Guy Cipriani), Heather Locklear (Grace Cipriani), David Warner (Barclay), Gerard Ismael (Villard), Paul Gleason (Pickett), Elise Neal (Paula). Directed by Brett Ratner and produced by Walter Coblenz and Tracy Kramer. Screenplay by Joel Cohen and Alec Sokolow.

How does a guy like Jim Carrey get his first chance to perform anarchic comedy in a movie? Now that he's a star, directors are of course happy to let him run wild. But how did he get his foot in the door in the first place? How did they know they should hand him the scenery and a knife and a fork? I wonder because in *Money Talks,* a comedian named Chris Tucker has his own foot jammed in the same door, and you can see his talent blossom right there before your eyes.

The movie is not distinguished. It's a clone of the black-and-white buddy pictures, with a little of *48 HRS* and *Lethal Weapon* and *Nothing to Lose.* The plot is so dumb that at one point terrorists blow up a prison bus so that their leader can escape, and no one even considers the possibility that, gee, maybe the leader could get blown up along with everyone else on the bus. He isn't, and that's just as well, because he's handcuffed to Franklin Hatchett, the Chris Tucker character, and we're going to need him for the rest of the movie.

You may remember Tucker from *The Fifth Element,* where his character went on endlessly, as an emcee in a nightclub on a space station. Watching that movie, I felt the Tucker role derailed the ending by continuing too long on the wrong note, as a distraction. But in *Money Talks,* where he has more of a chance to develop a character and experiment with his voice and style, Tucker has a personal triumph. He's funny in that cocky, free-fall way that Carrey and Jerry Lewis get away with: He's floating on inspiration and improvisation, like a musician.

Consider the scene where he is presented at a black-tie wedding party for a rich Italian-American, played by Paul Sorvino. Sorvino is dubious about this black man he's never seen before. But Tucker, who earlier in the day happened to watch a TV ad for the greatest hits of Vic Damone, has a brainstorm: He introduces himself as Vic Damone Jr., the son of the singer and Diahann Carroll. Sorvino embraces the Italian connection, ignores the African-American component, and is blissful as Tucker recalls a childhood spent among other juniors: "Junior Walker Junior, Sammy Davis Junior Junior . . ."

I'm not giving Tucker credit for this hilarious scene, which was written by Joel Cohen and Alec Sokolow. But I'm crediting him with how he sells it: The lines are funny, but Tucker runs with them, and there's a kind of wink to the audience as he relaunches himself as Vic Damone's son: We know he knows exactly what he's doing.

He was invited to the prewedding party by a TV newsman named James Russell (Charlie Sheen), who plays his sidekick through most of the movie. Russell is not a great newsman (and it doesn't help that nobody connected with the movie knows anything about how real TV news reporters talk or behave). In fact, he's just been fired by his weary, cynical boss (David Warner, very funny in an engaging, attention-getting role). But when there's a manhunt for the escaped terrorist, and the Tucker character is fingered as the mastermind behind the prison break, Tucker turns to Sheen for protection—and Sheen agrees to hide him for a weekend (under cover of his own wedding) in order to produce him in time for a sweeps ratings period.

Sheen has the most thankless role in the movie, as the straight man, and there are scenes where he seems to realize that Tucker, Sorvino, and Warner have all the best lines. He stands there while Tucker goes on wild verbal riffs and has the thankless task of appearing to take him seriously. Some critics have disliked Sheen's performance, but I think it's more or less what's called for: He provides the solid backdrop for the anarchy, and probably feels like Margaret Dumont to Tucker's Groucho Marx.

The movie is the directing debut of Brett Ratner, who has not made a flawless film but at least has made an interesting one, and who understands what Tucker is able to do, and helps him do it. And Tucker, like Carrey, comes on obnoxious and irritating at first, and then you see the smile and the intelligence underneath, and he begins to grow on you.

## Mother ★ ★ ★ ½

PG-13, 104 m., 1997

Albert Brooks (John Henderson), Debbie Reynolds (Beatrice), Rob Morrow (Jeff), Lisa Kudrow (Linda), Isabel Glasser (Cheryl, Jeff's wife), Peter White (Charles). Directed by Albert Brooks and produced by Scott Rudin and Herb Nanas. Screenplay by Brooks and Monica Johnson.

The mother in Albert Brooks's *Mother* knows how to push the secret buttons to drive her son up the wall. All it takes is a slight intonation, a little pause, a wicked word choice no outsider would notice. And she's so sweet while making her subtle criticisms; why, you'd almost think she didn't know what she was doing.

*Mother* opens with John Henderson (Brooks) in despair because his second marriage has ended in divorce. In the lawyer's office, his ex-wife holds herself apart from him like the survivor of a long and exquisitely unpleasant experience. "She brought a lot of great furniture to the marriage," Henderson reflects, returning to a house now furnished with one chair, which he spends the afternoon rearranging. Then he telephones his mother, tells her his problems with women all started with her, and says he wants to move back home and get it right this time.

Beatrice Henderson (Debbie Reynolds) is not pleased. She's paid her dues, raised her children, and embraced the solitude of widowhood. She doesn't really seem to be focusing on his anguish; she constantly interrupts his emergency telephone call with call waiting, even though she doesn't know how it works. We see the nature of the difficulty: A mother who insists on her right to do things wrong is a torture to a perfectionist son.

Brooks is working with materials which look like the stuff of a sitcom; there is an *Odd Couple* spin-off here, waiting to happen. But Brooks, who cowrote (with Monica Johnson) and directed as well as starred, is much too smart to settle for the obvious gags and payoffs. All of his films depend on closely observed behavior and language, on the ways language can refuse to let us communicate no matter how obsessively we try to nail things down. In his scenes with Reynolds, they talk quietly, conversationally; they're not pounding out punch lines, and that's why the dialogue is so funny.

The experiment begins. John moves in with Beatrice and their first battles are joined over the issue of food. Beatrice puts salads in the freezer along with ancient blocks of Swiss cheese large enough to feed a day-care center. She buys the cheapest brands of everything, including "Sweet Tooth" orange sherbet, which has been hibernating in the freezer for years, growing what she happily describes as a "protective ice coating." ("This tastes," he tells her, "like an orange foot.") When he says he's a vegetarian, she offers to "scrape the top off the meat loaf."

Reynolds, who has not had a leading role in twenty-seven years, has two scenes with Brooks which are triumphs of perfect tone and timing. One is the scene just mentioned, where she tries to feed him dinner. Another is when they go shopping and get into arguments about everything that goes into the shopping cart; when she selects a generic brand of peanut butter, he cries out, "Just once, I want an experience where we throw away ninety-one cents together."

These tussles over superficial issues reveal underlying problems. Yes, Beatrice is maddening. But if John wants to improve his track record with women, he's going to have to learn not to be maddened. And the screenplay has some sly tricks up its sleeve: Perhaps, for example, it is absolutely true that Beatrice favors her other son (Rob Morrow) over John. The Morrow character is handled with a sharper edge than Beatrice and John. We see him at home with his wife (Isabel Glasser) in a scene that is deadly serious, as they argue over his possessiveness and insecurity about his mother.

The dialogue in *Mother* is written so carefully that some lines carry two or three nuances. That's especially so when John discovers that his mother has a gentleman friend (Peter White) who comes to visit once a month or so for dinner and sex. John has by now moved back into the room he had in high school (and decorated it with all the same old posters and sports pennants). His mother tiptoes down the corridor to be sure he's asleep, while the friend waits eagerly in the foyer.

I've seen *Mother* twice, once at the Toronto

film festival and again with a capacity audience in Santa Monica. There was a lot of laughter both times, and the second time, listening closely, I recognized a certain quality in it. It wasn't the automatic laughter produced by slam-dunk punch lines, but the laughter of recognition, of insight, even sometimes of squirmy discomfort, as the truths hit close to home.

The audiences appreciated the film; they seemed grateful for its invention and intelligence, which didn't insult them, and on the way out they were repeating some of the best lines. I don't know if you can improve your romantic life by moving back in with your mother, but it might be a help to see this movie. Maybe with your mother. Maybe not. ☞

## Mother Night ★ ★ ½

R, 113 m., 1996

Nick Nolte (Howard Campbell), Sheryl Lee (Helga Noth), Alan Arkin (Kraft), John Goodman (Frank Wirtanen), Kirsten Dunst (Resi Noth), Arye Gross (Abraham Epstein), Frankie Faison (Black Fuehrer of Harlem), David Strathairn (Bernard B. O'Hare). Directed by Keith Gordon and produced by Gordon and Robert B. Weide. Screenplay by Weide, based on the novel by Kurt Vonnegut.

When Kurt Vonnegut, then in the U.S. Army, was being held in a German prison camp, he was asked by his guards why he was not fighting for the Germans—since he had a German name. Vonnegut later confessed in his introduction to his novel *Mother Night*, "If I'd been born in Germany, I suppose I would have been a Nazi." It is easy to lose sight of the fact that almost all of us take the side of that country where we are born or the tribe we are born into; for every person who takes sides for ethical reasons, a thousand or more take sides because of accidents of geography or birth.

*Mother Night*, a difficult movie made from Vonnegut's 1961 novel, is about a man whose life illustrates that reality. His name is Howard W. Campbell Jr. (Nick Nolte), and he is born in the United States but moves with his family to Berlin in 1919. He grows up, becomes a successful playwright, marries an actress, and by then the war clouds are gathering. Should he stay in Germany or return to America? An American agent (John Goodman) makes it easy for him by asking him to stay and deliver anti-Semitic and anti-American diatribes on Nazi radio. Through a subtly coded system of pauses and coughs, the broadcasts will also carry secret information of great use to the Allies.

I have no doubt that such systems were in fact used, but for the purposes of *Mother Night* this scheme is ideal: It puts Campbell on both sides of the same fence. As his German father-in-law tells him, "Even if you were a spy, you served Germany more than the enemy." Did he? The experience at the time indicates that none of the propaganda broadcasts (by Tokyo Rose, Lord Haw Haw, Ezra Pound, etc.) had much of an effect, since they were seen as exactly what they were.

Campbell's secret handler tells him that the American government will never claim him or come to his rescue. After the war is over, and he sees with his own eyes the horror of the death camps, Campbell is able to make his way to New York City, where he lives for almost fifteen years under his own name; no one can believe he is the same person as the notorious traitor.

If the movie had been played out in this tone, I might have felt it worked better. That tone would not, however, have been Vonnegut's, which is more daring but harder to film. He adopts a wry angle toward his material, hinting at the madness and evil that lurk just below the surface of civilization, and the movie follows its story into Vonnegut land. A neo-Nazi newspaper publishes his address, and Campbell finds himself consorting with American Nazis and assorted other fauna, including "the black fuehrer of Harlem" and the nice old man across the hall (Alan Arkin), who is a Nazi—or then again, perhaps he isn't. Helga, his German wife, thought dead in a Russian attack, turns up again—or then again, perhaps she doesn't.

This unwelcome publicity causes Campbell a dilemma: Which side was he on? Was he an American who inadvertently helped the Nazis? An American not reluctant to help the Nazis? A Nazi posing as an American? His old handler (Goodman) turns up again, but cannot help him, and eventually he finds himself standing stock-still in the street one day, because he has no reason to move in any direction.

His paralysis is broken by the Israelis, who arrest him and take him to Israel for trial as a war criminal. He is given a typewriter and three weeks to write his memoir (the cell scenes are the movie's framing device), and he can talk with, but not see, one of his fellow prisoners, Adolf Eichmann. His story concludes, I suppose, in the only way it should. It is a tribute to Nolte's performance that while we are confused about the meaning of the story, we never doubt the presentation of his character.

Walking out of *Mother Night,* I asked myself what statement, exactly, the movie had made. I could not answer. Campbell is a man without a country, without core beliefs. It is impossible to say for sure which side he was on, and which side he harmed more. He was a man prepared to take the most convenient course, and for him the ability to stay in Germany and become a famous propagandist (wined and dined by top Nazis) was very convenient, especially if he could pass along secret messages for the Americans, which was convenient too.

The convenience for Campbell ended when the Nazis lost the war. Since the Americans were never going to claim him, it would have been more convenient if Germany had won. I assume in that case that Campbell would have stayed in Germany, been celebrated as a hero, and eventually been given a plum job. The dilemma Vonnegut sets him in is that he cannot jump off the ship it was convenient for him to sail on through the war.

Vonnegut wants to show us a man very much like most of us, no smarter, no braver, who does what he does because it will contribute to his comfort and perhaps to his survival. There but for the grace of God go we, drifting through life having benefited from chance and convenience, hoping the day will not come when we have to risk everything by declaring ourselves. It takes an extraordinary man to stand outside his tribe and try to see what is objectively good and right. Campbell was not within miles of being that man.

Does the film work? Not really. It loses itself in comic caricatures of the loonies that Campbell meets in New York; and its melodramatic double-reverses, by making the plot seem arbitrary, rob it of importance. Nor does the film, within itself, make it clear what it thinks. We can think about it afterward and that is instructive, but *Mother Night* is like notes for a lecture that is not completed.

## Mouse Hunt ★ ★

PG, 97 m., 1997

Nathan Lane (Ernie Smuntz), Lee Evans (Lars Smuntz), Christopher Walken (Caesar), Vicky Lewis (April Smuntz), Eric Christmas (Lawyer), Maury Chaykin (Alexander Falko), Michael Jeter (Quincy Thorpe), William Hickey (Rudolph Smuntz). Directed by Gore Verbinski and produced by Alan Riche, Tony Ludwig, and Bruce Cohen. Screenplay by Adam Rifkin.

*Mouse Hunt* is not very funny, and maybe couldn't have been very funny no matter what, because the pieces for comedy are not in place. It's the story of two luckless brothers who inherit a priceless architectural treasure and hope to auction it for a big bundle, but are frustrated at every turn by the house's only inhabitant, a very clever mouse. Quick: Whom do we sympathize with? The brothers or the mouse?

The movie doesn't know, and as a result the payoffs are lost in a comic vacuum. Pratfalls, slapstick, and special effects are not funny in themselves (something Hollywood keeps forgetting). They're only funny when they apply to someone we have an attitude about, so that we want them to succeed or fail. A comedy that hasn't assigned sympathy to some characters and made others hateful cannot expect to get many laughs because the audience doesn't know who to laugh at, or with.

Consider the rodent itself. In appearance, it is a common field mouse. Sort of cute. It has been cinematically assembled from many sources (real trained mice, animated mice, an animatronic mouse for the close-ups), but it has never been given a goal in life, other than to function as a plot device. Is the mouse intelligent? Does it know and care what is happening? Or is it simply a movie prop to be employed on cue? We aren't told, and we don't know. Because the mouse has no personality or personal history, because it has no particular goals other than to continue being a mouse, it isn't a sympathetic character, but simply an ingenious prop.

Now what about the brothers Smuntz? Ernie (Nathan Lane) and Lars (Lee Evans) have inherited the string factory of their father (William Hickey), and also a run-down old Victorian mansion that turns out to be a lost masterpiece of a great architect. They can get rich by selling it, but first they have to make some repairs—and get rid of the mouse. To help themselves, they bring in an exterminator named Caesar (Christopher Walken).

At some point in the production, someone undoubtedly said, "Wouldn't it be great to get Christopher Walken as the exterminator!" But why? Yes, Walken is an actor who inspires strong audience reactions, and, yes, his baggage from previous roles makes him a plausible exterminator. But what is funny about the character *other* than that it's played by Walken? Are we supposed to laugh when he's humiliated by the mouse? Not unless we care about him—and we don't, since he's obviously as much a prop as the mouse.

What about the brothers? Are they funny? No. But it is supposed to be funny that they can't get rid of the mouse, which is able to set off all their traps, figure out all their plans, and anticipate all their schemes. Since we never believe the mouse is doing that (we believe the screenplay is doing it), we don't much care that it's done.

*Mouse Hunt* is an excellent example of the way modern advances in special effects can sabotage a picture (*Titanic* is an example of effects being used wisely). Because it is possible to make a movie in which the mouse can do all sorts of clever things, the filmmakers have assumed incorrectly that it would be funny to see the mouse doing them.

Years ago, a comedy with a similar theme would have established the mouse, but would have been about the people. The characters would have reacted to the simple presence of a mouse, not to the incredibly elaborate stunts the mouse performs. The brothers and their auctioneer could have been developed as desperate for money, as eager to deceive, as pathetic liars, as hapless victims. The mouse would have been there, but wouldn't have had more screen time than most of the characters.

*Mouse Hunt* is a film that has gone to incredible effort and expense in order to sidetrack itself from comic payoffs. Less mouse, better dialogue, and more strongly drawn characters might have made a funnier movie. I believe a mouse can be trained to pick up an olive and run with it, but I don't believe it's funny. Not unless I know the mouse.

## Mulan ★ ★ ★ ½

G, 98 m., 1998

With the voices of: Ming-Na Wen (Mulan), Lea Salonga (Mulan, Singing), Eddie Murphy (Mushu), B. D. Wong (Shang), Donny Osmond (Shang, Singing), Harvey Fierstein (Yao), Jerry Tondo (Chien-Po), Gedde Watanabe (Ling). Directed by Barry Cook and Tony Bancroft and produced by Pam Coats. Screenplay by Rita Hsiao, Christopher Sanders, Philip LaZebnik, Raymond Singer, and Eugenia Bostwick-Singer, based on a story by Robert D. San Souci.

*Mulan* charts a new direction for Disney's animation studio, combining the traditional elements (brave heroine, cute animal sidekicks) with material that seems more adventuresome and grown-up. Like Fox's *Anastasia*, this is a film that adults can enjoy on their own, without feeling an obligation to take along kids as a cover.

The story this time isn't a retread of a familiar children's classic, but original material, about a plucky Chinese teenage girl who disguises herself as a boy to fight the invading Huns. When the invaders and their implacable leader Shan-Yu (who looks alarmingly like Karl Malone) sweep down on the Great Wall, the emperor calls up all able men to defend the kingdom. Mulan's father is old and feeble, but throws away his crutch to volunteer. To spare him, Mulan steals the family sword, summons the family ancestors for aid, and secretly goes in his place.

Ah, but it isn't as simple as that. Mulan is defying not simply convention, but her family's desire that she abide by the plans of a matchmaker and marry whomever she selects for her. Opening scenes in the film show her botching the interview with the matchmaker (she sets her pants on fire, a nice Freudian touch), and asking, "When will my reflection show who I am inside?"

The message here is standard feminist empowerment: Defy the matchmaker, dress as a boy, and choose your own career. But *Mulan* has it both ways, since inevitably Mulan's heart goes pitty-pat over Shang, the handsome young captain she's assigned to serve under. The movie breaks with the tradition in which the male hero rescues the heroine, but is still totally sold on the Western idea of romantic love. (In an Eastern culture, the ending might have involved an arranged match between Mulan and Shang, which she has earned by her exploits.)

Disney movies since time immemorial have provided their leads with low-comedy sidekicks, usually in the form of animals, although teacups and chandeliers are not unheard-of. Mulan is accompanied on her journey by a scrawny dragon named Mushu, whose voice is performed by Eddie Murphy. It's a little disconcerting the first time we hear his street-smart lingo (a black dude in medieval China?), but Mushu quickly grows on us. Murphy, working in the tradition of Robin Williams's genie in *Aladdin,* is quick, glib, and funny. He is also offended when people doubt he is a real dragon and refer to him as a lizard.

The action plot involves Mulan training for battle (the song promises, "I'll make a man out of you"), and using quick thinking to save Shang's troops from certain defeat. There are a couple of scenes where she narrowly escapes detection, including one at a swimming hole, and then, when she's unmasked, Shang's snaky adviser whispers that to impersonate a man is "treason." The outcome manages somehow to be true simultaneously to feminist dogma and romantic convention.

The visual style breaks slightly with the look of modern Disney animation to draw from Chinese and Japanese classical cartoon art; in the depiction of nature, there's an echo of the master artist Hiroshige. In a scene where the Hun troops sweep down the side of a snowy mountain, I was reminded of the great battle sequence in Eisenstein's *Alexander Nevsky.* There are scenes here, indeed, where the Disney artists seem aware of the important new work being done in Japanese anime; if American animation is ever going to win an audience beyond the family market, it will have to move in this direction, becoming more experimental in both stories and visual style.

Animation often finds a direct line to my imagination: It's pure story, character, movement, and form, without the distractions of reality or the biographical baggage of the actors. I found myself really enjoying *Mulan,* as a story and as animated art. If the songs were only more memorable, I'd give it four stars, but they seemed pleasant rather than rousing, and I wasn't humming anything on the way out. Still, *Mulan* is an impressive achievement, with a story and treatment ranking with *Beauty and the Beast* and *The Lion King.*

## Mulholland Falls ★ ★ ★ ½

R, 107 m., 1996

Nick Nolte (Hoover), Melanie Griffith (Katherine), Jennifer Connelly (Allison Pond), Chazz Palminteri (Coolidge), Michael Madsen (Eddie Hall), Chris Penn (Relyea), Treat Williams (Colonel Fitzgerald), John Malkovich (General Timms), Bruce Dern (AEC Head), Andrew McCarthy (Jimmy Fields). Directed by Lee Tamahori and produced by Richard D. Zanuck and Lili Fini Zanuck. Screenplay by Pete Dexter.

They were called the Hat Squad. They were four beefy middle-aged guys who drove around in a black Buick convertible, wearing fedoras and chain-smoking, and throwing guys, mostly bad guys, over cliffs. They worked for the LAPD. This was in the early 1950s.

*Mulholland Falls* takes the idea of these licensed vigilantes and crafts it into a *Chinatown* of the early atomic age. When the body of a young woman is discovered at a construction site, pressed into the earth almost as if by a steamroller, the Hat Squad gets involved. More involved than they planned, because the leader of the squad, a cop named Hoover (Nick Nolte), knew the dead girl. Knew her and had knowledge of her, if you see what I mean.

This is the kind of movie where every note is put in lovingly. It's a 1950s crime movie, but with a modern, ironic edge: The cops are just a shade over the top, just slightly in on the joke. They smoke all through the movie, but there's one scene where they're disturbed and thoughtful, and they all light up and smoke furiously, the smoke lit by the cinematographer to look like great billowing clouds, and you smile because you know the scene is really about—itself.

In addition to Nolte, the squad is played by Michael Madsen, Chazz Palminteri, and Chris Penn. Palminteri is seeing a shrink because he has trouble sleeping at night, no doubt because of his job (the film opens with the guys throwing a gangster over the edge of Mulholland Drive with the helpful advice, "We don't want organized crime in L.A.!"). The other three guys look like they sleep all right. But Nolte's dreams are haunted after he sees the dead girl.

Her name is Allison Pond (Jennifer Connelly). She lives in an efficiency apartment in a postwar pool-and-bedroom building, and is one of those beautiful lost young Hollywood girls who is halfway between being discovered as a starlet and growing old as a hooker. Hoover met her the first time as she was being beaten by a hoodlum. He sapped the hood and then injected him with a needle full of his own medicine, causing a drug overdose. That led to his first conversation with Allison:

"That's an inventive way of dispensing justice."

"It's an integral part of the job. So, who are you?"

"Well, you won't find out by killing me."

She is breathtakingly beautiful, lush, carnal, and yet innocent. She could be a model for the covers of all those 1950s pulp detective magazines. When the cops find her body, Hoover feels a special pain, because he loved her for six months, and then finally left her because he loved his wife (Melanie Griffith) more.

The cops follow a trail of leads and clues through a strange cross section of southern California. Their search mirrors the method used by Raymond Chandler in his Philip Marlowe novels, where a crime requires an expedition into the psychological undergrowth of a sinful and greedy community. Hoover gets a film in the mail, showing him having sex with Allison. Tracking down the film leads to the possibility that there were other films, and that blackmail may be involved. And then tests show that glass in the dead girl's foot is radioactive, and the Hat Squad finds itself breaking onto a military atomic test range.

This Allison knew a lot of guys. Maybe she would have stayed with Hoover if he had stayed with her. But then her list grew longer, and as Hoover follows it, it leads him to the consumptive General Timms (John Malkovich), kingpin of U.S. atomic testing, who saw the girl on the last weekend of her life. And Timms, in turn, is connected to the unbending Colonel Fitzgerald (Treat Williams) and the snaky chief of police (Bruce Dern).

*Mulholland Falls* is the first movie directed by Lee Tamahori since his powerful *Once Were Warriors* (1995), the story of violence and abuse in a Maori family in New Zealand. It couldn't look and feel more different—it's a masterfully atmospheric *film noir*—and yet it sees a similar culture of men who define themselves violently by other men, and use women without knowing them. The film was photographed by Haskell Wexler, who finds a clean, hard-edged look to shots like one where the cops peer down into a nuclear crater in the sand, and others where the Hat Squad in their shiny Buick look like male action dolls out for a spin in *Toy Story*.

One of the key casting decisions was to use Jennifer Connelly as the wounded beauty at the heart of the story. Connelly is sexy in the way Marilyn Monroe was sexy—as if she doesn't quite believe it and can't quite help it—and she finds the right note, halfway between innocence and heedless abandon. The men around her are well cast to show the varieties of male ego and ruthless power, and it's no surprise that her best friend (Andrew McCarthy) is gay.

In the way the movie makes a tour through colorful locations—gangster nightclubs, lonely mountain roads, cheap apartment complexes, saloons, the desert—it reminds us of Chandler's famous line about the mean streets a man must walk down. It also seems to know something about how those streets got to be so mean.

## Multiplicity ★ ★ ½

PG-13, 110 m., 1996

Michael Keaton (Doug Kinney), Andie MacDowell (Laura Kinney), Zack Duhame (Zach Kinney), Katie Schlossberg (Jennifer Kinney), Harris Yulin (Dr. Leeds), Richard Masur (Del King), Eugene Levy (Vic), Ann Cusack (Noreen). Directed by Harold Ramis and produced by Trevor Albert and Ramis. Screenplay by Chris Miller, Mary Hale, Lowell Ganz, and Babaloo Mandel, based on the short story by Miller.

As *Multiplicity* opens, Doug Kinney is complaining that he's too busy to talk to himself. He's a construction executive, saddled with a foreman who rips up the wrong driveways. Home is a place he visits between emergencies. When he tells his wife, Laura, that they need a schedule, she wails, "We don't need a schedule. We need a miracle!"

They get one. Doug (Michael Keaton) is working on a job one day at the Gemini Institute, one of those California think tanks where no idea is too large to be enlarged. Its director, Dr. Leeds (Harris Yulin), listens to his complaints and offers a solution: Doug obviously needs to be cloned. Leeds explains his scientific method, and Doug gasps, "You Xerox people!" But if Doug—or two Dougs—could be in two places at one time, think of the scheduling breakthroughs he could make. And so he agrees to be cloned.

That's the setup for *Multiplicity*, the new reality-adjusting comedy from Harold Ramis, whose *Groundhog Day* (1993) starred Bill Murray as a weatherman condemned to repeat the same day over and over until he gets it right. *Groundhog Day* had a certain sweetness and even a sly philosophical depth, but *Multiplicity* is more of a ground-level comedy, in which we can usually anticipate the problems that Doug and his clones will encounter.

Of course the clone (Doug Two) doesn't think of himself as a clone; he is in every detail the duplicate of Doug One. Dr. Leeds helpfully provides tattoos behind the ears to tell them apart. One takes Two home with him and hides him in an apartment upstairs over the garage. Laura (Andie MacDowell) luckily never goes up there—which is just as well, since the entire plot depends on the clones running riot over the garage while the facade of normal family life is maintained in the house.

Keaton plays Dougs One and Two (and eventually Three and Four) fairly seamlessly, thanks to special effects. In his conversations with himself, he doesn't always have the precise timing that Eddie Murphy brought to the dinner-table scenes in *The Nutty Professor*, which used similar methods. But he's good at helping us tell the Dougs apart. From the moment of cloning, each Doug begins to develop individual traits. Doug One, who was such a workaholic, turns out to have an unsuspected domestic side. Doug Two is even more workaholic than the original. Three develops party-animal tendencies. And Doug Four is a simpleminded goof. (Dr. Leeds explains that Four was cloned from a copy, not the original, although with digital methods the copy should not have degraded—but we're not talking hard science here.)

Once the premise is established, the movie drifts into predictable waters. Discovery of the scheme will be narrowly averted. Laura will somehow remain oblivious to most of the bizarre and inexplicable things happening around her. One will wear himself out trying to keep Two, Three, and Four in line ("No sex with my wife!"). And there will be a lesson in life at the end, although I am not sure this material has earned such profundity.

Watching the film, I enjoyed a lot of it, especially Keaton's permutations on the theme of himself. But I wondered why the possibilities weren't taken to greater comic extremes. How about a gay Doug? A mean one? A blackmailing Doug who threatens to go public? How about Laura finding out what's going on (which she doesn't do during a long, long night with the clones)? How about elevating the material to true screwball, instead of staying at the level of sitcom and human comedy?

As it is, *Multiplicity*'s promising material gets awfully thin by the end of the film. It feels more like a short film grown long, which is death to a comedy. And why, oh why, does an anarchic spirit like Harold Ramis (who was once a resident anarchist at Second City) feel obligated to provide a sweet little moral at the end of this fable? Why not run wild and see what happens?

## Muppet Treasure Island ★ ★ ½

G, 99 m., 1996

Tim Curry (Long John Silver), Kermit the Frog (Captain Smollett), Kevin Bishop (Jim Hawkins), Miss Piggy (Benjamina Gunn), The Great Gonzo (Himself), Rizzo the Rat (Himself), Billy Connolly (Billy Bones), Jennifer Saunders (Mrs. Bluveridge). Directed by Brian Henson and produced by Martin G. Baker and Henson. Screenplay by Jerry Juhl, Kirk R. Thatcher, and James V. Hart, suggested by the Robert Louis Stevenson novel.

I was talking to a friend the other day who said he'd never met a child who liked reading Robert Louis Stevenson's *Treasure Island*. Neither have I, I said. And he'd never met a child who liked reading Stevenson's *Kidnapped*. Me either, I said. My early exposure to both books was via the Classics Illustrated comic books. But I did read the books later, when I was no longer a kid, and I enjoyed them enormously. Same goes for Stevenson's *Dr. Jekyll and Mr. Hyde*.

The fact is, Stevenson is a splendid writer of stories for adults, and he should be put on the same shelf with Joseph Conrad and Jack London instead of in between Pooh and Peter Pan. The Stevenson books have been pretty well swamped by the countless movie, TV, and stage adaptations of the stories. *Treasure Island* was made into four films between 1934 and 1990, with Long John Silver played by Wallace Beery, Robert Newton (the best), Charlton Heston, and Orson Welles. Meanwhile, the old peg-legged scoundrel has even spun off a chain of fast-food restaurants.

The original Stevenson version has been so thoroughly updated, retreaded, and revised, indeed, that it was probably only a matter of time until the Muppets got to it. After the success of *The Muppet Christmas Carol* (1992), the heirs to Jim Henson must have seen the road ahead: Take famous family stories and recast them with a mixture of humans and Muppets. How can it fail?

Basically, it can't. *Muppet Treasure Island*, directed by Brian Henson, son of the late Muppet genius, will entertain you more or less in proportion to your affection for the Muppets. If you like them, you'll probably like this. In the democratic tradition that has distinguished Muppet movies since the beginning, the credits list Muppets and humans interchangeably, in the order of the size of their roles, and so we note that the movie stars Tim Curry as Long John Silver, Kermit the Frog as Captain Smollett, Kevin Bishop as young Jim Hawkins, and Miss Piggy as Benjamina Gunn.

The story: An old salt named Flint buries untold treasure on an island. Young Jim is given a map to the treasure and sets sail (with The Great Gonzo and Rizzo the Rat) to find it. Kermit's character captains the ship, and also on board is Curry, as Long John Silver. Once on the island, they find, as in most of the other film versions of the story, that Flint has left someone behind.

In most versions, it's Ben Gunn. In this one, it's Benjamina Gunn, played with her usual panache by Miss Piggy, who is queen of the island's warthogs. (Don't quiz me on this, but I think there's a sneaky cross-reference here to *Lord of the Flies*, which has, of course, its own warthogs and a character named Piggy.)

Silver is determined to have the treasure, and is backed by fellow mutineers. Jim Hawkins feels betrayed and cheated of what's rightfully his. And Miss Piggy is the wild card, describing herself in the press book as ". . . a beautiful—correction—devastatingly beautiful pig," observing, "Although *moi*'s screen time is far below that of your average superstar, *moi* makes every moment count."

So does Tim Curry, who has more or less perfected the over-the-top put-on. Not for nothing was he cast in *Rocky Horror Picture Show*. It isn't easy, costarring with a Muppet, as actors as talented as Orson Welles and Michael Caine have discovered over the years, but Curry's strategy is to outact and outbluster them, and mostly he succeeds.

As I suggested, you're likely to enjoy the movie in proportion to how much you enjoy the Muppets anyway. *Moi*, I sort of like them sometimes, and I enjoyed the *Christmas Carol* movie, but this one seems less cleverly written, and for *moi* it's a near miss.

## Murder at 1600 ★ ★ ½

R, 106 m., 1997

Wesley Snipes (Harlan Regis), Diane Lane (Nina Chance), Alan Alda (Alvin Jordan), Daniel Benzali (Nick Spikings), Dennis Miller (Detective Stengel), Ronny Cox (President Jack Neil). Directed by Dwight Little and produced by Arnold Kopelson and Arnon Milchan. Screenplay by Wayne Beach and David Hodgin.

There is an opening sequence that's familiar from a lot of cop movies. A madman is waving a gun and threatening bystanders. He is surrounded by cops. Then the department's hot shot drives up, sizes up the situation, intuits how to push the madman's buttons, walks up to him unarmed, distracts him, disarms him, and the crisis is over.

That's how Eddie Murphy's *Metro* opened, and that's Wesley Snipes's big opening scene in *Murder at 1600*. This cliché serves useful purposes: (1) it opens the movie with an action scene, (2) it establishes the hero's credentials as a guy who doesn't play by the rules, and (3) it's the setup for a payoff later in the movie—usually in a minor comic key.

That's what happens this time. Turns out the guy waving the gun is a depressed government commissioner. Turns out Snipes has had problems with the same agency: It wants to tear down his apartment building and put up a parking lot. In a movie involving a White House murder, the odds are excellent that sooner or later the cop and the president are going to be chatting about that parking lot.

Snipes plays Harlan Regis, a Washington police detective who is assigned when a woman is found murdered in the White House. He gets into a territorial struggle with Spikings (Daniel Benzali), the head of the Secret Service detail, who gives him absolutely no cooperation.

"She was killed in my city," Regis barks.

"She was killed in my house," Spikings growls.

Why was a city cop assigned in the first place? "They got you in to make it look real," Regis is told, and indeed there seems to be a cover-up under way. Among the suspects: the president's son, who was a lover of the dead woman, and perhaps the president himself (Ronny Cox). A voice of reason seems to be the national security adviser (Alan Alda), who's a contrast to the demented Mr. Clean image of Spikings.

Because this is a cop movie, Regis is supplied with a partner (Dennis Miller). Miller serves no function except to take phone calls, but soon we understand: He's a seat-warmer, brought in to provide a virtual partner until the movie can supply a real one. Regis quickly meets Nina Chance (Diane Lane), a member of the Secret Service detail and an Olympic Gold Medal sharpshooter. Even though they're on opposite sides of the jurisdictional divide, they share the conviction that an innocent man is being framed.

A lot of *Murder at 1600* is well done. Characters are introduced vividly, there's a sense of realism in the White House scenes, and some of the dialogue by Wayne Beach and David Hodgin hits a nice ironic note. (In a briefing, White House spokesmen are told: "We would like you to avoid two words when talking to the media. The words are 'woman' and 'murder.'") The cop and the sharpshooter achieve an easy rapport; she likes it that his apartment is filled with incredibly elaborate reconstructions of Civil War battles.

But then the movie kicks into autopilot. The last third of the film is a ready-made action movie plug-in. Without giving away a single secret, I can tell you that Regis and Chance find it necessary to break into the White House. And to do this, they must traverse a forgotten series of tunnels that lead by labyrinthine twists into the White House basement. The movie does what too many thrillers do: It establishes an interesting premise, and then instead of following it, substitutes standard action clichés. Will there be water, rats, electricity, dangerous secrets, hazards, security traps, flames, explosions, and gunshots in the tunnel? If you think not, you haven't seen *The Rock* or all the other movies that inspire this sequence.

While our heroes are wading through the dangerous subterranean waters, let's step back and think. They need to tell the president something. He is walled off by a conspiracy. How can they get the information to him? I can think of two answers: (1) the president's son has a personal motive for wanting his father to get the information, and has complete access to him; and (2) the cop is surrounded by TV cameras every time he steps outside. He could simply blurt out the truth, since there is no need to keep it secret. Neither of these alternatives would be as much fun as breaking into the White House, but they would have a better chance of success.

The fact is, the entire movie is fiction, and so if it's entertaining me, then I'm grateful. It's only when a movie stops working that I ask questions. For example, in a later scene, Regis masquerades as a janitor and pushes a cart through the White House while holding his head down and whistling tunelessly. Doesn't he know that holding your head down and whistling tunelessly is what *all* suspicious characters do when they disguise themselves as janitors? Isn't that like wearing a neon sign saying IMPOSTOR?

I'd love to see a taut, competent police procedural based on a murder in the White House—one that followed standard procedures to see how they were warped by presidential power. *Murder at 1600* seems to have started in that direction, before the fatal decision was made to cut out large chunks of the story in order to import weary thriller clichés. If I want to see a movie about slogging through flooded tunnels, I'll watch *The Third Man*.

## My Best Friend's Wedding ★ ★ ★

PG-13, 105 m., 1997

---

Julia Roberts (Julianne Potter), Dermot Mulroney (Michael O'Neal), Cameron Diaz (Kimmy Wallace), Rupert Everett (George Downes), Philip Bosco (Walter Wallace), M. Emmet Walsh (Joe O'Neal), Rachel Griffiths (Samantha Newhouse),

Carrie Preston (Amanda Newhouse). Directed by P. J. Hogan and produced by Jerry Zucker and Ronald Bass. Screenplay by Bass.

When she dumped Michael as a boyfriend in college, Julianne made him her new best friend. And they made a pact: If they were still single at twenty-eight, they'd marry each other. Now they're almost twenty-eight. And Michael is in Chicago. And wants Julianne to call him. She's touched. She's always really loved the guy. But he's not calling to propose. He's calling to explain he's engaged to be married in three days—to a junior at the University of Chicago, whose father owns the White Sox and a cable TV empire.

This is not good news for Julianne. P. J. Hogan's *My Best Friend's Wedding* tells the story of how she tries to sabotage the wedding and win the man she should have married all along. And since Julianne, a famous food critic, is played by the luminous Julia Roberts, we know how the movie will end, right? Not necessarily.

One of the pleasures of Ronald Bass's screenplay is the way it subverts the usual comic formulas that would fuel a plot like this. It makes the Julia Roberts character sympathetic at first, but eventually her behavior shades into cruel meddling. It gives Kimmy Wallace (Cameron Diaz), the fiancée, goodness and warmth instead of a ditzy facade. It makes Michael (Dermot Mulroney) an intelligent player in the drama, rather than the easily manipulated male we might expect. And out of left field it brings in another character, George (Rupert Everett), who is Julianne's editor, gay, and playfully wise.

The movie takes place over a few days in summer in Chicago. Julianne is devastated to learn that Michael is marrying this rich young beauty, and her strategy is simple: Put on a happy face, pretend to go along, and destroy from within. Kimmy knows she's got a formidable opponent, and her strategy is niceness: "You win. He's got you on a pedestal and me in his arms." She asks Julianne to be maid of honor.

How does Michael feel? He's a sportswriter who's always working, whose idea of a honeymoon is taking his bride on a baseball road trip, whose occupation, as Julianne observes, involves spending a great deal of time in places like College Station, Texas. He loves Kimmy. Truly loves her. The fact that her dad is a zillionaire sports owner isn't relevant because Michael, of course, would never accept a job from him. And Kimmy's dad (Philip Bosco), of course, would never offer him a job—not until the scheming Julianne convinces Kimmy to ask her dad to do that.

The fight over the job offer is a disaster, because it ends in reconciliation and forgiveness. It is also a bad idea when Julianne forces Kimmy to sing in a karaoke bar. Will Michael see his fiancée in a different light when he discovers what a lousy singing voice she has? Not at all, because she has moxie, and saves her bad performance with showmanship. That's when Julianne gets the idea of forging an e-mail from Kimmy's rich dad to the editor of Michael's sports magazine.

The e-mail is the movie's turning point. Until then, we've been more or less on familiar ground, in a tables-turned romantic comedy. But the e-mail is really sneaky, and really mean, and we realize with a little start that Julia Roberts is not the heroine of this movie. We were identifying with the wrong person. We hope, guiltily, that Michael and Kim will get married.

That makes the movie's third act surprisingly interesting: We don't have any idea what will happen. The screenplay has never been on autopilot; it just fooled us into thinking it was, in order to sneak up on the unpredictability. Ronald Bass, who wrote this as an original, has credits including some of the best recent women's roles: *Sleeping with the Enemy, The Joy Luck Club, When a Man Loves a Woman, Dangerous Minds, Waiting to Exhale.* Here he takes a romantic formula, turns it inside out, and adds a wild card in the character of George, who is played by Rupert Everett as a man comfortable with himself and insightful about others (he gives Julianne the only advice that could ever work—"tell him you love him!"—even though it may come too late).

Stories like this are tricky for the actors. They have to be light enough for the comedy, and then subtle in revealing the deeper tones. Roberts, Diaz, and Mulroney are in good synch, and Roberts does a skillful job of negotiating the plot's twists: We have to care for her even after we stop sharing her goals. I was wondering, toward the end, how the story could possibly stay true to itself and still contrive a happy ending. It does, but not at all the one we're expecting. This is subtle writing, to end a movie not with a clear-cut plot resolution, but with the right note, struck and then held. ☞

## My Favorite Season ★ ★ ★

NO MPAA RATING, 120 m., 1995

Catherine Deneuve (Emilie), Daniel Auteuil (Antoine), Marthe Villalonga (Berthe), Jean-Pierre Bouvier (Bruno), Chiara Mastroianni (Ann), Carmen Chaplin (Khadija), Anthony Prada (Lucien). Directed by Andre Techine and produced by Alain Sarde. Screenplay by Claudine Taulere.

Here is a French movie about a family that is unhappy in so many different ways that death is not a defeat but an escape. It is about the way a hurt in childhood can bend and shape an adult life years later, and about how guilt may make us regret being selfish, but is unlikely to make us generous. It is a sad film, but not a depressing one; to some degree it is a comedy.

Andre Techine's *My Favorite Season* is one of those intriguing films that functions without a plot and uses instead an intense curiosity about its characters. As it opens, an old woman (Marthe Villalonga) has reached the point where she should no longer live alone. Her daughter (Catherine Deneuve) brings her home to live with her family, which includes a daughter (Chiara Mastroianni), an adopted son (Anthony Prada), and the son's uninhibited Moroccan girlfriend (Carmen Chaplin). There is also a husband (Jean Pierre Bouvier), who is remote from the others.

The mother is not happy in the family's bourgeois home in Toulouse. She sits by the swimming pool in the middle of the night, talking fretfully under her breath ("Sometimes I talk to myself—it's less exhausting than talking to someone else"). Deneuve goes to pay a visit on her unmarried younger brother (Daniel Auteuil), whom she has not seen for three years, since they quarreled at their father's funeral. He is invited to a Christmas dinner for the entire family. Soon we will find that Christmas is probably not anyone's favorite season.

Andre Techine, the former critic who directed this film from a screenplay by Claudine Taulere, doesn't set up the story in terms of goals and setbacks. He is content to sit on the sidelines and watch, bemused. For a time we watch the behavior of the children. Auteuil walks in on Prada and Chaplin as they are making love, and later Prada and Mastroianni repair to his bedroom with Chaplin and convince her to do a striptease. She is in the middle of it when their father walks in, distractedly, and leaves again. This family has so much on its mind that strange adolescent sexual behavior hardly registers.

There is, we gather, a lot of bad blood in the past. The husband is not pleased to see his brother-in-law. The brother-in-law locks himself in the toilet and makes resolutions ("Be nice, express an interest, don't get carried away"). The evening ends in a fistfight, and blood is shed—not much, but enough to convince the old mother that she should return to her home and no longer test her daughter's hospitality.

Now what about Deneuve and Auteuil? What happened in their childhood that has made them so skittish today? It becomes clear that Auteuil passionately loves Deneuve, probably not in an incestuous way, but more in a possessive way. She was like a mother and a heroine to him, and when she got married and left home, a wound was opened up in his soul that has never healed. He prays for an end to Deneuve's marriage, and nurses hopes that perhaps they can set up a household together. The fate of the mother seems forgotten at times.

We watch this movie with interest because it watches its characters with interest. They behave with the unpredictability of real people. At one point, angry and disturbed, Deneuve deliberately slides an expensive china clock off a mantel, allowing it to crash into pieces on the floor. Why? Because it's what she felt like doing. The movie feels no need to explain every action.

There are perfect little moments in the film. A woman in a café singing "One day, he will die." Deneuve's memory of how her mother could find mushrooms in the woods "like an animal." Auteuil dropping from the balcony of his room to deliberately break his leg (we are left to decide if he is acting out of self-loathing, or from a desire to inspire his sister's pity). You leave this movie in the same way you leave family gatherings, aware that years of old aches, torments, and resentments are simmering under the surface, and that it is probably wise to leave them there.

## My Fellow Americans ★ ★ ½

PG-13, 102 m., 1996

Jack Lemmon (Russell P. Kramer), James Garner (Matt Douglas), Dan Aykroyd (William Haney), John Heard (Ted Matthews), Wilford Brimley (Joe Hollis), Lauren Bacall (Margaret Kramer), Sela Ward (Kaye Griffin), Everett McGill (Colonel Paul Tanner). Directed by Peter Segal and produced by Jon Peters. Screenplay by E. Jack Kaplan, Richard Chapman, and Peter Tolan.

Only the thought that the same words will be used by every other reviewer in the country prevents me from referring to *My Fellow Americans* as "Grumpy Old Presidents." Or did I just do that? James Garner steps into the role usually played by Walter Matthau, Jack Lemmon plays his usual grump, and 102 minutes of insult humor rolls painlessly past.

The characters: Lemmon was president for four years, and then was defeated by Garner, who was president for four years before being defeated by Dan Aykroyd. Lemmon, such a penny-pincher that he wants to charge Garner for half a Tootsie Roll, is vaguely George Bushian. Garner, a ladies' man, is vaguely Clintonian. Aykroyd is not really presidential at all, but his vice president, played by John Heard, is aimed squarely at Dan Quayle.

Given this premise, *My Fellow Americans* could have been hard-edged political satire, but that's not what anybody connected with the film had in mind. Neither Republicans nor Democrats will find anything to really offend them, and although some audience members may be surprised at the salty language of the two ex-presidents, all the evidence indicates that the actual recent inhabitants of the White House, Jimmy Carter perhaps excluded, have had extremely well-developed vocabularies.

The story: The Aykroyd character, about to be skewered in a kickback scandal, finds a way to shift the blame to the two ex-presidents. They, of course, hate one another, but find themselves fighting for their lives after administration hit men blow up their helicopter (just after they've left it). Evidence to prove Lemmon's innocence may be in his presidential library in Ohio, but there are killers looking for the two men, and they escape only by the neat trick of posing as celebrity look-alikes of themselves.

A lot of the movie is, shall we say, not convincing (I was personally certain that I would never again see Jack Lemmon or James Garner leaping from a moving train, but I was wrong). Chase scenes involve the usual assortment of on-the-road types, including a colorful female truck driver, an Elvis imitator, illegal immigrants, and the "Dykes on Bikes" motorcycle club. These scenes are familiar from many another film.

What's entertaining, however, is the way the movie skewers the human weaknesses of the two old presidents. It's funny when Lemmon collects a big paycheck for giving a speech before a Japanese insurance company, and finds himself dancing with the company mascot, a giant panda. It's funny when Garner agrees to write his memoirs mostly in the hopes of sleeping with his sexy book editor. It's funny when Lemmon boasts of his eleven books in print, including a cookbook, *Hail to the Chef.* And touching when he confesses he only writes the books to remind people that he still exists.

Both actors have enormous charm, work easily together, and have enough parallels with real-life counterparts that we can amuse ourselves playing Spot-the-Chief Executive. I liked the moment, for example, when Garner (posing as his own celebrity impersonator) meets a blonde who tells him she slept with "the real guy." Garner is interested. "What was he, uh, like?" And I smiled as Lemmon drank vodka from hotel minibars and then refilled the little bottles with water to keep from being charged.

*My Fellow Americans* is a series of cheap shots and missed opportunities, but a lot of the cheap shots are funny, and maybe the climate is wrong for sharply barbed political satire. I dunno. This is not a great comedy and will be soon forgotten, but it has nice moments.

## My Giant ★ ★

PG, 107 m., 1998

Billy Crystal (Sammy), Kathleen Quinlan (Serena), Gheorghe Muresan (Max), Joanna Pacula (Lilianna), Zane Carney (Nick), Jere Burns (Weller), Steven Seagal (Himself). Directed by Michael Lehmann and produced by Billy Crystal. Screenplay by David Seltzer, based on a story by Crystal and Seltzer.

The posters for *My Giant* show the seven-foot, seven-inch basketball star Gheorghe Muresan holding Billy Crystal (who is at least two feet shorter) under his arm. That looks funny. Who could guess it's a heartfelt friendship?

We go into the movie and meet Crystal, who plays Sammy, a Hollywood agent visiting the set of his single remaining client, in Romania. He's not having a good day. His wife announces she's leaving him, his client fires him, and then his car swerves into a creek. It looks like he'll drown, until he is saved by two enormous hands.

Regaining consciousness later in a monastery, he discovers that the hands belong to Max (Muresan), a local giant who is the ward of the monks. In the monastery he reads Shakespeare and pines for his lost love, who jilted him and moved to New Mexico. He is a big, sweet guy. Very big. Muresan may not have heard of Rossellini's belief that everyone has at least one movie performance in him (playing himself), but he illustrates that principle nicely.

Sammy, a desperate hustler, sees Max as his meal ticket out of Romania and back into the business. Promising him an eventual reunion with his lost beloved, he flies the two of them back to America, where the plot grows mired in sentimentality and we gradually realize this is not a comedy after all, but a greeting card crossed with a guide to improved self-esteem. The movie, which could have been a funny send-up of Hollywood talent requirements, gets distracted by subplots: Can Sammy's marriage be saved? Will his son learn to trust him again? Will that heartless girl in New Mexico give a break to the big lug whose heart she shattered?

Why is it that comics are always the biggest pushovers when it comes to sentiment? Do people who are funny have a greater than ordinary need to be loved? Is that why they want to make us laugh in the first place? After its promising start, *My Giant* isn't a comedy about an agent and a giant, so much as the heartwarming tale of a guy who learns to be a better family man.

It's interesting, the way Muresan establishes himself on screen as a stable area of calm, while the plot scurries around him. His English is not the best, but we believe he is who he's playing, and that's a test not every actor can pass. There are a few attempts to insert him into the world of showbiz, and they provide the movie's biggest laughs. There's a talk show sequence, a wrestling gig, and a funny send-up of Steven Seagal, in which Seagal does a good job of cheerfully skewering himself. That comes as Sammy tries to get Max a job on the new Seagal thriller, being shot in Las Vegas, and suggests how the whole movie could have worked, if it hadn't headed straight for the heart-tug department.

But most of the movie is lugubrious. Way too much dialogue is about whether Sammy forgot his son's birthday, and whether his wife (Kathleen Quinlan) can trust him to ever remember it again, and whether Max's lifelong happiness really does depend on the coldhearted woman in New Mexico. Do you know anyone who wanted to see a heartwarming story about Gheorghe Muresan helping Billy Crystal get in touch with his better nature? I don't think I do.

## Mystery Science Theater 3000: The Movie ★ ★ ★

PG-13, 73 m., 1996

Trace Beaulieu (Dr. Forrester), Michael J. Nelson (Mike Nelson), Jim Mallon (Gypsy), Kevin Murphy (Tom Servo), Trace Beaulieu (Crow T. Robot), John Brady (Benkitnorf). Directed and produced by Jim Mallon. Screenplay by Michael J. Nelson, Trace Beaulieu, Mallon, Kevin Murphy, Mary Jo Pehl, Paul Chaplin, and Bridget Jones.

I doubt if any television show in the history of the medium has inspired more traffic on the Internet than *Mystery Science Theater 3000*, the show that elevates to an art form the ancient practice of talking during a movie. On CompuServe, in just one week, I noted more than 800 messages posted. If you add AOL and Prodigy and the Web and the Usenet, there must be thousands. It's as if the sight and sound of all those ad libs inspires fans to log in with their own.

Now there is a movie to go along with the TV show—or, more accurately, to act as a rebuke to the Comedy Channel, which chose the very time of the movie's release to announce that it would not renew *MST3K* (as its fans call it). Although *MST3K* found a new home on the Sci-Fi Channel, its loss would have been bearable, if only because we can do at home what the stars of the show do on the tube, which is to provide a running commentary on some of the worst movies ever made.

But perhaps you are not familiar with the

show. I've described it to any number of people who told me they'd never heard of it, only to have them say, "Oh, yeah—that show with the funny silhouettes down at the bottom of the screen. I always wondered what that was." Those who have never seen the show will find it easy to get up to speed for the movie, which explains the whole premise at the top. We learn about the diabolical Dr. Clayton Forrester, a twisted scientist who hopes to rule the world by frying our brains with the worst movies ever made. Will his plan work? To find out, he conducts experiments on the Satellite of Love, where the innocent Mike Nelson is his psychological subject. Mike fights back against brainwashing by using his sense of humor—he wisecracks all through the horrible movies, and is flanked by his robot pals, who join in.

*MST3K* looks easy enough that anyone could do it. But although we can all shoot a basket, not all of us are Michael Jordan, and the key to the program is in the scripting. My guess is that the show's hypothetical audience consists of brainy techno-nerds with a wide and eclectic familiarity with pop culture, politics, literature, and the movies. And to keep the audience on its toes, the program occasionally throws in esoteric references, which may be completely meaningless to all but a few viewers.

Part of the appeal of the program is in the wisecracking. But the movies themselves are also crucial. They are so incredibly bad (many of them are not only out of copyright but perhaps were never worth copyrighting in the first place) that they get laughs twice—once because of what they are, and again because of what is said about them.

The odd thing about *MST3K: The Movie* is that its target is *not* that bad—or at least, not *all* that bad. On second thought, maybe it is. Let's put it this way: I liked it a lot more when I was twelve than I do now. The movie is *This Island Earth* (1955), starring Jeff Morrow, Rex Reason, and Faith Domergue. It got fairly good reviews forty years ago, although today the props and makeup are ludicrous, and whoever gave Morrow his towering forehead was seriously overestimating the credulity of the audience.

As the film opens, Reason is saved from a plane crash by a mysterious and cheesy green ray, and soon receives a mysterious shipment of strange scientific parts, which he assembles with the assistance of a TV-like device that functions about as helpfully as the directions that come with mail-order bookshelves. The equipment allows him to contact an alien (Morrow), who invites him to dinner (much hilarious comment from Mike and the robots about good manners in seeming not to notice that the aliens look weird). Soon the humans board an airplane which looks from the outside like a DC-3, and from the inside like a plywood set. Mike boasts, "I'm fully instrument-rated for Microsoft Flight Simulator!" They fly to alien headquarters, where they discover only they can save Earth from the evil plans of one of the alien factions.

*This Island Earth* was eighty-seven minutes long, but *MST3K: The Movie* is itself only seventy-three minutes long, and since it has scenes of its own, we see only about fifty-five minutes of the original movie. Nothing I saw made me want to see more.

The problem with attending a movie like this is that it makes everyone into a comedian, and there's the temptation to wisecrack right along with Mike and his friends. Some people will find that alarming, since there's already too much talking in movie theaters. My own feeling is that movies get pretty much the audiences they deserve: People tend to be quiet for good movies and noisy during bad ones, and *This Island Earth* gets just about what it has coming.

## The Myth of Fingerprints ★ ½

R, 90 m., 1997

Blythe Danner (Lena), Hope Davis (Margaret), Laurel Holloman (Leigh), Brian Kerwin (Elliot), James LeGros (Cézanne), Julianne Moore (Mia), Roy Scheider (Hal), Noah Wyle (Warren), Arija Bareikis (Daphne), Michael Vartan (Jake). Directed by Bart Freundlich and produced by Mary Jane Skalski, Tim Perell, and Freundlich. Screenplay by Freundlich.

Some families cannot be saved. The family in *The Myth of Fingerprints* is one of them. There have been a lot of movies where dysfunctional families return home for uneasy Thanksgiving weekends (*Home for the Holidays* and *The Ice Storm* come to mind), but few in which the turkey has less to complain about than anyone else at the table.

The film takes place in chilly light at a farmhouse somewhere in New England, where angry and sullen grown children return for Thanksgiving, bringing along apprehensive lovers and angry memories. Waiting to welcome them is their mother, Lena (Blythe Danner), whose relative cheer under these circumstances is inexplicable but welcome, and their father, Hal (Roy Scheider), who, like so many WASP fathers in recent films, is by definition a monster (aware of his pariah status, he walks and talks like a medieval flagellant).

The family drags itself together like torture victims returning to their dungeons. The dialogue, wary and elliptical, skirts around remembered wounds. Angriest of all is Mia (Julianne Moore), who glowers through the entire film, nursing old grudges, and lashes out at her hapless fiancé, Elliot (Brian Kerwin), a psychotherapist who, if he were any good at all, would prescribe immediate flight for himself. Mia's younger sister, Leigh (Laurel Holloman), seems relatively unscathed by the family experience, maybe because her siblings exhausted the family's potential for damage before she grew into range.

Also in the family are two sons. Warren (Noah Wyle) is interested to learn that the great love of his life, Daphne, is back in town. Jake (Michael Vartan) has brought along his fiancée, Margaret (Hope Davis), who has an alarming taste for immediate sexual gratification ("anywhere, anytime," as Travis Bickle once said).

During the weekend, two of these characters will meet people from their pasts. For Warren, the reunion with Daphne (Arija Bareikis) will be a chance to explain why he broke off their warm relationship so suddenly and seemed to flee. Mia meets an old schoolmate who now calls himself Cézanne (James LeGros), and who represents, I think, a life principle the family would be wise to study.

Frequently in the movies, when an alienated, inarticulate, and depressed father starts cleaning his rifle, we can anticipate a murder or a suicide by the end of the film. Here we're thrown off course when Hal, the dad, buys a turkey at the grocery store and then shoots it with his rifle, so his family will think he hunted it down himself. (I would have appreciated a scene where he explained the plastic bag with the gizzards.)

The movie is not unskillful. The acting is much better than the material deserves, and individual scenes achieve takeoff velocity, but the movie ends without resolution, as if its purpose was to strike a note and slink away. *The Myth of Fingerprints* makes one quite willing to see the same actors led by the same director—but in another screenplay. This one is all behavior, nuance and angst, seasoned with unrelieved gloom. Some families need healing. This one needs triage.

## Nelly and Monsieur Arnaud ★ ★ ★ ½

NO MPAA RATING, 106 m., 1996

Emmanuelle Béart (Nelly), Michel Serrault (Monsieur Arnaud), Jean-Hughes Anglade (Vincent), Claire Nadeau (Jacqueline), Francoise Brion (Lucie), Michèle Laroque (Isabelle), Michel Lonsdale (Dollabella), Charles Berling (Jerome). Directed by Claude Sautet and produced by Alain Sarde. Screenplay by Sautet, Jacques Fieschi, and Yves Ulmann.

What a delicate dance they perform in *Nelly and Monsieur Arnaud.* It is a matter of great erotic fascination when two people are intrigued by the notion of becoming lovers, but are held back by the fear of rejection *and* the fear of involvement. Signals are transmitted that would require a cryptographer to decode. The difficulty is to send a message that can be read one way if the answer is yes, and the other way if the answer is no.

Nelly (Emmanuelle Béart) is young and beautiful, and poor, and married to an unemployed slug who is stuck in front of the television set all day. Monsieur Arnaud (Michel Serrault) is old and rich, and married to a woman who has been living in Switzerland for years with another man. One day Nelly meets her older friend Jacqueline in a café, and they are joined by Arnaud, who was once Jacqueline's lover.

Arnaud makes it clear he remembers meeting Nelly before: "Two years ago your hair was shorter, and lighter." When Jacqueline leaves the table for a moment, he asks her personal questions, discovers she is in debt, and offers her money. She turns it down. "It was an honest offer," he says. "I hope so," she says. They part, but a connection has been made. Arnaud has declared his interest, and Nelly has started to think. She tells her husband that Arnaud offered the money and she accepted it. She is testing him. He fails. She explains that she is leaving him. "You understand?" He nods. He does.

Arnaud gives Nelly the money, and she goes to work for him, editing his memoirs. He was once a judge, and then grew wealthy in real estate, "making Paris ugly." They work day after day in his vast, book-filled apartment. She criticizes his manuscript. He quietly enjoys the attention. She makes changes. "You butchered my text!" he cries. "You're turning my book into a brochure!" They become like a married couple. No, not like a married couple, but like two halves of a strange whole: Despite their age difference, they fit. It's not love. It's an infinitely delicate emotional and intellectual dance.

Nelly is one of those women who is so beautiful that everything she does is about her beauty. Arnaud knows how beautiful she is. So do his friends. One night he takes her to a restaurant and buys a bottle of wine older than she is. They talk about the possibility that Arnaud's friends, across the room, assume she is a prostitute. They would be wrong. To begin with, there is no sex. Although money is involved, Nelly is not with Arnaud because of money; it is simply that money makes it possible for her to be there.

But what do they want? Arnaud clearly wants to live with Nelly and be her lover, if he is not (as he fears) too old for that. On the other hand, equally clearly, he doesn't want to make a fool of himself, either by being rejected or by being accepted and then finding he is unwilling to make the changes that a relationship would require. As for Nelly, she wants—well, you will have to decide for yourself. I think she finds Arnaud enormously attractive, not least because of his great reserve. She is attuned to the fact that she attracts him, and she enjoys attracting him. But does she want him to declare his attraction or leave them suspended in their state of exquisite erotic tension?

And then there are others. Arnaud's handsome young editor Vincent (Jean-Hughes Anglade), for example. He sees Nelly at Arnaud's house and immediately asks her out. Arnaud is too proud to object to either one of them. But he is possessive and jealous. In response to his questions, Nelly tells him she has slept with Vincent. She has not. She is setting him a test, just as when she told her husband about the money. Does Arnaud pass it? The question is too simple. It is more a case of whether he agrees to take the test.

*Nelly and Monsieur Arnaud* won two Cesar awards, the French Oscars, for best director and best actor. For Claude Sautet, the director, it is a return to the subject of romantic restraint; in his *Un Coeur en Hiver* (1993), also starring Béart, he dealt in a different way with a man who will not declare himself, who plays it safe and canny. These are films of great fascination. Béart is as talented and subtle as she is beautiful, and in this role, where so much goes unsaid, nothing goes uncommunicated.

Serrault, who is sixty-eight, made his first movie in 1955 (no less than *Diabolique*). He has done a lot of comedy (he was in all three *La Cage aux Folles* movies), but here he finds a gravity and intelligence that are indispensable to the character. And he avoids all temptations toward sentimentalizing the situation; he gives us no way to feel sorry for Arnaud, who demonstrates, especially at the end of the story, that he is quite able to take care of himself.

A movie like this is likely to appeal to the same kinds of people who admire the novels of Henry James. It is about the emotional negotiations of people who place great value on their status quo, yet find it leaves them lonely. Sometimes, of course, the alternatives to loneliness are not worth the price, and that is something to think about, especially for Monsieur Arnaud, and perhaps even for Nelly.

## Nenette et Boni ★ ★ ★

NO MPAA RATING, 103 m., 1997

Gregoire Colin (Boni), Alice Houri (Nenette), Valeria Bruni-Tedeschi (Baker-Woman), Vincent Gallo (Baker), Jacques Nolot (Mr. Luminaire), Gerard Meylan (Uncle), Alex Descas (Gynecologist), Jamila Farah (Wise Woman). Directed by Claire Denis and produced by Georges Benayoun. Screenplay by Jean-Pol Fargeau and Denis.

There's an offhand cockiness to the characters in *Nenette et Boni* that reminded me of *Jules and Jim* and the other early Truffaut films where characters acted tough but were really emotional pushovers. Boni, a dreamy nineteen-year-old kid in Marseilles, shoots his pellet gun at a neighbor's cat, but has untapped reserves of romanticism and tenderness. It's Nenette, his fifteen-year-old sister, who's been tempered by life.

Claire Denis, the gifted French director, tells their story as if we already knew it. There are throwaway details, casual asides, events that are implied rather than shown. This creates a paradoxical feeling: We don't know as much, for sure, as we would in a conventional film, but we somehow feel more familiar with the characters because of her approach.

Nenette and Boni are the survivors of an apparently ugly divorce. After the breakup, Nenette (Alice Houri) lived with her father, and Boni (Gregoire Colin) with his mother. Now Boni lives alone, and one day Nenette turns up, seven months pregnant. She doesn't want the baby, but it's too late for an abortion, and so she accepts approaching motherhood with a grim indifference. Boni, on the other hand, is thrilled; he cares tenderly for the young mother-to-be, and dotes on every detail of the pregnancy.

They form, if you will, a couple. Not one based on incestuous feelings, but on mutual need and weakness: Boni provides what emotional hope Nenette lacks, and her pregnancy adds a focus and purpose to his own life. It is something real. And reality is what he's been lacking in a love life based largely on his inflamed fantasies about the plump wife (Valeria Bruni-Tedeschi) of the local baker (Vincent Gallo, playing an American in France).

*Nenette et Boni* is one of those movies that is saturated with sensuality but not with explicit detail. One of the most extended sex scenes involves Boni kneading pizza dough; what he does to the dough he does, in his imagination, to the baker's wife, and that is going to be one happy pizza.

Boni is sort of a moony kid, who keeps a pet rabbit and is apt to fall thunderstruck into long reveries of speculation or desire. The approaching childbirth is a reality check for him; we sense it will be one of the positive, defining moments of his life. About Nenette we aren't so optimistic. There are vague, alarming possibilities about the father of her child—the film acts like a family member that knows more than it says—and it may be years before Nenette recovers her emotional health.

Claire Denis, born in French Africa, is a director who seems drawn to stories about characters who want to build families out of unconventional elements. I have never forgotten the haunting emotional need in her first film, *Chocolat* (1988), about a mother and daughter living in an isolated African outpost, the father absent, and finding themselves drawn to an African foreman whose ability and stability offered reassurance.

With *Nenette et Boni,* she makes a more delicate film. She feels affection for the characters, especially Boni, and is very familiar with them. Maybe that's why she feels free to tell the story so indirectly. This isn't a chronicle of events in two lives told one after another. It's more like an affectionate, fond chat. "And Boni? How is he?" you imagine the audience asking her just before the movie begins. And Denis replying, "Oh, you know that Boni . . ."

## The Newton Boys ★ ★

PG-13, 122 m., 1998

Matthew McConaughey (Willis Newton), Skeet Ulrich (Joe Newton), Ethan Hawke (Jess Newton), Julianna Margulies (Louise Brown), Dwight Yoakam (Brentwood Glasscock), Vincent D'Onofrio (Dock Newton), Gail Cronauer (Jess Newton), Chloe Webb (Avis Glasscock). Directed by Richard Linklater and produced by Anne Walker-McBay. Screenplay by Linklater, Claude Stanush, and Clark Lee Walker, based on the book by Stanush.

The Newton boys were the most successful bank robbers in American history, up until the savings and loan bandits of the 1980s. Operating in the Roaring Twenties, they hit as many as two hundred banks, and then pulled off the nation's biggest train robbery, a mail train heist in northern Illinois. Despite their remarkable record, they never became as famous as John Dillinger or Bonnie and Clyde. On the basis of this movie I suspect it was because they were too respectable.

*The Newton Boys* tells the story of the four brothers and a friend who knew how to handle nitroglycerine. Operating mostly at night, blowing up safes that were no match for their skill, they worked under a simple code: no killing, no stealing from women and children, and no snitching. According to the film, they actually managed to complete their criminal careers without shooting anybody except for one of their own brothers, by accident.

The brothers are played by a roll call of gifted young actors: Matthew McConaughey (Willis, the oldest), Skeet Ulrich (Joe), Ethan Hawke (Jess), and Vincent D'Onofrio (Dock). Dwight Yoakam is Brentwood Glasscock, their explosives expert, who pours nitro as if intensely curious about what it would feel like to be vaporized in the next nanosecond. Julianna Margulies plays Louise, the cigar-store girl who hitches up with Willis without knowing his real name or occupation, and Chloe Webb is Glasscock's approving wife. It's not an enormous cast, and yet somehow the Newtons are hard to tell apart—not in appearance, but in personality. Their dialogue mostly strikes the same musing, loquacious note.

The film chronicles their criminal career in a low-key, meandering way; we're hanging out with them more than we're being told a story. There are a lot of conversations about the profession of bank robbery—which, as a topic for conversation, is not a whole lot more interesting than double-entry bookkeeping. And when there is action (as in a scene where they're unexpectedly chased by bank guards), it plays like a pale shadow of this film's master, *Bonnie and Clyde.*

The *B&C* influences are everywhere: in the period, the clothes, the cars, the banjo music on the sound track, the reunions between brothers, the suspicions of girlfriends, and even in the character of Texas Ranger Frank Hamer, who arrests the Newtons. Hamer was the ranger forced to pose for photos with Bonnie and Clyde; to be fair, his inclusion is probably a deliberate in-joke by Richard Linklater, the director and cowriter, but the film as a whole seems drained of thrust and energy—especially compared to his earlier films.

Linklater is the talented maker of *Slacker, Dazed and Confused, Before Sunrise,* and the underrated *subUrbia.* Those have all been pigeonholed as Gen-X movies, although there's a wide range of material. What none of them lack is energy: He's intensely involved in the lives of his characters, whether the preppies of *Before Sunrise* or the losers hanging out in a strip-mall parking lot in *subUrbia.*

He just doesn't seem as interested in the Newton Boys. Sure, they were great bank robbers—but their very success may help explain why their legend hasn't placed as high in the charts as Dillinger, Baby Face Nelson, or Pretty Boy Floyd. They were efficient professionals. And the movie sits there on the screen like a biopic of traveling salesmen who crack safes instead of prospects.

The most entertaining footage in the film comes at the end, during the credits, when we see the real Willis Newton, in his eighties, being interviewed by Johnny Carson, and see scenes from a home movie interview with the real Joe Newton. Willis makes a spirited defense of their trade to Carson. Since the insurance companies were crooks, too, and since the banks always exaggerated the amount of their losses, he says, it was "just one thief a-stealing from another."

## Niagara, Niagara ★ ★ ★

R, 93 m., 1998

Robin Tunney (Marcy), Henry Thomas (Seth), Michael Parks (Walter), Stephen Lang (Claude), John MacKay (Seth's Father), Alan Pottinger (Lot Cop), Sol Frieder (Pawn Broker), Candy Clark (Sally). Directed by Bob Gosse and produced by David L. Bushell. Screenplay by Matthew Weiss.

*Niagara, Niagara* is about two misfits who become lovers and hit the road, where the cruel world boots them toward a tragic conclusion. This is not a new idea, as the current revival of *Badlands* (1973) reminds us. But the movie contains three strong performances and a subject I haven't seen before: the affliction of Tourette's syndrome.

Marcy (Robin Tunney) and Seth (Henry Thomas) meet while shoplifting. In the parking lot outside the store, they share a broken conversation, until Marcy finally admits that she can't look at people while talking to them and notices that Seth can't either: "I like that." Outsiders and loners, they fall into one another's arms by default, and Seth is too shy or uncertain to show that he notices her sometimes strange behavior.

She levels with him: She has Tourette's syndrome, which in her case takes the form of sudden tics, contortions, arm-flailing, bursts of aggressive behavior, and acting out. There's medication to control it. And she constantly takes little drinks out of a flask because booze seems to help. "And sex helps. For some reason, sex helps."

We get a glimpse of their home lives. Seth lives with a violent, abusive father. Marcy lives in a cluttered school bus behind a mansion that I assume belongs to her parents. She has always wanted a "black Barbie head," but cannot find one on local shelves, so they decide to run away together. Maybe she can find one in Toronto.

The parabola of a road movie is as reassuring as a nursery rhyme. It is required that the heroes drive a full-sized American car, preferably an older model. That there be long shots showing them on the open road. That there be a montage of the roadside sights and signs. And eventually that there be a collision with the unbending requirements of society.

Marcy needs pills. They try to get them from a drugstore. They don't have a prescription. Since the medication she needs isn't a controlled substance, it's likely she could find someone to prescribe it for her, maybe in a free clinic, but no: They stick up the store that night, Seth is wounded, their car overturns in the getaway, and then the movie's strange, enchanted centerpiece begins.

They're found by an old geezer named Walter (Michael Parks) in a tow truck. He takes them to his ramshackle spread, tends the wound, and tells them of his late wife, whom he loved, and his favorite chicken, which he still loves. Seth is afraid of fish, but somehow finds the courage to go fishing with Walter. The writing and acting here blossom, and we get a glimpse of how the movie might have developed without the road formula to contain it.

What happens later in their journey I shall not reveal. We do indeed see Niagara Falls, which inspires some easy symbolism, and we do eventually see the rare Barbie head. But what disappointed me was the film's need to hold itself within the narrow requirements of the genre.

How many times have we seen Tourette's syndrome on the screen? Hardly ever. So why not devise a story that would be about these two characters and their problems, rather than plugging them into a road movie? They're packaged much as Barbie comes boxed in different roles. The movie is good, but could have been better if it has been set free to explore.

Robin Tunney is sometimes scary, she's so good at conveying her character's torment (she won the Best Actress Award at Venice). And Henry Thomas, who fifteen years ago was the little boy in *E.T.*, has developed into a fine actor, able to be quiet and absorbed. The materials were here for a different kind of film, in which the souls of the characters had an effect on the outcome. In *Niagara, Niagara*, we want to warn them there's no hope. They're in the wrong genre for that.

## Nick and Jane ½★

R, 96 m., 1997

Dana Wheeler-Nicholson (Jane Whitmore), James McCaffrey (Nick Miller), Gedde Watanabe (Enzo), David Johansen (Carter), Clinton Leupp (Miss Coco Peru), John Dossett (John Price). Directed by Richard Mauro and produced by Bill McCutchen III. Screenplay by Mauro, Neil William Alumkal, and Peter Quigley.

You don't want to watch *Nick and Jane;* you want to grade it. It's like work by a student inhabiting the mossy lower slopes of the bell curve. Would-be filmmakers should see it and make a list of things they resolve never to do in their own work.

The story involves Jane (Dana Wheeler-Nicholson), a business executive, and Nick (James McCaffrey), a taxi driver. She is unaware of the movie rule that requires that whenever a character arrives unannounced at a lover's apartment for a "surprise," the lover will be in bed with someone else. She finds the faithless John (John Dossett) in another's arms, bolts out of the building, and into Nick's cab. Then follow the usual scenes in which they fall in love even though two different worlds, they live in.

I call that the story, but it's more like the beard. Inside *Nick and Jane*'s heterosexual cover story is a kinky sex comedy, signaling frantically to be released. Consider. Nick's neighbor in his boardinghouse is Miss Coco Peru (Clinton Leupp), a drag queen. Nick's roommate is Enzo (Gedde Watanabe), whose passion for feet is such that he drops to his knees to sniff the insteps of complete strangers. The friendly black woman at the office is into bondage and discipline with the naughty boss. Carter (David Johansen), the boss's special assistant, is Miss Coco's special friend. Key scenes take place at a drag club where Miss Coco is the entertainer (her act consists of singing "The Lord's Prayer"—in all seriousness, and right down to the "forever and ever, Amen," I fear).

These elements could possibly be assembled into quite another movie (for all I know, they were disassembled from quite another movie). But they don't build into anything. They function simply to show that the filmmakers' minds are really elsewhere—that the romance of Nick and Jane is the bone they're throwing to the dogs of convention. I kept getting the strange feeling that if they had their druthers, director Richard Mauro and writers Neil William Alumkal and Peter Quigley would have gladly ditched Nick and Jane and gone with Miss Coco as the lead.

As for Nick and Jane, they have alarming hair problems. Dana Wheeler-Nicholson goes through the movie wearing her mother's hairstyle, or maybe it's Betty Crocker's. James McCaffrey starts out with the aging hippie look, but after an expensive makeover paid for by Jane, he turns up with his hair slicked back in the Michael Douglas Means Business mode. I think the idea was to show him ever so slightly streaked with blond, but they seem to have dismissed the stylist and done the job themselves, maybe over Miss Coco's sink with a bottle of something from Walgreen's, and Nick looks like he was interrupted in the process of combing yolks through his hair.

The camera work is sometimes quietly inept, sometimes spectacularly so. Consider the scene involving a heated conversation, during which the camera needlessly and distractingly circles the characters as if to say—look, we can needlessly circle these characters! The dialogue is written with the theory that whatever people would say in life, they should say in a movie ("This is a wonderful view!" "I've never been in the front seat of a cab before!").

There is one scene where Nick bashfully confesses to having studied art, and reluctantly lets Jane see some sketches he has done of her. The usual payoff for such scenes is a drawing worthy of Rembrandt, but what Nick shows her is one of those Famous Artist's School approaches where he drew an egg shape and then some crosshairs to mark where the ears and eyes should line up.

Nick's artistry knows no bounds. While masquerading as a business executive, he effortlessly absorbs the firm's current challenge, which apparently involves saving 25 percent on the importation of scrap metal from Surinam. He dispatches Enzo (wearing those L.A. Gear shoes with heels that light up) to collect lots of scrap metal from a junkyard, after which Nick dons a handy welder's helmet to fashion a sculpture, which he hauls into the CEO's office, explaining it is intended "to punctuate the enormity of the idea I'm about to present." Yes. That's what he says.

## Nico Icon ★ ★ ★

NO MPAA RATING, 75 m., 1996

Directed by Susanne Ofteringer and produced by Annette Pisacane and Thomas Mertens. Screenplay by Ofteringer.

*In the future everyone will be world famous for fifteen minutes.*

—Andy Warhol

That was too long for Nico. The most beautiful of Warhol's "superstars" was empty and disaffected, a woman who was given great natural gifts but could not enjoy them. *Nico Icon* is a documentary that tells the story of a woman who hated the natural beauty that landed her in *Paris Vogue* as a teenager, who was bored by life, love, and sex, who spent great portions of her life in a search for heroin, and who supported herself as a singer even though she hated singing and couldn't carry a tune. Death, when it came, must have been a relief.

Nico was born in 1939 in Cologne, Germany, christened Christa Paffgen. By the 1950s, she was in Paris, working as a fashion model, and she can be seen, ravishingly beautiful, in Fellini's *La Dolce Vita* (1959), joining Marcello Mastroianni on the Via Veneto and on a wild car ride to a decadent party. Even then her pose was one of ennui.

Bob Dylan introduced her to Andy Warhol in 1960. He used her in some of his movies (notably *Chelsea Girls*, where she endlessly snipped at her hair) and used her to draw attention to the Velvet Underground, a band he was promoting. She played tambourine and did vocals with Lou Reed, one of her many lovers.

After the Warhol scene faded, she drifted to Europe and fronted a band; those days are remembered in the film by her former drummer and manager, who says "she was the Sun and we were the planets" and their whole world centered on the van they used to drive from gig to gig. Nico, always in search of a fix, would pull knives and throw tantrums, and was "proud of her bad hair, rotted teeth, bad skin, and needle tracks . . . she was a middle-aged junkie." She switched from heroin to methadone in 1986, and died in 1988 of "too much sun," says her son, Ari. Uh-huh.

Since Nico apparently lived more or less the life she chose, and was either incapable or unwilling to imagine a happier one, it is hard to gather much sympathy for her. Ari is another matter. Nico conceived him with the French actor Alain Delon, who denied paternity, although Ari, seen in the film as an adult, is a dead ringer. Nico was not, to put it mildly, an ideal mother. She fed the infant on potato chips, and Ari was eventually rescued by Delon's mother, the only heroine in this film.

We meet her in her humble flat ("People think I live in a castle or something") and we learn that Delon gave her a choice: Ari or Alain. She chose the little boy, and has not spoken to Delon for seventeen years. Delon emerges from the episode as a right proper bastard, something that will not surprise those who have followed him over the years.

Nico reappeared in her son's life years later, hooked him on heroin, and when he was in a coma in the hospital she tape-recorded the sound of his life-support system and used it on her next album. Ari says his mother was a free spirit, a "gypsy." I say if he ever kills anybody, he's got a better defense than the Menendez boys.

Who was really there behind the beautiful, then crumbling, Nordic facade? It is hard to say. Nico was more than six feet tall, had perfectly chiseled features, spoke several languages, and took many lovers (Jim Morrison once tried to kill her during a sex ritual, she thought, and that endeared him to her). She had the Warholian fifteen minutes and more. We see her at the end in a 1986 interview, looking wasted. And in performance, clutching a mike and a cigarette, singing a low, mournful dirge. "Behind everything," a friend remembers, "was a desire for her own annihilation."

*Nico Icon* tells this story in a visual style that owes a lot to modern graphics (disjoined words appear on the screen just as they do in the Windows 95 ads) and a catchy editing style (music and dialogue are mixed so they comment on one another). Susanne Ofteringer, who directed the film, has found a lot of those who knew Nico, including aging Paris bohemians, Warhol director Paul Morrissey, and even Jackson Browne, her lover when he was seventeen. She has also managed, I sense, to be true to the spirit of Nico. The movie has no moral or message, does not attempt to rehabilitate Nico as an antiheroine, finds mostly emptiness and sadness in her life. I have a feeling Nico would have enjoyed it.

## Night Falls on Manhattan ★ ★ ★ ½

R, 114 m., 1997

Andy Garcia (Sean Casey), Lena Olin (Peggy Lindstrom), Richard Dreyfuss (Sam Vigoda), Ian Holm (Liam Casey), Ron Leibman (Morgenstern), James Gandolfini (Joey Allegretto), Shiek Mahmud-Bey (Jordan Washington), Colm Feore (Elihu Harrison), Paul Guilfoyle (McGovern). Directed by Sidney Lumet and produced by Thom Mount and Josh Kramer. Screenplay by Lumet, based on the novel *Tainted Evidence* by Robert Daley.

I see a slick, bemused man sitting behind a big desk in a dark room, flanked by his lieutenants. An evil man. I see a movie in which this sadistic puppet master devises diabolical schemes to destroy lives—until he is at last destroyed himself by the hero in a series of chase scenes and shoot-outs.

This man I see has absolutely nothing to do with Sidney Lumet's *Night Falls on Manhattan.* Why do I begin with him? Because he is not in the movie. Because a clone of him is at the center of so many films about police and criminals, law and order. Because he is an example of creative bankruptcy—the stereotyped villain who toys with a paperweight or a kitten, representing the inability of the filmmakers to find a good story in the world around them.

*Night Falls on Manhattan* is based on a book by Robert Daley, a New York writer who specializes in the shadowlands between right and wrong. It is about characters who have held onto what values they could while dealing in a flawed world. It has characters who do wrong and are therefore bad, but it doesn't really have "villains" in the usual movie sense of the word. It's too smart and grown-up for such lazy categories.

As the film opens, a lawyer named Sean Casey (Andy Garcia) is being trained as an assistant district attorney. Those scenes are intercut with some cops on a stakeout: Casey's father, Liam (Ian Holm), and the father's partner, Joey (James Gandolfini). They're after the biggest drug dealer in Harlem. But when they try to burst through his door, a barrage of gunfire answers them, and Liam is critically wounded. The call for help is answered by three precincts and ends in a fiasco: One cop is shot by another when a tire blowout is mistaken for gunfire, and the drug dealer ends up escaping in a squad car, while three cops are dead.

This creates a political hot potato for Morgenstern (Ron Liebman), the district attorney. His chief assistant, Harrison (Colm Feore), expects to be assigned the case, but instead, for publicity reasons, Morgenstern gives it to young Sean Casey, the hero cop's son. Leading the defense is hotshot Sam Vigoda (Richard Dreyfuss), who resembles Alan Dershowitz. One of the things Vigoda would like to reveal in court is why three precincts responded to the call when only one was supposed to: Were they turning up because they were all on the dealer's payroll?

Vigoda has a brilliant opening ploy: He produces his client (Shiek Mahmud-Bey) at a press conference and has him strip, so the reporters can be witnesses: "I am delivering my client in perfect condition. I want to be sure he turns up for trial in the same condition."

You see here how the complexities coil in upon themselves. The drug dealer is bad, yes, but are the cops heroes? Was the bust clean? Is there anything the young assistant D.A. doesn't know about his father, or his father's partner? There is a scene in a steam bath (where no one can wear a wire) between Casey and Vigoda, in which real motives and possibilities are gingerly explored. And as a result of the case, Casey finds himself sleeping with Peggy Lindstrom (Lena Olin), a lawyer in Vigoda's office, who frankly tells him, "I knew I was seeing the start of a great career and I knew I couldn't wait until I got you into bed."

Sidney Lumet is a director who is bored by routine genre filmmaking in which everything is settled with a shoot-out. In movies like *Dog Day Afternoon* (1975), *Prince of the City* (1981, also based on a Daley book), *The Verdict* (1982), *Running on Empty* (1988), and *Q & A* (1990), he shows how well he knows his way through moral mazes, where what is right and what is good may not coincide.

In this film he finds performances that suggest how tangled his characters are. Consider Liebman's scene-stealing work as the district attorney: The character (not the actor) is sort of a ham, who enjoys pushing his personal style as far as it will go, this side of parody. The way he speaks and moves fills all the volume of space around him. Is he a completely political animal? Not wholly. He has a very quiet, introspective late scene in which he reveals a deep, sad understanding of his own world. It is a fine performance.

Consider, too, James Gandolfini as Allegretto, one of the cops on the original bust. What does he know that he isn't telling? Young Sean has known his father's partner for a long time. Can he trust him? "I swear to God, Sean," the partner says, looking him straight in the eye, "your father is clean." But can he even trust his father? When asked why only two cops were on such an important bust, the old man testifies significantly, "In narcotics you gotta be careful. On a good lead you don't want too much word out."

*Night Falls on Manhattan* is absorbing precisely because we cannot guess who is telling the truth, or what morality some of the characters possess. In a lesser movie, we'd be cheering for the young assistant D.A. and against the slickster defense attorney. When the Lena Olin character climbed into bed with the hero, we'd suspect treachery or emotional blackmail. We'd assume the original cops were either heroes or louses. We'd assume that Harrison, the D.A.'s second-in-command, would be a schemer out to further his own career at any cost.

Here we don't know. Here intelligence is required from the characters: They're feeling their way. They've been around. They know movie courtrooms aren't like real ones, and that movies simplify life. They know that sometimes good people make mistakes, and that even those who break the law may be fundamentally committed to upholding it. That in a society where people find a choice between abject poverty and selling drugs, not everyone has the luxury of deciding in the abstract.

This movie is knowledgeable about the city and the people who make accommodations with it. It shows us how boring that obligatory evil kingpin is in so many other crime movies—sitting in his room, flanked by his henchmen, a signal that his film is on autopilot and we will not need to think.

## Nightwatch ★ ★

R, 105 m., 1998

Ewan McGregor (Martin Bells), Nick Nolte (Inspector Gray), Josh Brolin (James), Patricia Arquette (Katherine), Alix Koromzay (Joyce), Lauren Graham (Marie), Erich Anderson (Newscaster), Lonny Chapman (Old Watchman), Scott Burkholder (College Professor), Brad Dourif (Duty Doctor). Directed by Ole Bornedal and produced by Michael Obel. Screenplay by Bornedal and Steven Soderbergh, based on the film *Nattevagten* by Bornedal.

Horror films often bring out the best in a director's style but not in his intelligence. *Nightwatch* is an example. It's a visually effective and often scary film to watch, but the story is so leaky that we finally just give up: Scene after scene exists only to toy with us and prop up the impossible plot.

Ewan McGregor, from *Trainspotting,* stars as Martin Bells, a law student who takes a night watchman's job in the local morgue. It's a creepy building, not improved by two giant pine trees that flank the doors and have been wrapped in plastic, so that they look like swaying bodies in huge garbage bags.

Inside, we find the usual lighting problem: Corridors have small bulbs and are spooky, but the cold room for the corpses is brightly lit so we can see what we don't much want to see. The building itself has a certain eerie charm, with its large empty spaces and its institutional chill.

There's a nice sequence with Lonny Chapman as the retiring watchman, who shows the kid the ropes, filling him in on creepy old stories, and entreating, "Get a radio!" Much is made of the alarm that will go off if one of the corpses should suddenly come to life ("It's not going to happen," the old man assures Martin). The story is repeated about a watchman from "several years ago," who was dismissed in a messy scandal. There are murky shots of vats of chemicals, one of which, Martin is disturbed to discover, contains "feet—nothing but feet!"

Of course, the watchman's rounds include a time clock on the far wall of the cold room, which must be punched once an hour. (The morgue door has no handle on the inside, which if you really think about it makes sense, from the point of view of the corpses.) Each marble palette has a cord above it, within reach of a body that returns to life, although in the absolute dark of the storage room it would be a clever resurrectionist who thought to wave his hand in search of it.

The other characters: Martin's best friend,

James (Josh Brolin), who gets in bar fights because he likes the rush ("my tolerance level has increased"). Martin's girlfriend, Katherine (Patricia Arquette), who puts up with his bad breath, a by-product of working around formaldehyde. The creepy doctor (Brad Dourif) who works in the morgue. The frightened hooker (Alix Koromzay), who has a client who wants her to play dead. And the cop, Inspector Gray (Nick Nolte), who is sad, rumpled, and wise, and warns Martin that he is being framed for murder: "There's someone really dangerous standing right behind you."

One of these people is responsible for a series of murders of local prostitutes. I was able to guess which one in the opening credits, although I wasn't sure I was right for a while—and the movie gives him (or her) away in such a sneaky way that for a moment there even seems to be another explanation for his (or her) presence at the murder scene.

The movie is a remake of *Nattevagten*, a Danish film by Ole Bornedal, who also directed this English-language version. Dimension Films bought the original film, a hit in Europe, and kept it off the market here while producing the retread, no doubt to forestall the kinds of unfavorable comparisons that came up when the Dutch director George Sluizer remade his brilliant *The Vanishing* (1988) into a sloppy, spineless 1993 American film.

I haven't seen *Nattevagten*, and don't know how it compares with *Nightwatch*, but this film depends so heavily on horror effects, blind alleys, false leads, and red herrings that eventually watching it stops being an experience and becomes an exercise.

## Nil by Mouth ★ ★ ★ ½

R, 128 m., 1998

Ray Winstone (Raymond), Kathy Burke (Valerie), Charlie Creed-Miles (Billy), Laila Morse (Janet), Edna Dore (Kath), Chrissie Coterill (Paula), Jon Morrison (Angus), Jamie Forman (Mark), Steve Sweeney (Danny). Directed by Gary Oldman and produced by Luc Besson, Douglas Urbanski, and Oldman. Screenplay by Oldman.

Gary Oldman's *Nil by Mouth* descends into a domestic hell of violence, drugs, and booze, where a man can kick his pregnant wife and then, drunk, scrape out the words "My Baby" on the wallpaper with his bloody fingernails. It takes place in the pubs and streets of South London, where the actor grew up, and is dedicated enigmatically, "In memory of my father." We want to stand back out of the way; something primal, needful, and anguished is going on here.

Using a handheld camera and close-up style, Oldman plunges into the middle of this family as they spend a night at their local pub. At first we don't understand all the relationships, but Oldman uses the right approach: These people know each other so intimately and in such fearsome ways that any "establishing" scenes would dilute the impact.

The center of authority in the film is Janet (Laila Morse), the worn blond mother whose factory job is one of the family's few steady sources of income. Her own aged, feisty mother, Kath (Edna Dore), is still around. Janet's daughter is Valerie (Kathy Burke, who won the Best Actress award at Cannes). Val's husband, Ray (Ray Winstone), is a violent drunk whose rage alternates with self-pity. Val's brother, Janet's son, is Billy (Charlie Creed-Miles). He has a drug habit. Ray's best friend Mark (Jamie Forman) is emotionally dependent on him—maybe he's an excitement junkie, who feeds on the moments when Ray explodes.

This family weeps, bleeds, and endures. Billy, who lives with Val and Ray, is thrown out of the house after some money is missing; Ray beats him and bites his nose, and Billy staggers into a bleak dawn—homeless, although he still lives on the outskirts of the family, like a wounded wolf following the pack.

A day or so later, Ray walks into a pub and finds his wife, Val, playing pool with a casual friend. Ray seems cheerful at first, but he has the personality changes of the alcoholic, and orders her home, where he weeps and explodes in a jealous rage, sure Val (who is large with child) was having an affair with the man. She miscarries after his beating.

One of the film's key scenes comes after Val returns home and is seen, black, blue, and bandaged, by her mother. She tells Janet she was struck by a hit-and-run driver. Janet clearly knows Ray beat her daughter, but accepts the story. The dialogue here is precise in its observation; Val's details all have to do with the location ("You know, down by the shops"), as if the story is proven by the fact that the shops exist. Her mother vows revenge on the bastard driver who committed the hit and run; both women understand this is code for Ray. ("You know what it's like going to hospitals late at night," Janet says at one point. In most healthy families this is not something everyone knows.)

The film's portrait of street life in South London is unflinching and observant. Billy, drifting, looking for a fix, gets involved in a strange fight over a tattooed street person and his little pet dog. He goes to his mother's factory to borrow money for a fix, and then asks her to drive him to a dealer. Back in her van, he starts to shoot up, and she snaps, "Get in the back of the van where no one can see you." Just like a mother. The cost of Billy's habit is something Janet knows, just as in another family the mother would know the size of her son's paycheck.

Gary Oldman is clearly dealing here with autobiographical wounds. I saw him after the film played at Cannes, and he volunteered the information that a chair in the film is the same one his father sat in while drinking at home. He spoke in a flat voice, giving information, but I sensed that the chair was still occupied by the stabbing ghosts of days and words.

Yet *Nil by Mouth* is not an unrelieved shriek of pain. There is humor in it, and tender insight. After he almost kills himself on a bender, Ray is hospitalized, and Mark visits him. In a monologue brilliantly delivered by Winstone, Ray complains about the lack of love from his own father: "Not one kiss. Not one cuddle." In Ray's mind, he is the abused child. We sense Oldman's ability to understand, if not forgive.

At the beginning of *Nil by Mouth* we cannot understand the South London dialect very easily, and aren't sure who all the characters are. By the end, we know this family and we understand everything they say, and many things they do not say. And we remember another very minor character in the film, the small child of Ray and Val, who sits at the top of the stairs during a bloody fight and sees everything.

*Footnote: Dedicated to Oldman's father, the film is filled with personal touches. The actress who plays Janet, billed as "Laila Morse," is the author's sister; her stage name is an anagram of "my sister" in Italian. When Kath sings "Can't Help Lovin' That Man" over the closing credits, the voice dubbed onto the track belongs to Oldman's seventy-five-year-old mother. And that is his father's chair.*

## No Looking Back ★ ★

R, 96 m., 1998

Jon Bon Jovi (Michael), Edward Burns (Charlie), Lauren Holly (Claudia), Connie Britton (Kelly), Blythe Danner (Claudia's Mom), Jennifer Esposito (Teresa), Shari Albert (Shari), Kathleen Doyle (Mrs. Ryan). Directed by Edward Burns and produced by Ted Hope, Michael Nozik, and Burns. Screenplay by Burns.

Hobbies. That's what the characters in *No Looking Back* need. Bowling or yard sales or watching the Knicks on television. Anything. Although the movie wants us to feel sympathy for them, trapped in meager lives and empty dreams, I saw them as boring slugs. There is more to existence than moping about at bars and kitchen tables, whining about unhappiness while endlessly sipping from long-neck Budweiser bottles. Get a life.

The movie is the latest from Ed Burns, who won the Sundance Film Festival in 1995 with his rich and moving *The Brothers McMullen*, but has since made two thin and unconvincing films: *She's the One* (1996) and now this one, in which self-absorbed characters fret over their lives. I have no brief against that subject matter; I simply wish the characters and their fretting were more interesting, or their unhappiness less avoidable.

The film is set in the bleak, wintry landscape of Rockaway Beach, New York, where Claudia (Lauren Holly) works in a diner and lives with Michael (Jon Bon Jovi), a mechanic. They are engaged, in a sense, but with no plans for marriage; Michael wants to marry her, but she's "afraid to wake up ten years from now" still working in the diner.

As the film opens, Charlie (Edward Burns) returns to town on the bus after an absence of three years. He was once Claudia's lover, but ditched her without a farewell. Now he apparently hopes to pick up where they left off. He moves into his mother's house; she has his number and tells him to get a job. And then Michael, who was his best friend, comes over for more beer and conversation, and explains that he and Claudia are "together" now.

Will Claudia accept the dependable Michael? Or will she be swept off her feet once again by the flashier, more charismatic Charlie? "It's different this time," he tells her. "This time I need you. I love you." He's not the soul of eloquence, but she is willing to be persuaded.

The problem is, Charlie is an enigma. Where was he for three years? Why is he back? What are his skills, his plans, his strategies? His vision for the two of them is not inspiring: They'll leave town and go to Florida, where he has no prospects, and "start over." Still, Charlie paints a seductive picture.

Or does he? The film wants us to see Michael, the Bon Jovi character, as a boring, safe, faithful, but unexciting choice. But I sort of liked him; Bon Jovi plays the role for its strengths, which involve sincerity and a certain bottom line of integrity. Charlie, on the other hand, is one of those men who believe that true happiness, for a woman, consists of doing what he wants. He offers Claudia not freedom, but the choice of living in his shadow instead of her own.

The story plays out during overcast days and chilly nights, in lonely barrooms and rented houses. Some small life is provided by Claudia's family, which includes her mother (Blythe Danner) and her sister. The mother is convinced her husband, who has deserted her, will return someday. The sister is dating the local fishmonger. As the three women discuss the comings and goings of the men in their lives, they scheme like some of Jane Austen's dimmer characters, for whom the advent of the right man is about the most a girl can hope for.

It is extremely important to some men that the woman of their choice sleep with them. This is a topic not of much interest to outside observers, and often not even to the woman of their choice. *No Looking Back* is really only about whether Claudia will sleep with Charlie, stay with Michael, or leave town. As the characters unhappily circled those possibilities, I felt like asking Claudia to call me back when she made up her mind.

## Normal Life ★ ★ ★ ½

R, 104 m., 1996

Ashley Judd (Pam Anderson), Luke Perry (Chris Anderson), Bruce Young (Agent Parker), Jim True (Mike Anderson), Edmund Wyson (Darren), Michael Skewes (Swift). Directed by John McNaughton and produced by Richard Maynard and John Saviano. Screenplay by Peg Haller and Bob Schneider.

Sometimes a man and woman are drawn together precisely because they are perfectly wrong for one another. Consider Pam and Chris Anderson, the subjects of *Normal Life*. He is a Chicago suburban cop. She is a pothead who works in a factory, drinks too much, and dreams of falling into a black hole so that her image is forever imprinted on its event horizon.

They meet in a bar. Pam's with a guy. They have a fight. She smashes a glass and cuts herself. The guy leaves. Chris walks over, helps her bandage the cut, and says, "Want to dance?" It's a little awkward dancing with your hand held up in the air so the blood doesn't drip, but she accepts. It's love.

*Normal Life*, loosely based on a real-life crime story from the Chicago suburbs, is the new movie by John McNaughton, famous for *Henry: Portrait of a Serial Killer*. It's not as unremittingly painful as the earlier film, but it's just as fascinating in its portrait of criminal pathology. Just as Henry drew accomplices into the net of his madness, so does Pam (Ashley Judd) mesmerize Chris (Luke Perry). He's a straight-arrow policeman whose hobby is target practice. She's a space cadet whose hobby is astronomy, and who is reading, or pretending to read, *A Brief History of Time*.

Pam is one of those women who is forever pushing the edges of her own personal event horizon. She is drunk a lot, hysterical, manic-depressive, self-destructive. She tears up the apartment, mutilates herself, tries suicide, and specializes in embarrassing Chris (she walks into the police station dressed in hot pants, and turns up at his father's funeral on in-line skates).

Chris puts up with this because he must. Something in his makeup has addicted him to—what? The excitement? The abuse? The role of rescuer? "I just want to make you happy," he says. After he gets fired from the police department, he works a double shift at a security service, but she spends faster than he can earn. So he robs a bank. He's good at robbing banks, and soon he's able to show her the bright new townhouse in Lisle that he's bought with the money.

As for Chris, he gets his dream, too—which is to operate his own used-book store. Eventually, of course, she finds out what he's doing—and is so excited she has a sexual climax for the first time in her life. She wants to come along on the next job, and although Chris knows in his bones that this is a big mistake, he lets her. You may vaguely remember the outcome from headlines a few years ago.

This is one of those movies you watch with the same fascination as a developing traffic accident. Part of its success is because of the casting. Ashley Judd, so warm and likable in *Ruby in Paradise* (1993), here plays the kind of woman you would cross the room, or the state, to avoid. Luke Perry, who has a neat cop-style mustache and an obsession with control and order, is a perfect foil as a man who has never seen anything like her, and can't stop looking.

*Normal Life* takes place against the very normal backdrop of Chicago's western suburbs. Pam and Chris eat in fast-food places, shop in stores with BUY MORE painted on the walls, rob drive-up banks, and when they fight, they do it while stalking down the deserted sidewalks of a mall in the middle of the night. They look, at first glance, like your typical young married couple. But on the basis of this film, my guess is that after their crime spree ended and the press came to interview their neighbors, nobody said, "Gee, they were always so quiet and nice."

McNaughton seems fascinated by the ways in which lawlessness is infectious. In both *Henry* and *Normal Life*, there are characters who would never commit a crime on their own. But once they fall under the spell of a reckless or heedless outlaw, they are helpless to resist. The lesson, I guess, is that if you see someone in a bar cut themselves while breaking up with their last lover, let them bleed.

## Nothing to Lose ★ ★

R, 97 m., 1997

Martin Lawrence (T. Paul), Tim Robbins (Nick Beam), John C. McGinley (Davis "Rig" Lanlow), Giancarlo Esposito (Charlie Dunt), Kelly Preston (Ann), Irma P. Hall (Bertha), Michael McKean (Philip Barrow), Rebecca Gayheart (Danielle), Susan Barnes (Delores). Directed by Steve Oedekerk and produced by Martin Bregman, Dan Jinks, and Michael Bregman. Screenplay by Oedekerk.

*Nothing to Lose* is a five-peat: Buddy Movie, Fish-Out-of-Water Movie, Road Movie, Mistaken Identity Movie, and Corporate Espionage Movie.

Okay, so maybe the fifth one isn't a genre of its own yet, but it sure seemed familiar when the heroes were creeping around the halls of power, eluding security guards.

The writer-director, Steve Oedekerk, is at least an attentive student of what's been done before. Notice how subtly he sets up the plot as a Strange Bedfellows Movie and then slips into Buddy Movie mode. You can hardly hear the gears meshing as *Nothing to Lose* shifts between one set of obligatory scenes and another.

The film stars Tim Robbins as Nick Beam, a corporate executive who comes home one afternoon to find his wife (Kelly Preston) in bed with another man. Cufflinks in the living room provide a fatal clue: It's his boss. Angered and distraught, Nick drives out into the night, where before he can do something reckless he is carjacked by T. Paul (Martin Lawrence), an unemployed man who looks more dangerous than he is.

"You sure picked the wrong guy," Nick tells him, flooring the accelerator and taking T. Paul on a hair-raising wild ride. Through a series of plot devices, Nick is soon deprived of his wallet and credit cards, and the two men find themselves in the middle of the Arizona desert, living by their wits and an occasional stickup while having heartfelt conversations about life in America today.

Oedekerk's previous movie was *Ace Ventura: When Nature Calls*. This time he offers some of the same comic spirit, interlarded with messages about how T. Paul can't get a job, corporate America is racist, and Nick's life is built on a shaky foundation of unexamined assumptions.

The movie wants to be two or three things at once, and while I applaud the ambition, the result is kind of shapeless.

There are good moments. The biggest laugh in the entire film belongs to that splendid character actress Irma P. Hall, who plays T. Paul's mother and leaves no doubt about who is boss. Another wonderful scene features Patrick Cranshaw as a convenience-store clerk who, in the process of being stuck up, is asked to judge which of two approaches is the scarier, and offers some helpful suggestions. A third good scene belongs to a security guard in corporate headquarters who, in the middle of the night in what he thinks is an empty office, unleashes his disco spirit.

In a way, this is not as it should be. The biggest laughs shouldn't come from walk-on characters. But Robbins and Lawrence have been supplied with so much quasi-serious motivation that it's hard for them to free themselves from the requirements of the plot and seize the moment; there should be more scenes like the one where Robbins's shoes catch on fire.

Two other dependable character actors, Giancarlo Esposito and long-faced John C. McGinley, play a couple of stickup artists who trail Nick and T. Paul, trying to rob them—but their characters and scenes seem manufactured only for the convenience of the plot. (It's nice to have two antagonists who follow you around in a Road Movie, popping up when needed.)

Oedekerk's screenplay has serious ambitions, which it should have suppressed. A scene with T. Paul's family is sweet, but belongs in a different movie. And Nick's scenes with the good-hearted woman who runs the flower shop in his building don't seem consistent with how the movie turns out.

At the end, *Nothing to Lose* turns out to be a textbook example of our old friend the Idiot Plot, in which everything depends on a crucial but unconvincing misunderstanding that needs to be laboriously contrived. Sometimes you can watch movies in the spirit in which you solve Acrostics; the trick is in interpreting the clues. Advanced students of the genre will find their ears pricking up the moment Nick's wife mentions her sister. Catch that clue, and everything falls into place.

## The Nutty Professor ★ ★ ★

PG-13, 95 m., 1996

Eddie Murphy (Sherman Klump, Buddy Love, Lance Perkins, Papa Klump, Mama Klump, Grandma Klump, and Ernie Klump), Jada Pinkett (Carla Purty), James Coburn (Harlan Hartley), Larry Miller (Dean Richmond), Dave Chappelle (Reggie Warrington), John Ales (Jason), Patricia Wilson (Dean's Secretary), Jamal Mixon (Ernie Klump Jr.). Directed by Tom Shadyac and produced by Brian Grazer and Russell Simmons. Screenplay by David Shefield, Barry W. Blaustein, Tom Shadyac, and Steve Oedekerk.

Eddie Murphy's talent for comedy was in eclipse during the lean years of flops like *A Vampire in Brooklyn*—but in *The Nutty Professor* he came back with exuberance and energy, in a movie that's like a thumb to the nose for everyone who said he'd lost it. He's very good. And the movie succeeds in two different ways: It's sweet and good-hearted, and then again it's raucous slapstick and bathroom humor. I liked both parts.

The movie is inspired by a 1963 Jerry Lewis comedy, said by some to be Lewis's best, in which Jerry played a mild-mannered chemistry professor whose secret formula allowed him to transform himself into an obnoxious lounge lizard named Buddy Love. Some said Buddy Love was modeled on Lewis's former partner Dean Martin, allowing him to play both sides of their double act. Others said the Buddy Love character was an uncanny foreshadowing of Lewis's own personality in the years to come. Maybe it was a little of both.

The Murphy version follows the broad outlines of the Lewis film, with one inspired addition: It makes the hero fat, in addition to making him shy and inept, and that doubles the opportunities for physical comedy. Jerry Lewis's transformation from the professor into Buddy Love was a personality switch, but Murphy also goes through a complete physical morphing, from 400 pounds to average weight and back again, sometimes almost instantly.

As the movie opens, Murphy is Professor Sherman Klump, brilliant chemist and geneticist, and fat slob. He falls instantly in love with a new graduate student named Carla Purty (Jada Pinkett) and bashfully bumbles his way into asking her out on a date. Meanwhile, his position at school depends on raising new research funds, and the smarmy college dean (Larry Miller) puts on the pressure during a sarcastic meeting ("Anything I can get for you? Juice? Coffee? Rack of lamb?").

Sherman's tendency, when worried, is to eat, and so he settles down with relief to the Klump family dinner table. Every adult member of the Klump family—Sherman's parents, brother, and granny—is played by Murphy, who has always been a master of disguise (remember him as Gumby?) but here outdoes himself in a rising crescendo of vulgarity that would be disgusting if it weren't so funny (the audience laughed so hard at Papa Klump's approach to colon cleansing that I missed the next six lines of dialogue).

Not only does Murphy play the Klumps, but he also scores a lot of big laughs as a Richard Simmons clone on a TV exercise program.

The character of Sherman himself is a triumph of effective disguise, combined with good writing and acting. The makeup by three-time Oscar winner Rick Baker adds pounds to Murphy's face and neck so seamlessly that Sherman looks completely convincing. And as Murphy plays him, Sherman becomes one of his most likable characters, good-hearted, sympathetic, and funny. When Sherman morphs into Buddy Love, the thin character resembles some of Murphy's own abrasive stage incarnations; does this mean he'll be hosting telethons in ten years?

The plot, loosely inspired by the 1963 film, gets Sherman and the beautiful Carla to a trendy nightclub where Sherman is humiliated by a comic (Dave Chappelle) because he's fat ("I think I found where they hid Jimmy Hoffa"). Later Buddy Love returns to the club and gets revenge, although Carla's attraction to Buddy is never quite accounted for in the fast-moving plot.

Sherman's transformation into Buddy isn't all makeup; at times animation and visual tricks are used. And there are a couple of slick special-effects sequences, including a nightmare in which Sherman grows to the size of King Kong and strides through a terrified city. Buddy has a tendency to blow up into Sherman without notice, which leads to embarrassment: Fireman have to cut him out of a sports car. And Murphy plays both roles simultaneously in a scene where the two characters fight for control of his body. (The manic energy here is a reminder that the director, Tom Shadyac, also made *Ace Ventura: Pet Detective.*)

The ending is just as sentimental as in the original, with Sherman learning to accept himself (and to be loved by Carla). He delivers a heartfelt speech ("Buddy's who I thought I wanted to be—who I thought the world wanted me to be. But I was wrong"). Eddie Murphy looks straight at the camera as he hits the last line, and it occurred to me that maybe he was referring indirectly to some of his recent career miscues. There is a lot of Buddy Love in the Eddie Murphy screen persona. Maybe too much. And not enough Sherman Klump. But I've never doubted Murphy's comic gift, and *The Nutty Professor* shows him back on track, balancing two sides of a real talent.

# O

## The Object of My Affection ★ ★

R, 111 m., 1998

Jennifer Aniston (Nina Borowski), Paul Rudd (George Hanson), John Pankow (Vince McBride), Alan Alda (Sidney Miller), Tim Daly (Dr. Robert Joley), Nigel Hawthorne (Rodney Fraser), Allison Janney (Constance Miller), Amo Gulinello (Paul James). Directed by Nicholas Hytner and produced by Laurence Mark. Screenplay by Wendy Wasserstein, based on the novel by Stephen McCauley.

There is a movie fighting to get out of *The Object of My Affection*, and I like it better than the movie it's trapped in. It involves a wise old man who has arrived at some useful insights about life. If they did spin-offs of movie characters the way they do on TV, he'd be in a movie of his own.

Alas, this touching and fascinating character is mired in the worst kind of sitcom—a serious one (seriocom?). *The Object of My Affection* deals with some real issues and has scenes that work, but you can see the wheels of the plot turning so clearly that you doubt the characters have much freedom to act on their own.

The story involves a social worker named Nina (Jennifer Aniston) and a first-grade teacher named George (Paul Rudd). Nina is engaged to a creep named Vince (John Pankow), and George is living with a literary critic named Robert (Tim Daly), who, like all Bernard Shaw experts, can afford a BMW convertible and a luxurious apartment in Manhattan. At a dinner party, Nina finds out that Robert is leaving George, and tells George—alas, before Robert has. George is crushed, but soon has moved into Nina's Brooklyn apartment, where they will live as good friends.

Then Nina gets pregnant. Vince, the father, keeps talking about "our" baby until Nina announces it is her baby and she has no plans to marry Vince, and Vince stalks out after declaring, "I never want to see you again," a line that sounds for all the world like a screenwriter's convenience to get him out of the cluttered plot for a scene or two. Nina, who really likes George, asks him to share the fathering: They could be a couple in everything but sex. George agrees, but then he falls for Paul (Amo Gulinello), and Nina feels hurt and jealous.

All of this material, which is promising, is dealt with on that level where characters are not quite allowed to be as perceptive and intelligent as real people might be in the same circumstances. That's because they're shuttled hither and yon by the plot structure, which requires, of course, a false crisis and false dawn (Nina and George dance to "You Were Meant for Me") before the real crisis and real dawn. At least we're spared a live childbirth scene, although to be sure, we do get the listening-to-the-embryo's-heartbeat scene.

Aniston and Rudd are appealing together; however, Pankow's crudely written role puts him through bewildering personality shifts. But then, suddenly, a character walks in from nowhere and becomes the movie's center of interest. This is the aging drama critic Rodney, played by Oscar nominee Nigel Hawthorne of *The Madness of King George*. He is gay, and Paul is his young protégé. They do not have sex, Paul makes clear to George. But Rodney clearly loves the young man, and there are a couple of scenes in which he says and does nothing, and achieves a greater emotional effect than is reached by any dialogue in the movie.

He also offers Nina hard-won advice: In the long run, her arrangement with George will not work. "Don't fix your life so that you're left alone just at the middle of it," he says, and we sense that the movie has quieted down and found its focus and purpose. You ask yourself, what would the whole film have been like if it had been written and acted at this level? The answer, sadly, is—not much like *The Object of My Affection*.

## The Odd Couple II ★ ½

PG-13, 107 m., 1998

Jack Lemmon (Felix Ungar), Walter Matthau (Oscar Madison), Christine Baranski (Thelma), Barnard Hughes (Beaumont), Jonathan Silverman (Brucey Madison), Jean Smart (Holly), Lisa Waltz (Hannah Ungar), Mary Beth Peil (Felice). Directed by Howard Deutch and produced by Neil Simon, Robert W. Cort, and David Madden. Screenplay by Simon.

Watching Walter Matthau and Jack Lemmon make the talk show circuit, trading one-liners and barbs like a vaudeville team, I imagined a documentary simply showing them promoting this film. They're funny, familiar, edgy, and smart. *The Odd Couple II* is none of those things, and a much longer list could be made of other things it is not.

Lemmon and Matthau are perfectly suited for working together. In life as in fiction, they *are* a little like the original odd couple, Felix and Oscar: Lemmon concise and tidy, Matthau rambling, shambling, and gambling. When they're given a decent screenplay, as in the original *Odd Couple* (1968) or last year's engaging *Out to Sea*, they're fun to watch; their timing is impeccable, and you can sense their joy of work.

*Odd Couple II* is not, alas, such a screenplay. It has been written by the master, Neil Simon, who in this case is an emperor without any clothes. Did no one have the nerve to suggest a rewrite? To tell him that his story was slight, contrived and flat? Perhaps it seemed to the film's producers that the combination of Simon, Lemmon, Matthau, and the words "odd couple" were a sufficient guarantee of success. The difference between a creative executive and a contract signer lies precisely in the ability to see, in a case like this, that they were not. (Of course, Simon himself is one of the producers on this film, so in a way he was working without a net.)

The story opens seventeen years after Oscar and Felix last saw one another. (It's thirty years since the movie, but that would make their children middle-aged, so never mind.) Both now live in Florida, where Felix plays cards with old cronies and fusses over the snacks, while Oscar practices trying to hit his garbage can with a Hefty bag from an upper floor. They get calls: Oscar's son is engaged to marry Felix's daughter.

This inevitably requires them to fly to Los Angeles, where they plan to rent a car and drive to the town where the wedding is being held (it's "San something," but they can't remember what). Felix injures his foot while crashing into Oscar at the airport, they rent a car, the car rolls over a cliff and explodes, etc., and they find themselves in a road movie, complete with seamy motels and colorful characters along the way.

Simon's borscht-belt humor still prevails in the dialogue. ("My sister lost three pairs of dentures in the earthquake." "What did she do to eat?" "She sent out.") There are jokes about age, sex, and death, and a nice sight gag after they get a lift in a Rolls-Royce driven so slowly by a millionaire that they are passed up first by runners, and then by walkers.

But the movie has no purpose for being. That's revealed by the road movie premise: The genre is ideal for throwing characters and dialogue at situations without the bother of contriving any kind of a dramatic or comedic reason for them to be together. More honest, and maybe even funnier, would have been the story of the two old adversaries forced to be roommates in a retirement village. The movie slogs on and on, Matthau and Lemmon gamely delivering lines that may contain mechanical wit, but no impulse or dramatic purpose.

## Once Upon a Time . . . When We Were Colored ★ ★ ★ ★

PG, 111 m., 1996

Al Freeman Jr. (Poppa), Phylicia Rashad (Ma Ponk), Charles Earl (Spud) Taylor Jr. (Cliff at Five), Willie Norwood Jr. (Cliff at Twelve), Damon Hines (Cliff at Sixteen), Leon (Melvin), Iona Morris (Showgirl), Richard Roundtree (Cleve), Polly Bergen (Miss Maybry), Paula Kelly (Ma Pearl), Bernie Casey (Mr. Walter), Isaac Hayes (Preacher Hurn). Directed by Tim Reid and produced by Reid and Michael Bennett. Screenplay by Paul W. Cooper.

Tim Reid's *Once Upon a Time . . . When We Were Colored* re-creates the world of a black community in the rural South in the years from 1946 to 1962, as hard-line segregation gradually fell to the assault of the civil rights movement. It is a memory of the close bonds of family, friends, and church that grew up to sustain such communities, in a society where an American version of apartheid was the law.

The key word there is "community," and rarely has a film more movingly shown how people who work, live, and pray together can find a common strength and self-respect. There are eighty-three speaking parts in this ambitious film, which spans four generations and remembers not only the joy of Saturday night dances and Sunday church socials, but also the cruel pain of a little boy learning to spell his first words: "white" and "colored." By the end of the film, we feel we know the people in the "colored town" of Glen Allan, Mississippi, and we understand why such communities produced so many good and capable citizens.

The movie is based on a 1989 book by Clifton Taulbert, who published it with a small Kansas City firm and then saw it reach the best-seller lists after a strong review in the *New York Times;* it was the first book requested by Nelson Mandela after he was released from prison. One of its early readers was the television actor Tim Reid *(WKRP in Cincinnati, Frank's Place),* who determined to film it even though it seemed "commercial" in no conventional sense. He assembled the enormous cast, shot on location in North Carolina, and has made a film that is both an impressive physical production (the period looks and feels absolutely authentic) and a deeply moving emotional experience. In many ways this film compares with *The Color Purple,* although it has a simpler, more direct, less melodramatic quality; it is not about a few lives, but about life itself as it was experienced in the segregated South.

There are so many characters that to attempt a plot summary would be pointless. Better to remember some of the extraordinary scenes. Much of the story is told through the eyes of a young boy named Cliff (played at different ages by three actors), who is raised by his great-grandparents (Al Freeman Jr. and Paula Kelly). As he watches and learns, so do we, especially in a scene where Poppa, his great-grandfather, takes him to town for a treat. It is on this trip that he makes the mistake of going into the "white" washroom in a gas station, and Poppa carefully traces out the letters "C" and "W" and tells him what words they stand for, and why.

Few scenes in my memory have had a greater impact than the one where the boy, happily supplied with an ice-cream cone, joins his grandfather in watching silently as a Klan parade marches ominously down Main Street. Al Freeman's character never says a word, but his jaw tightens and his eyes compress with pain, and we feel as we seldom have before in the movies how personally hurtful racism is.

But there are happier moments. Many of them involve Cliff's adventures in the neighborhood, especially on a day when a carnival comes to town, and one of the dancing girls is boarded with a local woman named Ma Ponk (Phylicia Rashad). The dancer, played by Iona Morris, is basically no more than a sideshow stripper, but to young eyes she seems impossibly glamorous.

There is a scene that begins conventionally, as the dancer promises to "make over" Ma Ponk by doing her hair and makeup, and putting her in a fancy dress. But the payoff is extraordinary, as the local woman combs out the dancer's hair in front of a mirror and the touch of her hands reminds the dancer of her own mother, whom she has not seen in fifteen years. A wordless communication of understanding and sympathy passes between the women. It is one of those magical scenes you cannot account for; something happens that transcends story and acting, and reaches straight into the heart.

Segregation was wrong and hurtful, but the system did provide a benefit: The black community was self-sufficient, supporting its own tradespeople, schoolteachers, ministers, and craftsmen, who provided role models for young people growing up. The movie remembers one-room schoolhouses, and churches where gospel music and fiery sermons uplifted a congregation after its week of work in the fields. It remembers juke joints and church picnics (with the cards hidden under a hat when the preacher approaches) and the way that old people were respected and consulted.

There are also scenes to show that many of the local white people were good-hearted and well-meaning; a woman named Miss Maybry (Polly Bergen) gives young Cliff books to read, and encourages him to stretch his mind and develop his ambition. (There is a very funny scene where Cliff says things that Miss Maybry perhaps should not be told, and Miss Maybry's maid tries to signal him from behind her employer's back.)

When the civil rights movement first penetrates into this corner of Mississippi, not everyone in the black community is happy to see it come. Many people have a working arrangement with the old system, and are afraid of stirring up trouble, especially since they know that "agitators" can be beaten or killed. There is a meeting in the church that dramatizes that tension.

The changing times come to a head through the person of Cleve (Richard Roundtree), the local iceman, who has hired Cliff to help him on his rounds. A white ice company decides to take over the "colored route," and so the local ice wholesaler refuses to sell to Cliff. He goes to another dealer, miles away. Then the white field foreman announces that anyone not buying ice from the white company will lose their job. And that is when something cracks, and feeling that has been repressed for long years finally breaks through.

It is almost impossible to express the cumulative power of *Once Upon a Time . . . When We Were Colored.* It isn't a slick, tightly packaged docudrama, but a film from the heart, a film that is not a protest against the years of segregation so much as a celebration of the human qualities that endured and overcame. Although the movie is about African-Americans, its message is about the universal human spirit. I am aware of three screenings it has had at film festivals: before a largely black audience in Chicago, a largely white audience in Virginia, and a largely Asian audience in Honolulu. All three audiences gave it a standing ovation. There you have it.

## 187 ★ ★

R, 121 m., 1997

Samuel L. Jackson (Trevor Garfield), John Heard (Dave Childress), Kelly Rowan (Ellen Henry), Clifton Gonzalez Gonzalez (Cesar), Karina Arroyave (Rita), Jonah Rooney (Stevie Middleton), Lobo Sebastian (Benny Chacon). Directed by Kevin Reynolds and produced by Bruce Davey and Steve McEveety. Screenplay by Scott Yagemann.

*187* tells the story of a high school teacher who is driven mad by the system. We can well believe it, especially given the schools portrayed in the movie, where violent bullies control the classrooms, and the spineless administration—terrified of lawsuits—refuses to back up the teachers. But the movie ends in a way that will disturb its more thoughtful viewers.

Samuel L. Jackson stars as Trevor, a dedicated and gifted teacher who does a demonstration of centrifugal force that I, for one, wanted to try for myself. He finds the pages of his textbook defaced with the scrawl "187," which is police code for "homicide." It's a warning, he thinks, from a dangerous student. He gets no sympathy or support from his principal, who says: "You know what your problem is? On the one hand, you think someone is going to kill you, and on the other hand, you actually think kids are paying attention in your class."

The warning is real; Trevor is attacked and seriously wounded, and then the main story begins fifteen months later, after the teacher has switched coasts and is trying to make a fresh start as a substitute science teacher in the San Fernando Valley. Trevor is no longer quite the man he was. He confides in Ellen, a friendly fellow teacher, that the assault meant "the robbery of my passion, my spark, my unguarded self. I miss them."

This California school is no better than the one he left in New York. Thugs and gang-bangers challenge the teachers for control of the classroom and threaten lawsuits if teachers try to take firm measures. The administration gives no support. It's as if the whole system is engaged in a charade. The students pretend to study, the teachers pretend to teach, and nobody rocks the boat.

But Trevor is different. He really wants to teach. He draws closer to Ellen (Kelly Rowan), but she senses a wall that will always be there, and he quotes Thomas Wolfe's despairing cry that loneliness is the human condition. He does what he can. He offers to tutor a student named Rita, but she misinterprets his attention and offers him sex. He visits the home of a violent student named Benny, and wishes he hadn't. He is counseled by a disillusioned teacher named Childress (John Heard), who then finds out he's the famous teacher who was attacked out east, and says, "I'm giving advice to a guy with a purple heart."

And then all of the plot threads come together in a way I will not reveal, but which raised serious questions in my mind about motivation, about plausibility, and even about whether a climactic final scene should have been in the movie at all. The movie, written by Scott Yagemann and directed by Kevin Reynolds *(Waterworld),* has elements that are thoughtful and tough about inner-city schools, and other elements that belong in a crime thriller or a war movie.

At the end, I know, Trevor has come unhinged. I accept that and believe it. But it feels like the movie lost the nerve of its original story impulse and sought safety in elements borrowed from thrillers. Its destination doesn't have much to do with how it got there.

Too bad, because this is a strong and sympathetic performance by Samuel L. Jackson, who has so many different notes in his work and here is able to make the teacher come completely alive—right until the end, when the plot manipulations bury him. I also liked the tentative sweetness of Kelly Rowan as the friendly teacher, although the relationship isn't resolved very neatly. The young actors playing the dangerous students are focused and effective; they include Lobo Sebastian as Benny and Clifton Gonzalez Gonzalez as Cesar.

But . . . I dunno. If you see the movie, ask yourself if the last third is really satisfying. Was there another way to present the same kind of frustration and despair? Are they really proving anything in the final confrontation? What do they think they're proving? The motivation seems cloudy on both sides.

## One Fine Day ★ ★

PG, 108 m., 1996

Michelle Pfeiffer (Melanie Parker), George Clooney (Jack Taylor), Mae Whitman (Maggie Taylor), Alex D. Linz (Sammy Parker), Charles Durning (Lew), Jon Robin Baitz (Yates Jr.), Ellen Greene (Elaine Lieberman), Joe Grifasi (Manny Feldstein), Pete Hamill (Frank Burroughs). Directed by Michael Hoffman and produced by Lynda Obst. Screenplay by Terrel Seltzer and Ellen Simon.

"Cinema is the history of boys photographing girls."

Or so Jean-Luc Godard is claimed to have said. I thought of his words while watching *One Fine Day*, an uninspired formula movie with another fine performance by Michelle Pfeiffer. She does everything in this movie that a much better movie would have required from her, but the screenplay lets her down.

Since Pfeiffer is one of the executive producers, she can blame herself; she *wanted* to make this predictable fluff about two beautiful people who engage in a verbal sparring match for ninety minutes while we patiently wait for them to acknowledge that they have fallen hopelessly in love. She creates a three-dimensional, appealing character, and puts her in a lockstep plot.

The movie stars Pfeiffer as Melanie, a divorced mom who has some kind of a job involving big architectural projects. George Clooney plays Jack, a divorced columnist for the *New York Daily News*. Through a series of coincidences, both single parents are suddenly required to take care of their kids for the day, and then circumstances throw them together, again and again.

So, okay, what's going to happen? Consider this to be like a crossword puzzle. Get out your pencils.

The kids, Maggie and Sammy (like/dislike), each other. When their parents are distracted for a moment, they (run out of sight/stay where they're told to stay). When the parents try to find them, they (do, with great relief/lose them, and the movie turns into *Ransom*). When both parents use identical cellular phones, they (accidentally exchange phones and get each other's calls/keep their own phones and get all of their own calls). When Maggie grows attached to some kittens, her father (lets her keep them/tells her to forget them). After the Pfeiffer character criticizes the Clooney character for being late and irresponsible, she herself is (late and irresponsible/always on time). Toward the end of the film, when it appears certain they are in love, a silly misunderstanding (will delay this realization/will be ended in a kiss).

And so on. This is the kind of movie you can sing along with. I amused myself by trying to figure out Michelle Pfeiffer's job. She works for a big company, I guess, but her only colleague seems to be her elderly and powerful boss. When she trips and falls and breaks the model of a big architectural project, it's her job to take it downtown and hire a guy to glue it back together again, and yet she also seems to be the designer, or planner, or salesperson, or broker, or something, of this whole undertaking.

We don't know for sure because it's all flimflam. Her job scenes should be subtitled "Obligatory Scenes Necessary So Little Maggie Can Be Taken to the Office." Jack's newspaper job is easier to understand, especially after he explains it takes him "about an hour" to write a column, and the mayor is planning to sue him after yesterday's column. Everybody knows columnists like that.

Meanwhile, the two kids like each other, and the two parents like each other, and there are scenes at the docks, scenes in the park, scenes in toy stores, scenes in the streets, scenes in the rain, scenes in taxis, scenes where Ocean Spray Brand Cranberry Juice gets squirted on Michelle Pfeiffer's blouse, and similar scenes in which other garments are stained on a regular basis.

Pfeiffer looks, acts, and sounds wonderful throughout all of this, and George Clooney is perfectly serviceable as a romantic lead, sort of a Mel Gibson Lite. I liked them. I wanted them to get together. I wanted them to live happily ever after. The sooner the better.

## 101 Dalmatians ★ ★ ½

G, 103 m., 1996

Glenn Close (Cruella DeVil), Jeff Daniels (Roger), Joely Richardson (Anita), Joan Plowright (Nanny), Hugh Laurie (Jasper), Mark Williams (Horace), John Shrapnel (Skinner), Tim McInnerny (Alonzo). Directed by Stephen Herek and produced by John Hughes and Ricardo Mestres. Screenplay by Hughes.

The thing about animation is that it gives equal time to kids and animals. They get to be important, too—the simplified world of cartoons cuts the adult world down to size. The problem with the new live-action version of *101 Dalmatians* is that it's never really able to make the dogs as important as the people. We think we'll see the adventures of some cute puppies, and most of the time we're looking at grown-up intrigues and the schemes of a couple of bad guys recycled straight out of *Home Alone.*

Disney's new version of this good old story (made into a feature cartoon in 1961) stars Jeff Daniels as a London-based computer game author named Roger; Joely Richardson as a dress designer named Anita; and Glenn Close as the steel-edged Cruella DeVil, who admits early in the film, sincerely but desperately, "I worship fur." It is her only vice, but she makes it do the duty of a dozen.

The movie tells a simple tale. Roger's male Dalmatian (Pongo) cruises St. James Park, falls in love with Anita's female Dalmatian (Perdy) and drags his master's bicycle on a wild chase that ends with Roger being splashed in the lagoon. As the dogs nuzzle happily, the eyes of the owners meet, and it is true love times two. The chemistry between them is sweet and convincing.

Anita works for Cruella, who is not above using stolen pelts from murdered animals to adorn her high-fashion figure. Glenn Close is a skilled actress and looks right for Cruella (I like the touch of the gloves that have their own fingernails). She drives the snotty classic car, uses the long cigarette holder, strikes the flamboyant poses, and yet, somehow, she's only human. She isn't Cruella DeVil. No one of flesh and blood could be. If she's anyone, she's Norma Desmond from *Sunset Boulevard,* playing Cruella DeVil.

The plot, as you may recall from the earlier film, involves Pongo and Perdy having fifteen puppies, which Cruella covets as part of her plan to design a new coat out of Dalmatian skins. The birth of the puppies leads to the one big laugh in the movie: As Cruella visits the newlywed Anita and Roger at home, Roger boasts, "We're having puppies too!" and Cruella responds, "Puppies! You *have* been a busy boy."

Cruella has two henchmen named Jasper (Hugh Laurie) and Horace (Mark Williams), and they steal the pups and take them to her remote farmhouse, where she has eighty-four other puppies already in captivity. Then the barnyard animals help the pups escape, a kind of urban animal telegraph alerts Pongo and Perdy and their masters to the danger, and Jasper and Horace are subjected to a series of painful humiliations: electrocuted by fences, dumped off ladders, dunked in mud and other substances, bonked on the head, etc.

Their exploits are recycled directly out of the adventures of the hapless thieves in the *Home Alone* movies, and indeed *101 Dalmatians* has been written by the creator of the *Home Alone* films, John Hughes. It would be unfair to make the link with Hughes if he didn't force it by ripping himself off so obviously that he might just as well have gone ahead and *cast* the *Home Alone* villains in this movie and made an in-joke out of it.

What's funny in cartoons is not always funny in live action, and some of the dunkings in unsavory substances left me less than amused. Slapstick is a much-overused and misunderstood art form.

That's not to say the movie doesn't have its pleasures, and one of them is the unaffected, warm relationship between Roger and Anita (who looks so clean-cut you suspect she smells of clean sheets). I know a lot of little kids who can't wait to see this movie, and no doubt the cute Dalmatian puppies will enthrall them. It is certainly more innocent and less angry than *Jin-*

*gle All the Way,* and the kids will not be surprised to find that Cruella is a villain, while in the other film they might be alarmed by the sight of several Santas puffing on cigars and planning scams. For older viewers, *101 Dalmatians* may seem closer to the artistic level of the *Beethoven* dog adventures than the mid-level Disney classic that inspired it.

## One Night Stand ★ ★ ★

R, 105 m., 1997

Wesley Snipes (Max Carlyle), Nastassja Kinski (Karen), Ming-Na Wen (Mimi), Robert Downey Jr. (Charlie), Kyle MacLachlan (Vernon). Directed by Mike Figgis and produced by Figgis, Annie Stewart, and Ben Myron. Screenplay by Figgis.

*One Night Stand* is work in a minor key from Mike Figgis, whose previous film was the symphonic *Leaving Las Vegas.* The romance this time is lighter and more cheerful, but the result is peculiar: I liked almost everything about the film except for the central relationship, which struck me as just an excuse for everything else.

The story opens with a Meet Cute. Max (Wesley Snipes), a director of TV commercials, misses his flight out of New York. There are no rooms left when he returns to his hotel. Sitting in the lobby, he's told by a pretty blonde (Nastassja Kinski) that his fountain pen is leaking. They attend a chamber music concert, she touches his shoulder as the music weaves a romantic mood, she lets him use the extra bed in her room, and soon the extra bed is not required.

Max was in New York to visit his best friend, Charlie (Robert Downey Jr.), who is HIV-positive. He returns to Los Angeles and his wife, Mimi (Ming-Na Wen), his children, and the family dog, who growls softly while sniffing his crotch. You can't fool a dog. One year passes. Read no further unless you want to know that Charlie is in the hospital with weeks to live. Max flies back to New York, meets Charlie's brother Vernon (Kyle MacLachlan) and his wife, Karen—who is, of course, Kinski.

That's the setup. The central question would seem to be, how do Max and Karen handle this embarrassing development? The two adulterers go through the motions required by movie convention ("As far as I'm concerned," Karen says, "nothing happened"). And eventually all of the romantic problems are sorted out. But I didn't much care, because the real interest in the film is not the relationship between Max and Karen, and the Karen character is so underwritten that Kinski has to create it mostly out of surfaces and body language.

I did find myself caring about Charlie, the best friend with AIDS, who is played by Downey as a man determined not to go solemnly into that good night. He has a sense of humor even on his deathbed, and gets one of the movie's best laughs just by raising his eyebrows. I liked him, and I also liked the character of Max's wife, Mimi, who is written with much more detail than the Kinski character, and played by Ming-Na Wen as smart, observant, fiery and extremely clear about what she likes in bed.

The writing credit for *One Night Stand* goes to Figgis. The original screenplay was by Joe Eszterhas, who removed his name after reading Figgis's rewrite. (Figgis observed at the Toronto Film Festival that Eszterhas's partner Ben Myron still has a producer's credit—"although I never met him.") What Figgis liked, he said, was the three-act structure of the original script, by which I think he means the way that the lovers Meet Cute, part, and Meet Cuter. I wonder if the Eszterhas version paid more attention to Karen. This version adds several scenes that play well, but seem to belong in a movie about Max, not Max and Karen. For example, a discussion of an ad campaign for a pickle manufacturer, and a fight between Max and his wife.

In the last act of the movie, the romance essentially becomes a backdrop for the real drama, which involves Charlie's illness. There's a party in his hospital room and a celebration held by his friends, both recalling the tenderness of the 1996 movie *It's My Party,* where Eric Roberts was the dying man. Compared to the power of these scenes, the movie's ending plays as a Meet Cutest, with some sly exploitation of what we assume about a series of two-shots.

Strange, that these observations did not get in the way of my enjoyment of the movie as a whole. It is so well acted and written that it convincingly shoulders aside its central premise and works because of the subplots and the supporting characters. Even the Wesley Snipes character, presumably at the center of the action, acts more as a master of ceremonies, leading us from one diversion to another. And

Kinski, although underused, is warm and fetching, and gets maybe the movie's best line. "What do you do, Karen?" asks Mimi. And she replies: "I'm a rocket scientist."

## Operation Condor ★ ★ ★

PG-13, 92 m., 1997

Jackie Chan (Jackie), Carol Cheng (Ada), Eva Cobo De Garcia (Elsa), Shoko Ikeda (Momoko), Alfred Brel Sanchez (Adolf), Ken Goodman (Adolf's Guard). Directed by Jackie Chan and produced by Leonard Ho. Screenplay by Chan and Edward Tang.

The knowledge that Jackie Chan performs all of his own stunts brings a certain intensity to the act of watching his movies: A real person in real time is really doing something dangerous. There's an element of Evel Knievel to it. And also an element of Buster Keaton, because Chan is above all a silent comedian who depends on broad humor and timing to make action comedies in which the violence is secondary ("No guns!" he likes to shout).

Although Chan does his own stunts, they are, of course, stunts—safety precautions are taken, and camera angles are chosen to make things look more difficult than they are. Sometimes there is a certain clumsiness that makes the realism even more effective.

Early in *Operation Condor,* for example, Jackie straps on a hang-gliding outfit powered by an airplane engine, fires it up, and runs with mounting desperation across a meadow, trying to get airborne. Eventually, he does. In a slicker action picture, the flight would have been effortless. It's more fun to watch Chan sweating a little. And that's really him in the air.

There are a couple of other stunts in the film that had me seriously impressed. In one of them, Chan is hanging from a beam near the roof of a warehouse. A car catapults through the air, straight at him. He swings up out of the way and the car misses him. It looked to me as if trick photography wasn't involved; there was a real car and perfect timing. In another stunt, he leaps from a motorcycle speeding off of a pier and grabs a safe hold on a fisherman's net. And there's a wonderfully choreographed fight above odd, flat, moving steel platforms high above a hangar floor.

Even the little moments are a kind of perfection. Chan jumps against a wall, pushes off to the parallel wall, and leaps over a gate in the wall. The stunt combines an acrobat's skill with a dancer's grace. And there are scenes where he kids himself, as when he rescues a baby carriage in the middle of a breakneck chase, or when he makes a quick getaway by bouncing down a hill inside what looks like a large inflated volleyball.

*Operation Condor* was originally released in Asia in 1991 with the prefix *The Armor of God II.* Chan is the writer, director, and star. The plot is about as silly as most of his movies. A European count hires him on behalf of the United Nations to find Nazi loot—a fortune in gold buried in the North African desert near the end of World War II. Chan is supplied with a sidekick, an agent named Ada (Carol Cheng), and eventually collects two more bodacious babes: Elsa (Eva Cobo De Garcia), who is the granddaughter of the Nazi who hid the gold, and Momoko (Shoko Ikeda), an innocent soul they encounter in the desert, who is searching for the meaning of life and death, and keeps a pet scorpion.

It's a little dizzying, the way the movie switches locations from the desert to Arab bazaars to fleabag hotels to a really elaborate set representing some kind of long-lost Nazi headquarters with a built-in wind tunnel that stars in the final action scene. (There is a bomb in the buried headquarters, and in a nod to period detail, it has a countdown timer that uses analogue hands instead of a digital readout.) The screenplay pauses for as little dialogue as possible ("Look out behind you!" "Take this!"), and provides a couple of teams of bad guys whose motivations are barely described—but then, what do we really need to know, except that they want the gold and are enemies of Jackie?

Most action pictures are, at some level, a little mean-spirited: They depend upon macho brutes getting their way. Jackie Chan is self-effacing, a guy who grimaces when he's hurt, who dusts himself off after close calls, who goes for a gag instead of a gun. It adds to the amusement that he bears an uncanny resemblance to Tom Hayden. He brings that lighthearted persona to the fact that he is also a superb athlete and does amazing things in every film. There's a kind of innocence to it all, and a joy of performance. Half of the time, you find yourself wearing a silly grin.

## The Opposite of Sex ★ ★ ★
R, 105 m., 1998

Christina Ricci (Dedee Truitt), Martin Donovan (Bill Truitt), Lisa Kudrow (Lucia), Lyle Lovett (Carl Tippett), Johnny Galecki (Jason), Ivan Sergei (Matt Mateo), William Lee Scott (Randy). Directed by Don Roos and produced by David Kirkpatrick and Michael Besman. Screenplay by Roos.

*The Opposite of Sex* is like a movie with the *Mystery Science Theater 3000* commentary built right in. It comments on itself, with the heroine as narrator. Dedee Truitt, a trash-talking teenager from Louisiana, chats on the sound track during and between many of the scenes, pointing out the clichés, warning us about approaching plot conventions, and debunking our desire to see the story unfold in traditional ways.

Watching the movie is like sitting through a film in front of a row of wisecracking cult movie fans. It's also sometimes very funny. Dedee (the name may relate to her bra size) is played by Christina Ricci, who is having a very good year, and has left all memories of *The Addams Family* far behind with roles in movies such as *The Ice Storm* and *Fear and Loathing in Las Vegas.* Here she shows a cocky, smart-aleck side. She's the kind of actress who makes an audience sit up and take notice, because she lets us know she's capable of breaking a movie wide open.

In *The Opposite of Sex,* her sixteen-year-old character Dedee bails out from an unhappy home life in Louisiana and makes her way to Indiana, where an older half-brother named Bill (Martin Donovan) teaches high school. Bill is gay, and until recently lived with a stockbroker named Tom, who died of AIDS and left him all his money. Now he lives with a younger man named Matt (Ivan Sergei) and gets frequent visits from Lucia (Lisa Kudrow), who was Tom's sister.

It's a good thing we have Dedee to explain all of this to us, usually in cynical terms. Dedee is advanced sexually, if not intellectually, and soon sets about trying to convince Matt that he is not really gay at all, but has just been killing time while waiting for Dedee to come along. She has a good reason for snaring Matt: She got pregnant in Louisiana and is recruiting a partner.

Dedee and her brother Bill have obviously had quite different childhoods. Bill is quiet, civilized, accepting. When he finds a student writing a crude graffiti about him on the wall of the high school men's room, he suggests grammatical improvements. Dedee is loud, brash, and in your face—a hellion whose master plan includes seducing Matt and stealing $10,000 from Bill so she and Matt can flee to Los Angeles for the good of "their" baby.

Meanwhile, an obnoxious dropout named Jason (Johnny Galecki from *Roseanne*) claims Bill has molested him. It's a blackmail scheme, but the sheriff (Lyle Lovett) has to investigate anyway, even though he more or less sees through Jason. Working behind the scenes, Lucia, the Kudrow character, wonders if maybe Bill would like to live with her in whatever arrangement might seem to work. The sheriff likes Lucia in his earnest and plodding way, but she can't really focus on him.

In its plot outlines, *The Opposite of Sex* is an R-rated sitcom. But first-time director Don Roos (who wrote *Single White Female* and *Boys on the Side*) redeems it with Dedee's narration. When a gun turns up on the screen, Dedee tells us: "This is foreshadowing. Duh!" She likes to tell us she knows what we're thinking, and we're wrong.

The approach is refreshing. Most movies are profoundly conservative at the level of plot construction, no matter how offbeat their material may be. They believe that all audiences demand happy endings, and want to be led lockstep through traditional plot construction. When you've seen enough movies, alas, you can sense the gears laboriously turning, and you know with a sinking heart that there will be no surprises. The Dedee character subverts those expectations; she shoots the legs out from under the movie with perfectly timed zingers. I hate people who talk during movies, but if she were sitting behind me in the theater, saying all of this stuff, I'd want her to keep right on talking.

## Oscar and Lucinda ★ ★ ★ ★
R, 133 m., 1998

Ralph Fiennes (Oscar Hopkins), Cate Blanchett (Lucinda Leplastrier), Ciaran Hinds (Reverend Dennis Hasset), Tom Wilkinson (Hugh Stratton), Richard Roxburgh (Mr. Jeffris), Clive Russell (Theophilus), Bille Brown (Percy Smith), Josephine Byrnes (Miriam Chadwick), Geoffrey

**Rush (Narrator). Directed by Gillian Armstrong and produced by Robin Dalton and Timothy White. Screenplay by Laura Jones from the original novel by Peter Carey.**

"In order that I exist," the narrator of *Oscar and Lucinda* tells us, "two gamblers, one obsessive, one compulsive, must declare themselves." The gamblers are his grandparents, two oddball nineteenth-century eccentrics, driven by faith and temptation, who find they are freed to practice the first by indulging in the second. Their lives form a love story of enchantment and wicked wit.

When we say two people were born for each other, that sometimes means their lives would have been impossible with anyone else. That appears to be the case with Oscar and Lucinda. Their story, told as a long flashback, begins with Oscar as the shy son of a stern English minister, and Lucinda as the strong-willed girl raised on a ranch in the Australian outback. We see them formed by their early lives; he studies for the ministry, she inherits a glassworks and becomes obsessed with glass, and they meet during an ocean voyage from England to Australia.

They meet, indeed, because they gamble. Oscar (Ralph Fiennes) has been introduced to horse racing while studying to be a clergyman, and is transformed by the notion that someone will actually pay him money for predicting which horse will cross the line first. Lucinda (Cate Blanchett) loves cards. Soon they're playing clandestine card games on board ship, and Oscar is as thrilled by her descriptions of gambling as another man might be by tales of sexual adventures.

*Oscar and Lucinda* is based on a novel by Peter Carey, a chronicler of Australian eccentricity; it won the 1988 Booker Prize, Britain's highest literary award. Reading it, I was swept up by the humor of the situation and by the passion of the two gamblers. For Oscar, gambling is not a sin but an embrace of the rules of chance that govern the entire universe: "We bet that there is a God—we bet our life on it!"

There is also the thrill of the forbidden. Once ashore in Sydney, where Oscar finds rooms with a pious church couple, they continue to meet to play cards, and when they are discovered, they're defiant. Oscar decides he doesn't fit into ordinary society. Lucinda says it is no matter. Even now they are not in love; it is gambling that holds them together, and Oscar believes Lucinda fancies another minister who has gone off to convert the outback. That gives him his great idea: Lucinda's glassworks will fabricate a glass cathedral, and Oscar will superintend the process of floating it upriver to the remote settlement.

For madness, this matches the obsession in Herzog's *Fitzcarraldo* to move a steamship across a strip of dry land. For inspiration, it seems divine—especially since they make a bet on it. Reading the novel, I pictured the glass cathedral as tall and vast, but of course it is a smaller church, one suitable for a growing congregation, and the photography showing its stately river progress is somehow funny and touching at the same time.

*Oscar and Lucinda* has been directed by Gillian Armstrong, whose films often deal with people who are right for each other and wrong for everyone else (see her neglected 1993 film *The Last Days of Chez Nous*, about a troubled marriage between an Australian and a Frenchman, or recall her 1979 film *My Brilliant Career*, in which Judy Davis played a character not unlike Lucinda in spirit). Here there is a dry wit, generated between the well-balanced performances of Fiennes and Blanchett, who seem quietly delighted to be playing two such rich characters.

The film's photography, by Geoffrey Simpson, begins with standard, lush nineteenth-century period evocations of landscape and sky, but then subtly grows more insistent on the quirky character of early Sydney, and then cuts loose altogether from the everyday in the final sequences involving the glass church. In many period films, we are always aware that we're watching the past: Here Oscar and Lucinda seem ahead of us, filled with freshness and invention, and only the narration (by Geoffrey Rush of *Shine*) reminds us that they were, incredibly, someone's grandparents.

*Oscar and Lucinda* begins with the look of a period literary adaptation, but this is not Dickens, Austen, Forster, or James; Carey's novel is playful and manipulative, and so is the film. Oscar is shy and painfully sincere, Lucinda has evaded her century's strictures on women by finding a private passion, and they would both agree, I believe, that people who worship in glass churches should not throw stones.

## Out of Sight ★ ★ ★ ½

R, 123 m., 1998

George Clooney (Jack Foley), Jennifer Lopez (Karen Sisco), Ving Rhames (Buddy Bragg), Isaiah Washington (Kenneth), Don Cheadle (Maurice Miller), Steve Zahn (Glenn Michaels), Keith Loneker (White Boy Bob), Dennis Farina (Marshall Sisco), Albert Brooks (Ripley). Directed by Steven Soderbergh and produced by Danny DeVito, Michael Shamberg, and Stacey Sher. Screenplay by Scott Frank, based on the novel by Elmore Leonard.

Steven Soderbergh's *Out of Sight* is a crime movie less interested in crime than in how people talk, flirt, lie, and get themselves into trouble. Based on an Elmore Leonard novel, it relishes Leonard's deep comic ease; the characters mosey through scenes, existing primarily to savor the dialogue.

The story involves a bank robber named Foley (George Clooney) and a federal marshal named Sisco (Jennifer Lopez), who grow attracted to one another while they're locked in a car trunk. Life goes on, and in the nature of things, it's her job to arrest him. But several things might happen first.

This is the fourth recent adaptation of a Leonard novel, after *Get Shorty, Touch,* and *Jackie Brown,* and the most faithful to Leonard's style. What all four movies demonstrate is how useful crime is as a setting for human comedy. For example: All caper movies begin with a self-contained introductory caper that has nothing at all to do with the rest of the plot. A cop will disarm a hostage, or a terrorist will plant a preliminary bomb. *Out of Sight* begins with as laid-back a bank robbery as you'd want to see, as Clooney saunters up to a teller's window and politely asks, "This your first time being held up?" How he cons the teller is one of the movie's first pleasures. The point of the scene is behavior, not robbery.

It turns out that this robbery is not, in fact, self-contained—it leads out of and into something—and it's not even really the first scene in the story. *Out of Sight* has a time line as complex as *Pulp Fiction,* even though at first we don't realize that. The movie's constructed like hypertext, so that, in a way, we can start watching at any point. It's like the old days when you walked in to the middle of a film and sat there until somebody said, "This is where we came in."

Elmore Leonard is above all the creator of colorful characters. Here we get the charming, intelligent Foley, who is constitutionally incapable of doing anything but robbing banks, and Sisco, the marshal, who has already had a previous liaison with a bank robber (admittedly, she eventually shot him). They are surrounded by a rich gallery of other characters, and this movie, like *Jackie Brown,* takes the time to give every character at least one well-written scene showing them as peculiar and unique.

Among Foley's criminal accomplices is his criminal partner, Buddy Bragg (Ving Rhames, who played Marcellus Wallace in *Pulp Fiction*). He's waiting on the outside after the prison break. In prison, Foley met a small-time hood named Glenn (Steve Zahn), who "has a vacant lot for a head." They're highly motivated by one of their fellow prisoners, a former Wall Street leverage expert named Ripley, who unwisely spoke of a fortune in uncut diamonds that he keeps in his house. (Ripley is played by Albert Brooks with a Michael Milkin hairstyle that is not a coincidence.)

Then there's the threesome that join Foley and his friends in a raid on Ripley's house. Snoopy Miller (Don Cheadle) is a nasty piece of work, a hard-nosed and violent former boxer; Isaiah Washington plays his partner; and Keith Loneker is White Boy Bob, his clumsy but very earnest bodyguard. It's ingenious how the raid involves shifting loyalties, with Foley and Sisco simultaneously dueling and cooperating.

All of these characters have lives of their own and don't exist simply at the convenience of the plot. Consider a tender father-daughter birthday luncheon between Karen Sisco and her father (Dennis Farina), a former lawman who tenderly gives her a gun.

At the center of the film is the repartee between Jennifer Lopez and George Clooney, and these two have the kind of unforced fun in their scenes together that reminds you of Bogart and Bacall. There's a seduction scene in which the dialogue is intercut with the very gradual progress of the physical action, and it's the dialogue that we want to linger on. Soderbergh edits this scene with quiet little freeze-frames; nothing quite matches up, and yet everything fits, so that the scene is like a demonstration of the whole movie's visual and time style.

Lopez had star quality in her first role in *My Family,* and in *Anaconda, Selena,* and the underrated *Blood and Wine* she has only grown; here she plays a role that could be complex or maybe just plain dumb, and brings a rich comic understanding to it. She wants to arrest the guy, but she'd like to have an affair with him first, and that leads to a delicate, well-written scene in a hotel bar where the cat and mouse hold negotiations. (It parallels, in a way, the "time out" between De Niro and Pacino in *Heat.*)

Clooney has never been better. A lot of actors who are handsome when young need to put on some miles before the full flavor emerges; observe how Nick Nolte, Mickey Rourke, Harrison Ford, and Clint Eastwood moved from stereotypes to individuals. Here Clooney at last looks like a big-screen star; the good-looking leading man from television is over with.

For Steven Soderbergh, *Out of Sight* is a paradox. It's his best film since *sex, lies, and videotape* a decade ago, and yet at the same time it's not what we think of as a Soderbergh film—detached, cold, analytical. It is instead the first film to build on the enormously influential *Pulp Fiction* instead of simply mimicking it. It has the games with time, the low-life dialogue, the absurd violent situations, but it also has its own texture. It plays like a string quartet written with words instead of music, performed by sleazeballs instead of musicians.

## Out to Sea ★ ★ ★

PG-13, 106 m., 1997

Jack Lemmon (Herb), Walter Matthau (Charlie), Dyan Cannon (Liz), Gloria De Haven (Vivian), Brent Spiner (Godwyn), Elaine Stritch (Mavis), Hal Linden (Mac), Donald O'Connor (Jonathan). Directed by Martha Coolidge and produced by John Davis and David T. Friendly. Screenplay by Robert Nelson Jacobs.

The grumpys have never been funnier than they are in *Out to Sea,* which continues the comic relationship of Jack Lemmon and Walter Matthau on board a cruise ship. They are not, strictly speaking, the original grumpy old men—they're Herb and Charlie instead of John and Max—but they might as well be, since this movie uses a lot of the same elements, including romance in the sunset years.

The setup: Matthau is a gambler who is deeply in debt to various bookies and other shady associates. Lemmon is his brother-in-law. Lemmon's wife is dead, his life is empty, and Matthau thinks it's time for them to have a change of scenery. So he arranges free tickets for them on the cruise ship *Westerdam.* The only catch is, they have to work for their passage: They'll be professional dance partners for the widows on board.

Matthau and Lemmon have long since settled into comfortably comic persona: Matthau rumpled and raffish, Lemmon uncertain and fretting. That's how it goes on board the ship, where Lemmon tries to please the militaristic cruise director, while Matthau sneaks off to the high-stakes poker games.

Their fellow passengers include a sweet-faced widow (Gloria De Haven) and a brassy blonde (Dyan Cannon), whose mother (Elaine Stritch) is engineering her attempts to snag a Daddy Warbucks. It goes without saying that Lemmon falls at once into love with the widow, while Matthau lays siege to the gold digger.

It's hard to describe just why *Out to Sea* is so funny and charming. Part of it may be due to the tender touch of Martha Coolidge, the director, whose films *(Rambling Rose, Lost in Yonkers, Real Genius)* always find humor in the human aspects of her stories. There is sheer slapstick here, including an inevitable scene in a lifeboat, but the human comedy is funnier—especially when it involves Brent Spiner, as the cruise director who introduces himself in glowing terms, and tells his dance partners: "I'm your worst nightmare: a song-and-dance man raised on a military base."

Matthau, who can't dance, fakes injuries and tries to hide from his martinet boss. Lemmon, who can dance, finds himself in the arms of De Haven and starts feeling guilty about his own departed wife, to whom he pledged eternal love. De Haven's role would seem to be thankless, but this movie veteran (whose first role was in Charlie Chaplin's *Modern Times*) looks warm and dazzling and finds just the right note in several tricky scenes.

Matthau and Lemmon are easy together, and no wonder; this is their seventh major film together, not counting a few footnotes. "Years of insanity have made you crazy," Lemmon tells Matthau, but when Lemmon is afraid it's too late for him to find love again, Matthau offers sound advice: "There's no such thing as too late. That's why they invented death."

Is the movie's ending, involving not only a lifeboat but also a seaplane, preposterous? Of course. Do we care? Not at all. In an industry overwhelmed with $100 million special-effects pictures, here's an alternative: a classic romantic comedy with big laughs and a sweet story.

# P

## The Pallbearer ★ ★ ★

PG-13, 94 m., 1996

David Schwimmer (Tom Thompson), Gwyneth Paltrow (Julie DeMarco), Michael Rapaport (Brad), Toni Collette (Cynthia), Carol Kane (Tom's Mom), Bitty Schram (Lauren), Barbara Hershey (Ruth Abernathy). Directed by Matt Reeves and produced by Jeffrey Abrams and Paul Webster. Screenplay by Jason Katims and Reeves.

To begin with the obvious: *The Pallbearer* is a goofier, gloomier trek across some of the same ground covered in *The Graduate,* with David Schwimmer of TV's *Friends* in the Dustin Hoffman role. The filmmakers must have subjected the 1967 classic to minute scrutiny. And yet the movie is not simply a retread; it has its own originality and tone and a quirkier sense of humor, and the central role is ideal for Schwimmer's hangdog charm.

He plays Tom Thompson, twenty-five years old and unemployed, who hopes to be an architect but goes into job interviews with a manner that shouts, "I am not the leading candidate for this job." He still lives at home with his mother (Carol Kane), is hopelessly inept with women, and has the fashion sense of a person who, if blindfolded, would not be able to describe what he was wearing.

As the movie opens, he gets a strange telephone call from a Mrs. Abernathy, who informs him that her son, Bill, is dead. He is not sure who Bill Abernathy was, but since Mrs. Abernathy seems convinced that Tom was Bill's best friend, he makes plans to attend the funeral. That involves borrowing a suit. Then Mrs. Abernathy (Barbara Hershey) calls at his home with a personal request: She wants him to deliver the eulogy.

Tom is played by Schwimmer as a well-meaning pushover who will agree to anything rather than say what he really thinks. He looks up Bill's picture in the high school yearbook and discovers Bill was absent the day photos were taken. Under his name are the unhelpful words, "Chess Club." Tom's funeral oration is not a success: "Who was . . . Bill Abernathy? What memories I have! Chess Club . . ."

Mrs. Abernathy is an attractive woman, bleached blond, grieving, needy, and although she is not impressed by the eulogy, she blames herself. She seeks out Tom for more talk about her son, and one misunderstanding leads to another until they have become, amazingly, lovers. This is not what Tom had in mind, although he likes Mrs. Abernathy well enough. His heart is focused on Julie DeMarco (Gwyneth Paltrow), although with her, too, he seems ill-prepared. At one point, revving up for a date, he tries to borrow a fresh shirt: "I used to be in love with her. I haven't seen her since high school. Imagine if she sees me in the same shirt."

We now have all the elements in place for *The Graduate*'s triangle between the nerdish hero, the alluring older woman, and the sweet younger one. And *The Pallbearer* has fun with some of the same kinds of scenes, including a spectacularly awkward meeting with Julie's parents, who have no idea who he is or why he has joined them for dinner.

There are moments in *The Pallbearer* when the plot almost gets entangled in itself, but that's part of the fun; all the characters operate under fundamental misinformation about one another. That leads to missed romantic signals, as when Tom tries to kiss Julie and ends up head-butting her. (Later, when she decides she wants to kiss him, she issues a prudent warning: "I'm coming in.") The structure of the screenplay, by Jason Katims and director Matt Reeves, is screwball comedy, but then they slow it down, add some sincere emotion, and filter it all through Schwimmer's awkward, inarticulate charm.

One of the influences of *Pulp Fiction* on other recent movies is the notion that not every scene has to single-mindedly further the plot. Some scenes can exist simply for themselves (consider the date in *Fargo* between the pregnant police chief and the old high school buddy). In *The Pallbearer,* there are several scenes and even plot-threads like that, including the backstage role of Tom's mother, who is played by Carol Kane as superficially ditzy but fundamentally sound. At one point she enters Tom's room without knocking, and receives his outraged complaint about privacy, etc., before quietly saying: "I came to see if you want some ice cream." "A little," says Tom, instantly forgiving.

Barbara Hershey's role as Mrs. Abernathy is

also written with some freedom in it. At first she seems set up simply as a clone of Mrs. Robinson in *The Graduate,* but her character takes some unmarked turns and ends up less predictable, and much nicer, than we expect. Tom, too, is not locked into one mode of behavior, and in a way the movie is about how he grows up and learns to take charge of himself. And Gwyneth Paltrow fools us about who Julie really is, and what she really wants.

There were times during *The Pallbearer* when I felt the plot was too clever for its own good, that twists were being added simply to frustrate us. But the director, Matt Reeves, has a master plan, and it's amazing how a movie with so many detours can arrive so convincingly at its destination.

## Palmetto ★ ★

R, 113 m., 1998

Woody Harrelson (Harry Barber), Elisabeth Shue (Rhea), Gina Gershon (Nina), Rolf Hoppe (Felix Malroux), Michael Rapaport (Donnelly), Chloe Sevigny (Odette), Tom Wright (John Renick), Marc Macaulay (Miles Meadows). Directed by Volker Schlondorff and produced by Matthias Wendlandt. Screenplay by E. Max Frye, based on the novel *Just Another Sucker* by James Hadley Chase.

Florida is the ideal state for *film noir.* Not the Florida of retirement villas and golf condos, but the Florida of the movies, filled with Spanish moss and decaying mansions, sweaty trophy wives and dog-race gamblers, chain-smoking assistant DAs and alcoholic newspaper reporters. John D. Macdonald is its Raymond Chandler and Carl Hiaasen would be its Elmore Leonard, if Leonard hadn't gotten there first.

*Noir* is founded on atmosphere, and Florida has it: tacky theme bars on the beach, humid nights, ceiling fans, losers dazed by greed, the sense of dead bodies rotting out back in the Everglades. (Louisiana has even more atmosphere, but in *noir* you need a society where people are surprised by depravity, and Louisiana takes it for granted.)

*Palmetto* is the latest exercise in Florida *noir,* joining *Key Largo, Body Heat, A Flash of Green, Cape Fear, Striptease,* and *Blood & Wine.* The movie has all the elements of the genre, and lacks only pacing and plausibility. You wait through scenes that unfold with maddening deliberation, hoping for a payoff—and when it comes, you feel cheated. Watching it, I was more than ever convinced that Bob Rafelson's *Blood & Wine* was the movie that got away in 1997—a vastly superior Florida *noir* (with a Jack Nicholson performance that humbles his work in *As Good As It Gets*).

Both films depend on our sense of rich, eccentric people living in big houses that draw the attention of poor people. Both involve deception and hidden identities. Both heroes are once-respectable outsiders, driven to amateurish crime by desperation. Both involve older men blinded to danger by younger women with beckoning cleavage. *Blood & Wine* is the film that works. *Palmetto* is more like a first draft.

Woody Harrelson stars as Harry Barber, a newspaper reporter who tried to expose corruption in the town of Palmetto and was framed and sent to prison. After two years his conviction is overturned and he's released—by a judge who renders the verdict over closed-circuit TV. When Harry starts screaming that he wants his two years back, the judge dismisses him by clicking the channel-changer.

Harry wants to start over, anywhere but in Palmetto. But he's drawn back by his ex-girlfriend, Nina, an artist played by Gina Gershon. He looks for work, can't find it, and amuses himself by hanging around daytimes in bars, ordering bourbon and not drinking it (this is not recommended for ex-drinkers). One day a blonde named Rhea (Elisabeth Shue) undulates into the bar, makes a call, and outdulates without her handbag. Harry finds it in the phone booth, she reundulates for it, and they fall into a conversation during which Harry does not drink bourbon and Rhea holds, but does not light, a cigarette ("I don't smoke").

The sense that Harry and Rhea are holding their addictions at bay does not extend to sex, which Rhea uses to enlist Harry in a mad scheme. She's married to a rich old coot named Felix who is dying of cancer but may linger inconveniently; meanwhile, her stepdaughter, Odette (Chloe Sevigny, from *Kids*), is threatening to run away rather than be parked in a Swiss boarding school. Rhea's proposal: Harry fakes Odette's kidnapping, Felix pays $500,000 in ransom, Harry keeps 10 percent for his troubles,

Odette has her freedom with the rest. Lurking in the background: Michael Rapaport, as Felix's stern houseboy.

Well, what mother wouldn't do as much for a child? Harry's misgivings about this plot are silenced by Rhea's seductive charms, while Nina observes in concern (her role here reminded me of Barbara Bel Geddes in *Vertigo*—the good girl with the paint brush, looking up from her easel each time the bad boy slinks in after indulging his twisted libido).

Harry is, of course, spectacularly bad as a kidnapper (I liked the scene where he types a ransom note on his typewriter and flings it from a bridge, only to see that he has misjudged the water depth and it has landed in plain sight on the mud). While he busies himself leaving about fingerprints and cigarette butts ("DNA? They can test for that?"), there's a neat twist: The assistant DA in charge of the kidnapping case (Tom Wright) hires Harry as a press liaison. So the kidnapper becomes the official police spokesman.

All of the pieces are here for a twisty *film noir*, and Harry's dual role—as criminal and police mouthpiece—is Hitchcockian in the way it hides the perp in plain sight. But it doesn't crackle. The director, Volker Schlondorff *(The Tin Drum)*, doesn't dance stylishly through the genre, but plods in almost docudrama style. And screenwriter E. Max Frye, working from James Hadley Chase's novel *Just Another Sucker*, hasn't found the right tone for an ending where victims dangle above acid baths. The ending could be handled in many ways, from the satirical to the gruesome, but the movie adopts a curiously flat tone. Sure, we have questions about the plot twists, but a better movie would sweep them aside with its energy; this one has us squinting at the screen in disbelief and resentment.

The casting is another problem. Gina Gershon and Elisabeth Shue are the wrong way around. Gershon is superb as a lustful, calculating femme fatale (she shimmers with temptation in *Bound* and *This World, Then the Fireworks*). Shue is best at heartfelt roles. Imagine Barbara Stanwyck waiting faithfully behind the easel while Doris Day seduces the hero and you'll see the problem. Woody Harrelson does his best, but the role serves the plot, not his character, and so he sometimes does things only because the screenwriter needs for him to. *Palmetto* knows the words, but not the music.

## Palookaville ★ ★ ★

R, 92 m., 1996

Adam Trese (Jerry), Vincent Gallo (Russ), William Forsythe (Sid), Gareth Williams (Ed), Lisa Gay Hamilton (Betty), Bridgit Ryan (Enid), Kim Dickens (Laurie), Frances McDormand (June). Directed by Alan Taylor and produced by Uberto Pasolini. Screenplay by David Epstein.

One of my favorite moments in movie comedy comes in *Big Deal on Madonna Street* (1958), when a gang laboriously breaks through a wall, only to find one of their gang standing on the other side, baffled. They have broken through the wrong wall.

Alan Taylor's *Palookaville*, which obviously had that moment in mind, opens with an equally hapless gang of thieves, these in Jersey City, breaking through a wall into what should be a jewelry store but turns out to be a bakery, and then loading up on doughnuts. When the police arrive, one of the thieves hides behind a rack of baked goods, still helping himself.

Russ (Vincent Gallo), the leader of the gang, lives at home, where his brother-in-law, a cop, talks idly about "some jerk who tried to take a bakery," but fails to notice the powdered sugar on Russ's collar. One of the things that drives Russ wild is that he still lives under the thumbs of his mother and sister, not to mention his brother-in-law; a man his age should be on his own, but he doesn't have a job and can't afford to move out.

None of these guys have quite grown up. Russ sneaks out of his bedroom window for rendezvous with the teenager who lives next door. Jerry (Adam Trese) cautions them to use only plastic guns. And Sid (William Forsythe) is so sentimental about dogs that it sometimes endangers his life. He dreams up a scam involving taxi rides for the elderly, but they don't like sharing his car with all those dogs.

Jerry may have the brains, but they are unfocused. "Look," he says at one point, "we should just forget theft entirely, and concentrate on a life of ideas." When he finds his wife, Betty (Lisa Gay Hamilton), in the amorous arms of the manager of the grocery where she works, he causes a scene—and she makes him apologize because she needs the job.

They all need jobs; Jerry describes one of his pals as "self-unemployed." Then they stumble into the idea of robbery; an armored car driver has a heart attack, they take him to the hospital, and then start thinking about how much money they left behind. Studiously watching a movie named *Armored Car Robbery* on TV for tips, they plan their big heist so ineptly that at one point the cop is actually following them while they're tailing an armored car.

No doubt *Palookaville* will have the millstone of Tarantinoism tied around its neck; any urban crime movie with a lot of guys and a little humor is routinely linked these days with Q.T. But the movie's roots go back further, to a group of short stories by the Italian writer Italo Calvino, in the 1940s. And the feel of the movie is more like those older caper films, not only Italian but British *(The Lavender Hill Mob).*

*Palookaville* understands a kind of low-key humor based on human nature. It's not into cynicism, it's not hip, it's not *Reservoir Dogs,* nor does it want to be. Essentially these are guys who see the bright side, which is why they loaded up on the doughnuts.

## Paperback Romance ★ ★ ★

R, 89 m., 1997

Gia Carides (Sophie), Anthony LaPaglia (Eddie), Rebecca Gibney (Gloria), Jacek Koman (Yuri), Sioban Tuke (Kate), Lewis Fiander (Bruce Wrightman), Robyn Nevin (Anne-Marie LePine), Marshall Napier (George LePine). Directed by Ben Lewin and produced by Bob Weis. Screenplay by Lewin.

The voice describes images of passion in the words of lurid melodrama; we think this must be a dream sequence, and in a way we're right. *Paperback Romance* cuts to reveal that the words are being read aloud by a pretty woman writer in a large and almost empty library, and overheard by a man who asks her out because "conversation with you would be the most exquisite imaginable form of foreplay."

She turns him down. We might ask why, since a writer who reads soft-core pornography aloud in a public place usually does not wish to avoid attention. Then we find out why: After the man leaves, we see that the woman wears a leg brace and uses crutches. Later, we discover she had polio as a child.

My guess is that in the real world this woman would not feel the need to conceal her disability. But in the world of *Paperback Romance* she conceals it for an excellent reason: The entire plot depends on the misunderstandings that result.

The woman's name is Sophie, and she's played by Gia Carides, whom you may remember as the nasty rival in *Strictly Ballroom.* The man, Eddie (Anthony LaPaglia), runs a jewelry store in a mall, and Sophie, who is intrigued, tracks him down there. She wants to remain hidden, especially after she sees him with the attractive Gloria (Rebecca Gibney), but in trying to hurry out of view she stumbles on her crutches, falls into a baby carriage, and is hurtled over the edge of the balcony and into the arms of a rotund opera singer below.

She breaks her leg in the accident. It's the same leg that is crippled, so now she wears a crutch and has an alibi (it was a "skiing accident") as her relationship with Eddie proceeds uncertainly—very uncertainly, since he is scheduled to marry Gloria. Eddie finds himself in the grip of a mad passion involving Sophie, however, and during a sex scene, blind as a bat, he injures his lip on her cast and is unable to speak for several scenes. Sophie can understand his tortured mumblings, and helpfully translates for him with Gloria, adding her own spin to most of what he says.

The pratfall over the edge of the balcony caught me by surprise, since I thought the movie had started on a different kind of note. But the director, Ben Lewin, permits himself screwball comedy at the same time he develops his darker material, and the scenes involving the lip injury are truly funny. So are aspects of a subplot involving a Russian and a stolen necklace, although the setup is pretty conventional.

*Paperback Romance* comes from Australia, and I was more than mildly surprised to find out that LaPaglia does, too (he's married to Carides). On a quiz, I would have penciled in New Jersey, or maybe Manhattan. The movie's country of origin helps explain its screwy charm. For a long time I've been talking about "offbeat Australian comedies," but on reflection I realize there are no Australian comedies that are on beat. With *Love Serenade*, we had a very strange romance between two sisters and a fishy disk jockey, and of course there have been *Strictly Ballroom, Muriel's Wedding, Priscilla, Queen of the Desert*, and a lot of other films to suggest that perhaps this is more than a trend: Perhaps everyone in Australia *is* goofy.

## Paradise Road ★ ★
R, 130 m., 1997

Glenn Close (Adrienne Pargiter), Pauline Collins (Margaret Drummond), Cate Blanchett (Susan Macarthy), Frances McDormand (Dr. Verstak), Julianna Margulies (Topsy Merritt), Sab Shimono (Colonel Hiroyo), Jennifer Ehle (Rosemary Leighton-Jones), Elizabeth Spriggs (Mrs. Roberts), Joanna Ter Steege (Sister Wilhelminia). Directed by Bruce Beresford and produced by Sue Milliken and Greg Coote. Screenplay by Beresford.

Bruce Beresford's *Paradise Road* tells the story of a group of women who were held prisoner in a Japanese internment camp for most of World War II. If you were told this story by one of the survivors, you would shake your head in amazement and marvel at her courage. You would probably think it would make a good movie; after all, it's even true.

The film begins at Raffles Hotel in Singapore in 1942, at an elegant dinner dance. An alert arrives that Japanese forces are about to take the city. Women and some children are hurried aboard a transport ship, which is attacked a few days later by Japanese aircraft. Life rafts float ashore at Sumatra, where the survivors are taken to a POW camp, there to spend the rest of the war.

The movie now has a delicate balance to find. It is no longer acceptable to portray the Japanese as the embodiment of evil; the monsters of *The Bridge on the River Kwai* now have to be seen in a slightly better light, as harsh and cruel, perhaps, but not inhuman—and capable of sentiment when the prisoners form a choir and begin to perform classical choral works. (Earlier, the screenplay provides racist anti-Japanese slurs at the Singapore party, to show that the British, too, had their flaws; the film is set in 1942, but its attitudes are circa 1997.)

We meet the prisoners. They include a remarkable group of women: the British musician Adrienne Pargiter (Glenn Close); the Australian missionary Margaret Drummond, nicknamed Daisy (Pauline Collins); the nurse Susan Macarthy (Cate Blanchett); the German-accented Dr. Verstak (Frances McDormand); and an American painted in broad strokes, Topsy Merritt (Julianna Margulies).

Conditions are brutal in the tropical climate, food is scarce, living quarters are filthy, and the camp commandant (Sab Shimono) supervises cruel punishments, including one where a woman must kneel for hours in the hot sun, or fall over onto sharp spikes. Yet their music somehow redeems the conditions and elevates their spirits; the choir even soothes the Japanese to such an extent that guards sent to silence them cannot bring themselves to halt such a glorious sound (they, too, hate the war and are moved by beauty).

Told this story, and that it was true, you would think it would be enough for a screenplay. But would you be correct? I didn't want *Paradise Road* to be a melodrama—a *Great Escape*, say, or *Stalag 17* in which the sound of the music distracts from the digging of tunnels. There is not even the possibility of escape, because they are on an island in the middle of a sea controlled by Japan. We realize fairly early on that prison life, within boundaries, will remain much the same until the film's end. But what the movie lacks is a story arc to pull us through.

The performances are moving, especially Glenn Close's work as the strongest of the women, who conducts the choir. It was difficult for me to accept Frances McDormand with a German accent (*Fargo* was too fresh in my mind), but I admired Pauline Collins (of *Shirley Valentine*), whose character's remarkable memory allows her to write down classical music so that they can rehearse it.

There is a possibility in this material for a story that contains more drama. The women are offered an alternative to the prison camp: If they volunteer to be prostitutes and please Japanese officers, they can live in a hotel with clean sheets, hot meals, and nightly dances. (A lapse in the dialogue: When one woman seems tempted, another asks, "But what about the choir?") Some women in such a position did choose to become prostitutes (some women in Raffles in 1942 no doubt had made that career choice even earlier). If the film had intercut the camp scenes with the experiences of a woman who accepted the Japanese offer, it would have brought contrast into the story—and provided an ironic ending for her, no doubt.

Am I being a vulgarian? Given these brave, muddy women singing Dvorak, why am I not content? Why do I want to see one of them sell her body and soul to the Japanese? I think the film cries out for contrast, for tension, for choice. It is too linear. The women are captured, they go to the camp, they suffer and endure, they perform their music, and then the war is over. The movie is an anecdote, not a story.

## Paulie ★ ★

PG, 92 m., 1998

Gena Rowlands (Ivy), Tony Shalhoub (Misha), Cheech Marin (Ignacio), Bruce Davison (Dr. Reingold), Jay Mohr (Paulie/Benny), Trini Alvarado (Adult Marie), Buddy Hackett (Artie), Hallie Kate Eisenberg (Marie). Directed by John Roberts and produced by Mark Gordon, Gary Levinsohn, and Allison Lyon Segan. Screenplay by Laurie Craig.

*Paulie* tells the story of a parrot who can think like a human and talk like a stand-up comic, but a parrot who really had those gifts wouldn't have the problems this one does. He doesn't come across as a bird at all, but as a small, wisecracking person wearing feathers. He's just a little more interesting than the other guy with the same first name who also stars in—but no, that sentence was headed in an unkind direction.

The film is aimed at children, I suppose, although I don't think they'll like Paulie all that much. I didn't. I know there are people who love parrots, but they love them for being parrots. Would you want to live with a parrot who talked and thought like Buddy Hackett? You would? As long as he cleaned his own cage?

As the movie opens, Paulie is in "purgatory" in the basement of a research lab, where he's been banished for refusing to cooperate with an ambitious scientist (Bruce Davison). How did Paulie get there? After he's befriended by a Russian-American janitor (Tony Shalhoub), he offers to tell his story, and we see it in flashback as an odyssey across the country.

Paulie started, we learn, as the friend of a little girl named Marie. After he's blamed for her fall from a roof, he's dispatched to Buddy Hackett's pawnshop, where he picks up some of his vocal style before he's purchased by a lovable woman named Ivy (Gena Rowlands) who (kids! hide your eyes!) goes blind and dies. Then he travels cross-country to Los Angeles, where he has an unconsummated romance with a girl parrot, and no wonder: If you were as smart as Buddy Hackett, how long would you be able to sustain a relationship with a parrot? Cheech Marin makes a brief appearance as another of Paulie's owners, and the bird even becomes expert at stealing from ATM machines before he ends up in the hands of the scientist.

The movie's slant is that it's wrong to keep animals in cages and do experiments on them, and Paulie makes some dramatic gestures toward this end, but by then my attention was drifting. Dogs and cats, horses and monkeys, and even bears make charismatic movie stars, but *Paulie*, I think, suggests that birds are more decorative than dramatic.

On the other hand, just to be fair, I should mention that parrots make great subjects for jokes. I know about a dozen, including the ones about the parrot in the deep freeze, the insulting parrot, the 300-pound parakeet, and the parrot whose last words were, "Who moved the ladder?"

I even made up a brand-new parrot joke while watching this movie. A parrot has a memory that will hold only the last two things it has heard. A guy buys him, puts him by the front door and tests him. "One, two," the man says. "One, two," the parrot says. "Three," says the man. "Two, three," says the parrot. "Four," says the man. "Three, four," says the parrot. Then the guy shouts to his wife: "So long, honey, I'm going to the office!" When the guy comes home, what does the parrot say?

I'd tell you, but this is a family movie.

## The Peacemaker ★ ★ ½

R, 122 m., 1997

George Clooney (Thomas Devoe), Nicole Kidman (Julia Kelly), Marcel Iures (Dusan Gavrich), Alexander Baluev (Alexsander Kodoroff), Rene Medvesek (Vlado Mirich), Gary Werntz (Hamilton), Randall Batinkoff (Ken), Jim Haynie

(General Garnett). Directed by Mimi Leder and produced by Walter Parkes and Branko Lustig. Screenplay by Michael Schiffer.

At first I wasn't going to mention the red digital readout. I've talked about them so often in the past I was afraid of boring you. Then I thought, hey, I was amazed when I saw it in this movie—so why shouldn't I share? I refer to the wheezy movie device requiring the hero to defuse a bomb or other dangerous device before it explodes. Such devices invariably have red digital readouts, so we can see the seconds ticking away with deadly precision.

RDRs have become a jarring cliché, but they survive because they're a quick, cheap device for manufacturing phony suspense. Already this year we've seen RDRs on a doomed ocean liner *(Speed II)* and onboard *Air Force One*, and now, in *The Peacemaker*, the whole climax comes down to whether Nicole Kidman and George Clooney can disarm a ticking nuclear bomb before it vaporizes Manhattan.

This is the first big release from the new DreamWorks studio, and it looks great. The technical credits are impeccable, and Clooney and Kidman negotiate assorted dangers skillfully. But it's mostly spare parts from other thrillers. There's one flash of originality (the villain is protesting that the world has ignored the killing in Bosnia). Much of the rest is retreaded, including the standard idea of teaming a macho military hero (Clooney) with a bright female government official (Kidman). "Give me a man who knows how to take orders from a woman," she barks, just before the scene where he marches into her briefing, interrupts her, corrects her, and then spends the rest of the film giving her orders.

Kidman plays the "acting head of the White House Nuclear Smuggling Group," and Clooney is an intelligence officer with Army Special Forces. The terrorist (Marcel Iures) is haunted by images of his loved ones slaughtered in the former Yugoslavia.

The film opens with a convincing sequence in which nuclear bombs are stolen from a Russian train carrying them to be defused. ("I didn't join the Russian Army to dismantle it for the Americans," one soldier grumbles.) The train is destroyed in a nuclear blast to make it look like all the bombs were destroyed by accident, but Clooney saves us ten minutes of screen time by seeing through the scheme at once.

The film then assembles off-the-shelf parts. These include such standbys as (1) beetle-browed enemy officials sitting in ornate offices and issuing imprecations; (2) preparations for an emergency mission by the good guys; (3) canned personality conflicts, quickly resolved; (4) exterior shots of ominous-looking places, with captions telling us what they are; (5) rat-a-tat military music over convoys to Iran, etc.; (6) high-tech displays of satellite surveillance; and (7) after a few subtitles, a Russian barking "speak English!" at a subordinate, after which they continue in English for no other reason than that they must realize they're in an American movie.

Everything comes down to a cat-and-mouse chase in Manhattan, where the terrorist hopes to explode his bomb. He's made a videotape arguing that he is not a bad man, but he remains such a cipher we don't know if he's sincerely misguided, or simply mad. No matter; the film goes on autopilot for its last act, with the usual canned chase scenes down Manhattan streets, heroes climbing over automobiles, sirens blaring, cars crashing, etc. This used to be known as "second unit" stuff. Now it's the centerpiece.

Finally we get the red digital readout scene, and I'm thinking—what? A movie this expensive was actually based on the bankrupt climax of the heroes dismantling a bomb while an RDR ticks down? Wasn't it possible to think up an original third act? Three other not dissimilar thrillers released at about the same time *(The Assignment, The Edge,* and *Kiss the Girls)* all featured real endings involving character developments and new surprises. DreamWorks shouldn't have settled for less.

At one point, trying to dismantle the bomb, the Kidman character tells a children's choir director, "Get those kids as far away from here as possible," and the kids scurry out the church door. A nuclear bomb is set to explode in under two minutes. If it does, it won't help that the kids are four blocks down the street. If it doesn't, the kids are safe where they are. A wittier screenplay might have had her say, "Let the kids watch this. They might learn something." And then a cherubic little choir boy hurrying over and saying, "Wow! A red digital readout! Just like in the movies!" ☞

## The People vs. Larry Flynt ★ ★ ★ ★

R, 130 m., 1996

Woody Harrelson (Larry Flynt), Courtney Love (Althea Leasure), Edward Norton (Alan Isaacman), Brett Harrelson (Jimmy Flynt), Donna Hanover (Ruth Carter Stapleton), James Cromwell (Charles Keating), Crispin Glover (Arlo), Vincent Schiavelli (Chester). Directed by Milos Forman and produced by Oliver Stone, Janet Yang, and Michael Hausman. Screenplay by Scott Alexander and Larry Karaszewski.

"This is it?" the Cincinnati printer asks dubiously, looking at the page proofs for the newsletter Larry Flynt wants him to print. "You've got to have text—like *Playboy*." Flynt is unyielding. He is interested in gynecological detail, not redeeming social merit. Soon his newsletter has blossomed into *Hustler* magazine, although not without difficulties (one editorial conference is devoted to a discussion of why the number of a magazine's pages must be divisible by two).

If you believe that *Hustler* is pornographic and in bad taste, you will not get an argument from Flynt. Flaunting the magazine's raunchiness, he became a millionaire while printing cartoons like the one where "Dorothy has a foursome with the Tin Man, the Cowardly Lion, and the Scarecrow—oh, and Toto." Emboldened by his success, Flynt grew more outrageous, until finally one of his parody ads inspired a $40 million lawsuit from the Rev. Jerry Falwell.

Was Falwell right to be offended? He certainly was; the parody of a Smirnoff ad was in outrageously bad taste. Did Flynt have a right to print the parody? The Supreme Court eventually decided that he did. No one in his right mind could believe that what the ad said was true (as Falwell himself admitted from the witness stand), and the right of free speech includes the right to offend.

The Supreme Court's ruling in the *Hustler* case came under attack at the time, but consider this: If Falwell had won his suit against Flynt, all newspapers would be fundamentally different. The editorial cartoons could not make fun of public officials. The op-ed columns could not risk offending. The lawyers might have questioned a recent review in which I said a film should be cut up into ukulele picks; after all, that might have hurt the director's feelings. And Falwell himself might not have been able to broadcast his sermons, because they might have offended atheists (or you, or me).

"If they'll protect a scumbag like me, then they'll protect all of you," Flynt said after his 1987 court victory. Inelegant, but true. Milos Forman's *The People vs. Larry Flynt* argues that the freedom of speech must apply to unpopular speech or it is meaningless. Beginning with this belief, Forman constructs a fascinating biopic about a man who went from rags to riches by never overestimating the taste of his readers.

If you question the dimensions of *Hustler*'s success, reflect that a modern skyscraper towers in Los Angeles, proclaiming FLYNT PUBLICATIONS from its rooftop. Even if he's only leasing, that's a lot of rent. When Flynt started *Hustler* in 1972, *Playboy* was already twenty years old and *Penthouse* was a success. He aimed below them—at the vulgar underbelly of the market—and offered pictorial details that *Playboy*, at least, has never been interested in printing.

For Flynt, *Hustler* was like winning the lottery. Played by Woody Harrelson, he was a Kentucky moonshiner's son who ran away from home and eventually ran strip clubs in Cincinnati. There he found the love of his life: Althea Leasure (Courtney Love), a bisexual stripper who bluntly told him, "You are not the only person who has slept with every woman in this club."

*Hustler*'s first publicity breakthrough came when Flynt printed nude photos of Jacqueline Onassis, a coup so sensational it forced the media (and the public) to notice the magazine. *The People vs. Larry Flynt* shows Flynt running a loose editorial ship in which his brother Jimmy (Brett Harrelson), hangers-on, and assorted strippers and hookers seem to publish the magazine by committee.

Very early, he meets a man destined to be a lifelong companion: his lawyer, Alan Isaacman (Edward Norton), who wins his spurs defending him in one action after another. An early antagonist is Charles Keating, then head of Citizens for Decent Literature, more recently a figure in the S&L scandals. "I'm your dream client," Flynt tells Isaacman. "I'm fun, I'm rich, and I'm always in trouble."

The movie shows Larry and Althea as a couple deeply into promiscuity; proposing marriage to him in a hot tub, Althea is shocked when

Larry thinks she means monogamy. Their marriage survives many tests, not least the one when Flynt is temporarily converted to religion by Ruth Carter Stapleton, sister of the president. (The movie never really makes it clear how sincere Flynt was in his born-again period.)

As the magazine grows, Flynt keeps it on the low road, eventually developing enemies. In 1978, during a trial in Georgia, both he and Isaacman are shot by an unknown gunman, and Flynt is paralyzed from the waist down. That leads to a long dark period, until 1983, when he and Althea hole up in a Los Angeles mansion, using painkillers and whatever other drugs come to hand. The magazine seems to run itself while they cower behind the steel door of their bedroom.

Flynt eventually has an operation that stops his pain, and he kicks drugs. Leasure, not as lucky, sickens and dies of AIDS. Then comes the suit by Falwell, and a journey that ends with Flynt pumping his wheelchair into the Supreme Court.

Larry Flynt is never likely to find his face on a postage stamp, but he has played a role in our era. A negative one, in contributing to the general decay of taste and decorum, and a positive one, in being the point man for a crucial defense of American liberties. As an individual, he seems to have been clueless some of the time and morose much of the time (he plays a cameo role in the film as a judge, and looks unhappy).

But like many another man he was fortunate to find the love of a loyal woman, and Althea, as played by Love, is a quirky free spirit. The product of a tragic childhood (she identified the bodies after her father murdered her family, then went to an orphanage where she was abused), she is made by Love into a kind of life force, misdirected but uncompromised. It is quite a performance; Love proves she is not a rock star pretending to act, but a true actress, and Harrelson matches her with his portrait of a man who has one thing on his mind and never changes it.

Milos Forman's other films have included *Amadeus* and *One Flew Over the Cuckoo's Nest,* both about inspired misfits with the courage of their eccentricity. Now Larry Flynt is another. Who else could have so instinctively combined idealism and cash, declaring at a press conference, "Americans for a Free Press is me. Who do you think is paying for this show?"

## A Perfect Candidate ★ ★ ★

NO MPAA RATING, 105 m., 1996

A documentary directed and produced by R. J. Cutler and David Van Taylor.

*A Perfect Candidate* is a documentary about the ugly, messy 1994 Virginia senatorial campaign between Charles Robb and Oliver North—who offered a choice one voter compares to "mumps, or the flu." The TV ads paint one candidate as a liar who cheats on his wife, and the other as a liar and closet racist, but the candidates themselves seem unable to articulate any issues at all. It is, says a reporter covering the campaign, "the triumph of anger over politics."

It was widely observed that the 1996 political conventions were not conventions at all in the traditional sense of the word, but carefully scripted infomercials; speeches were edited down to sound bites, prime time was devoted to audience-pleasers, and there was no debate on the issues. The 1994 Virginia race was an illustration in miniature of how our politics got this way. Personalities are being sold, not parties or philosophies, and *A Perfect Candidate* makes that process even more interesting because one candidate, Robb, apparently has no personality at all, while the other, North, has two.

Ollie North's fame rests on his role in the Iran-Contra affair, during which he lied to Congress about his role in illegally selling arms in the Middle East to finance right-wing forces in South America. His defense was patriotism: He did what he thought was right for his country. In Virginia, his campaign cloaked itself in "family values" and was the instrument of the Christian right wing. To his supporters, North was a patriot, a Christian, an upholder of conservative social beliefs. His supporters were almost all white. His opponents branded him a racist, linked him with David Duke and the Ku Klux Klan, and ran TV ads hammering his perjury before Congress.

That created two Norths, a devil and an angel. Charles Robb, in contrast, hardly seems to be present at all. He wanders forlornly through a supermarket, seeking a voter, and when he finds one his approach is so inept the voter seems unsure why this stranger is talking to him. One dawn Robb campaigns outside a factory gate and is asked by a reporter for his position on workers hired to replace strikers.

"My position hasn't changed," he says. "Well," says the reporter, "are you for it?" "I have not changed my position." "Are you against it?" "I have the same position I have always had." The reporter turns to a Robb handler and asks, "Can we have a simultaneous translation here?"

Midway through the campaign, when Robb is linked with a former *Playboy* model named Tea Collins, there is almost a sense of relief: If he is an adulterer, at least that is *something* interesting about him. North's handlers work the angle for all it's worth; if both candidates have lied, that makes the honesty issue a wash.

The hero of the film is the reporter who has that perplexing exchange with Robb outside the factory gate. He is Don Baker of the *Washington Post,* a man who tirelessly drives up and down the state chronicling the cheerless campaign, and provides a stream-of-consciousness commentary for the documentary cameras. He thinks North is a demagogue ("I don't know if he really believes all that Christian stuff") but a skillful politician. Robb he considers sort of a political black hole. The campaign is finally tilted when a politician who does deal with the issues—former Virginia governor Douglas Wilder—endorses Robb (even though he privately detests him) and helps solidify the black vote.

There is a fascinating moment when Baker muses on what might happen if North were elected: "Maybe then we'd get a showdown—not just a middle-of-the-road compromiser." It might be fun and even useful, in other words, to have someone in the Senate actually articulating the loony quasi-issues that drive the underbelly of American politics.

Because this film was obviously not going to be released until long after the campaign was over, some of the campaign strategists are frank with the filmmakers. One of them is North's master planner, Mark Goodin, who does a brilliant job of overcoming North's negatives and bringing him almost to victory. On the day after the election, when Robb has somehow won, Goodin observes, "In the end, the negative stuff sticks and it works. I should never ever have forgotten that." He blames himself for being too much of a good guy.

Those over a certain age in America can remember campaigns where the politicians debated the issues in some detail, and voters were trusted to be able to follow along. They remember conventions that actually decided who would be a party's candidate, and platform fights that went on all night, as parties decided what they believed. This year we are given a choice between a bridge to the past and a bridge to the twenty-first century, and both bridges look a little like unfinished exit ramps, ending in midair.

## A Perfect Murder ★ ★ ★

R, 107 m., 1998

Michael Douglas (Steven Taylor), Gwyneth Paltrow (Emily Bradford Taylor), Viggo Mortensen (David Shaw), David Suchet (Detective Karaman), Constance Towers (Sandra Bradford), Sarita Choudhury (Raquel Martinez). Directed by Andrew Davis and produced by Arnold Kopelson, Anne Kopelson, Christopher Mankiewicz, and Peter MacGregor-Scott. Screenplay by Patrick Smith Kelly, based on the play *Dial M for Murder* by Frederick Knott.

Michael Douglas is about as good as anyone can be at playing greedy, coldhearted SOBs. He's also good at playing nice guys and victims—he's a versatile pro—but when he goes into his Gordon Gekko mode there's an extra charge on the screen, because we know everything his character says and does will be deceitful and self-interested.

Consider an early scene in Andrew Davis's *A Perfect Murder.* Douglas plays Steven Taylor, a wealthy currency trader. Gwyneth Paltrow plays Emily, his wife. She comes home to their designer apartment to find him dressed for a museum opening. They kiss. She says how nice he looks: "I'll hurry and get dressed so I can catch up." Throughout this entire scene, dislike hangs in the air. There's nothing overt. It's simply a way Douglas has of pronouncing his words, as if he wants to say all the proper things even though he doesn't mean them.

The Paltrow character is an heiress who is having an affair with an artist named David Shaw (Viggo Mortensen). We learn that in the first scene. *A Perfect Murder* doesn't fool around with a misleading opening charade to deceive us. This is not a happy marriage and the movie never pretends otherwise, and when the husband confronts the artist in his studio, there is a kind of blunt savagery to the way he cuts to the bottom line. ("You steal the crown jewel of a man's life, and all you can come up with is some candy-ass Hallmark sentiment?")

A murder is arranged in the movie, but for once the TV ads leave you with a certain doubt about who is doing what and with which and to whom, so I won't reveal the secret. I will say that Paltrow does a convincing job of playing a chic wife who considers love to be a choice more than a destiny. Viggo Mortensen undergoes an interesting transformation in his key scene with Douglas; we believe him when he's a nice guy, and we believe him even more when he's not; he doesn't do a big style shift, he simply turns off his people-pleasing face.

The screenplay, by Patrick Smith Kelly, is based on the play *Dial M for Murder* and the Hitchcock film of the same title. It has little in common with its predecessors. It's about negotiation more than deception, money more than love. Everybody's motives are pretty much clear from the beginning, and when the body is found on the kitchen floor the only mystery is how long it will take the survivor to find the key to the scheme.

Surprisingly, the movie got some negative early reviews. I think it works like a nasty little machine to keep us involved and disturbed; my attention never strayed, and one of the elements I liked was the way Paltrow's character isn't sentimentalized. She says she's in love with the artist, yes, but she gets over it in a hurry; it takes her about one line of dialogue. And there is a moment when it appears that husband and wife will put adultery and violence behind them, and continue their pragmatic liaison as a rich guy and his multilingual trophy wife. Who wouldn't want to keep living in that great apartment?

But there's another problem: Steven is having a portfolio meltdown (his adviser tells him, "Think Chernobyl"). Steven is driven not only by jealousy but by need and greed. Emily has a $100 million trust fund that would help Steven cover those margins (although the markets move a lot faster than probate, and the inheritance is unlikely to arrive in time to do much good).

The movie is a skilled example of what I call the Fatal Basic Genre. Like *Fatal Attraction, Basic Instinct* and all of their lesser imitators, it's about sex between bad people who live in good houses. Nobody is better at Fatal Basic than Michael Douglas, who doesn't need to read *GQ* because he instinctively knows what clothes to wear and which cigars to smoke.

My only real disappointment with the movie comes at the end, when various differences are resolved with gunshots. This is such a tired story solution. I realize that the Hollywood bylaws require all action movies to end in shoot-outs, but is a gun really necessary in a Fatal Basic movie? I'd prefer the chessmaster approach to the problem, in which a single line of logical dialogue seals a character's fate, and then we get a big close-up of him realizing he's screwed. Gunshots release tension, but they don't provide audience pleasure, because the victim is dead and therefore cannot feel as bad as he deserves to.

## The Phantom ★ ★ ★ ½

PG, 105 m., 1996

Billy Zane (Phantom/Kit Walker), Kristy Swanson (Diana Palmer), Treat Williams (Xander Drax), Catherine Zeta Jones (Sala), James Remar (Quill), Cary-Hiroyuki Tagawa (Kabai Sengh), Bill Smitrovich (Uncle Dave), Casey Siemaszko (Morgan). Directed by Simon Wincer and produced by Robert Evans and Alan Ladd Jr. Screenplay by Jeffrey Boam.

*The Phantom* is one of the best-looking movies in any genre I have ever seen. I suppose people don't go to the movies just to drink in the production design, but here is a movie that would reward a visit by someone who loves art but is indifferent to adventure movies and comic book superheroes. It uses the visual materials of 1930s pulp fiction, adds a touch of *film noir,* and paints everything in a palette of reds, browns, golden yellows, creams, greens, blacks—and purples, of course.

The movie is also smashingly entertaining on the story level. The Phantom, created in 1936 by Lee Falk, is said to be the first of the superheroes, and the movie is true to his origins. He doesn't have the absurd powers of Superman or the catlike grace of Batman, and when he lands on the hood of a speeding truck, he doesn't do it with a light pounce, but with a heavy thud, as of muscle meeting metal.

Although he's known to those who fear him as

"the Ghost Who Walks," he isn't immortal; he's the twenty-first in a line of Phantoms, who trace their heritage back to the first Phantom's vow to fight evil and piracy. (How the Phantoms have found twenty brides willing to live in the Skull Cave is a question not answered in this film.)

The film stars Billy Zane as the Phantom, a.k.a. mild-mannered Kit Walker. His fury is roused when an evil industrialist named Xander Drax (Treat Williams) schemes to bring together three priceless skulls which, when assembled, will give him power over mankind. Fighting against Drax's schemes is a heroic newspaper publisher (Bill Smitrovich), who dispatches his niece, Diana Palmer (Kristy Swanson), to the jungle in search of one of the skulls. Phantom fans of course know Diana eventually becomes Mrs. Phantom, but here they are meeting again for the first time after a college courtship that ended when the Phantom mysteriously disappeared.

The movie's plot is essentially a series of adventure sequences. There's an aerial dogfight between a Pan American Clipper and two red biplanes. Two perilous crossings by truck over a disintegrating suspension bridge. A strangling by skeleton. A chase in which the Phantom and Diana successfully drop from a plane and land on the back of Hero, the white stallion, just before the plane crashes into a mountain. And a showdown inside an eerie mountain cave, where members of the Singh Brotherhood and Drax battle for the skulls against the Phantom and the forces of good. At the end, as a bonus, there's a really neat miniature submarine.

The director, Simon Wincer, orchestrates these events just a hair this side of parody. He and Billy Zane find the right tone for the Phantom: bemused, all-knowing, wise, irreverent. "No smoking in the Skull Cave," he says at one point. And when Diana tries to run the show: "Fine, go ahead—it's your rescue." The movie's best line is said by a bad guy from the big city, who now finds himself, in brown suit and fedora, inside a menacing jungle cavern: "Skulls! Powers of darkness! This isn't right! I was an altar boy, for the love of Pete, at Saint Timothy's! The only power I believe in comes out of the barrel of a gun!"

Zane plays the Phantom as essentially an ordinary, if talented, human who wears a purple suit and an eye mask (of course, Diana can't recognize him when he's wearing the mask). He often functions as the calm center of the storm. Treat Williams, as Drax, is implacably evil (he blinds a librarian by hiding spring-loaded needles in a microscope) and also slick and oily in the best pulp tradition. Kristy Swanson (whose *Buffy the Vampire Slayer* is a cult favorite) is plucky and athletic as Diana, and develops an intriguing relationship with Sala (Catherine Zeta Jones), Xander's dragon-lady sidekick, who softens and changes sides.

What all of these people decided, I suppose, was that the great strength of *The Phantom* was style—which made the classic comic strips stand out from the crowd, and which might help define the Phantom franchise for modern audiences (since, let's face it, the Phantom is not as big a name as Batman or Superman). The production design by Paul Peters is tirelessly inventive, but also crucial is the photography by David Burr, whose framing creates montages defined like a comic strip, and sometimes uses color and composition in much the same spirit as the Glasgow artist Jack Vettriano, whose flashy gangster types and molls in red dresses regard each other in sullen lust.

*The Phantom* was written by Jeffrey Boam, who wrote *Indiana Jones and the Last Crusade,* and it has the breakneck energy of the Indiana Jones movies, and the same love of fedora hats and very big old trucks. But it's not Indy in a purple suit. It has its own distinctive tone and feel, and a certain innocence; the PG rating indicates it's suitable for families, and so it is, because it lacks unnecessary violence and sexuality—but that doesn't mean it's not red-blooded. It's in love with a period when there were islands not on any map, and one or two brave people could change history, and characters could shout out, "Have you heard the exciting news? We're going to the Devil's Vortex!"

## Phantoms ★

R, 91 m., 1998

Peter O'Toole (Timothy Flyte), Rose McGowan (Lisa Pailey), Joanna Going (Jenny Pailey), Liev Schreiber (Deputy Stu Wargle), Ben Affleck (Sheriff Bryce Hammond), Nicky Katt (Deputy Steve Shanning). Directed by Joe Chappelle and produced by Joel Soisson, Michael Leahy, Robert Pringle, and Steve Lane. Screenplay by Dean Koontz, based on his book.

Did you know that if a certain kind of worm learns how to solve a maze, and then you grind it up and feed it to other worms, the other worms will then be able to negotiate the maze on their first try? That's one of the scientific nuggets supplied in *Phantoms,* a movie that seems to have been made by grinding up other films and feeding them to this one.

As the movie opens, two sisters arrive by Jeep in a quaint mountain town that seems suspiciously quiet, and no wonder: Everybody in town seems to be dead. Some of them have died rather suddenly. The baker's wife, for example. Her hands still grip the rolling pin. Just her hands. The rest of her is elsewhere.

The sisters (Rose McGowan and Joanna Going) find more ominous signs. A dead deputy sheriff, for example. And phones that don't work—but then one does. The older sister picks it up. "Who are you? What do you want?" she asks. It is a test of great acting to be able to say those ancient lines as if you mean them. A test like many others that this movie fails.

The sheriff turns up. He is played by Ben Affleck, wearing an absurd cowboy hat that looks like the kind of unsold stock they unload on city slickers at the end of the season. He is accompanied by another deputy (Nicky Katt), who wears an identical hat. Don't they know it's a rule in the movies: Hero wears neat hat, sidekick wears funny hat?

Joining the two young women, they search the town and find a desperate message written in lipstick on a mirror, which (I'm jumping ahead now) leads them to Dr. Timothy Flyte (Peter O'Toole), an editor of the kind of supermarket rag that features babies with nine-pound ears. Dr. Flyte and U.S. Army troops soon arrive in the small town, dressed like ghostbusters, to get to the bottom of the mystery. "What kind of threat are we dealing with here—biological, chemical, or other?" he's asked. "I'm leaning toward 'other,'" he replies, with all the wisdom and poignancy of a man who once played Lawrence of Arabia and is now playing Dr. Timothy Flyte.

The movie quickly degenerates into another one of those Gotcha! thillers in which loathsome, slimy creatures leap out of drain pipes and sewers and ingest supporting actors, while the stars pump bullets into it. There are a few neat touches. In front of an altar at the local church, the heroes discover a curious pile of stuff: watches, glasses, ballpoints, pacemakers. At first they think it's an offering to the Virgin Mary. But no: "That's not an offering. Those are undigested remains."

How common are these films getting to be? Two out of the three films I saw today used the formula. With a deep bow (almost a salaam) to *Tremors,* they locate their creatures beneath the surface of the land or sea, so that most of the time, although not enough of the time, you can't see them.

Peter O'Toole is a professional and plays his character well. It takes years of training and practice to be able to utter lines like, "It comes from the deep and secret realms of our Earth" without giggling. It is O'Toole who gets to float the educated tapeworm theory. When these creatures eat a human, they learn everything it knows—and even everything it thinks it knows, so that since many humans think they are being eaten by the devil, the creatures think they are the devil too. If only we could learn to think more kindly of those who digest us, this movie could have ended happily.

## Phenomenon ★ ★ ★

PG, 117 m., 1996

John Travolta (George Malley), Kyra Sedgwick (Lace Pennamin), Forest Whitaker (Nate Pope), Robert Duvall (Doc), David Gallagher (Al), Ashley Buccille (Glory), Tony Genaro (Tito), Sean O'Bryan (Banes). Directed by Jon Turteltaub and produced by Barbara Boyle and Michael Taylor. Screenplay by Gerald DiPego.

The opening titles of *Phenomenon* plant a sly idea that the film does nothing to discourage. We see the star-filled sky, and then the letters of the title settle into place with a subtle *whoosh.* We pick up *Close Encounters* vibes. Not long after, the film's hero walks out under the stars and is startled to see some kind of a weird white light that zaps him from the heavens. Has he been touched by a UFO? Maybe.

The hero is George Malley (John Travolta), a genial garage mechanic of average intelligence, well liked in his small California town. After the visitation from the sky, he begins to get smarter. A lot smarter. He starts taking out six books a day from the local library and figuring out things that had previously been beyond him. He's able to learn a foreign language by riffling through a textbook. This is not the George people know.

It is the lament of *Phenomenon* that people do not like the unexpected. They want George to continue to be George, no more, no less, so that he continues to fill the same predictable place in their lives. A brilliant new George, winning at chess, predicting earthquakes, picking up strange vibes, is disturbing.

"What is going on, George?" asks Lace (Kyra Sedgwick), the pretty divorced woman George would like to be dating. "I need the simple truth!" She has the thankless role of the woman who demands an explanation that the audience knows is impossible to give: "I just asked you for one thing, George, and you couldn't handle it!"

It's about the only thing George can't handle; matters of the heart are just as difficult to solve when you're a genius. The only people in town who can easily accept the new George are Doc (Robert Duvall), who considers him like a son, and Nate (Forest Whitaker), his best friend. With them, George is able to share his enthusiasm for the daily cascade of new discoveries.

This is a good role for Travolta, who has an underlying sweetness and enthusiasm that is well used here. There's not an ounce of circumspection in his character, and when he gets his unexpected gift, he wants to share it. He contacts scientists and universities, and is startled when the FBI turns up in its obligatory role as paranoid sniffer after suspicious behavior. (His interview with a federal agent is a small gem.)

We know the general outlines of the story, having been through somewhat similar territory with Cliff Robertson's *Charly* (1968). Although Charly was retarded and George is average, they are both transformed through their blooming intelligence, and then in the third act something happens that is not foreseen. I will not reveal what that is, except to say that the film will leave you with questions that it does not quite resolve. Maybe that's the best thing. We know what happened to George, but not precisely why, and who's to say if a UFO was involved or not?

The heart of the story is in George's character and his relationship with Lace (who, apart from her obligatory demands for an explanation, is a good and understanding woman). The film is essentially a good-hearted story about the rhythms of small-town life and the meaning of friendship, and if George's gift is a mystery even to him, at least it inspires a lot of conversation. Like many small towns (or movies set in small towns), this one has a bar where the locals provide a chorus for all of the action, and after George begins spinning paper clips in midair and breaking mirrors, they have the material for many a long beery discussion.

*Phenomenon* could have been more, I think. It might have pushed the edges of its story a little harder, and found out things that would be more challenging, or threatening, to George and the world he lives in. But that's not what it's about. It's about change, acceptance, and love, and it rounds those three bases very nicely, even if it never quite gets to home.

## Picnic ★ ★

PG, 115 m., 1955 (rereleased 1996)

William Holden (Hal Carter), Kim Novak (Madge Owens), Rosalind Russell (Rosemary Sidney), Susan Strasberg (Millie Owens), Arthur O'Connell (Howard Bevans), Cliff Robertson (Alan Benson), Betty Field (Flo Owens), Verna Felton (Helen Potts), Reta Shaw (Linda Sue), Nick Adams (Bomber). Directed by Joshua Logan and produced by Fred Kohlmar. Screenplay by Daniel Taradash, based on the play by William Inge.

"What good is it only being pretty?" the nineteen-year-old girl asks her mother. "I get tired of only being looked at." To which her mother can only reply, "What a question!" In Kansas in 1955, being a pretty girl was pretty much a lifestyle in itself, and when Madge (Kim Novak) is crowned Queen of Neewollah (that's Halloween spelled backward), all she can do is clutch the bouquet of roses and promise not to get too conceited.

It is hard to believe that *Picnic* was considered hot stuff in 1955. Clunky and awkward, with inane dialogue, it's a movie to show how attitudes have changed. It's easy to see why 1950s audiences responded to it—William Holden and Kim Novak look great and generate a certain dutiful chemistry—but hard to see how, in a time when the sexual boldness of movies like *A Streetcar Named Desire* was well known, people could sit through this with a straight face.

The movie, now restored in a handsome new wide-screen print, takes place on a long Labor Day and the night and morning that follow. It begins as Hal Carter (Holden) hops off a freight train and goes looking for his old college roommate, Alan (Cliff Robertson). Hal was a football hero but now he's a bum and needs a job. Alan takes him up atop one of his family's grain elevators, and Hal explains what he has in mind: "A nice little office where I can have a sweet little secretary and talk over the telephone about enterprises and things."

He's promised the job. Meanwhile, he's fallen into the orbit of the Owens family, who run a boardinghouse. There's mom (Betty Field), and the beautiful Madge, and her kid sister, Millie (Susan Strasberg), who sneaks puffs on cigarettes and is college-bound and has apparently read the same page of her Flannery O'Connor novel so often that it's creased and dog-eared (if we notice things like that, why can't the prop department?).

Mrs. Owens is pushing her daughter's romance with Alan, the rich kid from the right side of town. But then Madge lays eyes on Hal, who first appears to the Owens women while burning trash for kindly ole Mrs. Potts next door. Holden, who spends much of the film stripped to the waist and much of the rest with his shirt torn from one shoulder, stands behind the trash can so that the flames wrinkle the air in front of him, and looks like a Chippendale boy on yard duty.

The center section of the film takes place at the Labor Day picnic, where the Halloween queen begins her reign. The director, Joshua Logan, who was among the worst filmmakers of his time, spends so much footage on the picnic you'd think this was a documentary: There are crying babies, laughing babies, frowning babies, three-legged races, pie-eating contents, balloon drops, concerts, and boy-girl contests that involve the women trying to throw rubber canning rings over popsicle sticks held in their menfolks' mouths.

The Owenses gather with several friends, including Rosalind Russell as an old-maid schoolteacher, Arthur O'Connell as her cigar-chomping beau, and Alan, who watches uneasily as sparks fly between Hal and Madge. This scene, like several others involving a lot of characters, is composed awkwardly. All of the actors are lined up from one edge of the Vista Vision screen to the other, seemingly not noticing that they're all facing in the same direction (ours).

As night falls Madge and Hal begin to dance together sensuously, in the movie's famous sexy scene. Madge, dizzy with passion, tells him, and I quote, "You remind me of one of those statues—one of those old Roman gladiators. All he had on was a shield." Meanwhile, the Rosalind Russell character gets drunk and hysterically demands that her old coot marry her and save her from spinsterhood.

The actual subject of *Picnic* is the utter irrelevance of women in that place and that time, unless they were young and pretty and not too smart. Madge says wistfully that she wishes she were as smart as her kid sister and were going to college, but her mom gives her hardheaded advice: Marry the rich kid, quick. ("A girl gets to be twenty, twenty-one, and then she's forty.")

The movie is possibly not aware of two ironies in its examination of the female dilemma. One is that Madge, "tired of only being looked at," falls instantly for Holden, who only looks at her. When he talks, it is of his own dreams, his own past, his own desires. To hear him explain it, the best thing about Madge is how much he loves her.

The second irony is that the Holden character is treated exactly like the women in the movie. Like them, he's not considered to be very smart. Like them, he's physically attractive. Like them, he's displayed in beefcake poses (the memory of Marlon Brando's T-shirt in *Streetcar* in 1952 is never far from mind). He should listen to Mrs. Owens and marry a rich kid himself.

The movie doesn't have the self-awareness to know that Hal faces the same dilemma as Madge; it's blinded by the fact that he's a man. At the end, he hops a freight to Tulsa, where he'll get a job as a bellboy. And Madge rebelliously follows him on the bus (which conveniently stops right in front of her house). When they get together in Tulsa, they're gonna get mighty tired of only being looked at.

## Picture Perfect ★ ★

PG-13, 101 m., 1997

Jennifer Aniston (Kate), Jay Mohr (Nick), Kevin Bacon (Sam), Olympia Dukakis (Rita), Illeana Douglas (Darcy), Kevin Dunn (Mr. Mercer), Anne Twomey (Sela), Faith Prince (Mrs. Mercer). Directed by Glenn Gordon Caron and produced by Erwin Stoff. Screenplay by Arleen Sorkin, Paul Slansky, and Caron.

Sometimes a movie will include a subversive line of dialogue that shows somebody was paying attention. In *Picture Perfect,* that line comes when the devious woman tells the good guy: "This sounds like something out of *The Patty Duke Show.*" That hits the nail on the head. And it's a shame the plot is so contrived, because parts of this movie are really pretty good.

The film has Jennifer Aniston of TV's *Friends* in her first leading movie role, as Kate, an ad executive who has good ideas but projects the wrong image. She dreams up a campaign for Gulden's mustard, but when the client buys it, she's not included on the account team. Why not? Mercer (Kevin Dunn), the agency head, says it's because she's not engaged and not in debt, so there's nothing to stop her from leaving the agency. So her best friend, Darcy (Illeana Douglas), dreams up a scheme: She should claim to be engaged to a guy from Boston.

She has met this guy from Boston just once. His name is Nick (Jay Mohr), he videotapes weddings for a living, and he's in love with her. In a nice, subtle touch, we can sense the moment he first notices her, because we're looking through the POV of his viewfinder at a wedding when his camera focuses on her and freezes. Kate contacts him and offers him $1,000 to come to New York for a weekend, pose as her boyfriend, and break up with her publicly. That way she'll get the job and be able to explain her freedom. It's at this point that she uses the Patty Duke line and he turns down the money.

I'm not sure *Picture Perfect* paints a very accurate portrait of the requirements that modern ad agencies have for their employees; it sounds more as if Kate is being considered for a job as a deaconess. But never mind. The plot thickens when she immediately has an affair with the office bad boy (Kevin Bacon), who thought she was "too nice" until she got "engaged," but is now attracted by the thought that he's stealing her away from her fiancé.

The movie has some nice dialogue touches in it. I like how Darcy justifies her bright idea about the Boston boyfriend to Kate: "We're in advertising, Kate. I didn't lie—I sold." I liked the way Kate prepared a "study guide" so that Nick would know all about her if anybody asked specific questions. And I liked Nick's sweet little speech about why he feels so privileged to videotape the most important moments in his clients' lives.

But against those moments are some huge distractions. One is the plot, which has Kate being so incredibly crass and rude toward Nick that we almost fall out of sympathy with her—and lose respect for Nick for putting up with it. Another is the character of Kate's mother (Olympia Dukakis), who pops up regularly to do things that, frankly, she seems too bright to do.

And the third, which becomes a distraction during at least the last third of the movie, is Jennifer Aniston's neckline. After the agency boss advises her to buy a new dress, she appears in a series of plunging frocks that seem designed to advertise the powers of the WonderBra. Aniston is pretty and she has a swell body, but these dresses get to be a joke after a while; is she auditioning for *Playboy*'s Girls of Summer? It was W. C. Fields who hated to appear in the same scene with a child, a dog, or a plunging neckline—because nobody in the audience would be looking at him. Jennifer Aniston has the same problem in this movie, even when she's in scenes all by herself.

## The Pillow Book ★ ★ ★ ½

NO MPAA RATING, 126 m., 1997

Vivian Wu (Nagiko), Yoshi Oida (The Publisher), Ken Ogata (The Father), Hideko Yoshida (The Aunt/The Maid), Ewan McGregor (Jerome), Judy Ongg (The Mother), Ken Mitsuishi (The Husband), Yutaka Honda (Hoki). Directed by Peter Greenaway and produced by Kees Kasander. Screenplay by Greenaway.

Nagiko's father was a calligrapher, and when she was a little girl he would write his birthday greetings on her face. Her mother would read aloud from a 1,000-year-old manuscript, *The Pillow Book of Sei Shonagon,* which dealt among other things with the arts of love. Because children invest their birthdays with enormous importance, it's no wonder that when Nagiko grows up she finds a powerful link between calligraphy, human flesh, poetry, and sexuality.

Peter Greenaway, born in Australia, long working in England, is not so far from Nagiko himself. His films also work by combining images, words, quotations, and sexual situations. He uses the screen as Nagiko uses flesh, finding an erotic charge not just in the words, but in the surface they are written on. His new film *The Pillow Book*, starring Vivian Wu (from *The Last Emperor*), is a seductive and elegant story that combines a millennium of Japanese art and fetishes with the story of a neurotic modern woman who tells a lover: "Treat me like the pages of a book."

Early in Nagiko's life, she sees something she was not intended to see: her father's publisher (Yoshi Oida), forcing her father (Ken Ogata) to have sex as the price of getting a book published. On another occasion, when she is six or seven, she is introduced to the publisher's ten-year-old nephew and told this will be her future husband. These events set up fundamental tensions in her life, and as an adult, unhappily married to the publisher's nephew, she begins keeping her own pillow book. The nephew (Ken Mitsuishi) is a shallow dolt, who finds her book and in a jealous rage burns her papers and then their house.

Nagiko flees from Kyoto to Hong Kong, where eventually she finds work as a fashion model and begins to seek lovers who will fulfill her dreams. For her the appearance of a person's handwriting is more important than the surfaces of his face; she wants to be used as a book, to be written on, to be read.

Her fetish ties in with two ancient Japanese artistic practices. One is the art of tattooing, which can be much more elegant and artistic than in the West, and is used by the Yakuza as a way of bonding with their criminal brothers. It can be seen as a form of submission—to the will of the tattoo artist, to the will of the group dictating the tattoos, or simply in the willingness of a person to be used as an object.

The other practice is the long-standing Japanese tradition in art of deliberately exposing the artificiality of a work of art. Realism is less prized than style. Landscapes may use great realistic detail, and then have captions written on them, or the bright red artist's mark. Kabuki and Noh theater overlay their stories with ancient layers of style and tradition. To write a poem on a body is much the same as writing it on a landscape: The word and the image create a tension.

Greenaway, whose work includes *The Draughtsman's Contract; The Cook, The Thief, His Wife and Her Lover;* and *Prospero's Books*, uses an essentially Japanese technique. He likes to build up his images in layers, combining film and video, live action and paintings, spoken narration and visual texts. He shoots in color, black and white, and subtle tints. Here he tells a lurid story of sexuality, fetishism, and betrayal, in an elegant and many-faceted way.

The story itself is simple. In Hong Kong, Nagiko takes a British lover, Jerome (Ewan McGregor). He is a good lover and a bad calligrapher; certainly his handwriting is not good enough to decorate her body. Meanwhile, Nagiko's book has been rejected by the publisher (the very same publisher who has caused her so much unhappiness). Jerome hits on an inspiration: Why not use his body as her book, which he will then take to the publisher? She decorates his body, he goes to the publisher, and the publisher and Jerome end by making love—which for Nagiko is a betrayal that spirals back through all her memories.

One of the most elegant parts of the film comes toward the end, as Greenaway illustrates the pages of Nagiko's pillow book. She has used each part of the body for the appropriate texts, even writing on ears and tongues, and here the words (Japanese, English, printed, spoken, Kanji) take on a sort of mystical, abstract quality. The talkies chained pictures to words; Greenaway finds a way out by using words as pictures.

Greenaway once said something that perfectly describes his work: "I don't make pictures that have a sell-by date." Most new American movies have a limited shelf life. They're put in the theaters to sink or swim. If they haven't sold in a week or two, they're yanked like stale bread. Greenaway's notion is that his movies stand outside the ordinary distribution channels. You may see them today or in ten years, as you choose. And when you are ready.

## Pink Flamingos

STAR RATING: NOT RELEVANT
NC-17, 92 m., 1972 (rereleased 1997)

Divine (Divine/Babs Johnson), David Lochary (Raymond Marble), Mary Vivian Pearce (Cotton), Mink Stole (Connie Marble), Danny Mills (Crackers), Edith Massey (Mama Edie), Channing

Wilroy (Channing), Cookie Mueller (Cookie). Written, produced, and directed by John Waters.

John Waters's *Pink Flamingos* has been restored for its twenty-fifth anniversary revival, and with any luck at all that means I won't have to see it again for another twenty-five years. If I haven't retired by then, I will.

How do you review a movie like this? I am reminded of an interview I once did with a man who ran a carnival sideshow. His star was a geek who bit off the heads of live chickens and drank their blood.

"He's the best geek in the business," this man assured me.

"What is the difference between a good geek and a bad geek?" I asked.

"You wanna examine the chickens?"

*Pink Flamingos* was filmed with genuine geeks, and that is the appeal of the film to those who find it appealing: What seems to happen in the movie really does happen. That is its redeeming quality, you might say. If the events in this film were only simulated, it would merely be depraved and disgusting. But since they are actually performed by real people, the film gains a weird kind of documentary stature. There is a temptation to praise the film, however grudgingly, just to show you have a strong enough stomach to take it. It is a temptation I can resist.

The plot involves a rivalry between two competing factions for the title of Filthiest People Alive. In one corner: a transvestite named Divine (who dresses like a combination of a showgirl, a dominatrix, and Bozo); her mentally ill mother (sits in a crib eating eggs and making messes); her son (likes to involve chickens in his sex life with strange women); and her lover (likes to watch son with strange women and chickens). In the other corner: Mr. and Mrs. Marble, who kidnap hippies, chain them in a dungeon, and force their butler to impregnate them so that after they die in childbirth their babies can be sold to lesbian couples.

All of the details of these events are shown in the film—oh, and more, including the notorious scene in which Divine actually ingests that least appetizing residue of the canine. And not only do we see genitalia in this movie—they do exercises.

*Pink Flamingos* appeals to that part of our psyche in which we are horny teenagers at the county fair with fresh dollar bills in our pockets and a desire to see the geek show with a bunch of buddies, so that we can brag about it at school on Monday. (And also because of an intriguing rumor that the Bearded Lady proves she is bearded all over.)

After the restored version of the film has played, director John Waters hosts and narrates a series of outtakes, which (not surprisingly) are not as disgusting as what stayed in the film. We see long-lost scenes in which Divine cooks the chicken that starred in an earlier scene; Divine receives the ears of Cookie, the character who costarred in the scene with her son and the chicken; and Divine, Cookie, and her son sing "We Are the Filthiest People Alive" in Pig Latin.

John Waters is a charming man, whose later films (like *Polyester* and *Hairspray*) take advantage of his bemused take on pop culture. His early films, made on infinitesimal budgets and starring his friends, used shock as a way to attract audiences, and that is understandable. He jump-started his career, and in the movie business, you do what you gotta do. Waters's talent has grown; in this film, which he photographed, the visual style resembles a home movie, right down to the overuse of the zoom lens. (Amusingly, his zooms reveal he knows how long the characters will speak; he zooms in, stays, and then starts zooming out before the speech ends, so he can pan to another character and zoom in again.)

After the outtakes, Waters shows the original trailer for the film, in which, not amazingly, not a single scene from the movie is shown. Instead, the trailer features interviews with people who have just seen *Pink Flamingos,* and are a little dazed by the experience. The trailer cleverly positions the film as an event: Hey, you may like the movie or hate it, but at least you'll be able to say you saw it! Then blurbs flash on the screen, including one comparing *Pink Flamingos* to Luis Buñuel's *An Andalusian Dog,* in which a pig's eyeball was sliced. Yes, but the pig was dead, while the audience for this movie is still alive.

*Note: I am not giving a star rating to* Pink Flamingos, *because stars simply seem not to apply. It should be considered not as a film but as a fact, or perhaps as an object.*

## Player's Club ★ ★ ★

R, 103 m., 1998

Lisa Raye (Diana Armstrong), Bernie Mac (Dollar Bill), Chrystale Wilson (Ronnie), Adele Givens (Tricks), A. J. Johnson (Li'l Man), Larry McCoy (St. Louis), Jamie Foxx (Blue [DJ]), Monica Calhoun (Ebony). Directed by Ice Cube and produced by Patricia Charbonnet and Carl Craig. Screenplay by Ice Cube.

*Player's Club,* written and directed by the rapper Ice Cube, is a gritty black version of *Showgirls,* set in a "gentlemen's club" where a young college student hopes to earn her tuition. Rich with colorful dialogue and characters, it's sometimes ungainly but never boring, and there's a core of truth in its portrait of sex workers.

Thirty years ago this material would have been forced into the blaxploitation genre—dumbed down and predictable. But *Player's Club* is observant and insightful, and beneath its melodrama lurks unsentimental information about why young women do lap dances for a living, and what they think about themselves and their customers.

The movie stars a convincing newcomer named Lisa Raye as Diana, who has a fight with her father over what college to attend. Pregnant and jobless, she moves away from home, gets a job in a shoe store, and is fairly happy until her child's father wants "more space" and abandons her.

That's when she meets Tricks and Ronnie, two dancers at the Player's Club, who tell her there are ways to make a lot more money. They are correct, but the money comes at a price. The film is knowledgeable about details of the clubs: the camaraderie of the dancers, the flamboyance of the owner and grandiloquence of the doorman, the way the bartenders and the disk jockey keep an eye on the action, and the needy absorption of the customers. "The first dance is degrading," Ronnie (Chrystale Wilson) tells her, "but you get used to it." Her advice to the newcomer: Don't look at the customers, look at yourself in the mirror.

Onto this semidocumentary material, Ice Cube grafts a crime story involving the mysterious St. Louis, a gangster who is owed a lot of money by Dollar Bill (Bernie Mac), the club's fast-talking owner. St. Louis wants his money, Dollar Bill doesn't have it, and at one point Bill is actually inside a car trunk and we think we know what has to happen next, but the action tilts toward farce rather than tragedy. (A lot of people get shot at in the movie, but I don't think anyone ever quite gets killed.)

Problems for Diana begin when Ebony (Monica Calhoun), her eighteen-year-old cousin, comes to stay with her. She wants to keep Ebony away from the club, but "Ebony jumped headfirst into the lifestyle," and soon Diana, who has drawn the line at prostitution, finds that Ebony treats it more like a career goal. Ice Cube uses strong dramatic intercutting to build suspense in a scene where Ebony, hired as a dancer at a bachelor party, is uneasy to find there aren't any other girls there.

What's interesting about *Player's Club* is the way it moves through various tones and kinds of material. There's the documentary stuff, the crime story, Diana's shaky romance with a new boyfriend, Ebony's problems, and comic relief from the stylized dialogue of Dollar Bill and his doorman, L'il Man (A. J. Johnson). And then a strong underpinning of economic reality, as Diana works hard to pay her bills, and is encouraged by a professor after she finds herself falling asleep in class.

The movie has strong scenes for all its major characters, including a boozy after-hours party being held by some ATF agents who hire Ronnie and some of the other girls as strippers. Ronnie knows these guys from earlier parties and plays the role of dominatrix. (Slapping one officer on the behind with a paddle, she says, "That's one more for Rodney King.") The scene develops interestingly: At first we think Ronnie may be in danger, and when we see she knows what she's doing, Ice Cube resists the temptation to go for a comic put-down of the agents, and stays instead with the real tension of the tables being turned. The scene's effect depends on the way Wilson plays it; a less convincing performance, and we wouldn't buy it.

The movie doesn't preach, but it has values. It sees the Player's Club as a job, and the women there as workers, not sex objects. It's work that pays well, but at a price, and although Diana has rules about drugs and sex, Ebony seems like an excellent candidate to crash and burn. I liked Ice Cube's ambition in writing so many colorful characters and juggling them all at the same time. The movie isn't deep, but it's sophisticated about its people and places, and Diana and Ebony have the clarity of characters who seem drawn from life. It would be easy to dismiss *Player's Club* by looking only at its subject matter, but look a little harder and you see an ambitious filmmaker at work.

## Playing God ★ ★ ★

R, 93 m., 1997

David Duchovny (Eugene Sands), Timothy Hutton (Raymond Blossom), Angelina Jolie (Claire), Michael Massee (Gage), Peter Stormare (Vladmir), Andrew Tiernan (Cyril), Gary Dourdan (Yates). Directed by Andy Wilson and produced by Marc Abraham and Laura Bickford. Screenplay by Mark Haskell Smith.

*Playing God* opens with the hero deep in trouble. Eugene Sands (David Duchovny) is a former surgeon, now a druggie, who's in a scuzzy bar looking to score synthetic heroin. Shabby as he looks, he attracts the eye of a dazzling woman across the room—but then shots ring out and a man is gravely wounded.

Sands argues, not unreasonably, that someone should call 911. But there are reasons why the police should not be involved in this shooting, and soon the defrocked doc is reenacting one of those classic movie situations where he barks orders and prepares for instant surgery. A master of improvisation (few battlefield surgeons must be this creative), he fashions a breathing apparatus out of a plastic pop bottle and some tubing from the club soda siphon, cuts a hole in the guy's chest, plugs the tube into his lung, and restores vital signs. Of course, the beautiful woman, named Claire (Angelina Jolie), has the right stuff and could become an expert ER nurse.

It is a tribute of some sort to Duchovny, the *X-Files* star, that I was almost able to believe this was possible. He's a convincing actor. Among those his character convinces in the movie is Raymond Blossom (Timothy Hutton), a shady millionaire, who invites Sands to his home and gives him $10,000 for saving his colleague's life. Also at Blossom's home is, inevitably, Claire, a not-uncommon type in the movies: Living with a rich and dangerous man, she makes eyes at every poor schmuck who drifts into range.

In a flashback, we learn the sad story of ex–Dr. Sands. Up for twenty-eight hours straight and exhausted, he once tried balancing uppers and downers and did it so well that he came to a complete halt, losing a patient in the process. His license was lifted, and now he's a man without a career or future, until Blossom offers him one. The older man has a lot of pals who get shot, it appears. And none of them much want to go to the hospital. Blossom offers Sands a retainer to come on staff as the house specialist in gunshot wounds.

*Playing God,* directed by Andy Wilson, a former cameraman, tells a preposterous story in a way that almost makes it credible. It's based on three sound performances. Duchovny finds a delicate balance between action hero and moping antihero. Angelina Jolie (Jon Voight's daughter) finds a certain warmth in a kind of role that is usually hard and aggressive; she seems too nice to be Blossom's girlfriend, and maybe she is.

And the surprise in the movie is Timothy Hutton, as the villain. I sense the curtain rising on the next act of his career. Having outgrown the sensitive-boy roles that established him *(Ordinary People, Made in Heaven),* he returns to his dark side, to notes he struck in such films as *The Falcon and the Snowman* and *Q & A.* He shows here what sets the interesting villains apart from the ordinary ones.

Too many movie villains are simply evil. They sneer, they threaten, they hurt, but they do not much involve us, except as plot devices. The best villains are intriguing. They have a seductive quality, as when Blossom tells the doctor, "Eugene, you should embrace your criminal self." We can believe that beautiful women would be attracted to them. Thin, chain-smoking, with a fashionable two-day beard, Hutton creates a character instead of simply filling a space.

*Playing God* is David Duchovny's first starring role, unless you count the *Red Shoe Diaries* episodes on cable. It seems crafted to match his new stardom on *The X-Files,* and it does: He has the psychic weight to be a leading man and an action hero, even though his earlier TV and film roles might not have revealed it. And he also has a certain detachment, a way of standing above the action, that stars like Eastwood and Mitchum have. This may not be a great movie, but for both Duchovny and Hutton, it's a turning point.

## The Pompatus of Love ★ ★

NO MPAA RATING, 99 m., 1996

Jon Cryer (Mark), Tim Guinee (Runyon), Adam Oliensis (Phil), Adrian Pasdar (Josh), Kristen Wilson (Tasha), Kristin Scott Thomas (Caroline), Paige Turco (Gina), Dana Wheeler-Nicholson (Kathryn), Roscoe Lee Browne (Playwright). Directed by Richard Schenkman and produced by D. J. Paul and Jon Resnik. Screenplay by Jon Cryer, Adam Oliensis, and Schenkman.

The movie *The Pompatus of Love* begins, as indeed it should, with a discussion of what the pompatus of love is. We learn fairly quickly, if we didn't already know, that it is a line from a Steve Miller song. "Pompatus." That's the word. Don't look it up in the dictionary because it's not there. The characters in the movie spend a good five minutes discussing the word. Is it "impetus? prophetess?"

No, it's "pompatus," as anyone listening to the song can perfectly well tell, and the movie would have been much improved with a different title and no mention at any point of the word "pompatus." That would also spare us the ending, which reads like an exercise in a creative writing class—a reprise in which one character says, "What the (bleep) is the pompatus of love?" and another character replies, "Exactly!"

A lot of the movie consists of the characters speaking to each other in one-liners and epigrams. Less of this would have been a splendid idea; none would have been an inspiration. It is late in the day, I think, for anyone in a movie to talk about "the band that Paul McCartney was in before Wings" as if this is an original line. At the very least, any character using that ancient wheeze should indicate that he is quoting it ironically.

The story follows the adventures of four friends in their mid-thirties, who are having great difficulty in their relationships with women, possibly because they don't have their pompatuses screwed on straight. Mark (Jon Cryer) is a therapist, Runyon (Tim Guinee) is a writer, Josh (Adrian Pasdar) is a businessman, and Phil (Adam Oliensis) runs a hardware store. They're all single except for Phil. During the course of the movie they meet various women and have various relationships with them, and whenever the film is able to pause long enough to observe these relationships, it is interesting.

Unfortunately, both director Richard Schenkman and editor Dan Rosen can't leave well enough alone. This is an overdirected and overedited film, in love with the technique of short cuts in which characters finish each other's sentences. Since this is impossible in the real world, it suggests that the filmmakers consider technique—and indeed their own implied presence in the film—more important than their characters.

There are a couple of nice sequences. One involves Mark and Tasha (Kristen Wilson), who meet on a blind date, fall in love, and then fall out of love during the process of deciding where they want to live. (The movie is set in New York, and like a lot of New York films it more or less equates romance with apartment hunting.) Once again we get quick cuts of the characters starting a line in one apartment and ending it in another, but at least the sequence has a subject.

I also enjoyed the dilemma of Runyon, the playwright, who nurses an unrequited love for a woman who now lives in Los Angeles. He flies to L.A. to meet with some TV producers, and has an intriguing encounter on the plane with a seatmate (Jennifer Tilly) who describes herself as "Geena Davis's body double." In L.A., after endless agonizing about whether he should call his old flame, what he should say on the answering machine, etc., he climbs in through her bedroom window, finds her asleep with her significant other, wakes her, and has a conversation with her on the beach in which she explains how much of an idiot he is.

Nice, and also nice is the meeting Runyon has with the TV producers. It is a cliché that all producers are stupid and all writers are unrecognized geniuses, so it's refreshing to meet producers who are so much smarter than Runyon that he should have stayed home. Later he calls the Tilly character, who, in a moment the movie observes with perfect accuracy, won't consider a date with him until she finds out how the meeting with the producers went.

These scenes are a hint of what the movie might have been it if hadn't come down with the cutes. My suggestion to the filmmakers: If in doubt about what to do in a story, trust your characters, trust their dialogue, and get out of the way. It is some small consolation, I suppose, to know that after this film the word "pompatus" will never again be heard in a motion picture.

## Ponette ★ ★ ★ ½

NO MPAA RATING, 92 m., 1997

Victoire Thivisol (Ponette), Matiaz Bureau (Ponette's Cousin), Delphine Schiltz (Ponette's Cousin), Marie Trintignant (The Mother), Xavier Beauvois (The Father), Claire Nebout (The Aunt), Aurelie Verillon (Aurelie), Leopoldine Serre (Ada). Directed by Jacques Doillon and produced by Alain Sarde. Screenplay by Doillon.

*Ponette* enters the mystery of a little girl's mind at the age of four, when she has all of her intelligence but little experience and information. Ponette has been in a car crash. Her arm was broken. "Mommy may die," her father tells her. How does she deal with that information? What does death mean to a four-year-old? How can it be dealt with?

The most extraordinary thing about *Ponette* is the way it faces these questions while staying resolutely within the focus of the child's mind. It follows the little girl out of the hospital and to her aunt's house, where with two cousins about her own age she tries to puzzle out what is happening to her.

She doesn't get a lot of help from her father. "Mommy's dead," he tells her after a few days. "She was all broken. They couldn't fix her." He is preoccupied with his own grief. He makes her promise not to die. And he talks about how stupid his wife was to get in the car crash. "She's not stupid!" Ponette cries. "It wasn't her fault!"

Played by Victoire Thivisol, she is a small, blond, round-faced little girl, very solemn much of the time, and the film follows her with an intensity that requires her to give a real performance—not as a "child actor," but as a real actor who has to negotiate tricky dialogue and situations. She does. "In the matter of child acting," writes Stanley Kauffmann, "this is the most extraordinary picture I know." (Thivisol's performance won the Best Actress Award at the 1996 Venice Film Festival.)

In preparing the dialogue for Ponette and her young friends, Jacques Doillon, the writer-director, interviewed hundreds of young children, I understand. What he captures is the logical way that kids proceed from what little they know to what, therefore, must be the case. As Ponette copes with the fact that her mother is in a coffin and will soon be under the ground, her little friend explains about crucifixes and pillows under the head and what happens to bodies after a long time, and adds helpfully: "I like living above ground. I really hate skulls."

Whether Ponette understands the finality of death in an adult way is a good question. Certainly she misses her mother, and is not consoled by her aunt's stories about Jesus and resurrection. If Jesus gets to rise from the dead, she asks not unreasonably, why can't her mother? And if it's true, as she's told, that the dead sometimes like to have little gifts or keepsakes left in their coffin to remember things by, then why not offer her mother even larger gifts? There is a scene where Ponette stands fiercely under the empty sky, holding up the offerings she has selected, hoping her mother will come down for them.

The film is not entirely about the aftermath of death. Its real subject, actually, is the development of intelligence in childhood. How do kids interact with their environment and learn from their friends, and fashion theories and test them out? There is a sequence where the children play a game involving an empty dumpster. Is it dangerous? Perhaps. Do they benefit from the game? Yes. Because city streets are no longer considered safe for children, they're kept inside more than earlier generations. Street games are no longer played. In *Ponette* we see how through trial and error these children learn from the lessons and adventures of the neighborhood.

The theology in *Ponette* is direct and challenging. Given the consolations of the Christian faith, Ponette responds with reasonable questions a child might ask and a philosopher might not be able to answer. She also has to deal with the casual cruelties of childhood, as when a friend tells her: "You killed your mother." Applying logic, Ponette determines that if her mother died and went to heaven, then the best way to visit her would be to die and go to the same place. "I want you to make me die," she tells a friend.

The movie's one wrong step is a closing sequence reuniting Ponette with her mother. Is this a fantasy or a miracle? A miracle, I fear—and Ponette deserves better. In the real world, when mothers die they don't come back.

Ponette has just about dealt with that when the movie sneaks in a happy ending. She'll never learn that way.

But the ending is an imperfection in a film of great imagination and close observation. I can't even begin to imagine how Doillon obtained these performances from Thivisol and her friends (Matiaz Bureau and Delphine Schiltz). Watching this film is like eavesdropping on bright children and observing the process by which their intelligence builds their personalities, their beliefs, their strategies, and their minds.

## The Portrait of a Lady ★ ★ ★

PG-13, 144 m., 1997

Nicole Kidman (Isabel Archer), John Malkovich (Gilbert Osmond), Barbara Hershey (Madame Serena Merle), Mary-Louise Parker (Henrietta Stackpole), Martin Donovan (Ralph Touchett), Shelley Winters (Mrs. Touchett), John Gielgud (Mr. Touchett), Richard E. Grant (Lord Warburton), Shelley Duvall (Countess Gemini), Valentina Cervi (Pansy), Christian Bale (Edward Rosier), Viggo Mortensen (Caspar Goodwood). Directed by Jane Campion and produced by Monty Montgomery and Steve Golin. Screenplay by Laura Jones, based on the novel by Henry James.

For Henry James, who spent most of his life there, Europe was a snake pit for naive Americans, who were prey to the intrigues of more devious races. His Yankees disembark fresh-scrubbed from the land of Lincoln, only to tumble into the coils of greed. Isabel Archer, the heroine of *The Portrait of a Lady,* is one of his most loved and tragic characters; everything she does is inspired by idealism, and leads to heartbreak and ruin.

In Jane Campion's film of the James novel, we meet Isabel (Nicole Kidman) at what could have been the defining moment of her life. Orphaned in America, she visits rich English relatives and receives a proposal of marriage from Lord Warburton (Richard E. Grant). He is rich and titled, and even lives in a house with a moat. She rejects his proposal, although reassuring him that she does love moats.

Why does she turn down Warburton? Because he is too right, too safe and sure, and she seeks a spark of inspiration in her man. One of those astounded by her decision is her cousin Ralph (Martin Donovan), who also loves Isabel, but keeps that a secret because he is dying of consumption. "I shall have the pleasure," he muses, "of seeing what a young lady does who rejects Lord Warburton." It will be no pleasure.

Ralph lives with his parents, the rich Touchetts (John Gielgud and Shelley Winters). Knowing Isabel has rejected Warburton, aware of her poverty, he fears her spirit will be crushed by the hard realities of Europe. He wants her to have a chance to bloom. As his father lays dying, Ralph asks him to leave a large portion of his inheritance to the young woman. Ralph explains, "I call people rich when they are able to meet the requirements of their imagination."

Isabel, surprised by the bequest and never suspecting its reason, embarks on the grand tour. In Rome she swims into the net of Madame Merle (Barbara Hershey), an independent woman who knows everyone and is frank about her purpose: "I don't pretend to know what people are meant for. I only know what I can do with them."

Merle, knowing what she can do with Isabel, delivers her to the indolent expatriate artist Gilbert Osmond (John Malkovich). Osmond is a fake—a lazy fraud with more manner than means. But Isabel, who could see Lord Warburton's flaws, cannot see Gilbert's, and soon she is married. He has a daughter named Pansy; he explains vaguely that his first wife is deceased. Isabel comes to love Pansy, and soon she loves her a great deal more than Osmond.

The story leaps forward three years, to a time when Isabel and Gilbert coexist in a hateful truce. Her cousin Ralph, visiting Rome, sees through their marriage: "Weren't you meant for something better than to keep guard over the sensibilities of a sterile dilettante?" Then the noose tightens, as Isabel discovers the exact nature of her situation.

I will not reveal more. Yet I assume that most of the people going to see this movie will have read the book, and, frankly, you can't easily understand this film if you haven't. Too much is left out, glossed over, or implied.

Why, for example, does Isabel marry Osmond? In the novel there is no mystery. He is an "artist"—able to pose, at least during their courtship, as a man who lives on a higher plane. In Campion's film, Osmond is never allowed the slightest plausibility. Malkovich plays him as a snaky, sinister poseur, tobacco smoke coiling past his hooded eyes. The crucial distinction is: In the novel, Isabel marries him because she is an idealist, but in the movie because she is a masochist.

This difference is fatal to the development of the story. To Ralph, she must seem more stupid than brave. Madame Merle's manipulation becomes cynical, not simply opportunist. Even Osmond seems more a villain here (where he is not deceived by his intentions) than in the novel (where he half-believes his lies).

*The Portrait of a Lady* ends with a series of hammer blows. Anyone who believes Henry James is bloodless has never really read him. Beneath his meticulous prose are lusts and fears that his characters struggle to contain within the strictures of proper society. His conclusion of this novel is one of incredible power; Isabel is a good woman who has tried to do right, and who has done wrong, wrong, wrong—wrong to Ralph's faith, wrong to Warburton's love, wrong to herself.

In the movie, it just doesn't play that way. Isabel turns too hard in the years the film leaps over. By the time of the final revelations, she is no longer as deserving of Ralph's pity as she should be. By tilting the story at this angle, Campion and her writer, Laura Jones, are said to have brought a "feminist sensibility" to the film. I think the James version was more truly feminist and that this version sees Isabel more as a victim and less as a heroine gone astray.

Yet I think if you care for James, you must see it. It is not an adaptation but an interpretation. It gives us Isabel from a new angle. And it is well acted. Kidman has the bearing and quality of the intelligent young American. Barbara Hershey is magnificent as Madame Merle (who has her own heartbreak, and has worked with the means at her disposal). Martin Donovan is touching as Ralph, whose own love is bravely concealed. Only Malkovich seems wrong; we need an Osmond who seems worthier at first.

The value of Henry James is that he teaches us to consider our motives. Today we rush heedless into life. We believe in "love at first sight." We get our values from TV and film, where the plot exists only to hurry the characters into sex. All modern emotions can be expressed in a sound bite. James's people think before they commit. When they choose wrong, they eventually learn how, and why. Today's Isabel Archer would dump Osmond, sue for her money back, and head for a spa to recuperate. I imagine James's Isabel captured forever in the loveless tomb of her own choosing.

## Post Coitum, Animal Triste ★ ★ ★

NO MPAA RATING, 95 m., 1998

Brigitte Rouan (Diane), Boris Terral (Emilio), Patrick Chesnais (Philippe), Nils Tavernier (Francois), Jean-Louis Richard (Weyman-Lebeau). Directed by Brigitte Rouan and produced by Humbert Balsan. Screenplay by Santiago Amigorena, Jean-Louis Richard, Rouan, and Guy Zylberstein.

The first shot is of a cat writhing in lust. The second shot is of a woman writhing in emotional agony. Both feel the same animal need, according to Brigitte Rouan, who directed, stars in, and cowrote the astonishing psychodrama *Post Coitum, Animal Triste,* which is about a woman's transition from wild sexual excitement to love to fury at rejection.

Rouan plays Diane, a Parisian book editor in her forties, who is trying to guide a young author named Francois (Nils Tavernier) through the ordeal of his second novel. At his apartment, she meets Emilio (Boris Terral), Francois's roommate. Their eyes lock. They seem almost immediately to fall into a mutual sexual trance and are making love before they know each other. He is young, wild, reckless. She is a bourgeoisie intellectual with a husband and two children. "I'm a lifetime ahead of you," she complains. "Want to help me buy some socks?" he asks.

The first stage of their relationship is one of urgent risk taking, as they meet whenever and wherever they can. She races across streets, crying out his name. Kissing, they fall onto the hood of a car in the middle of traffic, oblivious. Once they become so reckless that they are requested to leave a restaurant. Diane is amazed to feel so strongly and deeply; at one point, she is literally seen floating on air. The bewitched Emilio seems in a tumescent daze.

Her husband, Philippe (Patrick Chesnais), of course, soon suspects an affair. He is a lawyer, not stupid, whose current client plunged a carving fork into the jugular of her husband; the older woman had put up with years of infidelity and abuse, but could not deal with her husband's threat to leave her. As Philippe quizzes his client about her crime, he senses a certain serenity in her manner; by murdering her husband, she has at last ended her lifetime of suffering. The film teases us with the possibility that Philippe may take the hint.

Then, gradually, in steps as small as a few words murmured to his grandfather, Emilio begins to lose his passion. He is a "hydraulic engineer in the Third World," on leave after mending dikes in Bangladesh, and now he informs Diane he is going to Africa for six months. She interprets this, correctly, as an attempt to get away, and has a breakdown that escalates for most of the rest of the movie.

It is not a pretty sight, seeing a dignified and attractive woman of a certain age as she goes completely to pieces. "I hurt all over and you feel nothing," she tells Emilio. He might have been willing to extend their relationship in a reasonable way, but is frightened by her frenzy. She drinks to oblivion. She starts a fire in her office. She loses her job. She lives on the sofa. She forgets to eat. She cries for hours. Her family moves out. She doesn't kill herself only because, perhaps, she masochistically enjoys her agony.

This breakdown went on too long, I thought; a little forlorn hysteria goes a long way. But by the end of the film, we have come to admire Rouan's courage as a performer and a filmmaker in following Diane's mania as far as it will go. And I liked the way the central drama is surrounded by small, observant moments involving the husband, the children, and even the accused murderer (at one point, Philippe plays tapes of his wife's secret phone calls to his client—to get the benefit of her more direct experience with adultery).

The title translates loosely as "After sex, animal grief." Is it autobiographical? I don't know. My guess is, either these events are inspired by an affair that Rouan once had, or they are a memorandum to herself: Never have one.

## The Postman ★ ½

R, 177 m., 1997

Kevin Costner (The Postman), Will Patton (Bethlehem), Larenz Tate (Ford Lincoln Mercury), Olivia Williams (Abby), James Russo (Idaho), Tom Petty (Mayor). Directed by Kevin Costner and produced by Costner and Steve Tisch. Screenplay by Erich Roth and Brian Helgeland.

There are those who will no doubt call *The Postman* the worst film of the year, but it's too good-hearted for that. It's goofy, yes, and pretentious, and Kevin Costner puts himself in situations that get snickers. And it's way too long. But parables like this require their makers to burn their bridges and leave common sense behind: Either they work (as *Forrest Gump* did), in which case everyone involved is a genius, or they don't—in which case you shouldn't blame them for trying.

In choosing *The Postman* as his new project, however, Kevin Costner should perhaps have reflected that audiences were getting to be over-familiar with him as the eccentric loner in the wilderness, coming across an isolated community and then joining their war against evil marauders. He told that story magnificently in *Dances With Wolves* (1990) and then did another version in the futuristic fantasy *Waterworld* (1995).

Now he sort of combines them, in a film that takes place in the post-Apocalyptic future like *Waterworld*, but looks and feels like it takes place in a Western.

The movie, based on an award-winning science-fiction novel by David Brin, takes place in 2013. The dust clouds have settled after nuclear war, and scattered communities pick up the reins of civilization. There is no central government. Costner is a lone figure in the wilderness, friendly only with his mule, named Bill. They support themselves by doing Shakespeare for bands of settlers. Bill can hold a sword in his mouth, and in *Macbeth* he plays Birnam Wood. His master recites lines like, "Life is a tale told by a moron," not the sort of mistake he'd be likely to make, especially with a woman helpfully prompting him by whispering, "Idiot! Idiot!" Or maybe she's a critic.

Costner is conscripted into a neofascist army run by General Bethlehem (Will Patton). He escapes, stumbles over an abandoned U.S. Mail van, and steals the uniform, cap, and letter bag of the skeleton inside. At the gates of a settlement called Pineview, he claims he's come to deliver the mail. Building on his fiction, he tells the residents of a restored U.S. government in Minneapolis. The sheriff spots him for a fraud, but the people want to believe, and the next morning, he finds letters pushed under his door. Walking outside, he discovers that all the people of the town have gathered in hushed silence in a semicircle around his lodging, to await his awakening and appearance—the sort of thing townspeople do in movies, but never in real life, where some helpful townsman invariably suggests, "Let's just wake the sonuvabitch up."

In a movie that proceeds with glacial deliberation, the Postman becomes a symbol for the survivors in their struggling communities. "You give out hope like it was candy in your pocket," a young woman tells him. It's the sort of line an actor-director ought to be wary of applying to his own character, but Costner frankly sees the Postman as a messiah, and there is a shot late in the film where he zooms high above a river gorge in a cable car that serves absolutely no purpose except to allow him to pose as the masthead on the ship of state.

That young woman (Olivia Williams), by the way, wants the Postman's semen. Her husband is infertile after the "bad mumps," and the couple desires a child. The Postman eventually obliges, and she makes love with him in a scene reminiscent of those good Victorian wives who closed their eyes and thought of the empire. Her husband is murdered, and she's kidnapped by General Bethlehem, who has seen *Braveheart* and knows about the feudal system where the lord gets first dibbies on the wedding nights of his vassals. She and the Postman eventually escape into the wilderness and spend the winter together while she comes full term. This is some frontier woman; in the spring, she burns down their cottage so they'll be forced to move on, and "we can find someplace nice for the baby."

In his absence, the Postman's legendary status has been magnified by young Ford Lincoln Mercury (Larenz Tate), who has named himself after an auto dealership and in the absence of the Postman has organized a postal service in exile. It is clear that the Postman and Bethlehem will sooner or later have to face each other in battle. When they do, the general produces a hostage he has captured—Ford L. Mercury—and the Postman pales and pauses at the prospect of F.L. Mercury's death, even though the Postman's army consists mostly of hundreds of women and children he is cheerfully contemplating leading to their slaughter.

The movie has a lot of unwise shots resulting in bad laughs, none more ill-advised than one where the Postman, galloping down a country lane, passes a gate where a tow-headed little tyke holds on to a letter. Some sixth sense causes the Postman to look back, see the kid, turn around, then gallop back to him, snatching up the letter at full tilt. This touching scene, shot with a zoom lens in slow motion to make it even more fatuous than it needed to be, is later immortalized in a bronze statue, unveiled at the end of the movie. As a civic figure makes a speech in front of the statue, which is still covered by a tarpaulin, a member of the audience whispered, "They've bronzed the Postman!" Dear reader, that member was me, and I guess I shouldn't have been surprised that I was right.

## The Preacher's Wife ★ ★ ★

PG, 124 m., 1996

Denzel Washington (Dudley), Whitney Houston (Julia Biggs), Courtney B. Vance (Henry Biggs), Gregory Hines (Joe Hamilton), Jenifer Lewis (Marguerite Coleman), Loretta Devine (Beverly), Justin Pierre Edmund (Jeremiah Biggs), Lionel Richie (Britsloe). Directed by Penny Marshall and produced by Samuel Goldwyn Jr. Screenplay by Nat Mauldin and Allan Scott, based on a screenplay by Robert E. Sherwood and Leonardo Bercovici.

*The Preacher's Wife* is a sweet and good-hearted comedy about the holiday season, and I suppose that is enough, although I would have liked it with more punch and bite. It tells the story of an inner-city pastor who grows discouraged with his never-ending struggle, asks God for help, and gets it in the form of an angel from above.

The preacher, Henry Biggs (Courtney B. Vance), is happily married to his childhood sweetheart, Julia (Whitney Houston). They have a cute little boy named Jeremiah, who narrates the story, apparently with his mouth full of gum. The angel is named Dudley (Denzel Washington), and he dresses in shades of gray and often consults his *Angel's Handbook*, and soon falls quietly in love with Julia.

Eagle-eyed theologians will have already asked themselves how an angel can fall in love. They have spotted a large hole in the story: Dudley is not, strictly speaking, an angel at all, but a human who died thirty years earlier and has now been sent from heaven on this aid mission. But he calls himself an angel, and one of the Three Laws of Angels is "Angels cannot lie," so either he (1) thinks he is an angel but is sincerely mistaken, or (2) is a human, and lying.

Surely the makers of this film do not believe that humans go to heaven and become angels. As we all know, angels were created by God as his first companions, and he created humans much later, presumably after tiring of companions who never lied.

In any event, what is sweet about the movie is that all of its characters, human, angel, or whatever, are good and kind and determined to make a contribution in the world. Even the villain, a property developer named Joe Hamilton (Gregory Hines), isn't really so evil. He is a board member of Henry's church, and secretly wants to tear it down and construct condos and tennis courts, while moving Henry to a splendid new suburban church with separate centers for youth and the elderly. This plan doesn't exactly put Joe Hamilton in league with Satan, and for much of the movie he qualifies as a villain only because anyone involved in real estate is always a villain in the movies.

Vance turns in a sound, touching performance as a pastor who spends much of his time visiting the sick, distributing food baskets, and helping an innocent young man defend himself against criminal charges. His weekly collection one Sunday is only $96, the church boiler has just exploded, and although he asked God for help, of course he doesn't believe the angel's story.

But his wife, Julia, is more interested in Dudley; she thinks he has been sent by the church council, welcomes him into her home, and before long is spending a lot of time with him; they go ice-skating and visit a jazz club. The club is one of several opportunities the movie finds to let Whitney Houston sing, and she is especially good when backed by the church gospel choir.

But Julia's mother (Jenifer Lewis) is quick to see the new love growing in her daughter's eyes, and warns her away from Dudley. "I can look in the window—even if I don't buy," Julia says. "Don't go window-shopping with money in your pocket," her mother snaps. And even saintly Henry eventually warns the angel away from his wife.

This is all done so nicely, though, that *The Preacher's Wife* doesn't produce much tension, even though it generates much warmth and light. The film is a remake of the 1947 *The Bishop's Wife,* which starred Cary Grant as the angel and David Niven and Loretta Young as the church couple. I haven't seen that version, but this one, directed by Penny Marshall, would have been better if the screws had been tightened.

I would have liked Dudley and Julia to be more in love, and for Henry to feel more threatened. I would have liked the urban developer to have a more evil scheme, and for more suspense to develop when the neighborhood kid is accused of a crime he didn't commit. Even small moments could have used more punch, as when the angel fixes Jeremiah's toy ambulance and it suddenly has a siren it didn't have before. In the hands of a Spielberg, this would have been a big laugh moment, but Marshall mutes it. (There's also not enough of a comic payoff in a nativity pageant where the doll representing baby Jesus turns out to have a pee function.)

Despite these reservations, I found myself enjoying *The Preacher's Wife* for its simple but real pleasures: for the way Houston sings, and for the glimpses of the people in the church congregation, and for the way the preacher tries his hardest to do the right thing. And also for Denzel Washington, who is able to project love without lust, and goodness without corniness. This movie could have done more, but what it does, it makes you feel good about. ☞

## Prefontaine ★ ★ ★

PG-13, 106 m., 1997

Jared Leto (Steve Prefontaine), R. Lee Ermey (Bill Bowerman), Ed O'Neill (Bill Dellinger), Breckin Meyer (Pat Tyson), Lindsay Crouse (Elfriede Prefontaine), Amy Locane (Nancy Alleman), Laurel Holloman (Elaine Finley), Brian McGovern (Mac Wilkins). Directed by Steve James and produced by Irby Smith, Jon Lutz, Mark Doonan, and Peter Gilbert. Screenplay by James and Eugene Corr.

Steve Prefontaine was one of the greatest runners produced in the United States, and one of the most abrasive. This film based on his life makes him seem fairly unlikable, and that's one of its best qualities: Here is a sports movie in the tradition of the best sportswriting, where athletes are portrayed warts and all. You do not have to be nice to win races, but you have to be good.

*Prefontaine* opens in the 1960s, with Steve (Jared Leto) as a kid whose short stature and "bad hand-eye coordination" make him the most hapless player on the football team. Determined to be good at something—to get even with those who dismissed him—he turns to track, and even though he's not built like a runner and one leg is shorter than the other, he uses sheer determination to win. Soon he's being scouted by the legendary Oregon coach Bill Bowerman (R. Lee Ermey), who manufactures track shoes in his garage, using his wife's waffle iron to mold the rubber treads. Bowerman goes on to cofound Nike, and Pre goes on to hold almost every American record at the longer distances.

Sports movies have traditionally tried to turn their heroes into demigods. Not *Prefontaine,* which sees Pre as a single-minded, self-centered, ruthless competitor. At one point, goofing around on the track with kids, he refuses to even pretend to let a nine-year-old beat him. He has to win even that race. When his girlfriend Nancy (Amy Locane) wonders if that's carrying things too far, he spits out: "All my life people have said to me, 'You're too small, Pre. You're not fast enough, Pre. Give up your foolish dreams, Steve!' They forgot something: I have to win. No fallback here, no great stride, no long legs—nothing!"

The movie follows Prefontaine to an NCAA championship he wins with twelve stitches in his foot (he runs an extra victory lap in his bloody shoe). It shows him arguing with Bowerman about distance (he wants the higher visibility of the mile); Bowerman correctly sees him at the longer distances, where stamina and guts count for more. He qualifies for the 1972 Olympics—and then the massacre of the Israeli athletes takes place the night before his big race. The race is eventually held, even though Pre tells his assistant coach (Ed O'Neill) he "can't run over the bodies of those dead athletes."

Does he win? You will have to see for yourself. What sets *Prefontaine* aside from most sports movies is that it's not about winning the big race. It's about the life of a runner. After he returns from Munich, Prefontaine supports himself by bartending and lives in a mobile home. Other nations support their athletes in style, but the rules of American amateur sports at that time essentially required a life spent in training and poverty. (Much is made of the shabby quarters supplied to U.S. athletes in Munich while 100 adult "officials" lived in splendor at a luxury hotel.)

After Munich, Bowerman retires to start his track shoe empire (Pre says the Nike trademark "looks like needless air resistance to me"). What Prefontaine eventually does is break the nerve of the American amateur athletic establishment by getting his teammates (including discus champion Mac Wilkins) to join him in an unsanctioned invitation for the Finnish national team to visit Oregon. Accused of betraying the U.S. national team, he tells a press conference, typically: "To hell with love of country; I'm looking out for me."

*Prefontaine,* which is smart, quirky, and involving, is the first fiction film by Steve James, who directed the great sports documentary *Hoop Dreams.* In a sense, this is a continuation of the same story, about how the sports establishment uses and then discards gifted young athletes with little regard for their personal welfare.

If the two young subjects of *Hoop Dreams* won a victory of sorts (they got college educations and were able to use basketball to better their prospects in life), Steve Prefontaine won one too. In the process he may have dismantled the idea of pure amateur athletics in this country, but the movie shows how much hypocrisy was masked by that ideal. By the end of the film we may not like Pre, but we understand and respect him. The movie shows an athlete for whom winning wasn't everything—but *having* to win was.

## A Price Above Rubies ★ ★ ★

R, 116 m., 1998

Renee Zellweger (Sonia), Christopher Eccleston (Sender), Julianna Margulies (Rachel), Allen Payne (Ramon), Glenn Fitzgerald (Mendel), Kim Hunter (Rebbitzn), John Randolph (Rebbe), Phyllis Newman (Mrs. Gelbart). Directed by Boaz Yakin and produced by Lawrence Bender and John Penotti. Screenplay by Yakin.

*A Price Above Rubies* tells the story of a woman who burns for release from the strictures of a closed society. We learn much about her during the film, but not much about her society—a community of Orthodox Hasidic Jews, living in Brooklyn. Perhaps that's in the nature of commercial filmmaking; there is a larger audience for a story about the liberation of proud, stubborn Renee Zellweger (from *Jerry Maguire*) than there is for a story about why a woman's place is in the home.

During the film, however, questions about the message were not foremost in my mind. I was won over by Zellweger's ferociously strong performance, and by characters and scenes I hadn't seen before: the world, for example, of Manhattan diamond merchants, and the parallel world of secret (untaxed) jewel shops in Brooklyn apartments, and the life of a young Puerto Rican who is a talented jewelry designer. The film also adds a level of magic realism in the character of an old homeless woman who may be "as old as God himself."

Zellweger plays Sonia, the daughter of gemologists who steer her away from the family business and into marriage with a young scholar named Mendel (Glenn Fitzgerald), who prefers prayer and study to the company of his wife. (During sex, he turns off the light and thinks of Abraham and Isaac.) Sonia's unhappiness makes her an emotional time bomb, and it is Mendel's older brother Sender (Christopher Eccleston) who sets her off. First he tests her knowledge of jewelry. Then he offers her a job in his business. Then he has sex with her. It's rape, but she seems to accept it as the price of freedom.

*A Price Above Rubies* is the second film by writer-director Boaz Yakin, whose *Fresh* (1994) was able to see clearly inside a black community; here, although he is Jewish, he is not able to bring the Hasidim into the same focus. All I learned for sure about them is that the men wear beards and black hats and suits, and govern every detail of daily life according to the teachings of rabbis and scholars. The women obey their fathers and husbands, and the group as a whole shuns the customs of the greater world and lives within walls of rules and traditions. There is not a lot of room for compromise or accommodation in their teachings, which is a point of tension in modern Israel between Orthodox and other Jews.

Sonia does not find this a world she can live in. She is rebellious when her husband insists their newborn son be named after the rabbi rather than after Sonia's beloved brother, who drowned when he was young. She is opposed to the boy's circumcision ("He's like a sacrifice!")—but, to be sure, her husband also faints at the sight of blood. She is as resentful at Mendel's long hours at study and prayer as another wife might be at a husband who spent all of his time in a bar or at the track. And there is that unquenched passion burning inside of her. (In equating her sexual feelings with heat, Yakin unwittingly mirrors the convention in porno films, where women complain of feeling "hot . . . so hot" and sex works like air-conditioning.)

After her brother-in-law sets her up in the jewelry business, she glories in her freedom. She wheels and deals with the jewelry merchants of the city, and runs his illicit store from a garden apartment. On a park bench one day, she sees a black woman with beautiful earrings, and this sends her on a search for their maker, Ramon (Allen Payne), a Puerto Rican who sells schlock in Manhattan to make money, and then does his own work for love.

This man is unlike any Sonia has ever met, but at first her love is confined to his jewelry. She encourages him, commissions him, reassures him that his work is special. But then Sender discovers their connection and tells Sonia's husband and family, and Sonia is locked out of her house, cut off from her child, and divorced.

It is hard to see why Sender would take that risk, considering what a powerful weapon Sonia has: She could accuse him of rape. But perhaps he knows she wouldn't be believed. His values are hardly those of his prayerful brother's; he believes we sin in order to gain God's forgiveness (or perhaps even his attention), and that "the quality of our sins sets us apart."

I was always completely absorbed in Sonia's quest. Zellweger avoids all the cute mannerisms that made her so lovable in *Jerry Maguire,* and plays this young woman as quiet, inward, even a little stooped. She knows she must find a different kind of life for herself, and does.

The film has been protested by some Hasidic Jews, who especially disliked the circumcision scene. Yakin did little for his defense by claiming it was "comedic"—which it is not remotely. Like the Amish of *Kingpin* and the Catholics of the early scenes in *Household Saints,* these Jews come across as exotic outsiders and holdouts in the great secularized American melting pot.

What may offend them as much as anything is that their community is reduced to a backdrop and props for Sonia's story. It would be an interesting challenge for a filmmaker to tell a story from inside such a community. *Witness* came close to suggesting the values of the Amish, I think, but then how would I really know?

## Primal Fear ★ ★ ★ ½

R, 131 m., 1996

Richard Gere (Martin Vail), Laura Linney (Janet Venable), Edward Norton (Aaron Stampler), John Mahoney (John Shaughnessy), Alfre Woodard (Judge Miriam Shoat), Frances McDormand (Dr. Molly Arrington), Andre Braugher (Tommy Goodman), Maura Tierney (Naomi Chance). Directed by Gregory Hoblit and produced by Gary Lucchesi. Screenplay by Steve Shagan and Ann Biderman, based on the novel by William Diehl.

Once it was cops who solved crimes. Then private eyes. In the Grisham Era, it has been lawyers. *Primal Fear,* based on a novel by William Diehl, stars Richard Gere as a flamboyant Chicago defense attorney who chases defendants instead of ambulances, and volunteers his services when a teenager from Kentucky is charged with murdering an archbishop.

Why? Because he knows the case will be the most sensational of the year, and he wants to be where the action is. And maybe because he thinks the kid might be innocent, although the movie's literate, pointed dialogue makes it clear that guilt isn't an issue with this lawyer: Every defendant deserves a competent defense, he believes (and defendants in sensational, highly publicized cases deserve a defense from him).

The attorney is named Martin Vail. In playing him, Gere creates one of the best performances of his career, nuanced and smart, although the conventions of the thriller genre distract from how good it really is. He's a hard-drinking, ego-driven man who recently broke up with a young assistant D.A. named Janet Venable (Laura Linney), who is now, inevitably, his opponent on the case.

As the movie opens, Martin Vail is seen moving smoothly through the centers of power in Chicago. He attends a benefit. He knows everybody's name. They behave toward him in a way that implies his importance. But there's something else going on. The director, Gregory Hoblit, is able to take a church benefit with a boys' choir performing, and somehow fill it with sinister undertones. There is more than meets the eye. An atmosphere of menace is created without a single word or shot you can put your finger on.

The archbishop is murdered in a grisly scene, and the suspect, Aaron Stampler (Edward Norton), is captured a short time later, after a foot chase with police that is telecast live. He's covered with the archbishop's blood, and the headlines call him "The Butcher Boy of St. Mike's." But did he commit the crime? A psychologist named Molly Arrington (Frances McDormand) examines him for the court and thinks the question has no simple answer, since the kid, under intense pressure, suggests there was another person in the room. There is a lot more to it than that, although I will not reveal the details.

The story develops against a backdrop of Chicago politics and corruption. The archbishop, we learn, was involved in land deals that created a lot of unhappiness among powerful Chicagoans who lost millions of dollars. He has received forty death threats. And his relationship with some of the members of the boys' choir was not strictly pastoral. A Latino alderman, who defends the building of a clinic on land intended to be "upscaled," gets into hot water. And Martin Vail seems to be at the center of all of these events. Is it possible that young Aaron is a fall guy for a much larger, more sinister plot?

The plot is as good as crime procedurals get, but the movie is really better than its plot, because of the three-dimensional characters. Gere is given several quiet scenes, including a half-drunken conversation with a journalist, to develop the complexities of his character. Laura Linney makes more of her fairly standard character than we might expect. And the supporting performances—from John Mahoney as the hard-bitten D.A., from McDormand as the psychologist, and from Alfre Woodard, who plays the judge and presides over a key scene in chambers—are strong and convincing. Edward Norton, as the "Butcher Boy," creates a character that is, as you will see, completely convincing in more ways than one.

The best crime movies, and novels, are not

about who did it or why. They are about how the characters feel about what happened. The screenplay for *Primal Fear,* by Steve Shagan and Ann Biderman, knows that, and uses the labyrinthine plot details as backdrop to issues of identity. Because this movie has a commercial destiny, of course the crime is sensational and the revelations are startling. But the character of Martin Vail is so well done that it could have supported a smaller, more plausible movie. Richard Gere's film choices could use more quality control, but at times, as in *Days of Heaven, American Gigolo, Pretty Woman, Internal Affairs, Miles From Home,* and *Mr. Jones,* he shows what an interesting actor he can be. *Primal Fear* contains some of his best work.

## Primary Colors ★ ★ ★ ★

R, 135 m., 1998

John Travolta (Governor Jack Stanton), Emma Thompson (Susan Stanton), Billy Bob Thornton (Richard Jemmons), Kathy Bates (Libby Holden), Adrian Lester (Henry Burton), Maura Tierney (Daisy), Larry Hagman (Governor Fred Picker), Diane Ladd (Mamma Stanton). Directed and produced by Mike Nichols. Screenplay by Elaine May, based on the novel by "Anonymous."

Here's the surprising thing: *Primary Colors* would seem just about as good, as tough, and as smart if there had never been a president named Bill Clinton. Of course the movie resonates with its parallels to the lives of Bill and Hillary Clinton, but it's a lot more than a disguised exposé. It's a superb film—funny, insightful, and very wise about the realities of political life.

The director, Mike Nichols, and the writer, his longtime collaborator Elaine May, have put an astonishing amount of information on the screen, yes, but that wasn't the hard part. Their real accomplishment is to blend so many stories and details into an observant picture that holds together. We see that Jack Stanton, the presidential candidate in the film, is a flawed charmer with a weakness for bimbos, but we also see what makes him attractive even to those who know the worst: He listens and cares, and knows how to be an effective politician.

John Travolta and Emma Thompson play Stanton and his wife, Susan, as a couple who, we feel, have spent many long hours and nights in mind-to-mind combat. Her true feelings about his infidelity remain unexpressed, but she is loyal to a larger idea of the man, and not as hurt that he fools around as that she's lied to about it. Much will be written about how much Travolta and Thompson do or do not resemble the Clintons, but their wisest choice as actors is to preserve their mystery.

By *not* going behind their bedroom door, by not eavesdropping on their private moments, the movie avoids having to explain what perhaps can never be understood: why a man is driven to self-destructive behavior, and how his wife might somehow remain at his side anyway. The movie wisely stays a certain distance from the Stantons. There are no important scenes in which they are alone together in a room.

Instead, *Primary Colors* centers its point of view in a character named Henry Burton (Adrian Lester), grandson of a civil rights leader, who doesn't join the campaign so much as get sucked into its wake. Before he has even agreed to join Stanton's team, he finds himself on a chartered plane to New Hampshire with the candidate asleep on his shoulder. Earlier, he saw Stanton at work. At an illiteracy class, a black man (Mykelti Williamson in a powerful cameo) tells of the pain of not being able to read. Stanton empathizes with him, telling the story of his Uncle Charlie, who was a Medal of Honor winner but passed up college scholarships because he was ashamed to admit his illiteracy, and instead "just laid down on his couch and smoked his Luckies."

Of course, the Uncle Charlie story may not be entirely true, and later that day Henry sees Stanton emerging from a hotel bedroom with the flustered woman who runs the illiteracy program, but for Henry and the other campaign workers it eventually comes down to this: All the candidates are flawed in one way or another, but some have good ideas, and of those only a few might be able to win.

John Travolta dominates the movie, in part, by his absence. Nichols and May must have decided it would be a mistake to put him into every scene: A man like Jack Stanton is important because of the way people talk, speculate, and obsess about him in his absence.

Through Henry, we meet the campaign's inner circle. Richard Jemmons (Billy Bob Thornton), obviously based on Clinton's strategist James Carville, is a cynical realist who provides running commentary on the stages of the campaign. Libby Holden (Kathy Bates), the "dust-buster," is a longtime Stanton confidant and recent mental patient who comes out of retirement, foul-mouthed and lusty, to dig up the dirt before the other side can. And Daisy (Maura Tierney), quiet and observant, is a scheduler who eventually finds herself in Henry's bed, not so much out of choice as default. Of the crowd, Bates is the dynamo, playing a hard-living lesbian with a secret center of idealism; it's an Oscar-caliber performance.

The movie ticks off episodes based on real life. There's a woman from the candidate's home state who claims to have had an affair with him and to have tapes to prove it. And a dramatic appearance on national TV, where Susan Stanton holds her husband's hand and defends him (her hand snaps away from his as the show goes off the air). It intercuts these with fiction, created in the novel by "Anonymous," now revealed as ex-*Newsweek* writer Joe Klein. There's the pregnancy of the teenage daughter of Stanton's favorite barbecue chef. And the populist Florida governor (Larry Hagman), who looks good against Stanton until his past returns to haunt him.

Much of the movie's ethical content revolves not around sex, but around how a primary campaign should handle damaging information it turns up about its opponent. Libby argues that they shouldn't use it. Jack says that if they don't, the other side will. Better to get it out before it does more harm.

In the way *Primary Colors* handles this issue, it shows more insight and maturity than all but a handful of recent mainstream movies: This is a grown-up film about real issues in the real world. Among its pleasures is the way it lets us examine the full frame, and observe how characters at the side or in the background react; whole characters are developed in asides.

It is also very funny at times, as when Stanton, Jemmons, and others get in a "momma-thon," praising their mothers into the night. Or when Susan snatches Jack's ever-present chicken drumstick out of his hand. Or when the candidate, his wife, and his aides search a roadside for a cell phone thrown from a car in anger. The movie is endlessly inventive and involving: You get swept up in the political and personal suspense, and begin to understand why people are engulfed in political campaigns.

Will *Primary Colors* hurt or help the Clinton presidency? To some degree, neither; it's a treatment of matters the electorate has already made up its mind about. The film has certainly not in any sense "softened" its portrayal of its Clintonesque hero—those rumors are exposed by its almost brutal candor. But in a strange way *Primary Colors* may actually work to help Clinton. While a lesser film would have felt compelled to supply an "answer," this one knows that the fascination is in the complexity, in the strong and weak qualities at war with one another. The secret of what makes Jack Stanton tick is as unanswerable as the meaning of Citizen Kane's "Rosebud." And the resemblance doesn't stop there. ☞

## Prisoner of the Mountains ★ ★ ★ ½

R, 99 m., 1997

Oleg Menshikov (Sacha), Sergei Bodrov Jr. (Vania), Jemal Sikharulidze (Abdoul-Mourat), Susanna Mekhralieva (Dina), Alexei Jharkov (The captain), Valentina Fedotova (The mother). Directed by Sergei Bodrov and produced by Boris Giller and Bodrov. Screenplay by Arif Aliev, Bodrov, and Giller.

An old man, the Muslim patriarch of a mountain village, takes two Russian soldiers prisoner because he wants to trade them for his own son. The mother of one of his prisoners comes to see him, to make a trade to save her son. "I know your son is a teacher," she tells him. "I am a teacher too." The old man shakes his head: "It doesn't matter. We are enemies."

Sergei Bodrov's *Prisoner of the Mountains*, a thoughtful and moving film about war, exists on the line between the individual and "the enemy." Because we have seen similar stories before, we expect that eventually the two Russian soldiers will become the friends of their captors, who will begin to see them as human beings. It is not going to be that simple. The war that brings them together—a war between the Russian central government and Muslim rebels in the Caucasus mountains—is based on a hatred so old and durable that this movie, set in the present day, is based on a short story written by Leo Tolstoy more than 150 years ago.

The soldiers are Sacha (Oleg Menshikov) and Vania (Sergei Bodrov Jr.). Sacha is older, more confident, dashing. Vania is an uncertain kid. They meet in training, go on a tank patrol, and are almost immediately captured by a freelance rebel ambush headed by old Abdoul-Mourat (Jemal Sikharulidze), the tall, intimidating leader of a mountain village. Placed in shackles, they are kept prisoner and put to hard labor. Abdoul's sweet, dark-eyed daughter (Susanna Mekhralieva), who is about twelve, soon begins to like them, although she never questions their captivity. "My dowry," she boasts complacently, "will include two Russian slaves."

This war zone seems so small that some of the participants know each other (in fact, Bodrov shot the whole movie within twenty miles of actual fighting). Abdoul sends off his ransom letter (learning that the mail delivery will take about ten days). But Vania's mother simply goes to the front, confronts her son's former commander, and says she wants to deal directly with the rebels. The commander discourages her ("You can't trust anyone here. Soldiers traded grenades for hash, and kids threw the grenades back at them."). The mother swings her purse at his head, and he ducks, apologizing, "Mother, you don't understand. We have casualties every day."

She sets off alone for a rendezvous with Abdoul in a café. They are two parents negotiating for the lives of their sons. The difference is that the Russian woman places her son above ideology, and the patriarch believes in the value of a glorious death. Meanwhile, the two soldiers, chained together, sing songs, drink smuggled booze, and one night are taken out on a patrol by regular troops, who force them to look for land mines.

When they are not blown up as expected, we get a scene which shows the greater maturity of this film, as opposed to standard Hollywood war movies. The Muslim troops have gathered on a bleak hillside for a little entertainment: all-in fighting, starring their defending champion, who leaves his opponents broken and bloody. We watch while the fighter wins his latest bout, and then one of the prisoners is ordered to fight him. Frightened, trembling, he approaches the champion. In most Hollywood films, this scene would end with the good guy being beaten to a pulp, yes, but then staging a comeback and hammering the champion. *Prisoner of the Mountains* is wiser about human nature: The champion, who is a fighter but not a murderer, takes one look at his puny challenger and dismisses him with a laugh. It is a special moment.

The movie has an acute sense of place and the passage of time. The mountain village seems unchanged over the centuries ("The wind frightens the hearts of strangers here," the children say). When we hear Louis Armstrong on a radio, it is like a signal from space. Modern methods of warfare are meaningless here; the rebels know the mountain passes, and fight with greater zeal. The little girl, who in a conventional film would befriend the soldiers, does befriend them, but after the style of her people: She promises them a proper burial. Because the film is about these specific characters and not about a formula with a happy ending, we are wrapped in the story: We have no way of knowing how it will turn out.

Movies can have a way of putting faces to headlines. I have been reading for years about the various obscure (to me) rebellions in the old Soviet Union, and now I can put faces to them and see what they come down to: bureaucracy against zealotry, weary regular troops against fierce men who burn with conviction. When your enemy considers his death a victory, it is impossible to defeat him. In a way, this movie is about how the two prisoners come to terms with that realization.

## Private Parts ★ ★ ★

R, 111 m., 1997

Howard Stern (Himself), Robin Quivers (Herself), Mary McCormack (Alison Stern), Paul Giamatti (Pig Vomit), Fred Norris (Himself), Jackie Martling (Himself), Gary Dell'Abate (Himself), Richard Portnow (Ben Stern), Kelly Bishop (Ray Stern). Directed by Betty Thomas and produced by Ivan Reitman. Screenplay by Len Blum.

Howard Stern has been accused of a lot of things, but he has never been accused of being dumb. With *Private Parts,* his surprisingly sweet new movie, he makes a canny career move: Here is radio's bad boy walking the finest of lines between enough and too much. His fans will find enough of the Howard whose maxims include "lesbians equal ratings." General audiences will be seduced by the film's story line, which exploits three time-honored

Hollywood formulas: (1) rags to riches, (2) I gotta be me, and (3) hey, underneath it all I'm really just a cuddly teddy bear.

The movie shows the coronation of a geek. In grade school, we learn, Howard's father made a more or less daily practice of calling him a moron. Howard was the only white kid in an all-black high school. He didn't date until college (even a blind girl turns him down, after feeling his nose), and he married almost the first woman who was nice to him. Played by Mary McCormack, his wife, Alison, plays a key role in the film, which asks as its underlying subplot, "How much will this woman put up with before she dumps him?" The answer, as Stern listeners know, is "a lot."

*Private Parts* is a biopic about an awkward kid with a bad radio voice and such shaky breath control that he was always running out of steam in the middle of the call letters. Working at a 40-watt station, he's promoted to program manager because he's such a lousy DJ, and told by the station owner: "Disc jockeys are dogs. Your job is to make them fetch." Fired from a country station he hates, Howard tells Alison: "I have to be myself on the radio, and tell the truth. I have to go all the way." He does. He reveals things about their marriage on the radio that would be grounds for divorce in any civilized land.

In 1981, Howard arrives at a Washington station and is paired for the first time with Robin Quivers, who plays herself in the movie and functions as ballast, steadying Howard in his manic phases and speaking for many members of the audience when she tells him, over and over, that this time he's gone too far. Stern and Quivers are both making their screen acting debuts here, and they do what seasoned actors claim is very difficult: They play convincing, engaging versions of themselves.

The final third of the movie shows Howard in his modern incarnation, as the shock jock who will say almost anything on the radio. He crowns himself King of All Media (tough to do, since by his account he rarely has both hands free at the same time). And he gets into trouble after WNBC, the network's New York flagship, hires him apparently without having listened to his show. His new boss is a program director quickly nicknamed Pig Vomit (well played by Paul Giamatti), who promises his superior, "Either I tame him or I make him so crazy he quits." The process includes lessons in the proper sing-song pronunciation of the call letters.

When one bit goes over the top, Howard makes Robin the fall guy and she's fired and feels betrayed. This episode, based on life, is played honestly; Howard acts like a creep and doesn't resign on principal, although perhaps he is right, strategically, to see the firing as a ploy to get him to resign.

The film has been directed by Betty Thomas *(The Brady Bunch, The Late Shift),* whose steadying hand makes it play like a movie and not a series of filmed radio shows. Many sequences are very funny, including one where Howard uses a listener's subwoofer to create effects for which it was not designed. Stern on-air regulars like Fred Norris, Jackie (the Joke Man) Martling, and Stuttering John play themselves, and producer Gary Dell'Abate hosts inserts that feel unrehearsed, including one where a donkey makes a surprise appearance.

Stern reportedly rejected some two dozen scripts before settling on this one, written by Len Blum. He made the prudent choice. The material is just outrageous enough to be convincingly Stern, but not so far out it will offend those likely to see this movie (*Booty Call,* by contrast, is more uninhibited). The movie successfully launches Stern's screen career, and it will be interesting to see how its inevitable sequel, *Miss America,* will develop. What is certain about Stern is that he will find a way to stretch the envelope without tearing it; he may have paid $1 million in fines to the FCC, as his publicity boasts, but he is still, after all, on the air. ☞

## The Proprietor ½★

R, 113 m., 1996

Jeanne Moreau (Adrienne Mark), Sean Young (Virginia Kelly), Sam Waterston (Antiques Dealer), Christopher Cazenove (Eliott Spencer), Nell Carter (Milly), Jean-Pierre Aumont (Franz Legendre), Austin Pendleton (Willy Kunst), Charlotte De Turckheim (Judith Mark), Josh Hamilton (William O'Hara). Directed by Ismail Merchant and produced by Humbert Balsan and Donald Rosenfeld. Screenplay by Jean-Marie Besset and George Trow.

*The Proprietor* is an astoundingly bad movie. I could hardly believe my eyes. Or my ears, or my memory. In its attempt to tell the story of the life of a legendary French woman (perhaps, we gather, the greatest since Joan of Arc), it steps so wrong, so often, that even casting Jeanne Moreau is of no avail. If anyone can play the greatest French novelist of modern times, it is she, but not here.

Moreau plays Adrienne Mark, formerly Markowsky, a French Jewish writer whose 1960 novel, modestly titled *My Name Is France,* was an intellectual, artistic, social, publishing, and paper-manufacturing landmark. It was made into a great French film and remade into a bad Hollywood film *(Call Me French),* and now she lives in New York in an apartment filled with her memories.

But she wants to return to Paris after thirty years, and buy the apartment she was raised in as a child. Clumsy flashbacks show that her mother was betrayed to the Nazis by a rich lover after putting the apartment in the lover's name to keep it from being taken over. Now Adrienne fantasies Nazis everywhere: Even her doorman seems to have a swastika on his sleeve. Adrienne's best friend is her faithful black maid, Milly (Nell Carter), who tsks-tsks her and breaks into song (she used to sing backup for Wilson Pickett).

Adrienne hires an auctioneer to assess the contents of her apartment (Sam Waterston is the victim of this role). Meanwhile, a handsome young man (Josh Hamilton) sees her at an opening, falls instantly in love, and follows her around like a puppy with a video camera. (The movie seems to have been written by a puppy with a typewriter.) Adrienne goes to Paris to bid on the apartment, and the young man, having won a contest for a Slurpy Peaches promotional film, pursues her to Paris, declares his love, and gets as his only reward a chaste kiss on the forehead, to our immense relief.

Oh, and then Adrienne's son turns up with a Hollywood producer (Sean Young), a cheerful vulgarian who tells her, "You changed demographics forever!" Young seems to think she is in another movie, which is an excellent strategy. She and the son kiss, a fountain erupts, and the son sings "If I Didn't Care" in the Ink Spots arrangement while splashing about in the pool. Yes.

More flashbacks. Adrienne accidentally knocks a hole in the wall while hanging pictures, and finds a cache of her mother's letters, indicating that maybe the mother's lover did not betray her to the Nazis. It is suggested that the mother offered to turn in other Jews to save herself, but the lover wouldn't let her. Or maybe not. It is all very murky. Eventually the mother appears in a fantasy, but only dances with her daughter, alas, instead of explaining anything.

There is more. The returned novelist is hailed as a national heroine and appears on opening night of the Cannes Film Festival while commentators breathlessly describe France in ecstasy. These scenes were actually shot at the Cannes Film Festival, where the real Moreau, of course, got an ecstatic ovation. They are realistic except for one detail: Why would the author of *My Name Is France,* the greatest cultural figure of her century, choose John Waters as her escort? I'm as big a fan of *Pink Flamingos* and *Polyester* as anybody, but still . . .

*The Proprietor* is such a mess that when it was over I was still not sure who the proprietor was. I think maybe the title refers to Adrienne's return to her old apartment, in which case the title should have been *The Occupant,* which may have been where the screenplay was originally addressed.

## Public Housing ★ ★ ★ ★

NO MPAA RATING, 210 m., 1997

A documentary by Frederick Wiseman.

If I told you I've seen a documentary about public housing in Chicago, you might immediately assume it shows poverty, illiteracy, welfare, drugs, and crime. If I told you that the documentary had moved me almost to tears with the kindness, courage, tenacity, and hope that it displayed, you might wonder what miracle the filmmaker had witnessed—or evoked. But all Frederick Wiseman has done is point his camera, and look and listen.

His new film *Public Housing,* is the record of a lot of time spent among the residents of the Ida B. Wells homes on the South Side. These are poor people, mostly unemployed, one step from homelessness, preparing for the coming changes in the welfare system.

Watching the film, I came to the uneasy conclusion that the Chicago Housing Authority bureaucracy is a pyramid of jobholders balanced precariously on the backs of the poor. Residents speak helplessly of the steps necessary to get anything done. There's a woman who needs an ink cartridge for a copying machine: Her request has to go through four levels of authorization to be approved. Then it has to be put out for three bids. Then the lowest bid has to go through an approval process. "I finally went out and just bought the thing myself," she says.

Yet many of the people involved at ground level in the system, including maintenance men, residents, volunteers, social workers, and police officers, are so generous and patient in their efforts that their everyday lives take on a sort of quiet heroism.

Yes, heroism. The news is filled with stories about bad cops. But look at the cops in *Public Housing.* Two stand for fifteen minutes on a street corner with a young woman who is apparently involved in the drug business. They find no drugs, but they, and eventually we, can see what's up. Finally one cop tells her: "Six months from now you're gonna have all your teeth broken out, and your eyeball hanging down on your cheek. You still got a life ahead of you. You can beat these drugs. I'm gonna remember you. You're gonna be my special project. Every time I see you I'm gonna pull over."

Then there are two other cops, evicting an old man who is being sent to a nursing home. Look at their tenderness. The old man is surrounded by the scant remains of a lifetime. One cop sighs and shakes open a brown paper bag, and begins to fill it with canned goods.

There's an exterminator, patiently giving a woman tips on how to catch bugs off guard. A plumber, fixing a leaking drain and obviously concerned about a young man who seems to wander through an old woman's apartment at will. A police captain, talking quietly with a man who owes $80 to drug dealers; they both know the man will be beaten later that night. "Have you got any relatives you could go to?" the cop asks. And, "Well, your wife hung in there for a while, huh?"

There is a woman named Helen Finner, who has been president of the Ida B. Wells Resident's Association for twenty years, and who works the phone in her office while a sad young girl sits huddled in a blanket. "You have 200 vacancies waiting for somebody to move into them, and you have mothers with children, homeless, sitting around in the lobby of the hospital, who can't find a place to spend the night," she says into the phone. "If I haven't heard from (you) by one o'clock Monday, then I'm gonna call down there and act crazy."

There are meetings. The Men of Wells sit behind folding tables and discuss commitments for volunteer work. A teacher from a junior college explains ways residents can qualify for funds to start small businesses. There's a meeting about the Child Family Preservation Center, and the speaker tells a story I will not forget. She has just seen a young mother's children taken away from her in court. When her own mother tries to comfort her, the younger woman tells her frankly, "If they had taken me away from you, I wouldn't be here today."

And on and on. Frederick Wiseman has spent his lifetime filming the institutions of society: hospitals, high schools, mental homes, even a monastery. He doesn't bring an attitude to his work. He visits, looks, and listens. To watch his films is to spend some time in the lives of other people.

Those who do not live in public housing have a lot of ideas about those who do. Most of them are formed by crime reports in the news. What you see in *Public Housing* is a neighborhood with many people, some bad, some devastated by drugs, yes—but most just sincerely trying to get by, live right, improve themselves, and stick together. If you were in big trouble, these might be neighbors you would be happy to have.

## Purple Noon ★ ★ ★

PG-13, 119 m., 1960 (rereleased 1996)

Alain Delon (Tom Ripley), Marie Laforet (Marge), Maurice Ronet (Phillippe Greenleaf), Bill Kearns (Freddy Miles), Erno Crisa (Inspector Riccordi), Frank Latimore (O'Brien), Ave Ninchi (Gianna), Viviane Chantel (Belgian Tourist). Directed by Rene Clement and produced by Robert Hakim and Raymond Hakim. Screenplay by Clement and Paul Gegauff, based on the novel *The Talented Mr. Ripley* by Patricia Highsmith.

If you've read Patricia Highsmith's novels about Tom Ripley, you know they can make your skin crawl. Ripley is a criminal of intelligence and cunning who gets away with murder. He is charming and literate, and a monster. It's insidious, the way Highsmith seduces us into identifying with him and sharing his selfishness; Ripley believes that getting his own way is worth whatever price anyone else might have to pay.

*The Talented Mr. Ripley* was the first of the Ripley novels, published in the 1950s when Highsmith was already famous for writing *Strangers on a Train,* adapted by Hitchcock into one of his best films. In both stories, one man is strongly attracted to another one and expresses his obsession through crime. Although it is never directly stated, there is obviously a buried level of homoerotic attraction; the criminal in both stories essentially wants to become the other man.

*Purple Noon* is Rene Clement's 1960 French adaptation of the first Ripley novel, starring a young Alain Delon as Ripley, a man who is just learning that he can get away with almost anything. As the film opens, Ripley has been sent to Rome to find his longtime friend Phillippe (Maurice Ronet), a rich playboy whose parents want him to return to San Francisco. Ripley is in no hurry to return to the States, and enjoys letting Phillippe introduce him to the sweet life. (The movie's opening scenes are on Rome's Via Veneto, immortalized just a year earlier by Fellini's *La Dolce Vita,* and Nino Rota composed the music for both films.)

Phillippe is dating Marge (Marie Laforet). Soon Tom Ripley wants to be dating Marge, too, and there is an odd little scene when he dresses in Phillippe's clothes and kisses the mirror in Phillippe's bedroom, whispering as if he were Phillippe, "My Marge knows I love her and won't go with that nasty Tom to San Francisco." The three begin to travel around Italy, and the men at one point strand Marge while they fly back to Rome for drinks and womanizing.

Eventually they all end up on a boat, sailing toward Sicily, and by now it is fairly clear that Marge is superfluous, and that the two men, unable to acknowledge their erotic attraction, are growing hostile. Ripley overhears Phillippe's plans for putting him ashore. Phillippe mistreats Ripley, to see how much he'll put up with. Ripley moves on Marge. Phillippe banishes Ripley to a rowboat, and while Marge and Phillippe make love the tow-rope splits and Ripley is marooned alone in the ocean, the sun blistering his skin. Ripley is rescued. Marge is put ashore.

And then—read no further if you'd rather not know—there is a scuffle and Ripley kills Phillippe and disposes of his body—safely, so he thinks. All of these events are essentially just the setup for the real story, which is about how Ripley, improvising brilliantly, plans to get away with the murder and win not only Phillippe's fortune but even Marge.

The fascination in Highsmith's Ripley novels resides in the way Ripley gets away with his crimes. In most of them, his advance planning is meticulous; only in this first adventure does he have crime thrust upon him. Ripley in the later novels has become a committed hedonist, devoted to great comfort, understated taste, and civilized interests. He has wonderful relationships with women, who never fully understand who or what he is. He has friendships—real ones—with many of his victims. His crimes are like moves in a chess game; he understands that as much as he may like and respect his opponents, he must end with a checkmate. The best thing about the film is the way the plot devises a way for Ripley to create a perfect cover-up, a substitution of bodies (for which a second corpse comes in handy). Ripley's meticulous timing, quick thinking, and brilliant invention snatch victory out of the hands of danger.

When he made it, Rene Clement may have been inspired by Clouzot's *Diabolique* (1955), another famous story of devious plotting and double-crossing. The films have certain similarities. *Diabolique*'s two women have unexpressed lesbian feelings, just as *Purple Noon*'s men suppress their homosexuality. Both stories involve drowned corpses that do, or do not, appear or disappear on demand. And both have less-than-satisfactory endings. *Diabolique* can end as it does only because the police inspector doesn't act on all of the knowledge he has. And *Purple Noon* ends as it does only because Clement doesn't have Highsmith's iron nerve. Do you want to know if Ripley finally gets caught? All I will tell you is that there were more Ripley novels than you would expect on the basis of this movie's ending.

# Q

## Quest for Camelot ★ ★

G, 83 m., 1998

With the voices of: Jessalyn Gilsig (Kayley), Andrea Corr (Kayley Singing), Cary Elwes (Garrett), Bryan White (Garrett Singing), Gary Oldman (Ruber), Eric Idle (Devon), Don Rickles (Cornwall), Jane Seymour (Juliana), Celine Dion (Juliana Singing). Directed by Frederik Du Chau and produced by Dalisa Cooper Cohen. Screenplay by Kirk De Micco, William Schifrin, Jacqueline Feather, and David Seidler, based on the novel *The King's Damosel* by Vera Chapman.

*Quest for Camelot* is still another big-studio attempt to wrest the crown of family animation away from Disney. It's from Warner Bros., which scored with the bright and amusing *Space Jam*, but now seems to fall back into the pack of Disney wannabes. The animation isn't vivid, the characters aren't very interesting, and the songs are routine.

*Space Jam* and Fox's *Anastasia* are the only recent non-Disney features to steal some of the magic from Walt's heirs. Since *Quest for Camelot* cost a rumored $100 million and yet lacks the sparkle of a *Beauty and the Beast*, perhaps it's time for Warners to explore a different approach—perhaps animation aimed at the teenage and adult market, which does so well in Japan.

*Quest for Camelot*, like so many animated features, is a template into which superficially new characters are plugged. We need a young hero, and get one in Kayley, the brave teenage daughter of Lionel, one of Arthur's knights. Lionel, of course, is killed in an early scene while defending Arthur, because the heroes of animated films must always lack at least one parent (later, Kayley's mother is conveniently kidnapped).

We also need—let's see, a villain (Ruber, the evil and jealous knight), a villain's cruel sidekick (the wicked griffin), and a villain's good-hearted sidekick (Bladebeak the chicken). We need a young man to help the heroine on her quest (Garrett, the blind forest dweller), a hero's noble friend (a silver-winged falcon), and the hero's low comedy team (Devon and Cornwall, the two-headed dragon). Then have Ruber steal the magic sword Excaliber, and have Kayley and Garrett try to recapture it, throw in some songs and a lot of animated action, and you have your movie.

I'm not putting the formula down. Done well, it can work, and some version of these ingredients now seems to be required in all feature-length animated films. But *Quest for Camelot* does a fuzzy job of clearly introducing and establishing its characters, and makes them types, not individuals. Their personalities aren't helped by the awkward handling of dialogue; in some of the long shots, we can't tell who's supposed to be speaking, and the animated lip synch is unconvincing. Another problem is the way the songs begin and end abruptly; we miss the wind-up before a song and the segue back into spoken dialogue. The movie just doesn't seem sure of itself.

Will kids like it? I dunno. I saw it with a theater filled with kids, and didn't hear or sense the kind of enthusiasm that good animation can inspire. The two-headed dragon gets some laughs with an Elvis imitation. But there's a running joke in which one head is always trying to smooch the other one, and the kids didn't seem sure why they were supposed to laugh. There's also the problem that Ruber is simply a one-dimensional bad guy, with no intriguing personality quirks or weaknesses; he pales beside Rasputin in *Anastasia* or Scar in *The Lion King*.

Of the supporting animals, the falcon has no particular personality, and Bladebeak is a character in search of a purpose. Even the vast, monstrous dragon that ends up with Excaliber (as a toothpick) is a disappointment. When the heroes find him in a cave, he doesn't exude much menace or personality; he's just a big prop.

The most interesting character is Garrett, who (we learn) was rejected from Camelot because he was blind, and now lives in the forest with the falcon. "I stand alone," he sings, but his friendship with Kayley is the only meaningful one in the movie. It's also curious that the plants in his forest are more interesting than most of the animals. There are eyeball plants that snap at people, and helicopter plants that give free rides (more could have been made of these), and plants that snap at ankles and elbows.

Really good animation can be exhilarating; I remember the "Under the Sea" sequence from

*The Little Mermaid,* and "Be Our Guest" from *Beauty and the Beast.* In *Quest for Camelot* there are no sequences that take off and soar, and no rules to give shape to the action scenes (if Excaliber is really all-powerful, how is its power exercised, and why can its bearer be defeated?). The movie's underlying formula is so familiar that there's no use bothering with a retread unless you have compelling characters and good songs. Enormous resources went into the making of this film, but why wasn't there more stretching and creativity at the screenplay level? Why work so hard on the animation and run the plot on autopilot?

## Race the Sun ★ ½

PG, 105 m., 1996

Halle Berry (Sandra Beecher), James Belushi (Frank Machi), Bill Hunter (Commissioner Hawkes), Casey Affleck (Daniel Webster), Eliza Dushku (Cindy Johnson), Kevin Tighe (Jack Fryman), Anthony Ruivivar (Eduardo Braz). Directed by Charles T. Kanganis and produced by Richard Heus and Barry Morrow. Screenplay by Morrow.

I have no doubt that a group of brilliant students from Konaweana High School on the Big Island of Hawaii built a solar-powered car that distinguished itself in a six-day race across Australia in 1990. What amazes me is that their real-life experiences inspired a movie that is exactly like every other movie about plucky underdogs who prevail against the rich and powerful.

*Race the Sun* tells the story of a group of science students who design, build, and race a solar car inspired by the aerodynamics of a cockroach. About how their new teacher (Halle Berry) believes in them, even though a veteran teacher (James Belushi) thinks they're quitters. About how a shy fat kid gets the confidence to drive the car. About how a troubled girl learns to face her problems. And about how a rich corporate sponsor of the race does all he can to make the team lose.

All of these ingredients are recycled out of countless other movies, such as the one about the plucky Jamaican bobsled team, or the plucky Texas soccer team, or the plucky California hockey team. Even the villains in these movies are standard: They always have expensive equipment and a snotty leader, and their team color is always black. This time, the enemy (it almost goes without saying) is the German team, complete with a driver named Hans who is insulting and supercilious. (I kinda liked the one where the villains were from Iceland: That was an original touch. God forbid the villains would be anything but whites from a rich country.)

But let's not get too worked up here. *Race the Sun* is nothing if not ambitious to please—a pleasant, unchallenging, predictable formula film about a bunch of kids who build a car out of a pile of junk and enter it in the big race. The film's only real problem is how to create suspense out of its mundane materials.

It tries hard. On the first day of school, when Halle Berry enters the teacher's lounge filled with hopes and plans for the new year, Belushi jumps all over her. He's a veteran teacher, you see, and knows these kids can't be expected to achieve anything. It might have helped Belushi if the script had given him a more gentle curve—had allowed him to build up to his peak of negativity. But time is at a premium since Belushi has to do a U-turn and become a good guy by the end of the movie.

Building the solar car proceeds along lines laid down years ago in all those movies about the Soap Box Derby. I was waiting for one scene in particular, and yep, the movie didn't disappoint me: When a car is taken for a trial run, it falls to pieces. Literally. It breaks down and parts fall off. This is not possible in the real world, since such cars are not held together by spit. It takes a lot of clever prop work to build a car that falls to pieces, but movies like this always have one.

Once the kids build the car and get to Australia, we get the plot by the rich (white) corporate sponsors to sabotage them. In the real world, of course, a corporate sponsor would like nothing better than to back a car by a bunch of high school science students, but *Race the Sun* has been blinded by movie clichés about monolithic corporate villains. *Race the Sun*'s real ambition is not to win the race but to be a Michael Crichton movie.

Now to the race. Of course there are setbacks along the way, as the evil Germans race ahead with their expensive technology. One scene I especially noticed, however, had a young team member running beside the car, shouting "Go! Go!" and "You can do it!" to the driver. Since at this point the speed of the car is determined only by the solar batteries and gravity, the driver is essentially a passenger, and it is hard to see how encouragement is going to help him.

Am I being too hard on the movie? Probably. But as I said up top, I'm sure there really was a team like this from Konaweana High School in 1990, and what they achieved might have made a good movie. Too bad they decided to substitute exhausted old clichés.

## The Rainmaker ★ ★ ★

PG-13, 137 m., 1997

Matt Damon (Rudy Baylor), Danny DeVito (Deck Shifflet), Claire Danes (Kelly Riker), Jon Voight (Leo F. Drummond), Mary Kay Place (Dot Black), Teresa Wright (Miss Birdie), Mickey Rourke (Bruiser Stone), Danny Glover (Judge Tyrone Kipler), Virginia Madsen (Jackie Lemanczyk), Red West (Buddy Black), Johnny Whitworth (Donny Ray), Dean Stockwell (Judge Hale). Directed by Francis Ford Coppola and produced by Michael Douglas, Steven Reuther, and Fred Fuchs. Screenplay by Coppola and Michael Herr, based on the novel by John Grisham.

Rudy Baylor, the hero of *The Rainmaker,* works the other end of the scale from the legal superpowers in most of John Grisham's stories. He's a poor kid who has scraped through law school by the skin of his teeth, is living in his car as the film begins, and signs on with a firm where most of the work is done by a paralegal, and the boss wears the kinds of cufflinks you can get rid of in a hurry at a pawn shop.

Francis Ford Coppola, who wrote and directed the film, has made the most of Grisham's ground-level realism. This is not a film that loves the legal profession, and yet it loves some of those who labor in it—not only Baylor, played by Matt Damon with the earnestness of an Eagle Scout, but also Deck Shifflet (Danny DeVito), the kind of courthouse handyman who has never passed the bar exam, perhaps because a license would slow him down. Their give-and-take is the soul of the film; they form a desperate democracy made possible because *The Rainmaker,* unlike most Grisham films, doesn't have to drag a high-paid superstar around and give him all the best lines. DeVito's role is in the fading tradition of the star character actor.

The movie takes place in Tennessee, where Baylor has just graduated from a second-rate law school, and goes to work for Bruiser Stone (Mickey Rourke), a flashy fraud with charm where his morals should be. The law is closing in on Bruiser. Deck Shifflet sees the end coming and convinces Rudy to open a storefront office, with Deck as the legman who knows all the ropes. (Deck's credo: "A lawyer should fight for his client, refrain from stealing money, and try to tell the truth.") One of Baylor's first clients is Miss Birdie (Teresa Wright), a sweet old lady who plans to leave her money to a TV preacher ("he needs it for his airplane"), and who rents Rudy a cheap apartment. She doesn't actually have much money, but Rudy observes that her son treats her better after being told she does.

Soon Baylor and Shifflet are involved in trickier cases. One involves Kelly Riker (Claire Danes), whose husband plays softball and likes to practice his swing on her. The other involves Dot and Buddy Black (Mary Kay Place and Red West), whose son Donny Ray (Johnny Whitworth) is dying of cancer and has been refused treatment by his insurance company.

Coppola juggles these three cases with side stories involving the insurance company's amoral, high-paid lawyer (Jon Voight) and the continuing threat to Kelly from her husband. Along the way, Rudy finds it necessary to violate what he understands of legal ethics, particularly when he gets personally involved with Kelly and she convinces him there is only one right thing to do in a desperate situation.

Kelly and Rudy don't have a romance, exactly; Coppola's screenplay is too smart to stop the action for obligatory love scenes, and Rudy's legal life has become so complex that there's no time for personal matters. Hey, he hasn't even had time to be sworn in—a service the judge (Dean Stockwell) obligingly performs before his first case. The DeVito character is like a wise, profane little shadow, stage-managing his court appearances and finding the crucial evidence.

Coppola assigns Michael Herr, one of his screenwriters on *Apocalypse Now* (1979), to write a narration that casts all of these events in a jaundiced light; Rudy Baylor's tone throughout is that of a man who has drifted into a profession that makes his skin crawl. Much is made of the hourly billing rates of the insurance company's lawyers, and Voight does a quietly masterful job of being elegantly sleazy. One strong scene is blindsided by a woman (Virginia Madsen) who knows more about the inner workings of the insurance company than perhaps she should.

I have enjoyed several of the movies based on Grisham novels *(A Time to Kill, The Pelican Brief, The Firm),* but I've usually seen the storyteller's craft rather than the novelist's art being reflected. Coppola says he picked up *The Rainmaker* in an airport, was intrigued by the story, and asked to direct it. What attracted him, I imagine, was the richness of the supporting characters: Miss Birdie, Deck, Bruiser, Kelly, and the scorned woman from the insurance company. The gallery is so colorful this could almost be a movie based on a Carl Hiassen story. By keeping all of the little people in focus, Coppola shows the variety of a young lawyer's life, where every client is necessary and most of them need a lot more than a lawyer.

## Ransom ★ ★ ★

R, 121 m., 1996

Mel Gibson (Tom Mullen), Rene Russo (Kate Mullen), Brawley Nolte (Sean Mullen), Gary Sinise (Jimmy Shaker), Delroy Lindo (Agent Lonnie Hawkins), Lili Taylor (Maris Connor), Liev Schreiber (Clark Barnes), Donnie Wahlberg (Cubby Barnes). Directed by Ron Howard and produced by Scott Rudin, Brian Grazer, and B. Kipling Hagopian. Screenplay by Richard Price and Alexander Ignon, based on a story by Cyril Hume and Richard Maibaum.

*Ransom* is a smarter-than-usual kidnapping thriller, starring Mel Gibson as an airline owner whose child is kidnapped, and who tries to outsmart the kidnappers with a risky plan that might work, or might lead to the loss of his child. Everything depends on his hunch that the child is doomed anyway—unless his desperate scheme pays off.

Gibson plays a former fighter pilot who has built up an airline from scratch, and is now under investigation for bribing union officials. He lives with his wife (Rene Russo) on Central Park, where they take their young son (Brawley Nolte) to a science fair. The boy is kidnapped, a ransom note arrives by anonymous e-mail, and the FBI is called even though, as Gibson observes, "The FBI just spent three months trying to bury us."

The movie makes little mystery about the identity of the kidnappers; we need to know who they are in order to appreciate the cat-and-mouse game that takes place. The gang is masterminded by Gary Sinise, a crooked police detective, and includes his girlfriend (Lili Taylor), who once worked for Gibson and knows the family's routine. Other members include a computer whiz and a couple of low-life thugs.

The FBI kidnapping expert (Delroy Lindo) wants Gibson to pay the ransom. He tries to, but an FBI helicopter interrupts the ransom drop, and Gibson becomes convinced (by the look in a gang member's eyes) that the kidnappers have no plans to return the child alive. That's when he devises his daring plan, which horrifies his wife and angers the FBI, but puts the ball squarely in Sinise's court.

Instead of developing this material along pure thriller lines, *Ransom* also involves intriguing side issues. It's clear, for example, that Gibson *did* bribe a union official (who becomes one of the kidnapping suspects). At one point, talking to Sinise, he asks the question that eventually occurs to everyone in such a situation: Why me? "Because you buy your way out of trouble," Sinise tells him. "You're a payer. You did it once, and now you're gonna do it again."

The movie spends a lot of time examining the dynamics inside the kidnap gang, but there's the feeling that scenes have been dropped that might have made things clearer. When Sinise and Lili Taylor confront each other at the end of the film, for example, we would have liked to know more about the real nature of their relationship.

The screenplay, by Richard Price and Alexander Ignon (based on the 1956 Glenn Ford movie of the same name), also hints at depths of Gibson's character: He's a self-made man with a temper, who needs to control it in order to win. But the movie sets up more elements than it deals with.

And a final scene—the closing confrontation between Gibson and Sinise—has the potential to be more clever and suspenseful than it is. The director, Ron Howard, obviously has a notion of how to handle the material, but somehow the timing and the logic are off. Without giving away the situation, I'll point out that Gibson's moment of realization is hammered too hard (there are too many close-ups of narrowing eyes), and the charade inside a bank has ironic promise, but could have been great and is only adequate.

Still, Gibson gives an interesting performance, showing a man trying to think his way out of a crisis, and Sinise makes a good foil: Here are two smart men playing a game with deadly stakes. (The plot evokes Kurosawa's great 1962 film *High and Low*, based on an Ed McBain novel about kidnappers who think they have a millionaire's son—but have mistakenly kidnapped the son of his chauffeur.)

Howard is a director who specializes in movies about tension within large groups of people (his credits include *Backdraft, Apollo 13,* and *The Paper*). Here again he chooses a large canvas and fills it with a lot of characters. The movie would have benefited from a tight rewrite (it is too ambitious in including plot threads it doesn't have time to deal with), but Gibson's strong central performance speeds it along.

## The Real Blonde ★ ★ ★

R, 107 m., 1998

Matthew Modine (Joe), Catherine Keener (Mary), Daryl Hannah (Kelly), Maxwell Caulfield (Bob), Elizabeth Berkley (Tina), Marlo Thomas (Blair), Bridgette Wilson (Sahara), Buck Henry (Dr. Leuter), Christopher Lloyd (Ernst), Denis Leary (Doug), Kathleen Turner (Dee Dee). Directed by Tom DiCillo and produced by Marcus Viscidi and Tom Rosenberg. Screenplay by DiCillo.

Tom DiCillo's *The Real Blonde* is a meandering movie that usually meanders in entertaining directions. It has too many characters and not much of a plot, but that didn't bother me while I was watching it. It's a sketchbook in which the director observes certain types he seems familiar with. A lot of them are actors and models, who are understandably confused because they don't know if they're being paid to be someone else, or just because of who they are.

The central couple are Joe (Matthew Modine) and Mary (Catherine Keener), who have been together so long they feel they should either break up or get married. Not that it isn't working the way it is, but they feel embarrassed, somehow, by not having chosen one path or the other. Joe is an actor with such high standards that he never works. Mary is a makeup artist in the fashion industry, skilled at calming restless models before they go in front of the camera.

The movie proceeds as a sort of tag game, as each new character introduces other ones. Through Mary we meet a famous photographer (Marlo Thomas) and an insecure model named Sahara (Bridgette Wilson). Through Joe we meet the punctilious caterer (Christopher Lloyd) he works for, and Joe's best friend Bob (Maxwell Caulfield), a soap opera actor obsessed with dating a real blonde. And then through Bob we meet a real blonde named Kelly (Daryl Hannah) and, full circle, Bob also meets Sahara.

Meanwhile, Mary's therapist (Buck Henry) leads her to discover a self-defense instructor (Denis Leary), while Joe's agent (Kathleen Turner) gets him a job in a Madonna video directed by Steve Buscemi, where he meets Madonna's body double (Elizabeth Berkley) and almost has an affair with her, while Mary is almost having an affair with the karate teacher.

You see what I mean. There are so many characters that none of them is really developed, except to a certain degree Joe and Mary. But the film isn't about psychological insight. It has about the same depth as many real relationships in the same circles, where ego and job demands fit right into the lifestyle: People meet and feel like they know one another because they share the same jargon and reference points. They flirt, talk, and dart away like mayflies who must mate before the end of the day—or the current shoot, whichever comes first.

DiCillo is a quixotic director, who began as a cinematographer for directors like Jim Jarmusch, and whose take is always a little skewed. His credits include the ambitious, oddball but not compelling *Johnny Suede* (an early Brad Pitt film); the satirical *Living in Oblivion,* about a cheap horror movie production; and *Box of Moonlight,* about a man who goes in search of... well, in search of something to go in search of.

Here he devises brief, sharply observed scenes. He notices, for example, the way a makeup artist makes up not only a model's face but also her attitude. The way the karate instructor, playing an aggressor, takes a sly pleasure in using sexist insults. The way people talk knowledgeably about movies they haven't seen. The way a guy who's embarrassed to be in a porno store will brazen it out. All of the actors are right for their roles, because a degree of typecasting has been done, but Daryl Hannah brings a particularly focused energy to the role of a soap opera actress who is not impressed that a guy is impressed by her. And Catherine Keener brings a kind of wry wit to her character; she sees models in billboards on Times Square and knows what it took to get them there.

The film's opening titles are a visual tease: We see parts of two torsos, gradually revealed, like shards of a giant sculpture, until finally they resolve themselves into a blonde with a man who kneels to embrace her. Later in the film, we see the Marlo Thomas photographer taking that shot, and we learn the real story: The model, a European Fabio clone, is embarrassed because he "released the gas," as he puts it, and the model consoles him. Thus are legends born.

As for Joe and Mary, their threatened relationship and their temptations to stray: *The Real Blonde* is so much more adult in its attitudes than a shallow film like, say, *Kissing a Fool.* The characters are articulate enough to talk about what really moves them; they don't play sitcom games. DiCillo never puts two and two together, but somehow it all adds up.

## Red Corner ★ ★

R, 119 m., 1997

Richard Gere (Jack Moore), Bai Ling (Shen Yuelin), Bradley Whitford (Bob Ghery), Byron Mann (Lin Dan), Peter Donat (David McAndrews), Robert Stanton (Ed Pratt), Tsai Chin (Chairman Xu), James Hong (Lin Shou). Directed by Jon Avnet and produced by Avnet, Jordan Kerner, Charles B. Mulvehill, and Rosalie Swedlin. Screenplay by Robert King.

*Red Corner* is a contrived and cumbersome thriller designed to showcase Richard Gere's unhappiness with Red China, which it does with such thoroughness that story and characters are enveloped in the gloom. The Chinese do this better to themselves. Unlike such Chinese-made films as *The Blue Kite, To Live,* and *The Story of Qui Ju,* which criticize China with an insider's knowledge and detail, *Red Corner* plays like a xenophobic travelogue crossed with *Perry Mason.*

Gere plays an American TV executive with a bathetic life story, who has been reduced to wandering the globe, living in anonymous hotel rooms and selling syndicated TV programming that one character describes, probably overoptimistically, as "pornographic, violent, and superstitious" (sounds like *Xena* reruns to me). He meets a pretty girl in a bar, they go back to his hotel, and the next morning he's awakened by the police, who point out disapprovingly that the girl is dead and Gere is covered with her blood. Still worse, the dead girl is the daughter of an important general.

Gere protests his innocence, and, of course, we believe him, but if it's all a setup (a) did the girl volunteer to be killed, or (b) were the conspirators not clever enough to find a victim with less clout? No matter; Gere is soon inside the Chinese legal system, which is portrayed as biased, brutish, and slanted in favor of the prosecution.

He is assigned a lawyer (another pretty young woman, well played by Bai Ling), who advises him to plead guilty because, "It can be more easy if you confess your crime." Given the dead body and the blood, he might get similar advice in the United States, especially since his attorney sincerely believes he's guilty.

I have no doubt that the Chinese court system could use reform. It does, however, have the advantage of allowing the hero of a movie considerable latitude to cross-examine witnesses, spring surprise developments, and generally run the show from the defendant's box—even being able to return to the courtroom and pick up the reins after an escape attempt. Chinese courts also add the interesting touch of "people's assessors"—two ordinary citizens who flank the judge and can express their own opinions, speaking for the People. Amazing that so fiendish a conspiracy was not able to control them along with everyone else. Haven't they ever heard of jury-tampering in China?

There are billions to be made for whoever gets the license to sell pornography, violence, and superstition (not to mention ESPN) to the Chinese via satellite TV, and so perhaps Gere has been framed by his business competitors. Before the movie explores this possibility, we get scenes of Gere in solitary confinement, Gere having his glasses stepped on, Gere having his law books taken away, and a ludicrous scene in which he escapes from his guards in a chase down crowded alleyways and across rooftops. He was, as I recall, handcuffed during this chase. It must not be easy to outrun dozens of cops across rooftops while handcuffed.

He gains the safety of the U.S. Embassy, only to discover that his attorney gave her personal guarantee of his return, and will lose her license as a result. Rather than have this happen to her, he voluntarily returns to what looks like certain and quick execution. What a great guy. Then what happens is worthy of a *Perry Mason* showdown, involving secret photos inside lockets, surprise last-minute confessions, and suspicions about the odor of chloroform. Only the portentous music keeps this silliness earthbound.

Red China has indeed been guilty of human rights violations, the criminal mistreatment of Tibet, persecution of minority religions, and general surliness. What is interesting, as I mentioned, is that Red Chinese films have done a good job of portraying some of those evils (particularly the nightmare of the Cultural Revolution). To some degree, Richard Gere set himself up by appearing in this film; as an outspoken critic of China and follower of the Dalai Lama, he has a case to plead. It's surprising, then, that he chooses to do it so lamely in such a lugubrious movie.

## The Relic ★ ★ ★

R, 110 m., 1997

Penelope Ann Miller (Margo Green), Tom Sizemore (Lieutenant Vincent D'Agosta), Clayton Rohner (Hollingsworth), Linda Hunt (Ann Cuthbert), Chi-Muoi Lo (Greg Lee), James Whitmore (Dr. Frock), Audra Lindley (Coroner), Robert Lesser (Mayor Owen). Directed by Peter Hyams and produced by Gale Anne Hurd and Sam Mercer. Screenplay by Rick Jaffa, Amy Holden Jones, John Raffo, and Amanda Silver, based on the novel by Lincoln Child and Douglas Preston.

*The Relic* begins with a boiling cauldron deep in the Amazonian jungle, and includes not only a cat that leaps out and frightens someone but such other horror film standbys as kids locked into a museum after hours, a lucky bullet, a hard-boiled coroner who thinks she has seen everything (but is wrong), and the mayor of Chicago fleeing with socialites through waist-deep water in a tunnel linking the Field Museum of Natural History to Lake Michigan.

He is not simply fleeing, but being chased by a monster that decapitates its victims and chews a hole in their skulls to suck out their thalamus and pituitary glands. A monster, mind you, that has genes combining human, insect, and reptile DNA, and might be the product of an "evolutionary leap that causes grotesque and short-lived aberrant species." The species looks plenty aberrant to me: It's twice the size of a raptor, looks like a cross between a kangaroo and Godzilla, has teeth the size of fence pickets, and a long, red, forked tongue it uses to lick the face of the pretty young anthropologist.

Her name is Dr. Margo Green (Penelope Ann Miller). She works at the museum, where two large crates have arrived from a colleague in South America. Not long after, a security guard is found dead (decapitated, hole in skull, pituitary missing, etc.). The cop assigned to the case is Lieutenant D'Agosta (Tom Sizemore), who makes a quick link between this death and the mysterious case of a South American freighter found floating in Lake Michigan with a bilge full of corpses (all missing their pituitaries, etc.). When he discovers there is a tunnel from the lake to the museum, he asks ominously if it would be possible to enter the museum from the lake that way.

Why would a monster from a ship want to go to all that trouble? Maybe because one of the crates in the museum contains the leaves he likes to eat. Or maybe because the beast was in the crate with the leaves, escaped, and nailed the crate shut again, so people would think it was merely a crate of leaves. This is a clever monster. At one point, even though steel security doors have slammed down and isolated all parts of the museum from each other, the monster seems capable of simultaneously chasing the mayor and his friends down the tunnel, terrorizing scientists in the museum basement, and chewing up cops who are trying to attack it from the skylights. It gets around.

All of this is actually a lot of fun, if you like special effects and gore. To see this movie in the same week as the hapless and witless *Turbulence* is to understand how craft and professionalism can let us identify with one thriller heroine and laugh at another. Peter Hyams is a skillful action director, working here with the veteran "creature-effects" specialist Stan Winston and so many special-effects technicians that they could have played the entire sound track album under the end credits.

It's clever the way the movie combines the conventions of the horror and disaster genres. Although this is technically a science-fiction movie about a mutant monster, Hyams adds another level by having the mayor insist that a black-tie charity benefit proceed inside the museum as planned, even though the cops are convinced that it's not safe. After the steel doors slam shut, the sprinkler system drenches everyone, and decapitated bodies start dropping from above, the guests are in roughly the same predicament as in a disaster movie: trapped, in danger, and helpless to escape.

The level of horror and violence in *The Relic* is a notch or two above the industry average. There's a scary scene where a flaming monster pursues Dr. Green down a corridor of exploding specimen bottles. And a gory scene involving an autopsy, with Audra Lindley chillingly effective as the coroner. And scenes where cops get half their bodies chewed off, and a lot of scenes involving heads and brains, and lots of scientific double-talk to go with it. *The Relic* is not for younger viewers.

There are a few loose ends. Early in the film, Dr. Green tells Lieutenant D'Agosta about the tanks of chemicals they use to strip the flesh from rhino bones. Later in the film, she hides in such a tank herself, yet emerges with all her flesh. I am not sure what connection the monster has with the little red fungus pellets on the imported leaves. And there is the matter of the relic itself—a stone devil that was damaged in shipment. For most of the movie, a restoration expert is ominously piecing it back together, but I don't think the relic actually has anything to do with the man-lizard-insect creature.

I know Chicago mayor Richard M. Daley is a movie fan, and I imagine he will check out this one. He'll be disappointed by Robert Lesser as the mayor (instead of using a Chicago accent, he talks much like Al Pacino). But Daley might enjoy some of the other stuff, including city cops using acetylene torches to burn through the steel doors of the museum and rescue the terrified millionaires inside—proving Chicago is "the city that works." And he will reflect that in the real world, no Chicago mayor would ever be so reckless as to order a society benefit to proceed in a museum still being scoured for vicious decapitating pituitary-suckers. A guy gets his pituitary sucked out, he's not going to contribute to your next campaign.

## Rendezvous in Paris ★ ★ ★ ½

NO MPAA RATING, 100 m., 1996

Clara Bellar (Esther), Antoine Basler (Horace), Mathias Megard (The Flirt), Judith Chancel (Aricie), Aurore Rauscher (The Woman), Serge Renko (The Man), Michael Kraft (The Painter), Benedicte Loyen (The Young Woman), Veronika Johansson (The Swedish Woman). Directed by Eric Rohmer and produced by Francoise Etchegaray. Screenplay by Rohmer.

Paris is a city for lovers not because you can love better in it, but because you can walk and talk better in it. Lesser cities with fewer resources require their lovers to spend too much time loving, which tires and bores them, while in Paris the whole city is foreplay. It cannot be a coincidence that although we have the word "meeting" in English, we also borrow the French word "rendezvous." A rendezvous is to a meeting as a rose is to a postage stamp of a rose.

Eric Rohmer, who is now in his seventies, has dedicated most of his career to making films about men and women talking about love: the flirtations, the suggestions, the analysis, the philosophy, the quirks, the heartfelt outpourings, the startling revelations.

*Rendezvous in Paris,* which tells three stories in one film, is one of the best of his works. In it there are no sex scenes, and you could even make the case that there are no lovers—or two, at the most. Paris is such an inspiration for these characters that they *play* lovers even when their hearts aren't in it. Ideally, you should have your true love at your side for walking through the parks, sitting on benches, and having deep conversations. But if that is not possible, then you should annex whoever is available, and pretend.

In the first story, a girl (Clara Bellar) is told her boyfriend (Antoine Basler) is cheating on her—seeing another girl at times when he claims he is "busy." Walking through the market, she is approached by a stranger (Mathias Megard) who has become instantly attracted to her, but is on his way to the dentist. Can they meet later? Yes, she says—at the café where she's been told her boyfriend is having his secret rendezvous. The outcome of this story, which I will not reveal, is typical Rohmer in that she's wrong about both men—and wrong in two different ways about the second.

In the second story, a woman (Aurore Rauscher) leads her would-be suitor (Serge Renko) on a series of daily walks through Paris, while they talk and talk about love. She is in the process of breaking up with her former lover, and tells this new candidate with brutal frankness: "I used to love him more than I do you now, but I don't love him any more." Finally they have almost talked themselves into a position where they have to make love or stop talking. Then she discovers that her former lover has a new woman in his life. This makes her own new lover unnecessary, since only if the old lover still cared about her would he (and she) care about the new lover. The more you think about this logic the more French it becomes.

In the third story, an artist (Michael Kraft) has a visitor (Veronika Johansson) who bores him, so he suggests a visit to the nearby Picasso museum. At the museum, he notices a woman (Benedicte Loyen) looking at a painting. He explains the painting to his own date, loudly enough so the other woman can hear him, which is the point. (Someone once said that all female speech is explanation and all male speech is advertisement.) He succeeds in ridding himself of the first woman and catches up with the other woman in the street, only to discover she is on her honeymoon. But she asks to be shown his paintings, and in his studio their conversation takes a painfully analytical turn. In an exquisite twist, he is later stood up by the first woman.

Did you spot the two real lovers? They are the woman from the first story and the man she is told is cheating on her. Of all the dialogue in this film, they have the least. Is that the point? That talk is seduction and becomes redundant after it serves its purpose? I don't think Rohmer is that simple. I think he believes that love is love and that flirtatious conversation is an entirely separate pleasure, not to be confused with anything else.

What the people in *Rendezvous in Paris* are really saying, underneath all of their words, is: "I am not available. You are not available. But let us play at being available, because it is such a joy to use these words and tease with these possibilities, and so much fun to be actors playing lovers, since Paris provides the perfect set for our performance." Rohmer splendidly illustrates the theory that Parisians all possess two means of sexual intercourse, of which the primary one is the power of speech.

## The Replacement Killers ★ ★ ★

R, 88 m., 1998

Chow Yun-Fat (John Lee), Mira Sorvino (Meg Coburn), Michael Rooker (Stan "Zeedo" Zedkov), Kenneth Tsang (Terence Wei), Jurgen Prochnow (Michael Kogan), Til Schweiger (Ryker), Danny Trejo (Collins), Clifton Gonzalez Gonzalez (Loco). Directed by Antoine Fuqua and produced by Brad Grey and Bernie Brillstein. Screenplay by Ken Sanzel.

*The Replacement Killers* is all style. It's a high-gloss version of a Hong Kong action picture, made in America but observing the exuberance of a genre where surfaces are everything. The characters are as flat as figures on a billboard, but look at the way everything is filmed in saturated color, and anything that moves makes a metallic whooshing sound that ends in a musical chord, and how when the hero walks down a corridor at a car wash, it's done with a tilt and a zoom. In a movie like this, the story is simply a device to help us tell the beginning from the end.

The film is the American debut for Chow Yun-Fat, a popular star in Asia for twenty years and for the last ten a frequent collaborator with John Woo, the Hong Kong action wizard also now working in Hollywood (he produced this film). Chow is good-looking, open-faced, with a hint of sadness that reminded me of Charles Bronson in repose. Here he plays a Chinese immigrant to America, who owes a favor to the drug lord Terence Wei (Kenneth Tsang), whose son has been killed by a cop (Michael Rooker).

Chow's assignment: Kill someone important to the cop. But with the target framed in his telescopic sights, Chow just can't do it. "I went against Mr. Wei," he tells a wise Buddhist monk. "There will be consequences." He knows Wei will go after his mother and sister in Shanghai, and he needs a forged passport to fly home and protect them. That leads him to the lair of Meg Coburn (Mira Sorvino), a master forger whose first appearance is a good example of the movie's visual lushness: Leaning over her computer, she's in red lipstick and a low-cut dress in a hideaway that looks like a cross between Skid Row and a cosmetics ad.

Meg is a tough girl, played by Sorvino with a nice flat edge (while Chow's posing for his passport picture, she says "Smile, and say, 'Flight from prosecution.'"). She wants no part of his troubles, but soon they've teamed up as Wei throws squadrons of killers at them, including two "replacements" flown in to kill the cop's son.

In movies like this, everyone knows everyone.

Chow and Sorvino go into an amusement arcade, and she's hit on by a gold-toothed creep. Her reaction: "I try to stick to my own species." The creep of course is in the hire of Wei, and soon a gun battle rages through the arcade. Other elaborately choreographed shoot-outs take place in a car wash, and in a theater where the cop has taken his son for a cartoon festival (the gunfire is intercut with Mr. Magoo).

There's a moment in the recent *Desperate Measures* where violence erupts as a father tries to save the life of his son, and a cop asks, "How many people are gonna have to die here tonight so that kid of yours can live?" I had the same thought in *The Replacement Killers.* Because Chow spares Wei's target, approximately two dozen people die, or maybe more (in the dark it's hard to see what happens to all the Magoo fans).

What I liked about the film was its simplicity of form and its richness of visuals. There's a certain impersonality about the story; Chow and Sorvino don't have long chats between the gunfire. They're in a ballet of Hong Kong action imagery: bodies rolling out of gunshot range, faces frozen in fear, guys toppling off fire escapes, grim lips, the fetishism of firearms, cars shot to pieces, cops that make *Dragnet* sound talky. The first-time director, Antoine Fuqua, is a veteran of commercials and music videos; with cinematographer Peter Lyons Collister he gets a sensuous texture onto the screen that makes you feel the roughness of walls, the clamminess of skin, the coldness of guns. *The Replacement Killers* is as abstract as a jazz instrumental, and as cool and self-assured.

## Restoration ★ ★ ★ ½

R, 118 m., 1996

Robert Downey Jr. (Robert Merivel), Sam Neill (Charles II), David Thewlis (John Pearce), Polly Walker (Celia), Meg Ryan (Katherine), Sir Ian McKellen (Will Gates), Hugh Grant (Finn). Directed by Michael Hoffman and produced by Cary Brokaw, Andy Paterson, and Sarah Ryan Black. Screenplay by Rupert Walters.

Michael Hoffman's *Restoration* plunges us into the heart of seventeenth-century England and the court of Charles II, who followed the austere Cromwell years with a riotous time of sensual excess. The film has many virtues, but for me the most enchanting is simply the lust with which it depicts a bold and colorful era in history.

Never before in the movies have I seen such a riotous depiction of period London: the overwhelming excess of the royal court, the teeming traffic on the Thames, the bridges groaning with buildings and people, the streets jammed with life and lowlife, the delight in all the pleasures of the flesh—and then, like two grim wake-up calls, the Black Plague and the Great Fire. It is remarkable that this movie, which creates a world, cost only about $19 million and never seems to cut a corner; credit goes to production designer Eugenio Zanetti and costumer James Acheson.

Then there is the story itself, sometimes as rambunctious as *Tom Jones,* sometimes morbid and dour. The movie stars Robert Downey Jr. in a remarkable performance as Robert Merivel, a serious young physician who, in an opening scene, is seen solemnly palpitating the exposed heart of a patient who sits proudly (cheerfully, even) in an operating theater. Merivel is summoned away from his studies by the king (Sam Neill), and his first entry into the Stuart court is an astonishing progression through ornate decoration and the heedless display of excess.

The king is morose. His beloved Lulu is dying. Lulu, Merivel eventually discovers, is a spaniel. The young doctor cures the dog, more by luck than skill, and is appointed on the spot as physician to the king's dogs. He accepts, although it means abandoning his serious medical studies and the respect of his best friend, a Puritan named John Pearce (David Thewlis).

Life at the court in the 1660s is presided over by a king who can only be called the world's most committed amateur. He is a hobbyist at everything: He parades down avenues of architectural models, he peers through telescopes, he breeds animals, and he beds his extensive collection of mistresses. Finally the most spirited of them, Celia (Polly Walker), grows troublesome, and so the king determines to marry her off to Merivel. The deal is straightforward: The doctor gets the mistress, a knighthood, and a country estate in Suffolk, but no sex: "No intimacy!" the king warns. "You are a keeper!"

The wedding scene is one of unbridled excess; a lagoon is constructed, and Merivel's bride floats toward him on a vast horse while playing the lute. To see such a scene is to revel in the vulgarity. Merivel settles into the life of a country knight (aided by the advice of a servant cunningly played by Ian McKellan), and yet he is not happy, because of course he wants the one thing he cannot have, Celia. His passion leads to disgrace and banishment, and for much of the second half of the movie he is reduced to living in poverty with his friend Pearce.

These scenes teem with the same kind of life you experience in a Dickens novel. The plague has spread from Europe, the hospitals are bursting at their seams, the streets are filled with dead and dying, and the living walk through the city wearing fearsome beaked masks. They look like birds of prey, but the beaks are stuffed with herbs to fight the plague. It is at about this time that Merivel meets a wandering woman (Meg Ryan), who is said to be mad, but who provides a center for his life. (Ryan, who has played many kinds of scenes in her career, here definitively ups the ante in the childbirth sweepstakes by undergoing an unanesthetized Caesarian section.)

Some reviews of *Restoration* faulted it for trying to cram too much in. I don't see it that way. There may have been a temptation to limit the story to the private affairs of Robert Merivel, but I would not want to do without the plague and the Great Fire, which bring to vivid visual life the kinds of events described in Pepys's diary. The scope also gives room for the key emotional arc in the film, which is the maturation of Merivel, who grows up into a worthy man. (Even the king is older and wiser by the end.)

*Restoration* is based on a 1989 novel by Rose Tremain, unread by me, but my guess is she covers as much ground as the movie does, since her story is titled *Restoration* and not *Merivel.* What the film evokes is an age that must have been supremely *interesting* to live in. Sometimes I think that modern travel and communication have destroyed the mysteries by which we live. The people in this film occupy a world of unlimited choice, playing flamboyant roles, relishing in theatricality, mixing science with superstition, discovery with depravity. And by capturing that energy, *Restoration* avoids the pitfalls of pious historical reconstructions and plunges right into the cauldron.

## Return of the Jedi
(Special Edition) ★ ★ ★ ★
PG, 133 m., 1983 (rereleased 1997)

Mark Hamill (Luke Skywalker), Harrison Ford (Han Solo), Carrie Fisher (Princess Leia), Billy Dee Williams (Lando Calrissian), Anthony Daniels (C-3PO), Peter Mayhew (Chewbacca), Sebastian Shaw (Anakin Skywalker), Ian McDiarmid (Emperor). Directed by Richard Marquand and produced by Howard Kazanjian. Screenplay by Lawrence Kasdan and George Lucas, based on a story by Lucas.

*Return of the Jedi* completes the epic Star Wars cycle with the final destruction of the Empire and the inevitable face-off between Luke Skywalker and the evil Darth Vader, now revealed, as we surmised, to be his father. The film has a tone of its own. If *Star Wars* was a brash space opera and *The Empire Strikes Back* was a visual feast, *Return of the Jedi* is a riot of character invention. We get a good look at Jabba the Hutt and his court, we meet the fuzzy-wuzzy Ewoks, and we are confronted by two wonderfully loathsome creatures—the beast in the dungeon beneath Jabba's throne room, and the desert monster made of teeth and gullet.

If I had to choose, I would say this is the least of the Star Wars films. It lacks the startling originality of the first two: It's more concerned with loose ends and final resolutions. It was the correct decision for George Lucas to end with a trilogy and then move to another point in time for the continuation of the saga; to return to these characters a fourth time would destroy the mythic structure of the story and turn it simply into a series.

Still, there are inspired things here. The early scenes are dominated by Jabba the Hutt, whose cavern is populated with lots of small, obnoxious creatures in the corners, and with a grotesque intergalactic jazz band that seems to have been improvised along with its music. Secure in his lair, Jabba has Han Solo frozen in a sculpture on the wall, and eventually takes all of our heroes captive. His gurgling voice is wonderfully reprehensible, and he squats beneath his cavern ceiling like a stalagmite of slime. (It has been observed that Jabba seems much larger here than in *Star Wars.* Some say it is because he is on a platform, some say it is an optical illusion; I suggest that a hutt is a slug, and slugs continue to grow all of their lives.)

The monster in the dungeon, made of teeth and scales, is the embodiment of disgusting aggression, and yet its death provides one of the movie's finest moments. The creature is crushed beneath a heavy door, and then we see its keeper come forward, weeping to have lost his pet. It's a throwaway moment, but typical of the film's richness.

An extended sequence takes place in the desert, where Jabba's hovercraft positions itself over the creature in the sand, which seems to consist primarily of a large digestive system. He intends to force his captives to walk the plank, but the tables are nicely turned. I have always felt Lucas lost an opportunity here; since Jabba obviously must die at some point, why not feed him to the sand thing? I can envision the hutt's globular body slithering along the plank and plopping down into the big open mouth—and then being spit up again, as too unsavory even for this eating machine. Final shot: Green gooey Jabba-stuff dissolving in the monster's digestive juices under a pitiless sun.

The Ewoks (never referred to by name in the film) are as cute as stuffed animals, and bring a kind of innocence to the Forest Moon, where the power station for the orbiting Death Star is located. Their forest provides the location for the movie's most inexplicable sequences, in which characters chase each other on high-speed hover-scooters. As you know if you have seen the film (and *USA Today* assures us the average American has seen it several times), bad guys regularly get wiped out by running their scooters into trees. Question: Isn't a thickly forested area the wrong venue for these vehicles? How about flying above the treetops, where there's nothing to run into?

This third movie lacks the resonance that Obi-Wan and Yoda brought to the second one (they make cameo appearances, but are not major players). We see a great deal more, however, of Darth and the Emperor, who looks uncannily like Death in *The Seventh Seal.* There is, of course, the climactic moment when Vader reveals his real face, allowing the character to become the first in movie history to be played by three actors (body by David Prowse, voice by James Earl Jones, face by Sebastian Shaw). By this third installment, I think, we've seen quite enough of the swordplay with laser beams, and those scenes could be shortened. The Sharper Image catalog, I see, is offering replicas of the lightsabers for $350 to $450—pricey, when you consider the original prop was a photoflash grip.

At the end of it all, after the three movies, we've taken an epic fantasy journey. George Lucas has in common with all great storytellers the ability to create a complete world; these films may spring from space opera, science fiction, and Saturday serials, but they are done so superbly that they transcend all genres, and become a reverberating place in our imaginations.

Thinking back over the three, I find that the most compelling characters are Darth Vader, Yoda, and Obi-Wan Kenobi. That is because their lives and thoughts are entirely focused on the Force. To the degree that characters have distance from the Force, they resonate less: Skywalker is important although boyishly shallow, and Princess Leia harbors treasured secrets, but Han Solo, for all his importance to the plot, is not very interesting as a person, and a little of Chewbacca, as observed earlier, goes a long way.

The droids, R2-D2 and C-3PO, play much the same role here as their originals did in the movie that inspired them, Kurosawa's *The Hidden Fortress.* They're a team, Laurel and Hardy or Vladimir and Estragon, linked together by fate and personality. The other characters—Lando, Jabba, the Grand Moff Tarkin, and the many walk-ons and bit players—function, in Eliot's words, to swell the progress of a scene or two.

At the end, what are we left with? Marvelous sights: the two Death Stars, the lumbering war machines on the snow planet, space warfare, the desert monster, buccaneering action. Marvelous sounds: the voices of Darth Vader, Jabba, and the chirpy little R2-D2. And an idea—the Force—that in encompassing everything may, perhaps, encompass nothing, and conceal another level above, or beneath. I'm guessing that will be the subject of the next trilogy.

## The Rich Man's Wife ★ ★ ½

R, 95 m., 1996

Halle Berry (Josie Potenza), Christopher McDonald (Tony Potenza), Clive Owen (Jack Golden), Peter Greene (Cole), Charles Hallahan (Dan Fredricks), Frankie Faison (Ron Lewis),

Clea Lewis (Nora Golden), Loyda Ramos (Grace). Directed by Amy Holden Jones and produced by Roger Birnbaum and Julie Bergman Sender. Screenplay by Jones.

I wish we could simply dispense with a review and handle things this way: You go see the movie, and then we'll sit down and have a long and very detailed talk. And you will try to explain to me how the last scene in the movie, the one that is supposed to provide the key, fits in with what has gone before.

Because I don't think it does. Or can. Or should. I suppose the final twist is some sort of attempt by the writer-director, Amy Holden Jones, to pull the same kind of trick on the audience that *The Usual Suspects* did. I don't pretend to fully understand that film, either, but I am at least prepared to give its plot the benefit of the doubt: I believe that close story analysis would not find any actual or absolute impossibilities.

With *The Rich Man's Wife,* what we are given is the twist without the twister or the twistee, if you see what I mean. (Don't for a moment fear I am going to give anything away, since in my current state I would be incapable of knowing what to give away, or how to do it.) The movie proceeds more or less satisfactorily for ninety-four minutes, and then in the last sixty seconds expects us to revise everything we thought we knew, or guessed, or figured out—just because of an arbitrary ending. That went against my grain. It wasn't playing fair. Not even fair by *The Usual Suspects* rules.

Here is the story as we have reason to believe it. A blustering, hard-drinking business executive named Tony (Christopher McDonald) is married to an attractive younger wife named Josie (Halle Berry). Worried about him, she persuades him to take a vacation in the woods, but when he's called back to town, she goes to a local bar to console herself, and soon her path crosses that of a man named Cole (Peter Greene).

He follows her home into the deep, dark woods. Her Jeep breaks down. He is there to help. He is threatening but ingratiating. He gathers that she is unhappy with her husband. Well, tonight she is. But when he says he'll fix things by killing Tony, she's horrified. Tony met her, Josie explains, when she was a confused seventeen-year-old runaway. He asked her to marry him on their first date. Yes, he drinks too much, and there are other problems, but she is still grateful to him and has hopes for their future.

Cole doesn't seem to hear her, and eventually the situation grows into a nightmare. Tony is killed. Josie is a suspect. There is more: Josie has been conducting an affair with Jake (Clive Owen), Tony's partner in a failing restaurant. Josie stands to inherit a lot of money—or does she? If she does, she'll bail out Jake—or will she? How much does Jake's wife, Nora (Clea Lewis), know? What about those compromising Polaroids of Josie and Jake that she delivers to the police? Can the police really believe Josie's story that Cole acted on his own?

And so on. This plot is not blindingly original; its elements are familiar from many other crime stories. But it does become intriguing, because the writing is good and the characters are original—especially two cops in key supporting roles, who argue over whether Josie is a suspect only because she's a black woman married to a white man. There are also amusing scenes involving Nora, who is played by Lewis as a ditzy goofball with a mind of her own.

Halle Berry is convincing, too, and I cared about her, especially as the plot began to turn against her. Was she innocent or guilty? Innocent, I thought, although maybe guilty if the evidence is looked at in a certain way. What I was not prepared for was the twist at the end, which doesn't seem to follow from anything that went before, and makes all of my speculation irrelevant.

Am I holding the ending against the entire movie? Yes, I suppose I am. *The Rich Man's Wife* is not a great movie but it's competent and effective enough, and I might have been tempted to give it a marginal recommendation if I hadn't felt so cheated at the end. Somehow a movie like this establishes a contract with us, an unspoken agreement that some things cannot be doubted even though others are up for grabs. When a few of the sure things turn out to be tricks, that's part of the fun. But when *everything* is smoke and mirrors, I walk out wondering, where is Keyser Soze when we really need him?

## Richard III ★ ★ ★ ½

R, 105 m., 1996

Ian McKellen (Richard III), Annette Bening (Queen Elizabeth), John Wood (King Edward),

Matthew Groom (Young Prince), Nigel Hawthorne (Clarence), Maggie Smith (Duchess of York), Robert Downey Jr. (Rivers), Kristin Scott Thomas (Lady Anne), Jim Broadbent (Buckingham). Directed by Richard Loncraine and produced by Lisa Katselas Pare and Stephen Bayly. Screenplay by Ian McKellen and Loncraine.

One of the most audacious proposals in all of literature occurs in Shakespeare's *Richard III,* when the misshapen Richard, who has caused the death of King Henry VI, proposes to his widow, Anne, as she accompanies the corpse of her husband through the streets. Here Shakespeare was collapsing events separated in time to underscore Richard's evil impudence. Of course, in the fifteenth century, royal marriages were more a matter of politics and strategy than of romance, and by the end of the scene Anne is actually considering his proposal.

Now look at a small touch added to the scene by *Richard III,* the new film by Richard Loncraine and Ian McKellen. Richard (McKellen) softens up Anne (Kristin Scott Thomas) with flattery, sophistry, and lies, and finally offers her a ring, which she accepts. All very well. But in this version, he first removes the ring from his own finger by sticking it in his mouth and lubricating it with saliva, so that as he slips it on her finger she cannot help but feel the spit of her husband's murderer.

That extra measure of repulsive detail scuttles through the entire film, making this *Richard III* not just a seductive telling of Shakespeare's story but also a perversely entertaining one. I've seen it twice, the second time with a large audience that chuckled the way people did during *The Silence of the Lambs;* Richard, like Hannibal Lector, is not only a reprehensible man, but a smart one, who is in on the joke. He relishes being a villain; it is his revenge on the world that twisted his body, his face, and his smile, and placed him below men who were better shaped to rule and love.

The movie, based on a London stage production that also starred McKellan, advances the action 500 years, to the 1930s, while keeping Shakespeare's words. The first ten minutes of the film set the stage almost without dialogue, as Richard shoots a rival and then addresses a political rally. When the famous opening lines arrive ("Now is the winter of our discontent"), we slip easily into the language. (More fiendishness: Richard begins his speech in public glory, and then concludes it in private, standing at a urinal, speaking directly to the camera, enlisting us in his scheme.)

The movie is set in the kind of England that might have resulted if Edward VIII, instead of abdicating, had been able to indulge his fascist fantasies, summon Oswald Mosley to lead a government, and lead his people into an accommodation with Hitler. Much of the popular appeal of Nazism grew out of the costumes, settings, and architecture of the Hitler cult, and in *Richard III* the men strut in black and red, in leather and tailored wool—their politics an expression of their fetishes. Many of the scenes are placed inside and outside a vast 1930s Art Deco power station, which looks like the set for an Ayn Rand wet dream.

And they smoke constantly. Of course, everyone smoked in the 1930s, but the smoking behavior in *Richard III* is particular: Richard's consciousness in many scenes seems to center on his cigarette, which he returns to obsessively, as if through its tube he is inhaling the venom that enables him to carry on. All of the others smoke, too—the women using cigarette holders and gloves to maintain a dainty distance between themselves and the poison they crave.

Richard's progress to the crown is hastened by a steady stream of murders, orchestrated with the aid of a couple of blank-faced hit men and the advice of the plump, sleek Buckingham (Jim Broadbent), who beams benignly over the slaughter and dreams of being paid off with a country estate. All of the deaths are gruesome, particularly the way Richard's brother, Clarence (Nigel Hawthorne), is dispatched in his bath, and Queen Elizabeth's brother, Rivers (Robert Downey Jr.), experiences a most unanticipated form of interruptus.

Annette Bening plays Elizabeth solidly, but without the deftness she brought to a movie like *The American President;* there is the hint that she is too impressed to be in a play by Shakespeare. Maggie Smith is right at home; as Richard's mother, and the grandmother of his victims, she curses him so venomously that even Richard has pause.

The movie is really McKellen's, and with director Loncraine, his cowriter, he comes up with one sly touch after another to make Richard a satisfactory villain. Given an apple to feed to a pig, he throws it at the animal and nods with quiet satisfaction at its squeal. When a child jumps up playfully and knocks against his hump, he crumbles to the ground, lets out a beastial snarl, and then clambers to his feet with the oddest little smirk. And in a final scene, done to Al Jolson's "I'm Sittin' on Top of the World," he embraces the hellfire of his destiny.

Released a month before this movie was a traditional adaptation of Shakespeare, *Othello*, which was reverent but yet not filling. Now here is that bane of the purists, a modern-dress Shakespeare, which works in the way the play should work. Perhaps that is because the 1930s period and decor match the tone of the play: decadent royalty strutted on the European stage, having a last dance before the Nazi beast pounced.

## Ridicule ★ ★ ★ ½

R, 103 m., 1996

Charles Berling (Ponceludon de Malavoy), Jean Rochefort (Marquis de Bellegarde), Fanny Ardant (Madame de Blayac), Judith Godreche (Mathilde de Bellegarde), Bernard Giraudeau (Abbot de Vilecourt), Bernard Dheran (Monsieur de Montalieri), Carlo Brandt (Knight de Milletail). Directed by Patrice Leconte and produced by Gilles Legrand, Frederic Brillion, and Philippe Carcassonne. Screenplay by Remi Waterhouse.

Imagine a time when all compliments are two-faced, when every truth is tinged with irony, when insults are the currency of humor. We have more in common with the eighteenth century than we might imagine. *Ridicule* is a movie that takes place at the court of Louis XVI, circa 1783, but its values would be at home around the Algonquin Round Table or in modern comedy clubs. Wit is all. Sincerity is an embarrassment.

The movie tells the story of a provincial baron with a scientific cast of mind. The people of his district are dying because of the pestilent waters that breed mosquitoes and disease. He has a scheme for draining the marshes and making the land tillable. He needs the help of the king, and so he journeys to Versailles to press his case. But the king values verbal wit above all, and lives mostly to be entertained. If the baron cannot develop a savage tongue, he has no chance.

The baron, named Ponceludon de Malavoy (Charles Berling), is like all provincials inclined to give his rulers credit for being better than they are. In Versailles he witnesses shocking displays of public humiliation, which are all part of the game. He seems to have no chance at all, but then he is taken under the wing of the wise old Marquis de Bellegarde, played by Jean Rochefort, that tall, long-faced master of sly intrigue. "Be witty, sharp, and malicious," the marquis tells him, "and never laugh at your own jokes."

The baron somehow stumbles into success; his honesty plays like rudeness, and he doesn't laugh because he doesn't know he has told jokes. He gains admission to court circles, where he finds that in romance, as well as politics, wordmanship is more crucial than swordsmanship.

*Ridicule* has been directed by Patrice Leconte, a name not well known in this country unless you have had the good fortune to see *Monsieur Hire* (1989) or *The Hairdresser's Husband* (1990). Those films were about erotic fixations carried to uncomfortable extremes: about a little man who becomes solemnly obsessed with the young woman he can see across the courtyard, and about a fetishist (Rochefort) who loves hairdressers so much he marries one and hums with bliss every time she administers a shampoo.

In *Ridicule* the characters are faced with the exquisite torture of seducing one person while desiring another. The baron quickly falls in love with Mathilde (Judith Godreche), the kindly marquis's daughter, and she with him. But she is determined to marry a distasteful old rich man (they are only waiting for his wife to die), so that he can finance her researches into diving bells. Meanwhile, the baron, for matters of expediency, pays court to the powerful and beautiful Madame de Blayac (Fanny Ardant), who can do him good at court.

She likes him. Well, he likes her. She understands almost everything about the motives of the people in her life, and at one point, while he is going through the motions of wooing her, she looks at him in amusement and advises, "Learn to hide your insincerity so that I can yield without dishonor." After all, she is not a woman without stature; her own official lover is the abbé of Vilecourt.

The kind old marquis sees all and keeps his counsel. He does not have the money to support his daughter's researches, and sees how much she treasures her diving bells. He rather prefers the baron as a son-in-law, but realizes that no swamps are going to get drained that way. And the king? He has peepholes installed so that he can secretly observe the real goings-on in his court, the better to savor the ridiculous posturings of his petitioners when they come into his presence.

*Ridicule* reminded me of the equally fascinating *Restoration* (1995), with Robert Downey Jr., as an ordinary man embraced by the king after he treats his beloved dogs. It was set a century earlier at the equally colorful but somewhat less mannered British court of Charles II. Both films show a monarch using his personal style to set the agenda for his nation, and both are about lifestyles as a work of art. Both, too, are about simpler men from scientific backgrounds, who find that being straightforward gets them points at court that they haven't really earned.

What is fascinating about *Ridicule* is that so much depends on language, and so little is really said. The characters come and go, polishing their one-liners, memorizing their comebacks, desperately walking the line between delectable rudeness and offending the king. None of what they say means anything. It is all words. The eyes carry the meaning. Watch the way the characters look at one another, and you can follow the real plot, while they spin their tortured fancies.

## The Rock ★ ★ ★ ½

R, 129 m., 1996

Sean Connery (Patrick Mason), Nicolas Cage (Stanley Goodspeed), Ed Harris (General Francis X. Hummel), David Morse (Major Tom Baxter), John C. McGinley (Marine Captain Hendrix), Bokeem Woodbine (Sergeant Crisp), Jim Maniaci (Private Scarpetti), Greg Collins (Private Gamble). Directed by Michael Bay and produced by Don Simpson and Jerry Bruckheimer. Screenplay by David Weisberg, Douglas S. Cook, and Mark Rosner.

*The Rock* is a first-rate, slam-bang action thriller with a lot of style and no little humor. It's made out of pieces of other movies, yes, and not much in it is really new, but each element has been lovingly polished to a gloss. And there are three skillful performances: Sean Connery is Mason, an intelligence expert who's been in prison for thirty years; Nicolas Cage is Goodspeed, an FBI scientist; and Ed Harris is General Hummel, a war hero with a mad scheme to wage chemical warfare against San Francisco.

The plot hook is a mission to break into Alcatraz. Harris and his men have occupied the former prison island, taken civilian hostages, and threatened to fire deadly rockets at San Francisco unless their demands are met. What are the demands? Hummel, who has three Purple Hearts, two Silver Stars, and the Medal of Honor, is angered that eighty-three men have died under his command and never been recognized because they were on secret missions that the government denied even existed. He wants $100 million in payments to their next of kin.

Hummel is known and respected in Washington, and his demands are taken seriously. A news blackout is imposed while the Pentagon assembles a team to break into Alcatraz and neutralize the poison gas missiles. We've already seen Goodspeed think fast while sealed into an airtight chamber with a deadly chemical bomb; now he's assigned to join the task force, even though he's basically a lab rat with minimal field or combat experience.

Another key member of the team is Mason, a British spy who, we learn, successfully stole all of J. Edgar Hoover's secret files ("even the truth about JFK's assassination") before being secretly jailed for life without a trial. Mason's qualification: He is a jailbreak expert who is the only man to ever successfully escape from Alcatraz.

Movies like *The Rock* progress from one action sequence to another. Sometimes it doesn't even matter much how they fit together. Consider, for example, the highly entertaining way in which Mason turns a haircut into an opportunity to dangle one of his old enemies by a cord from a top floor of a hotel. And how that leads to a San Francisco streetcar chase inspired by *Bullitt,* leading to a crash almost as sensational as the train crash in *The Fugitive.*

Strange, isn't it, that after going to all that trouble to escape, Mason allows himself to be recaptured almost passively—probably because unless he joins the team, there's no movie. Strange, too, that although it has time for unlimited action, *The Rock* never slows down enough for a scene you might have thought was obligatory, in which Mason has the plan explained to him, along with a pitch about why he should go along. (He has a motive, all right—his only child is in San Francisco, and could be one of the poison victims. It's just that the movie never quite bothers at this stage to formally tell him about the poison.)

The break into Alcatraz owes something to Don Siegel's *Escape from Alcatraz,* the 1979 Clint Eastwood movie. While that one negotiated the maze of tunnels under Alcatraz in murky darkness, however, *The Rock* provides Alcatraz with a subterranean labyrinth as large and well-lighted as the sewers in *The Third Man* and as crammed with props and unidentified metallic machinery as the *Alien* movies.

The plot moves efficiently among firefights, explosions, torrents of water, hand-to-hand combat, interrogation, torture, imprisonment, escape, and scientific mumbo-jumbo, as the infiltrators try to stop Harris's men from wiping out 70,000 San Franciscans, and the Pentagon prepares to firebomb the island with planeloads of Thermite Plasma, which sure sounds neat. All of these elements are standard issue for action thrillers, but the script adds some deft touches (asked if he knows why he has been released from prison, Connery wryly said, "I've been locked up longer than Nelson Mandela. Maybe you want me to run for president").

What really works is the chemistry between Connery, as a reluctant warrior who has all the skills necessary to outsmart and outfight the occupying force, and Cage, as the nerd who can disarm the rockets but is not much in the killing department. And then there is an intriguing complexity added to the Ed Harris character, who is not as one-dimensional as he seems (early in the film, he advises some small children touring Alcatraz to return to their tour boat).

There are some loose ends. Cage and Connery keep turning up dry when they should be wet. A White House aide gently says, "We need a decision, Mr. President"—*after* the deadline has passed—and gets a speech long enough it could have cost the 70,000 lives. And of course the heroes are allowed to eavesdrop as needed on any conversations containing information they need to know.

In a movie that borrows from all the movies I've already listed (plus secondhand filching from *Die Hard* and related epics), there are two particularly obvious steals: The old hypodermic-needle-plunging-into-the-heart trick, from Quentin Tarantino's *Pulp Fiction,* and the Mexican standoff in which everybody has a gun pulled on everyone else (from QT's *Reservoir Dogs* and *True Romance,* courtesy of old Westerns). Two lifts from Tarantino? Maybe the producers, Jerry Bruckheimer and the late Don Simpson, were getting their revenge for the famous Tarantino monologue in *Sleep With Me,* where he analyzed their *Top Gun* as a homosexual parable.

No matter. Director Michael Bay *(Bad Boys)* orchestrates the elements into an efficient and exciting movie, with some big laughs, sensational special-effects sequences, and sustained suspense. And it's interesting to see how good actors like Connery, Cage, and Harris can find a way to occupy the center of this whirlwind with characters who somehow manage to be quirky and convincing. There are several Identikit Hollywood action stars who can occupy the center of chaos like this, but not many can make it look like they think they're really there. Watching *The Rock,* you really care about what happens. You feel silly later for having been sucked in, but that's part of the ride.

## Rocket Man ★ ★ ★

PG, 93 m., 1997

Harland Williams (Fred Z. Randall), Jessica Lundy (Julie Ford), William Sadler ("Wild Bill" Overbeck), Jeffrey DeMunn (Paul Wick), James Pickens Jr. (Ben Stevens), Beau Bridges (Bud Nesbitt), Peter Onorati (Gary Hackman). Directed by Stuart Gillard and produced by Roger Birnbaum. Screenplay by Craig Mazin and Greg Erb.

The thought never occurred to me that Jim Carrey made grown-up films—until halfway through *Rocket Man,* when I realized that Harland Williams was basically a Jim Carrey for the six-to-fourteen set. Filling the void in our national life left by the retirement of Pee-wee Herman, he plays the kind of guy who lands on Mars and tells Mission Control: "Look! I'm the first man to walk backward on Mars!"

Williams (from TV's *Simon*) plays Fred Z. Randall, computer nerd, whose dream since childhood has been to be an astronaut. We see him first inside a washing machine, pretending the window is a spaceship porthole. (He sets the machine to spin, which may give kids dangerous ideas, but pays off with a big laugh when his mother liberates him and he tumbles onto the floor explaining, "I come in peace!")

As an adult, Randall is responsible for a computer guidance program for the manned mission to Mars. The ace pilot, however, keeps crash-landing in training simulations, and Fred is able to prove it's because the pilot's feeding in the wrong figures. Fred's helpful demonstration lands the pilot in a cast, and there's only one other person qualified to join the three-man crew: Fred himself.

*Rocket Man* is cheerfully oblivious to any scientific discoveries about Mars more advanced than that the planet is red. (It assumes, for example, that instantaneous two-way communication could take place with a lander on the Martian surface.) But this is not a science movie, to put it mildly. It's a wacky comedy in the Jerry Lewis–Jim Carrey mold, with lots of jokes about two astronauts who share the same air hose while one of them passes enormous volumes of gas. Guess which one.

Harland Williams comes across uncannily like a man born to annoy you with everything he says. The movie exploits this. After the mission lands on Mars and he gets into an explorer vehicle with the mission commander (William Sadler), he badgers the commander with little-kid questions: "Are we almost there? Can I drive?" He bungles the dramatic moment when they plan to raise the American flag on Mars by dropping it over a cliff—but he saves the day with his own substitute flag, which waves proudly on TV for the folks at home: his pair of stars-and-stripes boxer shorts.

Jessica Lundy and Sadler, who play his fellow crew members, are deployed mostly as foils. And the movie has fun with the obligatory shots of Mission Control, with rows of men in white shirts and ties, stationed solemnly at computers but jumping up on cue to cheer successful developments. (There's a bald-headed actor playing a Mission Control guy here who has had similar roles, I'll bet, in half the space pictures made; no, not Clint Howard, but you get the idea.) Most of the technical dialogue is right out of other space movies, but there's the occasional zinger, such as "Your promises are worth about as much as dental floss at a Willie Nelson concert."

*Rocket Man* is not inspired or brilliant or original, but it's the kind of movie that gives you a goofy grin half of the time. A lot of the credit goes to Williams, who has the knack of almost making you think he doesn't know how obnoxious his character is. "It wasn't me!" he shouts, every time he screws up. For example, when he falls out of the lander door and inadvertently becomes the first man on Mars. And when his air hose is linked to Sadler's, and Sadler realizes someone has cut the cheese.

## Romy and Michele's High School Reunion ★ ★ ★

R, 91 m., 1997

Mira Sorvino (Romy), Lisa Kudrow (Michele), Janeane Garofalo (Heather), Alan Cumming (Sandy Frink), Camryn Manheim (Toby), Justin Theroux (Cowboy). Directed by David Mirkin and produced by Laurence Mark. Screenplay by Robin Schiff.

"I just get really happy when they let her shop," Michele tells Romy, tears in her voice, as they watch the video of *Pretty Woman* for the umpteenth time. Romy agrees. The two women, curled up on their beds, have been pals since high school, and now, in Los Angeles and pushing thirty, they're still single but still making the dance club scene and still looking for Mr. Okay. Here they are in front of the mirror: "I can't believe how cute I look."

"Don't you love how we can say that to each other and we know we're not being conceited?"

"No, we're just being honest."

The two women have been friends so long they talk the same way, sounding a little like the *Saturday Night Live* version of Tori Spelling. Romy (Mira Sorvino) is a cashier at a Jaguar dealership, and Michele (Lisa Kudrow) is unemployed at the moment, but, honestly, they think their lives are pretty darn exciting.

Memories of their painful and dreadful days in high school are all but obliterated until one day an old classmate named Heather (Janeane Garofalo) walks into the Jaguar shop, is recognized by Romy, and tells her their tenth reunion is coming up at Sagebrush High in Tucson. Will she be there?

Romy and Michele at first decide not to go. They recall nothing but agony. They were labeled as "kooks" and persecuted by the popular girls.

But then . . . then . . . they start thinking maybe they could go and make a different impression. Romy can borrow a used Jag from the dealership. And they can pose as business executives. What business? They decide to tell everyone they invented Post-It Notes. "Well, I invented them," Romy tells Michele, "but you were instrumental in the development and marketing."

There have been a lot of high school reunion movies, and they all hinge on long-lasting insecurity. Apparently *everyone* was miserable during high school, and even the popular kids didn't seem successful to themselves. (I recently got a note from a high school classmate who described herself as painfully shy and dyslexic. Looking at the signature, I recognized the name of a woman I'd always thought of as the epicenter of popularity.)

*Romy and Michele's High School Reunion,* written by Robin Schiff (based on her play) and directed by David Mirkin, is one of the brightest and goofiest comedies in a while, a film that has a share of truth, but isn't afraid to cut loose with the weirdest choreography I have seen outside of a 1960s revival.

It alternates scenes from the reunion with flashbacks to real memories of high school and fantasy scenes (the funniest is when Michele is challenged to explain how she invented Post-It Notes, and responds with a detailed and technical explanation that sounds pretty good to me).

In high school, Romy and Michele were scorned by a trio of the most popular girls. Romy had a crush on cute Billy Christiansen, who wouldn't give her the time of day. Michele had scoliosis and had to wear an unsightly neck brace that squeaked every time she moved. Times were not good, especially when the popular girls stuck refrigerator magnets to her brace.

For everyone who is unpopular, there is someone more unpopular still. Sandy Frink (Alan Cumming), the class nerd, had such a hopeless crush on Michele that he carried a giant notebook with him everywhere, for camouflage in case of unwanted physical responses to her mere presence. And there was plump, plain Toby (Camryn Manheim), who exuded school spirit but was always ignored.

Now Sandy has become incredibly wealthy (he's a Bill Gates clone) and arrives by helicopter. He even looks better: "When I made my first million, my present to myself was a new face," he tells Michele during a dream sequence. He still carries a torch for her, which helps set up the funny closing sequences at the reunion dance, where old wrongs are righted and old enemies are slighted.

Mira Sorvino and Lisa Kudrow work easily and wickedly together, playing conspirators who are maybe just a little too dense to realize how desperate they are, or maybe just a little too bright to admit it. Janeane Garofolo, looking fearsomely hard-boiled, is the *really* successful businesswoman from the class, chain-smoking and blurting out the truth, and at the reunion she, too, runs into an old nemesis: Cowboy (Justin Theroux), who she used to meet when she slipped behind the building to sneak a cigarette. He has a secret, too.

Comedies are hard to make well. The proof is in how many are made badly. *Romy and Michele's High School Reunion* is light as a feather and cheerfully inconsequential, and most of the developments are predictable, but it has charm, a sly intelligence, and the courage to go for special-effects sequences like a weird run-in with a limo. And then there's that three-way dance number at the reunion. I can't believe how cute they look. Honest.

## Rosewood ★ ★ ★ ½

R, 142 m., 1997

Jon Voight (John Wright), Ving Rhames (Mann), Don Cheadle (Sylvester Carrier), Bruce McGill (Duke), Loren Dean (James Taylor), Esther Rolle (Sarah Carrier), Elise Neal (Scrappie), Catherine Kellner (Fannie Taylor), Michael Rooker (Sheriff Walker). Directed by John Singleton and produced by Jon Peters. Screenplay by Gregory Poirier.

John Singleton's *Rosewood* re-creates the story of a shameful event in American history, the race riot by whites against blacks in 1922 in the small Florida town of Rosewood, that left the town a smoking ruin while dozens of its residents were shot, burned to death, or lynched. But if the movie were simply the story of this event, it would be no more than a sad record. What makes it more is the way it shows how racism breeds and feeds, and is taught by father to son.

Early in the film we see a young white boy named Everett whose best playmate is a black boy about the same age. His father forbids him to "pal around with that little nigger boy." During the course of the film, this father will show his son how to tie a hangman's noose, and he will shove others aside, crying out "make way for a boy to look!" so his son can peer down into a mass grave filled with the bodies of African-Americans—some of them babies.

We do not need to be told that many of the white men in the mob had similar childhood experiences, and that their own guilt was mixed with fear, envy, and the intoxicating frenzy of the mob to create the bloodbath of Rosewood. "Between 70 and 250 African-Americans" were killed during the violence, according to recent reconstructions (state authorities at the time estimated "2 to 6"). But Rosewood remained a secret until newspaper reports in the *St. Petersburg Times* and a recent ABC news documentary on the Discovery channel—perhaps because there were few survivors, or they were too frightened to talk.

As the film opens in 1922, we see a prosperous town owned by its African-American residents, who have only a few white families living among them—the grocer, Mr. Wright (Jon Voight), whose affection for his neighbors extends to sexual relations with his pretty seventeen-year-old clerk. The black families own their own land and run their own businesses, and are resented by poorer whites living in a neighboring town. ("Why does that nigger have a piano when I don't?" one man asks; he is offended on principle, since he can't play the piano.)

Early in the film, Singleton and his screenwriter, Gregory Poirier, introduce a key story element not based on fact: the character of Mann (Ving Rhames), who rides into town on a handsome horse, has money, and bids at auction for five acres of land coveted by the white grocer. A black convict has just escaped from a chain gang in the area: Is Mann the escapee? Almost certainly not, although rumors feed the fires of suspicion when a local white woman claims she was beaten (but not raped, she is careful to add) by a black man who invaded her home.

We saw the event and know what happened. She was beaten by her own white lover, and has made up the story to explain her bruises to a jealous husband. Two local black women also know the story, but remain silent until it is too late because they fear retribution. The white woman's report inspires white mob violence.

One of the crucial figures in these events is the white sheriff (Michael Rooker), who has a good idea of what really happened and tries ineffectually at times to cool the mob, but is powerless because he is the creature of its collective will. He makes attempts to warn blacks—especially the stubborn, courageous Sylvester Carrier (Don Cheadle)—to get out of town and save their lives, but their understandable desire to protect their property causes them to delay until it is too late. (The older woman who witnessed the original attack, played by Esther Rolle, was midwife to half the local whites, and perhaps has a misplaced belief that people who were so lovable as babies could hardly grow up to attack her family.)

The character named Mann is also aware of the dangers ("If I stay I'm sure to be hung"), but he becomes the leader of the defense, especially in a sequence where he leads women and children to a train—operated by friendly whites—that will help them escape. Although the train escape is based on historical events, this sequence plays a little too much like an action movie to fit convincingly with the rest of the story.

Singleton is the young director who burst onto the scene with *Boyz N the Hood* (1991). *Rosewood* represents an important step in his growth; it's a period picture painted on a large canvas, and he handles his large cast effortlessly, establishing a good sense of the community's life.

The *Rosewood* project began with the screenplay by Poirier; Singleton was brought in at a time when a more "positive" black lead than Ving Rhames was being sought (that's Rhames's own word). But his performance here finds the right note, and is essential to the film. Rhames became famous as the mob boss in *Pulp Fiction* and played a South African drug lord in *Dangerous Ground*. He is a powerful, direct actor, who takes up considerable psychic space. Here, in a partly symbolic role, as the strong independent counterpoint to the local blacks who are reluctant to fear the worst, he convinces at first sight and keeps on convincing. Rhames at this point has an element of mystery and unfamiliarity that's effective.

*Rosewood* was expensive, and a box office disappointment. It didn't obviously appeal to either blacks (since it documents such a depressing chapter) or whites (depicted as murderous or ineffectual). Perhaps on video it will appeal to people looking for a well-made film that tells a gripping, important story. Now there's a notion.

## Rough Magic ★ ★

PG-13, 104 m., 1997

Bridget Fonda (Myra Shumway), Russell Crowe (Alex Ross), Jim Broadbent (Doc Ansell), D. W. Moffett (Cliff Wyatt), Kenneth Mars (Magician), Paul Rodriguez (Diego), Andy Romano (Clayton), Richard Schiff (Wiggins), Euva Anderson (Diego's Wife/Tojola). Directed by Clare Peploe and produced by Laurie Parker and Declan Baldwin. Screenplay by Robert Mundy, William Brookfield, and Peploe, based on the novel *Miss Shumway Waves a Wand* by James Hadley Chase.

If ever there were two genres that don't seem to fit together, they're *film noir* and magic realism. The one grovels in gritty reality, the other dissolves into clouds of butterflies. Clare Peploe deserves credit for the uncompromising way in which she stage-manages a head-on collision between them in *Rough Magic,* an oddly enchanting fantasy that almost works.

The story, set in 1952, follows a magician's assistant named Myra (Bridget Fonda) as she flees from a Los Angeles murder scene and the arms of an arranged marriage. Her fiancé, a Howard Hughes type named Wyatt (D. W. Moffett), sends a private eye named Alex (Russell Crowe) after her, and then flies down himself, piloting his private DC-3. But by then she's fallen in love with Alex, and fallen into the clutches of a quack named Doc Ansell (Jim Broadbent), who sells a constipation cure (not that it doesn't work). The doc realizes she's the real thing. So he arranges for her to go on a solo mission: She crosses a lake and engages in rituals with ancient shaman women, drinks a secret potion, and finds that she possesses real magic (she also lays a blue egg).

It can be dangerous, being a genuine magician. At one point she unintentionally turns an ominous Mexican bandit into a sausage, which is gobbled up by Doc Ansell's beloved terrier. At another point, she makes love with Alex so enthusiastically that they levitate. She kills someone without meaning to, but not to worry: Hardly anyone is dead for long in this movie.

My favorite dialogue exchange comes after she turns the guy into a sausage: "Those guys would have made a hamburger out of me," Alex says. She frowns and says thoughtfully, "Don't say things like that."

*Rough Magic* is based on a novel by the *noir* novelist James Hadley Chase, best known for *No Orchids for Miss Blandish.* I haven't read it, but I'll bet nobody lays a blue egg in it. The screenplay, written by Peploe with Robert Mundy and William Brookfield, is curiously serious even in its most absurd moments; Bridget Fonda looks at times as if she thinks she may be in a comedy, but can't be sure. Neither can we. A whimsical fantasy may be the correct description.

Peploe, who is married to Bernardo Bertolucci, cowrote his *Luna* (1979) and Antonioni's *Zabriskie Point* (1970), and has directed one previous feature, *High Season* (1987), an engagingly goofy comedy set on a Greek island and involving tourists and spies. Nothing she has done before is anything like *Rough Magic,* which seems to be a visitor from a parallel time line: If *film noir* had developed in South America instead of California, maybe we would have seen more films like this.

Apart from anything else, the movie is wonderful to look at. It's a cliché to talk about great visuals, since if you point a camera in the right direction you can make almost anything look good. But John J. Campbell and Peploe create painterly compositions with rich Mexican colors, and there are landscape shots and atmospheric effects here that are astonishing.

The acting is quirky in an engaging way. Moffett is dry and opaque as the ambiguous Hughes clone, Broadbent is a likable scoundrel as the snake oil salesman, and Russell Crowe is steady in the Mitchum role, as a guy hired to do a job who falls in love with the dame. At one point in the movie he starts calling Bridget Fonda "Slim," and indeed her hairstyle and costumes are intended to evoke Lauren Bacall, but it's hard for her to maintain an air of mystery while laying eggs.

In casting the lead, Peploe obviously leaned toward the *noir* side of her material, and went for an actress who could project 1950s allure. Maybe she should have tilted toward the Latin elements of magic realism, and picked somebody like

Maria Conchita Alonso or Jennifer Lopez—somebody who, when presented with a mysterious green goblet of liquid prepared by an ancient priestess on the slopes of a volcano, would be able to look eager to taste it. Or maybe the project was so weird it was doomed from the start. Give *Rough Magic* credit, however, for possessing all the pieces necessary to make two other movies that both might have worked.

## Roujin-Z ★ ★ ★

PG-13, 80 m., 1996

An animated film directed by Hiroyki Kitabuko and produced by Yoshiaki Motoya. Screenplay by Katsuhiro Otomo.

Japanese animation, or "anime," as its fans call it, is an enormous but almost invisible phenomenon in this country. There has never been a wide-platform U.S. release of an animated film from Japan, and even those few titles that have won acceptance *(Akira, My Neighbor Totoro, The Wings of Honneamise)* have played mostly in art theaters, often as midnight shows. Most North Americans have no exposure at all to made-in-Japan animation except on TV cartoon programs—which, although they have their fanatic fans on the campuses, don't show the genre at its best.

In Japan, animation is not automatically considered entertainment for children and families. Adult themes, violence, and sexuality are often dealt with in animated films, as in the incredibly popular comic books you can see half the subway population reading every day. Walt Disney did a great service to animation by popularizing it at feature length, and his heirs continue to find enormous audiences for the art form, but the very success of Disney and its imitators has prevented the development of animation as a fully rounded art form.

So if that's the case, then where does anime thrive in North America? On video, mostly. Every video store has a shelf devoted to Japanimation, often under examination by intense young men who hold detailed conversations in what sounds like code. The stores devoted to comic books and trading cards all have shelves of video anime for sale. Almost every campus has an anime club, where even animated daytime kiddie serials are analyzed and deconstructed. Anime films are booked by campus film societies. There are lots of anime fanzines. And the Internet is crawling with hundreds of anime Web pages and thousands of newsgroup messages.

All of this is taking place out of sight of conventional entertainment channels, but occasionally one of the better feature-length films does find a theatrical booking. Two have been released in the United States: *The Ghost in the Shell* and *Roujin-Z.*

A film like *Roujin-Z* shows how animation can liberate filmmakers to deal with themes that would be impossible in a conventional movie. It was written by the major anime figure Katsuhiro Otomo, whose *Akira* (1990) was an animated vision of a nightmare future urban world. His new film is a quite different but equally savage satire, about health care for the aged in the twenty-first century.

As the story opens, scientists are alarmed that there are too many old people. Ambitious medical students resent them, because geriatric care is seen as a career dead-end. A computerized machine, named the Z-100, is invented to provide a permanent home for the elderly. It's a walking, talking combination of a hospital bed, a robot, and a computer, and once a patient is installed in one, he's expected to stay there until he dies.

This is quite a machine. It bathes its occupants, massages them, shows them movies and video games, attends to their bathroom functions, diagnoses their ills, and administers medicine. It's powered by an atomic reactor, and even has a built-in safety device: Should its onboard reactor fail, the machine is programmed to instantly bury itself in concrete. What happens to the patients? I guess they go down with their ships.

Most everybody likes the Z-100, except for a few humanistic types like a young nurse who feels sympathy for the old man who is berthed in one of the prototypes. Japanese folklore teaches that there can be spirits in almost anything, and in the case of this machine, the computer seems to have been inhabited by the spirit of the old man's dead wife, who wants to visit the sea. So, the powerful machine makes an effort to break out of the hospital and visit the seaside, with catastrophic results.

I cannot imagine this story being told in a

conventional movie. Not only would the machine be impossibly expensive and complex to create with special effects, but the social criticism would be immediately blue-penciled by Hollywood executives. Health care for the aged may be big on Capitol Hill, but it doesn't sell movie tickets. What's interesting, as you watch *Roujin-Z,* is how quickly the story itself becomes as interesting as the fact that the movie is animated. Perhaps because of our training with Disney movies, we accept cartoon characters as "real," and these characters—especially the hapless old man—have a curiously convincing quality.

The level of the dialogue is also intriguing. Dubbed into English, it ranges from standard comic book slang to the thoughtful, literate, and controversial. Speech of this level would be dumbed down in a studio rewrite. The animation, on the other hand, is not technically sophisticated by Hollywood standards; the filmmakers are economical with their animation of backgrounds and secondary characters. But here again, there is a gain as well as a loss: They break the film down into storyboarded shots as a comic book might, using unexpected angles and perspectives, shadows and light, surrealism and visual invention, so that the animation, while not as "realistic" as in, say, *Pocahontas,* feels rich and complex.

I am not sure *Roujin-Z* is the film to start with if you're curious about animation. It's more for devotees. My recommendation would be *Akira*—or, for family viewing, the delightful *My Neighbor Totoro,* which, like *Babe,* might actually appeal more to adults than children.

## Rudyard Kipling's Second Jungle Book: Mowgli and Baloo ★ 1/2

PG, 88 m., 1997

Jamie Williams (Mowgli), David Paul Francis (Chuchandra), Bill Campbell (Harrison), Dyrk Ashton (Karait), Roddy McDowell (King Murphy), Gulshan Grover (Buldeo). Directed by Duncan McLachlan and produced by Raja Patel. Screenplay by Bayard Johnson and Matthew Horton, inspired by the book by Kipling.

One of the reasons to make a movie is to tell a good story, which makes it all the more mysterious that so many storytelling opportunities are lost in *Rudyard Kipling's Second Jungle Book: Mowgli and Baloo.* The move is in no sense authored by Kipling, who knew how to tell a story; its primary connection to the *Jungle Books* is the name of the hero and the name of the bear. But it has a promising premise: Boy is raised in the jungle by animals, lives with them as an equal, then falls afoul of evil civilized men who want to exploit him.

Can you imagine a film involving a boy, animals, and the jungle? I can. It would involve a lot of storytelling imagination, since there would presumably be no dialogue. And it would be hard to photograph the animals convincingly. But a film could be made—maybe a good one.

*Rudyard Kipling's Second Jungle Book: Mowgli and Baloo* (which has the longest movie title since *Swept Away by an Unusual Destiny in the Blue Sea of August)* is not the one. It gives us a child actor whose acting is limited largely to looking agog in close-ups, while the editor cuts to shots of animals. Adult characters are thrown in for broad comedy and manufactured thrills. Great effort was obviously expended on the film—some of these sequences could not have been easy to shoot, and they look good—but the filmmakers were content with a limp story, one of those ready-made combinations of chases that aren't exciting and pratfalls that aren't funny.

Consider Chuchandra (David Paul Francis), the major Indian character. He's a caricature, a collection of Indian stereotypes. When we first see him, he's aghast because his pet monkey has escaped and is frolicking with Mowgli (Jamie Williams) on a train. The monkey is referred to as dirty. "He is not filthy!" the Indian cries. "I am picking off his fleas every day!" Ho, ho. Later Chuchandra exhibits exaggerated fright at sounds he must have been long familiar with (thunder, and animal roars) and races about waving his hands like a silent comedian.

The film opened with Mowgli swinging through the treetops like a junior Tarzan. He comes upon a railway track and tries to stop the train, only to be chased through the car (he may be small, but he's strong enough to drag a grown man the length of a carriage). Among those coveting him: Harrison (Bill Campbell), who works for P. T. Barnum and intends to exhibit the boy in the circus. Harrison teams up with Buldeo (Gulshan Grover), a local with a secret:

Mowgli is probably his lost nephew, and Buldeo has stolen his hereditary fortune.

An even more villainous character is Karait (Dyrk Ashton), who has trained a snake to hunt; the snake can wrap itself around the sleeping Mowgli—who, after years in the jungle, doesn't have instincts that awaken him. The snake then helpfully drops Mowgli into a net. After Mowgli escapes and stumbles upon a lost city, there is the character of King Murphy (Roddy McDowell), who lives half-mad in a jungle ruin, expecting visits from royalty.

All of these adult characters are arbitrary. They have little to do with Mowgli or with one another, they are invented out of whole cloth and put into a series of lame chases, double takes, frights, surprises, sinister developments, and contrived escapes.

It is not easy to get a movie made, and even harder to make one for young audiences. If you're going to the effort, why not make a smart one? Young moviegoers, in my experience, are sharp and observant: Bored by countless hours of brainless television, they don't want the same old stuff on a movie screen. At a time when a film like *Shiloh* is playing in theaters, there is no reason to see *Rudyard Kipling's etc., etc.*

# S

## The Saint ★ ★

PG-13, 117 m., 1997

---

Val Kilmer (Simon Templar), Elisabeth Shue (Dr. Emma Russell), Rade Serbedzija (Ivan Tretiak), Valery Nikolaev (Ilya). Directed by Phillip Noyce and produced by David Brown, Robert Evans, and Mace Neufeld. Screenplay by Jonathan Hensleigh and Wesley Strick.

---

*The Saint* is a James Bond wannabe, which is an irony, since James Bond in a way is a Saint clone. Leslie Charteris created his gentleman crook in 1926 and wrote about him in dozens of novels before his death in 1993. The Saint also inspired fourteen movies and a 1960s TV series starring Roger Moore, a future Bond. When Ian Fleming began writing his Bond stories, he must have had the Saint in mind: The two characters share a debonair sophistication, a gift for disguise, a taste for beautiful women, a fetish for expensive toys, and a thorough working knowledge of fine wines and fast cars.

If the Saint inspired Bond, the Bond films have obviously inspired *The Saint,* which stars Val Kilmer as Simon Templar, a man of constantly shifting appearances and identities. "Who *are* you?" asks the woman who loves him. "No one has a clue," he says. "Least of all me."

The movie opens with the Saint's origination story, although the time line seems a bit askew. The man who was to name himself after the Knights Templar spent his boyhood, we learn, in a Dickensian orphanage somewhere in the Far East. When the cruel headmaster locks all the food in a storage cart as a punishment, young Simon picks the lock, and is launched on his life of adventure.

What does he do? Steals things for people, sometimes with legal sanction, more often not. This Saint is more high-tech than his pulp predecessors, and uses a Mac Powerbook and a palmtop to dial the Internet and check on his Swiss bank account, which is creeping toward $50 million. His latest assignment is to steal the secret of cold fusion from an unsuspecting Oxford scientist named Emma Russell (Elisabeth Shue).

Cold fusion, of course, would provide unlimited free power, and that is of great interest to the man who has hired the Saint, Ivan Tretiak (Rade Serbedzija). He was once a communist boss, is now an oil billionaire, and is secretly withholding vast stores of heating oil in an attempt to freeze Russian citizens into an uprising that would sweep him into office. The Saint's assignment involves a trip to Moscow in midwinter, some impressive location shots of Red Square, and a scene where he sneaks into what I guess is the Kremlin, wearing goggles and a black ski mask so that anyone who sees him will instantly know he's up to no good.

Most of his costumes are more wisely chosen. When he goes to Oxford, he poses as an Austin Pendleton lookalike—a chatty egghead who attends Shue's lectures and learns that she is on the verge of providing Earth with free energy. Then he poses as an artist to win her trust, gets her drunk, inveigles his way into her arms, and is on the brink of learning the secret of cold fusion when an inconvenient thing happens: He falls in love with her.

All of this involves some of the same ingredients that have been road tested in Bond movies, and indeed there's speculation that *The Saint* is also the first of a series. If so, they'll have to wind the plot a little tighter. Compared to the sensational stunts and special effects in the Bond series, *The Saint* seems positively leisurely. The fight scenes go on too long and are not interesting, the villains aren't single-minded enough, and the Saint seems more like a disguise fetishist than a formidable international operative. What does work is the chemistry between Kilmer and Shue, whose scenes have a certain charm, especially the one where she says she'll give away the secret of cold fusion to avoid anyone getting rich with it.

I've been trying to put my finger on the movie's key problem, and I think it may be that Kilmer plays the Saint too realistically. If you take a step back and really think about James Bond, you will realize that he is mad. So is Batman. So is the Phantom (the most unfairly overlooked recent movie superhero). They live in fantasy worlds of their own creation, and bring a certain style to their delusions. The Saint still harbors ordinary human emotions, and that will not do.

## Scream ★ ★ ★

R, 100 m., 1996

David Arquette (Dewey), Drew Barrymore (Casey), Neve Campbell (Sidney), Courteney Cox (Gale Weathers), Jamie Kennedy (Randy), Matthew Lillard (Stuart), Rose McGowan (Tatum), Liev Schreiber (Cotton), Skeet Ulrich (Billy), Henry Winkler (Principal). Directed by Wes Craven and produced by Cathy Konrad, Cary Woods, and Marianne Maddalena. Screenplay by Kevin Williamson.

Wes Craven's *Scream* violates one of the oldest rules in movie history: It's about characters who go to the movies. They've even heard of movie stars. They refer by name to Tom Cruise, Richard Gere, Jamie Lee Curtis. They analyze motivations ("Did Norman Bates have a motive? Did Hannibal Lecter have a reason for wanting to eat people?").

True, the characters went to the movies in *The Last Picture Show,* and the heroes of *Clerks* worked in a video store. Even Bonnie and Clyde went to the movies. But those movies were about the *act* of going to the movies. *Scream* is about *knowledge* of the movies: The characters in *Scream* are in a horror film, and because they've seen so many horror films, they know what to do and what not to do. "Don't say, 'I'll be right back,'" one kid advises a friend, "because whenever anybody says that, he's *never* right back."

In a way, this movie was inevitable. A lot of modern film criticism involves "deconstruction" of movie plots. "Deconstruction" is an academic word. It means saying what everybody knows in words nobody can understand. *Scream* is self-deconstructing; it's like one of those cans that heats its own soup.

Instead of leaving it to the audience to anticipate the horror clichés, the characters talk about them openly. "Horror movies are always about some big-breasted blonde who runs upstairs so the slasher can corner her," says a character in *Scream.* "I hate it when characters are that stupid."

The movie begins, of course, with a young woman (Drew Barrymore) at home alone. She gets a threatening phone call from an evil Jack Nicholson soundalike. She is standing in front of patio doors with the dark night outside. She goes into a kitchen where there are lots of big knives around. You know the drill.

Later, we meet another young woman (Neve Campbell). Her father has left for the weekend. Her mother was murdered . . . why, exactly a year ago tomorrow! Her boyfriend climbs in through the window. At high school, rumors of cult killings circulate. The killer wears a spooky Halloween costume named "Father Death." There are more phone calls, more attacks. The suspects include the boyfriend, the father, and a lot of other people. A nice touch: The high school principal is The Fonz.

All of that is the plot. *Scream* is not about the plot. It is about itself. In other words, it is about characters who *know* they are in a plot. These characters read *Fangoria* magazine. They even use movie-style dialogue: "I was attacked and nearly filleted last night."

The heroine has been rejecting her boyfriend's advances, and just as well: As another character points out, virgins are never victims in horror films. Only bad boys and girls get slashed to pieces. Realizing they're in the midst of a slasher plot, the characters talk about who could play them: "I see myself as sort of a young Meg Ryan. But with my luck, I'll get Tori Spelling."

The movie itself, for all of its ironic in-jokes, also functions as a horror film—a bloody and gruesome one, that uses as many clichés as it mocks. One old standby is the scene where someone unexpectedly enters the frame, frightening the heroine, while a sinister musical chord pounds on the sound track. I love these scenes, because (a) the chord carries a message of danger, but (b) of course the unexpected new person is always a harmless friend, and (c) although we can't see the newcomer because the framing is so tight, in the real world the frightened person would of course be able to see the newcomer all the time.

The movie is also knowledgeable about the way TV reporters are portrayed in horror films. The reporter this time, played by Courteney Cox of *Friends,* asks wonderful questions, such as "How does it feel to almost be the victim of a slasher?" Savvy as she is, she nevertheless suggests to a local deputy that they shouldn't drive to an isolated rural setting when it's a nice night to walk down a deserted country road in the dark while a slasher is loose.

What did I think about this movie? As a film

critic, I liked it. I liked the in-jokes and the self-aware characters. At the same time, I was aware of the incredible level of gore in this film. It is *really* violent. Is the violence defused by the ironic way the film uses it and comments on it? For me, it was. For some viewers, it will not be, and they will be horrified. Which category do you fall in? Here's an easy test: When I mentioned *Fangoria*, did you know what I was talking about? ☞

## Scream 2 ★ ★ ★

R, 122 m., 1997

Neve Campbell (Sidney Prescott), David Arquette (Dewey Riley), Courteney Cox (Gale Weathers), Liev Schreiber (Cotton Weary), Sarah Michelle Gellar (Cici), Jamie Kennedy (Randy Meeks), Elise Neal (Hallie), Jerry O'Connell (Derek), Jada Pinkett (Maureen), Omar Epps (Phil). Directed by Wes Craven and produced by Cathy Konrad and Marianne Maddalena. Screenplay by Kevin Williamson.

Wes Craven's *Scream* (1996) was a revolutionary film, the first horror movie in which the characters had seen other horror movies, knew all the clichés, and tried not to make the obvious mistakes. Now comes *Scream 2,* in which the characters have seen a movie based on the first killings, and are trapped once again in a slasher nightmare.

Like all sequels, this one is a transparent attempt to cash in on the original—but, of course, it *knows* it is, and contains its own learned discussion of sequels. The verdict is that only a few sequels have been as good as the originals; the characters especially like *Aliens* and *Godfather, Part Two.* As for *Scream 2,* it's . . . well, it's *about* as good as the original.

Both movies use a Boo Machine, a plot device for making the audience jump and scream and clutch each other's forearms. The scares this time come from a mad slasher in a curiously unsettling Halloween ghost mask, who stalks a bunch of college freshmen who survived the original slashings. The killer is also interested in such groupies as a TV newsman and a crippled former deputy sheriff.

I have witnessed a lot of slashers jump out of a lot of shadows. When Alan Arkin pounced on Audrey Hepburn in *Wait Until Dark,* that pretty much defined, for me, how scary such an event could be. I was not frightened by the Boo Moments in *Scream 2,* and I found the violence kind of inappropriate; this movie is gorier than the original, and that distracts from the witty screenplay by Kevin Williamson.

His premise this time is that violence is quickly translated into marketable form by the media; since he is doing that very thing in *Scream 2,* there are ironies within ironies here. The movie is so articulate about what it's doing, indeed, that you can't criticize it on those grounds—it gets there first.

The film opens with a showing of *Stab,* a movie based on the killing in the first film, and at the screening two audience members (Jada Pinkett and Omar Epps) are . . . well, see for yourself. Soon the slasher has moved to a nearby campus, where survivors, including Sidney Prescott (Neve Campbell), are students, and the wounded Deputy Riley (David Arquette) has found a job as a security guard. Also hanging around is TV newswoman Gale Weathers (Courteney Cox), who covered the first murders and wrote a best-seller about them, which became *Stab* and has now inspired the new murders. Also moping about is Cotton (Liev Schreiber), accused by Gale in the first film but found innocent, and now demanding a second helping of his fifteen minutes of fame.

Who gets killed, and why, and how, I will not reveal, except to register a useless complaint that there is no way to guess who's doing the killing, and everyone who seems suspicious is (almost) sure to be innocent. Idea: In *Scream 3,* the man behind the mask is a movie critic, trying to discredit horror movies so he won't have to sit through any more.

The Williamson screenplay uses the horror platform as a launching pad for a lot of zingers; I'd like to see his work in a more mainstream film. When the TV newswoman is asked about her nude photos on the Internet, for example, she replies, "It was just my head. It was Jennifer Aniston's body." And a killer says he *wants* to be caught because he's already mapped out his strategy: "The movies made me do it," he'll argue, and he plans to have Bob Dole testify for the defense. ("I'll get Dershowitz! Cochran! The Christian Coalition will pay for my defense!")

Wes Craven was born to direct this material. One of the most successful of horror filmmakers, he made *The Hills Have Eyes* and the *Nightmare on Elm Street* movies, and was already headed in the same direction as the Williamson screenplay when he wrote and directed *Wes Craven's New Nightmare* in 1994. That was a movie (better than either *Scream* picture, I think) in which the cast and crew of a horror film found deadly parallels between the plot and their lives.

Do movies cause people to act violently? *Scream 2* seems to think so—or is that an ironic stance, to make the movie scarier? Will a movie like this, by educating its audience to the conventions and silly clichés of horror films, defuse the violence and make them less likely to be influenced? Now there's an intriguing notion. ☞

## Screamers ★ ★ ½

R, 107 m., 1996

Peter Weller (Hendricksson), Roy Dupuis (Becker), Jennifer Rubin (Jessica), Andy Lauer (Ace), Charles Powell (Ross), Ron White (Elbarak), Michael Caloz (David). Directed by Christian Duguay and produced by Tom Berry and Franco Battista. Screenplay by Dan O'Bannon and Miguel Tejada-Flores, based upon the short story "Second Variety" by Philip K. Dick.

Once on CompuServe there was a discussion about the most depressing movie of all time. The finalists included *Johnny Got His Gun, Testament,* and *Midnight Express.* If there'd been a sci-fi category, *Screamers* would be right at the top of the list. It's not exactly a bad movie; it's made with a certain imagination and intelligence. But its future is so grungy and grim it makes our current mess look like a utopia.

The year, 2078. The planet, Sirius 6B, source of a substance that solves all of Earth's energy problems. The problem is that obtaining this substance can be fatal to the miners, who die of radiation poisoning. For years there has been a cold war on Earth and a hot war on Sirius 6B between the miners' union and the energy company. As the story opens, Henricksson (Peter Weller) is leading a group of miners holed up in a vast bunker in the side of a hill in the middle of a landscape that looks like Death Valley after being strip-mined.

A man staggers out of the desert. They're ready to shoot him, but a Screamer gets him first. Screamers are weapons used by the miners. They're nasty little automatons that burrow under the surface of the sand, have razor-sharp saws to cut off arms and legs, and are guided by tiny onboard computers. Their full name: Autonomous Mobile Swords.

The messenger is quickly sliced up, but his message is intriguing: The other side wants to enter peace talks immediately. That sounds suspicious and Henricksson is wary, but meanwhile we absorb details of life on Sirius 6B, which mostly consists of looking out of slits in the concrete and smoking. Most of the time, the miners smoke Earth cigarettes. Occasionally, when the radiation level creeps too high, they smoke special pink antiradiation cigarettes. Ho, ho.

A spaceship crash-lands in front of the bunker, and its lone survivor adds to the confusion: Is the war on or off? And what *is* the alarming new development hinted at in the message from the other side? Henricksson, now joined by a freelance black marketer named Jessica (Jennifer Rubin), leads the group on an expedition to enemy headquarters, which appear to be deserted, and then there is a labyrinthine subplot involving new models of the Autonomous Mobile Swords, which can look like humans, or nasty little midget dinosaurs.

These creatures, smart as they are, can luckily be blasted to smithereens by the guns the humans carry. (Like a lot of the guns in futuristic films, they're about the size of Jet Skis.) The technology here is disappointing; you'd expect the Screamers to be more invulnerable, and you'd also expect the good guys would have developed a more sophisticated way of dealing with them. As a Screamer comes burrowing under the sand and a human blasts it with his weapon, thoughts of Bill Murray killing gophers come to mind.

Some of the elements in *Screamers* seem recycled out of *Alien,* especially the basic situation of humans creeping through a vast abandoned outpost on another planet, while threatened by evil little sharp-toothed creatures that leap out of nowhere. Although the film is based on a short story by Philip K. Dick, the *Alien* connection is persuasive since the same man, Dan O'Bannon, was a writer on both films.

The look is much the same, too: the familiar postindustrial wasteland of abandoned machinery, rusting pipes, moldy walls, underground passages, and rats—lots of rats. The look of this movie is so gray, green, brown, shadowy, gloomy, and dirty that shooting it in black and white would have cheered it up. And Peter Weller (*Robocop, Buckaroo Banzai*) fits the look with his worn heroism: He looks like a man who has been forgotten on this miserable planet for so long that death would be a welcome change.

The look and the basic plot elements are not original, but what makes the film somewhat intriguing is its *Blade Runner*–like ambiguity, and who is, and isn't, a human being. (Without revealing too much of the plot, I can say that advanced models of the Autonomous Mobile Swords can look a great deal like anyone else in the film.) The dialogue is often effective, too, as when one Sword fights another, and Weller observes, "You're coming up in the world. You know how to kill each other now."

## The Secret Agent ★

R, 95 m., 1996

Bob Hoskins (Verloc), Patricia Arquette (Winnie), Gérard Depardieu (Ossipon), Robin Williams as George Spelvin (Professor), Jim Broadbent (Chief Inspector Heat), Christian Bale (Stevie), Eddie Izzard (Vladimir), Elizabeth Spriggs (Winnie's Mother). Directed by Christopher Hampton and produced by Norma Heyman. Screenplay by Hampton.

I have been wondering ever since I read it why someone doesn't make a movie out of Joseph Conrad's novel *Victory.* It tells the story of a proud, lonely man, the young woman who comes to share his hideaway on an island, the murderers who invade their solitude, and the way he must choose between philosophy and violence. I see John Malkovich as the man and Lili Taylor as the woman.

In a more perfect world, I could go on to describe the movie, its surprises and riches, its depths of character, its marriage of ideas and action. But in this world I am forced instead to review *The Secret Agent,* an overcast film made from a different novel by Joseph Conrad (from, indeed, perhaps the least filmable novel he ever wrote).

The action takes place mostly in 1890s London—or in a small, rainy corner of London represented by a claustrophobic studio set. In a shabby street-corner shop, a man named Verloc (Bob Hoskins) sells pornography to furtive men. "Would you like to have a look at . . . something more interesting?" he asks, insinuating himself, as all pornographers must, into the needs of his clients.

Pornography is not his real business. He is a member of an anarchist cell. Its members meet upstairs in Verloc's flat, planning the destruction of society. But anarchy is not his real business, either; he is a double agent, paid by the Russians to infiltrate exile groups. (These are the czarist Russians, of course, although the Soviet version also hated anarchists.)

Verloc lives with a ripe young woman (Patricia Arquette) who has married him for only one reason: to find a home for her little brother (Christian Bale), who is retarded. She pours tea uneasily for her husband's friends, and reduces all of the film's politics into an angry statement to her mother ("The police are there so that them as have nothing can't take nothing away from them as have a lot").

Conrad wrote his novel soon after an actual attempt to blow up the Royal Observatory at Greenwich, and in *The Secret Agent* the Russian ambassador (Eddie Izzard) orders Verloc to blow up the observatory in order to discredit the anarchists. But the plot goes horribly wrong, revealing the whole shabby worthlessness of Verloc and all of his enterprises.

Conrad made *The Secret Agent* a character study, and although it is not one of his great novels, it is a good one. The movie deals more with externals, and since there are few of any interest, it drags and finally sighs and expires. The performances are as good as the material permits, and I liked jolly Jim Broadbent as the police inspector (the kind of man who studies dirty postcards very carefully before arresting them as is connected with 'em). Robin Williams is grim and effective as the Professor, who walks the city with bombs strapped to his body.

The film was directed by Christopher Hampton, also a playwright, whose film *Carrington* was one of 1995's best. This project is dead in the water. Read the book. Better still, read *Victory.*

## Secrets and Lies ★ ★ ★ ★

R, 142 m., 1996

Timothy Spall (Maurice), Marianne Jean-Baptiste (Hortense), Brenda Blethyn (Cynthia), Phyllis

**Logan (Monica), Claire Rushbrook (Roxanne), Elizabeth Berrington (Jane), Michele Austin (Dionne), Lee Ross (Paul). Directed by Mike Leigh and produced by Simon Channing-Williams. Screenplay by Leigh.**

Moment after moment, scene after scene, *Secrets and Lies* unfolds with the fascination of eavesdropping. We are waiting to see what these people will do next, caught up in the fear and the hope that they will bring the whole fragile network of their lives crashing down in ruin. When they prevail—when common sense and good hearts win over lies and secrets—we feel almost as relieved as if it had happened to ourselves.

Mike Leigh's best films work like that. He finds a rhythm of life—not "real life," but real life as fashioned and shaped by all the art and skill his actors can bring to it—and slips into it, so that we are not particularly aware we're watching a film; he has a scene here, set at a backyard barbecue, that shows exactly how family gatherings are sometimes a process of tiptoeing through minefields. One wrong word and the repressed resentments of decades will blow up in everyone's face.

It would be easy, but wrong, to describe the plot of *Secrets and Lies* as being about an adopted black woman in London who seeks out her natural birth mother, discovers the woman is white, and arranges to meet her. That would be wrong because it sidesteps the real subject of the film, which is how the mother and her family have been all but destroyed by secrets and lies. The young black woman is the catalyst to change that situation, yes, but her life was fine before the action starts and will continue on an even keel afterward.

Given the deep waters it dives into, *Secrets and Lies* is a good deal funnier and more entertaining than we have any right to expect. It begins with the black woman, a thirtyish optometrist with the quintessentially British name Hortense Cumberbatch (Marianne Jean-Baptiste). After the death of her adoptive mother, she goes to an adoption agency to discover the name of her birth mother, and thinks there must have been a mistake, since the papers indicate her mother was white. There was no mistake.

We meet the mother, named Cynthia, who is played as a fearful nervous wreck by Brenda Blethyn (who won the Best Actress award at Cannes for this performance). She lives in an untidy council house with her daughter, Roxanne (Claire Rushbrook), who works as a street sweeper, is in a foul mood most of the time, and has a boyfriend whom she has thoroughly cowed. Cynthia mourns the fact that her beloved younger brother, Maurice (Timothy Spall), hasn't called her in more than two years, and blames Maurice's wife, Monica (Phyllis Logan), that "toffee-nosed cow," for the long silence.

The phone rings. It is Hortense. "Oh, no, no, no, no, no, dear—there's been some mistake!" says Cynthia. But Hortense persists. Cynthia hangs up. The phone rings again, and she approaches it like an animal sure the trap is set to spring. But she agrees to meet Hortense, and the scene of their meeting—outside a tube station and then in a nearby café—is one of the great sequences in all of Mike Leigh's work, based on incredulity, disbelief, memory, embarrassment, and acceptance. "But you can't be my daughter, dearie!" Cynthia exclaims. "I mean . . . just look at you!" She claims she has never even slept with a black man, and thinks she is telling the truth, but then a moment comes when she arrives at a startling revelation, and we don't know whether to smile or hold our breaths.

Much of the film is devoted to the domestic life of Maurice and Monica. He is a photographer specializing in wedding pictures; she is a loving woman whose life becomes unbearable for herself and her husband every twenty-eight days. Spall, who you may remember as the proprietor of the doomed French restaurant in Leigh's *Life Is Sweet,* is a born conciliator, wanting to make everyone happy and usually failing.

The movie arrives at its magnificent conclusion at the family reunion, the barbecue where Cynthia brings Hortense and introduces her as a "friend from work." Soon the family is trying to puzzle out why an eye doctor would be employed at a cardboard box factory. Leigh and his actors (who develop the characters and dialogue together, in collaboration) play this scene in one unbroken take, in which six characters eat, drink, talk, and stumble across secrets and lies.

I have admired the work of Mike Leigh ever since 1972, when his *Bleak Moments* premiered in the Chicago Film Festival. For many years he was an outcast of British cinema; it's hard to get financing when you don't have a script or even the idea for a film, but Leigh stubbornly persisted in his method of gathering actors and working with them to create the story. In the 1970s and 1980s, he worked mostly in London theater and for the BBC, and then came *High Hopes* (1988), *Life Is Sweet* (1991), and *Naked* (1993).

Now *Secrets and Lies,* which won the Palme d'Or at Cannes, is a flowering of his technique. It moves us on a human level, it keeps us guessing during scenes as unpredictable as life (the visit, for example, of the former owner of the photography studio), and it shows us how ordinary people have a chance of somehow coping with their problems, which are rather ordinary too. One intriguing aspect of the film is the way Leigh handles race: The daughter is black, the mother is white, the family has no idea she had another child, and yet race is not really on anybody's mind in this film. They think they have more important things to worry about, and they're right.

## Selena ★ ★ ★ ½

PG, 130 m., 1997

Jennifer Lopez (Selena), Edward James Olmos (Abraham Quintanilla), Jon Seda (Chris Perez), Constance Marie (Marcela Quintanilla), Jacob Vargas (Abie Quintanilla), Lupe Ontiveros (Yolanda Saldivar), Jackie Guerra (Suzette Quintanilla), Becky Lee Meza (Young Selena). Directed by Gregory Nava and produced by Moctesuma Esparza and Robert Katz. Screenplay by Nava.

*Selena* brings freshness and heart to the life story of a little girl from Corpus Christi, Texas, who had big dreams and was lucky enough to realize almost all of them before her life was cut short. Selena Quintanilla was poised to become the first female singer to cross over from Spanish to English markets when she was shot dead on March 31, 1995.

By the time she died, the English-speaking Selena (Jennifer Lopez) had conquered the Spanish charts, dominated Mexican-American pop music, and even won acceptance in Mexico, despite her shaky Spanish and an American accent. She'd had No. 1 hits, won a Grammy award, and was about to go on tour to promote her first English album. "Everybody's gonna wonder how I learned English so fast," she joked. Then it all ended when an employee shot her in an argument over theft.

*Selena,* written and directed by Gregory Nava *(El Norte, My Family),* places her firmly inside a close, loving family. From the very beginning, "Selena y Los Dinos" was a family act, guided by her father, Abraham (Edward James Olmos), and including sister Susie (Jackie Guerra) on drums and brother Abie (Jacob Vargas) on guitar. They toured county fairs and played school dances, and Abraham even opened a restaurant just so he could book his kids as the entertainment (Selena's big crowd-pleaser was "Over the Rainbow"). It was slow going at first, and when Abraham insisted Selena start singing in Spanish, the young teenager rebelled: "I don't want to learn to sing in Spanish! I don't even *like* Spanish music. I like Donna Summer."

Abraham tells her she has to sing from the inside, from what she is, and she is Mexican-American, between two worlds, and that's tough: "The Americans jump all over us because we don't speak perfect English, and then the Mexicans jump all over us because we don't speak perfect Spanish." So Selena learns from her father to sing Spanish and eventually to speak it, and becomes a regional star of Tejano music—the unique South Texas blend that formed in the early 1900s when Mexican bands mixed in the accordion music of their Czech and Polish neighbors.

The movie opens with Selena singing "I Will Survive" to a packed house in the Houston Astrodome, and then flashes back to the early life of her father, who formed a rock 'n' roll group named "The Dinos." Like his daughter many years later, he found himself caught between two worlds: Anglo clubs didn't want Chicano bands, and Mexican clubs wanted Spanish dance music. After one appearance ends in a fight, a cop asks Abraham, "What'd y'all do?" He answers, "We sang 'We Belong Together.'"

Abraham's band fails, but he starts again, bringing home secondhand instruments to begin a family group, despite the doubts of his wife, Marcela (Constance Marie). In one of the movie's most charming scenes, the family has hit bottom. Abraham promises Selena someday she'll be a big star "and go to Disneyland." Then Marcela hears a familiar song on the radio, and teaches her daughter to dance to it, giving her the trademark of perpetual motion onstage.

Young Selena is played by Becky Lee Meza, who has a big smile and a lot of energy. The teenage and adult Selena is played by Lopez in a star-making performance. After her strong work as the passionate lover of Jack Nicholson in *Blood and Wine,* here she creates a completely different performance, as a loyal Quintanilla who does most of her growing up on a tour bus with her dad at the wheel.

She's very close to Susie and Abie, and finds a trusted confidante in her mother, but when a talented young guitarist named Chris Perez (Jon Seda) joins the band and she falls in love with him, there's trouble. "This stops right now!" Abraham thunders, firing the kid. But it's true love, well written and acted here, and after Selena and Chris elope, the family accepts him. Olmos's scene with his daughter, when she brings her new husband home, is one of the movie's most touching.

The biographical scenes are intercut with a lot of music; Selena's original recordings are used, with Lopez lip-synching and doing a convincing job of being Selena on stage; she has the star presence to look believable in front of 100,000 fans in Monterrey, Mexico. Some of the songs build real power, but others are undercut, I think, by unnecessary visual gimmicks like Woodstock-style double and triple split screens, and cutaways to the Moon, roses, and other symbols. In one montage late in the movie, the same song is shown being performed at several concerts, to showcase the many different costumes Selena designed for herself; the costumes come across, but the performance is lost in the cutting. When Lopez (and Selena) are left alone to simply sing, the results are electrifying.

*Selena* is smart in not letting the singer's death dominate the story of her life. We meet her killer, Yolanda Salvidar (Lupe Ontiveros), almost obliquely, when she's introduced as the manager of Selena's new boutique and the former president of her fan club. Soon there's a discrepancy over missing money, and then the shooting, which the movie wisely deals with only through its aftermath.

*Selena* succeeds, through Lopez's performance, in evoking the magic of a sweet and talented young woman. And, like Nava's *My Family,* it's insightful in portraying Mexican-American culture as a rich resource with its own flavor and character. It's ironic that the most successful modern Latina female singer could once have had a talk with her dad where he sighed, "You like Donna Summer; I like doo-wop." But he also said, "You gotta be who you are." She was.

## A Self-Made Hero ★ ★ ★

NO MPAA RATING, 105 m., 1998

Mathieu Kassovitz (Albert Dehousse), Anouk Grinberg (Servane), Sandrine Kiberlain (Yvette), Albert Dupontel (Dionnet), Nadia Barentin (Mme Louvier/Mme Revuz/General's Wife). Directed by Jacques Audiard and produced by Patrick Godeau. Screenplay by Alain Le Henry and Jacques Audiard, based on the novel by Jean-Francois Deniau.

"The past only drags you down," the Captain advises Albert, who is a beggar at the time. Albert takes him at his word and reinvents himself as a hero of the French Resistance—so successfully that men who really were heroes have tears in their eyes when they think of his bravery. *A Self-Made Hero* is inspired by the way that some French belatedly recalled that they were always against the Nazis in World War II, but it is not simply an attack on hypocrisy. In a larger sense, it's about our human weakness for inventing stories about ourselves and telling them so often that we believe them.

Albert Dehousse (Mathieu Kassovitz) is schooled in deception at his mother's breast. From her he learns that his father was a hero in the first war: Doesn't she have his veteran's pension to prove it? From nasty local urchins Albert learns the more likely story, that his father was a drunk who died of liver failure, and his mother made the whole thing up.

Albert himself is an idle daydreamer, a blank slate on which various versions of a life story can be sketched. He reads romantic novels, and then tells a girl he is a novelist. She believes him and marries him, but her family so mistrusts him that it is only after the war he discovers they were in the Resistance, and sheltered Allied pilots who were shot down.

Albert spends the war as a salesman, having evaded the draft. From his father-in-law he learns that to make a sale, you must determine what a customer wants to believe, and confirm it.

Fleeing his first marriage after the liberation, he is penniless in Paris when he meets the Captain (Albert Dupontel), a heroic Resistance parachutist who assumed so many fake identities during the war that he perhaps lost touch with himself and identified only with his deceptions. He bluntly counsels Albert to invent a new past.

This process comes easily to Albert because he has no present. Like Chance, the hero of *Being There,* he is such a cipher that other people see what they want. Albert studies papers on the Resistance, memorizes lists, even inserts himself into old newsreel footage. Some of his skills he learns during a period as private secretary to the enigmatic Mr. Jo, who survived the war by supplying both the Nazis and the Resistance with what they wanted. Albert, indeed, has a gift for finding those who can tutor him in deception: He even learns about the artifices of love from a prostitute.

*A Self-Made Hero* is not an angry exposé, but a bemused, cynical examination of human weakness. Not a week goes past without another story of an ambassador who invents wartime heroism, an executive who awards himself fictitious degrees, a government official who borrows someone else's childhood trauma and calls it his own. I myself have told stories so often they seem real to me, and can no longer be sure whether my friend McHugh really slapped King Constantine on the back in that hotel bar in Rome. All children tell you with great solemnity about adventures that never happened. Some children don't stop when they grow up.

As it must to all men, some degree of maturity eventually comes to Albert, and with it an uneasiness about what he has done. Even deception has its responsibilities, as when fate requires Albert to decide the fates of six Frenchmen who served in the German army. And then there is a woman he begins to love; he is seized by a great need to tell her the truth.

Albert is played by Mathieu Kassovitz, whose own films as a director *(Cafe au Lait, Hate)* skate along the cutting edge of France's racial tension. In those films he can seem brash, quick, violent. Here he's more of a wraith, and the parallel with Chance is appropriate. Resistance heroes embrace him because his experience enhances their own; the real reason anyone listens to your story is so that you will have to listen to theirs.

Jacques Audiard, who directed the film and cowrote it (the screenplay won an award at Cannes), is of course aware of the way many French collaborationists suddenly discovered Resistance pasts after the war. But that process is too well known to need repeating. His film is more subtle and wide reaching, the story of a man for whom everything is equally unreal, who distrusts his own substance so deeply that he must be somebody else to be anybody at all.

## Senseless ★ ★ ½

R, 88 m., 1998

Marlon Wayans (Darryl Witherspoon), David Spade (Scott Thorpe), Matthew Lillard (Tim LaFlour), Rip Torn (Randall Tyson), Tamara Taylor (Janice), Brad Dourif (Dr. Wheedon), Kenya Moore (Lorraine). Directed by Penelope Spheeris and produced by David Hoberman. Screenplay by Greg Erb and Craig Mazin.

*Senseless* is a Jim Carrey movie fighting to be a Penelope Spheeris movie, and losing. In this corner is Marlon Wayans, another of the large and talented Wayans family, playing a college student who becomes the pawn of a mad scientific experiment. And in the other corner, Spheeris *(The Decline of Western Civilization, Wayne's World, Black Sheep).*

Wayans does Jim Carrey–style berserk physical comedy, and does it pretty well. Spheeris fills the crannies of the film with Gen-X counterculture stuff, including Wayans's college roommate, who is so deeply into body piercing that he not only wears studs in his eyebrows, tongue, and lower lip, but wears a gold chain linking those two parts of the anatomy which any prudent man would most hope to keep unbound.

Wayans plays Darryl Witherspoon, who is being dunned for past-due tuition, and in desperation seeks out Dr. Wheedon (Brad Dourif), an owlish scientist whose experimental potion enhances the five senses beyond belief. Darryl hires on as a guinea pig, and the movie's gags involve what he does with his supersenses.

This is a promising idea, and *Senseless* has some fun with it. The slightest sound drives Darryl mad, and side effects make him too itchy to sit through an exam. But soon he's able to see, hear, taste, smell, and feel better than anyone else. That makes him a star on the hockey team, and a virtuoso in other areas too. (He's been raising money by donating blood and sperm, and now asks the sperm bank for a quote on two gallons.)

The film's villain is the supercilious Scott (David Spade), who maneuvers to keep Darryl out of his fraternity. That's important because an important alum of the fraternity (Rip Torn) might help a bright economics major get a job with a Wall Street firm. Darryl and Scott are finalists when tragedy strikes: Darryl incautiously takes a double dose of the magic potion and finds that his senses are cycling out of control. He can count on only four of the five at any given moment, and when Torn takes him to a Knicks game, his hearing cuts out during the national anthem and his eyesight fails as he sits next to an unamused Patrick Ewing.

This is not great comedy, and Wayans doesn't find ways to build and improvise, as Carrey does. But he's talented and has unbounded energy, a plastic face, and a rubber body. I liked him. And I liked his flirtation with Janice (Tamara Taylor), a co-ed who accepts his bizarre misadventures. I was not so fond of a subplot involving Lorraine (Kenya Moore), Janice's buxom sorority sister, who seems written in to supply an awkward and pointless seduction scene.

Penelope Spheeris, whose *Wayne's World* remains one of the funniest of recent movies, never finds a consistent tone here. The broad physical humor of the main plot contrasts weirdly with the character of the roommate (Matthew Lillard), who doesn't seem to vibrate in the same universe. His character could be funny in a different movie, but he seems at right angles to this one.

## Set It Off ★ ★ ★ ½

R, 121 m., 1996

Jada Pinkett (Stony), Queen Latifah (Cleo), Vivica A. Fox (Frankie), Kimberly Elise (Tisean), John C. McGinley (Detective Strode), Blair Underwood (Keith). Directed by F. Gary Gray and produced by Dale Pollock and Oren Koules. Screenplay by Kate Lanier and Takashi Bufford, based on a story by Bufford.

*Set It Off* is advertised as a thriller about four black women who rob banks. But it's a lot more than that. It creates a portrait of the lives of these women that's so observant and informed, it's like *Waiting to Exhale* with a strong jolt of reality. The movie surprised and moved me: I expected a routine action picture, and was amazed how much I started to care about the characters.

The action sequences—the robberies, the close calls, the shoot-outs—are all well handled (this movie has the first chase scene I've seen in a long time that I cared about). But what makes the film special is the way it shows the motivations of its four women, whose lives are in economic crisis. It doesn't justify bank robbery, but it makes a convincing case for the mixture of desperation, impulsiveness, and thrill seeking that catapults its characters from minimum-wage jobs to the TV news bulletins.

As the film opens, Frankie (Vivica A. Fox) is a teller in a bank that's in the process of being robbed by a gang of armed men. She recognizes one of them from her neighborhood: "Darnell! What are you doing?" Afterward, Frankie is grilled by the cops and bank authorities. "What's the proper procedure for dealing with this situation?" asks a detective (John C. McGinley). She's fired. "The fact that you knew the perpetrator," a bank executive coldly tells her, "doesn't sit well with us."

These scenes are immediately believable. Although Frankie and Darnell come from the same milieu, their lives have taken completely different paths, until today. Meanwhile, we meet Frankie's friends, including Stony (Jada Pinkett), who has a problem: Her kid brother has been accepted at UCLA, but didn't get a scholarship. This looks like a plot gimmick (will she rob banks to pay his tuition?) until the screenplay, by Kate Lanier and Takashi Bufford, provides a convincing, realistic twist to his story.

The other friends include Cleo (Queen Latifah), a tall, broad, strong woman, a lesbian who delights in buying gifts for her girl-toy; and Tisean (Kimberly Elise), who has a young child and is struggling to raise him as a single mother. They work for a janitorial service, and that's where Frankie ends up, too; being fired has cost her the references she needs for bank employment.

All four women know Darnell, and the word quickly spreads that he got away with $20,000. They draw an obvious conclusion: "If crackhead Darnell can rob a bank, we can." They begin planning a bank job, more on a dare than anything else, but after some false starts they actually do rob a bank; hesitating, almost deciding not to, and then following an impulsive decision.

But life has unexpected turns. Casing a bank for a possible robbery, Stony is approached by a black bank executive (Blair Underwood) who likes her looks and suggests she needs her own "personal banker." She starts dating him, but won't tell him where she lives; it's as if this relationship is taking place on a separate track from the rest of her life.

The movie is more aware of the economic struggles of its characters than most American films allow themselves to be; the director, F. Gary Gray, also made the underrated *Friday,* about unemployment and anger. There's a wonderfully written scene where the women sit on a rooftop, smoking pot, looking at a factory, and observing wistfully, "Before they started laying people off, they were paying $15 an hour at that place."

These women can't hold much of a household together on the minimum wage. Tisean brings her young son to work with her because she can't find child care and can't afford to lose a day's pay. The kid is injured—not seriously, but enough so that a social worker takes custody of the child, and Tisean is devastated. Sure, she can get her child back when she proves she can provide an adequate home and child care. But how, in her economic reality, is that possible?

One scene after another surprised me with its invention. I loved a moment when the four women sit around a conference table in the office building they clean, and do imitations from *The Godfather* while discussing their plans. The scene where Cleo lives it up with the girlfriend she dotes on. The scene where Stony's banker takes her to a black-tie dinner and she says it's "the best night of my life." And the subtle, unspoken reasons that a white woman refuses to pick Cleo out of a police lineup.

There is even a scene where the four women hold a planning session at a coffee shop, discover they don't have enough money to pay the bill, and sneak out—stiffing the waitress. The waitress, by the way, is black. So is the social worker. The movie is not about overt racism, but about the buried realities of an economic system that expects these women to lead lives the system does not allow them to afford.

The movie is not perfect; its most obvious error is that the characters do not react to the violence in the way that real women would. The movie provides perfunctory reaction shots and then moves on. The movie is so psychologically accurate in its other scenes that it should have given more thought to how the reality of death would affect these women, who are not killers.

One clue to the depths of *Set It Off* may come from a previous credit of cowriter Kate Lanier, who wrote the Tina Turner biopic *What's Love Got to Do With It.* That was grounded in close observation of harsh women's realities, and so is *Set It Off.* Reviewing *Waiting to Exhale,* which I enjoyed, I wrote: "There are times when the material needs more sharpness, harder edges, bitter satire, instead of bemused observation." Here is the film I was thinking of.

## Seven Years in Tibet ★ ★ ½

PG-13, 131 m., 1997

Brad Pitt (Heinrich Harrer), David Thewlis (Peter Aufschnaiter), B. D. Wong (Ngawang Jigme), Lhakpa Tsamchoe (Pema Lhaki), Mako (Kungo Tsarong), Danny Denzongpa (Regent), Victor Wong (Chinese "Amban"), Ingeborga Dapkunaite (Ingrid Harrer), Jamyang Jamtsho Wangchuck (Dalai Lama [fourteen years]). Directed by Jean-Jacques Annaud and produced by Annaud, John H. Williams, and Iain Smith. Screenplay by Becky Johnston, based on the book by Heinrich Harrer.

Jean-Jacques Annaud's *Seven Years in Tibet* takes the true story of a bright and powerful young boy who meets a stranger from a different land, and buries it inside the equally true but less interesting story of the stranger. The movie is about two characters, and is told from the point of view of the wrong one.

As it opens, we already understand or guess much of what there is to know about Heinrich Harrer (Brad Pitt), an Austrian obsessed by mountain climbing. We know next to nothing about the early life of the Dalai Lama. We know all about the kind of events that occupy the first half of the movie (mountain climbing, POW camps, wilderness treks). We know much less about the world inside the Forbidden City, where lives a fourteen-year-old boy who is both ruler and god.

*Seven Years in Tibet* is an ambitious and beautiful movie with much to interest the patient viewer, but it makes the common mistake of many films about travelers and explorers: It is more concerned with their adventures than with what they discovered. Consider Livingstone and Stanley, the first Europeans to see vast reaches of Africa, who are remembered mostly because they succeeded in finding each other there.

Vienna, 1939. Harrer is preparing an assault on the difficult Himalayan peak of Nanga Parbat. War is about to break out, but he is indifferent to it, and cold to his pregnant wife ("Go—leave! I'll see you in four months!"). He and a guide named Peter Aufschnaiter (David Thewlis) are soon on the peaks. The mountain-climbing scenes (shot in the Andes) are splendid but not very original; Heinrich saves Peter despite a broken ankle, they are nearly killed by an avalanche, the war begins, and they're interred in a British POW camp, from which they finally escape.

This material occupies the first half of the movie, and yet strictly speaking, it has nothing to do with it. The story proper (the seven years mentioned in the title) begins after they stumble into Tibet and are welcomed uncertainly by the peaceful and isolated civilization they find there.

From the moment of the first appearance of the Dalai Lama (Jamyang Jamtsho Wangchuck), the film takes on greater interest. He stands on the parapet of his palace in Lhasa and surveys his domain through a telescope. He is fascinated by the strangers who have arrived in his kingdom, and soon sends his mother to invite Harrer to visit.

"Yellow Head," he calls him, touching the European's blond hair with fascination, and soon protocol falls aside as he asks Harrer to build him a movie theater and teach him about the world outside. This makes an absorbing story, although I suspect the relationship between pupil and teacher did not feel as relaxed and modern as it does in the film.

Aufschnaiter, the guide, meets a local woman tailor (Lhakpa Tsamchoe) and marries her, and we gather from soulful looks that Harrer would have liked to marry her himself, but the Harrer character is not forthcoming. Brad Pitt plays him at two speeds: cold and forbidding at first, and then charming and boyish. He might have been more convincing if he'd been played by, for example, Thewlis. But *Seven Years in Tibet* is a star vehicle: Pitt is required to justify its $70 million budget, and it would be churlish to blame him for his own miscasting since the movie would not have been made without him.

The film shows the behavior of the Red Chinese toward Tibet as cruel and gratuitous. Why the Chinese so valued this remote, sealed-off kingdom is a mystery; maybe it was a threat to self-righteous, lockstep Marxism. The film shows how Tibet was betrayed from without and within, and then the Dalai Lama, now twenty-one, flees into long years of exile.

He has a more complex face for me, now that I have seen the tortuous journey from his childhood. I wish I had learned more about Tibet: What were the ethnic ramifications, for example, of the marriage between the tailor and the mountain climber? How easily was the language barrier overcome? Why were the Dalai Lama's advisers willing to allow him to come under the influence of a foreigner? How did the boy overcome his godlike upbringing to become open and curious to the outside?

These questions are not exactly answered. But the film does deal with one issue that has been publicized recently: the fact, unknown to the filmmakers when they began, that Harrer had been a Nazi Party member since 1933. Voice-over dialogue establishes him as a Nazi early in the film, and another line later says he "shuddered to recall" his early errors. The information about Harrer should have come as no surprise; would the Nazis have risked letting a nonparty member win the glory of conquering Nanga Parbat?

## Shadow Conspiracy ★

R, 103 m., 1997

Charlie Sheen (Bobby Bishop), Linda Hamilton (Amanda Givens), Donald Sutherland (Conrad), Stephen Lang (The Agent), Sam Waterston (President), Ben Gazzara (Vice President Saxon), Henry Strozier (Treasury Secretary Murphy). Directed by George P. Cosmatos and produced by Terry Collis. Screenplay by Adi Hasak and Ric Gibbs.

*Shadow Conspiracy* is a simpleminded thriller that seems destined for mercy killing in the video stores after a short run before appalled audiences. There isn't a brain in its empty little head, or in its assembly-line story, which is about how Charlie Sheen pauses occasionally between ludicrous action scenes, some of them ripped off from better films.

Sheen plays a special assistant to the president of the United States. After a dozen people are shot dead in Washington (five victims at a conspiracy center, several reporters at the local paper, etc.), he catches on that something is not right. "Remember that article you wrote about a shadow government?" he askes his former lover, a reporter played by Linda Hamilton. "A conspiracy in the highest levels of government?" She does.

The president (Sam Waterston) threatens to call a halt to all federal spending. His chief of staff (the ominous Donald Sutherland) can't have that. An expert killer (Stephen Lang) is dispatched to kill those who would expose Sutherland's conspiracy. Lang is expert, but not subtle; he pulls women's hair, knocks over laundry carts, runs through public places firing his gun, and tries to assassinate the president with a toy helicopter that fires real machine guns. (If any students of Newton's second law are reading this, I hope they will explain why a toy weighing five pounds would not be disabled by the recoil from these weapons.)

The movie starts with the assault on the center for conspiracy studies, where all of the researchers are apparently deaf, since none of them hear a thing when Lang shoots his first victim through a plate glass window. Later Sheen twigs to the conspiracy and is chased through Washington by Lang; the chase leads into one of my favorite cliché locations, a Steam and Sparks Factory—so named because all it apparently produces are steam and sparks. From the factory Sheen dives into a river, escapes over a waterfall, and dries off with the hot-air blower in a men's room (I will not soon forget him directing the jet of air down the front of his pants). Oh, I almost forgot that the sequence began with Sheen surviving a fall from a high-rise window-washer's platform. ("It's funny how twenty-four hours in this town can put you on the other side of the fence," he philosophizes.)

I especially doubted some of the technical details. Sheen hacks into a top secret National Security database to discover the fate of a colleague, and reads on the screen: "Terminated With Extreme Prejudice. Authorized by Jacob Conrad." Conrad is the Sutherland character. I'm sure secret government agencies carefully enter all of their murders into their databases.

Then there's the matter of the surveillance satellites used by the White House conspirators to track down Sheen and Hamilton in her Jeep. Starting with a view of the hemisphere, the spy cameras can apparently scan every license plate in Washington, and find hers—not once but several times. I'm thinking (a) how come the car is never parked in a garage, or pointing the wrong way, or under a tree? and (b) is this tracking method really the easiest way of spotting two famous people driving around central Washington in an open Jeep?

Such quibbles do not easily slow the director, George P. Cosmatos, whose credits include *Rambo II, Cobra,* and *Leviathan.* His movie contains a scene with Lang riding a motorcycle that chases Sheen into the subway system and onto the tracks. Moviegoers with long memories will recall this sequence in its original, much superior incarnation, in *Diva* (1982). Only moviegoers with very, very short memories, however, should attempt to see *Shadow Conspiracy.*

## Shall We Dance? ★ ★ ★ ½

PG, 118 m., 1997

Koji Yakusyo (Shohei Sugiyama), Tamiyo Kusakari (Mai Kishikawa), Naoto Takenaka (Tomio Aoki), Eriko Watanabe (Toyoko Takahashi), Akira Emoto (Toru Miwa), Yu Tokui (Tokichi Hattori), Hiromasa Taguchi (Masahiro Tanaka), Reiko Kusamura (Tamako Tamura). Directed by Masayuki Suo and produced by Yasuyoshi Tokuma, Shoji Masui, and Yuji Ogata. Screenplay by Suo.

One night as he is taking the train home after work, a man sees a beautiful woman standing alone at a second-floor window, lost in thought.

The second night, she is there again. The sign on the window advertises ballroom dancing lessons. The third night, the man gets off the train at an unaccustomed stop and climbs the stairs to the dance studio.

With these simple and direct shots, Masayuki Suo establishes loneliness, mystery, and allure. Later, all will become clear, but it is more intriguing this way: A man seeking not so much a woman as an answer to his question. Why is she sad? What is she thinking?

In Japan the opening scenes would play with an even greater charge. Opening titles, probably added by the distributor, tell us, "Ballroom dancing is regarded with great suspicion, in a country where couples don't go out hand in hand, or say 'I love you.'" The hero of *Shall We Dance?* named Shohei Sugiyama (Koji Yakusyo), is married, a salaryman who works late at night in an office. For him to take dance lessons is as shocking as taking a mistress.

Japan is in some ways still a Victorian society, which makes its eroticism more intriguing. Repression, guilt, and secrecy are splendid aphrodisiacs. Sugiyama creeps up the staircase like a man sneaking into a brothel, and enters a brightly lighted room where other students are already taking their lessons. He is disappointed to learn that his instructor will not be the mysterious stranger at the window (Tamiyo Kusakari), but a friendly, plump, middle-aged woman who teaches him the fundamentals of the fox-trot, and warns him: "She's all the sweeter when viewed from afar."

*Shall We Dance?* is not about love with a tantalizing mirage, then, but about a man losing his inhibitions and breaking out of the rut of his life. Even Sugiyama's wife thinks he should get out more. "He's working too hard," she tells her daughter; we get a glimpse of the Japanese salaryman's home, where the wage earner often arrives late at night and leaves early in the morning, and may have more important relationships at work than with his own family.

The little crowd at the dance studio has its regulars, including a chubby man who will forever be uncoordinated, and a "wild and crazy" little guy with a mop of hair whose identity provides one of the movie's best moments. Eventually Sugiyama learns that the beautiful woman is embittered because of a breakup with her dance partner, and slowly he is introduced to the world of ballroom dancing competitions, which seem to be the same the world over (the scenes have some of the same feel as the contests in the Australian *Strictly Ballroom*).

There are puzzles at Sugiyama's home. His wife smells unfamiliar perfume on his shirt. His daughter catches him rehearsing alone, late at night. Is he having an affair? Not with the mysterious woman he's not: When he asks her out for dinner, she explains sternly that dancing is her life, and that she certainly hopes he didn't take lessons just in the hopes of meeting her.

The last third of *Shall We Dance?* provides audience-pleasing payoffs that could make this the most successful Japanese film at the Western box office since *Tampopo* ten years ago. But it is the opening material that fascinates. To seek out the secret of a beautiful woman in a window is much more interesting than to discover the secret. Familiarity dissipates eroticism. But of course I realize I am asking the impossible, because of course Sugiyama will mount the stairs, and so of course there must be a story.

Masayuki Suo's direction combines the psychological and intriguing with comedy bits that might be found in a lesser movie. This is often a characteristic of Japanese art; between the moments of drama and truth, lowbrow characters hustle onstage to provide counterpoint. The result is one of the more completely entertaining movies I've seen in a while—a well-crafted character study that, like a Hollywood movie with a skillful script, manipulates us but makes us like it.

As for the happy ending: Well, of course there is one. And it is happy not just for the characters in the movie, but for me, as well, because I imagine the mysterious woman will again appear at her place in the window, gazing out, lost in thought, an inspiration to us all.

## Shanghai Triad ★ ★

NO MPAA RATING, 109 m., 1996

Gong Li (Xiao Jingbao), Li Baotian (The Godfather), Li Xuejian (Liu Shu), Wang Xiao Xiao (Shuisheng), Shun Chun (Number Two). Directed by Zhang Yimou and produced by Jean Louis Piel. Screenplay by Bi Feiyu, adapted from a novel by Li Xiao.

*Shanghai Triad* may be the last, and is certainly the least, of the collaborations between the Chinese director Zhang Yimou and the gifted actress Gong Li. The story of a gang boss in 1930s Shanghai and his willful, troublesome mistress is seen through the eyes of a small boy from the country, who loses his innocence in eight bloody days.

Zhang Yimou and Gong Li's great works together, starting in 1987, were *Red Sorghum, Ju Dou, Raise the Red Lantern, The Story of Qui Ju,* and *To Live.* These five films represent one of the great actor-director collaborations, but the couple ended their romantic involvement in February 1995, and now plan to work apart.

This last film, which is never involving and often pointless and repetitive, is about the powerful boss (Li Baotian) of a Shanghai crime triad and his mistress, Xiao Jingbao (Gong Li), a nightclub singer who mocks and taunts him, and whose nickname is Bijou. The true nature of their relationship emerges only gradually, because the point of view is supplied by a fourteen-year-old named Shuisheng (Wang Xiao Xiao), who comes from the country under the sponsorship of his uncle, a gangster.

Shuisheng's assignment is to work as a personal servant for the glamorous Bijou, but almost before he has his feet on the ground he witnesses a gangland execution. And he overhears troubling conversations between the woman and the godfather (as the film calls him, perhaps in a bow to Brando by the subtitles). The godfather's word is law in his little world, but he cannot bend Bijou to his will.

Shuisheng is naive and inexperienced (asked by a gangster if he's ever slept with a woman, he replies helpfully, "Yes, with my mother, when I was little"). He views the world of the godfather and the mistress incompletely, through doors slightly ajar, through overheard conversations, through the implications of statements he does not fully understand.

Yimou is one of the best visual stylists of current cinema, and *Shanghai Triad* is a good-looking film. The scenes set in Bijou's nightclub have a nice smoky, decadent, sensuous look, and Bijou is in the great tradition of gangster movies where the boss's girlfriend is the lead singer: She does not sing nearly as well as the boss thinks she does. But the nightclub production numbers go on so long they break the rhythm and seem to occupy a movie of their own.

Trouble strikes. A rival gang attacks the godfather's house, killing many people, including the boy's uncle ("his open eyes call out for vengeance," the boy is told). The boss gathers his gang members, his mistress, and the little boy, and removes them all to a small island. Shuisheng now begins to suspect that his mistress is in special danger, but any tension is dissipated in the island's foggy atmosphere. An annoying childhood song is sung again and again (and again), as characters wander through the mist, and we discover that the plot is not at all what we thought.

*Shanghai Triad* plays like a movie in which some scenes are missing and others have been stretched out to make up the difference. It was made by Zhang Yimou under difficult conditions; his *To Live* was entered in the Cannes Film Festival against the wishes of the Chinese government, which then slapped restrictions on this production. But even if the film had been more fully realized, I wonder if it would have been much better.

There are two basic weaknesses. One is that the boy supplies the point of view, and yet the story is not about him, so instead of identifying with him, we are simply frustrated in our wish to see more than he can see. The other problem is that Gong Li's character is thoroughly unlikable. She can be the warmest and most charismatic of actresses, but here she always seems mad about something. Maybe about her director?

## She's So Lovely ★ ★ ★

R, 112 m., 1997

Sean Penn (Eddie), Robin Wright Penn (Maureen), John Travolta (Joey), Harry Dean Stanton (Shorty), Debi Mazar (Georgie), Gena Rowlands (Miss Green), James Gandolfini (Kiefer), Kelsey Mulrooney (Jeanie). Directed by Nick Cassavetes and produced by Rene Cleitman. Screenplay by John Cassavetes.

At first I didn't understand some of the behavior in the second half of *She's So Lovely,* but then I found the explanation, which is that two of the characters are mad. They often are in the films of John Cassavetes, and this is the last that will bear his credit: Cassavetes, who died in 1989, wrote the screenplay, which has been directed by his son, Nick.

The presence in a small role of Cassavetes's widow, Gena Rowlands, is a reminder of all the characters she played in her husband's movies. Most of them were also mad-deranged, alcoholic, obsessive wives, lovers, or eccentric dames, driven crazy by love and need. Narrow your eyes a little, imagine Rowlands, Cassavetes, and Peter Falk in the roles played here by Robin Wright Penn, Sean Penn, and John Travolta, and you have the key that unlocks the film. Otherwise, you're likely to leave the theater frustrated and confused, asking yourself how any mother could make the choice that the woman in this film makes.

As the story opens, the woman, named Maureen (Wright Penn), lives in a transient hotel with her lover, Eddie (Sean Penn). He has been missing for three days. She seeks him out (and also free drinks and smokes) in a Skid Row bar, and ends up in the room of Kiefer (James Gandolfini), a neighbor across the hall. Through a very large, alcoholic misunderstanding, he assaults her, and Maureen is afraid that when Eddie finds out, he'll kill the guy.

She is nearly right. Eddie, also drunk, succeeds in accidentally shooting a member of an emergency response team, and is sent to prison. At this point, halfway through the movie, everything has advanced according to a certain logic, and we understand that Maureen and Eddie are alcoholics who are obsessively in love, and whose lives, as they say, have become unmanageable.

Ten years pass, handled and explained only with a title on the screen. Maureen is now serenely married to Joey (John Travolta), and lives in a suburban home with her three children, the oldest by Eddie. Then Eddie is released from prison, and the madness begins all over again. Eddie still loves her and wants to see her. In a sequence that has a scary fascination, Joey takes Eddie's daughter, Jeanie, to meet Eddie at a downtown hotel. Would a stepfather do such a thing? Yes, but in such a place? "Shut up and drink your beer," Eddie tells Jeanie at one point, not unkindly.

I was reminded of the Cassavetes film about an obsessive gambler who took his child with him to Vegas and left him in a room at a casino while he disappeared for hours to gamble. Or another where kids are yanked out of school for a weird day at the beach. The families in Cassavetes films are always dysfunctional, the children confronted with irresponsible, deranged adults and trying to make sense of them. Cassavetes's films spun at such a pitch of emotional chaos that no behavior seemed unbelievable, although a lot of it seemed unwise.

The crucial late scene in *She's So Lovely* involves Eddie's visit to the suburban home of Joey and Maureen. This scene will raise questions among logical viewers, but it works as drama, and we cannot look away. Eddie and Maureen are not given a lot of choices (they're locked into a compulsive replay of old tapes), but Travolta finds ways to introduce dark humor into the scene, and we smile sometimes, as we did with so many Cassavetes films, because the characters are mad in such a verbal, screwy, almost pathetic way.

Watching *She's So Lovely,* it's helpful to remember that movies can show behavior without recommending it—that the highest purpose of a movie is not to reflect life realistically, but to filter it through the mind of the artist. *She's So Lovely* does not depict choices most audiences will condone, or even understand, but the film is not boring, and has the dread hypnotic appeal of a slowly developing traffic accident (in which we think there will probably be no fatalities).

Robin Wright Penn and Sean Penn are locked into Maureen and Eddie with a savage zeal; the characters play less implausibly than they sound, because the actors believe in them. Penn is one of our best actors, and his wife (who was so solid as Jenny in *Forrest Gump*) is able to stay with him in these harrowing situations. Travolta finds a way to somehow be outside firing range—his Joey is a man with his own goofiness, who only seems to be ordinary. And there are nice side roles, including one for Harry Dean Stanton, as a drinking buddy who has the classic line, "Nobody brought a piece—it's not that kind of an evening."

Nick Cassavetes, now in his thirties, has been an actor (as indeed anyone with his parents would almost have to be) and is now a director. In *Unhook the Stars* (1996) he directed his mother, Gena Rowlands, as a sensible woman trying to deal with the dysfunctional young mother (Marisa Tomei) across the street, and now here he directs his father's last script.

As a filmmaker, he lacks his father's untidy emotional wildness; he makes films that are more carefully crafted and lack the anarchic spirit. But he understands the territory, and in *She's So Lovely* what he especially understands is that if you want to see true weirdness, you don't look along Skid Row, where the motives are pretty easy to understand, but out in suburbia, where those green lawns can surround human time bombs.

## She's the One ★ ★

R, 97 m., 1996

Edward Burns (Mickey), Maxine Bahns (Hope), Cameron Diaz (Heather), Mike McGlone (Francis), John Mahoney (Mr. Fitzpatrick), Jennifer Aniston (Rene). Directed by Edward Burns and produced by Ted Hope, James Schamus, and Burns. Screenplay by Burns.

Early in *She's the One,* a beautiful woman named Hope (Maxine Bahns) gets into a cab driven by a feckless bachelor named Mickey (Edward Burns). They fall into conversation. She likes him. She's on the way to the airport but doesn't like planes, and so she hires him to drive her to New Orleans. A day later they are married. Uh, huh. Not likely—especially not in a New York cab—and yet Meet Cutes like this have been fueling romantic comedies since time immemorial, and so we go along with the gag.

Once they return to New York, reality intrudes. Mickey's brother, Francis (Mike McGlone), is angry because Mickey got married without a best man. Meanwhile, Francis is cheating on his wife, Rene (Jennifer Aniston, from *Friends*), with Heather (Cameron Diaz).

Now about this Heather. She used to date Mickey, who knew that she worked her way through college as a hooker. They were engaged, but it ended, and now Heather is dividing her time between Francis and Poppa, a very old, very rich man we never see. Heather is described as working on Wall Street, but her job description may not be precisely what Francis envisions.

Mickey and Francis are Irish-American brothers, who along with their father (John Mahoney) like to call themselves the Fighting Fitzpatricks. They have a mother, but she is never seen in the movie, only talked about. Their father, who likes to call the boys "sister" and "Barbara," believes that even at their age there's no better way to settle a family fight than by putting on the gloves and stepping into the backyard.

*She's the One* was written and directed by Edward Burns, who won the Sundance Film Festival in 1995 with his beguiling comedy *The Brothers McMullen.* The Brothers Fitzpatrick are not quite so beguiling, and the movie feels like material from the same pot, stirred and shaken, with a touch of screwball. If this were exclusively a screwball comedy—involving romantic misunderstandings and revolving doors—it might have worked better, but unfortunately Burns allows an element of Sincerity and Psychological Insight to take over, and the movie bogs down in earnestness.

The two big moral issues in the movie seem rather contrived. One involves Hope, who, having married Mickey within twenty-four hours, now wonders how to tell him she plans to leave for Paris in the fall to study at the Sorbonne and expects him to come along. My own notion is that a part-time cab driver so unattached he can get married in twenty-four hours is probably not going to balk at the idea of a trip to Paris with his beautiful new wife. But the movie treats Paris as a feminist issue: Is Mickey comfortable with the idea that Hope has these plans, etc., or does he have tiresome old ideas that since he's the man, etc? (Of course, Hope perhaps should have mentioned Paris during the whirlwind courtship, but never mind.)

The other moral issue involves brother Francis, who is a successful Wall Street investor, making lots of money and plotting to dump his wife for his mistress. But the mistress is not so sure she wants to be married to Francis, and there's Poppa waiting in the wings. He may pack a colostomy bag, but he knows how to treat a woman, which is, in a movie like this, something the hero will never, ever understand. Cameron Diaz, as the mistress, proves again that she is a real actress in addition to being one of the most beautiful women in the movies; it's interesting how she lets Heather maintain a certain privacy and reserve, so that we can't make easy assumptions about her.

Around they go, the Fighting Fitzpatricks, with the action punctuated by fishing trips during which Dad imparts wisdom that it takes all of John Mahoney's considerable skill to keep from sounding as if it had just been downloaded from Edward Burns's word processor. Many of the scenes will create a sense of déjà vu if you've seen *The Brothers McMullen;* Burns and McGlone play roles very similar to their characters in the earlier movie, and Bahns's character is not a million miles removed.

Although the movie disappointed me, it did not dishearten me about Edward Burns as an actor or filmmaker. He knows how to move a scene, and he has a nice feel for the ground-level human touches that make his characters real.

His real future, however, may be as an actor: He and Bahns both have genuine star power, and it would be interesting to see them in the hands of a director more willing to exploit their attractiveness and charisma.

If Burns wants to continue at the helm, however, I hope he expands his reach. By that I don't mean abandoning his Irish-American world view and the characters he finds there, but deepening and pushing and testing. *She's the One* plays like an overhaul of *The Brothers McMullen* with a larger budget, and it's time for him to move on.

## Shine ★ ★ ★ ★

PG-13, 105 m., 1996

Geoffrey Rush (David [adult]), Noah Taylor (David [young man]), Alex Rafalowicz (David [boy]), Armin Mueller-Stahl (Peter), Lynn Redgrave (Gillian), John Gielgud (Cecil Parkes), Googie Withers (Katharine Prichard), Nicholas Bell (Ben Rosen). Directed by Scott Hicks and produced by Jane Scott. Screenplay by Jan Sardi.

Wandering in the rain, the man looks like one of the walking wounded. His talk is obsessive chatter, looping back on itself, seizing on words and finding nonsense associations for them. He laughs a lot and seems desperately affable. When he sits down at a piano in a crowded restaurant, he looks like trouble, until he starts to play. His music floods out like a cry of anguish and hope.

This is the central image in Scott Hicks's *Shine,* based on the true story of an Australian pianist who was an international prodigy, suffered a breakdown, and has gradually been able to piece himself back together. The musician's name is David Helfgott. His life story is not exactly as it is shown here, but close enough, I gather, for us to marvel at the way the human spirit can try to heal itself.

The movie circles in time, using three actors to play Helfgott. Alex Rafalowicz is young David, encouraged to excel at music and chess by a domineering father who slams the chessboard and shouts, "You must always win!" He is savage when his son places second in a national competition. Noah Taylor, so good in *Flirting,* plays the adolescent David, who blossoms at the piano but is forbidden by his father from accepting a scholarship offered by Isaac Stern. Geoffrey Rush plays David as an adult who goes mad and then slowly heals with the help of an understanding woman.

But it is all so much more complicated than this makes it sound. We should begin with David's father, Peter (Armin Mueller-Stahl), a Polish Jew who survived the Holocaust but lost most of his family. Now resettled in Australia, he places family above everything; refusing to let David study at the Royal College of Music in London, he screams, "You will destroy your family!" Peter is capable of violence but also tenderness and love; his family is in the grip of his tyranny, and it is little wonder that David comes unglued, torn between his father's demands that he be perfect at the piano, and his refusal to let him follow his musical career where it will lead.

David finds friendship and support from an old woman (Googie Withers) who encourages his music and helps him find the courage to go to London, where his tutor is played wonderfully, with dryness and affection, by Sir John Gielgud. There he is happy for a time, but during a performance of the formidable Rachmaninoff Piano Concerto no. 3, he comes apart.

We see him next as a middle-aged man, a wanderer back in Australia, talking nonsense, his name forgotten by all but a few. I understand that Scott Hicks got the idea for this film when he came across Helfgott playing in a restaurant, and heard his story.

One of the buried motifs of *Shine* is the war that goes on between David's parent figures. His father is a monster and his mother is weak, but the old woman in Perth helps him, and so does the piano teacher (Nicholas Bell). His key helper is a middle-aged astrologer (Lynn Redgrave), who meets him through a friend toward the end of his restaurant days. They fall in love, and love saves him.

Music is one of the areas in which child prodigies often excel; two others are mathematics and chess. All three have the advantage of not requiring much knowledge of life or human nature (for technical proficiency, anyway). David's piano playing is at first a skill that comes naturally to him; only later does it become an art, a way of self-expression.

What is terrifying for him is that the better he gets, the closer he comes to expressing feelings that his father has charged with enormous guilt.

The "Rach 3" is a tumult of emotion, and what happens is that David cannot perform it without being destroyed by the feelings it releases.

The father is undergoing a process similar to the one he has inflicted on his son. He, too, cannot deal with the emotions unleashed by his son's playing, which is why he forbids David to study in Europe; if the son becomes good enough, he will fly away on the wings of the music, breaking up the sacred family unit and reopening the father to all the terrors of the Holocaust—terrors against which he has raised up as a bulwark his family in its little suburban house. The last scene of the movie (filmed, I have been told, at Peter Helfgott's actual grave) tries to acknowledge some of these truths: Peter is a man whose life inflicted great damage, not least upon himself.

There has been much talk about films that said they were based on true stories but were kidding *(Fargo)* and films that said they were based on true stories but might have been lying *(Sleepers).* Here is a movie that is based on the truth beneath a true story.

The fact that David Helfgott lived the outlines of these events—that he triumphed, that he fell, that he came slowly back—adds an enormous weight of meaning to the film. There was controversy over his subsequent concert tour of North America, but I can understand why many of those who saw the film wanted to hear him—not for the "comeback drama" so much as to hear the music he kept on playing during his years in the wilderness, and which led him back again to his true calling. ☞

## Sick: The Life & Death of Bob Flanagan, Supermasochist ★ ★ ★ ½

NO MPAA RATING, 90 m., 1997

A documentary directed and produced by Kirby Dick. Featuring Bob Flanagan and Sheree Rose.

A few months before he died, Bob Flanagan and Sheree Rose had an argument. She was angry with him for refusing to submit to her sexual discipline. He was angry because she couldn't see that he was dying—drowning in the fluids of cystic fibrosis—and could hardly breathe.

This bare outline makes Rose seem like a monster, but the reality was much, much more complicated. Years earlier, in 1982, Flanagan had signed a contract giving Rose "total control over my mind and body." They had a sadomasochistic relationship lasting fifteen years. At the end she was not being cruel, so much as expressing her fear of losing him. It sounds cruel because she speaks in the terms they used to express their love.

*Sick: The Life & Death of Bob Flanagan, Supermasochist* is one of the most agonizing films I have ever seen. It tells the story of a man who was born with cystic fibrosis, a disease that fills the lungs with thick, sticky mucus, so that breathing is hard and painful, and an early death is the prognosis. He was in pain all of his life, and in a gesture of defiance he fought the pain with more pain. With Sheree Rose as his partner, he became a performance artist, using his own body as a canvas for museum shows, gallery exhibits, lectures, and performances. He was the literal embodiment of the joke about the man who liked to hit himself with a hammer because it felt so good when he stopped.

Flanagan's masochism began early in life. He recalls forcing himself to sleep under an open window in the winter, and torturing himself by hanging suspended from his bedroom ceiling or the bathroom door ("My parents could never figure out why all the doors were off the jambs"). By the time he made it formal with Sheree Rose, he had already been a masochist for years. "Where was I?" his mother asks herself. "Did we only give him love when he was in pain? I don't know. He was in pain so much of the time."

How do you develop a taste for sticking nails into yourself? His parents recall that as a small child he had pus drained from his lungs by needles; since he felt better afterward, perhaps he identified the pain with relief. Later it became a sort of defiant gesture. His father says: "He's saying to God—'I'll show you!'" In Sheree Rose he found a woman who was a true dominatrix, not just a kinky actress with bizarre costumes. He also found a life partner, and the closeness of their relationship seems frightening at times; they seemed to live inside each other's minds.

What makes *Sick* bearable is the saving grace of humor. Apart from the pain he was born with and the pain he heaped on top of it, Bob Flanagan was a wry, witty, funny man who saw the irony of his own situation. We see video footage of his lectures, his songs, his poems. He takes one of those plastic "Visible Man" dolls they use in science class, and modifies it to illustrate his own special case. As he jokes, kids himself, and makes puns about pain, we are aware of the plastic tubes leading into his nose: oxygen from a canister he carries everywhere.

We are a little surprised to discover that from 1973 to 1995 he was a counselor at a summer camp for kids with CF, and around the campfire we hear him singing his version of a Dylan song, "Forever Lung." He was "scheduled" to die as a child, but lived until forty-two (two of his sisters died of the disease). He was a role model for CF survivors. We meet a seventeen-year-old Toronto girl named Sara who has cystic fibrosis and tells the Make-a-Wish Foundation her wish is to meet Bob Flanagan. She does. How does she deal with his sex life? "Bondage. I can relate to that. Being able to control *some*thing."

Flanagan and Rose collaborated on this film with the documentarian Kirby Dick. It is a last testament. He was very sick when the filming began, and he died in January 1996, almost literally on camera. We see and hear him gasping for his last breaths. If that seems heartless, reflect on his (unrealized) plans for a final artwork: "I want a wealthy collector to finance an installation in which a video camera will be placed in the coffin with my body, connected to a screen on the wall, and whenever he wants to, the patron can see how I'm coming along."

There are scenes in *Sick* that forced me to look away. I could not watch as Flanagan pierced his penis with a nail. But the scenes I did watch were, if anything, more painful. At the end, as Bob fights for breath and Sheree weeps and cares for him, what we are seeing is a couple that had something, however bizarre, that gave them the roles they preferred, and mutual reassurance. Now death is taking it all away.

After his death, Sheree Rose holds a large canister filled with the contents of Bob's lungs, removed at the time of the autopsy. There are pints of liquid there, manufactured by his disease in its determination to kill him. No one can say that Bob Flanagan, after his fashion and in his own way, did not fight back.

## A Simple Wish ★ ½

PG, 95 m., 1997

Martin Short (Murray), Kathleen Turner (Claudia), Mara Wilson (Anabel), Robert Pastorelli (Oliver), Amanda Plummer (Boots), Francis Capra (Charlie), Ruby Dee (Hortense), Teri Garr (Rena). Directed by Michael Ritchie and produced by Sid, Bill, and Jon Sheinberg. Screenplay by Jeff Rothberg.

*A Simple Wish* has assembled all the trinkets and effects necessary for its story, without bothering to tell one. Here are the ingredients for a funny family movie about an incompetent fairy godperson (Martin Short), but there's nothing much to really care about, and characters go off on their own without it much mattering.

The movie stars Short as a trainee male godmother named Murray. We see him apparently flunking his godmother's exam in the funny opening credits, but evidently he passed it, because when a little girl needs a godmother, there he is. The girl's name is Anabel (Mara Wilson), and she's the eight-year-old daughter of a Central Park carriage driver (Robert Pastorelli) who dreams of being cast for the lead in the new Broadway musical *A Tale of Two Cities.*

Can Murray help him? Will he be able to edge out the less talented but more famous front-runner for the job? Not necessarily. Short, who comes across in some scenes amazingly like Pee-wee Herman, is a willing but incompetent godmother who lands them in Nebraska and is indirectly responsible for Mara's dad being turned into a bronze statue in Central Park.

Meanwhile, at cross-purposes to this plot, there's another story involving an evil former godmother named Claudia (Kathleen Turner) and her devoted sidekick Boots (Amanda Plummer), who looks like a regular in a punk bar. ("One night, in a weak moment," Claudia sighs to her, "I chose to tolerate your companionship.") Their objective is to steal lots of wands at the annual gathering of the fairy godmother's association, and in general take over the show. They see Murray as a gnat in the way of their plan.

The movie has been produced by three members of a famed showbiz family (Sid, Bill, and Jon Sheinberg), and the screenplay might be tilted a little too much in the direction of their interests. Most smaller children are not very familiar with Broadway musicals, auditions, sniffy producers, and egotistical stars, and while of course you can learn about such things and still enjoy a movie, *A Simple Wish* is sometimes a little too inside in its theatrical references.

Most of the children in the audience, alas, will never have seen a Broadway musical (given the quality of many of them, maybe I don't need that "alas"). When the movie's *Tale of Two Cities* goes for laughs with a big scene delivered from the guillotine, will kids know it's funny? Maybe the movie should have taken inspiration from the musical of *The Elephant Man* staged in the underrated comedy *The Tall Guy*.

Kathleen Turner can be very quirky, and Amanda Plummer is an eccentric original, but do they really have a purpose in this movie? When special effects are used to shatter Turner's mirror image into a thousand jagged pieces, the effect is sensational—but it would mean more if she and Plummer had been more carefully involved in the plot. Many of their scenes together read like a stand-alone double act.

Now. Will kids like it? I doubt it. When family audiences avoid inspired films like *The Secret Garden, The Little Princess,* and *Shiloh,* why would they choose a pallid exercise like this? One of the great fictions is that America has a large audience hungering for family films, which Hollywood won't supply. The truth is that Hollywood wants to make family films more than families want to see them. I imagine most of the kids in the target audience for *A Simple Wish* will see *Men in Black* instead.

## Six Days, Seven Nights ★ ★ ½

PG-13, 101 m., 1998

Harrison Ford (Quinn Harris), Anne Heche (Robin Monroe), David Schwimmer (Frank Martin), Jacqueline Obradors (Angelica), Temuera Morrison (Jager), Allison Janney (Marjorie), Douglas Westoh (Phillippe), Cliff Curtis (Kip). Directed by Ivan Reitman and produced by Reitman, Wallis Nicita, and Roger Birnbaum. Screenplay by Michael Browning.

Whenever pirates turn up in a romance set more recently than 1843, you figure the filmmakers ran out of ideas. *Six Days, Seven Nights* illustrates that principle. It's the kind of movie that provides diversion for the idle channel-surfer but isn't worth a trip to the theater. A lot of it seems cobbled together out of spare parts.

Harrison Ford and Anne Heche costar in an Opposites Attract formula that strands them on a South Pacific island. He once owned his own business, but simplified his life by moving to paradise as a charter pilot. She's a high-powered New York magazine editor (the third this month; Tina Brown should collect royalties). Heche and her would-be fiancé (David Schwimmer) arrive on the tropical isle, he proposes marriage, she accepts—and then hires Ford to fly her over to Tahiti for an emergency photo shoot.

When their plane crash-lands on an uninhabited island in a thunderstorm, Ford and Heche are thrown together in a fight for survival. (I would like to know what Ford's thoughts were in the scene where he dresses up in palm fronds to hunt birds). Back on the resort island, Schwimmer and Ford's friendly masseuse, an island seductress played by Jacqueline Obradors, mourn their missing lovers and seek consolation, or something, in each other's arms.

The screenplay by Michael Browning has little interest in the characters—certainly not enough to provide them with a movie's worth of conversation. It's devised along standard formula lines, and so desperate for a crisis that pirates conveniently materialize on two occasions simply to give the movie something to be about. If you want to see a movie that knows what to do with a man, a woman, and an island, see John Huston's *Heaven Knows, Mr. Allison,* in which Robert Mitchum and Deborah Kerr create atmosphere where Ford and Heche create only weather.

Not that they aren't pleasant enough to watch. Ford has a nice early drunk scene where he avoids the usual clichés and gives us a man who gets thoughtful and analytical in a sloshed sort of way. Heche is plucky and has unforced charm, and does a great job of looking searchingly into Ford's eyes while he talks to her. Meanwhile, Schwimmer and Obradors provide counterpoint, mirroring in low comedy what the stars are doing at a more elevated level.

Harrison Ford has an easy appeal in movies like this, and never pushes too hard. Anne Heche plays a nice duet with him. But their adventures on the island are like the greatest hits from other movies *(Butch Cassidy, Flight of the Phoenix),* and when they have a couple of well-written dialogue scenes toward the end, you wonder why two intelligent people like these need pirates in their movie.

## The Sixth Man ★ ½
PG-13, 105 m., 1997

Marlon Wayans (Kenny Tyler), Kadeem Hardison (Antoine Tyler), David Paymer (Coach Pederson), Michael Michele (R. C. St. John), Kevin Dunn (Mikulski), Gary Jones (Gertz), Lorenzo Orr (Malik Major), Vladimir Cuk (Zigi Hrbacek). Directed by Randall Miller and produced by David Hoberman. Screenplay by Christopher Reed and Cynthia Carle.

*The Sixth Man* is another paint-by-the-numbers sports movie, this one about a college basketball team that makes it to the NCAA finals with the help of the ghost of one of its dead stars. Let's not talk about how predictable it is. Let's talk about how dumb it is.

The film starts with the childhood hoop dreams of a couple of brothers, Antoine and Kenny, who are coached by their father and hope to be stars one day. The father dies before he can see them realize their dream: They're both starters for the University of Washington Huskies. Antoine (Kadeem Hardison) is the dominant brother, the playmaker who gets the ball for the crucial last-minute shots. Kenny (Marlon Wayans) is a gifted player, but in his brother's shadow.

Then tragedy strikes. Antoine dunks the ball, falls to the court, and dies of heart failure on the way to the hospital. Kenny is crushed, and the Huskies embark on a losing streak until, one day at practice, Kenny throws the ball into the air and it never comes back down again.

Antoine, of course, has returned, this time as a ghost that only Kenny can see. And eventually Antoine returns to the court as an invisible sixth man on the Huskies team. He deflects the ball, tips in close shots, gives a boost to the Huskies, and trips up their opponents, and soon the team is in the NCAA playoffs.

Presumably *The Sixth Man* is intended to appeal to basketball fans. Is there a basketball fan alive who could fall for this premise? I'm not talking about the ghost—that's easy to believe. I'm talking about the details of the game.

I was out at the United Center last week for a big overtime contest between the Bulls and the SuperSonics. Along with thousands of other fans, I was an instant expert, my eyes riveted on every play. If the ball had suddenly changed course in midair, do you think we would have noticed? What if a ball dropped all the way through the basket and then popped back up again? What if a player was able to hang in midair twice as long as Michael Jordan?

My guess is that any one of those moments would have inspired a frenzy of instant replay analysis, and all three of them together would have induced apoplexy in announcer Johnny (Red) Kerr. But in *The Sixth Man*, audiences and commentators don't seem to realize that the laws of physics and gravity are being violated on behalf of the Huskies. Finally a woman sportswriter (Michael Michele) for the student paper uses the stop-action button on her VCR to replay a game, and notices that Kenny never even touched a ball before it went in.

I don't want to belabor technicalities here. I know the movie's premise is that nobody notices that the ghost is affecting the game. Because nobody notices, that frees the movie to proceed with its lethargic formula, right to the bitter end. (Will the team decide it has to win on its own? Will the ghost and his brother have to accept the fact of death? Will the Huskies be way behind at halftime of the big game? Will they win? Will the Sun rise tomorrow?)

You can't even begin to enjoy this game unless you put your intelligence on hold, or unless you're a little kid. A real, real, little, little kid. Why do Hollywood filmmakers hobble themselves in this way? Why be content with repeating ancient and boring formulas when a little thought could have produced an interesting movie? What if Kenny and Antoine had worked out a strategy to *secretly* affect the outcome of the game? What if they were aware that obvious tactics would be spotted? What if Kenny didn't tell his teammates about the ghost? What if Antoine, for sheer love of the game, took the other side once in a while?

The possibilities are endless. Movies like *The Sixth Man* are an example of Level One thinking, in which the filmmakers get the easy, obvious idea and are content with it. Good movies are made by taking the next step. Twisting the premise. Using lateral thinking. I imagine a lot of studio executives are sports fans. Would any of them be *personally* entertained by this movie? If this answer is "no"—and it has to be—then they shouldn't expect us to be, either.

## Slappy and the Stinkers ★ ★
PG, 78 m., 1998

B. D. Wong (Morgan Brinway), Bronson Pinchot (Roy), Jennifer Coolidge (Harriet), Joseph Ashton (Sonny), Gary LeRoi Gray (Domino), Carl Michael Lindner (Witz), Scarlett Pomers (Lucy), Travis Tedford (Loaf), Sam McMurray (Boccoli). Directed by Barnet Kellman and produced by Sid, Bill, and Jon Sheinberg. Screenplay by Bob Wolterstorff and Mike Scott.

The opening moments of *Slappy and the Stinkers* filled me with shreds of hope: Was it possible that this movie, about five kids who kidnap a sea lion, would not be without wit? The story opens in music class, where the teacher (B. D. Wong) slogs through Gilbert and Sullivan while the kids in the chorus giggle at lines like "my bosom swells with pride."

A nice touch. And I liked the way the kids waved their hands desperately for permission to go to the washroom. That rang a bell. And the irritation of the teacher ("My big number is coming up!"). But the movie is not, alas, interested in continuing such social observation. It's really a retread of the *Little Rascals* or *Our Gang* comedies, in which lovable scamps—freckled, towheaded, and gap-toothed—get up to mischief.

The setup: The stinkers, so named because they're always in trouble, are poor kids on scholarship at a posh private academy. Everything they touch turns to trouble. In a long and spectacularly unfunny opening sequence, they attach a leaf blower to a hang glider and the headmaster's desk chair in an attempt to "go where no kid has ever gone before." The contraption of course goes exactly where the screenplay requires it to go for a long time after we have lost interest in whether it goes anywhere.

Then the kids sneak away for a visit to the aquarium. There they get involved with Slappy, a sea lion who passes a lot of gas and provides the kids with an excuse to say "fart," which, I recall from my own grade school days, is a word kids adore so much they are rarely happier than when saying it. The kids, who have seen *Free Willy*, decide Slappy should be stolen from the aquarium and returned to the sea, although they have some second thoughts: "There's Willy!" they say, seeing a familiar whale tail on the horizon. "Hey, don't killer whales eat sea lions?"

The spectacle of Willy making a meal of Slappy right in front of the horrified kids will have to wait, unfortunately, for the Leslie Nielsen version of this picture. The best horror *Slappy and the Stinkers* can come up with is an evil sea lion–napper named Boccoli (Sam McMurray), who dreams of Slappy starring in a circus act. Boccoli (who with just a little more trouble could have been called Broccoli) is an unshaven chain-smoker with a broken-down van, and a lot of stuff falls on him, and he falls on a lot of stuff. His function is to take a lickin' and keep on kidnappin'.

We actually see a snippet of the sea lion's circus act, in which Slappy jumps through a ring of fire. If you can visualize a sea lion, you might ask yourself, how easy would it be for one to jump through such a ring? The same thought occurred to me, and I studied the stunt closely. My best guess is that what we are actually witnessing is an arrangement between a catapult and a large black Hefty garbage bag.

Along with hilarities involving a cattle prod, and scenes in which it appears that Slappy has learned to understand, if not to speak, English, there are a lot of sight gags in the film involving the teacher getting slushy drinks in his face, and the kids getting peanut butter and jelly sandwiches on theirs, and many close-ups of the little tykes shrieking and trying manfully to get their tongues around the big words in the dialogue.

Yeah, but will kids like it? I dunno. I never much liked the *Our Gang* and *Little Rascals* movies. The kids seemed too doggone cute. The Bad News Bears were a lot more fun, but, mister, I've seen *The Bad News Bears*, and these ain't them.

## Sliding Doors ★ ★
PG-13, 105 m., 1998

Gwyneth Paltrow (Helen), John Hannah (James), John Lynch (Gerry), Jeanne Tripplehorn (Lydia), Zara Turner (Anna), Douglas McFerran (Russell), Paul Brightwell (Clive), Nina Young (Claudia). Directed by Peter Howitt and produced by Sydney Pollack, Philippa Braithwaite, and William Horberg. Screenplay by Howitt.

*Sliding Doors* uses parallel time lines to explore the different paths that a woman's life might take after she does, and doesn't, find her lover in bed with another woman. I submit that there is a simple test to determine whether this plot can work: Is either time line interesting in itself? If not, then no amount of shifting back and forth between them can help. And I fear they are not.

The movie stars Gwyneth Paltrow as Helen, a London publicity executive who is fired for no good reason, and stalks out of her office in mid-morning to take the underground train back home. In one scenario, she catches the train. In the other, she misses it because she's delayed, and the doors slide shut in her face. To save confusion, we will call these Scenarios A and B.

In A, Helen arrives home unexpectedly and finds her lover, Gerry (John Lynch), in the sack with his mistress, Lydia (Jeanne Tripplehorn). She confronts them, walks out, goes to a bar to get drunk, and runs into James (John Hannah). James recognizes her, because earlier he chatted her up on the train. Over the course of the next few days, Helen A is comforted by her best friend, gets her long hair cut and dyed blond, and begins to fall in love with James.

In Scenario B, Helen misses the train, and by the time she arrives home Lydia is already off the scene. But she begins to suspect things when she realizes two brandy glasses were on the dresser. Eventually Helen B finds out about Lydia, who is the kind of woman who gets a sadistic satisfaction out of popping up unexpectedly and threatening to blow Gerry's cover.

The film cuts backs and forth between A and B. It is clear that Gerry is a creep, Lydia is a Fatal Attraction, and James is a thoroughly nice bloke, although of course the requirements of Screenwriting 101 force the movie into a manufactured crisis in which it appears that James may have been lying to Helen A. There's even one of those scenes that madden me, in which James goes to Helen A's best friend's house, is informed of the misunderstanding, could say two or three words to clear it all up—but doesn't, because he is a puppet of the plot.

Gwyneth Paltrow is engaging as the two Helens, and I have no complaints about her performance. Pity about the screenplay. It requires her to appear to be unobservant, gullible, and absentminded as the faithless Gerry hems and haws through absurdly contrived emergencies. The worst moment comes when he opens the kitchen blinds and Lydia is standing right outside them, staring at him, and he slams them shut and tries to pretend nothing happened. What we have here is a particularly annoying movie gimmick in which the other person (Lydia, in this case) knows exactly when and where to position herself to create the shock effect. We aren't allowed to wonder how many hours, or days, she was posted outside, maybe in the rain, waiting for him to open the blinds.

I am grateful that the movie provides Helen A and Helen B with different haircuts, which helps tell the story lines apart (a bandage is used in the early scenes). But as we switched relentlessly back and forth between A and B, I found that I wasn't looking forward to either story. True, James is played by Hannah with warmth and charm, but to what effect? Is he interesting as a person? Does he, or anyone in the film, have much to say that's not at the service of the plot? I would have preferred Hypothetical Scenario C, in which Gwyneth Paltrow meets neither James nor Gerry, and stars in a smarter movie.

## Sling Blade ★ ★ ★ ½

R, 135 m., 1996

Billy Bob Thornton (Karl Childers), Dwight Yoakam (Doyle Hargraves), J. T. Walsh (Charles Bushman), John Ritter (Vaughan Cunningham), Lucas Black (Frank Wheatley), Natalie Canerday (Linda Wheatley), James Hampton (Jerry Woolridge), Robert Duvall (Karl's father). Directed by Billy Bob Thornton and produced by Brandon Rosser and David L. Bushell. Screenplay by Thornton.

*Sling Blade* begins with a remarkable monologue delivered straight to the camera. A man with a raspy speaking voice, an overshot jaw, and a lot of pain in his eyes says he reckons we might like to hear about his story, and so he tells it. His name is Karl Childers, he is retarded, and he has been in a state facility since childhood, when he found his mother with her lover and killed them both. But now, he says, "I reckon I got no reason to kill no one. Uh, huh."

Karl is talking to a newspaper reporter about his release from the institution. They reckon he has been cured. They are probably right. He is not a killer, would not kill without good and proper reason, and now understands how, as a child, he misinterpreted the situation. As he talks, we are struck by his forceful presence; he is retarded, yes, but he is complex and observant, and has spent a lot of time thinking about what he should and shouldn't do.

If *Forrest Gump* had been written by William Faulkner, the result might have been something like *Sling Blade*. The movie is a work of great originality and fascination by Billy Bob Thornton, who wrote it, directed it, and plays Karl Childers. He says that the character "came to him" one morning while he was shaving, and he started talking to himself in the mirror in Karl's voice.

Thornton is a former country musician turned screenwriter (he wrote the remarkable *One False Move* and *A Family Thing*). He plays Karl as a man of limited intelligence but great seriousness, who reasons as well as he can and feels deeply. There is pain, humor, irony, and sweetness in the character, and a voice and manner so distinctive he is the most memorable movie character I've seen in a long time. Uh, huh. And the way the story of his freedom unfolds has a terrible fascination: We can guess where events might be leading, and we can see how they cannot be changed.

On his release from prison, Karl is more or less at loose ends. He can fix most anything, and gets a job as a garage mechanic. He encounters and befriends a young boy named Frank (Lucas Black), and senses immediately that the boy has a wounded spirit. He meets the boy's mother, Linda (Natalie Canerday), who has a good heart and offers to let Karl live with them in quarters in the garage. Karl soon understands the wounded look in Frank's eyes, because he meets Linda's boyfriend, Doyle (country singer Dwight Yoakam), who likes to lounge in the living room drinking one longneck beer after another and ruling the roost with loud, boorish opinions. His criticisms of the boy are especially cruel.

Karl watches, and listens, and thinks. There is another key character in the story: Linda's boss, Vaughan (John Ritter), a homosexual who accepts his sexuality but seems sort of apologetic about it, and who is also Linda's best friend. It's hard to understand why Linda stays with the venomous Doyle; maybe it's a version of battered wife syndrome and she can't imagine leaving. Only Vaughan makes life bearable.

Karl settles into the new household and begins to savor the taste of freedom. He is not too sure how some aspects of the world work, and stands in front of a door for hours before he thinks of knocking. He repairs everything he puts his hands to, he makes new friends, and in one superb adventure he orders and eats french fries for the first time, and his delight, masked behind his usual gruff manner, is boundless. ("I reckon I'd like me some of them french fries, uh, huh.")

These characters are brought to life with a vivid strength. We see Linda's life from the outside, through Karl's eyes, who views it in a very literal way and tries to make sense of it. And we see it from the inside, through the eyes of Vaughan, the homosexual, who like Karl is only a witness, but feels the pain. One of the many pleasures of the movie is John Ritter's performance as Vaughan; the character has a complexity and sensitivity that seem to have come right out of his small-town time and place.

The movie's ultimate destination is not hard to guess, but we feel a certain satisfaction when it arrives there. And by then we have come to know Karl with a real understanding and fondness. He is a character unlike any other in the movies, an original, and in creating him, Billy Bob Thornton has made a place for himself among the best new filmmakers. And as an actor, he creates a difficult character and finds exactly the right way to play him. If there were the slightest justice and curiosity in the Academy Award process, Thornton's work here would get a nomination.

*There were, and it did—for Best Actor and Screenplay Adaptation, winning in the latter category.*

## Smilla's Sense of Snow ★ ★ ★

R, 120 m., 1997

Julia Ormond (Smilla), Gabriel Byrne (The Mechanic), Richard Harris (Tork), Vanessa Redgrave (Elsa Lubing), Robert Loggia (Moritz Jasperson), Jim Broadbent (Lagermann), Peter Capaldi (Birgo Lander), Emma Croft (Benja). Directed by Bille August and produced by Bernd Eichinger and Martin Moszkowicz. Screenplay by Ann Biderman, based on the novel by Peter Hoeg.

Here is a movie so absorbing, so atmospheric, so suspenseful, and so dumb that it proves my point: The subject matter doesn't matter in a movie nearly as much as mood, tone, and style.

*Smilla's Sense of Snow* is a superbly made film with one of the goofiest plots in many moons. Nothing in the final thirty minutes can possibly be taken seriously, and yet the movie works. Even the ending works, sort of, because the film has built up so much momentum.

*Smilla* stars Julia Ormond, who often plays sensuous women but here plays a cold and distant one, born in Greenland and now living in Copenhagen, where she keeps her distance and seems to be nursing an obscure wound or anger. Smilla's confidant is the little boy named Isaiah who lives in the building. He is an Inuit, a native Greenlander, and Smilla is half Inuit, and sometimes tells him stories based on the lore of their people.

One day she returns to her apartment building to find the boy's body crumpled on the ground. The official verdict is that he fell off the roof, but she has been to the roof and seen his footprints in a straight line running right over the edge. What was he running from? What frightened him so?

Smilla makes it her business to answer this question. The movie, which has so far been a character study, now becomes a crime procedural. She questions a helpful man at the coroner's, who notes mysteries about the autopsy. She discovers that the boy's father died in a mining accident, and learns from a retired mining company secretary (Vanessa Redgrave) of a secret company archive. She breaks into the archive by night and finds information about the accident and how it might be linked to events from 30 and 130 years ago.

She's aided in some of these investigations by her neighbor in the building, a man named The Mechanic (Gabriel Byrne). They are even drawn toward one another, although his motives are murky. What does it mean that she sees him at dinner with the head of the mining company (Richard Harris)? Less or more than it seems?

I cannot describe the impact of these scenes because they are so visceral. Ormond embodies Smilla—her iciness, her determination, her anger. She creates an interesting character, which is one of the hardest things to do in a movie: a character who intrigues us to such a degree that when she is doing nothing, we're reading motives into her inaction. Ormond has a beautiful face, less full here than in *Sabrina*, and the fact that she will not "let" it be beautiful—that she separates from the world around her with an almost painful defensiveness—makes her, paradoxically, more attractive. Byrne, who specializes in men that women love but shouldn't, plays a hesitant but smooth operator.

And then we arrive at the film's final passages. Smilla smuggles herself on board a ship to Greenland, and in one sequence hides inside a dumbwaiter with skills she must have learned from a Nancy Drew mystery. In Greenland . . . well, I wouldn't dream of telling you what's under the ice. But I sat in stunned amazement. I know *Smilla's Sense of Snow* is based on a best-selling novel by Peter Hoeg, and I assume all of this plot stuff must come from the book. But how absurd it all is. In the early 1960s, when American-International was cranking out a science-fiction thriller every other week, a plot like this would have been worthy of something like *Prehistoric Radioactive Worms from Outer Space.*

Never mind. The ending simply doesn't matter. The movie presents it, but isn't implicated in it. The movie is off somewhere else. *Smilla* was directed by Bille August, whose credits include *Pelle the Conqueror* (1988), and the strengths in both films are in the relationships between young children and adults who are moved by them. *Smilla* also works as a character study: We are intrigued by Smilla, by her quietness, by her strength. In a better world with more curiosity, we could have had this movie without any of the Greenland scenes. It could have been about Smilla and her neighbors. In our world movies need a plot, I guess, and so this one has one. Ignore it. It's irrelevant to the movie's power.

## Some Mother's Son ★ ★ ★

R, 111 m., 1996

Helen Mirren (Kathleen Quigley), Fionnula Flanagan (Annie Higgins), Aiden Gillen (Gerard Quigley), David O'Hara (Frank Higgins), John Lynch (Bobby Sands), Tom Hollander (Farnsworth), Tim Woodward (Harrington), Ciaran Hinds (Danny Boyle). Directed by Terry George and produced by Jim Sheridan, Arthur Lappin, and Edward Burke. Screenplay by George and Sheridan.

If the long struggle between the British and the Irish had been carried out only on movie screens, the Irish would long since have been the victors. The Irish film industry, one of the most creative and interesting in Europe, has returned time and again with fierce zeal to the Troubles, most recently with Neil Jordan's *Michael Collins,* and before that *In the Name of the Father, Cal,* and *Hidden Agenda.*

Now comes *Some Mother's Son,* a fictionalized account of the 1981 IRA hunger strikers of Belfast's Maze Prison, who broke the iron policies of Margaret Thatcher after ten of them died. (The issue: As self-proclaimed political prisoners, they did not want to wear criminals' prison uniforms.) One of the martyrs was Bobby Sands, who was elected to Parliament while in prison, and whose funeral procession attracted 100,000 mourners. The film is not really about him, however, but about two fictional hunger strikers and their mothers—who are asked, after their sons lapse into comas, to authorize intravenous feeding.

The mothers come from very different parts of the community. Kathleen Quigley (Helen Mirren) is a pacifist, a schoolteacher who doesn't know her son Gerard (Aiden Gillen) is even in the IRA. The other is Annie Higgins (Fionnula Flanagan), whose son Frank (David O'Hara) has been implicated in a fatal mortar attack on British troops. When both men join Sands and the other hunger strikers, the mothers become friends, even though Annie steadfastly supports her son's readiness to die and Kathleen cannot see how any mother could make that decision. (The dead British soldiers, she says, were also "some mother's son.")

The movie, directed by Terry George (who cowrote *In the Name of the Father*) intercuts three main strands: life inside the prison, life for the two mothers, and the attempts by Thatcher's government to hold firm in the face of mounting sentiment for the strikers. The face of Britain in the movie is represented by a man named Farnsworth (Tom Hollander), who takes a hard line and defends it with the least possible grace, sympathy, or intelligence. It might have made the movie more absorbing if Farnsworth had been allowed some human feelings, but George saves those for the chief IRA negotiator, Danny Boyle (Ciaran Hinds).

As the IRA plots its strategy, as London adopts a bunker mentality, as the hunger strike drags on to a worldwide chorus of publicity, the film's real story comes down to this: Is any political belief so important that it is worth sacrificing the life of your son? Millions of parents, of course, vote "yes!" every time they send their children off to war. The scenario for such sacrifices seems to be hard-wired into many people, and comes under the heading of giving your life for your country.

In war, in any event, you take your chances and try to give as good as you get. In a hunger strike, the strikers seek to bring about their own deaths. But when they lose consciousness, it is up to their parents to decide whether to allow them to die. Death by hunger takes weeks or months, during which all of the relevant morality is agonized over, priests offer advice, arguments are heard, and there is always the hope that the other side will cave in at the last minute. What it comes down to, finally, in *Some Mother's Son,* is what it always comes down to: Hate the enemy enough, and any sacrifice is justified. See the other side as "some mother's son," and you are less willing to sacrifice your own.

For Annie, there is no question. Her husband was killed by the British, and she shares her son's convictions. Kathleen is not so sure, and it is Helen Mirren's performance, so closely observed, with so much depth and urgency, that embodies the central questions of the movie. It is fascinating to see Kathleen's independent intelligence shining in the midst of other characters, on both sides, who are true believers.

The movie is, of course, completely on the side of the IRA, but Kathleen's dilemma succeeds in allowing a subversive notion to sneak through: Although Protestants and Catholics have been killing each other for years in Northern Ireland, can any god who permits war between sides that both seek to worship him be a god worth dying for?

## Sonatine ★ ★ ★ ½

R, 89 m., 1998

Beat Kitano (Murakama), Tetsu Watanabe (Uechi), Aya Kikumai (Miyuki), Masanobu Katsumura (Ryoji), Susumu Terashima (Ken), Ren Ohsugi (Katagiri), Tonbo Zushi (Kitajima), Kenichi Yajima (Takahashi). Directed by Takeshi Kitano and produced by Masayuki Mori, Hisao Nabeshima, and Takeo Yoshida. Screenplay by Kitano.

"Maybe you're too rich for this business," a friend tells Murakama, the stone-faced gangster hero of *Sonatine.* Murakama, who rarely says anything, has let it slip that he is tired. Very tired. When he is not actually engaged in the business of being a yakuza, he simply stops moving at all and sits, staring into space, sometimes with a cigarette, sometimes not.

He is tired of living, but not scared of dying, because death, he explains, would at least put an end to his fear of death, which is making his life not worth living. When he explains this perfectly logical reasoning, you look to see if he is smiling, but he isn't. He has it all worked out.

*Sonatine* is the latest film to be released in this country by Takeshi Kitano, who wrote, directed, and edited it—and stars in it under his acting name, Beat Kitano. It arrives here only a month after *Fireworks,* his 1997 Venice Film Festival winner, but was made in 1993, the fourth of his seven films. He is the biggest star in Japan right now, and as a filmmaker one of the most intriguing.

This film is even better than *Fireworks.* It shows how violent gangster movies need not be filled with stupid dialogue, nonstop action, and gratuitous gore. *Sonatine* is pure, minimal, and clean in its lines; I was reminded of Jean-Pierre Melville's *Le Samourai* (1967), another film about a professional killer who is all but paralyzed by existential dread.

Neither movie depends on extended action scenes because neither hero finds them fun. There is the sense in a lot of American action movies that Bruce Willis or Arnold Schwarzenegger enjoy the action in the way, say, that they might enjoy a football game. Murakama and the French samurai (Alain Delon) do jobs—jobs they have lost the heart for, jobs that have extinguished in them the enjoyment of life.

As the film opens, Murakama and his crew are being assigned by a yakuza overlord to travel to Okinawa as soldiers on loan to an ally who is facing gang warfare. They sense that something is phony about the assignment. "The last time you sent us out," Murakama tells his boss, "I lost three men. I didn't enjoy that." Murakama is correct in his suspicions: The district he controls has become so lucrative that the boss wants to move in and take over.

These yakuza live by a code so deep it even regulates their fury. Murakama administers a brutal beating to the boss's lieutenant, but they remain on speaking terms. Later, one yakuza stabs another in the stomach. Yet they sit side by side on a bus in Okinawa. "Ice cream?" says the guy who had the knife. "You stabbed me in the belly and it still hurts," the other replies, and we are not quite sure if he is rejecting the ice cream out of anger, or because he doesn't think it will stay down.

In Takeshi's universe, violence is as transient as a lightning bolt. It happens and is over. It means nothing. We sense that in a scene where three men play "paper, rock, scissors" to see who will get to point a pistol at his head and pull the trigger to see if there is a round in the chamber. We see it again in a chilling sequence where a gambler, who didn't want to pay protection, is dunked into the sea; Murakama gets into a conversation and almost forgets to notice how long the guy has been under. And we see it in the climactic battle scene, which is played entirely as flashes of lights against the windows of an apartment: Who else would have the wit, or the sadness, to leave the carnage offscreen?

Kitano was in a motorcycle accident a few years ago that paralyzed half his face. This film was made before the accident, but there's little difference between the way he appears here and in *Fireworks.* If ever there was an actor who could dispense with facial expression, he's the one.

The less he gives, the less he reveals, the less he says and does, the more his presence grows, until he becomes the cold, dangerous center of the story. And in his willingness to let characters languish in real time, to do nothing in between the moments of action, he forces us to look into their eyes and try to figure them out. Films that explain nothing often make everything clear. Films that explain everything often have nothing to explain.

## Soul Food ★ ★ ★ ½

R, 115 m., 1997

Vanessa L. Williams (Teri), Vivica A. Fox (Maxine), Nia Long (Bird), Irma P. Hall (Big Mama), Michael Beach (Miles), Mekhi Phifer (Lem), Brandon Hammond (Ahmad), Jeffrey D. Sams (Kenny), Gina Ravera (Faith), Carl Wright (Reverend Williams), Mel Jackson (Simuel), John M. Watson Sr. (Uncle Pete). Directed by George Tillman Jr. and produced by Tracey E. Edmonds and Robert Teitel. Screenplay by Tillman Jr.

*Soul Food* tells the story of a big African-American family from Chicago with warm-hearted good cheer; in the way it cuts between stories of romance and trouble, it's like *Waiting to Exhale,* but more down-to-earth and believable—and funnier. It knows about how black families stay in constant communication down three or four generations and out to third cousins—how when a matriarch like the movie's Big Mama (Irma P. Hall) hosts a holiday dinner, there are going to be a lot of people in the house, and a lot of stories to catch up with.

The story is told through the eyes of Big Mama's grandson, Ahmad (Brandon Hammond), who introduces us to the key players, especially his mother and her two sisters. His mom and dad are Maxine (Vivica A. Fox) and Kenny (Jeffrey D. Sams). The oldest sister is Teri (Vanessa L. Williams), a successful attorney married to Miles (Michael Beach), who is also an attorney but wants to leave the law and follow his first love, music. The youngest sister, Bird (Nia Long, from *love jones*), has just married Lem (Mekhi Phifer) and opened a beauty shop with a loan from Teri.

Ahmad is young but observant, and starting with his clues we learn that Teri and Miles's marriage has lost its spark—Teri is a workaholic who's not interested in her husband's music. Bird and Lem are struggling, not least because of the shadowy presence of her former boyfriend (Mel Jackson). The whole family is apprehensive about the arrival back in town of Faith (Gina Ravera), who is thought to have been a stripper in California, and is well remembered for several loans she still hasn't paid back.

Oh, and the family extends further: It's a tribute to the script and direction by George Tillman Jr. that he makes them memorable, including the Reverend (Carl Wright) who is a faithful anchor at Big Mama's Sunday dinners, and the mysterious Uncle Pete (John M. Watson Sr.) who hasn't left his room in years. All of these people and more—including neighbors, church friends, and sometimes even the homeless—turn up at Big Mama's on Sundays for her famous soul food feasts, at which long-simmering family issues sometimes come to the boil before Big Mama puts the lid on.

"Big Mama" is not a nickname but an honorary title in a lot of African-American families, indicating a woman who has lived long, worked hard, and acted as an inspiration for many generations. That certainly describes my own mother-in-law, Mrs. Johnnie Mae Hammel, the first Big Mama I met, and it also describes the unforgettable character played by Irma P. Hall in this movie. She has an uncanny gift for seeing right to the heart of her family's strengths and weaknesses, and dishing out firm advice, spiritual sometimes and practical always.

That's until she has a stroke and is hospitalized in a coma. In one of the movie's key scenes, young Ahmad goes to visit her, and in a low-key, unemphasized way, seems to communicate telepathically. (He agrees with her about plans for the garden, even though she, of course, cannot speak.) Later, in the film's closing sequence, it is Ahmad who understands Big Mama's desires for the family and brings them about through some sneaky planning of his own.

The heart of the movie involves the three sisters, their stories and their marriages. The work of all the actors in these sequences—those playing the three couples, plus the two troublesome outsiders—is a reminder of how rich the African-American acting community has grown in recent years, with the renaissance in black-themed films. Williams does an observant job of playing Teri, the most successful woman in her family—ambitious, competitive, tired of picking up bills. She's happy to loan money to Bird (Long), but has a lifelong competition with Maxine (Fox) because she senses a happiness and marital security she'll never know.

Drama comes when Bird's ex-boyfriend pretends to help Lem get a job—and uses the opening to humiliate him. There's more trouble when Faith, the ex-stripper, needs a piano player and finds Teri's husband, Miles, available. It's unfortunate, in a way, that some of these developments lead to sexual situations that make this wonderful family film unsuitable for younger viewers.

Watching *Soul Food,* I reflected that in many ways it depicts a world that white audiences will find unfamiliar. Oh, Big Mama's family shares the same kinds of values, problems, worries, successes, and failures as whites. But movies and TV often focus only on a narrow wedge of black America, showing pimps and junkies, outlaw teenagers and con men, but ignoring the vast and substantial African-American middle and working classes. George Tillman says *Soul Food* is based in part on his own family, and I believe him, because he seems to know the characters so well; by the film's end, so do we.

## Sour Grapes no stars

R, 92 m., 1998

Steven Weber (Evan), Craig Bierko (Richie), Jennifer Leigh Warren (Millie), Karen Sillas (Joan), Jack Burns (Eulogist), Viola Harris (Selma), Scott Erik (Teenage Richie), Michael Resnick (Teenage Evan). Directed by Larry David and produced by Laurie Lennard. Screenplay by David.

*Sour Grapes* is a comedy about things that aren't funny. It reminded me of *Crash*, an erotic thriller about things no one finds erotic. The big difference is that David Cronenberg, who made *Crash*, knew that people were not turned on by auto accidents. Larry David, who wrote and directed *Sour Grapes*, apparently thinks people are amused by cancer, accidental castration, racial stereotypes, and bitter family feuds.

Oh, I have no doubt that all of those subjects could be incorporated into a great comedy. It's all in the style and the timing. *Sour Grapes* is tone-deaf comedy; the material, the dialogue, the delivery, and even the sound track are labored and leaden. How to account for the fact that Larry David is one of the creators of *Seinfeld*? Maybe he works well with others.

I can't easily remember a film I've enjoyed less. *North*, a comedy I hated, was at least able to inflame me with dislike. *Sour Grapes* is a movie that deserves its title: It's puckered, deflated, and vinegary. It's a dead zone.

The story. Two cousins (Steven Weber and Craig Bierko) go to Atlantic City. One is a designer who wins a slot jackpot of more than $436,000. He was playing with quarters given him by the other guy. The other cousin, a surgeon, not unreasonably thinks he should get some of the winnings. If not half, then maybe a third. The winner offers him 3 percent.

This sets off several scenes of debate about what would be right or wrong in such a situation. Even a limo driver, hearing the winner's story, throws him out of the car: "You were playing with his money!" The losing doctor nevertheless gives his cousin a blue warm-up suit for his birthday, only to discover that the louse has given the suit away to an African-American street person.

So far all we have is a comic premise that doesn't deliver laughs. Now the movie heads for cringe-inducing material. We learn about the winner's ability to perform oral sex while alone. He's alone a lot because his wife is mad at him, but that's an opening for stereotyped Jewish mother scenes. The feud heats up until the enraged doctor lies to the winner: "You have terminal cancer. It's time to set your house in order." Ho, ho.

The winner wants to spare his mother the misery of watching her son die. So he gives her house key to the black bum in the warm-up suit and tells him to make himself at home. His plan: His mother will be scared to death by the sight of the black home invader. After she screams, we see the bum running down the street in Steppin' Fetchit style. Was there no one to hint to David that this was gratuitous and offensive?

Further material involves the surgeon getting so upset in the operating room that he reverses an X-ray film and removes the wrong testicle from a TV star—who then, of course, has to be told that they still had to go ahead and remove the remaining testicle. The star develops a castrato voice. Ho, ho.

This material is impossible to begin with. What makes it worse is the lack of lightness from the performers, who slog glumly through their dialogue as if they know what an aromatic turkey they're stuck in. Scene after scene clangs dead to the floor, starting with the funeral service that opens the film. The more I think of it, the more *Sour Grapes* really does resemble *Crash* (except that *Crash* was not a bad film). Both movies are like watching automobile accidents. Only one intended to be.

## Space Jam ★ ★ ★ ½

PG, 87 m., 1996

Michael Jordan (Michael Jordan), Wayne Knight (Stan Podolak), Theresa Randle (Juanita Jordan), Billy West (Bugs's voice), Danny DeVito (Swackhammer's voice). Directed by Joe Pytka and produced by Ivan Reitman, Joe Medjuck, and Daniel Goldberg. Screenplay by Steve Rudnick, Leo Benvenuti, Timothy Harris, and Herschel Weingrod.

*"I thought I thaw—I did! I did! I thaw a Michael Thjordan!"*

—Tweetie Pie in *Space Jam*

*Space Jam* is a happy marriage of good ideas—three films for the price of one, giving us a comic treatment of the career adventures of Michael Jordan, crossed with a Looney Tunes cartoon and some showbiz warfare. It entertains kids at one level while giving their parents a lot to smile at too. It's an inspired way to use, and kid, Jordan's image while at the same time updating Bugs Bunny & Company for doing battle in the multizillion-dollar animation sweepstakes.

The story begins with young Michael Jordan shooting baskets with his father in the backyard of their home, and dreaming of his path to happiness: North Carolina . . . the NBA . . . and finally the ultimate goal, pro baseball. Then we flash forward to very funny sequences showing Jordan in the midst of his baseball career.

He's not a very good baseball player (a TV newscast is frank about that), but everyone around him is starstruck by his sports stardom anyway. ("He looks good in a uniform," one player enthuses. "You can't teach that.") An opposing catcher is such a fan that he tells Michael what pitches to expect, and Jordan is having a great time realizing his childhood dream when suddenly he finds himself yanked down a hole on the golf course and into Looney Tunes-land.

A parallel story has filled us in on the situation in an alternate cartoon universe, where an amusement park in outer space has desperate need for new attractions. To bolster ticket sales, the alien Nerdlucks, who run the park, kidnap the Looney Tunes stars (the stellar roster includes Bugs, Daffy, Elmer Fudd, Porky Pig, Tweety and Sylvester, the Tazmanian Devil, Speedy Gonzales, Yosemite Sam, Foghorn Leghorn, and the sexy newcomer Lola Bunny). The desperate Bugs and friends have cut a deal: They'll get their freedom if they can defeat the Nerdluck "Monstars" in a basketball game. But the Monstars suck up the basketball talent of such stars as Charles Barkley and Patrick Ewing (leaving them unable to even catch a ball, and telling it all to therapists). In desperation, the Looneys kidnap Michael as their secret weapon.

"I'm a baseball player now," Jordan protests. "Right!" says Bugs. "And I'm a Shakespearean actor!" Rising to the occasion Jordan coaches the Looney Tunes squad in a series of high-energy games and action sequences that combine his live scenes with state-of-the-art animation. The cartoon sequences employ traditional animation techniques and newer approaches such as the three-dimensional computer animation used in *Toy Story*.

You can watch the movie on the sports and cartoon levels, and also appreciate the corporate strategy that's involved. A successful feature-length animated family film can roll up astronomical grosses (more than $1 billion from all sources for *The Lion King*). But the problem for the rest of Hollywood is only Disney seems to have the key and the cachet to make those films. Animated movies from other sources tend to do disappointingly at the box office.

Warner Bros. has historically been a studio with a rich legacy in animation; such great cartoon directors as Chuck Jones helped fashion their stable of stars. But six-minute cartoons are a neglected art form, and *Space Jam* looks like a Warners vehicle to catapult their Looney Tunes characters into the feature-length arena to do battle with Disney.

There are hints of the rivalry all through the film. The outer space amusement park is named "Moron Mountain," perhaps a tribute to Space Mountain at Walt Disney World. And when a professional hockey team is mentioned, Bugs sputters, "The Ducks? What kind of a Mickey Mouse organization would name their team the Ducks?"

Will the Warners strategy work? It will if they can keep costars like Michael Jordan on board. It is difficult for an actor to work in movies that combine live action with animation, because much of the time he cannot see the other characters in a scene with him. But Jordan has a natural ease and humor, an unforced charisma, that makes a good fit with the cartoon universe. By not forcing himself, by never seeming to try too hard to be funny or urgent, Jordan keeps a certain dignity; he never acts as if he thinks he's a cartoon, too, and that's why he has good chemistry with the Tunes. He's a visitor to Looneyland, not a resident.

There are other funny live-action scenes involving Jordan and Hollywood's favorite unbilled guest star, Bill Murray, and scenes, too, with Wayne Knight, as a baseball publicist who comes along as an adviser and confidant. The film was produced by Ivan Reitman *(Ghostbusters)* and directed by Joe Pytka, who has directed Jordan in a lot of his best TV commercials; their work was blended with the animation of a team headed by Ron Tippe, and the result is delightful, a family movie in the best sense (which means the adults will enjoy it too).

## The Spanish Prisoner ★ ★ ★ ½

PG, 112 m., 1998

Campbell Scott (Joe Ross), Rebecca Pidgeon (Susan Ricci), Steve Martin (Jimmy Dell), Ben Gazzara (Klein), Ricky Jay (George Lang), Felicity Huffman (McCune), Richard L. Freidman (Businessman). Directed by David Mamet and produced by Jean Doumanian. Screenplay by Mamet.

There are really only two screenwriters working at the moment whose words you can recognize as soon as you hear them: Quentin Tarantino and David Mamet. All of the others, however clever, deal in the ordinary rhythms of daily speech.

Tarantino we recognize because of the way his dialogue, like Mark Twain's, unfurls down the corridors of long inventive progressions, collecting proper names and trademarks along the way, to arrive at preposterous generalizations—delivered flatly, as if they were the simple truth.

Mamet is even easier to recognize. His characters often speak as if they're wary of the world, afraid of being misquoted, reluctant to say what's on their minds: As a protective shield, they fall into precise legalisms, invoking old sayings as if they're magic charms. Often they punctuate their dialogue with four-letter words, but in *The Spanish Prisoner* there is not a single obscenity, and we picture Mamet with a proud grin on his face, collecting his very first PG rating.

The movie does not take place in Spain and has no prisoners. The title refers to a classic con game. Mamet, whose favorite game is poker, loves films where the characters negotiate a thicket of lies. *The Spanish Prisoner* resembles Hitchcock in the way that everything takes place in full view, on sunny beaches and in brightly lighted rooms, with attractive people smilingly pulling the rug out from under the hero and revealing the abyss.

The hero is Joe Ross (Campbell Scott), who has invented a process that will make money for his company—so much money that when he writes the figure on a blackboard, we don't even see it, only the shining eyes of executives looking at it. ("The Process," he says. Pause. "And, by means of the Process, to control the world market." The missing words are replaced by greed.)

He works for Mr. Klein (Ben Gazzara), who has convened a meeting in the Caribbean to discuss the Process. Also on hand is George, a company lawyer played by Ricky Jay—a professional magician and expert in charlatans, who is Mamet's friend and collaborator. And there is Susan (Rebecca Pidgeon, Mamet's wife), whose heart is all a-flutter for Joe Ross, and who is very smart and likes to prove it by saying smart things that end on a triumphant note, as if she expects a gold star on her report card. ("I'm a problem solver, and I have a heart of gold.")

To the Caribbean island comes a man named Jimmy Dell (Steve Martin), who may or may not have arrived by seaplane. We see how Mamet creates uncertainty: Joe thinks the man arrived by seaplane, but Susan thinks he didn't and provides photographic proof (which, as far as we can see, proves nothing), and in the end it doesn't matter if he arrives by seaplane or not; the whole episode is used simply to introduce the idea that Jimmy Dell may not be what he seems.

He seems to be a rich, friendly New Yorker, who is trying to conceal an affair with a partner's wife. He says he has a sister in New York, and gives Joe a book to deliver to her ("Might I ask you a service?"). Joe has thus accepted a wrapped package from a stranger, which he plans to take on board a plane; you see how our minds start working, spotting conspiracies everywhere. But at this point the plot summary must end, before the surprises begin. I can only say that anything as valuable as the Process would be a target for industrial espionage, and that when enough millions of dollars are involved, few people are above temptation.

*The Spanish Prisoner* is delightful in the way a great card manipulator is delightful. It rolls its sleeves to above its elbows to show it has no hidden cards, and then produces them out of thin air. It has the buried structure of a card manipulator's spiel, in which a "story" is told about the cards, and they are given personalities and motives, even though they are only cards. Our attention is misdirected—we are human and invest our interest in the human motives attributed to the cards, and forget to watch closely to see where they are going and how they are being handled. Same thing with the characters in *The Spanish Prisoner.* They are all given motives—romance, greed, pride, friendship, curiosity—and all of these motives are inventions and misdirections; the magician cuts the deck, and the joker wins.

There is, I think, a hole in the end of the story big enough to drive a ferry boat through, but then again there's another way of looking at the whole thing that would account for that, if the con were exactly the reverse of what we're left believing. Not that it matters. The end of a magic trick is never the most interesting part; the setup is more fun, because we can test ourselves against the magician, who will certainly fool us. We like to be fooled. It's like being tickled. We say, "Stop! Stop!" and don't mean it. ☞

## Spawn ★ ★ ★ ½

PG-13, 93 m., 1997

Michael Jai White (Al Simmons), John Leguizamo (Clown), Martin Sheen (Jason Wynn), Theresa Randle (Wanda), Nicol Williamson (Cogliostro), D. B. Sweeney (Terry Fitzgerald). Directed by Mark Dippe and produced by Clint Goldman. Screenplay by Alan McElroy, based on the comic books by Todd McFarlane.

*Spawn* is best seen as an experimental art film. It walks and talks like a big-budget horror film, heavy on special effects and pitched at the teenage audience, and maybe that's how it will be received. But it's more impressive if you ignore the genre and just look at what's on the screen. What we have here are creators in several different areas doing their best to push the envelope. The subject is simply an excuse for their art—just as it always is with serious artists.

Still, we can begin with the story. A man named Al Simmons (Michael Jai White) is happily married and at peace with himself, when he's recruited on a mission to destroy a biological warfare factory in North Korea. The mission is a setup. He is horribly burned and disfigured, and made captive of the forces of darkness. They offer him a deal: Lead the army of evil and he can see his wife again. He loves her, and he agrees.

That's what comic book writers call the "origination story," and *Spawn,* of course, is based on a famous series of comic books by Todd McFarlane, who made "Spiderman" the top-selling comic in history before jumping ship at Marvel to start his own company. After the setup, five years pass before the evil ones make good on their promise. Simmons by now is Spawn, seen either grotesquely scarred, or in an elaborate costume. He goes to his old home, sees his wife (Theresa Randle), now happily remarried, and is mistaken as a homeless man by everyone except his faithful little dog Spaz.

Most of the movie involves Spawn's efforts to break loose from his bargain with the devil, whose representative is Clown, a fat, wisecracking midget played with brilliant comic timing by John Leguizamo (who has little but his timing left to recognize after the special effects and makeup people have finished disguising him). Other key characters include Martin Sheen as Jason Wynn, a diabolical government agent who hopes to control the earth with biological blackmail, and Nicol Williamson as Cogliostro, Clown's enemy and a counterforce for good. Spawn has agreed to lead Armageddon for the powers of hell, but now finds himself trapped between good and evil.

And so on. I am sure there will be some who get involved at the plot level, but in comic books, and movies spawned by comic books, few things are ever really settled forever; the ending has to be left open for a sequel, and of course whole story lines can be negated (as happened at Marvel recently) just by explaining that impostors were at work. What matters is style, tone, and creative energy.

*Spawn* is the work of some of the most inventive artists now working in the area of digital effects. Its first-time director, Mark Dippe, worked on the dinosaurs of *Jurassic Park* and the shape-shifting villain of *Terminator 2.* The visual effects coordinator is Steve "Spaz" Williams, once a resident genius at Industrial Light and Magic. They've gathered an expert creative team, and what they put on the screen are vivid, bizarre, intense images—including visions of hell that are worthy of Hieronymus Bosch.

Spawn himself is an extraordinary superhero, with smoking green eyeballs and two looks—scarred skin, or a uniform that makes Batman look underdressed. Clown is a shape-shifter who can impersonate almost anyone else in the movie; Leguizamo's features are buried in fat makeup and then transplanted by animation onto a grotesque clown's body. There is a dragonlike thing, the beast of hell, that is all tooth, eyeball, and disgusting, coiling tongue (an "overgrown gekko," it's called). And there are vast vistas of the expanse of hell, with countless souls writhing on clouds of flame, tortured by the very anonymity of their suffering.

Against this, and preventing the film from being even better, is a pretty sappy plot. Yes, I said that the subject is just an excuse for the art, but audiences don't always see it that way, and some are likely to complain that *Spawn* is basically just shallow setups for virtuoso special-effects sequences. And so it is. Michael Jai White (who once played Mike Tyson on TV) makes a powerful Spawn with a presence both menacing and touching, and Clown is an inspired villain with one wicked one-liner after another ("You're Jimmy Stewart—and I'm Clarence"). But the Sheen and Williamson characters exist primarily just to nudge the plot along, and Theresa Randle's wife is underwritten; we want more about her feelings.

So the way to view the movie, I think, is to consider the story as the frame—necessary, but upstaged by what it contains, which in this case is some of the most impressive effects I've seen. The disciplines blend into one another: animation, makeup, costuming, process shots, morphing. They create a place and a look as specific as the places evoked in such films as *Metropolis* and *Blade Runner.* As a visual experience, *Spawn* is unforgettable.

## Special Effects ★ ★ ★

NO MPAA RATING, 40 m., 1996

A documentary directed by Ben Burtt and produced by Susanne Simpson.

The summer of 1996 may go down in history as the first movie season when machines did better than men at the box office. Computers may not always be able to defeat the world chess champion, but they are out-grossing movie stars. Consider *Twister, Mission: Impossible, The Rock, Eraser, The Nutty Professor,* and *Independence Day.* There is a natural tendency to think of them as starring, say, Tom Cruise, Sean Connery, Arnold Schwarzenegger, or Eddie Murphy. But really they star special effects.

Audiences like it when the helicopter chases the train into the Chunnel, when deadly missiles head for a football game, when flying saucers zap the White House, and when Eddie Murphy's body bulges out of control. Special effects are as old as the movies. But my hunch is that we passed some kind of turning point in the summer of 1996, and that from now on the big-audience blockbusters will belong to the f/x experts.

We've always been aware of special effects in movies where they were obviously being used—in the *Star Wars* trilogy, for example. But we're less aware in films where they fit in more quietly. *Forrest Gump* removed an actor's legs so realistically that many moviegoers assumed he was an amputee. *A Walk in the Clouds* created an idealized California valley of beautiful vistas and heart-stopping sunsets, and few audiences realized the landscapes were being created in the workshop, not the camera. And although many shots in *Jumanji* are obviously special effects, what about the wild animals? They're real, aren't they? With trainers hovering just out of camera range?

Not necessarily. A new documentary named *Special Effects* shows me things about *Jumanji* I never suspected. There is a lion, for example, that looks completely realistic. But it is an animatronic creation—a detailed, life-size puppet with a man inside and dozens of remote controls. That is a special effect. So is an animal created entirely in a computer, such as the hippo that gobbles up the kid's parents in *James and the Giant Peach.*

*Special Effects* is a documentary directed by Ben Burtt and produced by Nova and WGBH, the Boston PBS station. Theatrically, it was made for the big Omnimax and IMAX screens. It opens with footage of *King Kong* made specifically for this film, and continues in a superficial but entertaining way to reveal the tricks behind a lot of movies.

Five-story-high Omnimax/IMAX screens aren't really necessary for this film, which is mostly concerned with effects in ordinary movies. But there is one sequence that will buckle your shoes. George Lucas and his people at Industrial Light and Magic have re-created the opening of *Star Wars* for the giant screen, which curves over the head of the audience, so that you feel like you're suspended in space as the vast interstellar spacecraft looms overhead. The effect is awesome.

One is tempted to wonder why Lucas, who at the time was preparing a twenty-fifth-anniversary rerelease of the *Star Wars* trilogy, didn't just go ahead and release the whole thing in the MAX format. The unfortunate answer is he'd have to have issued barf bags to every customer. The big-screen process is so disorienting to our sense of balance that audiences can't take quick-cutting in it. Films made for MAX theaters are usually long shots connected by dissolves. Even in *Special Effects,* there are a couple of sequences from ordinary films that, blown up so big, gave me a twinge of vertigo.

In *Special Effects,* we see that the camera's ability to fool the eye was grasped even by the earliest cinema pioneers. The Frenchman George Méliès, an admirer of the famous magician Robert Houdin, did magic tricks on screen as early as 1896, and you can see him leap off a table and change into a woman in midair. His *Voyage to the Moon* (1902) shows a rocket ship leaving Earth and landing in the Man in the Moon's eye. Every trick in *Independence Day* is implied in the work of Méliès, except for the notion that effects could be created in a computer instead of from paint, backdrops, miniatures, animation, and optical printing techniques.

As a film, *Special Effects* doesn't dig very deep (in general terms, audiences will already know everything the film tells them) and doesn't reach very far: It includes footage from such films as *Independence Day* and the *Star Wars* retread that promoted the movies. But it is entertaining and interesting to see Lucas's teams out in the desert rephotographing *SW* sequences, and to learn that the twenty-fifth-anniversary edition will not simply be "restored," but in some scenes will be reshot to give life to alien beasts that didn't move in the original.

It is also revealing to learn how big and detailed the doomed model of the White House was on the *Independence Day* set. How did they do that shot where the death ray blows it up? Simple: They built a big White House and literally blew it up (we see the safety preparations). In that sequence and many from *Star Wars,* we see how slow motion and sound help make the miniatures seem real.

The day is still ahead when filmmakers can create a "real life" movie entirely with special effects. But not that far ahead. *Toy Story* was all done with computer animation, and its characters could easily have been made to look more realistic than they did. There are moments in *The Nutty Professor* when Eddie Murphy's character is on screen but Eddie Murphy the human being is not.

Is this a bad thing? Not at all, as long as the stars are willingly involved in the process. I think it's unethical to "steal" a likeness of a dead star (I don't like those soft drink ads with Bogart in them), but if living stars can extend their performances by using technical tricks—well, that's what they've been doing from the beginning.

## Speed 2: Cruise Control ★ ★ ★

PG-13, 125 m., 1997

Sandra Bullock (Annie), Jason Patric (Alex), Willem Dafoe (Geiger), Temuera Morrison (Juliano), Brian McCardie (Merced), Christine Firkins (Drew), Michael G. Hagerty (Harvey), Colleen Camp (Debbie). Directed by Jan De Bont and produced by De Bont, Steve Perry, and Michael Peyser. Screenplay by Randall McCormick and Jeff Nathanson, based on a story by De Bont and McCormick.

I love the summertime. I love strolling down Michigan Avenue on a balmy June evening, past the tourists and the shoppers and the lovers and the people dawdling on their way home from work, and I love going into a theater for a sneak preview of a summer movie and buying popcorn and settling back in my seat and enjoying a movie containing:

—A chainsaw.

—An explosive device with a red digital readout that nobody will ever be able to see (this one is concealed inside a fake golf club).

—A villain who travels with jars of leeches to suck the copper poisoning from his blood.

—A sweet girl and her lover on a Caribbean cruise. He just happens to be a member of an LAPD SWAT team.

—The other passengers on the cruise, who just happen to include members of a diamond dealer's association, who have filled the ship's vault with treasure.

—The villain's plot to hijack and destroy the ship, steal the diamonds, and get revenge on the computer company whose "electromagnetic fields gave me copper poisoning," after which he was fired and cast aside.

All of these pleasures, and more, are in *Speed 2: Cruise Control,* which is a sequel to *Speed* in name only—since even the basic premise is different. In the first movie, if the bus stopped, everyone would get killed. In this one, if the ocean liner doesn't stop, everyone will get killed. It's a small twist, I grant you, but a decisive one.

The movie stars Sandra Bullock, from *Speed,* and Jason Patric as her boyfriend. (The dialogue explains that she split up with the Keanu Reeves character from the earlier film for a lot of reasons, one of them possibly being that he did not want to appear in the sequel.) They go on a cruise and are unlucky enough to pick the boat targeted for revenge by a villain named Geiger (Willem DaFoe), whose laptop computers can take over the ship's own systems and control them.

Bullock plays the same fetching character she played the first time: warm, likable, stuttering a little, calm under pressure. Unfortunately, considering that she was crucial to the success of *Speed,* the screenplay gives her a secondary role and hands most of the best scenes to Patric, who handles them like a traditional action hero. At one point he puts on scuba gear and dangles inches from the giant spinning props of the ocean liner, and at another point he shoots a seaplane with a speargun and reels himself in. These stunts make the original *Speed* look plausible.

The ship itself is, of course, supplied with a cross-section of typical passengers, who in addition to the diamond dealers include a fat-acceptance group and a deaf girl who gets trapped in an elevator and can't hear the abandon-ship alarm. The captain is thrown overboard early in the film, after Geiger explains his grievance. (Seems like a waste, somehow, to go to the trouble of lodging your complaint with someone you immediately kill.) Then it's up to the hero and his girlfriend to save the day.

I will leave you in suspense as to whether they succeed. I will observe, however, that it's not every day (unless you live in New Orleans) that you get to see a ship crashing into a pier. The special-effects sequences in the movie are first-rate, especially that one. I know some of the houses on shore were models and that all kinds of fancy techniques were used, but the progress of the ship, as it crushes piers and condos, restaurants and trucks and cars, looks surprisingly real. And I was grateful to Jan De Bont, director of this film and the first one, for not overlooking such touches as The Dog Who Survives.

I chortled a few times. The first was at the digital readout. Why do mad bombers always go to the trouble of supplying them? There's not much room inside the head of a golf club (even a wood), so why waste space on a digital readout? I also chortled a few moments later, when the villain pulled out a piece of equipment labeled FIBER OPTIC CONVERTER in letters so large they could be read across the room. Doesn't mean much, but it sure looks good. And I will long treasure a moment when a computer asks Geiger, "Time to initiate?" and he types in, "Now."

Is the movie fun? Yes. Especially fun when the desperate Bullock breaks into a ship's supply cabinet and finds a chainsaw, which I imagine all ships carry. And when pleasure boaters somehow fail to see a full-sized runaway ocean liner until it is three feet from them. Movies like this embrace goofiness with an almost sensual pleasure. And so, on a warm summer evening, do I. ☞

## Sphere ★ ½

PG-13, 120 m., 1998

Dustin Hoffman (Dr. Norman Goodman), Sharon Stone (Beth Halperin), Samuel L. Jackson (Harry Adams), Peter Coyote (Barnes), Liev Schreiber (Ted Fielding), Queen Latifah (Fletcher). Directed by Barry Levinson and produced by Levinson, Michael Crichton, and Andrew Wald. Screenplay by Stephen Hauser and Paul Attanasio, based on the novel by Crichton.

Michael Crichton is the science-fiction author people read if they think they're too good for "regular" science fiction. Too bad. What they get in *Sphere,* now filmed by Barry Levinson, is a watered-down version of the sci-fi classic *Solaris,* by Stanislaw Lem, which was made into an immeasurably better film by Andrei Tarkovsky.

The underlying idea is the same: Humans come into contact with an extraterrestrial presence that allows their minds to make their thoughts seem real. The earlier novel and film challenged our ideas about human consciousness. *Sphere* functions more like a whodunit in which the plot's hot potato is tossed from character to character.

As the movie opens, an expert team is brought to the middle of the Pacific, where an amazing thing has been found on the ocean floor: a giant spacecraft, apparently buried for nearly 300 years, that still emits a distant hum—suggesting it is intact and may harbor life. The members of the team: a psychologist (Dustin Hoffman), a mathematician (Samuel L. Jackson), a biochemist (Sharon Stone), and an astrophysicist (Liev Schreiber). In command of a navy "habitat" on the ocean floor next to the ship is Peter Coyote. The habitat's small crew includes radio operator Queen Latifah, from *Set It Off,* who is on hand to illustrate Hollywood's immutable law that the first character to die is always the African-American.

The descent to the ocean floor, accompanied by much talk about depressurization, will be a disappointment to anyone who remembers the suspense in similar scenes in James Cameron's *Abyss.* And the introduction of the spacecraft is also a disappointment: Instead of the awe-inspiring first glimpses we remember from *Close Encounters* or even *Independence Day,* it's a throwaway. No wonder. The ocean-floor special effects are less than sensational, and the exteriors of the descent craft and the spacecraft are all too obviously models.

No matter, if the story holds our attention. At first it does. As long as we're in suspense, we're involved, because we anticipate great things. But *Sphere* is one of those movies where the end titles should be Peggy Lee singing "Is That All There Is?" The more the plot reveals, the more we realize how little there is to reveal, until finally the movie disintegrates into flaccid scenes where the surviving characters sit around talking about their puzzlements.

I have been careful to protect most of the film's secrets. I can be excused, I suppose, for revealing that what they find inside the spacecraft is, yes, a sphere. Where does this sphere come from? Who or what made it? How does it function? I am content to let it remain a mystery, so long as it entertains me, but after a promising start (it generates a *2001*-style hurtle through space and time), it just sits there, glowing and glowering, while the humans deal with the dangers of undersea life.

Hoffman, Jackson, Stone: These are good actors. How good is illustrated by how much they do with the flat, unyielding material. The last twenty minutes of the film are a slog through circular explanations and speculations that would have capsized lesser actors. They give it a good try, with dialogue that sounds either like characters analyzing the situation, or actors trying to figure out the plot.

*Sphere* feels rushed. The screenplay uses lots of talk to conceal the fact that the story has never been grappled with. The effects and the sets are pitched at the level of made-for-TV. The only excellence is in the acting, and even then the screenplay puts the characters through so many U-turns that dramatic momentum is impossible.

There are ideas sloshing around somewhere in the rising waters aboard the undersea habitat. The best one is an old science-fiction standby: Are humans mature enough to handle the secrets of the universe? Or are we but an infant species, whose fears and phobias prevent us from embracing the big picture? The last scenes are supposed to be a solemn confrontation of these questions, but they're punctuated by a special effects shot so puny and underwhelming that the spell is broken. That's all, folks. Put your hands together for Miss Peggy Lee. ☞

## Spice World ½★

PG, 93 m., 1998

Spice Girls (Themselves), Richard E. Grant (Clifford, the Manager), Claire Rushbrook (Deborah, the Assistant), Alan Cumming (Piers Cutherton-Smyth), Roger Moore (The Chief), George Wendt (Martin Barnfield), Meat Loaf (Dennis), Naoko Mori (Nicola). Cameos: Stephen Fry, Bob Hoskins, Elvis Costello, the Dream Boys, Bob Geldof, Elton John, Jonathan Ross. Directed by Bob Spiers and produced by Uri Fruchtmann and Barnaby Thompson. Screenplay by Kim Fuller.

The Spice Girls are easier to tell apart than the Mutant Ninja Turtles, but that is small consolation: What can you say about five women whose principal distinguishing characteristic is that they have different names?

They occupy *Spice World* as if they were watching it: They're so detached they can't even successfully lip-synch their own songs. During a rehearsal scene, their director tells them, with such truth that we may be hearing a secret message from the screenwriter, "That was absolutely perfect—without being actually any good."

*Spice World* is obviously intended as a ripoff of *A Hard Day's Night* (1964), which gave the Beatles to the movies. They should have ripped off more—everything they could get their hands on. The movie is a day in the life of a musical group that has become an overnight success, and we see them rehearse, perform, hang out together, and deal with such desperately contrived supporting characters as a trash newspaper editor, a paparazzo, and a manipulative manager.

All of these elements are inspired in one way or another by *A Hard Day's Night.* The huge difference, of course, is that the Beatles were talented—while, let's face it, the Spice Girls could be duplicated by any five women under the age of thirty standing in line at Dunkin' Donuts.

The Beatles film played off the personalities of the Beatles. The Spice Girls have no personalities; their bodies are carriers for inane chatter. The Beatles film had such great music that every song in it is beloved all over the world. The Spice Girls' music is so bad that even *Spice World* avoids using any more of it than absolutely necessary.

The film's linking device is a big double-decker bus, painted like a Union Jack, which ferries the Girls past London landmarks (so many landmarks I suspect the filmmakers were desperately trying to stretch the running time). This bus is of ordinary size on the outside but three times too wide on the inside; it is fitted with all the conveniences of Spice Girlhood, except, apparently, toilet facilities, leading to the unusual sight of the Girls jumping off for a quick pee in the woods. (They do everything together.)

So lacking in human characteristics are the Girls that when the screenplay falls back on the last resort of the bankrupt filmmaking imagination—a live childbirth scene—they have to import one of their friends to have the baby. She at least had the wit to get pregnant, something beyond the Girls since it would involve a relationship, and thus an attention span. Words fail me as I try to describe my thoughts at the prospect of the five Spice Girls shouting "push!"

## The Spitfire Grill ★ ★

PG-13, 111 m., 1996

Alison Elliott (Percy Talbott), Ellen Burstyn (Hannah Ferguson), Marcia Gay Harden (Shelby Goddard), Will Patton (Nahum Goddard), Kieran Mulroney (Joe Sperling), Gailard Sartain (Sheriff Gary Walsh), John M. Jackson (Johnny B./Eli). Directed by Lee David Zlotoff and produced by Forrest Murray. Screenplay by Zlotoff.

*The Spitfire Grill* won the audience award at the 1996 Sundance Festival, which says less for the movie than for the audience. It's an unabashedly manipulative, melodramatic tearjerker with plot twists that Horatio Alger would have been embarrassed to use, and the fact that it's so well acted only confuses the issue.

The movie takes place in Gilead, Maine, another one of those small towns like Salome, Texas, and Whistle Stop, Alabama, where everybody knows each other and they all gather every day to trade the latest news. Towns like this don't much exist anymore except in sitcoms, where the characters are constantly "dropping in" on one another in order to prod the plot and explain the latest developments.

Gilead, so far north that the locals call other Americans "flatlanders," has just had a stranger come to town. Her name is Perchance Talbott, Percy for short, and she has chosen it after getting out of prison. In a nice little scene, the local sheriff (Gailard Sartain) lines up a job for her as a waitress at the local restaurant, which is run by an older woman named Hannah (Ellen Burstyn) and already has a veteran waitress named Shelby (Marcia Gay Harden). It also has a regular customer named Joe (Kieran Mulroney).

Sometimes as a movie critic you have to knock yourself sharply on the ear to dislodge the last movie you've seen and pay attention to this one. Watching this plot unfold, I was remembering *Heavy,* which also premiered at Sundance; its café was run by an older woman (Shelley Winters) and had a veteran waitress (Deborah Harry) and had a young waitress (Liv Tyler) and had a regular customer whose name was Leo, not Joe, although he *was* played by Joe Grifasi. Also echoing in the caverns of my memory were several other movies about stalwart women running cafés and striding above the local gossip: *Ballad of the Sad Café, Fried*

*Green Tomatoes, Staying Together,* and of course *Bagdad Cafe.*

In *Spitfire Grill,* which weaves several fairly overworn feminist strands into its quilt, everyone of course immediately gossips about where Percy came from and why she would want to settle in Gilead. (Ever notice how in the movies people who believe they live in the best place on earth are always resentful when an outsider wants to move there?) Percy puts an end to the gossip by making a loud announcement at lunchtime: "I've been in prison. So now you know."

Yes, but what was she in prison for? I wondered. And then my Automated Mental Plot Analyzer hummed to life and suggested that in a movie of this sort it is almost inevitable that she committed her crime in self-defense against an abusive man. Is that what did happen? My lips are sealed.

Percy is soon asked out by Joe. She grows unhappy at his questions and blurts out the worst part of her past history (such characters of course never blurt out the best parts). Then Hannah breaks a leg and is laid up in her room, and so Percy and Shelby have to run the restaurant together, and Shelby's husband, Nahum (Will Patton), is unhappy, because he thinks this outsider is angling to take over the restaurant.

Meanwhile, Percy learns that Hannah puts canned goods in a sack and leaves them outside by the old stump where they are picked up at dawn by a mysterious hooded figure. No points for wondering if the mystery man has any connection to Hannah's son who fought in Vietnam. What's clear is that Hannah can no longer run the café, and so Percy suggests one of those essay contests like she saw on TV, where people send in $100 and say why they deserve to get the café, and the winner takes over.

The last half-hour of the movie is more than one movie can bear, as sacks of mail arrive, townspeople help judge the entries, and Joe's old father is so moved by one of them that he leaves the house for the first time in years; meanwhile there is skullduggery involving the money, and a misunderstanding involving the sack of canned goods, and a scientist thinks he can extract a cancer cure from the local trees, and if I told you that someone is swept down the river and into the rapids, you wouldn't believe me, would you?

It is impossible to believe the events manufactured so prodigiously by *The Spitfire Grill,* and yet there is no hint of a smile: Lee David Zlotoff, who wrote and directed it, means it seriously. What redeems it somewhat is the level of the acting. You can see how good actors can make almost anything believable. Alison Elliott is a calm, strong presence at the center, and all of the others are good, too—especially the sheriff, Gailard Sartain, and Will Patton as the mean husband (although the screenplay gives him a speech to deliver that even Tammy Faye Bakker would have found over the top). They make a lot of their moments work very nicely. But the movie as a whole is preposterous.

## Sprung ★ ½

R, 105 m., 1997

Tisha Campbell (Brandy), Rusty Cundieff (Montel), Paula Jai Parker (Adina), Joe Torry (Clyde), John Witherspoon (Detective), Jennifer Lee (Veronica), Clarence Williams III (Grand Daddy), Loretta Jean (Bride's Mother). Directed by Rusty Cundieff and produced by Darin Scott. Screenplay by Cundieff and Scott.

Sometimes it takes one movie to show you how good another movie was. *Sprung* provides that service for *Booty Call.* Both movies are sexcoms about two black couples. Both are cheerfully vulgar. Both have lots of sex and slapstick. *Booty Call* works. *Sprung,* despite containing a sweet relationship, doesn't.

The film begins with a manhunting woman named Adina (Paula Jai Parker) who convinces her somewhat shy friend Brandy (Tisha Campbell), a law clerk, to go partying. At a party, Adina exhibits her laserlike ability to calculate a man's worth by running an inventory on what he's wearing, while mental cash registers ring. She's fooled, though, by Clyde (Joe Torry), manager of a fast-food store, who flashes the keyring of a borrowed Porsche and "drops" a phony bank receipt.

When Adina and Clyde pair off, that leaves Brandy with Clyde's friend Montel (Rusty Cundieff, the film's director and cowriter). Cut to Clyde's apartment where, in the movie's worst miscalculation, he and Adina make love in a disturbingly animalistic scene that runs on and on and on to the world's loudest simultaneous orgasm—surpassing any possible comic purpose and simply becoming porno without the close-ups.

That scene throws the whole opening of the movie out of whack: In tone, effect, and length it breaks the rhythm and disturbs the tone, and it's a long time before we realize it had nothing to do with the rest of the plot. The other couple, Montel and Brandy, fall in love, and they're charming with one another—it would be a nice story if it weren't always being interrupted. But that happens regularly; Adina and Clyde plot to trick their friends to break up. Why? Because otherwise the couples will always be double-dating, and Adina and Clyde will have to spend too much time together.

Don't worry if you don't follow this. It has no connection to human life, and exists only in the terms of screenplay clichés. All that redeems it is the characters of Montel and Brandy; we care about them even though the movie does little to help us. There are well-written scenes in which Brandy, who's studying to be a lawyer, has to get over her snobbery and realize that Montel may indeed have a future in fast food.

Unfortunately, the good vibes in the movie are undermined by the dialogue, which makes a running gag out of the ability to put together long, ugly sentences full of insulting epithets; "pimp" and "buckwheat" are two I can print here. Why are there so many racial insults in black-oriented movies; isn't it time to declare a moratorium on insulting language?

Thinking back over the film, I can see how it might have been better. The plot might have worked if the characters had been allowed to emerge as halfway convincing people. Instead, there's a hyper quality to *Sprung,* as if Cundieff was concerned that a moment's pause or silence would sink the picture. It's amusing when he uses special effects (stars spin around Clyde's head, and Adina's inventory scene has cute visuals). But desperation created the sequence where Clyde plots to get Montel drunk and seduced by an old flame; Brandy's heart is broken when she overhears what she thinks are the sounds of love.

There is a nice extended sequence when Brandy and Montel first meet for lunch in the park. They like each other, they eat an obligatory hot dog, they talk and walk, and then, that evening, they happen upon a ballroom dancing party of middle-aged African-Americans, and spin onto the dance floor. Afterward they walk in the moonlight—and the next morning they're *still* in the park! It's like getting *Before Sunrise* as a bonus in the middle of a different movie.

## Star Kid ★ ★ ★

PG, 101 m., 1998

Joseph Mazzello (Spencer Griffith), Joey Simmrin (Turbo Bruntley), Alex Daniels (Cyborsuit), Arthur Burghardt (Cyborsuit Voice), Brian Simpson (Broodwarrior), Richard Gilliland (Roland [Dad]), Corinne Bohrer (Janet Holloway), Ashlee Levitch (Stacey [Sister]), Lauren Eckstrom (Michelle). Directed by Manny Coto and produced by Jennie Lew Tugend. Screenplay by Coto.

How would you like to climb inside a glistening metallic superhero suit and be partners with the intelligent cyborg that controls it? If you were a shy twelve-year-old boy, picked on by bullies and your brat of a sister, you'd love it. *Star Kid* develops that fantasy in a lively action movie that young boys may especially enjoy—if their innocence hasn't already been hammered down by too much R-rated violence.

The movie stars Joseph Mazzello *(Jurassic Park, The River Wild)* as Spencer, a bright student whose imagination is centered on the adventures of a comic book hero named Midnight Warrior. He's got a hopeless crush on a girl at school named Michelle (Lauren Eckstrom), who also likes Midnight Warrior, and who would probably be his friend if he weren't paralyzed by shyness every time he tries to talk to her. At home, he has a preoccupied dad (Richard Gilliland) and a mean older sister (Ashlee Levitch) who gets resentful when she's required to baby-sit "the little scab juice."

One night everything changes for Spencer, when he sees a rocket land in a nearby junkyard. He scampers inside and finds the ship, still steaming, as it opens up to reveal a tall, glistening robotic cyborg inside. This creature, who looks like a detailed version of the visitor in *The Day the Earth Stood Still,* is inhabited by an intelligence that is quickly able to communicate with Spencer, inviting him to step inside and occupy his body.

We've already learned the back story. The creature was built by a race named the Trelkans, who look like Yoda with eczema, and are engaged in a struggle with the evil Broodwarriors. Spencer, once inside the suit, communicates face to face with a holographic image representing the cyborg's intelligence, and before long he's calling him Cy.

The movie's appeal is obvious: Inside the suit, Spencer becomes unbelievably strong and can do all kinds of neat stuff, like give the school bullies their comeuppance, impress Michelle, and let his sister see he's not a little scab juice anymore. There are comic scenes as Spencer awkwardly learns to control the suit, and then a climax when a Broodwarrior arrives on Earth for a final showdown.

Spencer is essentially living inside a comic book. A lot of action comics originate from the same premise—an ordinary guy like Clark Kent or Peter Parker is transformed into a paragon of strength and power. Adolescent readers like that; it suits their fantasies. *Star Kid,* written and directed by Manny Coto, has a sweet heart and a lot of sly wit, and the symbiosis between boy and cyborg is handled cleverly. For kids of a certain age, it pushes the right buttons.

## Star Maps ★ ★

R, 95 m., 1997

Douglas Spain (Carlos), Efrain Figueroa (Pepe), Kandeyce Jorden (Jennifer), Martha Velez (Teresa), Lysa Flores (Maria), Annette Murphy (Letti), Robin Thomas (Martin), Vincent Chandler (Juancito). Directed by Miguel Arteta and produced by Matthew Greenfield. Screenplay by Arteta, based on a story by Arteta and Greenfield.

Sometimes while channel-surfing I'll linger with envy on the Spanish-language stations, where the dramas always seem steamier and more dramatic. I wish I spoke the language. I have the feeling I wouldn't be as bored. Characters make emotional declarations, bosoms heave, eyes flash, hair is tossed, faces are slapped, and there's lots of weeping, especially during emotional partings.

*Star Maps* is a movie that exists in the same emotional range, but it's in English, which is not necessarily an advantage, since you can almost always imagine better dialogue than the actors come up with in soft-core melodrama. The movie tells the story of a malevolent father named Pepe (Efrain Figueroa) who controls a string of young men on Hollywood street corners, who pretend to be selling maps to the stars' homes, but are actually male prostitutes.

As the film opens, Pepe's son Carlos (Douglas Spain), who dreams of being an actor, has returned from Mexico, where he was in amateur productions. He hopes his father's "connections" in showbiz will help him get his career started. His father immediately puts him out on the street as a hustler. It's a family tradition: Pepe's own father did the same to him.

Meanwhile, at home, life is chaotic. Pepe's wife, Teresa (Martha Velez), spends most of her time in bed, allegedly dying of cancer. Sometimes she has hallucinations in which she smiles and jokes with Cantinflas, the famous comedian. It was Teresa who sent young Carlos to her family in Mexico to get him away from the evil Pepe, and now that Carlos is back, Teresa has retreated into madness. Her daughter Maria (Lysa Flores), who has somehow escaped the family curse, warns Carlos that their father will destroy him. Meanwhile, another brother spends most of his time on the couch, eating. Occasionally he rouses himself to put on an S&M superhero costume and enact private fantasies.

Carlos doesn't much mind being a hustler, since for him it is good practice for the acting profession. But one day his luck changes when he meets Jennifer (Kandeyce Jorden), a TV star who is, she says, "looking for a nice little Mexican boy." The sex is good, and she decides she wants him around all the time, so she demands that he be written into her show. ("You're a Mexican stud. I'm helpless and white.") Jennifer's husband, who produces the show, is not pleased by this development.

Meanwhile, one of the better subplots involves the relationship between Pepe and Letti (Annette Murphy), his mistress, whom he also has working as a hooker. Letti, for some reason, trusts this monster, who exists on the fringes of Hollywood respectability, finding clients through bartenders (and promising clients "a guide to show you the more intimate parts of Hollywood"). Pepe is thrown out of a bar where he gets a lot of business after he beats up Letti, and that causes changes in the family's fortunes.

And there's more. Much more. *Star Maps* reads like a collision involving three or four scripts in different stages of development. It's a comedy, especially as Jennifer's writers try to rewrite a script to make use of Carlos. It's a tragedy, because Pepe is unspeakably evil and brutal. It's magic realism, as the mother chats with Cantinflas. And there are times when I think it's trying for parody, as when the sister, Maria, brings home the nice pharmacist who likes her, and Pepe puts on a horror show around the dinner table. (The pharmacist says, "Sir! This is no way to treat your daughter!" The father says, "I think she is probably a virgin. It's gonna cost you $50.")

*Star Maps* is not, to be sure, boring. But it is wildly unfocused. Is it about family abuse, prostitution, show business, dreams of fame, or what? It was written and directed by Miguel Arteta, who shows great energy and a dramatic drive, and with a more considered screenplay might have made a better movie. Walking out of the theater, I found myself wondering how this film is going to affect the lives of the people who really do sell maps to the stars' homes.

## Star Trek: First Contact ★ ★ ★ ½

PG-13, 112 m., 1996

Patrick Stewart (Jean-Luc Picard), Jonathan Frakes (William Riker), Brent Spiner (Data), James Cromwell (Zefram Cochrane), Alfre Woodard (Lily Sloane), LeVar Burton (Geordi La Forge), Alice Krige (Borg Queen), Michael Dorn (Worf), Gates McFadden (Beverly Crusher), Marina Sirtis (Deanna Troi). Directed by Jonathan Frakes and produced by Rick Berman. Screenplay by Brannon Braga and Ronald D. Moore, based on *Star Trek*, created by Gene Roddenberry.

*Star Trek: First Contact* is one of the best of the eight *Star Trek* films: Certainly the best in its technical credits, and among the best in the ingenuity of its plot. I would rank it beside *Star Trek IV: The Voyage Home* (1986), the one where the fate of Earth depended on the song of the humpback whale. This time, in a screenplay that could have been confusing but moves confidently between different levels of the story, the crew of the *Enterprise* follows the evil Borg back in time to the day before mankind made its first flight at warp speed.

That flight, in 2063, was monitored by an alien race, the Vulcans, who took it as evidence that man had developed to the point where it deserved to meet another race. But now the Borg, starting from the twenty-fourth century, want to travel back through a temporal vortex (how I love the Star Trek jargon!), prevent the flight and rewrite history, this time with Borg populating Earth instead of humans.

The latest edition of the starship is the *Enterprise E* (and there are plenty of letters left in the alphabet, Captain Picard notes ominously). It is patrolling deep space when it learns the Borg are attacking Earth. The *Enterprise* is ordered to remain where it is—probably, Picard (Patrick Stewart) notes bitterly, because he was a prisoner of the Borg some six years ago, and "a man who was captured and assimilated by the Borg is an unstable element."

These Borg are an interesting race. They are part flesh, part computer, and they "assimilate" all the races they conquer into their collective mind, which organizes their society like a hive. There is even a queen (Alice Krige), although she is not fat and pampered like an ant or a termite, but lean, mean, and a student of seduction. One of the movie's intriguing subplots involves Data (Brent Spiner), the *Enterprise*'s android, who is captured and hooked up to a Borg assimilating machine—which fails, because it can't crack his digital defenses. Then the queen tries some analog methods all her own.

The central plot takes place as the *Enterprise* follows a Borg ship back through time to Earth, which, the Trekkers are dismayed to learn, is now populated by Borg. To turn history around again, they need to be sure man's first warp flight succeeds. Earth is recovering from the Third World War, and a brilliant inventor named Cochrane (James Cromwell, the tall farmer from *Babe*) has adapted a missile for this historic flight.

He leads a commune that seems to be part hippie, part survivalist, and spends much of his time listening to rock 'n' roll and drinking, to the despair of his associate Lily (Alfre Woodard). These two do not believe the weird story they get from the starship crew, and at one point Lily nearly fries Picard with a stolen gun. (He: "Maximum setting! If you had fired you would have vaporized me." She: "It's my first ray gun.")

The plot moves deftly between preparations for the Earth launch, Data's assimilation tortures on the Borg ship, and a fight against a Borg landing party on the *Enterprise,* which Picard personally directs, overruling doubts expressed by his second in command, William Riker (Jonathan Frakes), and their own assimilated Klingon, Worf (Michael Dorn).

Some of the earlier *Star Trek* movies have been frankly clunky in the special effects department; the first of the series came out in 1979 and looked pale in comparison to *Star Wars.* But this one benefits from the latest advances in f/x artistry, starting with its sensational opening shot, which begins so deep inside Picard's eyeball it looks like a star-speckled spacescape, and then pulling back to encompass an unimaginably vast Borg starship. I also admired the interiors of the Borg probe, and the peculiar makeup work creating the Borg Queen, who looks like no notion of sexy I have ever heard of, but inspires me to keep an open mind.

*Star Trek* movies are not so much about action and effects as they are about ideas and dialogue. I doubted the original *Enterprise* crew would ever retire because I didn't think they could stop talking long enough. Here the story gives us yet another intriguing test of the differences between humans, aliens, and artificial intelligence. And the paradoxes of time travel are handled less murkily than sometimes in the past. (Although explain to me once again how Earth could be populated with millions of Borg who are expected to vanish—or never have been—if the *Enterprise* succeeds. Isn't there some sort of law of conservation of energy that requires their physical bodies to come from, or be disposed of, somewhere, somehow?)

*STFC* was directed by Jonathan Frakes, who did some of the *ST Next Generation* shows for television, and here achieves great energy and clarity. In all of the shuffling of time lines and plotlines, I always knew where we were. He also gets some genial humor out of Cromwell, as the inventor (who never wanted fame but simply enough money to go off to a "tropical island with a lot of naked women"). And there is such intriguing chemistry between Picard and the Woodard character that I hope a way is found to bring her onboard in the next film. *Star Trek* movies in the past have occasionally gone where no movie had gone, or wanted to go, before. This one is on the right beam. ☞

## Star Wars (Special Edition) ★ ★ ★ ★

PG, 125 m., 1977 (rereleased 1997)

Mark Hamill (Luke Skywalker), Harrison Ford (Han Solo), Carrie Fisher (Princess Leia), Peter Cushing (Grand Moff Tarkin), Alec Guinness (Ben (Obi-Wan) Kenobi), James Earl Jones (Vader's voice), Anthony Daniels (C3PO). Directed by George Lucas and produced by Gary Kurtz. Screenplay by Lucas.

To see *Star Wars* again after twenty years is to revisit a place in the mind. George Lucas's space epic has colonized our imaginations, and it is hard to stand back and see it simply as a motion picture because it has so completely become part of our memories. It's as goofy as a children's tale, as shallow as an old Saturday afternoon serial, as corny as Kansas in August—and a masterpiece. Those who analyze its philosophy do so, I imagine, with a smile in their minds. May the Force be with them.

Like *Birth of a Nation* and *Citizen Kane, Star Wars* was a technical watershed that influenced many of the movies that came after. These films have little in common, except for the way they came along at a crucial moment in cinema history, when new methods were ripe for synthesis. *Birth of a Nation* brought together the developing language of shots and editing. *Citizen Kane* married special effects, advanced sound, a new photographic style, and a freedom from linear storytelling. *Star Wars* combined a new generation of special effects with the high-energy action picture; it linked space opera and soap opera, fairy tales and legend, and packaged them as a wild visual ride.

*Star Wars* effectively brought to an end the golden era of early-1970s personal filmmaking and focused the industry on big-budget special-effects blockbusters, blasting off a trend we are still living through. But you can't blame it for what it did; you can only observe how well it did it. In one way or another all the big studios have been trying to make another *Star Wars* ever since (pictures like *Raiders of the Lost Ark, Jurassic Park,* and *Independence Day* are its heirs). It located Hollywood's center of gravity at the intellectual and emotional level of a bright teenager.

It's possible, however, that as we grow older we retain within the tastes of our earlier selves. How else to explain how much fun *Star Wars* is, even for those who think they don't care for science fiction? It's a good-hearted film in every single frame, and shining through is the gift of a man who knew how to link state-of-the-art technology with a deceptively simple, really very powerful, story. It was not by accident that George Lucas worked with Joseph Campbell, an expert on the world's basic myths, in fashioning a screenplay that owes much to man's oldest stories.

By now the ritual of classic film revival is well established: An older classic is brought out from the studio vaults, restored frame by frame, rereleased in the best theaters, and then relaunched on home video. With this "special edition" of the *Star Wars* trilogy (which includes new versions of *Return of the Jedi* and *The Empire Strikes Back*), Lucas has gone one step beyond. His special effects were so advanced in 1977 that they spun off an industry, including his own Industrial Light & Magic Co., the computer wizards who do many of today's best special effects.

Now Lucas has put IL&M to work touching up the effects, including some that his limited 1977 budget left him unsatisfied with. Most of the changes are subtle; you'd need a side-by-side comparison to see that a new shot is a little better. There's about five minutes of new material, including a meeting between Han Solo and Jabba the Hut that was shot for the first version but not used. (We learn that Jabba is not immobile, but sloshes along in a kind of spongy undulation.) There's also an improved look to the city of Mos Eisley ("a wretched hive of scum and villainy," says Obi-Wan Kenobi). And the climactic battle scene against the Death Star has been rehabbed.

The improvements are well done, but they point up how well the effects were done to begin with: If the changes are not obvious, that's because *Star Wars* got the look of the film so right in the first place. The obvious comparison is with Kubrick's *2001: A Space Odyssey,* made ten years earlier, in 1967, which also holds up perfectly well today. (One difference is that Kubrick went for realism, trying to imagine how his future world would really look, while Lucas cheerfully plundered the past; Han Solo's Millennium Falcon has a gun turret with a hand-operated weapon that would be at home on a World War II bomber, but too slow to hit anything at space velocities.)

Two Lucas inspirations start the story with a tease: He sets the action not in the future but "long ago," and jumps into the middle of it with "Chapter 4: A New Hope." These seemingly innocent touches are actually rather powerful; they give the saga the aura of an ancient tale, and an ongoing one.

As if those two shocks were not enough for the movie's first moments, as the camera tilts up, a vast spaceship appears from the top of the screen and moves overhead, an effect reinforced by the surround sound. It is such a dramatic opening that it's no wonder Lucas paid a fine and resigned from the Directors' Guild rather than obey its demand that he begin with conventional opening credits.

The film has simple, well-defined characters, beginning with the robots R2D2 (childlike, easily hurt) and C3PO (fastidious, a little effete). The evil Empire has all but triumphed in the galaxy, but rebel forces are preparing an assault on the Death Star. Princess Leia (pert, sassy Carrie Fisher) has information pinpointing the star's vulnerable point, and feeds it into R2D2's computer; when her ship is captured, the robots escape from the Death Star and find themselves on Luke Skywalker's planet, where soon Luke (Mark Hammil as an idealistic youngster) meets the wise, old, mysterious Ben Kenobi (Alec Guinness) and they hire the freelance space jockey Han Solo (Harrison Ford, already laconic) to carry them to Leia's rescue.

The story is advanced with spectacularly effective art design, set decoration, and effects. Although the scene in the intergalactic bar is famous for its menagerie of alien drunks, there is another scene, when the two robots are thrown into a hold with other used droids, which equally fills the screen with fascinating throwaway details. And a scene in the Death Star's garbage bin (inhabited by a snake with a head curiously shaped like E.T.'s) is also well done.

Many of the planetscapes are startlingly beautiful, and owe something to Chesley Bonestell's imaginary drawings of other worlds. The final assault on the Death Star, when the fighter rockets speed between parallel walls, is a nod in the direction of *2001,* with its light trip into another dimension: Kubrick showed, and Lucas learned, how to make the audience feel it is hurtling headlong through space.

Lucas fills his screen with loving touches. There are little alien rats hopping around the desert, and a chess game played with living creatures. Luke's weather-worn "Speeder" vehicle, which hovers over the sand, reminds me uncannily of a 1965 Mustang. And consider the details creating the presence, look, and sound of Darth Vader, whose fanged face mask, black cape, and hollow breathing are the setting for James Earl Jones's cold voice of doom.

Seeing the film the first time, I was swept away, and have remained swept ever since. Seeing this restored version, I tried to be more objective, and noted that the gun battles on board the spaceships go on a bit too long; it is remarkable that the Empire marksmen never hit anyone important; and the fighter raid on the enemy ship now plays like the computer games it predicted. I wonder, too, if Lucas could have come up with a more challenging philosophy behind the Force. As Kenobi explains it, it's basically just going with the flow. What if Lucas had pushed a little further to include elements of nonviolence or ideas about intergalactic conservation? (It's a great waste of resources to blow up star systems.)

The films that will live forever are the simplest-seeming ones. They have profound depths, but their surfaces are as clear to an audience as a beloved old story. The way I know this is because the stories that seem immortal—the Odyssey, the Tale of Genji, Don Quixote, David Copperfield, Huckleberry Finn—are all the same: a brave but flawed hero, a quest, colorful people and places, sidekicks, the discovery of life's underlying truths. If I were asked to say with certainty which movies will still be widely known a century or two from now, I would list *2001,* and *The Wizard of Oz,* and Keaton and Chaplin, and Astaire and Rogers, and probably *Casablanca* . . . and *Star Wars,* for sure. ☞

## The Starmaker ★ ★ ★

R, 114 m., 1996

Sergio Castellitto (Joe Morelli), Tiziana Lodato (Beata), Franco Scaldati (Brigadiere Mastropaolo), Leopoldo Trieste (Mute), Clelia Rondinella (Anna's Mother), Tano Cimarosa (Grandpa Bordonaro), Nicola Di Pinto (Communal Functionary). Directed by Giuseppe Tornatore and produced by Vittorio and Rita Cecchi Gori. Screenplay by Tornatore and Fabio Rinaudo.

Don't we all sometimes believe, in some secret recess of our being, that if we were only seen correctly we could be stars? Joe Morelli (Sergio Castellitto), the hero of *The Starmaker,* feeds on that folly. In the years after World War II, he tours the backwaters of Sicily in a truck plastered with movie posters, posing as a talent scout for Universal Studios of Rome. He sets up his tent in the town square, and films screen tests of the locals, charging them a "service fee," which they are happy to pay.

Of course he is a fraud. We know that almost from the moment we see him, but his clients are trusting. "Mother of God, what faces!" he says, as he photographs them reading lines from *Gone With the Wind.* Some are paralyzed with fear. Some cannot stop talking. Some break down and confess their deepest fears and griefs. A mother seduces him to win a screen test for her daughter. He is like Miss Lonelyhearts, the hero of the Nathanael West novel; he knows he is a phony, but he becomes transformed by the weight of the needs that these people bring to him.

*The Starmaker,* directed and cowritten by Giuseppe Tornatore, is a companion film to his *Cinema Paradiso* (1990). Both films take place in Sicily at about the same time, as television is replacing the big screen. Both films are about cinema professionals—a projectionist and a "talent scout"—who understand in an instinctive way how ordinary people nourish themselves from dreams of the movies. In both films, the professionals befriend young outcasts in need.

In *Cinema Paradiso,* it was the young boy from an unhappy home, who made the projectionist his surrogate father, and the movies, in a way, his mother. In *The Starmaker,* it is a simple but beautiful young girl (Tiziana Lodato), who works in a village cleaning and bathing the old and the sick, and makes money by letting lecherous old men look at her body. She believes the talent scout can rescue her from her life, and stows away in his truck. Although he is far from a celibate, he returns her to the village, only to find that their lives are entangled in ways he does not foresee.

The film in Joe Morelli's camera may be out of date. The "screen tests" are certainly going nowhere near "Universalia Studios di Roma." He may not be seriously filming his subjects—but he is seriously looking at them. Through the camera, he sees their souls. There is a humble shepherd who comes down from the hills and tells the camera, "The best thing about being a shepherd is that you can reason with the stars." There is an old man in a cloak, in one village, who has not spoken since the war. He enters Morelli's tent one night for a test and finds, as the camera rolls, that he can speak again: "Oh, Fifth Regiment of my life!"

And there are stories all around Morelli that could be made into movies. Like the men who bring him to a shuttered room to photograph the dead body of a Mafia don, who was never photographed in life. They want something to remember him by. And the Count of Montejuso, whose beautiful wife brings him once a month in their Rolls-Royce to the bombed-out village that was once his: "All I have left is here." Morelli, himself a con man, believes these people as if he is the most trusting man on earth.

In the period Tornatore tells his stories about, the movies had not become so familiar to their audiences—had not lost their mystery. There was still a barrier of glamour between the audience and the film. It was believed that movie stars, in some way, had transcended the mundane lot of the rest of us, and ascended to a more glorious plane. And that (here is the crucial part) the movies themselves had caused that glorification. To be touched by the movies was perhaps to be sanctified.

Those beliefs are a heavy burden for Joe Morelli to bear. He cannot help seeing that somehow he is not entirely a fraud; that his subjects are getting their money's worth, sitting in front of the camera that allows them to express their dreams, and then waiting patiently for the call from Rome.

*The Starmaker* is not quite the film that *Cinema Paradiso* was, if only because the purity of the friendship between the projectionist and the young boy is not equaled here by the bond between Joe Morelli and the naive Beata. There are some uncomfortable moments when we sense that Tornatore, by asking his actress to reveal her body, is placing himself, and us, in the same position as the old man who pays her to remove her blouse.

And he doesn't find a perfect ending for *The Starmaker,* as he did for *Cinema Paradiso.* In that film, we saw a montage of all of the movie kisses that had been snipped from the movies over the years by the censorious local priest. In this one, there is a reunion between Morelli and Beata that does not quite ring true. And then a montage of some of the "screen tests" he filmed, which seems too obviously a replay of the kisses. It's as if Tornatore is trying to make the same movie again, when in fact *The Starmaker* has its own right to be told. The movie is not as special as *Cinema Paradiso,* but in its own way it is enchanted too. Mother of God, what faces.

## Starship Troopers ★ ★

R, 129 m., 1997

Casper Van Dien (Johnny Rico), Dina Meyer (Dizzy Flores), Denise Richards (Carmen Ibanez), Michael Ironside (Jean Rasczak), Jake Busey (Ace Levy), Neil Patrick Harris (Carl Jenkins), Clancy Brown (Sergeant Zim), Seth Gilliam (Sugar Watkins), Patrick Muldoon (Zander Barcalow). Directed by Paul Verhoeven and produced by Jon Davison and Alan Marshall. Screenplay by Ed Neumeier, based on the novel by Robert A. Heinlein.

*Starship Troopers* is the most violent kiddie movie ever made. I call it a kiddie movie not to be insulting, but to be accurate: Its action, characters, and values are pitched at eleven-year-old science-fiction fans. That makes it true to its source. It's based on a novel for juveniles by Robert A. Heinlein. I read it to the point of memorization when I was in grade school. I have improved since then, but the story has not.

The premise: Early in the next millennium, mankind is engaged in a war for survival with the Bugs, a vicious race of giant insects that colonize the galaxy by hurling their spores into space. If you seek their monument, do not look around you: Bugs have no buildings, no technology, no clothes, nothing but the ability to attack, fight, kill, and propagate. They exist not as an alien civilization but as pop-up enemies in a space war.

Human society recruits starship troopers to fight the Bugs. Their method is to machine-gun them to death. This does not work very well. Three or four troopers will fire thousands of rounds into a Bug, which like the Energizer Bunny just keeps on comin'. Grenades work better, but I guess the troopers haven't twigged to that. You'd think a human race capable of interstellar travel might have developed an effective insecticide, but no.

It doesn't really matter, since the Bugs aren't important except as props for the interminable action scenes, and as an enemy to justify the film's quasi-fascist militarism. Heinlein was, of course, a right-wing saber-rattler, but a charming and intelligent one who wrote some of the best science fiction ever. *Starship Troopers* proposes a society in which citizenship is earned through military service, and values are learned on the battlefield.

Heinlein intended his story for young boys, but wrote it more or less seriously. The one redeeming merit for director Paul Verhoeven's film is that by remaining faithful to Heinlein's material and period, it adds an element of sly satire. This is like the squarest but most technically advanced sci-fi movie of the 1950s, a film in which the sets and costumes look like a cross between Buck Rogers and the Archie comic books, and the characters look like they stepped out of Pepsodent ads.

The film's narration is handled by a futuristic version of the TV news crossed with the Web. After every breathless story, the cursor blinks while we're asked, "Want to know more?" Yes, I did. I was particularly intrigued by the way the Bugs had evolved organic launching pods that could spit their spores into space, and could also fire big globs of unidentified fiery matter at attacking spaceships. Since they have no technology, these abilities must have evolved along Darwinian lines; to say they severely test the theory of evolution is putting it mildly.

On the human side, we follow the adventures of a group of high school friends from Buenos Aires. Johnny (Casper Van Dien) has a crush on Carmen (Denise Richards), but she likes the way Zander (Patrick Muldoon) looks in uniform. When she signs up to become a starship trooper, so does Johnny. They go through basic training led by an officer of the take-no-prisoners school (Michael Ironside), and then they're sent to fight the Bugs. Until late in the movie, when things really get grim, Carmen wears a big, wide, bright smile in every single scene, as if posing for the cover of the novel. (Indeed, the whole look of the production design seems inspired by covers of the pulp space opera mags like *Amazing*, *Imagination*, and *Thrilling Wonder Stories*.)

The action sequences are heavily laden with special effects, but curiously joyless. We get the idea right away: Bugs will jump up, troopers will fire countless rounds at them, the Bugs will impale troopers with their spiny giant legs, and finally dissolve in a spray of goo. Later there are refinements, like fire-breathing beetles, flying insects, and giant Bugs that erupt from the earth. All very elaborate, but the Bugs are not *interesting* in the way, say, that the villains in the *Alien* pictures were. Even their planets are boring; Bugs live on ugly rock worlds with no other living species, raising the question of what they eat.

Discussing the science of *Starship Troopers* is beside the point. Paul Verhoeven is facing in the other direction. He wants to depict the world of the future as it might have been visualized in the mind of a kid reading Heinlein in 1956. He faithfully represents Heinlein's militarism, his Big Brother state, and a value system in which the highest good is to kill a friend before the Bugs can eat him. The underlying ideas are the most interesting aspect of the film.

What's lacking is exhilaration and sheer entertainment. Unlike the *Star Wars* movies, which embraced a joyous vision and great comic invention, *Starship Troopers* doesn't resonate. It's one-dimensional. We smile at the satirical asides, but where's the warmth of human nature? The spark of genius or rebellion? If *Star Wars* is humanist, *Starship Troopers* is totalitarian.

Watching a film that largely consists of interchangeable characters firing machine guns at computer-generated Bugs, I was reminded of the experience of my friend McHugh. After obtaining his degree from Indiana University, he spent the summer in the employ of Acme Bug Control in Bloomington, Indiana. One hot summer day, while he was spraying insecticide under a home, a trap door opened above his head and a housewife offered him a glass of lemonade. He crawled up, filthy and sweaty, and as he drank the lemonade, the woman told her son, "Now Jimmy—you study your books or you'll end up just like him!" I wanted to tell the troopers the same thing.

## Stealing Beauty ★ ★

R, 102 m., 1996

Liv Tyler (Lucy Harmon), Carlo Cecchi (Carlo Lisca), Sinead Cusack (Diana Grayson), Jeremy Irons (Alex Parrish), Jean Marais (M. Guillaume),

Donal McCann (Ian Grayson), D. W. Moffett (Richard Reed), Stefania Sandrelli (Noemi), Rachel Weisz (Miranda Fox). Directed by Bernardo Bertolucci and produced by Jeremy Thomas. Screenplay by Susan Minot.

*I wait and wait so patiently.*
*I'm quiet as a cup . . .*
*I hope you'll come and rattle me . . .*
*Quick! come and wake me up!*

This is one of several poems written by Lucy, the Heroine of *Stealing Beauty,* as she drifts through an endless house party in Tuscany. I quote Lucy's poetry because I want to set you a test question. Reading it, how old would you guess Lucy is? Nine? Fourteen? The notion of being "quiet as a cup" is not bad. "Rattle me" is better than "drink from me." Those double exclamation points, however . . .

Pencils up. Lucy is nineteen. If this poetry seems unsophisticated for a wordly nineteen-year-old, you should read some of her other poems, which are superimposed on the screen in her own handwriting, and (I am afraid) her own spelling.

Lucy is a creature without an idea in her head. She has no conversation. No interests. No wit. She exists primarily to stir lust in the loins of men. After the death of her mother, a poet who visited these Italian hills twenty years ago, Lucy has come back to an artist's home with two things on her mind: She wants to discover the identity of her real father, and she wants to lose her virginity. Experienced moviegoers can assess the risk that she will solve these problems simultaneously.

*Stealing Beauty* is the new film by Bernardo Bertolucci *(Last Tango in Paris, The Last Emperor),* who like many of middle-aged man before him has been struck dumb by the beauty of a nubile young girl, and has made the mistake of trying to approach her on what he thinks is her level. The movie plays like the kind of line a rich older guy would lay on a teenage model, suppressing his own intelligence and irony in order to spread out before her the wonderful world he would like to give her as a gift. Look at these hills! The sunsets! Smell the herbed air! See how the light catches the old rose-covered villa! The problem here is that many nineteen-year-old women, especailly the beautiful international model types, would rather stain their teeth with cigarettes and go to discos with cretins on motorcycles than have all Tuscany as their sandbox. (For an example of a cannier May–December seduction strategy, consider *Nelly and Monsieur Arnaud,* in which an older man fascinates a young woman by emphasizing his age and experience and pretending to be beyond her charms.)

Lucy is played by Liv Tyler, a young actress who has been profiled in all the glossies by writers who find it delightful that she thought her father was one rock star when in fact he was another. Thus there is an autobiographical component to her search among the artistic layabouts at the Tuscan villa for the man who seduced her mother twenty years ago. Tyler is indeed attractive, and looks enough like Lili Taylor to be her sister. But Lili Taylor usually plays smart women, and if she were in this movie her BS alarm would be ringing constantly.

The villa is occupied by a sculptor (Donal McCann), who starts on a tree trunk with a chain saw and is soon sandpapering the curve of Lucy's chin. His earth-mother wife (Sinead Cusack) is tired after twenty years of cooking and keeping house for a continual house party, and no wonder. The most interesting guest is a gay playwright (Jeremy Irons) who is dying of AIDS and attracts Lucy because he is not after her. Other guests include an art dealer (Jean Marais), an advice to the lovelorn expert (Stefania Sandrelli), a designer (Rachel Weisz), and an entertainment lawyer (D. W. Moffett), who sighs, "I think it would be great, you know, to just sit around all day and express yourself." Neighbors drop in, including assorted young men, one of whom may have sent Lucy a letter, which she thinks was romantic and poetic—as indeed anyone who writes like Lucy would.

The movie is great to look at. Like all those other Brits-in-Italy movies *(A Month at the Lake, Enchanted April, A Room With a View),* it makes you want to find this place and go there. In this case, however, you hope the movie characters have moved out before you get there. There is a simmer of discontent beneath the surface of everyday life in the villa, a sort of sullen, selfish unhappiness that everyone has about his or her lot in life.

The purpose of the Lucy character, I guess, is to act like a catalyst or a muse, shaking up old patterns and forcing these exiles to decide where their homes really are. She is fresh and they are decadent narcissists. Only the Jeremy Irons character, absorbed in his dying, and the Donal McCann character, absorbed in his art, have lives of any meaning.

The young men who buzz about Lucy are of no substance whatever. The older men are of similar substance, but can make better conversation, which would be useful if there were any evidence that Lucy was a conversationalist. Actually she serves for Bertolucci more as a plot device than as a person. She represents some kind of ideal of perfect virgin beauty, and the film's opening shots, in which a photographer on a plane sees her sleeping and takes close-ups of her lips and crotch, set the tone. The sad thing is that, sleeping, she embodies what she represents to this movie just as well as when she's awake.

## Stonewall ★ ★ ½

NO MPAA RATING, 98 m., 1996

Guillermo Diaz (LaMiranda), Frederick Weller (Matty Dean), Brendan Corbalis (Ethan), Duane Boutte (Bostonia), Bruce MacVittie (Skinny Vinnie). Directed by Nigel Finch and produced by Christine Vachon. Screenplay by Rikki Beadle Blair, based on the book *Stonewall* by Martin Duberman.

Homosexuality, which Lord Alfred Douglas called "the love that dare not speak its name," spoke its name loudly in the summer of 1969 when the clients of the Stonewall, a bar in Greenwich Village, fought back against police who were engaging in ritual gay-bashing. The police were caught off guard: This wasn't in the script, which called for their targets to flee or submit to ritual bookings for such crimes as not dressing to reflect their gender.

On that day, the gay liberation movement was born, and homosexuals began to assert their sexuality instead of concealing or denying it. *Stonewall* re-creates that time and place in a docudrama that looks through the eyes of a naive young man who comes to New York from a small town and is dismayed to find the situation little better than the one he left behind.

His name is Matty Dean (Frederick Weller), and he is comfortable with his sexuality—more easy with it, indeed, than most of the men he meets at the Stonewall. That includes its owner, Vinnie (Bruce MacVittie), who is in love with a drag queen named Bostonia (Duane Boutte) but keeps it a secret and poses as a straight businessman. Matty's first night at the Stonewall ends with a police raid, and he watches as customers are beaten up, booked, or dunked in the dishwater. For the regulars, it's an old story; drag queens quickly hide their wigs and wipe off their makeup, or race for the exit doors.

Matty doesn't see why his lifestyle should be against the law. Neither does LaMiranda (Guillermo Diaz), the drag queen he begins to date. Like all drag queens, LaMiranda is more inclined to flaunt sexuality than to conceal it; that's a contrast to the members of the Mattachine Society, a cautious gay group that's planning a protest march in Philadelphia and has strictly enforced regulations: suits and ties for the men, conservative dresses for the women.

When Matty is asked to go to the Philadelphia march by Ethan (Brendan Corbalis), he doesn't tell LaMiranda, "because I was afraid to tell you about the dress code." He was also, perhaps, more comfortable in public with the straight-looking Ethan than the flamboyant LaMiranda. LaMiranda, who prides herself on never taking emotional chances, has taken a chance and seems to have lost.

*Stonewall* follows its characters during a summer when life for gays follows a long-established pattern: Pretend to be straight except among friends. Ethan takes Matty to Fire Island, then as now a homosexual enclave, but even there Matty is astonished when he goes to a dance and finds that "local ordinances" require men to dance while standing side by side, not facing one another.

The movie, directed by Nigel Finch, a British filmmaker who died last year of AIDS, is serious about its subject but not about its style. Dramatic scenes are intercut with musical interludes in which three drag queens lip-synch to songs that comment, often wryly, on the action.

Some of the movie's most interesting scenes involve the relationship between Vinnie, the mob-connected bar owner who wants to be seen as straight, and Bostonia, the black queen he loves. Vinnie supplies Bostonia with a chauffeured limousine, but is paranoid about meeting her; one of their conversations takes place at dawn on top of a deserted building.

What Vinnie wants, he has decided, is for

Bostonia to have a sex-change operation so that they can move to "Arizona or someplace" and "live like normal people." This is a curious plan, considering that in 1969 an interracial couple might not be accepted in Arizona any more warmly than a gay couple, and that in any event only Vinnie would presumably be familiar with Bostonia's genital landscape. It becomes clear later in the film, however, that the person Vinnie most wants to appear normal to is himself.

This is all interesting material—especially since the world it represents is ancient history for many young people. But *Stonewall* handles its characters as pawns in a soap opera; there is little particular insight and much emotional drama. Like many docudramas, it sacrifices the intensity of the foreground by always making us aware of the historical backdrop. And each of the characters is such a basic type that we sometimes feel they're following a formula instead of feeling for themselves. My guess is that the movie began as a "gay film" instead of being character-driven; the message is more important than the messengers, and that limits the story's depth.

The film's climax is the Stonewall Riot, now immortalized in story and song, but then a disorganized response by gay men who were fed up and not going to take it anymore. Watching the film, I was reminded of how circumspect society was about homosexuality in the 1960s. As a graduate student of English, I remember professors suggesting that there was something unusual about W. H. Auden and Willa Cather, but they never quite said what it was. With Oscar Wilde, of course, there was no doubt, but then he was always ahead of his time.

## Striptease ★ ★

R, 115 m., 1996

Demi Moore (Erin Grant), Burt Reynolds (David Dillbeck), Armand Assante (Al Garcia), Ving Rhames (Shad), Robert Patrick (Darrell Grant), William Hill (Jerry Killian), Paul Guilfoyle (Malcolm Moldovsky), Jerry Grayson (Orly), Rumer Willis (Angela). Directed by Andrew Bergman and produced by Mike Lobell. Screenplay by Andrew Bergman, based on the book by Carl Hiaasen.

Carl Hiaasen's *Striptease* was a novel that thought all of its characters were hilarious. Now here is the Demi Moore movie version, in which all of the characters are hilarious except for Demi Moore's. Her character, named Erin Grant, is a woman who has lost her children in a crooked custody battle and goes to work in a strip club to earn enough to win her children back. The woman is brave, heroic, and stacked, but she's not funny. The movie's fatal flaw is to treat her like a plucky Sally Field heroine. That throws a wet blanket over the rest of the party.

The point of the Hiaasen story was that everyone was funny: He cast a dubious eye on the strippers, the bar management, the customers, the sex-mad congressman, the sneaky sugar baron, Erin's ex-husband—on everyone. They were all part of the same comic world. When you extract one of those characters from the mix and treat her seriously, it throws off the timing and it undermines the rationale of the whole undertaking.

My guess is that when Demi Moore and the writers started musing about how Erin Grant would "really feel" in a situation, or how the audience would be able to "identify" with her mother's urge to win her children back, someone should have stepped in to gently say: It's a comedy, honey, and when it's not a comedy, it's a satire. Everything in this movie should be for laughs, including the ex-husband, the kids, and the brave Erin Grant.

As *Striptease* opens, custody of Erin's children is being given over to her worthless husband (Robert Patrick), who may be a convicted criminal but was, as the Florida judge recalls fondly, "a great tailback." Erin needs work, and starts stripping at the Eager Beaver, a "gentleman's club"—so called because most of its customers are never called one anywhere else. We meet the fellow strippers, including the buxom Urbana Sprawl (Pandora Peaks), who is named after my hometown and so, of course, deserves a mention here. The bouncer is Shad, played by Ving Rhames, who was Marcellus Wallace in *Pulp Fiction* and this time provides a strong shoulder for a vulnerable girl to cry on.

The club customers include the Erin-worshipping Jerry Killian (William Hill), who thinks he may know how to help Erin win her children back, and the perpetually drunk and randy Congressman David Dilbeck (Burt Reynolds), who is capable of leaping onto the stage in mid-grind to protect one of the dancers from an annoying customer. Among the other threats to the dancers are boa constrictors that wrap themselves around their necks, and a management that is always thinking up bright new ideas. One stripper protests against the latest proposal, which is corn-wrestling: "No chance I'm gonna roll around in creamed corn with a bunch of yahoos trying to push Niblets up my hoo-hah."

There is in that dialogue a suggestion of the direction *Striptease* might have taken. Certainly the director, Andrew Bergman, is capable of making a satirical laughfest; his credits include *Honeymoon in Vegas* and *The Freshman*. But the problem is with Erin Grant, who interrupts the comic rhythm with her underlying seriousness. When she's not on the screen, the characters are free to float into satire, and Burt Reynolds has some splendid scenes as the tool of the local sugar cartel. But when Erin returns, the other actors have to match her more somber energy level, and there goes the comedy.

The sex business is certainly ripe for satirical treatment. But not here. That leaves the movie's much-advertised nudity and eroticism, which for me were disappointing. The stripteases are choreographed to present the strippers as seasoned pros, indifferent to their nudity and disdainful of their customers. To be erotic, a striptease must seem to mean something to the person disrobing: There must be the illusion that nudity is a meaningful decision, which the stripper is taking reluctantly. Most striptease gimmicks and props are therefore counterproductive. A stripper who needs to perform with a snake, or demonstrate dexterity in making tassels twirl in opposite directions, is essentially saying that she realizes her unclothed body is of no interest unless she also does parlor tricks.

The strippers in *Striptease* are at pains to show that stripping in public is without psychic risk to them. This is true even of the Erin Grant character, who claims at one point she gets nauseous before she goes on stage, but is a pro the moment the spotlight hits her. The attitude she projects in the TV ads is the same one that carries through the movie: I'm doing this so brazenly that you'll never know how I really feel about it.

The greatest stripper of all time was probably Tempest Storm, who is, I gather, still active in her 60s. Perhaps no one alive has taken it off more often. Yet on the two or three occasions when I saw her (including once in a sleazy Times Square theater) she was able to create the illusion that she was reluctant—all but a blushing novice—and there was a certain sweet delight in the way she finally disrobed. The strippers in *Striptease* would possibly find her act too revealing; their impersonality is a shield protecting them from the suckers.

Hiaasen is a very funny writer, whose work needs to be respected if it is to work on the screen. Like Elmore Leonard, who Hollywood finally got right in *Get Shorty*, Hiaasen is not a writer whose books you film for the plot. You film him for the dialogue and the attitude. Forget that, and why bother? ☞

## The Substance of Fire ★ ★ ★

R, 102 m., 1997

Ron Rifkin (Isaac Geldhart), Timothy Hutton (Martin Geldhart), Tony Goldwyn (Aaron Geldhart), Sarah Jessica Parker (Sarah Geldhart), Eric Bogosian (Gene Byck), Lee Grant (Cora Cahn), Ronny Graham (Louis Foukold). Directed by Daniel Sullivan and produced by Jon Robin Baitz, Randy Finch, and Ron Kastner. Screenplay by Baitz.

*The Substance of Fire*, like *Shine*, involves a father who is descending into madness. In both films, the process is a result of the psychic wounding done by the Holocaust. And in both films we are not quite sure how we are expected to deal with the illness, which results in cruelty to the next generation. It would be simpler without the madness: A man is damaged by the Holocaust and visits his pain on his children. That is possible to understand. But insanity brings with it a certain license: Does it matter, after a point, what a mad person does? Can we blame them?

The fact that we ask such questions makes both movies more interesting. The Holocaust is often used in fiction as pure evil, to which our moral response is immediate and direct. In these films it is more complicated. The father in *The Substance of Fire* is Isaac Geldhart (Ron Rifkin), who as a child saw the Nazis burn books. Now he heads one of New York's most respected publishing houses and wants to publish a four-volume study of Nazi medical atrocities. This would seem destined to be a scholarly or academic work, but Isaac wants to print it like an art book and sell it for hundreds of dollars. He rejects an entire printing—at $200 per set wholesale—because the paper is not good enough.

What's going on here? Why must the book be so beautiful and expensive when its contents are as well contained in a paperback? Where is the market? Will the book appeal to those sometimes slightly ambivalent collectors of Nazi memorabilia? Isaac apparently wants the set to be handsome as a tribute to the aging scholar who spent his life writing it. He saw the Nazis burn books; now he will publish an elegant book about the Nazis. There is symbolism here, but hard to sort out.

Like Lear, Isaac has three children and is of an age to divide his kingdom among them. His oldest son, Aaron (Tony Goldwyn), who is gay, works with him in the publishing house. His other son, Martin (Timothy Hutton), teaches landscape architecture at Vassar. His daughter, Sarah (Sarah Jessica Parker), is an actress on a children's TV series ("I sing songs about trichinosis").

"Everybody in town knows your company is on the rocks," an agent (Eric Bogosian) tells Aaron. There's talk of a merger with Japanese interests, but they find the Nazi book "too morbid" and shy away from Isaac's developing mania. Aaron hopes to make some money by publishing a steamy novel by his lover. The father calls it "meretricious crap—a trashy novel by a sicko hipster. I wanted my time back after I read it." Isaac is probably right. But a business cannot be run as a charity.

The children, who all own stock in the company, meet with their father, and the meeting degenerates into a tirade against them. He fires his son. His daughter sides with her brother. The family is in disarray. At the same time it's clear that Isaac is losing his sanity. In the early scenes he's a literate, tart-tongued iconoclast. In the last scenes, like Lear, he ranges across the blasted heath of his office, denouncing his children and clinging to his fool—or, in this case, his faithful secretary. Soon he is holding imaginary conversations with his wife and offering to buy a man's shoes off his feet.

A line has been crossed, and we as viewers have to decide when it was crossed and how that affects our feelings. Was Isaac ever wholly sane? Was the four-volume edition ever a good idea? Certainly we like the old man (Ronny Graham) who wrote it. Does the Holocaust stop being a relevant factor in Isaac's life after he loses his mind—or is it, as the cause of the madness, more relevant than ever? What about Aaron's homosexuality? Does his father reject the lover's book as a way of rejecting his son's sexuality?

*The Substance of Fire* was written by Jon Robin Baitz, based on his stage play, which according to some reports was not as ambiguous. The film, directed by Daniel Sullivan, is brave, I think, to offer us a complicated scenario without an easy moral compass. *Shine,* by contrast, is much simpler: The young pianist's father lost his family in the Holocaust, is terrified of losing a family again, and thus becomes insanely possessive of his son. The son, torn between ambition and guilt, goes mad. Cut and dried. In *The Substance of Fire,* more complex issues lurk in the corners of the material.

It would be useful to know, for example, whether the four-volume work about medical atrocities contains any information likely to be of scientific benefit. Will it save lives? Or does it simply record sadistic experiments and their results? If so, what is the purpose of publishing it and reading it? Everything depends on context and tone; *Schindler's List* and *Ilsa, She-Wolf of the SS* both contain concentration camp commandants.

Leaving this movie, we want answers, and there aren't any (apart from an answer of sorts in a silly epilogue that plays like it was tacked on in a sentimental fit). Because the film is well written and acted, it holds our interest. Because its ideas remain murky, it frustrates our expectations. It's not a satisfying film, but that doesn't make it a bad one.

## The Substitute ★

R, 103 m., 1996

Tom Berenger (Shale), Ernie Hudson (Claude Rolle), Diane Venora (Jane Hetzko), Glenn Plummer (Mr. Sherman), Marc Anthony (Juan Lacas), Raymond Cruz (Joey Six). Directed by Robert Mandel and produced by Morrie Eisenman and Jim Steele. Screenplay by Roy Frumkes and Rocco Simonelli.

I am so very tired of this movie. I see it at least once a month. The title changes, and the actors change, and the superficial details of the story change, but it is always about exactly the same thing: heavily armed men shooting at each other. Even the order of their deaths is preordained: First the extras die, then the bit players, then the featured actors, until finally only the hero and the villain are left.

The name of the movie this time is *The Substitute.* It stars Tom Berenger as Shale, a mercenary soldier who has just returned after a raid on a Cuban drug depot. He goes to visit Jane (Diane Venora), a high school teacher he met on vacation in Latin America. She teaches in a Miami high school that is dominated by thugs. Her boss, Principal Rolle (Ernie Hudson), doesn't seem willing to do anything about them.

These are dumb thugs. They call attention to themselves when there is no need to. They keep a high profile when they should be trying to blend into the woodwork. Why? Because they are all working for Principal Rolle's multimillion-dollar drug importing business. He uses school buses to move the drugs, stores a fortune in cocaine in the school's boiler room, and sells to students. It's a very efficient business model.

One of the thugs beats up Jane on the beach because she is dissing his buddies in school. Her leg is broken. Shale, who knows all about falsifying records, poses as a substitute teacher, takes over her class, and is soon in the middle of a violent war over drugs.

Of course there are a few human moments, spaced out sparingly, to lend the formula interest. I found a real warmth in the scenes between Venora and Berenger, a feeling genuine enough it could have graced a better movie. And Glenn Plummer, as the heroic teacher Mr. Sherman, puts in an interesting performance. There is nothing wrong with Ernie Hudson's evil principal either, except for the screenplay he finds himself in.

The movie's problem is that it's not interested in these characters—not even as interested as we are. They are all simply a means of getting to the payoff scenes. Shale gets shot at on a highway, and throws some thugs out of the high school library window, and finds out about the drugs, and engages in two lengthy shoot-outs, one in Jane's apartment, the other one in the corridors of the high school.

The architecture of a routine movie shootout is by now well rehearsed. A man appears in frame, holding a gun. We can see down a corridor next to him. He jumps out, shoots, jumps back again. Variations of this move are done a dozen ways. It's like a computer game. Occasionally dialogue is added: "You don't teach history any more! You are history!"

It's all so boring. During *The Substitute,* I idly noted that about twenty men had been firing heavy automatic weapons for half an hour, and that they had also used a bazooka and a grenade. Didn't the neighbors call the cops? In the final moments of the film, Shale and a sidekick answer my objection: The drug kingpin had paid off the cops.

But the explosions also set off the sprinkler system and so presumably the school's fire alarms were triggered. Had Rolle paid off the fire department too? Do firemen routinely shrug and let high schools burn? You see how desperately the mind seeks out interesting topics as a distraction, while an exhausted genre wheezes out one more lap around the track.

## subUrbia ★ ★ ★ ½

R, 118 m., 1997

Jayce Bartok (Pony), Giovanni Ribisi (Jeff), Nicky Katt (Tim), Steve Zahn (Buff), Ajay Naidu (Nazeer), Samia Shoaib (Pakeesa), Amie Carey (Sooze), Dina Spybey (Bee-Bee), Parker Posey (Erica). Directed by Richard Linklater and produced by Anne Walker-McBay. Screenplay by Eric Bogosian, based on his play.

"Don't tell us about private property—this is America!" So says one of the slackers who hang out endlessly at the minimart of a strip mall in "subUrbia." He's shouting at the owners of a store, a Pakistani couple who feel, reasonably, that the constant presence of a half-dozen beer-swilling teenagers is not good for business. What the Pakistani store owner sees (and tells one of them in a devastating speech) is that the lives of these young people are on hold. They have no plans and few skills, and resentment is a poison in their souls.

*subUrbia* has been directed by Richard Linklater, whose movie *Slackers* gave a name to part of a generation, and whose *Dazed and Confused* caught much of its tone. Now, working from a screenplay by Eric Bogosian, he takes the despair of *Waiting for Godot* and tops it: His heroes aren't waiting as a mission, but as a lifestyle.

The movie is dark, intense, and disturbing. It takes place during a long night when the slackers in the parking lot are awaiting the appearance of a friend of theirs who has made it. His name is Pony (Jayce Bartok), and the last time they saw him he was the geek who was singing folk songs at the senior prom. Now, suddenly, amazingly, he is a rock star. He has promised to drop by and see them after his concert.

Among the slackers leaning against the brick wall, the dominant figure is Jeff (Giovanni Ribisi). He is darkly handsome, sardonic, intelligent, and utterly clueless. The depth of his alienation is established the first time we see him: He lives in a pup tent in his parents' garage, and communicates with his friends by cell phone.

He has been dating Sooze (Amie Carey), but that's about to end because she plans to move to New York and attend an art school. The fact that she has plans is a rebuke, in a way. In one of the movie's best scenes, she does a performance piece by the cold light of a bakery window, attacking testosterone as the enemy of civilization (her hit list ranges from Pope John Paul II to Howard Stern).

Their friends in the lot include Tim (Nicky Katt), an air force dropout who is hard at work perfecting his alcoholism; Sooze's best pal Bee-Bee (Dana Spybey), who is out of rehab but very shaky; and Buff (Steve Zahn), who cherishes his reputation as a nut who will do anything for attention. As they wait for Pony to arrive, they shift restlessly against the wall, perch on an iron bar, and sometimes fight new engagements in their running battle with the Pakistanis (Ajay Naidu and Samia Shoaib), who in this movie represent traditional American values.

Their conversation, originally written by Bogosian for a stage play, is talky, but I like that. It doesn't seem too theatrical to me, because these characters have absolutely nothing else to do except talk, and this barren corner of a suburban wasteland is literally their stage: They make their entrances and exits with a certain dramatic flair, as if reality stops when they are not here to watch it. Their suburb is perfectly named: Burnfield.

Pony eventually arrives, accompanied by his publicist (Parker Posey). They size up the situation but go with it; Pony tries to be nice, and the publicist tries to get lucky. One of Bogosian's inspirations is to avoid the predictable line in which Pony is a jerk or a big shot. He seems like a decent enough guy, unimpressed with his success, who only wants to hang out with the old gang. His chances of fitting in are destroyed immediately, of course, by his stretch limo, which underlines the fact that he's made it (however improbably) and they have not. Jeff's inferiority complex is painful in its twists and evasions, and it is revealing to watch him while Pony sighs about the thankless life of a rock star: "It's just airport, hotel, show, airport, hotel, show . . . you still living at your mom's house?"

This is the fourth Linklater film I've seen (he also made the smart, romantic *Before Sunrise*). All of them take place within a twenty-four-hour period, and involve characters who are between engagements. There is, I believe, a seductive quality to idleness. To be without ambition or plans is to rebuke those who have them: It is a refusal to enlist in the rat race, and there may even be a sad courage in it. But what Linklater sees is that it is so damned boring. Life without goals reduces itself to waiting. What it finally comes down to is airport, hotel, show—but without the airport, the hotel, or the show.

## Sunday ★ ★ ★

NO MPAA RATING, 93 m., 1997

David Suchet (Matthew/Oliver), Lisa Harrow (Madeleine Vesey), Jared Harris (Ray), Larry Pine (Ben Vesey), Joe Grifasi (Scotti Elster), Arnold Barkus (Andy). Directed by Jonathan Nossiter and produced by Nossiter, Alix Madigan, and Jed Alpert. Screenplay by James Lasdun and Nossiter.

*Sunday* opens like a documentary, watching the residents of a halfway house get up for the day, shave, dress, pour coffee, and continue what seem to be eternal arguments about what is or isn't "community property." Then it cuts outside, to the wintry gray streets of Queens, and what appears to be a large green plant walking down the street. The plant is in the arms of a woman who spots a man, walks up to him, and calls him Matthew Delacorta. He is, she says, the famous movie director, whom she met in London.

He is not. He is Oliver (David Suchet), a middle-aged man who lives in the shelter, where he is generally disliked, and spends his days wandering the streets. But he is so astonished to be addressed in this way that he goes along with the misunderstanding, pretending to be the director. The woman's name is Madeleine (Lisa Harrow), and she is a British actress, once a member of the Royal Shakespeare Company, but now reduced, she confesses, to playing "mutant zombies."

They talk. Their talk will occupy most of the movie—the best parts, certainly—as they sit in a diner, drink wine at her nearby home, and eventually have sex. But *Sunday* is not a romance, and they are not flirting but crying for help, for companionship, for another voice against the loneliness.

*Sunday* won the screenwriting award at the 1997 Sundance Festival (it also won the Grand Jury Prize), and its writing, by James Lasdun and the director, Jonathan Nossiter, is its best quality. It is about two people who were once good at what they did, who were "downsized" in one way or another, and who now feel stranded and worthless. "When they ask what do you do," he says, "they mean, who are you?" He eventually tells her who he was once, and what he is now.

She had a crisis in her career—a loss of voice, or perhaps a loss of the will to speak on stage—and notes that her agent mostly sends her horror roles: "I guess I'm too old to play a human being." Oliver could, in a way, make the same statement.

The movie plays a subtle game with the information they share with each other. "Tell me one of your stories," she says, over a glass of wine, and he tells her the literal story of this day in his life, which we have already glimpsed as it began in the shelter. It is the truth. Does she accept it as the truth, or continue to deceive herself that he is Matthew Delacorta?

We have to decide as the movie continues; some moments we would answer one way, some moments another. It's intriguing, how they play games with their dialogue; at times it's like a conversation with an artificial intelligence program, especially when the "director" uses her questions to inspire his answers—not so much confirming that he's Delacorta as letting her assert it.

One of the things the movie accepts without apology or question is the substantial flesh of these two middle-aged people. Suchet (who plays Hercule Poirot on television) has a potbelly, and Harrow (unforgettable in Gillian Armstrong's *The Last Days of Chez Nous*) has a tummy, smaller but definite. In one scene she lies on a bed, frankly revealing herself to his gaze, looking like a model for a Francis Bacon portrait—but Madeleine isn't ugly, as Bacon's subjects were made to seem; she is lovely, and more at home in her body than in her life.

The film takes this strong, simple material and surrounds it with a little too much artiness. There are cutaway shots to the dismal streets, shots of a fellow resident of the shelter singing for coins in the subway, and flashbacks to Oliver's daily routine. When Madeleine's husband and adopted daughter return home, there are hints that all is not right in their house—hints that add an unnecessary subtext.

But the heart of the film is strong. It is about two people who would rather build and share a fantasy together than do whatever else would have occupied them on this empty Sunday. "The hardest thing is having nothing to do," Oliver says about unemployment. "Every day is Sunday."

## Sunset Park ★ ★

R, 100 m., 1996

Rhea Perlman (Phyllis Saroka), Fredro Starr (Shorty), Carol Kane (Mona), Terrence DaShon Howard (Spaceman), Camille Saviola (Barbara), De'Aundre Bonds (Busy-Bee), James Harris (Butter), Anthony Hall (Andre). Directed by Steve Gomer and produced by Danny DeVito, Michael Shamberg, and Dan Paulson. Screenplay by Seth Zvi Rosenfeld and Kathleen McGhee-Anderson.

*Sunset Park* tells the story of a middle-aged gym teacher named Phyllis (Rhea Perlman) who needs a new challenge and more money in her life. When the job of basketball coach opens up at her inner-city high school, she applies for it and gets it—maybe because no one else applied.

The ancient traditions of this genre require that she inherit a team of losers. What is a little different about *Sunset Park* is that her players are not untalented; they have the skills to be champions, if they can rise above their personal problems and personality quirks.

Phyllis is not much of a coach. In fact, the big credibility problem in the opening scenes of the movie involves her lack of knowledge about basketball. Most gym teachers of both sexes are jocks who follow sports and have done some coaching in their lives. Phyllis doesn't seem to know as much about basketball as your average

Bulls fan who watches a few games on TV. When the team asks for her advice on defense, she replies, "Play the defense you played last year." In a tough game situation, she shouts helpfully from the bench: "Rotate!"

We meet the players on the team, each one packaged with his own problem. The leader is Shorty (Fredro Starr), who has romantic problems that get him in trouble with the law. Spaceman (Terrence DaShon Howard) is a psychopath when he's on drugs.

Other players are badly motivated, mistrustful, or defeatist. Most of them take one look at their coach and decide, not unreasonably, that if she is all the coach they deserve, they must not have much of a future as a team.

Meanwhile, Phyllis has problems of her own. A faithless lover bails out of her life with her TV and VCR. Her best friend (Carol Kane) observes, "In one year you have been dumped by more guys than have dated me in ten years." Phyllis tells herself she'll coach the team for one year and then retire to her dream, which is to run a restaurant on St. Croix. No points for guessing whether (a) she learns to be a good coach, (b) wins the team's trust, and (c) puts the restaurant plan on hold.

Rhea Perlman makes an unusual and appealing heroine for this story. She's feisty, direct, and unadorned, and she looks a lot more like your average high school teacher than, say, Michelle Pfeiffer in *Dangerous Minds.* There is a bedrock truth and directness to the way she plays her scenes. There's also a good performance by Fredro Starr, a former rapper, who tries to explain the facts of his life to the coach, including the complex chain of events that led up to his arrest on a weapons charge.

But the movie is not written or directed very skillfully. Especially in early scenes, there are inept reaction shots and uncertain timing that make us aware of the film's technique just when we should be focusing on the story. And there's some continuity confusion at the end, where it seems, unless you are paying very close attention, that the coach is able to go to court with Shorty in the time between the warm-up for a big game and the opening whistle.

I also suspect there was some desperation at the screenplay level in the scene where Phyllis gets drunk in order to find the courage to confront Shorty (and herself). Finding courage in a bottle is a standby cliché in countless stories, but Phyllis simply doesn't seem like the kind of person who would drink like that (she's too old to do it as an experiment, and if she has a pattern of doing it, she'd be an alcoholic).

*Sunset Park* begins with good intentions, and the cast manages some convincing moments together, but the movie never really jells. It's not slick enough to work as a conventional sports movie, and too distracted by its sports conventions to focus on its drama. And beneath everything is an uncertainty about camera setups, editing pace, and the overall structure of the film: Like the team, it seems coached by people who want the job but aren't really prepared for it.

## The Sweet Hereafter ★ ★ ★ ★

R, 110 m., 1997

Ian Holm (Mitchell Stephens), Sarah Polley (Nicole Burnell), Bruce Greenwood (Billy Ansell), Tom McCamus (Sam Burnell), Gabrielle Rose (Dolores Driscoll), Arsinee Khanjian (Wanda Otto), Alberta Watson (Risa Walker), Maury Chaykin (Wendell Walker). Directed by Atom Egoyan and produced by Egoyan and Camelia Frieberg. Screenplay by Egoyan, based on the novel by Russell Banks.

A cold, dark hillside looms above the Bide-a-Wile Motel, pressing down on it, crushing out the life with the gray weight of winter. It is one of the strongest images in Atom Egoyan's *The Sweet Hereafter,* which takes place in a small Canadian town, locked in by snow and buried in grief after fourteen children are killed in a school bus accident.

To this town comes a quiet man, a lawyer who wants to represent the residents in a class-action suit. Mitchell Stephens (Ian Holm) lacks the energy to be an ambulance chaser; he is only going through the motions of his occupation. In a way he's lost a child, too; the first time we see him, he's on the phone with his drug-addicted daughter. "I don't know who I'm talking to right now," he tells her.

There will be no victory at the end, we sense. This is not one of those Grisham films in which the lawyers battle injustice and the creaky system somehow works. The parents who have lost their children can never get them back; the school bus driver must live forever with what happened; lawsuits will open old wounds and betray old secrets. If the lawyer wins he gets to keep a third of the settlement; one look in his eyes reveals how little he thinks about money.

Egoyan's film, based on the novel by Russell Banks, is not about the tragedy of dying but about the grief of surviving. In the film the Browning poem about the Pied Piper is read, and we remember that the saddest figure in that poem was the lame boy who could not join the others in following the Piper. In *The Sweet Hereafter,* an important character is a teenage girl who loses the use of her legs in the accident; she survives but seems unwilling to accept the life still left for her.

Egoyan is a director whose films coil through time and double back to take a second look at the lives of their characters. It is typical of his approach that *The Sweet Hereafter* neither begins nor ends with the bus falling through the ice of a frozen lake, and is not really about how the accident happened, or who was to blame. The accident is like the snow clouds, always there, cutting off the characters from the sun, a vast fact nobody can change.

The lawyer makes his rounds, calling on parents. Egoyan draws them vividly with brief, cutting scenes. The motel owners, Wendell and Risa Walker (Maury Chaykin and Alberta Watson), fill him in on the other parents (Wendell has nothing good to say about anyone). Sam and Mary Burnell (Tom McCamus and Brooke Johnson) are the parents of Nicole, the budding young C&W singer who is now in a wheelchair. Wanda and Hartley Otto (Arsinee Khanjian and Earl Pastko) lost their son, an adopted Indian boy. Billy Ansell (Bruce Greenwood) was following the bus in his pickup, and waved to his children just before it swerved from the road. He wants nothing to do with the lawsuit, and is bitter about those who do. He is having an affair with Risa, the motel owner's wife.

This story. It is not about lawyers or the law, not about small-town insularity, not about revenge (although that motivates an unexpected turning point). It is more about the living dead: About people carrying on their lives after hope and meaning have gone. The film is so sad, so tender toward its characters. The lawyer, an outsider who might at first seem like the source of more trouble, comes across more like a witness, who regards the stricken parents and sees his own approaching loss of a daughter in their eyes.

Ian Holm's performance here is bottomless with its subtlety; he proceeds doggedly through the town, following the routine of his profession as if this is his penance. And there is a later scene, set on an airplane, where he finds himself seated next to his daughter's childhood friend, and remembers, in a heartbreaking monologue, a time in childhood when his daughter almost died of a spider bite. Is it good or bad that she survived, in order now to die of drugs?

Egoyan sees the town so vividly. A hearing is held in the village hall, where folding tables and chairs wait for potluck dinners and bingo nights. A foosball table is in a corner. In another corner, Nicole, in her wheelchair, describes the accident. She lies. It is too simple to say she lies as a form of getting even, because we wonder—if she were not in a wheelchair, would she feel the same way? Does she feel abused, or scorned?

"You'd make a great poker player, kid," the lawyer tells her.

This is one of the best films of 1997, an unflinching lament for the human condition. Yes, it is told out of sequence, but not as a gimmick: In a way, Egoyan has constructed this film in the simplest possible way. It isn't about the beginning and end of the plot, but about the beginning and end of the emotions. In his first scene, the lawyer tells his daughter he doesn't know who he's talking to. In one of his closing scenes, he remembers a time when he did know her. But what did it get him? ☞

## Sweet Nothing ★ ★ ★

R, 88 m., 1996

Michael Imperioli (Angel Gazetta), Mira Sorvino (Monika Gazetta), Paul Calderon (Raymond). Directed by Gary Winick and produced by Rick Bowman and Winick. Screenplay by Lee Drysdale.

The rewards of selling drugs are so small compared to the risks you run and the price you pay. That is the remorseless lesson of *Sweet Nothing,* which tells the story of a Wall Street worker who wants a little more money for his family, and ends up broke, addicted, sought by the police, and without his family.

One of the key images in the early part of the

movie shows him smoking crack for the first time and saying, "So *that's* what I was missing." One of the key images from the closing scenes shows him huddled against a wall, sucking on a piece of candy, waiting for drugs while watching the clock advance one excruciating second at a time. Here is a man who had no idea at all how much he could be missing.

The film is about Angel (Michael Imperioli), who in the opening scenes celebrates the birth of his second child. He visits his wife, Monika (Mira Sorvino), in the hospital and then goes out to celebrate. His friend Raymond (Paul Calderon) offers him a hit from a cocaine pipe, and he likes it. "Give me another," he says, perhaps unaware of George Carlin's famous line, "What does cocaine make you feel like? It makes you feel like having some more cocaine."

Raymond tells him the truth: "People sell their front doors for this stuff." Angel doesn't care, because already he is ready to sell his own front door. Before long he's doing some dealing, finding customers at work, talking about how he can clear $1,000 a week. One night he puts a pearl necklace around Monika's neck and she glows with delight. She allows herself to think that maybe this thing will work—that Angel can make extra money, the family can benefit, and somehow nobody will get hurt.

One characteristic of all addictions is that they create a state of compulsive self-monitoring. The user is constantly asking, How do I feel? Have I had enough? Too much? Can I get more? Am I in trouble? Although using the drug or drink of choice seems to create a state of benevolence and relaxation, in fact it builds a wall that closes out other people. When a user is high he smiles at you, but it's because of how he feels about himself, not because of how he feels about you.

*Sweet Nothing* understands this process. Gary Winick, who directed, and Lee Drysdale, who wrote the screenplay, subtly mark out the stages in the progress of Angel's addiction. He defends himself by claiming the best motives (he is dealing drugs to help his family), even though his real motive is to get high, and the family obviously suffers. They move to a shabby apartment ("just for a little while"). There is no food in the house. Monika cannot cope by herself. Eventually even the small son knows that the man on the corner is a drug dealer. One night, desperate for drugs, Angel dumps his kids at his in-laws' house, terrifying them in the process.

Nor are drugs kind to Raymond, the friend. He seemed better able to handle them than Angel. Perhaps he was wise enough to balance his business against his addiction. But eventually the cops are looking for him, and someone is dead, and everything is coming to pieces. Angel's life in the closing stages of his addiction can be symbolized by that guy on the old TV shows who tried to keep a lot of plates spinning on the tops of poles all at once.

Michael Imperioli has been in some two dozen movies, often playing a tough kid, an outsider, troubled, complex. In *Sweet Nothing* he shows a new maturity and command in his acting, maybe because he is given a key role that runs all the way through. He doesn't fall for the actor's temptation of making too many emotional choices; he understands that many of Angel's problems are very simple: He wants to use more drugs than he can afford. For Mira Sorvino, this is a new kind of role, and she is very good in it, as a woman who wants to hold her marriage and family together, who is willing to give her husband the benefit of the doubt, who believes more than she should, stays longer than she should, and finally finds the strength to act for herself.

Winick uses an interesting narrative device—the story is told in a journal being kept by Angel—and the journal segments suggest Angel has arrived at some sort of end to his journey. Wisely, the movie doesn't spell out the details. We can arrive at our own conclusions. "If I were still using," addicts say, "I would be dead." There is a logical paradox there, but the message is clear enough.

## Swept From the Sea ★ ★

PG-13, 114 m., 1998

Rachel Weisz (Amy Foster), Vincent Perez (Yanko), Ian McKellen (Dr. James Kennedy), Kathy Bates (Miss Swaffer), Joss Ackland (Mr. Swaffer), Tony Haygarth (Mr. Smith), Fiona Victory (Mrs. Smith), Tom Bell (Isaac Foster). Directed by Beeban Kidron and produced by Polly Tapson, Charles Steel, and Kidron. Screenplay by Tim Willocks.

*Swept From the Sea* is a plodding retelling of *Amy Foster,* not one of Joseph Conrad's best short stories. It follows the original more or less faithfully, except for the addition of a subtle element of homosexuality—which, if it had been less subtle, might have made the movie more intriguing.

The story involves a doomed love affair between a simple country girl and a Russian peasant who is swept onto the Cornish shore in 1888, after his emigrant ship sinks on its way to America. The peasant, whose hair, beard, and rags make him look like a wild man, speaks no English. He is feared by the locals—except for Amy Foster (Rachel Weisz), a local girl born in scandal and working for the Swaffers, a farm family. Amy is thought to be retarded, but it is more complicated than that; she was a student at the parish school for years, we learn, without making the slightest effort to read and write. Then she read and wrote for a month, to prove a point, and then stopped again.

Amy and the castaway, whose name is Yanko (Vincent Perez), fall in love, court, are married, and have a child. These events are closely monitored by James Kennedy (Ian McKellen), the local doctor, who shares the general feeling that Yanko is simpleminded until the Russian whips him at chess. With quiet hints and lingering looks, the film makes it clear that the doctor becomes attracted to the well-built Yanko, and resentful of Amy Foster for possessing his time and love.

Conrad's original story was narrated by Dr. Kennedy, who is not shy in describing Yanko's physical beauty, so the filmmakers are not unjustified in making his feelings more overt. Conrad has Kennedy speaking to the author of the tale, so that we got a narration within a narration. In the film, the doctor tells it instead to the bedridden Miss Swaffer, creating an unnecessary question: Why does he need to tell her things she already knows at firsthand? Better to simply eliminate the narrator and the flashbacks, and just tell the story from beginning to end.

The director is Beeban Kidron, whose films *(Antonia & Jane, To Wong Foo, Thanks for Everything, Julie Newman)* have been miles away from this sort of overwrought historical melodrama. She enters into the spirit of the enterprise with one of the most remarkable opening shots I have seen, as the camera sweeps over miles of ocean before rising to the top of a cliff and to the lonely figures of a mother and a child. There are also effective storm scenes, and the landscape is evoked as Conrad described it, as low and flat, a depressing setting for a population devoted enthusiastically to the hatred of outsiders.

This drabness is relieved by Amy's secret grotto, where she keeps treasures given to her by the ocean, and where she takes Yanko, also a gift of the sea; when they make love in the grotto's waters, however, I couldn't help wondering about the source of the shimmering underwater illumination.

I suppose the film can be excused for casting the slender and beautiful Rachel Weisz as Amy, described by Conrad as squat and dull-faced. The story is about two outsiders who find one another, and the movie remains faithful to that idea while adding another outsider, the doctor, who is never quite said to be homosexual but goes out of his way to be as near to Yanko as he can, as often as possible, and whose dislike of Amy extends to rudeness. At the end of the film, after the doctor has told Miss Swaffer (Kathy Bates) all that he knows about the histories of the two unfortunate people, she asks, "Did your own love blind you to hers?"

Kidron and her screenwriter, Tim Willocks, are not reaching in making Kennedy homosexual (certain lines in the story point in that direction). But why make his sexuality so understated many viewers will miss it? For fear of offending an audience that has turned up for a conventional period romance?

McKellen plays the character subtly and with restraint, even deliberate repression; there is the possibility the doctor has not acknowledged his sexuality and is responding only to unexamined feelings. But at the end, when the sad story has played out, there is a moment in which Dr. Kennedy lashes out, and the moment would play better and provide more of a dramatic shock if the movie had been clearer about the nature of the feelings he is expressing. As it is, *Swept From the Sea* is a disappointment, a film in which good and evil dutifully go through their paces, while the character who could have added complexity and intrigue remains, unfortunately, unrealized.

## Swingers ★ ★ ★

R, 95 m., 1996

Jon Favreau (Mike), Vince Vaughn (Trent), Ron Livingston (Rob), Patrick Van Horn (Sue), Alex Desert (Charles), Heather Graham (Lorraine), Deena Martin (Christy), Katherine Kendall (Lisa), Brooke Langton (Nikki). Directed by Doug Liman and produced by Victor Simpkins and Jon Favreau. Screenplay by Favreau.

Sometimes I get this Whitmanesque vision of America. But instead of wheat fields and mighty cities and deep lakes stretching from sea to sea, I imagine a vast number of coffee shops. And in these coffee shops, urgent conversations are taking place. Here's Mickey Rourke talking with Kevin Bacon in *Diner.* And Quentin Tarantino, on Santa Monica Boulevard, writing down ideas for *Pulp Fiction.* And Andy Garcia in Denver, rehearsing for *Things to Do in Denver When You're Dead.* And Pacino and De Niro, out near the L.A. airport, acting in their first scene together in *Heat.* And Marc Andreesson in Urbana, Illinois, inventing a surfer for the World Wide Web . . .

I doubt if there will ever be a movie named *Netscape 3.0,* but no matter; the new American frontier is the all-night diner, with Formica tops and ketchup and sugar on every table, and a waitress who writes down your order on a green-and-white Guest Check. And in these coffee shops, which reach out like an endless progression of stops on the highway to fame, there are countless young men like the heroes of *Swingers,* who are so near to stardom they can reach out and touch it, and so far away they can't afford to pick up the check.

*Swingers* is about a loosely knit group of friends who hang out in Hollywood and hope to make it big in the entertainment industry. "The hottest 1 percent of guys from all over the world come to our gene pool," they assure one another, although that gives them better prospects for reproduction than success. One of the guys, named Trent (Vince Vaughn), uses the word "money" as an adjective: "That's really money. They'll see how money you are." This is inspired, since in Hollywood absolutely everything comes down to money. Intelligence, beauty, talent, and fame go through a kind of universal currency exchange, and come out converted into money, less 15 percent.

The film's hero is Mike (Jon Favreau), who wants to be a stand-up comic but has no job prospects. A friend at least is weighing an offer to play Goofy at Disneyland ("Hey, at least it's Disney," Trent observes). He mopes about Michelle, the girlfriend he left behind back East, and Trent spends long hours with him in the coffee shop of a Best Western, advising him that you cannot get a woman to come back unless you're willing to forget her, after which, of course, you don't care if she comes back.

The movie follows Mike, Trent, and a shifting cast of other friends through several days during which they drive through the Hollywood Hills looking for parties at which Trent promises there will be lots of Honey Babies to pick up. They spend a lot of time playing an advanced version of video hockey. They go looking for hot clubs ("All the cool bars in Hollywood have to be real hard to find and have no signs"). They try to pick up girls (Mike claims he's in showbiz, but the woman remembers seeing him in Starbucks, picking up an employment application).

In the middle of his angst, Mike more or less shuts down, cowering in his half-furnished apartment. Trent blasts him out with a midnight drive to Las Vegas, where Mike has difficulty finding conversation openers (it doesn't help to drop insights about the Age of Enlightenment). Amazingly, they pick up a couple of waitresses, who take them home (an Airstream trailer), where of course Mike blubbers about his former girlfriend.

They say you should write about what you know. Doug Liman, who directed *Swingers,* and Favreau, who wrote it, obviously know a lot about young guys in Hollywood sitting around in coffee shops talking about making it in show business. If you had entered that Best Western coffee shop a year or two ago, you might actually have seen them planning this movie. It's not a terribly original idea, but then as one of the guys says, "Everybody steals from everybody" (this observation is closely followed by shots cheerfully stolen from Scorsese's *GoodFellas* and Tarantino's *Reservoir Dogs*). The movie is sweet, funny, observant, and goofy (with a small "g," which means you don't get paid, but at least you don't have to wear the suit).

## Switchback ★ ★
R, 121 m., 1997

Danny Glover (Bob Goodall), Dennis Quaid (Frank LaCrosse), Jared Leto (Lane Dixon), R. Lee Ermey (Sheriff Buck Olmstead), William Fichtner (Chief Jack McGinnis), Ted Levine (Deputy Nate Booker). Directed by Jeb Stuart and produced by Gale Anne Hurd. Screenplay by Stuart.

*Switchback* is not a good movie, but it does an admirable job of distracting us from how bad it is. If they'd thrown out the two leading characters and started all over with the locations, the lore, and the supporting actors, they might have had something here. Time and again the movie fascinates us with digressions, only to jerk back to the helpless main story line.

There are two threads to the action. One involves a long car journey through the West by Bob, a former railroad worker (Danny Glover), and Lane (Jared Leto), a hitchhiker with a secret in his past. The other involves Sheriff Buck Olmstead (R. Lee Ermey) of Amarillo, Texas, and Frank LaCrosse, an FBI agent (Dennis Quaid), who has just turned up in town.

The agent is on the trail of a serial killer. They've been involved in a cat-and-mouse game for months or years, but now the rules have changed: The killer has kidnapped the agent's young son, and so the bureau has pulled the agent off the case, because it would be a conflict of interest. Would it ever.

The rules of movies like this require that the serial killer must be one of the characters onscreen. We easily narrow the suspects to the railway worker or the hitchhiker—unless the FBI agent is an impostor, which is also a possibility. Clues are scattered prodigiously. The killer knows how to sever arteries with a scalpel. So does the hitchhiker, Lane, a former medical student. The killer is maybe driving a Cadillac lined with centerfold pinups. So is Bob. And what about Frank, the FBI man: How can he be so sure that the violent hostage-taker just arrested in Amarillo, who was driving another car linked to the serial killer, isn't the right man?

All of this is plot stuff, and unreels as plot stuff does. None of it is very interesting, especially since we know too soon who the serial killer is, and he's not very convincing. Yes, there's suspense about whether he'll kill again. But let's put it this way: After two of the possibilities save each other's lives, we doubt they'll go on to kill each other in the next act.

What I liked about the movie had nothing to do with any of the above. I found Dennis Quaid's FBI agent a monotonous bore (he plays the role with a flat monotone that sounds affected). I found Danny Glover's character too chatty and genial. I was, however, persuaded by Lane, the Jared Leto character, who can't be blamed for a strange movie coincidence: A guy in a bar collapses on the floor and Lane cries, "I'm a doctor!" and proceeds to use a knife, a soda siphon, and a plastic bottle to perform the exact same weird emergency surgery performed by David Duchovny in *Playing God*. I guess it was the luck of the draw which movie came out first.

But the real center of the movie is occupied, not by the nominal leads Glover and Quaid, but by Ermey as the Amarillo sheriff, who is in the middle of a tough reelection campaign. Ermey is the former Marine drill instructor who was hired by Stanley Kubrick as a technical adviser on *Full Metal Jacket*, and then given the role he was advising on. He plays a fully drawn, colorful, convincing character, whose dialogue rings with an authenticity the others lack. He steals every scene and what is left of the movie; he's so tough and authentic he can get away with dry understatements like, "You can see this whole experience has just devastated me."

I also liked the use of winter locations in Texas, New Mexico, and Utah. And the railroad lore involving getting trains through snowbound mountain passes. I liked the culture of the truck stops and the railroad bunkhouses, and the old rail workers warming their hands over stoves in cabooses. I liked the faces of the bit players—guys in bars and locomotives. And I liked the way a climactic scene was played out on a train (the film's writer-director, Jeb Stuart, cowrote *The Fugitive*, which also made good use of a train and the cold light of winter locations).

If we lived in a more venturesome and curious world, *Switchback* would have been about a sheriff fighting for reelection in Amarillo, and about some rail workers trying to get a train through a blizzard. No serial killers, no obsessed FBI agents, maybe just enough of a crime for the sheriff and his opponent (the slimy local police chief) to fight over. What we have here is a potentially good movie swamped by the weight of Hollywood formulas it is forced to carry.

*Footnotes: I was amused to see Stuart recycling the always reliable "It's Only a Cat!" gimmick in an early scene. And the convention that whenever a stranger walks into a Western saloon, all the regulars immediately beat him senseless. Late in the film, when a character falls backward from a train, he shouts "Yee-ha!" and both the shot and the shout are homage to Kubrick's* Dr. Strangelove.

## Switchblade Sisters ★

R, 90 m., 1975 (rereleased 1997)

Robbie Lee (Lace), Joanne Nail (Maggie), Asher Brauner (Dominic), Monica Gayle (Patch), Marlene Clark (Muff), Janice Karman (Bunny). Directed by Jack Hill and produced by John Prizer. Screenplay by F. X. Maier.

*Sooner or later, every girl's got to find out—the only thing a man's got below his belt is clay feet.*
*—Switchblade Sisters*

Insights like that were big in the exploitation movies of the 1970s. The dialogue clanked along from one dumb profundity to another, and the sentiments were as pious as political speeches. One of the characters in *Switchblade Sisters* (1975) quotes approvingly from Mao's *Little Red Book,* although enlightenment among the sisters is not universal: After the leader of a boy gang rapes a new member of a girl gang, he asks, "You all right? You were asking for it." She is inclined to agree.

*Switchblade Sisters* is one of the countless films viewed by Quentin Tarantino during his now-legendary employment at Video Archives in Manhattan Beach, California (the store owner should get a finder's fee based on QT's subsequent career). Now Tarantino has started a division of Miramax named Rolling Thunder Pictures to rerelease some of his discoveries. After *Switchblade Sisters* we are promised *Mighty Peking Man* (1977), the 1964 Italian horror film *Blood and Black Lace,* and the 1973 blaxploitation epic *Detroit 9000.*

Exploitation films could be a lot of fun. The director of *Switchblade Sisters,* Jack Hill, directed sixteen of them, including two of my favorites, the Pam Grier films *Coffy* and *Foxy Brown.* His other titles included *Swinging Cheerleaders, The Big Bird Cage, Snake People, Blood Bath,* and *Spider Baby.* Often they were released more than once under various titles; *Spider Baby* became *The Liver Eaters,* and *Switchblade Sisters* was also known as *The Jezebels* and *The Playgirl Gang.*

What made the Pam Grier pictures stand out from the others was Grier's own charisma; she was an authentic movie star, and even Hill's sleazy production values and slapdash photography and editing couldn't conceal her talent. The problem with *Switchblade Sisters* is that no one onscreen is any better than the talent behind the camera. The movie is badly acted, written, and directed, and while I was watching it I realized that in some unexplained but happy way, the basic level of cinematic talent has improved in the past two decades.

Few new directors today could make a film this bad. Low budgets have nothing to do with it. Consider Robert Rodriguez (whose *El Mariachi* cost $8,000), Matty Rich (*Straight Out of Brooklyn,* $24,000) and Edward Burns (*The Brothers McMullen,* $28,000). Despite their budgets, they are born filmmakers who know where to put a camera, how to write a script, how to cast and direct actors, and how to move things along. By contrast, *Switchblade Sisters* is a series of tableaux in which stiff actors are grouped in awkwardly composed shots to say things like "Freeze, greaseball!"

The greaseball, by the way, is a sadistic bill collector trying to collect $40 in back payments on a TV set owned by a tearful welfare mother in a building that is otherwise apparently occupied only by "switchblade sisters." As he takes the elevator to the street, another sister gets on at every floor (are they psychic, or did they phone ahead and plan the elevator ride?). When they reach the ground floor, the greaseball gets his tie cut off. Heavy.

The plot involves a girl gang named the Jezebels, which hangs out at a burger stand. Maggie (Joanne Nail), a new girl in the neighborhood, refuses to give her seat to Lace (Robbie Lee), the Jezebels' leader, and that leads to a fight but also to mutual respect. Soon Dominic (Asher Brauner), the leader of the Silver Blades, rapes Maggie—and since he is Lace's boyfriend, this leads to a certain tension.

One thing leads to another, as the script hurries from cliché to cliché. The Jezebels are thrown into jail, where they are mistreated by a lesbian warden before getting their revenge. Later there's a hilarious rumble in a roller rink—it's a shoot-out on skates with automatic weapons—that seems to leave dozens dead, although all but one of the key characters survives.

The movie is wallpapered with the slogans of the era. The cops are "pigs," the Black Power girl gang is the repository of revolutionary wisdom, there is solidarity between the girl gangs, and at some point we are astonished to be given the information that all of these characters are still in high school, and as juveniles cannot be tried for what seems like a citywide crime wave.

The only real reason for seeing *Switchblade Sisters* would be to condescend to it, to snicker at its badness. But there are degrees of bad, and this movie falls far below Pauline Kael's notion of "great trash." There is also some amusement to be had from the costumes: the mile-wide shirt collars, leather vests, and plaid pants on the men, and the hot pants and thigh boots on the women. But such pleasures are fleeting, and life is short.

## Synthetic Pleasures ★ ★ ½

NO MPAA RATING, 83 m., 1996

A documentary directed by Iara Lee and produced by George Gund III. Featuring Michio Kahu, Scott Bukatman, Jaron Lanier, John Perry Barlow, Timothy Leary, and others.

*Synthetic Pleasures* casts its net as wide as it possibly can to capture examples of the ways in which we humans are attempting to take conscious control of our environment and our bodies themselves. Director Iara Lee takes us on a roller coaster from the sublime to the ridiculous: from artificial intelligence to body piercing, from I.Q.-enhancing drugs to indoor ski slopes, from on-line dating services to the possibility of having virtual sex in our minds.

Lee has been criticized for bringing too large a shopping basket to the party. She has the same enthusiasm for scientists trying to develop intelligent robots, and a guy who travels the world on a recumbent bicycle with a solar-powered Macintosh mounted between the handlebars, and explains, "I live on the Internet." Surely, her critics have said, she could have zeroed in on one thing or another: on cybersex, or game theory, or artificial intelligence, or cryogenics, or Prozac, or a performance artist whose art is plastic surgery on her own body, or . . .

I think she's on the right track to be uncritical, to look at the countless bizarre ways that people are attempting to dictate the terms under which they live in this world. Evolutionary change takes place at the margins, not in the center. Something that works perfectly need not evolve. Only failures need to become better.

The checkout clerk with pierced eyelids may not seem to have much in common with Marvin Minsky, the guru of artificial intelligence, but both are saying that man need no longer play only the cards he has been dealt. The most significant discovery during the life span of human intelligence is the cracking of the genetic code, and with it the possibility that we need no longer be only the passive result of eons of evolution. Today, we cross a tomato with cod genes and get a vegetable that doesn't freeze. Tomorrow, we learn to live forever. (Or, maybe, the tomato turns us into fish. We take our chances.)

Lee's documentary is not a well-organized film, and it is sometimes maddening (she accepts everything that is told to her, and rarely questions anyone even when statements cry out for follow-ups). But what it lacks in precision and organization, it makes up for in a reckless, globe-trotting enthusiasm. A Korean raised in South America and now living in America, she traveled widely for three years to interview people who were trying to shape inner and outer environments.

In Japan, she finds vast indoor pleasure domes: ski slopes built with artificial snow, beaches washed by artificial waves, golf driving ranges where the players are stacked one above the other up to the sky. On the Internet, she visits Web pages where strippers perform on demand. It is a cliché to visit Las Vegas and find artificial volcanoes and pyramids—but what about the notion that someday society will be organized along similar lines, and like gamblers we will never go outside, or know night from day, or desire anything that cannot be ordered over the phone?

The underrated movie *Strange Days* suggests a future in which we can "jack in." Electrodes attached to our brains will give us the illusion of complete virtual reality; all of our senses will be involved, so that we will not be able to tell the difference between something we are really experiencing, and something we "only think" we are experiencing. (After all, even now, we "only think" we are having experiences.) What if we could jack in to computer-generated artificial sex and have a virtual orgasm? Would that constitute adultery? Would it be a sin? Would it be sex?

Lee visits a French performance artist who is having herself turned into a replica of the *Mona Lisa*. Is this any stranger than the countless women who are using plastic surgery to turn into younger replicas of themselves? She is fascinated by tattoos, not for their art, but because they reveal an impatience with the bodies we were issued. Transsexuals fascinate her for the same reason: Why must we be the same sex for an entire lifetime? For that matter, why must we die? Can we be frozen and resurrected later?

One stop she didn't make was in Sri Lanka, where Arthur C. Clarke has recently become fascinated with the idea of a Soul Machine—a computer with a memory so vast and fast that "we" could be downloaded into "it" and exist forever on a computer chip. And if the chip were fed virtual images to inform "us" that we were living in a "real" world, would we know we were not? (This is the same idea Clarke touched on years ago in his science fiction.)

*Synthetic Pleasures* raises these questions and many more. It does not deal deeply with any of them; it is not investigative, but evocative. Seeing it, you may be frustrated because Lee is essentially just a cheerleader. But it will make you think. Or at least you will think you are thinking. If, of course, that is really you.

# T

## The Tango Lesson ★ ★ ★ ½

PG, 101 m., 1997

Sally Potter (Sally), Pablo Veron (Pablo), Carlos Copello (Carlos), Olga Besio (Olga), Carolina Iotti (Pablo's Partner), Gustavo Naveira (Gustavo). Directed by Sally Potter and produced by Christopher Sheppard. Screenplay by Potter.

*The Tango Lesson* is a fictional film in which almost everything and everybody seems to be, in some sense, real. It's about a British film director named Sally, who is played by the British film director Sally Potter. She meets a great tango dancer named Pablo, who is played by the great tango dancer Pablo Veron. She says that if he gives her tango lessons, she will put him in a movie. She has put him in this movie. She is pretty damn fine at dancing the tango; she must have had some lessons somewhere.

For her pains in telling this story, Miss Potter has been slapped down by several critics. How dare she, a middle-aged woman, star herself in a love story where she falls in love with a tango dancer—and, even worse, is good enough to dance as his partner? This is "blatant narcissism" (Britain's *Empire* magazine), and "an act of wild hubris" *(The New York Times).* "Talk about self-indulgence!" says a critic on the Internet.

Political correctness is not my favorite pose, and so I will not go into detail about the countless movies in which middle-aged (and, indeed, elderly) men seduce twenty-two-year-old models and jump out of airplanes while throwing bombs. I will note, however, that Sally Potter really does dance the tango herself in this film; it's not a stunt woman or special effects, and my theory is, if you've got it, flaunt it.

She also does other things very well. One of them is to delicately examine the tension between a man and a woman who are not really sexually destined for one another, but go through a mad moment of thinking they are—simply because they have idealized one another. If power is the ultimate aphrodisiac, then what could be sexier than the power you yourself have granted to another person by mentally supplying them with those qualities you find most dazzling? Sally and Pablo have "no chemistry," I read, and are "passionless." These are words that could only have been written by critics whose own ideas of passion are limited to the narrow range of testosterone emissions seen in most movies. The typical movie love story is about characters so young that proximity triggers tumescence. *The Tango Lesson* is not intended as a story about romantic passion achieved, but about passion sighted in the near distance, considered, flirted with, and regretfully declined. "We should set some limits," Sally tells Pablo after he stands her up on New Year's Eve. "It's better to sublimate our relationship in our work." Those are words you will not hear for many years between Tom and Nicole, Matt and Minnie, Will and Jada, or Johnny and Kate.

Potter is best known in North America for *Orlando,* her 1993 film starring Tilda Swinton as a character who lives four centuries, half as a man, half as a woman. Now here is another film about a character who dares to reinvent herself—whose future is not defined by her past. As the film opens, Sally is working on an artsy movie named *Rage,* which involves beautiful models and a legless fashion designer who pursues them in a wheelchair, shooting at them. Not surprisingly, the work is not going well; the opening shot of *Tango Lesson* suggestively shows Sally wiping her worktable clean.

She goes to Paris, wanders into a theater, sees Pablo dancing, and is entranced—more, I think, by the intricate sexiness of the dance than by the man himself. (The tango strikes me as aggressive foreplay performed with legs instead of genitals.) She visits Pablo, suggests that she might put him in a movie in return for dance lessons, and begins to study the tango.

The scenes are broken down into "lessons." Some of them are about dance, and others are about life. We visit Argentina, London, Paris again. Sally gets good. They perform together, but there is tension: As a director, she is accustomed to leading. As a male dancer, so is he. "You should do nothing!" he tells her. "When you dance—just follow! Otherwise you destroy my freedom to move."

There is an interesting underlying question here: All good artists are the undisputed rulers of their art. Novelists or painters are godlike tyrants who create every molecule of their work out of their own beings. Can two artists therefore collaborate, or must one always be the brush and the other the canvas? When a man and a woman dance the tango, is the man the artist and his partner's response the work he is creating? "I did everything he did," Ginger Rogers once said about Fred Astaire. "And I did it backwards, and in high heels."

*The Tango Lesson* considers but does not answer these questions. It contains truly virtuoso dance sequences, photographed in black and white by Robby Muller (who must agree with Astaire's fierce belief that color only distracts from dance on the screen). The duel between Potter and Veron is all the more fascinating because it is about the wisdom of passion, rather than the temptation. The score, partly composed by Potter, is so seductive that for the first time in years I walked out of the screening and down the street and bought the sound track.

Most dances are for people who are falling in love. The tango is a dance for those who have survived it, and are still a little angry about having their hearts so mishandled. *The Tango Lesson* is a movie for people who understand that difference.

## The Taste of Cherry ★

NO MPAA RATING, 95 m., 1998

Homayon Ershadi (Mr. Badii), Abdolrahman Bagheri (Taxidermist), Afshin Khorshid Bakhtiari (Soldier), Safar Ali Moradi (Soldier), Mir Hossein Noori (Seminarian). Directed and produced by Abbas Kiarostami. Screenplay by Kiarostami.

There was great drama at Cannes in 1997 when the Iranian director Abbas Kiarostami was allowed, at the last moment, to leave his country and attend the festival premiere of his new film, *The Taste of Cherry*. He received a standing ovation as he entered the theater, and another at the end of his film (although this time mixed with boos), and the jury eventually made the film cowinner of the Palme d'Or.

Back at the Hotel Splendid, standing in the lobby, I found myself in lively disagreement with two critics I respect, Jonathan Rosenbaum of the *Chicago Reader* and Dave Kehr of the *New York Daily News*. Both believed they had seen a masterpiece. I thought I had seen an emperor without any clothes.

A case can be made for the movie, but it would involve transforming the experience of viewing the film (which is excruciatingly boring) into something more interesting, a fable about life and death. Just as a bad novel can be made into a good movie, so can a boring movie be made into a fascinating movie review.

The story: A man in a Range Rover drives through the wastelands outside Tehran, crisscrossing a barren industrial landscape of construction sites and shantytowns, populated by young men looking for work. The driver picks up a young serviceman, asking him, at length, if he's looking for a job: "If you've got money problems, I can help." Is this a homosexual pickup? Kiarostami deliberately allows us to draw that inference for a time, before gradually revealing the true nature of the job.

The man, Mr. Badii (Homayon Ershadi), wants to commit suicide. He has dug a hole in the ground. He plans to climb into it and take pills. He wants to pay the other man to come around at 6 A.M. and call down to him. "If I answer, pull me out. If I don't, throw in twenty shovels of earth to bury me."

The serviceman runs away. Badii resumes his employment quest, first asking a seminarian, who turns him down because suicide is forbidden by the Koran, and then an elderly taxidermist. The older man agrees because he needs money to help his son, but argues against suicide. He makes a speech on Mother Earth and her provisions, and asks Badii, "Can you do without the taste of cherries?"

That, essentially, is the story (I will not reveal if Badii gets his wish). Kiarostami tells it in a monotone. Conversations are very long, elusive, and enigmatic. Intentions are misunderstood. The car is seen driving for long periods in the wasteland, or parked overlooking desolation, while Badii smokes a cigarette. Any two characters are rarely seen in the same shot, reportedly because Kiarostami shot the movie himself, first sitting in the driver's seat, then in the passenger's seat.

Defenders of the film, and there are many, speak of Kiarostami's willingness to accept silence, passivity, a slow pace, deliberation, inactivity. Viewers who have short attention spans will grow restless, we learn, but if we allow ourselves to accept Kiarostami's time sense, if we open ourselves to the existential dilemma of the main character, then we will sense the film's greatness.

But will we? I have abundant patience with

long, slow films, if they engage me. I fondly recall *Taiga,* the eight-hour documentary about the yurt-dwelling nomads of Outer Mongolia. I understand intellectually what Kiarostami is doing. I am not impatiently asking for action or incident. What I do feel, however, is that Kiarostami's style here is an affectation; the subject matter does not make it necessary, and is not benefited by it.

If we're to feel sympathy for Badii, wouldn't it help to know more about him? To know, in fact, *anything at all* about him? What purpose does it serve to suggest at first he may be a homosexual? (Not what purpose for the audience—what purpose for Badii himself? Surely he must be aware his intentions are being misinterpreted.) And why must we see Kiarostami's camera crew—a tiresome distancing strategy to remind us we are seeing a movie? If there is one thing *The Taste of Cherry* does not lack, it is such a reminder: The film is such a lifeless drone that we experience it *only* as a movie.

Yes, there is a humanistic feeling underlying the action. Yes, an Iranian director making a film on the forbidden subject of suicide must have courage. Yes, we applaud the stirrings of artistic independence in the strict Islamic republic. But is *The Taste of Cherry* a worthwhile viewing experience? I say it is not.

## Taxi Driver: 20th Anniversary Edition ★ ★ ★ ★

R, 112 m., 1976 (rereleased 1996)

Robert De Niro (Travis Bickle), Jodie Foster (Iris), Harvey Keitel (Sport), Albert Brooks (Tom), Peter Boyle (Wizard), Leonard Harris (Senator Palatine), Cybill Shepherd (Betsy). A restored version of a film directed by Martin Scorsese and produced by Michael Phillips and Julia Phillips. Screenplay by Paul Schrader.

*Are you talkin' to me? Well I'm the only one here.*
—Travis Bickle in *Taxi Driver*

It is the last line, "Well I'm the only one here," that never gets quoted. It is the truest line in the film. Travis Bickle exists in *Taxi Driver* as a character with a desperate need to make some kind of contact somehow—to share or mimic the effortless social interaction he sees all around him, but does not participate in.

The film can be seen as a series of his failed attempts to connect, every one of them hopelessly wrong. Bickle (Robert De Niro) asks a girl out on a date, and takes her to a porno movie. He sucks up to a political candidate, and ends by alarming him. He tries to make small talk with a Secret Service agent. He wants to befriend a child prostitute, but scares her away. He is so lonely that when he asks, "Who you talkin' to?" he is addressing himself in a mirror.

This utter aloneness is at the center of *Taxi Driver,* one of the best and most powerful of all films, and perhaps it is why so many people connect with it even though Travis Bickle would seem to be the most alienating of movie heroes. We have all felt as alone as Travis. Most of us are better at dealing with it.

Martin Scorsese's 1976 film, which is now being rereleased in a restored color print, with a stereophonic version of the Bernard Herrmann score, is a film that does not grow dated or overfamiliar. I have seen it dozens of times. Every time I see it, it works; I am drawn into Travis's underworld of alienation, loneliness, haplessness, and anger.

It is a widely known item of cinematic lore that Paul Schrader's screenplay for *Taxi Driver* was inspired by *The Searchers,* John Ford's 1956 film. In both films, the heroes grow obsessed with "rescuing" women who may not, in fact, want to be rescued. They are like the proverbial Boy Scout who helps the little old lady across the street whether or not she wants to go.

*The Searchers* has Civil War veteran John Wayne devoting years of his life to the search for his young niece Debbie (Natalie Wood), who has been kidnapped by Comanches. The thought of Debbie in the arms of an Indian grinds away at him. When he finally finds her, she tells him the Indians are her people now, and runs away. Wayne then plans to kill the girl for the crime of having become a "squaw." But at the end, finally capturing her, he lifts her up (in a famous shot) and says, "Let's go home, Debbie."

The dynamic here is that Wayne has *forgiven* his niece, after having participated in the killing of the people who, for fifteen years or so, have been her family. As the movie ends, the niece is reunited with her surviving biological family, and the last shot shows Wayne silhouetted in a doorway, drawn once again to the wide, open spaces. There is, significantly, no scene showing us how the niece feels about what has happened to her.

In *Taxi Driver,* Travis Bickle is also a war veteran, horribly scarred in Vietnam. He encounters a twelve-year-old prostitute named Iris (Jodie Foster), controlled by a pimp named Sport (Harvey Keitel). Sport wears an Indian headband. Travis determines to "rescue" Iris, and does so, in a bloodbath that is unsurpassed even in the films of Scorsese. A letter and clippings from the Steensmans, Iris's parents, thank him for saving their girl. But a crucial earlier scene between Iris and Sport suggests that she was content to be with him, and the reasons why she ran away from home are not explored.

The buried message of both films is that an alienated man, unable to establish normal relationships, becomes a loner and wanderer, and assigns himself to rescue an innocent young girl from a life that offends his prejudices. In *Taxi Driver,* this central story is surrounded by many smaller ones, all building to the same theme. The story takes place during a political campaign, and Travis twice finds himself with the candidate, Palatine, in his cab: Once, the candidate is with a hooker, and the next time, with campaign aides. Travis goes through the motions of ingratiating flattery on the second occasion, but we, and Palatine, sense something wrong.

Shortly after that Travis tries to "free" one of Palatine's campaign workers, Betsy, a blonde he has idealized (Cybill Shepherd), from the Palatine campaign. That goes wrong with the porno movie. And then, after the fearsome rehearsal in the mirror, he becomes a walking arsenal and goes to assassinate Palatine. The Palatine scenes are like dress rehearsals for the ending of the film. With both Betsy and Iris, he has a friendly conversation in a coffee shop, followed by an aborted "date," followed by attacks on the men he preceived as controlling them; he tries unsuccessfully to assasinate Palatine, and then goes gunning for Sport.

There are undercurrents in the film that you can sense without quite putting your finger on them. Travis's implied feelings about blacks, for example, which emerge in two long shots in a taxi driver's hangout, when he exchanges looks with a man who may be a drug dealer. His ambivalent feelings about sex (he lives in a world of pornography, but the sexual activity he observes in the city fills him with loathing). His hatred for the city, inhabited by "scum." His preference for working at night, and the way Scorsese's cinematographer, Michael Chapman, makes the yellow cab into a vessel by which Travis journeys the underworld, as steam escapes from vents in the streets, and the cab splashes through water from hydrants—a Stygian passage.

What is the purpose, the use, of a film like *Taxi Driver*? It is not simply a seamy, violent portrait of a sick man in a disgusting world. Such a portrait it is, yes, but not "simply." It takes us inside the mind of an alienated fringe person like those who have so profoundly changed the course of recent history (Oswald, Ray, Bremer, Chapman). It helps us to understand these creatures who emerge, every so often, guns in their hands, enforcing the death penalty for the crime of celebrity. Sick as he is, Travis is a man. And no man is an island.

## Telling Lies in America ★ ★ ★

PG-13, 101 m., 1997

Kevin Bacon (Billy Magic), Brad Renfro (Karchy Jonas), Maximilian Schell (Mr. Jonas), Calista Flockhart (Diney), Paul Dooley (Father Norton). Directed by Guy Ferland and produced by Ben Myron and Fran Kuzui. Screenplay by Joe Eszterhas.

Cleveland, 1960. "I haven't been Billy Magic since Fort Worth," says the lanky, chain-smoking disc jockey. He has the grin of a man who is getting away with something. He is. *Telling Lies in America,* based on the memories of America's top-paid screenwriter, Joe Eszterhas, is about the kid who helps Billy get away with it, and does a lot of growing up in the process. He gets a break and loses his innocence at the same time.

Karchy Jonas (Brad Renfro) is a student at a Catholic high school attended mostly by rich kids, who call him "white trash." His father (Maximilian Schell) is a Hungarian immigrant, who was a professor in the old country but is a janitor in this one. Karchy works for an egg dealer in the local produce market, and has a crush on a girl who tells him she'll date him, but only if he's picked for Billy Magic's "High School Hall of Fame."

Hall of famers are supposed to be nominated by their classmates, but Karchy forges the signatures, sends them in, and wins. What he doesn't know is that Billy Magic is *looking* for a cheater. "You lie good, kid," Billy tells him, but even after he gives Karchy $100 a week, the kid won't admit he was lying. That's good. It's the time of the payola scandals, and Billy needs an underage bag man who can't be forced to testify.

Eszterhas, who has made a fortune with screenplays like *Basic Instinct* and *Showgirls*, has had this story in the works for fifteen years. Himself a Hungarian immigrant who came to Cleveland as a child, he remembers what success looked like from the outside. To Karchy, Billy Magic is a star. And the kid soon centers his life on the radio station, letting his grades slip because high school is no longer where he expects to find his future.

Kevin Bacon's work as the disc jockey is one of his best performances. He never pushes it too far: His style is laid-back cool rather than frantic. His lazy announcer's drawl suggests a cynicism developed during a career on too many stations under too many names. When the kid tells him he's got it made, Billy explains about his ex-wives, his child support payments, and the fact that his red Cadillac convertible is leased. He's one jump ahead of his next market.

Brad Renfro is assured and involving as Karchy. Amazingly, he's playing over his age; Renfro (so good as the young boy in *The Client* in 1994) was fourteen or fifteen when he played this seventeen-year-old; it is a nuanced performance, showing a character who has been so wounded by life (his mother is dead, his father embittered) that, yes, he'll lie to get what he wants. And in an unexpected twist at the end of the film, lying pays off. (At one point, he advises the girl to read *Huckleberry Finn*—a nod to his previous role, as Huck in *Huck and Jim*.)

The movie's weak point is Karchy's father, as played by Schell. Mr. Jonas is a weary assortment of clichés about immigrant dads; he always wears his hat in the house, has stringy hair, and needs a shave. We are told this man was a professor and famous doctor in Hungary. It is more likely that he would dress according to Old World standards, however old his clothes. He wouldn't seem so self-demeaning and clueless, forever moping around at home waiting for his son to walk in. A smarter character would have led to a better relationship.

But that's a small point. I liked this movie a lot—not just for Bacon and Renfro, but also for the work of the wonderfully named Calista Flockhart, as the girl who dates Karchy even after he unwisely tries to give her Spanish fly. What I'll remember best about the film is Billy Magic, who does what he does, knows what he knows, and is intimately familiar with the underside of fame.

## Temptress Moon ★ ★

R, 115 m., 1997

Leslie Cheung (Zhongliang), Gong Li (Pang Ruyi), Kevin Lin (Pang Duanwu), He Saifei (Yu Xiuyi [Zhongliang's Sister]), Zhang Shi (Li Niangjiu), Lin Lianqun (Pang An), Ge Xiangting (Elder Qi), Zhou Yemang (Zhengda). Directed by Chen Kaige and produced by Tong Cunlin and Hsu Feng. Screenplay by Shu Kei, based on the story by Kaige and Wang Anyi.

Chen Kaige's *Temptress Moon* opens like one of those nineteenth-century novels with a cast of characters on the first page. In a helpful sequence added by Miramax, the film's U.S. distributor, we are introduced to the three central characters, first as children, then as adults, with their names printed on the screen under their faces. There is also a prologue, which scrolls up the screen as it is read aloud.

This is not window dressing. *Temptress Moon* is a hard movie to follow—so hard, that at some point you may be tempted to abandon the effort and simply enjoy the elegant visuals by the Australian cinematographer Christopher Doyle, who mirrors the labyrinthine story with his treatment of city streets and shadowed corridors, all circling back upon themselves.

Like almost all modern Chinese films, this one is ravishing to look at, but it is impossible to care deeply about, because Kaige's characters, once we have them straight, are not sympathetic or even very interesting. I found myself more absorbed in the backgrounds and contexts of the action—in the ceremony, for example, by which a family aide informs its members of a change of leadership.

The story centers on Zhongliang (Leslie Cheung), who as a boy was raised on the decadent country estate of the Pang family, where his playmate was Ruyi (Gong Li). Now follow this closely. In 1911, the family is headed by Old Master Pang. His son, Zhengda (Zhou Yemang), is married to Xiuyi (He Saifei), who is Zhongliang's sister—which is why Zhongliang is invited there in the first place. (Ruyi is Zhengda's sister.) Zhongliang's duties include preparing the opium pipes for the Pangs, father and son, and for his own sister. There is a murky flashback later in the film indicating that Zhengda forced Zhongliang to kiss Xiuyi—and there are shadowy implications of additional incest.

Whatever. Time passes. Zhongliang flees, eventually finding work in Shanghai as a gigolo who kisses women while stealing their pearls. Old Master Pang dies. Young Master Pang (Zhengda) becomes a witless basket case through opium addiction, and so Zhengda's sister, Ruyi, is made the acting head of the family. Knowing that Ruyi and Zhongliang were playmates as children, Zhongliang's criminal boss orders him back to the Pang estate, where the scenario is that he will use his skills as a gigolo to seduce Ruyi and gain control of the family's assets.

Ruyi is envisioned as a sort of caretaker until a suitable male heir can be groomed, but she seizes firm control immediately, and orders her late father's concubines out of the house (everyone is scandalized; surely they deserve a serene retirement?). But Ruyi is also addicted to opium, and the entire family seems bemused by its fumes.

Why do I feel like I'm sitting in an opera house, trying to absorb the convoluted synopsis before the curtain goes up? Somehow it seems as if Kaige could have covered the essential elements of his story with fewer characters, especially since the flashbacks mean that the key characters are played both by children and adults, further complicating things.

Bewildered, I turned to the Web to see what Asian critics of the film had written, and was relieved to find I was not alone: "This dazed and confused viewer found it hard to make out what the story was about" (S. Young, Singapore). "He has to be ambiguous and obscure. The man has a thing or two to say. You bet. But he (doesn't) say it straight. He has to say something by not saying it, say something that has something else inside it, or say one thing and mean another" (Long Tin, Hong Kong).

The film is, in any event, beautiful to behold—as is Gong Li, although by making her an opium addict Kaige requires her to be unfocused and addled, and that undercuts the intelligence that is key to her beauty.

The film and its director ran into difficulties with the Chinese government, as did Kaige's *Farewell My Concubine* (1993), which also starred Gong Li and Leslie Chueng. The earlier film depicted homosexuality and suicide, which were frowned upon. I am not sure why *Temptress Moon* got into trouble. It presumably wouldn't concern the current regime that the 1920s are portrayed as a period of decadent capitalist excess, but I suspect there is a level of allegory in the story that eludes me. The film opens with the abdication of the old emperor in 1911; could we move the entire action forward to the death of Mao and decode the symbolism? You tell me.

## Tetsuo II: Body Hammer ★ ★ ★

NO MPAA RATING, 83 m., 1997

Tomoroh Taguchi (Tomoo Taniguchi), Nobu Kanaoka (Kana), Shinya Tsukamoto (Guy), Sujin Kim (Taniguchi's Father). Directed by Shinya Tsukamoto and produced by Fuminori Shishido, Fumio Kurokawa, Nobuo Takeushi, and Hiromi Aihara. Screenplay by Tsukamoto.

When Shinya Tsukamoto was growing up in Tokyo, there were still green and open spaces in the city—but now he sees it transformed into a towering, compacted mass of steel and concrete. This is not altogether a bad thing, he believes; both visions of the city attract him. But the inhabitants of the new Tokyo need to adapt in order to survive—have to become steel and concrete themselves—and that is what happens in the gruesomely fascinating images of *Tetsuo II: Body Hammer.*

The movie has many points in common with the original *Tetsuo* (1989), a black-and-white cult classic that became a fetish for some fans. The second film is not a sequel so much as another run at the same material, this time with more money, better special effects, and color (although the palate is mostly limited to dark grays and blues). Tsukamoto has an image in his mind of a human terrifyingly morphed into a machine and a weapon, and he creates nightmarish visions from this idea with only the most casual attention to plot.

The story involves a salaryman named Taniguchi (Tomoroh Taguchi), sort of a Clark Kent wearing horn-rimmed glasses and a neatly pressed shirt, whose child is kidnapped by skinhead cyborgs. Pursuing them, he mysteriously undergoes an experience in which his flesh mates with steel, and his body undergoes a transformation into a fearsome creature that looks like a dirty concrete block with arms and guns extruding from it, and exhaust pipes for ribs.

*Tetsuo II* doesn't rise (or stoop) to the level of conventional action or suspense; it's a design concept, a director's attempt to take some of the ideas in *Blade Runner* and some of the Schwarzenegger films and the Japanese animated films like *Akira* and extend them into grotesquerie. Japanese art has since the earliest times been fascinated by the possibilities in shape-changing, in creatures who take first one form and then another. Here we have the changes forced upon the ordinary hero by the very terms of his environment: Tokyo has reached some sort of critical mass in which flesh and steel combine, just as atomic reactions are created in the center of the Sun.

The movie's look is grim and grungy—heavy metal punk cyber-surrealism with undertones of S&M. Dialogue is scattered here and there, mostly in the form of cries, threats, and imprecations, but the bulk of the film consists of horrific confrontations between Taniguchi and his persecutors (led by Tsukamoto himself). There is an odd flashback, late in the film, that provides some sort of psychological underpinning for the events, but it's superfluous: Tsukamoto is painting a canvas, not a narrative, here—the vision is as complex, detailed, and obsessive as a painting by Bosch.

I assume that some of the shots are animation, or involve animation, but I can't be sure. Much of the action takes place at night, or in shadow, or in rain, and a typical shot will show a cyborg mutant monster lumbering piteously toward us, helpless to do anything except kill and maim. The film plays like an extended heavy-metal music video, and the sound track, insidious and hypnotic, is part of the effect.

Does *Tetsuo II: Body Hammer* succeed? Those who see it are not likely to forget it, and its images will linger as a warning of postapocalyptic urban critical mass. We already act for several hours every day like the extensions of our automobiles, telephones, computers, and television sets, so I suppose it is only a matter of time until we also take architecture and weaponry on board, and join Tsukamoto's future. It looks more like fate than destiny, but you can't have everything.

## That Old Feeling ★
PG-13, 105 m., 1997

Bette Midler (Lilly), Dennis Farina (Dan), Paula Marshall (Molly), Gail O'Grady (Rowena), David Rasche (Alan), Jamie Denton (Keith), Danny Nucci (Joey). Directed by Carl Reiner and produced by Leslie Dixon and Bonnie Bruckheimer. Screenplay by Dixon.

Remember those little Scotty dogs kids used to play with? They were glued to magnets. If you pointed them one way, they jumped toward each other, and if you pointed them the opposite way, they jumped apart. Carl Reiner's *That Old Feeling* is an entire movie based on the dance of the Scotty dogs, and the characters in it act as mechanically as if they had big magnets strapped to their thighs.

The premise: A senator's son (Jamie Denton) gets engaged to the daughter (Paula Marshall) of a movie star and a journalist. He wants a big wedding. Her parents have been divorced for fifteen years and both have remarried. He insists on inviting everyone. She warns against it: "My parents hate each other with a nuclear capacity."

She is right. In no time at all her parents (Bette Midler and Dennis Farina) are insulting each other on the dance floor ("I could have had the entire rock 'n' roll hall of fame!" Bette shouts. "I turned down a Beatle for you."). This is, of course, painful to their current spouses: Farina's wife (Gail O'Grady) and Midler's husband (David Rasche). But not nearly as disturbing as when the fighting couple suddenly fall into each other's arms.

Okay. So now we have Farina and Midler fighting and loving and fighting and loving. The wheezy screenplay by Leslie Dixon now works out the other combinations with almost mathematical precision. First it must be established that the young groom is a prig. Then the plot must contrive to lock the bride into a hotel room with a paparazzo (Danny Nucci) who has been following her movie-star mother. Then Farina's wife must get drunk with the groom, with predictable consequences.

And so on. There is not a moment that is believable, but of course the movie is not intended as realism. It is intended as comedy. So consider this "funny" scene: Marshall and Nucci, locked in the hotel room, try to attract attention by dropping fruit from a balcony. Cops see them, but nod indulgently and walk on. Jeez. So the two continue to drop fruit, finally dropping a whole lot of fruit. End of scene, with a whole lot of fruit on the sidewalk. At least when David Letterman was dropping watermelons off of buildings he showed them hitting the sidewalk in slow motion.

What's in slow motion here is the progress of the plot. Every development is exhausting because we have arrived at it long, long before the characters. There are only two saving graces. One is that Bette Midler sings "Somewhere Along the Way" to Farina in a piano bar, very nicely. The other is that David Rasche has some funny dialogue. He is a self-help counselor with smarmy little slogans at his command: "It is important to dialogue and to language each other," he says, and he recommends "emotional valet parking" and says to Farina's wife: "Is any part of your body original? You are so at odds with your shadow self."

I liked his dialogue because it was smart and satirical. I liked the two young actors—Denton and Marshall—because they were fresh and appealing. Hell, I liked Farina and Midler too. I liked everyone: O'Grady, Nucci . . . make a list. They all seemed way too nice to have done anything to deserve this screenplay.

## That Thing You Do! ★ ★ ★

PG, 110 m., 1996

Tom Everett Scott (Guy Patterson), Liv Tyler (Faye), Johnathon Schaech (Jimmy), Steve Zahn (Lenny), Ethan Embry (Bass Player), Tom Hanks (Mr. White), Bill Cobbs (Del Paxton), Rita Wilson (Margueritte). Directed by Tom Hanks and produced by Gary Goetzman, Jonathon Demme, and Edward Saxon. Screenplay by Hanks.

*That Thing You Do!* is the first film written and directed by Tom Hanks, and not surprisingly it is as sunny and guileless as many of the characters he's played. The movie may be inconsequential, but in some ways that's a strength. Without hauling in a lot of deep meanings, it remembers with great warmth a time and a place.

The time, the summer of 1964. The place, Erie, Pennsylvania, where life for young people centers around music, around records, around the radio, and especially around the incredible phenomenon of the Beatles. It's the kind of world where the owner of an appliance store can say, "I don't think I want to live in a country where you have to work on Sunday" without suspecting he will ever have to.

The owner's son, named Guy (Tom Everett Scott), lurks in the store after hours to play records loudly on the turntables and accompany them on the drums. His friends have started a band, and when the drummer breaks an arm, Guy joins the band just before it gets its big breaks—a gig at a high school prom that leads to a gig at a bowling alley. By picking up the tempo, Guy changes the band's sound until they resemble the Beatles, a little, as so many bands did then.

They have one song, written by their lead vocalist, Jimmy (Johnathon Schaech). It's called *That Thing You Do!* and it's a good thing it's a good song (written by Adam Schlesinger) because boy, are we familiar with it by the time the movie is over. As they get better as a band, the song gets better, too, and soon they're being signed to tour Pennsylvania by a so-called manager who pulls up outside the store in his camper.

*That Thing You Do!* is a rags-to-riches-to-oblivion story, the saga of the kind of band known in the industry as one-hit wonders. Appropriately enough, the name of the band is the Wonders, although it starts out as the "One-ders" and the name gets changed only because so many fans insist on pronouncing it "O-need-ers."

The band really picks up steam when the head of Play-Tone records (Tom Hanks) hears them, signs them to a state fair tour, and pilots them toward Hollywood. Meanwhile, their first record is chasing the Rolling Stones up the *Billboard* charts, and in Hollywood they get their big break, a spot on a TV showcase.

Meanwhile, maybe inevitably, the band members are developing problems with one another. Jimmy, the lead singer, brings along his girlfriend (Liv Tyler) but treats her coldly. When the band appears on TV, the words "Careful, girls—he's engaged!" appear beneath his shot, and that enrages him. ("Jimmy," she says, "I've wasted thousands and thousands of kisses on you.") One band member enlists in the service, another runs off to Vegas to get married, and the veteran recording executive accepts this as a fact of life: Maybe they were only meant to have one hit. There are other bands.

My favorite scenes take place in Hollywood as the band is breaking up and Guy has time on his hands. He meets his longtime idol, the jazz great Del Paxton (Bill Cobbs), gets to join him in a session, and learns from him a basic lesson: "Bands come and go." And he meets a friendly waitress (Rita Wilson) who subtly offers herself, and just as subtly takes back the offer.

In the annals of pop music, 1964 was a fairly innocent time. Bands broke up because of girlfriend problems, not drugs and murders. A guy could still run a record company out of his briefcase and get airtime by personal visits with disc jockeys. It wasn't all organized, it wasn't all big time, and if it was all hype, well, it's always been all hype.

## A Thin Line Between Love and Hate ★ ★ ½

R, 108 m., 1996

Martin Lawrence (Darnell), Lynn Whitfield (Brandi), Regina King (Mia), Bobby Brown (Tee), Della Reese (Ma Wright), Malinda Williams (Erica), Daryl Mitchell (Earl), Roger E. Mosley (Smitty). Directed by Martin Lawrence and produced by Douglas McHenry and George Jackson. Screenplay by Lawrence, Bentley Kyle Evans, Kenny Buford, and Kim Bass.

Most of the men who believe they are God's gift to women are right only if God plays dirty tricks. Consider Darnell Wright (Martin Lawrence), the hero of *A Thin Line Between Love and Hate.* He is a self-proclaimed ladies' man who haunts the nightclubs and coffee bars, picking up prey. He lies, he connives, he strings them along, and he even does what no man should do unless he really means it: He tells them he loves them. He's the kind of man who keeps the *Waiting to Exhale* generation waiting.

Nothing turns on a man like this more than a woman who resists him. Consider Brandi (Lynn Whitfield). From the moment Darnell sees her getting out of her limousine, it appears to his libido that she moves in slow motion, like the objects of lust in Martin Scorsese films. He is struck down with desire, but she wants nothing to do with him. When he tracks her to her office and presents her with a bouquet of flowers, she calls security to have him thrown out.

But Darnell will not be dismissed. He plots a campaign. Discovering that Brandi is a real-estate agent, he arranges for her to show him a house. He talks sweet. He convinces her to go out on a date. They attend gallery openings and have fancy dinners, and gradually her detachment melts. Darnell is blissful, but he would be less happy if he could see her in a private moment, regarding her mirror and repeating to her own image: "I *cannot* be hurt. It would *not* be good if I were hurt."

She is going to be hurt. Darnell and his buddy Tee (Bobby Brown) continue to play the field, and soon Darnell is rediscovering an old passion for Mia (Regina King), a girl he's known since childhood. One night Darnell invites Brandi to dinner—it's her birthday—and as she waits over a candlelit table, Darnell stands her up and spends the night with Mia. In the morning, he finds the birthday cake on Mia's doorstep with a knife stuck in it. This is not a good sign.

*A Thin Line Between Love and Hate* is an African-American version of *Fatal Attraction* and the other female slasher movies, with the twist that it's harder on the man than on his dangerously scorned woman. It's a morality play, in a way, warning that it's dangerous to trifle with a woman's affections. That's the movie's main line, and if it had stuck to it and developed it more relentlessly, this might have been a better movie. But Lawrence, who directed and cowrote it, is sidetracked by his own ambition. He wants to include more than the plotline—like so many post–*Pulp Fiction* filmmakers, he likes asides and excursions—and he drifts away into character studies, subplots, and passages where the clever dialogue is the only point. This can work (it worked for Tarantino), but the further you swing away from the center, the stronger the center needs to be. Here the central story about Darnell and Brandi sometimes seems misplaced altogether, as if we've drifted into a parallel movie.

What the movie does show is that Martin Lawrence (who previously made the performance film *Martin* and the not-very-good cop comedy-thriller *Bad Boys*) is an interesting filmmaker with some insights into male behavior that aren't often seen in the movies. Not many director-writer-stars would place themselves in a screen situation so critical of their characters. This *Fatal Attraction* scenario isn't just a retread of the scorned woman with the butcher knife; the man more or less deserves what he gets, and the movie violates its genre by revealing a certain sympathy for the wronged woman. At last we see God's gift to women in the hands of an angry God.

### Things to Do in Denver When You're Dead ★ ★ ½

R, 104 m., 1996

Andy Garcia (Jimmy the Saint), Christopher Walken (Man with the Plan), Gabrielle Anwar (Dagney), William Forsythe (Franchise), Treat Williams (Critical Bill), Christopher Lloyd (Pieces), Bill Nunn (Easy Wind), Jack Warden (Joe Heff), Steve Buscemi (Mister Shhh), Fairuza Balk (Lucinda). Directed by Gary Fleder and produced by Cary Woods. Screenplay by Scott Rosenberg.

I've been back and forth on *Things to Do in Denver When You're Dead.* At the 1995 Cannes Film Festival, I thought it had more spirit and audacity than most of the films in a slow year. But then, seeing it again, I found myself focusing on its cuteness and contrivance: It's so overwritten it becomes an exercise in style rather than a story about its characters. On balance, I think it's an interesting miss, but a movie that you might enjoy if (1) you don't expect a masterpiece, and (2) you like the dialogue in Quentin Tarantino movies.

I hasten to add that *Things to Do in Denver When You're Dead* has apparently *not* been directly influenced by QT. When I suggested in a dispatch from Cannes that it was "Quentonian" (or should it be "Tarantinesque"?), I got a note from Gary Fleder, who directed it, pointing out that the screenplay by Scott Rosenberg was written long before *Reservoir Dogs* saw the light of day.

I can believe that. Rosenberg's screenplay, however, probably springs from some of the same impulses that inspired Tarantino. The characters talk like they were raised on 1940s *noir* movies and then given a quick course in advertising copywriting. Every other line sounds like a would-be catch phrase: "Most girls, they plod. You glide along." "I want you to brace this guy." "I lost a toe the other day." "Maybe not today and maybe not tomorrow, but someday soon." Sorry—that one's from *Casablanca*. But Andy Garcia uses it here.

As the movie opens, Garcia plays Jimmy the Saint, who is running a service where dying people can videotape advice to their loved ones. ("Treat them like dirt, and they come running," one dad tells his son about women.) The service is losing money, and the notes are held by the Man with the Plan (Christopher Walken), a right-wing homophobe who runs the Denver crime scene from his breath-powered wheelchair (one wonders exactly where Walken would begin if he ever wanted to satirize himself).

The M.W.T.P. will forgive the debt if Jimmy the Saint does a job for him. The Man's son has been charged with child molesting after a daylight raid on a school playground, and the Man thinks he might settle down if he got his old girlfriend back. Therefore, Jimmy's job is to intercept the old girlfriend's new boyfriend on his way into town, and "brace" him.

Jimmy is a former criminal now trying to go straight, but he's forced to take the job. So he rounds up some old associates who make Tarantino's reservoir dogs look like brush salesmen. They include Critical Bill (Treat Williams), who hasn't beaten up a live person in years—"not since I found myself that exercise program," which consists of beating up corpses in the morgue; Pieces (Christopher Lloyd), a porno projectionist with leprosy, whose toes and other parts are falling off; and Franchise and Easy Wind (William Forsythe and Bill Nunn), who are marginally more mainstream.

Can these five guys "brace" the boyfriend? They devise a plan worthy of the Brinks Job, including a stolen police cruiser and the impersonation of police officers. Unfortunately, the boyfriend isn't too impressed by Pieces when he's hauled over on the road into town. In the movie's funniest scene, he wonders why the police department hasn't issued him a rain hat, and then notices the missing fingers and calls the bluff ("Tell me, Officer Leper . . .").

The movie has not one but two romances, both involving Jimmy the Saint. He falls hard for Dagney (Gabrielle Anwar) in a bar, smelling her hair and informing her, "Girls who glide need guys to make them thump." But when the situation gets dangerous, he returns to an old friend, Lucinda (Fairuza Balk), a hooker with a face like a wounded Judy Garland—but a heart, of course, of gold.

All of this action is carefully monitored from a local diner by a retired hood named Joe (Jack Warden). He supplies sort of a Greek chorus of commentary on the action, not really necessary, although it provides for dialogue while Jimmy the Saint is gulping down milk shakes for his bad stomach.

*Things to Do in Denver When You're Dead* is not a successful movie on its own terms. It's too cute and talky, and too obviously mannered to develop convincing momentum. But as an exercise it's sometimes funny and always energetic, and it shows that Rosenberg can write and Fleder can direct. Now if they can just dial down a little.

## A Thousand Acres ★ ★

R, 104 m., 1997

Michelle Pfeiffer (Rose Cook Lewis), Jessica Lange (Ginny Cook Smith), Jason Robards (Larry Cook), Jennifer Jason Leigh (Caroline Cook), Colin Firth (Jess Clark), Keith Carradine (Ty Smith), Kevin Anderson (Peter Lewis), Pat Hingle (Harold Clarke). Directed by Jocelyn Moorhouse and produced by Marc Abraham, Lynn Arost, Steve Golin, Kate Guinzburg, and Sigurjon Sighvatsson. Screenplay by Laura Jones, based on the novel by Jane Smiley.

*A Thousand Acres* is an ungainly, undigested assembly of "women's issues," milling about within a half-baked retread of *King Lear.* The film is so unfocused that at the end of its very long 104 minutes, I was unable to say who I was supposed to like and who I was supposed to hate—although I could name several characters for whom I had no feelings at all.

The movie is set on the 1,000-acre Cook farm in Iowa, where the weathered and wise old patriarch, Larry (Jason Robards), is the most powerful farmer for miles around. Then he announces he has decided to retire and to divide his farm into three parts, giving shares to each of his daughters.

That's fine with Rose (Michelle Pfeiffer) and Ginny (Jessica Lange), who are married farm women—but Larry's youngest and most favored daughter, Caroline (Jennifer Jason Leigh), a lawyer, questions the wisdom of the plan. Larry instantly disowns her and later slams a door in her face, and as the other two daughters and their husbands begin running the farm, we figure it's only a matter of time until old Larry is out there in a raging storm, cursing the heavens.

We are correct, but *A Thousand Acres* wants only to borrow plot elements of *King Lear,* not to face up to its essentials. We are denied even the old man's heartbreaking deathbed scene—that goes to one of the daughters after her second bout with breast cancer. The movie repeats the currently fashionable pattern in which men are bad and fathers are the most evil of all; there is not a single positive male character in the movie, unless you count the preacher who says grace before the church supper.

The husbands of the two older daughters, indeed, are written so thinly that when one of them (Kevin Anderson) kills himself, we're not sure why (until it's belatedly explained) and don't much care, and when the other (Keith Carradine) goes off to Texas to work on a hog farm, his wife scarcely seems to notice he's gone. Along the way, in a development so badly handled it seems to belong in another movie, Caroline gets married in Des Moines and lets her sisters find out about it only through a wedding announcement in the local weekly; as nearly as I can recall, we never meet her husband, nor is he ever referred to again.

All white male patriarchs must be guilty of something in modern women's fiction, preferably the sexual abuse of their children, and I was not surprised to find out that Larry visited the bedrooms of Rose and Ginny. Rose describes the visits in lurid detail, but Ginny cannot remember, although they took place as late as her sixteenth year; her memory lapse, I think, serves to prolong the breathless scenes of description. ("Daddy might be a drinker and a rager," Ginny says, "but he goes to church!") The youngest daughter was apparently not molested, maybe because (in the movie's laborious Lear parallels) she was the most favored.

Among the other subjects dutifully ticked off are a husband's rejection of his wife after she has a mastectomy; a woman who has five miscarriages because no one told her the local drinking water was poisoned with pesticides; the alcoholism of the father and one of the husbands; the inadequate sexual performance of both husbands; the betrayal of Rose and Ginny by a handsome neighbor man (Colin Firth), who is such a cad he sleeps with both of them but tells only one about the other; and a man who buys a tractor that is three times bigger than he needs—a clear case of phallic compensation. Toward the end we get the tragedy of Alzheimer's, the heartlessness of banks, the problem of unnecessary lawsuits, and the obligatory "giant agricultural conglomerate."

All of these subjects are valid and promising and could be well-handled in a better movie. In *A Thousand Acres,* alas, they seem like items on a checklist. The movie is so distracted by both the issues and the Lear parallels that the characters bolt from one knee-jerk situation to the next.

Then there is the problem of where to place our sympathy. In *King Lear,* of course, we love Lear and his daughter Cordelia, and hate the two older sisters and their husbands. In *A Thousand Acres,* it cannot be permitted for a man to be loved or a woman to be hated, and so we have the curious spectacle of the two older sisters being portrayed as somehow favorably unfavorable, while the youngest, by eventually siding with her father, becomes a study in tortured plotting: She is good because she's a woman, suspect because she's a lawyer, bad because she sues the others, forgiven because her father evolves from monstrous to merely pathetic. Many of the closing scenes are set in a courtroom, providing the curious experience of a movie legal case in which the audience neither understands the issues nor cares which side wins.

The movie is narrated by Ginny, the Lange character, apparently in an effort to impose a point of view where none exists. But why Ginny? Is she better than the others? At the end of the film she intones in a solemn voice-over: "I've often thought that the death of a parent is the one misfortune for which there is no compensation." Say what? She doesn't remember her mother and is more than reconciled to the death of a father who (thanks to recovered memory) she now knows molested her. What compensation could she hope for, short of stealing him from his deathbed to hang him on a gallows?

*A Thousand Acres* is so misconceived it should almost be seen just to appreciate the winding road it travels through sexual politics. Many of the individual scenes are well acted (Michelle Pfeiffer and Jessica Lange are luminous in their three most important scenes together). But the film substitutes prejudices for ideas, formula feminism for character studies, and a signposted plot for a well-told story. The screenplay is based on a novel by Jane Smiley, unread by me, which won the Pulitzer Prize—which means that either the novel or the prize has been done a great injustice.

## Three Lives and Only One Death ★ ★ ★

NO MPAA RATING, 123 m., 1997

Marcello Mastroianni (Mateo, Georges, Butler, Luc), Anna Galiena (Tania), Marisa Paredes (Maria), Melvil Poupaud (Martin), Chiara Mastroianni (Cecile), Arielle Dombasle (Helene), Feodor Atkine (Andre), Jacques Pieller (Tania's Husband), Jean-Yves Gautier (Mario), Pierre Bellemare (Radio Narrator), Lou Castel (Bum). Directed by Raul Ruiz and produced by Paulo Branco. Screenplay by Ruiz and Pascal Bonitzer.

I never tire of quoting Godard, who said the way to criticize a movie is to make another movie. For those left unsatisfied by David Lynch's *Lost Highway,* I offer Raul Ruiz's *Three Lives and Only One Death.* The fact that they both opened in Chicago on the same day was one of those serendipitous events that, according to Ruiz, happens all the time.

*Three Lives* stars Marcello Mastroianni in one of the last and most enchanting of his screen appearances. As if aware that time was running out, he plays four roles—or so we think, although by the end we learn there was perhaps only one. In a series of stories that first seem separate and then seem entwined, Mastroianni plays a man who shifts roles, costumes, and identities as readily as a street performer, moving effortlessly through his many lives.

In *Lost Highway,* one character disappears halfway through the film and another appears. How this happens and whether the characters are related (or perhaps are even the same person) I leave for you to discover—not because I hesitate to reveal the plot, but because I do not understand it. *Three Lives and Only One Death* is more complicated, but also more understandable; its complications are not added out of whimsy or the desire to frustrate, but as part of Ruiz's delightful storytelling game.

The first part of the film could be a story by Kafka; a man named Andre (Feodor Atkine) wakes up feeling out of sorts, says good-bye to his wife and daughter, and wanders out in search of cigarettes. He meets an engaging stranger (Mastroianni) who buttonholes him, plies him with champagne, and even pays him 1,000 francs an hour just to listen to his story.

And what a story. "I lived in your apartment twenty years ago," Mastroianni tells the man. "But," the man says, "my wife was living there then, with her first husband. . . ." Exactly. Mastroianni was the first husband. And now he wants to take up where he left off, back before . . . before . . . well, it's hard to explain precisely what happened, but it involves another apartment he moved into, one with strangely shifting walls and ceilings, which was inhabited by tiny fairies living in speeded-up time. When Andre doesn't seem eager to trade his own apartment for this magic place, he ends up with a hammer embedded in his head. Although this is not immediately fatal, it certainly indicates which way the wind is blowing.

The second story involves a man (Mastroianni again) who lectures at the Sorbonne. One day on his way to class he pauses, thinks, and abandons his teaching career to become a beggar. He is assaulted and then befriended by a prostitute, although it turns out she is not who, or what, she appears to be, either. (I like the moment when the professor's demanding mother spies on him through binoculars and discovers he makes more as a beggar than as a professor.)

In the third story, a young couple (played by Melvil Poupaud and Chiara Mastroianni, who is Mastroianni's daughter by Catherine Deneuve) receive a mysterious offer to occupy a luxurious chateau, where they are waited on by a butler (Mastroianni). And then there is a concluding segment in which a wealthy industrialist (Mastroianni) has invented a fictitious family, only to discover that its members are coming to visit him. It is here that the film reveals its overall plan: Perhaps Mastroianni has been playing only one man all of this time. Perhaps all of the roles were performances. Perhaps, I say. You tell me.

The movie has been compared to films by Luis Buñuel, the Spanish surrealist who loved to tell matter-of-fact stories about ordinary people who tried to behave in an everyday way while finding themselves in extraordinary circumstances. There is a bit of Buñuel here, and a little of *Groundhog Day*, too: Mastroianni's characters are never anything but sweet, calm, and reasonable as they negotiate life's bizarre twists. The movie works in two ways. Each of the "stories" has its own interior logic and charm. And then the overall picture, as it gradually develops, adds level upon mysterious level.

Ruiz seems to be an altogether more mature and complete filmmaker than the Lynch of *Lost Highway*. He is not simply toying with paradoxes and mysteries, but arranging them lovingly into a wicked pattern. Both directors are playing games, but Ruiz knows the rules. Comparing the two films, I am struck by the way both involve sexuality and violence, but in Ruiz such elements grow naturally out of the characters' lives, while in Lynch there is a rush toward lurid melodrama: pounding *noir* music, ominous rumbles, screams, distorted close-ups, fires, stabbings, shootings, rapes, sexual humiliation, all burying the characters beneath a flood of exhibitionism. Ruiz has more confidence in his story—and, it must be said, in his technique.

## 'Til There Was You ★ ½

PG-13, 114 m., 1997

Jeanne Tripplehorn (Gwen), Dylan McDermott (Nick), Sarah Jessica Parker (Francesca), Jennifer Aniston (Debbie), Craig Bierko (Jon), Nina Foch (Sophia Monroe), Alice Drummond (Harriet), Christine Ebersole (Beebee). Directed by Scott Winant and produced by Penney Finkelman Cox, Tom Rosenberg, and Alan Poul. Screenplay by Winnie Holzman.

Here is the most tiresome and affected movie in many a moon, a 114-minute demonstration of the Idiot Plot, in which everything could be solved with a few well-chosen words that are never spoken. The underlying story is a simple one: A man and a woman who are obviously intended for each other are kept apart for an entire movie, only to meet at the end. We're supposed to be pleased when they get together, I guess, although the movie ends with such unseemly haste that we never get to experience them as a couple.

*'Til There Was You*, directed by Scott Winant with a screenplay by Winnie Holzman, plays like

half-digested remnants of a dozen fictional meals. We have flashbacks to the love stories of parents, college love affairs, shocking revelations about sexuality and parentage, a maladjusted former sitcom star, an architect who is a "perfectionist with low self-esteem," a ghostwriter who falls in love with a colorful old apartment building, not one but two colorful old ladies who stick to their guns, a restaurant that's an architectural nightmare, zoning hearings, bad poetry, endlessly falling rose petals, chain-smoking, gays in the closet, traffic accidents, and at the end of it all we have the frustration of knowing that 114 minutes of our lives have been wasted, never to be returned.

Oh, and we have disastrous casting decisions. I find it helpful, as a general rule, to be able to tell the characters in a movie apart. Several of the characters in this film (a gay college professor, an architect, and another guy) look so much alike I was forever getting them confused. They were all sort of would-be Pierce Brosnan clones. Since the plot depends on coincidental meetings (and close misses) involving people who should know each other but don't, and people who do know each other but shouldn't, the look alikes grow even more confusing. The casting director no doubt thought that since several of the leads have appeared on TV sitcoms, the audience would recognize them and not be distracted by superficial physical similarities. Sorry.

The plot: A former sitcom star (Sarah Jessica Parker) owns a wonderful old apartment complex that has been earmarked for replacement by a condo. She begins to date the architect (Dylan McDermott) who will design the condo. His hero is an old lady architect (Nina Foch) who is apparently the Frank Lloyd Wright of her generation. She designed the colorful old apartment complex, but he doesn't know that. (How likely is it that an architect would be unfamiliar with one of his famous mentor's key buildings in the city where he lives? Not very.)

Meanwhile, a ghostwriter (Jeanne Tripplehorn) is hired by the sitcom star to write her autobiography. The ghostwriter and the architect met when they were children at summer camp. They are destined to meet again, but keep missing each other by inches or minutes. Some of their near misses take place in a restaurant the architect designed.

This restaurant, of frightening ugliness, seems designed to keep personal injury lawyers in work. When Tripplehorn enters it for the first time, she can't get the door open. Then it flies open and she staggers across the entire room and bangs into something. Later, she beans herself on a low-flying sculpture, trips over a waiter, catches her heel in the floor, falls over a chair, etc. Did she train for a Three Stooges movie?

All of the movie's heartfelt scenes are tangential. They involve major characters talking to minor ones instead of to each other. There is the heartfelt talk between the architect and his mentor. The heartfelt talk between the ghostwriter and a dotty old lady (Gwen Verdon) who lives in the colorful old building (which the writer staggered into after a coincidental car crash). There is the heartfelt talk between the writer and her old father, who tells her the childhood legends the movie began with were all fiction. There is the heartfelt love scene between the writer and her college professor, who is later revealed to be gay, and then disappears from the movie just when we thought the story would be about him.

Many details are just plain wrong. Since the Tripplehorn character is a literature student, we expect her to be a fairly sophisticated writer. Yet when we hear one of her poems read (after it accidentally sticks to the bottom of an architectural model thrown out of a window—but never mind), it turns out to be written in rhyming couplets of the sort found beneath the needlework column in women's craft magazines. All of the characters smoke unpleasantly and want to stop, and one of the movie's near misses, where they almost meet, is an "N.A." meeting, which is described as "Nicotine Anonymous." Warning: Before dropping "N.A." into your conversation, be aware that most people think it stands for something else.

And what about those rose petals? Or lilac petals, or whatever they are? The courtyard of the colorful old building, we can clearly see, has no foliage above it. Yet petals drift down in endless profusion for days and weeks during every scene—so many, I sat through the end credits in the futile hope there would be mention of the Petal Dropper.

All comes together at the end. Landmarks are saved, hearts are mended, long-deferred love is realized, coincidences are explained, the past is healed, the future is assured, the movie is over. I liked the last part the best.

## Tin Cup ★ ★ ★

R, 130 m., 1996

Kevin Costner (Roy "Tin Cup" McAvoy), Rene Russo (Dr. Molly Griswold), Cheech Marin (Romeo Posar), Don Johnson (David Simms), Linda Hart (Doreen). Directed by Ron Shelton and produced by Shelton, Gary Foster, and David Lester. Screenplay by John Norville and Shelton.

When you hit a perfect golf swing, "a tuning fork goes off in your heart." So says Tin Cup McAvoy, the "club pro" at a $2-a-bucket golf driving range in Salome, Texas—a range so pitiful that in the course of this movie he has only one customer. But when he sees her, a tuning fork goes off in his heart, and elsewhere.

Tin Cup (Kevin Costner) was once a golf champion at the University of Houston, but his career has gone to hell, mostly because he'll throw away a safe situation to take crazy shots on a dare. Now he lives in a woebegone Winnebago overlooking the desolate wasteland of the driving range. He spends his days with a crowd of beer-swilling cronies, taking bets on such events as which bug will be the next to light up the zapper. And he commiserates with his friend Romeo (Cheech Marin), who remembers Tin Cup from the good old days.

Then one day he sees a dream walking. She's Dr. Molly Griswold (Rene Russo), new in town, a psychologist who wants to take golf lessons. There is a problem. She wants to learn golf because her new boyfriend is on the pro Tour. Worse, her boyfriend is David Simms (Don Johnson), the arrogant jerk who has been Tin Cup's rival and nemesis since college days. How bad is Simms? "He hates women, children, and dogs," Tin Cup tells Molly. Romeo backs him up.

That's the setup for *Tin Cup,* a formula sports comedy with a lot of nonformula human comedy. We can anticipate the broad outlines of the plot (Tin Cup knows he must rehabilitate himself to win the woman and enters the U.S. Open, which of course ends in a showdown between himself and Simms). But the U.S. Open doesn't end quite the way we might have predicted, and the movie itself isn't even about who wins—it is, as they say, about how you play the game. And the game is love.

Costner is unshaven, creased, weather-beaten, and in need of a bath during much of *Tin Cup.* That's more or less how he looked in *Waterworld,* too, but this time there's charm. In his desperation to win Dr. Griswold, he turns himself in for therapy, only to discover to his horror that she wants to discuss personal matters ("I didn't know it was that kind of therapy"). She is true to her fiancé, but has some sympathy for this forlorn loser, and agrees to help him get his head into shape for a comeback. ("You don't have inner demons. What you have is inner crapola.")

The movie was written and directed by Ron Shelton, a onetime minor league baseball player whose credits include writing and directing *Bull Durham* and writing *White Men Can't Jump* and *Cobb.* He knows sports, and he especially knows the world of the hanger-on—the world of the girlfriends, cronies, gamblers, broadcasters, and businessmen who like to get close to sports heroes. Some of the funniest scenes in *Tin Cup* involve unlikely bets with amateurs who think they should be professionals (Tin Cup plays one round using a baseball bat and a shovel instead of clubs).

*Tin Cup* is well written. The dialogue is smart and fresh, and when Tin Cup and Molly are talking to each other they savor the joy of language. The movie is strong in supporting characters. Don Johnson finds the right blend for the villain: He's likable, tanned, and ingratiating when it suits him, and a jerk the rest of the time. Cheech Marin is crucial in a couple of sequences in which he is the caddie and *knows* Tin Cup is calling for the wrong club. And an actress named Linda Hart has some nice moments as the local stripper who is the landlady of the driving range.

Shelton's gift is to take the main lines of the story, which are fairly routine, and add side stories that make the movie worth seeing. I liked the scene where Molly explains how she got into the therapy business. The scene where Simms tells off some fans who want his autograph. The scene where Romeo tries emergency surgery on Tin Cup's golf swing ("It feels like an unfolded lawn chair"). And the ending, which flies in the face of convention and is therefore all the more satisfactory.

## Titanic ★ ★ ★ ★

PG-13, 194 m., 1997

Leonardo DiCaprio (Jack Dawson), Kate Winslet (Rose DeWitt Bukater), Billy Zane (Cal Hockley),

Kathy Bates (Molly Brown), Bill Paxton (Brock Lovett), Gloria Stuart (Rose Calvert), Frances Fisher (Ruth DeWitt Bukater), Bernard Hill (Capt. E. J. Smith), David Warner (Spicer Lovejoy), Victor Garber (Thomas Andrews), Jonathan Hyde (Bruce Ismay). Directed by James Cameron and produced by Cameron and Jon Landau. Screenplay by Cameron.

Like a great iron Sphinx on the ocean floor, the *Titanic* faces still toward the West, interrupted forever on its only voyage. We see it in the opening shots of *Titanic,* encrusted with the silt of eighty-five years; a remote-controlled TV camera snakes its way inside, down corridors and through doorways, showing us staterooms built for millionaires and inherited by crustaceans.

These shots strike precisely the right note; the ship calls from its grave for its story to be told, and if the story is made of showbiz and hype, smoke and mirrors—well, so was the *Titanic.* She was "the largest moving work of man in all history," a character boasts. There is a shot of her, early in the film, sweeping majestically beneath the camera from bow to stern, nearly 900 feet long and "unsinkable," it was claimed, until an iceberg made an irrefutable reply.

James Cameron's 194-minute, $200 million film of the tragic voyage is in the tradition of the great Hollywood epics. It is flawlessly crafted, intelligently constructed, strongly acted, and spellbinding. If its story stays well within the traditional formulas for such pictures, well, you don't choose the most expensive film ever made as your opportunity to reinvent the wheel.

We know before the movie begins that certain things must happen. We must see the *Titanic* sail and sink, and be convinced we are looking at a real ship. There must be a human story—probably a romance—involving a few of the passengers. There must be vignettes involving some of the rest, and a subplot involving the arrogance and pride of the ship's builders—and perhaps also their courage and dignity. And there must be a reenactment of the ship's terrible death throes; it took two and a half hours to sink, so that everyone aboard had time to know what was happening, and to consider his actions.

All of those elements are present in Cameron's *Titanic,* weighted and balanced like ballast, so that the film always seems in proportion. The ship was made out of models (large and small), visual effects, and computer animation. You know intellectually that you're not looking at a real ocean liner—but the illusion is convincing and seamless. The special effects don't call inappropriate attention to themselves, but get the job done.

The human story involves an eighteen-year-old woman named Rose DeWitt Bukater (Kate Winslet) who is sailing to what she sees as her own personal doom: She has been forced by her penniless mother to become engaged to marry a rich, supercilious snob named Cal Hockley (Billy Zane), and so bitterly does she hate this prospect that she tries to kill herself by jumping from the ship. She is saved by Jack Dawson (Leonardo DiCaprio), a brash kid from steerage class, and of course they will fall in love during the brief time left to them.

The screenplay tells their story in a way that unobtrusively shows off the ship. Jack is invited to join Rose's party at dinner in the first-class dining room, and later, fleeing from Cal's manservant, Lovejoy (David Warner), they find themselves first in the awesome engine room, with pistons as tall as churches, and then at a rousing Irish dance in the crowded steerage. (At one point Rose gives Lovejoy the finger; did young ladies do that in 1912?) Their exploration is intercut with scenes from the command deck, where the captain (Bernard Hill) consults with Andrews (Victor Garber), the ship's designer, and Ismay (Jonathan Hyde), the White Star Line's managing director.

Ismay wants the ship to break the transatlantic speed record. He is warned that icebergs may have floated into the hazardous northern crossing, but is scornful of danger. The *Titanic* can easily break the speed record, but is too massive to turn quickly at high speed; there is an agonizing sequence that almost seems to play in slow motion, as the ship strains and shudders to turn away from an iceberg in its path, and fails.

We understand exactly what is happening at that moment because of an ingenious story technique by Cameron, who frames and explains the entire voyage in a modern story. The opening shots of the real *Titanic,* we are told, are obtained during an expedition led by Brock Lovett (Bill Paxton), a documentary filmmaker. He seeks precious jewels but finds a nude drawing of a young girl. In England, an ancient woman sees the drawing on TV and recognizes herself. This is Rose (Gloria Stuart), still alive at 101. She visits Paxton and shares her memories ("I can still smell the fresh paint"). And he shows her scenes from his documentary, including a computer simulation of the *Titanic*'s last hours—which doubles as a briefing for the audience. By the time the ship sinks, we already know what is happening and why, and the story can focus on the characters while we effortlessly follow the stages of the *Titanic*'s sinking.

Movies like this are not merely difficult to make at all, but almost impossible to make well. The technical difficulties are so daunting that it's a wonder when the filmmakers are also able to bring the drama and history into proportion. I found myself convinced by both the story and the saga. The setup of the love story is fairly routine, but the payoff—how everyone behaves as the ship is sinking—is wonderfully written, as passengers are forced to make impossible choices. Even the villain, played by Zane, reveals a human element at a crucial moment (despite everything, damn it all, he does love the girl).

The image from the *Titanic* that has haunted me, ever since I first read the story of the great ship, involves the moments right after it sank. The night sea was quiet enough so that cries for help carried easily across the water to the lifeboats, which drew prudently away. Still dressed up in the latest fashions, hundreds froze and drowned. What an extraordinary position to find yourself in after spending all that money for a ticket on an unsinkable ship. ☞

## To Gillian on Her 37th Birthday ★ ★

PG-13, 93 m., 1996

Peter Gallagher (David Lewis), Michelle Pfeiffer (Gillian Lewis), Claire Danes (Rachel Lewis), Laurie Fortier (Cindy Bayles), Wendy Crewson (Kevin Dollof), Bruce Altman (Paul Wheeler), Kathy Baker (Esther Wheeler), Freddie Prinze Jr. (Joey Bost). Directed by Michael Pressman and produced by Marykay Powell and David E. Kelley. Screenplay by Kelley based on the play by Michael Brady.

*To Gillian on Her 37th Birthday* is one of those movies in which nosy but well-meaning relatives try to force a reluctant family member to embrace a truth that is obvious to everyone except him. In this case, the truth is that we cannot allow ourselves to be paralyzed forever by grief over the death of a loved one. Why do I always root for the recalcitrant family member?

The movie takes place two years to the day after Gillian (Michelle Pfeiffer) has fallen from the mast of a sailboat and died. It is also her birthday. Her husband, David (Peter Gallagher), has since then lived as a recluse on Nantucket Island with his sixteen-year-old daughter, Rachel (Claire Danes). She suspects that he fantasies his wife is still alive and goes for long walks and talks on the beach with her. She is correct.

To observe "Gillian's Day," as it is known in the family, Gillian's sister Esther and her husband, Paul (Kathy Baker and Bruce Altman), arrive with a woman friend named Kevin (Wendy Crewson). She is intended as a blind date, although when she finds out it is Gillian's Day, she wants to return immediately to the mainland—and so she should, since she plays such an unnecessary role in the drama to follow.

The movie, written by David E. Kelley and directed by Michael Pressman, is well versed in the cinematic symptoms of excessive grief. David drives too fast, gets in fights with other motorists, plays the radio too loud, and goes off a lot by himself. Esther believes it's time for him to get a grip on himself. Worse, she plans to sue for custody of Rachel, who she fears is having an inadequate adolescence because of having to spend the off-season on Nantucket.

The movie cannot see that Esther is a deranged nuisance who should mind her own business, that David is entitled to his grief, that Rachel is happy living on the island, and that if Gillian appears to David, so much the better. (She also appears to us, and since we can see and hear her I guess she is "really" there, which gives David an excellent reason for not wanting to leave.)

The movie lurches to its sentimental conclusion via several dead ends of plot ideas that are introduced but not developed. During the course of the long day and night, Rachel goes out on her first date with a kid she meets on the beach who has rings piercing his nose, ears, and who knows what all, and dyes the sides of his head blond, which is proof in any court of law that he is cool, or, if not cool, definitely a teenager. David doesn't like the kid, but allows the date, during which Rachel gets drunk, comes home, barfs, goes to bed, has a nightmare, and then has a heartfelt talk with her aunt and her dad. The subplot (including the dance they go to) is all filler.

So is Kevin, the blind date, who sees she is not needed, says she is not needed, acts as if she is not needed, and is not needed. I was also underwhelmed by a side plot having to do with the marital history of Paul and Esther, since this, too, has no bearing on David's problem.

And what of David? How does he spend his time as a recluse? Well, he's a literature professor and claims he's using his free time to write a book. This sounds like a splendid idea, but not to Esther, who believes he should return to the mainland and go back to his old job. With people like this, how many books would ever get written?

We have a national compulsion to insist that people deny their grief. A friend loses a loved one, and three weeks later we're asking, "Are you okay?" And we want them to say, "Why, yes, I'm doing just fine," so we can nod in approval. If we were really friends, we'd say, "I imagine you still feel miserable," so they could say, "Sometimes it's worse than ever."

As to whether David is able to bid good-bye to his ghost on the beach and return to the mainland, or whether Esther succeeds in tearing his daughter from his side, I will leave you to guess. Here's fair warning: A movie that hasn't had an original idea in eighty-three minutes is unlikely to develop one in the last ten.

## Tomorrow Never Dies ★ ★ ★

PG-13, 120 m., 1997

Pierce Brosnan (James Bond), Jonathan Pryce (Elliot Carver), Michelle Yeoh (Wai Lin), Teri Hatcher (Paris Carver), Goetz Otto (Stamper), Judi Dench (M), Desmond Llewelyn (Q), Samantha Bond (Miss Moneypenny). Directed by Roger Spottiswoode and produced by Barbara Broccoli and Michael G. Wilson. Screenplay by Bruce Feirstein.

James Bond has battled evil commies and megalomaniac madmen; perhaps it was only a matter of time until he faced off against a media baron—the only sort of figure in today's world that actually does seek global domination. His enemy in *Tomorrow Never Dies* wants to start a war in order to create headlines for the launch of his latest news channel. Just imagine what Rupert Murdoch and Ted Turner would like to do to each other and imagine either one of them doing it to the Chinese, and you'll get the idea.

Bond, played confidently and with a minimum of fuss by Pierce Brosnan, stumbles into the middle of the plot, masterminded by Elliot Carver (Jonathan Pryce), who owns newspapers, TV stations, and a gigantic Stealth warship that's invisible to radar. Carver's plan is ingenious: He'll use his satellites to draw a British warship off course, sink it with the Stealth ship, steal its nuclear warheads, and fire one at China, which will think it is under attack from the West. The only flaw in this plan, as far as I can see, is the likely nuclear destruction of most of Carver's biggest markets.

Bond films traditionally open with an elaborate scene built of stunts and special effects, and *Tomorrow Never Dies* doesn't break with custom: We see British military officials monitoring a "Terrorist Arms Bazaar on the Russian Border" (which border? who cares?). A hothead British general gives an order that leads to the likely detonation of nuclear weapons. Then Bond appears, steals the plane containing the warheads, uses its missiles to destroy all of his enemies, and takes off in it before . . .

But I dare not reveal too much. The plot has a lot of fun with the Carver character, played by Pryce in a platinum crew cut. He likes to write headlines and design front pages in advance of big news events, and then make them happen, although more than once he's premature in reporting the death of Bond. His wife, Paris (Teri Hatcher), happens to be a former lover of 007, and M (Judi Dench), head of the British secret service, makes a few tart suggestions about how Bond might make use of the connection.

The other Bond woman this time is a departure from many of 007's former teammates. She's Wai Lin, an agent for the "Chinese External Security Force," and she's played by Michelle Yeoh as a karate expert with formidable fighting and intelligence skills. Yeoh, of course, is a star in her own right, having toplined many Asian martial arts movies, and her presence in the movie is so effective that she'd be a natural to add to the other regulars, like M, Q, and Miss Moneypenny.

In its thirty-fifth year, the long-running Bond series has settled into a dependable formula, based on gimmicks, high-tech toys, chases, elaborate stunts, and the battle to foil the madman's evil schemes. The toys this time are a couple of BMW products: a motorcycle, used during an incredible chase scene over rooftops, and a car, which is remote-controlled by a handheld device with a touch pad. In one ingenious chase scene, Bond crouches in the backseat of the car while guiding it with the remote control.

All Bond movies include at least one Fruit Cart Scene, in which market stalls are overturned in a chase, and this one sets some kind of a record by having the carts destroyed by the blades of a helicopter that's chasing Bond and Wai Lin. There is also the obligatory Talking Killer Scene, in which the madman explains his plans when he should simply be killing Bond as quickly as possible ("Caesar had his legions, Napoleon had his armies, and I have my divisions—TV, newspapers . . .").

Is Pierce Brosnan better or worse as Bond than Connery, Lazenby, Moore, and Dalton? This is one of those questions (like why doesn't tomorrow ever die?) that can be debated but never answered. Basically, you have Connery, and then you have all of the rest. I enjoyed Brosnan in the role, although I noticed fewer Bondian moments this time in which the trademarks of the series are relished.

Yes, we have the usual double entendres and product placements (I find product placement distracting in most movies, but sort of anticipate them as part of the Bond formula). There's a high gloss and some nice payoffs, but not quite as much humor as usual; Bond seems to be straying from his tongue-in-cheek origins into the realm of conventional techno-thrillers.

Still, *Tomorrow Never Dies* gets the job done, sometimes excitingly, often with style. The villain, slightly more contemporary and plausible than usual, brings some subtler-than-usual satire into the film, and I liked the chemistry between Bond and Wai Lin (all the more convincing because the plot doesn't force it). The look of the film is authoritative; the scenes involving warships and airplanes seem sleek and plausible. There's gorgeous photography as a junk sails in a sea filled with peaks, and astonishing action choreography in the rooftop motorcycle chase. On the basis of this installment, the longest-running movie series seems fit for the twenty-first century.

## Touch ★ ★ ½
R, 97 m., 1997

Christopher Walken (Bill Hill), Skeet Ulrich (Juvenal), Gina Gershon (Debra Lusanne), Bridget Fonda (Lynn Faulkner), Janeane Garofalo (Kathy Worthington), Lolita Davidovich (Antoinette Baker), LL Cool J (LL Cool J). Directed by Paul Schrader and produced by Lila Cazes and Fida Attieh. Screenplay by Schrader, based on the novel by Elmore Leonard.

There is a moment in Paul Schrader's *Touch* when all of the conflicting forces of this strange film seem to come together at once. It involves a young man named Juvenal, a former Franciscan who is able to heal people by touching them. On his body he bears the five stigmata—the marks of the wounds of Christ. He has met a woman named Lynn, who cares for him, and she is trying to bring order to his solitary existence by doing some laundry. "Do you think it's all right?" she asks him. "Stigmata blood going through the wash?"

Here we have a moment which probably reads as if it were intended to be funny or satirical. Probably it was written that way by Elmore Leonard, whose most bizarre novel inspired the screenplay. But it plays as if Lynn is asking the question in all seriousness. There's no attempt by the actress Bridget Fonda to punch up the moment, and it almost slips by without registering. A few people in the audience snickered uncomfortably, and fell silent: We are more comfortable with postcard angels than with saints who bleed like Christ.

The plot of *Touch* sounds like a comedy. But the experience of seeing the film is subduing; the movie plays in a muted key. Actors like Tom Arnold, who approach their characters more broadly, sound like they're talking too loudly in church. The dominant note is set by Skeet Ulrich, as Juvenal: He's sweet, soft-spoken, not sure what it all means. Schrader has said his movie has "a whole cast of ironic characters, with an existential character in the center." If the viewer doesn't figure this out, some scenes play very oddly.

As the movie opens, Juvenal finds himself comforting a blind woman (Conchata Ferrell) who has been beaten. He touches her, and she can see. This miracle excites a man named Bill

Hill (Christopher Walken), who had a thriving evangelism business in the south, but moved it to Los Angeles, went broke, and was reduced to selling recreational vehicles. He thinks maybe Juvenal could put him back in business, but can't find out his last name because Juvenal is in a rehab center, and A.A. rules require anonymity. Bill recruits Lynn (Fonda) to pose as an alcoholic and infiltrate the center. (They're old friends; she was a baton twirler at his services.)

Juvenal sees through Lynn instantly. He touches her breast and says, "You were gonna tell me you have a lump here—maybe a tumor—and if it was malignant, would I help you?" That is what she was going to do. She falls under his spell. Also drifting through this milieu is a militant Catholic conservative (Tom Arnold) who heads a group called "Outrage!" which demonstrates in favor of the discarded Latin rite.

Elmore Leonard, whose novels have fueled such films as *Get Shorty* and *52 Pickup*, has never written a story with more possibilities and hazards. I'm not sure why Schrader was drawn to it. There may be a connection with his own background. Raised in a strict religion, he didn't see his first movie until he was seventeen. His writing credits include *Taxi Driver* and *Raging Bull*, but two of his directing credits might provide clues: *Mishima* is about a Japanese novelist who commits suicide as a statement of his medieval ideals, and *Hard Core* is about a fundamentalist father who seeks his daughter among the porn and drug users of San Francisco.

Schrader is serious about religion. He may no longer be a formal believer, but the lessons are in his blood, and in *Touch* I believe he was drawn to the serious implications of the story, not the comic possibilities. It is not in him to generate jokes with the stigmata. He correctly sees Walken and Arnold as figures of fun: Anyone who uses religion as an avenue to publicity and self-aggrandizement is missing the point, and that is always funny. But Juvenal does bleed from the wounds of Christ, and so must be approached in another way.

The story is cluttered by two unnecessary filler characters: Gina Gershon plays a TV talk show host, and Janeane Garofolo plays a newspaper reporter. They get involved with the Walken and Arnold stories and stumble into the possibility that Juvenal may be for real. But their subplots, using standard media-bashing techniques, don't pay off. Much more interesting (in a fascinating pure dialogue scene) is Lolita Davidovich as Antoinette, a stripper who figures in a brilliantly written barroom conversation about religion. It basically asks: What do you do when your religion calls your bluff and turns out to be real, and you can't get away with safe middle-class piety any more, but are called to behave like those fanatics in the Lives of the Saints?

*Touch* is not successful in any way I can easily describe. Its effect is like that of a ghost at a banquet. Comic actors deliver one-liners, and the screenplay serves up the usual easy shots against phony evangelists, and then this tender, sweet, confused young man wanders in and doesn't know what to make of his frightening power.

How should a reviewer rate a film like this? I am not "recommending" the picture because I don't think it delivers what any reasonable filmgoer is likely to expect from it. Unreasonable filmgoers are another matter. You know who you are.

## Traveller ★ ★ ★

R, 100 m., 1997

Bill Paxton (Bokky), Mark Wahlberg (Pat), Julianna Margulies (Jean), James Gammon (Double D), Luke Askew (Boss Jack), Nikki Deloach (Kate), Danielle Wiener (Shane), Michael Shaner (Lip), Vincent Chase (Bimbo). Directed by Jack Green and produced by Bill Paxton, Brian Swardstrom, Mickey Liddell, and David Blocker. Screenplay by Jim McGlynn.

One of the pleasures of *Traveller* is trying to figure out how the scams work. Some of them are easy, like the con where they take worthless crankcase oil and sell it to homeowners as driveway sealant or to farmers as roofing tar. But the last one—a final scam involving two teams of con men dealing in counterfeit money—is so twisted that only later, after the movie, do you understand it.

Travellers are con men of Irish descent who belong to a tightly knit clan based in the American South and travel the highways looking for easy marks. As the film opens, a young man named Pat (Mark Wahlberg), whose father married outside the clan, has returned with his body for burial. His father was banished, but Pat wants back in. The head of the clan, Boss Jack

(Luke Askew), won't have anything to do with him, but a traveller named Bokky (Bill Paxton) takes him under his arm, and they set out together for a life of crime.

If that's all there was to it, *Traveller* would be a standard road picture with a twist. There's more to it. Bokky and Pat pull a complicated scam on a bartender named Jean (Julianna Margulies), and then Bokky regrets it—she's a nice woman—and violates all of his own principles by returning her money. He likes her, and it's headed in the direction of love.

Meanwhile, the two men pick up a fellow traveller (James Gammon). They cooperate on some scams and like to exclaim, "This is the life!" while sitting in a cheap motel room drinking beer (there doesn't seem to be a lot of money in travelling). When Jean needs money for an operation for her daughter, Bokky winds up the incredibly complicated scam involving two kinds of money: real counterfeit money and phony counterfeit money. His intended mark is a bald fat man named Bimbo, played by Vincent Chase with a silky, insinuating quality; like Sydney Greenstreet, Chase is able to suggest he knows all about the sin and has no interest in salvation.

Chase in a way is the most interesting character in the movie. Paxton has an everyman quality that makes it possible to overlook his skill, but here he finds the right way to be true to his criminal career while still scamming: His heart is in the right place, even if his hand is in your pocket. As producer, he supervised the sound track, which has a lot of country swing. And Julianna Margulies, from *ER,* is able to make her bartender tired and hard-pressed, yet filled with promise for the future.

The movie is the directorial debut of Jack Green, the Oscar-winning cinematographer of many Clint Eastwood films (and of *Twister,* where he worked with Paxton). The screenplay by Jim McGlynn, which plays a little like something Eastwood might have made, is subtle and observant; there aren't big plot points but lots of little ones, and the plot allows us the delight of figuring out the scams. Too bad the ending is a surprisingly violent confrontation; that seems to be obligatory these days. The movie should have ended as it began, slyly.

## Trees Lounge ★ ★ ★ ½

R, 96 m., 1996

Steve Buscemi (Tommy), Mark Boone Jr. (Mike), Chloe Sevigny (Debbie), Michael Buscemi (Raymond), Anthony LaPaglia (Rob), Elizabeth Bracco (Theresa), Carol Kane (Connie), Bronson Dudley (Bill), Eszter Balint (Marie), Kevin Corrigan (Matthew). Directed by Steve Buscemi and produced by Kelley Forsyth, Sarah Vogel, Brad Wyman, and Chris Hanley. Screenplay by Buscemi.

If anybody ever wrote a *Field Guide to Alcoholics,* with descriptions of their appearance, sexual behavior, and habitats, there would be a full-color portrait on the cover of Tommy, the hero of *Trees Lounge.* Steve Buscemi, who plays Tommy and wrote and directed the film, knows about alcoholism from the inside out and backward, and his movie is the most accurate portrait of the daily saloon drinker I have ever seen.

Tommy is thirty-one years old, an unemployed auto mechanic. For eight years he dated Theresa (Elizabeth Bracco), but recently she dumped him, married his ex-boss, and is having a baby (maybe Tommy's, but who knows?). Tommy, who lives in an unremarkable section of Long Island, spends his days in Trees Lounge, a corner bar that is perfectly established in an early shot showing Bill, an aging alcoholic, gazing blankly into space before rousing himself to use sign language to order another double shot. The close-up of Bill's face is a complete portrait of a man whose world has grown smaller and smaller, until finally it has defined itself as the task of drinking.

Tommy has a stubborn spirit. He goes through the motions of having fun, but everything in his life is breaking down, including his car, which stalls whenever he removes his foot from the pedal. As a mechanic, you'd think he could fix it, but he uses more direct methods, asking a friend to keep a foot on the gas while Tommy dashes into the lounge for "just one drink." The bartender, who knows him, bets him $10 he can't have just one.

*Trees Lounge* doesn't paint a depressing portrait of Tommy, just a realistic one. Any alcoholic knows that life is not all bad, that there comes a moment between the morning's hangover and the night's oblivion when things are balanced very nicely, and the sun slants in through the bar windows, and there's a good song on the jukebox, and the customers might even start dancing. Tommy makes some headway one afternoon with a woman he meets in the bar; like a lot of drinkers, she can dance better than she can stand.

When I met Buscemi at the 1996 Cannes Film Festival, where *Trees Lounge* premiered, he said the movie was a portrait of a direction his life was going in before he started acting. He remembers it well; remembers such perfect details as a scene where Tommy's drinking buddy, Mike, is fascinated by a stupid bar trick that Johnny is performing ("I'll bet I can drink two beers before you can drink one shot"). Mike's wife, who sees him only during pit stops from his drinking, walks into the bar and essentially wants to tell him she's taking the kid and leaving, but Mike is too interested in the bar trick to focus on this news.

Tommy makes money occasionally by driving a Good Humor truck, although he does not look like a Good Humor man. On his rounds he encounters a seventeen-year-old girl he knows, Debbie (Chloe Sevigny, from *Kids,* who finds just the right note for the role). They spend some time together that leads to a wrestling match at his house. "Nothing happened—we just made out like a couple of teenagers," he later says, but Debbie's father is understandably enraged and destroys the Good Humor truck with a baseball bat.

All of this seeking, drinking, dancing, and wrestling is centered on Tommy's pain because his former girlfriend dumped him. The film comes to its epiphany when he visits Theresa in the maternity ward, and apologizes for being a geek when he dated her, and cries and thinks maybe he could straighten out if he had a kid. Drunks always think that if they could fix all the things that are wrong, then they could stop drinking. It never occurs to them to stop drinking first.

Buscemi is the house act of American independent films. He was the talkative killer in *Fargo,* and Mr. Pink in *Reservoir Dogs,* and has been in more than thirty other recent movies. Critics love to describe him ("skinny, bug-eyed, twitchy"—*New York Times;* "caffeinated downtown geek whose feelings seem to bleed right through his pale vampire skin"—*Entertainment Weekly;* "oyster-eyed"—*Mr. Showbiz*). He is above all able to project the quality of bone-weariness. It is almost a little noble, the way he endures what the disease of alcoholism is putting him through. He keeps planning, dreaming, hoping. And always there is Trees Lounge, where the living dead sit at the bar, waiting for him to return with news of the world.

## Trial and Error ★ ★ ★

PG-13, 106 m., 1997

Michael Richards (Richard Rietti), Jeff Daniels (Charles Tuttle), Alexandra Wentworth (Tiffany), Rip Torn (Benny Gibbs), Charlize Theron (Billie), Jessica Steen (Elizabeth Gardner), Austin Pendleton (Judge Graff). Directed by Jonathan Lynn and produced by Gary Ross and Lynn. Screenplay by Sara Bernstein and Gregory Bernstein.

There is a moment in *Trial and Error* when a woman in love finds out her man is engaged to another woman, and she handles it by telling him she understands. "Look," she says, "it's not a federal case." Then she walks outside his room and starts to cry. What I liked about that scene—especially in a comedy—is that it looked for the truth and not just for the easy sitcom laugh.

In a lazier or more routine movie, the woman—a waitress in a Nevada backwater town—would have exploded, or thrown things, or insulted the guy's fiancée, or done anything other than to react the way a real person might really react. That's why so many comedies aren't funny: They don't go for the humor of truth, but for the kind of machine-made insult comedy that sitcoms extrude by the yard.

*Trial and Error* has some very funny scenes in it—funny because they reflect the natures of the characters. (It has some other scenes that aren't so funny, when characters trip over things and knock things over and we doubt any human being would be so clumsy.) By the end of the film, we actually care what happens to the people in the film, and in a modern comedy, that's rare.

The movie is the starring debut of Michael Richards, a *Seinfeld* regular, who plays a so-so actor named Richard Rietti. He's planning to be the best man at the wedding of his friend Charles Tuttle (Jeff Daniels), a lawyer. Tuttle is engaged to marry the daughter of his boss at the law firm. He's dispatched to Nevada to defend the boss's distant relative, Benny Gibbs (Rip Torn), who is a con man and has been for fifty years. His latest stunt: selling "genuine copper engravings of the Great Emancipator" for $17.99 through the mail, and sending his victims a penny.

Richard sneaks ahead to the small town to throw a surprise bachelor party for Tuttle. Tuttle gets so drunk he can't appear in court the next day. Rietti pretends to be the lawyer, and when a continuance plea is rejected, he ends up facing a desperate choice: continue the masquerade and defend the client, or be arrested for impersonating a lawyer. The two friends work out a makeshift arrangement involving flash cards, horn toots, and other signals by which Tuttle tries, and fails, to control the phony lawyer.

A promising premise. And the director, Jonathan Lynn, has already proven he knows how to handle comedies about fish out of water in the courts of a small town: He made *My Cousin Vinny* five years ago. That was the film that won an Oscar for Marisa Tomei, and again this time he has a key role for a newcomer: Charlize Theron plays Billie, the waitress at the local hotel, who falls in love with Tuttle.

Rip Torn, all guilt and phony wounded dignity, makes the con man into a defendant who obviously should go to jail. Austin Pendleton has a lot of fun playing the judge, a man who finds the case increasingly incredible and hilarious. Jessica Steen has the key but thankless role of playing the prosecuting attorney, but the screenplay saves her from a one-note role by giving her priceless scenes where she cross-examines two of the defense witnesses: One is a "psychiatric expert" who is glib but seems to be about eighteen, and the other, the keystone of Rietti's Twinkie defense, is a "nutritional expert" who explains that the only difference between sugar and cocaine is a few molecules here and there.

The movie reminded me a little of some of Billy Wilder's work in the way he took the characters seriously, or at least as seriously as the material allowed, and got a lot of the laughs by playing scenes straight.

Jeff Daniels is invaluable in films like this (as he was in *Dumb and Dumber*) because he doesn't overplay or sound like he's going for a laugh. And Michael Richards makes the wise decision to play the courtroom scenes not as a buffoon, but as an intelligent guy who's seen too many courtroom movies.

I liked the love affair between the Daniels and Theron characters. I liked the way they seemed comfortable with one another, and the way she projected both love and sympathy. And in a crucial scene, where her eyes are filled with love and forgiveness, and she runs in slow motion across the street toward him, I liked the little touch that she looked both ways first. You'd be surprised how many movie heroines would run across the street without looking in a scene like that. Surprising more of them aren't traffic victims.

## Troublesome Creek: A Midwestern ★ ★ ★

NO MPAA RATING, 88 m., 1997

A documentary directed and produced by Jeanne Jordan and Steven Ascher. Screenplay by Jordan and Ascher. Featuring Russel and Mary Jane Jordan and their family.

There were 6 million family farms in 1960, but there are only 2 million now. That is a fact. Mary Jane Jordan saw her beloved Ethan Allen dining room table sold at auction for only $105. That is an experience. The gift of every good reporter is to turn the facts into experiences, so that we can understand what they mean and how they feel. *Troublesome Creek: A Midwestern* sees the disappearance of the family farm through the eyes of one Iowa family, the Jordans, who have been farming the same land since 1867.

The movie is narrated by their daughter Jeanne and filmed by her husband, Steven Ascher. They codirected it during a series of several trips back to the farm from their home in Cambridge, Massachusetts. They present the story of her parents, Russ and Mary Jane Jordan, not as a tragedy but as a response to very hard times.

The Jordan place is what we all think of as a farm: It could be a movie set. There's a big clapboard house, lots of well-tended outbuildings, silos, hogs, cows, and rich flat fields. Russ worries about the livestock and crops, and Mary Jane worries about the bills; we often see her on the telephone, talking to her contact at the bank about another short-term loan. The Jordans are both about seventy. She was state 4-H president in high school. He once placed second in an Abe Lincoln look-alike contest.

They have a son, Jim, who is farming rented land nearby. "What many people fail to realize," Jeanne explains on the sound track, "is that sons have to move off the farm where they were born and work a rented farm until their father retires or dies and they can inherit the family place." Jim is the obvious heir since the other Jordan children have moved into town; there isn't a living for a big family from this land.

As the film begins, the Jordans face a crisis. Farm prices have fallen and they've gotten $70,000 in debt to the bank, in addition to their annual $150,000 loan. The local bank has been absorbed into a megabank named Norwest, which has a tower in Des Moines from which tidy young men telephone with news of "risk ratios." It is unlikely the Jordans can get more credit.

We see flashbacks to better days and photographs of all the Jordans who have worked this land, including the great-great-grandfather who came out to Iowa from Ohio after the Civil War. During a visit home, Jeanne and her husband join her parents in visiting the farm where she was raised—the rented farm her father worked while waiting for *his* father to retire. "When I was a child I didn't even know we rented this farm," she says. "I thought of it as home." The clothesline trees are still in the yard and a closet door still shows signs of an unwise orange paint job, but the farm is abandoned. "I wouldn't think a place could go down this bad in fifteen years," says Russ.

He looks a little like Gary Cooper. Mary Jane could pose for Bisquick commercials. They like to watch Westerns on TV, and their daughter casts their story as a "Midwestern," a last stand by heroic figures against the onslaught of the bankers.

Then more bad news arrives; the farm Jim rents is being sold. He owns equipment, but has no place to use it. Russ devises a plan. He and his wife will sell everything—their livestock, farm machinery, house, possessions, everything—to pay off the bank debt and keep the land. They'll move to town (they know a little house that's walking distance from Van's Chat and Chew) and Jim will work the land with his machinery.

The film follows the preparations for the big auction sale with details that will be familiar to many who have never been on a farm. Mary Jane cannot bring herself to part with certain items—a plant stand, her collections of saucers and spoons—but she believes fondly that her treasured Ethan Allen dining room set, protected from scratches all these years with pads, will get a good price. I remember my mother speculating about the untold fortune she was convinced her Hummel figurines would bring.

The table goes for almost nothing. Mary Jane bites her lip in disbelief. But the plan keeps the wolf from the door for the time being, and Jim takes up the struggle of all the Jordans before him.

The underlying lesson is clear: Our state and federal farm policies do not really allow for family farms anymore. Corporations and conglomerates now farm the land, with men paid by the day or the week. Big banks don't much care. Small banks are sold to big banks. When Russ calls up Des Moines to tell the bankers he can pay off the loan, he says they're happy to hear the good news. "Daddy, that's just guilt!" his daughter tells him. "You don't have to make it so easy for them!"

In Gary Sinise's *Miles From Home* (1988), Richard Gere and Kevin Anderson starred as two brothers unable to make a go of their family's Iowa farm, which had been visited by Khrushchev as the "farm of the year" in 1959. Filled with drama and action, it was a pretty good film. Now here is the everyday face of the same story. Should we make it easier for family farms? Yes. Why? Because they represent something we think America stands for. Strange how for all the talk of individualism and resourcefulness from politicians, our country drifts every year closer to a totalitarianism of the corporation.

## The Truman Show ★ ★ ★ ★

PG, 104 m., 1998

Jim Carrey (Truman Burbank), Laura Linney (Meryl), Noah Emmerich (Marlon), Natascha McElhone (Lauren/Sylvia), Holland Taylor (Mother), Ed Harris (Christof), Brian Delate (Kirk), Paul Giamatti (Simeon). Directed by Peter Weir and produced by Scott Rudin, Andrew Niccol, Edward S. Feldman, and Adam Schroeder. Screenplay by Niccol.

*The Truman Show* is founded on an enormous secret, which all of the studio's advertising has been determined to reveal. I didn't know the secret when I saw the film, and was able to enjoy the little doubts and wonderings that the filmmakers so carefully planted. If by some good chance you do not know the secret, read no further.

Those fortunate audience members (I trust they have all left the room?) will be able to appreciate the meticulous way director Peter Weir and writer Andrew Niccol have constructed a jigsaw plot around their central character, who doesn't suspect that he's living his entire life on live television. Yes, he lives in an improbably ideal world, but I fell for that: I assumed the movie was taking a sitcom view of life, in which neighbors greet each other over white picket fences, and Ozzie and Harriet are real people.

Actually, it's Seaside, a planned community on the Gulf Coast near Panama City. Called Seahaven in the movie, it looks like a nice place to live. Certainly Truman Burbank (Jim Carrey) doesn't know anything else. You accept the world you're given, the filmmakers suggest; more thoughtful viewers will get the buried message, which is that we accept almost everything in our lives without examining it very closely. When was the last time you reflected on how really odd a tree looks?

Truman works as a sales executive at an insurance company, is happily married to Meryl (Laura Linney), and doesn't find it suspicious that she describes household products in the language of TV commercials. He is happy, in a way, but an uneasiness gnaws away at him. Something is missing, and he thinks perhaps he might find it in Fiji, where Lauren (Natascha McElhone), the only woman he really loved, has allegedly moved with her family.

Why did she leave so quickly? Perhaps because she was not a safe bet for Truman's world: The actress who played her (named Sylvia) developed real feeling and pity for Truman, and felt he should know the truth about his existence. Meryl, on the other hand, is a reliable pro (which raises the question, unanswered, of their sex life).

Truman's world is controlled by a TV producer named Christof (Ed Harris), whose control room is high in the artificial dome that provides the sky and horizon of Seahaven. He discusses his programming on talk shows, and dismisses the protests of those (including Sylvia) who believe Truman is the victim of a cruel deception. Meanwhile, the whole world watches Truman's every move, and some viewers even leave the TV on all night as he sleeps.

The trajectory of the screenplay is more or less inevitable: Truman must gradually realize the truth of his environment and try to escape from it. It's clever the way he's kept on his island by implanted traumas about travel and water. As the story unfolds, however, we're not simply expected to follow it; we're invited to think about the implications. About a world in which modern communications make celebrity possible, and inhuman.

Until fairly recently, the only way you could become really famous was to be royalty, or a writer, actor, preacher, or politician—and even then, most people had knowledge of you only through words or printed pictures. Television, with its insatiable hunger for material, has made celebrities into "content," devouring their lives and secrets. If you think *The Truman Show* is an exaggeration, reflect that Princess Diana lived under similar conditions from the day she became engaged to Charles.

Carrey is a surprisingly good choice to play Truman. We catch glimpses of his manic comic persona, just to make us comfortable with his presence in the character, but this is a well-planned performance; Carrey is on the right note as a guy raised to be liked and likable, who decides his life requires more risk and hardship. Like the angels in *City of Angels,* he'd like to take his chances.

Ed Harris finds the right notes as Christof, the TV Svengali. He uses the technospeak by which we distance ourselves from the real meanings of our words. (If TV producers ever spoke frankly about what they were really doing, they'd come across like Bulworth.) For Harris, the demands of the show take precedence over any other values, and if you think that's an exaggeration, tell it to the TV news people who broadcast that Los Angeles suicide.

I enjoyed *The Truman Show* on its levels of comedy and drama; I *liked* Truman in the same way I liked Forrest Gump—because he was a good man, honest and easy to sympathize with. But the underlying ideas made the movie more than just an entertainment. Like *Gattaca,* the previous film written by Niccol, it brings into focus the new values that technology is forcing on humanity. Because we can engineer genetics, because we can telecast real lives—of course we must, right? But are these good things to do? The irony is, the people who will finally answer that question will be the very ones produced by the process. ☞

## The Truth About Cats and Dogs ★ ★ ★ ½

PG-13, 97 m., 1996

Janeane Garofalo (Abby), Uma Thurman (Noelle), Ben Chaplin (Brian), Jamie Foxx (Ed), James McCaffrey (Roy), Richard Coca (Eric), Stanley DeSantis (Mario). Directed by Michael Lehmann and produced by Cari-Esta Albert. Screenplay by Audrey Wells.

*The Truth About Cats and Dogs* is one of those warmhearted, quick-footed comedies that's light as a feather, fueled by coincidence, and depends above all on the luminosity of its performers. Janeane Garofalo in this movie, like Sandra Bullock in *While You Were Sleeping*, is so likable, so sympathetic, so revealing of her character's doubts and desires, that she carries us headlong into the story.

Garofalo plays Abby, a veterinarian who gives advice to pet owners over a talk radio station in Santa Monica. Her callers have the sorts of problems I suspect all pet owners secretly have. One is concerned about a cat that won't stop licking its owner's face. Another has depressed fish. A third is trying to deal with a Great Dane on roller skates. The dog is a pretty good skater, but it has understandably grown disturbed and won't let anyone near it.

This last caller is Brian (Ben Chaplin), and as he talks we see his Great Dane whizzing past on skates. It's the kind of surrealistic image that blindsides you; beyond language, beyond logic, it's intrinsically funny. As Abby dispenses advice about roller-skating dogs, Brian finds himself strangely attracted to her voice—to its intelligence and tone, and to a quality that calls out to some need within him.

He asks Abby to meet him. "Why," she asks, "would I meet a listener I know nothing about except that he puts roller skates on his dog?" But there is something in his voice, maybe in his British accent, that appeals to a need in her, and God knows she's needy, since her social life is in disrepair. She agrees to meet him. He asks how he will recognize her. Abby is struck with an attack of insecurity; she doesn't think of herself as attractive, and so she describes a person who is her opposite: "I'm tall and blond."

She knows such a person: Noelle (Uma Thurman), her neighbor, whose romantic life is crumbling (Noelle has a bully for a boyfriend, who thinks nothing of breaking the bow of Abby's violin over his knee). When Brian calls for her at the radio station, Abby in desperation begs Noelle to go out with him—to pretend to be her. But poor Noelle is not very bright. At least not when she is with Brian and pretending to be Abby. When Brian goes home and calls Abby on the phone, however, a miraculous transformation seems to take place; Abby becomes a delightful, seductive, witty conversationalist, and one night she and Brian talk for hours, until dawn, gradually drawing a web of seduction and passion around themselves.

This story is yet another retooling of the legend of Cyrano de Bergerac, the pudding-faced dreamer who loved the great beauty Roxanne, and wrote her inspired love letters while stage-managing a courtship by his handsome but doltish friend Christian. The story of Cyrano was first told in the seventeenth century, and was made into an enduring play by Edmond Rostand in 1897. It has been remade countless times; José Ferrer won an Oscar as Cyrano in 1950, Steve Martin updated the story in *Roxanne* (1987), and Gérard Depardieu got an Oscar nomination for best actor for his version in 1990. Now here is Janeane Garofalo in a gender switch for the story, which plays just as well, because who cannot identify with it? Who does not like to believe that true love exists between two hearts and minds, not between two faces, and that love can overleap such trifles as physical appearance?

*The Truth About Cats and Dogs* is not simply another version of the old story, however. It includes a lot of humor that is generated by its specific situation. Much of it does indeed have to do with cats and dogs (and with a convincing demonstration of how to get a tortoise to stick its head out of its shell). And then there is the matter of Noelle, the best friend. In Uma Thurman's hands she does not simply become a pawn, a false front for Abby. There is a poignance in her situation, because she loves Brian too, in her way, and handles a difficult situation with unexpected sweetness.

Of course, all movies like this toy a little with the odds. The movie is based upon the presumption that Janeane Garofalo is not pretty, and of course she is. She has never been allowed to appear particularly appealing on screen, however; after an apprenticeship on *Saturday Night Live* she broke into the movies as the date from hell in *Bye Bye Love* and Winona Ryder's best friend in *Reality Bites.* In both roles she was blunt, abrasive, and took no hostages—although she was more likable in the second. Here we see an entirely other side to her personality; a smartness, a penetrating wit, that takes this old story and adds a wry spin to its combination of romance, sweetness, and hope.

## Turbulence ★

R, 100 m., 1997

Ray Liotta (Ryan Weaver), Lauren Holly (Teri Halloran), Brendan Gleeson (Stubbs), Hector Elizondo (Detective Aldo Hines), Catherine Hicks (Maggie), Rachel Ticotin (Rachel Taper), Ben Cross (Captain Sam Bowen). Directed by Robert Butler and produced by Martin Ransohoff and David Valdes. Screenplay by Jonathan Brett.

*Turbulence* thrashes about like a formula action picture that has stepped on a live wire: It's dead, but doesn't stop moving. It looks like it cost a lot of money, but none of that money went into quality. It's schlock, hurled at the screen in expensive gobs.

The plot involves an endangered 747 flight from New York to Los Angeles. It's Christmas Eve, and there are only about a dozen passengers on board, including two prisoners and their federal marshals (anyone who has flown around Christmastime knows how empty the planes always are). One prisoner gets a gun and shoots some of the marshals, after which the other prisoner—the really dangerous one—gets a gun and kills the rest, including both pilots and one flight attendant. He locks the remaining hostages in the "crew quarters," where they are forgotten for most of the picture.

This prisoner is Ryan Weaver (Ray Liotta), a.k.a. the Lonely Hearts Killer. He claims the evidence against him was faked by an L.A. cop (Hector Elizondo). In a performance that seems like an anthology of possible acting choices, Liotta goes from charmer to intelligent negotiator to berserk slasher to demented madman. My favorite moment is when he's covered with blood, the plane is buckling through a Level 6 storm, bodies are littered everywhere, and he's singing "Buffalo Gals, Won't You Come Out Tonight?"

This is one of those movies where you keep asking questions. Questions like, how much money does an airline lose by flying a 747 from New York to L.A. with a dozen passengers on board? Like, do passengers board 747s from the rear door? Like, can a 747 fly upside down? Like, have you ever seen Christmas decorations inside an airplane (lights and wreaths and bows and mistletoe)? Like, why don't the oxygen masks drop down automatically when the cabin depressurizes—and why do they drop down later, during a fire? Like, do storms reach as high as the cruising altitude of a transcontinental flight?

The big conflict involves the Lonely Hearts Killer and two flight attendants. One of them (Catherine Hicks) is strangled fairly early. The other (Lauren Holly) wages a heroic fight after both pilots are killed. It's up to her to fend off the madman and somehow land the big plane. Holly's performance is the key to the movie, and it's not very good: She screams a lot and keeps shouting "Ooohhh!" but doesn't generate much charisma, and frankly I wish the killer had strangled her and left the more likable Hicks to land the plane.

The 747 spends much time weathering a big storm ("It's a Level 6!" "Is that on a scale of 1 to 10?" "No! It's on a scale of 1 to 6!"). The storm causes all of the lights inside the plane to flash on and off, including the Christmas lights. That lends to extended sequences in which the attendant and the madman crawl around the aisles in darkness illuminated by lightning bolts—and then there's the big moment when the plane flies upside down and they get to crawl on the ceiling.

On the ground, events are monitored in the Los Angeles control tower. The pilot of another 747 (Ben Cross) talks the brave attendant through the landing procedure, while a stern FBI agent argues that the plane should be shot down by the Air Force before it crashes in an inhabited area. Eventually he orders a fighter plane to fire—although by then the plane is already over Los Angeles and looks as if it would crash more or less into Disneyland.

There are more questions. Like, if a 747 sheers off the roof of a high-rise restaurant, wouldn't that cause it to crash? Like, if a 747 plows through an outdoor billboard, wouldn't that cause it to crash? Like, if it sweeps all the cars off the roof of a parking garage, wouldn't that cause it to crash? Like, if it gets a truck caught in its landing gear, what would happen then? ("It's a Ford!" a sharp-eyed observer says, in a line that—for once—I don't think represents product placement.)

Oh, yes, there are many moments I will long remember from *Turbulence*. But one stands out. After Lauren Holly outsmarts and outfights the berserk killer and pilots the plane through a Level 6 storm, the FBI guy still doubts she can land it. "She's only a stewardess," he says. To which the female air traffic controller standing next to him snaps, "She's a—flight attendant!"

## Twelfth Night ★ ★ ★ ½

PG, 125 m., 1996

Imogen Stubbs (Viola/Cesario), Helena Bonham Carter (Olivia), Richard E. Grant (Sir Andrew Aguecheek), Nigel Hawthorne (Malvolio), Ben Kingsley (Feste), Mel Smith (Sir Toby Belch), Imelda Staunton (Maria), Toby Stephens (Orsino), Stephen Mackintosh (Sebastian). Directed by Trevor Nunn and produced by Stephen Evans and David Parfitt. Screenplay by Nunn, based on the play by William Shakespeare.

Shakespeare's *Twelfth Night* bears something of the same relationship to his serious romances (like *Romeo and Juliet*) that, if you will forgive the comparison, *Airplane!* bears to *Airport*. Adjust for period, genre, and style, and acknowledge the fact that Shakespeare occupies a different creative universe than, say, David Zucker, and the intention is the same: Elements that are heartbreaking when handled seriously become funny when they're pushed over the top.

Trevor Nunn's new film version of *Twelfth Night*, a lighthearted comedy of romance and gender confusion, creates a romantic triangle out of the same sort of mistaken sexual identities that inspired *Some Like It Hot*. And Nunn directs it in something of the same spirit; the film winks at us while the characters fall in love. To be sure, Imogen Stubbs makes a better boy than Jack Lemmon made a girl, but nobody's perfect.

The period has been moved up to the eighteenth century, and the dialogue has been slightly simplified and clarified, but Shakespeare's language is largely intact (and easier to understand than in Baz Luhrmann's new *Romeo and Juliet*). Also intact is the elaborate low-comedy subplot involving the servants, which gets too much screen time relative to the main story, but supplies showcases for a ribald cast of character actors.

The story: A great storm at sea capsizes a ship. A young woman named Viola (Imogen Stubbs) is washed ashore, but believes her twin brother, Sebastian, has drowned. Finding herself in the unfamiliar kingdom of Ilyria, where a young woman might be at hazard, she dresses in her brother's uniform, cuts her hair, pastes on a false mustache, and poses as a young man named Cesario.

Soon she wins a position at the court of young Count Orsino (Toby Stephens), who is desperately in love with the lady Olivia (Helena Bonham Carter). The count sends his new page to stand before Olivia's gate and press his case. But there are complications: Viola falls in love with Orsino, and Olivia falls in love with Viola. Since Viola cannot tell either one she is really a woman, almost every situation involving her is rich with double meaning.

*Twelfth Night* has been directed by Trevor Nunn, for twenty years a stalwart of the Royal Shakespeare Company. He knows the material and knows the right actors to play it. Shakespeare's language is not hard to understand when spoken by actors who are comfortable with the rhythm and know the meaning. It can be impenetrable when declaimed by unseasoned actors with more energy than experience (as the screaming gang members in *Romeo and Juliet* demonstrate).

Nunn's casting choices make for real chemistry between Imogen Stubbs and Helena Bonham Carter (whose film debut was in Nunn's film, *Lady Jane*, in 1986). Bonham Carter, who has grown wonderfully as an actress, walks the thin line between love and comedy as she sighs for the fair youth who has come on behalf of the count. She wisely plays the role sincerely, leaving the winks to the other characters.

Shakespeare's comedies all offered two levels, high and low, and here the bawdy is handled by Mel Smith as Olivia's kinsman Sir Toby Belch, Richard E. Grant as his foppish and absurd friend Sir Andrew Aguecheek, and Ben Kingsley as the troubadour Feste. But the downstairs action is stolen by Nigel Hawthorne *(The Madness of George III)* as Malvolio, Olivia's chief of staff, who convinces himself Olivia loves him. Swollen with his self-importance, proud that he is impervious to the failings of mortals, he falls hard, and Shakespeare is just barely able to save his heart from breaking.

Nunn sets up all of these tensions and misunderstandings in an enchanting, beguiling style, and then lobs in a grenade with the unexpected arrival of the twin brother, Sebastian. The last scenes are exercises in double takes and sly timing. All's well that ends well, of course, but the full title of the play provides a better key: *Twelfth Night, or, What You Will.* Since the notion of romantic love is what all of the characters are really in love with, it matters not so much who they love as that they love, allowing for the quick adjustments of focus at the end.

The movie's key player is Imogen Stubbs, who was Emma Thompson's rival in the 1995 *Sense and Sensibility* (she was the character Hugh Grant was engaged to, against his druthers). Here she has just that reserve that makes her character's ridiculous situation work. She must contain her feelings about both Orsino and Olivia, even in such touchy situations as when scrubbing her employer's back in the bath. It calls for perfect tact, which she was born with, along with a twinkle in her eye.

## 12 Monkeys ★ ★ ★

R, 130 m., 1996

Bruce Willis (James Cole), Madeleine Stowe (Kathryn Railly), Brad Pitt (Jeffrey Goines), Christopher Plummer (Dr. Goines). Directed by Terry Gilliam and produced by Charles Roven. Screenplay by David and Janet Peoples.

Terry Gilliam's ambitious *12 Monkeys* was coauthored by David Peoples, who wrote *Blade Runner,* and it has the same view of the near future as a grunge pit—a view it shares with Gilliam's own *Brazil.* In this world everything is rusty, subterranean, and leaks. The movie uses its future world as a home base and launching pad for the central story, which is set in 1990 and 1996, and is about a time traveler trying to save the world from a deadly plague.

The traveler is Cole (Bruce Willis), who in the opening shots lives with a handful of other human survivors in an underground shelter put together out of scrap parts and a lot of wire mesh. The surface of the planet has been reclaimed once again by animals, after the death of five billion people in a plague in 1996.

Cole is plucked from his cage and sent on a surface expedition by the rulers of this domain, who hope to learn enough about the plague virus to defeat it. Later he is picked for a more crucial mission: He will travel back in time and gather information about the virus before it mutated. (The movie holds out no hope that he can "stop" it before it starts; from his point of view, the plague has already happened, and so the future society is seeking treatment, not prevention.)

Cole lands in 1990, bruised, bleeding, and dripping sweat and mucus from every pore (a large percentage of Bruce Willis's total screen career has been spent in this condition). He's thrown in jail, and assigned a psychiatrist (Madeleine Stowe), who believes he's delusional when he says he's a visitor from the future ("You won't think I'm crazy when people start dying next month"). He pulls off an inexplicable jail break, and reappears in her life in 1996, kidnapping her because he needs help in finding twelve monkeys in Philadelphia that have the virus in its "pure" form before it mutated, later that year, into a killer of humans.

Cole discovers that a mental patient named Jeffrey (Brad Pitt), whom he met in 1990, is an animal rights activist with a father (Christopher Plummer) whose laboratory may be harboring the deadly virus. Does Jeffrey want to unleash the virus, returning the earth to the animals? Or does his father, or another member of the team . . .

All of this is just the plumbing of the plot. What the movie is really about is its vision. The decor of the movie looks cobbled together from the debris of the twentieth century. Cities are either scabby skid rows or towering skyscrapers. Scientists still work in laboratories that look like old postcards of Edison, inventing. Bizarre killers and villains are hurled at Cole and the psychiatrist, and there are many bloody fights. And gradually the psychiatrist comes to believe, after Cole makes a series of accurate predictions, that he may be from the future after all.

The movie is not, however, a straight forward action thriller. Much of the interest comes from the nature of the Cole character. He is simple, confused, badly informed, exhausted, and shot through with feelings of betrayal. Nothing is as it seems—not in his future world, not in 1990, and not in 1996. And there is another factor, one hinted at in the opening shot of the movie and confirmed in the closing: He may have already witnessed the end of the story.

The plot of *12 Monkeys,* if you follow it closely, involves a time travel paradox. Almost all time travel movies do. But who cares? What's good about the film is the way Gilliam, his actors, and his craftspeople create a universe that is contained within 130 minutes. There are relatively few shots in this movie that would look normal in any other film; everything is skewed to express the vision.

Gilliam's *Brazil* was praised by a lot of critics, but I didn't get it, even after repeated viewings. *12 Monkeys* is easier to follow, with a plot that holds together and a solid relationship between Cole and the psychiatrist. But even here, Gilliam allows the anarchic flywheel of madness to spin: The Brad Pitt character, spewing compulsive visions of paranoia and dread, is a powerful influence, suggesting that logic cannot solve the movie's problems. And other characters—those in charge of the subterranean future world, as well as the conspirators around the Plummer character—behave like villains pumped in from an H. G. Wells science-fiction fantasy. Wild overacting takes place on bizarre sets that are photographed with tilt shots and wide-angle lenses, and we begin to share the confusion and exhaustion of Cole. Like him, we're wrenched back and forth through time, and dumped on the concrete floor of reality.

One of the most intriguing sequences is completely arbitrary. Cole and the woman hide out in a movie theater playing Hitchcock's *Vertigo,* and later, in their own lives, replay the movie's key scene, with the same music on the sound track. What is Gilliam doing here? Not simply providing a movie in-joke. The point, I think, is that Cole's own life is caught between rewind and fast-forward, and he finds himself repeating in the past what he learned in the future, and vice versa.

I've seen *12 Monkeys* described as a comedy. Any laughs that it inspires will be very hollow. It's more of a celebration of madness and doom, with a hero who tries to prevail against the chaos of his condition, and is inadequate. This vision is a cold, dark, damp one, and even the romance between Willis and Stowe feels desperate rather than joyous. All of this is done very well, and the more you know about movies (especially the technical side) the more you're likely to admire it. But a comedy it's not. And as an entertainment it appeals more to the mind than to the senses.

## TwentyFourSeven ★ ★

R, 96 m., 1998

Bob Hoskins (Alan Darcy), Frank Harper (Ronnie Marsh), Pamela Cundell (Auntie Iris), Danny Nussbaum (Tim), James Hooton (Knighty), Darren O. Campbell (Daz), Justin Brady (Gadget), Jimmy Hynd (Meggy). Directed by Shane Meadows and produced by Imogen West. Screenplay by Meadows and Paul Fraser.

I've never been able to understand why boxing is so often recommended as a worthwhile pastime for idle lads in depressed areas. As a possible avenue to future employment, it ranks well below the chances of making it in the NBA, and has the added inconvenience that you get hit all the time. There is, in fact, almost no legitimate job that depends on boxing skills, unless it be nightclub bouncing.

And yet there's a whole body of films about earnest reformers who look around the neighborhood, see young men who are unemployed and aimless, and decide that what they need is a boxing club. Just this year we've had Jim Sheridan's *The Boxer,* with Daniel Day-Lewis as an ex-IRA man who starts a club in Belfast, and now Shane Meadows's *TwentyFourSeven,* with Bob Hoskins starting a club in the British Midlands.

Although both seem to feel that practicing the manly art will help their members develop self-confidence and personal goals, I'm more persuaded by the theory that if they spend all day beating up each other they'll be too tired in the evening to beat up civilians. Another motive, in *The Boxer,* is to run the club along nonsectarian lines, so that Catholics and Protestants can pound each other without regard for sect or creed.

*TwentyFourSeven* takes place in a desolate postindustrial wasteland in England, where the unemployed are warehoused in government housing and spend their days watching the telly, visiting the pub, and weighing the possibilities of petty crime. Their idea of amusement is to spit in a friend's chips when he isn't looking.

Into this bleak prospect comes Bob Hoskins, a former local lad who remembers when there was a boxing club and times were better. He determines to start the club again, and recruits the local louts, including one who's better off than the others because his dad is a gangster. The gangster is happy to see his son's days fruitfully occupied and helps underwrite the club, although in an excess of zeal (or bad timing) he manages to knock Hoskins unconscious against his car, and then complains about the blood on his paint job.

Hoskins, as he often does, brings a sweetness and conviction to his character. He conducts an inarticulate romantic campaign aimed at a local shop girl who is not interested, and in one of the film's best scenes he takes an aged aunt dancing. There's a certain humor in the boxing sequences (the first match turns into a brawl), and a good feeling for local color. But the personal tragedy of the Hoskins character evolves unconvincingly from the story of the boxing club, and I was left with the curious impression that the director would have rather made a documentary and not told a story at all.

## Twilight ★ ★

R, 104 m., 1998

Paul Newman (Harry Ross), Susan Sarandon (Catherine Ames), Gene Hackman (Jack Ames), Stockard Channing (Verna), Reese Witherspoon (Mel Ames), Giancarlo Esposito (Reuben), James Garner (Raymond Hope), Liev Schreiber (Jeff Willis), Margo Martindale (Gloria Lamar), John Spencer (Captain Phil Egan), M. Emmet Walsh (Lester Ivar). Directed by Robert Benton and produced by Arlene Donovan and Scott Rudin. Screenplay by Benton and Richard Russo.

Before a concert, the orchestra members warm up by playing snatches of difficult passages from familiar scores. *Twilight* is a movie that feels like that: The filmmakers, seasoned professionals, perform familiar scenes from the world of *film noir.* They do riffs, they noodle a little, they provide snatches from famous arias. But the curtain never goes up.

The reason to see the film is to observe how relaxed and serene Paul Newman is before the camera. How, at seventy-two, he has absorbed everything he needs to know about how to be a movie actor, so that at every moment he is at home in his skin and the skin of his character. It's sad to see all that assurance used in the service of a plot so worn and mechanical. Marcello Mastroianni, who in his humor, ease, and sex appeal resembled Newman, chose more challenging projects at a similar stage in his life.

The other veterans in the cast are Gene Hackman, Susan Sarandon, and James Garner. They know as much about acting as Newman does, although the film gives them fewer opportunities to display it. Garner, indeed, is the man to call if you need an actor who can slip beneath even Newman's level of comfortability. But the movie's story is too obvious in its message, and too absurd in its plotting.

The message: The characters are nearing the end of the line. They know the moves but are losing the daylight. "Your prostate started acting up yet?" Garner asks Newman. After Newman's character is shot in the groin, the rumor goes around that he's no longer a candidate for the full monty. What kind of a private eye doesn't have any privates? For all of the characters, this is the last hurrah, and that's especially true for Hackman's, who is dying of cancer.

The plot: Harry, the Newman character, is described as "cop, private investigator, drunk, husband, father." He has failed at all of those roles, and now, sober, broke, single, and retired, he lives on the estate of Jack and Catherine Ames (Hackman and Sarandon), movie stars who are old friends. One day Jack gives him a package to deliver. At the address he's sent to, he discovers Lester, a dying man (M. Emmet Walsh) whom someone has already shot. When he goes to the man's apartment, he finds newspaper clippings from twenty years ago, about the death of Catherine Ames's first husband.

Were Catherine or Jack involved in the murder? Who was paying for the investigation? Harry wants to know. His trail leads him to Raymond Hope (Garner), a guy he knew on the force, who has made a lot of money as a studio security chief, and lives very well. It also leads to Catherine's bedroom. He's had a crush on her for years, but no sooner is there a romantic breakthrough than the intercom rings: Jack is having an attack.

Jack discovers Catherine's infidelity through the kind of clue (she's wearing Harry's polo shirt) that seems left over from much older films. Harry knows Catherine was at the apartment where Lester died, because he smelled her perfume there. These are clues at the Perry Mason level, but the complete explanation, when it comes, doesn't depend on them. It's lowered into the film from the sky.

The screenplay, by director Robert Benton and his cowriter, Richard Russo, is bits and pieces. The movie appeals because we like the actors, not because we care about their characters. They're like living beings caught in a clockwork mechanism. Also caught are several characters who hang around the periphery without enough to do: Stockard Channing as a cop Harry's fooled around with in the past, and Giancarlo Esposito as a limo driver who turns up out of nowhere and becomes an inexplicable sidekick. Reese Witherspoon plays the sexpot Ames daughter.

Newman's previous film, *Nobody's Fool,* was also written and directed by Benton, based on a novel by Russo. It gave Newman one of his great roles, as an aging failure, still able to dream, hope, and repair the wreckage of a life. Here we have essentially the same character description, including the same roguish, unflagging sexuality, but the payoff isn't a rich human portrait, it's a contrived manipulation of arbitrary devices from old crime stories. Who cares?

## Twin Town ★ ★

NO MPAA RATING, 99 m., 1997

Llyr Evans (Julian), Rhys Ifans (Jeremy), William Thomas (Bryn Cartwright), Dorien Thomas (Greyo), Dougray Scott (Terry), Biddug Williams (Mrs. Mort), Ronnie Williams (Mr. Mort), Huw Ceredig (Fatty), Rachel Scorgie (Adie). Directed by Kevin Allen and produced by Peter McAleese. Screenplay by Allen and Paul Durden.

When Bill Clinton warned the fashion industry about heroin chic, perhaps he could have steered it toward films like *Twin Town* from Wales or *Trainspotting* from Scotland—two films in which drugs play a role and chic definitely does not.

*Twin Town* is a grotty examination of sordid lives, a reminder that many colorful characters are colorful only from a distance. The movie takes place in Swansea, Wales, a town that the Welsh poet Dylan Thomas once referred to as "the graveyard of ambition"—and he was a local boy, mind you. I have friends who live there, and who assure me that most of the creeps in the film live on the other side of town. I hope for their sake they are right.

The story involves two families who work up an extremely unpleasant disagreement after the father of one clan falls off a ladder while working on a roof. Fatty (Huw Ceredig) is injured, and his twin grandsons see that as a golden opportunity for an out-of-court settlement. The roof belongs to Bryn Cartwright (William Thomas), a contractor, property developer, and occasional cocaine dealer, who takes great pride in the greens of the local football club, which he controls along with most of the rest of the town. Cartwright won't pay, and that leads to an undeclared war in which pet dogs are beheaded and house trailers are set on fire.

The twins are Julian (Llyr Evans) and Jeremy (Rhys Ifans). They're actually not twins, only brothers, but everyone calls them twins (and they are played by brothers, despite the difference in the spellings of their names). How to describe them? If you saw them coming, you'd lock up your daughters, your sheep, and perhaps even your turtles. Swansea is not the graveyard of their ambition, only because they never had any.

They live in a trailer on the outskirts of town, where the arts are manifested only in nail-painting. The Cartwrights live in a nicer house, where Bryn plays with model trains. The mothers in both families are dim-witted, and the children have not turned out well.

The plot veers uneasily between comedy and pathos, with episodes of gore. There are beatings, a murder, lots of drugs, two crooked and dim-witted cops, the savage destruction of a soccer field, a particularly unpleasant hanging method, and also, lest we forget, karaoke sessions, a massage parlor, and a peculiarly poetic ending involving a local choir (one can just glimpse, at times, what must be the very pleasant other side of town).

I was not sure where the movie wanted to go and what it wanted to do; this despite the fact that it goes many places and does too much. Somewhere buried within it is a sweeter, more lighthearted story about its feckless lads, and then the hard-edged *Trainspotting* angle seems to have been added. But while *Trainspotting* had a clear vision and found a way to move confidently between comedy and the appalling, *Twin Town* is less surefooted.

The movie's executive producers are Danny Boyle and Andrew McDonald, who were the director and producer of *Trainspotting.* Its director, Kevin Allen, is the brother of Keith Allen, an actor in *Trainspotting.* The connection is obvious: This film wants to do for (or to) Wales what the other did for Scotland. Some audiences will have trouble with the accents, but I find that in films like this (and Gary Oldman's much superior *Nil by Mouth*) it isn't the words but the music, and you can nearly always sense pretty easily what is being said. *Twin Town* makes things easier by using variations of the same four-letter word as roughly a sixth of its dialogue.

## Twister ★ ★

PG-13, 117 m., 1996

Helen Hunt (Jo Harding), Bill Paxton (Bill Harding), Cary Elwes (Dr. Jonas Miller), Jami Gertz (Melissa), Lois Smith (Aunt Meg), Alan Ruck (Rabbit), Philip Hoffman (Dusty). Directed by Jan De Bont and produced by Kathleen Kennedy, Ian Bryce, and Michael Crichton. Screenplay by Crichton and Anne-Marie Martin.

Melissa is not happy. One minute she's engaged to handsome young Bill Harding, who has a promising career as a TV weatherman ahead of him. The next minute, she's cowering in a pickup truck while tornadoes blow houses at her. And Bill can't wait to find another tornado. "When you told me you wanted to chase tornadoes," she tells him, "I thought that was a metaphor."

It is a metaphor, Melissa, but not for Bill's dream. It's a metaphor for *Twister,* a movie that chases tornadoes with such single-minded dedication that plot, character, dialogue, and even your engagement all disappear into the Suck Zone—which is, we learn, that part of the tornado that sucks up everything in its path. By the end of the film, we have seen trees, TV towers, drive-in theaters, trucks, houses, barns, and even cows sucked up by the Zone. Well, maybe only one cow. "I think it's the same one, coming past again," Bill tells Jo.

Jo (Helen Hunt) is his first wife. Jo and Bill (Bill Paxton) worked happily together as storm chasers for several years, before something went out of their marriage (the movie is too breathless to ever tell us what that was) and Bill filed for divorce. Jo still loves Bill. Hell, Bill still loves Jo. Even Melissa (Jami Gertz) can see that.

As the film opens, Bill wants Jo to sign the divorce papers, and so he visits her out in a field where she's staked out with their old team, waiting for twisters to come by. Also staked out is the oily Jonas Miller (Cary Elwes), the "Night Crawler," who is also a storm chaser—an evil one, we can tell, because all of his vehicles are black, and, even worse, he has "corporate sponsorship."

Before Bill and Jonas can exchange more than a few heated words and some wild swings ("Your temper hasn't gotten any better," Jo observes), they're all careening across the countryside in pursuit of twisters. It's a good day for them. By the end of the movie, we will have seen five, including a double twister ("The Sisters") and a dreaded Level 5 tornado ("The Finger of God"—no prizes for guessing which one).

Before they split up, Bill and Jo invented "Dorothy," which is a machine for studying tornadoes. Listen carefully and I will tell you how Dorothy works. Dorothy contains hundreds of little plastic spheres that have sensors inside. "You put Dorothy in the path of a tornado, and run like hell," another storm chaser helpfully explains. In theory, the spheres are swooped up into the Suck Zone, and send back lots of rare information on conditions inside a twister.

The evil Jonas has ripped off Dorothy (his copycat machine is called D.O.T. 3). But the spheres don't seem to work too well. They spill in the road and stay there, until Jo takes a second look at the wind sculptures created by her Aunt Meg (Lois Smith), and realizes that each sphere needs a little wing. Then follows one of the movie's unforgettable lines: "I need every aluminum can you can find! And duct tape!" Well, wouldn't you know that every single aluminum can they can find is a Pepsi can, although it's beyond me why Pepsico thinks disappearing into the Suck Zone qualifies as advantageous Product Placement.

*Twister,* directed by Jan DeBont, is tireless

filmmaking. It lacks the wit of his *Speed,* but it sure has the energy. If the actors in this movie want to act, they have to run to catch up with the camera, which is already careening down a dirt road to watch while an oil tanker truck spins into the air, crashes, and explodes. The movie is wall-to-wall with special effects, and they're all convincing, although it's impossible for me to explain how Bill and Jo escape serious injury while staring right up into the Suck Zone of the Finger of God.

I think the movie has to be graded on two scales. As drama, *Twister* resides in the Zone. It has no time to waste on character, situation, dialogue, and nuance. The dramatic scenes are holding actions between tornadoes. As spectacle, however, *Twister* is impressive. The tornadoes are big, loud, violent, and awesome, and they look great. Even "Dorothy" looks good, until you realize the entire machine, including its flashing red lights and little gizmos sticking up into the air, is essentially just a garbage can filled with plastic balls.

The movie, which is classified PG-13, clarifies that rating with one of the greatest single explanations in the history of the MPAA Code and Ratings Board, and I quote: "For intense depiction of very bad weather." That means, for you kids under thirteen, that in the opening scene Jo, as a child, sees her daddy disappear into the Suck Zone. Is this movie too intense for kids? You bet. But say you're over thirteen. You want loud, dumb, skillful, escapist entertainment? *Twister* works. You want to think? Think twice about seeing it.

## Two Bits ★ ½

PG-13, 93 m., 1996

Jerry Barone (Gennaro), Mary Elizabeth Mastrantonio (Luisa), Al Pacino (Grandpa), Patrick Borriello (Tullio), Andy Romano (Dr. Bruna), Donna Mitchell (Mrs. Bruna), Rosemary DeAngelis (Mrs. Conte), Alec Baldwin (Narrator). Directed by James Foley and produced by Arthur Cohn. Screenplay by Joseph Stefano.

*Two Bits* is an exercise in the kind of nostalgia that gives old memories a bad name. Told through the eyes of a boy of about twelve, it recalls a long-ago summer in Philadelphia when his grandfather was dying and a new movie theater was opening, and there was no doubt in his mind which was the more exciting event.

Young Gennaro (Jerry Barone) lives with his mother (Mary Elizabeth Mastrantonio) and his grandfather (Al Pacino) in a small house; or, more exactly, he and his mom live in the house, and Grandpa camps out in the backyard, where he has an easy chair set up under a tree and sits all day, listening to the radio, reading the paper and, mostly, going on interminably about his own approaching death. No wonder Gennaro loses interest.

What the kid wants to do is attend opening night at La Paloma, a new movie palace which in its glitter and glamour is a stark contrast to the Depression era. To buy a ticket, he needs twenty-five cents. And to earn the money, he must get involved in a series of scenes that are pointless because we are so aware they have been fabricated for the purposes of the plot.

This is the kind of movie so desperate for incident that it will grasp at any straw. Consider, for example, an early scene in which a funeral and a wedding arrive simultaneously to use the same church, and a fistfight breaks out. Who are these people? What happened then? We never find out. The scene is simply there for atmosphere.

Later, the kid is sent by a doctor to clean the ashes out of his basement—an excuse, we learn, for Gennaro to be eyeballed by the doctor's sex-starved wife. No payoff there, either. No payoff at all, indeed, until so late in the movie that we are actually hoping for Grandpa to die just so something will have happened.

*Two Bits* was directed by James Foley, who has made some splendid films, including *At Close Range* (1986) and *Glengarry Glen Ross* (1992). That last film, with a screenplay by David Mamet, starred Pacino in one of his best performances. Presumably Foley and Pacino decided to work again almost immediately and made *Two Bits,* which then sat on the shelf for two years before finally being released on the coattails of Pacino's vastly more successful film *Heat.*

Not only does the film feel false and contrived, but we resent the way the threads are all so neatly brought together at the end: Is it absolutely necessary for Grandpa's fate, Gennaro's coming of age, and the opening of La Paloma to take place on the same day? Not to mention

Gennaro's mission to the woman Grandpa once loved and lost?

All of that is excess enough, without the crowning touch, a scene in which the backyard is filled with candles. Dozens of candles. Hundreds of candles. The availability of countless candles is a movie conceit I've noticed before, in films as different as *Taxi Driver* and *Interview With the Vampire.* You want to ask how a poor family in the Depression happened to have hundreds of dollars of candles available to burn—not to mention, who lit them all? But never mind. It's the kind of question you're not supposed to ask. Here's another one: Do you think Grandpa would live longer if they ever brought him inside at night?

## Two Deaths ★

R, 102 m., 1996

Michael Gambon (Daniel Pavenic), Sonia Braga (Ana Puscasu), Patrick Malahide (George Bucsan), Ion Caramitru (Carl Dalakiss), Nickolas Grace (Marius Vernescu), John Shrapnel (Cinca), Ravil Isyanov (Lieutenant). Directed by Nicolas Roeg and produced by Carolyn Montagu and Luc Roeg. Screenplay by Allan Scott, based on the novel *The Two Deaths of Senora Puccini* by Stephen Dobyns.

*Two Deaths* is a labored political and moral allegory, I guess, although I am not sure what parallels to draw or what lessons to learn. It takes place during a long night in 1989 in Bucharest, in the midst of the Romanian overthrow of the hated dictator Ceaușescu. A wealthy doctor has invited guests to dinner, but only three of them arrive, their taxis dodging gunfire. They settle in for a long night of eating, drinking, deep conversation, and interruptions from the fighting outside.

Although the director, Nicolas Roeg, has gone to some pains to establish the events in Bucharest at a crucial moment, the movie is not about Romania, dictators, revolutions, or warfare, as nearly as I could tell. (The original novel, *The Two Deaths of Senora Puccini,* by Stephen Dobyns, is set in South America.) The fighting outside simply provides a backdrop.

Inside the house, the host is a fleshy, self-assured doctor named Daniel (Michael Gambon), who has had his blind cook prepare a feast of indescribable luxury. As his guests eat and drink, they talk. They are intrigued by the photograph of an attractive woman on the doctor's mantelpiece. Surely he has never married? This cannot be wife or daughter? Daniel explains that it is his maid, Ana (Sonia Braga), pictured when she was much younger. As he speaks, Ana moves silently among them, dispensing food, drink, and vibrations of great silent portent.

The topic for the evening turns to sexual obsession, as it often does in a Nicolas Roeg film. Daniel confesses that as a younger man he became obsessed with Ana, and events transpired that allowed him to make her his slave. She lives in his house and does his bidding, because of a horrifying secret (which I will not reveal) involving the man she truly loved.

The others, emboldened by the doctor's example and his wine, make their own confessions, which run toward sexual humiliation. Since none of these men look like finalists in any form of sexual steeplechase, we guess that their obsessions are primarily mental. Soon the topic of sexuality blends into the topic of power over others, and over ourselves.

Like Polanski's *Death and the Maiden* and Tornatore's *A Pure Formality,* most of the film takes place in conversation against the background of outside and earlier events. The men talk and talk. Occasionally a wounded man from outside is brought to the doctor for treatment. Sometimes the guests stand on the rooftop and survey the fighting below. Long-buried issues in the relationship between Daniel and Ana surface. The secret of a hidden room in the house is revealed. And so on.

I am at a loss to know what to make of the film. Well acted, crisply directed, it did not engage me on any level. It seemed like an exercise rather than a drama. Perhaps the conversations have an interest, but it is an interest limited to the words; such material would work better on the printed page. Very occasionally, a film made mostly of dialogue does work; consider *My Dinner with André.* Here it is all slow, relentless, unrewarding.

## Two Girls and a Guy ★ ★ ★

R, 92 m., 1998

Robert Downey Jr. (Blake), Natasha Gregson Wagner (Lou), Heather Graham (Carla). Directed by James Toback and produced by Edward R. Pressman and Chris Hanley. Screenplay by Toback.

Sometimes the story behind a movie can bring an angle to what's on the screen. Consider *Two Girls and a Guy*, written and directed by James Toback, and starring Robert Downey Jr. The story involves a two-timing actor who returns to his Manhattan apartment to be confronted by both of his girlfriends, who've just found out about each other.

Here's the background:

—Toback and Downey worked together before, in *The Pick-Up Artist* (1987), where Downey played a compulsive womanizer who bounded through the streets of New York, fast-talking pretty girls. He was a cad and a liar, but likable; Pauline Kael wrote that "Downey, whose soul is floppy-eared, gives the movie a fairy-tale sunniness."

—James Toback himself is, or was, a notorious pickup artist. How notorious? The late *Spy* magazine once printed a double fold-out chart of his activity during just one month. With the names of his female targets running down the left-hand side of the page, the magazine used a grid to chronicle his various approaches, and how many of his favorite pickup lines ("I work closely with Warren Beatty") he used on each woman.

—When Downey was shown on television, being led to jail in handcuffs on drug charges, Toback was watching, and says he sat down immediately to write a screenplay for his old friend. "When I saw him in that orange jail jumpsuit, I knew he was ready to play this role," Toback told me at the 1997 Toronto Film Festival. Of course, perhaps Toback (whose screenplays include *The Gambler* and *Bugsy*) was also ready to write it; the film is confessional and contrite.

—*Two Girls and a Guy* was written in four days and filmed in just eleven, mostly inside a single apartment in SoHo. Not long after, Downey went back to court and eventually to jail, only to be released this month.

Downey is not floppy-eared or sunny in the new film, but he is resilient and unbowed. Confronted with both of his girlfriends (Heather Graham and Natasha Gregson Wagner), he talks and thinks quickly, saying he meant it when he told them both he had "never experienced real love" before.

"He decided consciously to start with both of us at the same time!" Lou (Wagner) says. And as they work it out, it appears he did meet them at about the same time. He saw each girl three nights of the week, excusing himself on the other nights because of the illness of his mother, whom neither one ever met.

The two women meet on his doorstep, break into his apartment, and are hiding there when he returns from a trip and leaves phone messages for them both. When he sees them, he's at a loss for words, but soon they come tumbling out; Toback in person is a torrential talker, and here Downey is as persuasive as a snake oil salesman and Wagner (Natalie Wood's daughter) fires out high-energy dialogue like Robin Williams.

What can be said, really? He's a cheating, lying SOB, and both women find even more colorful terms to describe him, both as a person and in terms of his various parts. The movie is essentially a filmed stage play, one of those idea-plays like Shaw liked to write, in which men and women ponder their differences and complexities. Is it true that men are polygamous by nature? It's much more complex than that, the movie suggests, especially after Lou suggests that her interest in Blake might expand to include Carla (Graham).

Downey, whatever his problems, is a fine actor, smart and in command of his presence, and he's persuasive here as he defends himself: "I'm an actor. And actors lie." There is a showstopping scene when he looks at himself in a mirror and warns himself to get his act together. There are some notes in the movie that I could have done without, including an offstage gunshot and a tearjerker ending. But I enjoyed the ebb and flow of their time together.

What shows Toback has learned something since his days as a *Spy* cover boy is that the movie doesn't pretend any of these three people is *really* in love. They're playing at being in love, but essentially all three are soloists, looking out for themselves, and the women can sustain outrage only so long before they begin to seek additional amusements and possibilities. As for the man, well, he always told them his favorite song was "You Don't Know Me."

## Two Much ★ ½

PG-13, 118 m., 1996

**Antonio Banderas (Art/Bart Dodge), Melanie Griffith (Betty Kerner), Danny Aiello (Gene), Daryl Hannah (Liz), Joan Cusack (Gloria), Eli Wallach (Sheldon). Directed by Fernando Trueba and produced by Cristina Huete. Screenplay by Fernando Trueba and David Trueba, based on the novel by Donald E. Westlake.**

The longer I'm a movie critic and the more films I see, the more I believe that screwball comedy is the most difficult of all film genres. It is a truism among actors that comedy is harder to play than drama, even though serious performances are routinely more honored and praised. But straight comedy is a cinch, I think, compared to screwball, which is an art so exacting and difficult that when it works it's a miracle.

But what, I hear some readers asking, what exactly *is* screwball comedy? James Monaco's invaluable *How to Read a Film* defines it as: "A type of comedy prevalent in the 1930s, typified by frenetic action, wisecracks, and sexual relationships as an important plot element. Usually about middle- and upper-class characters and therefore often involving opulent sets and costumes as visual elements. . . . Highly verbal, as opposed to its predecessor, the slapstick comedy."

Given this definition, *Two Much* is a screwball comedy in every ounce of its being. A bad one, true, but screwball all the same. It has the action, the sex, the wisecracks, the costumes, and the sets, and the key characters are all very rich. All except for the hero, the well-named Art Dodge (Antonio Banderas), who is a dishonest art dealer who specializes in convincing widows that their recently departed husbands had just purchased expensive artworks.

Art rings the bell one day at the mansion of a deceased Mafia boss, and the boss's son and heir (Danny Aiello) sees through the con and orders his goons to tear the fraudster to pieces. Art sneaks out of the house, hides in the back of a Rolls convertible, and thus meets the new boss's former wife, Betty (Melanie Griffith). She takes an instant liking to him (as who would not, since Banderas comes across as an intelligent Favio), and immediately starts making wedding plans.

Art is happy to marry Betty, who is rich and sexy, but then he meets Betty's sister, Liz (Daryl Hannah). Liz wins his love in a heartbeat: She is sweet, smart, beautiful, and without Betty's edge of what can only be called vulgarity. But Art can't see how he can extricate himself from his situation, and so he invents a twin brother, named Bart, to be Liz's lover. To change between characters, he has Bart wear glasses and removes the rubber band from his ponytail.

One of the conventions of screwball comedy is observed when no one ever realizes that Art and Bart are the same person. (When they have a "conversation" with one another, they are glimpsed only through a doorway, and no one, of course, enters the room and finds that only one person is there.) Art/Bart's situation grows more desperate as the wedding grows closer, his love for Liz more earthshaking, and the threats from Aiello's goons more dangerous.

There are some supporting characters. To explain Art's Spanish accent, we get his father (Eli Wallach), who was a Spanish civil war veteran. That leads to a chase scene also involving three other old comrades from the Abraham Lincoln Brigade. There is also Gloria (Joan Cusack), Art's assistant at the failing art gallery, who offers advice and counsel, thanklessly.

The elements are here, I suppose, for a successful comedy. But elements don't count in screwball, because nobody takes them seriously anyway. What counts is energy, tone, and timing. Banderas has an extended scene where he races between the bedrooms of the sisters, past a swimming pool, while frantically changing bathrobes. It's not funny. It goes on and on and still doesn't become funny, and I don't know why it doesn't: This is a classic screwball situation, but the fuse doesn't light.

The whole deception is unsuccessful, indeed, because it leaves the two sisters as essentially passive foils. Screwball is funnier when the characters are smart—when everyone is thinking fast. Liz, the Hannah character, is obviously intelligent (the sister played by Griffith is supposed to be a little denser), and it is simply not possible to believe she would be taken in by the deception. That means we're watching contrivance instead of invention.

Other scenes imitate their betters, and fail. Two run-ins with an angry wine steward (Vincent Schiavelli) are supposed to give us a brilliant little cameo, but the scenes drag on, repeat themselves, and resemble nothing so much as a character actor pushing his role further than it will go. It's better to adapt the strategy used by Griffith, Hannah, and Aiello, who simply play their roles straight, and let the screenplay take care of the comedy. It doesn't, unfortunately, but that's not their fault.

# U

## Ulee's Gold ★ ★ ★ ½

R, 115 m., 1997

Peter Fonda (Ulee Jackson), Patricia Richardson (Connie Hope), Jessica Biel (Casey Jackson), J. Kenneth Campbell (Bill Floyd), Christine Dunford (Helen Jackson), Steven Flynn (Eddie Flowers), Dewey Weber (Ferris Dooley), Tom Wood (Jimmy Jackson). Directed by Victor Nunez and produced by Nunez, Sam Gowan, and Peter Saraf. Screenplay by Nunez.

Peter Fonda was never an action hero in the first place. Tall, introverted, and sensitive, he was best cast in his breakthrough role as Captain America, a hippie motorcyclist on an odyssey in *Easy Rider* (1968). His films since are an undistinguished collection of action and exploitation pictures; the rare good film like *The Hired Hand* (1971) looks lonely in such company. Now, at fifty-seven, he has found the role of a lifetime—perhaps the role that points the way to a reborn career.

In *Ulee's Gold,* he plays Ulysses Jackson, a beekeeper in the Florida panhandle who has a lot on his mind. He was the only survivor of his Vietnam unit. His wife died six years ago. His son is in prison on a robbery charge, and he is raising his two granddaughters as best he can. He is a very lonely man, but he loves his work: "The bees and I have an understanding."

He hasn't spoken to his son, Jimmy (Tom Wood), in two years when one day a call comes. He goes to visit the boy in prison. The son asks for help: His wife, Helen (Christine Dunford), has turned up in bad shape, and is staying with Eddie and Ferris, the two guys Jimmy pulled the robbery with. Jimmy wants Ulee to get Helen and take care of her.

"She can just stay gone," Ulee says.

"She's sick, Dad," says Jimmy.

So Ulee drives his pickup truck down to where Ferris and Eddie (Dewey Weber and Steven Flynn) are holed up in a flophouse with Helen, who is strung out on drugs and madness. And he hauls Helen home, although not before the two men tell him they believe Jimmy hid $100,000 from the robbery, and they want it back—or they will come after the grandchildren.

A woman named Connie (Patricia Richardson, from *Home Improvement*) lives across the street from Ulee. She's a nurse, divorced twice, no children. The granddaughters like her, and when they see the shape their mother is in, they drag her across the street to help. Helen needs a lot of help: sedatives, restraints, the whole detox process. Ulee tries to thank her. "It's what I do," she says.

The elements are in place here for a fairly standard story in which Ferris and Eddie come looking for the money, and Ulee must defend his family, while falling in love, of course, with Connie—while the girls bond once again with their mother. But to look at events in that way would miss the whole purpose of *Ulee's Gold,* which is not about who prevails, but about what Ulee learns about himself.

The movie was written, directed, and edited by Victor Nunez, who sets all of his films in Florida and goes from strength to strength. His films include *Gal Young 'Un* (1979), about a backwoods widow's run-in with a con man; *A Flash of Green* (1984), with Ed Harris as a newspaper reporter, in one of his finest roles; and then, after too long a wait, the wonderful *Ruby in Paradise* (1993), with its luminous performance by Ashley Judd.

Nunez has a gift for finding the essence, the soul, of his actors; that's why Harris and Judd were so good, and why Peter Fonda here reveals a depth of talent we did not suspect. Nunez is attentive to the quiet in Fonda's nature, to the deeply buried anger, and to the intelligence. There is a situation late in this film that involves a gun, and the Fonda character handles it like a chessmaster, figuring out what the real threat is and how his opponents will react. Raised on routine movies, we figure Ulee will grab for the gun. Ulee is smarter and deeper than that.

The scenes between Fonda and Richardson are charged with quiet tension. Obviously she likes him. He tells her he is no longer good at—well, getting along with people. She understands. What happens between them happens slowly and tactfully. And Nunez is just as careful in the way he introduces Ulee's profession. We learn something about bees in this movie, and a lot about beekeepers, but *Ulee's Gold* is not a documentary; all of the information is put to the use of the story, especially in a scene where one of the granddaughters uses bees in a parable she tells her mother. Basically, it comes down to: You take care of them, and they'll take care of you.

## Ulysses' Gaze ★

NO MPAA RATING, 180 m., 1997

Harvey Keitel ("A"), Erland Josephson (Film Library Curator), Maia Morgenstern ("Ulysses' Wives"), Thanassis Vengos (Taxi Driver), Yorgos Michalakopoulos (Journalist Friend), Dora Volanaki (Old Woman). Directed by Theo Angelopoulos and produced by Eric Heumann. Screenplay by Angelopoulos, Tonino Guerra, and Petros Markaris.

Because it is a noble epic set amid the ruins of the Russian empire and the genocide of what was Yugoslavia, there is a temptation to give *Ulysses' Gaze* the benefit of the doubt: to praise it for its vision, its daring, its courage, its great length. But I would not be able to look you in the eye if you then went to see it, because how could I deny that it is a numbing bore?

A director must be very sure of his greatness to inflict an experience like this on the audience, and Theo Angelopoulos was so sure that when he won only the Special Jury Prize at the 1995 Cannes Film Festival, he made his displeasure obvious on the stage. He thought he should have won the Palme d'Or, which went instead to *Underground,* by Emir Kusturica, which was also three hours long and also set in the wreckage of Yugoslavia, but had at least the virtue of not being almost unendurable.

*Ulysses' Gaze* stars Harvey Keitel as a Greek movie director named "A," who returns to his roots thirty-five years after leaving for America. He seeks, he says, some rare old film footage: the first film ever shot in the Balkans. His odyssey (for so we must describe any journey in a movie with "Ulysses" in the title) takes him by taxi from Greece to the Albanian border, and then by boat to the cities of Skopje, Bucharest, and Sarajevo. ("Is this Sarajevo?" he asks at one point. If you have to ask, you're in the wrong place.) Along the way there are flashbacks to 1945 and 1946 when, as a friend in Belgrade tells him, "We fell asleep in one world and were rudely awakened in another."

You might be tempted to wonder why old film footage would be so important to "A" that he would risk his life traveling unprotected through a war zone to find it. Since Angelopoulos in fact directed this movie about such a man, and filmed it in the very same war zones, he would probably not be the man to ask.

The initial "A" undoubtedly stands for Angelopoulos, but why he chose Harvey Keitel to portray him is a mystery. Keitel is a great spontaneous actor, able to think on his feet and move around quickly in dialect, but here he acts as if someone has injected him with crazy glue. He's slow, measured, portentous, tedious, and his dialogue sounds like readings from an editorial translated imperfectly through several languages.

There are several women in the movie (the credits call them "Ulysses' Wives"), and they find themselves powerfully attracted to "A," a mystery only partly explained by the fact that they are all played by the same actress, Maia Morgenstern. They see him, he sees them, and soon the two of them are looking greatly pained. I was reminded of Armando Bo's anguished 1960s Argentinian soft-core sex films, which starred his wife, Isabel Sarli, whose agony was terrible to behold and could only be slaked in the arms of a man. "A" and the women make love in this movie as if trying to apply unguent inside each other's clothes.

There are some remarkable images. They are spaced throughout the film at roughly twenty-minute intervals. One shows a thin line of police separating demonstrators with torches, and other people with umbrellas. When the torch-bearers press forward, the umbrellas undulate backward, in a scene reminiscent of the umbrella scene in Hitchcock's *Foreign Correspondent.* Similar crowds with umbrellas stand in squares, and in fields, and along the banks of rivers. One wonders if the umbrellas are important to the shots, or if the extras demanded them.

Another big image involves a huge statue of Lenin, which has been disassembled and placed aboard a barge. (For shipment . . . where? Where is there a demand for used Lenin statues these days?) The vast stone head looks forward, and Lenin's giant finger points the way, as "A" travels on the same barge. The image is so powerful that even its banality cannot diminish it.

The closing passages of the film have an immediacy; they're set in the middle of a war zone, and characters important to "A" are endangered. But one can easily think of much better films also shot under wartime conditions, particularly *Circle of Deceit,* shot by Volker Schlondorff during the fighting in Beirut, or Milcho Manchevski's *Before the Rain,* shot near the fighting in Yugoslavia.

What's left after *Ulysses' Gaze* is the impression of a film made by a director so convinced of the gravity and importance of his theme that he wants to weed out any moviegoers seeking interest, grace, humor, or involvement. One cannot easily imagine anyone else speaking up at a dinner table where he presides.

It is an old fact about the cinema—known perhaps even to those pioneers who made the ancient footage "A" is seeking—that a film does not exist unless there is an audience between the projector and the screen. A director, having chosen to work in a mass medium, has a certain duty to that audience. I do not ask that he make it laugh or cry, or even that he entertain it, but he must at least not insult its goodwill by giving it so little to repay its patience. What arrogance and self-importance this film reveals.

## The Umbrellas of Cherbourg ★ ★ ★ ½

NO MPAA RATING, 91 m., 1964 (rereleased 1996)

Catherine Deneuve (Genevieve), Nino Castelnuovo (Guy), Anne Vernon (Mme. Emery), Marc Michel (Roland Cassard), Ellen Farner (Madeleine), Mireille Perrey (Tante Elise), Harald Wolff (M. Dubourg). Directed by Jacques Demy and produced by Mag Bodard. Screenplay by Demy.

Has there ever been an actress in the history of the movies who has changed as little and aged as slowly as Catherine Deneuve? Here she is in *The Umbrellas of Cherbourg,* her first major film, made in 1964 and now restored. Thirty-one years later, I met her at the 1995 Cannes Film Festival. To the degree that she had changed, it was simply to ripen, to add experience and sympathy to the raw beauty of a teenager. I am not making empty compliments. Her beauty, then and now, is like a blow to the eyes.

When she made *Umbrellas* for the French director Jacques Demy, Deneuve was twenty, and her work in this film was a flowering that introduced one of the great stars of modern French cinema. The film itself was a curious experiment in which all of the words were sung; Michel Legrand wrote the wall-to-wall score, which includes not only the famous main theme and other songs, but also Demy's sung dialogue, in the style of the lines used to link passages in opera. This style would seem to suggest a work of featherweight romanticism, but *Umbrellas* is unexpectedly sad and wise, a bittersweet reflection on the way true love sometimes does not (and perhaps should not) conquer all.

Demy's film was a worldwide hit when it was first released, but if its star did not age, its film stock did. Like many of the movies shot in the 1960s, it was released in a version of Eastmancolor that did not remain true to the original colors. The greens and blues lost their strength, leaving the film looking pink, as if it had faded in a bright sun. Demy regained control of the film a few years before his death in 1990, and I remember a summer day in 1989 when I sat with Demy and his wife, the director Agnes Varda, in the garden of their house in Paris, and they talked of restoring the film's original color. That task was finally finished by Varda in 1994, and now here is *The Umbrellas of Cherbourg* again, looking as bright and fresh as on the day it premiered.

The story is a sad one, yes, but it ends on a note we can only conclude is the right one. (Do not read further until you see the film.) Deneuve plays a young woman named Genevieve, who is head-over-heels in love with a local garage mechanic named Guy (Nino Castelnuovo). Her mother (Anne Vernon) runs a little local shop, and is desperately in need of money to save her business. A rich man (Marc Michel) walks into the shop, falls in love with the daughter, and begins a slow, indirect process that might lead to a proposal of marriage. Genevieve has eyes only for Guy, but he is drafted for two years by the army. And although they pledge to love one another forever, she receives only one letter from him in two months.

Meanwhile, almost inevitably, Genevieve finds she is pregnant. The rich man proposes, is told of this development, and offers to marry Genevieve anyway and raise the child as their own. And then there is an epilogue, in which Guy returns to the town, discovers what has happened, turns to drink and dissolution, and then is rescued by Madeleine (Ellen Farner), the young woman who was the companion for Guy's aunt, and has secretly loved him for a long time. The very last scene, of a final meeting between Guy and Genevieve, is one of such poignancy that it's amazing the fabric of a musical can support it.

I had forgotten many of the details of the story in the thirty-two years since first seeing it; my mental images were of smiling garage mechanics and Catherine Deneuve happily singing with her lover. The film is incomparably richer and more moving than that. And although the idea of having the actors sing (or, more exactly, lip-synch) every single line might sound off-putting, it's surprising how quickly we accept it.

*The Umbrellas of Cherbourg* did not initiate a new movie style (although Demy tried it again in *The Young Girls of Rochefort* in 1968, with Deneuve, her sister Francois Dorleac, and Gene Kelly). But it is remembered as a bold, original experiment, and now that it is restored and back in circulation, it can also be remembered as a surprisingly effective film, touching and knowing and, like Deneuve, ageless.

## Unhook the Stars ★ ★ ★

R, 105 m., 1997

Gena Rowlands (Mildred), Marisa Tomei (Monica), Gérard Depardieu (Big Tommy), Jake Lloyd (J.J.), Moira Kelly (Ann Mary Margaret), David Sherrill (Ethan), David Thompson (Frankie), Bridgett Wilson (Jeannie). Directed by Nick Cassavetes and produced by Rene Cleitman. Screenplay by Cassavetes and Helen Caldwell.

If Gena Rowlands were getting a makeover on one of the chat shows, they'd tell her to cut her hair to a sensible length and stop trying to look like a 1950s sex bomb, but what her look tells you is that you get the whole package: She's bringing along the past, the glamour, and all those blowzy, confused, desperate women she played for her husband, the late John Cassavetes. You want my theory about the hairstyle? John liked it that way.

In *Unhook the Stars*, the directorial debut of their son, Nick Cassavetes, Rowlands plays a calmer version of the high-energy, neurotic heroines of *Opening Night, Love Streams, Minnie and Moskowitz, A Woman Under the Influence,* and all those other Cassavetes dramas in which the characters drank and smoked and tried to settle—right now!—things that could never be settled at all. In the current movie, she's a widow named Mildred, comfortably well-off, living in a house that's too big for her now that her husband has died. Her son is prospering in San Francisco, and her daughter has angrily moved out.

One day there's a knock on the door, and she opens it to find a neighbor she doesn't know, Monica (Marisa Tomei), with her small son J.J. (Jake Lloyd) in tow. Monica is obviously at the end of her rope, and we know why: Her husband, who likes to slap her around, has made life impossible, and she needs emergency baby-sitting, right now.

That's the setup for a film of gentleness and low-key romance. Mildred finds herself caring for a small child once again, and volunteers to do it on a daily basis. There's a hint of the old Cassavetes compulsiveness in a scene where she settles the kid down with the encyclopedia and begins to read, starting with "a, for a capella." Soon she and J.J. are best friends, and Mildred is tactfully trying to bring some order into Monica's life.

Monica is played by Tomei as the kind of borderline manic that the senior Cassavetes filled his films with. Nick sees her with more dimensions. Yes, she has a problem with anger. Yes, she drinks too much. Yes, she dates men as if they're a quick fix. ("This guy I'm going out with," she giggles to Mildred, "I don't even like him. Good thing I'm drinking.") But she is also a loving mom who is determined to raise her son as best she can, and who deals with an abusive spouse in a direct and decisive way.

Meanwhile, other issues are churning in Mildred's life. Her daughter (Moira Kelly), sullen and angry, has moved out to live with her boyfriend, in a relationship that clearly will not survive. Her son (David Sherrill) invites her out to San Francisco for a tour of his luxury townhouse, which includes a "mother-in-law apartment" just for her. But is she ready to sell her rambling house and move in with him?

And then there is the most unexpected development of all. Monica takes her to a bar one night, and she is picked up—yes, at her age!—by a French-Canadian truck driver (Gérard Depardieu) who seems to have fallen in love with her. They go on a date, he delivers her back home in his giant rig, and there is a kissing scene that only these two accomplished actors could have made work quite the way it does.

*Unhook the Stars* doesn't create a lot of contrived plot problems and then resolve them with dramatic developments. Each element of the screenplay (written by Nick Cassavetes and Helen Caldwell) is taken only as far as it will willingly go. Monica's husband doesn't go berserk, Mildred's daughter is rebellious but not insane, the truck driver is tactful in declaring his love, and even the inevitable separation between Mildred and J.J. is handled as the next step, rather than the last straw. The outcome is nicely open-ended, instead of insisting that Mildred do something concrete to provide a happy ending.

*Unhook the Stars* feels as if it may have been written for Rowlands, but who better to write for? What's interesting is how developed all of the characters are; Tomei doesn't have a supporting role but sort of a parallel one, and young Jake Lloyd is blunt and direct as J.J., zeroing in as children do on the subject at hand. Like his father, Nick Cassavetes has made a movie about a slice of life. But it is about manageable, not unmanageable, life. It has an underlying contentment.

## Up Close and Personal ★ ★ ★

PG-13, 124 m., 1996

Robert Redford (Warren Justice), Michelle Pfeiffer (Tally Atwater), Stockard Channing (Marcia McGrath), Joe Mantegna (Bucky Terranova), Kate Nelligan (Joanna Kennelly), Glenn Plummer (Ned Jackson). Directed by Jon Avnet and produced by Avnet, David Nicksay, and Jordan Kerner. Screenplay by Joan Didion and John Gregory Dunne.

*Up Close and Personal* reminds me of nothing so much as those career novels for teenagers in which a plucky youngster rises to the top, guided by a helpful mentor. The movie could as well be titled, *Tally Atwater, Girl Broadcaster.*

It tells the story of a poor young woman from Reno with an unhappy background (Michelle Pfeiffer), who fakes her résumé to get a job on a TV station, and then plugs away until she's a network anchor. (To be sure, she's only the anchor on Saturdays—but she's still young.) During the years of her rise, which seem more like weeks or months, she's guided by a handsome local news director (Robert Redford), who was once a White House correspondent before he made the mistake of trusting a woman he loved.

If this sounds contrived and corny, it's because it is. We're in romance novel territory. And yet alert readers will have noticed that I've appended three stars to my review, a sign of approval. The temptations are great to mock the clichés and melodrama in *Up Close and Personal,* but the movie undeniably works as what it really is—a love story.

It didn't start out that way. It began as a screenplay by two tough cookies, Joan Didion and John Gregory Dunne, about the life of the late NBC correspondent Jessica Savitch, who climbed fast, partied hard, and died when her car landed upside down in a stream.

*Up Close and Personal* is so different from the facts of Savitch's life than if Didion and Dunne still have their first draft, they could probably sell it as a completely different movie. Tally Atwater, the Pfeiffer character, doesn't party much, doesn't do drugs, and doesn't die. (I am reminded of the time Samuel Goldwyn ordered a screenplay about the Lindbergh kidnapping: "Only, it can't be about kidnapping, which is against the Code. For legal reasons, we have to change the name from Lindbergh. And the kid's father shouldn't fly.")

As the movie opens, Redford's character, subtly named Warren Justice, is a news director at a Miami TV station. He looks at a demo tape sent in by Tally Atwater, guesses that large parts of it are faked, and decides to give her a chance anyway—because if she wants it that much, she may have something.

Atwater turns up in Miami wearing the wrong hair and dress, obviously a naive outsider (at her first Meet Cute with Justice, she drops her purse and a Tampax spills out). But Tally works hard and listens fast, is willing to make coffee and fetch laundry, and is very ambitious, angling for the weathergirl job even though, when she gets it, she throws up before airtime and freezes on the air. Justice doesn't care: "She eats the lens."

He brings her along slowly, with practical tips and lots of lectures about covering the news. And all the time a tension grows, between them and within us, because they are apparently falling in love, and yet for a long time they do not act on their feelings. This is an effective device too little used in modern movies, where one significant exchange of glances can substitute for months of courtship. Because they are good and attractive people and we like them, we want them to fold into each other's arms, and when they do not, that makes the movie better—more romantic.

When it comes to its insights into television news, *Up Close and Personal* is superficial. It knows something about talent consultants and ratings services that advise stations on how to package their newscasts. It knows a little about how a local newscast goes on the air ("If it bleeds, it leads," Justice tells her). But large parts of it play as if the filmmakers learned about television by watching it. *Broadcast News* and *Network* are much more knowledgeable.

But this isn't really a movie about television. It's a movie about love. You could change the careers of the Pfeiffer and Redford characters and still have essentially the same movie. The director, Jon Avnet *(Fried Green Tomatoes)*, is almost consciously going here for the broad movie star approach to movie romance.

Redford smiles a lot, as the camera lingers, to show his sincerity. Pfeiffer gets the obligatory makeover scene; she's blond as the movie opens, then becomes brunette so her on-camera image will seem more serious—and of course the first brunette scene has her looking all wrong, after which she looks ravishing for the rest of the movie. There are many lush backdrops for their conversations: the surf, sunsets, skylines. There are sweet little things that happen between them that they cherish. And there is sadness, of course, because bittersweet love is the best kind of all, especially for audiences who would rather feel sorry for characters they like than happy for them.

The supporting cast is first-rate. Stockard Channing plays a hard-as-nails older anchor who is pushed aside by young Tally, and goes off uncomplainingly to a station in Cincinnati. ("It's nobody's fault. That's how it works.") Kate Nelligan (who could have been the lead in a movie based on the real Jessica Savitch) plays one of Redford's former wives, a Barbara Walters clone, in a role that avoids almost all the usual clichés about former wives. Joe Mantegna is a crab leg–sucking broadcast agent, using clout and connections to win better deals for his "talent" (the TV word for on-air newspeople). And Glenn Plummer fills the obligatory role of the little guy who admires the heroine and is a loyal sidekick. He's the cameraman who gets locked inside a prison with Tally; they stay on the air live during a riot, and that's her break into the big time—although, truth to tell, she doesn't do a very good job of covering the riot.

The distributors of *Up Close and Personal* are wise. In their ads for the movie, they're downplaying the TV aspects of the movie and underlining the romance. Who knows? Maybe the film will play like those old *Girl Reporter* books, and a future Connie Chung, now thirteen, will go to see it and decide to become an anchorwoman. At some point, she should probably also read up on Jessica Savitch.

## U.S. Marshals ★ ★ ½

PG-13, 123 m., 1998

Tommy Lee Jones (Marshal Sam Gerard), Wesley Snipes (Sheridan), Robert Downey Jr. (John Royce), Joe Pantoliano (Deputy Marshal Cosmo Renfro), Kate Nelligan (U.S. Marshal Walsh), Irene Jacob (Marie), Daniel Roebuck (Biggs), Tom Wood (Newman). Directed by Stuart Baird and produced by Arnold Kopelson and Anne Kopelson. Screenplay by John Pogue, based on characters created by Roy Huggins.

I didn't expect *U.S. Marshals* to be the equal of *The Fugitive,* and it isn't. But I hoped it would approach the taut tension of the 1993 film, and it doesn't. It has extra scenes, needless characters, an aimless plot, and a solution that the hero seems to keep learning and then forgetting.

The hero is U.S. Deputy Marshal Sam Gerard, played by Tommy Lee Jones in a reprise of his costarring role in *The Fugitive.* The fact that they made this quasi-sequel without its original star (Harrison Ford) is a tribute to the strength of Jones's presence in the earlier film, where he had more dialogue than the lead. Jones made a big impression there, and won an Oscar. Here he hits the same marks with the same razor-edged delivery; everything's right about his performance except that it's in a rambling movie.

Take the opening sequence, where Jones disguises himself as a fast-food chicken to supervise a stakeout of a wanted man. There's a break-in, a fight, some violence, an arrest, TV interviews, a jailing, a tavern scene to celebrate, a reprimand by his superior (Kate Nelligan)—and all for what? So that the guy they caught can be put on a plane to a Missouri prison, and Sam Gerard can be put on the same flight—but not to guard the guy. No, Sam is flying on to Washington. The guy they caught and fought with is utterly unnecessary for the rest of the movie.

But also on that plane to Missouri is another character, played by Wesley Snipes. When we first see him he's a Chicago tow-truck driver. Another driver causes a crash, he's hospitalized, his prints are checked, and he's arrested and charged with the murders of two agents in New York. He protests that it's a case of mistaken identity. Is it?

Never mind that for a moment. Stop to consider. All you need for the movie to get rolling, is to establish the Snipes character and get him on that plane with Marshal Gerard. The marshal doesn't need a lot of establishing because (1) we know him from the earlier movie, and (2) Tommy Lee Jones can establish himself with three lines of dialogue, as he did in the first film.

By lingering over the chicken-suit raid, the movie has wasted time. More time is wasted by supplying a girlfriend for Snipes, played by Irene Jacob. This character is utterly superfluous. Example: She turns up at a cemetery in the middle of a shoot-out, flees with Snipes, can't make it over a wall, and is left behind. (That wall . . . hmmm. How can Snipes leap high enough to get atop the wall, but Jacob can't even jump high enough to reach his outstretched hand lowered to her?)

The movie gets rolling at around the twenty-five-minute mark, with a spectacular plane crash, reminding us of the train crash in *The Fugitive.* One prisoner escapes: Snipes. The marshal coordinates a manhunt that looks like it costs millions (helicopters, roadblocks for a twenty-mile radius, teams combing the woods, etc.). "We got a fugitive," he barks, in a line supplied as a convenience for the producers of the TV spots.

The State Department gets involved, revealing that Snipes is a bigger fish than anybody thought. And the marshal is supplied with a shadow: an agent named Royce (Robert Downey Jr.), who will follow him everywhere. They spar. "You sure you wanna get cute with me?" the marshal asks him. And, "I love that nickel-plated sissy pistol." Royce falls under the Law of Economy of Characters: A seemingly unnecessary sidekick will inevitably turn out to be—but you know how it goes.

The movie settles into a chase structure, with set pieces: a confrontation in a swamp, a cat-and-mouse game in a cemetery, and a chase through an old folks' home. It's there that the Snipes character commits the Fallacy of the Climbing Fugitive (fleeing man climbs stairs, tower, scaffold, etc., even though he can't possibly escape at the top unless he can fly). There is, however, a reason for him to climb—a spectacular escape that would have made Batman proud.

There is an explanation for all of this. We know or guess its outlines early in the film. The marshal figures it out, too ("This is a 'ruthless assassin' who keeps going out of his way to let people live"). He even discovers videotape evidence revealing the real story. And yet, in the cemetery, even when the evil Chinese agent tries to kill the fugitive, the marshal and his men still chase Snipes. It's like Gerard keeps absentmindedly overlooking what he's learned earlier in the film.

The result is unconvincing and disorganized. Yes, there are some spectacular stunts and slick special-effects sequences. Yes, Jones is right on the money, and Snipes makes a sympathetic fugitive. But it's the story that has to pull this train, and its derailment is about as definitive as the train crash in the earlier film.

## U-Turn ★ ½

R, 125 m., 1997

Sean Penn (Bobby Cooper), Billy Bob Thornton (Darrell), Powers Boothe (Sheriff), Jennifer Lopez (Grace McKenna), Nick Nolte (Jake McKenna), Julie Hagerty (Flo), Joaquin Phoenix (Toby N. Tucker), Jon Voight (Blind Man), Claire Danes (Jenny), Laurie Metcalf (Bus Clerk), Liv Tyler (Girl in Bus Station). Directed by Oliver Stone and produced by Dan Halsted and Clayton Townsend. Screenplay by John Ridley.

Only Oliver Stone knows what he was trying to accomplish by making *U-Turn,* and it is a secret he doesn't share with the audience. This is a repetitive, pointless exercise in genre filmmaking—the kind of movie where you distract yourself by making a list of the sources. Much of the story comes from *Red Rock West,* John Dahl's 1994 film about a man and a wife who both try to convince a drifter to kill the other. And the images and milieu are out of Russ Meyer country;

his *Cherry, Harry and Raquel* and *SuperVixens* contain the same redneck sheriffs, the same lustful wives, the same isolated shacks and ignorant mechanics and car culture. *U-Turn* and *Cherry* both end, indeed, with a debt to *Duel in the Sun.*

I imagine Stone made this movie as sort of a lark, after the exhausting but remarkable accomplishments of *Nixon, Natural Born Killers, Heaven and Earth,* and *JFK.* Well, he deserves a break—but this one? Stone is a gifted filmmaker not afraid to take chances, to express ideas in his films and make political statements. Here he's on holiday.

Watching *U-Turn,* I was reminded of a concert pianist playing "Chopsticks": It is done well, but one is disappointed to find it done at all.

The film stars Sean Penn, in a convincing performance all the more admirable for being pointless. He plays Bobby, a man who has had bad luck up the road (his bandaged hand is missing two fingers) and will have a lot more bad luck in the desert town of Superior, Arizona. He wheels into town in his beloved Mustang convertible, which needs a new radiator hose, and encounters the loathsome Darrell (Billy Bob Thornton), a garage mechanic he will eventually be inspired to call an "ignorant inbred turtleneck hick."

While Darrell works on the car, Bobby walks into town. Superior is one of those backwater hells much beloved in the movies, where everyone is malevolent, oversexed, narrow-eyed, and hateful. There are never any industries in these towns (except for garages, saloons, and law enforcement) because everyone is too preoccupied by sex, lying, scheming, embezzling, and hiring strangers to kill each other.

Bobby quickly finds a sultry young woman named Grace (Jennifer Lopez) and is invited home to help her install her drapes and whatever else comes to mind. Soon her enraged husband, Jake (Nick Nolte), comes charging in, red-eyed and bewhiskered, to threaten Bobby with his life, but after the obligatory fight they meet down the road and Jake asks Bobby to kill his wife. Soon Grace will want Bobby to kill her husband (the *Red Rock West* bit), and the film leads to one of those situations where Bobby's life depends on which one he believes.

Superior, Arizona, is the original town without pity. During the course of his brief stay there, Bobby will be kicked in the ribs several dozen times, almost be bitten by a tarantula, shot at, and have his car all but destroyed—and that's all before the final scenes with the vultures circling overhead. Bobby comes across almost like a character in a computer game; you wipe him out, he falls down, stars spin around his head, and then he jumps up again, ready for action.

The film is well made on the level of craft; of course it is, with this strong cast, and Stone directing, and Robert Richardson as cinematographer. But it goes around and around until, like a merry-go-round rider, we figure out that the view is always changing but it's never going to be new. There comes a sinking feeling, half an hour into the film, when we realize the characters are not driven by their personalities and needs but by the plot. At that point they become puppets, not people. That's the last thing we'd expect in a film by Oliver Stone.

# V

## The Van ★ ★ ★

R, 100 m., 1997

Colm Meaney (Larry), Donal O'Kelly (Bimbo), Brendan O'Carroll (Weslie), Ger Ryan (Maggie), Ruaidhri Conroy (Kevin). Directed by Stephen Frears and produced by Lynda Myles. Screenplay by Roddy Doyle, based on his novel.

In three novels made into three movies, Roddy Doyle has brought to life the comic, poignant, resourceful people of a fictitious North Dublin suburb he calls Barrytown. They live so close together they're almost in each other's pockets, and are chronically short of cash (although there is somehow always money for drink). And they weather life's crises with imagination and resiliency.

*The Van* is the third of the trilogy, the story of two good buddies whose friendship is almost wrecked by their decision to go into business with an ancient and filthy fast-food truck they find rotting in someone's backyard. It has no engine and is caked with grease ("It's like the inside of a leper"), but as "Bimbo's Burgers," it embodies all their hopes.

The friends are Larry (Colm Meaney) and Bimbo (Donal O'Kelly). Meaney has been in all three of the Doyle films; he was the exasperated father of the pregnant teenager in *The Snapper* (1993) and the father of the young band leader in *The Commitments* (1991), and is underused as the mad-dog DEA agent in *Con Air.* He's a large man with a face that exudes goodwill in spite of everything—and the characters he plays usually have a lot of everything to be in spite of. As the film opens, he's locked in unemployment and consoling Bimbo over a pint of Guinness after Bimbo has been fired at the bakery.

One of the quiet gifts of all the Doyle films (the first directed by Alan Parker, the next two by Stephen Frears) is the richness of Dublin life you can spot in the margins. Consider Larry's home life. He presides uneasily over a household consisting of a daughter with a baby but no husband, and a son with a sharp tongue ("Who paid for that dinner in front of you, son?" "The state."). But there is an underlying happiness in the film, added to by his much-loved wife, Maggie (Ger Ryan), who is taking night school literature classes. The perfect note is struck by a subtle decorating touch: the framed portrait of John Wayne on the kitchen wall. (When the van is finally cleaned up and ready to be moved, it's to the call of "Take 'em to Missouri, men! Yee-haw!") Another touch: the kitchen "swear jar," where a contribution frequently has to be made because of the words that are the cornerstones of Larry's vocabulary.

The movie's action takes place during the summer of 1990, fondly remembered in Dublin because the Irish soccer team made it to the semifinals of the World Cup, defeating England and Romania along the way. Larry and Bimbo and all of their friends gather to watch the matches in pubs, cheering passionately and with utter conviction ("I love Ireland, Maggie!" a beery Larry cries, kissing his wife).

Their venture into business is inspired after they leave a pub after one match and the usual fast-food van, owned by Vietnamese, is gone. (The explanation is matter-of-fact: "They've got to be gone by dark or they'll get bricked by the kids.") Larry and Bimbo figure to clean up after the cup matches and down at the beach. And so they do, for a while, despite several problems (a breaded and deep-fried diaper is served to one customer in place of cod, and when another is ten pence short of the price for a burger, Larry takes a ten-pence bite out of it and hands it to the man).

The movie builds its comic scenes by close observation. Consider, for example, the Christmas dinner sequence, which combines Guinness with "Frosty the Snowman" and a mute, disapproving mother-in-law, and involves the theft of a candy bar from a child's Christmas basket. Or the scene where the two friends combine golfing and baby-sitting, taking along a snapper (baby) in its rainproof little stroller. Characters on the edges contribute to the overall atmosphere, especially Brendan O'Carroll as Weslie, a little man in a long plaid coat who always seems to know where he can get you a better price.

When I saw *The Van* for the first time at the Cannes Film Festival in 1996, I felt it was the least of the three films, and I still do, but it was trimmed of about five minutes of footage after Cannes and, seeing it again a year later, I found it quicker and more alive. It is also the most thoughtful, in a way, and the ending has a poignancy and an unresolved quality that is just right: These disorganized lives would not fit into a neat ending.

## A Very Brady Sequel ★ ★ ½

PG-13, 90 m., 1996

Shelly Long (Carol), Gary Cole (Mike), Tim Matheson (Roy), Henriette Mantel (Alice), Christopher Daniel Barnes (Greg), Christine Taylor (Marcia), Jennifer Elise Cox (Jan), Paul Sutera (Peter). Directed by Arlene Sanford and produced by Sherwood Schwartz, Lloyd J. Schwartz, and Alan Ladd Jr. Screenplay by Harry Elfont, Deborah Kaplan, James Berg, and Stan Zimmerman.

The mystery of Carol Brady's hair is not quite solved in *A Very Brady Sequel,* even after she visits a punk beauty shop where the stylist requires a chain saw to cut through the layers of hair spray. He promises a complete makeover, but she emerges still wearing that strange flap of hair down her neck, the one that makes her coif look modeled on ancient Teutonic helmets.

It takes more than a chain saw to cut through the Bradys' enduring family style, which has carried the 1970s intact into the future. In *A Very Brady Sequel,* however, there is a shock to the system that very nearly disrupts their time capsule. Carol's first husband, Roy, who was thought to be lost at sea, rings the doorbell one day and claims to be very much alive. "You look so different," Carol muses. "An elephant stepped on my face in Kuala Lumpur," he explains.

Mike Brady, the current husband, is a good sport. "We Bradys are known for our hospitality," he says, giving Roy the sofa bed in his den. What we know and the Bradys don't is that Roy (Tim Matheson) is an impostor—a smuggler who killed the real Roy, and is trying to get his hands on the priceless Thai sculpture that adorns the Brady living room.

Carol (Shelley Long) hardly seems fazed by the appearance of Roy, but then she hasn't been fazed by anything in a very long time. Mike (Gary Cole), is untroubled by jealousy, perhaps because he is serene in the knowledge that no man of the 1990s could find a way to communicate with his wife. But the newcomer does intrigue the kids, especially the two older stepsiblings, Greg and Marcia (Christopher Daniel Barnes and Christine Taylor), who muse, "If Roy really is mom's husband—does that mean we're not brother and sister?" This possibility arises at a delicate time, since Mike Brady has just declared that "fair's fair," and has decreed that Marcia must share the "far-out pad" that Greg has established for himself in the attic.

As this plot thickens, and does it ever, *A Very Brady Sequel* flirts cheerfully with the gulf between the innocence of the Bradys and the hazards of contemporary life. Before the film is over, Alice the housekeeper will have served hallucinogenic mushrooms in the spaghetti sauce, RuPaul will have appeared as the high school guidance counselor, and Roy will have imparted a few words of fatherly wisdom ("Lie, cheat, steal, and kill").

Although I am still not a convert to the Brady universe, I did find myself enjoying *A Very Brady Sequel* more than *The Brady Bunch Movie* (1995). For one thing, it takes more notice of the real world the Bradys live in, and gets more humor from the contrasts between their unchanging 1970s starshine and today's harsher life. The director, Arlene Sanford, and her four writers have explored the darker side of a family that Mike and Carol think is all sunshine (when Cindy tells a kidnapper he can't take her mom, Marcia cries, "Cindy's right! Take Jan!").

There is also humor in Jan's attempts to use such modern inventions as Dial-a-Hunk to create a fictitious boyfriend for herself, as well as such timeless Brady touches as Mom using needlepoint to write a call for help. And we get some reaction shots of how the real world responds to the Bradys' giddy togetherness, as when flight attendants try to restrain them during a flight to Hawaii.

I didn't laugh much during *A Very Brady Sequel,* but I did smile a lot. It's possible that I'm simply not in full sympathy with the material (I was not a fan of the television program). I did think this movie was better than the first one, though, and in a curious way I'm hoping there will be a third: I think they're getting somewhere.

## The Visitors ★ ★
R, 106 m., 1996

Christian Clavier (Jacquouille/Jacquart), Jean Reno (Godefroy), Valerie Lemercier (Frenegonde/Beatrice), Marie-Anne Chazel (Ginette). Directed by Jean-Marie Poire and produced by Alain Terzian. Screenplay by Christian Clavier and Poire.

*The Visitors* begins in the twelfth century, in swashbuckling style, as a knight saves the king's life and is rewarded with the hand of his daughter. Alas, a magician's potion so addles the knight that he then mistakes the king for a bear and slays him. Having killed the king he can hardly marry the daughter, and so he pledges that he will never marry; small consolation, but it's the thought that counts.

So opens the most popular film in French history—the film that outgrossed *Jurassic Park* and left Frenchmen helpless with laughter. I didn't find it very funny, but then I didn't find *Black Sheep* or *The Cable Guy* very funny either, so maybe the problem is with me or, more likely, maybe all three films need to be sealed into capsules and shot into space.

The twelfth-century stuff is the setup for the story, which mostly takes place in modern France after the knight, Sir Godefroy (Jean Reno), is catapulted into the future along with his vassal Jacquouille, known in the subtitles as Jacquasse (Christian Clavier). That happens as the result of a miscalculation by a friendly magician, who offers to send Godefroy back in time just far enough to save the king's life, but instead drops him into the twentieth century.

Godefroy and Jacquasse handle modern times as best they can. They do war with an automobile, they steal steaks from the grill of a roadside café, they eat the plastic wrappers along with the sandwiches, and eventually Godefroy is befriended by the gentle Beatrice (Valerie Lemercier), who looks exactly like the gentle Frenegonde, whom he left behind. When they seek out Godefroy's castle, they find it has been converted into a hotel, run by Jacquart (Clavier again), who is the vassal's descendant.

Some of the jokes are clever, as when the time travelers receive strong hints about their body odor and take baths while fully clothed, after pouring thousands of francs of expensive perfume into the water. Other jokes run toward bathroom humor, goofy slapstick, and the sorts of things you'd expect from a *Naked Gun* clone. There is much goofiness involving priceless rings and hidden dungeons.

Watching the movie, I was reminded of a poignant luncheon I attended at the Cannes Film Festival. It was hosted by two French film executives who lamented to their guests (North American film critics) that French films could not get entrée into the American market. The dilemma: (1) Most Americans refuse to attend subtitled films, but (2) all Americans who do attend foreign films insist that they be subtitled.

Obviously a film like *The Visitors* is aimed at a mass market—at the *Ace Ventura* crowd. It should logically be dubbed into English, just as *Ace Ventura* was dubbed into French. But after the box-office catastrophe of *Little Indian, Big City*, the distributors were unwilling to risk that. So they have released it subtitled and sent it to art theaters, where it is exactly the sort of movie that audiences go to art theaters to escape from. "Zut alors," as the French say. "Quel dommage. Mais . . . c'est la vie."

## Volcano ★ ½
PG-13, 104 m., 1997

Tommy Lee Jones (Mike Roark), Anne Heche (Dr. Amy Barnes), Don Cheadle (Emmitt Reese), John Corbett (Norman Caldwell), Keith David (Lieutenant Fox), Gaby Hoffman (Kelly Roark), Jacqueline Kim (Dr. Jaye Calder), John Carroll Lynch (Stan Olber), Michael Rispoli (Gator). Directed by Mick Jackson and produced by Andrew Davis and Neal H. Moritz. Screenplay by Jerome Armstrong and Billy Ray.

I expected to see a mountainous volcano in *Volcano*, towering high over Los Angeles. But the movie takes place at ground level; it's about how lava boils out of the La Brea Tar Pits, threatens a stretch of Wilshire Boulevard, and then takes a shortcut through the city sewer system. The ads say, "The Coast Is Toast," but maybe they should say, "The Volcano Is Drano."

This is a surprisingly cheesy disaster epic. It's said that *Volcano* cost a lot more than *Dante's Peak*, a competing volcano movie, but it doesn't look it. *Dante's Peak* had better special effects, a more entertaining story, and a real mountain.

*Volcano* is an absolutely standard, assembly-line undertaking; no wonder one of the extras is reading a paperback titled *Screenwriting Made Easy.*

The movie stars Tommy Lee Jones, professional as always even in this flimsy story, as the chief of the city's Office of Emergency Management. He races through the obligatory opening scenes of all disaster movies (everyday life, ominous warnings, alarm sounded by hero scientist, warnings poo pooed by official muckety-mucks, etc.). Soon manhole covers are being blown sky-high, subway trains are being engulfed by fireballs, and "lava bombs" are flying through the air and setting miniature sets on fire.

Jones is at ground zero when the La Brea Tar Pits erupt and lava flows down the street, melting fire trucks. Like all disaster movie heroes, he's supplied with five obligatory companions:

1. His daughter (Gaby Hoffmann), who comes along for the ride, gets trapped by a lava flow, is rescued, is taken to a hospital, and has to be rescued from the path of a falling skyscraper that her dad has blown up to redirect the lava flow.

2. The blond female scientist (Anne Heche), who warns that the first eruption is not the last, predicts where the lava will flow next, and at a crucial point explains to Jones that it will flow downhill, not uphill. He tells her at a critical moment: "Find my daughter!" She should have replied, "Hey, I'm the one who told you what the lava was going to do! Find her yourself! I'm needed here."

3. The African-American sidekick (Don Cheadle), whose function is to stand in the middle of the Office of Emergency Management and shout at Jones through a telephone. I don't know what he *did* at the office, but nobody else did anything either. One wall was covered by a giant screen showing hysterical anchors on the local TV news. Rows of grim technicians faced this wall, seated at computer terminals that showed the very same TV news broadcast. (All of the anchors are so thrilled to be covering a big story that they can scarcely conceal the elation in their voices.)

4. The Asian-American female doctor (Jacqueline Kim), who arrives at the scene, gives first aid to firemen and hero's daughter, and organizes the evacuation of Cedars-Sinai Hospital as the lava flows toward it. (She doubles as the wife of the man who builds the high-rise tower that Jones blows up.)

5. The dog. In a tiny subplot, we see a dog barking at the lava coming in the front door, and then grabbing his doggy bone and escaping out the back. When that happened, not a single dog in the audience had dry eyes.

Tommy Lee Jones is a fine actor, and he does what he can. Striding into the OEM control center, he walks briskly up to a hapless technician and taps on his computer keyboard, barking: "See that, that, and that? Now watch this!" He sounds like he means business, but do you suppose someone was actually paid for writing that line?

Various subplots are rushed on and off screen at blinding speed. At one point a troublesome black man is handcuffed by police, who later release him as the lava flow approaches. He's free to go, but lingers and says, "You block this street, you save the neighborhood—right?" The cops nod. Then he pitches in and helps them lift a giant concrete barrier. The scene is over in a second, but think how insulting it is: It doesn't take a rocket scientist to figure out they're trying to save the neighborhood, so the dialogue is for our benefit, implying that the black dude cares merely for "the neighborhood," and volunteers only when his myopic concerns have been addressed.

The lava keeps flowing for much of the movie, never looking convincing. I loved it when the firemen aimed their hoses way offscreen into the middle of the lava flow, instead of maybe aiming them at the leading edge of the lava—which they couldn't do, because the lava was a visual effect, and not really there.

I also chortled at the way the scientist warns that the first eruption "is not the last," and yet after the second eruption (when it is time for the movie to end), the sun comes out, everyone smiles, and she offers Jones and his daughter a lift home. Hey, what about the possibility of a third eruption? What about that story she told about the Mexican farmer who found a mountain in his cornfield?

The movie has one perfect line: "This city is finally paying for its arrogance!" Yes, and *Volcano* is part of the price. ☞

# W

## Waco: The Rules of Engagement ★ ★ ★ ½

NO MPAA RATING, 135 m., 1997

A documentary directed by William Gazecki and produced by Gazecki and Michael McNulty.

Like many news-drenched Americans, I paid only casual attention to the standoff at Waco between the Branch Davidians and two agencies of the federal government. I came away with the vague impression that the "cult," as it was always styled, was a group of gun-toting crackpots, that they killed several U.S. agents, refused to negotiate, and finally shot themselves and burned down their "compound" after the feds tried to end the siege peacefully with tear gas.

Watching William Gazecki's remarkable documentary *Waco: The Rules of Engagement*, I am more inclined to use the words "religion" than "cult," and "church center" than "compound." Yes, the Branch Davidians had some strange beliefs, but no weirder than those held by many other religions. And it is pretty clear, on the basis of this film, that the original raid was staged as a publicity stunt, and the final raid was a government riot—a tragedy caused by uniformed boys with toys.

Of course, I am aware that *Waco* argues its point of view, and that there is, no doubt, another case to be made. What is remarkable, watching the film, is to realize that the federal case has not been made. Evidence has been "lost," files and reports have "disappeared," tapes have been returned blank, participants have not testified, and the "crime scene," as a Texas Ranger indignantly testifies, was not preserved for investigation, but razed to the ground by the FBI—presumably to destroy evidence.

The film is persuasive because:

1. It presents testimony from both sides, and shies away from cheap shots. We feel we are seeing a fair attempt to deal with the facts.

2. Those who attack the government are not simply lawyers for the Branch Davidians or muckraking authors (although they are represented) but also solid middle-American types like the county sheriff, the district Texas Rangers, the FBI photographer on the scene, and the man who developed and patented some of the equipment used by the FBI itself to film devastating footage that appears to show its agents firing into the buildings—even though the FBI insists it did not fire a single shot.

3. The eyes of the witnesses. We all have built-in truth detectors, and although it is certainly possible for us to be deceived, there is a human instinct that is hard to fool. Those who argue against the government in this film seem to be telling the truth, and their eyes seem to reflect inner visions of what they believe happened, or saw happen. Most of the government defenders, including an FBI spokesman and Attorney General Janet Reno, seem to be following rehearsed scripts and repeating cant phrases. Reno comes across particularly badly: Either she was misled by the FBI and her aides, or she was completely out of touch with what was happening.

If the film is to be believed, the Branch Davidians were a harmless if controversial group of religious zealots, their beliefs stretching back many decades, who were singled out for attention by the Bureau of Alcohol, Tobacco and Firearms for offenses, real or contrived, involving the possession of firearms—which is far from illegal in Texas. The ATF hoped by raiding the group to repair its tarnished image. And when four of its agents, and several Davidians, were killed in a misguided raid, they played cover-up and turned the case over to the FBI, which mishandled it even more spectacularly.

What is clear, no matter which side you believe, is that during the final deadly FBI raid on the buildings, a toxic and flammable gas was pumped into the compound even though women and children were inside. "Tear gas" sounds innocent, but this type of gas could undergo a chemical transition into cyanide, and there is a pitiful shot of an eight-year-old child's body bent double, backward, by the muscular contractions caused by cyanide.

What comes through strongly is the sense that the attackers were "boys with toys." The film says many of the troops were thrilled to get their hands on real tanks. Some of the law-enforcement types were itching to "stop standing around." One SWAT team member boasts he is "honed to kill." Nancy Sinatra's "These Boots Are Made for Walking" was blasted over loudspeakers to deprive those inside of sleep (the memory of that harebrained operation must still fill the agents with shame).

When the time came, on April 19, 1993, the agents were apparently ready to rock and roll. Heat-sensitive film taken by the FBI and interpreted by experts seems to show FBI agents firing into the compound, firing on an escape route after the fires were started, and deliberately operating on the side of the compound hidden from the view of the press. No evidence is presented that those inside started fires or shot themselves. Although many dead Davidians were indeed found with gunshot wounds, all of the bullets and other evidence have been impounded by the FBI.

Whatever happened at Waco, these facts remain: It is not against the law to hold irregular religious beliefs. It is not illegal to hold and trade firearms. It is legal to defend your own home against armed assault, if that assault is illegal. It is impossible to see this film without reflecting that the federal government, from the top on down, treated the Branch Davidians as if those rights did not apply.

## Wag the Dog ★ ★ ★ ★

R, 97 m., 1998

Dustin Hoffman (Stanley Motss), Robert De Niro (Conrad Brean), Anne Heche (Winifred Ames), Woody Harrelson (Sergeant William Schumann), Denis Leary (Fad King), Willie Nelson (Johnny Green), Andrea Martin (Liz Butsky), Kirsten Dunst (Tacy Lime). Directed by Barry Levinson and produced by Jane Rosenthal, Robert De Niro, and Levinson. Screenplay by David Mamet and Hilary Henkin, based on the book *American Hero* by Larry Beinhart.

So, why *did* we invade Grenada? A terrorist bomb killed all those Marines in Beirut, the White House was taking flak, and suddenly our Marines were landing on a Caribbean island few people had heard of, everybody was tying yellow ribbons 'round old oak trees, and Clint Eastwood was making the movie. The Grenadan invasion, I have read, produced more decorations than combatants. By the time it was over, the Reagan presidency had proven the republic could still flex its muscle—we could take out a Caribbean Marxist regime at will, Cuba notwithstanding.

Barry Levinson's *Wag the Dog* cites Grenada as an example of how easy it is to whip up patriotic frenzy, and how dubious the motives can sometimes be. The movie is a satire that contains just enough realistic ballast to be teasingly plausible; like *Dr. Strangelove,* it makes you laugh, and then it makes you wonder. Just today, I read a Strangelovian story in the paper revealing that some of Russia's nuclear missiles, still aimed at the United States, have gone unattended because their guards were denied their bonus rations of four pounds of sausage a month. It is getting harder and harder for satire to stay ahead of reality.

In the movie, a U.S. president is accused of luring an underage "Firefly Girl" into an anteroom of the Oval Office, and there presenting her with opportunities no Firefly Girl should anticipate from her commander in chief. A presidential election is weeks away, the opposition candidate starts using "Thank Heaven for Little Girls" in his TV ads, and White House aide Winifred Ames (Anne Heche) leads a spin doctor named Conrad Brean (Robert De Niro) into bunkers far beneath the White House for an emergency session.

Brean, a Mr. Fixit who has masterminded a lot of shady scenarios, has a motto: "To change the story, change the lead." To distract the press from the Firefly Girl scandal, he advises extending a presidential trip to Asia, while issuing official denials that the new B-3 bomber is being activated ahead of schedule. "But there *is* no B-3 bomber," he's told. "Perfect! Deny it even exists!"

Meanwhile, he cooks up a phony international crisis with Albania. Why Albania? Nobody is sure where it is, nobody cares, and you can't get any news out of it. Nobody can even think of any Albanians except—maybe the Belushi brothers? To produce the graphic look and feel of the war, Brean flies to Hollywood and enlists the services of a producer named Stanley Motss (Dustin Hoffman), who is hard to convince at first. He wants proof that Brean has a direct line to the White House. He gets it. As they watch a live briefing by a presidential spokesman, Brean dictates into a cell phone and the spokesman repeats, word for word, what he hears on his earpiece. (I was reminded of the line in *Broadcast News:* "Goes in here, comes out there.")

Motss assembles the pieces for a media blitz. As spokesmen warn of Albanian terrorists skulking south from Canada with "suitcase bombs," Motss supervises the design of a logo for use on the news channels, hires Willie Nelson to write the song that will become the conflict's "spontaneous" anthem, and fakes news footage of a hapless Albanian girl (Kirsten Dunst) fleeing from rapists with her kitten. (Dunst is an American actress, and the kitten, before it is created with special effects, is a bag of Tostitos.)

But what about a martyr? Motss cooks up "good old Shoe," Sergeant William Schumann (Woody Harrelson), who is allegedly rescued from the hands of the Albanians to be flown back for a hero's welcome. Shoe inspires a shtick, too: Kids start lobbing their old gym shoes over power lines, and throwing them onto the court during basketball games, as a spontaneous display of patriotism.

It's creepy how this material is absurd and convincing at the same time. Levinson, working from a smart, talky script by David Mamet and Hilary Henkin, based on the book *American Hero* by Larry Beinhart, deconstructs the media blitz that invariably accompanies any modern international crisis. Even when a conflict is real and necessary (the Gulf War, for example), the packaging of it is invariably shallow and unquestioning; like sportswriters, war correspondents abandon any pretense of objectivity and detachment, and cheerfully root for our side.

For Hoffman, this is the best performance in some time, inspired, it is said, by producer Robert Evans. (In power and influence, however, Motss seems more like Ray Stark.) Like a lot of Hollywood power brokers, Hoffman's Motss combines intelligence with insecurity and insincerity, and frets because he won't get "credit" for his secret manipulations. De Niro's Brean, on the other hand, is a creature born to live in shadow, and De Niro plays him with the poker-faced plausibility of real spin doctors, who tell lies as a professional specialty. Their conversations are crafted by Mamet as a verbal ballet between two men who love the jargon of their crafts.

"Why does a dog wag its tail?" Brean asks at one point. "Because the dog is smarter than the tail. If the tail was smarter, it would wag the dog." In the Breanian universe, the tail is smarter, and we, dear readers, are invited to be the dogs. ☞

## Waiting for Guffman ★ ★ ★

R, 84 m., 1997

Christopher Guest (Corky St. Clair), Eugene Levy (Dr. Allan Pearl), Fred Willard (Ron Albertson), Catherine O'Hara (Sheila Albertson), Parker Posey (Libby Mae Brown), Matt Keeslar (Johnny Savage), Lewis Arquette (Clifford Wooley), Bob Balaban (Lloyd Miller). Directed by Christopher Guest and produced by Karen Murphy. Screenplay by Guest and Eugene Levy.

Blaine, Missouri, was founded, we are told, 150 years ago by settlers who were trekking to the West Coast and stopped when their leader "smelled the salt air." Its place in history has been assured by two events: a wooden stool made in Blaine, presented to President William McKinley, led to the city becoming "stool capital of America." And in 1946, a flying saucer landed nearby. Within its radius it was "always sixty-seven degrees with a 40 percent chance of rain." Local residents were invited aboard for a potluck supper, and one of them still has no feeling in his buttocks.

Obviously such events cry out for dramatic treatment, and for its 150th anniversary Blaine obtains the services of Corky St. Clair (Christopher Guest), a "relocated" Broadway director who will stage an amateur theatrical pageant. Corky's credits include *Backdraft*, a musical based on the film about firemen. He allegedly has a wife named Bonnie, who has never been seen, although he buys all of her clothing and knows a great deal about depilatories.

Such is the setup for *Waiting for Guffman*, directed and cowritten by Guest, who was also the cowriter for *This Is Spinal Tap*, the very funny 1981 mock-documentary about a failing rock group. *Guffman* is not as insistently funny, perhaps because it has a sneaking fondness for its characters (*Spinal Tap* ridiculed its heroes with a true zeal). In a sequence that, I gather, was improvised by the actors themselves, a group of locals audition for Corky and the local music teacher (Bob Balaban), and we see Parker Posey's extremely literal interpretation of "Teacher's Pet."

Others in the audition include the local travel agents (Fred Willard and Catherine O'Hara), who have never been out of town but have travelers' imaginations and perform "Midnight at the Oasis." They consider themselves "the Lunts of Blaine."

The movie doesn't bludgeon us with gags. It proceeds with a certain comic relentlessness from setup to payoff, and its deliberation is part of the fun (as when it takes its time explaining the exact nature of the travel agent's plastic surgery). Some of the better laughs are deadpan, as when the travel agent and his wife take the local dentist (Eugene Levy) and his wife to dinner at a Chinese restaurant. It has a neon sign two stories high that announces CHOP SUEY; the travel agent asks, "How did you find this place?"

Much of the fun comes from the songs composed for the pageant (music and lyrics by Guest, Harry Shearer, and Michael McKean). They have the sound and the brio of 1940s musicals, and the literal-mindedness of people determined to shoehorn cosmic significance into a perspective. Tension is generated when it becomes known that a man named Guffman, a famous New York producer's agent, will attend opening night with the thought that "Red, White . . . and Blaine" might travel well to Broadway.

The comic tone of *Waiting for Guffman* has grown out of Second City (where most of the actors once worked) and the classic SCTV television show. Attention is paid not simply to funny characters and punch lines, but to small nudges at human nature. Consider, for example, Bob Balaban in an understated role as the long-suffering local teacher who knows how outrageous Corky St. Clair is, but never quite acts on his knowledge. Or listen to small touches as when the descendant of Blaine's original settlers sighs, "I know how the Kennedys must feel." Some of the laughs are so subtle you almost miss them, as when Corky warns the dentist that his horn-rimmed glasses would be out of place in a scene set in 1846—but neglects to remember his own earring.

If you see the film, don't leave before the closing credits, which include several "movie collectibles" that provide maybe the loudest laughs in the movie.

## Warriors of Virtue ★ ★

PG, 103 m., 1997

Angus Macfadyen (Komodo), Mario Yedidia (Ryan), Marley Shelton (Elysia), Chao-Li Chi (Master Chung), Dennis Dun (Chef Ming), Michael John Anderson (Mudlap), Jack Tate (Yun), Doug Jones (Yee), Don W. Lewis (Lai), J. Todd Adams (Chi), Adrienne Corcoran (Tsun). Directed by Ronny Yu and produced by Dennis Law, Ronald Law, Christopher Law, Jeremy Law, and Patricia Ruben. Screenplay by Michael Vickerman and Hugh Kelley.

I have always been amazed by the recuperative powers of young heroes who are snatched away from home and family and sent to struggle in distant fantasy worlds. Consider young Ryan (Mario Yedidia), the hero of *Warriors of Virtue.* One moment he's balancing above a drainage whirlpool on a bet from a bully on the football team, and the next he's on the planet Tao, helping a race of kangaroo warriors fight the evil Komodo for control of the Lifespring.

Does he weep? Does he worry about his parents? Is he homesick? Not for a moment. He's a comic book fan who intuits, I guess, that he's been magically transported into a fantasy adventure, and soon he is getting briefed by the beautiful Princess Elysia (Marley Shelton) and wise old Master Chung (Chao-Li Chi) about the desperate state of affairs on Tao, where all but one Lifespring have been exhausted, and the vile Komodo (Angus Macfadyen) wants it for himself.

The key to this dilemma lies with Ryan, who in real life has a friend named Ming who is a virtuoso chef in a Chinese restaurant (he can land a ladle full of fried rice on a platter at ten paces). Ming is wise in the Zen master tradition, and shows Ryan an empty cocoon: As a child he released a beautiful moth from it, only to see the moth die because "I interrupted its journey" and it "needed its struggle." Likewise, Ryan must continue his journey. If he feels inadequate as the water boy on the football team, then he must prove himself. Ming gives him an old book that may contain the answers.

*Warriors of Virtue* is ambitious in its production, if not especially original. Its set design is by Eugenio Zanetti, who won an Oscar for "Restoration," and he does a good job of creating a forest planet with towering trees and an Everglades-like landscape that looks not unlike Yoda's setting in *The Empire Strikes Back.* The *Star Wars* movies are evoked in more than the setting; when Ryan opens the old book Ming gave him, he finds its pages blank, and on the sound track we hear, "The answer lies within you, Ryan"—which sounds uncannily Force-like.

On the planet of Tao, he finds Elysia and Master Chung (a Mr. Miyagi clone) helped by a group of five creatures who look like kangaroos but behave like a cross between Power Rangers and Ninja Turtles. The kangaroos represent the elemental forces of fire, metal, wood, water, and earth (the movie informs us these forces are more powerful than "guns, lasers . . . morphing"). As the evil Komodo schemes to drop the Roo Warriors through a trapdoor into death by spinning blades, only Ryan can save the day—if he can wrest the book from the scheming little person Mudlap (Michael John Anderson).

And so on. The movie looks better than it plays, and gets rather tiresome, especially since there is a limit to a Roo personality, Ryan is resolutely one-dimensional, and Angus Macfadyen (who played Robert the Bruce in *Braveheart*) makes Komodo into a villain who goes through the motions of evil but doesn't seem to have his heart in it.

At one point, Komodo wearily intones, "The center cannot hold; things fall apart." It's a slight misquotation from W. B. Yeats's poem "The Second Coming," but one is surprised to hear it at all, since everything said on the planet Tao presumably comes from within Ryan's mind, and he shows no signs of having read any book—except, of course, for Chef Ming's. The Yeats poem continues, "Mere anarchy is loosed upon the world." Call me a dreamer, but that sounds like an even more promising story idea than *Warriors of Virtue.*

## Washington Square ★ ★ ★

PG, 115 m., 1997

Jennifer Jason Leigh (Catherine Sloper), Albert Finney (Dr. Austin Sloper), Maggie Smith (Aunt Lavinia), Ben Chaplin (Morris Townsend), Judith Ivey (Mrs. Almond). Directed by Agnieszka Holland and produced by Roger Birnbaum and Julie Bergman Sender. Screenplay by Carol Doyle, based on the novel by Henry James.

So often in Henry James it comes down to the same contest: On the one side, the yearnings of the heart, and on the other side, money. Usually it is old family money and the old family that controls it, sometimes hoping to restrict the freedom of a character *(The Ambassadors)*, sometimes hoping to grant it *(Portrait of a Lady)*. In James's short novel *Washington Square*, a rich doctor cannot believe anyone would value what he considers his plain and graceless daughter, and so assumes that the man she loves is after her money. That he may be right is, for her, no consolation.

Agnieszka Holland's new movie *Washington Square* makes of this situation a sad story about a young woman named Catherine (Jennifer Jason Leigh), who spends much of her life seeking the love of two men who do not deserve it. Her father, the wealthy Dr. Austin Sloper (Albert Finney), resents her because his wife died in giving birth to her. Her suitor, Morris Townsend (Ben Chaplin), likes her well enough if she comes with her father's money, but not so well otherwise. Her challenge is to find some measure of self-respect in a life where everyone seems to value her because of someone else's accomplishments.

Her father is an orotund monster who demands, and even receives, the love and obedience of his daughter. He sees her as a loyal helpmate, waiting with tea when he returns from work, content to spend the rest of her days as her father's meek little companion. Her lover is poor, must marry money or make it, and knows which course he prefers, although he is handsome and agreeable enough to feel his "attributes" are the equal of her own.

And the girl? "I've never thought of her as delightful and charming," the doctor says on one occasion, astonished that anyone else should. He is capable of astonishing cruelty, as when he tells her, "How obscene that your mother should give her life so that you can inhabit space on this earth." She is so intimidated that when asked, as a little girl, to give a recital for her father's friends, she can do no more than pee on the floor.

There are, however, weapons in her arsenal. She is not as plain as her father thinks, nor as lacking in spirit. And she has an ally in her father's sister, Aunt Lavinia (Maggie Smith), who is thrilled by romantic intrigue and does everything she can to further the courtship—if only because it provides her entertainment by allowing her to sneak off as a secret emissary.

The movie is set in the years before the Civil War in a newly prosperous section of Manhattan, where Dr. Sloper, as James tells us in his book, "was what you might call a scholarly doctor, and yet there was nothing abstract in his remedies—he always ordered you to take something." Sloper earns a good income, but came into his fortune by marrying a rich woman, and so is uniquely prepared to judge the motives of young Mr. Townsend.

For Catherine, Townsend's attention is liberating, offering a way out of her father's house. Still, she agrees to a year's European journey with her father, during which she is to reconsider her position. At the very summit of the Alps (how did they get there, dressed as they are?), her father asks, "Should you like to be left in such a place as this to starve?" He warns that Townsend will someday abandon her in just such a place, literally or figuratively. She cannot believe this, and we are not sure. Townsend is no worse, probably, than most of the young men produced by his materialistic society. The problem is, he is not nearly as good as Catherine thinks.

Jennifer Jason Leigh often plays women of brassy boldness *(Last Exit to Brooklyn, Kansas City,* and Dorothy Parker in *Mrs. Parker and the Vicious Circle).* What is remarkable is how she can also play a recessive character like Catherine so that every assertion seems like an act of courage. Her Catherine is based on quiet determination: She can either collapse or grow.

Holland is a director interested in the secrets behind family walls, as in her wonderful *The Secret Garden.* Here she takes a story that, in a modern rewrite, would be about child abuse, and she makes it into the story of how the doctor's fortune seems to shrink even as it grows—until it loses all its power to destroy Catherine's life. Henry James saw more humor in the story than Holland does (although Aunt Lavinia remains comic), but what they both understand is that in a family like this, everything depends on the money—unless nothing does.

## The Wedding Singer ★

PG-13, 96 m., 1998

Adam Sandler (Robbie), Drew Barrymore (Julia), Christine Taylor (Holly), Allen Covert (Sammy), Matthew Glave (Glenn), Ellen Albertini Dow (Rosie), Angela Featherstone (Linda), Alexis Arquette (George). Directed by Frank Coraci and produced by Robert Simonds and Jack Giarraputo. Screenplay by Tim Herlihy.

*The Wedding Singer* tells the story of, yes, a wedding singer from New Jersey, who is cloyingly sweet at some times and a cruel monster at others. The filmmakers are obviously unaware of his split personality; the screenplay reads like a collaboration between Jekyll and Hyde. Did anybody, at any stage, give the story the slightest thought?

The plot is so familiar the end credits should have issued a blanket thank-you to a century of Hollywood love-coms. Through a torturous series of contrived misunderstandings, the boy and girl avoid happiness for most of the movie, although not as successfully as we do. It's your basic off-the-shelf formula in which two people fall in love, but are kept apart because (a) they're engaged to creeps; (b) they say the wrong things at the wrong times; and (c) they get bad information. It's exhausting, seeing the characters work so hard at avoiding the obvious.

Of course, there's the obligatory scene where the good girl goes to the good boy's house to say she loves him, but the bad girl answers the door and lies to her. I spent the weekend looking at old Astaire and Rogers movies, which basically had the same plot: She thinks he's a married man, and almost gets married to the slimy bandleader before he finally figures everything out and declares his love at the eleventh hour.

The big differences between Astaire and Rogers in *Swing Time* and Adam Sandler and Drew Barrymore in *The Wedding Singer* is that (1) in 1936 they were more sophisticated than we are now, and *knew* the plot was inane, and had fun with that fact, and (2) they could dance. One of the sad by-products of the dumbing-down of America is that we're now forced to witness the goofy plots of the 1930s played sincerely, as if they were really deep.

Sandler is the wedding singer. He's engaged to a slut who stands him up at the altar because, sob, "the man I fell in love with six years ago was a rock singer who licked the microphone like David Lee Roth—and now you're only a . . . a . . . wedding singer!" Barrymore, meanwhile, is engaged to a macho monster who brags about how he's cheating on her. Sandler and Barrymore meet because she's a waitress at the weddings where he sings. We know immediately they are meant for each other. Why do we know this? Because we are conscious and sentient. It takes them a lot longer.

The basic miscalculation in Adam Sandler's career plan is to ever play the lead. He is not a lead. He is the best friend, or the creep, or the loser boyfriend. He doesn't have the voice to play a lead: Even at his most sincere, he sounds like he's doing stand-up—like he's mocking a character in a movie he saw last night. Barrymore, on the other hand, has the stuff to play a lead (I commend you once again to the underrated *Mad Love*). But what is she doing in this one—in a plot her grandfather would have found old-fashioned? At least when she gets a good line (she tries out the married name "Mrs. Julia Gulia") she knows how to handle it.

The best laughs in the film come right at the top, in an unbilled cameo by the invaluable Steve Buscemi, as a drunken best man who makes a shambles of a wedding toast. He has the timing, the presence, and the intelligence to go right to the edge. Sandler, on the other hand, always keeps something in reserve—his talent. It's like he's afraid of committing; he holds back so he can use the "only kidding" defense.

I could bore you with more plot details. About why he thinks she's happy and she thinks he's happy and they're both wrong and she flies to Vegas to marry the stinker, and he . . . but why bother? And why even mention that the movie is set in the mid-1980s and makes a lot of mid-1980s references that are supposed to be funny but sound exactly like lame dialogue? And what about the curious cameos by faded stars and inexplicably cast character actors? And why do they write the role of a Boy George clone for Alexis Arquette and then do nothing with the character except let him hang there on screen? And why does the tourist section of the plane have fewer seats than first class? And, and, and . . .

## Welcome to Sarajevo ★ ★

R, 102 m., 1998

Stephen Dillane (Henderson), Woody Harrelson (Flynn), Marisa Tomei (Nina), Emira Nusevic (Emira), Kerry Fox (Jane Carson), Goran Visnjic (Risto), James Nesbitt (Gregg), Emily Lloyd (Annie McGee). Directed by Michael Winterbottom and produced by Graham Broadbent and Damian Jones. Screenplay by Frank Cottrell Boyce, based on the book *Natasha's Story* by Michael Nicholson.

My confidence in *Welcome to Sarajevo* was undermined by the film's uncertain air of improvisation. Like Haskell Wexler's *Medium Cool,* which plunged into the midst of the riots at the 1968 Democratic Convention in Chicago, it combines fact and fiction, real and fake news footage, and actors side-by-side with local people. Wexler pulled it off. Michael Winterbottom, who made this film about a 1992 Sarajevo where the smoke seems to be still rising from the latest shellings, doesn't quite.

The movie centers itself on a group of journalists who take harrowing risks to cover a war that their editors and viewers back home aren't very interested in. Stephen Dillane plays Henderson, a British reporter who finds his latest big story has been pushed off the front page by the divorce of the Duchess of York. And Woody Harrelson plays Flynn, a high-profile news star on American TV, who walks into the range of sniper fire to aid a wounded altar boy—after first making sure, of course, that the cameras are rolling. His reasoning: "Well you know, oddly enough, back home no one has ever heard of Sarajevo and everyone has heard of me."

The story of Henderson forms the core of the movie. He's in anguish over the fates of children who are war victims, and narrates footage of a big UN plane taking off: "Children are dying in the most dangerous corner of the most dangerous city on earth—but this plane is flying out of here empty." He eventually takes things into his own hands, smuggling a young girl orphan out of Sarajevo by quasi-legal means, so that he and his wife can adopt her. This story thread is based on fact—British TV reporter Michael Nicholson and his wife adopted an orphan, and he wrote a book about it.

One can imagine a strong film about that part of the story. One can also imagine a film about war correspondents under fire and frustrated by an indifferent world. The problem is that Winterbottom has imagined both stories and several others, and tells them in a style designed to feel as if reality has been caught on the fly. What it more often feels like, alas, is the venerable Second City formula for improvisation—"Something wonderful right away!"—and too often we sense that the actors are drifting and the story is at sea.

That's especially true of the Woody Harrelson scenes. He's an interesting, intense actor, and a good choice for a character living recklessly under fire. But too often I got the feeling that Winterbottom, having imported American stars (Marisa Tomei is also in the cast), tried to plug them into spur-of-the-moment, spontaneous situations that didn't fit with the rest of the film. There's the feeling that the central characters don't really know each other as well as they should. The film arrives in fragments, without a sense of destination.

Films like this, of course, lament for the children—for helpless orphans and altar boys gunned down by partisan and sectarian snipers. But the snipers were altar boys only a few years ago, and altar boys grow up to become snipers. The film decries "violence" but doesn't name names: Much of the evil that has descended on this part of the world is caused by tribalism and religious fanaticism (when one group kills another in the name of their God, that is fanaticism).

So often there is a style of reporting events like the Bosnian tragedy in which words like "partisans" are used instead of "religious fanatics," because although a man might kill others for worshiping the wrong god, of course we must not offend his religion. *Welcome to Sarajevo* tiptoes around that awkwardness with easy pieties, in which an orphan is spared, a man is a hero, cynicism masks bravery—and the underlying issues are not addressed. A better and braver film about this part of the world is Milcho Manchevsky's *Before the Rain* (1995), which shows clearly how the circle of killing goes around and around, fueled by the mindless passion that my God, my language, my ancestors, give me the right to kill you.

## When the Cat's Away ★ ★ ★

R, 95 m., 1997

Garance Clavel (Chloe), Zinedine Soualem (Jamel), Renee Le Calm (Madame Renee), Olivier Py (Michel), Arapimou (Gris-Gris), Romain Duris (Drummer). Directed by Cedric Klapisch and produced by Aissa Djabri, Farid Lahouassa, and Manuel Munz. Screenplay by Klapisch.

Here is a movie about a young woman named Chloe, who has no luck with men, considers herself desperately lonely, and then finds out what loneliness is when she loses her cat. She's a little mouse, and *When the Cat's Away* tells the story of how she plays. But it is all so much more tricky than that.

The French love to make these pictures that are about attitude and personal style. The one thing you know is that the movie is not going to be about the cat's loss, or the cat's return, or even the cat's life or death.

In an American movie the heroine would think the cat's fate was terribly important, and so would the filmmakers. But Cedric Klapisch, who wrote and directed *When the Cat's Away,* realizes that the movie is really about a woman who has nothing better to do than obsess about her cat.

Chloe (Garance Clavel) lives in a district of Paris that was until recently rather shabby and neglected, which meant that people could count on spending their lives there without being annoyed. When she decides to go on vacation, she needs someone to look after the cat (named Gris-Gris), and the waiter in the local café suggests Madame Renee (Renee Le Calm), an elderly cat woman who lives in an apartment nearby.

Chloe parks Gris-Gris with Madame Renee, goes on vacation (the director compresses the entire holiday into one postcard shot), and returns to find Madame Renee in distress because the cat has run away. Chloe now sets about finding the cat, aided by Madame Renee's network of cat ladies, and by a simpleminded fellow named Jamel (Zinedine Soualem), who helpfully risks his life on rooftops, usually in search of the wrong cat.

The disappearance of Gris-Gris compounds Chloe's isolation. "Why am I all alone?" she asks her gay roommate, who is lonely himself. "Guys scare you," he says. "That's why you have a roommate who's gay." She goes awkwardly into a bar, but doesn't know any of the right pickup behavior, and ends up being accused in the toilet of trying to steal another woman's boyfriend. Not that Chloe's love life is quite that adventuresome; in one scene, the guy seems to hurry through the mechanics of sex because he's eager to make a phone call.

All of this takes place in a kind of casual, offhand way: Chloe exudes the sense of living in her city, of being rooted in the neighborhood, of being not a character in a movie but someone you might see or hear about. And many of the other characters really do live in the district, and are playing themselves—particularly Madame Renee, a short, frizzy-haired, strongly opinionated little woman who is so uninhibited and convincing you'd never guess she's a real cat lady, playing herself.

The movie reminds us of what it must have been like to live in cities before air conditioning sealed the windows and television ended leisurely conversations on the front steps. Now we live in containers, like cargo on a ship. In Chloe's Paris, people have a good sense of who lives next door and upstairs, and when she finally meets the neighborhood rock 'n' roll musician, she and everyone else have been listening to his drums for weeks. Of course, this is changing; the district is being gentrified, and familiar old merchants are being replaced by high-priced shops.

The movie is made in the tradition of Eric Rohmer, who is the master of this sort of film. In his many movies, most recently *Rendezvous in Paris,* he follows people into the casual moments of their lives, and allows them coincidences and mistakes. Klapisch does the same thing. *When the Cat's Away* is like a very subtle, curious, edgy documentary in which we get interested in Chloe because she has lost her cat, and by the end almost have to be reminded that the cat is missing.

## When We Were Kings ★ ★ ★

PG, 85m., 1997

A documentary film directed by Leon Gast and produced by David Sonenberg, Gast, and Taylor Hackford. Featuring Muhammad Ali, George Foreman, James Brown, B. B. King, Don King, Spike Lee, Norman Mailer, Miriam Makeba, George Plimpton, and Mobutu Sese Seko.

The heavyweight title fight between Muhammad Ali and George Foreman in Zaire on October 30, 1974—the "Rumble in the Jungle"—is enshrined as one of the great sports events of the century. It was also a cultural and political happening. Into the capital of Kinshasa flew planeloads of performers for an "African Woodstock," TV crews, Howard Cosell at the head of an international contingent of sports journalists, celebrity fight groupies like Norman Mailer and George Plimpton, and, of course, the two principals: Ali, then still controversial because of his decision to be a conscientious objector, and Foreman, now huggable and lovable in TV commercials but then seen as fearsome and forbidding.

"I'm young, I'm handsome, I'm fast, I'm strong, and I can't be beat," Ali told the press. They didn't believe him. Foreman had destroyed Joe Frazier, who had defeated Ali. Foreman was younger, bigger, and stronger, with a punch so powerful, Norman Mailer recalled, "that after he was finished with a heavy punching bag it had a depression pounded into it." Ali was thirty-two and thought to be over the hill. The odds were seven-to-one against him.

The Zaire they arrived in was a country much in need of foreign currency and image refurbishment. Under the leadership of Mobutu Sese Seko ("the archetype of a closet sadist," said Mailer), the former Belgian Congo had became a paranoid police state; the new stadium built to showcase the fight was rumored to hold 1,000 political prisoners in cells in its catacombs.

Don King, then at the dawn of his career as a fight promoter, had sold Mobutu on the fight and raised $5 million for each fighter. The "African Woodstock," featuring such stars as B. B. King, James Brown, and Miriam Makeba, was supposed to pay for part of that. For Ali, the fight in Africa was payback time for the hammering he'd taken in the American press for his refusal to fight in Vietnam. For Foreman, it was more complicated. So great was the pro-Ali frenzy, Foreman observed, that when he got off the plane the crowds were surprised to find that he was also a black man. "Why do they hate me so much?" he wondered.

Leon Gast's *When We Were Kings* is like a time capsule; the original footage has waited all these years to be assembled into a film, because of legal and financial difficulties. It is a new documentary of a past event, recapturing the electricity generated by Muhammad Ali in his prime. Spike Lee, who with Mailer and Plimpton provides modern commentary on the 1974 footage, says young people today do not know how famous and important Ali was. He is right. "When I fly on an airplane," Ali once told me, "I look out of the window and I think, I am the only person that *everyone* down there knows about." It is not bragging if you are only telling the truth.

The original film apparently started as a concert documentary. Then the fight was delayed because of a cut to Foreman's eye. The concert went ahead as scheduled, and then the fighters, their entourages, and the press settled down to wait for the main event. No one really thought Ali had a chance—perhaps not even Ali, who seems reflective and withdrawn in a few private moments, although in public he predicted victory.

How could he have a chance, really? Hadn't the U.S. government taken away his prime years as a fighter after he refused to fight in Vietnam? ("I ain't got no quarrel with the Viet Cong," he explained.) Wasn't Foreman bigger, faster, stronger, younger? History records Ali's famous strategy, the "Rope-a Dope Defense," in which he simply outwaited Foreman, absorbing incalculable punishment until, in the eighth round, Foreman was exhausted and Ali exploded with a series of rights to the head, finishing him.

Was this, however, really a strategy at all? The film gives the impression that Ali got nowhere in the first round and adopted the "Rope-a-Dope" almost by default. Perhaps he knew, or hoped, that he was in better condition than Foreman and could outlast him if he simply stayed on his feet. It is certain that hardly anyone in Zaire that night, not even his steadfast supporter Cosell, thought Ali could win; the upset became an enduring part of his myth.

*When We Were Kings* captures Ali's public persona and private resolve. As heavyweight champion during the Vietnam War, he could easily have arrived at an accommodation with the military, touring bases in lieu of combat duty. Although he was called a coward and a draft dodger, surely it took more courage to follow the path he chose. And yet it is remarkable how ebullient, how joyful he remained even after the price he paid; how he is willing to be a clown and a poet as well as a fighter and an activist.

Seeing the film today inspires poignant feelings; we contrast young Ali with the ailing and aging legend, and reflect that this fight must have contributed to the damage that slowed him down. It is also fascinating to contrast the young Foreman with today's much-loved figure; he, too, has grown and mellowed. When the movie was made all of those developments were still ahead; there is a palpable tension, as the two men step into the ring, that is not lessened because we know the outcome.

## White Squall ★ ★ ★

PG-13, 128 m., 1996

Jeff Bridges (Sheldon/"Skipper"), Caroline Goodall (Dr. Alice Sheldon), John Savage (McCrea), Scott Wolf (Chuck Gieg), Jeremy Sisto (Frank Beaumont), Ryan Phillippe (Gil Martin), David Lascher (Robert March), Eric Michael Cole (Dean Preston). Directed by Ridley Scott and produced by Mimi Polk Gitlin and Rocky Lang. Screenplay by Todd Robinson.

*White Squall* is the sort of red-blooded young man's adventure movie that Jack London might have penned, although not quite in this way. Said to be based on fact, it's about a group of high school students who sign on aboard the brigantine ship *Albatross* for their senior year at sea. They'll sail to the tip of South America and back, learning along the way to be sailors, accept responsibility, and grow up.

The skipper: Sheldon (Jeff Bridges), a skilled sailor and schoolmaster who believes in firm onboard discipline. His wife: Dr. Alice Sheldon (Caroline Goodall), who will teach science and be ship's nurse. The English and history teacher: McCrea (John Savage), whose approach to instruction is to wake the lads every morning with loud doses of Shakespeare and Coleridge. There is also a Cuban cook, who, true to type, pops up in an opening scene to darkly warn the boys to stay out of his galley. And a ship's motto: "Where we go one, we go all."

The emphasis on one for all and all for one, coupled with the high value placed on discipline, adds up to a program designed to make good soldiers, and indeed the cruise seems at times a little like boot camp, with Bridges as drill instructor (a student with vertigo is forced to climb the rigging). Yet Bridges is a likable type who runs a fairly loose ship; he's the kind of skipper to whom a father might say, "I give you the boy. Give me back the man."

For Bridges, that includes turning a fairly blind eye on the boys' smoking (not all that common among sixteen-year-olds in 1960), drinking, and whoring around in port (his wife matter-of-factly administers stabs of penicillin). It also involves trust that the young sailors will learn and do their jobs. We sense that he is an expert seaman, although the movie is thin on details so that in a crucial late scene we are not sure if it was Bridges or one of his young sailors who made the correct decision.

The movie has been directed by Ridley Scott, whose brother Tony's *Top Gun* (1986) provides a model: Assemble a group of young men, distribute good and bad qualities among them, and have them learn through hard lessons that it is best to stick together and follow orders. Women play a secondary role (in this case, limited to the transmission and healing of VD). The underlying orientation of the movie, common enough in the 1960s, is that boys grow up to be men who do neat things together and then go out on Saturday night looking for easy action.

Movies in this genre almost always have one kid with a rich, obnoxious father who turns up unexpectedly, embarrasses his son, and expects impossible things of him. Also a kid with a secret phobia. And a kid who is terrified he is inadequate. All such characters appear here, although they are a little hard to tell apart, because instead of helpful typecasting, Scott has manned his crew with muscular, bronzed young types with keen haircuts, who look as if they hang out in Calvin Klein ads. (When I was fifteen or sixteen, most kids were scrawny and had pimples and cowlicks, and they didn't look a bit like movie stars.)

Those weaknesses—the vague moral mission, the interchangeable crew members, and the obligatory assortment of personal problems—keep the movie from taking wing as it might have, say, in a story by Jack London or Joseph Conrad. They would have focused more on individual characters and have been less interested in the goal of forming team players. But they might have liked the good things in the movie, and so did I: the feel of the ship itself, the spectacular photography, the delicious sense of liberty during nights in port, and especially the storm sequence near the end.

About this storm I will not say much, except to observe that a *White Squall*, according to the dictionary, is a sudden storm that comes unaccompanied by clouds. And so it does, in storm footage of great fury and effectiveness (save one shot where you can see that Bridges and two others are in fact standing on the bottom of a tank). One of the storm's outcomes is a hearing held by the Coast Guard, at which positions are taken and speeches are made that will sound very familiar to anyone who recalls the climax of *Scent of a Woman* (1992).

The movie could have been smarter and more particular in the way it establishes its characters. Its underlying values are better the less you think about them. And the last scene not only ties the message together but puts about three ribbons on it. And yet, I enjoyed the movie for the sheer physical exuberance of its adventure. It is magnificently mounted and photographed. I sat up close to the screen, and was immersed in the glory of the sailing ship and the exhilaration of the voyage.

## The Whole Wide World ★ ★ ★

PG, 105 m., 1997

Vincent D'Onofrio (Robert E. Howard), Renee Zellweger (Novalyne Price), Ann Wedgeworth (Mrs. Howard), Benjamin Mouton (Clyde Smith), Chris Shearer (Truett). Directed by Dan Ireland and produced by Carl-Jan Colpaert, Kevin Reidy, Ireland, and Vincent D'Onofrio. Screenplay by Michael Scott Myers, based on the memoir "One Who Walked Alone" by Novalyne Price Ellis.

The pulp magazines that flourished from the 1920s through the 1950s were one of the great trashy entertainment media of our century. I got in at the end of the period, as the big-format classic pulps like *Thrilling Wonder Stories* were being pushed aside by television and replaced on the newsstands by more respectable digest-sized mags like *Analog*, *Galaxy*, and *F&SF*. But I haunted used bookstores and brought home old pulps in cardboard boxes strapped to the back of my bike, and late into the night I'd read their breathless stories and feel faint stirrings of unfamiliar emotions as I examined their covers, on which desperate women in big titanium brassieres squirmed in the tentacles of bug-eyed monsters.

The great pulps came in four flavors: science fiction, Westerns, romance, and crime. Of these, the brand-new genre was SF, baptized by Hugo Gernsback in his pioneering magazine *Amazing Stories*. The skilled pulp writers could move from one genre to another, sometimes using pseudonyms because they had more than one story in an issue. The crime mags gave birth to *film noir* and the great writers like Hammett, Chandler, and their heirs. They also gave rise to the image of the writer as romantic loner, slaving at his typewriter in a rented room, a cigarette in his mouth and a bottle on the floor, working for peanuts.

Robert E. Howard bought that image lock, stock, and truncheon. He was by his own admission "the greatest pulp writer in the whole wide world," a mainstay of the famous fantasy/horror magazine named *Weird Tales.* The best of his creations was Conan the Barbarian, who had a rebirth in the 1970s in two Schwarzenegger movies and in some fifty Conan paperbacks written under license by modern-day hacks. By then Howard was long dead.

*The Whole Wide World* is based on a 1988 memoir of Howard, written by a woman named Novalyne Price Ellis, who was a retired Louisiana schoolteacher when the Conan boom came along. Disturbed by portraits of Howard as some kind of loony loner, she wrote the book to recall her own romance with Howard more than fifty years earlier. Her memories have served him well, even though he was probably loony and a loner given to statements like "the road I walk, I walk alone," which are not designed to inspire confidence in the bosom of a potential fiancée.

Howard is played in the film by Vincent D'Onofrio as a tall, broad, open-faced Texas boy who likes to wear white shirts and suspenders. Novalyne is Renee Zellweger, who was magical as Tom Cruise's romantic partner in *Jerry Maguire* and is charming here, too, as a small-town schoolteacher who dreams of being a writer and talks her date into taking her to meet his friend Bob Howard, who really was one.

Bob and Novalyne like each other immediately, but Bob comes with a great deal of emotional baggage. He lives at home with an almost invisible father and an ailing mother he dotes upon. In another sense he lives in his head and in his stories; Novalyne hears him at his typewriter, pounding the keys while shouting out his prose at the same time: "When women felt those tree-trunk arms around their waists, they melted like butter!"

The two young people have a sweet, innocent courtship, with much talk but little sex; Howard appreciates her as an audience but does not quite seem to see her as a woman until, realizing they have no future, she starts dating a more conventional young man in town. Then he is betrayed, not because she left him, but because she abandoned their vision—a vision that had him promising her he could deliver the best sunsets in Texas right on order, as if he were God. Somehow in his film Ireland implies the tenderness that an old woman might still feel for the boy she once loved; there is an echo here somewhere of Joyce's short story "The Dead."

Howard's inner emotional life is obviously in turmoil. "Robert is real close to his mother," the family doctor observes, and Bob changes her soiled linen, combs her hair, and coos to her in between banging out bloodcurdling adventures on his typewriter. Novalyne sees him striding down the street trying out new dialogue, and Ireland uses subtle devices on the sound track to suggest that Howard's fantasy world was as real to him as any other.

Howard was not a great writer, but he was a great storyteller, like Edgar Rice Burroughs, Doc Smith, and the other masters of pulp. For a teenage boy his stories were so enthralling that I can only pity today's kids who have to make do with tamer fiction. His books indeed still sell, maybe because readers can sense the utter conviction behind the muscular prose. The pulps "don't pay much," he tells Novalyne, "a half-cent a word, mostly—so I stretch my yarns." It was the kind of writer's bravado he loved, to discuss his work in mercenary terms. He knew, and she guessed, he stretched them because he didn't want to leave them. He was afraid to.

## Wide Awake ★ ★

PG, 90 m., 1998

Joseph Cross (Joshua Beal), Timothy Reifsnyder (Dave O'Hara), Dana Delany (Mrs. Beal), Denis Leary (Mr. Beal), Robert Loggia (Grandpa Beal), Rosie O'Donnell (Sister Terry), Julia Stiles (Neena Beal). Directed by M. Night Shyamalan and produced by Cary Woods and Cathy Konrad. Screenplay by Shyamalan.

In an opening scene of *Wide Awake,* the fifth-grade kids in a Catholic school have a spirited discussion about whether the unbaptized can get into heaven. This rang a bell. Morning religion class in my grade school was much the same; the nuns tried to teach us principles, and we were always getting sidetracked on technicalities.

When *Wide Awake* observes moments like these in the classroom, it's an entertaining film. I liked, for example, Rosie O'Donnell's performance as Sister Terry, a Philadelphia Phillies fan, and was reminded of my own teacher, Sister Marie Donald, who was also our basketball coach. A film accurately remembering Catholic school in the pre–Vatican II era could be a charmer.

But the movie has higher and, I'm afraid, more contrived goals. Its hero is young Joshua (Joseph Cross), who has been depressed ever since his beloved grandfather (Robert Loggia) died of bone marrow cancer. He mopes about his granddad's room, he doesn't want to get up for school, he is the despair of his parents (Dana Delany and Denis Leary) and annoys his sister (Julia Stiles). Finally he announces to his best friend, Dave (Timothy Reifsnyder), that he's going on a mission to find out if his grandfather is okay.

Joshua's mission, which occupies much of the movie, involves his demand for a sign from heaven. Along the way, he also sneaks into a girls' school to cross-examine a cardinal and holds a photo of the pope hostage in the rain. Does he get his sign? The movie is rated PG, a tip-off that it does not end with Joshua taking a tough position in favor of existential nothingness. (It is clever how the movie hides the "sign" in plain view all along.)

I wonder who the movie was made for. Smaller kids, I'm afraid, will find it both slow and depressing, especially the parts about why God allows bad things to happen. The health problems of Dave, the best friend, may also come as an unsettling shock. Older kids, on the other hand, are likely to find it too cute, and adults are better advised to see the French film *Ponette*, a more intelligent treatment of a child asking hard questions about heaven.

The film does have some pleasures, however. One of them is Rosie O'Donnell's performance. Although I can relate to her cheerful energy on television, I've not been a fan of her work in movies—especially not in *Exit to Eden* (1994), where she played a dominatrix as if her whip didn't fit.

In *Wide Awake*, however, she finds a role that she seems comfortable in and creates a character I would have liked to see more of. Becoming a nun is sometimes seen as a renunciation of independence and freedom, but for some women it is liberating—a role they feel relaxed in, allowing them to express themselves. Movies give us priests and nuns who are tortured and neurotic, but O'Donnell's Sister Terry seems happy and fulfilled; her role suits her personality.

As for the rest of the movie: Well, Joseph Cross is an effective and convincing little performer, but I always felt I was looking at a movie, not the actions of a real little boy. At the end of his film, when he reads his essay to his class, I asked myself if fifth-graders really thought and wrote like that. No, I decided, they don't. But screenwriters do.

## The Wife ★ ★ ★

R, 101 m., 1997

Julie Hagerty (Rita), Tom Noonan (Jack), Wallace Shawn (Cosmo), Karen Young (Arlie). Directed by Tom Noonan and produced by Scott Macaulay and Robin O'Hara. Screenplay by Noonan.

Jack's eyes dart around the table like a cat waiting to pounce. He looks at his wife and their guests, shields his own thoughts, and occasionally drops another word into the conversation just to see what effect it will have. He is as frightening as a madman with a knife—curious about whether he can goad the others to an explosion, a damaging revelation, or self-destruction.

Jack (Tom Noonan) is supposed to be a therapist. Well, so is his wife, Rita (Julie Hagerty). They practice those brands of therapies you learn out of best-sellers on the counter near the scented candles and the angel bookmarks. Jack's secret is that he gets off on manipulation and control. He has manipulated Rita into becoming his cotherapist, although we suspect she doesn't much believe in herself or their practice. She has ludes and booze stashed around the house like magic talismans. They talk in gentle tones to one another, as if recovering from much damage in the past.

Their house is a comfortable cabin in the country, near a frozen lake that Jack sometimes visits, even late at night in the winter, carrying a torch. This is the kind of house where every decorating touch seems planned for its secret effect; the dining room table has a four-sided triangular lamp in its center—a low lamp, so that everyone at dinner is lit from beneath, as in a horror movie. When the lamp is turned brighter, it hums.

As the movie opens, indeed, dinner guests have arrived. Cosmo (Wallace Shawn), one of their clients, has brought his wife, Arlie (Karen Young), to meet his therapists. He has a hidden motive: He wants them to see that he's telling the truth when he says how hostile and crazy she is. Arlie is a onetime topless dancer who is still proud of her body; we dread, correctly, that at some point in the evening she will display her still-marketable assets. (Ever notice how the more a woman wants to show you her breasts, the less you want to see them?)

Rita is unhappy about the unexpected company, but then she's unhappy about everything. Jack is delighted, and insists on an impromptu dinner party. The conversation races through the conventional niceties at a breakneck speed, as Jack steers it into verbal games of truth and pain. And watch his eyes, as he feasts on the unhappiness he inspires. Arlie does her topless act, and Cosmo at one point does a dance that looks for all the world like an animated version of a Thurber drawing.

*The Wife* can be compared to *Who's Afraid of Virginia Woolf?* in the sense that it consists of two couples, much booze, and a long evening. There is a key difference. Here, only one character is the gamemaster and the other three are his victims. It makes for a whole new set of possible moves.

Tom Noonan is an actor and writer whose name you may not recognize, although his face and body might ring a bell. He's tall, balding, and born to play Death in *The Seventh Seal.* This is his second film based on probing conversational fun and games. His *What Happened Was . . .* , in 1993, was about a blind date between two people so desperate that eventually each can hardly bear to look upon the other. Here he ups the stakes.

One could say this is a filmed version of a stage play, and so it is (the stage version was named *Wifey*). But I think this material benefits from being filmed. It craves the close-ups. Four people on a stage would be too far away. We need to be trapped in the eerie light of that dinner table, or the flickering torch, or the candles, or the headlights; all of the illumination in this film seems like a last stand against all-encroaching darkness.

## Wild America ★ ★

PG, 107 m., 1997

Jonathan Taylor Thomas (Marshall Stouffer), Devon Sawa (Mark Stouffer), Scott Bairstow (Marty Stouffer), Frances Fisher (Agnes Stouffer), Jamey Sheridan (Marty Stouffer Sr.). Directed by William Dear and produced by James G. Robinson, Irby Smith, and Mark Stouffer. Screenplay by David Michael Wieger.

A lot of movies begin with the information that they're based on true stories. *Wild America* ends with that information—wisely, since it would be impossible to watch the movie without hooting and hollering if you had the slightest suspicion you were supposed to believe the stuff on the screen.

The film tells the story of the three irrepressible Stouffer brothers—Marshall, Mark, and Marty—who dream of growing up to make movies about wild animals. In the late 1960s, when the two older boys are teenagers and the youngest is maybe eleven or twelve, they buy a used 16mm camera and talk their parents into letting them make a wildlife photo odyssey from their southern home to the mountains of the West. They have only a few weeks, because it's August and they have to be back for school in the fall. We follow them through a series of adventures that I, for one, (a) doubt ever happened, (b) doubt could happen in a two- or three-week period, and (c) doubt could happen without one, two, or perhaps all three young Stouffers ending up like their namesakes, as reheatable entrées.

First stop, Alligator Hell, an alligator preserve where the boys rent a boat and head into the swamp at night with flashlights. Needless to say, they find alligators. They also find themselves overboard—splashing in the water as the giant beasts attack them and flashlight beams reflect off rows of wicked alligator teeth. They all escape alive. Whew!

After a brief respite with some skinny-dipping British girls (who do not endanger the PG rating), the boys head out West, where a subtitle informs us they have arrived at the "High Country." Why do we need to be told it's the High Country? Because there's snow on the ground. Of course, there is snow on mountain peaks even in August, but my rudimentary knowledge of wild animals leads me to believe that hibernating bears and snakes, etc., head for warmer climes farther down on the slopes. A bear that is still hibernating in August is dead, or agoraphobic.

Not in this movie. The boys are searching for the Cave of the Sleeping Bears. Most bears hibernate alone, but this legendary cave is sort of like a dorm. From a mysterious woman with a scarred face, who lives in a cabin, they get secret information, and soon they have found the very cave itself. Film footage of this could make their fortune.

Alas, the mouth of the cave is guarded by dangerous snakes. Thinking fast, the boys throw snow into the cave to cool the snakes and neutralize them. Now hold on a second. Wouldn't the temperature inside a cave be the same as outside? If there's snow on the ground, wouldn't the cold-blooded snakes be asleep, unless they built campfires for themselves?

Not in this movie. The lads venture into the cave, which, sure 'nuf, is filled with sleeping bears (who do not know that farther down the mountain it's summertime and the livin' is easy). They make a lot of noise and shine their flashlights around and wake the bears, which rumble and roar alarmingly and loom over the lads until (I am not making this up) the lads lull them back to sleep by singing that popular bear lullaby, "Mountain Dew."

More adventures ensue. Back home, the youngest boy goes on a solo flight in his dad's restored antique aircraft, while Dad (in the hospital after a truck accident) looks on with horror and pride. It's a stunt to demonstrate to strict old Dad, in the words of a son, that "I doubt this family is gonna stay together unless you let every one of us be who he needs to be."

It seemed to me that Dad was less a curmudgeon than a sensible father. There is a difference between letting a teenage boy realize his dream, and letting him wake sleeping bears and rassle with gators. (I won't even mention the moose attack, or the adventure on the air force bombing range.)

The film ends with the Stouffers showing their film footage to a crowd in the local gymnasium, and a few years later, on "Aug. 6, 1977," their first nature film premiered on NBC-TV, "narrated by Robert Redford." All of the boys have since gone on to careers as photographers and naturalists, for which I applaud them, while wondering how much of *Wild America* can be true. I imagine the animal hijinks in the film will be entertaining for younger viewers, as true-life adventures often are. But—caution, kids! Do not experiment with throwing snow at deadly snakes. And if you find yourself in the Cave of the Sleeping Bears, go out the same way you came in, as quietly as you possibly can.

## Wild Man Blues ★ ★ ★

PG, 104 m., 1998

A documentary film directed by Barbara Kopple and produced by Jean Doumanian. With Woody Allen, Soon-Yi Previn, Letty Aronson, Eddy Davis, and others.

Early in *Wild Man Blues,* as they arrive in Europe, a subtitle identifies one of the women with Woody Allen as "Letty Aronson, Woody Allen's sister," and the other simply as "Soon-Yi Previn." One can only speculate how long a subtitle it would have taken to explain *her* presence. "Theoretically, this should be fun for us," Allen observes at the start of a tour with his New Orleans jazz band. Theoretically, it should, but the greatest pleasure for Woody seems to be having his worst fears confirmed. An omelet in Spain seems "vulcanized." A gondola ride in Venice leads to seasickness. An audience in Rome is "anesthetized, like a jury." In Milan he worries that the hotel might bread their laundry.

*Wild Man Blues,* Barbara Kopple's documentary about the tour, could be retitled *The Innocents Abroad*—although Woody, sixtyish, not Soon-Yi, twenty-fiveish, is the innocent. What was I expecting from this scrutiny of Allen on tour with the adopted daughter of his former companion Mia Farrow? Perhaps something slightly scandalous—the aging rake flaunting his Asian girlfriend in continental hot spots. But it's not like that at all.

Woody and Soon-Yi, who was soon to become his wife, seem to have a stable and workable relationship, in which Allen plays his usual role as the dubious neurotic, and Miss Previn is calm and authoritative—a combination of wife, mother, and manager. She seems to be good for him. Whether he is good for her, of course, has been a matter of controversy, but this film supports what Allen said when their affair was first revealed: "The heart has its reasons."

Soon-Yi seems more like the adult in the partnership. At one point, she advises him to be more animated when he appears on stage with his band. "I'm not gonna bob my head or tap my feet," he says. "They want to see you bob a little," she says, and he gets defensive: "I'm appropriately animated for a human being in the context in which I appear." But at the next concert, he bobs a little.

Little romantic passion is revealed onscreen, perhaps because of mutual reticence. At one point, checking into another of the vast hotel suites they occupy, Woody looks around hopefully for a real king-size bed, instead of two twin beds pushed up against each other. No luck. He frets that he could fall into the crack between the two beds and get stuck. Here is an example of their morning conversation: She: "The shower was excellent, wasn't it?" He: "Yes, great pressure."

The ostensible purpose of the documentary is to showcase Allen's seven-piece band and its music. But the audiences come to see Woody more than to listen to the music, and so do we. The music is entertaining, and the crowds like it (except for the stone-faced concertgoers in Rome, who look like they paid for their benefit tickets by donating blood). Eddy Davis, the banjo player and musical director, remembers that he first met Allen at Mister Kelly's in Chicago in the 1960s, and even then "he was a serious clarinetist."

Apparently terrified that he might say something funny and betray his serious calling as a musician, Allen introduces the numbers with the gravity of a heart surgeon announcing his next incision. Forced to attend a series of receptions before or after the concerts, he deals graciously with some fans, impatiently with others. When an official in black tie announces, "I present to you my wife," Allen nods and says, "This is the notorious Soon-Yi Previn."

Kopple made the Oscar-winning documentaries *Harlan County, USA* and *American Dream,* both about labor disputes. She might seem an unlikely choice for this material, but no doubt her track record gained Allen's trust. To his credit he hasn't exercised veto power over the results (if he had, he probably would have removed his observation that as a child Soon-Yi "was eating out of garbage pails").

In a closing sequence, Woody and Soon-Yi visit the director's elderly parents in New York. His father, examining various trophies presented to Woody on tour, seems more interested in the quality of the engraving than in the honors. His mother admits she would have preferred "a nice Jewish girl" to Soon-Yi, and wonders if her son might not, after all, have been more successful as a pharmacist.

Woody seems at times to be inviting his parents' comments with leading questions, and the reunion has been interpreted by some as illustrating his "Jewish self-hate," but that's a charge sometimes misused to punish anything other than perfect piety and filial regard. So Woody didn't like Hebrew school? I was bored during Catechism. A lot of Protestant kids would rather play baseball than go to Sunday school. That's not self-hate; it's human nature.

## Wild Things ★ ★ ★

R, 113 m., 1998

Kevin Bacon (Ray Duquette), Matt Dillon (Sam Lombardo), Neve Campbell (Suzie Toller), Theresa Russell (Sandra Van Ryan), Denise Richards (Kelly Van Ryan), Daphne Rubin-Vega (Gloria Perez), Robert Wagner (Tom Baxter), Bill Murray (Ken Bowden), Carrie Snodgress (Ruby). Directed by John McNaughton and produced by Rodney Liber and Steven A. Jones. Screenplay by Stephen Peters.

*Wild Things* is lurid trash, with a plot so twisted they're still explaining it during the closing titles. It's like a three-way collision between a softcore sex film, a soap opera, and a B-grade *noir.* I liked it. This being the latest example of Florida *noir* (hot on the high heels of *Palmetto*), it has a little of everything, including ominous shots of alligators looking like they know more than they're telling.

The movie solidifies Neve Campbell's position as the queen of slick exploitation, gives Matt Dillon and Kevin Bacon lots of chances to squint ominously, and has a sex scene with Denise Richards (of *Starship Troopers*) that is either gratuitous or indispensable, depending on your point of view. Plus it has Bill Murray as a storefront lawyer who delivers twenty minutes of hilarity, which at the time is the last thing we're expecting.

Movies like this either entertain or offend audiences; there's no neutral ground. Either you're a connoisseur of melodramatic comic vulgarity, or you're not. You know who you are. I don't want to get any postcards telling me this movie is in bad taste. I'm warning you: It *is* in bad taste. Bad taste elevated to the level of demented sleaze.

The plot: Matt Dillon plays Lombardo, a high school teacher who was "educator of the year" and has an engraved crystal goblet to prove it. As the movie opens, he writes SEX CRIMES on the board at a school assembly, and introduces speakers on the subject, including police officers Duquette (Bacon) and Perez (Daphne Rubin-Vega). In the back of the room, a student named Suzie (Neve Campbell) stalks out, suggesting which part of her anatomy one of the speakers can kiss. I wasn't sure if she was referring to Bacon or Dillon, but this is the kind of plot where it works either way.

Then we meet Kelly Van Ryan (Denise Richards), the richest kid in the upscale Florida enclave of Blue Bay. She's got the hots for Mr. Lombardo. She follows him home, asks for rides, washes his Jeep, and turns up in his living room so thoroughly wetted-down she reminds us of the classic Hollywood line about Esther Williams: "Dry, she ain't much. Wet, she's a star!" Later, we see her leaving the teacher's humble bungalow, looking mad.

Why is she mad? I will tread carefully; a publicist was stationed at the door of the screening, handing out letters begging the press not to give away the ending. The problem is, the ending of this film begins at the forty-five-minute mark and is so complicated, I doubt if it *can* be given away. What sets up everything, in any event, is Kelly's testimony that she was raped by Mr. Lombardo—and the surprise testimony of Suzie that she was too.

Suzie lives in a trashy trailer out behind an alligator farm run by Carrie Snodgress. But Kelly lives on the right side of town, in manorial splendor, with her bikini-wearing, martini-drinking mom (Theresa Russell), who has had an affair with Lombardo. Hearing her daughter has been raped by him, Mom is enraged, and snarls, "That SOB must be insane to think he can do this to me!" That's the kind of dialogue that elevates ordinary trash into the kind that glows in the dark. Here's another line, after a murder: "My mother would kill me if she knew I took the Rover!"

Bill Murray lands in the middle of this pie like a plum from heaven. Wearing a neck brace as part of an insurance scam, Murray runs his shabby storefront law office like a big downtown spread; when he asks his secretary to "show Mr. Duquette his way out," all she needs to do is look up and say, "Good-bye," since the door is in arm's reach of everything else in the office.

Without giving away the ending, that's about all I can tell you. See the movie and you'll understand how very much I must leave unsaid. The director is John McNaughton, whose work includes two inspired films, *Henry: Portrait of a Serial Killer* and *Normal Life*. He likes to show audiences how wrong their expectations are by upsetting them. That worked in *Henry* as grim tragedy, and it works here as satire.

Don't leave when the end titles start to roll. Credit cookies (those little bonus scenes they stick in between Key Grip and Location Catering) are usually used for outtakes showing Matthau and Lemmon blowing their lines, or Jackie Chan breaking his legs. In *Wild Things*, McNaughton does something new: flashbacks, showing us stuff that was offscreen the first time around. The movie is still explaining itself as the curtains close, and then the audience explains it some more on its way out of the theater.

## Wilde ★ ★ ★ ½

R, 116 m., 1998

Stephen Fry (Oscar Wilde), Jude Law (Lord Alfred Douglas), Vanessa Redgrave (Lady Speranza Wilde), Jennifer Ehle (Constance Wilde), Gemma Jones (Lady Queensberry), Judy Parfitt (Lady Mount-Temple), Michael Sheen (Robert Ross), Zoe Wanamaker (Ada Leverson), Tom Wilkinson (Marquis of Queensberry). Directed by Brian Gilbert and produced by Marc Samuelson and Peter Samuelson. Screenplay by Julian Mitchell, based on the book *Oscar Wilde* by Richard Ellmann.

"Wickedness," Oscar Wilde said, "is a myth invented by good people to account for the curious attractiveness of others." Wilde himself was considered in some quarters the most wicked man of his time, in others the most attractive—a gifted artist who was a martyr to convention.

At the very peak of his fame, after his play *The Importance of Being Earnest* opened to wild success in 1895, Wilde was convicted of "gross indecency," and spent his few remaining years in prison or decline. A century later his reputation, personal and professional, could not stand higher, and this new biopic joins two new stage productions in celebrating his rise, fall, and immortality. If he were alive today he would no doubt describe his homosexuality as a good career move.

Wilde's personal tragedy would be of little lasting interest were it not for the enduring popularity of his work, and the sensational nature of his fall. There were no doubt as many homosexuals in Wilde's day as there are now, but most of them either repressed their feelings or kept them secret. Homosexual behavior was, after all, against the law. It was Wilde's misfortune to fall in love with a reckless and vain young man who hated his pigheaded father, and wanted to use Wilde's fame as a taunt.

Worse luck that the father was the marquess of Queensbury, a famous figure in boxing and horse racing. Still worse luck that when the marquess left an insulting message at Wilde's club, Wilde unwisely sued him. And dashedly bad luck that the marquis's attorneys were able to produce in court "rent boys" from a male brothel, who testified that the marquis was correct in describing Wilde as a sodomite.

Consider that a century later gay men are being knighted, and you see what bad timing it was to be born in 1854. In another sense, Wilde's genius required a backdrop of Victorian stuffiness. Many of the people in his audiences understood what he was writing between the lines, but accepted it as funny and daring—as long as it stayed between the lines. ("Earnest," for example, was in Wilde's time a synonym for "gay.") Wilde was famous for his quips and one-liners, which survive because they almost always contain a center of truth. With immense self-enjoyment, he punctured hypocrisy ("I never take any notice of what common people say, and I never interfere with what charming people do").

Brian Gilbert's *Wilde*, with a screenplay by Julian Mitchell, based on Richard Ellmann's famous biography, has the good fortune to star Stephen Fry, a British author, actor, and comedian who looks a lot like Wilde and has many of the same attributes: He is very tall, he is somewhat plump, he is gay, he is funny, he makes his conversation into an art. That he is also a fine actor is important, because the film requires him to show many conflicting aspects of Wilde's life: How he loved his wife and children, how his homosexuality was oriented not so much toward the physical as toward the idealistic, how he was so successful for so long in charming everyone in his life that he actually believed he could charm an English courtroom out of a sentence for sodomy.

Wilde was the dandy as superstar; in the years before mass media, he wrote best-sellers and long-running plays, and went on enormously popular lecture tours (the film opens with him down in a silver mine in Nevada, reading poetry to the miners and beaming upon their muscular torsos). He invented the type exploited by the later Elvis Presley: the peacock in full plumage, kidding himself.

Born in Dublin, he came out of Ireland more or less expecting to behave as a heterosexual, and was sincere in his marriage to Constance (Jennifer Ehle). He loved his children, and the movie uses one of his children's stories as a counterpoint. But when a young Canadian houseguest named Robbie (Michael Sheen) boldly approached him in the parlor late one night, Wilde responded. He might have settled into an existence of discreet bisexuality had it not been for his meeting, some years later, the beautiful young Lord Alfred Douglas (Jude Law), known as "Bosie"—who was, if Wilde had only realized it, more interested in his fame than his body.

Bosie liked to flirt and flaunt. There is a scene in a restaurant where the two men smoke, smile, and hold hands, while all of London seems to look on. Bosie did that to shock. Wilde did it because he was a genuinely sweet man who believed in expressing his feelings, and was naive about how much leeway he'd be given because of his fame. Bosie's physical interest in Wilde soon waned, and he took the playwright to a famous male brothel, which Wilde seems to have seen as an opportunity to expose handsome working-class lads to the possibilities of higher culture.

It is so sad how ripe Wilde was for destruction. We can see the beginning of the end in an extraordinary scene in a restaurant, where Wilde calmly charms the tough, angry marquess of Queensbury (Tom Wilkinson). The marquess is happy to exchange tips about fly-fishing, but warns Wilde to stay away from his son (ironic, since Wilde was the seduced, not the seducer). Soon it all comes down to a humiliating courtroom scene, despite the desperate advice of loyal Robbie to stay far away from the law. Those who know of Wilde at thirdhand may be under the impression that the marquess hauled him into court; actually, it was Wilde who sued the marquess for slander.

Stephen Fry brings a depth and gentleness to the role that says what can be said about Oscar Wilde: That he was a funny and gifted idealist in a society that valued hypocrisy above honesty. Because he could make people laugh, he thought they always would. Bosie lived on for years, boring generations of undergraduates with his fatuous egotism. He grew gross and ugly. Wilde once said that he could forgive a man for what he was, but not for what he became.

## William Shakespeare's Romeo & Juliet ★ ★

PG-13, 130 m., 1996

Claire Danes (Juliet Capulet), Leonardo DiCaprio (Romeo Montague), Harold Perrineau (Mercutio), Pete Postlethwaite (Father Laurence), Paul Sorvino (Fulgencio Capulet), Brian Dennehy (Ted Montague), Diane Venora (Gloria Capulet), Miriam Margolyes (Nurse), M. Emmet Walsh (Apothecary), Vondie Curtis-Hall (Captain Prince). Directed by Baz Luhrmann and produced by Gabriella Martinelli and Luhrmann. Screenplay by Luhrmann and Craig Pearce, based on the play by William Shakespeare.

I've seen Shakespeare done in drag. I've seen Richard III as a Nazi. I've seen *The Tempest* as science fiction and as a Greek travelogue. I've seen Prince Hal and Falstaff as homosexuals in Portland. I've seen *King Lear* as a samurai drama and *Macbeth* as a Mafia story, and two different *Romeo and Juliets* about ethnic difficulties in Manhattan *(West Side Story* and *China Girl),* but I have never seen anything remotely approaching the mess that the new punk version of *Romeo & Juliet* makes of Shakespeare's tragedy.

The desperation with which it tries to "update" the play and make it "relevant" is greatly depressing. In one grand but doomed gesture, writer-director Baz Luhrmann has made a film that (a) will dismay any lover of Shakespeare, and (b) bore anyone lured into the theater by promise of gang wars, MTV-style. This production was a very bad idea.

It begins with a TV anchor reporting on the deaths of Romeo and Juliet while the logo STAR-CROSSED LOVERS floats above her shoulder. We see newspaper headlines (the local paper is named *Verona Today*). There is a fast montage identifying the leading characters, and showing the city of Verona Beach dominated by two towering skyscrapers, topped with neon signs reading MONTAGUE and CAPULET. And then we're plunged into a turf battle between the Montague Boys (one has "Montague" tattooed across the back of his scalp) and the Capulet Boys. When, in an early line of dialogue, the word "swords" is used, we get a close-up of a Sword-brand handgun.

If the whole movie had been done in the breakneck, in-your-face style of the opening scenes, it wouldn't be Shakespeare, but at least it would have been something. But the movie lacks the nerve to cut entirely adrift from its literary roots, and grows badly confused as a result. The music is a clue. The sound track has rock, Latin, and punk music, a children's choir, and a production number, but the balcony scene and a lot of the later stuff is scored for lush strings (and not scored well, either; this is Mantovani-land, a dim contrast to Nino Rota's great music for the Zeffirelli *Romeo and Juliet* in 1968). Much of the dialogue is shouted unintelligibly, while the rest is recited dutifully, as in a high school production.

Leonardo DiCaprio and Claire Danes are talented and appealing young actors, but they're in over their heads here. There is a way to speak Shakespeare's language so that it can be heard and understood, and they have not mastered it. The only actors in the film who seem completely at home, indeed, are Pete Postlethwaite as Father Laurence, and Miriam Margolyes as the Nurse. They know the words and the rhythm, the meaning and the music, and when they say something, we know what they've said. The other actors seem clueless, and Shakespeare's lines are either screamed or get all mushy. (Brian Dennehy, as Romeo's father, "Ted Montague," would have been able to handle Shakespeare, but as nearly as I can recall he speaks not a single word in the entire movie—a victim, perhaps, of trims in postproduction.)

Not that there is much Shakespeare to be declaimed. The movie takes a "Shakespeare's greatest hits" approach, giving us about as much of the original as we'd find in *Bartlett's Familiar Quotations.* And even then it gets nervous and tarts things up. What can we make of a balcony scene that immediately leads to Romeo and Juliet falling into a swimming pool and reciting their best lines while treading water? I think back to the tender passion of the 1968 version, and I want to shout: "Romeo! Quick! Poison yourself!"

The film's climactic scenes are more impressed by action-movie clichés than by the alleged source. Romeo pumps Tybalt full of lead while shouting incomprehensible lines. He tenderly undresses Juliet and they spend the night together. Shakespeare's death scene in the tomb lacked a dramatic payoff for Luhrmann, who has Juliet regain consciousness just as Romeo poisons himself, so that she can use her sweet alases while he can still hear them.

No doubt I will receive mail from readers accusing me of giving away the story's ending by revealing that Romeo and Juliet die. I had my answer all prepared: If you do not already know what happens to the star-crossed lovers, then you are not the audience this movie is aiming for. But, stay, my pen! Perhaps you are.

## Wings of Courage ★ ★ ★

G, 40 m., 1996

Craig Sheffer (Henri Guillaumet), Elizabeth McGovern (Noelle Guillaumet), Tom Hulce (Saint-Exupery), Val Kilmer (Jean Mermoz). Directed and produced by Jean-Jacques Annaud. Screenplay by Alain Godard and Annaud.

If *Wings of Courage* had not been filmed in the 3-D IMAX process and projected onto a five-story screen—if it had been, in short, an ordinary movie—there wouldn't have been much in the acting or screenplay to recommend it. But the dramatic credits are beside the point. The only reason to see the movie is to experience the process, and that's reason enough.

I've been watching 3-D movies since my father took me to the first one, *Bwana Devil,* in 1952. I've seen *Amityville 3-D, Jaws 3-D,* and even *The Stewardesses in 3-D,* a soft-core porn film with stars whose body parts loomed alarmingly over the audience. All of them had one thing in common: The 3-D wasn't very good.

Now IMAX has developed 3-D projected on the world's largest screens with a process that uses a wider film gauge, more intense light, and a brighter screen (five coats of silver). And instead of those flimsy little glasses with the red and green lenses, you get space-age goggles that wrap around your head and make you look like Tom Corbett, Space Cadet.

The goggles are high-tech; they have liquid crystal lenses that are controlled by radio waves, and each lens blinks forty-eight times a second, in sync with the projected image. The result is breathtakingly good: The picture at last looks truly three-dimensional. Because the screen is so large, the illusion isn't constantly being shattered when an object touches the edge of the screen. And because the light source is so strong, the picture isn't dim and washed-out.

I saw the movie at the IMAX theater at Navy Pier in Chicago, which shut down to install the new projectors necessary for the process. It was one of the few theaters in the country capable of showing IMAX 3-D (another was the Sony flagship on Broadway in New York City). But then the whole 'max empire jumped on the bandwagon.

IMAX movies are more or less limited to a forty-minute running time because of the huge size of their film reels (you need a block and pulley to lift one). *Wings of Courage* finds that more than long enough for its thin story, which involves the early days of commercial aviation in South America. A company is established by aviation pioneer Antoine Saint-Exupéry (Tom Hulce) to extend airmail service over the Andes, and Henri Guillaumet (Craig Sheffer) is the brave pilot who flies his flimsy little craft into mountain storms. Elizabeth McGovern plays his wife, and Val Kilmer is Jean Mermoz, the heroic pilot who is his inspiration.

The story: Guillaumet takes off, crashes, and spends several days trekking back through breathtaking mountain scenery to civilization.

Meanwhile, Saint-Exupéry searches for him, and his wife waits fearfully at home.

That's it, but it's enough. Because IMAX screens are so large, quick cutting between close-ups can actually cause disorientation and even nausea in an audience. Outdoor scenes with lots of long shots are best. The director, Jean-Jacques Annaud, captures the vastness and beauty of the mountains (actually the Canadian Rockies) in shots of incredible clarity, which allow us to see for miles. The film's opening shots, in which a plane seems to hover in the center of the theater space, are far beyond anything 3-D has ever achieved before. Other shots, of the biplane in a storm, are not quite as impressive because it's pretty clear that a model is being used.

There are a few straight dramatic scenes—in a nightclub, in the airline headquarters, and with the wife at home—and they're so detailed and realistic they're almost distracting. There's so much in each scene to look at that I found it hard to focus on the characters because I was checking out other details.

One subtle touch I enjoyed was the effect of an "inner voice" on the sound track. In addition to the giant IMAX theater speakers, the process builds tiny individual speakers into each headset, right next to the viewer's ears. In *Wings of Courage,* Annaud uses those speakers to allow Sheffer's private thoughts to be whispered into our ears.

*Wings of Courage* is a technical, rather than an artistic achievement, but then so was *The Jazz Singer*—which wasn't a great film, but by golly you sure could hear Al Jolson singing. Because of its 3-D process, its amazing scenery, and its simple story thrillingly shown, it's worth experiencing. Younger viewers will probably find it especially entertaining.

## The Wings of the Dove ★ ★ ★ ½

R, 103 m., 1997

Helena Bonham Carter (Kate Croy), Linus Roache (Merton Densher), Alison Elliott (Millie Theale), Charlotte Rampling (Aunt Maude), Elizabeth McGovern (Susan), Michael Gambon (Kate's Father), Alex Jennings (Lord Mark). Directed by Iain Softley and produced by Stephen Evans and David Parfitt. Screenplay by Hossein Amini, based on the novel by Henry James.

What happens in Henry James takes place deep within stories where, on the surface, the characters go languidly about their lives of privilege. They subscribe to a code of what is done and what is not done. They know exactly what it means to be a gentleman or a lady; those titles are like decorations, to be worn invisibly at social occasions. And then in the privacy of their souls, some of James's characters darkly contemplate getting their way no matter what.

*The Wings of the Dove* is the cold-blooded story of two British lovers who plot to deprive a rich American girl ("the richest orphan in the world") of her heart and her inheritance. What makes it complicated—what makes it James—is that the two lovers really do like the rich girl, and she really does like them, and everyone eventually knows more or less precisely what is being done. The buried message is that when it comes to money, sex, love, and death, most people are prepared to go a great deal further than they would admit. There is, if you know how to look for it, incredible emotional violence in the work of Henry James.

This new film of his famous novel makes two significant changes. It moves the action up slightly, from 1902 to 1910. And it makes the British woman a little more sympathetic than she was in the original. The second change flows from the first. James's story, which he began writing in 1894, embedded the characters in the world of Victorian propriety. By 1910, the actions they contemplate, while still improper, were not unthinkable; modern relativism was creeping in. Kate Croy, whose desire fuels the story, was more selfish and evil in the James version; the film softens her into someone whose actions can almost be defended as pragmatism.

Kate, played with flashing eyes and bold imagination by Helena Bonham Carter, is a poor girl with a tenuous foothold in society. Her father is a penniless drunkard. Her mother is dead. She is taken in by her wealthy Aunt Maude (Charlotte Rampling), who wants to marry her off to the best advantage—perhaps to Lord Mark (Alex Jennings). But Kate loves Merton Densher (Linus Roache), an ill-paid journalist who cheerfully admits he doesn't believe the things he writes. Maude forbids the marriage, and even threatens to cut off the weekly shillings she pays Kate's father.

What is Kate prepared to do? Characters talk a

great deal in Henry James, but are sometimes maddeningly obscure about what they mean (does any other novelist use the word "intercourse" more frequently, while not meaning by that word or any other what we immediately think of?). They talk much less in this film, where facial expressions imply the feelings that are talked around in the novel. My guess is that Kate might have eventually married the odious Lord Mark, while continuing quietly to see Merton Densher.

But that is not necessary. At a dinner party, she meets Millie Theale (Alison Elliott), the rich young American, and discovers that Millie has an unnamed disease, possesses hardly a protector in the world except for her traveling companion (Elizabeth McGovern), and intends to see Europe and die. One of the things Millie wants to experience in Europe is romance; she doesn't say so, but she is looking for a man, and when she sees Merton, she asks Kate about him.

"He's a friend of the family," Kate replies—a lie of omission, because Kate and Merton are secretly engaged. Kate's plan is clear. She will accompany Millie to Venice. Merton will join them there. Millie will fall in love with Merton, marry him, die, and leave him her fortune. Merton will then have the money he needs to marry Kate. This scheme unfolds only gradually in the James novel, emerging from behind leisurely screens of dialogue and implication. It is more clear in the film, especially in a dark, atmospheric scene where Kate and Merton walk down deserted Venetian passages. She tells him she is returning to London, and outlines what she expects him to do. Then, to seal the bargain, they have sex for the first time. (They do it standing up against the old stones of Venice; one imagines the ghost of James turning aside with a shudder.)

Iain Softley's film, written by Hossein Amini, emphasizes Kate's desperation and downplays her cold calculation. It softens the villainy of Merton by making it clear how desperately Millie does want to be involved in a romance with him; is he simply granting her dying wish? There is another fugitive strand of affection in the film that I did not sense in the book: Millie and Kate genuinely like one another, and it's almost as if they strike an unexpressed bargain, in which Kate lets Millie have the use of Merton—lets her find what she came to Europe for. The money is crucial, of course, but too vulgar to be discussed.

In its stark outlines, this plot would be at home on a daytime talk show ("Sold her lover to a dying rich girl"). But the film sets it at a time when standards were higher, when society had clear expectations of moral behavior. The reason we're so fascinated by the adaptations of James, Austen, Forster, and the others is that their characters think marriage, fidelity, chastity, and honesty are important. In modern movies many characters have no values at all.

In *The Wings of the Dove* there is a fascination in the way smart people try to figure each other out. The film is acted with great tenderness. If the three central characters had been more forthright, more hedonistic, we wouldn't care nearly as much. But all three have a certain tact, a certain sympathy for the needs of the others. At the end, when Millie knows the score, she can at least be grateful that she got to play the game.

## The Winter Guest ★ ★ ½

R, 110 m., 1998

Phyllida Law (Elspeth), Emma Thompson (Frances), Gary Hollywood (Alex), Arlene Cockburn (Nita), Sheila Reid (Lily), Sandra Voe (Chloe), Douglas Murphy (Sam), Sean Biggerstaff (Tom). Directed by Alan Rickman and produced by Ken Lipper, Edward R. Pressman, and Steve Clark-Hall. Screenplay by Sharman Macdonald.

Winter in Scotland is as muted as a wake. So far north the sun is slow to rise and early to set, and a day can be blindingly bright or always seem like twilight. *The Winter Guest* follows four sets of characters through a day in a Scots village, and its purpose is not to draw a lesson or tell a story, but to evoke a mood. To see this film is like spending a day in a village near St Andrews, and with a shock I realized I had once lingered for an afternoon in this village, or one much like it—in August, when the days were long and the trees were green.

Everything is different in winter. The people disappear inside and count on one another. The film opens with a well-coifed woman in her sixties, in a long fur coat, making her way across a field in bitter cold. This is Elspeth (Phyllida Law), and she is on her way to the house of her daughter Frances (Emma Thompson). She fears losing her. Frances's husband has died, and she has retreated into an angry silence beyond mourning. Perhaps she will leave Scotland and move to Australia with her teenage son, Alex (Gary Hollywood).

Alex has an admirer. Her name is Nita (Arlene Cockburn), and she has a crush on him. Early on the day of the film she ambushes him with a snowball, and at first they scuffle but then they begin to talk, and by the end of the day they will be boyfriend and girlfriend, with all the uncertainty that that means at their age.

There are two boys walking by the frozen sea. It is a school day, but they have stayed away, and no one will look for them here. They are Sam (Douglas Murphy) and Tom (Sean Biggerstaff), and the emptiness of the town and the quiet of the weekday has made them a little more serious than they planned; they look about twelve or thirteen, and tentatively talk about more serious things than they would have six months ago.

Two old ladies wait for a bus. They are Lily (Sheila Reid) and Chloe (Sandra Voe), and they are connoisseurs of funerals. Like the girl in *Huckleberry Finn* who loved to mourn, they find something cheerful about the rituals of death. They scour the death notices and compare notes on funerals past; they are old enough and ordinary enough that no one ever questions them when they attend a funeral; they look like the relatives you are sure you have forgotten.

*The Winter Guest,* based on a play by Sharman Macdonald, follows these four couples and listens to them. There isn't a lot of interaction between them, although Alex does bring Nita home, and she does talk with Frances. Since there is no plot engine to drag them all to the same station, we're forced to decide why they find themselves in this film, and what connection they have. Is the Winter Guest death? Do these couples represent four stages of life? Childhood, courtship, parenthood, and old age?

The central strands involve Elspeth and Frances. Phyllida Law and Emma Thompson are mother and daughter in real life, and in the film they have the familiarity of a lifelong couple. They know each other's speech rhythms. They look alike. When Frances closes herself off and refuses to talk, the worry lines between Elspeth's eyes seem real—the stress of a mother who loves a daughter and cannot reach her. Frances at one point buries her ears in the bathwater to block out words she doesn't want to hear, but it's hard to ignore someone if you're also concerned about them—and Frances is worried that Elspeth is growing older and soon will not be able to take care of herself.

The other three couples have defined roles. They are sure who they are, and more or less clear on how they should be acting on this winter day. But Elspeth and Frances are unsprung. The death of Frances's husband has changed everything, redefined it, ended a stage of life. There is so much pain that talking about it is unbearable, and so the mother and daughter talk around it.

*The Winter Guest* is the directing debut of Alan Rickman, an actor who makes intelligent British films *(Truly, Madly, Deeply; Sense and Sensibility)* and makes big money as a villain in American films *(Die Hard).* He has great command here of look and tone, and I felt I knew what it would be like to wander the streets of that village in Scotland. But the film left me feeling strangely hollow. Perhaps it was meant to. At the end there is an emptiness, like stepping into air, or like a play interrupted after the first act.

## Woo ★ ½

R, 80 m., 1998

Jada Pinkett Smith (Woo), Tommy Davidson (Tim), Duane Martin (Frankie), Michael Ralph (Romaine), Darrel M. Heath (Hop), Dave Chappelle (Lenny), Paula Jai Parker (Claudette), LL Cool J (Darryl). Directed by Daisy V. S. Mayer and produced by Beth Hubbard and Michael Hubbard. Screenplay by David C. Johnson.

*Woo* is about a collision between black lifestyles when a sexpot looking for "someone impulsive and exciting" ends up with a middle-class professional, and puts him through a severe psychosexual test-drive. When the smoke clears, she's revealed as not quite as streetwise as she pretends, and he turns out to have a few personality secrets concealed behind that white collar. Along the way, the movie touches on subjects usually sidestepped in African-American films, including the discomfort of black professionals around "country" behavior.

Jada Pinkett Smith stars as Woo, a girl who likes to party and is looking for a man. Her transvestite psychic friend predicts that a dynamic Virgo is in her future, but she doubts it. That night, she drops in on her cousin Claudette

(Paula Jai Parker) and her boyfriend, Lenny (Dave Chappelle), but they want to be alone together, so Lenny talks his friend Tim (Tommy Davidson of *In Living Color*) into taking her out. Tim is a law clerk, studying for the bar; Woo suspects a bore, but agrees to the date when she finds out he's a Virgo.

That's the setup for a movie constructed so loosely that I had the feeling some of the characters were introduced after we'd already met them. The film is a series of episodes in which Woo and Tim demonstrate to each other's satisfaction (and certainly to ours) that they have no business being out on a date with one another—although, of course, after they survive assorted bizarre adventures a certain camaraderie grows up between them. As hostages of each other, they develop reciprocal Stockholm syndrome.

The running joke is that Tim doesn't know much about women or, for that matter, black culture. Fixed up on the blind date with Woo, he goes across the hall to get tips from his neighbor Darryl (LL Cool J), who supplies him with a kit containing various stimulants and preventives, and a cassette of absolutely guaranteed romantic music ("by the time you get to side B, you should be naked").

Woo is not in the mood to be wooed, however, and the evening breaks down into episodes like the one in an Italian restaurant, where polite Tim doesn't get very far with the waiter, but Woo (who turns out to speak Italian) does. Then she sees an old friend through the window, and their reunion essentially demolishes the restaurant.

Movies like this don't really establish their characters and draw much of the humor out of their personalities; they go for quick payoffs, easy slapstick and in-jokes based on insults and code words. It's harmless and sometimes entertaining, but compared to Tommy Davidson's previous film, *Booty Call* (1997), or for that matter Jada Pinkett Smith's work in *Set It Off* and *The Nutty Professor*, it's lightweight and disposable.

## The X Files: Fight the Future ★ ★ ★

PG-13, 122 m., 1998

David Duchovny (Agent Fox Mulder), Gillian Anderson (Agent Dana Scully), Martin Landau (Kurtzweil), Armin Mueller-Stahl (Strughold), Blythe Danner (Cassidy), Mitch Pileggi (Director Skinner), William B. David (Cigarette-Smoking Man), John Neville (Well-Manicured Man). Directed by Rob Bowman and produced by Chris Carter and Daniel Sackheim. Screenplay by Carter.

As pure movie, *The X Files* more or less works. As a story, it needs a sequel, a prequel, and Cliffs Notes. I'm not sure even the filmmakers can explain exactly what happens in the movie and why. It doesn't make much difference if you've seen every episode of the TV series or none: The film is essentially self-contained, and that includes its enigmas. X-philes will probably be as puzzled at the end as an infrequent viewer like myself.

Puzzled, but not dissatisfied. Like *Mission: Impossible,* this is a movie that depends on surface, on mystery, on atmosphere, on vague hints and murky warnings. Since the underlying plot is completely goofy, it's probably just as well that it's not spelled out. If it were, this would play more like a seminar on the works of Whitley Strieber. Instead, producer-writer Chris Carter, who conceived the TV series, reassembles his basic elements in a glossy extravaganza that ends, apparently, with humankind facing precisely the same danger it did at the beginning.

The story involves, of course, Mulder and Scully, who call each other "Mulder!" and "Scully!" so often they must be paid by the word. FBI agents Fox Mulder (David Duchovny) and Dana Scully (Gillian Anderson) have been investigating a cover-up of aliens among us. Yanked off their X-files and assigned to an antiterrorism unit, they get involved in the explosion of a Dallas high-rise.

The alien conspiracy theorist Kurtzweil (Martin Landau) tells Mulder some of the bombing victims were already dead, and the blast was a plot to account for their bodies. (There is a shot of the ruined building, its front blasted away, that evokes disturbing memories of the Oklahoma City tragedy; that shot could have been removed from the film with absolutely no loss.)

We already know something about the dead bodies. The film opens in "North Texas, 35,000 B.C." (a long time before it was north Texas), with prehistoric men encountering violent, creepy, leaky beings in a cave. In "Present Day: North Texas," a kid falls into the same cave, and sluglike beings slither into his nose and eye sockets. What are these?

"The original inhabitant of this planet," we eventually learn, and a mighty patient inhabitant, too, if it had to wait for us to evolve. The alien creatures are a "virus," and yet they also seem to have bodily form, unless they inhabit hijacked bodies, which they can indeed do, although that begs the question of what they were to begin with, who built the large object we see in the final scenes, etc.

It's tricky work, not giving away the plot of a movie you don't understand. The story is less concerned with the aliens than with the cover-up, and there are several scenes (maybe one too many) of agents Scully and Mulder being grilled by an FBI panel about their misdeeds. I can't fault the FBI here. If I were investigating unreliable field agents and they told me they spent the weekend in Antarctica, I'd want to know what they were smoking.

Speaking of smoking, the Cigarette-Smoking Man (known on the Web as the Cancer Man) is in the movie, of course. Has there ever been a more thankless role? William B. David, who plays him, has to inhale, exhale, or light up every time we see him. The Well-Manicured Man (John Neville) has more to do, as does Director Skinner (Mitch Pileggi), but the best supporting performance is by Landau, as a desperate man who lurks in the back booths of shady bars, passing info to the X-agents.

What does he know? What's being covered up? Why are all the powerful men having the secret meeting in London? If you watch the show you will guess it has something to do with covering up the Aliens Among Us. What are they doing here? What are their hopes and plans? There's dialogue in which we get the answers to these questions, I guess, but they didn't fit together for me. And when the large unnamed object appears at the end, I wanted to know where it came from, where it was going, what it was leaving behind, and why. I also wanted a better look at it (the special effects are too cloudy).

There is little real drama, as such, in *The X Files.* Mulder and Scully are in love with one another, but sublimate all their feelings into their work. Do they kiss? Would I tell you? Do their lips meet? Is that one question, or two? They spend much of their time gaining unchallenged entry into vast installations that should be better guarded. One of these installations involves corn and bees. Why? We are told, but I didn't believe it. Nor do I understand why humans cooperate with the aliens; what sort of Faustian bargain has been struck?

Much has been made of the fact that *The X Files* is not so much a film based on a TV series as a continuation of that series in film form. The movie feeds out of last season and into the next one. No final answers are therefore provided about anything; it's as if, at the end of *Casablanca,* the airplane circled around and landed again. But I liked the way the movie looked, and the unforced urgency of Mulder and Scully, and the way the plot was told through verbal puzzles and visual revelations, rather than through boring action scenes. And it was a relief to discover that the guys in the black helicopters are just as clueless as the rest of us.

# Y

## Year of the Horse ★
R, 108 m., 1997

Featuring Neil Young, Billy Talbot, Poncho Sampedro, Ralph Molina. Directed by Jim Jarmusch and produced by L. A. Johnson.

*Year of the Horse* plays like *This Is Spinal Tap* made from antimatter. Both films are about aging rockers, but *Year of the Horse* removes the humor and energy, portraying Neil Young and Crazy Horse as the survivors of a death march. There are times, indeed, when Young, his hair plastered flat against his face with sweat, his eyes haunted beneath a glowering brow, looks like a candidate for a mad slasher role.

The film, directed by Jim Jarmusch, follows a 1996 concert tour and intercuts footage from 1986 and 1976 tours. It's all shot in muddy earth tones, on grainy Super 8 film, Hi Fi 8 video, and 16 mm. If you seek the origin of the grunge look, seek no further: Young, in his floppy plaid shirts and baggy shorts, looks like a shipwrecked lumberjack. His fellow band members, Billy Talbot, Poncho Sampedro, and Ralph Molina, exude vibes that would strike terror into the heart of an unarmed convenience store clerk.

This is not a fly-on-the-wall documentary. Jarmusch's interviews take place in a laundry room where the band members and Young's father sit on straight chairs and meditate on the band's long and lonely road. Young muses on "the trail of destruction I've left behind me," and there is solemn mention of departed band members ("Neil once said they were dropping like flies").

These séances are intercut with concert footage, during which the band typically sings the lyrics through once and then gets mired in endless loops of instrumental repetition that seem positioned somewhere between mantras and autism. The music is shapeless, graceless, and built from rhythm, not melody; it is amusing, given the undisciplined sound, to eavesdrop later as they argue in a van about whether they all were following the same arrangement.

The older footage is not illuminating. One high point, from a visit to Glasgow in 1976, is a meal in a restaurant that is interrupted when the fabric flowers in the centerpiece catch fire. The band members try smothering the flames with napkins and extinguishing them with orange juice, and eventually they join the woman who owns the place in sadly eyeing the ashes.

Later in the film, Jarmusch himself appears on camera, reading to Young from the Old Testament, a book the musician seems unfamiliar with. Jarmusch reads the parts where an angry God tells his people how he will punish them, and Young looks like God's tribulations are nothing he hasn't been through more than once.

If there is a theme to the band's musings, it is astonishment that they have been playing together for so long. They play with other groups, but when they come together, they say, there is a fusion. With touching self-effacement, Young tells Jarmusch, "The band is called 'Neil Young and Crazy Horse,' but I know it's really 'Crazy Horse.' My new jacket says 'Crazy Horse.' The others say 'Neil Young and Crazy Horse,' but mine just says 'Crazy Horse.'" Yes, but wouldn't the point come across a little better if theirs just said "Crazy Horse" too?

## The Young Poisoner's Handbook ★ ★ ★ ½
NO MPAA RATING, 99 m., 1996

Hugh O'Conor (Graham), Antony Sher (Dr. Zeigler), Ruth Sheen (His Stepmother), Roger Lloyd (His Father), Charlotte Coleman (Pack Winnie), Paul Stacey (Dennis), Samantha Edmonds (Sue), Vilma Hollingbery (Aunt Panty). Directed by Benjamin Ross and produced by Sam Taylor. Screenplay by Jeff Rawle and Ross.

"I was very young when I discovered I had a gift for chemistry," the hero of *The Young Poisoner's Handbook* tells us. "Life at home was a stale affair." His dreary London suburb of Neasden crouches beneath a sullen sky, and his family sits stupefied before the telly. But up in his room, Graham Young lives in another world entirely, a world of brightly colored chemicals and arcane instructions, and the exciting possibility that a test tube might blow up at any moment.

So begins the story of a young man whose bizarre secret life engendered one of the most famous British criminal cases of the century. Graham Young fatally poisoned his stepmother, caused many others to become ill, was sentenced to prison, bamboozled the prison psychiatrist, was set free, and went in for experiments on a larger scale when he was unwisely given the responsibility for preparing the tea at his new job.

Graham is a very sick young man. (In real life he was sicker—a neo-Nazi with dreams of genocide.) But *The Young Poisoner's Handbook* is not a grim record of crime; it's a wickedly satirical view of ambition in a gifted, if misguided, youth. Graham is played by Hugh O'Conor, seen in 1989 as the young Christy Brown in *My Left Foot.* O'Conor has now grown into a gangly teenager who makes a convincing nerd as he hunches in his upstairs room, making careful entries in his notebooks.

"Every king needs a queen—and I had mine," Graham tells us, after a girl at the library allows him to check out restricted books on poisons. The friendly local chemist allows him to buy chemicals best not trusted to young hands. At home, things remain grim: "Have you been using the cups and saucers again for your bloody experiments?" his father asks, although actually it is his sister who has been mixing up face creams.

Graham's stepmother (Ruth Sheen) finds nude pinups in the house, and punishes Graham by scrubbing him raw in the bath and burning his chemistry set. Graham has his revenge as his stepmother grows ill. Medicine is prescribed, and Graham adds a little touch of this and that, until the poor woman has been reduced to a bald skeleton. He makes careful records of his experiments in his journals with the detachment and intellectual curiosity of a born scientist. When the stepmother dies, Graham's dad rises to the level of his mediocrity by observing that his wife's death "smells like death."

Benjamin Ross, who directed and cowrote with Jeff Rawle, somehow finds the right tone for this material; the events in the movie are dismaying, but the effect is darkly comic. When I reviewed *Getting Away With Murder,* a comedy about justice for a Nazi war criminal, I observed that anything *can* be made funny, "but humor depends on tone, timing, and even on taste, and when a comedy starts on the wrong foot, it is hard to regain balance." *Getting Away With Murder* was not at all funny, but *The Young Poisoner's Handbook* is both funny and creepy, like an accident that is tragic and absurd at the same time (I am reminded of the famous Second City sketch in which mourners at a funeral discover that their friend drowned in a large can of pork and beans).

I am not sure how closely the film follows the facts, but it doesn't really matter. Graham is found out, tried and convicted, and given a life sentence as an "incurable psychopath." Then he comes under the wing of "the famous Dr. Zeigler" (Antony Sher), who is impressed by his command of Latin and asks him to start recording his dreams. Graham does not dream, so he makes up dreams, but Dr. Zeigler sees through them. So Graham begins waking up his cellmate every hour on the hour to write down *his* dreams.

After three months of this the cellmate hangs himself, but the dreams have done the trick, and after a brilliant performance before a parole board, Graham is back on the streets and working in a firm where, of course, a mysterious illness starts to go around. Graham has a complicated system for keeping track of his secret experiments on the employees; everything depends on each one getting the correct teacup, which leads to a scene of screwball complexity.

George Orwell would have loved this film. In his famous essay "The Decline of the English Murder" he complained, "You never seem to get a good murder nowadays." The ingenious murderers of the nineteenth and early twentieth centuries dispatched their victims with subtle poisons and disposed of them in acid baths, or buried them in the garden, or ground up the bones—presenting the police with a bit of a challenge. Modern murderers, he lamented, simply bashed away with guns and knives and showed no imagination at all. Graham Young is at bottom a monster, but as Hugh O'Conor plays him he is also peculiarly beguiling. It is easy to sympathize with a bright young man who wants to get ahead in his chosen field.

# Z

## Zero Effect ★ ★ ★ ½

R, 115 m., 1998

Bill Pullman (Daryl Zero), Ben Stiller (Steve Arlo), Ryan O'Neal (Gregory Stark), Kim Dickens (Gloria Sullivan), Angela Featherstone (Jess), Hugh Ross (Bill), Sara Devincentis (Daisy), Matt O'Toole (Kragen Vincent). Directed by Jake Kasdan and produced by Lisa Henson, Janet Yang, and Kasdan. Screenplay by Kasdan.

*Zero Effect* opens with the key character offscreen. His name is Daryl Zero, he's the best private detective in the world, and he's a recluse who prefers to be represented in public by a hireling. Sounds like the setup for a comedy, but this is one of those movies that creeps up on you, insidiously gathering power. By the end, I was surprised how much I was involved.

The hireling, named Steve Arlo, is played by Ben Stiller as a dry, detached functionary. He represents Zero at a meeting with a millionaire named Stark (Ryan O'Neal), who wants to find some lost keys—one of them to a safe-deposit box. Stark is being blackmailed by someone who may have access to the secret of dark deeds in the past.

Arlo enjoys spinning amazing tales about Zero. He's the kind of guy who feels personally enhanced by his boss's qualities. "He has a deeply nuanced understanding of human nature," Arlo says of Zero, but when we see Zero he looks more like a case for treatment. He lives behind a steel door with six locks on it. He eats little except for tuna fish from a can. And he likes to bounce on the bed while singing very bad folk songs of his own composition.

Yet this man is indeed an investigative genius, and soon he's meeting a young woman named Gloria (Kim Dickens) and using his sense of smell to tell her she's a paramedic. Zero is strangely split: He's hopelessly incompetent in his personal life, but when he goes into P.I. mode he's cool, competent, suave, and self-confident. Using Arlo as his assistant, he begins to unravel a murder that took place more than two decades ago, and leads to a trail of hidden identities.

To describe the details of the case would be wrong. They lead to surprises and reversals that are among the movie's pleasures (the last scenes force us to rearrange almost everything we thought we knew about the plot). The movie was written and directed by Jake Kasdan, son of the writer-director Lawrence Kasdan, and it's an exercise in devious construction—like one of those Ross Macdonald novels in which the sins of the fathers are visited upon the children.

If the plot is ingenious, it's the personal stuff that makes the movie increasingly delightful. Daryl Zero is baffled and challenged by Gloria, who is one of the few people he's ever met whose mind he can't more or less read. She fools him. She's shielded. She intuitively understands him the way he understands other people. When he claims to be in town at an accountant's convention, she finds a way to check that: She asks him to do her income tax.

Midway through the movie, I was being nudged by echoes of another story, and then I realized that *Zero Effect* was probably inspired by the relationship between Sherlock Holmes and the faithful Watson—Holmes, who could sit in his study and use pure deduction to solve a crime. When Zero describes his methods, he sounds Holmesian: "Objectivity . . . and observation. The two obs."

If Zero is like Holmes, Gloria is certainly like Irene Adler, from *A Scandal in Bohemia.* She was the one woman for Holmes, the one who got under his skin and into his mind. And as Gloria begins to have that effect on Zero, a softening and humanizing takes place: He becomes less weird, less insistent on his peculiar rituals, more like a guy.

*Zero Effect* begins, as I said, like a comedy—one not a million miles away from the kind of private-eye parody David Spade or Mike Myers might make. The Bill Pullman character, the first time we see him, seems like a goofy, off-the-shelf weirdo. But Pullman, from *While You Were Sleeping* and *Independence Day,* can drop the facade and let you see the complications inside. He also costarred in *Sleepless in Seattle,* and it's uncanny, by the end of *Zero Effect,* how much this private-eye caper has started to touch some of the same notes.

# The Best Films of 1997

## 1. *Eve's Bayou*

This is the astonishingly assured debut film by writer-director Kasi Lemmons, who explores the secrets of a Louisiana family through the not always understanding eyes of a ten-year-old girl (Jurnee Smollett). She has a strong affection for her father, a local doctor—and is jealous when he seems to favor her older sister. The doctor (Samuel L. Jackson) is also a womanizer, and when Eve sees him with a local woman, all sorts of half-understood emotions come churning into her heart.

The film evokes a time and place as well as any movie released all year, and it creates vivid characters—for example, Eve's aunt (Debbi Morgan), who can foretell everyone's future except for her own.

Released with little fanfare on a limited budget, *Eve's Bayou* became the top-grossing art-house film of the year, mostly because people told one another about it. It takes us into a realm of poetry and dreams and shows us how deceptive memory can be. In the way it examines a family's emotional life, it reminded me of the family dramas of Ingmar Bergman.

## 2. *The Sweet Hereafter*

Atom Egoyan's heartbreaking drama takes place in a small Canadian town in the dead of winter, as a cloud of grief settles over it. Fourteen children are killed in a school bus accident, and a lawyer (Ian Holm) arrives to interview possible clients for a class-action suit. He may seem to some like an ambulance chaser, but he's only going through the motions; his own daughter may die any day from drug abuse, and he shares more with the grieving parents than they know.

Egoyan's story circles around the central fact of the accident, moving back and forth in time as the lawyer and the audience come to know the people in the town. Some of them have secrets that the accident will betray. All have a deep hopelessness, evoked by the film's sad, beautiful cinematography.

Egoyan, whose last film was the seductive (and also sad) *Exotica,* is a director whose films see human weakness with a special poignancy.

## 3. *Boogie Nights*

Set in the late 1970s world of X-rated porno films, this ambitious drama by Paul Thomas Anderson wasn't about sex so much as about need: the need to belong, the need to be famous, the need to be part of the Hollywood movie industry—however small and disreputable that part might be. Burt Reynolds, in one of his best performances, plays a pornmaker who discovers a kid (Mark Wahlberg) in a nightclub and makes him into an X-rated star.

The rich supporting cast includes Julianne Moore as Reynolds's companion and frequent star; drugs have lured her away from her husband and family, but here she tries to create a surrogate family in scenes of tenderness and desperation. *Boogie Nights* was an unsentimental, detached, analytical look at sex films that was a surprise for those anticipating winks and nudges: This was about business and failure, not fantasies.

## 4. *Maborosi*

There was no more beautiful film this year. Makiko Esumi, a fashion model with a quiet grace and introspection, played a woman who loses her husband, raises their baby until he is a small boy, and then marries again—to a man who lives in an isolated fishing village. Ignoring all the conventional ways in which this story could unfold, the movie is about how the woman adjusts to her new life while she continues to mourn her old one. How and why, exactly, did her young husband, who was so happy with her and their baby, die? She does not know.

The director, Hirokazu Kore-Eda, films sequence after sequence with such a sure eye for light and composition that your eyes drink in the screen. His camera is tactful; he tells us what we need to know about this woman and lets us intuit the rest, in long, silent passages in which she goes about her daily life, or cares for the child, or learns to know her new husband, or simply sits and thinks.

## 5. *Jackie Brown*

The best films in 1997 were sad. Here is the first comedy, a triumphant encore for Quentin

Tarantino more than three years after his influential *Pulp Fiction*. Pam Grier and Robert Forster, two actors whose careers have been in eclipse, are perfectly cast here—she as a weary stewardess who smuggles money for a gun dealer, he as the bondsman who gives her bail. An unspoken affection grows between them, as Grier improvises a brilliant scam that will prevent the gun dealer (Samuel L. Jackson) from killing her, while separating him from his money.

The movie is based on *Rum Punch*, a novel by Elmore Leonard, who is known for his dialogue. So is Tarantino, and here they mesh smoothly in a film that is a delight to simply listen to: The characters are savvy, quick, and colorful, and they talk in specifics that help establish their personalities. The film's special quality is its sense of freedom over time and space: Unlike most genre characters, these are not limited to plot mechanisms, but can meander, as we circle more widely into the details of their lives.

### 6. *Fast, Cheap & Out of Control*

Errol Morris's visionary, free-form documentary considers the lives of four people who have dedicated themselves to controlling that which cannot or should not be controlled. There is a lion tamer, whose profession consists of making animals behave contrary to their nature; a topiary gardener, who wants to clip shrubs so they look like animals or geometric designs; a robot designer, who wants machines to move instinctively like animals or people do; and an expert on the naked mole rat, who wants to build habitats in which they will reveal their lifestyle to the patrons.

Tying his images together with an evocative sound track, Morris never forces his theme but lets us discover it: When these four lifetimes are over, everything they have accomplished will snap back to the way it was before. And perhaps that's true of all of man's efforts in the face of nature's vast indifference, and the tendency of all things to behave as they are predisposed to.

### 7. *L.A. Confidential*

Set in the Los Angeles of the 1950s, when lines often crossed between cops, criminals, and celebrities, Curtis Hanson's twisted melodrama was about sleaze in the land of dreams. Two young cops (Guy Pearce and Russell Crowe) approach ethics from different viewpoints, but find themselves on the same side in a messy case involving a dead cop, a high-priced call girl ring, and corruption in high places. Kevin Spacey finds the right note as a cop intoxicated by his role as "adviser" to a TV police show, and Danny DeVito has diabolical energy as the publisher of a scandal sheet. Kim Basinger is a beautiful hooker who has the misfortune to fall in love.

The film inhabits its period so effortlessly that it seems like a time capsule; the plot reveals layer after layer; the characters are richly drawn, and there is often a thin line between the top and the bottom. (When one cop says a hooker looks like Lana Turner, his partner corrects him: "She *is* Lana Turner.")

### 8. *In the Company of Men*

No film this year was more cruel or unforgiving. Neil LaBute's hard-edged, perceptive film was about two men in a faceless corporation who are assigned to an out-of-town branch office. One (Aaron Eckhart) nurses a special grudge against women, and enlists the other (Matt Malloy) in a plan to play a cruel practical joke on a woman (Stacy Edwards) at the new location—a woman who turns out to be deaf, which only underlines the cruelty.

The dialogue is harsh and contemptuous, the scheme is diabolical, and the plot turns out to have more surprises than we, or some of the characters, anticipated. This is the kind of film that demands to be discussed afterward—or fought about, as the case may be.

### 9. *Titanic*

What a superb achievement this was! Blending special effects with strong melodrama and an element of docudrama, writer-director James Cameron made a film in the tradition of classic Hollywood epics. His special effects are astonishingly convincing, re-creating the *Titanic* in all her splendor, and then spending more than an hour of screen time on the story of her sinking. But it was an equal technical achievement to tell the story so clearly, thanks to modern characters who set up the sequence of the tragedy so that, when it happens, we're always clear about what is taking place, and why.

### 10. *Wag the Dog*

Barry Levinson's savage political satire may inspire me to read the papers in a slightly new light. After a U.S. president is caught in a sex scandal, a spin doctor (Robert De Niro) is brought in by the White House, and hires a Hollywood producer (Dustin Hoffman) to produce a phony international crisis—to distract attention. The details are precise and unforgiving, the dialogue is priceless, ironies abound, and at the end we wonder how much could be true, or half-true. Isn't it strange, after all, how modern armed conflicts so quickly generate their song, their symbol, their logo, and their poster child?

## I, the Jury

At international film festivals, there is always a "Special Jury Prize," sort of a glorified second place. A few years ago I started a similar category.

—*Donnie Brasco* centered on Al Pacino's best performance in years, as an aging hood named Lefty who develops a strong affection for a younger man (Johnny Depp) and sponsors him for the mob—a bad decision, as it turns out. Directed by Mike Newell, it also had effective work by Michael Madsen as Lefty's superior, in a story that made the life of crime seem like a boring, unrewarding, and deadly career choice.

—*Ice Storm* was Ang Lee's bleak drama about families in the Connecticut suburbs in the early 1970s. A companion piece to *Boogie Nights,* in a way, it also shows unconvincing family units struggling to hold together against the flood of drugs, sexual license, and permissiveness. Kevin Kline, Sigourney Weaver, and Joan Allen were standouts.

—*Kundun,* by Martin Scorsese, told the story of the fourteenth Dalai Lama from his childhood to his handling of the crisis between Tibet and China. A voluptuously beautiful film, with a lush score by Philip Glass and—unusual for Scorsese—a center of spiritual serenity.

—*Oscar and Lucinda,* directed by Gillian Armstrong *(My Brilliant Career)* and starring Ralph Fienes and Cate Blanchett, is based on the brilliant, comic, romantic novel by Peter Carey about a nineteenth-century English clergyman who loves to gamble—and meets his counterpart in Sydney, Australia. Together, they conceive a mad scheme to float a glass cathedral upriver to the outback.

—*Shall We Dance,* written and directed by Masayuki Suo, told the story of a Tokyo salaryman who is enchanted by the image of a beautiful woman standing alone in the window of a dance studio. He goes in, signs up for ballroom lessons, and gets more of a life-changing experience than he counted on.

## Top Ten Sleepers

Readers sometimes tell me, "Hey, I haven't even heard of half the films on your year-end list." I tell them, "That's what I'm for. Now you have." Here are ten superb 1997 films that you may have missed if you weren't playing close attention. Some were made on shoestrings, others have stars like Jack Nicholson or Helena Bonham Carter. Look for them at the video store.

—*Bang,* written and directed by Ash (that's his name), stars Darling Narita (that's her name) as a Japanese-American actress who is hassled by a Los Angeles cop, manages to handcuff him, steals his uniform and motorbike, and spends a day finding out how people treat you when you wear the badge.

—*Bliss,* written and directed by Lance Young, takes sex seriously, which makes people squirmy, because it senses their fears and secrets. It's grown-up, thoughtful, and surprisingly erotic, and has strong performances by Craig Sheffer and Sheryl Lee, as a couple that seeks help from two very different sex therapists, played by Spalding Grey and Terence Stamp.

—*Blood and Wine,* directed by Bob Rafelson, contains the best Jack Nicholson performance of the year, more focused and fascinating than *As Good As It Gets.* He's a wine dealer who gets involved with an ailing British crook (Michael Caine in one of his best performances) in a theft that goes desperately wrong. Inspired supporting work by Judy Davis, Stephen Dorff, and Jennifer Lopez.

—*Chasing Amy,* written and directed by Kevin Smith *(Clerks),* was a joyous job of writing and construction, in a plot that keeps us fascinated by its human dimensions. It's a comedy about two buddies (Ben Affleck and Jason Lee) who write comic books. Affleck falls in love with a woman (Joey Lauren Adams), only to discover she's a lesbian. What to do? Not what you might think, or guess. Evidence that Smith's talent continues to grow.

—*Female Perversions* was sort of the other side of the coin from *In the Company of Men.* Cowritten and directed by Susan Streitfeld, it starred Tilda Swinton *(Orlando)* as a successful attorney whose career and sexuality are in unacknowledged conflict. Amy Madigan's supporting performance as her sister casts both women in a strange light, poised between perfection and madness.

—*Hard Eight* was one of two wonderful films this year by Paul Thomas Anderson *(Boogie Nights)* and featured a flat-out great performance by that underappreciated actor Philip Baker Hall, as an older man who takes a down-and-out younger one (John C. Reilly) under his wing and shows him the ropes of Reno casinos. Also with Gwyneth Paltrow and Samuel L. Jackson.

—*Margaret's Museum* starred Helena Bonham Carter in a sad, stunningly beautiful film shot in a 1940s Nova Scotia that looks like a Wyeth painting. She plays a local waitress who marries a young man who serenades her with bagpipes. The house he builds her is a wacky masterpiece; the ending is a heartbreaker.

—*Pillow Book* is another of the visually elegant, intellectually challenging films by Peter Greenaway, about a woman named Nagiko (Vivian Wu) who finds a powerful link connecting calligraphy, human flesh, poetry, and sexuality. In a complex plan designed to atone for a loss by her father, she uses parts of the human body to write a book and prove a point.

—*Shiloh* was a heartwarming and surprisingly complex story about a boy and his dog—and family values. It starred Blake Heron as a kid who befriends a dog that an alcoholic neighbor abuses; his father (Michael Moriarity) explains why he has to return the dog, and the movie is like a G-rated seminar in situational ethics. Wonderfully entertaining for all ages—not just kids.

—*The Tango Lesson*, written and directed by Sally Potter, stars her as a British director who takes tango lessons from a master (Pablo Veron) and falls almost in love with him, before they quarrel over who should lead. A fascinating study of dance, music, power, and sexuality, with one of the year's best scores.

## Five Documentaries

I've just finished teaching a semester of documentaries at the University of Chicago's downtown center, after which we observed that, film for film, a doc is likely to be more fascinating than almost any fiction film. Here are five that prove it.

—*4 Little Girls* was Spike Lee's heartrending, historically fascinating story of the Birmingham church bombing. Using historical footage and news interviews with parents and other observers, he shows how the death of the four little girls was a turning point in the civil rights movement.

—*Microcosmos* was a stunningly well-photographed French film about the insect life in a meadow, seen magnified hundreds of times.

—*Public Housing*, by the *cinema verité* master Frederick Wiseman, takes us inside Chicago's Ida B. Wells homes and shows us the problems, the hope, and the human resources in a "project."

—*Sick, the Life and Death of Bob Flanagan, Supermasochist*, by Kirby Dick, tells the story of a cystic fibrosis victim who fought pain with pain; he and his dominatrix lover, Sheree Rose, made works of art out of his suffering. Agonizingly unwatchable at times; brutally honest, and with a stubborn wit and courage.

—*Waco: The Rules of Engagement*, by William Gazecki, raises disturbing and so far unanswered questions about the standoff between the feds and the Branch Davidians. Did the FBI lie about its methods? Were all of those deaths necessary? The film uses heat-sensitive aerial footage to show firepower where there shouldn't be any, and makes a strong case against the government's methods.

## The Next Ten

*Anaconda* was one of the year's great entertainments, not least because of Jon Voight's wink. *Anastasia* proved that a studio other than Disney could make a good animated feature. Robert Duvall's *Apostle* featured his inspired performance as a man of God who sins but is redeemed. Robert Zemeckis's *Contact* was the provocative, challenging film about first contact with extraterrestrial intelligence, starring Jodie Foster as a radio astronomer. Woody Allen's *Deconstructing Harry* cut close to the bone in a story where the characters say about the hero what some people are saying about him.

Judi Dench played Queen Victoria as a woman with a needy heart in *Mrs. Brown*, and Billy Connolly was the one man who stood up to her. Gregory Nava's *Selena* starred Jennifer Lopez in a luminous performance as the late Mexican-American singer. *Soul Food*, written and directed by George Tillman Jr., was the surprise hit about an extended black family, their hopes and setbacks, all centering on the rock-solid presence of their "Big Mama" (Irma P. Hall). Victor Nunez's *Ulee's Gold* had that quiet, nuanced performance by Peter Fonda as a Florida beekeeper who kept to himself—until he couldn't anymore. And Iain Softley's *Wings of the Dove,* from the Henry James novel, starred Helena Bonham Carter in the story of a woman who can't afford to marry the man she loves—unless he marries her new friend first.

## Runners-Up

Here are some of the year's other good films: *Absolute Power, Amistad, The Assignment, Crash, G.I. Jane, The Game, Gattaca, Good Will Hunting, Kiss the Girls, Kolya, Marvin's Room, Men in Black, Mimic, My Best Friend's Wedding, Night Falls on Manhattan, Ponette, Prisoner of the Mountains, Rosewood, She's So Lovely, Smilla's Sense of Snow, SubUrbia,* and *Telling Lies in America.* They're mostly on video by now, and so are almost all of the other films on my list.

# Interviews

## Paul Thomas Anderson

*Chicago,* October 1997—Paul Thomas Anderson has made one of the best films of 1997, and at age twenty-seven is getting the kind of attention no young director has had since Quentin Tarantino erupted. His *Boogie Nights,* which follows a cast of colorful characters through six eventful years in the adult film industry, is the year's best-reviewed film—a hit at the Toronto and New York Film Festivals.

Although the film's subject matter is touchy, *Boogie Nights* is not a sex film; porno supplies the backdrop to a traditionally structured Hollywood story about an unknown kid (Mark Wahlberg) who is discovered by a director (Burt Reynolds), encouraged by an older actress (Julianne Moore), and becomes a star—until his ego and drugs bring everything crashing down.

Apart from anything else, the film is about *filmmaking.* It captures the familial atmosphere of a filmset as well as any film since Truffaut's *Day for Night.* The focus is not on sex but on loneliness and desperation, leavened with a lot of humor, some of it dark, some of it lighthearted.

*Boogie Nights* is Anderson's second feature. When I saw the first one in 1996 at the Cannes Film Festival, I felt I was watching the work of a born filmmaker. *Hard Eight* starred John C. Reilly and Philip Baker Hall in the story of a relationship between an old gambler who shows the ropes in Nevada to a broke kid. As characters played by Gwyneth Paltrow and Samuel L. Jackson get involved, the story reveals hidden connections. It is a riveting debut film.

Reilly and Hall also have important roles in *Boogie Nights*—Reilly as the young porno star's sidekick, Hall as the shadowy figure who finances the films. And the big cast also includes such actors as William H. Macy (the car salesman in *Fargo*) and Don Cheadle *(Devil in a Blue Dress).* In a year of often disappointing films, here at last is a great one.

On his way from Los Angeles to the New York Film Festival, Anderson stopped for a few hours in Chicago, and we sat outside on a perfect October day and talked about how he had accomplished so much, so quickly.

RE: So you made a shorter version of this film as a kid, right?

PTA: Yeah. When I was seventeen, I wrote a half-hour short called the *The Dirk Diggler Story.* I was so influenced by *Spinal Tap* at the time that it was in my brain, so it was like, "Let's play it as a documentary." I'd seen this piece on *A Current Affair* on (porn actress) Shauna Grant, which was the clichéd-but-true story of a girl from Iowa who comes to Hollywood on the bus, looking for dreams.

RE: So this is basically a Hollywood story, except it's about the porn industry . . .

PTA: It's a Busby Berkeley movie. The reason things are clichés is because they're true.

RE: The whole period of X-rated filmmaking was over before you had an experience of it.

PTA: A lot of those people are still around, you know. And not happy, although they were probably not that happy to begin. What they had was a little dignity by shooting on film, and now it's just video assembly-line crap. There are still certainly people who consider themselves mavericks, and once in a while there will be a porno film shot on film. And it's really like a big selling point—not that the public cares, if you know what I mean.

RE: I interviewed Gerard Damiano at the time. He was probably the best of the hard-core directors, and he went through a period of believing he could make art films about sex. Home video came along in 1979 and destroyed that illusion. The golden age on film was from about 1969 to 1979.

PTA: It's like there could have been a new genre. We've had sci-fi, murder mysteries, Westerns, and there could have been a sex genre . . .

RE: But isn't it true that if you make a hard-core film, the sex scenes will derail whatever else there is?

PTA: There was a movie called *Amanda by Night* that kinda came close, and some of the early John Holmes stuff came really close, not only in terms of structure but—you could see different characters have sex in different ways. I think sometimes you can watch a character in a movie and you wonder what their sex life might be like. I get sick to death of totally unnecessary sex scenes, but there are movies where I do want to see what it's like behind doors for a movie character.

RE: The adult film industry is kind of like a shadow version of the mainstream industry. They have adult film awards, they have their own trade magazines, their own stars.

PTA: It *is* filmmaking. When you go on porn sets there's a shock for a minute, but then it's just like any other set. It's like, let's get the shot, let's get in focus. And they have ceremonies to celebrate what they're doing; who else is going to celebrate it but them?

RE: There's a character in the film who I guess is from the Mafia?

PTA: With a name like Floyd Gondolli, and played by Philip Baker Hall, there's a hint of that.

RE: I've been told the Mafia wasn't involved in the films, but they used porno theaters to launder money. They'd sell 1,000 tickets and say they'd sold 10,000 tickets. That gave them a way to get rid of all those $5, $10, and $20 bills.

PTA: It was never really clear in my research how involved the Mafia was. I could never get a straight answer. I guess they were for a time, but apparently not now.

RE: Porno acting, in a way, is Method acting taken to its extreme. If the Method actor recollects an emotional event to re-create that emotion, maybe porno actors think of things that turn them on . . .

PTA: The Method times fifty. Some of them told me they put themselves somewhere else mentally to be successful in making it look like they're having a good time. A lot of the acting is stiff and uninvolved. But good sex in pornos is probably some of the best acting there has ever been.

RE: There are rumors that Burt Reynolds is unhappy about the film. Here's a guy who willingly trashed his career with *Stroker Ace* and *Cannonball Run* and *Smokey and the Bandit*. Doesn't he know this is one of his best performances?

PTA: I haven't talked to him since we finished, so I don't know. He's a good guy. He has a good heart and he's a good actor. He told me: "I was an actor first. I became a celebrity second. Please just remember that I'm an actor." Sort of this weird parallel to Jack Horner, the character he plays, who's always insisting he's a filmmaker.

RE: Except for what they do at work, there's very little sex in the world of these people. They've burned it out for themselves, right?

PTA: I saw a mixture of people that did it when they went to work and couldn't otherwise, and then people that were just twenty-four-hour sex maniacs. In the film there's that set-piece sex scene, where we see Julianne Moore's and Mark Wahlberg's characters have sex, and to me that was enough to take care of showing how it's usually done.

RE: The one character who *is* sex-mad is William H. Macy's wife, played by Nina Hartley, who was a porno star.

PTA: Still is. She makes a lot of money doing pornos and she also makes a lot of money from lecturing. She's a sexologist and registered nurse, and she gives incredibly wonderful, frank, odd lectures on sex.

RE: Now, the last shot of the movie, showing Dirk Diggler's penis. Real or not?

PTA: Absolutely, 100 percent real.

RE: I read somewhere else it's a prosthesis.

PTA: I've gotta say it's real.

RE: Is it the same actor? The same human being? Or do you substitute people as you cut away from the mirror?

PTA: No, there's no cut. There's no cut in the short.

RE: In other words, to be direct, that is his penis.

PTA: That is Mark Wahlberg's penis. The funny thing is that we did a press junket and Mark, maybe out of embarrassment, started telling people that it was my penis. You could just watch the gears turn in everyone's head, then a couple of hours later these people said, "So that's your penis at the end of the movie?" A couple of times I said, "Yeah, it is." Mark's just embarrassed.

RE: You're only what, twenty-seven? And you made *Hard Eight* when you were twenty-five. You bypassed the film school route?

PTA: Yeah, pretty much. I did enroll for a couple of days at NYU, but I went into it with a bad attitude. I was enrolling just so I could garner enough ammunition to bad-mouth what I knew was not a good situation. I made a short film, and then went to the Sundance Director's Lab and worked on *Sidney*, which became *Hard*

*Eight*. I had some money that I'd won gambling, funnily enough, and I had my girlfriend's credit card, and my dad set aside $10,000 for college for me and I said, "Listen, I'm not going. This twenty-minute short will be my college."

RE: *Hard Eight* had a quality that I hunger for in movies: It knew a lot about something and told me about it. I found out how to take $150 and convince a casino to comp me for the night.

PTA: When I went to Sundance, all I had written was this wonderful long scene between John C. Reilly and Philip Baker Hall in a car, where Sidney's telling him that there is a way with $50, $100, he can get a bed and a meal and be set up for a couple of days. So I got to Sundance and Richard LaGravenese (screenwriter of *The Bridges of Madison County*) says, "Why isn't that in the movie? You just explained this wonderful scam to me! Why aren't you *showing* it?"

RE: I saw it at Cannes two years ago and loved it. But then it was one of those stories like *Normal Life* or *The Last Seduction* or *Red Rock West*. The distributors didn't know what they had. Some of the best movies made in America recently have been misunderstood by studios, dumped on cable and video.

PTA: For me, it was a wake-up call that making a good movie, unfortunately, is only 50 percent of the job. The other half is dealing with studio politics. The company that paid for it didn't like the movie that I'd made and went to test screenings with it. I mean, you can't test-screen a movie like *Hard Eight*. And when those cards come back and people were asking where the action was, and why wasn't Gwyneth Paltrow naked, then the studio just kinda gave up. You'd think that with the budget so small they'd at least try to recoup costs. But they looked at it as a nice little experiment, like a rat in a cage.

RE: Getting back to *Boogie Nights*—do you think that this film is going to have problems with people who are offended by its subject matter? If a movie gets an NC-17, it can't play in a lot of theaters or theater chains. You have an R. Will they *still* say they can't play it? Just as Blockbuster drops certain movies even though they're R's?

PTA: I know for a fact that Blockbuster has recut movies that they stock as R's. I know friends who rented *Scarface*, came home and saw cuts clearly made by some kid behind a counter—from VCR to VCR—which you can recognize in the way the image loses quality for a minute or two. So they're even attacking films that are R-rated. The main reason that I contractually couldn't make an NC-17 was because of Blockbuster.

RE: You're gonna have some people amazed that you got an R.

PTA: Ultimately we only cut about forty seconds out of the movie. There are one or two that still bother me just slightly, but not enough that it affects the story, so I'm cool. The biggest thing that we had to deal with was when Bill Macy first discovers Nina Hartley in bed with the man. And the MPAA said I can't show sexual movement and talking at the same time. So I got a flat and put it up, got a light in the camera and I put Nina on the bed and I said, "Just move once, stop, and say the lines."

RE: The scene at the end is amazing, where they're doing the drug deal and the guy is throwing firecrackers around. Where did that come from?

PTA: First is my mild obsession for firecrackers. That came from my dad, who hosted late-night horror shows in Cleveland. He would show these terrible movies and introduce them as this cult figure called "Ghoulardi." And he would set off firecrackers. That stuck with me. And in *Putney Swope*, there's background action where this guy throws firecrackers. And I called Robert Downey Sr. and I said, "This is brilliant. I wanna take this and run it through this whole scene. Is that cool with you?" And he said, "Absolutely."

RE: Los Angeles is filled with people who want to direct films. They're always asking, "How do I get started, what do I do?" You have somehow managed to negotiate a path to that point. What do you tell people who want to be directors?

PTA: That there is nothing else I can do, and nothing else I will do. "No" is not an option. I have to do this or I will die. I only get to direct because I can write—that's the key. The scary thing is, if you can write, you hold a lot of cards. They're starving for material. Starving. ☞

## James Cameron

*Chicago*, December 1997—There is a shot in *Titanic* that I watched like a hawk. The point of view is from above, as the great ship steams to its destiny. In one apparently uninterrupted piece of celluloid, we see the ship from bow to stern, every foot of it, with flags flying and smoke coiling from its stacks, and on the deck hundreds of passengers strolling, children running, servants serving, sportsmen playing.

I watched it because I knew, logically, that this shot was a special effect. They did not rebuild the *Titanic* to make the movie. I knew, in general, what to look for—what trickery might be involved—and yet I was fooled. The shot looks like the real thing.

"That was a model shot," James Cameron said, smiling. "The people were all computer graphics. The way we did it was, we had people act out all of those individual behaviors in what we call a 'motion capture environment.' So, a steward pouring tea for a lady seated on a deck chair—that was all acted out and then that motion file was used to drive and animate those figures. The end result is like you said: We pull back down the full length of *Titanic*, and you see 350 people all over the decks, doing all those different things. The same technique was used for the sinking, when you see hundreds of people on the ship jumping off or rolling down the decks."

So it's all f/x. Well, I didn't expect them to build the *Titanic* and sink it again. But what I also didn't expect was a film so completely convincing in its details. There are a few moments the viewer doubts (the portholes look suspiciously bright at night), but in general Cameron's film is a triumph of reconstructed realism: Inside and out, in good times and bad, when it is launched and when it goes to its grave, the *Titanic* in this movie looks like a real ship.

James Cameron is, of course, a director who specializes in special effects, and he's been at the cutting edge since *Aliens* (1986), still the most disturbing of the *Alien* series. Before that he worked valiantly in films where the budget and the technology were not yet there for him (*Piranha II* in 1981, *The Terminator* in 1984). After, he was the king of f/x, with such credits as *The Abyss* (1989), *Terminator II* (1991), *True Lies* (1994), and such producer credits as Kathryn Bigelow's *Strange Days* (1995).

There has always been the choice in Cameron's work to insist on a story; he doesn't lazily throw cardboard puppets into explosions and chases. When time ran out on the production schedule for *The Abyss*, and he had to make a deadline decision about what to finish for the release print, he kept the relationship story between aquanauts Ed Harris and Mary Elizabeth Mastrantonio. Not until the release of the Director's Cut could we see the spectacular special effects (a city rising from the sea, a tidal wave) that he was willing to surrender before he shortchanged his story.

In *Titanic*, there are three stories: The historic story of the sinking of the grandest ship of its time; the fictional story of a young female passenger and the men in her life; and the modern story of the *Titanic* in its grave, two and a half miles beneath the sea.

There is a lot of footage of the real *Titanic* on the bottom, and some fake footage, and some footage that dissolves from one to the other. Cameron wasn't content to buy up footage from the various documentaries about the search for the *Titanic;* he shot the film's undersea footage himself, new for this film: "It's all our own. I made the dives and operated the camera, and we lit it and everything."

You saw the *Titanic,* I said.

"Yes. Sat on the deck twelve times. The IMAX film stuck the camera inside the sub; it shot out of the view port, which was very limiting. We built a camera that went outside the sub and could pan and tilt and do all the normal movie camera-type stuff. Ironically, we totaled the number of hours that we spent at *Titanic* during the course of those dives and it was more than the number of hours that the passengers spent on board."

That last shot, I said, where we float on the bottom along the wrecked ship's deck, and then . . .

"In that particular case, it's a model," he said, "but we did generate a lot of footage of the real ship that's in the film. Also interiors of the ship as it sits right now on the bottom of the ocean, and then fake interiors as well."

It's all so seamless.

"It's consistent with what *Titanic* looks like. We couldn't explore the whole interior of the ship. We could only get a glimpse into some areas. We went down some corridors to the D Deck level and saw a lot of the remaining hand-carved woodwork, the wall paneling, the beautiful, ornate carved doors. A lot of it is still there. It's very, very cold, which helps preserve things. There are marine organisms that will eat wood, but in certain areas the wood was covered with white leaded paint that protected *Titanic.*"

"*Titanic,*" he calls it. Not "the *Titanic.*"

"That's how they referred to liners in those days. The great ships were places, not things. They were an entity almost. You'd say, 'I'm crossing in *Mauritania.*'"

I was sitting in a Chicago hotel, drinking coffee with a man who had been as close to the *Titanic* as he was to me.

"It was eerie," Cameron said. "I love to dive and I love shipwrecks, so the adrenaline was spiking. But there's something about *Titanic* that's sort of mythic, that's storylike and you don't quite believe it. It's almost more like a novel than an event that really happened—and yet here's the wreck. It really happened. People died here. That was the thing I had to take away. Not just the images of a wreck. I had to take away the sense of responsibility to do it right and to honor *Titanic.* The film that resulted is an expression of what happened there."

*Titanic* is said to be the most expensive film ever made. Perhaps it is. Few films contemplate financing an expedition to the bottom of the Atlantic just to get things rolling. When *Titanic* missed its original opening date, there were rumors that the film was in trouble, that it would be a disaster in the tradition of *Raise the Titanic!* (1980), a film that inspired its producer, Lord Grade, to observe, "It would have been cheaper to lower the ocean."

But the film's world premiere at the Tokyo Film Festival was a triumph, and soon the word was trickling forth from press screenings that, whatever its cost, *Titanic* was value for money, a marriage of imagination and technology in the Hollywood tradition of well-crafted epics.

The framing story involves an old lady, a *Titanic* survivor, who sees TV documentary footage of a sketch drawn on board all those years ago. She visits the documentary filmmakers and tells her story, which is reconstructed in flashbacks. Kate Winslet plays the survivor as a young girl, Billy Zane is her rich and arrogant fiancé (who loves her all the same), and Leonardo DiCaprio is the kid from steerage who becomes her lover and, eventually, her savior.

Around their story all of the details are fashioned of fact and fiction. The real *Titanic* took a long time to sink, and the film re-creates an eerie feeling of how that time was spent by the passengers—both first-class ticket holders and those with cheaper tickets who are temporarily locked below, because there were not enough lifeboats for everyone.

"Many died in terror, you know," Cameron said. "When you look at the numbers, if you were a third-class male on *Titanic,* you stood a one-in-ten chance of survival. If you were a first-class female, it was virtually a 100 percent survival rate. It broke down along lines of gender and class. If you were a first-class male, you stood about a fifty-fifty chance of survival. And the crew took it hardest. Of the 1,500 who died, 600 or 700 of them were crew members. The people who stayed in the dynamo room and the engine room, to keep the lights on so that the evacuation would not become panicked—who stayed till the end and missed their opportunity to leave the ship—that's something you'd see less of today."

I can only imagine, I said, what kind of conditions prevailed on the set when you were filming the scenes where *Titanic* is almost vertical and people are sliding straight down and bouncing off air vents and deck walls.

"That was our most dangerous work," Cameron said. "The stunt team worked for weeks in advance, videotaping each one of those stunts and rehearsing them and showing me the tapes. It was all intensely preplanned, and the set was made about 50 percent out of rubber at that point, all padded up. But there's always an X-factor. We had 6,000 stunt person days on this film—the equivalent of one man doing stunts seven days a week for sixteen years. But it was all happening at once.

"We did have a guy break his leg, which I hated. I don't think anybody should get hurt for a film. So I decided to do more of it with computer graphics. Here was a case where the effects actually stepped in and took the place of some of the more dangerous stunts—like the guy falling who hits the propeller of the ship and bounces off. But a lot of those other stunt falls are real. If you look at our stunt credits in the film it's like the Manhattan phone book."

It was such a blow to human confidence, I said, that this great ship, unsinkable, the largest ever built, would . . .

"The great lesson of *Titanic* for us, going into the twenty-first century," he said, "is that the inconceivable *can* happen. Those people lived in a time of certainty; they felt they had mastered everything—mastered nature and mastered themselves. But they had mastered neither. A thousand years from now *Titanic* will still be one of the great stories. Certainly there have been greater human tragedies during this century, but there's something poetically perfect about *Titanic*, because of the laying low of the wealthy and the beautiful people who thought life would be infinite and perfect for them."

Anyone seeing this movie, I said, will have to ask themselves this question: Would I have fought to get on a lifeboat? Would I have pushed a woman or a child out of the way? Or would I have sat down in the lounge and called for a brandy, like Guggenheim, and faced the inevitable with grace?

"The sinking of *Titanic* took two hours and forty minutes. People had time to think about their doom and to make choices. It wasn't instantaneous like the crash of the *Hindenberg*. This was about moral choices, and so it asks every member of the audience to question their own moral choices, their own courage, their own kind of fiber."

He sighed. "I don't know what I would have done. Well, I know what I would have done if I had been taken back on a time machine and put on the deck of *Titanic*. I know exactly how I could have survived without hurting anybody else. But if I was really there, with my personality but without my current knowledge, I don't know what I would have done."

What would the time traveler have known to do?

He smiled. "Oh, it's very simple. You just wait until Boat No. 4 is pulling away from the ship and dive in at the front off the B Deck level and swim to it, because it was only half full anyway."

## Jim Carrey

*(Note: If by any chance you do not know the secret of* The Truman Show, *even though all of the TV ads revealed it, give yourself a treat and see the movie before reading this or any other article about the movie. If you do know, read on.)*

*Chicago,* April 1998—A few weeks before *The Truman Show* opened, I was talking with its director, Peter Weir, about the idea of a man whose life is lived entirely on television. He doesn't have a single private moment. And Weir quietly observed, "Princess Di lived a life like that."

A few days later, I mentioned this to Jim Carrey, the star of the movie, and he nodded: "Oh, yeah, sure. In fact, I've lived a life a little bit like Truman in the last few years."

And so he has. After half a dozen enormous comedy hits in a row, Jim Carrey is one of the few stars able to pull down a $20 million paycheck and deserve it; his movies open strongly and have legs, and it is becoming increasingly clear that he's not a goofball one-hit wonder but an enormously talented man who, like him or not, is a fact of life. That gets him a lot of publicity.

I haven't liked all (or even most) of his movies, but I have almost always liked him in them; his energy is a natural force, he takes an obvious joy in entertaining, and for a guy who played Dumber in *Dumb and Dumber*, he is very smart.

Now he's opening in *The Truman Show*, which is gathering the kind of reviews and advance audience responses that *Forrest Gump* received a few years ago. It's not a typical Carrey performance (he doesn't have any entrances through the hindquarters of a hippopotamus), but a skilled exercise in satire and light comedy, and it could win him an Oscar nomination.

The opening scenes seem carefully modulated to orient the audience, which on the opening days is likely to contain a lot of Carrey fans: Weir and Carrey let the audience know it's okay to laugh, but that this isn't your typical Carrey movie.

"It was a very carefully thought out thing with Peter and I as to how much humor should be shown up front," Carrey told me. "We didn't wanna mislead the audience. I believe that *The Cable Guy* kinda misled the audience—the marketing most of all. The audience thought they were going to *Ace Ventura* and it was a dark-edged comedy. But in this one, Peter was amazing at finding the right note. I come full-bore, but I am directable, you know."

Although Truman Burbank, the Carrey character, is the most famous person in the world, the movie isn't really about the pressures of celebrity because Truman, of course, doesn't know he's on TV.

"For me," Carrey said, "the media is only a backdrop for this person who needs to separate himself from the safe things in life and go into the abyss. Which we all have to do if we wanna end up doing something we love and being with someone we love."

Was there a little window, I asked, between when you were trying to become famous and when you were trying to get shelter from your fame? You start out, you're unemployable, nobody's heard of you, and then you're living in a fishbowl.

"There was a thrilling moment when, in fact, I was here in this very hotel in Chicago when *Ace Ventura* opened up. And it was like suddenly, you know: 'Okay! I got their attention!' And things were okay."

Before that was a time when you were always referred to as "the white guy on *In Living Color.*" You were doing terrific work and people weren't quite sure exactly who you were.

"I thought I was going to hell half the time. Literally. After the first Fire Marshal Bill sketch I did, I walked home just thinking, well, I've brought evil into the world; now I'm gonna suffer for it."

We were talking in a room of the Four Seasons, drinking coffee, reviewing his career, and I was thinking that Carrey was being rather civil to a critic who wrote of *Ace Ventura* that "Carrey plays Ace as if he's being clocked on an Energy-O-Meter, and paid by the calorie expended."

"You ripped me, totally," he said, somehow smiling nostalgically. "That's your prerogative. I don't feel bad about those things at all. When I read it I was in a restaurant with my gang and I was reading the review and I was going, oh man, that's brutal. But at the same time, I have this automatic thing, maybe it's a defense mechanism, but I really like to look at the negatives as things to learn from, and I went, well, I hope the movie does good but, wow, a lot of people aren't going to like it."

A lot of people didn't, but it still grossed more than $200 million. And then came *Dumb and Dumber,* and *The Mask,* and *Ace Ventura: When Nature Calls,* and *Batman Forever,* and *Liar, Liar,* and although some of them didn't work for me (I liked *The Mask* and *Liar Liar,* and Carrey's Riddler in the *Batman* movie), I began to suspect that I had approached *Ace Ventura* with the wrong set of expectations. Carrey had to do what all original artists have to do: inform his audience that he exists as a fact and not as a copy of anything else. I wish I could claim that I knew that from the first, but even the closest scrutiny of my 1994 review reveals no such insight.

"Before *Ace* came out," Carrey was telling me, "I spent fifteen years in the comedy clubs and I had promises of fame and promises of glory that faded away. The next thing you hear is, studio executives go, no, you've had your chance. I've been up and down like that a good five or six times in my life, so that when success came in my thirties I just thanked God. Because I don't think I'd wanna be where Leonardo DiCaprio is right now. That's very confusing, to be so successful so young. It's so hard to deal with ego-wise."

It's strange, looking at your filmography and finding that you had a whole career before people knew who you were. You were in eight movies. You were the guy in *Pink Cadillac.*

"Yeah, the wacky cousin or something like that."

I was watching one of your films on an airplane once with the earphones off.

"I hate the way they cut the films for airplanes. I won't do the looping, either."

Where you have to change all the four-letter words?

"Yeah. I get in the dubbing booth and something wells up inside me. I'm having a love scene and they want me to say, 'I'd love to kiss your sandwich,' or whatever. I'd rather they bleeped it and just left it to the audience's imagination."

Anyway, I said, watching you on this airplane, without the dialogue or the plot, I could see that you moved like a character in a cartoon. You know? They don't just start here and run there.

"They go 'sproooinggg!'"

Yeah. They back up before they run. They kind of have to cock themselves first.

"Yeah, absolutely."

And I thought, Carrey doesn't hold anything back. He is totally up there.

"I am willing to make an idiot of myself."

Like a six-minute cartoon.

"Absolutely. I think in cartoons. I used to walk down the street when I was a kid and see the coyote's Acme blueprint on top of things, you know. I'd see a pile of garbage, and I'd see the little dots going over it and the little line and I'd somehow figure out whether or not I could leap over it. That's how I'd think. Like a Wile E. Coyote cartoon."

Sometimes your body language on the screen is the body language of a cartoon character. Not by using gimmicks such as fast motion, but because you physically go into hyperdrive. Like in

*Liar, Liar,* when you bang yourself with the toilet seat.

"Well, *The Truman Show* is a much thicker soup, but I believe that the characters I've done so far have been totally appropriate to the tone of the films. Ace Ventura was a cartoon; when this guy who's like no one else on the planet enters a room, he's the fly-in-the-ointment guy."

Did that begin to take form when you were a kid?

"I've always been trying to be somebody special. That's how it started out. As a kid, I was in my room when everybody was out playing. I was trying to get Johnny Mathis down, so that I could entertain people at Christmastime or whatever. But at a certain point, when I was about nineteen, I had to go off on my own and find my own way. I quit doing what was working for me and I used to go up to the Comedy Store to find something new. I promised myself that I wouldn't repeat a word that I said the night before. Two-thirds of the time it was garbage, but sometimes things would come out that were really kinda beautiful, and nice. That's the abyss, you know. You have to go right to the edge."

## Helena Bonham Carter

*Toronto,* September 1997—She is the queen of the British period pictures, the forceful heroine with the flashing eyes and the knack of looking as if she's worn those costumes all her life. Helena Bonham Carter has played Lady Jane Grey and Ophelia, and the heroines of Forster's *Room With a View* and *Howards End,* and the evil doctor's lover in *Mary Shelley's Frankenstein,* and Olivia in *Twelfth Night,* and if she somehow missed starring in one of the Jane Austen adaptations, now here she is as Kate Croy, a woman prepared to loan out the man she loves, in Henry James's *The Wings of the Dove.*

It is one of her best performances, making her a likely candidate for an Academy Award nomination, and yet, like all of her work, she cannot bear to watch it. She slipped out of the gala premiere at the Toronto Film Festival: "I didn't particularly want to see it with 1,200 people. I'm totally unmoved by the whole thing. But then I'm never moved by anything that I'm in. It's too excruciating. You know it's only you, you know the drama behind the whole thing, you know the story, everything always seems so long and boring and unsympathetic and uninvolving when it's something I'm in . . ."

But she does like to watch other people in other movies: "Oh yes, absolutely. Sometimes I can even watch myself, when I have something to hide behind; an accent, or it's a character part. But mostly it's a painful process and not one that I enjoy."

I believe her. I believe she is impatient with herself, and doesn't enjoy looking at herself in a mirror, and spends her days off wearing jeans with holes in the knees, and sees acting in the British way, as more of a job or a craft than an art or a calling. That's why I like her in her period roles: She plays her characters as if she's not impressed with them, as if she knows their weaknesses all too well. She doesn't, like some actors, behave as if she knows she's in a Great Literary Classic.

Consider Kate Croy. Here is one of James's most complicated characters. She is a poor girl who wants to marry a poor boy. Her aunt wants her to marry a lord. To get her way, Kate needs money. She meets a rich American orphan named Millie Theale, who has a fatal disease and has come to Europe to live before she dies. Millie likes Kate's poor boy, whose name is Merton Densher. Slowly, subtly, revealing her hand one card at a time, Kate unfolds a scheme in which, to put it bluntly (which James never does), Merton will marry Millie, Millie will die, and Merton will inherit her money and be able to marry Kate.

This could be a soap opera. James makes it a romantic tragedy by the brilliant expedient of making the three characters like one another. In his novel, their liking is more bittersweet and ironic; the film version deepens it, which has the effect of making Kate's character more sympathetic. It is a wonderful role for Helena Bonham Carter, leaving her always at the crucial apex of the triangle, so that even when she is offscreen, Merton and Millie are following her design.

We sat in a restaurant on the balcony of a vast Toronto hotel, the escalators running past us into the sky, and talked about the worlds of London and Venice in the early years of the century. I observed that she had many famous authors attached to her work: Forster, Shakespeare, Shelley, even George Orwell, whose novel about a wretched bookseller, *Keep the Aspidistra Flying,* also premiered at Toronto, and also starred Bonham Carter. (It's been retitled *A Merry War.*)

"Literary adaptations are sort of the whole industry in England," she mused. "You either get put into films of novels, or you get adopted by the Ken Loachs or the Mike Leighs. That's pretty much the range of the films we produce. I get a new project and I think—been there, done that. But if you look beyond the costumes, they *do* come from great authors, and the characters are subtly drawn and three-dimensional, and women tend to be the protagonists in period costume dramas. They offer a better stock of female parts than contemporary screenplays."

Your characters aren't typecast, I said, but your sources are.

"It's either literature, or some kind of grotty, gritty, working-class, street sort of thing. Which I would love to do. Although in England there's a sort of chippiness if you try to move out of your assigned niche. Much has been made of my double-barreled name and my so-called illustrious background. I mean, I'm not particularly aristocratic. I'm sort of comfortably, I guess, upper-middle, as they say. But I'm not trendily working class. And I'm associated with Merchant and Ivory; after having only done two of their films, I have become synonymous with them."

She does have a famous name in England; Bonham Carters have been prominent in politics and the arts for generations.

"You're punished for it," she said. "The thing's beyond your control, you know. Looks too. You don't choose your parentage, you don't choose your class, you don't choose a hell a lot of things that you're saddled with which will inspire a certain reaction from people that will not necessarily be friendly."

Sometimes she leaves the cycle, as when she came to New York three years ago to play Woody Allen's wife in *Mighty Aphrodite.* More often she plays one of those wonderful literary heroines. Certainly Kate Croy is one of the best roles in literature. The film's director, Iain Softley, has made a bold choice by taking James, whose novels are told in a flow of sentences sinuously coiling back upon themselves, and adapting his story into a film of spare dialogue and suggestive silences.

"I think *The Wings of the Dove* was the most unwordy film that I've ever done," she said. "There's very little dialogue in it. We had to concentrate on what was not being said."

The peculiar thing about the relationship between Kate and Millie, I said, is that they really like each other. The heiress more or less understands the exact situation—that the man she loves needs her money to marry the woman he loves.

"Oh, everyone knows. Kate may be seen as the immoral character, but I think she's the one who has the most moral courage. She comes up with a plan, and she implements it. Merton tries the moral high ground, he tries being outraged, but he goes along with it, and Millie at the end goes along with it too."

To some degree doesn't Millie come to Europe knowing she's dying and hoping to have a fling?

"That's all she wants. She wants to live."

The scenes in Venice, I said, were so atmospheric. Venice in the summer is filled with tourists, but Venice in the winter, when the movie is set, is such a dark, romantic backdrop.

"We had four weeks there," she said. "Unfortunately, it was actually August."

You're kidding!

"We made it look like winter. It was, as you can imagine, a logistical nightmare."

The shot, for example, where the camera sweeps into the café in San Marco in the rain.

"It's just one rain machine. We had a very odd shooting schedule. We'd shoot through the night, and then we'd have an hour and a half of daylight at the beginning, just after dawn, before the square filled up. Suddenly the tourists would arrive en masse, and we'd have to stop.

"When Merchant and Ivory made *Room With a View,* they pulled some strings in Florence, and bought the plaza for the day. So they could be imperialistic and keep everyone out, including irate tourists who had traveled so far and couldn't go in to see the loggia and all that. But you can't rent Venice for the day, so it was an absolute sort of nightmare."

I would have never guessed in a thousand years that you shot in August.

"There was a lot of rain in that film, wasn't there? I felt seasick for about the first two weeks. It took me an age to find my sea legs because we were always on gondolas. But on the gondola you feel fine; it's when you get on the ground that the swaying doesn't stop."

In the film Millie rents a palazzo, and for the

film they used the same palazzo on the Grand Canal that Henry James lived in. Speaking of palazzos, I said, because I love phrases like "speaking of palazzos," what about the one Woody Allen was thinking of buying? The bad luck palazzo? Everyone who has ever owned it has met an untimely end. It's haunted, and they all commit suicide or fall into the canal or something.

"Woody loves traveling," she said, "but as long as it's in five-star hotels with all his little creature comforts around him."

That was sort of an unexpected departure for you, playing Woody Allen's wife.

"I auditioned without knowing what the part was. I just had some pages of dialogue. I didn't read very well, and I had no idea what I was meant to be projecting. It was like some spy movie. They said the script would be in a brown envelope in such and such a hotel. I was to pick it up there, read it an hour, and then meet Woody for an hour's conversation, and then hand back the script."

Sounds like working for Kubrick.

"There is a degree of paranoia there. Although it was very nice working with him."

After Toronto she was going to go home to London, she said, and unpack. She had bought a house in a sort of bohemian neighborhood down the hill from artsy Hampstead, and after a year she still hadn't moved in. Too much travel, too many locations; she's made three films since *The Wings of the Dove.*

"I have a lot of work to do on it. I've got an interesting relation with the pub in front, because that's where you park. The trouble is, in the summer at least, they use it as a bit of a beer garden, so you've got this immediate audience."

You mean you have to walk through a beer garden to get to your front door?

"They're regulars."

## Francis Ford Coppola

*Chicago,* November 1997—There is a kind of shyness, a modesty, about Francis Ford Coppola that is so surprising. Here is the director of *The Godfather,* and the epic *Apocalypse Now,* and the paranoid psychodrama *The Conversation,* and he talks about whether he has the *right* to put his name above the title. Kids out of film school put their names on their first films, and here he is explaining why his movies are called *Mario Puzo's The Godfather* and *Bram Stoker's Dracula* and *John Grisham's The Rainmaker.*

"Someday," he was saying, "I really dream to make a movie that's 'Francis Coppola's.' But I can only do that if I write it from scratch. With those other films, my job is to make *their* work come alive, as I tried to do with Mario or John Grisham. I really believe that I should not put in my own two cents other than as an interpretive artist. Right now I'm writing something original, and I am totally willing to use all the money from *The Rainmaker* to make that happen, and then I would put my name above the title."

Other directors sign movies they didn't write. They do it all the time. Coppola doesn't say that's wrong. It's just that . . . he couldn't.

"I know all about everything there is in a film," he told me, "but what makes me different, I think, from even some of my very great colleagues, is I really can write from nothing."

He can, and has, and yet here he is sitting in the Chicago Ritz-Carlton talking about his new movie, which has John Grisham's name above the title. I wonder if, in a sense, he puts Grisham's name there as a way of *not* putting on his own name. But, no, he likes the film and likes the novel it was based on.

"I'd never read a Grisham novel before. I saw *The Rainmaker* in an airport. I got it and enjoyed it. It had a lot of humor. In some ways it sort of reminded me of *The Godfather.* People like the idea that if injustice has happened, they can go to somebody and get it remedied. In *The Rainmaker,* they've been paying premiums to an insurance company for twenty years and then the company says, 'Well, your policy doesn't apply to that.' And here's this idealistic kid, with a good heart but hardly any equipment, and he wants to see justice done."

The kid is played by Matt Damon, as a new graduate of a second-tier law school, who ends up in a storefront office with a hustling paralegal (Danny DeVito) as his sidekick. The large, deep, and rich supporting cast includes Teresa Wright as a widow who rents the kid a room, Claire Danes as a battered wife, Mary Kay Place as the mother of a dying son, and Jon Voight as the slimy insurance company lawyer. It's a good movie, but you can kind of see why it's "John Grisham's" and not "Francis Ford Coppola's."

I was talking not long ago with Tom Luddy, who has been Coppola's friend and a producer for his company for many years, and he told me *The Rainmaker* is the last film Coppola has had to do for money, in order to finally get completely out of debt and be able to make his own work. I asked Coppola point-blank if that were true.

"To write your own film takes a year," he said, "and while you're writing, what does everyone else do? How do you pay your company? There's a tremendous force that says, the second I go to work, then everyone works and the money flows. I'm the elder of the community—my own fault, since I aspired to have a company and employ people in the first place. Only now after all these years am I in a position to say—'You know, I'm gonna write something and I'm not going to make another film for a while.'"

Few directors have had a more unremitting struggle than Coppola. To the glory of his Oscars you have to match the dark side of his career. He literally almost lost his health and his mind in the nightmare of filming *Apocalypse Now.* (If you think I exaggerate, look at the documentary about that experience, *Hearts of Darkness,* and listen to the despairing conversations his wife, Eleanor, secretly recorded.) Then he founded his own studio, American Zoetrope, to produce the film *One From the Heart,* using still-experimental video and editing techniques. Coppola felt the distributor tested it incompetently, before the wrong audiences, and pulled it out of release. It never had a proper theatrical run, and buried Coppola and Zoetrope in a mountain of debt. Then there was his decision to buy a vineyard in the Napa Valley and go into the wine business. Still more debt. There was a day, he recalled, when process servers were knocking on the door to evict his family from their home, and he and Ellie were hiding upstairs while his daughter Sofia boldly ordered the strangers off the property. And there was the 1986 death of his son Gio in a boating accident.

"Things happened," he said, "so that I will never be the same. It was a test of my will and resiliency. *Apocalypse* obviously was a scary situation, because I not only was making this strange movie that looked like it was going straight down the tubes, but my family's home was mortgaged to pay for it. I was in a state of fear. And I had to come up with $2 million a year for the bank in New York and I didn't know where to get it from.

"I never made a film where I didn't find something that I loved. But I did make films that I wouldn't have made had I not had to work. Time does heal a lot of feelings. I never felt burnt out; I always felt alive—but my mind wasn't on film in the same way it was when I was a kid. If I made any mistakes in my life, it was that I allowed the success of *The Godfather* to sweep me off the course that I had set for myself as a young man, which was to always creatively write original material."

Now the bad times are at least behind him.

"I'm out of the dire financial straits, and with this movie, I'm ahead—which is why I did it. I've made my family secure with the wine business, and so with the money I've made on *The Rainmaker,* I have my wife's permission, everyone's permission, to invest in my own next movie. The only way you can make unusual movies is if you put your money where your mouth is."

We are sitting, talking, drinking coffee so casually it is necessary to recall that this is Francis Ford Coppola, and not some struggling would-be auteur. He is all but apologizing for films that would crown anybody else's career. He thought the script for *Peggy Sue Got Married* (1986) was kind of dumb, he says, and I reflect that I thought it was one of the year's best films. *The Outsiders* (1983) was not a box-office hit—but it was Coppola's eye that picked out Tom Cruise as a promising unknown.

Of *The Rainmaker,* he said, one of the joys was playing games with the actors. Literally, games. Exercises from the classic acting book *Game Theater* by Viola Spolin of Chicago, who was once his teacher, and whose son, Paul Sills, founded Second City.

"I tried every trick in the book. The stunts we pulled on these people! You don't get life from actors by smothering them. You lay around opportunities for them to go to themselves. The joke was that when I worked with Marlon (on *The Godfather*), I put around Italian cigars and Italian cheese, and just the smell on your fingers starts making you feel a certain way.

"A week before *The Rainmaker* we began playing Viola's games. They break the ice. But also teach concentration. We played games with the actors the whole time we shot. You know how on a movie the photographer will say, 'Uh, oh—there's a glare,' and then everything will stop for the lighting department? Well, on this movie I said we were going to have an *acting* department. I had a dialogue coach and an acting coach, and we'd take half an hour and do improvisations. Or stage little scenarios. At one point, for example, I told Matt Damon: 'Gee, Matt—I just got a call from Paramount, and they're looking at the dailies and they're not real happy with your work. Apparently Ed Norton is available . . .' Then he had to go and play a scene where he got fired from his job. He knew I was making it up, but in a way, it got him in touch with the feelings."

The movie is unusual, I said, in the way it gives good screen time to so many different characters. In the movies with the $20 million paychecks, we seem to get the same two people in every scene.

"It's very much economics. If you paid $20 million for someone, you'd want to use them. Also you don't have any money left for anyone else. Grisham has written a lot of great characters and that meant I could have a wonderful cast and focus on the acting."

Coppola's eye for actors has paid off time and again. He created the third act of Marlon Brando's career with *The Godfather.* He was there at the beginning for Al Pacino, Robert Duvall, Diane Keaton, Robert De Niro. Look at the cast of *The Outsiders.* These are the unknowns he cast in 1983: Matt Dillon, Ralph Macchio, C. Thomas Howell, Patrick Swayze, Rob Lowe, Emilio Estevez, Diane Lane, and, yes, Tom Cruise.

"I really felt this Tom Cruise kid was gonna be incredible," he said. "I don't know him now, but he was such a hardworking kid. I mean, he'd do anything for his character, and I understand even today when they work on films he's extremely hardworking."

He's certainly getting his ultimate test right now, I said. He and Nicole Kidman have entered the eleventh month of shooting on Stanley Kubrick's *Eyes Wide Shut.* The contract says they have to work as long as Kubrick needs them.

Coppola nodded. "I wish I could do a movie and all these stars would stay around for a year. I'd have them all stomping on grapes. 'Okay, crew, that's it for today. Actors, you're going to work. We've got a lot of grapes to pick.'"

## Stephen Fry

*Philadelphia,* April 1998—"Why is America such a violent country, Mr. Wilde?"

"Because the wallpaper is so ugly."

Oscar Wilde was famous for his one-liners, but lurking beneath the surface was a serious purpose. That's what Stephen Fry was arguing the other night in Bookbinder's, where he tucked into a lobster and talked about the doomed wit and playwright.

"What he was saying, I think, is that nature reflects perfection, but if you replace it with the ugliest artifacts of man, you must be violent," Fry explained. "If you rip the earth open into quarries, only to stamp out tin ornaments, of course you hate yourself."

Fry talks like a man who could dictate polished prose. He eats like a man who knows what a good lobster is, and he spreads butter on his bread like a man for whom the recommended daily dietary allowance of saturated fat is a record to be broken. We talked one night during the Philadelphia Film Festival; his new film *Wilde* was not in the festival, but that was a minor technicality.

In the film, he gives a much-praised performance as the celebrated writer, who produced a series of wildly successful plays and novels, and then unwisely sued the marquess of Queensbury for libel. The marquess's attorneys were able to prove in court that Wilde was indeed, as the libel claimed, a homosexual, and Wilde was convicted to two years' hard labor from which he never recovered.

A century later, Wilde is more popular than ever. Just as the film is going into national release, Liam Neeson has opened in a Broadway play based on the playwright, whose books are all in print and whose plays flourish in countless revivals.

Fry plays Wilde with tenderness, as a man who loved his wife and children but loved even more an ideal of masculine youth. For the young men, both willing and paid, who entered his arms, he felt more like a mentor than a lover. There is the sense that the sex itself was never the real point.

Fry at forty is a very tall man, a master of table chat, an entertainer. He writes as much as he acts; he wrote a column in the *London Telegraph* for years, and has produced novels and memoirs. Like Wilde, he is a homosexual, although he has made it a point to say he is celibate, suggesting in some of his writings that the messiness of sexual intimacy is not to his taste.

Why, I asked him, is Wilde so popular right now?

"As we arrive at the end of our century," he said, "we seem to look down a long corridor to the end of the previous century, asking what will last and make a difference. My generation put up posters of Che and Dylan and somehow felt rock music *might* do something to make a difference. We no longer believe that it might. We look back to see whose attitudes and ideas still seem relevant, and with Wilde and Einstein, their authority is still there. He was the crown prince of Bohemia. He was always curious. The best of us want to be students for the rest of our lives. He fills a need. Even cheap detective writers create heroes out of what their time is lacking, and we lack the intelligence and wit of Wilde, who doesn't buy into the whining, sanctimonious culture in which we live."

Yes. He talked about Wilde in the deep, plummy tones that first became famous when he starred in the BBC series *Jeeves and Wooster*. It was not exactly conversational, but it was more entertaining than most conversation, and more coherent.

"Take an Englishman like myself, visiting America. I'm told that I'm driving past the Empire State Building, but as I look out the window all I can see is the next building, which stands in the way. As we continue down the street, however, the Empire State Building reemerges, and when I get far enough away it towers above all of the others. Something like that has happened to Wilde. The further away we've got from him, the more he's grown."

Fry bears a certain physical resemblance to Wilde: "As I broke the membrane of my thirties and began to develop interesting new chins and a spreading waistline," he mused, "I began to be told I should play Wilde. And he meant a lot to me. If you knew you were gay in the early 1970s, you felt very alone. You went to the movies about Wilde, and of course they were never very explicit; you wondered why that man was sent to jail for patting people on the head. But you knew that in Wilde you'd found a sympathetic sensibility."

The conversation strayed.

We talked about the new movie *The Truman Show*, about a man who discovers his whole life is being lived on television: "Of course I felt exactly like that when I was growing up," Fry smiled. "I used to think—a-ha! I saw that woman 200 miles ago, in another town! The assistant director has confused his extras!"

We talked about the Bad Sex Prize, awarded every year by *Literary Review* magazine for the worst prose description of sex in the year's novels: "I was supposed to present this year's prize, but I got the date wrong," he said. "I attended one year, when it was won by a writer named Philip Kerr, and everybody in the room went into contortions, trying to twist themselves into the positions he described."

And we talked about the writings of Shirley MacLaine: "The day life has so little to offer that I read the next Shirley MacLaine book, disembowel me."

## Pam Grier

*Los Angeles*, December 1997—I walked in to talk to Pam Grier with these words of Quentin Tarantino fresh in my mind:

"In the 1970s they talked about Jim Brown being the black Burt Reynolds, or Shaft being the black James Bond, but Pam Grier wasn't the black anybody, because there was nobody else, black or white, who was like her. And there still isn't. She founded her own genre."

She did. In more than a dozen movies like *Coffy, Foxy Brown,* and *Sheba Baby,* she played a tough chick who could handle a gun and her fists, and not only beat up drug dealers but do things to them even their worst (male) enemies wouldn't have dreamed of. Some of those movies weren't very good, but Grier's presence and personality stood above them; like Jackie Chan or Bruce Lee, she *was* the movie, and such trifles as plot and direction were irrelevant to her fans.

After the blaxploitation movies ran out of steam, she moved back to Denver to be near her family, but continued to work in two or three pictures a year—some of them good roles like the cop-killer in *Fort Apache, the Bronx* (1981), some of them throwaways like *Mars Attacks!* (1996). For those who remembered her early work, however, there was always something incomplete about her career; she made such a strong impression that somehow she should still be playing the title roles.

She wasn't just a strong, dynamic woman, but a great-looking one, with those high cheekbones and full breasts and hurdler's legs and . . . shoulders. Yes, a movie critic this week was actually complaining in print that Tarantino's new film doesn't show off Grier's shoulders, which he has apparently treasured in his memory for more than twenty years.

Quentin Tarantino, who used to clerk in a video store and is famous for having absorbed all of modern film history more or less as an uninterrupted download, was one of the countless fans who had not forgotten Pam Grier. He decided to film the Elmore Leonard novel *Rum Punch,* and in his screenplay changed a blonde named Jackie Burke into an African-American woman named Jackie Brown, and renamed the movie for her.

Grier remembers how it happened: "He says, 'Pam, I'm writing something about you.' Then I bumped into him a year later, and I thought, he's not gonna; he's so big, everybody's gonna come to him and pay him big bucks to write for them. And he says, 'No, I got something for you. I've been writin' on it.' 'Okay,' I say, 'but before my teeth fall out and my breasts sag? Quentin, when is this gonna happen?' And he says, 'No, I'm gonna . . .'

"So he calls me at my boyfriend's house, who says, 'Hey, there's some black guy on the phone named Quentin.' Cause I know Quentin probably said, 'Yo! Whassup?' And he says he's sending me something. It comes a week later, by mule train, and I'm reading it and I'm going 'Oh, my God, you can tell who's been reading Elmore Leonard.' I aspire to write like Elmore Leonard. He writes so well, you can smell his characters.

"I didn't call Quentin back right away. I loved it and I'm like, it's not gonna get done and I'll be so disappointed. Kevin, my boyfriend, says, 'You better call him before he hires somebody else.' So I called him and said, 'Quentin, you did an excellent job, you really did, because Elmore Leonard writes so well and it's your style.' He says, 'Well, I'm glad you like it because you're Jackie Brown.' I say, 'I am?' He says, 'Yeah. I wrote it for you. No one else could do it but you.' I say, 'You mean no one's crazy enough to do it but me.' He says, 'No one could do it but you.' I say, 'Watch my back and I'll watch yours and don't let me fall.' He says, 'Don't you let me fall.' And we did it."

Pam Grier is telling me this in one dramatic monologue, playing the parts, doing the dialogue, and it's not like she's providing information, it's like she's acting it out in case you weren't there at the time. While she talks, I'm checking her out, and I'm remembering a line from the movie, where Max Cherry the bail bondsman (Robert Forster) tells her, "I'll bet that except for the Afro you used to have, you look about the same now as when you were twenty-nine." And she does. She looks gorgeous, which is important to note, because there are times in *Jackie Brown* when she plays someone who just got out of jail after forty-eight hours.

"I was raised with very little vanity," she told me, when I said something about how good she looked. "One person is not prettier than the other. That's how I was brought up. If your eyes work and your mouth, you know, if everything works—that's fine. Hollywood told me, you're prettier with makeup. Be on screen with all the makeup and look great because that's how you get your next role. Now in *Jackie,* with maturity and confidence, when I come outta jail, I have on no makeup and I got a kitchen—you know, the naps. My hair has gone home and there I am on screen before the world, raw, because everything's been stripped away and I'm down to . . . this is it. It's me. Am I gonna let them get me? Am I gonna be victimized? The survivor in the mature woman is so evident and, oh, so much a part of me."

In the film, she's running illegal cash in from Mexico for a gun dealer (Samuel L. Jackson) when the feds bust her. She's smart enough to know that the dealer will kill her before she can testify against him. She's bailed out by the Forster character, and begins an elaborate scam to save her life, and eventually the bondsman starts to help her, because he has a crush on her. ("The biggest crush," Tarantino told me, "is the one you get after you think you've had your last crush.")

For both Grier and Forster, these are life-changing roles, allowing Hollywood to see them anew. But Grier told me she never stopped acting: "I didn't get into the business to become famous or to make a lot of money, to see my face on the screen. That's not my agenda." She began in Hollywood as a secretary at American-International Pictures, was cast at twenty-one in *The Big Doll House* (1971) more or less because she was standing right there, and didn't consider herself much of an actor until *Greased Lightning* (1977), opposite Richard Pryor and Beau Bridges.

"Every time after I did a film, I went back to work at a daytime job, which drove my agent crazy. He said, 'You're an actress. You're supposed to sit by the phone waitin' for me to get your next job. Why are you back working in the accounting department at Thrifty's?' In our family the work ethic is very important. You're never unemployed. You always work. So after I did *The Big Doll House* and *The Big Bird Cage*, I went back to work and they said, 'What are you doin'? You're an actress.' I am? I didn't think I was a real actress until I started doing theater."

She did a lot of stage work: *Piano Lesson* at the Denver Center for Performing Arts, and *Frankie and Johnnie in the Claire De Lune* in San Diego, and Sam Shepard's *Fool for Love* when it opened in 1986 at the Los Angeles Theater Center. She's written a play called *Heartbreak Row*, which she said is "about a religion and how my sister suffered and died because of it and how it made our family go crazy." She said all the theater prepared her for working with Tarantino, "who does a scene that's nine minutes long, and there's no cutting. You keep the energy going, like in theater."

So when the call came from Tarantino, she was ready. But was she willing? "Kevin my boyfriend says, 'Forget about how you'll feel about getting your feelings hurt if it doesn't go; you call him back.'"

This is a big romance? You're known for never having married.

"Yes, with Kevin Evans. He's a senior VP at RCA Music, and he's also from Denver, and listen to this. You're not going to believe this. He lived in the same house I lived in! His bedroom was my bedroom! Ten years after I moved out, his family moved into my old house in Denver!"

Karma, I said.

"I'm thinking that eventually we'll, you know, marry and have babies and adopt and take care of kids and dogs and birds and trees. I've always wanted to but you have to be with people in the right situation, right place, right time. You have to wait. I was asked many times, 'How come you're not married? Something wrong with you?' No, I'm pretty healthy; I'm fine. 'Well, are you gay?' I say, No, I'm not gay. I'm very straight; I love men and their fuzzy little chests, you know, and mustaches and it's just that when I'm ready I'll know."

What was it? I asked her. What was it, in the early 1970s, that you tapped into so strongly? What nerve were you striking?

Grier starts answering, and it's like earlier; she isn't just talking, she's performing, evoking, recreating, in a stream of memory:

"Well, I'm a part of that 1970s movement of women's independence. I just happened to bring it to film. The seventies were basically rewards for the political gains in the fifties and sixties. We had all those freedoms now. Jimi Hendrix was allowed to play rock 'n' roll and not be called an Uncle Tom. Whites could go to black concerts and not be called nigger-lovers. Blacks were becoming Buddhists as opposed to being Baptists, and we were seeing who had the biggest 'fro and running naked through Woodstock, and we were redefining ourselves, experiencing, exploring. Women could say, we wanna be able to work on a construction job because we like construction; we like being outdoors and then go home and put on a dress or cook for our children. Fifties women were told, don't pick up tools, women don't do this—women stay home. And we were really tired of people telling us. I think there's a Foxy Brown in every woman and a Coffy and a Jackie Brown, and I evolved from all of that. I get my womanhood from talking to them and listening to them in the beauty shop, you know. Or gettin' my nails done and being in the hood, goin' home and listening, looking and getting the characterizations.

"In real life, I don't put on makeup. My hair is not this nice, and I have overalls and I'm covered in dog hair and dog slobber, and I'm out there doin' it, you know. Bob Vila was my idol. Thank you for *This Old House* for teaching me skills that I'm not ashamed to do because I'm a woman. And I wanna show all that in my work. Or I'm gonna bore people, and they're not gonna come."

You know what, Pam? I said. I don't think you have to worry about boring people.

## Spike Lee

*Chicago*, April 1998—Walking into Spike Lee's *He Got Game*, I expected a couple of things. I expected that the movie would be a docudrama, gritty and real, and I expected that, like just about all sports movies, it would end with a big game. I was wrong on both counts.

No big game. Just a very little one, one-on-one between a father and his son. And no docudrama. Oh, there's a lot of information in the movie—few nonplayers have access to more inside information than Lee. But the information is contained within a larger story, which is about a lot more than basketball.

The film stars Ray Allen of the Milwaukee Bucks, as a high school senior who's the most sought-after college prospect in the country. Denzel Washington plays his father, doing up to fifteen years for manslaughter. His crime: He pushed his wife during an argument, and she fell and hit her head and died.

The son still hates his father for that. So it's going to be hard for the father to convince the son to sign a letter of intent with Big State University. And yet the state governor has promised that if the kid signs with Big State, the father will get paroled a lot sooner.

That's part of the story. The other parts involve the way star athletes are recruited by colleges and by the poaching of professional sports agents. The kid, named Jesus, is offered $10,000 by his own high school coach. A relative is given a Lexus to "hold" for him. Women are thrown at him. His own girlfriend turns out to be under the thumb of the high-powered agent. And here's his dad, one more person badgering him for information about "his plans."

Spike Lee was in Chicago a week ago to show the movie to a theater full of high school basketball players, including the championship teams from Whitney Young and Martin Luther King high schools—and, not incidentally, to watch his beloved Knicks play the Bulls. We talked one afternoon.

RE: The movie's last image is wonderful. It sums everything up in one bold gesture, as a basketball connects a father with his son.

SL: I think we'd been laying the groundwork for that type of ending from the very beginning, from the opening credits where you hear Aaron Copland's music and you see images of basketball being played all over this country.

RE: All through your films you reach for big images. I feel that so many modern directors just photograph the characters telling the story; they don't realize that movies are made of images.

SL: The person who really taught me that was Ernest Dickerson [the cinematographer on his early films]. When we were in film school, his expertise in getting the picture to say what the script said was much more advanced than mine. I knew that one day Ernest was not gonna be shooting for me. And it was gonna come down on me.

RE: Why do you love basketball so much?

SL: Well, to be honest, I thought baseball would be my first movie. *Jackie Robinson.* We still can't get the financing. With football, with all their equipment, you don't get to know the players. Basketball, those guys are out there running around practically naked; you can tell someone's personality just by the way they dribble.

RE: Watching the film, I was reminded of your speech to the players in *Hoop Dreams.*

SL: That was a great film. But what we wanted to show even more is how these guys—they're not being exploited; they're being pimped. The NCAA needs to enter the twentieth century because their thinking is backward; they make millions of dollars, make the sneaker companies rich, make the networks rich. Everybody gets rich but the guys out there killing themselves in the Division One big-time basketball and football schools. As long as they give the players tuition, room and board, they think they should be thankful.

RE: You think they should pay them? At the college level?

SL: If they got a stipend, I don't think you woulda had this point-shaving scandal at Northwestern. And I don't think these guys would be signing with agents while they were still playing. I don't think they'd be taking money under the table. These kids are not stupid. They see everybody's making money. The coaches make money 'cause they determine whether they're gonna wear Adidas, Nike, Converse, whatever. And the schools use those deals to pay for the coaches' contracts. But the student athletes get room and board, tuition . . . tough!

RE: Is everything in this movie based on stories you've heard or things you've seen?

SL: We just scratched the surface about what really goes on. I mean, people might think this stuff was wild in this film, but it gets a lot wilder.

RE: They really do hire women to seduce these kids?

SL: Yes.

RE: They supply girls in the dorm rooms, they offer cars?

SL: Yes! And jobs—they give their family members jobs. Women, money, cars, gold, sneakers, clothes. They know what these kids want.

RE: If an agent is found doing that, is he barred from any more dealings in professional basketball?

SL: Yes, he gets debarred. I think that happened with Marcus Canby where Marcus signed with this agent, so once he graduated, about to go in the draft, Marcus decided he didn't wanna have this guy for his agent so the agent tried to blackmail Marcus by saying, "If you don't sign with me, I'm gonna blow the whistle." So Marcus said, "Go ahead." They blew the whistle; the guy got disbarred and UMass, where he was playing, those games got voided and he had to give back like $250,000 to the tournament, because those games were forfeited because he's ineligible because he had an agent at that time. But he wasn't the only one. I would say half these guys playing today have agents.

RE: And the agents, if they're exposed, are out of the business?

SL: But they have buffers. You can't get to them very easily. And we're trying to show that the women are being exploited also. The women use their bodies. That's not to say all women are like that. But in this case they're gonna use what they have and that's been like that since the beginning of civilization.

RE: The girlfriend has a nice speech on the bench.

SL: Lala, played by Rosario Dawson. This is what I was trying to explain to my wife, who was wondering about the depiction of some of the women. I said, look, we're in the Coney Island section of Brooklyn, New York. High-rise projects, stuck on the edge of Brooklyn facing the Atlantic Ocean. They see no way out. For the guys—I'm gonna be a rapper, I'm gonna make it in the NBA, or I'm gonna sell drugs. For the women—I'm gonna hook up with one of these guys whether he's a rapper, going for pro athlete, or drug dealer. To them, that is the perception. Those are the only options they have. And Lala, she truly loves Jesus, but as she sees him being torn in more directions, it dawns on her that when he leaves, that's it. When he goes away to college, that's it—she's lost him forever. And if that's the case, she's gonna cash in like everybody else and try to get a piece of Jesus.

RE: Ordinarily, with a movie that is about a sport like basketball, we expect that the last scene is gonna be a big game. You must have made a decision that wasn't what you wanted to do.

SL: I made that decision because there's no way we would've been able to duplicate what people see for free in the NBA.

RE: So you use one-on-one instead.

SL: Right. And I give a nod to *The Great Santini* for that memorable scene where Robert Duvall and Michael O'Keefe go at it, and at the end of the game, Duvall's bouncing the ball off O'Keefe's head and they go back to the house.

RE: I was disappointed you didn't win an Oscar this year for *4 Little Girls.* How did you feel?

SL: We were not disappointed. The minute I found out there was a Holocaust film, we knew what was what. Automatic. Shoo-in. Better odds than saying the Bulls will win the NBA championship. When they're talking about the Holocaust, I was with them, but when they switched gears and became a propaganda piece for the state of Israel, and it's put out by the Wiesenthal Center, I mean, how you gonna win against that?

RE: I was disappointed *Eve's Bayou* didn't get any nominations. I've been getting a lot of letters lately from people who've rented it and really liked it.

SL: Kasi Lemmons should've been nominated for Screenplay. Debbi Morgan should've got Best Supporting Actress.

RE: I've read that you had problems with Samuel Jackson's use of the N-word in Tarantino's *Jackie Brown.*

SL: I never really talked about Sam. I talked about Quentin Tarantino and Sam turned on me, which was disappointing, but I understood why he did that. I never said that Tarantino can't use the N-word. The N-word is in *He Got Game.* My problem was, he killed it. It was excessive. And go back to *Pulp Fiction,* same thing. Go back to *Reservoir Dogs,* same thing. Include his screenplay for *True Romance,* same thing. This is not just one film. We're talking about the man's entire body of work. And the stuff Quentin says. Statements like, "Me and Rosie O'Donnell are the most well-liked white celebrities in the black community." Is there a fried chicken poll that he took? To get those results?

Then he tries to hide behind, "I'm an artist." Okay, you're an artist, fine. But my counterpoint is—okay, you're an artist. You've directed three films. Well, Michael Jackson's been an artist thirty years. Michael does a song called "They Don't Care About Us." Has the lyrics, "Jew me, sue me, kick me, kike me." What happens? Whole brouhaha. Michael has to recall all the CDs and tapes in the stores. Rerecord new lyrics and issue apologies. There's something wrong here. Why can the word "nigger" be out there in a film thirty-eight times, and that's all right? Okay, we know Quentin Tarantino's an artist. But is not Michael Jackson an artist? Why is Michael Jackson anti-Semitic? I called Harvey Weinstein, who runs Miramax with his brother Bob. Miramax releases Tarantino's films. I said, "Harvey, let me ask you a question. If I submitted a script to you with thirty-eight Jewish slurs, would you make that film?" You know what he said? "No." I don't know if I'm crazy or what. But something's wrong here.

RE: Tarantino has a black guy say it and it's supposed to take the curse off.

SL: Black people weren't saying that in *Reservoir Dogs.* Black people weren't saying that in *True Romance.* The way I saw it, Michael Jackson's use of those words in that song—I mean, it wasn't *him* saying that. Scorsese, my favorite filmmaker, he can make a film like *Taxi Driver.* Nobody says he's Travis Bickle. Why can't Michael Jackson be allowed to reflect the world like other artists are?

RE: What are you going to do next?

SL: Don't know. But I gotta do a musical pretty soon. I want the artist, the right music, and the lyrics. A full-out singing and dancing musical.

## Kasi Lemmons

*Toronto,* September 1997—There has been no more assured and powerful film debut this year than *Eve's Bayou,* the first film by Kasi Lemmons. Reviewers have compared it to work by Tennessee Williams, Carson McCullers, and other southern Gothic writers; it reminded me of a family drama by Ingmar Bergman. It's made of memories that still have the power to wound. Its shadows contain secrets that will always hurt.

Lemmons has been working as an actress for ten years, since she had a small part in Spike Lee's *School Daze.* Among her fifteen roles, she was Jodie Foster's roommate in *The Silence of the Lambs,* and the doomed researcher in *Candyman.* She's married to Vondie Curtis Hall, himself a gifted actor and director *(Gridlock'd).* Now, with a screenplay she worked on for a decade, she has made a great film.

The opening words set the ominous tone: "The summer I killed my father, I was ten years old." The speaker is Eve Batiste (Jurnee Smollett), the bright and sensitive younger daughter of a charming doctor (Samuel L. Jackson) and his elegant wife (Lynn Whitfield). Eve has an older sister named Cisely (Meagan Good), just on the edge of adolescence, who is the apple of her father's eye, and Eve, who like many older women has a crush on her father, looks on with hurt and asks, "Daddy, why don't you ever ask me to dance?"

The film takes place in Louisiana bayou country, in a black community where Cajun French patois is still sometimes spoken, and modern life still finds corners to harbor fortune-tellers like Eve's aunt Mozelle (Debbi Morgan) and the voodoo practitioner Elzora (Diahann Carroll). Filmed with dark beauty and grace by Lemmons and her cinematographer, Amy Vincent, *Eve's Bayou* builds slowly to an intersection between love, desire, and misunderstanding. I am astonished by its subtlety and power.

How does a first-time director make a film of such maturity? I am not exaggerating when I say it reminded me of Bergman's family dramas, like *Fanny and Alexander,* where adults live in a mysterious world that children perceive in incomplete and frightening ways. It sees its family not in the relaxed, everyday way of *Soul Food,* but in the forms of classic family tragedies by Bergman, Chekhov, or Eugene O'Neill.

And there is a touch of the magic of Bergman's cinematographer, Sven Nykvist, in scenes like the one where Aunt Mozelle tells of her unlucky past life; she and the girl Eve stand in front of a mirror, and behind them, in one unbroken shot, the mirror reflects the images she is describing. That is as great a single shot as any movie has given us in a long time—great not just because of the technique, but because the technique illuminates the material.

One morning at the Toronto Film Festival, Kasi Lemmons (she pronounces it "Casey"), small, sparkling, and thirtyish, sat in a coffee shop and talked about the film. I was surprised to find it was not very autobiographical; I assumed she was drawing from memory, but it is memory transposed in the service of fiction. I'd assumed she was from Louisiana.

"My father has Louisiana in his background. But no, I picked it simply because it was an ideal setting for this story. The bayou is a character in the piece—secretive and beautiful and oppressive. That's what I wanted, that kind of closeness that is frightening but gorgeous. My Eve-type memories come from Alabama, where my grandmother lived."

The secrets in this movie, I said, are so deep they're even secrets from the people themselves. The story doesn't seem to have been written out from beginning to end, so much as been allowed to accumulate around feelings.

"It started around the characters," she said. "I wrote short stories about these people. I knew they were members of the same family, and then it all came together and I started to dream about them. I could hear them talking; I knew everything about them. I could talk for hours about the Batiste family. Finally it was starting to be uncomfortable to hear these people in my head. I needed to get it out on paper; I wrote it really as kind of a cathartic experience, without thinking about having to show it to anybody. So I was kinda braver than I might have been if I'd overanalyzed it and said, oh, wow, am I being too melodramatic? Am I being too operatic? Is it too poetic? I was very free with it."

What emerges is a story based on memories in conflict, seen through the eyes of a child with imperfect understanding of adult behavior. Whether Eve really did kill her father the summer she was ten depends on many things, including the degree to which we are prepared to believe in the supernatural.

As a writer, I said, you could have told us just one version—the version you thought happened. Instead, more points of view are introduced; you back up and look at events again.

"That's absolutely what I set out to do," she said. "If two people look back at the childhood they shared, they have two completely different takes. For instance, there's something that happened to me when I was a kid that I can describe—but other people who were there say, 'No, you weren't there.' Okay, is it just because I've heard the story that I think I was there? But I can describe it so well! That happens to everybody. There's something you can remember vividly and your mother says, 'Oh, you were too young to remember that. You were just a baby; you must have been six months old.'"

And who knows what really happened on that crucial night that *Eve's Bayou* leads up to? Whose version is correct? As Eve says in the narration, "Memory is a selection of images, some elusive, others printed indelibly on the brain." What is remembered is more important than what really happened.

"Right. When something horrifying happens, the mind puts a spin on it because the reality's too painful. In your mind you flee to a safer position, and that position becomes your memory."

*Eve's Bayou* just doesn't seem like a first film, I said, and I meant it. It has the confidence of an accomplished director. It seems like you already knew how to direct.

"I study films as an audience member," she said. "But as an actress I was kind of oblivious. I just thought about acting. I went away to film school, and that was helpful."

Where to?

"The New School of Social Research, because I couldn't afford NYU. But it's a great school; they give you the camera and let you drop-kick it; send you out with a camera and crew and you learn on your feet, which is great. And after (producer) Caldecot Chubb got attached to the movie I woke up one day and said, 'You know, if we're gonna look at first-time directors, then I should direct it. I *know* this script.' He wisely said that first I should warm up with a short dramatic piece. So I directed a short with the big crew and the big cameras, and so that was really the first time that I asked, am I any good at this? I think it helps that I have a wild imagination; I'm a visual person."

How, for example, did you come up with the wonderful mirror shot with Eve and Aunt Mozelle, where they're in front of the mirror and we see her husband and her lover reflected in the background, and then she turns and walks into the past? That shot is beautiful, but it's not just a pretty picture; it's an elegant moment of storytelling.

"Well, the scene was always written as a monologue for Debbi Morgan, and when you take a piece of prose to the screen, it's like, okay—they can't just stand there and talk. We gotta do something visually exciting. I didn't wanna use a trick like blue screen (back projection) or have images superimposed on her face. I wanted something really simple and classy. And I was on a plane with my director of photography, Amy Vincent, going down to Louisiana. And we started talking about it and put it together on the plane. We drew it out: 'Okay, this is what happens . . . here's the mirror, she turns and then she walks back toward them . . .' Amy said. 'Well, we'll need an 11-to-1 zoom, and if we don't get it, we can't do the shot.' It became imperative to make sure everything was at exactly the right angle and distance. Technically, it was a bit of a problem, but there are no tricks. We did it with the mirror, the camera, and the actors, all in one shot."

There's the surface realism of the story, I said, and then a sublevel of the supernatural. Aunt Mozelle is pretty good at telling fortunes; at one point she tells a mother her son is going to be in St. Michael's Hospital in Detroit next Tuesday. Now that's pretty good. But then you have Elzora, the voodoo priestess, who is also tapping into something.

"Yeah, she was accurate too."

People say if you believe in voodoo, it believes in you.

"In Haiti, you know, somebody waves a stick at you and says you're gonna die and you shrivel up and die. Voodoo is a very serious religion, and it's not that I mean to make light of it, but the interesting thing about it, in the film, is the southernness of it, the casual everyday belief in the supernatural. But who knows what Elzora thinks? When Eve pays her $20 and asks for that event to happen, is she just taking the money and messing with the kid's head?"

Maybe it's up to Eve; she's the one who decides whether the actions become real or not.

"As for Mozelle," Lemmons said, "she can't see her own life. She can look at a stranger and know about the fight she had with her boyfriend last night. But she can't tell that her husband's gonna die. That's what drives her crazy; that these tragic events happen in her own life over which she has no control. She feels she's cursed."

A waiter arrived with bran muffins. You are never more than five minutes or two blocks away from a bran muffin in Toronto. We started talking about families. Lemmons's husband, Vondie Curtis Hall, has a small but crucial role in *Eve's Bayou* as the one man Aunt Mozelle truly does love. He directed *Gridlock'd*, earlier this year, a lively thriller starring Tim Roth and the late Tupac Shakur on an action-packed journey through the Detroit social services labyrinth.

Being a movie director is one of the most time- and soul-consuming jobs in the world. How can one family find room for two of them?

"We've talked a lot about how we're gonna manage that. We're gonna try not to do it at the same time, so that one of us can parent. And we're gonna work together as much as possible because that's how we get to see each other."

But there's gonna be a little professional competition, right?

"We have no professional competition. We actually weep with pride with each other. I just can't believe sometimes that I'm married to him, and I think he feels the same way. Vondie and I are writing a film together right now for him to direct. Let's see what happens."

## David Mamet

*Toronto,* September 1997—Some directors and writers won't talk about their work. You suggest a theory and they elevate an eyebrow and nod and drum their fingers, and imply that no such thing as a thought ever crossed their minds about the work in question.

David Mamet is not such a person. He and Sidney Lumet are the only two active directors who have written books about the craft of making movies. With them, there's a lot of theory. They like to talk about how the thing goes together.

You can see that in Mamet's other obsessions, which include magic and con games. Every card trick is a three-act drama in miniature; the cards are introduced and explained, the problem is outlined, the audience's sympathy is engaged, the outcome seems assured, and then something amazing happens: Hamlet is poisoned, or the ace turns up inside the balloon you've been holding the whole time.

When you take the buried structure of a card trick and expand it into a screenplay, here's what you keep: You manipulate the audience so that they are *not* trying to figure out what's happening, but they're trying to figure out the *secret purpose* for what's happening. In dumb movies, the director tries to fool the audience with the event itself. In smart movies, like

Mamet's, he tries to fool them into believing they've seen through it. By the same token, in clever card tricks, at the moment of deception there is another piece of business, suspicious-looking but irrelevant: "A-ha!" they think, looking at the scarf, "it's hidden in the folds!" Meanwhile, the magician is surreptitiously blowing up the balloon.

Mamet's new film, *The Spanish Prisoner,* is about just such a con game. Even to tell you that may be cheating. I walked in not *knowing* it was a con game, but suspecting it was, because a lot of Mamet's movies *(House of Games, Things Change, The Edge)* are about deception, and because the cast included Ricky Jay, the bearded wizard who always seems at Mamet's side when elaborate deception is involved.

So it's a con game. It stars Campbell Scott as a man who has invented "The Process," and it's going to make millions for a company headed by Ben Gazzara. They're in the Caribbean to iron out the details. Ricky Jay is a company attorney, Rebecca Pidgeon (Mamet's wife) is a secretary with a crush on Scott, and Steve Martin is a mysterious stranger who arrives on the island by a seaplane. Or does he? See, that's how it works: We're figuring that he probably wasn't in that seaplane at all, but only seemed to be, and actually it doesn't make the slightest difference if he bicycled to the island.

"Shakespeare said nothing's either good or bad, but thinking makes it so," Mamet told me. This was last September, right after the movie's world premiere at the Toronto Film Festival. He had written two other movies set to open first *(The Edge* and *Wag the Dog),* and then this film, which he wrote and directed, would open in the spring.

"People will be watching TV and a picture comes on of a brooding guy, maybe he's got a beard. And the anchor says, 'The young child was abducted by the gunman and held at gunpoint for three hours.' And you're looking at the bearded guy and thinking, 'Why would they even let this guy near a child?' And then the news continues, 'Then this heroic young clergyman walked in.' And now you're looking at the guy and thinking, well, obviously, he's a hero.

"What we're told about something so absolutely influences what we 'know' about it. And that's what a confidence game is about, and also what a lot of drama is about. We're told something about the hero—or more important, we allow ourselves to understand something."

In *The Spanish Prisoner,* which contains no prisoners and no Spanish, we're allowed to think whatever we want. From time to time Mamet leads us to think we see the card going up his sleeve, to see through the deception and spot the trick, which nevertheless conceals the real deception inside.

Mamet is so fascinated by this process that he wrote and directed the celebrated off-Broadway show by Ricky Jay, who is considered the greatest card manipulator in the world. The show also played Chicago and went on a national tour, and I remember watching it one night next to a professional magician who said quietly, "I know what he's doing and how he's doing it, but I can't see him do it."

"You've known Ricky Jay a long time," I said to Mamet.

"Yeah," he said.

"I was startled to find out I've known him longer than you have. We went to college together."

"You did? At Cornell?"

Now there was a little pause.

"At Illinois," I said. "Now that's interesting, that you said Cornell."

Did Ricky Jay even go to Illinois *or* Cornell? With Ricky Jay you can't be sure.

"I think he went to Cornell hotel school," Mamet said.

"When he told me we met at Illinois," I said, "I told him I didn't remember his name. And he said, 'My name wasn't Ricky Jay then. And I didn't look like this.'"

Perfect.

"So let me tell you how it works," Mamet said. "We were on the set of *Things Change* and a guy comes up to me and says, 'Dave, Dave.' I said 'Hi.' He says, 'Don't you recognize me?' I say, 'I beg your pardon.' He says, 'It's Pat. Pat Kelly.' I say, 'Oh, hi.' He says, 'Pat Kelly from Chicago.' I say, 'Where do I know you from?' He starts telling me about the times he worked with me at the St. Nicholas Theatre and I absolutely don't remember this guy and he's an actor. And he says, 'You got anything on the movie for me?' I say, 'Well, probably . . . sure; I'm sure I can find something for you to do in the movie. . . . I'll give you a part in the movie, you know, but just off the record, I've never met you, have I?' 'Come on, Dave,' he says, 'of course you remember me.'

"I've always loved that process," Mamet said. "To make someone go along with an idea, or even make them think it's their idea. I think it really hardened when I was living in Chicago and selling Walton carpets over the telephone. W-A-L-T-O-N is what you dial, remember that? And then I was selling real estate up at Lincoln and Peterson, and I got fascinated by the skill that it took to convince someone to do something which was absolutely against their interest and absurd into the bargain. The moral implications aside, it was an act of such personal courage to be able to force, to convince, to cajole another to do your bidding, and in such a way that they weren't aware of it. It wasn't their own idea. I thought that it was astounding, that it was the essence of drama."

Mamet treated the real estate days in *Glengarry, Glen Ross,* his Pulitzer Prize–winning play about salesmen seducing clients into buying property they didn't need, didn't want, and couldn't afford. And *The Spanish Prisoner,* beneath all the levels of differences, does the same thing.

What's being sold is hope. Or sex. Or greed. Depends on how you look at it. The weakness of the protagonist becomes the strength of his enemies.

"This has to work like a Swiss watch," Mamet told me, "because it's a confidence game, not on the characters, but on the audience. You put in one piece of information too many, they're gonna get bored. You put in one piece of information too little, they aren't gonna have enough to intuit ahead of you. What you want is to constantly try to make them guess wrong. Just like in magic."

## Errol Morris

*Chicago,* October 1998—Errol Morris is a truly odd man. I say this because he wears a disguise of normality. I have never seen him without a sport coat and a tie, his hair neatly cut, a briefcase nearby. He talks soberly and with precision, almost as if students are taking notes. And then he invents a device called the Interitron and uses it to interview lion tamers and experts on the naked mole rats.

His new film is *Fast, Cheap & Out of Control.* It is endlessly fascinating, the kind of film you are compelled to discuss afterward. It is about people who have chosen strange career avenues: a gardener who makes animals out of plants, a designer of robots, an animal trainer, and a man who spends a good deal of time trying to figure out where and how naked mole rats prefer to defecate.

This film is by the same man who made films about a possibly innocent man on Death Row in Texas; and about Stephen Hawking, the man almost trapped inside his own brain; and about a parrot who was the only witness to a murder (could the court believe that it was repeatedly squawking out the killer's name?). The Interitron is an invention that allows his subjects to stare straight into the camera while simultaneously making direct eye contact with him.

I met Errol Morris long before I was ever in the same room with him. I met him in 1978 when I was watching his first film, *Gates of Heaven.* I met him by inference, because of what he put on the screen and what he left off. His selection process gave me a sense of the man.

By choosing to make a film about two pet cemeteries, he staked his claim to the sidelines of the American mainstream. By making the film in such a challenging way, he refused to commit himself: You could see it as cruel or caring, as satirical or poker-faced, as cynical or deeply spiritual. Watching it, I knew that when I finally laid eyes on Morris, he would be wearing a quizzical grin.

He was. I met him in the 1980s at Facets, the video and repertory shrine in Chicago, where they showed *Gates of Heaven* in a tribute to Morris. It so happens that the theater at Facets begins with a flat floor, and then abruptly tilts upward. I sat at the dividing line, and noticed that those in front of me were silent, while those behind were laughing.

Of course they were, Morris explained. It is best to look up at drama, and down at comedy. We need to feel above comedy. Drama needs to feel above us. *Gates of Heaven* was so finely balanced between comedy and drama that the altitude of the seats determined the reaction of the audience members. Was he serious? I couldn't tell. Years later, Buddy Hackett told me he turned down big bucks in Vegas rather than play a room where the stage was higher than the audience. "They won't laugh unless they're looking down at you," he explained.

Having made *Fast, Cheap & Out of Control,* Morris is now touring the country to flog it. It has no stars and no big ad budget, and cannot be explained in a snappy line of advertising copy. If I had to describe it, I'd say it's about people who are trying to control things—to take upon themselves the mantle of God.

"There is a Frankenstein element," Morris said. "They're all involved in some very odd inquiry about life. It sounds horribly pretentious laid out that way, but there's something mysterious in each of the stories, something melancholy as well as funny. And there's an edge of mortality. For the end of the movie I showed the gardener clipping the top of his camel, clipping in a heavenly light, and then walking away in the rain. You know that this garden is not going to last much longer than the gardener's lifetime."

The gardener's name is George Mendonca. He makes topiaries—gardens like you see at Disney World, where shrubs have been trimmed to look like camels or giraffes. He circulates endlessly in the private garden of a rich woman, trimming and waiting and trimming. A good storm will blow everything away. When he dies, the shrubs will grow out and destroy his work in a season.

Then there is Ray Mendez, the naked mole rat expert. Mole rats live in Africa and were discovered only a few years ago; they are hairless mammals whose society is organized along insect lines.

"Ray tells you," Morris said, "that he's seeking some kind of connection with 'the other,' which he defines as that which exists completely independent of ourselves. And then he talks about looking into the eye of a naked mole rat and thinking, 'I know you are, you know I am.' It occurred to me that all of my movies are about language. About how language reveals secrets about people. It's a way into their heads."

That was true right from the start, I said. *Gates of Heaven* is filled with lines that could not possibly have been written. As when that woman says, "Death is for the living and not for the dead."

"I like to transcribe my own interviews," Morris said. "I'm really fascinated by how people speak. And there are so many strange lies that I've heard over the years. There's this idea that documentary filmmaking is a kind of journalism. So *Gates of Heaven* becomes a movie about pet cemeteries. It's about something different altogether. There's this sense of having one foot in the real world and another foot in some dreamscape."

Did you know *Fast, Cheap & Out of Control* was going to be about these four people or did you find the film shaping itself?

"Well, Dave Hoover, the lion tamer—I filmed his act in 1985 in Texas. There was this money from PBS to make a movie about Dr. James Gregson, the so-called Death Row doctor (who could always be counted on to testify that a killer would kill again). And I thought, I'll bet there's a similarity between theories of how to control wild animals and theories about how to deal with violent criminals. There was. There are all these different schools of wild animal training; there's a touchy-feely school, there's an 'I'm okay, You're okay' school, transactional analysis . . ."

But then you show that young woman who takes over as the animal trainer, and she seems to be more the master of her beasts than the older man. Her lions look better; they don't look all ratty and shopworn, and she puts her head in their mouths, and cuffs them around . . ."

"Although as Dave points out, these are tigers, not lions."

Admittedly a good point, I said.

"There's supposedly a big difference. He says anybody can do that with a tiger. I asked him, I said, 'Dave, how come the head-in-the-mouth thing, why aren't you doing that?' He said, A, it's a tiger, not a lion, and B, he wouldn't have anything to do with that sort of thing because there's a problem with halitosis. Their breath's real bad. Dave lives in this universe of his own devising. When he talks about what goes on inside a lion's head when it's facing him in the ring—well, is that what's really going on in the lion's brain, or is it Dave Hoover's crazy dreamscape?"

His lions look a little mangy.

"Periodontal difficulties, mange, gout . . ."

Maybe they won't bite him because it would hurt their gums.

"It's his world. It's his crazy universe and he says, 'Outside the cage is the cage.' And I have that shot of him at the very end of the movie, exiting the cage and firing his gun into the night, as if outside was the enemy. I like all four of the characters a lot."

I do too.

"There was a review in *Entertainment Weekly*

where I was taken to task for ridiculing these four. I certainly understood the criticism. A lot people said *Gates of Heaven* was poking fun of the people. I think it's far more complicated than that. I love those people. They're all such wonderful characters in their own right."

So you shot Dave in 1985. He must have acted as a magnetic attraction that drew the other three.

"The strange attractor."

He was trying to control that which in its nature is not to be controlled. They all are. But they're all very happy people, aren't they? The gardener is a little melancholy that his work will come to an end, but they're all absorbed in what they do.

"They're committed; that's how I would describe them. They're obsessed; they're involved. To me all of the stories are sad. In two of the stories there's a world coming to an end: the topiary garden and the lion taming. In the other stories there's a glimpse into a future that excludes us. Ray Mendez talks about the mole rat's world as the ultimate kibbutz, depending on the expandability of the individual. It's the insect-mammal future. And with Rodney Brooks, the robot designer, it's a world without us altogether, without carbon-based life. Just thinking machines."

Have you got another film in the works?

"I'm preparing a film," he said, "about an electric chair repairman."

## Martin Scorsese

*New York*, December 1997—There is no greater American filmmaker right now than Martin Scorsese, and hasn't been for some time, perhaps since Welles and Hitchcock and Ford died. And yet to talk with him is like meeting this guy who hangs out all the time at the film society.

We spoke for an hour or two about *Kundun*, his new film, and our conversation kept jumping the tracks and heading for his loves and enthusiasms. When I mentioned, for example, that his life story of the fourteenth Dalai Lama reminded me of the lives of the saints that we read in Catholic grade school, that started him on Rossellini's *Flowers of St. Francis*, and when I talked about how he got interested in the subject matter—the fall of Tibetan culture to Chinese imperialism—he began telling me about a 1952 film named *Storm Over Tibet*, and Frank Capra's *Lost Horizon*, and the Tyrone Power version of *The Razor's Edge*. We started on his camera moves in *Kundun*, and that led to his camera moves in *Taxi Driver*, and how its greatest influence was the way Hitchcock moved his camera in *The Wrong Man*.

This is a voluptuary, a sensualist. Instead of describing beautiful women or old masters, exotic cuisines or great wines, hordes of jewels or the effects of forbidden potions, he is describing movies. Scorsese tells you about a shot in an old film, and it's like listening to Sidney Greenstreet telling Bogart that he *must* have the Maltese falcon. Perhaps the reason he is the greatest director is because he has spent the most time learning from those who went before him. Listen to him here, in a breathless passage that I supply for you word by word.

"I heard that the opening shot in *Boogie Nights* is like the shot in *GoodFellas* where the camera tracks through the nightclub. Well, why not? I mean, we did tons of that. Myself and DePalma and Spielberg and Coppola; in so many of our films we did things that relate to earlier films. There are several shots in *Taxi Driver* that are inspired by *Shane*. It's homage—the self-consciousness of saying, hey, here's a little nudge in the ribs to Truffaut; that's a nudge to Fellini; that's one to George Stevens; that's one to John Ford. You find yourself looking at old films a lot. The Hitchcock pictures I like looking at repeatedly, repeatedly, repeatedly. Very often without the sound. The Powell-Pressburger films, John Ford, Welles of course.

"What happens is that you find, through these images, a way of writing with the camera that stays in your mind. *The Wrong Man* by Hitchcock has more to do with the camera movements in *Taxi Driver* than any other picture I can think of. It's such a heavy influence because of the sense of guilt and paranoia. Look at the scenes where Henry Fonda has to go back to the bank with the police and just walk up and down while the tellers look at him. They're deciding a man's fate. And watch the camera moves. Or the use of color in Michael Powell and Emeric Pressburger's *The Red Shoes*. I think there's that kind of . . . influencing. It's not necessarily direct stealing. Each film is interlocked with so many other films. You can't get away. Whatever you do now that you think is new was already done in 1913."

Scorsese is sitting in the screening room of his offices in midtown Manhattan. This is not simply the room were he looks at his daily rushes or the rough cuts assembled by his editor, Thelma Schoonmaker. It's also where he screens old movies, many of them rare prints from his own archive. Who else among active directors would take the time he did to assemble and narrate a long television documentary on great films, and then write a book to go with it?

Now that *Kundun* is being released, Scorsese is in the same strangely objective mind-set he often is after finishing a movie. I've been talking with him since his first film thirty years ago, and I suspect that if I looked back through all of my notes I would find him saying the same thing after every film: "I don't know if anyone will want to see this." He truly doesn't, and there is a reason for that: He doesn't *make* a film just because people will want to see it.

Most filmmakers work in a two-stage process: (1) read public's mind; (2) duplicate findings in next movie. Not Scorsese. "We're making this film for ourselves," he told Schoonmaker during *Raging Bull,* which was widely considered the best film of the 1980s. "It's a home movie."

*Kundun* would seem to be at right angles to most of his work. It's about the childhood and young manhood of Tibet's spiritual leader, who is believed to have lived thirteen times before his present reincarnation. This looks like a radical departure for Scorsese, whose films are often about Italian-Americans, not infrequently mobsters, living on the mean streets. Upward mobility for his characters means moving to Vegas *(Casino)* or Miami *(Raging Bull)* and continuing to lead the same lives.

But there is another thread to Scorsese's work that is perfectly consistent with *Kundun,* and that's his obsession with spirituality—which is usually linked with guilt, but not (significantly) this time. His hero in *Mean Streets* holds his hand in the flame of a votive candle, trying to imagine the fires of hell. The overhead shots in *Taxi Driver* are inspired by how priests array the implements of the Mass on an altar. *The Last Temptation of Christ* is the story of man's struggle between the carnal and the exalted (for if God became man, did he not feel the same lust as any other man?).

*Kundun* is the story of a man who has achieved mastery over his ignoble emotions, who has found spiritual peace, and who carries that treasure out into a hostile world. The film begins with a small child being chosen by monks who are seeking the new human vessel into which the thirteenth Dalai Lama, having died, will reappear. There is a magical scene in which the little boy tries to pick out "his" possessions from the earlier life, as they are scattered on a tabletop with others. As a young man he grows serene in the practice of his faith, and then must deal with postwar Red China, whose leaders covet the territory of Tibet and are scornful of its religion and tradition.

"I always wanted to make a series of films on the lives of the saints," Scorsese mused. "To try to understand their choices. I remember a film by Maurice Cloche, *Monsieur Vincent* (1947), about St. Vincent DePaul. The greatest one is Rossellini's *Flowers of St. Francis* (1950), which is daunting because of its simplicity and compassion and heart. I've been watching that film for twenty-five years, and I always wanted to make something like it, about a human being who by exemplary action shows us how to live. Where nonaction becomes action; where a decision not to make a decision is the decision. It may not be what Western audiences expect, but I believe the Dalai Lama and Gandhi and Martin Luther King, people who stood on the line for passive resistance and got hit for it, have a lotta guts."

Scorsese, who has made so many films about violent men, erupting tempers, and sudden death, told a "little parable" he came across while preparing this film: "An army came into town and marched up to the monastery door and the general took his sword out, and the head of the monastery opened the door and just stood there. The general looked at him and said, 'Don't you realize I can kill you without blinking an eye?' And the monk replied, 'Don't you realize I can die without blinking an eye?' That's where I'd like to get to."

Now watch the way Scorsese's mind works, how all of his films, even those that seem opposites, are directed by the same man. His parable would seem to be far outside the universe of Jake La Motta, the hero of *Raging Bull,* but a little later as we talked he said:

"I want to feel like Jake does at the end of *Raging Bull,* a stage I've never gotten to. He's at peace with himself by the end, looking at himself in the mirror, rehearsing his act, repeating 'my kingdom for a horse.' I knew when I was doing it that I wasn't there. Up to that point I was with him, but I couldn't get beyond that point until finally, maybe, oh, when I did *Color of Money* (1986), I kind of got used to myself. I realized, I'm gonna be this way all my life, and I better calm down, take it easy, don't waste the energy and burn up that fuel of yourself and everybody else around you. So I just got used to myself, and what can I do? I'm stuck."

He looked content to be stuck, at that place already occupied by Gandhi, Dr. King, La Motta, and the Dalai Lama, who apart from anything else would be the makings of an interesting dinner party.

"It has always made me feel a little comfortable that human beings may be capable of evolving spiritually," he said. "The Tibetans are not the only ones. There are modern people who have a compassionate heart, like Dorothy Day in New York, or Mother Teresa. There was a book recently that was critical of her, but the people who write that stuff, I wonder when was the last time they helped somebody to die?"

Scorsese cast his film only with nonactors, including many Tibetans who knew the Dalai Lama. And from them, he said, he absorbed some of the spirit that he tried to communicate in *Kundun*.

"Some of the older ones had been part of his retinue back in 1949, before they left Tibet. So they understood everything, and very often in the picture I'd walk onto the set and they'd be meditating and it was like a painting out of the Renaissance. There was a reverence and a spirituality that pervaded the set, which was interesting. I wanted to be part of that world. Whether I took something away with me, I'm not sure, but I think I have.

"And then working with the little boy who played the Dalai Lama as a child, that was a contact with reality. The kid was terrific; he had a great face. But we had to do a lot of tricks to get that performance. Like the scene where they put him in front of the table and ask him to choose 'his' possessions, from his previous reincarnation, so they'll know it's really him.

"The Tibetans in the scene, and his own mother and the father and the other kids really helped out a lot. But if a two-year-old kid doesn't want to play, he doesn't want to play; that's it. He wants to take a nap, the crew waits until he wakes up. But I found that I was anchored in his behavior, because he wasn't acting, and neither were the other Tibetan actors. Some of the best acting in the movie takes place at the edges of the screen, with the extras, because you look at their faces and you see they are really truly in the moment."

And so here is this film about peace and spirituality, filmed in the lush colors that Scorsese has always loved in the older films he studies, and expressing his own sense of connection and growth. And now what will he make next? He is discussing a film about the life of Dean Martin. Now that would seem like an absolute change in direction, a fundamental shift in tone. But if he makes it, we will, I suspect, still be able to sense the same vision, the same search, the same filmmaker. Come on in, Dino; have you met everyone else here tonight? Mother Teresa, you know . . .

## Quentin Tarantino

*Los Angeles,* December 1997—Has any other movie director become this famous after making only two movies? Well, yes, Orson Welles. But Welles was already a star when he went to Hollywood. Quentin Tarantino came out of next to nowhere and became famous because he made two of the most influential movies of the 1990s, and because . . . well, because he tickles people.

There's something so enthusiastic and unguarded about him that his personality has impressed itself even in this city of egos. Oh, and he's appeared in about a dozen movies, too; there was a time when no indee director felt right unless QT popped up in a cameo to provide his film with an imprimatur.

*Reservoir Dogs* (1992) announced Tarantino's talent and *Pulp Fiction* suggested his genius. And then for forty-three long months—from the 1994 Cannes Film Festival until this week—there was no new film from QT. There were rumors and sightings and a lot of publicity, especially when he slugged that guy in the restaurant, but no film. That wasn't tragic, but it was curious. What was he waiting for?

Now comes *Jackie Brown,* which confirms that Quentin Tarantino is the real thing, a genuinely talented filmmaker, not a two-picture wonder. It is a film of subtle and engaging gifts that lurk beneath the surface of its crimes, scams, murders, drugs, and colorful Tarantinian dialogue. It will entertain his fans, but it will also reward thoughtful analysis: It is a more revolutionary film than it appears.

It is also a showcase for two rediscovered talents, Pam Grier and Robert Forster. Tarantino has been given credit for rescuing the career of John Travolta in *Pulp Fiction.* The actor was fresh from, uh, *Look Who's Talking Now* when QT put him in the role that made him, again, into one of Hollywood's top stars. In *Jackie Brown,* he stars the legendary Pam Grier in the title role, and it's the kind of evocative, sympathetic performance that gets attention and job offers. But it doesn't take place in a vacuum; Robert Forster, another veteran whose career was drifting, gets the role of his lifetime opposite Grier, and together they create a poignant, understated romance—one of the most curiously convincing love stories of the year.

Grier plays a forty-four-year-old airline stewardess who is busted by the feds for bringing $50,000 in cash into the country from Mexico. Forster plays Max Cherry, her bail bondsman. Samuel L. Jackson plays Ordell, the illegal gun merchant who was using her as a money carrier. Robert De Niro plays Louis, his ex-con partner. Bridget Fonda is Ordell's spaced-out southern California beach bum girlfriend. Michael Keaton is the agent from Alcohol, Tobacco and Firearms. Another director might have made Forster the ex-con and given De Niro the much larger role of the bondsman, but that would have been the wrong use of both actors.

"I have more of a memory than most of the people in this town," Tarantino told me last weekend during a couple of conversations. "They have a short list of actors and they use them over and over again. I don't mean just the A-list actors like Harrison Ford. Even the supporting roles—they have a list of the A-list character actors. I've seen the old movies. I know who the actors are. I have a better memory than they do. I don't cast anyone out of sentiment. There's not an actor in this town who could have done better in these two roles than Pam Grier and Robert Forster."

He may be right. They play such specific, convincing, plausible people. Grier (who is gorgeous in person) plays Jackie Brown as a tired, discouraged woman who is barely hanging onto a job with the worst airline in North America, and doesn't have a lot of time and money to spend on her hair. Forster plays Max Cherry as a fifty-six-year-old man who knows his work and knows the law, and does a good job of being a bail bondsman, but is getting tired, he tells Jackie, of sitting on a bond-jumper's couch at 2:00 A.M., waiting for the guy to come home, and smelling the cat pee all over the room.

I don't know what I expected from *Jackie Brown,* but it wasn't a thoughtful, impeccably timed caper picture with the room in it for enough dialogue and development, enough unexpected scenes and peripheral characters, so that the people in the movie seem to live in the real world. Just one example: In most movies, the characters know only the other people necessary to the plot. In *Jackie Brown,* we keep meeting more people—their friends, lovers, hangers-on, confidants.

The characters suggest that they have corners and compartments they haven't revealed to us. A lot of that quality comes from the source material, Elmore Leonard's novel *Rum Punch.* Leonard is perhaps the most respected of living crime writers, famous for his dialogue, which somehow manages to be high comedy and low realism at the same time.

"I've always felt a kinship with Elmore Leonard," Tarantino told me. "I called him up and said, 'I'm not trying to sound bigheaded or anything, but I think I was the man born to translate your novels into film.' And he said, 'Well, I could have told you that after *Reservoir Dogs.*'"

And he could have too. Reading a novel by Leonard, you don't race ahead to see how the plot turns out; you savor the texture of the pacing and dialogue, and you look around at the world they inhabit. In *Jackie Brown,* as in the book, Max Cherry isn't a "bail bondsman" but a *bail bondsman*—his words, his knowledge, his experience, and his attitude all suggest that he actually works at this job. At the end of the movie, when we meet Max's office partner, a guy whose job it is to go out and find people, an agent asks how the guy found someone, and his answer is, "I find people. It's my job."

Tarantino told me he was conscious that he would be leaving his own universe and entering "Dutch" Leonard's: "Dutch's universe is a lot larger than mine, all right? Because he has more characters and more stories. But there're a lot of similarities and affinities, and probably the number one thing I'm proudest of is that 50 percent of the dialogue in that movie is mine and 50 percent of it is Dutch's, and I think it's seamless. I think you really can't tell."

One thing I enjoyed is the way the movie gives itself the luxury of apparently gratuitous scenes. Like *Pulp Fiction*, it has moments that don't serve the plot but simply serve the characters, or the atmosphere.

"I never have an issue of rushing things, all right?" he said. "I like the characters to hang out and be who they're being; there's no page-count limit. Like for instance, all those Ordell and Max Cherry bail bond scenes? That's pure Elmore Leonard. You could drop this and you could drop that, but it wouldn't quite have the right tone and feel."

While Tarantino is talking to me, I'm observing a curious thing about him: He seems calmer than ever before, more lucid, more content. There isn't that nonstop exuberance that runs right off the rails that he's sometimes known for. Has he grown up a little? Is he happier?

I know I have to ask about the infamous Beverly Hills restaurant incident, in which he threw punches at a producer and now faces a lawsuit. Are you, I say, gonna get into any more fights at lunch?

"I hope not. If people stop picking fights with me I'll stop defending myself."

Most of the witnesses seemed to see QT throw the first punch. But he's talking long term: "The guy's damn near been stalking me for three years. I could have had a feud with him in the press. That's his dream; that's exactly what he wants. That makes him the happiest man in the world. Or I could be like a real gangster and go looking for him. Nah, I'm not gonna do that either. It's a small town. Some day, I thought, I'll walk into a place and he'll be there. And that's what happened."

He paused, and then decided maybe he shouldn't say any more, what with the lawyers and all. So we moved on to the next thing I knew I had to ask him about his acting.

Between *Pulp Fiction* and *Jackie Brown* he was in maybe a dozen movies, both in cameos and in larger roles (as in *From Dusk Till Dawn* and *Four Rooms*), and in my reviews I criticized him for it—said Hollywood had lots of mediocre actors but not enough great directors.

"There'll come a day I believe you'll respect my acting," he said. "I think I'm in the way. I don't think you're seeing the work because you're just seeing me."

We should all do what we can do best, I suggest.

"I thought I got a very bum rap," he said, "when you gave me a Dubious Career Award, or whatever it was, for acting—and you gave the opposite award to Steve Buscemi, for directing. It was like actors can direct but directors can't act! It was like you were applauding him for stretching out and I was being criticized. Maybe those small parts got in the way, but I'm as proud of my work in *From Dusk Till Dawn* as I am of anything I've done."

But if you were to write a role for yourself and direct yourself in it, as Buscemi did, that would be another matter, I said.

"That's coming up. That'll happen probably in the next movie, actually. But I'm not—I didn't put myself in *Jackie Brown*, you know, I didn't give myself some silly cameo. But as far as my acting is concerned, I just want you to know I'm serious about it. It's not me screwing around, all right? It's not some ego thing. It's a need—all right? It's one of my colors; it's one of my palettes."

Maybe I'll see your performance in the next movie and love it, I said. I'm open to that.

"You don't have a problem with me going on Broadway, do you? I wouldn't be doing a movie in the next six months anyway."

You're going on Broadway?

"You didn't know about it?"

Are you gonna cut an album one of these days too? What about you as a painter?

"See, you're belittling my acting aspirations."

I am not.

"It's not Chad Everett doing an album. I'm doing a revival of *Wait Until Dark* with Marisa Tomei."

Hey, I said, I'm for anyone who has the balls to go out there and put themselves on the line and try something.

"It's not ego, Roger. I just want you to know that."

It's okay with me if it is, I said.

# Essays

## David Bradley (In Memoriam)

My first memory, when I heard that David Bradley was dead, was of him drop-kicking a footstool across the living room. Bradley, who died December 19, 1997, in Los Angeles, at the age of 77, was one of the legendary eccentrics of the film world, irascible and beloved. He launched the early career of Charlton Heston, amassed one of the great private film archives, and toasted the survivors of silent films at his legendary New Year's Day parties.

David Shedd Bradley was the son of a wealthy Chicago family that gave the city its Shedd Aquarium and was a major supporter of the Chicago Symphony. As a student at Northwestern in the 1940s, long before independent films came into fashion, he directed two 16mm features starring a fellow undergraduate, Charlton Heston. They were nothing if not ambitious: Ibsen's *Peer Gynt* and Shakespeare's *Julius Caesar* (where Bradley played Caesar and assigned Heston the Marc Antony role).

"They were shot on location around Chicago, wherever they could find a building that looked Greco-Roman," recalls the character actor Ken Du Main, Bradley's friend for more than forty years. Locations included the steps of the downtown post office, and the portico of the Elks' National Headquarters.

The films helped open Hollywood doors for Heston, and also for Bradley, who was signed up for a training program at MGM and directed *Talk About a Stranger* (1952), with George Murphy and Nancy Davis (Reagan). "On the lot, he was whispered about as a demigod of the avant-garde," Du Main remembered. "The idea of just going out and making your own films was new. And he was a friend of Orson Welles—that impressed them."

Bradley made a few other films but fought with the studio over the reedit of *12 to the Moon* and moved on to his real vocation, which was to hold strong opinions and express them at every opportunity. At a time when silent films were being forgotten and the studios were ignoring their archives, he began collecting prints of films. He had thousands, many the only surviving copies, and originally planned to leave them to Northwestern, but feuded with its film school. He was then teaching at UCLA, and decided to leave them there, but had another feud, switched to Santa Monica City College, and willed the films, Du Main said, to "Indiana University."

Visitors to the home he shared with Du Main in the Hollywood Hills would be treated to private screenings of rare treasures. I remember seeing the original version of Howard Hawks's *The Big Sleep* some twenty years ago, at a time when Bradley had the only known copy; this version of the film, which was reshot with more scenes for Lauren Bacall, was publicly seen only in 1997.

One day Bradley took me behind his house, to the concrete-block bunker that housed his archive. Row upon row of film cans and boxes towered overhead. "I brought Joseph von Sternberg back here one day," Bradley recalled, "and he started clawing his way up the shelves, crying out, 'My films! My films!'"

A visit to Bradley's home was invariably an occasion for him to take center stage in his living room and lecture his guests. His lifelong passion was the Chicago Symphony. "He loved Fritz Reiner and liked Georg Solti," recalled his friend Gregory Nava, the movie director. "But he hated Jean Martinon. He would play different versions of the same piece of music and shout out a note-by-note criticism, and then put on Reiner, and everything was glorious."

He was playing a record by the despised Martinon when he kicked the footstool into the record player, prompting Du Main to caution, "Careful, David—you'll need that record for future outbursts."

On New Year's Day, Bradley and Du Main would invite silent stars and directors to a party also attended by younger film folks eager to meet them. The guest lists over the years included von Sternberg, Fritz Lang, Claire Windsor, Madge Bellamy, Mae Murray, Allen Dwan, and Mary Miles Minter, who I met there on the day when she was fighting eviction from her home. "Look at this picture," she told me, holding a clipping from the *Los Angeles Times* of her sitting on her front steps. "How do I look?" I said I thought she looked wonderful. "What a kidder," she said. "I look like a bag lady." Well, she did, a little, and I reflected that she had once been a famous beauty whose lover, the director William Desmond Taylor, was murdered in one of Hollywood's notorious scandals.

Bradley filmed every one of his New Year's Day parties, including one at which Mary Philbin, star of the 1925 *Phantom of the Opera,* reenacted the unmasking of the phantom (played by Lon Chaney in the original and by Bradley, of course, in the reenactment). Every party's climax was the screening of a surprise treasure from Bradley's archive, starring one of his guests. The stars typically hadn't seen their films in fifty years, and would be moved to tears. Bradley would kiss their feet in the closing shot of each home movie.

In recent years the party faded away, as the guests died. "It is so sad," Bradley told me at one of his later parties, "to look around the room and wonder who will still be here next year."

"He made those people feel wonderful when the world was ignoring them," remembers writer-producer Anna Thomas, Nava's wife. "He made a fuss over them. A lot of people didn't see it, because he was so cranky, but David had such a great big heart."

## Frank Sinatra (In Memoriam)

When the book of twentieth-century popular entertainment is written, Frank Sinatra will get a chapter as the best singer of his time. As an actor, he will be remembered for the good films, and for a distinctive screen persona as a guy who could win a heart with a song.

The image that lingers is from *Young at Heart,* where he pushed back his hat, lit a cigarette, sat down at a piano, and sang to Doris Day and broke her heart. He never had the looks to be a matinee idol, but he had a voice—The Voice—and he had a screen presence, and for a time in the 1950s, Frank Sinatra was one of the most interesting and successful actors in American movies.

But he will not be remembered as one of the greatest movie stars of his time, maybe because he simply never cared enough to make it his business. What is remarkable is that he made more than sixty films, was often at the top of the box-office charts, won two Oscars (one the honorary Hersholt Award) and was nominated for another, and had starring roles spanning five decades—even though during most of that time movie acting, for Sinatra, was basically a sideline.

The saga of how he got into the movies in the first place has become a show-business legend. By 1953, his singing career was (temporarily) on the skids and he was considered a has-been, but he persuaded Harry Cohn, the boss of Columbia Pictures, to let him play the supporting role of Maggio, a wise-guy enlisted man, in *From Here to Eternity.*

How and why he got that role has been the subject of speculation ever since. The version absorbed by most people is the one fictionalized by Mario Puzo in his novel *The Godfather,* where a Sinatralike character named Johnny Fontaine was friendly with the Corleone family, which made a Hollywood mogul an offer he couldn't refuse, and backed it up with a special-delivery package: the severed head of his beloved racehorse, slipped between his sheets while he slept.

Those events, of course, never happened, and Sinatra and his family bitterly resented the popular belief that they contained an element of truth. But did the mob have anything to do with Sinatra getting the role that turned his career around? There is no evidence at all that it did, but throughout his career, it was informally understood that Sinatra had powerful "friends," and that image did his career no harm. It enhanced, indeed, his raffish aura as a weathered veteran of many a late night in a smoky saloon ("It's quarter to three . . ."), a glass of whiskey in his hand, singing the love ballads of a lonely fighter who could get up off the mat for one more bout with romance.

In a way, you wanted to believe Sinatra was "connected," because the clout was part of the appeal. The legends that collected about him often involved his influence, his feuds, his ability to get things done, or keep them from being done. There were two Sinatra images that overlapped, like a 3-D picture if you're not wearing the glasses: the beloved entertainer, and the power broker with an element of menace. Henry Kissinger observed that power is an aphrodisiac, and certainly Sinatra's power, real and imagined, magnified his sexiness. A famous *Esquire* cover in the 1960s showed him with a cigarette to his lips; the rest of the cover was filled with outstretched hands holding cigarette lighters.

No matter how Sinatra got cast in *From Here to Eternity,* it was the event that lifted the curtain on the long second act of his remarkable career. With that Oscar-winning role, and the films and songs that followed it, he put to rest his image as a crooner and teenage idol and began to fashion his mature image, as the singer who was better with a lyric than anyone else ever had been. Sammy Cahn, who wrote a lot of songs that Sinatra sang, told me that he'd write a lyric, hear Sinatra perform it, and think, "Oh, yeah, *that's* what I wrote."

After *From Here to Eternity,* Sinatra cemented his reputation as a film actor in a remarkable series of box-office and critical hits in 1954 and 1955: the *film noir Suddenly, Guys and Dolls, The Man With the Golden Arm, Not As a Stranger, The Tender Trap,* and *Young at Heart.*

These were all roles crafted for, and suited to, his emerging image as an underdog with a heart. Sinatra was nominated for best actor for *The Man With the Golden Arm,* Otto Preminger's controversial version of the Nelson Algren novel, which defied the Production Code's ban on movies depicting drug addiction. In *Guys and Dolls,* he was Damon Runyon's professional gambler Nathan Detroit, the operator of "the oldest established permanent floating crap game in New York," and sang about "ever-loving Adelaide."

*Young at Heart* is not Sinatra's best film, but it's one of my personal favorites, because it moves so deftly between two Hollywood icons that seemed miles apart: Sinatra and Doris Day. Day plays a cheerful, wholesome daughter in a musical family who meets Sinatra, a talented songwriter with a crippling inferiority complex. She tries to build him up, but he feels unworthy; she loves him, and he can't believe that, either.

For Sinatra in the mid-1950s, being a movie actor was central to his career. Before and after that golden period, he had his mind on other things.

In 1941, when he made his film debut as a saloon singer in *Las Vegas Nights* and sang "I'll Never Smile Again," he was, of course, the top singing idol in the world—the Beatles of his time. It was Sinatra, indeed, who inaugurated the twentieth-century spectacle of screaming, orgiastic fans; bobby-soxers jitterbugged in the aisles during his concerts, creating a tradition that was mirrored for every musical superstar since.

His voice was lighter and higher then; listen to his "Night and Day," and you almost think you're listening to another singer. He had the presence and the way with a lyric, but he was still working in the tradition of the proto-crooner, Bing Crosby.

Sinatra's 1940s films all referred, in one way or another, to his offscreen image as a matinee idol and popular singer. The best of them was probably Gene Kelly's *On the Town* (1949), with Sinatra and Kelly as sailors with twenty-four-hour passes in Manhattan. The Leonard Bernstein score evoked a giddy sense of freedom, which Kelly exploited with a Hollywood first: He left the sound stages for a week of location shooting in New York City, the first time a musical had done that, as the characters played by him and Sinatra pursued Vera-Ellen, Ann Miller, and Betty Garrett around the town.

There were other big titles for Sinatra in the 1940s, including *Anchors Aweigh* (1945), *Till the Clouds Roll By* (1946), and *Take Me Out to the Ball Game* (1949), but by the early 1950s, despite a few minor roles, his career was not thriving. The youthful stardom was over, and Sinatra went through the only real dip in his long career. Then came *From Here to Eternity* and other mid-1950s hits, and as a singer he reinvented himself, creating an image that would endure; he began to refer to himself as a "saloon singer."

As his musical career entered into its richest period, from the mid-1950s to the mid-1960s, his films sometimes became less remarkable. But there were some good ones.

One of his best performances was as a would-be writer in Vincente Minnelli's *Some Came Running* (1958), a project that signaled the rise of the Rat Pack movie, in which he joined with friends, especially Sammy Davis Jr., Dean Martin, Angie Dickinson, and Shirley MacLaine, to make movies in which the relaxed ambience betrayed the presence of a director who had been hired, rather than one who had hired him. There's fun to be had in *Ocean's Eleven* (1960), with the Pack again, but it's relaxed and self-congratulatory; Sinatra had entered a middle age of great power and influence, in which he didn't need to try as hard on the screen, or care as much about every movie.

But there was still one great film left: John Frankenheimer's *The Manchurian Candidate* (1962), with its chilling cold war plot about Sinatra and Laurence Harvey as U.S. soldiers brainwashed by the communist Chinese in Korea, as part of a plot to "activate" Harvey to assassinate a president. This was perhaps the best single film Sinatra ever made. But, typically, its artistry took second place in his thinking to its personal implications; when his friend, John F. Kennedy, was assassinated in 1963, Sinatra, as its producer, held it out of release for many years "out of respect." Only after twenty-five years had passed, in 1988, did he once again allow it to be shown.

If Sinatra had never made another film after *The Manchurian Candidate*, his ultimate reputation as a movie star would have remained much the same. He made some well-crafted crime movies, including *Tony Rome* (1967) and *The Detective* (1968), but already he had the reputation of wanting to work fast, of allowing his directors just a few takes. During the 1970s, he made not a single film, but in 1980 he returned for *The First Deadly Sin*, a hard-boiled crime melodrama in which he turned in an effective performance. He was coasting, however, in the dreadful *Cannonball Run II* (1984), where he appeared only in one-shots, never in scenes with the other actors (sharp-eyed viewers claimed that his over-the-shoulder shots were done with a double).

I received a letter from Sinatra once. I'd written a piece about his career, suggesting (not with blinding originality) that he did it "his way."

"That would have to be the most flagrant lie," Sinatra wrote, "because if I listed everybody who helps me every day and whom I need, this letter would run ninety pages." Sinatra was playing with the lyric. True, he didn't do it alone. But he did it his way.

## A Memory of *Blue Velvet*

What was it about that specific shot in *Blue Velvet* that forced me to take it so personally? When David Lynch's film was released in 1986, it was hailed as a masterpiece. But I rated it at one star, and my review expressed discomfort with the way that Lynch presented painful material and then pulled back to pretend it was all a joke.

My feelings were illustrated by one shot in particular, in which a character played by Isabella Rossellini appears naked. Now, eleven years after first seeing the film, I think I understand what I was feeling, and why it disturbed me so. Rossellini's new autobiography, *Some of Me* (Random House, $29.95), provides the information I was lacking.

The scene in question required Rossellini to walk naked in public in *Blue Velvet*'s small town, and although I'm sure we were intended to feel that was painful, somehow it was more—a violation of her own privacy and dignity. I sensed vaguely that some sort of boundary had been crossed, that the film was using its star in a way that went beyond the role. I felt Rossellini was hurt during the scene, and I felt sympathy for her; the spell of the movie's story was broken, and feelings were generated that colored my review.

I wrote: "In one scene, she's publicly embarrassed by being dumped naked on the lawn of the police detective. In others, she is asked to portray emotions that I imagine most actresses would rather not touch. She is degraded, slapped around, humiliated, and undressed in front of the camera. And when you ask an actress to endure those experiences, you should keep your side of the bargain by putting her in an important film."

I felt Lynch let her down by leading her down a garden path of honesty, pain, and revelation, and then leaving her hanging out to dry.

Here is what Rossellini writes in her new book about the night she shot that particular scene:

"Once when he was a kid, he (Lynch) told me, coming home from school with his older brother, they had seen a naked woman walking down the street. The sight had not excited them, it had frightened them, and David had started to cry. My 'model-trained' brain flashed me an image: the photo by Nick Ut of the girl in Vietnam walking in the street naked, skin hanging from her arms after a napalm bomb attack. That devastated, helpless, obscene, frightening look seemed to me what David wanted, and I adapted it for my scene . . .

"I wish I'd found some other approach for the scene in *Blue Velvet;* I did not like being totally exposed. I kept worrying about what my family would think when the film came out, and I searched and searched for other solutions until the last moment—also because people were gathering around the set to watch the making of the film.

"People came out with blankets and picnic baskets, with their grandmothers and small children. I begged the assistant director to warn them it was going to be a tough scene, that I was going to be totally naked, but they stayed anyway. I went out and talked to them myself, but they were already in the mood of an audience and just stared at me without reacting to my plea and warning . . ."

Extraordinary. It is customary in movies to clear the set before nude scenes. Here we have the general public settling down with picnic baskets to watch Rossellini enact humiliation. But Rossellini was being humiliated not only in the film, but by the film. Where was Lynch? Why did he film the scene with total strangers watching? Did he feel it would enhance her sense of embarrassment?

*Blue Velvet* was in some ways a remarkable movie, and my one-star rating probably reflects personal aversion to that particular scene more than a balanced judgment of its artistry. But now that I've read Rossellini's book I feel more than ever that a compact between actor and director was violated, and that what I was feeling was really there—painful, humiliating, and unwarranted.

## Thoughts on Barnacle Bill

I look at the photos with a sense of astonishment. I am looking at the surface of Mars. As long as man has been man, we have looked up into the sky at that familiar point of light and wondered what could be found there.

Now we know. Now the pictures are in our homes. With every picture comes a caption. And with every caption my blood boils. The publicity-mad popularizers at the Jet Propulsion Laboratory are hard at work trivializing their great achievement by packaging it like a theme park. Is the American public so juvenile and shallow that we cannot be interested in Mars unless it has names like Disneyland?

Consider "Barnacle Bill," one of the rocks they hope to study. It is a rock. It seems to contain about a cubic foot of matter. It has a rough exterior. It has been waiting for billions of years. It has no barnacles on it, because as nearly as we know there have never been barnacles on Mars.

Or anyone named Bill.

Another rock is named Yogi, because it looks to the JPL publicists like a bear. It looks like a rock to me. A third newly famous rock is named Flat Top, because it has one. That's not quite so offensive, since it's descriptive; they could have called it Jerry Lewis, since he had one too.

Describing an encounter between the *Sojourner* exploration vehicle and a rock, Dr. Matthew Golombek, the chief project scientist, told reporters: "It nestled up and kissed Barnacle Bill affectionately." When *Sojourner* sticks a probe into Bill to perform a spectroscopic analysis, I wonder how Dr. Golombek will describe that.

The problem with this cute naming system is that it's so patronizing. The JPL honchos obviously hope American taxpayers will spend millions more to underwrite additional Mars missions. So do I. Our future as a race depends on exploring the universe we inhabit. What I do not believe is that we need another Mars mission so that Barnacle Bill won't get lonely without us.

What the scientists are telling us is that they don't trust us to be impressed intellectually by the sheer wonder of their achievement. I, for one, would find Barnacle Bill even more impressive if it were known as Rock No. 1. There is a cold, objective ring to that name that helps express how strange, distant, and mysterious the surface of Mars really is.

There is a tendency throughout American life to reduce things to childish terms, as if, gee, we're all kids at heart. Recently, for example, I was told that the dinosaurs in *Lost World: Jurassic Park* should have been more "lovable." My feeling is that dinosaurs were selected through evolution to kill and eat in order to survive. They were not nice. It was not in their nature.

When we encourage children to diminish and personalize dinosaurs—to turn fearsome omnivores into Barney—that's one thing. When we as adults cannot gaze with awe on the surface of Mars without growing fond of good old Barnacle Bill, there is something weird going on.

## A Pulitzer for the Movies

The movies turned one hundred years old in 1997, and the Pulitzer Prizes were seventy. It's about time they got together. In addition to the journalism categories, Pulitzers are awarded in the areas of music, drama, and literature—but they have never been given to the movies, where they might actually have a greater influence.

The Tonys, Emmys, Oscars, Grammys, National Book Awards, and Obies are all insider prizes, run by the industries they honor. The Pulitzers have always stood outside and a little above, convening panels of independent experts to look for the best work in a field without regard for popularity, sales, or sentiment.

A Pulitzer Prize for film would presumably go to the kind of good film that doesn't often get nominated for an Oscar. It would not be inhibited, as the Oscars are, by a tendency to select films that reflect favorably on the industry. It would consider documentaries and made-for-TV movies, as well as theatrical fiction films.

In 1997, for example, Pulitzer candidates might have included a film like *In the Company of Men,* with its searing portrait of male corporate culture. Or Spike Lee's *4 Little Girls,* about the Birmingham church bombing. Or *Gattaca,* about a fearsome new world of genetic discrimination. Or *Eve's Bayou,* a Louisiana child's rich and tragic family memory. Or *Waco: The Rules of Engagement,* which offers a revisionist portrait of what happened in the Branch Davidian siege. Or *George Wallace,* the made-for-cable biography of the troubling politician.

The Pulitzer's board members meet at Columbia University in New York once a year to consider changes in the prizes. Surprisingly, 1997 was the first time they seriously considered adding movies, according to Kristen McCary of Hollywood Hills, California, who is leading a campaign for the change.

One tricky question they have to settle is: Who would the Pulitzer Prize for Best Film go to? The Pulitzer in drama goes to the playwright, not the production. The Pulitzers in music go to the composers, not the conductors or recording artists. Literature prizes, of course, go to the authors—but who is the author of a film?

That question has occupied the movie industry almost since its inception. The Oscar for Best Film is presented to a film's producer, in keeping with the Hollywood tradition that studios and producers are the only true begetters. The top prizes at film festivals are generally accepted by the directors, in keeping with the ascendant "auteur" theory, which holds that the director is the ultimate author of a film. But French critics first proposed the "auteur" theory because in France until the late 1950s the screenwriter was considered the true author. And in the case of the adaptation of a great work of literature—the 1996 *Hamlet,* say—who is more the author? William Shakespeare or Kenneth Branagh? Do not answer too hastily; Branagh won an Oscar nomination for his screenplay of *Hamlet,* even though he proudly filmed Shakespeare's uncut text.

Movies are children with many parents. It is impossible to untangle the contributions of the collaborators on a film—also including the actors, cinematographer, editor, composer, set designer, and special-effects artists. It is obvious, I think, that Pulitzer judges should consider only the excellence of a film, and not get involved in sorting out its pedigree. The Pulitzer Prize for film should be awarded to the film itself, period, end of discussion.

Consider. The Pulitzer for Drama goes to the playwright because his play is the underlying reality on which all productions must be based. The judges cannot see or imagine all productions, but they will all reflect the same text. It's the same with a musical composition.

But a film is seen everywhere in the same form. It will not feature different actors or costumes for its run in Chicago than it had on Broadway. All of the collaborators have come together once, made the film, and gone their separate ways. No matter who made what contribution to a great film, together they made this film and no other. They did not make a bad film, although they might have. The film itself should be honored, and Pulitzer's glory shine on all the contributors.

What practical good would the Pulitzer Prize for Film be? Would it be just one more award? Not at all. The Pulitzers are seen as more informed and disinterested than the honors given within each art form. They are the most prestigious awards in America. The annual debate over Pulitzer "finalists" would draw attention to many worthy films. The prize winner would be booked into more theaters and win a larger audience, and its life on television and on video would be greatly enhanced.

The American film industry today straddles a great divide. On the one side are the multimillion-dollar blockbusters, the thrillers and special-effects pictures. On the other, the renaissance in the world of independent and alternative films. The Oscars will usually be tilted toward the mainstream films—and above all toward successful films; it is easier for a film to pass through the eye of a needle than for a box-office flop to win the Oscar.

The Pulitzers might help restore the balance between success and quality—might even act as an inspiration or a rebuke for the Oscar voters. It's time for America's most important honor in the arts to be extended to America's most important contribution to the arts.

## Spielberg at Fifty

Steven Spielberg celebrated his fiftieth birthday December 18, 1997. If he never directed another film, his place in movie history would be secure. It is likely that when all of the movies of the twentieth century are seen at a great distance in the future—as if through the wrong end of a telescope—his best will be in the handful that endure and are remembered.

No other director has been more successful at the box office. Few other directors have placed more titles on various lists of the greatest films. How many other directors have bridged the gap between popular and critical success? Not many; one thinks of Chaplin and Keaton, Ford and Hitchcock, Huston and DeMille, and although the list could go on, the important thing is to establish the company that Spielberg finds himself in.

Now he owns his own studio, DreamWorks. A few other directors have grown so powerful that they could call their own shots: In the silent days, Griffith, Chaplin, DeMille, and Rex Ingram. Since then, not many, and those who have founded studios, like Francis Coppola, have lived to regret their entry into the world of finance. But Spielberg's success has been so consistent for so many years that even the mysteries of money (in some ways, so much more perplexing than the challenge of making a good film) seem open to him.

Consider some of his titles (Spielberg has made a dozen films known to virtually everyone): *E.T., Jaws, Close Encounters of the Third Kind, Raiders of the Lost Ark, Indiana Jones and the Temple of Doom, Indiana Jones and the Last Crusade, The Color Purple,* the two *Jurassic Park* movies, and his 1993 Oscar winner for Best Picture, *Schindler's List.* Consider his most recent releases, *Amistad* and *Saving Private Ryan;* he has used his success to buy the independence to make films that might not otherwise seem bankable.

If Spielberg had never directed a single film, however, he would still qualify as one of Hollywood's most successful producers. Look at these titles: *Who Framed Roger Rabbit,* the three *Back to the Future* movies, *An American Tail, Gremlins, Twister,* and many more. Yes, he's had failures *(1941, Always, Hook),* but more often than not when Spielberg makes a movie it finds one of the year's largest audiences.

To make a good movie is very difficult. To make a popular movie is not easy. To make both, time after time, is the holy grail that Hollywood seeks with the same fervor that Indy Jones devoted to the Ark of the Convenant. Talking to Spielberg over the years, and particularly during a four-hour conversation in the spring of 1996, I got the feeling that his success is based on his ability to stay in touch with the sense of wonder he had as a teenager—about the world, and about movies.

"I'm greedy about trying to please as many people, all in the same tent, at the same time," he told me. "I've just always wanted to please, more than I've wanted to create controversy and exclude people. And yet, when I made *E.T.,* I really thought I was making it, not for everybody in the world, but for kids. I actually told George Lucas that parents would drop their kids off at *E.T.* And the parents would go off and see another movie playing a block away."

And yet he made a movie that more people have seen, perhaps, than any other. What deeper need did it fill than simple entertainment? Why does the story of a little boy and a goofy-looking extraterrestrial make people cry who never cry at the movies?

"From the very beginning," Spielberg said, "*E.T.* was a movie about my childhood—about my parents' divorce, although people haven't often seen that it's about divorce. My parents split up when I was fifteen or sixteen years old, and I needed a special friend, and had to use my imagination to take me to places that felt good—that helped me move beyond the problems my parents were having and that ended our family as a whole. And thinking about that time, I thought, an extraterrestrial character would be the perfect springboard to purge the pain of your parents splitting up."

It's that deeper impulse, that need, that operates under the surface of *E.T.*, making it more emotionally complex than the story itself might suggest. And in the third *Indiana Jones* movie, there's that bond between Indy (Harrison Ford) and his father (Sean Connery). In *Close Encounters,* the hope that alien visitors might be benign, not fearsome as they always were in science-fiction movies. And in *The Color Purple,* again the impulse to heal a broken family.

Spielberg may begin with a promising idea, but in his best films he doesn't proceed with it unless there is also a connection to his heart. That may be why his Holocaust film, *Schindler's List,* is not only about horror, but about help, about man's better nature even in the worst times.

Spielberg told me that he got into the movies by sneaking onto the lot at Universal. He'd buy a ticket on the tour bus, jump off the bus, and hang around. After a while the guards had seen him so often (always dressed in his bar mitzvah suit, not T-shirt and jeans, so that he didn't look so much like a kid) they waved him through.

By then he had already made a lot of movies. His first involved his Lionel train set. "The trains went around and around, and after a while that got boring, and I had this 8mm camera, and I staged a train wreck and filmed it. That was hard on the trains, but then I could cut the film a lot of different ways, and look at it over and over again."

And what boy wouldn't rather make a movie than have a train set?

## On Wagging the Dog

*Chicago,* January 22, 1998—The newscasts I heard on Thursday weren't yet using the phrase "wagging the dog," but they will be. The parallels between the satirical movie *Wag the Dog* and the Affair of the White House Intern are so uncanny that the words are sure to enter our political vocabulary. And the film is likely to color perceptions of how the White House handles the situation.

*Wag the Dog,* opens with a president accused of behaving improperly in an Oval Office anteroom with a "Firefly Girl." This is presumably the same anteroom in which President Clinton and Monica Lewinsky are said to have met. Speeding to contain the crisis, the White House brings in an expert spin doctor (Robert De Niro). His advice: "Change the lead, and you change the story."

The De Niro character advises the White House to deny the story and distract the nation with a crisis—a war with Albania would be a good idea, he thinks, because it's almost impossible to check on what's really happening there.

De Niro hires a Hollywood producer (Dustin Hoffman) to "produce" the crisis, complete with a threat (Albanian terrorists with suitcase bombs), a hero (Woody Harrelson as an American soldier shot down and rescued), and a theme song (written by Willie Nelson).

Watching the film a month ago, I was amused by parallels with current events. The Paula Jones case was heating up, and so was a confrontation with Saddam Hussein. Coincidence? I'm sure it was, but the movie teases you: *Wag the Dog* observes that after the deaths of Marines in a Lebanon terrorist bombing, the Reagan White House regained stature by invading Grenada.

Now parts of the movie's scenario seem to be repeating themselves in real life. The administration is in turmoil. Charges of misconduct and a cover-up dominate the news. If *Wag the Dog* is correct, the White House, which has already issued denials, will act to "change the lead" by putting emphasis on an international crisis and positioning the president in leadership mode.

Problem is, people who have seen the movie may be tempted to discount the wagging. Clinton's luck is not good: First Paula Jones, then Monica Lewinsky, and now *Wag the Dog* to undercut the spin control. It's only a matter of time until a White House spokesman is asked if the president is "wagging the dog."

What does "wag the dog" mean? The film, written by playwright David Mamet and directed by Barry Levinson, has the De Niro character explain: "Why does a dog wag its tail? Because the dog is smarter than the tail. If the tail was smarter, it would wag the dog." As gloom and uncertainty envelop the presidency, it is hard to avoid the possibility that the tail may indeed be smarter than the dog.

## *Titanic*'s Triumph

When the numbers were crunched, *Titanic* officially became the top-grossing film at the worldwide box office, passing *Jurassic Park*'s record of $914 million on its way north of a billion.

Of course, the total doesn't account for ticket price inflation, and many more people have seen *Star Wars,* which opened in 1977 when prices were less than half their current levels. But *Titanic* will steam on and on, and seems on course to be seen by more people than any other movie of modern times.

Why? What it is about this high-tech melodrama that has created not just success, not just popularity, but genuine and heartfelt enthusiasm?

I ask because I hear the warmth in people's voices when they discuss it, and I see the light in their eyes. Strangers are forever telling me about this or that movie they've just seen, and I can guess by their manner how enthusiastic they really are. *Titanic* moves them. They feel real affection for it.

Those who love it are taking others—insisting that they go. Hollywood talks about "word of mouth" as the best advertising, because people believe it when a friend likes a movie. But with *Titanic,* people aren't just talking. The movie is doing an unusually high rate of repeat business because many repeaters are dragging along friends, insisting they share the experience.

Is there something buried and mythic in *Titanic* that strikes a deep chord and makes it into a quasi-ritual for those who love it? I think so. I know there are those who go because they like the love story, or are fans of Leonardo DiCaprio, or admire the special effects. But I think the breadth of the film's success is better explained by the way it touches universal feelings.

One key to the film's impact is the way director James Cameron incorporates the real *Titanic,* in its watery grave, in his fictional story. The opening footage from the bottom of the Atlantic is eerie in its impact; it gives the film weight and gravity. We look at a real ship that really sank, and we feel like intruders into its ghostly silence. The solemnity of those scenes lends authenticity to everything that follows; in a film constructed out of special effects, Cameron starts with the ultimate reality of the *Titanic* itself.

Then there's the romance. It's like an interlude in an opera, the moment of heedless abandon before tragedy comes crashing down. Leonardo DiCaprio and Kate Winslet, as Jack and Rose, are an attractive and likable couple, but they don't have the presence of, say, Clark Gable and Vivien Leigh in *Gone With the Wind.* Their romance is effective primarily because it is doomed; every moment has a bittersweet undertow because we know what's coming.

Jack and Rose began to grow in stature during the scenes re-creating what it was like once the *Titanic* struck the iceberg. Who hasn't wondered what such a situation would be like? I remember today, clearly, the first time I ever had the phrase "women and children first" explained to me, and I realized it meant my father would go down with the ship (I had never seen a ship, but no matter). Do we believe that today? Would men still stand aside for women and children? What a test of character in a society where a man will not even give his seat to a woman on the bus.

People on a sinking ship are presented with an ultimate test to determine what they are really made of. I would admire anyone giving up a place so another might live, but I would also understand a person scrambling desperately for the last lifeboat. I would want to behave heroically—but I would also not want to drown. The romance in *Titanic* is inconsequential, but the sacrifice at the end is incredibly moving; by the time the two young lovers are clinging to the floating debris, we are completely and truly inside the film, sharing their experience and identifying with it.

*Titanic*'s appeal is made of many things. It is exciting, glorious to look at, intelligent in the way it explains the tragedy—and one of the best *made* films in cinema history. But the heart of its appeal, I'm convinced, comes in the power of the sacrifice at the end—which Jack makes for Rose because he loves her.

We identify with films. A powerful movie can be an out-of-the-body experience, in which we are sharing the events on the screen; in a sense they are happening to us. In the clarity of the way *Titanic* prepares us for the ship's sinking, and in the inexorable way the tragedy progresses, the film places us in a situation with fewer and fewer choices, until finally there is only one.

Do we identify with Jack or Rose? With both, I argue. With Jack, because we would like to be brave and to sacrifice ourselves for the one we love. And with Rose, because it is a good thing to find true love—to know that someone loved you enough to die for you. That is why the modern story, of Rose when she is 101 years old, is so important. One wants to think that one will be well remembered, and for a long time.

The buried power of *Titanic* comes, not because it is a love story or a special-effects triumph, but because it touches the deepest human feelings about living, dying, and being cherished. For many viewers, it is their story, if only they were as lucky as Rose—or, yes, as Jack.

## Notes from the Toronto Film Festival

*Now in its twenty-third year, the Toronto Film Festival is considered the most important festival in North America, and on a global scale it ranks behind only Cannes, Berlin, and perhaps Venice. Its Canadian rival, Montreal, is also very important; both festivals benefit from high levels of government support. In America, the only festival to gain a comparable stature as a required industry destination is Sundance. In September 1997, I wrote a daily diary-type column from Toronto; here are some of the entries that still seem of interest, including my first glimpses of films that would later be much discussed, such as* Eve's Bayou *and* Boogie Nights.

* * *

We have come finally to the end of the long, hot summer of explosions and chases, fireballs and terrorists, and crashes involving ships, planes, trains, and automobiles. The autumn movie slate kicks off Academy Awards season, and here at the Toronto Film Festival some 300 films will unspool—many of them pretty good, and most of them at least sincere in trying to do something original or memorable.

Even the thrillers step up a notch in quality when summer is over. Consider *The Edge*. It's mostly about men in the northern wilderness, pursued by a man-eating bear, yes. But because this is September and we are at Toronto, the screenplay is by the playwright David Mamet, the bear's potential suppers are portrayed by Sir Anthony Hopkins and Alec Baldwin, and the macho dialogue is enlivened by lawyer jokes and discussions of the meaning of life.

You have to hit the ground running here. Toronto has more press screenings—in six different theaters—than other festivals have screenings. "This is the most important festival in North America," says Warner Bros. publicity honcho Stu Gottesman; "it's even become more important than New York."

That's because it lasts longer, shows five times as many films, and attracts more journalists—some 300 at last count, ranging all the way from the hotshot hosts of the TV entertainment magazines to James Berardinelli of New Jersey, who is considered the best of the Internet-based critics but was not having much luck landing the interview he wanted, with *Drive, She Said* star Moira Kelly. ("I understand she talked to her priest before doing nude scenes, and I want to ask her about that," said Berardinelli, who may be the only critic here who has a philosophical motive for discussing nude scenes.)

The opening weekend was overshadowed by the funeral of Princess Diana, and the TV sets in the press suites, usually devoted to playing the same promotional clips over and over again, were tuned to the coverage. Earl Spencer's remarks about the life and death of his sister probably received more comment than the films, and the stars themselves were in a thoughtful mood, none more so than Alec Baldwin, who with his wife Kim Basinger has received his share of attention from the trash press.

"I am here meeting the press to represent a film produced by 20th Century-Fox," he told me. "The studio is part of the News Corporation, which is owned by Murdoch, and the News Corporation is in the tabloid business. They own the *New York Post*, for example. So on the one hand Murdoch's film company wants me to be of service to them as a movie actor while another arm of the Murdoch empire is burying me in the tabloids they own. And they run those gossip TV shows: I ran into George Clooney on the Fox lot, and he told me he was working for them on stage 17 while they were ripping him to shreds on stage 19."

* * *

Sir Anthony Hopkins was calmer, even though the tabloids ripped him for a brief marital infidelity a few years ago.

"If someone becomes a celebrity, it's part of the territory, I guess. I dunno. Diana was wonderful with publicity, and yet it must sometimes have been very painful for her. I'm trying to be objective. The press has a job to do as well. People buy the papers; they want to see the pictures. The public pick up the *National Enquirer*, the *Globe* . . . are they guilty? I don't know.

Aren't we all responsible? Everyone wants to be famous, I guess."

## Lunch with George Christy

We are all gathered here at the Four Seasons hotel for the thirteenth annual running of George Christy's Toronto Film Festival luncheon. We know it is the thirteenth year because that's what it says on the handcrafted leather passport cases from Roots that are this year's favors. We are pretty sure the menu will center around chicken pot pie.

Christy, a columnist for the *Hollywood Reporter,* throws this party every year and we all attend every year, although we are not quite sure what the occasion is. George says it is the annual meeting of our "extended family," but I am not sure my family includes Kim Basinger, Gary Oldman, and Atom Egoyan. No matter. It is always lots of fun, and you get to hear great gossip.

For example, just now I am learning that James Ellroy doesn't wear underwear beneath his kilt. Ellroy of course is the best-selling crime novelist whose *L.A. Confidential* has been made into a big autumn movie. There he is in the corner, the tall drink of water with thinning hair and a defiant mustache, looking like Nelson Algren on steroids.

"I was with him when the movie premiered at the Cannes Film Festival," confides a publicist, "and he was wearing his kilt because the premiere is formal attire, and he was all wound up in telling me about the Blue Dahlia Murder, which he is utterly obsessed with, and he laid right down on the sidewalk to show me the position the corpse was found in."

"And that's when you found out he doesn't wear underwear under his kilt?" I asked.

"Uh, huh," she said.

I wandered over to Ellroy, who talks like a race track tout with a Ph.D. in criminology.

"Once you picture your characters in your mind," I said, "how does it affect you when you see them on the screen? Kevin Spacey and Kim Basinger—do they replace the people in your mind?"

"It's confusing," he said. "It's parallel. My people are still there. These new people are there now too. They exist uneasily side by side, trying to nudge each other out of my attention. I think my characters remain and I deal with the actors by thinking that they are playing my characters, although paradoxically the actors are of course real and my characters exist only in my imagination."

They claim the test of friendship is, can you take a three-day bus ride with the person? I think I would like to sit next to Ellroy on the Greyhound for three days. It would be more entertaining than a TV set screwed to the back of the seat in front of me.

Danny DeVito is in the corner, gesticulating. He is such a great gesticulator he looks like a conductor deprived of his orchestra. I wander over to him.

"I was just thinkin' the other day," he says, "that Ellroy could be an actor. No kiddin'. He's got that kind of weird light in his eyes, and that voice, and he's so articulate. The right kinda guy, he could play him."

DeVito and I fall into a deep discussion of the merits of DVD disks, and then a gong sounds and it is time to file into the dining room for the luncheon. I am seated next to the actor Matthew Modine, who is about as nice a person as you would want to meet, and who is worried about what to do with his father's collection of movie coming-attractions trailers.

"Dad ran a drive-in theater," he said, "and they'd send him all of these trailers. Science fiction, Westerns, classics, big pictures, *Night of the Living Dead,* everything. I've run into Jack Lemmon and told him I have the trailer for *Save the Tiger,* which he has never seen. But prints decompose if you don't take care of them. I'd like to donate them to some museums, but I don't know where."

We discuss the merits of the UCLA Film Archive and then he starts talking about working with Stanley Kubrick on *Full Metal Jacket.*

"He doesn't believe in waste," Modine said. "He uses the smallest possible crew. Sometimes only six people. One day he had a set lit, and he told the electrician, 'Okay, this set is lit and it's not going to change so I don't need you here anymore,' and he sent the guy over to work on the wiring on his house."

"They say he likes to make a lot of takes of every scene," I said.

Modine looked like I didn't know the half of it. "He told me that on *The Shining* Jack Nicholson would arrive on the set sort of knowing his lines. After six takes he would know them. After twenty takes he would know what they meant.

After fifty takes he would start to play around with them in interesting ways."

"And then it got good?" I asked.

"No . . . then, Stanley said, after one hundred takes, he begins to really feel them."

"Yeah," I said, "I heard he really works his actors."

"At the end of *Full Metal Jacket,*" Modine said, "there's a scene where all the soldiers have to march together. We did it over and over and over. Like 150 yards, and then back up, and then do it again and again, because he wasn't satisfied. Finally at the end of yet one more take, I shouted out, 'I am Spartatus!' And then all the others took it up, 'No, I am Spartacus!' And 'We are all Spartacus!' Because Stanley hates *Spartacus.*"

"There's supposed to be a scene where you can see one of the Roman soldiers wearing a wristwatch," I said.

"I kept a diary on the set of *Full Metal Jacket,*" Modine said. "I knew Kubrick had a reputation for working his actors hard. In the early weeks, I kept writing down, 'He is a great director. He is a great director.'"

"And toward the end of the film?"

"I wrote down, 'Stanley Kubrick is the Devil.'"

We are jerked back to reality by the arrival of our chicken pot pie. It is about the best chicken pot pie you can imagine. The menu used to change every year, but four or five years ago Garth Drabinsky, the theater mogol, told George Christy how much he liked the chicken pot pie, and so George has served it every year since. Garth Drabinsky did not attend the luncheon this year, but we ate the chicken pot pie, and thought of him.

## David Mamet and the State Fair

"I was trying to think what the summer movie season was like," David Mamet said, "and I realized it was like the state fair."

It was the first cup of coffee for both of us, in a Toronto hotel room that was furnished, oddly, with four straight chairs. We sat with our knees crossed, like men trying to appear at ease during an interrogation.

"First of all, what's the prime attraction at a state fair? The equipment! You go to see the new models of tractors. Same with summer movies. The new technology. The new vehicles and airplanes. The special effects. Then, of course, at a state fair you want a glimpse of the hoochie-koochie show. And the food: candy, hot dogs, pop, nacho chips. The same at the state fair and at the movies."

He took a sip of his coffee.

"Oh, and of course the livestock judging. Everyone wants to see the cow that sold for a record price. In the summer movies, the movie stars are the prize bulls, and everybody is just fascinated by how much money they were paid."

Mamet was here at the Toronto Film Festival to help launch the autumn movie season. The playwright and director, who made his name in Chicago, now lives in Vermont ("where I just laugh at the winters after Chicago") with his wife, Rebecca Pidgeon. She stars in *The Spanish Prisoner,* his new movie about an elaborate con game. Mamet also wrote *The Edge,* a Toronto entry about men lost in the wilderness.

*The Spanish Prisoner* weaves a hypnotic labyrinth of deception, as they say in the movie ads. Campbell Scott plays a man with a formula worth millions to an international conglomerate, and there are a lot of people who would like to get it away from him. More I must not reveal.

* * *

If summer is the state fair at the movies, then autumn is quality time, when we get the prestigious costume adaptations of great novels. The works of Jane Austen have been picked over in recent years, and now Henry James is the preferred literary source. After last year's *Portrait of a Lady* comes now *Wings of the Dove* and, later in the festival, *Washington Square,* starring Jennifer Jason Leigh as a bright but plain daughter of a rich doctor (Albert Finney), who is courted by a dashing man (Ben Chaplin) who may be after her money; Maggie Smith plays her wary aunt.

After James, the next distinguished source may be Virginia Woolf, whose *Mrs. Dalloway* has been made into a film at this year's festival. Vanessa Redgrave stars as a woman giving her annual party, which inspires thoughts of the man she might have married, and the man she did marry. What is always enjoyable about all of these movies, apart from their costumes, their locations, their skill, and their ambition, is their language: It is a pleasure to hear passion expressed by the literate, because they have so many more ways of putting it.

## Discovering *Eve's Bayou*

Kasi Lemmons was Jodie Foster's roommate in *The Silence of the Lambs,* she was the doomed researcher in *Candyman,* and one of Nicholas Cage's victims in *Vampire's Kiss.* I mention these credits because they are from another, earlier life; Lemmons emerged at this year's Toronto Film Festival as one of the most gifted young American writer-directors.

Her *Eve's Bayou,* which had its premiere at an opening weekend gala here, is one of the best films of the year—elegant, sensuous, haunting. It's the story of a Louisiana family and its secrets, with supernatural undertones; Tennessee Williams has been evoked in reviews, but it reminded me in ways of Ingmar Bergman's later family dramas, with their fathers, distant and mysterious, their women, confiding and conspiring, and their children, who interpret everything in their own ways.

The film is one of the big successes here, one everyone mentions when talking about the festival's discoveries. Lemmons wrote the screenplay, which is told through the eyes of a young girl named Eve (Jurnee Smollett), whose opening narration tells us, "I was ten the summer I killed my father." But if and how she killed him are questions the movie only gradually answers.

Unlike a lot of first films, which are overeager to impress, *Eve's Bayou* is serenely confident. The story introduces us to Eve's father, a successful, womanizing physician (Samuel L. Jackson), her long-suffering but loving mother (Lynn Whitfield), and her aunt, in some ways the most complex character in the movie, brilliantly played by Debbi Morgan, who is a very accurate psychic and (the doctor mentions) "not unfamiliar with the inside of a mental hospital." Diahann Carroll, at first unrecognizable behind creepy makeup, plays a voodoo woman.

The film is set largely in and around a large house in bayou country, which Lemmons and her cinematographer, Amy Vincent, paint in dreamy, sometimes scary detail: There is one extraordinary shot in which a mirror is used to blend past and present, and others in which flashbacks show how emotional shock can be remembered in different ways.

Lemmons (whose first name is pronounced like "Casey") is married to the actor and director Vondie Curtis Hall, whose own directorial debut, the dynamic and funny *Gridlock'd,* with Tupac Shakur and Tim Roth, came out earlier this year. They represent a lot of talent to live under one roof. *Eve's Bayou* will represent a marketing challenge, because the Creole and voodoo material will suggest it's a genre picture—when in fact it's a legitimate contender for an Oscar nomination as Best Picture.

* * *

My hotel concierge was back on duty today. "I took off three days and saw eleven films," she told me. The woman sitting in front of me at *Ma Vie en Rose* this afternoon was a travel agent who has taken off a week and is clocking four films a day.

The film festival preoccupies Toronto. Maybe it's because almost all the theaters are along the major subway lines, and maybe it's because Toronto has the highest per capita movie attendance in North America. Films unspool in some sixteen theaters, from the vast Roy Thompson Hall to the funky little Backstage twins. Moviegoers all seem to be carrying liters of water, in case they're stranded in line. There are parties every night, and you know you're at a hot one when one of the gate-crashers is Mick Jagger, in town to rehearse for the upcoming Rolling Stones tour.

Why does Toronto have a festival like this and Chicago, which got a ten-year head start, doesn't? Maybe it's because the city and provincial governments have sunk millions of dollars into support and subsidies, and have seen their investment grow into a global tourist attraction. No movie festival can turn a profit on its income alone, but in Canada they think about the spillover effect. "The festival," the maître d' at Bistro 990 told me last night, "is a lovely time to be in the restaurant business."

## On Discovering *Boogie Nights*

*Boogie Nights,* a sprawling, sloppy masterpiece of a movie, unspooled here Wednesday and Thursday before sharply divided audiences. Some walked out muttering imprecations. Others stayed to cheer. The movie features a big-name cast in a surprisingly frank treatment of the hard-core film industry during its last hurrah, in the late 1970s and early 1980s.

In energy and willingness to shock, it reminded me of an Oliver Stone film; in scope and the complexity of the supporting characters, like something by Robert Altman. And the sex scenes reminded me of. . .well, of porno, although the movie aims mostly above the waist until a final shot in which we see the full monty.

*Boogie Nights,* written and directed by Paul Thomas Anderson, is the kind of grimy, intense, passionate film we identify more with the 1970s than with today's slick productions. It stars Mark Wahlberg (a.k.a. Marky Mark) as a kid named Eddie Adams from the San Fernando Valley, whose remarkable genitals win him roles in the adult film industry until he becomes a top porn star—and then begins a slide into drug addiction, arrogance, and impotence. His career begins when he's seventeen and is more or less over by the age of twenty-three.

Burt Reynolds, in one of the best performances of his career, plays Jack Horner, a porno film producer who dreams of making a dirty movie so good that the audience will actually stay in their seats because of the plot. Reynolds plays Horner not as a sleaze merchant (although the character certainly is one) but as a man who sincerely wants to make the best porn around; the character is possibly inspired by the hardcore auteur Gerald Diamiano.

The cast includes many familiar faces, including William H. Macy (from *Fargo*) as a crew member whose wife sleeps with everyone in sight; Julianne Moore, as Horner's sweet but tearful wife; Don Cheadle (from *Devil in a Blue Dress*) as a black porn star who likes to dress as a cowboy; magician Ricky Jay as the cinematographer; and Philip Baker Hall as a producer who clearly sees that home video is the death of theatrical porn.

*Boogie Nights* is the second film by Paul Thomas Anderson, whose first, *Hard 8* (1997) also starred Hall, as a wise, sad-eyed gambler who shows a broke kid (John C. Reilly) how to con the casinos. Reilly turns up again here, as a sidekick to Eddie Adams, who renames himself Dirk Diggler, and becomes as famous as, say, Linda Lovelace or John Holmes.

The movie follows the classic showbiz rise and fall formula, but rises to where the others fall; Reynolds has a quiet little scene where he tells Wahlberg about the costs of casts, crews, camera, film, sound, lights, dubbing, labs, prints, and so forth, and ends with a sigh: "A film can easily end up costing $20,000." The last acts of the epic film (147 minutes) deal with suicides, drug deals, stickups and other dead ends that real-life porn stars also experience.

Like last year's *The People vs. Larry Flynt,* although much raunchier and more observantly sociological, *Boogie Nights* is sure to offend a lot of people. But its raw energy, its untidy morality, and its shocking juxtaposition of violence and comedy will wake up audiences lulled by the dozey movies of recent months; like *Pulp Fiction,* this is a reminder that movies can rattle and surprise.

## The Semiautobiography of Joe Eszterhas

Joe Eszterhas hasn't become history's highest paid screenwriter by penning quirky little stories about coming of age in Cleveland—but one of the big hits of the Toronto Film Festival's closing weekend is just such a film.

Guy Ferland's *Telling Lies in America,* based on a somewhat autobiographical script by Eszterhas, tells the story of a seventeen-year-old kid, the son of a Hungarian immigrant, who gets a job as a personal assistant to a shady local disk jockey. His prime attributes, although he doesn't know it, are that he is underage and a good liar—which makes him ideal for the purpose of accepting the DJ's payola payments.

The kid is played by Brad Renfro, in a coming-of-age performance of his own, and the DJ, who calls himself "Billy Magic," is played by Kevin Bacon in one of his best performances—as a man who is weary, cynical, and yet has an affection for the kid and wants to show him the ways, however sad, of his world.

Eszterhas, himself a first-generation American, specialized in sex and treachery *(Basic Instinct, Showgirls).* He obviously wrote this one from the heart, but also with a rich vein of humor and period color; it's an unlikely combination of sex, booze, rock 'n' roll, and a kid who believes that if he ever learns to pronounce "the" like an American, he might be a disk jockey himself some day. Or a screenwriter.

* * *

For Robert Downey Jr., the past year has been a publicity nightmare of stories about drug problems, rehab centers, and probation terms. But he also worked steadily, and now his comeback begins with two remarkable performances, filmed in the shadow of personal troubles but filled with life and intelligence.

Downey starred here in two Toronto premieres. In James Toback's *Two Girls and a Guy,* he's a pickup artist who returns to his luxurious Manhattan apartment to find that his two girlfriends, who are not supposed to know about one another, have met by accident, let themselves in, and are waiting for him. For an hour and a half, they all fight, argue, and theorize about men, women, sex, and honesty—in a tough, thoughtful script that completes a circle, since Toback and Downey also collaborated on the 1987 film *The Pick-Up Artist,* which cast a much more forgiving eye on male behavior.

The other Downey performance comes in *One Night Stand,* Mike Figgis's well-received drama about a man and a woman (Wesley Snipes and Nastassja Kinski) who meet by chance, have a brief and tender fling, and then meet again a year later under much different circumstances. Downey plays a dying AIDS patient, who despite playing the entire role from a hospital bed manages to fill it with life and humor; it's not easy for a dying man to get a laugh by lifting one eyebrow, but Downey does it.

"When I saw him being led away in handcuffs, wearing an orange prison suit, that's when I knew it was time to work with him again," Toback told me after the screening of *Two Girls and a Guy.* Days after Downey was released on parole for drug charges, he was working with Toback on an eleven-day shoot with actresses Heather Graham and Natasha Gregson; "I felt Bob was ready to reveal some truths about himself," Toback said.

* * *

This comes under the heading of backstage gossip, but I am happy to pass it along: Dame Maggie Smith may have saved Jennifer Jason Leigh's life, or at least her intestines, during the filming of *Washington Square.* The Henry James adaptation stars Leigh as a rich heiress who is courted by a poor young man (Ben Chaplin). Her father (Albert Finney) disapproves, but her aunt (Smith) schemes behind the scenes as a matchmaker.

"I had no idea what it was like to wear a corset," Leigh told me: An understatement, since she has specialized in playing women who need corsets the way a fish needs a bicycle. "I was dying the first three weeks. I wore the corsets the way women did in those days—right under my ribcage. They gave me a nineteen-inch waist, but I couldn't breathe, I couldn't move, I couldn't even go to the bathroom by myself."

Smith, who has appeared in many a costume role, advised her to loosen the corset and move it down to her natural waistline. Then Leigh did research on the subject, "and I found out why women were always fainting in those days. They were being squeezed to death. In one book I even read about a plug that was used to keep their intestines from falling out!"

The bright side? "Under all those petticoats, no one can figure out what's going on," she said. "I could play a scene looking formal and composed, and actually be sitting cross-legged, and no one would know."

* * *

Many of the festival types are staying at the Four Seasons Hotel, where three times in recent days there have been false fire alarms. After piercing bleats and whistles, a voice announces, "The situation has been rectified," which is the last thing you want to know. (A hint to the management: You want to know one of two things: (1) there is no fire; or (2) the fire is out.)

Fire alarm specialists were on the job Saturday. Perhaps they should have talked to New York superpublicist Leslee Dart. Her theory: "Paparazzi knew Brad Pitt was staying in the hotel, and set false alarms hoping to get pictures of him standing in the driveway in his bathrobe."

## The Winners

*The Hanging Garden,* a Canadian film by Thom Fitzgerald about a gay man's return home after ten years, won the Air Canada People's Choice Award at the twenty-second Toronto Film Festival.

The award is decided by festival patrons, who mark their ballots on leaving the theaters. The runners-up were Curtis Hanson's *L.A. Confidential,* a *film noir* about a police scandal in the 1950s, and *The Edge,* starring Anthony Hopkins and Alec Baldwin as two enemies stranded in the wilderness.

The Toronto festival has no jury and gives no awards, but over the years its sponsors and several other groups have established awards, which are announced on the closing day.

The Toronto-Citytv Award for Best Canadian Feature, with a $25,000 prize from the Toronto-based TV network and the city of Toronto, was shared by *The Hanging Garden* and Atom Egoyan's *The Sweet Hereafter,* based on the

Russell Banks novel about a town devastated by a school bus crash.

The Citytv Award for Best Canadian First Feature, with a cash prize of $15,000 from the Toronto-based TV network, went to Vincenzo Natali's *Cube*, about six people trapped in a diabolical maze.

The Metro Media Award, which can be voted on by the 740 reporters and critics at the festival, was shared by Paul Thomas Anderson's *Boogie Nights*, a harrowing portrait of the rise and fall of the adult film industry, and *L.A. Confidential*. The runners-up were *The Spanish Prisoner*, a thriller about a con game written and directed by David Mamet, and *The Sweet Hereafter*.

The Rothmans World Film International Critics Award, selected by a jury of the International Federation of Film Critics, went to Carine Adler's *Under the Skin*, a British film about a nineteen-year-old whose mother's death inspires a grief-stricken asexual odyssey.

For *The Hanging Garden*, the People's Choice Award is likely to launch a successful release for a film that was obscure before it became a festival hit. Shot in Halifax, Nova Scotia, and financed by Fitzgerald with the proverbial credit card cited by so many young directors, it stars Chris Leavins as a man who fled home, and returns to his sister's wedding to find that little has changed.

Although the exit polling that determines the People's Choice is admittedly unscientific, over the years Toronto audiences have been prescient in selecting films that went on to great success, like *Diva*, *Chariots of Fire*, and *Shine*.

# The Floating Film Festival 1998

*I met Dusty and Joan Cohl for the first time in 1977, on the terrace of the Carlton Hotel, during the Cannes Film Festival. He was easy to spot with his cowboy hat and big cigar—a lawyer from Toronto, now determined that Toronto, like Cannes, should have its own film festival. So he founded one, with Bill Marshall as his partner.*

*Since then the Toronto festival has grown to be the largest in North America. Dusty handed over leadership of the festival some fifteen years ago, but festivals were in his blood, and in 1990 he started the more-or-less semiannual Floating Film Festival, on board a series of Caribbean cruise ships. I've attended them all. Here are journal entries from the 1998 edition.*

* * *

*St. Thomas, Virgin Islands*—"I told my wife the only way she'd get me on a cruise ship would be if it was a film festival," said Dr. Richard Gaylord, a physicist from the University of Illinois-Urbana, who watches five to ten movies a week when he's not simulating social interactions on computers. "Here we are," said his wife Carole, a nutritionist.

They're among the 200 cinematic sailors on board the fifth "almost annual" Floating Film Festival, a ten-day marathon of movies aboard the MS *Statendam* of the Holland-America lines. The festival is the brainchild of Dusty Cohl, a retired Canadian lawyer who cofounded the Toronto Film Festival and came up with this idea while watching cruise ships sail past his Key Biscayne home.

It's a strange way to cruise, staggering out into the Caribbean sunlight after a plunge into *film noir*. Past festivals have included premieres of *Silence of the Lambs*, *Howards End*, and *Hoop Dreams*, and this one includes new films by Robert Altman, David Mamet, the Coen brothers, and Robert Towne, who was on board to discuss his *Without Limits*, about the legendary runner Steve Prefontaine.

The festival has developed traditions, setting it aside from the events at Cannes, Venice, and Sundance, and one of them is karaoke night, devoted mostly to songs from movies. At the first festival, a *Toronto Sun* ad salesman named John McDermott took the microphone to do "Danny Boy," and was so impressive that Dusty's cousin, Michael Cohl, tour impresario for the Rolling Stones, offered on the spot to produce an album. The rest is history: McDermott is now a star performer of Celtic songs, whose albums have gone platinum in Canada, the United Kingdom, and down under, and who still emcees karaoke night.

Films on the FFF are presented and discussed by a panel of critics, including Richard Corliss of *Time* magazine; his wife, Mary, of the New York Museum of Modern Art; Kathleen Carroll of Film Scouts; Jim Emerson of Microsoft Cinemania; the Canadian broadcast personality Brian

Linehan; and myself. Guest of honor this year is Charles Champlin, arts editor emeritus of the *Los Angeles Times.*

Robert Towne, whose credits include the scripts for *The Last Detail, Chinatown,* and *Shampoo,* and who directed *Personal Best,* unveiled his new *Without Limits,* starring Billy Crudup as Steve Prefontaine, and Donald Sutherland as his coach, Bill Bowerman. Regretting the passing of the kinds of more personal films he made in the 1970s, Towne speculated that, paradoxically, the success of movies like *Titanic* might be a predictor of a return to more personal films: "I think perhaps audiences are tiring of impersonal superheroes, and are interested again in individual people and the decisions they make."

*Without Limits,* the second biopic this year (after *Prefontaine*) about the great but abrasive runner, focused on his relationship with Bowerman, who invented Nike running shoes and struggled for years to get his most talented runner to plan a race intellectually instead of just heading for the front of the pack and staying there. Intercutting new footage with documentary footage of the real Prefontaine (who Crudup uncannily resembles), he paints a moving portrait of a kid who was invincible on the track and sometimes helpless off of it.

Robert Altman's *The Gingerbread Man,* starring Kenneth Branagh as not your usual John Grisham lawyer, had its world premiere on opening night. I was impressed by the way Altman takes the straight-ahead story line of genre fiction and enriches it with observant character touches, the atmosphere of an approaching storm, and the quirky, evasive personality of the Branagh character.

Also on opening night was *Me and My Matchmaker,* by Mark Wexler, a doc about the unexpected results when he focused on Chicago matchmaker Irene Nathan and her work. Under her maternal and possessive eye, he interviewed some of her clients and ended up dating a few of them, as Mrs. Nathan subtly shifted the emphasis of the film from herself to him.

Another world premiere on the first weekend was *God Said, "Ha!"* an extraordinary performance film by Julia Sweeney, the *Saturday Night Live* veteran best known for her omnisexual character "Pat." In a film that would be tragic if it weren't so funny, Sweeney tells of buying a house of her own in Hollywood, only to immediately lose her privacy when her brother Mike developed a dangerous cancer, and he, her parents, and a brother moved into her tiny house for the duration of the illness.

Sixteen years after she'd moved away, Sweeney reports, it was weird to be living with her parents again—especially since she'd inherited a lot of their old furniture, and so the setting was like their old home. She charts the advance of Mike's illness, and another sudden blow to the family, with loving but critical observations about her parents and siblings. The film is like a cross between stand-up comedy and one of Garrison Keillor's bittersweet reports from Lake Woebegone.

One of the biggest hits so far is *The Spanish Prisoner,* a new film directed and written by David Mamet, whose screenplay for *Wag the Dog* has uncanny parallels to the current White House crisis. Ever since his wonderful first film *House of Games* (1987), Mamet as a director has been fascinated by con games and deception, and this film unspools his most labyrinthine plot to date. Campbell Scott stars as the young inventor of an unexplained "Process" that could make millions for millionaire Ben Gazzara's corporation, and Steve Martin is a friendly guy who floats ashore onto a Caribbean island and into Scott's life, with dizzying results. Rebecca Pidgeon, Mamet's wife, plays a perky young woman who thinks Martin may be a deceiver. That's not the half of it.

The opening night film at Sundance this year played a week later on the FFF. It was Peter Howitt's *Sliding Doors,* from England, starring Gwyneth Paltrow as in a story that cuts between two alternative time lines. In one of them, she arrives home early, and discovers her husband's adultery. In another, she misses her train, is mugged, and . . . but a synopsis cannot summarize the twists of this plot, which, as one festivalgoer observed, provides Paltrow with "the role every actress dreams about: two marriages, two love affairs, two hospital scenes, and two hairstyles."

* * *

*Trinidad, West Indies*—It is now clear where Christina Ricci is headed. After becoming famous as the dark-eyed moppet of the Addams family, she has negotiated the neverland between child star and grown-up, and now arrives fully formed as a gifted comic actor in *The Opposite of Sex,* which just premiered at the Floating Film Festival.

The film, written and directed by Don Roos, is one of those outrageously in-your-face comedies that has audiences laughing, ducking, and not believing their ears. It's about sex, in a way, but also about selfishness and lives out of control, and it has as much fun with the stupidity of some of its characters as *Beavis & Butt-Head* did.

Ricci is the narrator. At one point, when we think she's dead, she breaks in to remind us that the narrator can't die. Duh! She plays Dedee, a sixteen-year-old runaway from the South who turns up at the home of her half-brother (Martin Donovan) in South Bend. He's a teacher with a live-in boyfriend (Ivan Sergei) that Dedee immediately sets about seducing, by trying to argue with him intellectually about his homosexuality.

Other characters: Lisa Kudrow, from *Friends,* wonderfully pruny as the uptight sister of Donovan's former lover, who tries to protect him from blackmail by an obnoxious high school kid who takes body-piercing to lengths we'd rather not think about. Ricci's performance is right on the money, as a bold, brazen, smart, pulchritudinous nymphet with a bad attitude, and *Time* magazine's Richard Corliss, who presented it at the festival, was quite right in comparing its wit and insight to last year's *Chasing Amy.*

* * *

A day ago I triumphantly concluded the second part of a marathon shot-by-shot analysis of Hitchcock's masterpiece *Vertigo,* with Chicago film critic Norman Mark acting as the designated phallic symbol spotter (notice the position of Jimmy Stewart's knee as he's seated in the late hotel room sequence, just as Kim Novak asks, "Is that the best you can do?"). The film strikes me more than ever as Hitchcock's best, and the emotional complexities of its key shot (Novak, remade as the woman of his dreams, approaching Stewart across the room) are so many that one can only wonder at how the screenplay assembles so many meanings at the same moment.

* * *

Other films I've enjoyed during the festival's outward-bound leg:

—*Off the Menu: The Last Days of Chasen's* is a documentary about the decline and fall of the last of the legendary Hollywood eateries. Filmed during the restaurant's closing days, including its last Oscar party and its closing night, the film includes lots of footage from the days when royalty (Hollywood and otherwise) flocked there for the chili, the carnivorous beef bones, and steak flamed at tableside.

Directed by Robert Pulcini and Shari Springer Berman, the doc is much more, however, than just the record of Chasen's closing. It is also the life story of the people who worked there—some for forty years—and made it more a vocation than a job. We meet Tommy Gallagher, the famous waiter who told customers what they shouldn't eat, called Sinatra "Frank," and once posed with two presidents on either side (for his encore, he posed with the pope). When he was buried a month after the closing, it was with a RESERVATIONS REQUIRED sign on the coffin, and a Chasen's menu in his arms.

There's also the banquet manager, Raymond Bilboul, such a stickler for perfection that a former employee once wrote a book attacking him. ("Then he married a woman with a mustache," Raymond sniffs.) And Onetta Johnson, the ladies' room attendant who inspired the Donna Summer hit "She Works Hard for the Money." And lots of witnesses describing the old days, including Fay Wray, Tom Snyder, and Ed McMahon, who has Pepe the bartender make his famous potion of love. ("That's okay if you have twenty minutes to wait for a drink," Raymond sniffs again.)

—*Comrades,* by Peter Chan, is the biggest hit from Asia in recent months—winner of nine Hong Kong Film Awards, including those for Picture, Actress, Director, and Screenplay. It stars Maggie Cheung, a frequent Jackie Chan costar who has broken out into art films such as *Irma Vep.* She and Leon Lai costar as two mainland Chinese who arrive in Hong Kong on the same day in 1986, and whose lives are destined to intersect for the next ten years, finally in New York's Chinatown.

The film is more mainstream and sentimental than we might expect, which could bode well for its chances of finding a distributor. It's a love story with a great deal of perception about the everyday lives of emigrants to Hong Kong—including their incredibly cramped living quarters, their menial jobs, and their limitless ambition.

—*Keep the Aspidistra Flying,* based on the novel by George Orwell and later retitled *A Merry War,* tells the story of Gordon Comstock, a young advertising man (Richard E. Grant) who quits his job in the midst of the Depression because he fondly imagines himself to be a writer. Supporting himself with a job in a used-book store, he quickly descends to poverty level and resents it bitterly—especially when that places limits on his love life with his girlfriend (Helena Bonham Carter, in a role miles away from *Wings of the Dove*).

Grant is an interesting choice for the lead. Angular and good at projecting unhappiness, he captures the essence of Orwell's sour hero more easily than an actor who might make him seem merely plucky and unfortunate. And there is no romance in his used-book trade: Gordon considers books to be his captors, not his inspiration, and seems almost to cringe inside his shiny suit and frayed shirt collars.

Tomorrow is Karaoke Night, for which I have been rehearsing "Young at Heart" every day in the shower.

* * *

*St. Kitts, West Indies*—"The American Dream was born in eastern Europe," argues the documentary *Hollywoodism: Jews, Movies and the American Dream*. The six greatest Hollywood studios were all founded and run by eastern European Jewish emigrants, who, according to the film, took assimilation as their goal and translated their experiences into American terms; the pogroms became Westerns, and anti-Semitic prejudice was displaced into films about treatment of blacks.

The film, which played aboard the Fifth Floating Film Festival, is a fascinating compilation of material, based on Neal Gabler's important book *An Empire of Their Own: How the Jews Invented Hollywood*. Refreshingly, it takes a strong point of view, and isn't just a tour through film clips. But it sees everything through the same lens, and overlooks facts that don't fit into its thesis.

The film is best in its portrait of the 1910s through the 1930s, when Jews such as Harry Cohn, Samuel Goldwyn, the Warner brothers, Louis B. Mayer, Adolph Zukor, Barney Balaban, and William Fox invented Hollywood by transforming the nickelodeons into the first great communications industry. Many of them, the film says, sought to lose their Jewish roots; they Americanized their names, took Gentile wives, even sent their children to Catholic schools. Their generation had been formed by the pogroms of Russia, where government hooligans swept down in fire and terror, and the film argues that the underlying thesis of the Western—a few good men standing up for civilization in the face of armed barbarians—is a retelling of that memory.

But Hollywood mogols rarely dealt with overtly Jewish themes. "Jews trying to pass as Gentiles made films about blacks trying to pass as whites," the film says, even enlisting blackface performers such as Al Jolson in this theory. In the years before World War II, there were only two anti-Nazi films from Hollywood, and the film tells us that ambassador Joseph Kennedy warned the mogols in a private meeting that Jews would be blamed for the coming war if they "stood out" by opposing Nazism.

The fact of that meeting is remarkable. But surely Hollywood's reluctance to attack Hitler had more to do with the Hitler-Stalin Pact and the reluctance of communists in the film industry to attack Russia's ally. After the war, the film says, six mogols were taken on a tour of the Nazi death camps, but none of them made films based on what they witnessed. Indeed, the only two postwar films about anti-Semitism (*Crossfire* and *Gentleman's Agreement*) were made by Gentiles, and the film says the mogols as a group offered $1 million to Daryl F. Zanuck, producer of *Gentleman's Agreement*, if he would destroy the film. (He refused, and had the incident written into the script.)

These stories fit into the film's thesis, that the rush to assimilation on the part of the mogols, fueled by self-hatred, helped form many of their decisions. But *Hollywoodism* is on shaky ground when it examines the postwar hearings into Hollywood communism by the House Un-American Activities Committee. In the *Hollywoodism* version, the mogols, by proclaiming their Americanism and throwing their left-wing employees to the dogs of HUAC, "helped anti-Semites rid Hollywood of Jewish intellectuals."

Then, "like the Wizard of Oz," the film tells us, "having been exposed as fearful refugees fleeing from themselves, they couldn't go on being mogols." Within a few years, the founding Hollywood giants were dead or deposed. This theory, while it fits neatly with the film's thesis, ignores three other factors in the fall of the mogols: Some of them had simply grown old, television had stolen Hollywood's monopoly on popular entertainment, and the Justice Department had made it illegal for the studios to own their own theaters—changing forever the pattern of movie distribution. In the face of these reasons, what the mogols said or didn't say to HUAC is relatively insignificant.

*Hollywoodism,* written and directed by Simcha Jacobovici, is most questionable in the sweeping assertions of its narration. Gabler himself, often seen on screen, makes much more sensible arguments, and so do the film's many other witnesses, including film critics J. Hoberman and Jonathan Rosenbaum, and many descendants of the original mogols.

Documentaries often fail to ignite the box office, but when people see them they are likely to get quite involved in them, and both *Hollywoodism* and *Off the Menu: The Last Days of Chasen's,* have been among the most-discussed films on the Floating filmfest. Both deal with the rise and fall of Hollywood generations, one from above, one from below: A splendid double feature.

Among other films screened in the last few days:

—*Bad Manners,* which also played at the Chicago Film Festival, is a sharp-edged, dark, witty drama involving an older academic couple (David Strathairn and Bonnie Bedelia) who are visited by younger houseguests (Saul Rubinek and Caroleen Feeney). The situation resembles *Who's Afraid of Virginia Woolf?* but a subplot involving the travels of a $50 bill owes more to David Mamet's fun with con games. Directed by Jonathan Kaufer, written by David Gilman.

—*Noose* tells the story of the lives and deaths of Irish-American hoods in a Boston suburb. Dennis Leary stars as a kid too smart for his milieu who comes up against a sadistic drug kingpin who has instituted a reign of terror. Directed by Ted Demme, written by Demme and Leary. (The title is in flux; the film was seen at Sundance as *Snitch.*)

—*Suicide Kings* stars Christopher Walken as a mob boss who is kidnapped by a group of rich kids who think he can use his power to get back one of the kid's sisters, who has earlier been kidnapped. The nature of Walken's dilemma occurs to him as he learns that the sister's little finger has been mailed in with a ransom demand, and that for every body part she loses, Walken loses one too. The screwball plot is harnessed to a dark vision. Directed by Peter O'Fallen.

* * *

*Ft. Lauderdale, Florida*—I have seen this year's *Full Monty,* and its name is *The Castle.* If this endearing human comedy from Australia doesn't turn into a sleeper hit, I'll be very surprised—because, like the box-office winner *The Full Monty,* it combines high humor with the kind of little-guy pluckiness that audiences applaud.

*The Castle,* which won the Jay Scott Award as the best of the eighteen entries in the fifth Floating Film Festival, tells the story of the Kerrigans, whose home is their castle, even though it's situated inches from the edge of an airfield where jumbo jets shatter the calm. When local authorities try to condemn their four little homes on Harvey Crescent, they spring into action, hiring a spectacularly incompetent lawyer and taking the case all the way to the Supreme Court.

Michael Caton stars as Dad, described by his son as a beloved all-around good guy who sees the upside of everything. Even the giant power pylons towering over their home "are a reminder of man's ability to generate electricity." Domestic life in chez Kerrigan is a beloved routine: "When we eat, the television is definitely turned down."

Dad Kerrigan hires a lawyer who protests he only handles "conveyances and small cases like that." "But you handled my son's burglary case," Dad protests. "Yes, and he's doing eight years." In a hilarious courtroom scene, the lawyer asks the judge for "an angle," and in his summation explains, "It's no one question, your honor; it's the vibe of the thing."

Directed by Rob Sitch, *The Castle* had an uproarious premiere on the Floating filmfest, which led to a "public screening" for the general public aboard the MS *Statendam.* This cross section of Middle America and Canada laughed, wept, and applauded their way through the film, and you could feel the electrifying populist energy of *The Castle* surging through the room: like *The Full Monty,* it's about little guys who stick it to the system.

The film, which cost only $300,000, is reportedly in the process of being acquired by Miramax, although a group of investors on the Floating filmfest, led by property tycoon John Daniels, worked the phones over the weekend trying to buy the rights themselves. Look for a summer opening and a crossover success.

The Jay Scott Award, decided by popular vote, is named in memory of the respected late film critic of the *Toronto Globe and Mail*. Second place in the balloting went to *Sliding Doors*, starring Gwyneth Paltrow, the story of a woman who experiences two possible fates. In third place was *Without Limits*, Robert Towne's biopic about runner Steven Prefontaine. A Critics' Prize was voted on by the professional film critics on board. First place was a tie between David Mamet's *The Spanish Prisoner*, with Steve Martin and Joe Mantegna caught in a con game, and *The Opposite of Sex*, starring Christina Ricci as a bayou big mouth who visits her gay half-brother in the North. Second prize from the critics went to *Forgotten Light*, a Czech film about a priest struggling under communist bureaucracy, and third place was *Comrades*, the Hong Kong film starring Maggie Cheung in the story of mainland Chinese who immigrate first to Hong Kong, then to America.

The film I voted for as the festival's best was *Bad Manners*, by Jonathan Kaufer, which on a second viewing seemed even more devious and intelligent than before. Telling the story of a game of sexual and professional one-upmanship when a professor and his younger lover visit an older academic couple, the movie centers on two possible frauds, one involving an elusive $50 bill, the other involving a few lines of medieval music found in the middle of a randomly generated computer program. Is this a message from God? Or a hoax?

The festival's closing film was *Under Heaven*, directed by Meg Richman, a close but uncredited retelling of Henry James's *Wings of the Dove*, updated to contemporary Seattle. Joely Richardson is quietly powerful as a rich girl dying from cancer, Molly Parker is a young woman hired as her companion, and Aden Young is Parker's boyfriend. They've never had enough money to make plans or to get an education, and when Parker see that Richardson is attracted to Young, she begs her lover, "Save me!" The interesting difference between this version and both the James novel and the recent Helena Bonham Carter film is that everyone's motives are explicitly acknowledged midway through the film. In James, they are only implied.

The Floating filmfest docked Sunday and floats again in 2000. And for the second festival in a row, the championship-level trivia contest was won by Bill and Thalia Zane of Chicago, whose son Billy's success in *Titanic* apparently did nothing to discourage them from boarding a cruise ship.

# Notes from the Cannes Film Festival

*It is the largest and most famous film festival in the world—in size and length, said to be second only to the Olympics as a global gathering. Cannes brings together some 45,000 people and some 500 films for nearly two weeks of screening, wheeling, and dealing. I filed a daily journal in May 1998, and here are some of the entries.*

* * *

Good news for Godzilla: The screen at the Cannes Film Festival is wider than your billboard. You won't feel cramped when your movie closes the festival on May 24. Neither will any of the other films.

The Auditorium Lumiere of the Palais at Cannes is arguably the best place in the world to see a movie, with the biggest screen, the best sound, and the most knowledgeable audience. And starting Wednesday, with the European premiere of Mike Nichols's *Primary Colors*, it will be home again to the most important event in the world of cinema.

For twelve days every spring, the festival showcases the best of the new films, while the marketplace surrounds them with the rest. Stars and great directors ascend the red carpet to the black-tie premieres of their movies, while in the back streets of Cannes deals are struck to sell exploitation films by the carload. The class and the crass coexist cheerfully here, as tourists descend on the Riviera for Europe's cross between the Oscars and Mardi Gras.

Most of the 45,000 people who visit Cannes stay a few days, showing their films or doing business. The critics are the true regulars, coming every year, staying the whole time, seeing four or five films a day. It gets to be an endurance run.

The first press screening is at 8:30 A.M., and it's always for one of the official entries. Miss this, and you never catch up for the rest of the day—which can end with dinners and parties far into the night, some of them even held after midnight screenings.

The audiences at Cannes hold strong opinions, and aren't shy about booing films they don't admire. And then there's the Thunk Index. Every time someone gets up out of their seat in the Lumiere, it thunks into an upright position. When a film is intensely disliked by a lot of people (as David Cronenberg's *Crash* was a few years ago), you hear first one thunk, then another, and then a whole lot at once; the timing is a little like when popcorn gets popping.

* * *

Gilles Jacob, the man who selects the films for the Cannes official competition, is not a booster. Unlike North American festival chiefs, who inevitably praise their latest discoveries, he has a certain French bluntness about his selections. At a press conference opening the fifty-first Cannes Film Festival, he announced that this was going to be a good year, that last year had been not so good, and that "every other year you seem to get a good selection."

What is refreshing is that Jacob did not wait until this year to dis last year's anniversary festival, but said the same thing a year ago. In appearance he is like a prosperous businessman, in a tailored grey suit. In manner, he is like a man brought in to soothe the warring parties: quiet, calm, even a little shy. In influence, he is a tiger, a man not afraid to stand up to studios and nations and say *oui* or *non* to their most cherished films.

It is said that Jacob viewed 1,074 films in choosing the two dozen in this year's official selection. I myself saw 400 films last year and called it a full-time job. No wonder he doesn't have a tan.

His program for the 1998 Cannes festival is being called the "fiftieth-anniversary festival a year late." Last year Jacob was unable to persuade Ingmar Bergman, the Swedish eminence, to journey south and stand on the stage with thirty other winners of the Palme d'Or. But this year he has a new Bergman film, more than a decade after the master announced his retirement.

And he has Martin Scorsese, considered the greatest living American director, as the chairman of his jury. Asked at the opening press conference what he was looking for in a Palme winner, Scorsese replied modestly, "A film that will change my life." Tell me about it.

* * *

The French kiss each other on the cheeks when meeting. Or near the cheeks. You reserve such kissing for friends. A friend is anyone you think you possibly recognize. You would, for example, air-kiss a person to whom you would not advance the price of a phone call.

This year there is an escalation in air-kissing behavior. Two kisses are not enough. Three are required. The third kiss is applied to the same cheek as the first one. There is a rule about which cheek you start with. I think each person begins by going to the left. But your left or their left? I am paralyzed by indecision, and the French spend a lot of time merrily kissing my nose.

* * *

The opening screening was the European premiere of Mike Nichols's *Primary Colors,* with Nichols, his wife Diane Sawyer, John Travolta, and Emma Thompson waving to the multitudes from atop the red-carpeted stairs. I did not attend; I avoid opportunities to put on a tuxedo in order to have a two-hour nap in public.

Jet lag, of course, means that the visiting North American critic is drowsy for a few days. Your body thinks it is either late yesterday or early tomorrow. If I were a distributor I would not let my film be shown on the weekend. Or I would screen it at 5:00 A.M., an hour when the body wickedly insists on providing a little window of alertness.

* * *

As usual, I awoke before dawn and made my ritual visit to the Café St. Antoine, across from the old yacht harbor, for café au lait while watching the sunrise above millions of dollars' worth of boats.

Then off to the 8:30 A.M. press screening of the first official entry, Patrice Chereau's *If You Love Me Take the Train,* from France, which was about a large number of people taking the train to the funeral of an irascible old painter who had, I think, committed suicide. The plot left doubts about that point. I lean toward the suicide theory, however; anyone with these relatives would find suicide an attractive option.

The highlights: A beautiful boy gets on the train and has sex with one of the men, who discovers the boy has been the lover of another relative, after which there is further confusion when the son of still another man turns up as his preop transsexual daughter. The father tries to pick him up in the train station, and slaps him when he realizes his error. Later, the son of the deceased delivers a bitter oration over his father's grave, observing that his father did not believe in children but had him inadvertently, and since life stinks, the son will honor his father's memory by having no children of his own. Still later, the dead man's brother, a bankrupt shoe manufacturer, spends an enchanting quarter-hour trying to fit the transsexual with a pair of red high heels.

Jet lag was intended for movies like this. An hour into the story, just as the station wagon carrying the coffin ran off the road and into a wheat field, I closed my eyes hopefully. But sleep would not come. Suggested blurb: "The film I could not sleep through."

* * *

Charity comes linked with a certain tackiness here at Cannes. For several years we've had the benefit auction for AmFAR, Elizabeth Taylor's worthy anti-AIDS foundation. One year Harvey Weinstein, head of Miramax, got into a big-cajones bidding battle with arms dealer Adnan Khashoggi over Naomi Campbell's navel ring, despite Ms. Campbell's protestation that it was not for sale. All for a good cause.

This year the National Women's Cancer Research Alliance is sponsoring a fund-raiser, chaired by Scorsese. Another worthy cause. But while AmFAR holds its events at a black-tie dinner at the famed restaurant Moulin des Mougins, this fund-raiser will take the form of a live telecast from a local brasserie on the QVC shopping network, which will donate half the proceeds from its sales of sunglasses, etc. We're in a downward spiral here. How many years until Jerry Springer hosts a charity chair-toss between Weinstein and Khashoggi?

* * *

It rained late in the day Saturday, but that didn't slow down a battle of the bands at the fifty-first Cannes Film Festival. A parade of saxophonists in black suits and dark glasses played to promote *Blues Brothers 2000,* which arrived here fresh from its failure in America; Dan Aykroyd and John Goodman were present for the premiere, and performed at the Casino party afterward with B. B. King. Meanwhile, an Algerian group played a free concert of desert rock on a big outdoor stage in the shadow of the Palais des Festivals, where a tent offered free screenings of new Algerian films.

Well, of course there is an Algerian tent. When John Ringling North declared "the tented circus is a thing of the past," he couldn't have had Cannes in mind. When I first started coming here, everything was held inside permanent structures. Then the British put up a tent by the beach and called it their Pavilion. You could get a cup of tea between screenings. Very nice. Soon came the American Pavilion, the Kodak Pavilion, the *Variety* Pavilion, and the MIF Pavilion (purpose still to be discovered), until now from a yacht in the bay the shoreline looks like a nomad city, huddled in the shadow of the Majestic Hotel.

I have a friend who refuses to eat fast food away from home, on the grounds that he has not traveled halfway around the world to monitor the consistency of McDonald's quality control. The pavilions would test his policy. They're for the homesick, I guess, and so the American Pavilion not only sponsored a satellite telecast of *Seinfeld*'s last show, but even has a booth where you can get a cup of American coffee (since, as everyone knows, the French simply don't know how to make a cup of coffee).

* * *

I have fallen into the rhythms of the daily screenings, and am up for the 8:30 press preview every morning. In the afternoon it's down the beach to the Noga Hilton (universally called the Naugahyde Hilton), where a vast cavern in the basement hosts the Director's Fortnight.

So far the festival has two qualified hits, Claude Miller's *The Class Trip* and Ken Loach's *My Name is Joe,* and one generally agreed-upon bomb, Terry Gilliam's *Fear and Loathing in Las Vegas,* with Johnny Depp. The latter stars Depp as Dr. Hunter S. Thompson, dean of gonzo journalism, who is joined by his Samoan attorney (Benecio Del Toro) on a drugged expedition to Vegas to cover a motorcycle race and a district attorney's convention. The problem with a hero who is constantly stoned is that he only has one note and two velocities (speeding and crashing). The movie helps explain why it is much more entertaining to hear a guy tell you what he did when he was drunk than to watch him doing it.

* * *

*The Class Trip* sees through the eyes of a timid eleven-year-old whose protective, menacing father insists on driving him to the ski lodge where his class will have a session away from home. The boy is deeply disturbed, and we gradually learn the reasons why, but the strength of the film is in the way the kid uses his imagination to create a fantasy world that helps him deal with the real one—and then describes his fantasies so colorfully that the class bully becomes his friend.

* * *

The most talked-about film so far, from the Director's Fortnight, is *Happiness,* by Todd Solondz, whose *Welcome to the Dollhouse* was a tough, bittersweet comedy about an unpopular girl's sexual semiawakening. This new film, set in New Jersey, is about an series of glum, stupid, and often perverted losers who are locked in loneliness and solitary pleasures. The characters include a therapist with sick tastes, a dirty phone call artist, the obligatory unpopular woman, and her popular sister, who is just as miserable. Some of the scenes (including a breakup in a restaurant) are very funny. Others are so disturbing I am not sure they can be justified. This movie is going to require a lot of thought.

* * *

Ken Loach is the gifted British director of working-class dramas and comedies *(Raining Stones, Ladybird, Ladybird, Riff Raff).* His new film, *My Name is Joe,* set in Scotland, stars a newcomer named Peter Mullan, who looks a little like Paul Newman and plays a recovering alcoholic who falls in love with a social worker and then tries to bail out a friend in trouble with drug dealers. The plot, for a Loach film, develops into a somewhat conventional crime story, although the details of the romance are touching and true.

Loach is known for his practice of filming in British accents so impenetrable that the audience is usually at sea. I'm usually able to understand most of what's said, but this time I had to rely on the French subtitles. Since there is nothing in this particular story that *requires* the characters to be incomprehensible to 98 percent of the world's English speakers, I can only attribute the accents to admirable artistic stubbornness.

* * *

I've also seen *Lulu on the Bridge,* the new film directed by writer Paul Auster, with Harvey Keitel as a saxophonist whose career is ended by a madman, but who finds a mysterious blue stone that levitates and fills him with contentment. The stone comes connected with the phone number of a young woman (Mira Sorvino), and they fall in love under the influence of its ethereal glow, which is as good an explanation as any for the surge of stories in which girls in their twenties fall in love with guys old enough to be, well, aging movie stars.

* * *

There was also *The Hole,* the official entry from Taiwan, about a virus that strikes on the eve of the year 2000. In the midst of general evacuation and a rainstorm so noisy that the English translation couldn't be heard over the festival earphones, an alcoholic merchant has a hole pounded through his floor by a plumber repairing a pipe. Later that night the merchant vomits through the hole into the apartment of the young woman who lives below him. This suggested the possibility of even more alarming bombing runs; I slipped out of the theater, preferring to wait for the Disney remake.

## Discovering Benigni's *Life Is Beautiful*

The festival has its biggest hit and controversy, both rolled into one. Roberto Benigni's *Life Is Beautiful* inspired a ten-minute standing ovation on Sunday night, with cries of "bravo!" rolling likes waves across the Auditorium Lumiere. Monday's editions of *Figaro,* the Paris daily, declared it the "sure winner" of the Palme d'Or. But its star and director, Italy's best-known comic actor, was accused at his press conference of making light of the Holocaust.

Benigni plays a goofy Jewish optimist who, in the first hour of the film, woos and wins the woman of his dreams and outsmarts the fascist leaders of his small Italian town with his wit and good nature. In the film's second hour, the man and his small son are sent to a concentration camp, and his Gentile wife insists on going along with them.

In the camp, the father, whose only gifts are as a clown, tries to shield his little boy from the horror of their situation by turning it into a game. The child is promised he will get a real tank if he amasses 1,000 points, and is awarded points for such "tricks" as remaining hidden from the camp guards—who have sent the other children to the gas chambers.

At the screening I attended, the audience reaction was emotional and positive; many film professionals were reduced to tears. The film is already an enormous hit in Italy, and has been picked up for American distribution by Miramax—whose president, Harvey Weinstein, vows it will be nominated for an Oscar as one of the year's best films. Although few subtitled foreign films make it into the top five, recall that it was Miramax's *Il Postino,* another Italian film with a strong emotional appeal, that last did the trick.

At lunch the day after their film's premiere, Benigni and his wife, Nicoletta Braschi, who plays the wife in the movie, talked about how the idea for this film has been forming in their minds for more than ten years. Benigni is a physical comedian of the Red Skelton and Jim Carrey school, whose films and TV shows have made him one of Italy's top stars (he was in the Jim Jarmusch movie *Down by Law*). Inspired by Chaplin's anti-Hitler comedy *The Great Dictator,* he began to think about a clown who used the tools of his trade as his only possible weapon against the horror of the camps. Benigni, who is not Jewish, was inspired in part by his own father, who spent the war imprisoned in a fascist work camp (for the crime of being in the wrong army unit).

"I fell in love with the idea of a clown in an extreme situation," he said, "and when you are in love, you are vulnerable. Of course I was afraid." He showed his script to Jewish friends, who urged him to go ahead with it, observing that the film's hero sees nothing funny about the concentration camps, but only pretends to, as a means of shielding his child.

At the press conference, a French journalist accused Benigni of taking too light an approach to the Holocaust. The conference moderator tried to reject the question, but in a dramatic moment Benigni insisted on answering it, in quiet French that was a contrast to his excited Italian, and said he was glad the question had been asked, "because there is a risk that some people will see the film this way, and I must answer them."

Then he quoted a poet who said, "After the Holocaust, no poetry is possible"—and observed that the statement itself was poetic. "No one can take from another man his belief that life is beautiful, right up to the final moment," he said.

No other film I've seen here is likely to find a warmer reception with North American audiences. Those who are offended by it are tone-deaf, I think, to its heart and nuance.

* * *

There is a wonderful Canadian film playing in the Director's Fortnight that acts as a quiet rebuke to the overwrought end-of-the-world dramas like *Deep Impact.* While Hollywood uses special effects to turn final disaster into a gimmick, Don McKellar's *Last Night* illustrates a deeper, more affecting approach.

In his film, it is 6:00 P.M. and the world is going to end at midnight for reasons that the film wisely never explains. A Toronto radio station advertises "The Top 500 songs on the planet—we're with you till the end!"

The story intercuts a small group of characters who deal with certain death in their own ways. One has a checklist of sexual experiences he hasn't yet had. A family has an early Christmas dinner. A young man wants to spend the last hours all by himself. A woman is stranded on the wrong side of town and can't get home to her husband. In a public park, thousands have gathered for a New Years' Eve–type party. Prayer groups meet in other parks.

McKellar's writing is the key to the movie's effectiveness (he wrote the acclaimed *Thirty-Two Short Films About Glenn Gould*). He suggests the depths of his characters with a few words, as when an old lady tells her friend, "I've heard enough about the young. I've invested eighty years in this life. They don't even begin to know what they're missing."

A film like *Last Night* is an adult film, for intelligent audiences; it doesn't deal in the shallow conventions of *Deep Impact,* where relationships are seen in easy soap-opera terms. There's a real poignancy in the way these people count down their final hours, and we realize how the standard disaster movie formula simply can't approach such truths.

## Living above the Planet

Howls and screams are welling up from beneath my hotel window. Bruce Willis was scheduled to arrive at Planet Hollywood late tonight, after a screening of preview footage from his new movie *Armageddon,* and it must be him. As a major stockholder in the restaurant chain, no doubt he wants to make sure the waiters aren't gravy-stained.

Faithful readers will know that for years while attending the Cannes Film Festival, I have stayed at the peaceful and serene Hotel Splendid. Last year, alas, the little cafeteria built into the hotel's waterfront side was replaced by the new Cannes branch of Planet Hollywood.

On party nights, the thud of the sound system shakes the walls of my room. New this year: The Planet has constructed an open-air stage in front of the restaurant, with bleachers that look directly into my window. Now I know how the Cubs feel about the bleachers across the street from Wrigley Field. I pay for the room, and the Planet customers get to watch my TV for free.

The Planet was kind enough to send me an "Official Press Card" with a forgery-proof 3-D holograph on it. When I presented this valuable card earlier tonight in an attempt to get at some brownies à la mode, I was informed by the gorillas at the door that it is useful only during hours when the restaurant is open to the public. I am forced to the conclusion that the only difference between an Official Press Card holder and a member of the public is that the cardholder gets to look like a doofus as he waves his card.

Some readers were so cynical that they doubted I was positioned directly above the Planet's powerful woofers and tweeters. I have two photos on file with my editors as evidence. One shows the letters "HS," which are on the awning outside my room. The other shows the view of the bleachers from my window.

Of course I am not without sympathy for the restaurant's point of view. Very loud music is crucial to the success of Planet Hollywood, which thrives by attracting people who have nothing at all they want to talk about with their dinner companions. It's a godsend for dining out with former spouses, sullen teenagers, and the stars of *Attack of the Rabid Grannies.*

## Moulin I: A Night with Depardieu

Most movie stars at Cannes make a fetish of invisibility. They're whisked about in official limos with curtained windows, and move behind a human wall of publicists.

But not the beloved Gérard Depardieu. France's biggest movie star is also the friendliest, plunging into the festival like a teenager thrilled to have a free ticket. The other night during an exclusive dinner at Moulin des Mougins, the most famous restaurant on the Riviera, I watched him operate.

He was attending an event sponsored by Bravo and the Independent Film Channel, which had flown about seventy-five American cable operators to Cannes for a look at the festival. He was thrilled to be there, he said, in order to announce his new film on Balzac, which was being financed by members of the group.

These members had not quite decided in their own minds to finance his film, but they *had* decided in Depardieu's mind, and he seized the microphone from Kathy Dore, president of Bravo/IFC, and thanked them profusely for their wisdom. "The world, it loves American films!" he cried, implying that the world would love them even more if they were all about Balzac.

Then he plunged into the crowd like an alderman. "What a beautiful necklace!" he told my wife, Chaz, plucking it from her décolletage like a boy who has found the plum in his pudding. He caressed her hair. "Marvelous!" I am translating from the French. He whispered softly and rapidly into her ear, and Chaz, who has just completed four weeks at Berlitz, looked like a woman who felt that her lessons had been an excellent investment.

"You are lucky, lucky man," he told me sorrowfully, before continuing his tour. "What a great beauty!" he told the wife of a cable operator from Atlanta. "Are you a model?" he asked a jolly lady from Omaha. Little sighs and cries of joy wafted back to us as he receded into the crowd, and a woman emerged from the crush to tell us, "His eyes ran up and down my body, and I could see him trying to decide what to say without repeating himself."

Photographers appeared, to take Depardieu's picture with the visitors. He gazed upon every wife with moonstruck eyes. Chef Roger Verge, whose cuisine is world famous, circulated among us, his little white mustache bristling with joy as he cooed that the dinner, she was ready. A shriek went up in the vicinity of the photographer, and soon a scout from that part of the room arrived in ours: "Now Depardieu is tongue-kissing them!"

"For the camera?"

"Not entirely."

That was on Sunday night. Today I read in the *International Herald-Tribune* that Depardieu had a motorcycle accident on Monday, near Paris, when his bike skidded on wet roads. He fractured his hip, and had to be taken to the hospital. If the medic was a woman, I picture him rising from his stretcher to caress her stethoscope.

## Observations on Lolitas

Lolitafest, they could call it, on the basis of three controversial films about child sexual abuse that are playing at this year's Cannes Film Festival. Two of them are more extreme than the much-debated *Lolita.*

*The Class Trip,* an official selection directed by Belgium's Claude Miller, is seen through the eyes of a young boy whose father drops him off at a ski lodge for a class ski holiday, and then goes on to kidnap and murder another small boy. The young hero, who has been abused by his father and half-suspects him of being capable of murder, survives by displacing his fears into fantasies, and building an active dream life.

The Miller film has gathered mostly respectful reviews. But *Happiness,* by Todd Solondz, and *Babyface,* by Canada's Jack Blum, have sharply divided audiences.

*Babyface* tells the story of an alcoholic, promiscuous mother in her thirties; her weak-willed boyfriend, who is in his early twenties; and her thirteen-year-old daughter, who in the movie's opening scene is suggesting to the school bus driver that they spend some quiet time together.

By the end of the film, the boyfriend and the young girl will be sharing an active sex life, and the mother will be floating down the river inside a deep freeze. The film is a no doubt accurate portrait of adult irresponsibility and a troubled, sexually precocious child, and can be defended for its sociological insights. But there were a lot of walkouts at its first screening in the Directors' Fortnight, and some felt the line between comment and exploitation had been crossed.

*Happiness,* which I've written about before, is one of the most challenging films in the festival. Written and directed by Solondz, whose *Welcome to the Dollhouse* was a brilliant portrait of an unpopular junior high school girl, this one includes a chilling portrait of a father who drugs and rapes his son's young friend.

All week I've found myself in discussions about *Happiness* and *The Class Trip,* and the arrival of *Babyface* has brought the topic to a boil. Does it go too far? Does it have "socially redeeming value"? Will some people see it for the wrong reasons? Is it the filmmakers' fault if they do? I think there may be a continuum here between artistic insight and social irresponsibility, with *The Class Trip* on the high end and *Babyface,* despite its undeniable sociological accuracy, shading toward exploitation.

* * *

My candidate for the festival's Best Actor Award: Brendan Gleeson, star of John Boorman's *The General,* the life story of Dublin master criminal Martin Cahill, who was assassinated by the IRA in 1994 after trying to sell some stolen paintings to Protestant provisionals.

Cahill pulled off fancy capers, including Ireland's biggest jewelry and art thefts, and was a figure of great fame, especially after the police started following him everywhere he went. But *The General* is not a caper or crime thriller in any conventional way; it's a character study of a man who forthrightly describes himself as a criminal, and tries to do his job the best he can, like any hardworking man. Gleeson brings a certain gentle lovability to the character—yes, even in the scene where he nails a colleague to a snooker table.

* * *

I looked up and there was Jerry Berliant. In a strange way it was a pleasure to see him. Berliant is Chicago's famed gate-crasher, who has been an uninvited guest at prize fights, political conventions, and the Oscars, and here he was inside the American Pavilion of the Cannes Film Festival—which is sort of impressive, considering the gorillas at the door who minutely examine everyone's photo credentials.

But Berliant is the Houdini of gate-crashers. I remember one year when Gene Siskel and I were presenting some awards at the NATPE syndicated television convention. Tickets and credentials were required at the door. But we were taken backstage, where security was even tighter, because big stars were set to be on the show. After a publicist passed us through two guarded doors, we were delivered safely to the Green Room—where, there to greet us, was Jerry Berliant, who had appointed himself bartender.

## Moulin II: Raising Money with Sharon

There are no taxis to be had in the whole of Cannes. The hotel clerk, she throws up her hands in despair. One cannot walk all the way to the Moulin de Mougins, which is in the hills above town. Violà! Here is ze taxi! But it is ordered for Catherine Verret of the French Film Office. She however is also going to the Moulin, although first she must stop at the Martinez Hotel to see if Jeanne Moreau, the great film star, has found a ride.

We pile into the backseat and race off to the Martinez, where a human sea of movie fans surges against the barricades, and police direct the taxis at their toes, a traditional French crowd-control device. Madame Moreau, she has already departed. We set off down the winding back streets. All of Cannes is on the move, up the hill to the famous AmFAR charity auction, dinner, and celebrity mob scene.

There is serious money at this event. The dinner tickets alone have raised $500,000. To be sure, the dinner is worth such a fortune. It is by Chef Roger Verge, whose forced zucchinis are admired wherever zucchinis are violated, and whose pea soup is so splendid that if it needs a little salt you simply weep into it with gratitude.

We begin in a huge tent in the garden of the Moulin. Bleachers have been erected for the TV cameras. Sharon Stone, Winona Ryder, Sigourney Weaver, and Lena Olin pose for the cameras. So do Elton John, Jeanne Moreau, Hugh Grant, Elizabeth Hurley, Rupert Everett, and Chiara Mastroianni, whose parents are Marcello Mastroianni and Catherine Deneuve, which if she were a horse would make her the Derby favorite.

Here is Ringo Starr with his wife Barbara Bach. "We live down the road in Monte Carlo," he mentions. Here is Pat Riley, who concedes that he would rather be coaching the Miami Heat in the NBA playoffs, and explains that the plot of the Jerrys to alienate the Chicago Bulls is brilliant: "If everything was peaceful, the team might lose its edge. So the management insults them, and the team pulls together into a bunker mentality. Inspired!"

A band is playing. Sharon Stone mounts the podium and introduces the auctioneer from Christie's, who is going to raise huge sums of money for AIDS research. His strategy is to tell first one side of the room and then the other side of the room that they are not rich enough to bid against the big boys. Everybody here is a big boy. Soon we (by "we" I mean "they") are bidding for solid gold amulets, a necklace "encrusted with emeralds, rubies, sapphires, and diamonds," and a tennis lesson with Marcelo Rios.

My wife and I examine the offerings in the silent auction, which are a little cheaper, ranging from a haircut by Jose Eber to a nude photograph by Francesco Seavullo of Burt Reynolds crouching on a bear rug ("value $3,500"). We bid on the thirteen-day luxury holiday in Thailand, which we agree will really give us greater pleasure over the years than the Reynolds photograph.

I drift to the rear of the tent, where Kieran Culkin and Elden Hanson are studiously pretending not to be seriously interested in Chiara Mastroianni, who looks like she could take the boy and give you back the man. Kieran and Elden are the two teenage stars of *The Mighty*, the film we have all just seen. Sharon Stone plays Kieran's mother. No jokes, please, about how after you make *Basic Instinct* you qualify to be a Culkin parent.

The kids are really nice. The movie is more than nice: Based on the enormously popular children's book *Freak the Mighty*, it is about a kid who is big and dumb, and another kid who is small and twisted but bright, and how through teamwork they deal with the world. We are discussing the movie when a shout goes up: Ringo Starr's drumsticks have just been auctioned off for $100,000.

Sharon Stone announces that Ringo and Sir Elton will play a duet. Everyone crowds around the stage. "Let's play 'Twist and Shout'," says Sir Elton. "Why not one of your songs?" asks Ringo. "They might have heard of it." They play "Twist and Shout." Sharon Stone dances seductively in front of the piano. Harvey Weinstein, the president of Miramax, which cosponsors the AmFAR auction, sings along. The only lyrics he knows are when you go "Ah . . . ah . . . ah . . . AH!!!" He might be able to raise another $100,000 just by stopping. Stone announces $1.1 million was raised in the auction.

We go in to dinner. We are seated next to a window overlooking the garden. I recall thrillers in which men in ski masks burst into gatherings of rich people in tuxedos, and steal their emerald-, ruby-, sapphire-, and diamond-encrusted necklaces. Sometimes they take them all hostage. I can imagine the movie: "Moulin! They fought for the zucchini—and their lives!" In the garden, I see gendarmes and plainclothesmen lurking in the shrubbery with rifles and cell phones. Next to them are rich people, lurking in the shrubbery with cigarettes and cell phones. In France you do not have to go outside to smoke, but to call. This confuses the Americans, who are always answering their cigarettes.

We are given pea soup, stuffed zucchini, lamb chops, and a towering dessert that looks inspired by a World's Fair pavilion (the Profiterole of the Future). Harvey Weinstein comes to our table, which is where all the journalists are sitting, and subtly pumps us for information. We agree that the official competition is so weak that a better time can be had by staying in the hotel room and watching television.

How bad? We play a game, quoting the worst lines from this year's movies. Janet Maslin of the *New York Times* wins, with this line from the Russian film: "But—your mattress stinks of sausage!"

My losing entry is from *Meet the Deedles,* a film starring Dennis Hopper as a man who trains prairie dogs to tunnel under Old Faithful in order to steal the geyser. He explains how he gets the rodents to do it: "Inject the soil with liquid kibble, and a-tunneling they will go!" I am disqualified because *Meet the Deedles* is not an official entry, although if it were, it might have a chance of winning something. If not the Palme d'Or, then maybe a photograph of Burt Reynolds.

## Two Winners, Two Styles

No films could be more different than the two top prize winners in this year's Cannes Film Festival. And no directors could have accepted the awards more differently—one with joy, the other almost defiantly.

The Palme d'Or for Best Film went to *Eternity and a Day,* by Theo Angelopoulos, of Greece. Climbing morosely to the stage, he said, "If I had not won, I would have made the same speech." Everyone in the Palais knew what he was referring to; how, three years ago, when his *Ulysses' Gaze* was passed over for the Palme and given the Grand Jury Prize instead, he spat into the microphone: "I have prepared a speech—but not for this prize!"

This year, the Grand Jury Prize, which is essentially second place, went to *Life Is Beautiful,* by the Italian comic actor Roberto Benigni. And *his* acceptance had the entire theater rolling with hilarity, and the jury laughing and crying at the same time.

Benigni, a thin, hyperactive clown with an unruly head of hair, used all of his gifts to show how happy he was. He threw his arms in the air. He crossed them over his chest. He blew kisses to the balcony. He kissed the feet of Martin Scorsese, the president of the jury. He embraced all the members of the jury—and for good measure all the members of the short film jury, who were also on the stage. He pretended he thought he had won the Palme d'Or. He got a standing ovation.

And then came the award for Angelopoulos, which played more like an anticlimax. It was as if Benigni had demonstrated the correct way to win second prize.

But it is not that simple, because Angelopoulos and Benigni are not, after all, the same person. And the differences in their personalities are reflected in the contrasting natures of their films.

*Eternity and a Day* tells the story of a man who expects to check into a hospital tomorrow, and probably will die there. It stars Bruno Ganz (of Wenders's *Wings of Desire*) as a great Greek writer who has abandoned his hopes of writing an epic poem, and now faces the possibility that in working so hard on his art, he missed his own life.

And then something happens to keep him from leaving life too easily. In a masterful single shot, Angelopoulos shows "red-light boys"—poor kids with squeegees who clear windshields at traffic signals—racing out to wash some windows. Then the hero's car enters from the right, and drives a block to another light. It stops, and another gang of boys come to wash his windshield. Behind him, as the camera rises up, we see several boys from the previous light running down the street, chased by police. The hero opens the door of his car and gestures for a boy to get in. They drive off, and he has saved the boy from arrest.

This boy turns out to be a homeless refugee from Albania. The dying poet and the boy will cross paths during the day, until finally the demands of the boy's life take precedence over those of the poet's death. There is a lot more, but that is the heart of the film, which is muffled in darkness, rain, and fog.

Now consider *Life Is Beautiful,* which was written and directed by Benigni, and stars him as an Italian Jew who, in the 1930s, woos and wins the woman of his dreams. Gradually, almost as a surreal intrusion into normal life, the horror of World War II slips into a story that began as a romantic comedy. Anti-Semitic laws are passed; Jewish stores are closed. Finally the father and his son are herded into a train for the concentration camps, and the wife, who is a Gentile, insists on coming along with them.

In the camps, the father, whose only gifts are as a clown, uses humor and fantasy to try to shield his little boy from the horror of the Holocaust. He invents a game: For 1,000 points, the kid will win an army tank. The game includes hiding from the guards, and the kid plays so well that he becomes the only surviving child in the camp.

Both films, then, are about similar themes: Adult men using their art and experience to protect little boys from a world that wants to kill them because of their ethnic identity. But the Benigni uses laughter and satire, and the Angelopoulos uses existential defiance; it tries to cut a deal with despair.

Thinking of the films, I understand completely why the two men accepted their awards in such different ways. Angelopoulos, like his hero, is weighted down with his art and his mortality. Benigni, like his hero, whistles defiantly into the face of catastrophe. For one, horror confirms the tragic human condition. For the other, it exists to be defied. Both films are true to the natures of the men who made them.

## The 1998 Cannes Winners

*Eternity and a Day,* a Greek film by Theo Angelopoulos, won the Palme d'Or here Sunday night at the fifty-first Cannes International Film Festival. The film stars Bruno Ganz as a writer who plans to check into a hospital, probably for the last time, on the next day—but finds that even as he prepares to leave his life, it reaches out and embraces him.

The Grand Prize of the Jury, which is essentially second place, went to Roberto Benigni of Italy, who wrote, directed, and starred in *Life Is Beautiful,* a film in which a man uses his powers of comic invention to try to shield his young son from the horrors of the Holocaust. The award was wildly popular; the audience cheered as Benigni, a popular figure, embraced jury president Martin Scorsese, kissed the other members of the jury, and gave himself over to ecstasy.

His joy held a message for festivalgoers with memories, because two years ago Angelopoulos won the Jury Prize, and sourly said, "I came prepared with a speech for the Palme d'Or, but not for this." Benigni's joy in the second prize upstaged, in a way, Angelopoulos's victory.

"We have decided to give a lot of prizes," Scorsese told actress Isabelle Huppert, the mistress of ceremonies. The winners included two ties, one for Best Actress, which was shared by Elodie Bouchez and Natacha Regnier, costars of *The Dream Life of Angels,* a French film about an unlikely friendship between a drifter and a troubled woman her own age.

The Best Actor Award went to Peter Mullan, star of Ken Loach's *My Name is Joe,* the story of a recovering alcoholic from Glasgow and his romance with a social worker.

A Jury Prize tie was declared between two other films, Claude Miller's *The Class Trip* (France), about a troubled young boy, and Thomas Vinterberg's *Festival* (Denmark), about a family reunion.

The Camera d'Or, for Best First Film, went to Mark Levin's *Slam,* a slice of life from the District of Columbia jail, which also won the Sundance Film Festival in January.

This year's Best Director Award was given to John Boorman, for *The General,* which starred Brendan Gleeson in a remarkable performance as Martin Cahill, a legendary Dublin thief shot dead by the IRA in 1994. American independent director Hal Hartley won for Best Screenplay, for his *Henry Fool,* about a hapless man who finds direction through poetry.

The jury honored Todd Haynes's *Velvet Goldmine,* about the mystery of a David Bowie-esque glitter rock star, for Best Artistic Contribution. And cinematographer Vittorio Storaro won the Grand Technical Prize for his work on Carlos Saura's *Tango.*

There is also a Critics' Prize at Cannes, voted on by members of the international film critics federation. Of the films in the official competition, the critics selected *The Hole,* by Taiwan's Tsai Ming-liang, about two neighbors who coexist in a time of plague and death. And as the best film shown in any category at the festival, the critics selected Todd Solondz's *Happiness,* a widely admired but much-debated film about a group of lonely inverts who seek happiness in strange ways.

Scorsese's jury included four actresses (Chiara Mastroianni, Lena Olin, Winona Ryder, and Sigourney Weaver), a Cuban writer (Zoe Valdes), a French rap artist (MC Solaar), and three other directors (China's Chen Kaige, Britain's Michael Winterbottom, and France's Alain Corneau).

* * *

*The festival closed with the European premiere of* Godzilla; *my review is in the main body of the book, along with the observation:*

*"Going to see* Godzilla *at the Palais of the Cannes Film Festival is like attending a satanic ritual in St. Peter's Basilica. It's a rebuke to the faith that the building represents."*

# American Film Institute's Top 100 Films

Orson Welles's *Citizen Kane* held off challenges from more famous, more recent, and more popular films, and placed first in the American Film Institute's blue-ribbon balloting for the title of Greatest American Film.

The other titles on the top ten, in order, were *Casablanca, The Godfather, Gone With the Wind, Lawrence of Arabia, The Wizard of Oz, The Graduate, On the Waterfront, Schindler's List,* and *Singin' in the Rain.*

The AFI's winners were revealed on a CBS-TV special. How were they selected? The institute compiled a list of 400 "finalists," including every film that ever won the Oscar for Best Picture, and then asked a group of directors, producers, screenwriters, actors, critics, and prominent citizens to vote on them. Those polled included President Clinton and Vice President Gore, both movie fans, although the AFI did not confirm that they had actually voted.

For *Citizen Kane,* the victory represents an upset. Although Orson Welles's 1941 masterpiece is routinely named the "best film of all time" in polls of film industry professionals, the general public is not nearly as familiar with *Kane* as with such titles as *It's a Wonderful Life* (eleventh place in the voting), *Star Wars* (fifteenth), *2001: A Space Odyssey* (twenty-second), *E.T.* (twenty-fifth), or *Snow White and the Seven Dwarfs* (forty-ninth).

One reason *Citizen Kane* is such a favorite of cineastes is that it represents a triumph of the individual filmmaker over the studio system. Welles was a golden boy of twenty-five, a star of radio and the stage, when he was summoned west to make the film and given an unprecedented "final cut" by RKO Radio Pictures. When he saw the studio lot, he's said to have exclaimed, "It's the best train set a boy could have."

The movie stars Welles in the life story of Charles Foster Kane, a media magnate who builds an empire of newspapers, magazines, radio networks, movie studios, and wire services. The screenplay, widely thought to be inspired by the life of publisher William Randolph Hearst, was written by Welles and Herman Mankiewicz, a confidant of Hearst's mistress, the actress Marion Davies.

Kane's story is told in a series of interlocking flashbacks, as those who knew him share their memories with a newsreel reporter. The film centers around the mystery of Kane's dying word, "Rosebud." Rumor had it that Mankiewicz was making a wicked in-joke, since "rosebud" was said to be Hearst's nickname for Davies. Louella Parsons, Hearst's famous gossip columnist, led an outraged campaign against the film, and all mention of it was forbidden in Hearst papers. Fearing his wrath, the major theater chains did not book the film, and although it was nominated for an Oscar as Best Picture (and won for Best Screenplay) it played mostly in independently owned houses.

Although *Citizen Kane* is beloved within the film community, it was not expected to win the AFI title. Indeed, when the AFI's Website asked the public to predict the winners, *Kane* placed third behind *Casablanca* and *Gone With the Wind,* and just ahead of *The Godfather* and *Star Wars.* I voted for *Kane,* but would have put my money on *GWTW.*

Admirers of Welles are no doubt pleased, and relieved, that *Citizen Kane* has won yet another poll. Yet the actual significance of the AFI title is clouded by three factors: (1) The finalists were limited to American films; (2) they were selected by a murky formula involving "critical recognition, major award winners, popularity over time, historical significance, and cultural impact"; and (3) the voters were chosen somewhat arbitrarily.

The primary purpose of the AFI event was to fuel the TV special, which raised funds for the institute. One positive spin-off is that Blockbuster Video, a cosponsor of the project, will feature most of the finalists in its stores, making classic videos more widely available. Other video stores will probably follow suit.

The most authoritative poll of great films is the one taken every ten years by *Sight and Sound,* the magazine of the British Film Institute. That is a global poll of directors, producers, other film professionals, critics, festival heads, and film archivists. In 1952, the first time it was conducted, Charlie Chaplin's *City Lights* placed first. Every ten years since then, *Citizen Kane* has been the clear winner.

In 1992, when the critics and directors were split into separate polls, *Kane* won both. It was, indeed, the only one of the top ten AFI titles even mentioned by the critics; the directors did include *The Godfather*. (The highest-ranking American films were Hitchcock's *Vertigo*, which placed fourth on the critics list and sixty-first on the AFI list, and Scorsese's *Raging Bull*, which tied for second with the directors, and was twenty-fourth on the AFI list.)

* * *

Here is the complete list of the AFI's top 100 American films:

1. *Citizen Kane*, 1941
2. *Casablanca*, 1942
3. *The Godfather*, 1972
4. *Gone With the Wind*, 1939
5. *Lawrence of Arabia*, 1962
6. *The Wizard of Oz*, 1939
7. *The Graduate*, 1967
8. *On the Waterfront*, 1954
9. *Schindler's List*, 1993
10. *Singin' in the Rain*, 1952
11. *It's a Wonderful Life*, 1946
12. *Sunset Boulevard*, 1950
13. *The Bridge on the River Kwai*, 1957
14. *Some Like It Hot*, 1959
15. *Star Wars*, 1977
16. *All About Eve*, 1950
17. *The African Queen*, 1951
18. *Psycho*, 1960
19. *Chinatown*, 1974
20. *One Flew Over the Cuckoo's Nest*, 1975
21. *The Grapes of Wrath*, 1940
22. *2001: A Space Odyssey*, 1968
23. *The Maltese Falcon*, 1941
24. *Raging Bull*, 1980
25. *E.T.—The Extra-Terrestrial*, 1982
26. *Dr. Strangelove*, 1964
27. *Bonnie and Clyde*, 1967
28. *Apocalypse Now*, 1979
29. *Mr. Smith Goes to Washington*, 1939
30. *The Treasure of the Sierra Madre*, 1948
31. *Annie Hall*, 1977
32. *The Godfather, Part II*, 1974
33. *High Noon*, 1952
34. *To Kill a Mockingbird*, 1962
35. *It Happened One Night*, 1934
36. *Midnight Cowboy*, 1969
37. *The Best Years of Our Lives*, 1946
38. *Double Indemnity*, 1944
39. *Doctor Zhivago*, 1965
40. *North by Northwest*, 1959
41. *West Side Story*, 1961
42. *Rear Window*, 1954
43. *King Kong*, 1933
44. *The Birth of a Nation*, 1915
45. *A Streetcar Named Desire*, 1951
46. *A Clockwork Orange*, 1971
47. *Taxi Driver*, 1976
48. *Jaws*, 1975
49. *Snow White and the Seven Dwarfs*, 1937
50. *Butch Cassidy and the Sundance Kid*, 1969
51. *The Philadelphia Story*, 1940
52. *From Here to Eternity*, 1953
53. *Amadeus*, 1984
54. *All Quiet on the Western Front*, 1930
55. *The Sound of Music*, 1965
56. *M*A*S*H*, 1970
57. *The Third Man*, 1949
58. *Fantasia*, 1940
59. *Rebel Without a Cause*, 1955
60. *Raiders of the Lost Ark*, 1981
61. *Vertigo*, 1958
62. *Tootsie*, 1982
63. *Stagecoach*, 1939
64. *Close Encounters of the Third Kind*, 1977
65. *The Silence of the Lambs*, 1991
66. *Network*, 1976
67. *The Manchurian Candidate*, 1962
68. *An American in Paris*, 1951
69. *Shane*, 1953
70. *The French Connection*, 1971
71. *Forrest Gump*, 1994
72. *Ben-Hur*, 1959
73. *Wuthering Heights*, 1939
74. *The Gold Rush*, 1925
75. *Dances With Wolves*, 1990
76. *City Lights*, 1931
77. *American Graffiti*, 1973
78. *Rocky*, 1976
79. *The Deer Hunter*, 1978
80. *The Wild Bunch*, 1969
81. *Modern Times*, 1936
82. *Giant*, 1956
83. *Platoon*, 1986
84. *Fargo*, 1996

85. *Duck Soup*, 1933
86. *Mutiny on the Bounty*, 1935
87. *Frankenstein*, 1931
88. *Easy Rider*, 1969
89. *Patton*, 1970
90. *The Jazz Singer*, 1927
91. *My Fair Lady*, 1964
92. *A Place in the Sun*, 1951
93. *The Apartment*, 1960
94. *GoodFellas*, 1990
95. *Pulp Fiction*, 1994
96. *The Searchers*, 1956
97. *Bringing Up Baby*, 1938
98. *Unforgiven*, 1992
99. *Guess Who's Coming to Dinner*, 1967
100. *Yankee Doodle Dandy*, 1942

# Questions for the Movie Answer Man

## *Addicted to Love*

Q. In your review of *Addicted to Love* you question the plausibility of the opening scene, in which astronomers can see the stars through their telescope at high noon—and then lower their sights so that Matthew Broderick can look at his girlfriend. This is kind of weird. Even weirder is what they actually say. The professor chap comments that Broderick has predicted that Alpha Orionis will go supernova. Alpha Orionis, better known as Betelguese, is one of the brightest stars in the sky. If it were to go supernova this would be the most spectacular astronomical event in recorded history. It isn't impossible that it might rival the Sun in brightness for a few days. Of course, if such an event did occur, most astronomers would be so excited about it that they would likely not sleep, eat, focus their telescopes at their girlfriends, or even notice that their girlfriends had left them for weeks. Anyone who successfully predicted such a thing would win fellowships, professorships, prizes, and celebrity, and would, I think, be rather too busy to be involved in the events in the rest of the movie.

—Michael Jennings, Department of Applied Mathematics and Theoretical Physics, The University of Cambridge, England

A. Do you mean to say that would be an even bigger deal than being jilted by Kelly Preston? Man, you guys are serious.

## *Air Bud*

Q. In your review of *Air Bud* you left the impression that trick photography was used in the scenes where the dog shoots baskets. I saw this particular dog on TV, and he is capable of everything he did in the movie.

—Carol Otakis, Skokie, Illinois

A. The movie is about a dog that plays basketball. To my amazement, I learn from Michael Strange of Keystone Productions that you are absolutely right, and the dog did indeed shoot all of those baskets itself, bouncing the ball off its nose. The dog's name is Buddy, and *Late Show News* correspondent Thomas Allen Heald tells me he was a star performer for David Letterman's Stupid Pet Tricks.

*Footnote: Buddy died, alas, some months after completing the film.*

## *Air Force One*

Q. You should switch your reviews of *Air Force One* and *Spawn* around. *Spawn* sucked. We should have left the theater (the last time we left a movie was *Hudson Hawk*—enough said). *Air Force One* was enjoyable from beginning to end. It was made to be a summer action fun movie and that's what it accomplished. I wanted to leave *Spawn* during the opening credits, which actually hurt my eyes. Maybe closing my eyes during the opening credits actually saved my mind; you watched the credits and received the brainwashing effects from them. That's the only reason for a favorable review on this movie.

—Paul Berker, Lake Villa, Illinois

A. *Air Force One* was a movie that has been done, in one form or another, many times before. *Spawn* tried for originality and for a consistent, creative style reflecting the groundbreaking comic book it is based on. *AF1* is basically the old "it's up, it's in trouble—now how do we get it down?" formula used in *Airport, Turbulence,* and so many other movies. Just this summer the formula was better handled in *Con Air,* which had more interesting characters on board instead of the standard Noble Wife, Threatened Child, Sinister Double Agent, etc. It had a better villain, too, and superior special effects.

Q. In your review of *Air Force One* you wondered whether it was actually possible to phone Moscow from Washington, D.C., with a cellular phone. Last year I used a cellular phone to call one of our sons, who was working as an accountant in Vladivostok, from the right field stands of Jacobs Field. I described the last of the ninth against the California Angels. Reception was so good he put it on the speaker phone at work. The call cost me over $70, but it was worth it, since Manny Ramirez hit a three-run homer to win it, 5 to 4. The crowd cheered for the next two or three minutes. One of the Russians at the office asked, "How can so many people be so happy for so long?"

—Jim Rozmajzl, Akron, Ohio

**A.** For your next experiment, why not place a call from a White Sox game, so the Vladivostokians can wonder why so many people can be so sad?

**Q.** Rush Limbaugh said on the radio that *Air Force One,* depicting the president as a hero, is a subtle plug for President Clinton. Limbaugh also said *Siskel and Ebert* would trip all over themselves to give top ratings to a movie depicting Braveheart Clinton.

—Baxter Wolfe, Arlington Heights, Illinois

**A.** Funny, but I gave *Air Force One* only two and a half stars, or thumbs down, and it never occurred to me that the Harrison Ford character was supposed to represent Bill Clinton. Limbaugh and Michael Medved have made a cottage industry out of attacking Hollywood liberalism, but even when Hollywood creates a conservative president (such as the Ford character in *AF1*) they find a hidden pro-Clinton message. I agree that Hollywood movies tend toward the liberal agenda, because artistic and creative types in general tend to be liberal. Here are two questions for Limbaugh and Medved: (1) Why aren't conservatives more drawn to the arts? and (2) Why have Hollywood's conservatives avoided making political movies?

**Q.** The total muddle of the script of *Air Force One* was highlighted in a recent interview of one of the supporting actors (the one who threw himself into the bullet in the big fight scene). He described the bad guys as "right wing"—yet we heard the general marching out of prison to the strains of the "Internationale."

—Jay Walker, Nashville, Tennessee

**A.** What? Left-wing villains? Plus a conservative president? Don't tell Limbaugh and Medved.

## Alan Smithee

**Q.** Joe Eszterhas is making a movie named *Directed by Alan Smithee,* in honor of the pseudonym used by directors who want to remove their names from a film. Who was the first person to use the pseudonym Alan Smithee, and for what movie? Any reason why the name Alan Smithee was chosen?

—Gary Currie, Montreal, Quebec

**A.** According to Theresa Fitzpatrick of the Directors Guild of America, research in the August-September 1992 issue of *DGA Magazine* reports that the pseudonym was first used in 1969 for *Death of a Gunfighter,* which had two directors, neither one wanting to claim it. The name was coined by DGA council member John Rich, who recalled, "It was going to be Alan Smith. I added the 'ee' at the end to make it more unusual sounding." In return for DGA authorization to use the "Smithee" name, "a director who feels maligned must not air his grievance in the press."

**Q.** Apparently there is a new movie coming out named *An Alan Smithee Film,* written by Joe Eszterhas and directed by Arthur Hiller, and it has led to a lot of publicity about "Alan Smithee" and his checkered career. What is your favorite Alan Smithee film?

—Casey Anderson, Schaumberg, Illinois

**A.** Easy. That would be *The Man in the Moon* (1991), directed by Robert Mulligan, which was released under Mulligan's name and made my list of the year's best. He insisted his name be removed from the airline version, which was so severely censored that all sense was lost. "Alan Smithee," of course, is the pseudonym used to replace the name of a director who has removed his name from a film in protest against changes he has no control over.

Now here is an irony. *An Alan Smithee Film* was indeed directed by Arthur Hiller, but during a dinner at the Cannes Film Festival, Hiller told me he had serious objections to changes ordered by Eszterhas, who has final cut. So serious, said Hiller, "that I am removing my name from the film." That means *An Alan Smithee Film* will indeed be directed by none other than Alan Smithee.

## *An American Werewolf in Paris*

**Q.** In *An American Werewolf in Paris* a young man leaps off the Eiffel Tower in pursuit of the fetching Julie Delpy (who jumped from the same point moments before). During the couple's free fall, the young man overtakes Ms. Delpy and grabs her before she smacks the pavement. Duh? Isn't this another case of film people snoozing through a high school physics class? I thought that all objects fall to earth at a constant rate (assuming that gravity is the dominant force) regardless of their weight. And I don't think that Ms. Delpy's clothing would offer enough resistance to allow the young man to catch up to her. I know that movies are something like dreams and that the laws of physics do not apply to the dream world. Maybe if I can provide the suspension of disbelief for werewolves I can also put aside Newton's Mechanical Universe.

—James B. Stevens, Lisle, Illinois

**A.** Close study of the Eiffel Tower reveals that it slopes out from a narrow top to a very broad base, so that even if Tom Everett Scott *could* have grabbed Delpy in midair, they would both have slammed into the girders of the tower's sides, and continued on down to the ground doing a passable imitation of carrots being diced in a Veg-a-Matic.

**Q.** While watching the end credits for *An American Werewolf in Paris,* I caught the name "Boris Karloff" listed for a Carpenter Technician. This can't be real, can it? Is it Boris Jr., or did someone change their name specifically for this project? Or were the sets so bad that the technician used the name, à la Alan Smithee, to hide?

—Robert Haynes-Peterson, Boise, Idaho

**A.** A Hollywood Pictures spokesman tells me: "This person was hired as a trainee during the filming, and thus was a noncontract person. He may have been on the set for only a week. They did list his name on the credits because he did work on the film; however, they are unable to track him down. Chances are this is his real name, but we cannot confirm it."

## Astaire and the Vacuum

**Q.** What'd ya think of that commercial on the Super Bowl showing Fred Astaire dancing with the vacuum cleaner?

—Harris Allsworth, Chicago, Illinois

**A.** Not much. Special effects were used to remove Astaire from *Royal Wedding* (1951), where he danced with a coatrack, and insert him in a TV commercial, where he danced with a Broom Vac. Rights to use Astaire's image were sold by his estate. I was reminded that when the late Ginger Rogers was honored at the Kennedy Center, Astaire's widow refused permission to use any clips of Astaire in the tribute. What would Astaire have thought about those two decisions? A man who could dance on the ceiling would have no difficulty spinning in his grave.

**Q.** Regarding the TV commercial where Fred Astaire dances with the Broom Vac. My best friend's wife is angrily adamant that if a company wants to use a dead celebrity in their advertising, the only legal way is to dig up the corpse and prop it next to that box of cereal. While I appreciate that point of view, I'm not unusually bothered by the Fred Astaire ad. It's really no different from almost any other use of a dead celeb's image. If I saw an Astaire T-shirt—a natty image from the "Dancin' Man" number from *The Barkleys of Broadway,* say—I'd have my wallet out in a flash. The only thing that bothered me about the Dirt Devil ads was that they were so poorly done. They looked like old footage with a bunch of digital effects embroidered in. Compare it to the wonderful Diet Coke ad of a few years ago, which featured Paula Abdul dancing with a dozen film legends. Exceptional job, and a perfect mating of subjects.

—Andy Ihnatko, Westwood, Massachusetts

**A.** Many actors are happy to appear in commercials because they enjoy the work and can use the money. They make a living by acting for hire, after all. But when great work of the past is recycled into TV ads, isn't that breaking a compact with their own art? And when their heirs sign the contract and pocket the change after they're dead, isn't that a little like selling their gold teeth?

**Q.** What irks me about that Astaire ad is that for two years now we have tried to license a Fred Astaire movie clip for the Cinemania CD-ROM. Our intention was to present the clip with the utmost affection and respect—a real tribute to his artistry in an encyclopedic multimedia showcase devoted to the love of movies. Imagine my surprise when I saw that

Mr. Astaire's likeness had been licensed to sell vacuum cleaners!

—Jim Emerson, editor, Microsoft Cinemania, Seattle, Washington

A. Maybe you should have tried to license Astaire for one of your ads. He could be dancing with a giant CD-ROM disc.

## Austin Powers

Q. Austin Powers, International Man of Mystery, says: "This is my happening, and it freaks me out!" Now I just wonder how many people (other than true *Beyond the Valley of the Dolls* mainliners) will catch that reference.

—Paul Kedrosky, London, Ontario

A. Ahem. It is always an honor for one artist to be quoted by another, and for Mike Myers, a true auteur, to refer to my 1970 screenplay is just one more evidence of his (and its) greatness. Did you notice that *Austin Powers* also used the original Strawberry Alarm Clock sound track song?

## *Babe*

Q. I was appalled when I read the story summary of the sequel to *Babe,* called *Babe in Metropolis.* It involves a bank threatening foreclosure on the Hoggett farm, and the pig traveling to a city to demonstrate his shepherding skills once again. The joy of *Babe* was watching the pig triumph against "all odds." This contrived plot will likely ruin the spirit of the original. Unless the Metropolis that Babe visits is anything like Fritz Lang's, I don't see any potential. What was James Cromwell thinking when he signed up for *Babe in Metropolis*?

—Rhys Southan, Richardson, Texas

A. He was probably thinking that his contract required him to. The problem the sequel will have to address is that now we know what Babe can do, and then we didn't. So suspense is replaced by impatience. If they have Babe visit a city that looks like the sets in Lang's silent classic, however, the film would have the distinction of being two unnecessary sequels instead of only one.

## Beavis and Butt-Head

Q. When I went to the Beavis and Butt-Head movie, I wasn't expecting them to be sitting in front of me. You may remember the scenes in which our erstwhile heroes are crawling through the desert, dying of thirst. Beavis takes that big bite of "cactus," and things start happening. Well, at that point, the two morons in front of me said (in stereo), "Dude, 'shrooms!"

—Katherine Keller, Las Vegas, Nevada

A. Heh, heh.

Q. I saw *Beavis and Butt-Head Do America* and noticed most of the dubbed voices were not credited. Reportedly some of the dubbers were famous friends of the filmmaker, Mike Judge. Can you confirm this?

—Charlie Smith, Chicago, Illinois

A. Aaron Barnhart of Kansas City, who produces the *Late Show News* netzine, wrote in a recent issue: "Sharp-eyed moviegoer Collin Cannaday reports that the voice of 'Motley Crue Roadie #1' in the new major motion picture, *Beavis and Butt-Head Do America,* is supplied by none other than 'Earl Hofert,' a.k.a David Letterman, who just might be the No. 1 fan of the toonful twosome. Letterman's 1994 cameo in *Cabin Boy* was also attributed to 'Hofert,' which happens to be the name of one of his Indiana uncles."

Q. In a recent Answer Man you had an item about the mystery voices in *Beavis and Butt-Head Do America.* As you know, a lot of celebs lend their voices anonymously, but now the Internet Movie Database has blown their cover. The uncredited voices include Greg Kinnear as FBI agent Bork; David Letterman (under the pseudonym Earl Hofert) as Motley Crue Roadie #1; Demi Moore as Dallas; and Bruce Willis as Muddy Grimes. David Spade is also in the movie, although I'm not sure what character he played.

—Robert Haynes-Peterson, Boise, Idaho

A. Given the ten characters listed in the credits and the four you've identified, how many are left? And why has David Spade grown so modest all of a sudden?

## Benevolent Blurbsters

Q. I had a weird sense of déjà vu while reading the ads for *Breakdown,* the new Kurt Russell thriller. Not the ads after the movie opened—the advance ads, which featured your old favorites, the "Benevolent Blurbsters," who can always be counted on for praise. Here are some of their quotes: "It keeps you on the edge-of-your-seat from start to finish" (Taylor Baldwin, CBS). "Edge-of-your-seat gripper that delivers" (Bonnie Churchill, National News Syndicate). "Edge-of-your-seat suspense" (Jim Ferguson, Prevue Channel). "An edge-of-your-seat suspense gem" (David Gillin, NBC-TV). Can this be mere coincidence?

—Baxter Wolfe, Arlington Heights, Illinois

A. Obviously, a faulty search-and-replace program in the studio's word processor accidentally replaced the brilliant prose of the Blurbsters with the words "edge-of-your-seat." Here is the clue: "Edge-of-your-seat" is only hyphenated when the phrase is used as an adjective. It should not have hyphens when used as Taylor Baldwin does when he writes "it keeps you on the edge-of-your-seat." Proof that Benevolent Blurbsters can actually be much more versatile in their word choices comes from Ron Brewington of the American Urban Radio Networks. The advertising campaign for *The Saint* used the following quotes from Brewington: "Loads of nail-biting excitement!" "Way over-the-top action!" "You'll really love this film!" "*The Saint* is the bomb!" "This picture has all the right ingredients!" Translated out of Blurbspeak, here is what Brewington, always a perceptive critic, is telling us: "It's good! But it didn't glue me to the edge-of-my-seat!"

Q. I caught the NPR report on quote whores—the "critics" who eagerly supply film studios with favorable quotes long in advance of a movie's opening. It included an interview with Susan Granger. They didn't talk to Jeff Craig of *Sixty Second Preview,* but I imagine he thought the report was "a riveting, nonstop thrill ride!" There was much debate over why studios solicit quotes like this. Seems to me if it wasn't making money for them, they wouldn't do it, despite the smug assurances of some of the interviewees that the silly quotes "aren't fooling anyone." No?

—Leon Lynn, Milwaukee, Wisconsin

A. In the old days, movies ads simply stated their bold claims. "Passion! Adventure! Excitement! The Most Thrilling Adventure of the Decade!" These days the ad guys figure such claims are more convincing if they come in quotes and were allegedly said by "critics." As a rule of thumb, any critic quoted in an ad more than a week before the movie opens is a quote whore—unless he works for a monthly or weekly publication with an early deadline, or actually made his statement in print or on the air. Legitimate critics do not supply quotes directly to publicists, nor do they scoop their own reviews by sharing the highlights before publication day.

## Best Bad Guys

Q. I saw something on the Internet about a poll of the top movie bad guys of all time, but forgot where I saw it and can't find it again. I remember Hannibal Lecter placed first.

—Pet Danforth, Oak Park, Illinois

A. Lecter, as played by Sir Anthony Hopkins, did indeed place first, in a poll by the British magazine *Total Film,* which I found with a Web search engine, as you could perfectly well have done for yourself. Second place went to the title character in *Henry, Portrait of a Serial Killer,* played by Michael Rooker. The rest of the top five: John Doe (Kevin Spacey) in *Seven,* Tommy DeVito (Joe Pesci) in *GoodFellas,* and Frank Booth, the gas-sniffing weirdo played by Dennis Hopper in *Blue Velvet.* The top female villain was Kathy Bates's enthusiastic literary fan in *Misery;* she placed fifteenth. My own choice? Count Orlok (Max Schreck) in Murnau's *Nosferatu,* who makes Hannibal Lecter look like a guidance counselor. Runners-up: Harry Lime (Orson Welles) in *The Third Man* and Norman Bates (Anthony Hopkins) in *Psycho.*

## Best Films of All Time

Q. If you could create a "must-see" list of films for the ardent film fan, what would they be? Films that are so important that it is impossible to have an intelligent discussion about the cinema without having seen these seminal works? The list could include films that are important to the history of film, and to film as it exists today, not necessarily just films that are still popular, or 100 percent grand.

—Robert Haynes-Peterson, Boise, Idaho

A. What are the basic films that everyone must absolutely have seen in order to avoid appearing completely out of the loop? The first five that come to mind are *Citizen Kane, Casablanca, 2001: A Space Odyssey, Battleship Potemkin,* and *Star Wars.* Then something by Keaton, something by Chaplin, something by Fellini, something by Hitchcock, and something by Bergman. (For example, *The General, City Lights, La Dolce Vita, Vertigo,* and *Persona.*)

*See the American Film Institute's list of the 100 greatest American films, elsewhere in this volume.*

## Blood

**Q.** When I cut myself shaving, the blood comes out bright red. However, in movies, when somebody is bleeding, the blood is usually a dark purple. I have never seen anybody bleed that color in real life, although I have never seen an actual gunshot wound. Why do movies use that color? Does red look too fake? I recall from high school biology that blood turns the brighter color upon contact with oxygen, such as in the atmosphere.

—Steven Stine, Buffalo Grove, Illinois

**A.** I asked Dr. Robert Kushner, of the University of Chicago Center for Advanced Medicine, who replies: "Arterial blood (pulsating arteries) is bright red because it carries oxygen from the heart and lungs to the rest of the body. Venous blood is darker red, almost purple, because it returns oxygen-drained blood back to the heart and lungs. So, a cut through an arm vein will look dark red and ooze out, while a severed artery (like the carotid artery in the neck) will pump out bright red blood. Can I be a movie critic now?"

**Q.** I am a fifteen-year-old movie geek, and I need an answer to a question that has confused me since my love affair with the movies began. In action and horror movies, whose decision is it whether or not blood will be shown when characters die or are wounded? I ask this because I have noticed that in some of Jerry Bruckheimer's films such as *Con Air,* blood is shown during almost every action scene. However, in some of his other films, such as *The Rock,* almost no blood is spilled. It only makes me more confused when I see Director Andrew Davis's *Under Siege* stained with squibbage, while his version of *The Fugitive* is blood-free. Is the screenwriter to blame or is it some overzealous effects technician who figures that blood is what people want to see?

—Wes Mize, Crescent City, California

**A.** I put your query to the director Gary Fleder, whose credits include *Things to Do in Denver When You're Dead* and *Kiss the Girls.* His reply:

"The amount of blood you see onscreen has little to do with bloodstained studio meetings and everything to do with the relationship between director and makeup artist. If one's shooting an aftermath of a fight scene (think of the *Rocky* flicks), the director and makeup artist must decide on the nature of the actor's bruises, abrasions, and oozing wounds days or weeks in advance. It's not uncommon to try out the blood makeup on film well before shooting the scene. Also, cinematography can accent or downplay blood by the quality of light (hard light, soft light, backlight, sidelight, etc.). Editing can 'cut around' too much blood in a sequence (the opposite might be said of Joel Silver flicks).

"Squibs add several people to the chain of command. When filming squibs, the stunt coordinator and the special-effects coordinator meet with the director (and, subsequently, the actor in the crosshairs) to conceptualize the sequence. A few big questions: How many squibs? How big the charge? And, naturally, how much blood do you want to see?

"As for the final question, obviously John Woo and Walter Hill (think *The Long Riders*) answer, 'As much blood as possible!' Oftentimes, squibs are shot at higher frame rates (48fps–120fps) to show all (Tony Scott loves it this way). The editor can either cut the squib sequence quickly and abstractly (the finale of *Bonnie and Clyde*) or with an over-the-top flair (*The Long Riders,* an homage to Peckinpah). So the director is the 'plasma auteur.'

## *Boogie Nights*

**Q.** At the end of *Boogie Nights,* in the montage, we get a throwaway laugh when Maurice Rodriguez (Luis Guzman) and his brothers unveil their nightclub sign to find out that the sign is spelled "Rodriquez." It's an unexpected laugh, and I wondered why Anderson bothered. My theory was that they ordered a Rodriguez sign, and it came back misspelled, just a happy accident.

—Steven Sherman, Toronto, Ontario

A. The laugh wasn't planned in advance. Director Paul Thomas Anderson says he misspelled the name in his screenplay, the sign was constructed that way, and when it arrived he decided to go with it.

Q. My friend Nina Hartley appeared in a small part in *Boogie Nights*. I was very surprised not to see any mention of Nina in New Line's publicity and press materials for the film. Nina is so smart and articulate she would make a great spokesperson. Plus she would be able to attest to the authenticity of the "scene" the movie explores. It would seem that they should be capitalizing on having a real-life porn star in their film, which is about the porn industry. Could it be that New Line wanted to distance themselves from the real porn industry? That would be so hypocritical given the film's subject.

—Dorna Khazeni, San Francisco, California

A. Hartley plays the wife of the William H. Macy character, and has one of the best lines in the movie: "You're embarrassing me!" It's possible the studio's snub of Hartley is part of a strategy to downplay the movie's subject matter; the ads dance all around it.

Q. Okay, for once and for all: In *Boogie Nights*, the last shot shows Mark Wahlberg displaying the full monty. Is that really him, or only a prop? I've heard it both ways.

—Ronnie Barzell, Los Angeles, California

A. I don't know. And it's not for lack of asking. The generally accepted opinion is that we are looking at a prosthesis; that's the verdict in most of the articles about the film. But *Boogie Night*'s director, Paul Thomas Anderson, swore it is absolutely, positively Mark Wahlberg's own precious bodily part we are gazing upon. Anderson was sitting on my back deck and drinking my iced coffee and looking me straight in the eye when he said, "That is Mark Wahlberg's penis." Not a special effect? "No." Not a double who is substituted in the shot? "No." My own opinion? It's a prosthesis.

Q. Regarding your Answer Man column about the controversial final shot in *Boogie Nights:* The director told you it was positively Mark Wahlberg, but you still thought it was a prosthesis. I have a theory. Wahlberg was interviewed on-line, and described the shot as "augmented by Hollywood smoke and mirrors." He added: "I didn't use a stand-in, but it's a trick." Since Wahlberg is standing in front of a mirror in the scene, I'm wondering if perhaps the mirror was distorted like the old funhouse mirrors—the ones that can make you look taller or shorter. If the mirror was distorted in just the right place, and his clothes were tailored to offset the effect, it might create the effect, even though it would still be him that we were seeing. Note that he stood very still in the scene—any movement would have caused the distortion to be obvious.

—Tom Crosley, San Jose, California

A. Too complicated (although there could be a big home market for a mirror with that ability). I've been trying to reconcile the apparent trickery with Paul Thomas Anderson's flat-out statement to me that the famous appendage was "absolutely, 100 percent real." It would seem that someone had to be lying, but try this on for size: What if Anderson were telling the truth, but neglecting to add that the full monty, although real, was enhanced through special effects? Not a trick mirror, but perhaps through digital technology?

Q. Why is there all of this confusion about the last scene in *Boogie Nights*? Doesn't anybody listen to Howard Stern? Four weeks ago Howard had on the special-effects team of Kurtzman, Nicotero, and Berger, who designed the prosthetic prop for Mark Wahlberg, not to mention the ear in *Reservoir Dogs* and Uma Thurman's chest plate in *Pulp Fiction*. Howard even got to live out a lifelong dream by wearing the thing in the studio. I hope this clears up this mystery.

—Bradley D. Richman, Flushing, New York

A. The mystery is not so much whether the final shot is real, as about the contradiction between what director Paul Thomas Anderson says ("Absolutely, 100 percent real") and what everyone else says. By the way, how did they get Howard to give the thing back?

Q. Is it just me or was the John C. Reilly character, Mark Wahlberg's main buddy, doing a Quentin Tarantino impression all during *Boogie Nights*? He gives an interview at one point during the movie explaining the use of violence in films that I could have sworn was word for word from Tarantino's comments after *Pulp Fiction* won the Cannes Film Festival.

—Joseph J. Elizondo, Las Vegas, Nevada

A. Hard to say whether it's a riff on Tarantino, or whether that's a prevailing mode of speech in Los Angeles showbiz circles.

Q. On your Oscars show you were discussing Julianne Moore's character in *Boogie Nights,* and said, "The people she's surrounded by are all sad." I spent the last two years as a stripper, (gay) porn star, and prostitute, while I got my M.A. in creative writing, and I have to tell you it was not all sad. There were definitely some ugly moments, but for me, on balance, it was really positive. As far as my peers, there were definitely some sad tales, but most of the time, it was a real blast. Why do you think people do it? Sure, because "they have to," some of them—with prostitutes in general, that might even be the norm, but in the porn business, that's clearly the exception. So I found the whole portrayal of the industry really disturbing and one-sided.

—Name Withheld

A. But the characters in *Boogie Nights are* sad. I do not doubt that your experience has been better than theirs, but the task of a movie critic is to describe what is on the screen. You do not find porn sad and are concerned that I thought *Boogie Nights* was sad. I refer you to Ebert's Law, which states: *A movie is not about what it is about, but about how it is about it.*

## Breakdown

Q. In your review of *Breakdown,* you wrote, "I noticed, interestingly, that no one in the audience cheered when that final death took place. I felt a kind of collective wince. Maybe that indicates we still have an underlying decency that rejects the eye-for-an-eye values of this film." On May 2 at the 7:30 P.M. showing at Movies 6 in McAllen, Texas (lower Rio Grande Valley)—the audience applauded when the truck ended the movie along with J. T. Walsh. I was surprised, not shocked, when I saw Kathleen Quinlan pull the gearshift to flatten him, but the audience here is less sophisticated than yours. For what it's worth, I've lived in Texas twelve years and have never seen the kinds of stereotypical Texas villains portrayed in the movie. Texas is mostly a friendly place.

—Paul Gabriel, McAllen, Texas

A. At the end of the film, the villain is totally incapacitated and barely alive, and the heroine gratuitously drops a truck on him to crush him. This would not have happened in an action thriller made ten or twenty years ago; the rules were that the villain had to represent some kind of final threat before he was killed. To squash a dying and powerless man seemed, to me, a violation of generally-held values. If your Texas audience cheered, that doesn't make them monsters; they were going along with the conventions of movie violence without thinking them through. But the filmmakers had lots of time to think about them. Why couldn't they at least have had the bad guy reach for a gun, or something? Since movies are one way that we discover our generally-held values, this movie ending plays for me like a disturbing omen.

## Breaking the Waves

Q. Have you seen the Criterion laser disc of *Breaking the Waves*? It includes four deleted scenes—three of which are dreadful. In one of the scenes (which takes place after Bess's sister-in-law calls her stupid) we learn that Bess can't read. In another that takes place after her husband tells her to have sex with other men to keep him alive, the husband tells his best friend (the guy with the weird sideburns) that he only told Bess to do this to drive her away. The strange part about the scene is that his buddy stays in character throughout, smiling and laughing inappropriately. The worst scene of all takes place after Bess escapes police custody. She confronts the doctor, asking him not to send her away because she must keep her husband alive. At the end of the scene, she pulls a gun on the doctor. Von Trier showed good judgment keeping these scenes out of the movie. He preserved the film's mystery and in the case of the gun scene, saved himself from a bad plot device. But why did he ever let these clips see the light of day? By deconstructing a film that worked (for me at least) on an allegorical level, he has taken something away. I don't know if I'll ever be able to watch the film again without having these terrible scenes in my mind.

—Daniel M. Conley, Chicago, Illinois

**A.** My guess is that the additional scenes are included in the "supplementary materials" section of the laser disc simply so that buyers can feel they are getting a bonus. They do not make the disc into a "director's cut" because Lars von Trier of course exercised his final cut in the film as it was seen in theaters. To see wrongly removed scenes is one thing. To see outtakes of scenes that were unwise or unsuccessful is something else altogether.

## *Bulworth*

**Q.** I saw *Bulworth* this weekend and liked it a lot. But could you answer a question for me? At the end, a homeless man tells the audience that it's better to be a spirit than a ghost. I consider myself an intelligent man but wasn't sure what the message here was. Could you shed some light?

—Paul Chinn, Columbia, Tennessee

**A.** I think that means it is better to leave behind your spirit than your ghost: to be a living presence rather than a dead memory. But the homeless man, who appears from time to time throughout the movie like the Spirit of Christmas Past, is an imperfectly realized idea, and most of the reviews of the film haven't even mentioned him. He resembles a similar character in *Mickey One,* a film Beatty made in 1965.

## Cannes

**Q.** Now that you're back from Cannes, what was the single funniest thing that happened?

—Susan Lake, Urbana, Illinois

**A.** At his party at Planet Hollywood for *She's So Lovely,* Miramax chief Harvey Weinstein was told by a publicist, "Harvey! Prince Albert of Monaco is here! Want to meet him?" And Weinstein replied, "Sure. Send him over."

**Q.** I enjoy your coverage from the Cannes Film Festival, and I've often thought that one day I would like to attend the festival. Would it be worth it for someone without connections to the movie industry or the press? Would one have any chance to attend the various screenings? Are there restrictions on local hotels, restaurants, bars, and beaches owing to the large celebrity contingent?

—Donald J. Lazo, Chicago, Illinois

**A.** It's a trade show, not really open to the public, but a limited number of tickets go on open sale every day, and moviegoers line up for them in front of the Palais des Festivals at 8 A.M. Also, you might run into someone who'll give you tickets to one of the market screenings. In addition, there's a lot of people-watching, with weirdos and street entertainers strolling along the Croisette. Every night big crowds surge against the barricades as the stars parade into the Palais. It can be fun, although if actually seeing movies is your objective, you'd be better off at the best festivals in North America, which are in Montreal in August, Telluride over Labor Day, and Toronto in September (Sundance is also hard to crack). As for Cannes hotels and restaurants, etc., they welcome anyone prepared to pay their startling prices. Of course, the regulars book their favorite rooms and tables a year in advance, but there's always room at La Pizza, down by the old yacht harbor, which probably has the best food in town anyway.

## *Chasing Amy*

**Q.** Went to see *Chasing Amy* and enjoyed it immensely. As the credits rolled, the nitwit sitting behind me said to his girlfriend: "I didn't like it. It started out funny, but by the end they weren't funny anymore" (insert open-faced palm-slap to own forehead here).

—Ed Slota, Warwick, Rhode Island

**A.** To which the nitwit's girlfriend replied:

(1) "Like, totally."

(2) "Yes, it's wonderful how, as Roger Ebert wrote, it starts out like a 'setup for an empty-headed sexcom, but develops into a film of touching insights.'"

(3) "Hey, nitwit, see the guy in front of us who just slapped his forehead? I'm leaving with him."

**Q.** Do you know why Ben Affleck is pictured without a beard in the newspaper ads for *Chasing Amy* while he definitely sports a beard in the movie?

—B. F. Helman, Chicago, Illinois

**A.** Robin Jonas from Miramax replies: "We weren't able to take a picture during production. The official photo was taken well after shooting was completed. By then Ben Affleck had shaved off his beard. It's hard to fake a beard so we used him without it."

## Chinese Takeaway

**Q.** Why has it become an increasingly common cliché for movies to always decorate dingy old apartments with Chinese take-out boxes? And why Chinese food? Is there something about the way those little boxes look?

—Joseph Tsai, West Covina, California

**A.** Yes, as a matter of fact, there is. They are white, stand up straight, photograph easily, and "read" well—which means, you can look at one and see instantly what it is. Other take-out options include pizza (comes in flat brown boxes that blend into surfaces), brown paper bags (could be holding anything), and little aluminum foil trays with cardboard covers (a nightmare to light because of the reflections). By a process of elimination, Chinese food is the movie takeaway of choice. Second place goes to Dunkin' Donuts, with the giant pink letters that leave no doubt what's in the box.

## Cinematic Motion Sickness

**Q.** I do not get carsick, seasick, or airsick. Am I the only person who suffers from "handheld camera sickness"? I was forced to sit through Woody Allen's *Husbands and Wives* back in 1992, in spite of intense nausea. Fortunately, I was able to make it home that night, before having to visit the bathroom. In 1995, I left my husband alone with *Crumb* on three separate occasions for trips to Mr. Toilet. Last night, the coup de grâce: *Breaking the Waves.* I knew I was in trouble after the opening scene. By the time they rolled Jan into the operating room, I had already lost my dinner and my M&M's, and had to go home. I am curious to know if you have heard of anyone else who suffers from this syndrome. Perhaps a support group could be started.

—Denise Leder, Las Vegas

**A.** Several people have told me they got "motion sickness" while watching *Breaking the Waves,* in which many scenes are shot with a handheld camera. According to clinical audiologist Marla Lappe, of Audio Vestibular Associates in Evanston, Illinois, when you're dizzy you get "nystagmus" eye movement, which makes the brain feel like you're on a ship. To fight the illusion, she says, pick a fixed point and stare at it. But since there's no fixed point in a movie, she says Dramamine will help. On television, with its smaller screen size, the effect does not take place, so if you don't want to take Dramamine I advise you to wait for the video.

**Q.** Re the problem of motion sickness in films that make use of handheld cameras: Actually the easiest way to get over it is just close your eyes and the sensation passes quickly.

—Doug Fletcher, RN, *Journal of Nursing Jocularity,* Mesa, Arizona

**A.** What do you suggest for Pauly Shore movies?

## *City of Angels*

**Q.** I'm all for the willing suspension of disbelief, but to paraphrase Kevin Kline's character in *A Fish Called Wanda,* don't consider me stupid. Case in point: *City of Angels.* An attractive female doctor is in a large metropolitan hospital late at night. She encounters a strange man lurking in a hallway who has no good reason for being there, and the man unaccountably knows her name. Does she: (a) yell "get out!" and dial 911 at the nearest security phone; or (b) engage the stranger in marginally upscale, Meet-Cute pleasantries that will be mined as intellectual ore in subsequent scenes? This is Hollywood, so the answer, of course, is (b). To my mind this incomprehensible scene captures everything that is subsequently wrong with the unromantic, uninteresting, underthought, and overschematized *City of Angels.*

—Paul Kedrosky, Vancouver, British Columbia

**A.** That's almost plausible compared to *Mercury Rising.* In that one, Bruce Willis, who is sweaty and smelly, wearing a torn T-shirt, and with an autistic kid under his arm, enters a café in Chicago and encounters Kim Dickens, who is in sales. He asks her to forget about her job in order to watch the kid for him, because he is really an FBI agent but the FBI is after him because of a big conspiracy. Of course she immediately agrees.

## *Contact*

Q. I am disappointed with *Contact*. The use of President Clinton and CNN kills the overall effect of diving into a fantastical voyage into space. For *Forrest Gump*, I accept the use of real people as tongue and cheek. But this movie makes Clinton a player in *Contact*'s White House. I find that disrespectful and unethical. I cannot imagine using Roosevelt in *Mr. Smith Goes to Washington*. Also, how can the entire CNN news team be for sale? How can journalists feel their integrity is not compromised when they are being paid to act out a script? I expect a news company to do one thing, to report the news. That is how they earn my trust.

—Beth Landau, Washington, D.C.

A. The Clinton White House has reacted with strong disapproval to director Robert Zemeckis's clever integration of fictional Clinton footage into fictional scenes in *Contact*. In my review of the movie I called those scenes "distracting," and so they were, because they were so obviously faked. (Oddly enough, it was the sheer effrontery of the fakery in *Gump* that made it so entertaining.) As for CNN allowing its newsmen to appear in the film: Network president Tom Johnson has stated that the experiment was a bad idea, and will not be repeated. The CNN footage reminded me of the classic line, "I'm not a newsman, but I play one on television." None of these side issues detract from *Contact*'s considerable impact.

Q. In your review of *Contact*, you refer to the late Carl Sagan, who spoke optimistically of "billions of billions of stars." Despite popular myth he never said "billions and billions." I think Johnny Carson just always kidded that he did. While updating the *Cosmos* TV series, Sagan watched the whole series to see if he ever spoke that phrase, and indeed it never happened. "It's so imprecise," he observed. "How many is billions and billions? One or two? A hundred?" As explosively as he pronounced the word, one utterance would have been enough for the whole thirteen episodes.

—Chris Rowland, Plainsboro, New Jersey

A. On the other hand, how many is "billions"? Two? A hundred? Sagan discusses this very subject in the introduction to his last book, titled *Billions and Billions*.

Q. Just before Ellie (Jodie Foster) departs on her expedition in *Contact*, one of the scientists gives her a vial containing a single pill. He tells her if she's faced with death, this pill will end her life painlessly and quickly. He also says all our astronauts have been given this pill in the event of capture, torture, or being helplessly lost in space. Is this based on fact?

—Deborah Ann Keith, Lakeland, Florida

A. A Warner Bros. rep replies: "According to Steve Starkey, producer of *Contact*, Carl Sagan told him and director Robert Zemeckis that the space program had provided pills of this type to astronauts. However, Gerry Griffin, the NASA consultant for *Contact*, denies that such pills were used by NASA. According to him, there are other ways an astronaut can easily end his life if he is stranded in space—such as cutting off his oxygen supply." The studio source adds: "It seems unlikely NASA would ever confirm the existence of such a pill, so we are left to draw our own conclusions."

## *Crash*

Q. Ted Turner delayed the release of the movie *Crash*, expressing fears that its exhibition in the United States would unleash a series of copycat car crashes. Well, now that the movie has been in American theaters for a while, I keep looking for news stories about this, without success. Just how has Mr. Turner done as a predictor of modern social trends?

—Don Baird, Chicago, Illinois

A. Not so well in this case. No deaths or injuries have been linked to *Crash*. And no wonder. There have been anecdotal stories over the years about people driving like crazy after seeing movies with great chase scenes *(Bullitt, The French Connection, Diva, The Rock)*, but in *Crash* what you mostly see are people who are horribly injured in crashes, bleed a lot, and limp around wearing casts and braces. I would expect patrons leaving after the show to drive slowly and thoughtfully.

Q. Has David Cronenberg's controversial *Crash* been censored for its current release on video? That's what I heard.

—Charlie Smith, Chicago, Illinois

A. Only at Blockbuster stores. The film, about a very literal form of auto-eroticism, was rated NC-17 when it was released, and Blockbuster won't handle movies with that rating. So Fine Line Pictures put a clause in Cronenberg's contract requiring him to deliver a "Blockbuster cut" for home video. All other video stores will carry the uncut version. Of the Blockbuster version, Cronenberg cheerfully told *Wired News:* "It'll probably run about an hour and make no sense at all."

## Credits

Q. *Evita* lists its screenwriters as Alan Parker and Oliver Stone. I find it interesting that lyricist Tim Rice is not credited as a screenwriter (although he does, of course, get the "lyrics by" credit). Since *Evita* is a sung-through musical, doesn't this mean that the author of all of the film's dialogue is not credited as a screenwriter? In the past, have sung-through movies typically credited the lyricist as one of the film's writers, or is this standard procedure?

—Jeffrey Graebner, Los Angeles, California

A. Interesting question. *The Umbrellas of Cherbourg* (1964) is another of the rare films that is sung all the way through. Director Jacques Demy gives himself a solo credit for the screenplay, and a different solo credit for the lyrics, indicating he thinks they are two different things.

Q. Today's film credits include such banal things as:
—who did the travel arrangements?
—who did the catering?
—who signed the film completion bond?
My question is, why does this appear in the film credits? Does it help to round out the sound track with enough time to play one more song?

—Rob Rosenberger, O'Fallon, Illinois

A. Everybody wants a little reflected glory. You somehow overlooked my favorite credit, for the "trout wrangler" in *A River Runs Through It.*

Q. Is it my imagination, or are the numbers of producers credited per film on the rise? *Michael,* for example, has no fewer than ten producers, executive producers, and associate producers listed. Similarly, *Jerry Maguire* credits eight such people. What gives?

—Jonas Grant, Van Nuys, California

A. Some kind of producer credit is now a perk written into the contracts of agents, managers, and lawyers, especially those associated with big stars who have the clout to say, "give my guy a credit." The "real" credits include "executive producer" (the person who raised some or all of the money), "line producer" (who cracked the whip and ran the physical side of the show), and just plain "producer." One way to tell a real producer from a perk producer is that the perk producer can be heard halfway across the cigar store saying, "I produced the new John Travolta/Tom Cruise/Mel Gibson picture." Real producers are usually too proud to say that, or too powerful to need to.

Q. In the end credits for *Batman & Robin* they listed "Dr. Fries Hairstylist." Since Arnold's character is bald for 99 percent of the movie was this an "in-joke" or was it a legitimate credit?

—Gary Currie, Montreal, Quebec

A. A Warner Bros. spokesperson reassures me: "The credit 'Dr. Fries Hairstylist: Peter Toth Pal' is legitimate. Before Arnold Schwarzenegger fell into the vat, he was Dr. Fries and he did have hair. After he fell into the vat, he became Mr. Freeze and he didn't have hair. So the credit for Dr. Fries hairstylist is correct."

Q. The end credits for *Greedy* inform us that Michael J. Fox had three assistants. How much bottled water did this man require?

—Greg Brown, Chicago, Illinois

A. Nanci Ryder, Fox's publicist, replies: "Michael J. Fox had two assistants while working on the 1994 film *Greedy,* one on the West Coast, another on the East Coast. They were employed by Michael. In addition, as with most films, the studio hired a personal assistant for Michael while filming." In other words, Fox required no more bottled water than the average movie star. He is not known in the industry for making unreasonable demands.

Q. I just saw *The Game* and thought it was terrific fun, though because it was directed by

Evil Dave Fincher *(Seven)*, I kept anticipating the arrival of another head in a box. But you want to know the best thing about it—what really makes it work? No opening credits. Just the title, that's all, and then the movie begins. I wish more filmmakers understood the importance of establishing this immediate sense of illusion, rather than trying our patience with a long résumé of actors and production people. Can't they wait to see their names until the end?

—Craig Simpson, Reynoldsburg, Ohio

A. Depends on the movie, I think. I enjoyed the way *Fargo* started out without credits, but with many movies I enjoy the credit sequences, which tip me off to actors I might not recognize (I hate spending a whole movie wondering—who *is* that guy?).

Q. Why don't more movies offer us "credit cookies" over the closing credits to munch on? Outtakes, party scenes, blown dialogue, scenery, something! They have a choice between blackness and something; why not use the more entertaining something?

—Steven D. Souza, Honolulu, Hawaii

A. Credit cookies, those bonus scenes over the end titles, are appropriate for some movies but not for others. *Dead Man Walking* would hardly be improved by outtakes of Sean Penn giggling in the death chamber. Mary Jo Kaplin of the CompuServe Showbiz Forum says TV networks, fretting that viewers will start surfing during lengthy credits, are starting to *require* Credit Cookies—or even previews for their upcoming shows!

## Cruelty to Cockroaches

Q. I saw *Starship Troopers* this weekend, and paid particular attention to the scene in which school kids stomp a bunch of cockroaches. It appeared to me that at least some of the beasties that got stomped were real, since they were walking around, but the film had the usual SPCA thingy at the end. Was this a special-effects shot? Or did the SPCA lower their standards after *Men in Black*?

—Dominick Cancilla, Santa Monica, California

A. First of all, Gini Barrett of the American Humane Association wants you to know: "There is no such thing as the 'usual SPCA thingy' at the end of films. While there are many Societies for the Prevention of Cruelty to Animals (SPCAs), only the American Humane Association is authorized to monitor the handling of animals on production, and is the only organization empowered to issue an end-credit disclaimer." As for *Starship Troopers*—no, the AHA has not lowered its standards. "The cockroaches were fake," she says, "and the only live animals used during filming were ferrets, frogs, and a cow."

Q. I noticed that in the credits for *Men in Black* there was the standard mention of Humane Society monitoring but it did *not* say "no animals were harmed." Is this because cockroaches were killed?

—Dan Sachs, Merrick, New York

A. You can rest easy. Not a single bug was squished. "No cockroaches were killed for *Men in Black*," I am told by Gini Barrett of the American Humane Association in Encino, California. "When Will Smith was 'stomping' on the cockroaches, rubber cockroaches were used. Mustard packets were used to get the colored squished-bug effect. The cockroaches were counted after each scene."

## *Dangerous Beauty*

Q. Your characterization of *Dangerous Beauty* as "lighthearted" is so puzzling that I am compelled to write. *Dangerous Beauty* is a biography of a woman who lived in sixteenth-century Venice, a time when "decent" women were illiterate chattel and the "best" life a smart, beautiful woman could make for herself—as long as youth and beauty lasted—was as a high-class prostitute. Veronica Franco become a courtesan because her mother lacked the dowry and social status necessary to marry her to the man she loved. She was ultimately denounced to the Inquisition, incarcerated, and almost burnt at the stake. In between she risked pregnancy, disease, and disfigurement in the beds of any number of distasteful if not revolting men and, when Venice went to war and plague swept the city, she and the other courtesans were made the whipping girls for its devastation. What is "lighthearted" about any of this?

—Lynn Hecht Schafran, New York City, New York

**A.** You have described the plot of the film but have not captured its tone, which is a good deal more lighthearted than the sordid docudrama you describe. I was reviewing the movie, and you are essentially discussing the profession of prostitution.

### *Deconstructing Harry*

**Q.** I saw Woody Allen's *Deconstructing Harry* the other day and enjoyed it. One thing I noticed at the end, when he's dreaming and all of his characters are assembled to forgive him, there are two or three quick shots of an actress who looks just like Mia Farrow. If this is true, it seems that Woody is wishing that someday Mia will forgive him. Can you confirm if this actress is supposed to be Mia Farrow?

—Jon Pietrowski, Genoa, Ohio

**A.** According to a representative of Allen's, any similarity was purely coincidental: "Woody does not choose his extras and had nothing to do with it." My opinion: If Allen had thought one of the extras looked like Farrow, he would not have used her.

### *Devil's Advocate*

**Q.** Toward the end of *Devil's Advocate* there was a scene (quite popular with the crowd) in which Al Pacino as Satan repeats some of Keanu Reeves's lines in Reeves's voice. My wife and I disagree about whether this was actually Pacino imitating his coactor, or if he was simply lip-synching to playback. Can you set the record straight?

—Dominick Cancilla, Santa Monica, California

**A.** It's even more devilishly complex. A Warner Bros. source says Al Pacino is not imitating Keanu Reeves's voice nor is he lip-synching to a playback. Instead, Pacino spoke the original lines during production. Later Reeves, during postproduction, looped the lines (spoke them, matching his voice to Pacino's original lip movements).

### *The English Patient*

**Q.** I thought *The English Patient* was a great film, but something about the central romance really bugs me. By coincidence, I'd seen *Casablanca* at a revival house just the night before. In that film, Bogart gives up the woman he loves for the higher purpose of defeating the Nazis. In *The English Patient,* the Ralph Fiennes character deals with the Nazis in order to get back to the woman he loves. Some of my women friends are captivated that Fiennes's character subordinates everything to his passion for this woman; that includes her husband and the fate of the free world, to name two. Am I a wet blanket to be totally turned off by this? Are some women actually leaving the theater wondering "Would my man sell out the world to the fascists to be with me?"

—John Miller

**A.** My guess is that few viewers of the film think it through in the way you have. Yes, the Fiennes character betrays the Allies and provides maps to the Nazis because of the woman he loves. Perhaps he was inspired by the decision a few years earlier by the duke of Windsor, who also put a woman above a kingdom, his responsibility, and his heritage. Your questions are precisely the ones, I think, that bother Caravaggio, the Willem Dafoe character, although he keeps his thoughts to himself for a long time, primarily for the convenience of the screenplay.

### *Fargo*

**Q.** I've spoken to several knowledgeable filmgoers and no one has given me a satisfactory explanation as to why the scene with Chief Gunderson (Frances McDormand) and her Asian high school friend Mike Yanagita (Steve Park) was included in the film *Fargo.* Your comments?

—Kerry Glicken, Highland Park, Illinois

**A.** This is the most common question asked about the film, and now that it's out on video, people are asking again. The scene functions in several ways. (1) It works on its own terms, as a wonderful little human drama. (2) It shows that Marge Gunderson, so competent as a police officer, is still capable of being thrown in a social situation. (3) Most important, it separates her two crucial meetings with the suspect Jerry Lundegaard (William H. Macy). She interviews Jerry almost as an afterthought at the car dealership (where she went looking for Shep Proudfoot). Then she has dinner with her old friend Mike. The next morning, she learns in a phone call that everything he told her was a fabrication. Then we see her looking thoughtful in her squad car. Then she returns to the dealership to ask Jerry more questions—and this time he cracks and flees the interview. Being deceived by the school friend nudged her to replay her original interview with Jerry. Imagine the Lundegaard interview as one unbroken scene, and you can see how much less effective it would have been. The delay between the scenes also allows us to imagine Lundegaard marinating in his guilt and fear, setting up his extreme nervousness when she returns.

## *Fast, Cheap & Out of Control*

Q. Did you see the latest story out of Los Angeles? It says that Errol Morris's *Fast, Cheap & Out of Control* failed to make the cutoff for this year's top fifteen documentaries, and therefore will not be considered for an Oscar nomination as Best Documentary!!! Can this possibly be true?

—Greg Nelson, Chicago, Illinois

A. It certainly can. The Academy has a long and consistent reputation for carefully overlooking the best documentaries, year after year—to such an extent that to fail to win a nomination is a badge of honor. Morris's film, the most widely-hailed doc of the year, now joins *Hoop Dreams, Roger and Me, Shoah, Crumb, Paradise Lost,* and Morris's own *Thin Blue Line* among films that the Academy's taste-dead selectors have overlooked. This time, though, there is outrage, not least from producer Frank Marshall *(The Color Purple, Who Framed Roger Rabbit),* who says there's something wrong with the system and has joined a rising tide of protest against the sadly out-of-touch volunteers who generously donate many hours of their time to ignoring good documentaries.

## *Fifth Element*

Q. What language is Milla Jovovich speaking in *Fifth Element*? Is it a real language? What is her native tongue?

—John McFarlane, Orlando, Florida

A. It was a special language created by director Luc Besson, according to a Columbia spokesman. Besson and Jovovich grew so fluent, they could communicate with each other using it. Her native tongues are Ukrainian and Russian.

## *The Full Monty*

Q. I saw *The Full Monty,* and while I ultimately thoroughly enjoyed it, I doubt that I actually understood more than 5 percent of the working-class dialogue—though I was able to follow the basic story, of course. There were sometimes periods of many minutes where they could just as well have turned off the sound. I can understand sentences that contain no vocalized consonants when they are spoken slowly, but no' a' the brea'ne' cli' tha' were oft' th' case in thi' fil'. A few people in the theater seemed to do much better, but I think a lot of people in theaters must laugh just because everyone else laughs. I think the film needs subtitles.

—Ira D. Flax, San Francisco, California

A. *The Full Monty* is the season's top art-house hit, and yet I'm sure a lot of audience members share your feelings. I had no difficulty with the dialogue because I've grown accustomed to British accents over the years, but it's true that there's an enormous difference between English as spoken by Lawrence of Arabia and by unemployed steelworkers in Sheffield. Subtitles would be a distraction, though. It's not the words, it's the music, and most of the time I think we catch the drift even if a word eludes us. It's a two-way street; I imagine they had trouble understanding *Deliverance* in Sheffield.

## Future Flicks

Q. The Amazing Kreskin is working on a "Millennium" book for release on January 1, 1999. He would like for you to provide insight into what could possibly lie ahead in the film world in the next millennium.

—Tom Coyne, Assistant to the Amazing Kreskin

A. Within the next 1,000 years, the "feelies" of science fiction will become a reality, and movies will take place entirely inside our heads. The computerized technology will be able to directly access and control those brain zones dealing with pleasure, thought, and the five senses. In these films of the future, we will all be incredibly smart, good-looking, and brave. Our fantasies will become so addictive that opium dens will pale by comparison, and "moviegoers" will return to their real lives only reluctantly. The human race will gradually die out, as fantasy becomes easier, more pleasant, and safer than reality. The last surviving human will die with a smile at a very old age, still plugged in and thinking he is enjoying great sex.

## *Gattaca*

**Q.** Saw *Gattaca* and found it very thought provoking. But either they never said or I missed it: What does Gattaca mean?

—Emerson Thorne, Chicago, Illinois

**A.** *Variety* film critic Emanuel Levy says the title is inspired by the four key chemicals in DNA: Guanine, Adenine, Thymine, and Cystosine.

## Getting Started

**Q.** Somebody who works in the film industry has given me advice about how to "move up the ladder of success." He said in no uncertain terms that "anyone who doesn't want to remain a production assistant for the rest of their career needs to have sex with the right people." He then elaborated on who I should have sex with (example: don't have sex with a director, but the casting director is okay). He explained how he had to do this to move from a location scout to a location manager. He said that *everyone* in the industry does this and there is no way around it. I will not prostitute myself. What should I believe?

—Debbie Vanden Dungen,
Abbotsford, British Columbia

**A.** I forwarded your message to Nancy De Los Santos, who began in Chicago as a production assistant on the *Siskel and Ebert* program, moved up to producer, and then moved to Hollywood, started as a production assistant, and climbed the ladder again; her most recent credit was as associate producer of *Selena*. She writes:

"Is it necessary to sleep with someone in order to be a success in Hollywood? Absolutely not. If only it were that easy! I don't know anyone who is successful who had to sleep with someone in order to succeed. To be successful in Hollywood, you need three things: talent, tenacity, and confidence in yourself. Being intimate with someone higher on the food chain might get you an 'in,' but it won't keep you there. You also have to consider what you think is 'successful.' I feel it's when you are respected and sought after for your work. I also have to question your contact's theory regarding sleeping with the 'casting director' but not the director. The director is the most powerful person (next to a high-priced star) on a film. If someone wanted to exchange sex for a chance at job advancement, the director would be a good choice, but only if he or she is currently in production. Your contact's route of advancing from location scout to location manger because he slept with someone only makes me think he must not have been a very good location scout. Delivering what you're hired to do is how to succeed in Hollywood. Don't let anyone tell you different."

## Giving Away the Ending

**Q.** I was fortunate enough to be invited to an early screening of *The Jackal*, and the one thing I liked about it was the fact that they didn't tell you who the target was until the climax—a nifty little touch. So you can imagine how stunned I was when you spilled the beans on TV and in print—and you can imagine how really p.o.'d I would've been if I hadn't yet seen the picture. To loathe a film, that's your right, but you still have a responsibility not to reveal surprises. There are plenty of ways to dissuade people from seeing a movie without trying to ruin it for them.

—Studio Executive, Name Withheld

**A.** I wrote, "This new *Jackal* considers a potential victim who is obviously supposed to be Hillary Clinton, and that made my heart sink." I felt it was my duty as a critic and, frankly, as a citizen, to register my protest against this story decision. As I added, "The next time Bruce Willis or Richard Gere complains about the invasion of their privacy by the media, I hope someone remembers to ask them why their movie needed to show the First Lady under fire." We live in a time when there are a lot of nuts out there. The movie could easily have made the intended target a generic first lady—not pleasant, I suppose, but not as dangerous as deliberately making her a lookalike and having her dedicate the "New

Hope" hospital, named no doubt after the "man from Hope." If I diminished your pleasure in the "nifty" surprise of seeing shots fired at a Hillary Clinton lookalike, well, that's a responsibility I'm willing to accept.

## *Godzilla*

**Q.** According to a report in the current issue of *Slate,* the upcoming *Godzilla* movie features a "Mayor Ebert" who gets "crushed like a bug." The screenwriters' previous film credits were *Independence Day* and *Stargate,* both of which you panned. Does this kind of silliness make you feel flattered or just annoyed? Will it affect the way you view the film?

—Sue Trowbridge, Albany, California

**A.** I am deeply honored to be working with Mr. Godzilla in his first major Hollywood film.

**Q.** There are a few things you got wrong in your *Godzilla* review that might have added a tenth of a star to that one-and-a-half-star rating. (1) Godzilla doesn't "breathe" fire. In the two shots where that appears to happen, I'm pretty sure it's exploding vehicles that provide the flames. (2) They don't say Godzilla's female. In fact, they make it clear that his reproduction as a male is paradoxical, which leads to all that silliness about asexual reproduction. Of course that's crap writing in itself, since it's only there to explain how they could get a Godzilla's-Nest plot without a second adult giant mutant lizard and without rewriting forty years of Godzilla lore (Godzilla's always been a guy).

—Blair P. Houghton, Phoenix, Arizona

**A.** I think Godzilla does indeed breathe fire, and have checked it with a couple of other people who saw the movie. The problem is, the fire-breathing is used as atmosphere, not as a plot point, and has no consistency, so that two intelligent people (such as ourselves) are left unsure about whether the centerpiece of a multimillion-dollar epic does or does not breathe fire. The movie should leave no doubt on this point. As for (2), my contention is a creature that lays eggs is a female, but I concede there is dialogue explaining why this does not apply in Godzilla's case, so I was wrong. If Godzilla is indeed a male, however, we are left perplexed by his apparent lack of reproductive equipment, although of course if he can impregnate himself it may be all built in.

**Q.** I just saw *Godzilla,* and I thought the spoof of you and Gene Siskel was pretty funny! Boy, they really didn't try to hide the symbolism in those characters! It's surprising they didn't get killed! I'll bet if you guys give it two thumbs up, Devlin and Emmerich will bring them back for the sequel, but if you give it two thumbs down, they'll probably kill them off in the sequel!

—Chad Polenz, Schenectady, New York

**A.** I think we got off pretty easy. I expected to be squished like a bug. I liked the way Mayor Ebert of New York makes all the obligatory wrongheaded decisions, including not wanting to evacuate Manhattan; he's obviously inspired by the real-estate mogols in *Jaws,* who didn't want to clear the beaches.

**Q.** I'd like to add one more dumb thing about *Godzilla* that most people likely didn't notice when watching it. Producer Devlin and director Emmerich need to learn or at least identify Japanese (or Korean) first before they remake a Japanese movie (or any other). When Broderick's character reaches the boat destroyed by Godzilla in Panama, he picks up a can of tuna on the ground in front of the wreckage. This can of tuna was made in Korea, and it clearly says "Dong-won Chamchi (tuna)" in Korean on it. First of all, let me tell you that there are plenty of tuna cans produced in Japan, and they don't need another tuna can imported from Korea. And second, wasn't it a fishing boat? Then why do they need to carry a can of tuna when they can fish for fresh? Maybe it doesn't matter to Americans, but it's insulting to me as a Korean.

—Min Woong Lee, Irvine, California

**A.** Whoa! I've heard a lot of mean things said about *Godzilla,* but yours is the first attack on the movie's use of Korean canned tuna. Insulting? Hey, the Japanese prefer Korean tuna! Be proud.

**Q.** You asked in your review of *Godzilla* how could they could miss Godzilla's being male. It's actually pretty easy. Lizards have semi-internal genitalia. All you see outside is a little slit, even for a male lizard.

—Susan Alderman, Cambridge, Massachusetts

**A.** At last I know why lizards always wear towels in shower scenes.

## *Good Will Hunting*

**Q.** In *Good Will Hunting,* the character of Will comes up with the names of twelve nonexistent brothers. Are the names of some significance to Will, or to the filmmakers? You know, like the Red Sox starting lineup?

—Paul Cormier, Leiden, Netherlands

**A.** A publicist for the film says "there's no significance." The names are listed, by the way, in a transcript of the movie posted on the Web by Dana Franklin. They are Marky, Ricky, Danny, Terry, Mikey, Davey, Timmy, Tommy, Joey, Robby, Johnny, and Brian.

*I offered a free copy of last year's edition of this book to the reader who could suggest the most plausible link among them.*

Tor C. Swanson of Minnetonka, Minnesota, suggested they're the names of the Ramone family, of "Ramones" fame. And Brad Richman of New York City wrote, "I remember thinking that they were the names of the Wahlberg family, whose members include Mark *(Boogie Nights)* and Donny (New Kids on the Block). I remember reading that the Wahlbergs were from a large family, and they are from Boston, where the story takes place."

Neither suggestion fits. Mark and Donnie Wahlberg have four other brothers (Arthur, Paul, Bobbo, and Jimbo) and three sisters (Debbie, Michelle, and Tracey). The Ramones include Johnny, Joey, Marky, C.J., Dee Dee, and Tommy. I haven't been able to get the names of nonband members of the family.

The search went on. A La Grange, Illinois, reader thought they were Twelve Apostles with a "y" added to each name (St. Brian?). The winning theory came from Gina Dante of Minneapolis, who wrote:

"I think the brothers are named after the film directors whom Ben Affleck and Matt Damon would like to work with—and whose movies they were possibly up for parts in. I've listed the director's name, a recent movie he directed, and the name of a Ben/Matt contemporary who acted in the movie. You may see a pattern forming here. Perhaps the brothers are a wish list."

1. Marc Rocco/*Murder in the First*/Christian Slater
2. Richard Attenborough/*Chaplin*/Robert Downey Jr.
3. Danny Boyle/*Trainspotting*/Ewan McGregor
4. Terry Gilliam/*12 Monkeys*/Brad Pitt
5. Mikael Soloman/*Hard Rain*/ Christian Slater
6. David Fincher/*Seven*/Brad Pitt
7. Tim Burton/*Edward Scissorhands*/Johnny Depp
8. Tom Hanks/*That Thing You Do!*/The Band Members
9. Joel Schumacher/*Batman Forever*/Chris O'Donnell
10. Robert Redford/*A River Runs Through It*/Brad Pitt
11. John Woo/*Broken Arrow*/Christian Slater
12. Brian De Palma/*Ambrose Chapel*/Brad Pitt

## *Hamlet*

**Q.** I can't understand how Kenneth Branagh gets nominated for Best Adapted Screenplay when he took Shakespeare's play and filmed it verbatim! It was an excellent and original adaptation, but how can he be nominated for what Shakespeare wrote? Methinks the screenwriters nominated him based on his direction of the movie, not on any writing.

—Steven Sherman, Montreal, Quebec

**A.** A screenplay is something more than dialogue. Consider, for example, that Alan Parker got a screenplay credit for *Evita,* even though virtually every word in the movie was in the form of a Tim Rice and Andrew Lloyd Webber lyric. Screenplays also cover construction, scene choices, character treatments, and, in the case of a writer-director like Branagh, the visual strategy. Yet the fact remains that this was an uncut text by Shakespeare. Screenwriter W. C. Martell tells me: "The staging of the soliloquy in front of the two-way mirror was brilliant! And there were other visuals that had to come in the script stage, rather than the direction. But I would question if there were enough new visual elements added to the original text to qualify Branagh as a cowriter. Had Shakespeare been alive, his agent would have surely pushed this through Writers Guild Arbitration, and they would have awarded the Bard sole script credit. Branagh would have to have added over a third new material to get his name on the screen."

## Hong Kong Subtitles

Q. As part of my efforts as a morning show host out here, I stumbled across this from the ABC newsroom. It's the translation of American films in Hong Kong. Some actual English subtitles:

"I am damn unsatisfied to be killed in this way."

"A normal person wouldn't steal pituitaries."

"This will be of fine service for you, you bag of the scum. I am sure you will not mind that I remove your manhoods and leave them out on the dessert flour for your aunts to eat."

"Take my advice, or I will spank you without pants."

"Yah-hah, evil spider woman! I have captured you by the short rabbits, and can now deliver you violently to your gynecologist for a thorough extermination!"

"Beat him out of recognizable shape!"

"How can you use my intestines as a gift?"

"Greetings, large black person. Let us not forget to form a team up together and go into the country to inflict the pain of our karate feets on some ass of the giant lizard person!"

—Bruce Maiman, Monterey, California

A. This list has been circulating on the 'Net, and on reading it I was convinced it was phony. It's just "too good." Through Norman Wang, an expert on Asian films, I got an authoritative opinion from Shu Kei, the Hong Kong–based writer *(Temptress Moon)* and director *(Queer Story, Stage Door).* While not judging the authenticity of these example, he writes: "Ninety-nine percent of the English subtitles of HK films are translated and done in HK. They are usually translated by the subtitling companies (there are only three) who hire inept translators or ask their sons to do the job. Production companies or directors almost never check the translators—actually almost no one cares. Worse still, the translators just listen to an audiotape of the sound track and never watch the film so most of the time they are just guessing at the meaning of the dialogue."

## *The Ice Storm*

Q. In *The Ice Storm,* there's a big ice storm on the Friday of that Thanksgiving weekend in Connecticut. I was wondering if this actually occurred there, or if it was just artistic license.

—Edward Matthew Prigge, Philadelphia, Pennsylvania

A. According to Darren Soldikoff of Fox Searchlight Pictures, "There was an actual ice storm in 1973 at Thanksgiving. The movie was filmed in the summer, however, so the ice storm had to be re-created. The book is not based on any true story nor is it based on that ice storm—but in the novel, it's written that way." And director Ang Lee adds that the "ice" was actually a special effect made of a gelatinous substance.

## *In and Out*

Q. Just saw and enjoyed *In and Out* but couldn't listen fast enough during the funny Oscar scene. In addition to the Matt Dillon character, who were the other nominees for Best Actor, and what were their film's names?

—Susan Lake, Urbana, Illinois

A. The other nominees were (the envelope, please!) Clint Eastwood for *Codger,* Paul Newman for *Coot,* Michael Douglas for *Primary Urges,* and Steven Seagal for *Snowball in Hell.*

Q. In your review of *In and Out,* you say the screenplay was by Paul Rudnick, "who under the pen name Libby Gelman-Waxner writes a funny column for *Premiere* magazine." What are you telling me—*there's no Libby Gelman-Waxner?? Paul Rudnick???* I am stunned. The column is just so . . . so . . . *female.* How could *he* possibly have such an insight into my feelings for Kevin Costner and Mel Gibson? I'm hoping that he's gay, therefore, as it would give me at least some small comfort.

—Denise Leder, Las Vegas, Nevada

A. From what I understand, you have reason to hope.

Q. The *In and Out* time line has me puzzled. As we all know, the Academy Awards are always held on the fourth Monday in March. In the film, Howard's wedding is held the next weekend (that's okay), but then the high school graduation is held a few days later—which would put it about mid-April!

—Ed Slota, Warwick, Rhode Island

A. Chalk it up to poetic license, according to Rob Hahn, the film's cinematographer. He adds that the exteriors were shot in October, and "sometimes we had to paint the leaves green." The interiors were shot in winter, with artificial light to suggest sunshine outdoors.

## *Independence Day*

Q. Usually the movies compress time, but sometimes they expand it, and that annoys me. For example, in *Independence Day,* Jeff Goldblum and Will Smith are told that the nuclear warhead they are carrying will explode thirty seconds after impact. When I recently watched this movie on video, I checked on the index counter. The explosion was at 1:35. If they want a certain series of events to occur, can't they figure out how long they would actually take, then use that amount of time in the script?

—Steven Stine, Buffalo Grove, Illinois

A. If the movie's working, you don't think about things like that. And there's a reason. The "logical" left hemisphere of the brain is aware of time; the "artistic" right brain much less so (you know how long you've been working on a spreadsheet, but not how long you've been painting a landscape). If a movie has completely absorbed you, the right brain takes over and you have a sensuous, escapist experience. If the movie doesn't grab you, then the left brain is aware of flaws and other details. For that reason I'm much more forgiving of clichés in movies that are really working—because then even the clichés work.

## *Jackie Brown*

Q. Am I crazy, or is the voice on Jackie Brown's answering machine ("You have one new message") belong to Quentin Tarantino himself?

—Leigh Emshey, Innisfail, Alberta

A. That is indeed Tarantino's voice. When I interviewed QT about the movie, he said he deliberately didn't give himself a cameo role, "because I didn't want people to take me for granted anymore, as far as that kind of stuff is concerned." But with your eagle ears you have discovered his hidden cameo.

Q. Just saw Tarantino's *Jackie Brown.* When Max Cherry (Robert Forster) is leaving the movie theater, we hear a song from the movie he was seeing. It is "Monte Carlo Nights," which is also the last song on the *Jackie Brown* sound track. What movie was Max watching?

—Brad Beall, Cedar Rapids, Iowa

A. *Jackie Brown,* obviously.

## *Inventing the Abbotts*

Q. I stood for a long time in front of the poster for *Inventing the Abbotts,* which shows five or six of the major characters piled into the front seat of a car. Something was wrong. Suddenly I realized: There isn't room in the front of that car for all the bodies connected to the heads! The heads are so close together that they apparently do not possess shoulders, arms, chests, torsos, etc. What's up?

—Emerson Thorne, Chicago, Illinois

A. I also stood for a long time in front of the poster. I think you are right. The beautiful Jennifer Connolly is in the center of the pile, smiling right at us, but if you study the layout she seems to have no body; it looks like her face was popped into the middle of the artwork like a cherry in a fruit cocktail. The wonders of computer graphics.

## John Gregory Dunne

Q. In John Gregory Dunne's new book about the screenwriting adventures of he and his wife, Joan Didion, he takes a really nasty crack at you and Siskel. Your response, please? He begins by describing the annual Academy Awards parties held at Spago by the legendary agent Irving "Swifty" Lazar and his wife, Mary. He says the earlier part of the evening was a "family party," as the big stars watched the Oscars on TV. After the ceremony was over, he says, "many of the older stars would depart," and people who had been at the Oscars would arrive. Then he writes, "The more presentable press also gained late entry, acting for all the world as if they were members of the community, and not its parasites. I remember Siskel and Ebert late that evening, at the corner window table, greeting and being greeted, with that extravagance of word and gesture affected by public people who know they are the object of attention. What they did not know was that they were seated in places recently vacated by Jim and Gloria Stewart—in the community, real stars."

—Andrea Gronvall, Chicago, Illinois

A. What Dunne did not know was that Siskel and I were both invited by the Lazars for the earlier dinner. My wife and I arrived late because I covered the Oscars. Gene and his wife arrived for the "family party" and were seated at James and Gloria Stewart's table by Mary Lazar herself. I am surprised Dunne did not see them sitting there all through the dinner. Perhaps his table was not well placed for observing the main room.

## *Jurassic Park: The Lost World*

Q. Rented *Jurassic Park: The Lost World,* and during the "Support Vehicle Falling over the Cliff" sequence I thought I was watching something I'd seen before, but couldn't put my finger on it. Then I saw Chaplin's *The Gold Rush* and there it was—this time in black and white, silent, and with computer-free special effects, but essentially the same event: Chaplin is in a cabin that's seesawing on the edge of a mountain, he grabs onto a rope that's tied off outside the cabin, the cabin falls out from under him, he holds onto the rope, and survives. I don't recall any of the reviews of *The Lost World* mentioning the sequence as a homage to Chaplin, but perhaps I missed one or two. By the way, who was it who said, "You call it stealing; the French call it homage"?

—Robert Atkinson, Portland, Oregon

A. The parallel is perfectly obvious, now that you mention it. And in a follow-up you mentioned another homage: The opening sequence of *Jackie Brown* is a lengthy shot of Pam Grier on a people-mover at an airport. Dustin Hoffman is shown in a similar shot in the opening of *The Graduate.*

## *La Bohème*

Q. Whatever happened with the all-cat version of *La Bohème*? The idea, as I recall, was a film featuring live feline "actors" while the sound track played the Puccini opera as performed by the likes of Freni and Pavarotti. Has this project ever been realized?

—Dix Sudquai, Chicago, Illinois

A. James Cameron decided to go ahead with *Titanic* instead.

## Letterboxing

Q. I am a fan of the letterbox format on video. I went all over town tonight to get a copy of *Independence Day* in letterbox and found none. With this movie, it's not the story, it's the special effects! The "pan-and-scan" version is missing a lot of neat stuff, chopped off of each shot. Is the general public so uneducated that it doesn't understand what they are missing? Am I alone out here? Twentieth-Century Fox just lost a sale.

—Brett Peters, Tallahassee, Florida

A. Major video rental chains don't like letterboxing because, as I was told once, it's too difficult to educate the clerks to explain it to customers. Steve Feldstein of Fox Video says the widescreen version of *Independence Day* will probably be released in March 1997. Strange, since it takes *more* time to pan and scan a movie than to simply transfer the existing widescreen version.

Q. Way back when *Schindler's List* was released on video, I wrote to the Answer Man about a newspaper article I had read about Blockbuster Video's policy against carrying letterboxed videos. The article mentioned that the corporate policy was never to carry letterboxed videos if a nonletterboxed version was available since letterboxing tended to confuse customers. Well, I was in a local Blockbuster store yesterday and thought you might be interested in what I discovered. In both the sales and the rental sections, they had large displays of nothing but letterboxed videos. They had professionally printed signs with "Widescreen" in big letters and the slogan "See what you have been missing." A large selection of letterboxed VHS tapes were available for either rental or purchase.

—Jeffrey Graebner, Los Angeles, California

A. Inexorably, the tide is turning, as increasing numbers of viewers request letterboxing. Since many cable channels have a policy of showing the widescreen letterbox versions instead of the despised pan and scan, people have grown more familiar with the format. Most of new DVD discs offer a choice between letterbox and p&s, where applicable, and that will accelerate the process; when you can sit at home and see for yourself how much of the total picture area you're missing with p&s, it's very persuasive. A Blockbuster person once told me it was too difficult to educate clerks to explain letterboxing to customers. My observation was that both clerks and customers understood it better than many Blockbuster executives.

## *Liar, Liar*

**Q.** I have yet to see this hidden joke from *Liar, Liar* mentioned anywhere, and was wondering if you had noticed it: When Jim Carrey's character first tries to overcome his inability to lie, he has an amusing tug-of-war with a blue pen. At the end of his futile battle, Carrey rises from behind his desk with the word "BLUE" written repeatedly all over his face. Among those scribbled BLUEs was the name "B. B. King." down by his chin. For some reason, I felt there was a reason to look for a "blues" joke there, and I found it!

—Matt Webb Mitovich, New York City, New York

**A.** You've got me so worked up, I'm searching for the *Dragnet* reference in your name.

## *The Long Way Home*

**Q.** We were deeply moved by the Oscar-winning documentary *The Long Way Home,* but had a question about the scenes of the Jewish refugees trekking across the Alps. Was this authentic footage? Why did there happen to be a camera there?

—Casey Anderson, Schaumberg, Illinois

**A.** Mark Harris, director of the film, replies: "The footage of the refugees crossing the Alps in *The Long Way Home* comes from Meyer Levin's film, *The Illegals.* Levin followed a group of refugees from Poland on their way to Palestine, across the Alps, and then aboard the ship the *Unafraid,* trying unsuccessfully to evade the British naval blockade. The British board the boat, tow it into Haifa, and then send all the refugees to Cyprus. The film was an early docudrama, somewhat like Haskell Wexler's *Medium Cool,* in that Levin structured the film around a fictional story, in this case a couple making their way illegally to Palestine. (The actress later became his wife.) But just as Wexler filmed his story in the midst of the Democratic Convention in Chicago, Levin put his fictional couple in a real group of Jewish refugees escaping from eastern Europe, so the footage of them crossing the Alps is all authentic, as are the out-of-focus shots we later used of the British boarding the *Unafraid.* In his autobiography *The Search,* Levin describes this clandestine journey and the dramatic effect the survivors had on him."

## Mafia and the Movies

**Q.** Watched *Bound* on video. Pretty good. I've liked Joe Pantoliano since I saw him in *Risky Business,* but now I understand he has a Mafia handle, "Joey Pants." I got this info from the former girlfriend of a guy who carries the bag from South Beach to Chicago. If you knew his name, your life wouldn't be worth a plugged nickel. This handle thing may have more to do with Joey's role on television's *EZ Streets* rather than his exceptional performance in *Bound.* Do you know if any other actors have a similar honor?

—R. P. Boblett, Collins, Mississippi

**A.** Yes, but if I told you, I'd have to kill you.

## *The Man in the Iron Mask*

**Q.** I saw *The Man in the Iron Mask* the other day. Is it just me, or do you highly doubt they used the word "tits" in seventeenth century France?

—Chad Polenz, Schenectady, New York

**A.** The *Oxford English Dictionary* says the word originated in Old English, so it was in use at the time—but in England, of course. No doubt the Musketeers would have used the French equivalent. I somehow have no doubt that Musketeers talked like that.

## May–September

**Q.** My local alterna-weekly reviewed *Horse Whisperer* and *Bulworth* this week, and in both cases the critic observed how incredulous the relationships between the grizzled actor-director and his decades-younger love interest were. I think *Titanic* pretty much made it clear that women would rather see the heroine fall in love with someone her own age than someone old enough to be her dad. (It wouldn't have been anywhere near as big a hit if the DiCaprio role had been filled by, say, Kevin Costner.) It's partly a generational thing: A lot of women my age have fathers who left their mothers for a younger woman. There's a growing intolerance toward that kind of behavior in the media, like the Tea Leoni subplot in *Deep Impact* and the sitcom *Just Shoot Me,* though in both cases, the dad gets off the hook pretty easy.

—Lucius P. Cook, Dallas, Texas

**A.** Incredulous, they were. Incredible, maybe not. I am reminded of a TV news feature I saw when *Indecent Proposal* came out—the movie where Demi Moore has to decide whether to accept $1 million for spending a night with Robert Redford. The reporter was asking a young woman in a shopping center if she would sleep with Redford for $1 million. "Sure," she said. How about $500,000? "Sure," she said. How about $100,000? "Let's cut to the chase," she said. "I'd do it for fifty cents."

## *Men in Black*

**Q.** In your review of *Men in Black,* you mention the celebrities that are shown on a chart and described as being alien. Besides the ones you've noted, I was also able to spot filmmaker George Lucas and self-improvement guru Tony Robbins.

—Mark Dayton, Costa Mesa, California

**A.** The complete list of "aliens among us" in *Men in Black,* according to Columbia TriStar's Danielle McLaughlin, includes Sylvester Stallone, Dionne Warwick, Al Roker, Newt Gingrich, Isaac Mizrahi, Danny DeVito, Steven Spielberg, George Lucas, Anthony Robbins, director Barry Sonnenfeld, and his daughter Chloe.

## *Midnight in the Garden of Good and Evil*

**Q.** Just saw *Midnight in the Garden of Good and Evil.* The setting is Savannah, Georgia, at Christmastime. I question all the fully-leafed trees. I thought trees lost their leaves because of the reduced amount of daylight, not because of the absence of warm weather. The scenic background was a glaring inconsistency for me.

—James C. Halas, Park Ridge, Illinois

**A.** Clint Eastwood filmed on location in Savannah in the months of May and June 1997.

## Misleading Ads

**Q.** You said in your review of *Persuasion* that it may take a while before we figure out that the story is about Amanda Root and Ciaran Hinds. Now the movie is on video, and, yes, it took me an inordinately long time to figure this out, largely because the couple pictured in a passionate embrace on the cover of the box are not Root and Hinds! The woman appears to be Ione Skye, and the man's head is down, so all we can see are his (very nineties) floppy bangs. Is it legal to put people on a video box who don't even appear in a video?

—Sheila Casey, Los Angeles, California

**A.** Making big but baseless claims for movies is an art form that goes back to the birth of the cinema. I've seen several video boxes that misrepresented the contents, including *Picture Bride,* which made the Asian-American heroes look Caucasian, and *The Journey of August King,* which made both of the leading characters look black even though one was white. The theory seems to be, "Give the customers what you think they want, even if you don't have it."

## *Mother*

**Q.** I saw *Mother* and enjoyed it, but I was puzzled by one scene early in the movie. When Albert Brooks is at dinner with the underinformed date, the wine in their glasses on the table is dancing all over the place without quite spilling. It looks like an earthquake is going on, but nothing else in the restaurant is bouncing like the wine. What is happening?

—Fr. Hal Weidner, Honolulu, Hawaii

**A.** Albert Brooks replies: "The reason that the wine was shaking is that he was so nervous on the date that his leg was shaking uncontrollably under the table. The lettuce was shaking too, but you couldn't see it."

## Movies on TV

**Q.** To the best of my knowledge, the telecast of *Schindler's List* was the first TV-M program on the broadcast networks. Personally, I was glad to see it, since it opens the door for more uncut movies (and less-censored original material), but I wonder if NBC has painted themselves into a corner by debuting with such a significant film? I'm sure a lot of people will say that this was okay because of the subject matter, but another R-rated movie of similar length (say, *Pulp Fiction*) wouldn't fly. What do you think?

—Allen Braunsdorf, Purdue University, Lafayette, Indiana

**A.** By justifying its decision to show the film uncut because of its importance and significance, the network was trying to have it both ways. It should have taken a stand on principle, instead of tacitly arguing that an exception should be made in this particular case. Broadcast standards should be applied consistently. I supported the telecast of *Schindler's List* and I would also support the airing of *Pulp Fiction.*

## *My Best Friend's Wedding*

**Q.** What do you think of my theory that *My Best Friend's Wedding* is really a guy movie in disguise, and not so much a chick flick. Romantic comedy is for women what action is for men—audiences desire a predictable ending that will push the right buttons and give them exactly the thrill and satisfaction they pay for. But *MBFW* undermines and subverts just about every romantic comedy convention there is. Usually the man starts out pigheaded, mistakenly involved with the wrong woman, and when he finally realizes the error of his ways, he has to diligently pursue the female lead. Here, Julia Roberts winds up chasing the man, in complete opposition to "the rules," and to underscore this unusual turn of events, Rupert Everett rubs it in, asking her "Who's chasing you?" *MBFW* is ironic and subversive, and it pays off from a guy's POV—the male lead gets the perfect woman—not from a woman's, which would have her getting the perfect guy.

—Paul Idol, Ft. Lee, New Jersey

**A.** So deeply embedded is our conviction that the heroine will get her man that when I wrote that the movie had a surprising ending, I was accused of giving it away. Screenwriter Ron Bass did a brilliant job of playing both with and against convention. Is it a guy film or a chick film? The interesting thing is that it keeps both camps guessing.

**Q.** I happened to read the screenplay for *My Best Friend's Wedding.* The movie follows the script closely, except for a greatly expanded scene between Julia Roberts's character and a hotel bellboy. In that scene, the two smoke a cigarette and revel in the pleasure of it. The dialogue and filming are bold—the bellboy blows smoke in our face—and you could feel the surprise in the audience at the screening I attended. Marlboro's products are featured elsewhere in the film. Would you know if the company paid to have this scene added? (I realize the male lead tells Julia to "stop smoking this s———, it'll kill you," but that's just equivalent to the surgeon general's warning.)

—Carl Marziali, Chicago, Illinois

**A.** A Columbia spokesperson says there was no product placement of any kind in *My Best Friend's Wedding.*

## *Nixon*

**Q.** In looking over your new book *Questions for the Movie Answer Man,* I was surprised to read a misconception that has arisen about my behavior on *Nixon.* Certain journalists have no shame about spreading negative rumors about me. In this case, a San Francisco critic included these comments in her rage-ridden review about the film, and probably this was passed around the critic community. The fact is we rushed the film through a difficult and hurried postproduction by early December that culminated in New York City in front of a huge press audience. This hardly qualifies as holding the film back. We provided full cooperation to the Golden Gloves and all of us, the actors and myself, attended their press conference. *Nixon* was ignored for the most part. The critics were mixed on the film, often having made up their mind, I believe, before they even saw the movie.

—Oliver Stone, Los Angeles, California

**A.** This is in reference to a question about why Stone's *Nixon* did not win more Golden Globe nominations. I wrote in my answer: "Oliver Stone may have lost the 'director' nomination for himself. In behavior that seemed positively Nixonian, he took personal control of the preview press screenings of the movie, insisting on approving every name. In most cities he allowed only a handful of 'leading' critics to attend. The Golden Globe membership is made up of Hollywood foreign correspondents—few of them on Stone's A-list

. . . Stone's policy may have aced him out a nomination." Whatever happened, *Nixon* certainly deserved more recognition and praise than it received.

## Oh, Gosh!

**Q.** Watching the film *Oh, God!* on the Family Channel, I noticed that it had been subtly edited, perhaps for philosophical reasons. John Denver plays a man who talks with God (played by George Burns). I sensed something was missing on the broadcast version, so I rented the video. I discovered that the Family Channel had edited out a moment when Denver asks Burns, "Was Jesus the son of God?" Burns responds: "Jesus was my son, Buddha was my son. The man who said, 'There's no room at the inn'—he was my son too. Let's move on." Was this dialogue edited out because the Family Channel broadcasts many Christian fundamentalist programs, and didn't want to show a scene suggesting there is more than one path to salvation?

—Michael West, Gloucester, Massachusetts

**A.** Ann Abraham, publicity manager for the Family Channel, replies: "The Family Channel does not follow a written policy for editing decisions. Programs are cut for time and/or content based on the assigned editor's discretion. In the case of *Oh, God!* the editor had to cut four minutes out of the movie. The segment in question, along with another short segment, fit the time constraints and was not considered integral to the story."

I asked her if the Family Channel might consider cutting a different four minutes the next time, and she replied that the channel doesn't have the movie on its upcoming schedule.

## Oscar

**Q.** The Oscars should be done like the Cable ACE Awards: All judges have to view all entries at the same time and can't discuss them with each other.

—Luigio Salmo, New York City, New York

**A.** What, and eliminate politics, cronyism, and guesswork? The Academy hasn't even gone so far as to require that voters actually *see* the films they vote for.

**Q.** I read that Steven Spielberg bought Clark Gable's *Gone With the Wind* Oscar for $550,000, and then donated it to the Motion Picture Academy. He did this to make a statement against the practice of selling Oscars, which is against Academy bylaws. What is your take on his action?

—Baxter Wolfe, Arlington Heights, Illinois

**A.** It was a fine and noble gesture, although by setting a new market record for famous Oscars, Spielberg may have inspired deep thoughts on the parts of other Oscar owners, who may be wondering if they would rather have the statuette, or the money. One thing's for sure: Now that we know what an Oscar can be worth, stars are going to stop leaving them around as paperweights and doorstops.

**Q.** You suggested that Steven Spielberg, who brought Clark Gable's Oscar for $550,000 and then donated it to the Motion Picture Academy as a gesture against the selling of Oscars, may in fact have helped establish a lucrative market for additional sales. However, as I'm sure you recognize, just because Clark Gable's Oscar sold for more than $500,000 doesn't mean that any other Oscar (or, at least, most Oscars) would sell for anywhere near that amount.

—Evan Zucher, San Diego, California

**A.** True. What would you take for yours? $50,000? $10,000? Actually, I think there's nothing wrong with selling an Oscar, should you be lucky enough to have one. In an industry that sees nothing wrong with spending $500,000 on a campaign to win an Oscar, what moral principle is being defended here?

**Q.** On a recent *Geraldo* show, Rex Reed made a serious allegation regarding the Academy of Motion Picture Arts and Sciences. Mr. Reed alleged there has been a massive cover-up involving the winner of the 1992 Best Supporting Actress Award. According to Reed, a blunder by presenter Jack Palance erroneously resulted in the awarding of the statue to Marisa Tomei for *My Cousin Vinny*, instead of Vanessa Redgrave. Reed explained a "stoned" or "drunk" Palance read the last name on the TelePrompter and did not properly open the envelope and name the winner as Redgrave. Can you shed any light on this alleged incident, which Reed described as Hollywood's best-kept secret?

—James Berg, Chicago, Illinois

**A.** Yours is one of several queries on this topic, and the "secret" is everywhere on the Internet. To nail this story for once and all, the Answer Man turned to Bruce Davis, executive director of the Academy, for an official statement, to wit:

"The legend of Marisa Tomei's 'mistaken Oscar' has appeared in various forms over the last four years and in that short time has achieved the status of urban myth. There is no more truth to this version than to any of the others we've heard. If such a scenario were ever to occur, the Price Waterhouse people backstage would simply step out on-stage and point out the error. They are not shy."

To which the Answer Man can add: If the story is true, how did Reed find out the winner was Vanessa Redgrave?

**Q.** Something has been bugging me. Female performers are now called "actors." What does that do to the "Best Actress" and "Supporting Actress" categories of the Oscars? Can they really have it both ways? What's wrong with being called an "actress"? Lest you think I'm a conservative antifeminist, know that I'm a knee-jerk liberal, but enough is enough!

—Marilyn B. Signer, Lakeland, Florida

**A.** The politically correct line is that gender distinctions should not be applied when a job is not gender-specific. An actor is an actor is an actor. It is only a matter of time, I suppose, until the Academy category is renamed "Best Female Actor." Of course to be truly consistent there should be no separate categories for men and women, and they should all compete equally for "Best Actor." After all, there isn't a category for "Best Female Director."

**Q.** When you were talking to Charlton Heston on TV as he arrived at the Oscars, you asked about the possibility that *Titanic* could beat *Ben Hur*'s record for number of awards. He made a decent point: Any comparison between the two epics would be unfair because there are now more Oscar categories than when *Ben Hur* was released in 1959. If that's the case, then those declaring "a tie" between the films are wrong.

—L. D. Paulson, Sacramento, California

**A.** In 1959, there were also categories that were later dropped, such as "Black-and-White Cinematography." But if you add up the categories in which both films were *eligible* to be nominated, it was fourteen for *Ben Hur* and seventeen for *Titanic*. Thus *Ben Hur* batted .785 and *Titanic* batted .647.

## *The Peacemaker*

**Q.** In your review of *The Peacemaker*, you failed to mention the most flagrant technical scientific error. The heroes save the day by preventing a nuclear explosion. But in the process a smaller explosion blows plutonium to bits in midtown New York City. I remember from high school physics that plutonium is the most lethal inorganic material known, and that a softball-size sphere, properly distributed, could kill everyone on Earth. Granted that the sphere in the movie was only baseball-size, George Clooney and Nicole Kidman should have been in the last throes of radiation poisoning at the end of the movie.

—Dave Jackson, Pekin, Illinois

**A.** And when she told the priest to get the choir boys "as far from here as possible," he should have had a jet plane parked outside.

## *The Preacher's Wife*

**Q.** In your review of *The Preacher's Wife* you state: "Surely the makers of this film do not believe that humans go to heaven and become angels. As we all know, angels were created by God as his first companions, and he created humans much later . . ." Perhaps you meant this comment ironically. I do not think Hollywood filmmakers take their theology from catechisms, serious theological works, or (God forbid) the Bible. Rather I presume their view of God, angels, the afterlife, etc., comes mostly from other movies, and television. The defining example for most filmmakers is, I suppose, *It's a Wonderful Life*, where Clarence (who has yet to earn his wings) is identified as a clock maker who had died 200 years before.

—Alan K. Scholes, Crestline, California

**A.** As I pointed out in a recent article on this very question, it is universally agreed among those religions that believe in them that angels have no sexual feelings, no bodies, no gender, and can love only God. They are *not* former humans who have returned from heaven for a visit to Earth. Angels like

Clarence, John Travolta's *Michael,* and the Denzel Washington character in *The Preacher's Wife* represent just plain sloppy theology from Hollywood.

## *Primary Colors*

Q. I noticed that Universal Pictures changed the tag line on the posters for *Primary Colors* from the double-entendre "What went down on the way to the top" to the much tamer "How much spin does it take to win?" They weren't afraid of offending someone, were they?

—Ed Slota, Warwick, Rhode Island

A. My suggestion would have been the tag line from *Alien:* "In space no one can hear you scream."

## *Private Parts*

Q. Went to see Howard Stern's *Private Parts.* Can't tell you how pleased I was to see scenes featuring "Kenny," the program director teaching Howard to pronounce "W-NNNN-BC!" I was an intern at WNBC during my senior year in college in 1980, and while there I gave a demo tape to "Kenny," whose real name was Kevin Metheny. He listened to it and trashed it, which would've been okay, except he did it in a hallway in front of my girlfriend (who despite this became my wife). Despite his predictions, I went on to have a pretty good on-air career, including doing morning radio with my wife. My question: Since Howard mentions people like Don Imus in his movie by name, and has already referred to Metheny as "Pig Virus" on the air, why couldn't he use the guy's actual name in the movie?

—Jim Crossan, Columbia, South Carolina

A. It is permissible to mention a real person in the context of commentary, but when a person is represented in a work of fiction and the depiction is negative, that person can sue. Imus is not really trashed in *Private Parts* (and besides, the chances are zero that he would sue). "Kenny" is one of the movie's major targets. And isn't it possible that the movie Kenny has been exaggerated from his real-life counterpoint, for comic purposes?

Q. When all is said and done, was *Private Parts,* the Howard Stern movie, a success? I saw it in maybe the fourth weekend of its release and sharing a screen with earlier screenings of some *Power Rangers* flick. It was only showing at 10 P.M. by that time. I had to complain twice (once to Beavis, once to Butt-head) before they got the movie started, a half-hour late.

—Jim Crossan, Columbia, South Carolina

A. It was a success, but is not perceived as one within the industry, because it is a victim of its own high expectations. The film opened like gangbusters, no doubt because Stern's listeners stormed the box office. But he has a finite number of listeners. The industry question was: Will it "cross over" to the mainstream public? It was carefully tailored to do so, and indeed most mainstream types who saw it liked it. But many apparently were kept away by Stern's reputation, so the movie didn't exhibit the "legs," or staying power, to maintain its opening pace. It was profitable, but not a monster hit. It will no doubt get good TV and cable ratings because of its curiosity value, and when home viewers see that Stern doesn't have horns, they may be more willing to test his next picture. Meanwhile, I ran into Stern at the Cannes Film Festival, where he is selling the film internationally. There's a big question mark about his market outside the United States: Will the film flop because he's unknown, or do well because it gets good reviews and there's no built-in antipathy to him in say, Belgium? Stay tuned.

*Footnote: It did only fairly well.*

## *Psycho*

Q. In your new *Roger Ebert's Book of Film* there is a selection by Janet Leigh in which she denies reports that the title designer Saul Bass actually directed the famous shower scene in Hitchcock's *Psycho.* This has sparked several letters to my Film 100 Website. I wrote that Hitchcock used Bass as a visual consultant on *Vertigo* and *North by Northwest* and that Bass so impressed the master of suspense with the storyboards for *Psycho*'s shower sequence, that Hitchcock rewarded him by allowing Bass to take the director's seat during the famous scene. Scouring through Bass obituaries, Hitchcock books, and *Los Angeles Times* archives, I found dozens of articles where crew members working the scene claimed Bass's account was correct. In your book, you leave the issue to Ms. Leigh, who was obviously there. But I wonder if her deference to the director has clouded her recollection.

—Scott Smith, www.film100.com

A. It seems unlikely that a perfectionist with an ego like Hitchcock's would let someone else direct such a scene. Janet Leigh was there every day and she is adamant, indeed furious, about Bass's claims to have directed it. "Absolutely not!" she writes. "I've said it in his [Bass's] face in front of other people. . . . I was in that shower for seven days, and, believe you me, Alfred Hitchcock was right next to his camera for every one of those seventy-odd shots." And here is Hilton Green, the assistant director and cameraman: "There is not a shot in that movie that I didn't roll the camera for. And I can tell you I never rolled the camera for Mr. Bass." Also check out pages 100–110 of the book *Alfred Hitchcock and the Making of Psycho,* by Stephen Rebello, in which he quotes numerous people who were on the set, and are certain Bass did not direct a single frame of the final film. Bass's participation may be one of those urban legends that gains credence because of the number of times it is repeated by people who learned it from each other.

## Ratings System

Q. I was quite disturbed by *Starship Troopers,* which is obviously marketed at children. You mentioned the violence, but what about the nudity and sex? I saw it yesterday with my eleven-year-old son (with many other parents and kids) and was shocked by the shower scene. The nudity served no purpose in the story line. I'm no prude and I don't believe in censorship but they know kids are going to be watching. Everyone likes to point a finger and blame Hollywood for everything that's wrong with society, but some criticism is fair. What were they thinking?

—Bob Cauttero, Harrington Park, New Jersey

A. The movie was rated "R" by the MPAA, which is a signal it is not appropriate for eleven-year-olds. Yet the film is obviously pitched at young teenage boys. It's hypocrisy: They take the "R" rating, knowing kids will find a way to see it, without or without an "adult guardian." As for the shower scene: It was a tongue-in-cheek satire of similar scenes in countless other movies, except, of course, that in this future world it's a co-ed shower. Just today a friend told me about seeing the movie in a packed house with "hundreds" of kids under seventeen, and seeing one parent telling his kids to cover their eyes during the shower scene, although of course they were free to drink in the gore, vivisection, and violence. We live in a strange world, when female breasts are considered a more offensive sight than men being cut in two.

Q. Re your Answer Man exchange about the parent who took his eleven-year-old to the R-rated *Starship Troopers* and then was offended by the shower scene: What you describe is exactly what happened to me! At a screening last week there were some kids, between the ages of six and ten, sitting behind me with their parents. During the aborted sex scene, when the actress took off her shirt, the mom said, "Tanner—don't look at this." Of course, the kid had already seen people screaming in agony as their bodies were pulled apart and blood and guts flew all over the place; then watched hundreds of dismembered corpses rot in the sun. If I'd seen *Starship Troopers* when I was a kid, I'd still be in a coma.

—Jim Emerson, editor, Microsoft Cinemania, Seattle, Washington

A. It illustrates the cynicism of the rating system that studios make R-rated movies while aiming their pitches at a prime audience including young teenagers. The same people who wonder if Joe Camel attracts fourteen-year-olds should note the *Starship Troopers* hoopla in young teen media.

Q. I loved *Secrets and Lies* now that it has finally made it to video, but why did it get an "R" rating? No nudity, no violence, not even much profanity.

—Christopher Hanley, Galesburg, Illinois

A. The MPAA's official explanation is that the film was rated R "for language." It must be one of the milder R-rated films of recent years, but the MPAA doesn't take context into account and basically just counts the four-letter words and applies its guidelines.

## Red Digital Readouts

Q. I always hate it when a movie plot goes into autopilot. Therefore, inspired by your review of *Peacemaker,* I would like to offer my comments about two clichés: RDR (Red Digital Readout) and its companion WCW (Which Color Wire?). A movie hero defusing a bomb always tries to guess the color-mnemonics of the builder. As a former electronics technician, if I was faced by this situation, I would simply look for the battery, make sure it was the only one, and cut *its* leads.

—Steven Stine, Buffalo Grove, Illinois

**A.** Why didn't Harrison Ford think of that in *Air Force One*? And Keanu Reeves in *Speed*? And Nicole Kidman in *Peacemaker*? Think of the screen time that could have been saved.

### *Scream*

**Q.** I saw Wes Craven's *Scream* last week. At the very end of the credits, it says, "No thanks whatsoever" to the school at which *Scream* was partially filmed. Did Craven and the school have a falling out? Or was this an inside joke? I've never seen a movie with end credits saying *No Thanks!*

—Michael Hatch

**A.** Janet Hill of Miramax tells me, "The Santa Rosa School District reneged on a verbal agreement to allow the production to film in that school. At the eleventh hour, Craven had to find another location. The school in the movie was filmed at the Sonoma Community Center in Sonoma, California." Robin Warder of the CompuServe Showbiz Forum adds: "What made Craven really mad was that the very week after, the same school allowed Ron Howard to film a movie there. Apparently, they were happier to accomodate Opie than the creator of Freddy Krueger!"

### *Scream 2*

**Q.** On the poster for *Scream 2,* two girls loom over the cast. One looks like Neve Campbell with blue eyes, when she clearly has brown eyes in the cast photo. The other looks like Jada Pinckett—but white. What's the deal behind changing Neve's eyes and Jada's race?

—T. Lehmann, Honolulu, Hawaii

**A.** A Miramax representative says the process used to "blue out" the photo for the poster to make it look cool had the result that all skin colors lost some of the grey tones; it happened to both Jada and Neve. They did play with the color of the eyes to make them more contrasting because both had such similar eye color. "Both Jada and Neve were crazy about the photo on the poster," I'm assured.

### Sequels and Remakes

**Q.** The movie *Three Men and a Baby* was based on a French film with the same theme. But was the French version based on an earlier American film, *Three Godfathers,* starring John Wayne?

—Rene Roy, Saskatoon, Saskatchewan

**A.** Funny you should ask. Yes, *Three Men and a Baby* (1987) was a remake of the French film *Three Men and a Cradle* (1985)—and represents one of the few cases where the remake was dramatically better than the original. But in my original review of the French film, I wrote: "It is clear as day that *Three Men and a Cradle* has been stolen—lock, stock, and barrel—from John Ford's Western classic *Three Godfathers,* a 1948 masterpiece in which outlaws John Wayne, Harry Carey Jr., and Pedro Armendariz find an abandoned baby in the desert and try to get it to safety. The sight of Wayne applying wagon grease to the little tyke's behind is all by itself worth more than every foot of this miserable French retread."

**Q.** When it comes to titles for sequels, Hollywood loses count. The first *Rambo* film was *First Blood.* Then followed *Rambo: First Blood II.* But next came *Rambo III.* What happened to *Rambo II*? Then there was *Mad Max,* followed by *The Road Warrior,* followed by *Mad Max III: Beyond Thunderdome.* What happened to *Mad Max II*? Or why wasn't the third film *Road Warrior II: Beyond Thunderdome*? Then came *Alien, Aliens,* and *Alien 3. Star Trek: The Motion Picture* was followed by *Star Trek: The Wrath of Khan,* which was followed by *Star Trek III: The Search for Spock.* The *Godfather* series is also not without its problems. The second film tells of the events leading up to the first film, as well as the events that happened after the first film. So should *The Godfather* have been *Godfather, Part II,* and should *Godfather, Part II* have been *The Godfather, Parts I and III*? And then of course *The Godfather, Part III* would have been *Part IV.*

—Bruce Totten, Chardon, Ohio

A. You have put your finger on a real problem. I first noticed it when *Henry: Portrait of a Serial Killer* was followed by *Henry V,* with no II, III or IV.

Q. You will be delighted to know that *Jungle 2 Jungle,* starring Tim Allen and Martin Short in an American remake of the French film *Little Indian, Big City,* will be released on March 14. Since you selected *Little Indian* as one of the worst films of 1996, save space on the '97 worst list now.

—Michael Dequina, Los Angeles, California

A. Although remakes are usually inferior to the films that inspired them, no film could possibly be worse than *Little Indian, Big City,* so I am cautiously optimistic.

*Note: But it was a close call.*

Q. I read in Liz Smith that they're planning a remake of *Casablanca,* and the writer (Michael Walsh) wants Sean Penn in the Bogart role, Julia Roberts as Ilsa, and Ralph Fiennes as the brave Resistance leader. To me, remaking *Casablanca* falls between sacrilege and stupidity. To you?

—Emerson Thorne, Chicago, Illinois

A. *Casablanca* cannot be remade, any more than the *Mona Lisa* can be repainted. It is as near to perfect as a movie can possibly be. Lesser films can be remade. Great films can only be ripped off. *Havana* (1990), with Robert Redford and Lena Olin, was a recycling of the same underlying story, which only served to illustrate that the material is uniquely linked to the original stars. Sean Penn is one of the best of living actors, but I am sure he would be the first to agree that Bogart, he ain't. And if, for the sake of argument, you were casting the Ilsa role, how could you possibly consider Julia Roberts when Isabella Rossellini, Bergman's daughter, is available—and has the right look, the right accent, and is the right age? If Nevada can pass a law against chewing off ears, why can't California pass a law against remaking *Casablanca*?

## *Seven*

Q. Did you notice, near the end of *Seven,* that just one frame of Gwyneth Paltrow is flashed in, almost like subliminal advertising? I didn't see it when I first watched the movie, but a friend of mine thought he did, and so I played the tape back frame by frame by repeatedly hitting the pause button. It is flashed on the screen just as Brad Pitt realizes whose head is in the box. Is it commonplace for movie directors to slip a subliminal message into their pictures?

—William Nack, Washington, D.C.

A. Not common, but it's been done before. There are some single-frame superimpositions of satanic faces over the face of Linda Blair in *The Exorcist.*

## *Shine*

Q. What is the significance of the title in the movie *Shine*?

—Grace Jablow, Palm Springs, California

A. *Shine,* the story of the gifted pianist David Helfgott, who had an emotional breakdown and a slow recovery, is one of this year's top Oscar candidates, but the title bears no apparent relationship to the movie. Scott Hicks, its director, tells me: "I have a favorite piece of music from the seventies—Pink Floyd's 'Shine on You Crazy Diamond.' I hoped to use it in the film as the lyrics were so appropriate (being about Syd Barrett, founding member of Pink Floyd, who went off the rails and retired to the shadows very young). However, the cost was prohibitive. I told Jan Sardi, who wrote the screenplay, about the track, and he played it a lot during periods of waiting. When we were agonizing over a title, Jan (being a master of reduction) suggested *Shine.* It seemed to convey the feeling of optimism and uplift that I had felt when I first saw David play, and which I wanted to share with the audience. During the title search we toyed with dozens of ideas. My first draft of the script was called 'Flight of the Bumblebee,' for example. Later I tried 'The Piece for Elephants'(!) which was Rachmaninoff's name for his Third Piano Concerto. But *Shine* was destined to stick—thank goodness!"

Q. I recently saw *Shine* and loved it. I noted in the end credits that the "Rach 3" was played by David Helfgott himself. In the *London Independent,* however, the reviewer noted that the sound track music was from Helfgott's 1995 recording, more than a decade after his return to the concert stage. The reviewer said: "His technical control is forever losing ground, the bravura elements massively compromised, not least in the finale where smudged and missing notes (fistfuls of them) fracture and displace Rachmaninoff's complete rhythmic configurations." Needless to say, this review saddened me. If true, is it possible that the "worst" of his errors were excised from the performance of the adolescent Helfgott, which wins him the medal and precipitates his breakdown, or is it just that the director knew that most of us are not such discerning music critics?

—Donna Martin, Kansas City, Missouri

A. I referred your question to the expert Wynne Delacoma, music critic of the *Chicago Sun-Times,* who replies: "The concerto is a sprawling work and director Scott Hicks could easily have chosen only bits and pieces of Helfgott's performance, presumably the most accurate as well as the most exciting, for *Shine*'s final cut. The music is so fast-paced and dramatic, even the best pianists can't guarantee note-perfect playing. Most listeners, caught up in the music's drive, wouldn't catch minor mistakes anyway. Most recordings these days are doctored to repair flubbed notes and other lapses. Audiences come to expect the perfection they hear on CDs from live performances."

## Siskel and Ebert Blurbs

Q. The newspaper ad for *Mars Attacks!* consists of multiple one-word reviews, probably all taken out of context, such as "Wild!" "Hilarious!" and "Outrageous!" One of them, "Funny!" is attributed to *Siskel and Ebert.* Funny, but I thought Gene liked it but you gave it thumbs down.

—Rhys Southan, Richardson, Texas

A. Funnily enough, on the show in question, the word "funny" was used five times: Three times by Siskel, who thought it was funny, and twice by me, who thought it was not. I complained to the studio, and they rewrote the ad to attribute the quote to Siskel, thus giving credit (or, in this case, blame) where due.

Q. The ads for David Lynch's *Lost Highway* in New York and Los Angeles use the quote "Two Thumbs Down!—Siskel and Ebert." Your comment?

—Joe Demanowitz, *Entertainment Weekly*

A. It's creative to use the quote in that way. Obviously there's a lot of disagreement about the film, and by playing up the discussion, the filmmakers encourage people to go see it for themselves. These days quotes in movie ads have been devalued by the "quote whores" who supply gushing praise to publicists weeks in advance of an opening. By playing up the controversy, *Lost Highway* is making a legitimate use of critics' opinions.

Q. Just got the video for *Fargo* and saw a quote from you and Gene Siskel on the cover, saying, "There won't be a better film than this all year!" Is this a new thing, or something you have being doing for years? I noticed Gene had one on *Crumb,* where he also said he wouldn't see a better film all year. Is this like a little "in" game, that allows you at the end of the year to say "See, I was right!"?

—Erik Solberg, Des Plaines, Illinois

A. That was Gene's quote, and *Fargo* should not have quoted both of us. I had no way of knowing in March 1996 if I would see a better film all year. Gene must be psychic, however, since I didn't see a better film all year.

Q. I am fascinated by the legal issues that might come into play involving the marketing of *Hercules,* in which many of the ads, whether in print or on TV, depict the character "Hades" giving "two thumbs up." I imagine that Disney folks hoped, and perhaps not unreasonably expected, that *Hercules* would receive the coveted "two thumbs up" rating, and scripted the movie to include a clever self-referential line to take advantage of the fact. But, failing that, they apparently decided there was nothing wrong with giving *themselves* two thumbs up—simply by using a clip from the movie. The problem is, that while the phrase "thumbs up" is obviously in the public domain, the phrase "two thumbs up" insofar as it applies to movies was—correct me if I'm wrong—created by you and Mr. Siskel. I note, with interest, that today's *New York Times'* ad for *Hercules* contains a picture of *Hades* making the "two thumbs up" gesture, sandwiched in among the "other" movie reviews. I also note that your own positive review of the film is conspicuous by its absence—since that would alert readers to the fact that Mr. Siskel did *not* give it a favorable review. What's next? Perhaps a film could have a character exclaim "Janet Maslin loves us," and then air the clip over and over, regardless of what Ms. Maslin thought of the film.

—Scott Morgan, Houston, Texas

**A.** "Two thumbs up" as it applies to movies is a trademark registered by Siskel and myself. We try to keep it from being misused. When "Hades" says "two thumbs up!" in the movie that of course is fair comment and part of the fun. But when we saw the TV ads, we made our opinion known to a studio executive, who agreed that it was a misrepresentation and said the offending ads would be pulled. Then the print ads appeared (not just in the *New York Times* but in the *Sun-Times* and many other newspapers). The thumbs-up Hades artwork was obviously intended to be misinterpreted as a favorable review. Once again, we called the studio, and once again we were told the ads would be pulled. How do I feel? That the ads were misleading and unfair. How does Gene feel? "Make it two thumbs down."

**Q.** I was perusing this week's issue of that paragon of journalistic integrity, the *Star*, and I was quite shocked to see amid the celebrity gossip an item about you, of all people. It said that you're suffering from arthritis, and it hurts when you have to extend your thumb. You're quoted as "telling a pal," "I'm having a problem with the thumb thing; I don't know how much longer I can do this." Any truth?

—Michael Dequina, Los Angeles, California

**A.** First, I don't have arthritis. Second, I don't need my thumb to be a movie critic. Third, you don't have to be able to move your thumb to give "thumbs up"—you need to be able to move your wrist. Fourth, I am amazed that the *Star* would devote its valuable columns to boring errors about my allegedly arthritic thumb when it completely ignored the rumor about the evening that Elizabeth Taylor, Mickey Rooney, and I got naked, covered ourselves with talcum powder, and rode bareback around her backyard. What a night it was!

## *The Spanish Prisoner*

**Q.** At the end of your review of David Mamet's *The Spanish Prisoner*, you noted that there is "a hole in the end of the story big enough to drive a ferryboat through." What do you see the hole as being?

—Zachary Juarez, Austin, Texas

**A.** *(Spoiler warning.)* I think there is a possibility that the Campbell Scott character orchestrated the entire con himself, which would explain why everybody was coincidentally on the boat. But I'm not sure. I have received so many long and detailed discussions of the plot points of the movie that it threatens to surpass even *The Usual Suspects* in the complexity of its analyses. In the interests of my tranquillity I have decided to discuss it no more until I have the opportunity to subject it to shot-by-shot analysis, maybe at an upcoming film festival.

## Special Effects

**Q.** My roommate thinks they shut down that entire street in *Devil's Advocate* for the dramatic Keanu-Walks-onto-an-Empty-Street-in-New-York Shot. I think that's unlikely. Since it's a crane shot (involving a shift along the vertical axis), a glass painting (see the final shot of *Raiders of the Lost Ark*) wouldn't work. So I say the traffic was removed digitally. Is that a powerful shot, or what? It's got to be my favorite single shot in recent months. When digital effects are being touted for how incredible they are, it's usually when there are fifty different spaceships moving within the frame. But this effect, by taking all the activity "out" of the shot, in my opinion has a much stronger effect.

—Robert Atkinson, Portland, Oregon

**A.** Paul Idol of the CompuServe Showbiz Forum says your guess is right, and points out that the movie's final credits include one for "57th Street Digital Effects."

**Q.** Since film travels at twenty-four frames per second and video travels at thirty frames per second, how do they put computer generated effects on films such as *Twister* and *Titanic*? If movie film is transferred to video first before computer effects are done, is it then transferred back to film where there would almost certainly be a generation loss of some kind?

—David Innes, Hammond, Indiana

A. I asked cinematographer Steven Poster, editor of *American Cinematographer* magazine, to reply. He writes:

"The system for utilizing computer-generated effects in movies doesn't use video at all. What happens is that the original film elements (like backgrounds or foreground actors) are 'scanned' into a digital medium with a laser scanner frame by frame. Once these images exist as digital information they are manipulated and enhanced and then combined with the computer-generated parts of the images. This way many different layers of information can be combined into each frame of the movie. Once the work has been done in the digital environment the images are transferred back to film frame by frame with a laser film recorder. Because the work is frame by frame the original film speed is not a factor. And the quality is very close to that of the original film. One of the important advantages of this is that the cinematographer has much more control to manipulate and correct the images. My first use of these techniques was on a movie called *Cemetery Club.* I had to correct a problem where inadvertently there was a piece of equipment left in the shot. I was able to completely remove this piece of aluminum pipe from the shot without a trace."

## *Speed 2: Cruise Control*

Q. Lightly sidestepping the reason why I went to see *Speed 2: Cruise Control,* there was one part that really surprised me. During the final explosion on board that oil tanker, I was certain that, on the right-hand side of the screen, one of the bits of debris was distinctly cow-shaped. In fact, it looked suspiciously like the flying *Twister* cow. Is this true and just an in-joke, or were my eyes trying to bring some excitement to a dull film?

—Julian Callinan, Melbourne, Australia

A. Congratulations on apparently being the first person to spot this in-joke inserted by the special-effects wizards. Glenn Salloum, associate producer of *Speed 2,* replies: "You have it right! The effects company of Rhythm and Hues added the cow into the second shot of the explosion as a homage to Jan de Bont and ILM's work on *Twister. Twister*'s cow received so much attention that we thought it would be fun to keep the flying cow thing going in *Speed 2.* It happens so fast and there really isn't a full shot so only a really keen eye will see it on the first or even second pass. You'll be happy to know, no cows were harmed in the making of *Speed 2.*"

## *Sphere*

Q. Regarding your comments on where the plot of the SF novel and movie *Sphere* was stolen from—*Solaris,* hell! As I realized when I read Michael Crichton's novel, the idea of the alien device that brings the human subconscious to life was lifted directly from the classic SF flick *Forbidden Planet,* which predates both Lem's novel and Tarkovsky's movie. *Monsters from the Id,* remember?

—Jim Dickey, Alexandria, Virginia

A. Of course *Forbidden Planet* was lifted directly from Shakespeare's *Tempest.* What is past is prologue.

## Star Ratings

Q. What is your policy regarding ratings? My interest was piqued after reading your review of *The Godfather, Part II.* You gave this film three stars. My thoughts on the film aside, your review solidly justifies this rating. (You said the De Niro parts interrupt the structure.) But in recent weeks you have given *Private Parts* and *The Fifth Element* the same three stars. Given that three stars is certainly an accurate representation of the quality of these two films (okay, three is a little generous for *The Fifth Element*), what does this say about *The Godfather, Part II* by comparison? Do you have a de facto statute of limitations on your ratings? Or do you categorically stand behind them? What, short of rereviewing them (as in your "Great Movies" project, a wonderful section) can you say about these older films you have reviewed?

—Michael C. Kingsley, New York City, New York

A. Star ratings are of course relative to the genre of the film. What "three stars" means, essentially, is that I recommend you see the film if it is the sort of film you might be interested in. (Four stars means I recommend you see it no matter what.) On a scale where *The Godfather* rates at four stars, I think three stars is a fair rating for its sequel (I was more or less alone among critics in preferring *Part III* to *Part II,* although of course I would not want to do without all three films). In my "Great Movies" feature I am going back and reviewing classics from the past, most of which I have not reviewed before. Occasionally on these excursions I find that my opinion has changed over time, as it did with *The Graduate,* which I no longer find as exciting as I once did.

### *Star Trek: First Contact*

Q. While watching *Star Trek: First Contact* we noticed something strange. After Picard jumps from one level of the ship to the next level down, several crew members follow him through the hole. Although the shot is framed primarily on him, the audience sees the crew members come through the hole behind Picard. For some reason, the lens distorts the length of their bodies, making them appear unnaturally long when they come through the hole (specifically their legs). This phenomenon made their jump seem to take an unusually long time.

—Mark Edlitz and Jerry Kolber, New York City, New York

A. The Answer Man's expert on Star Wars/Trek questions is Andy Ihnatko of Westwood, Massachusetts, who replies: "It's simple. Starfleet uniforms are solid black from shoes to upper chest. As far as I could tell, the crewman climbed down through the ceiling and then hung on the edge for a moment before dropping down. Because his feet had already been obscured by foreground actors and his top hadn't entered the frame yet, I think the viewer 'read' that solid black shape as continuing to drop down when in fact it wasn't moving at all."

### *Star Wars*

Q. My take on the new Jabba the Hut scene in the refurbished *Star Wars* is, how come Jabba is so short? Did he double or triple his size in the next six years? 'Splain that one to me please, Mr. Answer Man. Eating too many froglets? All Huts do that? What?

—Don Howard, San Jose, California

A. You have a point. Jabba is a towering figure the next time he turns up, in *Return of the Jedi.* Perhaps he grew? Perhaps he just seems taller because of his elevated perch? Ever notice how much he looks like Don Rickles?

Q. Last night we paid our homage to the reissued *Star Wars.* It seemed to have aged badly. Or is it me? In the Death Star conference room I was constantly diverted by the *ball casters* on the chairs, cynically thinking, "They got those from some London office supply—just like ones I used to have in an office when I had an honest living."

—John Jakes, Hilton Head Island, South Carolina

A. Of course you wouldn't want ball casters on office chairs in space, unless the Death Star makes its own gravity; crew members would forever be rolling around and smashing computer screens. But remember that *Star Wars* was made for only $12 million, which was peanuts. Even so, Lucas ran out of money and the plug was almost pulled. The people in that conference room were lucky to *have* chairs.

Q. Tonight I saw *Star Wars: The Special Edition* and I hated hated hated it! The original is my favorite film and is what has inspired me, from the age of four, to become a filmmaker. I have seen it hundreds of times. Lucas was not attempting to bring the new version closer to his original vision, but was simply showing off. I have no problem with going back and tinkering with the original, but only if it adds to the picture. But there was absolutely no reason for Han and Jabba to meet. There was no dramatic tension in the new scene between them. It is too short and the dialogue is stupid. Jabba's character was completely different in *Return of the Jedi,* and more menacing. In the special edition he's a wimp who does nothing when Han stupidly steps on his tail. The computer-generated Jabba is the worst special effect I have seen in years. You would have thought someone at ILM would have said, "George! the damn thing looks like a hunk of Play-Doh!!!" Another stupid touch was to have Boba Fett walk up to the camera and all but wink at the camera at the end of the scene. If this movie is to have any hope of being remembered a hundred years from now,

Lucas should burn the special edition, or at least cut out the garbage scenes.

—Scott Clements, Toronto, Ontario

A. You've seen it hundreds of times, and now you hate it? Why do you remind me of a guy who doesn't want his girlfriend to ever change her hair? I think it's useful for Jabba to turn up here, because that helps establish the character for his larger role later, and helps the trilogy in its task of connecting the three episodes.

Q. In *Star Wars,* when Ben Kenobi dies, he fades away. In *Return of the Jedi,* when Yoda dies, he also fades away. But when Darth Vader dies in *Return of the Jedi,* he doesn't fade away. Am I to presume that only the good Jedis fade away?

—Jon Pietrowski, Genoa, Ohio

A. The Answer Man's *Star Wars* guru is Andy Ihnatko of Westwood, Massachusetts, who replies: "Well, Anakin Skywalker, by virtue of the fact that he personally killed the leading force of evil in the galaxy, definitely built up oodles of Good Karma points with that one act and died a Good Jedi. But realize that his uniform was a fully ambulatory life-support system, and so it can be expected that the machinery kept him alive past the point of consciousness, long enough that Anakin could die discreetly—and cheaply—off-camera."

## Steadicam

Q. There's a moment in Stanley Kubrick's *The Shining* when Jack Nicholson's little boy is riding a big wheel through the Overlook Hotel. Kubrick's technical prowess always amazes me, but particularly here—not to mention the use of sound (the difference between the wheels turning on the carpet and on the wood floor is beautiful). The scene seems so difficult that it must have been shot with a Steadicam. As the film was released in 1980, I wondered if that date is indeed too early for this technique. When did Steadicam shots start to crop up in films?

—Mark Collins, Auburn, Alabama

A. Steadicams, which are harnessed to a cameraman and counterweighted to minimize camera movement and vibration, were first used by Haskell Wexler in his Oscar-winning cinematography for Hal Ashby's *Bound for Glory* (1976). Another memorable early Steadicam use is in James Crabe's shot that follows Sylvester Stallone, as Rocky, up the steps of the art museum in Philadelphia.

## Stereotypes

Q. Last week I rented the sixtieth-anniversary video of *King Kong.* In an early scene Fay Wray is abducted and the Chinese cook wants to join the rescue party. In the original print, a crewman says, "This is no job for a slope-head." I was startled to hear the line changed to "This is no job for a cook." The original line was offensive but is changing it the right thing to do? Isn't that the same sort of tinkering with history we used to chide the Russians for? Couldn't the distributor have issued a disclaimer and presented the movie as is?

—D. A. Forte, Chicago Heights, Illinois

A. Old movies should be released in their original form, period. Rewriting history deprives us of the opportunity to learn from it. Seeing old movies is a way to put the present into a wider context. A reasonable viewer could look at the movie and reflect that the crewman's language is regrettably typical of racist attitudes at the time.

Q. In seeing *Booty Call,* I was offended by the caricatures of the Indian shopkeepers. I understand *SubUrbia* has more positive Indian characters, and if it does I'd be so excited because there's finally a film with people like us, Americans who happen to also be Indian. That's the problem. I shouldn't be so excited about it. It should be a common enough event where the possibility of an Indian character wouldn't immediately send me running to the theater. I'm sitting in one of my school's computer labs right now. Looking around, I see people of all different races. In fact, Caucasians seem to be the minority at this particular time. Why isn't this reflected in Hollywood? That's what I really have a problem with. We're all out there. Isn't that one of the things that makes America unique?

—Matthew C. Thomas, Austin, Texas

A. Enormous progress has been made in casting actors of many different races in supporting roles. But Ben Kingsley is the only leading actor with an Indian background, and he usually plays other ethnic groups. What's interesting about *SubUrbia* is that it's the Indian or Pakistani character, a recent immigrant, who expresses traditional American values.

Q. Big problem arose last night for me at Spielberg's *Lost World: Jurassic Park.* When T-Rex goes storming through San Diego, there's a brief shot of a group of Japanese businessmen fleeing along with the rest of the crowd. I laughed aloud (as did many others in the house). My spontaneous outburst, in appreciation of what I saw as Spielberg's tip of the hat to a convention of Japanese monster movies, set my fiancée off on a tear that began with an elbow in my ribs and a warning to behave myself, and a berating as soon as the houselights came up. Her reason: The folks seated to her left were Asian—and my applause was an indication of racism. Roger, look at that scene: It's shot from the same low, three-quarters behind the characters angle, with the characters' faces turned to look back as they flee (running slo-mo), just like any Godzilla, Rodan, or Mothra movie. It is a tribute to the genre; use of a cinematic convention. She says it's a stereotype—because bad monster flicks "are all they make in Japan" and that Spielberg is no better for including it than I am for liking it.

—Gerard Farrell, Bay City, Texas

A. I laughed too. Spielberg is obviously basing an affectionate in-joke on the Japanese monster movie genre, and no racism was intended or should be found. By the way, your financée should know that fans of Japanese monster movies think they're *better* than *Lost World.*

Q. I'm trivia editor for the Internet Movie Database. I just read your recent *Answer Man* bit on the shot of the fleeing Japanese businessmen in *Lost World: Jurassic Park.* I thought you'd find this interesting: When fleeing the T-Rex in San Diego, what one of the Japanese businessmen says in Japanese is, "I came to America to get away from all this," a reference to *Gojira* (1954) and other *Godzilla* films.

—Murray Chapman, Brisbane, Australia

A. Although I got a few letters (none from Japanese-Americans) complaining that the shot was offensive, I disagree. It was obviously done in fun, as good-hearted humor, and will no doubt be enjoyed as such in Japan. I hope political correctness hasn't gotten to the point where no group can be represented at all without stirring up a protest. See the next letter.

Q. The AP reported that the National Federation of the Blind has protested Disney's plans to make a new movie about the nearsighted Mr. Magoo. What do you say?

—Susan Lake, Urbana, Illinois

A. What I say is, this is a silly, knee-jerk, decision by a bunch of well-meaning people who got caught up in a fervor of passing resolutions. Let them decide after the movie comes out if it's offensive, and protest it then, if they dislike it. Mr. Magoo is described in their resolution as "an ill-tempered and incompetent blind man who stumbles into things and misunderstands his surroundings." That only partly describes Magoo, who is also brave, resolute, creative, and adaptable, loves his nephew, and is always revealed as a good guy at the end. (He is not blind, by the way, but nearsighted, which indicates how carefully the delegates have studied the films.) The AP story goes on to say some of the delegates were hurt as children by being called "Magoo." Lucky is the child who has never been hurt by being called a name—many of them much worse than "Magoo." Movies like *Mr. Magoo* help to defuse the tension, caused by ignorance, that develops when we are too inhibited to deal openly and frankly with aspects of the human condition.

### *Striptease*

Q. Thanks for reminding viewers on your annual "worst of" list that the awful *Striptease* is based on the nearly-perfect novel *Strip Tease,* by the wonderful crime novelist Carl Hiaasen. Since we both agree that Demi Moore's performance sinks the movie, my question is, if you could remake the film, who would you cast in the role of Erin Grant? I've always pictured Sandra Bullock in the role, myself.

—Lucius P. Cook, Chicago, Illinois

Q. I'd also have chosen a reality type, like Bullock, Lili Taylor, or Janeane Garofolo. It's a comic character role, not an overtly sexy heroine. In his novel, Hiaasen describes the "modest dimensions" of Erin's breasts, and says her appeal is based on her ability to connect with the audience, not on her looks. One of the unfortunate aspects of Moore's approach to stripping is that she strutted arrogantly on the stage, deliberately distancing herself from the audience. Not Erin's approach at all.

## *The Sweet Hereafter*

Q. Can you tell me what character in *The Sweet Hereafter* did Russell Banks play?

—Joaquin M. Fernandez, Miami, Florida

A. Banks, who wrote the novel the movie is based on, played Dr. Robeson. He's the good-looking middle-aged man with the white beard.

Q. In *The Sweet Hereafter,* during the legal hearing at the end, a woman seems to be breathing into some kind of a cone. Does she need oxygen, or what?

—Susan Lake, Urbana, Illinois

A. "That is a dictating device that allows her to take verbal notes without disturbing the others," the film's director, Atom Egoyan, told me at the Independent Spirit Awards. He added: "I wish I had just shown her taking shorthand, since so few viewers apparently knew what that was."

## *Titanic*

Q. With all the *Titanic* special-effects hoopla—well-deserved, I might say—I was wondering if you remembered a near-forgotten movie from the early 1960s called *The Last Voyage.* I saw it a long time ago and all I remember is the wonderful Woody Strode galloping through the ocean liner rescuing people as the big boat sank. And Robert Stack was in it. But here's what I seem to recall about that movie: They filmed it on a real ocean liner and the director actually sank it for the movie and filmed it. Could this be right?

—Lee Bey, Chicago, Illinois

A. I greatly doubted that could be true, but I looked it up in Cinemania, and discovered from Leonard Maltin that, indeed, "To heighten the realism of the film, they really sank a ship."

Q. You wrote in your review of *Titanic,* "At one point Rose gives Lovejoy the finger; did young ladies do that in 1912?" This very question came up during an American Dialect Society's on-line discussion of anachronisms in *Amistad* (where characters say "hello" despite the fact that the word was not used until the invention of the telephone). Apparently, the gesture has been used at least since the last century (there are photographs of nineteenth-century people giving the finger), although I'd say it's unlikely that a young lady would have done so in 1912.

—Alan Baragona, Staunton, Virginia

A. Now I have another challenge for the anachronism hunters at the American Dialect Society. It may be a little off their specialty, but ask them to do their best. In *The Wings of the Dove,* a film based on a Henry James novel, two of the characters make love outdoors while braced up against a pillar in Venice. The novel is set earlier, but the film moves the action up to about 1910. In what year, according to the society's best thinking, did young ladies of the sort Henry James writes about begin to participate in such practices?

Q. Does the character of Rose (as the old woman) die in her sleep at the end of *Titanic*? I've asked a few people who saw the movie, and none of them had that interpretation, but most agree once I've outlined it to them. She tells her story for the first time, and returns the necklace to the ocean and *Titanic*'s resting place, completing the circle of her life. Then, we see her asleep in bed, after the camera slowly moves through her photos, illustrating the full life that she lived. Then, through subjective camera we're welcomed back to the ship, looking new, and greeted by passengers who died when the ship went down. Then she has a big reunion kiss with Jack. Was this just a dream? Or does this scene represent her being welcomed by her fellow shipmates, who have been dead for decades, and her finally joining them? Is this the obvious interpretation, or was it purposely left vague?

—Scott Hoenig, Washington, D.C.

A. "It's open to interpretation," according to a Paramount source who spoke with director James Cameron. My feeling is that the scene provides emotional closure, and should be appreciated on that level; whether she has rejoined the voyage in her dreams or in the afterlife, it is equally a fantasy, providing the inspiration for one of the film's most evocative sequences, in which the shattered hulk on the ocean floor comes to life once again.

**Q.** Something I haven't seen anyone mention about the fictional story in *Titanic.* If Rose had only stayed in the lifeboat when she had the chance, then Jack would have been able to survive by floating on the debris that saved her life.

—Larry Boyers, Nashville, Tennessee

**A.** Do you suppose they edited out a shot of Rose banging her palm against her forehead as that thought belatedly occurred to her?

**Q.** I saw *Titanic* a second time to be sure I heard correctly. During the scene where the crew is trying to avoid the iceberg, they shout, "Hard to starboard!" Since they were frantically trying to turn the ship to port, I didn't understand the command. The scene clearly shows the ship veering left, and all of the damage was subsequently done to the starboard side. If someone told me "hard to starboard," I would turn the ship to the right. Maybe we have just discovered the real reason the ship hit the iceberg that night ("Oops! I meant 'port'!").

—Denise Leder, Las Vegas, Nevada

**A.** Don Lynch, who acted as the official historian for *Titanic,* says you heard correctly: "The order 'hard to starboard' stems from the old sailing days. If you are sitting at the back of a sailboat, facing forward, and want to turn the ship to the left (port), you push the tiller over to the right (starboard). The rudder then points to the left, and you turn left. A decade or so after the *Titanic* disaster the turning orders were updated and standardized to keep up with the times and eliminate confusion, if any."

**Q.** This involves the Answer Man exchange about the order in *Titanic* for the ship to turn "hard to starboard" when an iceberg was sighted off the "starboard bow." A large ship actually turns from the stern as a result of rudder action. The order to turn to starboard would cause the *Titanic*'s hull to move to port, thereby reducing the effect of the starboard side of the hull raking the iceberg. The vessel probably would have taken a glancing blow on the starboard bow, limiting the damage to a few forward watertight compartments. Apparently, the "hard to starboard" command was followed by an order to "back full," which reduced the turning effect of the rudder, resulting in fatal damage. The operation of a "tiller" on a small sailboat has nothing to do with the order given to turn the *Titanic* to starboard, which was the correct order.

—Cmdr. Roy E. Nichols (Ret), U.S. Coast Guard, Reno, Nevada

**A.** Thanks. I've had so many letters on this I feel like I'm taking a correspondence course in ship steering.

**Q.** In one of the initial scenes in *Titanic,* Kate Winslet goes on deck wearing an evening gown, and I noticed a small tattoo on her shoulder. Surely no respectable young lady in 1912 would include such a fashion statement!

—John M. Paull, Chicago, Illinois

**A.** If it was on her right shoulder I hope it said "starboard."

*Andy Ihnatko wrote me: "According to the 'goofs' section of the* Titanic *entry of the Internet Movie Database, that's a crescent-shaped bit of beading that has come off of her dress."*

**Q.** Re that scene at the end of *Titanic* when Rose throws the diamond necklace into the ocean. I have talked to people who thought it was really cheesy and bewildering. They don't understand why she would throw a diamond that expensive away and not give it to charity. My explanation is that the experience was such a personal and private experience, and she felt that this was her opportunity to "return it" to the ship.

—Paul Chinn, Columbia, Tennessee

**A.** Since the diamond was so famous, she couldn't give it to charity without revealing her lifelong secret. She could have left it in her will, of course. But would your friends prefer *Titanic* to end with a conference between Rose and her lawyers?

**Q.** I have been amazed by criticisms that Kate Winslet was overweight for her role in *Titanic.* A woman with her body type would have driven men mad in 1912. There are styles in body types. If you took a Jane Marsh and put her on the real *Titanic,* everyone would have concluded she had consumption and would have quarantined her. I'm still waiting for my body type to come into fashion.

—Rich Elias, Delaware, Ohio

**A.** Does that mean you are often mistaken for Leonardo DiCaprio?

## Titles

**Q.** Did you know that *That Darn Cat* is known as *That Damn Cat* in the novel by the Gordons on which the movie is based?

—W. C. Martell, Studio City, California

**A.** Funny. That's the same thing we've always called our cat.

## Trailers

**Q.** Speaking of dumb trailers, have you seen these Wesley Snipes trailers for *Murder at 1600*? He lands on the lawn of the White House in a police helicopter (as if the Secret Service would okay that) and then steps out and on an open radio channel he says, "I have a murder at 1600 Pennsylvania Avenue!" As he was summoned there and as there were twenty police cars there already, the dispatcher would probably know, but then—this kills me—he adds, "an address that changes all the rules!" Hoo boy, as if anyone in the world would actually say that, in person, on a radio, or the phone. Who do the screenwriters think are in the audience? Numbskulls?

—Eric M. Davitt, Toronto, Ontario

**A.** Yes.

**Q.** I ran across something in a recent Bill Gates column that I thought you'd enjoy. Gates writes, "It surprises me that movie studios can't spend, say, 10 percent of budget to create a trailer and then do focus groups to predict how popular the movie will be and whether production should continue. That must not work or somebody would have done it by now—but it stuns me that it doesn't."

—Paul Kedrovsky, London, Ontario

**A.** Trailers always feature the big stars and the most spectacular special effects (the White House being blown up, etc.). Think of the cost of hiring stars and doing special effects only for a trailer! It would be much more than 10 percent; I think the trailer for *Mission: Impossible* showed every big scene in the movie. Would a Tom Cruise sign up to do a trailer on spec? Gates's statement goes a long way, however, toward explaining the methods of the software industry.

**Q.** Is it just me, or have trailers of late all started to conform to a nifty little formula started by *Twister* last year? Remember that one? Clips of the most spectacular special effects and action sequences of the movie are shown with pounding music blaring over the sound track. Finally, credits are shown as the music jolts to silence. As the audience is catching its breath—*boom!* An additional shot of a falling tractor scares the life outta ya. The first time I saw it, I thought: pretty cool. But I have noticed it in *dozens* of trailers since! *Double Team, Dante's Peak,* and *Air Force One* (Harrison Ford hitting someone with a stool), have all used this structure.

—Mike Spearns, St. John's, Newfoundland

**A.** When a trailer finds a gimmick that works, it's instantly copied all over town—especially since many studios farm out their trailers to a handful of specialty ad shops. Another trick: Trailers will recycle music from similar movies that were hits, in order to subtly associate themselves with it.

**Q.** Where'd the word "trailers" come from? They don't follow (or "trail") the movie. Did they, at one time? Is that where the word came from? If not there, then from where?

—Binky Melnik, New York City, New York

**A.** David J. Bondelevitch, of the CompuServe Showbiz Forum, replies: "Trailers were the *last* thing to play before the movie. In the past, the feature was preceded by numerous shorts (newsreels, cartoons, other short subjects). The trailer was the *last thing* on that reel, hence it 'trailed' everything else. Then the projectionist switched reels to the feature."

**Q.** I've noted a recent practice that is perplexing: The use of other earlier film scores in the ads and trailers for new releases. At least three films *(Courage Under Fire, Rosewood,* and *Mercury Rising)* have used James Horner's music from *Glory.* Even a director as distinguished as Martin Scorsese used Philip Glass's music from *Koyannisqatsi* in his TV ads for

*Kundun*. If they skimp on such an important production value as the score, where else have they skimped?

—Thomas G. Hanson, St. Cloud, Minnesota

**A.** You have good ears. It is routine to borrow from older scores for previews and ads, because the new original score for a movie is often not ready when the trailers are prepared. Also, there's an element of subliminal advertising: They want to subtly suggest an earlier movie you may have liked.

## *The Truman Show*

**Q.** My wife showed me your review of *The Truman Show*, and I was crushed with chagrin to learn the movie is constructed to reveal its secret slowly to the viewer. I've already seen *The Truman Show* commercials revealing the secret. I feel betrayed. This is the third time when the advance info has ruined a surprise. The first was *Terminator 2*. On talk shows, Arnold Schwarzenegger beamed, "This time I'm a good terminator! The bad guy is a T-1000, made of liquid metal, which can look like anyone." In the theater, the details are calculatedly ambiguous right until the two terminators confront each other and Schwarzenegger suddenly turns and protects the kid. At that moment, I thought—I shouldn't have known the details beforehand! The same thing happened with *The Empire Strikes Back*. Magazines had cover photos: "Here's Yoda! He's an old, eccentric, funny-looking creature who's really a Jedi master!" In viewing the film I realized the audience wasn't supposed to know Yoda's identity until he started conversing with the disembodied voice of Obi-Wan. Now here's *The Truman Show*, with a marketing campaign spilling all the beans. My wife contends there is no other possible way for the studio to successfully advertise the movie, but I have to believe there's *some* way to do it.

—Chris Rowland, Plainsboro, New Jersey

**A.** And Denise Leder of Las Vegas writes, "I would estimate that my viewing enjoyment was cut by 87.6 percent just because I knew what was going on." Alas, almost all the Hollywood studios believe the best way to advertise a movie is to reveal as much of it as possible in the ads and trailers. Since movies live or die by their opening weekend grosses, there's no angle in waiting for audiences to discover the secrets for themselves. If *The Crying Game* came out today, it would open with the full monty. I myself am guilty of discussing *Truman*'s plot on a *Siskel and Ebert* special that aired a couple of weeks before the opening, and again during our review of the film. There was no way *not* to reveal the secret on TV, because most of the clips gave it away. But I backed off in my newspaper review, issuing a Spoiler Warning.

**Q.** I have a problem with *The Truman Show*. I am amazed how the critics sing such praise for such an "original concept" when it was done before, and better, thirty years ago on a CBS series called *The Prisoner*. Patrick McGoohan played a prisoner of a village where his every move was constantly monitored on TV by the keepers of the village. He too could not escape until the last episode. The scene of Ed Harris watching Carrey on a big screen monitor is exactly the same as the keeper (Leo McKern) in *The Prisoner*, who would walk up to the big screen and try to anticipate the Prisoner's every move.

—Larry Koehn, Antioch, Tennessee

**Q.** A friend of mine swears that the story for *The Truman Show* was taken from an episode of *The New Twilight Zone*.

—Joseph Tsai, West Covina, California

**A.** I've received letters mentioning four different possible sources. But basic story ideas are often pretty generic; this idea occurred in various forms in science fiction years before *The Prisoner* appeared. What makes one film different from another is the treatment, tone, dialogue, style, and acting. Remember Ebert's Law: *It's not what the movie is about, but how it is about it*. Of course, as with any hit movie, there will no doubt be plagiarism lawsuits.

**Q.** Just saw *The Truman Show* in a theater in lower Manhattan and was unnerved to see that the closing credits were all in French (as in, "Un film de Peter Weir, *Le Show Truman*"). I thought it was a silly joke (which, I seem to remember, was a favorite of the Zucker brothers). However, I later spoke to friends in Cleveland and Los Angeles who swore up and down that the closing credits were in English. I know

I wasn't hallucinating; I saw it with a group of friends, and we were all puzzled. We couldn't imagine that Peter Weir would try something so gratuitously silly, unless he was going for some kind of alienating effect. Was it something they put in the popcorn?

—Chris Dumas, New York City, New York

**A.** A Paramount spokesman tells me the movie's end titles were all in English, and the studio is at a complete loss to explain how, or if, French titles were appended to any print. Their investigation continues, he added sternly.

*Footnote: Mike Schlesinger of Sony Pictures Repertory solved the puzzle. He wrote me: "Re that* Truman Show *print that supposedly had French end credits—no big mystery. The answer is Quebec: All major films must be released up there in French as well as English. Reels occasionally do get switched, and somewhere along the line, either at the lab or during shipment, wires got crossed. It's rare, but not unprecedented; it happened to us last year, when half a dozen theatres in the L.A. area got prints of* Absolute Power *with a couple of reels in French. I'm pretty sure the same thing happened to this theater.*

## TV in the Movies

**Q.** Just saw *Mad City.* What bothers me is that actors like Dustin Hoffman can do such convincing roles with a great variety of parts, yet when it comes to sounding like a television reporter they just never sound quite right. Alan Alda had an interesting part as a slimeball network anchor, but when he did his stand-up it sounded awful. Is this why Hollywood keeps getting real reporters to play themselves?

—Bruce Worthen, Salt Lake City, Utah

**A.** Maybe. Here's why actors get it wrong. They memorize the lines and deliver them as an actor would. TV people, on the other hand, read live off a TelePrompTer, often without knowing when they begin a sentence how it is going to end. So they sort of suspend their verbal commitment, finding inflections that allow them to go wherever the copy takes them without getting stuck on the wrong note. It is against an actor's very nature to read that way.

**Q.** We've seen a summer full of *CNN Reports* in fictional movies, and just as much controversy (mostly in news circles) over the use of real CNN anchors. Them-there "serious" news folk seem to think using the real call letters in films destroys their credibility. Gimme a break. I, for one, have a problem seeing fictitious call letters like "CMN" when everyone knows damn well what the movie producers are getting at. I don't see it as product placement (though in some cases, like Fox, I know they ain't puttin' NBC up there); I see it as realistic. Apparently, CNN buckled to peer pressure and decided "no more cameos in the movies." But the new film *Kiss the Girls,* appeared to use real local TV stations in the Raleigh-Durham area, and I was glad to see that. What's your feeling about using real news reporters in film?

—Bruce Maiman, Monterey, California

**A.** Phony call letters, like phony brand names, are always a distraction. But real ones blur the line between news and entertainment. One compromise is to use retired but recognizable newsmen, like Edwin Newman, and put them on a realistic set but not identify it.

## *2001* and *2010*

**Q.** I had an intense meeting with some computer clients last week. We were discussing the huge effort required to get their computer systems ready for the year 2000. This problem is caused by systems storing the year of a date as a two-digit number instead of a four-digit number. It got me thinking about my favorite film, *2001.* For years people have speculated about why HAL the computer went crazy. One reason I've never seen: Is it possible that HAL was programmed with two-digit year fields? Sure, he worked fine in 1997. But when the year 2000 rolled around, he was a system crash waiting to happen.

—John Miller, Cambridge, Massachusetts

**A.** Not only did he try to kill the astronauts, he screwed up their payrolls.

**Q.** In your "Great Movies" rereview of *2001,* you wrote: "I learn from a review by Mark R. Leeper that this was the first film to pan the camera across a star field: 'Space scenes had always been done with a fixed camera, and for a very good reason. It was more economical not to create a background of stars large enough to pan through'." The opening of *Star Wars* is dramatic, but it is hardly the first film to pan across a star field. *2001: A Space Odyssey* used this technique extensively—most noticeably during the final scene, where the film cuts from a close-up of the monolith to a shot of a planet, then pans down (across a large star field) to the star child.

—Steve Ankrom, Findlay, Ohio

**A.** Mark Leeper's review appeared on the Internet. Contacting him, I learned he lives in Old Bridge, New Jersey, and he and his wife have run the Bell Labs' science-fiction club for almost twenty years. He replies to Ankrom: "I suppose you are mostly correct, probably because my language was a little more loose than it should have been. What I was reacting to in *Star Wars* was the fast (even dizzying) pan through what looks like ninety degrees or more of nothing but sky. In *2001: A Space Odyssey,* the camera does indeed pan. But it is a very limited pan. The camera always either follows an object or pans between objects which are close to the camera and in angle close to each other. The background has enough sky to support the camera movement. The background sky is never really the center of attention of the shot. I would guess that the camera does not pan an angle of starscape of more than ten or twenty degrees—a fairly small star field. They could have set up the scene with the camera panning considerably more and I would guess did not because the camera motions were slow and dreamlike and the viewer would end up gazing into empty space for a long time. Also prior to digital technology that much starscape would have been expensive to build."

**Q.** I was watching a telecast of Peter Hyams's sequel *2010* (1984) when it occurred to me that the voice of SAL 9000, the twin to the computer HAL 9000, sounded exactly like Candice Bergen. On the Cinemania CD-ROM, the voice is credited to Olga Mallsnerd. Is that a joke? Or is it actually Ms. Bergen ducking the credit?

—Jeff Young, Lake Elsinore, California

**A.** SAL's voice indeed belongs to Candice Bergen, whose pseudonym translates to "bad Snerd," a cruel dig at Mortimer. Isn't it time for her to forgive and forget, after all these years?

**Q.** You are quite right that Candice Bergen did the voice of SAL 9000, the computer in *2010,* under the pseudonym "Olga Mallsnerd." But in translating it as "bad Snerd" and interpreting it as a dig at poor Mortimer Snerd, you missed another pun. "Mallsnerd" also seems to suggest the last name of her beloved husband, Louis Malle.

—Brian Linehan, Toronto, Ontario

**A.** Without a doubt. Now I've set my sights on the deconstruction of "Olga."

## *Vertigo*

**Q.** Re Alfred Hitchcock's *Vertigo:* All sources say that the "vertigo effect" was done by zooming in while pulling the camera out, whereas what we can see on the screen is clearly the reverse: Pushing the camera forward while zooming out. Is it possible that Hitchcock perhaps "did" film it the way everybody says he did but the sequence was edited in backward?

—Jan Bielawski, Molecular Simulations, San Diego, California

**A.** You are referring to the shot looking down the steep staircase inside the old mission tower, during the film's climactic scene. I referred your theory to the two ranking experts on the film, James C. Katz and Robert Harris, who supervised the recent restoration of Hitchcock's masterpiece. They seem to think there may be something to your theory. Their reply, couched in the detail that film restorers love:

"This is a question that may never be answered for certain. As *Vertigo* lore has it, it's a forward zoom and reverse tracking shot. But on close examination of the shots it is possible that it was the reverse. We have examined the two shots on a Vista Vision print derived from the camera negative. The shots are not dupes, and therefore are not opticals created from other elements. They are both photographed on camera original. One can see more information on the full Vista frame than on the cropped 1.85:1 image, and from the positioning of the hands on the railing, and the overall depth of focus, the shots do seem to be produced with the camera moving forward while the lens is zoomed back to a wider view. The depth of field is greater at the end of the shots than at the beginning. It should be noted that the physical pullback of the camera is very limited, probably not more than a couple of feet, but the effect works. The shot was not edited in backward as that would have flopped the emulsion on the negative during printing, sending the shot out of focus. Hope this is helpful, but alas, we'll never know for sure."

**Q.** Was just watching the newly restored version of *Vertigo,* reviewed in your "Great Movies" series. In the opening credits, the camera pans across the face of a woman and then focuses in on her eye. Who was the model for that sequence? Was it Alfred Hitchcock's daughter, Patricia?

—Tom Norris, Braintree, Massachusetts

**A.** According to Robert Harris, who with James Katz restored the Hitchcock classic, "The name of the actress/model we see behind the main titles in *Vertigo* is Audrey Lowell. She lives in Los Angeles."

## Viewing Conditions

**Q.** There are far too many theaters which, in trying to cut down their overhead, show films with the projection bulbs running at 50 percent to 75 percent of their intended strength—greatly increasing the life of the expensive bulb, but at the expense of the moviegoer, who *does not see* the film that was made, but a darker, murkier version. This is rampant. While working on a movie location here in Memphis, we have already found two theaters, comprising sixteen screens, that do this routinely. Infuriating! Fraud! Moviegoers should first notify the theater manager, and ask for the regional manager's name and number and tell him too. At $5 to $9 a ticket, the moviegoer deserves to get to see the movie the producer intended they should.

—Barry A. Toll, St. Petersburg, Florida

**A.** I first heard about this shameful practice from Martin Scorsese, who actually visits theaters with a light meter to determine if the picture is being projected at the correct light intensity. I have taken friends to movies I enjoyed, only to find that the screen is so dim that details disappear into shadows, and the EXIT sign washes out part of the picture. Complaints to the studios and directors might bear more fruit than talking to theater chain employees.

**Q.** I recently saw *Evita* at my local theater. The projectionist loaded two of the reels in reverse order, so that Eva Perón toured Europe and returned to start her foundation before she and Juan Perón were married and Perón was elected to the presidency! I alerted the manager to this, who told me I was the first to bring this to his attention after four days in the theater, so several hundred people saw a major portion of the film out of chronological order. What's disturbing to me is that they weren't sufficiently aware of this glitch to report the error. What does this say about the quality of the screenplay of this show, and (horrors!) the knowledge of history of those in the audience? I saw the movie on Saturday, told the manager on Monday, and went to see it again Tuesday afternoon, and the problem still wasn't solved! Do you have any suggestions as to how I can convince the manager of the theater that I'm right and not just some crazy person?

—Thomas P. Pusateri, Dubuque, Iowa

**A.** I have no suggestions. Anyone who pays intelligent attention to the continuity and logic of a modern film is obviously deranged in some way.

**Q.** When watching a movie, how do you decide the best time to go to the bathroom, when you really have to go? My answer is this: I go during a scene when you can tell at the start how it is going to end. For instance, if a cop's boss says "I want you to go undercover one more time to try and catch this guy," and the cop says, "No, no, I told you, no more undercover work," well—that's a good time to go, because you know he will eventually agree to go undercover. And you will be back from the bathroom in time to see that happen.

—John Dempsey, Chicago, Illinois

**A.** Sometimes I can tell at the start how a movie is going to end, and am tempted to spend the entire movie in the bathroom. What I don't understand is how the average moviegoer sits through a two-hour film *without* going to the bathroom, since the large size of pop served in movie theaters contains about three times as much liquid as the human bladder can physically contain.

**Q.** Why is it that it's 1997 and I'm sitting in the theater watching a very expensive movie like *Batman and Robin,* and there appears to be schmutz on the screen (kinky hairs, dust, specks, etc)? I expect this when I'm watching a really old movie, but why is it still happening now? Does the film have all this crap on it (if so, how'd it get there?) or is it the projector (if so, why isn't the projection room cleaner)? I have always imagined that the projection booth is like a computer room: good ventilation, nice and cool, extra clean. The previous film I saw was *Liar, Liar,* and the last ten minutes of the film appeared to have Wheat Chex, trail mix, Spaghetti-Os, carpet lint, root beer, and smegma on it. It was appalling.

—Binky Melnik, New York City, New York

**A.** Your lazy oaf of a projectionist should get out his can of compressed air and blow the schmutz off the lens. Many projection rooms, by the way, look like the attic of your reclusive neighbor who rides his three-wheel bike around to all the garage sales.

**Q.** I was troubled by your response to the reader who asked about the crud on the screen. You blamed the "lazy oaf projectionist." I have been a union projectionist for over twenty years and have even shown you a movie or two. Not all the problems on the screen are the fault of the projectionist. I operate theaters in Naperville and Aurora and am proud of the service I perform. Most new releases are printed on film stock that sheds small particles which, by static, cling to the print. There are products on the market to help reduce this condition. These items cost money—money the theater chains will not part with. If you complain about the print, they blame the projectionist and give you a pass for a later date. You return and dish out more dollars at the candy counter and watch the same or maybe worse-contaminated movie. This can go on forever. They love to give out passes. It's money in the bank. As for the Filthy Attic Projection Booth, theater chains have decided this is an ideal place to store everything from candy to marquee letters to cleaning supplies. I would like you to visit a ten-plex or twenty-plex or soon a thirty-plex and keep pace with what a projectionist must endure.

—Al Cimino Jr., Lombard, Illinois

**A.** My answer about projectionists also inspired impassioned responses from Alan R. Melzer of Crestwood, Susan Dethlefsen of Carol Stream, and Kent Dickinson of Hazel Crest, Illinois. All argued that projectionists do the best they can, while trying to monitor many different screens at the same time under trying work conditions. I am sure this is true, and regret my crack about "lazy oafs." I was particularly amused by Cimino's observation that a free pass means another opportunity to sell more candy and popcorn.

**Q.** I saw *Dumb and Dumber* with my older brother, and I've never laughed harder or more continuously in a movie before or since. He saw it with his wife on video and was embarrassed. I saw *Hot Shots* with my dad in an almost empty theater, and felt I'd wasted $5. My friends saw the same movie in a large group of peers and thought that it was hysterical. I watched *Bill & Ted's Excellent Adventure* three times in one week and each time different lines got different laughs, and one night, hardly anyone laughed (the theater was equally filled each night). The same movie watched with my brother and sister-in-law evoked only a few forced chuckles. A lot of this depends on who you are with and how full the theater is (or how good the sound). For these reasons, I refuse to rewatch many films on video, such as *Schindler's List.* Just for grins, you ought to let your readers know about the context of your experience. Sometimes I wonder, did you see it in a packed theater on opening night, or on a prerelease in a private studio?

—Bart McNeely, Fort Worth, Texas

**A.** The chemistry of the viewing experience is a mystery that filmmakers would love to solve. Some of them, like Stanley Kubrick, go so far as to keep files on every individual theater where their films are playing. As for myself, I know that perfect viewing conditions—as at the Cannes Film Festival, for example—can only enhance an experience. But movies can create their own moods (that's what they're for) and I have seen movies under lousy conditions and still loved them. I think you're right that some movies just don't translate well to video, and need to be shared with an audience.

**Q.** This happened during a screening of *Titanic.* Just as the credits started and Celine Dion's award-nominated song began, a guy in a black suit gave an order through his walkie-talkie and the projectionist turned the lights on, rolled down the curtain, and stopped the projection. I demanded this guy turn the projector back on and resume the credits. He said it was not possible: Once the curtain is down and the projector off, you cannot restart it. Is this true? I demanded my money back but he refused, so I told him I was going to call the president of the company. Then he started lying to me, saying that there is a limited time programmed into the system and that *Titanic*'s credits are too long, and so is the movie, so the system automatically shuts down. Then he made the projectionist come down to tell me another tall tale; that the last roll of film had become entwined on the magnetic heads and would have snapped if he hadn't turned it off. Finally, they gave me four passes for another show. It's rude to interrupt the credits and worse to lie to a customer. Is the theater under any contractual obligation to show the whole movie, from start to finish, including the credits?

—Jose Luis Silva, Naucalpan, Mexico

**A.** David J. Bondelevitch of the CompuServe ShowBiz Forum, an expert on matters of exhibition, replies: "Yes, theater contracts require them to show the whole movie, although the credits are routinely cut off in many theaters. You could inform the distributor of the film, but they probably would not do anything." So what can you do? Stand up on your seat and inflame the audience by shouting, "Hey! They're cutting off Celine Dion's nominated song! Free passes for everyone!" There is strength in numbers.

## *Volcano*

**Q.** In your review of *Volcano,* you wrote, "I expected to see a mountainous volcano in *Volcano,* towering high over Los Angeles. But the movie takes place at ground level." We all know how to tell *Volcano* and *Dante's Peak* apart, right? *Dante's Peak* had an andesitic cone volcano, which occurs at a subduction zone (in this case where the Pacific plate is subducting beneath the North American plate). *Volcano* consists of a flood basalt system, which occurs over a "hot spot" on the continental crust. See? Completely different movies—right?

—Robert Haynes-Peterson, Boise, Idaho

**A.** Not entirely. They both had brave dogs.

## *Wag the Dog*

**Q.** Stanley Motss, the character played by Dustin Hoffman in *Wag the Dog,* has an oddly spelled last name. I wonder if you know that "MOTSS" is an abbreviation for "Member of the Same Sex," in Internet-talk and classified-ad-speak. Stanley Motss in *Wag the Dog* never seems to have a family, just his assistants, Manuel and Grace. During his obituary, there are no survivors mentioned. I wonder if this was a shot at closeted gay Hollywood big shots.

—Alex Christensen, Lexington, Virginia

**A.** The abbreviation also commonly stands for "More of the Same (bleep)," which would certainly fit the Motss character.

## Wet Streets

**Q.** I am tired of seeing every movie with streets covered with water at night. Why use this effect repeatedly in every film? It doesn't rain all the time. It virtually never rains in Las Vegas. I am beginning to think I live in Seattle. I don't need to see reflections of street lamps. Show some imagination out there and put this trick to rest!

—Arthur M. Yollin, Las Vegas

**A.** Wetting the streets for night photography is an ancient cameraman's trick, because it makes the streets more dramatic and visible, and exploits the reflections of lights and signs. It is used routinely in movies and on TV, and will be dropped the moment a director asks his cinematographer, "Is there something you can do to make this shot less interesting?"

## Who Is That Guy?

**Q.** I've seen all of Martin Scorsese's work, and have noticed that Frank Vincent appears in every Scorsese movie Joe Pesci is in. They begin as friends or at least accomplices, but in *Raging Bull* and *GoodFellas,* Pesci gives Vincent a torturous beating or kills him. In *Casino,* Vincent turns the tables, and gives Pesci a beating more extreme than in the other two films, getting his "screen revenge." Is this a coincidence, or an in-joke?

—Josh Korkowski, Minneapolis, Minnesota

**A.** Kim Sockwell of Scorsese's office replies; "Marty laughed when he read the question. He said it was not an inside joke, nor was it necessarily intentional that the characters ended up that way. It was more of a 'happy coincidence,' especially for Frank Vincent; Frank and his wife often joked with Joe Pesci on the set about Frank finally getting years' worth of revenge."

**Q.** In *Liar, Liar,* I swear I saw Jim Carrey in the background in a scene at the airport. He is lying on the stretcher and his family is being held back by a police officer. In the background, for only two or three seconds, I noticed Carrey wearing a fireman's suit and helmet. He's talking into a walkie-talkie and making a strange face that looks suspiciously like his "Fire Marshal Bill" character from *In Living Color.* If I'm right do I win a prize or something?

—Allen Reid, Houston, Texas

**A.** You're right. A Universal source confirms that is Carrey making a sneaky walk-on as Fire Marshal Bill.

**Q.** I'm told that in *Jurassic Park: The Lost World,* director Steven Spielberg can briefly be spotted reflected on a TV screen, showing him sitting on a sofa with Jeff Goldblum and eating popcorn. Is this true?

—Kelly MacNamara, Chicago, Illinois

**A.** Blair Finberg of Universal confirms that Spielberg is seen briefly reflected during a scene where characters are watching a CNN broadcast. David J. Bondelevitch of the CompuServe Showbiz Forum adds: "My memory of the shot is that it starts with Goldblum asleep on the couch with the daughter eating popcorn, and pans over to the TV set where they are reflected."

**Q.** I went to see Truffaut's *Day for Night* yesterday—it's in revival at a local theater—after lo these many years. Did I see Graham Greene in there in an uncredited cameo role? I could have sworn that he played the Englishman who gives Truffaut and the producer the bad news from the insurers after Alexander dies in a car crash. I believe that Greene was living on the Riviera at that time, and it is the kind of inside film reference (Greene—*The Third Man*—Orson Welles) that Truffaut would have enjoyed making.

—Gerry Howard, New York City, New York

**A.** That is indeed Graham Greene, according to the Internet Movie Database.

## Worst Movies of All Time

**Q.** You once wrote that you "hated, hated, hated, hated, hated" the zero-star movie *North.* Has the zero-star *Mad Dog Time* eclipsed even that high standard?

—(Please withhold my name and supply a creative pseudonym, because I work for the *Chicago Tribune*)

**A.** Dear Mark: When it comes to comparing zero-star movies, I am reminded of the Billy Preston song lyrics, "nothing from nothing leaves nothing." The Internet Movie Database, which catalogs some 25,000 films, asks its users to vote on the quality of each one. The IMDb recently released its *Bottom 100* of the worst movies of all time, of which the lowest-scoring ten were: *Manos, the Hands of Fate* (1966), *Santa Claus Conquers the Martians* (1964), *As Summers Die* (made for TV, 1986), *Leonard Part 6* (1987), *Police Academy 5: Assignment Miami Beach* (1988), *Police Academy 6: City Under Siege* (1989), *Shadowhunter* (TV, 1993), *Slaughter of the Innocents* (1994), *Highlander II: The Quickening* (1991), and *Jaws: The Revenge* (1987). To put this into context, *none* of these films scored zero; the lowest score, on a 1-to-10 scale, was 2.1.

**Q.** I hatehatehate people who walk out of movies because "they're bored" or "they don't understand it." The only time you should walk out is if: (a) the quality of the print being shown is unwatchable—in which case you demand your money back; (b) you've left the door open, not put the alarm on, left the stove on, etc.; (c) the film being shown is morally sickening and you don't want to waste your time with filth; or (d) you've fallen asleep and you want to watch the film properly—and intend to come back another time.

—Ian Mantgani, Liverpool, England

**A.** Don't forget (e) it stars Pauly Shore.

**Q.** I'd like to give you my nominee (early, I know) for worst film of the entire 1990s. It is *Weekend at Bernie's, Part II.* As you recall, the original film was a comedy about a weekend party with a corpse that nobody notices is dead. My favorite aspect was that "Sunday" in the first film took place in 1987 and "Monday" in the second film happened around 1993. Andrew McCarthy especially didn't age too well overnight! I remember saying to my wife, "What happened to *him?*"

—Jim Crossan, Columbia, South Carolina

**A.** And he wasn't even the corpse.

# Reviews Appearing in Previous Editions of the *Video Companion*

## A

About Last Night . . . , 1986, R, ★★★★ 1998
Above the Law, 1988, R, ★★★ 1995
Above the Rim, 1994, R, ★★★ 1995
Absence of Malice, 1981, PG, ★★★ 1998
Absolute Power, 1997, R, ★★★½ 1998
Accidental Tourist, The, 1988, PG, ★★★★ 1998
Accompanist, The, 1994, PG, ★★★½ 1998
Accused, The, 1988, R, ★★★ 1998
Ace Ventura: Pet Detective, 1994, PG-13, ★ 1998
Ace Ventura: When Nature Calls, 1995, PG-13, ★½ 1998
Addams Family, The, 1991, PG-13, ★★ 1997
Addams Family Values, 1993, PG-13, ★★★ 1998
Addicted to Love, 1997, R, ★★ 1998
Addiction, The, 1995, NR, ★★½ 1997
Adjuster, The, 1992, R, ★★★ 1998
Adventures of Baron Munchausen, The, 1989, PG, ★★★ 1998
Adventures of Ford Fairlane, The, 1990, R, ★ 1992
Adventures of Huck Finn, The, 1993, PG, ★★★ 1998
Adventures of Priscilla, Queen of the Desert, The, 1994, R, ★★½ 1998
After Hours, 1985, R, ★★★★ 1998
After the Rehearsal, 1984, R, ★★★★ 1998
Against All Odds, 1984, R, ★★★ 1998
Age of Innocence, The, 1993, PG, ★★★★ 1998
Agnes of God, 1985, PG-13, ★ 1989
Airplane!, 1980, PG, ★★★ 1998
Airport, 1970, G, ★★ 1996
Airport 1975, 1974, PG, ★★½ 1996
Aladdin, 1992, G, ★★★ 1998
Alex in Wonderland, 1971, R, ★★★★ 1998
Alice, 1990, PG-13, ★★★ 1998
Alice Doesn't Live Here Anymore, 1974, PG, ★★★★ 1998
Alien Nation, 1988, R, ★★ 1994
Aliens, 1986, R, ★★★½ 1998
Alien³, 1992, R, ★½ 1997
Alive, 1993, R, ★★½ 1997
All Dogs Go to Heaven, 1989, G, ★★★ 1998
Allegro Non Tropo, 1977, NR, ★★★½ 1995
Alligator, 1980, R, ★ 1990
All Night Long, 1981, R, ★★ 1986
All of Me, 1984, PG, ★★★½ 1998
. . . All the Marbles, 1981, R, ★★ 1986
All the President's Men, 1976, PG, ★★★½ 1998
All the Right Moves, 1983, R, ★★★ 1998
All the Vermeers in New York, 1992, NR, ★★★ 1998
Almost an Angel, 1990, PG, ★★½ 1995
Altered States, 1980, R, ★★★½ 1998
Always, 1989, PG, ★★ 1997
Amadeus, 1984, PG, ★★★★ 1998
Amarcord, 1974, R, ★★★★ 1998
Amateur, 1995, R, ★★½ 1996
American Buffalo, 1996, R, ★★½ 1998
American Dream, 1992, NR, ★★★★ 1998
American Flyers, 1985, PG-13, ★★½ 1995
American Gigolo, 1980, R, ★★★½ 1998
American Graffiti, 1973, PG, ★★★★ 1998
American in Paris, An, 1952, G, ★★★½ 1997
American Me, 1992, R, ★★★½ 1998
American President, The, 1995, PG-13, ★★★★ 1998
American Tail: Fievel Goes West, An, 1991, G, ★★½ 1998
American Werewolf in London, An, 1981, R, ★★ 1998
Amityville II: The Possession, 1982, R, ★★ 1988
Amos & Andrew, 1993, PG-13, ★★½ 1995
Anaconda, 1997, PG-13, ★★★½ 1998
Angel at My Table, An, 1991, R, ★★★★ 1998
Angel Heart, 1987, R, ★★★½ 1998
Angelo My Love, 1983, R, ★★★½ 1995
Angels and Insects, 1996, NR, ★★★½ 1998
Angels in the Outfield, 1994, PG, ★★ 1996
Angie, 1994, R, ★★½ 1997
Angus, 1995, PG-13, ★★★ 1998
Annie, 1982, PG, ★★★ 1998
Annie Hall, 1977, PG, ★★★½ 1998
Another 48 HRS, 1990, R, ★★ 1996
Another Woman, 1988, PG, ★★★★ 1998
Antonia and Jane, 1991, NR, ★★★ 1998
Antonia's Line, 1996, NR, ★★★★ 1998
Any Which Way You Can, 1980, PG, ★★ 1988
Apocalypse Now, 1979, R, ★★★★ 1998
Apollo 13, 1995, PG, ★★★★ 1998
Applegates, The, 1991, R, ★★ 1994
Apprenticeship of Duddy Kravitz, The, 1974, PG, ★★★ 1998
Arachnophobia, 1990, PG-13, ★★★ 1998
Aria, 1988, R, ★★★ 1998

Ariel, 1990, NR, ★★★ 1998
Arizona Dream, 1995, R, ★★★ 1998
Arrival, The, 1996, PG-13, ★★★½ 1998
Arthur, 1981, PG, ★★★½ 1998
Article 99, 1992, R, ★½ 1993
Assassins, 1995, R, ★½ 1997
Assault, The, 1987, NR, ★★★ 1995
Asylum, 1972, PG, ★★ 1991
At Close Range, 1986, R, ★★★½ 1998
At Play in the Fields of the Lord, 1991, R, ★★★½ 1998
At the Max, 1992, R, ★★★★ 1998
Au Revoir les Enfants, 1988, PG, ★★★★ 1998
Austin Powers: International Man of Mystery, 1997, PG-13, ★★★ 1998
Autumn Sonata, 1978, PG, ★★★★ 1998
Avalon, 1990, PG, ★★★½ 1998
Awakening, The, 1980, R, ★ 1986
Awakenings, 1990, PG-13, ★★★★ 1998

# B

Babe, 1995, G, ★★★ 1998
Babe, The, 1992, PG, ★ 1993
Baby Boom, 1987, PG, ★★★ 1995
Babyfever, 1994, R, ★★★ 1998
Baby, It's You, 1983, R, ★★★ 1998
Baby's Day Out, 1994, PG, ★½ 1996
Baby . . . The Secret of the Lost Legend, 1985, PG, ★ 1987
Bachelor Party, 1984, R, ★★★ 1995
Backbeat, 1994, R, ★★ 1997
Backdraft, 1991, R, ★★★ 1996
Back Roads, 1981, R, ★★ 1987
Back to School, 1986, PG-13, ★★★ 1998
Back to the Beach, 1987, PG, ★★★½ 1998
Back to the Future, 1985, PG, ★★★½ 1998
Back to the Future Part II, 1989, PG, ★★★ 1998
Back to the Future Part III, 1990, PG, ★★½ 1998
Bad Boys, 1983, R, ★★★½ 1998
Bad Boys, 1995, R, ★★ 1996
Bad Company, 1995, R, ★★★½ 1998
Bad Dreams, 1988, R, ½★ 1990
Bad Girls, 1994, R, ★½ 1996
Bad Influence, 1990, R, ★★★ 1998
Badlands, 1974, PG, ★★★★ 1998
Bad Lieutenant, 1993, NC-17, ★★★★ 1998
Bagdad Cafe, 1988, PG, ★★★½ 1998
Ballad of Little Jo, The, 1993, R, ★★★ 1998
Ballad of the Sad Café, The, 1991, NR, ★★★ 1998
Bambi, 1942, G, ★★★½ 1997
Bandit Queen, 1995, NR, ★★★ 1998
Bang the Drum Slowly, 1973, PG, ★★★★ 1998
Barb Wire, 1996, R, ★★½ 1998
Barcelona, 1994, PG-13, ★★★ 1998
Barfly, 1987, R, ★★★★ 1998
Bar Girls, 1995, R, ★½ 1997
Barton Fink, 1991, R, ★★★½ 1998
Basic Instinct, 1992, R, ★★ 1998
Basketball Diaries, The, 1995, R, ★★ 1996
Basquiat, 1996, R, ★★★½ 1998
Batman, 1989, PG-13, ★★ 1998
Batman & Robin, 1997, PG-13, ★★ 1998
Batman Forever, 1995, PG-13, ★★½ 1998
Batman Returns, 1992, PG-13, ★★ 1998
Bat 21, 1988, R, ★★★ 1995
Beaches, 1988, PG-13, ★★½ 1993
Bear, The, 1989, PG, ★★★ 1995
Beautician and the Beast, The, 1997, PG, ★★ 1998
Beautiful Girls, 1996, R, ★★★½ 1998
Beautiful Thing, 1996, R, ★★★ 1998
Beauty and the Beast, 1991, G, ★★★★ 1998
Beavis and Butt-Head Do America, 1996, PG-13, ★★★ 1998
Bed of Roses, 1996, PG-13, ★★ 1997
Beethoven, 1992, PG, ★★½ 1993
Beethoven's 2nd, 1993, PG, ★★ 1995
Beetlejuice, 1988, PG, ★★ 1998
Before Sunrise, 1995, R, ★★★ 1998
Before the Rain, 1995, NR, ★★★★ 1998
Being There, 1980, PG, ★★★★ 1998
Belle de Jour, 1967, R, ★★★★ 1997
Belle Epoque, 1993, NR, ★★★½ 1998
Benny and Joon, 1993, PG, ★★★ 1998
Best Boy, 1980, NR, ★★★★ 1998
Best Little Whorehouse in Texas, The, 1982, R, ★★ 1991
Betrayal, 1983, R, ★★★★ 1998
Betrayed, 1988, R, ★★ 1993
Betsy's Wedding, 1990, R, ★★ 1993
Beverly Hillbillies, The, 1993, PG, ½★ 1995
Beverly Hills Cop, 1984, R, ★★½ 1998
Beverly Hills Cop II, 1987, R, ★ 1995
Beyond Rangoon, 1995, R, ★★★ 1998
Beyond the Limit, 1983, R, ★★½ 1989
Beyond Therapy, 1987, R, ★ 1988
Beyond the Valley of the Dolls, 1970, NC-17, Stars N/A 1997
Big, 1988, PG, ★★★ 1998
Big Bang, The, 1990, R, ★★★ 1995
Big Brawl, The, 1980, R, ★½ 1986
Big Business, 1988, PG, ★★ 1993

Bugsy Malone, 1976, G, ★★★½ 1998
Bull Durham, 1988, R, ★★★½ 1998
Bulletproof Heart, 1995, R, ★★★ 1998
Bullets Over Broadway, 1994, R, ★★★½ 1998
'Burbs, The, 1989, PG, ★★ 1992
Burden of Dreams, 1982, NR, ★★★★ 1998
Burglar, 1987, R, ★ 1989
Buster, 1988, R, ★★★ 1998
Buster and Billie, 1974, R, ★★★ 1995
Butcher's Wife, The, 1991, PG-13, ★★½ 1997
Butley, 1974, NR, ★★★★ 1987
Bye Bye Brazil, 1979, NR, ★★★★ 1996
Bye Bye, Love, 1995, PG-13, ★★ 1996

# C

Cabaret, 1972, PG, ★★★½ 1998
Cable Guy, The, 1996, PG-13, ★★ 1998
Cactus, 1987, NR, ★★★ 1998
Caddyshack, 1980, R, ★★½ 1998
Cadillac Man, 1990, R, ★★ 1994
California Split, 1974, R, ★★★★ 1998
Caligula, 1980, NR, no stars 1990
Camille Claudel, 1989, R, ★★★½ 1998
Candyman, 1992, R, ★★★ 1998
Candyman: Farewell to the Flesh, 1995, R, ★★ 1996
Cannery Row, 1982, PG, ★★½ 1987
Cannonball Run, The, 1981, PG, ½★ 1991
Cannonball Run II, 1984, PG, ½★ 1988
Cape Fear, 1991, R, ★★★ 1998
Carlito's Way, 1993, R, ★★★½ 1998
Carmen, 1984, PG, ★★★★ 1998
Carmen (dance), 1983, R, ★★★★ 1995
Carnival of Souls, 1962, NR, ★★★ 1997
Carrie, 1976, R, ★★★½ 1998
Carrington, 1995, R, ★★★★ 1998
Car Wash, 1976, PG, ★★★½ 1995
Casablanca, 1942, NR, ★★★★ 1997
Casino, 1995, R, ★★★★ 1998
Casper, 1995, PG, ★★★ 1998
Casualties of War, 1989, R, ★★★ 1998
Cat People, 1982, R, ★★★½ 1998
Cat's Eye, 1985, PG-13, ★★★ 1986
Caught, 1996, R, ★★★ 1998
Caveman, 1981, PG, ★½ 1986
Celluloid Closet, The, 1995, NR, ★★★½ 1998
Cement Garden, The, 1994, NR, ★★★ 1998
Cemetery Club, The, 1992, PG-13, ★★★ 1998
Chain Reaction, 1996, PG-13, ★★½ 1998
Chamber, The, 1996, R, ★★ 1998
Chances Are, 1989, PG, ★★★½ 1998
Chaplin, 1993, PG-13, ★★ 1994
Chapter Two, 1980, PG, ★★ 1992
Chariots of Fire, 1981, PG, ★★★★ 1998
Chase, The, 1994, PG-13, ★★½ 1995
Chasing Amy, 1997, R, ★★★½ 1998
Chattahoochee, 1990, R, ★★½ 1992
Child's Play, 1988, R, ★★★ 1998
China Moon, 1994, R, ★★★½ 1998
China Syndrome, The, 1979, PG, ★★★★ 1998
Chinatown, 1974, R, ★★★★ 1998
Chocolat, 1989, PG-13, ★★★★ 1998
Choose Me, 1984, R, ★★★½ 1998
Chorus Line, A, 1985, PG-13, ★★★½ 1998
Christiane F., 1981, R, ★★★½ 1998
Christine, 1983, R, ★★★ 1998
Christmas Story, A, 1983, PG, ★★★ 1998
Christopher Columbus: The Discovery, 1992, PG-13, ★ 1994
Chuck Berry Hail! Hail! Rock 'n' Roll, 1987, PG, ★★★★ 1998
Cinderella, 1950, G, ★★★ 1997
Cinema Paradiso, 1989, NR, ★★★½ 1998
Circle of Friends, 1995, PG-13, ★★★½ 1998
Citizen Kane, 1941, NR, ★★★★ 1998
City Hall, 1996, R, ★★½ 1997
City Heat, 1984, PG, ½★ 1991
City of Hope, 1991, R, ★★★★ 1998
City of Joy, 1992, PG-13, ★★★ 1995
City of Lost Children, 1995, R, ★★★ 1998
City of Women, 1981, R, ★★½ 1991
City Slickers, 1991, PG-13, ★★★½ 1998
City Slickers II: The Legend of Curly's Gold, 1994, PG-13, ★★ 1995
Claire's Knee, 1971, PG, ★★★★ 1998
Clan of the Cave Bear, 1985, R, ★½ 1989
Clash of the Titans, 1981, PG, ★★★½ 1998
Class Action, 1991, R, ★★★ 1995
Class of 1984, The, 1982, R, ★★★½ 1995
Class of 1999, 1990, R, ★★ 1992
Clean and Sober, 1988, R, ★★★½ 1998
Clean, Shaven, 1995, NR, ★★★½ 1998
Clerks, 1994, R, ★★★ 1998
Client, The, 1994, PG-13, ★★½ 1998
Cliffhanger, 1993, R, ★★★ 1998
Clifford, 1994, PG, ½★ 1995
Clockers, 1995, R, ★★★½ 1998
Close Encounters of the Third Kind: The Special Edition, 1980, PG, ★★★★ 1998
Close to Eden, 1992, NR, ★★★ 1998
Clueless, 1995, PG-13, ★★★½ 1998
Coal Miner's Daughter, 1980, PG, ★★★ 1998
Cobb, 1994, R, ★★ 1996
Coca-Cola Kid, The, 1985, NR, ★★★ 1987

Cocktail, 1988, R, ★★ 1993
Cocoon, 1985, PG-13, ★★★ 1998
Cocoon: The Return, 1988, PG, ★★½ 1997
Code of Silence, 1985, R, ★★★½ 1998
Cold Comfort Farm, 1995, PG, ★★★ 1998
Cold Fever, 1996, NR, ★★★ 1998
Color of Money, The, 1986, R, ★★½ 1998
Color of Night, 1994, R, ★½ 1996
Color Purple, The, 1985, PG-13, ★★★★ 1998
Colors, 1988, R, ★★★ 1998
Coma, 1978, PG, ★★★ 1995
Come Back to the 5 & Dime, Jimmy Dean, Jimmy Dean, 1982, PG, ★★★ 1998
Come See the Paradise, 1991, R, ★★★ 1998
Comfort of Strangers, The, 1991, R, ★★½ 1994
Coming Home, 1978, R, ★★★★ 1998
Commitments, The, 1991, R, ★★★ 1998
Company of Wolves, The, 1985, R, ★★★ 1987
Competition, The, 1981, PG, ★★★ 1995
Compromising Positions, 1985, R, ★★ 1987
Con Air, 1997, R, ★★★ 1998
Conan the Barbarian, 1982, R, ★★★ 1998
Conan the Destroyer, 1984, PG, ★★★ 1998
Coneheads, 1993, PG, ★½ 1995
Congo, 1995, PG-13, ★★★ 1998
Contact, 1997, PG, ★★★½ 1998
Continental Divide, 1981, PG, ★★★ 1998
Conversation, The, 1974, PG, ★★★★ 1998
Cookie, 1989, R, ★★ 1992
Cook, the Thief, His Wife and Her Lover, The, 1990, NR, ★★★★ 1998
Cool Runnings, 1993, PG, ★★½ 1995
Cop, 1988, R, ★★★ 1998
Cop and a Half, 1993, PG, ★★★ 1995
Cops and Robbersons, 1994, PG, ★★ 1995
Copycat, 1995, R, ★★★½ 1998
Corrina, Corrina, 1994, PG, ★★½ 1997
Cotton Club, The, 1984, R, ★★★★ 1998
Country, 1984, PG, ★★★½ 1998
Country Life, 1995, PG-13, ★★★½ 1998
Coupe de Ville, 1990, PG-13, ★½ 1992
Cousins, 1989, PG-13, ★★★½ 1998
Cowboys, The, 1972, PG, ★★½ 1991
Crash, 1997, NC-17, ★★★½ 1998
Crazy People, 1990, R, ★★ 1992
Creator, 1985, R, ★★½ 1987
Creepshow, 1982, R, ★★★ 1995
Cries and Whispers, 1973, R, ★★★★ 1998
Crimes and Misdemeanors, 1989, PG-13, ★★★★ 1998
Crimes of Passion, 1984, R, ★½ 1994
Crimson Tide, 1995, R, ★★★½ 1998
Critters, 1986, PG-13, ★★★ 1998
Crocodile Dundee, 1986, PG-13, ★★ 1998
Cronos, 1994, NR, ★★★ 1998
Crooklyn, 1994, PG-13, ★★★½ 1998
Crossing Delancey, 1988, PG, ★★½ 1995
Crossing Guard, The, 1995, R, ★★½ 1997
Cross My Heart, 1987, R, ★★½ 1989
Crossover Dreams, 1985, PG-13, ★★★ 1995
Crossroads, 1985, R, ★★★½ 1998
Crow, The, 1994, R, ★★★½ 1998
Crucible, The, 1996, PG-13, ★★ 1998
Crumb, 1995, R, ★★★★ 1997
Crusoe, 1989, PG-13, ★★★½ 1995
Cry-Baby, 1990, PG-13, ★★★ 1998
Cry Freedom, 1987, PG, ★★½ 1997
Crying Game, The, 1992, R, ★★★★ 1998
Cry in the Dark, A, 1988, PG-13, ★★★ 1998
Cure, The, 1995, PG-13, ★★½ 1996
Curly Sue, 1991, PG, ★★★ 1998
Curse of the Pink Panther, 1983, PG, ★½ 1986
Cutthroat Island, 1995, PG-13, ★★★ 1998
Cutting Edge, The, 1992, PG, ★★½ 1994
Cyborg, 1989, R, ★ 1992
Cyrano de Bergerac, 1990, PG, ★★★½ 1998

# D

Dad, 1989, PG, ★★ 1993
Daddy Nostalgia, 1991, PG, ★★★½ 1998
Dadetown, 1996, NR, ★★ 1998
Damage, 1993, R, ★★★★ 1998
Dances With Wolves, 1990, PG-13, ★★★★ 1998
Dance With a Stranger, 1985, R, ★★★★ 1998
Dangerous Ground, 1997, R, ★★ 1998
Dangerous Liaisons, 1988, R, ★★★ 1998
Dangerous Minds, 1995, R, ★½ 1997
Daniel, 1983, R, ★★½ 1987
Dante's Peak, 1997, PG-13, ★★½ 1998
Dark Crystal, The, 1982, PG, ★★½ 1991
Dark Eyes, 1987, NR, ★★★½ 1998
Dark Half, The, 1993, R, ★★ 1994
Dark Obsession, 1991, NC-17, ★★★ 1998
D.A.R.Y.L., 1985, PG, ★★★ 1998
Date with an Angel, 1987, PG, ★ 1989
Daughters of the Dust, 1992, NR, ★★★ 1998
Dave, 1993, PG-13, ★★★½ 1998
Dawn of the Dead, 1979, R, ★★★★ 1998
Day After Trinity, The, 1980, NR, ★★★★ 1998
Day for Night, 1974, PG, ★★★★ 1998
Daylight, 1996, PG-13, ★★ 1998
Day of the Dead, 1985, R, ★½ 1992
Day of the Jackal, The, 1973, PG, ★★★★ 1998
Days of Heaven, 1978, PG, ★★★★ 1998

Days of Thunder, 1990, PG-13, ★★★ 1998
Dazed and Confused, 1993, R, ★★★ 1998
D.C. Cab, 1983, R, ★★ 1986
Dead, The, 1987, PG, ★★★ 1998
Dead Again, 1991, R, ★★★★ 1998
Dead Calm, 1989, R, ★★★ 1998
Dead Man Walking, 1995, R, ★★★★ 1998
Dead of Winter, 1987, PG-13, ★★½ 1993
Dead Poets Society, 1989, PG, ★★ 1998
Dead Pool, The, 1988, R, ★★★½ 1998
Dead Presidents, 1995, R, ★★½ 1998
Dead Ringers, 1988, R, ★★½ 1993
Dead Zone, The, 1983, R, ★★★½ 1998
Dear America: Letters Home from Vietnam, 1988, PG-13, ★★★★ 1998
Death and the Maiden, 1995, R, ★★★ 1998
Death in Venice, 1971, PG, ★★½ 1994
Deathtrap, 1982, R, ★★★ 1998
Death Wish, 1974, R, ★★★ 1998
Death Wish II, 1982, R, no stars 1993
Death Wish 3, 1985, R, ★ 1993
Deceived, 1991, PG-13, ★★ 1993
Deep Cover, 1992, R, ★★★½ 1998
Deer Hunter, The, 1978, R, ★★★★ 1998
Defence of the Realm, 1987, PG, ★★★ 1998
Defending Your Life, 1991, PG, ★★★½ 1998
Delta Force, The, 1985, R, ★★★ 1998
Dennis the Menace, 1993, PG, ★★½ 1995
Desert Hearts, 1985, R, ★★½ 1988
Desperado, 1995, R, ★★ 1997
Desperate Hours, 1990, R, ★★ 1992
Desperately Seeking Susan, 1985, PG-13, ★★★ 1998
Devil in a Blue Dress, 1995, R, ★★★ 1998
Devil's Own, The, 1997, R, ★★½ 1998
Diabolique, 1955, NR, ★★★½ 1997
Diabolique, 1995, R, ★★ 1997
Diamonds Are Forever, 1971, PG, ★★★ 1998
Diary of a Mad Housewife, 1970, R, ★★★ 1996
Dice Rules, 1991, NC-17, no stars 1992
Dick Tracy, 1990, PG, ★★★★ 1998
Die Hard, 1988, R, ★★ 1998
Die Hard 2: Die Harder, 1990, R, ★★★½ 1998
Die Hard With a Vengeance, 1995, R, ★★★ 1998
Dim Sum, 1985, PG, ★★★ 1998
Diner, 1982, R, ★★★½ 1998
Dirty Dancing, 1987, PG-13, ★ 1995
Dirty Harry, 1971, R, ★★★ 1998
Dirty Rotten Scoundrels, 1988, PG, ★★★ 1998
Disclosure, 1994, R, ★★ 1996
Discreet Charm of the Bourgeoisie, The, 1972, PG, ★★★★ 1998
Distinguished Gentleman, The, 1992, R, ★★ 1994
Diva, 1981, R, ★★★★ 1998
Divine Madness, 1980, R, ★★★½ 1998
D.O.A., 1988, R, ★★★ 1998
Doc Hollywood, 1991, PG-13, ★★★ 1998
Doctor, The, 1991, PG-13, ★★★½ 1998
Dr. Strangelove, 1964, PG, ★★★★ 1997
Doctor Zhivago, 1965, PG-13, ★★★ 1997
Dog Day Afternoon, 1975, R, ★★★½ 1998
Dogfight, 1991, R, ★★★ 1998
Dogs of War, The, 1981, R, ★★★ 1988
Dolores Claiborne, 1995, R, ★★★ 1998
Dominick and Eugene, 1988, PG-13, ★★★½ 1998
Don Juan DeMarco, 1995, PG-13, ★★ 1996
Donnie Brasco, 1997, R, ★★★½ 1998
Doom Generation, The, 1995, NR, no stars 1997
Doors, The, 1991, R, ★★½ 1998
Do the Right Thing, 1989, R, ★★★★ 1998
Double Life of Veronique, The, 1991, NR, ★★★½ 1998
Down and Out in Beverly Hills, 1986, R, ★★★★ 1998
Down by Law, 1986, R, ★★★ 1998
Dragnet, 1987, PG-13, ★★★ 1998
Dragonheart, 1995, PG-13, ★★★ 1998
Dragonslayer, 1981, PG, ★★★ 1989
Dragon: The Bruce Lee Story, 1993, PG-13, ★★½ 1995
Draughtsman's Contract, The, 1983, R, ★★★★ 1998
Dreamchild, 1985, PG, ★★★ 1998
Dream Lover, 1994, R, ★★★ 1998
Dreamscape, 1984, PG-13, ★★★ 1989
Dream Team, The, 1989, PG-13, ★★ 1993
Dream With the Fishes, 1997, R, ★★★ 1998
Dressed to Kill, 1980, R, ★★★ 1998
Dresser, The, 1984, PG, ★★★★ 1998
Drive, He Said, 1971, R, ★★★ 1998
Driving Miss Daisy, 1989, PG, ★★★★ 1998
Drop Zone, 1994, R, ★★½ 1997
Drowning by Numbers, 1991, NR, ★★ 1995
Drugstore Cowboy, 1989, R, ★★★★ 1998
Dry White Season, A, 1989, R, ★★★★ 1998
Dumb and Dumber, 1994, PG-13, ★★ 1998
Dune, 1984, PG-13, ★ 1988
Dutch, 1991, PG-13, ★½ 1993
Dying Young, 1991, R, ★★ 1994

# E

Earth Girls Are Easy, 1989, PG, ★★★ 1998
Easy Money, 1983, R, ★★½ 1994

# F

Fire in the Sky, 1993, PG-13, ★★½ 1994
Firestarter, 1984, R, ★★ 1987
Firm, The, 1993, R, ★★★ 1998
First Blood, 1982, R, ★★★ 1998
Firstborn, 1984, PG, ★★ 1987
First Deadly Sin, The, 1980, R, ★★★ 1986
First Knight, 1995, PG-13, ★★ 1997
First Wives Club, The, 1996, PG, ★★ 1998
Fish Called Wanda, A, 1988, R, ★★★★ 1998
Fisher King, The, 1991, R, ★★ 1994
Fitzcarraldo, 1982, PG, ★★★★ 1998
Five Easy Pieces, 1970, R, ★★★★ 1998
Five Heartbeats, The, 1991, R, ★★★ 1998
Flamingo Kid, The, 1984, PG-13, ★★★½ 1998
Flashback, 1990, R, ★★★ 1998
Flashdance, 1983, R, ★½ 1994
Flash Gordon, 1980, PG, ★★½ 1988
Flash of Green, A, 1985, NR, ★★★ 1987
Flatliners, 1990, R, ★★★ 1998
Fled, 1996, R, ★★ 1997
Flesh and Bone, 1993, R, ★★ 1995
Fletch, 1985, PG, ★★½ 1995
Fletch Lives, 1989, PG, ★½ 1995
Flintstones, The, 1994, PG, ★★½ 1997
Flipper, 1995, PG, ★★ 1998
Flirting, 1992, NR, ★★★★ 1998
Fly Away Home, 1996, PG, ★★★½ 1998
Fog, The, 1980, R, ★★ 1988
Fool for Love, 1985, R, ★★★ 1998
Fools Rush In, 1997, PG-13, ★★★ 1998
Footloose, 1984, PG, ★½ 1995
Forever Young, 1992, PG, ★★½ 1994
Forget Paris, 1995, PG-13, ★★★½ 1998
For Keeps, 1988, PG-13, ★★★ 1998
For Love or Money, 1993, PG, ★★ 1995
Formula, The, 1980, R, ★★ 1987
For Queen and Country, 1989, R, ★★ 1992
Forrest Gump, 1994, PG-13, ★★★★ 1998
Fort Apache, The Bronx, 1981, R, ★★ 1987
For the Boys, 1991, R, ★★ 1993
48 HRS, 1982, R, ★★★½ 1998
For Your Eyes Only, 1981, PG, ★★ 1998
Four Friends, 1981, R, ★★★★ 1998
Four Rooms, 1995, R, ★★ 1998
1492: Conquest of Paradise, 1992, PG-13, ★★★ 1996
Fourth Protocol, The, 1987, R, ★★★½ 1998
Fourth War, The, 1990, R, ★★★ 1998
Four Weddings and a Funeral, 1994, R, ★★★½ 1998
Fox and the Hound, The, 1981, G, ★★★ 1998
Foxes, 1980, R, ★★★ 1998
Frances, 1983, R, ★★★½ 1998
Frankie and Johnny, 1991, R, ★★½ 1995
Frankie Starlight, 1995, R, ★★★½ 1998
Frantic, 1988, R, ★★★ 1998
Fraternity Vacation, 1985, R, ★ 1990
Freeway, 1997, R, ★★★½ 1998
Free Willy, 1993, PG, ★★★½ 1998
French Kiss, 1995, PG-13, ★★ 1997
French Lieutenant's Woman, The, 1981, R, ★★★½ 1998
Frenzy, 1972, R, ★★★★ 1998
Fresh, 1994, R, ★★★★ 1998
Freshman, The, 1990, PG, ★★★½ 1998
Friday the 13th, Part II, 1981, R, ½★ 1993
Fried Green Tomatoes, 1992, PG-13, ★★★ 1998
Friends of Eddie Coyle, The, 1973, R, ★★★★ 1998
Fright Night, 1985, R, ★★★ 1996
Frighteners, The, 1996, R, ★ 1997
Fringe Dwellers, The, 1987, PG-13, ★★★½ 1996
From Dusk Till Dawn, 1996, R, ★★★ 1998
From the Journals of Jean Seberg, 1996, NR, ★★★½ 1998
Frozen Assets, 1992, PG-13, no stars 1994
Fugitive, The, 1993, PG-13, ★★★★ 1998
Full Metal Jacket, 1987, R, ★★½ 1998
Full Moon on Blue Water, 1988, R, ★★ 1992
Funeral, The, 1996, R, ★★★ 1998
Funny Farm, 1988, PG, ★★★½ 1998
F/X, 1985, R, ★★★½ 1998
F/X 2: The Deadly Art of Illusion, 1991, PG-13, ★★ 1993

# G

Gambler, The, 1974, R, ★★★★ 1998
Gandhi, 1982, PG, ★★★★ 1998
Garden of the Finzi-Continis, The, 1971, R, ★★★★ 1998
Gates of Heaven, 1978, NR, ★★★★ 1998
Gauntlet, The, 1977, R, ★★★ 1998
George of the Jungle, 1997, PG, ★★★ 1998
George Stevens: A Filmmaker's Journey, 1985, PG, ★★★½ 1996
Georgia, 1996, R, ★★★½ 1998
Germinal, 1994, R, ★★★ 1998
Geronimo: An American Legend, 1993, PG-13, ★★★½ 1998
Getaway, The, 1994, R, ★ 1995
Get on the Bus, 1996, R, ★★★★ 1998
Getting Away With Murder, 1995, R, ★★ 1997
Getting Even with Dad, 1994, PG, ★★ 1995
Getting It Right, 1989, R, ★★★★ 1998

# H

Heartbreak Kid, The, 1972, PG, ★★★½ 1998
Heartbreak Ridge, 1986, R, ★★★ 1998
Heartburn, 1986, R, ★★ 1993
Heartland, 1981, PG, ★★★★ 1998
Heart of Midnight, 1989, R, ★★½ 1993
Hearts of Darkness, 1991, NR, ★★★½ 1998
Heat, 1987, R, ★★ 1988
Heat, 1995, R, ★★★½ 1998
Heat and Dust, 1983, R, ★★★ 1998
Heathers, 1989, R, ★★½ 1994
Heaven, 1987, PG-13, ★★ 1990
Heaven and Earth, 1993, R, ★★★½ 1998
Heaven Help Us, 1985, R, ★★½ 1989
Heavenly Creatures, 1994, R, ★★★½ 1998
Heavenly Kid, The, 1985, PG-13, ★ 1987
Heaven's Gate, 1981, R, ½★ 1994
Heaven's Prisoners, 1995, R, ★★ 1997
Heavy, 1996, NR, ★★★½ 1998
Heidi Fleiss, Hollywood Madam, 1995, NR, ★★★★ 1997
Hellbound: Hellraiser II, 1988, R, ½★ 1990
Hell Night, 1981, R, ★ 1986
Henry and June, 1990, NC-17, ★★★ 1998
Henry V, 1989, NR, ★★★½ 1998
Henry: Portrait of a Serial Killer, 1986, NR, ★★★½ 1998
Her Alibi, 1989, PG, ½★ 1993
Hercules, 1997, G, ★★★½ 1998
Hero, 1992, PG-13, ★★ 1994
Hero and the Terror, 1987, R, ★★ 1991
Hidden, The, 1987, R, ★★★ 1996
Hidden Agenda, 1990, R, ★★★ 1998
Hidden Fortress, The, 1958, NR, ★★★★ 1997
Hideaway, 1995, R, ★★★ 1998
High Anxiety, 1978, PG, ★★½ 1995
Higher Learning, 1995, R, ★★★ 1998
High Hopes, 1989, NR, ★★★★ 1998
Highlander 2: The Quickening, 1991, R, ½★ 1993
High Road to China, 1983, PG, ★★ 1987
High Season, 1988, R, ★★★ 1998
History of the World—Part I, 1981, R, ★★ 1995
Hitcher, The, 1985, R, no stars 1990
Hocus Pocus, 1993, PG, ★ 1995
Hoffa, 1992, R, ★★★½ 1998
Hollywood Shuffle, 1987, R, ★★★ 1998
Home Alone, 1990, PG, ★★½ 1998
Home Alone 2: Lost in New York, 1992, PG, ★★ 1995
Home and the World, The, 1986, NR, ★★★ 1987
Home of Our Own, A, 1993, PG, ★★★ 1998
Home of the Brave, 1986, NR, ★★★½ 1998
Homeward Bound: The Incredible Journey, 1993, G, ★★★ 1998
Homicide, 1991, R, ★★★★ 1998
Honey, I Blew Up the Kid, 1992, PG, ★½ 1994
Honey, I Shrunk the Kids, 1989, PG, ★★ 1995
Honeymoon in Vegas, 1992, PG-13, ★★★½ 1998
Honkytonk Man, 1982, PG, ★★★ 1998
Hook, 1991, PG, ★★ 1994
Hoop Dreams, 1994, PG-13, ★★★★ 1998
Hoosiers, 1987, PG, ★★★★ 1998
Hope and Glory, 1987, PG-13, ★★★ 1998
Horseman on the Roof, The, 1995, R, ★★★ 1998
Hotel Terminus, 1988, NR, ★★★ 1996
Hot Shots, Part Deux, 1993, PG-13, ★★★ 1998
Hot Spot, The, 1990, R, ★★★ 1996
Household Saints, 1993, R, ★★★★ 1998
Housekeeping, 1988, PG, ★★★★ 1998
House of Games, 1987, R, ★★★★ 1998
House of the Spirits, The, 1994, R, ★★ 1995
House on Carroll Street, The, 1988, PG, ★★★ 1998
House Party, 1990, R, ★★★ 1998
House Party 2, 1991, R, ★★ 1993
Housesitter, 1992, PG, ★★★ 1998
Howards End, 1992, PG, ★★★★ 1998
Howling, The, 1981, R, ★★ 1992
Howling II, 1986, R, ★ 1987
How to Make an American Quilt, 1995, PG-13, ★★ 1997
Hudsucker Proxy, The, 1994, PG, ★★ 1997
Hugh Hefner: Once Upon a Time, 1992, NR, ★★★ 1996
Hunchback of Notre Dame, The, 1995, G, ★★★★ 1998
Hunger, The, 1983, R, ★½ 1991
Hunt for Red October, The, 1990, PG, ★★★½ 1998
Husbands and Wives, 1992, R, ★★★½ 1998
Hype!, 1997, NR, ★★★ 1998

# I

Iceman, 1984, PG, ★★★★ 1998
Idolmaker, The, 1980, PG, ★★★ 1998
If Looks Could Kill, 1991, PG-13, ★★★ 1995
I Like It Like That, 1994, R, ★★★ 1998
Il Ladro di Bambini, 1993, NR, ★★★★ 1998
I'll Do Anything, 1994, PG-13, ★★★ 1998
I Love You to Death, 1990, R, ★★★ 1998
I, Madman, 1989, R, ★★★ 1996
Imaginary Crimes, 1994, PG, ★★★½ 1998
Imagine: John Lennon, 1988, R, ★★★ 1997

Immediate Family, 1989, PG-13, ★★ 1992
Immortal Beloved, 1995, R, ★★★½ 1998
I'm Not Rappaport, 1997, PG-13, ★★½ 1998
Impromptu, 1991, PG-13, ★★½ 1994
Impulse, 1990, R, ★★★ 1998
In Country, 1989, R, ★★★ 1998
Incredible Shrinking Woman, The, 1981, PG, ★★½ 1991
Incredibly True Adventure of Two Girls in Love, The, 1995, R, ★★★ 1998
Indecent Proposal, 1993, R, ★★★ 1998
Independence Day, 1996, PG-13, ★★½ 1998
Indiana Jones and the Last Crusade, 1989, PG-13, ★★★½ 1998
Indiana Jones and the Temple of Doom, 1984, PG, ★★★★ 1998
Indian in the Cupboard, 1995, PG, ★★ 1997
Indian Runner, The, 1991, R, ★★★ 1996
Indian Summer, 1993, PG-13, ★★★ 1998
Indochine, 1993, PG-13, ★★½ 1994
I Never Promised You a Rose Garden, 1977, R, ★★★ 1996
I Never Sang for My Father, 1971, PG, ★★★★ 1998
Infinity, 1996, PG, ★★★ 1998
Infra-Man, 1976, PG, ★★½ 1996
Inkwell, The, 1994, R, ★★★ 1995
Inner Circle, The, 1992, PG-13, ★★★ 1996
Innerspace, 1987, PG, ★★★ 1996
Innocent, The, 1995, R, ★★★ 1998
Innocent Blood, 1992, R, ★★ 1994
Innocent Man, An, 1989, R, ★½ 1993
Insignificance, 1985, R, ★★★ 1996
Interiors, 1978, PG, ★★★★ 1998
Intersection, 1994, R, ★ 1995
Interview With the Vampire, 1994, R, ★★★ 1998
Intervista, 1993, NR, ★★½ 1995
In the Line of Fire, 1993, R, ★★★½ 1998
In the Mood, 1987, PG-13, ★★★ 1995
In the Mouth of Madness, 1995, R, ★★ 1996
In the Name of the Father, 1994, R, ★★★ 1998
Into the Night, 1985, R, ★ 1987
Into the West, 1993, PG, ★★★½ 1998
Invasion USA, 1985, R, ½★ 1987
Inventing the Abbotts, 1997, R, ★★ 1998
I.Q., 1994, PG, ★★★½ 1998
Ironweed, 1988, R, ★★★ 1998
Iron Will, 1994, PG, ★★ 1995
Irreconcilable Differences, 1984, PG, ★★★½ 1995
Ishtar, 1987, PG-13, ½★ 1994
I Shot Andy Warhol, 1995, NR, ★★★½ 1998
I Spit on Your Grave, 1980, R, no stars 1990
It Could Happen to You, 1994, PG, ★★★½ 1998
It's All True, 1993, G, ★★★ 1997
It's a Wonderful Life, 1946, NR, ★★★★ 1997
It's My Party, 1995, R, ★★★ 1998
It Takes Two, 1995, PG, ★★ 1997
I've Heard the Mermaids Singing, 1987, NR, ★★★½ 1998
I Wanna Hold Your Hand, 1978, PG, ★★½ 1994

## J

Jack, 1996, PG-13, ★½ 1998
Jackie Chan's First Strike, 1997, PG-13, ★★★ 1998
Jacknife, 1989, R, ★★★ 1996
Jack's Back, 1988, R, ★★★ 1996
Jack the Bear, 1993, PG-13, ★★★ 1996
Jacob's Ladder, 1990, R, ★★★½ 1998
Jacquot, 1993, NR, ★★★½ 1996
Jade, 1995, R, ★★ 1997
Jagged Edge, 1985, R, ★★★½ 1998
James and the Giant Peach, 1995, PG, ★★★ 1998
Jamon Jamon, 1994, NR, ★★★½ 1998
Jane Eyre, 1995, PG, ★★★½ 1998
Jason's Lyric, 1994, R, ★★★ 1998
Jaws, 1975, PG, ★★★★ 1998
Jaws the Revenge, 1987, PG-13, no stars 1993
Jazz Singer, The, 1980, PG, ★ 1987
Jean de Florette, 1987, PG, ★★★½ 1998
Jefferson in Paris, 1995, PG-13, ★★ 1997
Jeremiah Johnson, 1972, PG, ★★★ 1998
Jerry Maguire, 1996, R, ★★★ 1998
Jesus of Montreal, 1990, R, ★★★½ 1998
Jewel of the Nile, The, 1985, PG, ★★★ 1998
JFK, 1991, R, ★★★★ 1998
Jimmy Hollywood, 1994, R, ★★½ 1997
Jingle All the Way, 1996, PG, ★★½ 1998
Joe Vs. the Volcano, 1990, PG, ★★★½ 1998
Johnny Dangerously, 1984, PG-13, ★★ 1993
Johnny Got His Gun, 1971, R, ★★★★ 1998
Johnny Handsome, 1989, R, ★★★½ 1998
Johnny Mnemonic, 1995, R, ★★ 1996
johns, 1997, R, ★★★ 1998
Jo Jo Dancer, Your Life Is Calling, 1986, R, ★★★ 1998
Josh and S.A.M., 1993, PG-13, ★★ 1995
Journey of Hope, 1990, NR, ★★½ 1995
Journey of Natty Gann, The, 1985, PG, ★★★ 1998

Lethal Weapon, 1987, R, ★★★★ 1998
Lethal Weapon 2, 1989, R, ★★★½ 1998
Lethal Weapon 3, 1992, R, ★★★ 1998
Let Him Have It, 1992, R, ★★★½ 1998
Let's Spend the Night Together, 1983, PG, ★★½ 1994
Lianna, 1983, R, ★★★½ 1998
Liar Liar, 1997, PG-13, ★★★ 1998
Licence to Kill, 1989, PG-13, ★★★½ 1998
Life Is Sweet, 1991, NR, ★★★★ 1998
Life Stinks, 1991, PG-13, ★★★ 1998
Life With Mikey, 1993, PG, ★★ 1995
Lightning Jack, 1994, PG-13, ★★ 1995
Light of Day, 1987, PG-13, ★★★½ 1998
Light Sleeper, 1992, R, ★★★★ 1998
Like Father, Like Son, 1987, PG-13, ★ 1991
Like Water for Chocolate, 1993, R, ★★★★ 1998
Lion King, The, 1994, G, ★★★½ 1998
Listen Up: The Lives of Quincy Jones, 1990, PG-13, ★★★½ 1998
Little Big League, 1994, PG, ★★★½ 1998
Little Big Man, 1971, PG, ★★★★ 1998
Little Buddha, 1994, PG, ★★ 1995
Little Darlings, 1980, R, ★★ 1987
Little Dorrit, 1988, G, ★★★★ 1998
Little Drummer Girl, 1984, R, ★★ 1991
Little Indian Big City, 1995, PG, no stars 1997
Little Man Tate, 1991, PG, ★★★½ 1998
Little Mermaid, The, 1989, G, ★★★★ 1998
Little Nikita, 1988, PG, ★½ 1991
Little Odessa, 1995, R, ★★ 1996
Little Princess, A, 1995, G, ★★★½ 1998
Little Vera, 1989, R, ★★★ 1996
Little Women, 1994, PG, ★★★½ 1998
Living Daylights, The, 1987, PG, ★★ 1994
Local Hero, 1983, PG, ★★★★ 1998
Lonely Guy, The, 1984, R, ★½ 1995
Lonely Lady, The, 1983, R, ½★ 1988
Lonely Passion of Judith Hearne, The, 1988, R, ★★★ 1998
Lone Star, 1996, R, ★★★★ 1998
Lone Wolf McQuade, 1983, PG, ★★★½ 1995
Long Goodbye, The, 1973, R, ★★★ 1996
Long Good Friday, The, 1982, R, ★★★★ 1998
Longtime Companion, 1990, R, ★★★½ 1998
Long Walk Home, The, 1991, PG, ★★★½ 1998
Looking for Mr. Goodbar, 1977, R, ★★★ 1998
Look Who's Talking, 1989, PG-13, ★★★ 1998
Look Who's Talking Now, 1993, PG-13, ★ 1995
Loose Cannons, 1990, R, ★ 1992
Lord of Illusions, 1995, R, ★★★ 1998
Lords of Discipline, 1983, R, ★★ 1991
Lorenzo's Oil, 1993, PG-13, ★★★★ 1998
Losing Isaiah, 1995, R, ★★½ 1997
Lost Angels, 1989, R, ★★½ 1992
Lost Boys, The, 1987, R, ★★½ 1993
Lost Highway, 1997, R, ★★ 1998
Lost in America, 1985, R, ★★★★ 1998
Lost in Yonkers, 1993, PG, ★★★ 1998
Lost World: Jurassic Park, The, 1997, PG-13, ★★ 1998
Louie Bluie, 1985, NR, ★★★½ 1996
Love Affair, 1994, PG-13, ★★★ 1998
Love and Human Remains, 1995, NR, ★★½ 1997
Love Field, 1993, PG-13, ★★½ 1997
love jones, 1997, R, ★★★ 1998
Love Letters, 1984, R, ★★★½ 1998
Lover, The, 1992, R, ★★ 1996
Lovesick, 1983, PG, ★★★ 1989
Love Story, 1970, PG, ★★★★ 1998
Love Streams, 1984, PG-13, ★★★★ 1998
Love! Valour! Compassion!, 1997, R, ★★★ 1998
Lucas, 1985, PG-13, ★★★★ 1998
Lust in the Dust, 1985, R, ★★ 1990

## M

Maborosi, 1997, NR, ★★★★ 1998
Mac, 1993, R, ★★★½ 1998
Macbeth, 1972, R, ★★★★ 1998
McCabe and Mrs. Miller, 1971, R, ★★★★ 1998
Madame Bovary, 1991, NR, ★★★ 1998
Madame Sousatzka, 1988, PG-13, ★★★★ 1998
Mad Dog and Glory, 1993, R, ★★★½ 1998
Made in America, 1993, PG-13, ★★★ 1998
Mad Love, 1995, PG-13, ★★★ 1998
Mad Max Beyond Thunderdome, 1985, R, ★★★★ 1998
Madness of King George, The, 1995, NR, ★★★★ 1998
Major Payne, 1995, PG-13, ★★★ 1998
Making Love, 1982, R, ★★ 1988
Making Mr. Right, 1987, PG-13, ★★★½ 1998
Malcolm X, 1992, PG-13, ★★★★ 1998
Malice, 1993, R, ★★ 1995
Mambo Kings, The, 1992, R, ★★★½ 1998
Manchurian Candidate, The, 1962, PG-13, ★★★★ 1997
Manhattan, 1979, R, ★★★½ 1998
Manhattan Murder Mystery, 1993, PG, ★★★ 1998
Manhattan Project, The, 1986, PG-13, ★★★★ 1998

Money Pit, The, 1986, PG-13, ★ 1991
Money Train, 1995, R, ★½ 1997
Monkey Trouble, 1994, PG, ★★★ 1998
Monsieur Hire, 1990, PG-13, ★★★★ 1998
Monsignor, 1982, R, ★ 1987
Month by the Lake, A, 1995, PG, ★★★½ 1998
Monty Python's Meaning of Life, 1983, R, ★★½ 1995
Moonlighting, 1982, PG, ★★★★ 1998
Moon Over Parador, 1988, PG-13, ★★ 1993
Moonstruck, 1987, PG, ★★★★ 1998
Morning After, The, 1986, R, ★★★ 1996
Mortal Thoughts, 1991, R, ★★★ 1998
Moscow on the Hudson, 1984, R, ★★★★ 1998
Mosquito Coast, The, 1986, PG, ★★ 1993
Motel Hell, 1980, R, ★★★ 1996
Mother, 1997, PG-13, ★★★½ 1998
Mother's Day, 1980, R, no stars 1991
Mountains of the Moon, 1990, R, ★★★½ 1998
Much Ado About Nothing, 1993, PG-13, ★★★ 1998
Mulholland Falls, 1996, R, ★★★½ 1998
Multiplicity, 1996, PG-13, ★★½ 1997
Muppet Christmas Carol, The, 1992, G, ★★★ 1998
Muppet Movie, The, 1979, G, ★★★½ 1998
Muppets Take Manhattan, The, 1984, G, ★★★ 1998
Murder at 1600, 1997, R, ★★½ 1998
Murder in the First, 1995, R, ★★ 1996
Murder on the Orient Express, 1974, PG, ★★★ 1998
Muriel's Wedding, 1995, R, ★★★½ 1998
Murphy's Romance, 1985, PG-13, ★★★ 1998
Music Box, 1990, PG-13, ★★ 1993
Music Lovers, The, 1971, R, ★★ 1993
Music of Chance, The, 1993, NR, ★★★ 1998
My Beautiful Laundrette, 1986, R, ★★★ 1998
My Best Friend's Wedding, 1997, PG-13, ★★★ 1998
My Bodyguard, 1980, PG, ★★★½ 1998
My Brilliant Career, 1980, NR, ★★★½ 1998
My Cousin Vinny, 1992, R, ★★½ 1998
My Dinner with André, 1981, NR, ★★★★ 1998
My Fair Lady, 1964, G, ★★★★ 1997
My Family, 1995, R, ★★★★ 1998
My Father's Glory, 1991, G, ★★★★ 1998
My Father the Hero, 1994, PG, ★★ 1995
My Favorite Season, 1995, NR, ★★★ 1998
My Favorite Year, 1982, PG, ★★★½ 1998
My Fellow Americans, 1996, PG-13, ★★½ 1998
My Girl, 1991, PG, ★★★½ 1998
My Girl 2, 1994, PG, ★★ 1995
My Heroes Have Always Been Cowboys, 1991, PG, ★★ 1992
My Left Foot, 1989, R, ★★★★ 1998
My Life, 1993, PG-13, ★★½ 1995
My Mother's Castle, 1991, PG, ★★★★ 1998
My Own Private Idaho, 1991, R, ★★★½ 1998
My Stepmother Is an Alien, 1988, PG-13, ★★ 1993
Mystery Science Theater 3000: The Movie, 1996, PG-13, ★★★ 1998
Mystery Train, 1990, R, ★★★½ 1998
Mystic Pizza, 1988, R, ★★★½ 1998
My Tutor, 1983, R, ★★★ 1986

# N

Nadine, 1987, PG, ★★½ 1993
Naked, 1994, NR, ★★★★ 1998
Naked Gun, The, 1988, PG-13, ★★★½ 1998
Naked Gun 2½: The Smell of Fear, The, 1991, PG-13, ★★★ 1998
Naked Gun 33⅓: The Final Insult, 1994, PG-13, ★★★ 1998
Naked in New York, 1994, R, ★★★ 1998
Naked Lunch, 1992, R, ★★½ 1994
Name of the Rose, The, 1986, R, ★★½ 1995
Narrow Margin, 1990, R, ★½ 1992
Nashville, 1975, R, ★★★★ 1998
Nasty Girl, The, 1991, PG-13, ★★½ 1993
National Lampoon's Animal House, 1978, R, ★★★★ 1998
National Lampoon's Christmas Vacation, 1989, PG-13, ★★ 1995
National Lampoon's Loaded Weapon I, 1993, PG-13, ★ 1994
Natural, The, 1984, PG, ★★ 1995
Natural Born Killers, 1994, R, ★★★★ 1998
Navy Seals, 1990, R, ★½ 1992
Necessary Roughness, 1991, PG-13, ★★★ 1996
Needful Things, 1993, R, ★½ 1995
Neighbors, 1981, R, ★★★ 1996
Nell, 1994, PG-13, ★★★ 1998
Nelly and Monsieur Arnaud, 1996, NR, ★★★½ 1998
Net, The, 1995, PG-13, ★★★ 1998
Network, 1976, R, ★★★★ 1998
Neverending Story, The, 1984, PG, ★★★ 1998
Never Say Never Again, 1983, PG, ★★★½ 1998
New Age, The, 1994, R, ★★★½ 1998
New Jack City, 1991, R, ★★★½ 1998
New Jersey Drive, 1995, R, ★★★ 1998

Newsies, 1992, PG, ★½ 1993
New York, New York, 1977, PG, ★★★ 1998
New York Stories, 1989, PG, 1998
  Life Lessons, ★★★½
  Life Without Zoe, ★½
  Oedipus Wrecks, ★★
Nico Icon, 1996, NR, ★★★ 1998
Night and the City, 1992, R, ★★ 1994
Nightmare on Elm Street 3, A: Dream Warriors, 1987, R, ★½ 1990
Night of the Living Dead, 1990, R, ★ 1992
Night on Earth, 1992, R, ★★★ 1998
Nina Takes a Lover, 1995, R, ★★ 1997
9½ Weeks, 1985, R, ★★★½ 1998
Nine Months, 1995, PG-13, ★★ 1998
1984, 1984, R, ★★★½ 1998
Nine to Five, 1980, PG, ★★★ 1998
Nixon, 1995, R, ★★★★ 1998
Nobody's Fool, 1986, PG-13, ★★ 1991
Nobody's Fool, 1995, R, ★★★½ 1998
No Escape, 1994, R, ★★ 1995
Nomads, 1985, R, ★½ 1987
No Man's Land, 1987, R, ★★★ 1998
No Mercy, 1986, R, ★★★ 1996
Normal Life, 1996, R, ★★★½ 1998
Norma Rae, 1979, PG, ★★★ 1998
North, 1994, PG, no stars 1997
North Dallas Forty, 1979, R, ★★★½ 1998
Nosferatu, 1979, R, ★★★★ 1998
Nothing But a Man, 1964, NR, ★★★½ 1997
Nothing in Common, 1986, PG, ★★½ 1988
Not Without My Daughter, 1990, PG-13, ★★★ 1998
No Way Out, 1987, R, ★★★★ 1998
Nuns on the Run, 1990, PG-13, ★ 1993
Nuts, 1987, R, ★★ 1993
Nutty Professor, The, 1996, PG-13, ★★★ 1998

# O

Object of Beauty, The, 1991, R, ★★★½ 1998
Off Beat, 1986, PG, ★★★½ 1995
Officer and a Gentleman, An, 1982, R, ★★★★ 1998
Of Mice and Men, 1992, PG-13, ★★★½ 1998
Oh, God!, 1977, PG, ★★★½ 1998
Oh, God! Book II, 1980, PG, ★★ 1995
Oh, God! You Devil, 1984, PG, ★★★½ 1998
Old Gringo, 1989, R, ★★ 1993
Oleanna, 1994, NR, ★★ 1997
Oliver & Co., 1988, G, ★★★ 1998
Once Around, 1990, R, ★★★½ 1998
Once Upon a Forest, 1993, G, ★★½ 1995
Once Upon a Time in America, 1984, R,
  ★—short version
  ★★★★—original version 1998
Once Upon a Time . . . When We Were Colored, 1996, PG, ★★★★ 1998
Once Were Warriors, 1995, R, ★★★½ 1998
One False Move, 1992, R, ★★★★ 1998
One Fine Day, 1996, PG, ★★ 1998
One Flew Over the Cuckoo's Nest, 1975, R, ★★★ 1998
One from the Heart, 1982, PG, ★★ 1995
One Good Cop, 1991, R, ★★ 1994
101 Dalmatians, 1961, G, ★★★ 1998
101 Dalmatians, 1996, G, ★★½ 1998
One Magic Christmas, 1985, G, ★★ 1987
$1,000,000 Duck, 1971, G, ★ 1987
1,000 Pieces of Gold, 1991, NR, ★★★ 1996
One-Trick Pony, 1980, R, ★★★½ 1998
On Golden Pond, 1981, PG, ★★★★ 1998
Onion Field, The, 1979, R, ★★★★ 1998
Only When I Laugh, 1981, R, ★ 1987
Only You, 1994, PG, ★★★½ 1998
On the Edge, 1986, PG-13, ★★★½ 1989
On the Right Track, 1981, PG, ★★½ 1986
On the Road Again, 1980, PG, ★★★ 1998
Opening Night, 1978, PG-13, ★★★ 1998
Operation Condor, 1997, PG-13, ★★★ 1998
Ordinary People, 1980, R, ★★★★ 1998
Orlando, 1993, PG-13, ★★★½ 1998
Orphans, 1987, R, ★★½ 1993
Othello, 1952, NR, ★★★ 1997
Othello, 1995, R, ★★ 1998
Other People's Money, 1991, PG-13, ★★★½ 1998
Outbreak, 1995, R, ★★★½ 1998
Outlaw Josey Wales, The, 1976, PG, ★★★ 1998
Out of Africa, 1985, PG, ★★★★ 1998
Out of the Blue, 1982, R, ★★★½ 1998
Outrageous Fortune, 1987, R, ★★ 1993
Out to Sea, 1997, PG-13, ★★★ 1998
Overboard, 1987, PG, ★★★ 1995

# P

Pacific Heights, 1990, R, ★★ 1993
Package, The, 1989, R, ★★★ 1998
Pale Rider, 1985, R, ★★★ 1998
Pallbearer, The, 1996, PG-13, ★★★ 1998
Panther, 1995, R, ★★½ 1996
Paper, The, 1994, R, ★★★½ 1998
Paper Chase, The, 1973, PG, ★★★★ 1998
Paperhouse, 1989, PG-13, ★★★★ 1998
Paradise, 1991, PG-13, ★★ 1993

Paradise Road, 1997, R, ★★ 1998
Parenthood, 1989, PG-13, ★★★★ 1998
Parents, 1989, R, ★★ 1993
Paris Is Burning, 1991, NR, ★★★ 1996
Paris, Texas, 1984, R, ★★★★ 1998
Pascali's Island, 1988, PG-13, ★★★ 1998
Passage to India, A, 1984, PG, ★★★★ 1998
Passenger 57, 1992, R, ★★★ 1998
Passion Fish, 1993, R, ★★★★ 1998
Paternity, 1981, PG, ★★ 1986
Patriot Games, 1992, R, ★★½ 1995
Patton, 1970, PG, ★★★★ 1998
Patty Hearst, 1988, R, ★★★ 1998
PCU, 1994, PG-13, ★★ 1995
Peeping Tom, 1960, NR, ★★★½ 1997
Peggy Sue Got Married, 1986, PG-13, ★★★★ 1998
Pelican Brief, The, 1993, PG-13, ★★★ 1998
Pelle the Conqueror, 1988, NR, ★★★½ 1998
Pennies from Heaven, 1981, R, ★★ 1986
People vs. Larry Flynt, The, 1996, R, ★★★★ 1998
Perez Family, The, 1995, R, ★★★ 1998
Perfect, 1985, R, ★½ 1987
Perfect World, A, 1993, PG-13, ★★★★ 1998
Performance, 1970, R, ★★½ 1993
Permanent Record, 1988, PG-13, ★★★★ 1998
Personal Best, 1982, R, ★★★★ 1998
Personal Services, 1987, R, ★★★½ 1998
Persuasion, 1995, PG, ★★★½ 1998
Peter's Friends, 1992, R, ★★★½ 1998
Phantom, The, 1996, PG, ★★★½ 1998
Phantom of Liberty, The, 1974, R, ★★★★ 1998
Phenomenon, 1996, PG, ★★★ 1998
Philadelphia, 1994, PG-13, ★★★½ 1998
Physical Evidence, 1989, R, ★★ 1992
Piano, The, 1993, R, ★★★★ 1998
Picnic at Hanging Rock, 1980, PG, ★★★½ 1998
Picture Bride, 1995, PG-13, ★★★ 1998
Pillow Book, The, 1997, NR, ★★★½ 1998
Pink Cadillac, 1989, PG-13, ★ 1992
Pink Flamingos, 1997, NC-17, no stars 1998
Pinocchio, 1940, G, ★★★★ 1997
Pirates of Penzance, 1983, G, ★★ 1986
Pixote, 1981, R, ★★★★ 1998
Places in the Heart, 1984, PG, ★★★ 1998
Planes, Trains and Automobiles, 1987, R, ★★★½ 1998
Platoon, 1986, R, ★★★★ 1998
Playboys, The, 1992, PG-13, ★★½ 1995
Player, The, 1992, R, ★★★★ 1998
Play It Again, Sam, 1972, PG, ★★★ 1998
Play Misty for Me, 1971, R, ★★★★ 1998
Plenty, 1985, R, ★★★½ 1998
Plot Against Harry, The, 1970, NR, ★★★½ 1998
Pocahontas, 1995, G, ★★★ 1998
Poetic Justice, 1993, R, ★★★ 1998
Point Break, 1991, R, ★★★½ 1998
Point of No Return, 1993, R, ★★★ 1998
Poison Ivy, 1992, R, ★★½ 1994
Police Academy, 1984, R, no stars 1994
Poltergeist, 1982, PG, ★★★ 1996
Ponette, 1997, NR, ★★★½ 1998
Pope of Greenwich Village, The, 1984, R, ★★★ 1998
Popeye, 1980, PG, ★★★½ 1998
Porky's, 1982, R, ★½ 1993
Portrait of a Lady, The, 1997, PG-13, ★★★ 1998
Posse, 1993, R, ★★ 1994
Possession of Joel Delaney, The, 1972, R, ★★ 1991
Postcards from the Edge, 1990, R, ★★★ 1998
Postman, The (Il Postino), 1995, PG, ★★★½ 1998
Postman Always Rings Twice, The, 1981, R, ★★½ 1991
Powder, 1995, PG-13, ★★ 1997
Power, 1985, R, ★★½ 1988
Power of One, The, 1992, PG-13, ★★½ 1995
Powwow Highway, 1989, R, ★★★ 1995
Prancer, 1989, G, ★★★ 1998
Preacher's Wife, The, 1996, PG, ★★★ 1998
Predator, 1987, R, ★★★ 1998
Predator 2, 1990, R, ★★ 1993
Prefontaine, 1997, PG-13, ★★★ 1998
Prelude to a Kiss, 1992, PG-13, ★★★ 1998
Presumed Innocent, 1990, R, ★★★½ 1998
Pretty Baby, 1978, R, ★★★ 1998
Pretty in Pink, 1985, PG-13, ★★★ 1998
Pretty Woman, 1990, R, ★★★½ 1998
Prick Up Your Ears, 1987, R, ★★★★ 1998
Priest, 1995, R, ★ 1997
Prime Cut, 1972, R, ★★★ 1998
Prince of the City, 1981, R, ★★★★ 1998
Prince of Tides, The, 1991, R, ★★★½ 1998
Princess Bride, The, 1987, PG, ★★★½ 1998
Prisoner of the Mountains, 1997, R, ★★★½ 1998
Private Benjamin, 1980, R, ★★★ 1998
Private Parts, 1997, R, ★★★ 1998
Prizzi's Honor, 1985, R, ★★★★ 1998
Professional, The, 1994, R, ★★½ 1997
Program, The, 1993, R, ★★★ 1998
Project X, 1987, PG, ★★★ 1995

Road Warrior, The, 1982, R, ★★★½ 1998
Robin Hood: Prince of Thieves, 1991, PG-13, ★★ 1997
RoboCop, 1987, R, ★★★ 1998
RoboCop II, 1990, R, ★★ 1995
RoboCop 3, 1993, PG-13, ★½ 1995
Rob Roy, 1995, R, ★★★½ 1998
Rock, The, 1996, R, ★★★½ 1998
Rocketeer, The, 1991, PG-13, ★★★ 1998
Rocky, 1976, PG, ★★★★ 1998
Rocky II, 1979, PG, ★★★ 1998
Rocky IV, 1986, PG, ★★ 1993
Rocky V, 1990, PG-13, ★★ 1993
Rocky Horror Picture Show, The, 1975, R, ★★½ 1998
Roger & Me, 1989, R, ★★★★ 1998
Romancing the Stone, 1984, PG, ★★★ 1998
Romeo Is Bleeding, 1994, R, ★★ 1995
Romy and Michele's High School Reunion, 1997, R, ★★★ 1998
Rookie of the Year, 1993, PG, ★★★ 1996
Room with a View, A, 1985, PG-13, ★★★★ 1998
Rosalie Goes Shopping, 1990, PG, ★★★ 1998
Rose, The, 1979, R, ★★★ 1998
Rosewood, 1997, R, ★★★½ 1998
Rough Magic, 1997, PG-13, ★★ 1998
'Round Midnight, 1986, R, ★★★★ 1998
Roxanne, 1987, PG, ★★★½ 1998
Ruby, 1992, R, ★★ 1994
Ruby in Paradise, 1993, NR, ★★★★ 1998
Rudy, 1993, PG, ★★★½ 1998
Rudyard Kipling's The Jungle Book, 1994, PG, ★★★ 1998
Runaway Train, 1985, R, ★★★★ 1998
Run of the Country, The, 1995, R, ★★½ 1997
Running on Empty, 1988, PG-13, ★★★★ 1998
Running Scared, 1986, R, ★★★ 1995
Rush, 1992, R, ★★★ 1996
Russia House, The, 1990, R, ★★ 1995
Ruthless People, 1986, R, ★★★½ 1998

## S

Sabrina, 1995, PG, ★★★½ 1998
Safe, 1995, NR, ★★★ 1998
Safe Passage, 1995, PG-13, ★★ 1996
Saint, The, 1997, PG-13, ★★ 1998
St. Elmo's Fire, 1985, R, ★½ 1987
Saint Jack, 1979, R, ★★★★ 1998
Saint of Fort Washington, The, 1994, R, ★★★ 1998
Salaam Bombay!, 1988, NR, ★★★★ 1998
Salvador, 1986, R, ★★★ 1996
Sammy and Rosie Get Laid, 1987, R, ★★★½ 1998
Sandlot, The, 1993, PG, ★★★ 1998
Santa Claus: The Movie, 1985, PG, ★★½ 1987
Santa Clause, The, 1994, PG, ★★½ 1998
Santa Sangre, 1990, R, ★★★★ 1998
Sarafina!, 1992, PG-13, ★★ 1995
Saturday Night Fever, 1977, R, ★★★½ 1998
Savage Nights, 1994, NR, ★★½ 1995
Say Amen, Somebody, 1983, G, ★★★★ 1998
Say Anything, 1989, PG-13, ★★★★ 1998
Scandal, 1989, R, ★★★★ 1998
Scarecrow, 1973, R, ★★★ 1998
Scarface, 1983, R, ★★★★ 1998
Scarlet Letter, The, 1995, R, ★½ 1997
Scene of the Crime, 1987, NR, ★★½ 1988
Scenes from a Mall, 1991, R, ★ 1995
Scenes from a Marriage, 1974, PG, ★★★★ 1998
Scent of a Woman, 1992, R, ★★★½ 1998
Scent of Green Papaya, The, 1994, NR, ★★★★ 1998
Schindler's List, 1993, R, ★★★★ 1998
School Daze, 1988, R, ★★★½ 1998
School Ties, 1992, PG-13, ★★★ 1996
Scout, The, 1994, PG-13, ★½ 1996
Scream, 1996, R, ★★★ 1998
Screamers, 1996, R, ★★½ 1997
Scrooged, 1988, PG-13, ★ 1994
Sea of Love, 1989, R, ★★★ 1998
Searching for Bobby Fischer, 1993, PG, ★★★★ 1998
Secret Garden, The, 1993, G, ★★★★ 1998
Secret Honor, 1984, NR, ★★★★ 1998
Secret of My Success, The, 1987, PG-13, ★½ 1989
Secret of NIMH, The, 1982, G, ★★★ 1986
Secret of Roan Inish, The, 1995, PG, ★★★½ 1998
Secrets and Lies, 1996, R, ★★★★ 1998
Seems Like Old Times, 1980, PG, ★★ 1986
See No Evil, Hear No Evil, 1989, R, ★½ 1993
See You in the Morning, 1989, PG-13, ★★½ 1993
Selena, 1997, PG, ★★★½ 1998
Sense and Sensibility, 1995, PG, ★★½ 1998
September, 1987, PG, ★★★½ 1998
Serial Mom, 1994, R, ★★ 1995
Serpent and the Rainbow, The, 1988, R, ★★★ 1998
Set It Off, 1996, R, ★★★½ 1998
Seven, 1995, R, ★★★½ 1998
Seventh Sign, The, 1988, R, ★★ 1992
Sex, Drugs, Rock & Roll, 1991, R, ★★★ 1998

sex, lies, and videotape, 1989, R, ★★★½ 1998
Shadow, The, 1994, PG-13, ★★★ 1998
Shadowlands, 1994, PG, ★★★★ 1998
Shadow of the Wolf, 1993, PG-13, ★★ 1994
Shadows and Fog, 1992, PG-13, ★★ 1997
Shaft, 1971, R, ★★½ 1995
Shakedown, 1988, R, ★★★ 1996
Shakes the Clown, 1992, R, ★★ 1993
Shallow Grave, 1995, R, ★★ 1997
Shall We Dance?, 1997, PG, ★★★½ 1998
Shanghai Triad, 1996, NR, ★★ 1997
Sharky's Machine, 1981, R, ★★★ 1998
Shattered, 1991, R, ★★ 1994
Shawshank Redemption, The, 1994, R, ★★★½ 1998
She-Devil, 1989, PG-13, ★★★ 1998
Sheena, Queen of the Jungle, 1984, PG, ★ 1990
Sheltering Sky, The, 1991, R, ★★ 1994
She's Having a Baby, 1988, PG-13, ★★ 1993
She's Out of Control, 1989, PG, no stars 1992
Shine, 1996, PG-13, ★★★★ 1998
Shining Through, 1992, R, ★★ 1994
Shirley Valentine, 1989, R, ★ 1993
Shoah, 1986, NR, ★★★★ 1998
Shock to the System, A, 1990, R, ★★★ 1996
Shooting Party, The, 1985, NR, ★★★ 1987
Shootist, The, 1976, PG, ★★★½ 1998
Shoot the Moon, 1982, R, ★★★½ 1998
Shoot to Kill, 1988, R, ★★★ 1996
Short Cuts, 1993, R, ★★★★ 1998
Showgirls, 1995, NC-17, ★★½ 1997
Shy People, 1988, R, ★★★★ 1998
Sid & Nancy, 1986, R, ★★★★ 1998
Sidewalk Stories, 1989, R, ★★★½ 1998
Silence of the Lambs, The, 1991, R, ★★★½ 1998
Silent Movie, 1976, PG, ★★★★ 1998
Silent Running, 1972, G, ★★★★ 1998
Silkwood, 1983, R, ★★★★ 1998
Silverado, 1985, PG-13, ★★★½ 1998
Simple Men, 1992, R, ★★ 1995
Sing, 1989, PG-13, ★★★ 1996
Singin' in the Rain, 1952, G, ★★★★ 1997
Singles, 1992, PG-13, ★★★ 1998
Single White Female, 1992, R, ★★★ 1996
Sirens, 1994, R, ★★★½ 1998
Sister Act, 1992, PG, ★★½ 1996
Sister Act 2: Back in the Habit, 1993, PG, ★★ 1995
Sisters, 1973, R, ★★★ 1998
Sixteen Candles, 1984, PG, ★★★ 1998
Skin Deep, 1989, R, ★★★ 1998
Slacker, 1991, R, ★★★ 1998
Slaves of New York, 1989, R, ½★ 1993
Sleeper, 1973, PG, ★★★1/2 1998
Sleeping with the Enemy, 1991, R, ★½ 1994
Sleepless in Seattle, 1993, PG, ★★★ 1998
Sleuth, 1972, PG, ★★★★ 1998
Sling Blade, 1996, R, ★★★½ 1998
Slugger's Wife, The, 1985, PG-13, ★★ 1986
Small Change, 1976, PG, ★★★★ 1998
Smash Palace, 1982, R, ★★★★ 1998
Smilla's Sense of Snow, 1997, R, ★★★ 1998
Smoke, 1995, R, ★★★ 1998
Smokey and the Bandit II, 1980, PG, ★ 1986
Smooth Talk, 1986, PG-13, ★★★½ 1998
Snapper, The, 1993, R, ★★★½ 1998
Sneakers, 1992, PG-13, ★★½ 1994
Sniper, 1993, R, ★★★ 1996
Soapdish, 1991, PG-13, ★★★½ 1998
So I Married an Axe Murderer, 1993, PG-13, ★★½ 1995
Soldier of Orange, 1980, PG, ★★★½ 1986
Soldier's Story, A, 1984, PG, ★★½ 1993
Some Kind of Wonderful, 1987, PG-13, ★★★ 1998
Someone to Watch Over Me, 1987, R, ★★ 1992
Something to Talk About, 1995, R, ★★★½ 1998
Something Wild, 1986, R, ★★★½ 1998
Sometimes a Great Notion, 1971, PG, ★★★ 1998
Somewhere in Time, 1980, PG, ★★ 1988
Sommersby, 1993, PG-13, ★★ 1994
Songwriter, 1985, R, ★★★½ 1996
Son-in-Law, 1993, PG-13, ★★ 1995
Sophie's Choice, 1982, R, ★★★★ 1998
Soul Man, 1986, PG-13, ★ 1989
Sounder, 1972, G, ★★★★ 1998
South Central, 1992, R, ★★★ 1996
Southern Comfort, 1981, R, ★★★ 1996
Spaceballs, 1987, PG, ★★½ 1991
Space Jam, 1996, PG, ★★★½ 1998
Spartacus, 1960, PG-13, ★★★ 1997
Species, 1995, R, ★★ 1997
Speechless, 1994, PG-13, ★★ 1996
Speed, 1994, R, ★★★★ 1997
Spider's Stratagem, The, 1973, PG, ★★★ 1998
Spike of Bensonhurst, 1988, R, ★★★ 1998
Splash, 1984, PG, ★½ 1993
Spring Break, 1983, R, ★ 1988
Spy Who Loved Me, The, 1977, PG, ★★★½ 1998
Stairway to Heaven, 1946, PG, ★★★★ 1997
Stakeout, 1987, R, ★★★ 1996
Stand and Deliver, 1988, PG-13, ★★½ 1994

Stanley & Iris, 1990, PG-13, ★★½ 1993
Stardust Memories, 1980, PG, ★★ 1997
STAR 80, 1983, R, ★★★★ 1998
Stargate, 1994, PG-13, ★ 1997
Star Is Born, A, 1954 (1983), PG, ★★★★ 1997
Starmaker, The, 1996, R, ★★★ 1998
Starman, 1984, PG, ★★★ 1998
Stars Fell on Henrietta, The, 1995, PG, ★★ 1997
Star Trek: First Contact, 1996, PG-13, ★★★½ 1998
Star Trek: Generations, 1994, PG, ★★ 1997
Star Trek: The Motion Picture, 1979, G, ★★★ 1998
Star Trek II: The Wrath of Khan, 1982, PG, ★★★ 1998
Star Trek III: The Search for Spock, 1984, PG, ★★★ 1998
Star Trek IV: The Voyage Home, 1986, PG, ★★★½ 1998
Star Trek V: The Final Frontier, 1989, PG, ★★ 1997
Star Trek VI: The Undiscovered Country, 1991, PG, ★★★ 1998
Star Wars, 1977, PG, ★★★★ 1997
Star Wars (Special Edition), 1997, ★★★★ 1998
State of Grace, 1990, R, ★★★½ 1998
Stay Hungry, 1976, R, ★★★ 1996
Staying Alive, 1983, PG, ★ 1994
Staying Together, 1989, R, ★★ 1993
Stealing Beauty, 1996, R, ★★ 1997
Steel Magnolias, 1989, PG, ★★★ 1998
Stella, 1990, PG-13, ★★★½ 1998
Stepfather, The, 1987, R, ★★½ 1994
Stephen King's Silver Bullet, 1985, R, ★★★ 1988
Stepping Out, 1991, PG, ★★ 1994
Stevie, 1981, NR, ★★★★ 1998
Sting II, The, 1983, PG, ★★ 1986
Stir Crazy, 1980, R, ★★ 1987
Stop Making Sense, 1984, NR, ★★★½ 1998
Stop! Or My Mom Will Shoot, 1992, PG-13, ½★ 1994
Stormy Monday, 1988, R, ★★★½ 1998
Story of Qiu Ju, The, 1993, NR, ★★★½ 1997
Story of Women, 1990, R, ★★½ 1993
Storyville, 1992, R, ★★★½ 1998
Straight Out of Brooklyn, 1991, R, ★★★ 1998
Straight Talk, 1992, PG, ★★ 1994
Straight Time, 1978, R, ★★★½ 1998
Strange Days, 1995, R, ★★★★ 1998
Stranger Among Us, A, 1992, PG-13, ★½ 1994
Stranger than Paradise, 1984, R, ★★★★ 1998
Strapless, 1990, R, ★★★ 1998
Strawberry and Chocolate, 1995, R, ★★★½ 1998
Streamers, 1984, R, ★★★★ 1998
Streetcar Named Desire, A, 1951, PG, ★★★★ 1997
Street Smart, 1987, R, ★★★ 1998
Streets of Fire, 1984, PG, ★★★ 1988
Streetwise, 1985, R, ★★★★ 1998
Strictly Ballroom, 1993, PG, ★★★ 1998
Strictly Business, 1991, PG-13, ★★½ 1993
Striking Distance, 1993, R, ★½ 1995
Stripes, 1981, R, ★★★½ 1998
Stripper, 1986, R, ★★★ 1987
Striptease, 1996, R, ★★ 1997
Stroker Ace, 1983, PG, ★½ 1986
Stroszek, 1978, NR, ★★★★ 1998
Stuart Saves His Family, 1995, PG-13, ★★★ 1998
Stuff, The, 1985, R, ★½ 1987
Stunt Man, The, 1980, R, ★★ 1988
Suburban Commando, 1991, PG, ★ 1993
subUrbia, 1997, R, ★★★½ 1998
Sudden Death, 1995, R, ★★½ 1998
Sudden Impact, 1983, R, ★★★ 1998
Sugar Hill, 1994, R, ★★★★ 1998
Summer House, The, 1993, NR, ★★★ 1998
Summer of '42, 1971, R, ★★½ 1987
Sunday Bloody Sunday, 1971, R, ★★★★ 1998
Super, The, 1991, R, ★★ 1995
Supergirl, 1984, PG, ★★ 1988
Superman, 1978, PG, ★★★★ 1998
Superman II, 1981, PG, ★★★★ 1998
Superman III, 1983, PG, ★★½ 1998
Superstar: The Life and Times of Andy Warhol, 1991, NR, ★★★ 1997
Sure Thing, The, 1985, PG-13, ★★★½ 1998
Surrender, 1987, PG, ★★ 1989
Survivors, The, 1983, R, ★½ 1991
Suspect, 1987, R, ★★½ 1993
Swamp Thing, 1982, R, ★★★ 1998
Swann in Love, 1984, R, ★★★ 1996
Swan Princess, The, 1994, G, ★★★ 1998
Sweet Dreams, 1985, PG-13, ★★ 1988
Sweetie, 1990, R, ★★★½ 1998
Sweet Liberty, 1986, PG, ★★½ 1993
Swimming to Cambodia, 1987, NR, ★★★ 1998
Swimming With Sharks, 1995, R, ★★★ 1998
Swingers, 1996, R, ★★★ 1998
Swing Kids, 1993, PG-13, ★ 1994
Swing Shift, 1984, PG, ★★★ 1988
Switch, 1991, R, ★★½ 1994
Switching Channels, 1988, PG-13, ★★★ 1996

Swoon, 1992, NR, ★★★ 1996
Sylvester, 1985, PG, ★★★ 1988

# T

Table for Five, 1983, PG, ★½ 1986
Tale of Springtime, A, 1992, PG, ★★★½ 1998
Talk Radio, 1988, R, ★★★★ 1998
Tall Guy, The, 1990, R, ★★★½ 1998
Tall Tale: The Unbelievable Adventures of Pecos Bill, 1995, PG, ★★★ 1998
Tampopo, 1987, NR, ★★★★ 1998
Tango and Cash, 1989, R, ★ 1992
Tank Girl, 1995, R, ★★ 1996
Tap, 1989, PG-13, ★★★ 1998
Taps, 1981, PG, ★★★ 1998
Tarzan, the Ape Man, 1981, R, ★★½ 1993
Tatie Danielle, 1991, NR, ★★★ 1996
Taxi Blues, 1991, NR, ★★★ 1998
Taxi Driver, 1976, R, ★★★★ 1997
Taxi Driver: 20th Anniversary Edition, 1995, R, ★★★★ 1998
Taxing Woman, A, 1988, NR, ★★ 1992
Teachers, 1984, R, ★★ 1986
Teenage Mutant Ninja Turtles, 1990, PG, ★★½ 1994
Teenage Mutant Ninja Turtles II: The Secret of the Ooze, 1991, PG, ★ 1994
Teen Wolf Too, 1987, PG, ½★ 1989
Tell Them Willie Boy Is Here, 1970, PG, ★★★½ 1996
10, 1979, R, ★★★★ 1998
Tender Mercies, 1983, PG, ★★★ 1998
Tequila Sunrise, 1988, R, ★★½ 1994
Terminal Velocity, 1994, PG-13, ★★ 1996
Terminator 2: Judgment Day, 1991, R, ★★★½ 1998
Terms of Endearment, 1983, PG, ★★★★ 1998
Terror Train, 1980, R, ★ 1986
Tess, 1980, PG, ★★★★ 1998
Testament, 1983, PG, ★★★★ 1998
Tex, 1982, PG, ★★★★ 1998
Texas Chainsaw Massacre, The, 1974, R, ★★ 1995
Texasville, 1990, R, ★★★½ 1998
That Obscure Object of Desire, 1977, R, ★★★★ 1998
That Old Feeling, 1997, PG-13, ★ 1998
That's Dancing!, 1985, PG, ★★★ 1998
That's Entertainment!, 1974, G, ★★★★ 1998
That's Entertainment! III, 1994, G, ★★★½ 1998
That Thing You Do!, 1996, PG, ★★★ 1998
That Was Then . . . This Is Now, 1985, R, ★★ 1987
Thelma & Louise, 1991, R, ★★★½ 1998
Thelonious Monk: Straight, No Chaser, 1989, PG-13, ★★★½ 1998
Theremin: An Electronic Odyssey, 1995, NR, ★★★½ 1998
Therese, 1987, NR, ★★★½ 1996
They Call Me Bruce, 1983, PG, ★★ 1986
They Shoot Horses, Don't They?, 1970, PG, ★★★★ 1998
Thief, 1981, R, ★★★½ 1996
Thieves Like Us, 1974, R, ★★★½ 1998
Thin Blue Line, The, 1988, NR, ★★★½ 1998
Thing, The, 1982, R, ★★½ 1995
Things Change, 1988, PG, ★★★ 1998
Things to Do in Denver When You're Dead, 1996, R, ★★½ 1997
35 Up, 1992, NR, ★★★★ 1998
36 Fillette, 1989, NR, ★★★½ 1996
Thirty-two Short Films About Glenn Gould, 1994, NR, ★★★★ 1998
This Boy's Life, 1993, R, ★★★½ 1998
This Is Elvis, 1981, PG, ★★★½ 1998
This Is My Life, 1992, PG-13, ★★★ 1996
This Is Spinal Tap, 1984, R, ★★★★ 1998
Three Men and a Baby, 1987, PG, ★★★ 1998
Three Men and a Little Lady, 1990, PG, ★★ 1994
Three Musketeers, The, 1993, PG, ★★ 1995
3 Ninjas Kick Back, 1994, PG, ★★½ 1995
Three of Hearts, 1993, R, ★★★ 1996
Threesome, 1994, R, ★★★ 1996
3 Women, 1977, PG, ★★★★ 1998
Throw Momma from the Train, 1987, PG-13, ★★ 1993
Thunderheart, 1992, R, ★★★½ 1998
THX 1138, 1971, PG, ★★★ 1998
Ticket to Heaven, 1981, R, ★★★½ 1998
Tie Me Up! Tie Me Down!, 1990, NR, ★★ 1993
Tiger's Tale, A, 1988, R, ★★ 1989
Tightrope, 1984, R, ★★★½ 1998
'Til There Was You, 1997, PG-13, ½★ 1998
Tim Burton's Nightmare Before Christmas, 1993, PG, ★★★½ 1998
Time Bandits, 1981, PG, ★★★ 1998
Timecop, 1994, R, ★★ 1997
Time of Destiny, A, 1988, PG-13, ★★★½ 1998
Times of Harvey Milk, The, 1985, NR, ★★★½ 1997
Tin Drum, The, 1980, R, ★★ 1988
Tin Men, 1987, R, ★★★ 1998
To Be or Not To Be, 1983, R, ★★★ 1998

To Die For, 1995, R, ★★★½ 1998
Tokyo Story, 1953, G, ★★★★ 1997
To Live, 1994, NR, ★★★½ 1998
To Live and Die in L.A., 1985, R, ★★★★ 1998
Tom and Viv, 1995, PG-13, ★★½ 1996
Tommy, 1975, PG, ★★★ 1998
Too Beautiful for You, 1990, R, ★★★½ 1998
Tootsie, 1982, PG, ★★★★ 1998
Topaz, 1970, PG, ★★★½ 1998
Top Gun, 1986, PG, ★★½ 1998
Top Secret!, 1984, R, ★★★½ 1998
Torch Song Trilogy, 1988, R, ★★★½ 1998
To Sleep With Anger, 1990, PG, ★★½ 1993
Total Recall, 1990, R, ★★★½ 1998
Toto le Heros, 1992, NR, ★★½ 1994
Tough Enough, 1983, PG, ★★★ 1986
Tough Guys Don't Dance, 1987, R, ★★½ 1993
To Wong Foo, Thanks for Everything! Julie Newmar, 1995, PG-13, ★★½ 1997
Toys, 1992, PG-13, ★★½ 1994
Toy Story, 1995, G, ★★★½ 1998
Track 29, 1988, R, ★★★ 1996
Trading Places, 1983, R, ★★★½ 1998
Trainspotting, 1996, R, ★★★ 1998
Trees Lounge, 1996, R, ★★★½ 1998
Trespass, 1992, R, ★★½ 1994
Trial, The, 1994, NR, ★★½ 1996
Trial and Error, 1997, PG-13, ★★★ 1998
Tribute, 1981, PG, ★★★ 1996
Trip to Bountiful, The, 1985, PG, ★★★½ 1998
Tron, 1982, PG, ★★★★ 1998
Troop Beverly Hills, 1989, PG, ★★ 1994
Trouble in Mind, 1985, R, ★★★★ 1998
True Believer, 1989, R, ★★★ 1996
True Colors, 1991, R, ★★ 1994
True Confessions, 1981, R, ★★★ 1996
True Lies, 1994, R, ★★★ 1998
True Love, 1989, R, ★★★ 1996
True Romance, 1993, R, ★★★ 1998
True Stories, 1986, PG-13, ★★★½ 1998
Truly, Madly, Deeply, 1991, NR, ★★★ 1998
Trust, 1991, R, ★★ 1994
Truth or Dare, 1991, R, ★★★½ 1998
Tucker: The Man and His Dream, 1988, PG, ★★½ 1993
Tune in Tomorrow . . . , 1990, PG-13, ★★½ 1993
Turbulence, 1997, R, ★ 1998
Turk 182!, 1985, PG-13, ★ 1987
Turning Point, The, 1977, PG, ★★★½ 1998
Turtle Diary, 1985, PG-13, ★★★½ 1998
Twelfth Night, 1996, PG, ★★★½ 1998
12 Monkeys, 1996, R, ★★★ 1998
Twenty Bucks, 1994, R, ★★★ 1996
28 Up, 1985, NR, ★★★★ 1998
29th Street, 1991, R, ★★★ 1996
Twice in a Lifetime, 1985, R, ★★★½ 1998
Twilight Zone—the Movie, 1983, PG, ★★★½ 1998
Twins, 1988, PG, ★★★ 1998
Twin Town, 1997, NR, ★★ 1998
Twister, 1995, PG-13, ★★ 1998
Two English Girls, 1972, R, ★★★★ 1998
Two Jakes, The, 1990, R, ★★★½ 1998
Two of a Kind, 1983, PG, ½★ 1986
2001: A Space Odyssey, 1968, G, ★★★★ 1997
2010, 1984, PG, ★★★ 1996

# U

Uforia, 1985, PG, ★★★★ 1998
Ulee's Gold, 1997, R, ★★★½ 1998
Umbrellas of Cherbourg, The, 1996, NR, ★★★½ 1997
Unbearable Lightness of Being, The, 1988, R, ★★★★ 1998
Uncle Buck, 1989, PG, ★½ 1993
Un Coeur en Hiver, 1993, NR, ★★★½ 1998
Under Fire, 1983, R, ★★★½ 1998
Under Siege, 1992, R, ★★★ 1996
Under the Volcano, 1984, R, ★★★★ 1998
Unforgiven, 1992, R, ★★★★ 1998
Unhook the Stars, 1997, R, ★★★ 1998
Universal Soldier, 1992, R, ★★ 1994
Unlawful Entry, 1992, R, ★★★ 1996
Unmarried Woman, An, 1978, R, ★★★★ 1998
Unstrung Heroes, 1995, PG, ★★★½ 1998
Untamed Heart, 1993, PG-13, ★★★ 1996
Until September, 1984, R, ½★ 1987
Until the End of the World, 1992, R, ★★ 1994
Untouchables, The, 1987, R, ★★½ 1994
Unzipped, 1995, PG-13, ★★★ 1998
Up the Creek, 1984, R, ★★★ 1989
Up the Sandbox, 1973, R, ★★★ 1996
Used Cars, 1980, R, ★★ 1994
Used People, 1992, PG-13, ★★ 1994
Usual Suspects, The, 1995, R, ★½ 1997

# V

Vagabond, 1986, NR, ★★★★ 1998
Valley Girl, 1983, R, ★★★ 1998
Valmont, 1989, R, ★★★½ 1998
Vanishing, The, 1991, NR, ★★★½ 1998
Vanishing, The, 1993, R, ★ 1994
Vanya on 42nd Street, 1994, PG, ★★★½ 1998
Verdict, The, 1982, R, ★★★★ 1998

Willow, 1988, PG, ★★½ 1994
Wind, 1992, PG-13, ★★★ 1998
Wings of Desire, 1988, NR, ★★★★ 1998
Winter of Our Dreams, 1983, R, ★★★ 1998
Wired, 1989, R, ★½ 1993
Wise Guys, 1986, R, ★★★½ 1998
Wish You Were Here, 1987, R, ★★★½ 1998
Witches, The, 1990, PG, ★★★ 1998
Witches of Eastwick, The, 1987, R, ★★★½ 1998
With Honors, 1994, PG-13, ★★½ 1995
Withnail & I, 1987, R, ★★★★ 1998
Without a Trace, 1983, PG, ★★★½ 1998
Without You I'm Nothing, 1990, R, ★★★ 1996
Witness, 1985, R, ★★★★ 1998
Wiz, The, 1978, G, ★★★ 1998
Wizard, The, 1989, PG, ★ 1992
Wolf, 1994, R, ★★★ 1998
Woman's Tale, A, 1992, PG-13, ★★★★ 1998
Woman Under the Influence, A, 1974, R, ★★★★ 1998
Wonderful Horrible Life of Leni Riefenstahl, The, 1994, NR, ★★★½ 1998
Woodstock, 1969, R, ★★★★ 1997
Working Girl, 1988, R, ★★★★ 1996
Working Girls, 1987, NR, ★★★ 1998
World According to Garp, The, 1982, R, ★★★ 1998
World Apart, A, 1988, PG, ★★★★ 1998
Wrestling Ernest Hemingway, 1994, PG-13, ★★★ 1998
Wyatt Earp, 1994, PG-13, ★★ 1995

# X, Y, Z

Xanadu, 1980, PG, ★★ 1988
Year of Living Dangerously, The, 1983, PG, ★★★★ 1998
Year of the Gun, 1991, R, ★★★ 1996
Year of the Quiet Sun, 1986, PG, ★★★★ 1987
Yentl, 1983, PG, ★★★½ 1998
Youngblood, 1985, PG-13, ★★ 1987
Young Doctors in Love, 1982, R, ★★ 1991
Young Einstein, 1989, PG, ★ 1992
Young Frankenstein, 1974, PG, ★★★★ 1998
Young Sherlock Holmes, 1985, PG-13, ★★★ 1998
Zabriskie Point, 1970, R, ★★ 1991
Zelig, 1983, PG, ★★★ 1998
Zentropa, 1992, R, ★★★ 1996
Zorro, the Gay Blade, 1981, PG, ★★ 1991

Note: The right hand column is the year in which the review last appeared in *Roger Ebert's Video Companion.*

# Index

## A

# B

# C

# D

# E

# G

# H

# J

# L

# M

# N

# O

# P

# T

# U



# V

# X



# Y



# Z